The Price of Victory

The Price of Victory

A Naval History of Britain
1815–1945

N. A. M. RODGER

W. W. NORTON & COMPANY
Independent Publishers Since 1923

First American Edition 2025
First published in 2024 in Great Britain by Allen Lane.

For information about permission to reproduce selections from this book, write to
Permissions, W. W. Norton & Company, Inc., 500 Fifth Avenue, New York, NY 10110

For information about special discounts for bulk purchases, please contact
W. W. Norton Special Sales at specialsales@wwnorton.com or 800-233-4830

Manufacturing by Lakeside Book Company

ISBN 978-0-393-29222-0

W. W. Norton & Company, Inc.
500 Fifth Avenue, New York, NY 10110
www.wwnorton.com

W. W. Norton & Company Ltd.
15 Carlisle Street, London W1D 3BS

10 9 8 7 6 5 4 3 2 1

For Roger Knight, with much gratitude

CONTENTS

FOREWORD

This is the last of three volumes under the general title of *A Naval History of Britain*. It follows *The Safeguard of the Sea* and *The Command of the Ocean*, published in 1997 and 2004 respectively, and I am painfully aware that those readers who generously praised the earlier volumes had reason to look for the last one some time ago. I have no excuse to offer save a serious illness and an exciting episode of brain surgery from which it took me several years to recover. Now, as the long-overdue ship is at length in sight of port, my first duty is to name and thank the many friends and colleagues who have contributed their time and skills to keep it afloat and under way.

Any writer undertaking so long a voyage single-handed would expect to draw largely on the generosity of his friends and connections: I would have leant on them even if my health had not failed, and in the event, I had to depend on them much more and much longer than I had expected. First and most of all I must thank my beloved wife Susan, without whose fathomless devotion neither book nor author would have survived so long. I owe a renewed obligation to the wise advice of my editor Stuart Proffitt, with whom I have been connected even longer than Penguin Books have been my publisher. Next, I must mention my everyday companions for twenty years past, the other fellows of All Souls College; a deep well of knowledge and good humour which never failed to guide and cheer me. For obvious reasons I am especially grateful for the support of the college librarians Gaye Morgan and Gabrielle Matthews. The College has also generously provided research funds for this volume.

Next, I must warmly thank a group of old friends associated with one or both of two learned institutions in which I worked at earlier stages of my career: the National Maritime Museum and the University of Exeter. Professor Roger Knight, formerly Deputy Director of the Museum, has been with me since the inception of this project in the early 1990s, adding to his many crucial contributions to the earlier volumes by more recently coordinating author, publisher, research assistants and other contributors to this volume, skilfully guiding it to completion. Professor Geoffrey Till gave me invaluable advice on the structure of the Epilogue. Dr Michael Duffy has been a faithful ally and adviser from first volume to last. I am grateful once again to Mr John Gilkes for his elegant cartography; Mrs Jane Knight has contributed valuably to the maps in this volume. Dr Philip Weir and Dr Kate Nicholls at different stages undertook much of the labour of compiling the appendices; Dr Nicholls has also undertaken the picture research for this volume, with additional work by Bob Todd, formerly of the Museum.

In the wider scholarly world I am glad to record my obligations to Professor Andrew Lambert of King's College London; my West London friends Sarah Lenton and Andrew Bickley who read the manuscript at short notice; Professor John Hattendorf, Dr J. Ross Dancy and Dr Evan Wilson of the US Naval War College; Professor Olivier Chaline of the Sorbonne; Dr Agustín Guimerá, for many years a distinguished member of the Consejo Superior de Investigaciones Científicas in Madrid; the late Professor Jaap Bruijn of Leiden University and the late Rear-Admiral James Goldrick RAN. There must be more: the lapse of twenty years has not improved my memory, and it is all too likely that I have omitted some names which should have been recorded here, for which I can only beg pardon.

All Souls College, Oxford
Candlemas, 2024

A NOTE ON CONVENTIONS

NOTES AND REFERENCES

Every direct quotation has a specific reference, but with that exception I have thought it sufficient in most of this book to support passages of general description or argument, drawing on secondary sources and dealing with matters known to history, with a single composite note for each paragraph. Whenever I felt that the argument was too complex or too novel, however, I have provided references more densely.

QUOTATIONS

English quotations in the text are given in modern English spelling, capitalization and if necessary punctuation. Abbreviations used in the notes and text are listed on pp. 809 and 813. Other unambiguous abbreviations and contractions in quotations have been silently expanded. Editorial omissions are indicated thus . . ., additions [thus] and the original wording [*thus*]; other words in italic are emphasized in the original. Quotations from other languages are translated in the text (by the author unless otherwise indicated), with the original wording given in the notes. Where no original wording is given, the quotation has been taken already translated from the source indicated.

PROPER NAMES

Political and geographical names have been subject to numerous changes in the two centuries covered by this volume. My practice has been to choose the names or spellings most likely to be familiar to adult readers in the English-speaking world today, with any likely alternatives following in parenthesis. Examples would be Formosa (Taiwan); Navarino (Pylos); Reval (Tallinn); Sveaborg (Suomenlinna, Viapori); Canton (Guangzhou).

Chinese and Japanese personal names are printed here in the oriental style, family name first. Authors' names in the bibliography, however, follow whatever style was used by the original publication.

TONNAGE

It is and was during the nineteenth and twentieth centuries a common error to believe that ships are weighed, rather than measured by volume or capacity. The range and complexity of tonnage systems which have been and are still used is considerable, but the measures most relevant to this book are the following. Gross and Net Register are fixed by a ship's dimensions and recorded on her registration documents, but deadweight and displacement vary considerably with her state of loading and the density of the water in which she floats.

Displacement: A calculation of the weight of water displaced by a ship's hull, and hence (by Archimedes' Rule) the weight of the ship herself; normally used only for warships. For practical use it is necessary to specify the ship's state of loading, and whether the weight is given in long tons of 2,240lbs, short tons of 2,000lbs, or metric tons of 1,000kg (2,205lbs).

Gross Register: The enclosed volume of the ship's hull below the upper deck expressed in tons of 100cu.ft or 2.83cu.m. The commonest measure for commercial freighters.

Net Register: The enclosed volume of the ship's earning space (internal volume subtracting engine rooms, bunkers, ship's stores, crew accommodation, etc.), likewise expressed in tons of 100cu.ft or 2.83cu.m. Widely used for harbour dues and taxation.

Deadweight: The weight of cargo laden to bring the ship down to her loading marks. For ships which trade in a single commodity (oil tankers most obviously) this may be obtained by actual measure of the cargo, but in most cases it is a volume measure (again at 100cu.ft to the ton) inferred from the observed sinkage of the ship when fully loaded.

LIST OF ILLUSTRATIONS

LIST OF MAPS

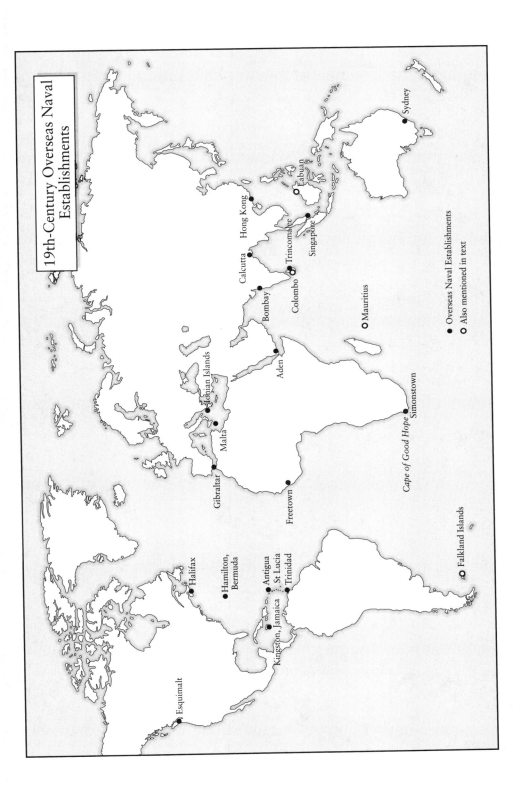

19th-Century Overseas Naval
Establishments

- Overseas Naval Establishments
- Also mentioned in text

Esquimalt
Halifax
Hamilton, Bermuda
Antigua
St Lucia
Kingston, Jamaica
Trinidad

Gibraltar
Malta
Ionian Islands
Freetown
Cape of Good Hope
Simonstown
Falkland Islands

Aden
Bombay
Calcutta
Colombo
Trincomalee
Hong Kong
Labuan
Singapore
Mauritius

Sydney

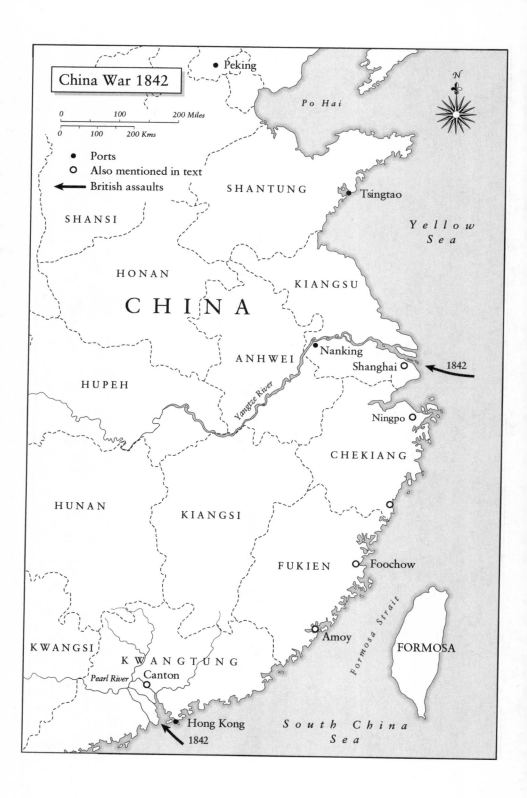

China War 1842

0 100 200 Miles
0 100 200 Kms

• Ports
○ Also mentioned in text
← British assaults

Peking

Po Hai

SHANTUNG

Tsingtao

Yellow Sea

SHANSI

HONAN

CHINA

KIANGSU

HUPEH

ANHWEI

Nanking

Shanghai ○ ← 1842

Yangtze River

Ningpo ○

CHEKIANG

HUNAN

KIANGSI

○

FUKIEN

Foochow ○

Formosa Strait

KWANGSI

KWANGTUNG

Amoy ○

FORMOSA

Pearl River

Canton ○

Hong Kong
1842

South China Sea

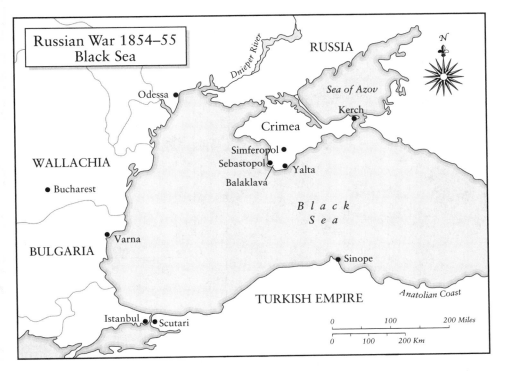

Russian War 1854–55
Black Sea

Dnieper River

RUSSIA

Sea of Azov

Odessa

Kerch

Crimea

Simferopol

Sebastopol

Yalta

Balaklava

WALLACHIA

Bucharest

Black
Sea

BULGARIA

Varna

Sinope

TURKISH EMPIRE

Anatolian Coast

Istanbul

Scutari

0   100   200 Miles

0   100   200 Km

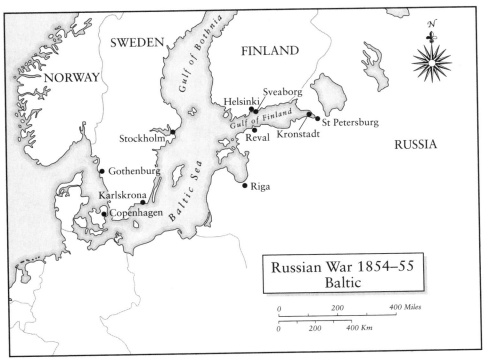

SWEDEN

FINLAND

NORWAY

Gulf of Bothnia

Helsinki

Sveaborg

St Petersburg

Gulf of Finland

Stockholm

Reval

Kronstadt

RUSSIA

Gothenburg

Baltic Sea

Karlskrona

Riga

Copenhagen

Russian War 1854–55
Baltic

0   200   400 Miles

0   200   400 Km

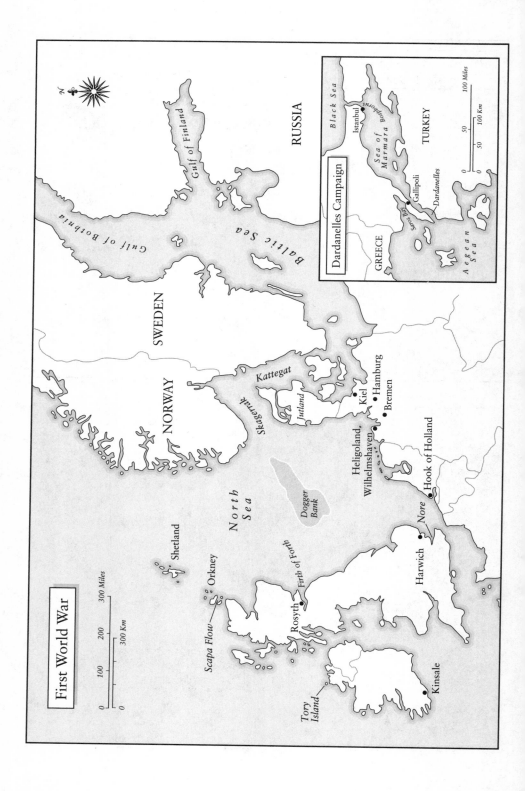

First World War

N

0 100 200 300 Miles
0 300 Km

NORWAY

SWEDEN

RUSSIA

Gulf of Bothnia

Gulf of Finland

Baltic Sea

Kattegat

Skagerrak

Jutland

North Sea

Dogger Bank

Shetland

Orkney

Scapa Flow

Firth of Forth

Rosyth

Kiel

Hamburg

Bremen

Heligoland, Wilhelmshaven

Hook of Holland

Nore

Harwich

Kinsale

Tory Island

Dardanelles Campaign

Black Sea

Sea of Marmara

Bosphorus

Istanbul

TURKEY

GREECE

Saros Bay

Gallipoli

Dardanelles

Aegean Sea

0 50 100 Miles
0 50 100 Km

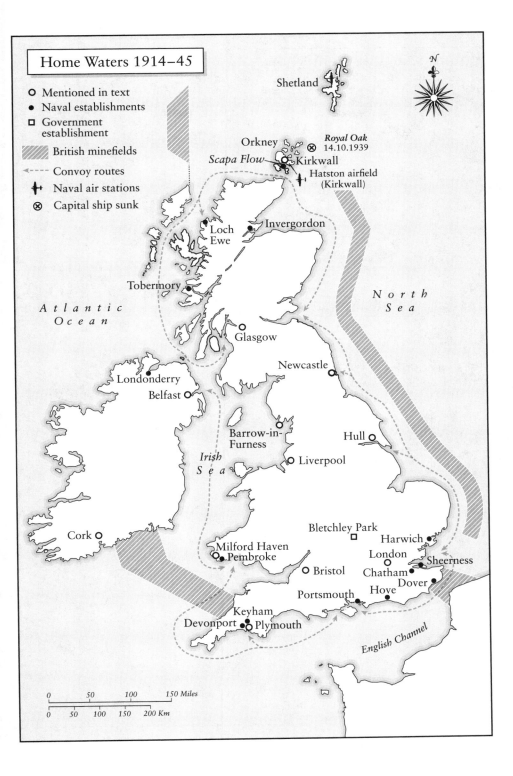

Home Waters 1914–45

- ○ Mentioned in text
- ● Naval establishments
- □ Government establishment
- ▨ British minefields
- ⊢ Convoy routes
- ✈ Naval air stations
- ⊗ Capital ship sunk

Shetland

Orkney
Royal Oak 14.10.1939 ⊗
Scapa Flow
Kirkwall
Hatston airfield (Kirkwall)

N

North Sea

Loch Ewe
Invergordon

Tobermory

Atlantic Ocean

Glasgow

Newcastle

Londonderry
Belfast

Barrow-in-Furness
Hull

Irish Sea
Liverpool

Cork

Bletchley Park
Harwich

Milford Haven
Pembroke
London
Sheerness

Bristol
Chatham
Dover

Portsmouth
Hove

Keyham
Devonport
Plymouth

English Channel

| 0 | 50 | 100 | 150 Miles |
| 0 | 50 | 100 | 150 | 200 Km |

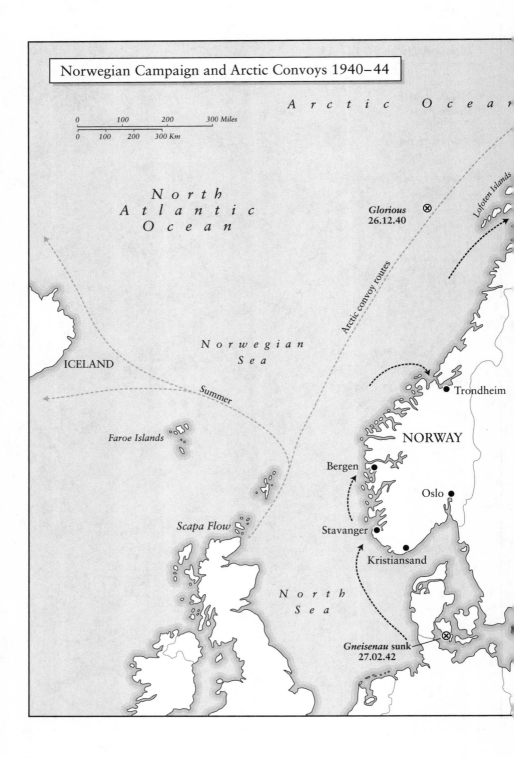

Norwegian Campaign and Arctic Convoys 1940–44

Arctic *Ocea*

0   100   200   300 Miles
0   100   200   300 Km

North
Atlantic
Ocean

Glorious
26.12.40 ⊗

Lofoten Islands

Arctic convoy routes

Norwegian
Sea

ICELAND

Summer

Faroe Islands

● Trondheim

NORWAY

Bergen ●

Oslo ●

Stavanger ●

Scapa Flow

Kristiansand ●

North
Sea

Gneisenau sunk
27.02.42 ⊗

Battle of the Atlantic

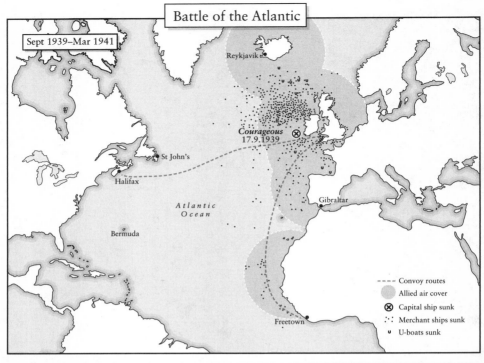

Sept 1939–Mar 1941

Reykjavik

Courageous
17.9.1939

St John's

Halifax

*Atlantic
Ocean*

Bermuda

Gibraltar

Freetown

- - - Convoy routes
Allied air cover
⊗ Capital ship sunk
∴ Merchant ships sunk
U U-boats sunk

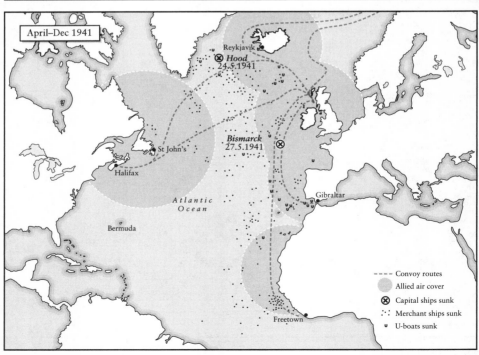

April–Dec 1941

Reykjavik

⊗ *Hood*
24.5.1941

St John's

Halifax

Bismarck
27.5.1941

*Atlantic
Ocean*

Bermuda

Gibraltar

Freetown

- - - Convoy routes
Allied air cover
⊗ Capital ships sunk
∴ Merchant ships sunk
U U-boats sunk

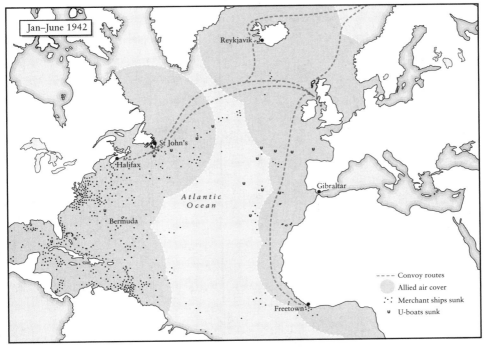

Jan–June 1942

Reykjavik

St John's

Halifax

Atlantic
Ocean

Bermuda

Gibraltar

Freetown

- - - Convoy routes
Allied air cover
Merchant ships sunk
U-boats sunk

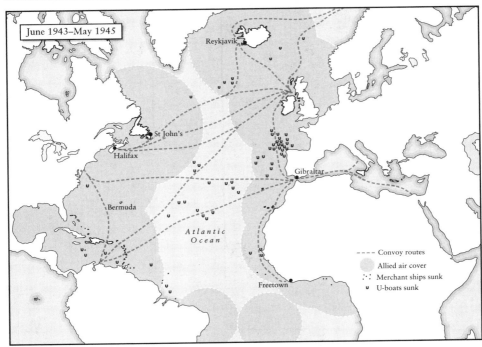

June 1943–May 1945

Reykjavik

St John's

Halifax

Bermuda

Atlantic
Ocean

Gibraltar

Freetown

- - - Convoy routes
Allied air cover
Merchant ships sunk
U-boats sunk

N

Bay of Biscay

FRANCE

ITALY

Genoa
La Spezi

Nice

Marseilles
Toulon
⊗
Provence
27.11.42

SPAIN

CORSICA

Roma ⊗
9.9.43

SARDINIA

Januar

Eagle ⊗   *Cape Spartivento*
11.8.42

Gibraltar   November 1942   *Cape Bon*

Ark Royal ⊗
13.11.41

Bretagne
3.7.40   Algiers   Bizerte

⊗
Oran
Mers-
el-Kebir

Tunis

MOROCCO

ALGERIA (Fr)

TUNISIA
(Fr)

⊗   Capital ships sunk

- - - ▶   Operation Pedestal 10–15 August 1942

───▶   Allied landings

0   100   200   300 Miles

0   100   200   300 Km

The Mediterranean, 1940–44

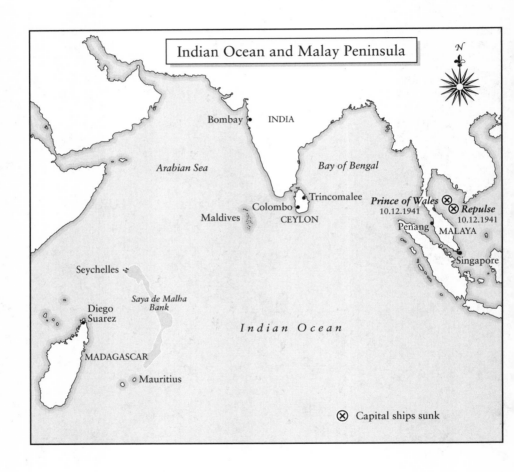

Indian Ocean and Malay Peninsula

N

Bombay
INDIA

Arabian Sea

Bay of Bengal

Trincomalee
Colombo
Maldives
CEYLON

Prince of Wales ⊗
10.12.1941

⊗ *Repulse*
10.12.1941

Penang
MALAYA

Singapore

Seychelles

Saya de Malha
Bank

Diego
Suarez

Indian Ocean

MADAGASCAR

Mauritius

⊗ Capital ships sunk

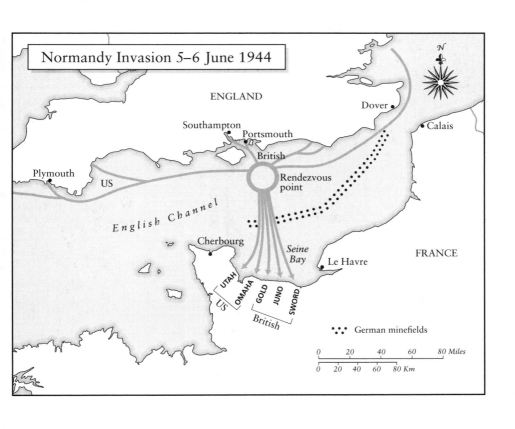

Normandy Invasion 5–6 June 1944

Sea of Japan

CHINA

JAPAN

Tokyo

Hiroshima

Haruna 28.7.45
Ise 18.7.45
Hyuga 24.7.45
Mutsu 8.6.45
Amagi 24.7.45

Nagasaki

Shinano
29.11.45

Yamato
7.4.45

Unryu 19.12.45
Shinyo 17.11.44

Kongo
21.11.44

Okinawa

Iwo Jima
Bonin Island

FORMOSA

MARIANAS
ISLANDS

Zuiho 25.10.44
Zuikaku 25.10.44

Shokaku 19.6.44
Hiyo 20.6.44
Taiho 19.6.44

Saipan
Tinian
Guam

⊗ *Princeton* 24.10.44

Musashi
24.10.44

Manila

PHILIPPINE
ISLANDS

South China
Sea

Leyte Gulf

Fuso 25.10.44
Yamashiro 25.10.44

Ulithi
Atoll

CAROLINA
ISLANDS

⊗ *Prince of Wales* 10.12.41
⊗ *Repulse* 10.12.41

Truk
Atoll

MALAYA

Singapore

BORNEO

NEW GUINEA

Manus Island

SUMATRA

Lae
Salamua

Port Moresby

PAPUA
NEW GUINE

Timor Sea

Darwin

AUSTRALIA

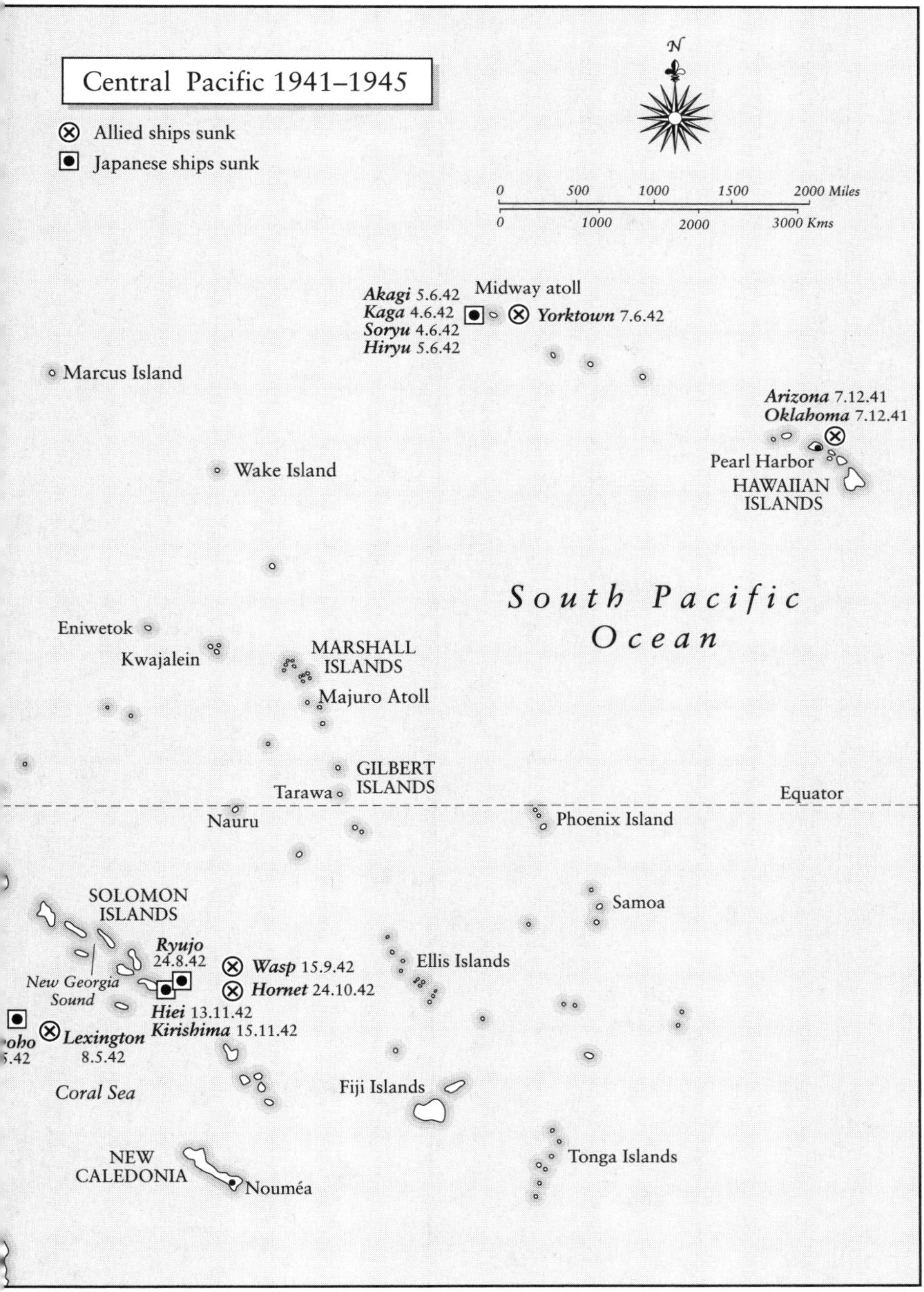

Central Pacific 1941–1945

⊗ Allied ships sunk

⊡ Japanese ships sunk

𝒩

0   500   1000   1500   2000 Miles

0   1000   2000   3000 Kms

Akagi 5.6.42   Midway atoll
Kaga 4.6.42   ⊡ ○ ⊗ *Yorktown* 7.6.42
Soryu 4.6.42
Hiryu 5.6.42

○ Marcus Island

Arizona 7.12.41
Oklahoma 7.12.41

○ Wake Island

Pearl Harbor ⊗
HAWAIIAN
ISLANDS

South Pacific
Ocean

Eniwetok ○
Kwajalein

MARSHALL
ISLANDS
Majuro Atoll

○ GILBERT
ISLANDS
Tarawa ○

Equator

Nauru   Phoenix Island

SOLOMON
ISLANDS

Samoa

Ryujo
24.8.42   ⊗ *Wasp* 15.9.42
New Georgia   ⊗ *Hornet* 24.10.42   Ellis Islands
Sound   *Hiei* 13.11.42
Kirishima 15.11.42
⊡ ⊗ *Lexington*
oho   8.5.42
5.42

Coral Sea

Fiji Islands

NEW
CALEDONIA
Nouméa

Tonga Islands

INTRODUCTION

This is the last volume of a three-volume work under the general title of *A Naval History of Britain*, which extends from 660 to 1945, with an Epilogue sketching post-war developments almost up to the present day. The dates alone will warn readers that this is not a history of the Royal Navy, which can scarcely be traced as a permanent English national organization before the sixteenth century and could not strictly be called 'British' (in the modern sense of the word) before the Union of England and Scotland in 1707. The earlier volumes have attempted to trace the progress of naval warfare as a core activity, firstly of the component states of the British Isles, and then in turn of England, Scotland and Great Britain. Readers who remember the earlier volumes will understand that this is not a self-contained 'company history' of the Royal Navy, but a survey of the contribution which naval warfare, with all its associated activities, has made to national history. That certainly includes the history of the Royal Navy as an institution, but it is not limited to that: its ambition is to link naval warfare to the many other aspects of history with which it was involved. As far as the limitations of a single work and a single author will allow, this is meant as a contribution to political, social, economic, diplomatic, administrative, agricultural, medical, religious and other histories which will never be complete until the naval component of them is recognized and understood. It is an attempt to spread the meaning of naval history well beyond the conduct of war at sea and the internal affairs of the Royal Navy, and to treat it instead as a national endeavour, involving many, and in some ways all, aspects of government and society.

It follows that this book, like its predecessors, tries to make connections, not all of which have been explored or even noticed, and about which we still know too little to reach definite conclusions. Specialists in the numerous aspects of national history on which this book trespasses will doubtless deplore the author's ignorance of them: his hope is that they will be stimulated to do it better. Readers whose primary interest is in war at sea may be disappointed that nearly half the book is devoted to the background rather than the foreground of naval history, but this is quite deliberate, for there is no understanding battle and campaigns otherwise. The book is arranged in four parallel narratives: policy and operations; government and administration, including all sorts of technical and industrial support; social history; and the material elements of sea power, ships, weapons and (in the twentieth century) air-craft. Chapters are devoted to each of these themes in turn, but they are not meant to be read in isolation. The author's intention is to unite rather than to divide.

The same applies to the national scope of the work. This is a naval history of Britain because it attempts to gather all the activities of the British state and society which had to do with making war at sea or preparing to do so. Implicitly or explicitly all history has a standpoint, and this work has a Brit-ish standpoint, but it is addressed to English-speaking readers everywhere, and it tries as far as possible to maintain an unpartisan and even-tempered position. The sea connects different nations both in friendly and hostile rela-tions. It is impossible to write a naval history of Britain without taking seri-ously the naval histories of the many nations which became her friends or enemies at sea. It is the historian's duty to seek out the truth about the past, which is invariably the first draft of prsent reality, and to compare and recon-cile the different narratives, which historians of different countries have left us. As far as his time and linguistic competence would allow, the author has tried to read widely in the histories of all the participants in the naval wars of the nineteenth and twentieth centuries, particularly those which were Brit-ain's friends or enemies, such as France, Spain, Russia, Ottoman Turkey, Ger-many, Italy, the Netherlands, Norway, Sweden, Denmark, Japan, Canada, Australia, New Zealand and the United States. All this is largely based on printed sources, as it must be in a work on this scale, very much enriched by unpublished theses and dissertations, and garnished in places with my own researches. Most of the facts and many of the ideas will be known to special-ists, but there remain many connections of cause and effect which are not generally understood.

Readers deserve a word of explanation of the title *The Price of Victory*. It may remind some readers of Rudyard Kipling's couplet, 'If blood be the price of admiralty, Lord God, we ha' paid in full!,'[1] but this was not what was in my mind. In fact, naval warfare in most ages and most countries has been an affair of high technology rather than mass slaughter. It has always been costly, but not in human life so much as in money and industrial resources. This volume will argue that Britain rose during the nineteenth century to a commercial and financial supremacy which depended on the command of the sea and the mer-chant fleet to exploit it. In the era of the world wars of the twentieth century, that supremacy was challenged by new enemies and weapons which were in the end defeated, but at a high price that weakened the national economy thereafter. This is the 'price of victory' to which my title refers.

I have explained at the beginning of the Epilogue my reasons for avoiding an abrupt end to the book in 1945. Instead, I have lightly traced naval history into the early years of this century, to build a bridge stretching from my detailed narrative almost into the current age. Further than this the historian cannot advance. It is time to pass the torch to others:

> Augescunt aliae gentes, aliae minuuntur,
> Inque brevi spatio mutantur saecla animantum
> Et quasi cursores vitai lampada tradunt.[2]

———•◆•———

ONE

Directing the March of Other Nations
Policy and Operations 1815–1840

In the modern popular imagination, nineteenth-century Britain was the superpower of the age, bestriding Europe and the world with its mighty empire and its unchallengeable industrial supremacy. Not much of this was true in 1815, when the powers which had defeated Napoleon gathered in Vienna to settle the future shape of Europe. As the war ended, the four leading allies (Austria, Prussia, Russia and Britain) were about equal in military strength, but the British had by far the largest fleet. Within a few years the British army had shrunk drastically, and the number of active ships likewise, though there remained a large fleet in reserve. The industrial 'revolution' was only in its early stages, and it seems to have been less a revolution than a gentle evolution, as yet contributing relatively little to British economic growth. The British economy was predominantly based on trade, not industry: a warehouse of the world rather than a workshop.[1]

As for empire, British statesmen were at pains to avoid it. The word reminded them of Bonaparte and military dictatorship; the catastrophe of the American War of forty years before was not forgotten, and its aftermath had taught them that trade and prosperity could be had without taking on the thankless burden of governing overseas territories. As the Duke of Wellington wrote in 1829, reacting against a proposal to annexe the Falkland Islands, 'We have possession of nearly every valuable post and colony in the world, and I confess I am anxious to avoid exciting the attention and jealousy of other powers by extending our possessions and setting the example of gratification of a desire to seize more territories.'[2] 'All we want is trade,' declared Lord Palmerston later, 'and land is not necessary for trade; we can carry on commerce on ground belonging to other people. Possession of land involves civil and military establishments and responsibility.'[3] Having conquered most of the colonial empires of France and the Netherlands during the Napoleonic Wars,

Britain handed them back at the peace, retaining only a small number of key naval bases. Malta, Ceylon, Mauritius and the Cape of Good Hope were of small or no economic value, but they made it possible to safeguard British shipping over much of the world. At the Vienna Congress in 1815, Lord Castlereagh, the British Foreign Secretary was at pains to ensure that the peace treaty left other European powers no scope to disturb the world beyond Europe.[4]

At home, however, Britain's situation was one of anxiety and instability. Britain had won the war by growing into a gigantic 'fiscal-military state' whose government swallowed about one-fifth of all national income (approximately the same as in 1944). Nobody thought this was economically or politically sustainable. The government's first priority was to protect liberty and property by reducing the state to something like its pre-war size, but there were no painless ways to get there. Against the wishes of Lord Liverpool's government, the House of Commons voted in 1816 to abolish income tax out of hand, cutting off the main source of wartime revenue when the Navy and army were only just beginning to demobilize. The result was a financial crisis, an enormous government deficit, and a chaotic collapse of economic activity with widespread unemployment and distress. Violent business cycles and frequent bank failures in the following years added to suffering and instability.[5]

The political situation was confused, public opinion disturbed and unpredictable. British government was controlled by Parliament, but both Houses essentially represented property rather than the people. It was therefore a matter of controversy whether, and if so how, the right to vote might be extended by enfranchising some of the areas (now including several big cities) which elected no MPs, or by reducing the property qualification for the franchise, which varied from place to place but was everywhere designed to keep voting rights in the hands of those with a stake in the country. 'God had ordained that the cream of British society would ultimately rise to the top through the accumulation of property, and popular government would topple the institutions that safeguarded this "natural" mechanism for the promotion of honest, responsible, efficient, and safe political leadership.'[6] The French Revolution, which had ruined France and plunged Europe into twenty years of destructive war, was an awful warning to the propertied classes of the dangers of change – but for the poor and powerless it offered many instructive lessons in how an established order might be overthrown.

There was as yet no stable party system in Parliament, but the various groups and personal followings fell roughly into a number of categories. Lord Liverpool and his Cabinet colleagues were the heirs of the younger Pitt's tradition of moderate, reforming Toryism, ready to adapt the structures of government and abolish obvious abuses in the interests of preserving stability. A great deal of its support came from the middle classes, most of whom did not yet have the vote. In the years after Waterloo, Tory ministries worked steadily to retrench government and eliminate waste. Opposed to them were the Whigs, the aristocratic party which in its own view had inherited the right and duty to rule the country and safeguard its freedom by checking the power of the Crown. The Whigs claimed to act on behalf of the liberty of the people, by which they meant their civil liberty to live in peace under the rule of law, safe from the fear of royal absolutism. They emphatically did not mean to extend political liberties such as the right to vote to the unpropertied: for them franchise reform meant enfranchising property-holders. It was the Whigs' duty to guard power in the interests of the country, not to share it with those whose birth and upbringing disqualified them from responsibility – which meant everybody, including even recent recruits to the peerage, who did not meet their exclusive standard of birth and wealth. In the 1820s a new group arose on the left wing of the Tories, almost a third party, often called the Peelites after their leader Sir Robert Peel. The Peelites were more open to political change than the 'ultra' Tories, and more open to social change than the Whigs. The Liberals were a more middle-class movement of opinion, many of them connected with commerce and industry, the first generation strongly influenced by Scottish intellectual currents. They were moved by a determination to reduce government to a minimum, promoting virtue and freedom in society. The Liberals embraced the new science of political economy as a guide to the reform of government, rather than leaving well alone if possible, as the Tories and Peelites preferred. In time the Liberals were to become closely identified with Evangelical religion, and an almost religious devotion to free trade not only as an economic policy, but as a moral movement rendering war impossible. The Whigs admitted the merits of some Liberal policies but tended to find the Liberals themselves socially unacceptable. The great difficulty of the Whigs was that they were so exclusive a caste that there were not many of them: by themselves they could form a Cabinet, but hardly a government. From the 1830s there was an increasing tendency for Whigs, Peelites and Liberals to occupy overlapping political territory, while remaining socially distinct groups. Those on the Radical left wing of the Liberals were especially aggressive in identifying 'corruption' in every area of administration. Indeed, if the only good government was a minimal government, any large expenditure, on the Navy and army for instance, was for them inherently corrupt. The Radical 'Manchester Party', led by the MPs Richard Cobden and John Bright, made a particular target of the aristocracy and the allegedly 'aristocratic' armed services as the means by which they helped themselves to public money, starting wars to line their own pockets. Naturally the Whigs, for whom aristocracy was the solution rather than the problem, did not share these views. Beyond the Radicals again were the Chartists, popular agitators demanding universal male suffrage.[7]

Much more fundamental to the nature of society than politics was religion, in which almost everybody was practically involved and emotionally committed. The late eighteenth-century revival and reform associated with John Wesley and others had convulsed the Church of England and set off shocks throughout English-speaking Protestantism which were still shaking church structures fifty years later. The most powerful movement to emerge from this was Evangelicalism, itself divided between various theologies and present in related forms in the Church of England, the Church of Scotland, the Church of Ireland, in Nonconformity (meaning Protestant denominations outside the established churches), and in a rapidly multiplying range of charismatic and apocalyptic sects. 'Vital religion', as it called itself, a faith of serious commitment and activity in the world, associated with a generally conservative political stance, had an enormous social and political impact on the nineteenth century. In politics it was especially present among Liberals and the Peelite wing of the Tories; in social terms it appealed most to the middle classes and to the propertied. Its first unifying cause was the ending of the slave trade, and then of slavery itself (abolished in most British territories in 1833): a great act of atonement to avert the wrath of God by redeeming the slaves from bondage and the slave-owners from sin. Few areas of national life were untouched by the Evangelical spirit of urgent moral commitment, but it certainly did not appeal to the Whigs, who emphasized their superiority over middle-class manners and morality by personal lives of ostentatious vice and decadence. 'It was generally held that to offer religion to a Whig was the equivalent of offering garlic to a vampire.'[8]

Religion in turn introduces another range of fault lines dividing British society. In Wales, Cornwall and much of the north of England, and in industrial districts everywhere, most of the working classes were Nonconformists rather than Anglicans, which implied that the religious as well as the political establishment would be threatened by any large increase in the franchise. In Ireland the choices were harder. The 1801 Act of Union had created the United Kingdom of Great Britain and Ireland, but the adjective 'united' was a prospectus rather than a description. Pitt the Younger's plan had been to bring lasting peace to Ireland by outflanking the political power of the Protestant 'ascendency' and forcing on them religious toleration for the Catholics who formed the majority of the common people of Ireland. His failure had left 'Catholic emancipation' as an open wound in the political system. If property was the foundation of political legitimacy, as Whigs and Tories agreed, then Irish politics had to be all Protestant (and largely all Anglican), since the Catholic propertied classes had been almost extinguished by prolonged persecution. If Catholicism was the enemy of freedom, as all Protestants had believed for centuries, then religious toleration was incompatible with political liberty. A figure like Granville Sharp, a founder of the Society for the Abolition of the Slave Trade and first chairman of the Protestant Union, was being completely consistent according to Evangelical lights in promoting the emancipation of slaves and opposing the emancipation of Catholics, for there could be no secure freedom for slaves or anybody else unless Catholicism were suppressed.[9] Very deeply rooted emotional and intellectual commitments stood in the way of compromising these principles, but without compromise there could be no peaceful political settlement in Ireland, and no united kingdom. Readers may think that politics and religion have nothing to do with naval history, but they had everything to do with the policies and purposes of government. The Navy was one of the most important agents of British policy, and it is impossible to explain what it was doing without explaining what British governments were trying to achieve.

The essential requirement for British safety was a stable European settlement with safeguards against any revival of French aggression. This could be assured so long as the victorious powers – the 'concert of Europe' as they called themselves – played in tune, but this harmony broke down quite rapidly. The reactionary outlook of the restored Bourbon monarchy made it a natural friend of Russia, and led it to support right-wing claimants to the thrones of Spain and Portugal. Even Tory governments were dangerously left-wing by continental standards, and found reactionary (and Catholic) governments distasteful; what was worse, with the support of such allies France might find an opening to restore her former power. The instability of much of Europe was a constant worry to British governments, and generated frequent employment for its warships. The ideal was never to have to open fire, but by the timely presence of powerful ships to remind other powers of the unwisdom of disturbing the status quo. 'Diplomats and protocols are very good things,' declared Lord Palmerston, 'but there are no better peacekeepers than well-appointed three-deckers.'[10] British naval policy in the immediate post-war years was based on building up the fleet to its pre-war strength of one hundred ships of the line and 160 frigates. As before, most of these ships would lie in reserve most of the time, but the capacity to mobilize them was the ultimate deterrent, and it was assumed from experience that the Navy would be able to raise sufficient men (about 100,000) in a year. Although not explicitly based on a 'two-power standard', this fleet would be adequate to match any alliance of France and Russia, which in 1818 Lord Castlereagh identified as 'the only one that can prove really formidable to the liberties of Europe'.[11]

At first the dangers to the post-war settlement came mainly from outside Europe. The United States was a potentially dangerous enemy. In 1816 Congress authorized a fleet of nine ships of the line and twelve heavy frigates. Building advanced very slowly, but British officers were impressed by the big new American ships. Sir Alexander Cochrane, meeting the *North Carolina* at Toulon in 1826, declared her the 'finest ship of her class I ever saw'.[12] The unsettled Canadian frontier was an obvious area of dispute, and another was the Caribbean, where the Spanish government's attempts to reassert its authority over Cuba generated much disorder and piracy. British governments feared American ambitions in both areas, but in the event the US government steered clear of provoking another war. Heavy expenditure on the frontier fortresses of Kingston, Montreal, Quebec, Halifax (and Bermuda) progressively put Canada out of danger of a sudden attack, and the 1817 Rush–Bagot agreement demilitarized the Great Lakes, so that by the late 1820s tensions had largely relaxed.[13] In South America, Britain was an officially neutral but highly interested spectator of the wars of independence against Spain. Spanish Catholic absolutism was odious to the British public, the rebel leaders (several of whom had lived in exile in Britain) mostly professed liberal principles, and the British were still wedded to their traditional faith in South America as the land of economic promise. The South American wars also attracted British participation. Captain Lord Cochrane, one of the most brilliant frigate captains of his generation but dismissed from the Royal Navy for fraud in 1814, made a second career in the navies of Chile and Brazil in succession. There he gained new reputations for boldness in the face of the enemy, and weakness in the face of temptation; the gallantry trumpeted by his Radical friends in Britain, the dishonesty more obvious to British officers on the spot. 'It is not difficult to foresee', wrote Commodore William Bowles from Buenos Aires in December 1818,

> that the class of foreigners entrusted with the principal naval commands are as likely to use their power and influence for the gratification of their private interests or feelings as for the advantage of the country which employs them. Their Lordships will judge what sort of conduct may be expected from Lord Cochrane . . .[14]

British involvement in South American trade made it impossible to ignore the war which broke out in 1825 between the new Empire of Brazil and the 'Republic of the United Provinces' (of Argentina). Mutual blockades, privateering and amphibious warfare in and around the River Plate estuary, conducted by fleets with many British and other foreign officers and men on both sides, drew in the leading trading powers, Britain, France and the United States, to protect their merchant shipping. To preserve neutrality but keep the seas and rivers open for trade without being drawn into a shooting war called for a considerable number of warships, as well as much restraint and diplomacy from their captains.[15]

British governments of the nineteenth century claimed, usually sincerely and occasionally correctly, to be running a moral foreign policy guided by the highest religious and political principles. It was painful to them to discover how often foreigners accused them of hypocrisy. The Congress of Vienna had scarcely assembled in 1815 when the Atlantic slave trade provoked the first of many such clashes. Apart from Britain, only Denmark of all the participants had abolished the slave trade, and the others were deaf to British suggestions that they should do the same. They had all suffered during the war from Britain's high-handed redefinition of 'belligerent rights', and had no intention of encouraging peacetime interference with their trade. Worse, they immediately reminded the British that there was another slave trade of which their own people were the victims, that conducted in the Mediterranean by the cruisers of the Barbary states (the three North African principalities or 'Regencies' of Algiers, Tunis and Tripoli), against the shipping and coastal regions of Christian states. The British were deeply complicit in this trade. After some fruitless attempts at suppression by force in the seventeenth century, they had made their peace with the Regencies, and throughout the eighteenth century paid tribute to buy immunity for their shipping, leaving other Christian states (Britain's commercial rivals) to bear the brunt of Muslim slaving. The Barbary powers had been especially helpful during the French wars in providing supplies for British squadrons operating in the Mediterranean.

To the surprise of the British, other European powers demanded that the abolition of slaving start closer to home, and the British government found it had to act on behalf of its new subjects in the Ionian Islands, a former Venetian territory now ceded to Britain. So Admiral Sir Edward Pellew, newly ennobled as Lord Exmouth, took a powerful squadron to the Mediterranean in 1816 in search of a settlement. Initially Exmouth's negotiations went well, but both sides miscalculated. The Algerines were prepared to ransom Neapolitan and Tuscan slaves for a good price, but had no idea of abandoning slaving for good. In May 1816 the capture of 200 Italian coral fishermen provoked a final rupture, and on 27 August Exmouth's nineteen ships, joined by a Dutch squadron of six under Baron van de Capellen, bombarded Algiers. Exmouth knew that the city was not a soft target, and planned with care to station his ships as far as possible out of the line of fire of the most powerful Algerine batteries, but his second in command, Rear-Admiral David Milne, anchored his ship in the worst possible position and suffered heavy casualties. The Anglo-Dutch force eventually withdrew, almost out of ammunition, having done enough damage to enforce a treaty and the release of 1,100 slaves. The Algerines, however, promised nothing for the future, and this was some way from the glorious triumph mentioned in English history books. Between 1817 and 1826 their cruisers took 26 prizes with 300 slaves. Naples, Sweden, Denmark and Portugal continued to pay tribute, and in 1824 Algiers declared war on Spain and the Netherlands again. This time the British limited themselves to a blockade, which achieved nothing.[16]

By this time corsairing was in decline, but mainly because the North African cruisers were busy elsewhere. As dependencies of the Ottoman Empire, the Regencies had been called to help suppress the Greek revolt against Turkish rule which broke out in 1821. In this almost roadless country, armies moved by sea, and the Greeks' main strength was in the cruisers of little ports like Hydra, Spetses and Psara, which harried Turkish warships and transports, and financed the war effort by the profits of unrestrained piracy. The British public was enthusiastic about the Greek cause, but British warships had to protect British (including Maltese and Ionian) shipping, and the British government's long-term objective was to strengthen the Ottoman Empire as a bulwark against Russian expansion towards the Mediterranean. These aims were not easy to reconcile, nor were the parties themselves easy to deal with. 'It appears to me,' wrote Sir Edward Codrington commanding the British Mediterranean squadron, 'that the Turks are neither to be trusted nor believed; that the Greeks prefer stealing and lying to telling the truth and acting honestly; and that of the Greeks, the Ionians . . . are the worst of all.'[17]

In 1827 Codrington found himself ordered to co-operate with French and Russian ships to protect Greek civilians from Turkish massacre without giving either France or Russia any advantage, and to suppress Greek piracy without damaging the Greek struggle. The three powers agreed to force the Turks to grant Greek self-government, 'taking extreme care that the measures you adopt against the Ottoman navy do not degenerate into hostilities', though it was obvious that the Turks would not yield to anything short of force.[18] In this all but impossible situation Codrington urgently needed political guidance, but he was a Whig serving a Tory government which did not trust him, the Prime Minister George Canning died in the middle of the crisis, and (for reasons to be explained later) there was no First Lord of the Admiralty in office. On 20 October the allies found the Ottoman fleet anchored in a strong defensive position in the bay of Navarino (Pylos) in western Greece, which the allies entered. They could scarcely stay longer in these waters with winter coming on, and whoever fired first, Codrington was happy to have cut the Gordian knot by bringing on an action. The battle was bloody and desperate, with a powerful Ottoman force fighting almost to the last ship (seventeen out of twenty large ships were destroyed with the loss of three or four thousand men), but Codrington, who was the senior of the three admirals and assumed command of the trinational force, placed his ships with skill and gained a complete victory. The British public was delighted, but the British government was not. Greek independence was secured in the end, not by the warships but by the Russian army invading and marching within forty miles of Constantinople – precisely the outcome the government had most wished to avoid.[19]

The first major disturbance of the 1815 settlement in Europe was the bloodless French revolution of July 1830, which replaced the Bourbon King Charles X with his cousin Louis-Philippe. A liberal in place of a reactionary monarch pleased British Liberals, especially as Tsar Nicholas I refused to have anything to do with the usurper, but there were obvious dangers lurking in an unstable, populist monarchy – exemplified by the French invasion of Algiers which was then actually in progress.[20] One month later the Parisian revolution was imitated in Brussels by a popular revolt against Dutch rule, to the alarm of British ministers and the delight of the French, both of whom took Belgian independence to mean Belgian dependence on France. A key element of the 1815 European settlement had been the creation of the strong new Kingdom of the Netherlands, made up of the old Dutch Republic, the (formerly Austrian) southern Netherlands, Luxemburg and Liège, and endowed with the restored Dutch Empire in the East Indies. This was intended to keep the French well away from the naval bases and building yards of Antwerp and the Scheldt, where Napoleon had tried to build a new navy to challenge Britain. Now they were once more available to the French, and all the more dangerous because Belgium was becoming the first industrial nation of continental Europe. This generated a prolonged diplomatic and military crisis lasting into 1833, which tied down much of the Royal Navy in a blockade of the Dutch coast. The eventual resolution of this crisis in 1839, with an international guarantee of Belgian neutrality and the rearrangement of frontiers in a manner acceptable to Britain, was a great achievement of Palmerston, the more notable as he was

Foreign Secretary of an uneasy coalition ministry in the midst of a major constitutional crisis – though it was to have unforeseen consequences seventy-five years later.[21]

Long before the Belgian crisis was resolved, the Navy had been drawn into the troubled internal affairs of Portugal. The Liberal revolution of 1820 brought in an anti-clerical government and indirectly led to the independence of Brazil under King John VI's son Dom Pedro, but Pedro's younger brother Dom Miguel led a rebellion aiming to restore autocratic government to Portugal. The result was a long civil war in which Britain sympathized with the Constitutionalists and deterred Spain from aiding the Miguelite cause, until in 1828 Wellington withdrew British warships from the Tagus, allowing the Miguelites to seize Lisbon. For the next four years both the Navy and the British government were too preoccupied elsewhere to pay much attention to Portugal. By 1832 Dom Pedro had succeeded his father as Emperor of Brazil, and his daughter Donha Maria represented the remnants of the Constitutionalist cause still holding out in the Azores. The Liberal ministry in London very much sympathized with her, as did Sir William Parker the Whig admiral commanding the British ships in the Tagus, but Britain's official policy was strictly neutral. Both sides in the Portuguese civil war had fleets; the Constitutional forces at Porto illegally commanded by a British officer, the Whig Captain Charles Napier, discreetly favoured by the Admiralty and supplied by Parker with intelligence on his Absolutist enemies in Lisbon. Palmerston was playing a delicate double game, ostensibly neutral though actually favouring Donha Maria. He had only three ships of the line to back his diplomacy, but Parker, his agent on the spot, was a skilful diplomat and strategist. On 5 July 1833 Napier captured almost the whole Miguelite fleet off Cape St Vincent, and the following year Donha Maria acceded to the throne. The whole campaign was a triumph of bold, risky and unscrupulous naval diplomacy in the Whig interest.[22] It was immediately followed by a more overt intervention in the Carlist War in Spain, where the government of Queen Isabel II was challenged by the conservative forces of her uncle Don Carlos. In this case Palmerston caused the Foreign Enlistment Act to be suspended, allowing the Radical MP Colonel George de Lacy Evans to raise a 'British Legion' which fought against the Carlists with the active support of detachments of Royal Marines.[23]

When Britain outlawed the slave trade in 1808, what ships could be spared from the war effort to suppress it could act as easily against foreign slavers as British ones, since almost all the nations active in the Atlantic slave trade were also Britain's enemies in the war. After 1814 other slaving countries could only be enlisted in the cause by diplomatic agreement, which was exceptionally difficult to obtain. The trade was highly profitable in itself, the supply of slaves essential to tropical agriculture in the Americas, and Britain's humanitarian pretensions easily dismissed as hypocrisy. Although Britain called for an international movement to suppress the trade, in practice only British ships were made available, and virtually nobody was ready to tolerate British cruisers stopping and searching their shipping as they had done in wartime. Most shipowning nations, even those which had declared against the trade, refused to allow their flag to be violated by foreign searches however strong the presumption of guilt in individual cases, so slavers had only to hoist, say, the French or American flag, and carry on unscathed. In any case there was no question of 'guilt' in countries which had not made the trade illegal. The United States had officially abolished the slave trade in 1808, but with no provision for enforcement. Slavery itself remained an untouchable institution fundamental to the political and economic constitution of the republic, and slaves continued to be discreetly imported through the Caribbean. American warships occasionally cruised in the Atlantic 'against the slave trade', but officers well understood that actually interfering with an American ship would be fatal to their careers.

By 1822 only three countries (Portugal, Spain and the Netherlands) had signed anti-slaving treaties, none of them effective. In 1818 Castlereagh tried to circumvent the legal obstacles by proposing that slaving be regarded as equivalent to piracy, but neither foreigners nor British lawyers agreed with this dubious idea, and it would only have transferred the problem to an even more uncertain area of law. The independence of nation states and the rule of law in international affairs were what distinguished civilized states from barbarians, but British public opinion insisted that slavery was sinful or barbarous, and trampled on international law. By the late 1830s Britain was paying a very heavy price in lives and money, and a heavier price in unpopularity and humiliation abroad, for a largely ineffective, inconsistent and seemingly hypocritical antislavery campaign.[24]

British action against pirates faced similar legal and diplomatic obstacles. In the Caribbean in the 1820s there was extensive piracy linked to the rebellions against Spanish rule. British and American ships officially co-operated against the pirates, but the US position was more supportive of the nascent South American republics. In Greek waters, as we have seen, it was acutely difficult to distinguish between Greek heroes fighting for national independence, and Greek pirates preying on the peaceful shipping of all nations, when in reality they were the same people doing almost the same thing.[25] In the East equally tricky questions presented themselves. In the Persian Gulf between 1800 and 1820 the ships and troops of the Bombay Presidency of the East India

Company fought a series of campaigns against the Qawasīm 'pirates', culminating in the storming of their capital of Ras-al-Khaimah in December 1819. It was and is a matter of some controversy whether these events should be understood as a righteous campaign against Arab pirates threatening the freedom of navigation, an unjustified interference in local tribal warfare, or an unprovoked aggression designed to seize Arab trade to the profit of Bombay.[26] In the East Indies tribal warfare afloat was endemic, and some rulers specialized in piracy and slaving. Their victims were chiefly the less warlike local populations, but European shipping was sometimes attacked. Radical critics in the House of Commons insisted that British warships had no right to waste public money interfering with local customs such as head-hunting, and the Royal Navy seems to have taken a detached view – until a statute of 1825 offered generous bounties: £20 for every pirate captured or killed, and £5 for each one who escaped. This sort of head-money was traditional for captured warships and privateers in European warfare, when the prize's papers or the oath of her officers would establish the numbers to the Admiralty Court's satisfaction.

In the Malay world where ship's papers were unknown there was a problem of evidence, which the 1825 Bounty Act solved by accepting the affidavit of the British officer making the claim. In 1844 the hydrographer Captain Sir Edward Belcher, surveying on the coast of Borneo in two boats with a total of twenty-six officers and men, was attacked, it seems, by 1,330 heavily armed pirates, of whom he claimed to have killed 350 (at £20 each) and driven off the remaining 980 (at £5 each). It is painful to report that the Treasury cast doubt on Belcher's claim, but happily the wording of the act did not allow for the possibility of disbelieving an officer's word of honour. Stephen Lushington, Judge of the High Court of Admiralty, took the view that anyone who fought against a British warship could be classified as a pirate automatically, while Captain Henry Keppel allowed himself and his ship to be enlisted by James 'Rajah' Brooke, a British adventurer who with the Navy's support carved out a principality for himself by a series of campaigns far upriver in Sarawak.[27] Between 1840 and 1847 bounties totalling £93,005 were paid for 151 Chinese pirates sunk or taken in eleven different actions. This act was then replaced by one less liable to abuse, under which £56,238 was paid for forty-five claims between 1851 and 1869.[28]

It is easy and tempting to write peacetime naval history as a series of episodes of active service, passing in silence over everything else. This would be a distortion of reality in any era, but especially so in the first half of the nineteenth century. Although the Navy was now barely one-sixth of its recent size (the numbers serving fell below 23,000 in 1817), there was all the more reason to justify the Service's existence by activities which satisfied Parliament, the public and, not least, naval officers themselves. It is rather too simple to reduce these activities to the single category of 'science', which involved a range of intellectual, social, political and religious considerations, and meant different things to various distinct (and often opposed) constituencies. Moreover, as contemporaries were slow to realize, the advancement of knowledge solved few problems by itself. Science had to be translated into innovation, practical technology adapted to real problems, a process which generated many tensions between the well-to-do 'gentlemen of science' who promoted the intellectual advance, and publicly funded bodies like the Admiralty which represented practical users. The period has traditionally been seen as dominated by Sir Francis Beaufort, Hydrographer of the Navy from 1829 to 1855, but in fact he was only one of several powerful figures, mostly in or near the Admiralty, who directed what we may broadly call 'naval science'. They had to bridge the often awkward gaps between independent gentlemen and government departments, between pure and applied science, which often met, and sometimes collided, at semi-official scientific institutions like the Royal Society, the Royal Institution and the British Association for the Advancement of Science.[29]

At the beginning of this period there were no reliable charts – and often no charts at all – of most of the world, including much of Britain's home waters; the first Admiralty Chart Catalogue of 1825 listed no chart of the west coast of England and Scotland north of Liverpool. In Beaufort's first full year, 1830, nineteen new Admiralty charts were published. In the early 1840s there were up to twenty-six survey ships in service at once; by 1849 charts issued had risen to seventy-nine in a year, and by 1855, to 130. From 1834 'Notices to Mariners' conveyed regular corrections to published charts, and Admiralty chart agents were obliged to correct their stock to keep them up to date. All this information, much of it of strategic value, was sold at low prices to the seafarers of the whole world. The first challenge of world hydrography was to discover sea level as a basis for triangulation. This was not simple. In the Irish Sea, for example, the tidal range at St David's Head was 30 feet, and fifty miles away on the Wicklow coast it was three feet. 'Mean Low Water Ordinary Springs', the proposed 'chart datum' or standard sea level, was apparently 14 feet different on opposite sides of the Irish Sea, which was impossible. Solving this problem involved addressing both theoretical and practical difficulties, inventing new instruments (tide gauges), organizing and financing an extensive international network of observers, and recruiting a large number of 'computers' (which meant skilled mathematicians, many of them women, ready to undertake a massive burden of tedious calculations for little or no reward).[30]

Hydrography was a fundamental science – without reliable charts common seafaring was perilous, free trade impracticable, and scientific study of the world impossible – but there was much more to hydrography than just navigation. In intellectual terms the naval officers of the early nineteenth century can be seen, and often saw themselves, as men of science in the late Enlightenment mould. Their task was to fill in the void of ignorance by collecting and classifying facts of every kind. They reported on climate, agriculture, zoology, botany, ornithology, mineralogy and tides. In 1849 the leading authority of the day was able to list twenty-five extensive surveys into terrestrial magnetism undertaken by naval officers within the last ten years. Officers were encouraged not only to conduct scientific research but to study the ethnology, history, languages and literature of the peoples they encountered, to take notes of inscriptions, sketch and measure ruins, collect coins and manuscripts. To those who produced 'eminently useful results' the Admiralty held out the promise of 'pecuniary reward or promotion', and several officers made their careers in scientific research: Sir Edward Parry and Sir James Clark Ross in the Arctic; Ross again on geomagnetism; Henry Foster on geodesy and magnetism; Frederick Beechey, William Hewitt and John Washington on tides; William Allen as an explorer of Africa; Robert FitzRoy on tides, meteorology and physical sciences; W. H. Smyth, Thomas Graves and Thomas Spratt as classical antiquaries; Smyth also as an astronomer; Philip Parker King as a naturalist. The Navy was substantially involved in a number of important archaeological expeditions, and Spratt was recommended for promotion by the trustees of the British Museum for his survey of the ruins of the Mausoleum at Halicarnassus. Between 1816 and 1855, eighty-five naval men became Fellows of the Royal Society, eighty-six of the Royal Astronomical Society and 181 of the Royal Geographical Society.[31]

In all these activities the naval officers were essentially imposing intellectual order on a disordered world. They were taming, civilizing and giving value to what had been chaotic and valueless. The Admiralty chart was both a symbol and an example of what they were doing; imposing a formal grid by which knowledge could be located and classified. It offered a world view; a view of the world from the seaward, a world reduced to the same conventions and symbols. This 'ordering' of the world meant both the uncovering of the underlying natural (and divine) order of creation, and the imposing of civilized order in the form of law and property rights. Order and progress were intimately linked (as they still are on the Brazilian flag), and provided a scale by which to classify the peoples of the world, from the most primitive to the most advanced and complex social structures. Naturally the most advanced were for the British those which most resembled their own, so they tended to favour stable societies ruled by a landed aristocracy. In Fiji, Lady Gordon, wife of the first British governor, alarmed her own servants by inviting the chiefs' wives to tea. 'Nurse can't understand it at all, she looks down on them as an inferior race. I don't like to tell her that these ladies are my equals, which she is not!'[32] Ranking the peoples they encountered by the sophistication of their societies, Charles Darwin and his contemporaries were remote from the genetic racialism of the late nineteenth century, because they regarded all peoples as created equal by God, and (at least in principle) equally capable of advancing to civilization. Education, toil, private property and free trade were the engines of progress, and Britain stood ready to point the way. A Commons Committee in 1837 expressed the hope that all countries might become 'partakers of that civilization, that innocent commerce, that knowledge and that faith with which it has pleased a gracious Providence to bless our own country'. 'We stand at the head of moral, social and political civilization,' declared Palmerston in 1848. 'Our task is to lead the way and direct the march of other nations.'[33]

Of course this was presented as an entirely altruistic and unselfish duty. As Sir John Barrow remarked of one of the Arctic voyages he sponsored, 'it may be truly characterized as one of the most liberal and disinterested that was ever undertaken, and every way worthy of a great, a prosperous and an enlightened nation; having for its primary object that of the advancement of science, for its own sake, without any selfish or interested views'.[34] Privately, however, British leaders were aware that their own country had benefited, and stood to benefit from the advance of civilization at least as much as any other. Moreover the voyages of exploration and survey had more than exclusively scientific motives. Scientific information shaded easily into intelligence on potential enemies; the presence of the Russians in Alaska was a significant encouragement to Arctic voyages. Botany often meant 'economic botany', the search for valuable crops such as tea, silk, rubber, sisal and cinchona (the source of quinine), which could be transplanted to British territory. As the Hydrographer of the Navy noted in 1874, 'the survey of a country prepares the way for commerce and civilization'.[35]

Prestige and international rivalry affected choices. Terrestrial magnetism was one of the great scientific subjects of the day, but there were rival schools of thought. On the Continent, Alexander von Humboldt, Carl Friedrich Gauss and others were associated with the 'Magnetic Union' (*Magnetisches Verein*) of Göttingen. Sir George Airy the Astronomer Royal was an ally, but his rival Captain Edward Sabine had the ear of Beaufort and the Admiralty. Sabine quite wrongly believed that only observation on the spot, in the northern Arctic, could fix the location of the North Magnetic Pole and win for Britain the prestige of mastering the subject. This (rather than the discovery of a 'North-West Passage', which was likely to be icebound and unusable) was the purpose of the large and costly expedition of Captain Sir John Franklin which sailed in 1845. The catastrophic result of this voyage, on which (including relief expeditions) at least 250 lives and seven British ships were lost, marked the end of an era. Parliament refused to squander more money on this sort of scientific endeavour, and the Navy found other things to do. But the essential part of its work was already done. The Navy had not created, nor tried to create, an empire of territory and overseas rule, but it had imposed a European intellectual order on the world, which was henceforth to be understood, and increasingly to understand itself, in terms of the European late-Enlightenment. Empires rose and sank like billows in the course of the nineteenth and twentieth centuries, but this empire of the mind still endures.[36]

TWO

Unity and Simplicity

Government and Administration 1815–1860

From many historical points of view, 1815 marks an obvious turning point: the end of the Napoleonic Wars and the start of a new international (or at least European) diplomatic order. From the narrower perspective of British government and administration, however, 1815 falls in the middle of a period of sustained interest in the reform of government which went back at least to the 1770s. The Whigs – in their own minds the sole proponents of reform – were out of office from 1783 to 1830, apart from the disastrous thirteen-month 'Ministry of All the Talents' of 1806–7, but the Tory governments of the intervening years were committed to pragmatic changes tending to save money and increase efficiency. That task became very urgent after the loss of the income tax in March 1816 left interest payments on the national debt consuming almost half of all government revenue, and annual deficits of up to 13 million pounds. For contemporaries this was not merely a practical danger, but a horrifying symptom of moral decay. The reality was that Parliament had abruptly abolished the revenue which had sustained the huge wartime growth of government: the public perception was that waste and corruption were rotting the fabric of society. The Whigs had more than twenty years in opposition to mature their grievances and nourish a political mythology according to which the reform of the Navy was the key to reforming government as a whole, and the first essential was to abolish the subordinate naval boards whose inefficiency and institutional conservatism had spoiled their plans in 1807.[1]

The Navy consumed 16 per cent of government revenue in 1816, and did not (briefly) fall below 10 per cent till 1823. It had to be at the centre of any attempt to balance the national books, and for many contemporaries, not only the Whigs, the obvious target was the complex structure of naval administration. The Admiralty Board in Whitehall, the 'Commissioners for

Executing the Office of Lord High Admiral', directly controlled only discipline, promotion and ship movements, but it received ministers' strategic
instructions, and in response generated administrative orders to the Navy
Board, a mile away in Somerset House, which ran the dockyards and built
ships, and to its neighbour the Victualling Board, which fed the Navy and
maintained substantial Victualling Yards at home and abroad. In 1816 the
Victualling Board absorbed the Transport Board, which had itself taken over
responsibility for the naval medical service and for prisoners of war in 1806 –
the reduction of five boards to three being of course driven by the search for
economy and efficiency. Beyond the naval administration proper, and beyond
Admiralty authority, the Ordnance Board was an independent department
responsible for supplying the Navy's guns, but also charged with responsibilities to the army which had grown during the Napoleonic Wars to dominate its business.[2]

The weakest part of naval administration and government lay at the centre.
The Admiralty Board was a political body made up of junior politicians early
in their careers, and officers chosen for political loyalty rather than familiarity
with naval or any other sort of administration. Lord Melville, First Lord with
one short break from 1812 to 1830, was a powerful politician who controlled
thirty Scottish M Ps, but after the 1830 Reform Act such figures largely disappeared. Later, First Lords were more often of the second rank, perhaps a bright
young man in his first ministerial post, or an experienced minister in his
declining years. There was no formal position of First Sea Lord, but in some
ministries one of the naval lords (not always the most senior) was politically
trustworthy and acted as 'confidential Sea Lord'. The most significant permanent figure in the Admiralty was the senior Secretary, the forceful Irish politician and man of letters John Wilson Croker, who in early 1816 (just before the
loss of the Income Tax) was able to push through a new career structure for
Admiralty clerks, with higher salaries, on an incremental scale with promotion on merit. In effect he had set up something foreshadowing a modern civil
service, forty years before it reached the rest of Whitehall. But Admiralty clerks
still spent most of their time on copying and drudgery, and even the most
senior of them had limited power to take decisions. In retirement in 1856,
Croker complained that the new civil service examination meant that only
university graduates would now be eligible for Admiralty clerkships: a 'system
of training race horses for the plough'.[3] The Admiralty's political and administrative ability to force unwelcome change on the Navy or Victualling Boards
was negligible – but the naval administration was a titan compared to the rest
of government. The Cabinet was of course composed of ministers chosen for

their political and social weight rather than for any knowledge of their departments, and they had much less assistance available than the Admiralty Board did. In 1815 the entire personnel of the Home Office numbered seventeen, and of the War and Colonial Department, fourteen. By comparison, the Admiralty Office had a staff of 65, the Navy Office 225, the separate Navy Pay Office 120, and the Victualling Office 209.[4]

In February 1827 Lord Liverpool's stroke led to a new government formed by the brilliant but distrusted George Canning, with whom Melville among others refused to serve. Casting about for an alternative, Canning took up the original idea (apparently proposed by Croker) of reviving the office of Lord High Admiral (which had been in commission since 1709), and bestowing it on Prince William Henry, the Duke of Clarence, whose naval career during and after the American War – fuelled by much enthusiasm, some talent, and no judgement at all – had caused not a little embarrassment to the Navy and to his father King George III. Canning's idea was to leave in place the former Admiralty Board, now renamed the Lord High Admiral's Council, to run the Navy under a distinguished royal figurehead with no authority to act on his own. Clarence was then heir to his ailing brother King George IV and constitutionally (as well as personally) unfit to sit in Cabinet, so one of the naval lords, Vice-Admiral Sir George Cockburn, was made a Privy Councillor to act as a quasi-minister, which indeed his powerful intellect and long Admiralty experience made him well capable of doing. Then Canning died in August 1827, the succeeding ministry fell apart, and not till January 1828 did the Duke of Wellington form a stable administration. Clarence had a year to play the Lord High Admiral according to his own ideas, which were not those of a powerless figurehead. With generous enthusiasm he entertained, ordered experiments and improvements – some of them sensible, all of them expensive – supported the Whig opposition against the king's government, warmly congratulated Codrington on his embarrassing victory at Navarino and gave promotions more generously than for Trafalgar. Clarence resented the existence of his Council and had no intention of being trammelled by it. Personally and politically he loathed the Tory Cockburn, whom he forbade to correspond with commanders-in-chief, thus depriving Codrington among others of the customary political and diplomatic guidance from government. In the summer of 1828 Clarence went down to Plymouth without telling anybody and took Sir Henry Blackwood's squadron to sea for exercises. The final straw was his demand that George IV dismiss Cockburn for offering unpalatable counsel. 'What becomes then of Sir George Cockburn's [Privy Council] oath,' the king wrote to his brother, his duty towards me, his sovereign, if he fails to offer such advice as he may think necessary to the Lord High Admiral? Am I, then, to be called upon to dismiss the most useful and the most important naval officer in my service for conscientiously acting up to the letter and spirit of his oath and his duty? The thing is impossible . . . you must give way.

So Clarence resigned, the Admiralty Board was restored under Melville, and all involved wondered uneasily what would happen when the duke became king.[5]

Earl Grey, the Prime Minister in the mainly Whig ministry of 1830, had briefly served as First Lord of the Admiralty in 1806, but he was one of the few ministers with any experience in government at all. Sir James Graham, the new First Lord, had made his reputation by his contribution to planning and passing the Reform Bill – the principal achievement of the ministry, and the greatest constitutional crisis of the era, in the course of which the new king William IV exercised his responsibilities with a degree of common sense which showed that he had learnt something as Lord High Admiral. Graham knew nothing about the Navy, and was as astonished as everyone else to find himself at the head of the Admiralty. The Navy was second only to the franchise in the Whig reform programme, indeed the two were essentially linked because the new ministry had to make massive economies to win Parliamentary support, but beyond the basic idea of abolishing the Navy Board, it had very little idea how to achieve them. Fortunately for Graham he could call on a good deal of bipartisan support and something like a ready-made plan. Melville had his own experience of the Navy Board's resistance to change, and in February 1829 had sharply reduced its autonomy, while John Barrow the second Secretary of the Admiralty, though a Tory in politics, had a scheme ready to offer to the new First Lord and remained in office to help. The main opposition came from the Controller of the Navy, Admiral Sir Thomas Byam Martin. He might have made a claim to be considered as a permanent official, but preferred to appear as a powerful Tory politician. Able and hard-working, after fifteen years at the head of the Navy Board he knew more about naval administration than anyone else in government or out of it; as an Admiral of the Blue and a Knight Grand Cross of the Order of the Bath he greatly outranked the entire Admiralty Board, whose senior naval member Sir Thomas Hardy was only a Rear-Admiral; he had been eighteen years MP for Plymouth where his family interest was reinforced by the dockyard's patronage – and he was an old friend and shipmate of the new king. All this made Byam Martin a dangerous opponent, but his uncompromising hostility to the 'noisy ignorant blockheads [who] seem to forget that the safety and glory of England depends upon her naval strength and her constant and ample state of naval preparation' – many of whom were of his own party – undermined his strong position and he was eventually forced out of office and the House of Commons.[6]

Byam Martin was one of the few opponents of Graham's reforms to resist them on principle from a real understanding of the issues. For most politicians it was enough that savings were desperately wanted, and getting rid of a lot of people would achieve them. The Benthamite principle of 'individual responsibility' provided the Whigs with a respectable cover for the visceral anger they had long felt towards a naval administration which they blamed for the failure of Earl St Vincent's 'reforms' thirty years before, and the collapse of their government in 1807.[7] Graham aimed to secure 'a just division of labour, an undivided control, and a due responsibility on the one hand, and, on the other, that unity and simplicity which he held to be the very essence and life of public business'.[8] The attack on boards as inherently inefficient and tending to dissipate responsibility had force, but Graham and the Whigs were not really much interested in administrative efficiency. They cared about power, which ought to belong only to themselves as ministers responsible to Parliament, not to officials many of whom were political enemies but not political appointments, and therefore neither answerable to Parliament nor dismissible on a change of government. 'The system which has hitherto been pursued', Graham wrote,

> although sanctioned by long usage, is in direct contradiction to the principle of undivided responsibility; and the whole history of the civil concerns of the Navy, from the first establishment of the dockyards to the present time, exhibits the fatal effects of clashing interests and rival powers – the consequence has been, inattention to the public welfare, gross neglect of important duties, a systematic counteraction of the supreme powers of the Board of Admiralty, an extravagant expenditure of stores, [and] gross peculation in a variety of instances . . .[9]

For Graham and most of his contemporaries an essential remedy was to confine naval expenditure strictly to the items voted by Parliament, rather than treating the Navy Estimates as a pool of money able to flow wherever it was needed, as the Navy Board had done. By 1818 the Treasury was requiring annual Estimates, approved in advance by the Cabinet and not to be exceeded without authority from the Prime Minister and the Chancellor of the Exchequer. This formalized the Cabinet's long-standing supremacy and expressed it in accounting terms; it meant that the First Lord had influence on the Estimates more as a Cabinet minister than as the head of the Admiralty. Wellington, who had imposed modern accounting on the Ordnance Board, fully approved, and Melville in 1829 replaced the Navy Board's unique and opaque accounting system. Graham changed the Navy's financial year to match the Parliamentary calendar, and made payments by cash or drafts rather than thirty-day Navy Bills, meaning that for the first time in history the Navy had no standing debt of its own. He divided the Estimates into numerous headings and forbade 'virement' (transfer) of money between them without Treasury approval. Not much of this was controversial. For most of the political nation, ensuring public money was spent only as Parliament had voted was a fundamental piece of political honesty, which would automatically promote the inseparable twin virtues of economy and efficiency. Not until much later in the century did it begin to dawn on some public men that ruthless economy and tight Parliamentary accounting might actually work against efficiency, and that efficiency and effectiveness might not be synonymous.[10]

Contemporary reformers were obsessed by Bentham's principle of personal responsibility, and largely unaware of its long-term consequences. Modern historians have tended to follow the arguments and personalities of the time, and overlook the degree to which large administrative machines depend on co-operation and co-ordination between individuals and departments – which the Benthamites in practice did a great deal to suppress. A more constructive instrument of administrative reform has been largely overlooked: the four reports of Peel's 1828 Parliamentary Committee on Public Income and Expenditure, and its chairman the eccentric Irish Whig MP Sir Henry Parnell, who did much to improve the quality of government accounts and reduce unproductive public offices. His work on the committee was continued and extended by his influential 1830 book *On Financial Reform*, and in 1835 he became the first Paymaster-General, replacing a considerable list of Treasurers and Paymasters and consolidating government financial control over the whole body of national revenue and expenditure, including of course the armed services. In the long run – in the era of the two world wars a century later – this made possible administrative reforms which the Benthamites never conceived of.[11]

Looking at the constitutional history of naval administration tends to give the impression of a great turning point in 1832 when the 'Reform ministry' abolished the Navy Board. This rather obscures the many other dimensions in which change and development were continuous. The Napoleonic Wars ended in 1815 in the middle of a major long-term programme of investment in naval infrastructure. The Plymouth Breakwater, providing a safe outer fleet anchorage in Plymouth Sound, was begun in 1812 and eventually completed fifty-three years and four million tons of stone later. A completely new dockyard, begun at Sheerness in 1813 to replace the cramped and almost ruinous seventeenth- and eighteenth-century yard, re-opened in 1823. The new building yard at Pembroke, begun in 1808, started work in the 1820s. A new naval yard on Haulbowline Island in Cork Harbour, started in 1806, was substantially complete by 1824. The year 1813 was also when the building slips began to be roofed over (copying the Swedish practice) so that ships could be built dry, and in all weathers – a key part of Byam Martin's largely successful campaign to eliminate dry rot from the Navy. A number of these bold, elegant timber canopies, some of them 100 feet in span, still stand at Devonport and at Chatham in Kent.[12]

It is remarkable that these costly wartime projects were carried to completion in a period of acute financial stringency, and more remarkable that they were followed by others on a yet bigger scale. The scattered and inadequate victualling stores at Plymouth had long been a source of expense and complaint, and in 1822 the Victualling Board began work on a consolidated depot at the mouth of Stonehouse Creek near Plymouth. Although no longer in naval use, the Royal William Victualling Yard still stands complete, a massive formal composition of fireproof buildings in dressed granite arranged around a basin, the whole covering fourteen acres. At almost the same time a similar process led to the building of the new Royal Clarence Victualling Yard at Weevil, opposite the dockyard on Portsmouth Harbour. This expensive scheme owes its existence to the support of the Lord High Admiral after whom it is named. On Bermuda a completely new naval yard, with Ordnance and Victualling yards and fortifications around them all, was built from the 1820s to 1860 to provide a base for the North America station in case of war with the United States. The geology of Ireland Island made a dry dock impossible, but in 1869 the Navy's first iron floating dock, with a lift of 10,000 tons (enough for any contemporary battleship), was towed across the Atlantic to complete the scheme.[13]

These costly projects were justified variously by administrative efficiency, strategic threats and the rapidly growing size of ships, but another significant driver was the coming of steam. The Navy's first steam vessels were tugs and dredgers employed in the dockyards. In the early 1820s the arrival of the first steam packets on the Irish Sea and cross-Channel routes presented the Post Office packet service with financial and technical challenges which it struggled to overcome. As a result the Navy took over the packet service (sail and steam) in stages, finishing it in 1837. By this time steam packets were already being used on routes to the Mediterranean and in the West Indies; the first transatlantic steam packet service was set up by the Canadian businessman

Samuel Cunard in 1840. The attraction of the packet service to the Navy was straightforward: it provided employment for some of the many hundreds of unemployed junior officers, and it gave the Navy the opportunity to learn how to handle steamers and to manage a steam fleet, at the General Post Office's expense. For this reason the initial proposal was warmly welcomed by Lord Melville and his successors. A new senior Admiralty position was created in 1837 to manage it, the Controller of Steam Machinery, first taken by the Arctic explorer Captain Sir Edward Parry. Within a few years, however, steam was becoming so important to all areas of naval activity that it was no longer appropriate or possible to segregate it, and in 1850 the Steam Department was abolished.[14]

Woolwich Dockyard, the oldest and smallest of the dockyards, with only a shallow basin and located far up the narrow and crowded Thames, was on the verge of closing in the 1820s when it was saved by the rise of steam. The early steam vessels were all small paddle steamers, shallow-draught and highly manoeuvrable, which had no difficulty in getting up to Woolwich, where most of the leading engine-builders lay near at hand. In 1836 Woolwich therefore became the Navy's first 'Steam Factory', where steam engines were repaired and engineers trained. Peter Ewart came from Boulton & Watt's Soho works in Birmingham as the first Chief Engineer and Inspector of Machinery, a new basin and docks were excavated and workshops erected. Almost at once it was clear that Woolwich was not going to be sufficient. Before it was even finished in 1844 new Steam Factories were begun at Portsmouth and Keyham, alongside but administratively separate from Portsmouth and Devonport dockyards, and there was a fourth steam factory at Malta. Already all the dockyards were using steam engines and employing millwrights and engineers to handle the new technology. The spacious basins and advanced industrial buildings of the Portsmouth and Keyham Steam Factories still stand as striking monuments to the first industrial age, and they would be better known if they were not still heavily used by the Navy and seldom open to public view. They were followed by a Steam Factory at Sheerness in 1854, the extensive Steam Yard at Chatham (built 1864–85), and a further large extension of Portsmouth in 1867.[15]

The Steam Factories maintained and repaired engines, but the Navy relied on private firms to design and build them. Although steam was a new technology, the Navy had always dealt in advanced technology, and the Navy Board handled contractors with the confidence born of three hundred years of experience. It was a 'wary pioneer', cautious but not at all conservative: it expected firms to innovate at their own expense and continually offer the Navy proven developments. It favoured established firms with a reputation for quality and reliability, which gave them an incentive to invest in new designs to retain the highly prestigious naval orders. At the same time it gave some orders to less established firms, and was always open to promising developments. All the engines were of the standard side-lever design until the steamer *Gorgon* of 1837 received John Seaward's direct-acting engine which promised higher power for lower weight. In the 1820s the leading naval contractors were Boulton & Watt, and Maudslays Sons & Field, but in 1831 Maudslays beat their rivals with a lower price and a promise of innovation, and by the 1840s the leading contractors were Maudslays, John Penn and John Seaward. All these firms were located on the Thames, close to Woolwich, to each other, and to the shipyards where the steamers were built. Scottish engineers alleged favouritism, but it is clear that the naval orders went to the best and most innovative firms, and by the early 1840s Clyde builders were gaining a prominent position in the new iron shipbuilding.[16]

The core of Graham's reform of the Admiralty followed Barrow's scheme to abolish the Navy and Victualling Boards and organize the whole naval administration into five departments, each headed by a 'Principal Officer' individually responsible to one of the Lords of the Admiralty, who in turn were politically responsible to the First Lord. The Principal Officers were the Accountant-General, the Storekeeper-General, the Comptroller of Victualling, the Physician (from 1843 Medical Director-General) of the Navy, and the Surveyor of the Navy. The Admiralty Board had little collective authority left, and its meetings served no obvious purpose. Formal chains of command now ran from individuals at the top downward, in writing, though important orders actually issued by the First Lord or one of his colleagues were still signed by the Secretary of the Admiralty 'by command of their Lordships', preserving the façade of a collective leadership which in reality had largely ceased to exist. The horizontal channels of communication formerly provided by conversation around the Board table were sharply restricted and replaced by the circulation of paperwork. At a time when the administrative load on the Admiralty was rising fast for other reasons (between 1827 and 1833 in-letters increased by 23 per cent, and out-letters by 88 per cent), the new system greatly increased the burden of correspondence laid on the Lords of the Admiralty, and especially the naval lords, who were almost the only naval officers in Whitehall, and therefore the only point of reference for all naval questions, however trivial. Barrow imagined that by leaving the dockyard and victualling administration in Somerset House, a mile away from the Admiralty, his scheme would save the Admiralty Lords from administrative details, but it only ensured that they would have to deal with them in writing. As Croker for one had foreseen, they ceased to be the responsible heads of a policy-making body and were swallowed up by routine.[17] 'It is an odd *system*,' noted the junior naval lord in 1848, 'everyone works independently in his own department and you know little of what is going on. This is all wrong, but I suppose cannot be remedied.'[18]

There were few ministers among the inexperienced Whigs who had much sense of the complexity and difficulty of government. As gentlemen, they took it for granted that it was their business to form policy and take charge, and when they encountered obstacles, they were liable to attribute them to political obstruction or the omnipresent 'corruption' which explained so many disappointments. Grey warned Graham to assert his authority over pretended experts: 'It is only in this way, and I know by experience, that any good is to be done with them. You must insist on their obeying you.'[19] For Graham it was fundamental that responsibility belonged to the First Lord alone. 'The whole system of the Admiralty is based on central superintendence and authority. Whatever impairs or impedes it is injurious.' He particularly disapproved of the presence of naval officers in Whitehall, and told a Parliamentary committee in 1861 that 'a Board only works well when the head of it makes it as unlike a Board as possible.'[20] Lord Ellenborough's brief experience as First Lord in 1846 taught him that 'the only real security for good conduct on the part of a public officer is the sense of entire and sole responsibility for everything that is done . . . [the Admiralty] is, without exception, the most inefficient [department], and the most incapable of doing good service to the public which at any time has come under my notice.'[21] Another First Lord, Sir Francis Baring, agreed that 'the entire responsibility of the administration of the Navy rests upon the First Lord.'[22]

Jeremy Bentham's principle of individual responsibility as the fundamental requirement for efficient and honest administration was generally admired, by ministers of other parties as much as by Graham and his successors. It is all the more strange to see how timidly they applied it to their largest and most costly management challenge, the dockyards. Until 1832 the management of the major home dockyards remained much as it had been since the mid-seventeenth century. The senior official was the Commissioner, usually a Captain on half-pay and always a member of the Navy Board on detached service, but he had almost no authority over the senior yard officers, who received their orders directly from the Navy Board in London. The Commissioner could supervise, advise, warn and report, but he could not command. His power to control the situation depended more on force of character than formal authority, and there was ample scope for conflict with the senior officers. They in turn were in the habit of delegating their management functions to subordinates.[23] 'Thus,' an Admiralty report of 1821 concluded,

> was this important branch of the dockyard duty (for the superintendence and control of which such high salaries are paid) for want of a proper and efficient system of control, actually carried on (in the main points of it) by individuals of the lowest class in the yard, to save trouble to the salaried officers . . . the greater number of the officers, receiving high salaries in the several departments, appeared to them [the Admiralty Board] an unnecessary and useless encumbrance, tending rather to afford a sanction to idleness than of any use in keeping the artificers to their labour. Indeed, it appeared that in proportion to the number of salaried officers in any department, was the quantity of useful labour diminished.[24]

Such an arrangement might almost have been designed to give a Benthamite apoplexy, yet Graham made it worse rather than better. The Commissioner's place was taken by the Superintendent, a captain on full pay rather than half, serving two or three years rather than fifteen or twenty, but in other respects not much changed. Instead of seeking orders from the Navy Board, the yard officers now had to apply to the Admiralty. The Surveyor of the Navy at Somerset House was responsible for ship design but could not act without written orders from the Second Naval Lord at the Admiralty. Other Admiralty lords and their principal officers had responsibilities for different activities in the yards and corresponded with different officials, but no one took responsibility for the yards as a whole. 'No one looks into their working, because it is no one's duty,' as the junior naval lord pointed out in 1852, 'and you must be aware that it is in the dock yards the large amount of naval money yearly voted by Parliament is sunk.'[25] Fifteen years later the situation had not changed. 'The management of the dockyards is vested in the Board of Admiralty, in the Senior Naval Lord, in one of two Junior Naval Lords, in the Controller of the Navy, in the Storekeeper General, and in some respects . . . in the Secretary of the Admiralty,' wrote the then Controller of the Navy, Sir Robert Spencer Robinson. 'How can there be unity of purpose, forethought or method in conducting these establishments?'[26] Lords of the Admiralty, like naval officers, were administrative amateurs, and their short terms of office left them little opportunity to learn their business. Superintendents were supposed to superintend the yards as a whole, without any authority over the individual activities which went on in them. As serving officers junior to the local commander-in-chief, they were at risk of having their nebulous authority undermined by the admiral. Whereas formerly the senior officers of the yard had met together every morning to read the Navy Board's incoming orders and arrange the work between them, from 1832 to 1847 they were forbidden to make contact with one another except in writing. When the separate Steam Factories were amalgamated with the dockyards in 1850 and the Admiralty Steam Department was put under the Surveyor, in the yards the Chief Engineers were left equal in authority to the Master Shipwrights, with no mechanism to co-ordinate their work or resolve disputes save by appealing to the Admiralty in writing.[27]

Throughout these years, indeed for most of the century, the management of the dockyard workforce was a continual difficulty. There were essentially two ways to pay the dockyardmen, by piece-work or by the day. To assess piece-work in a complex craft like shipwrightry was possible for shipbuilding (though scarcely for repairs), given tight supervision and an enormous force of measurers, highly skilled, highly impartial and applying very elaborate pricing schemes – but no First Lord was prepared to pay for so many unproductive hands, and in practice the men themselves and their foremen assessed their own work, with predictable results. Day wages avoided that problem, but the same weak management left the men to work as much, or as little, as they chose. The result in both cases was that the yards tended to work well, but not to work hard. Repeated changes of methods of payment were made without success. An almost unbroken series of committees and commissions of inquiry considered the dockyards and took voluminous minutes of evidence without discovering a solution. A very strong body of (mainly Liberal) political opinion took it for granted that the remedy to all management problems was 'business methods'; copying the practice of private shipyards. Several of the committees of inquiry were composed largely or entirely of private shipbuilders and were more or less directed to come to this conclusion, but in the real world the management of British private shipyards seems to have been if anything weaker than that of the dockyards, and their advantage lay mainly in being small and simple organizations. Moreover the dockyard shipwrights took great pride in their craft traditions and professional solidarity, and they loathed the attempts of Admiralty Boards to divide them into classes or groups according to productivity. In practice this meant rewarding the young and strong and punishing the senior and experienced, which outraged their sense of justice – the more so as yard appointments were still politicized, and there was no guarantee that any classifications would be applied fairly. Lifetime employment for established men, 'shoaling' shipwrights into gangs of mixed ability, or paying pensions to the long-serving, were regarded by Whigs like Graham as corrupt practices sheltering idleness, but by the shipwrights as integral to their way of life and labour. They were not without means of making their point, for these practices were the prime attractions of dockyard employment, and compensation for relatively low pay. In the late 1830s, after Graham had abolished superannuation and imposed a divisive scheme of classifying men into different wage groups, skilled men left the yards in such numbers as to create a crisis. Lord Minto, First Lord from 1835 to 1841, had to concede to many of the men's demands.[28]

The general opinion that the royal dockyards built to high standards but low productivity was very likely correct, but unfortunately for contemporary reformers (and modern historians) it is extremely difficult to prove. Although the yards had always expended a great deal of effort on accounts, they were seldom in a revealing form, and never available in time to be of help to management. Graham made things worse, if possible, by insisting on a form compatible with Parliamentary requirements. Richard Bromley, Accountant-General of the Navy from 1854 to 1863, instituted double-entry bookkeeping and did a good deal to improve the form of dockyard accounts, but they still provided little help to management.[29]

Graham's reforms centred almost all decisions on the individual members of the Admiralty Board, transacted all business in writing, and as far as possible removed all expert advice. In the past, policy and strategy had usually been made by the Cabinet, and it did not at first strike contemporaries as odd that the Lords of the Admiralty should be completely absorbed in routine administration. Until the late 1830s naval policy was driven mainly by domestic considerations, and economy was what Parliament demanded. Then the realities of a troubled world began to break in. With Radical MPs like Joseph Hume claiming that naval supremacy could be covered by half the existing Estimates, Whig governments demanded from the Navy more work for less money. In the 1840s the Navy was called upon to fight several naval wars (the reason Peel 'temporarily' restored income tax in 1842). In 1853 Sir James Graham returned as First Lord in the Earl of Aberdeen's administration shortly before the outbreak of a much bigger war, with Russia. His senior naval Lord Rear-Admiral Hyde Parker was crippled with gout, and the other admirals on the Board would have been of limited help, had Graham been inclined to consult them, so there was no official source of naval policy or strategy. Graham agreed entirely with his colleague W. E. Gladstone, Chancellor of the Exchequer, that war was no reason to borrow money, and consequently there was no relaxation of rigid economy. What money was available, Graham spent, not on the present war in alliance with France, but on a new fleet of steam battleships to fight France in the next war – which he expected shortly.[30]

Graham's successor as First Lord in 1834, and again from 1846 to his sudden death on 1 January 1849, was the Earl of Auckland, who 'administered the duties of his office with a sound judgement and impartiality that won him the golden opinions of the Service, in which I do not think he created an enemy'.[31] He did something to restore the Admiralty as a policy-making body, and in December 1847, with the consent of Lord John Russell the Prime Minister, he appointed Captain Alexander Milne as junior Naval Lord on an explicitly non-political basis. This had never been done before, though as junior member of the previous Board Rear-Admiral Sir William Parker had declined to become an MP and insisted on making promotions up to lieutenant from confidential reports alone. Milne's appointment was important both as a precedent for the future, and as the means of introducing a talented administrator into the Admiralty, where he remained for not less than twelve years, serving under six successive First Lords. Thoughtful, able and hard-working, Milne very soon became a sort of one-man naval staff, deploying the expertise which Graham had largely eliminated from the Admiralty. Already in 1852, still only a Captain but the sole member of the board with any experience of the Admiralty, Milne discreetly advised the incoming First Lord the Duke of Northumberland on his responsibilities.[32] Northumberland was an undistinguished naval officer who happened to have inherited a dukedom; his inexperience and the imprudence of Benjamin Disraeli, Chancellor of the Exchequer in the nine-month ministry of Lord Derby, involved them both in a scandal of political interference in dockyard appointments, which among other consequences gave Disraeli a life-long hatred of the Admiralty.[33]

On the outbreak of the Russian War in the autumn of 1853 Milne took on the entire charge of transporting a British army to the Black Sea, and later another for the Baltic, besides 44,000 Turkish troops, 15,000 Piedmontese and many French. In October 1854, as the government decided to improvise a winter campaign in the Crimea for which nothing had been prepared, the whole transport burden fell on Milne. Lord Raglan commanding the army ashore insisted that the bulk of the transport fleet be held on the spot, rather than returning for supplies. Steam transports were very scarce, but the twenty-five or so Milne was able to assemble did most of the work. For this he had to improvise colliers and a bunkering system, in the Mediterranean, the Black Sea and the Baltic. In the Crimea the only available port of Balaklava was a narrow creek too small to shelter all the needful shipping. It was urgent to unload ships as quickly as possible, but the Commissariat disintegrated into chaos and the naval Transport Agents had no authority over personnel ashore. With many essential cargoes delayed or shipwrecked, and many stores unloaded which never reached the troops three miles away on an exposed plateau, the British army passed a very hard winter. Much of this was cured by the new

Transport Board of 1855–6, on which representatives of the Navy, the army and merchant shipping worked together. Most of the weaknesses the campaign had exposed lay on the unreformed army side, but it was still somewhat ironic that an eighteenth-century administration had had to be revived to remedy the failures of a modern system, the naval part of which had just been reconstructed on the best Benthamite principles.[34]

THREE

The Shadow of a Great Name
Policy and Operations 1840–1860

In May 1839 Lord Melbourne's tottering Whig government resigned, both the Duke of Wellington and Sir Robert Peel failed to construct an alternative, and Melbourne returned to office yet weaker than before. The government was assailed by Chartist riots in England and a rising in South Wales, distress and agitation in Ireland, and revolts in Canada and Jamaica. Most worrying was the situation in the Levant. Egypt was the richest part of the Ottoman Empire; its ruler Mehmed Ali enjoyed semi-independence with his own armed forces (which had done most of the fighting in the Greek war), and French support to maintain his position against his nominal sovereign the sultan. Since Britain wished to sustain Ottoman power as a bulwark against Russia, and to keep free the overland route to India, the rise of Mehmed Ali seemed dangerous. In June 1839 his army heavily defeated the sultan's, whose fleet then defected. The French and Egyptian navies combined considerably outnumbered the British Mediterranean squadron, many of whose ships were small, old and undermanned. 'There is no doubt as you say,' Lord Minto the First Lord wrote to Admiral Sir Robert Stopford in the Mediterranean, 'that the French Squadron is ship for ship stronger than ours. This is a consequence of our having an old navy and they a wholly modern one. We must however use our old ships, and make numbers compensate for weight.'[1]

In the beginning of 1840 Stopford had twelve sail of the line to face seventeen French and nineteen Egyptian. The Cabinet was fearful of the outcome, but Lord Palmerston the Foreign Secretary kept his nerve. Austria agreed to join Britain and Turkey in restraining Mehmed Ali, and in September an Anglo-Turkish force was landed on the coast of the Lebanon, temporarily commanded by Rear-Admiral Sir Charles Napier. The situation suited Napier's genius for irregular land warfare; he attacked without orders, stormed Sidon,

and defeated an Egyptian army on Mount Lebanon. Then on 3 November Stopford's allied (British, Turkish and Austrian) squadron bombarded the strong
coastal fortress of Acre, held by the Egyptians. Stopford was an elderly Tory
(seventy-two years old and a flag officer of thirty years' standing), whom Palmerston despised as a 'superannuated twaddler . . . quite unfit for the mixed political and naval duties he had to perform'.[2] Palmerston longed to promote the
energetic Whig Napier in his place and kept in close touch with him behind
the commander-in-chief's back. But Stopford's methodical approach to Acre,
making full use of his steamers, paid dividends. The reefs surrounding the
town were supposed to make it impossible for attackers to close to an effective
range, but careful inshore surveying at night (it was Ramadan, and the garrison was not alert) revealed deep water inside the rocks, right under the walls.
At very close range the ships' gunfire was formidable even against stone walls,
and the explosion of the main magazine ended the defenders' resistance. 'It
is a glorious exploit,' Palmerston rejoiced, 'every country that has a fleet or
towns within cannon shot of the sea coast will treat us with much greater
respect in consequence.'[3] Palmerston himself was isolated in Cabinet and had
run big risks with inadequate forces, too late in the year for safety, but the warships' gunnery redeemed his judgement and restored Britain's reputation for
resolution.[4]

Meanwhile another crisis was developing in Chinese waters. The abolition
of the East India Company's monopoly in 1834 had incidentally disrupted the
regulated trade by which foreign barbarians were allowed to do business with
Chinese merchants in the single port of Canton (Guangzhou). The British government now appointed a series of 'commissioners of trade' with quasi-
diplomatic powers, whose misjudgements and mischief-making were a
principal cause of turning a trade dispute into a war. British ministers were
under heavy Parliamentary pressure to open China to free trade, and assumed
that Chinese reluctance masked the ill-paid mandarins' well-known tactic of
erecting barriers to trade in order to generate bribes. There was no contact
between the two governments, because the emperor did not admit any relationship with foreigners other than abject submission to provincial officials,
while the Foreign Office took no interest in a country which sent no ambas-
sadors. Each government was remote from events in South China, and badly
informed by officials on the spot who did not understand the language or the
motives of those they dealt with, and some of whom were actively deceiving
their masters. What news did reach London and Peking was months out of
date. The situation was further confused by the 'general superintendence of
our interests and operations in China' given to the Governor-General of India

as the British political authority 'on the spot', though Lord Auckland had no specific power to vary ministers' orders, and was himself a month away from events.[5] Although this is sometimes called the 'Opium War', Indian opium exports to China were only one among many factors tangled in the dispute. The British government disapproved of that trade, fully accepted that the Chinese emperor had the right to ban it, but had no legal power of its own to do the same. 'With respect to the smuggling of opium,' Palmerston wrote in June 1838,

> Her Majesty's Government cannot interfere for the purpose of enabling British subjects to violate the laws of the country to which they trade. Any loss, therefore, which such persons may suffer in consequence of more effectual execution of Chinese laws on this, must be borne by the parties who have brought that loss on themselves by their own acts.[6]

In Britain doctors regarded opium as a healthful medicine especially suitable for small children, and Chinese objections were dismissed as frivolous and dishonest by Radical critics in Parliament for whom free trade was 'God's diplomacy'; or in Cobden's words, 'the only human means of effecting universal and permanent peace'.[7] A weak government could not ignore them. There was no hope Parliament would pay for opium worth about two million pounds which had been confiscated by the British Trade Superintendent Captain Charles Elliot and handed over to the Chinese government, so ministers demanded that China pay instead.[8]

By the end of 1840 some agreement seemed to be in sight, but Elliot lost patience with diplomacy and ordered an attack. On 7 January 1841 the British force moved up the Pearl River towards Canton. The initial assault was a smashing success, in which a large share was borne by the East India Company's new iron steamer the *Nemesis*. Soon a ceasefire was followed by further talks in which the Chinese conceded to all the British demands, but once again Elliot was not prepared to take yes for an answer. On 26 February the British advanced again, storming the Bogue Forts, and on 18 March halting before Canton. All this bore no relation to Elliot's instructions, which were to apply pressure on the imperial government in Peking, not to punish the local inhabitants. 'Throughout the whole course of your proceedings,' Palmerston wrote to him, 'you seem to have considered that my instructions were waste paper, which you might treat with entire disregard, and that you were at full liberty to deal with the interests of the country according to your own fancy.'[9] Elliot was dismissed and a new Superintendent was appointed, Sir Henry Pottinger, who arrived in August 1841 in company with the new naval commander-in-chief, Sir William Parker. At the same time Melbourne's government finally fell, and the situation in China passed to the Earl of Aberdeen, Foreign Secretary in Sir Robert Peel's ministry, and to Lord Ellenborough the new Governor-General of India.[10]

Now the war moved to the north, as Palmerston had desired. Ellenborough had the good sense to leave the able and experienced Parker to handle the campaign. Unfortunately, Pottinger's status as plenipotentiary went to his head. Hoisting the flag of an admiral of the fleet and issuing a series of entirely illegal orders, he attempted to abstract ships from Parker's command, and encouraged captains to disobey the admiral's orders. Even as level-headed and tactful a flag officer as Parker was sorely tried, and though the Admiralty eventually upheld his authority, the ruling did not arrive until the campaign was long over. Nevertheless, under Parker's leadership, with 10,000 troops and plenty of steamers available, the 1842 campaign pushed up the Yangtze to capture Chiang-ning (Nanking) – the Chinese capital – on the way occupying Chingkiang (Zhenjiang), where the Grand Canal crossed the river, carrying northward the rice which fed Peking's population. In this position the warships could apply a remote but effective blockade of Peking, threatening the vital interests of the dynasty – though as yet no one at the Imperial Court had any conception of Western military power, and the shocking language of equality in the English version of the treaty was suppressed in translation. In the final Treaty of Nanking, China ceded Hong Kong for ever, paid an indemnity of $21 million, and opened five other ports (Canton, Amoy, Foochow, Ningpo and Shanghai) to foreign trade. There was no mention of opium.[11]

Peel's government took office in the summer of 1841 determined to adopt a policy of peace and economy, instead of which they found themselves embroiled in a long and expensive war in China. The public hardly noticed, because there were so many other wars and crises going on at the same time. The government of India, notionally responsible for British relations with China, was fully committed to a war of its own. In 1839 the Indian army had invaded Afghanistan and put a friendly candidate on the throne to repel Persian and Russian advances. Two years later the Afghans rebelled, and the British garrison of Kabul died almost to a man attempting a winter retreat to India. This disaster gravely damaged British prestige and weakened its position in India.[12]

In the River Plate the French were entangled in a local war between Argentina and Uruguay. Aberdeen intervened to safeguard freedom of navigation on the great rivers, and British warships were drawn into a complex and

dangerous situation, made worse by Aberdeen's characteristic style of instructions, firm in tone but vague in meaning, and by his Minister the inflamma-
tory Sir William Gore Ouseley. In November 1845 Captain Charles Hotham
with a joint Franco-British squadron forced the passage of the River Paraná at
Vuelta de Obligado, in the teeth of Argentine batteries manned largely by Englishmen. In the end the situation turned out better than British ministers
deserved; the interior was opened to trade, relations with France were preserved, and Britain avoided being drawn into the local wars of Argentina
against Uruguay.[13]

At the other end of Latin America the British-built iron paddle frigate *Guadalupe* played a leading role in the Mexican war of 1842–3 against Texas. As
this was the most advanced warship in the world, the Admiralty was happy to
receive unofficial reports from her captain, Commander Edward Charlewood,
though he was recalled before the United States became involved in the war
in 1846.[14] Meanwhile there were two crises in the Pacific. Fear of French intervention in New Zealand inspired the negotiations of 1840 which led to the
Treaty of Waitangi with the Maoris, but within five years British settlers had
provoked a war with them which drew in six warships. British naval officers
respected the Maoris and were openly hostile to many of the settlers.[15] In Tahiti
at the same time the rival activities of Catholic and Protestant missionaries
involved the French and British navies. Although instinctively anti-Catholic,
British officers tended to dislike many English Protestant missionaries as
ignorant lower middle-class troublemakers. 'What they really wish is that the
man of war should go to the islands and commit indiscriminate massacre,' as
Captain William Loring wrote to the First Lord in 1858.[16] Even so there was a
period of acute tension when the French Rear-Admiral Abel Dupetit-Thouars
annexed Tahiti without orders in September 1842 and expelled the British missionary and consul George Pritchard.[17] The only bright aspect of foreign affairs
was that diplomacy twice averted a serious risk of war with the United States:
in 1842 by the Webster-Ashburton Treaty which defined the Maine frontier,
and in 1846 by the settlement of the Oregon boundary to the Pacific coast on
the parallel of 49° North.[18]

All foreign alarms came home to add to the already agitated state of European and especially Anglo-French relations. Although King Louis-Philippe
and his Foreign Minister François Guizot professed friendship, and the fran-
cophile Aberdeen was ready to believe them, the public put no faith in French
stability. The lesson of the past half-century was that French politics were vol-
canic, and that the most peaceable policy might explode overnight into populist aggression. In the 1840s not only journalists and hysterics but such sober

and well-informed judges as Wellington thought that steamers had 'bridged the Channel' and permitted the strongest army in Europe instant free access to Britain. In May 1844 an anonymous pamphlet, 'Notes sur l'état des forces navales de la France', created a sensation when its author was discovered to be Louis-Philippe's naval son the Prince de Joinville. Those who actually read the pamphlet (including Queen Victoria) relaxed when they found it was a long list of essentials for a modern navy which France lacked; the much larger number who did not read the pamphlet took it for a plan of aggressive war if not an announcement of imminent invasion. That summer Joinville commanded a squadron on the coast of Morocco apparently practising large-scale landing operations. In this crisis Peel was appalled to discover that the Navy had only seven ships of the line in commission, of which precisely one was in the Mediterranean. 'Six millions of money and seven sail of the line!' he exclaimed to the Earl of Haddington, the First Lord,[19] not realizing that 6,000 men, enough to man another eight ships of the line, had since 1839 been diverted to anti-slavery, anti-piracy and the like. In December Sidney Herbert, the First Secretary of the Admiralty, produced a list of urgent deficiencies, including steamers, steam factories, dockyard defences, reserves, 'harbours of refuge' (a euphemism for protected anchorages intended as advanced bases for steamers in wartime), and admirals young enough to take command of them. The Navy Estimates for 1845 were increased by £1,250,000, and harbours of refuge were begun at Dover, Harwich and Portland.[20]

In 1844 Aberdeen and Guizot between them narrowly averted war, but after the revelations of the Royal Navy's weakness, no one was reassured. Early in 1846 the French Navy obtained a special vote of 93 million francs (3.6 million sterling) to remedy the worst of the deficiencies Joinville had identified. That summer Palmerston returned to office as Foreign Secretary in Lord John Russell's government, and judged that Britain and her empire 'existing only by sufferance, and by the forbearance of other Powers; and our weakness, being better known to others than it is felt by ourselves, tends greatly to encourage foreign states to do things calculated to expose us to war or to deep humiliation.'[21] 'The Channel is no longer a barrier,' he told the Commons in July. 'Steam Navigation has rendered that which was before impassable by a military force nothing more than a river passable by a steam bridge.'[22] In November he warned Russell that France 'has a million of muskets in store and probably 40 large steamers, each of which could carry 1,200 men. Comparing our present prepared means of defence with her means of attacks, we may say of England *stat magni nominis umbra*.'[23] A few months later Palmerston claimed that 'One single night would suffice to bring over from 20 to 30,000 men from French ports in steamers, and by midday they would be landed on our coast.'[24] He and Wellington pushed for better coastal, and especially dockyard, defences. By 1849 Britain and France were starting something like a naval race in the new steam ships of the line.[25]

British public opinion could be frightened by 'panics' (as Richard Cobden derisively called them), but tended to lose interest quickly. By 1848, the year when almost the entire naval force in home waters was in Ireland, overawing unrest and relieving famine, defence spending was once more unpopular. Prudent statesmen of all parties, Russell among them, knew this would happen, and modelled their policy accordingly. Moreover, these were the years of the greatest influence of Cobden and the 'Manchester Party', and of their greatest triumph, the 1846 repeal of the Corn Laws. For them the reduction of military spending and the establishment of universal peace were a single cause. It was a myth that pirates existed, Cobden proclaimed: Britain was the only disturber of the peace of the world. Excessive Navy Estimates, as the Radical MP Sir William Molesworth complained in March 1849, permitted Palmerston 'to meddle in every squabble that took place on the terraqueous globe – to teach constitutional maxims in Portugal – to contravert the "divine right" of kings in Sicily – to lead a crusade against the slave trade in Africa – and to do, he knew not what, in the Rio de la Plata.'[26] The Cobdenites were not enemies of British naval supremacy as such, but they were sure it could be maintained at half the cost if warships stayed in home waters and minded their own business. It was free trade, their sacred cause, which would teach the nations of the world to live in harmony.[27] 'How impossible it is to secure the peace of the world,' Cobden wrote in October 1846, 'and guarantee us against all the burdens which our present warlike attitude entails upon us by any means excepting a free commercial intercourse between all nations.'[28]

Free trade was one of the two great international moral causes of mid-Victorian Britain. The other was anti-slavery, and the two were flatly opposed to one another. The Atlantic slave trade was a fine example of a free trade with no government interference, joining willing buyers to willing sellers (albeit with very unwilling cargoes). It was impossible to eliminate the demand for slaves without international agreement not to consume the products of tropical agriculture (sugar, rice and cotton for example); it was equally impossible to eliminate the supply of slaves without conquering the whole of Africa and stilling its tribal wars. That left only one approach: the use of force in peacetime against foreign merchant ships at sea, in a manner which legally and practically looked uncomfortably like piracy. For Evangelicals, who provided so much of the impetus behind anti-slavery, true liberty was freedom from sin, and compatible with a high degree of social discipline – which in practice at sea meant a high degree of force, and a very low degree of respect for international law. Efforts to suppress the trade (just like modern efforts to suppress the drugs trade) made it vastly more profitable and threw it into the hands of ruthless criminals. Unlike legal slavers, whose profits had depended on delivering their slaves alive and well, these could and did throw slaves overboard if chased, for if there were no slave on board at the time of capture they could not be convicted. As Radical and Cobdenite proponents of free trade loudly argued, anti-slavery was brutal and ineffective. They had a good case, persuasive especially to Liberals, including Gladstone who voted to abandon the anti-slavery effort in 1848. Instead of spreading British prosperity across the Atlantic, the abolition of slavery in British colonies had simply reduced the wealthy and productive West Indies to a sort of tropical version of Sligo, with the former slaves turned into starving smallholders.

Meanwhile Cuba prospered, especially after the 1845 reduction in British sugar duties. It imported over half a million slaves between 1800 and 1860, and by 1870 exported 42 per cent of the world's production of tropical sugar. Cuba in turn sustained a Spanish Liberal government which Britain badly wanted to support, so British warships were sent to Cuba, not to suppress slaving but to deter American annexation. In a free-trading world, British goods, British capital and British merchants were still linked in many ways with the slave economies, but the profits now went elsewhere, and Britain reaped nothing but opprobrium for its efforts.[29] As Aberdeen wrote to Peel in October 1844:

> We are terribly hampered by this Slave Trade the questions about which meet us in every quarter and estrange us from our best friends. France, the United States, Spain, Portugal, Brazil all furnish matter for angry discussion every day. Never have a people made such a sacrifice as we have done to attain our object, and the payment of money is the least part of it.[30]

By the late 1840s the anti-slavery campaign was facing collapse. Existing treaties were hollow, since no trading nation would concede effective powers to British warships. The Portuguese-Brazilian trade in the South Atlantic was not covered by any treaty at all after Brazil's anti-slaving treaty expired in 1845. It would have been logical to abandon the effort to eradicate slavery, but British public opinion made that impossible. In 1850 the Radicals came close to carrying their argument in the House of Commons, but Lord John Russell held them off with an explicit appeal, not to law, which was out of the question, but to moral leadership:

It appears to me that if we give up this high and holy work, and proclaim ourselves no longer fitted to lead in the championship against the curse and the crime of slavery, that we have no longer a right to expect a continuance of those blessings, which, by God's favour, we have so long enjoyed.[31]

If failure was ruled out, the only alternative was success, and that (as a Lords Committee of 1849 frankly acknowledged) would require more force and fewer scruples. In 1845 Aberdeen had unilaterally declared Brazilian slavers to be pirates; now the Royal Navy began to take him at his word. In June 1850 the *Cormorant* took four slavers out of a Brazilian port, under fire from the batteries – an unambiguous act of war against a friendly nation. In December 1851, on Palmerston's orders and against the advice of the Admiralty, the Navy deposed the pro-slavery ruler of Lagos (whom Britain recognized as a legitimate sovereign) and forced a treaty ending the trade – which persuaded Dahomey to sign as well. It imposed a blockade on the Gallinas coast without declaration of war and arrested foreign merchantmen for breaking it. In all this the British bullied the weak, not the strong. The United States was untouchable, and the French, whose flag covered so much slaving in the Indian Ocean, were left alone. It was Britain's faithful ally, Sultan Seyyid Sa'id of Oman and Zanzibar, whose East African maritime empire depended heavily on the slave trade, who was subjected to intolerable pressure which steadily weakened his authority, and in the process undermined British policy in the region.[32]

British warships captured only about one Atlantic slaver in five and liberated only around one slave in sixteen. Since the British effort accounted for more than 85 per cent of all captures, it is evident that the direct effect of anti-slavery cruising was quite insufficient to suppress the trade. The ships were ineffective, however, because the slaving nations resisted British pressure to pass or enforce effective legislation. The greater British pressure grew, the more Britain was willing to override international law, the more dangerous it became to support slaving. One after another, the slaving nations, even France and Brazil, yielded to British pressure and to the shift of their own public opinion, until by 1857 only Cuba and the United States were still importing slaves across the Atlantic in large numbers, and the remaining trade was increasingly American-controlled.[33]

Over half a century, from 1816 to 1865, the British anti-slaving effort cost an average of a quarter of a million pounds a year. At its peak in 1845 it employed 4,445 men and cost £490,500 – about 13 per cent of the total for the Navy in each case, without considering the heavy casualties involved, which in the worst year of 1829 amounted to a quarter of the West African squadron dead.[34] In six months of that year, 110 of the 160 men of the *Eden* died:

> The whole of the officers with the exception of the First Lieutenant and the gunner are either dead or confined to bed; the men are dying almost daily amidst incessant rain and frequent tornadoes accompanied with much thunder and lightning; the main deck is crowded with sick and constantly wet. The moral effect of these scenes became palpable in every countenance; while for want of medical attendance, the surgeon and two assistant surgeons having died, it was impossible to pay attention to the ventilation of the ship, or even to the personal comfort of the sick.[35]

The blockade of the slaving coasts was 'beyond all question, the most wearisome, monotonous and thoroughly prostrating and dispiriting duty which the crews of Her Majesty's ships have to undergo in any part of the known world'.[36] Slavers usually sailed by night, aiming to be well offshore by dawn, when there was very little risk of detection in the vastness of the open Atlantic. Only patrols close inshore had a good chance of interception, and they exposed the crews to the highest risk of disease. Malaria (the African variety *plasmodium falciparum*, frequently fatal, rather than the 'remittent fever', *plasmodium vivax*, of the West Indies), yellow fever (the culprit in 1829) and dengue fever were all common; dysentery was caught from slaves; river blindness, Loa-Loa, guinea worms and septic wounds awaited those who landed even briefly. The US Navy kept its anti-slavery patrol well offshore, where there was little risk of meeting either mosquitos or slavers, and based its ships on the distant but healthy harbour of Porto Praya in the Cape Verde Islands, but the British wanted an effective blockade rather than a political token and did not have that option. Their base of Freetown in Sierra Leone was convenient but deadly; mortality among Europeans there was 50 per cent a year, and in 1825 86 per cent of the garrison died. Only in 1847 did the squadron acquire a healthy offshore base at Ascension Island. But every ship carried a surgeon, West Africa was an urgent laboratory of tropical medicine, and medical knowledge did advance. Quinine was isolated in the 1820s and grew rapidly in popularity; in the 1850s it was discovered to work as a prophylactic as well as a treatment, and to require a fortnight's follow-up course for a reliable cure. Bleeding and mercurials were now falling out of fashion. By the late 1850s the West Africa Squadron was losing fewer than 2 per cent a year to disease; in 1875 the Congo River expedition exposed 750 men to prolonged operations in swamps with only a few mild fever cases resulting.[37]

Throughout the nineteenth century, Britain kept her main fleet in the

Mediterranean because that was where the most serious threats tended to arise, that was where other powers noticed British naval strength, and it was not too far from home waters in the event of an emergency in the Channel. In 1844 Peel's Tory government appointed the moderate Whig Sir William Parker, just home from China, as commander-in-chief in the Mediterranean, because there was no Tory admiral left still fit to serve who had anything like his experience and judgement. Two years later Lord John Russell's Whig government tried to persuade Parker to join the Admiralty as senior naval lord, but he declined to risk the sight of his remaining good eye with long hours at a desk by candle-light. The unsatisfactory James Deans Dundas took his place, but ministers continued to consult Parker, and he kept up the standards of training and dis-cipline of the squadron. His prudence and wisdom, his willingness to take action without waiting for a weak government to issue instructions, supported friendly governments and solved repeated diplomatic crises: in Portugal in 1846, in Sicily in 1848, in the 'Eastern Crisis' of 1849 when Parker took the Mediterranean Squadron up the Dardanelles, in Greece with the 'Don Pacifico' affair of 1849–50. In the tumultuous year of 1848, when governments all over Europe were convulsed by popular revolutions, and Britain was convulsed by the 'Young Ireland' rising, the Irish famine and the largest-ever Chartist demonstration, Parker's ships appeared as an island of stability.[38]

The end result of 1848 in much of Europe was to strengthen authoritarian monarchies, but Louis-Philippe of France lost his throne to a revived repub-lic. Its first President was Bonaparte's nephew Louis Napoléon, who in Decem-ber 1851 proclaimed himself 'Prince-President', and one year later overthrew his own government and declared himself emperor as Napoleon III. The revival of this name, at a time when the French were making great efforts to strengthen their navy, was not calculated to calm British anxieties, though ministers were somewhat less liable to panic than the public and the newspa-pers. In December 1852 a new British government led by Aberdeen took office, an uneasy Whig-Peelite coalition with Palmerston as Home Secretary, Russell the Foreign Secretary, and Sir James Graham (who had done a lot to assemble the ministry) back at the Admiralty. Palmerston and Russell were rivals, and both anxious to unseat Aberdeen: 'a powerful team, but it will require good driving,' Graham commented.[39] Its first challenge was the 'eastern crisis', gen-erated (as it seemed) by fresh Russian aggression against the Ottoman Empire. In fact it was more the French who had stirred up the trouble; Tsar Nicholas I thought of himself as defending the sultan's persecuted Christian subjects, had no ambition to march on Constantinople, and was pained to find that other Christian monarchs did not support him. Britain and France found themselves thrown together in an uneasy alliance of convenience with divergent aims. 'I will tell you fairly,' Graham wrote to Palmerston in May 1853,

> that I can place no confidence in our French ally. We may be driven by force of circumstances to act with him: but unhappily at this moment France is one man; and that man is treacherous. Nicholas may be suspected, but Napoleon is known to set at naught all moral obligations . . . I place little confidence in princes; but I am disposed to place more reliance on the honour of Nicholas than on the broken faith of Napoleon . . .[40]

Austria, Prussia and Sweden declined to join the war, and the only allies of Britain and France were the Ottoman Empire, and later Piedmont-Sardinia.[41]

Britain and France had neither the desire, the means nor the plans for a major campaign against Russia. When their two Mediterranean fleets assembled at Besika Bay near the mouth of the Dardanelles in July 1853 they intended only to deter a Russian advance, and were at a loss to know what to do when deterrence failed and the Russians invaded the Ottoman Danube 'principalities' (roughly modern Romania). In October Turkey declared war on Russia, and the two fleets with some difficulty forced their way against the current up to Constantinople, while their governments groped for a policy. The British Cabinet contained no military men and took no military advice; no general staff existed, and after the death of the Duke of Wellington in September 1852 there were no competent generals available. Graham, clever, self-confident and familiar with the Navy, took the lead. Both France and Britain wanted a quick and painless victory. The Foreign Secretary Lord Clarendon declared in January 1854 that the 'object of the expedition . . . should be . . . to finish the Eastern question in the Euxine [i.e. Black Sea] before the Baltic opens and we can pay a visit to Cronstadt'.[42] Graham proposed a 'great raid' on Sebastopol, the Russian fortress and base in the Crimea, hoping to damage Russian sea power with French assistance: 'The Eye Tooth of the Bear must be drawn: and till his Fleet and Naval Arsenal in the Black Sea are destroyed, there is no safety for Constantinople, no Security for the Peace of Europe.'[43] Napoleon III aimed to win glory and efface the Vienna settlement which had destroyed his uncle's legacy. All assumed that Sebastopol was remote enough from European Russia to be ill-defended, and yet important enough to be a fatal loss to Nicholas I.[44]

The Imperial Russian Navy had two Black Sea squadrons: an eastern under Vice-Admiral Pavel Stepanovich Nakhimov, and a western under Vice-Admiral Vladimir Alexeyevich Kornilov, both energetic officers, based together at Sebastopol, close to the geographical centre of the sea, and much closer to the

Anatolian coast of Turkey than were the allied squadrons at Constantinople. Here lay the makings of a disaster, for the Turkish army on the Caucasus front depended on shipping moving along that coast, which was protected only by a weak squadron lying in the open bay of Sinope. Osman Pasha, the Turkish admiral, was an experienced officer and was warned of his danger, but the Turks seem to have been confident that the Russians would not dare to put to sea in the face of the allies (though Captain Muşaver Pasha – alias Captain Adolphus Slade, RN – vainly urged reinforcements). On 30 November Nakhimov's six ships of the line attacked and sank almost the whole Turkish force; only Slade's ship the steamer *Taif* escaped. It was subsequently claimed by Napoleon III, and has often been repeated, that the Russian ships owed their victory to French-manufactured shell guns, but they had only a few, and their overwhelming superiority in guns of all sorts more than accounts for the result.[45]

The allied fleets arrived in the Black Sea in January 1854, with nothing decided about strategy or command. In London every Cabinet member had his own proposal, while at Constantinople the long-serving British ambassador, Viscount Stratford de Redcliffe, had a broad authority over the fleet which he interpreted to include operational orders as well as political guidance. The four allied commanders-in-chief (six if the Turks were present) had equal voices on a council of war, but the French Vice-Admiral Ferdinand Hamelin was under the orders of Marshal Jacques St Arnaud, who was in the confidence of Napoleon III and as near a supreme commander as a dying man could be. Rear-Admiral Sir Edmund Lyons, the handsome and popular second-in-command of the British fleet, was a close friend of Graham, who corresponded privately with him and used him to undermine Deans Dundas his commander-in-chief. Lord Raglan was chosen to command the British army because of his tact, diplomacy and excellent French, not his force of character or military talents.[46]

Like Clarendon, Graham hoped to destroy the Russian Black Sea fleet during the winter in time to switch the attack to the Baltic when the ice melted, and seems not to have realized that the Black Sea in winter was no place for sailing ships. In practice much of 1854 was taken up with transporting the armies to Varna (in modern Bulgaria), reloading and preparing them for an assault, all in the midst of a serious cholera outbreak. The French troops, which sober observers had believed could be embarked in total secrecy in a few hours to attack England, actually required many months and a great deal of British help before they could sail for the Crimea. It was not until September that the allied invasion fleet put to sea, and it was fortunate that the Russian admirals were forbidden to attack (for fear of the British fleet), as the French ships, crammed with troops, were in no condition to fight.[47]

The embarkation and voyage were largely organized by Rear-Admiral Lyons' capable flag-captain William Mends. There were a total of 412 British, French and Turkish ships, the steamers towing the sailers, their funnels making the whole look like 'Manchester on the move'. Lyons, Mends wrote to his wife,

> puts confidence into all minds, explains away the misgivings of the croakers, and condemns the declaiming, rallying around him the sympathies and feelings of high and low, and yet he hates detail, and says so. He grasps the great features of any subject, knows the detail is necessary, but says to me sometimes, 'You and the general manage that, I see you understand it.'[48]

Although the army was completely unprepared for a campaign, Mends organized every detail of the successful landing near Eupatoria in September. A week later the allies defeated the Russians on the River Alma and might have rushed Sebastopol if they had co-ordinated any plans beforehand. The army insisted that the ships bombard the strong harbour defences on 17 October, though there was little chance of that contributing much to the assault (which in the event was cancelled anyway), and a considerable risk of losing enough ships to leave the armies cut off. Both fleets had already landed naval parties with heavy guns and much of their ammunition. The French ships chose to bombard at a long range (upwards of a mile) at which no damage could be done by either side; Lyons found a way through the shoals to approach the Russian batteries near enough for several British ships to be badly damaged by shells without achieving anything. Deans Dundas was blamed, with Graham's discreet encouragement. Time was now running out to seize the city, and the senior engineer General John Burgoyne insisted on a regular siege of the strong southern defences, condemning the army to a Russian winter under canvas for which little had been prepared.[49]

The British part of the siege was supplied from the safe but narrow harbour of Balaklava, with little room within and no safe anchorage outside. It was urgently necessary to unload supplies quickly and get them efficiently up to the siege works three miles away on the plateau, but here the military organization disintegrated, and the army suffered severely for want of stores, many of which had actually reached Balaklava. Naval observers were appalled at the British army on campaign:

The prevailing characteristics of the British Army officers are – apathy bordering on indifference to all the details of their profession; slowness and helplessness almost infantile in everything that does not accord with barrack routine; honourable and gentlemanly as a general rule; gallant and chivalrous to an utter regardlessness of their own safety when called into action. Discipline in many cases is lost sight of, so that very great demoralization prevails . . .[50]

The naval brigade collected their own supplies and fared reasonably well, the French were organized for the field and had a larger and more accessible harbour. But the British army suffered severely through the worst of a Crimean winter until the new Transport Service was formed in February 1855, and in March a light railway was built from Balaklava up to the siege lines.[51]

Sebastopol was never sealed off to the north, so supplies and reinforcements continued to make the three-month journey from European Russia, down the River Don and across the Sea of Azov. In the spring the French were at length persuaded to detach troops for an expedition which seized Kerch in May and opened the way for shallow-draught vessels to penetrate the Azov. Although the allied assault of 18 June was a bloody failure, the situation of the defenders was now getting worse. On 8 September the French took the Malakov Fort and the Russians evacuated the town. A month later (by chance on the exact anniversary of the unsuccessful bombardment of Sebastopol) the allies' new 'floating batteries' bombarded and captured the fort of Kinburn, guarding the mouth of the Dnieper (Dnipro). The first appearance ever of armoured warships in battle had opened a way into the interior of Russia, though neither ally was in any condition to exploit it.[52]

The Russian War involved major and minor campaigns spread over thousands of miles of land and sea, which makes the later title 'Crimean War' particularly misleading. Sir James Graham kept his eyes on the Baltic, where the Russians had their most modern and efficient warships, and detached ships to the Black Sea only after the Baltic froze in October 1853. He intended them to be back from their 'great raid' in time to attack Reval (Talinn) in the spring before the main fleet in Kronstadt was unfrozen. The fleet did not return in time, but fortunately for the allies, the Russians refused to risk fighting at sea and retreated into port in the Baltic as they had in the Black Sea.[53] Graham's first difficulty in the Baltic was to identify a commander-in-chief. He needed a flag-officer not below vice-admiral's rank with experience of handling a fleet. The only possibilities were Sir George Seymour, aged sixty-seven, who was in the West Indies; Lord Dundonald, who at seventy-nine had not lost his reputation for disobedience and 'desperate enterprises'; Sir William Parker, aged seventy-three, who declined the offer 'in justice to my country';[54] and Sir Charles Napier, who was available and only sixty-eight. Quarrelsome, boastful and slovenly, Napier had been a brilliant wartime leader when younger, but always an impossible colleague with an unmatched talent for losing friends. The Baltic command was to give him many opportunities to give offence, but few to take the offensive. The fleet mobilized slowly, with poor officers and insufficient men – partly because Graham and his friend W. E. Gladstone, the Chancellor of the Exchequer, were determined to show that they could wage war on a peacetime income. It turned out the Russians had abandoned Reval. An alternative plan to attack the incomplete Russian fortress of Bomarsund in the Åland Islands was intended to capture the islands (Swedish-speaking, and formerly part of the Swedish Empire) to enlist Sweden as an ally: 'she must become our suitor when we hold Åland, and we shall be enabled to command our future assistance on our own terms'.[55] Napier had already spoken with King Oscar I and knew that Sweden was not to be tempted. The isolated forts of Bomarsund were only brick faced with granite and were quickly overcome, but neither the French nor British, army nor Navy, could agree what to do next. The French general, Comte Achille Baraguey d'Hilliers, was a rival of Napoleon III who had sent the general to the Baltic to keep him out of the way; Baraguey d'Hilliers, Vice-Admiral Alexandre Parseval-Deschênes and Napier all loathed one another.[56]

In or out of the Admiralty, there was no effective mechanism for forming war policy other than Sir James Graham's intellect, and no machinery for inter-allied co-operation except mutual agreement among the admirals and generals on the spot. The First Lord was clever but allergic to responsibility and preferred to give hints rather than orders; Napier's official orders and his private instructions from Graham were at variance throughout. The upper Baltic is shallow, foggy and thickly strewn with rocks and islands; Napier would have been right to penetrate it with great caution even with younger and more practised captains. It took time to appreciate that he had two major assets. The first was steamers, and some steam line-of-battleships, which made navigation among the islands much easier and safer. The other was the presence of hydrographers led by Captain Bartholomew Sulivan of the steamer *Lightning*, who not only guided the fleet through the islands, but acted as a one-man planning staff. Sulivan showed the way to attack Bomarsund from the rear, and then led the fleet up the Gulf of Finland towards the island-fortress of Sveaborg (Suomenlinna, Viapori), beyond which lay Kronstadt and St Petersburg. To attack these, however, would require specialized ships and weapons, and it was not until October 1854, when the fighting season was over, that the government was persuaded to order floating batteries, gunboats and other vessels costing £600,000. The only other action that summer came from Rear-Admiral James Plumridge, who in May was sent with some steamers up the Gulf of Bothnia where Russian gunboats were supposed to be assembling. Assuming that everything he could see was Russian government property, Plumridge proceeded to burn towns, villages and export cargoes of tar and timber, most of them pre-sold to British merchants. This 'un-English and un-Christian proceeding' (Sulivan's words) outraged neutral and naval opinion equally: 'they signalized themselves by the destruction of half a million's worth of property, belonging, it is much to be feared, to inoffensive and friendly inhabitants . . . it has engendered a hatred of us on the part of the Finlanders, which will make them fight us *con amore*'.[57] It did: on 10 June a boat expedition to Gamla Carleby (Kokkola) was ambushed and incurred heavy casualties.[58]

Napier had taken the precaution of becoming a secret correspondent for the *Times*, which won him one friend where it mattered, but he lost all the others, both at home and in his fleet. His virulent attacks on the Admiralty alienated his supporters there, and most of the captains despised him. Graham, the Cabinet and even the *Times* united to blame him for the disappointments of the campaign.[59] His replacement for the 1855 campaign was Rear-Admiral Sir Richard Saunders Dundas, a good seaman and administrator, fluent in French, but pessimistic and irresolute. As a son of Lord Melville he had enjoyed every advantage: he was a Captain at twenty-two and reached flag-rank in July 1853, the first British admiral to have entered the Navy after the end of the French Wars. He was only fifty-one, but in his own mind already worn out. 'You are very kind, Mr Briggs,' he responded to an expression of congratulation,

> but it has come too late; had I been made an admiral ten years ago there was nothing I then felt I could not do, but now I have had forty year's [sic] service taken out of me . . . Few officers are really good for much after fifty or fifty-five years of age.[60]

Aberdeen's government fell in January 1855, and Palmerston formed an administration with Sir Charles Wood as First Lord. The Cabinet gave him no instructions about the war, and he had none for the admirals. The only strategy available for the Baltic in 1855 was that worked out by Sulivan, who wanted to go straight for the fortified island dockyard of Kronstadt, and the unprotected capital of St Petersburg beyond. In June some of the ships went up the Gulf of Finland as far as the Tolbukhin Light off Kronstadt, where they encountered

Russian 'infernals' (sea mines) for the first time. Rear-Admiral Michael Seymour examined one in person. 'Some of the officers remarked on the danger of its going off, and Admiral Seymour said, "Oh no; this is the way it would go off", and shoved the slide in with his finger . . . It instantly exploded, knocking down everyone round it.'[61] Dundas did exactly the same thing later that day. Luckier than they deserved, both admirals survived their first encounter with the new weapon, though Seymour was blinded in one eye.[62]

Reconnaissance of the much-reinforced defences of Kronstadt made it clear that they could not be attacked with the means available, but there was an intermediate target half-way up the gulf, the island fortress-dockyard of Sveaborg, which guarded the approach to Helsingfors (Helsinki) and the shipping route inside the islands along the Finnish coast. This was predominantly an earthwork fortress with no exposed walls like Bomarsund, and was only vulnerable to heavy mortars, but a fleet of gunboats and mortar-vessels was now ready. Between 8 and 11 August Sveaborg was bombarded and destroyed (much to the surprise of the pessimistic Dundas), the whole attack being planned and organized by Sulivan.[63] This was an encouraging precedent, the fall of Sebastopol on 9 September freed resources, the successful bombardment of Kinburn by the new ironclad floating batteries in October underlined what was now possible, and in November 1855 Palmerston and the Cabinet adopted Sulivan's plan to assault Kronstadt as their strategy for 1856. If Kronstadt could be taken, which Sulivan certainly believed possible, the Russian capital would lie under the guns of the allied fleet. Perhaps it was this threat which persuaded the Russians to open negotiations for peace in March 1856, though at the same time Sweden and Austria were threatening to enter the war, and Russia's essential supporter Prussia was under heavy pressure to close its borders.[64]

Russia had also been subject to a maritime blockade during the war, covering not only the Baltic and the Black Sea, but also the Pacific and even the Arctic, where a British squadron in the White Sea in 1854 and 1855 stopped the trade of Archangel.[65] It was difficult for Britain and France, with very different interests and traditions, to agree on a blockade policy. As usual in war, neutrals had power and had to be conciliated. Sweden and Denmark threatened a new 'armed neutrality', seventy years after the last one, and it would be impossible to campaign in the Baltic without their support. The United States was a friend of Russia and a likely source of Russian privateers; Prussia was a neighbour through whose ports and railways Russia could easily import what it needed. France herself needed to import Russian grain, and Britain expected to be the greatest and most vulnerable of all neutral shipowners in a future

war. In Parliament the Manchester School insisted on free trade with the
enemy, as the best method of paying for war, and the sanctity of private property as the best bulwark against tyranny. Clarendon, the Foreign Secretary,
thought it would be better to make a virtue of necessity. 'It is quite clear that
we can never again reestablish our ancient doctrine respecting neutrals, and
that we must in any future war adhere to the exception to our rule which we
admitted at the beginning of the present war, under pain of having all mankind against us.'[66]

All concerned were thinking not only of the present war, but of the
precedents they were establishing for the future – including, in the case of
Britain and France, a potential future war between them. They compromised
by offering the principle of 'free ships, free goods' (meaning no capture of neutral ships carrying enemy cargo), no right of privateering, and a blockade covering only contraband of war (traditionally understood as weapons and
ammunition, but potentially capable of elastic definition). At the end of the
war in April 1856 the allies issued this agreement, the 'Declaration of Paris', as
an international treaty open to any nation to join without formality so long as
it accepted the whole document. It was an important innovation in international law which in time became an almost universal voluntary legal agreement, establishing principles of international law by treaty rather than just by
precedent. Against critics who accused the government of throwing away a
powerful weapon of sea power, Clarendon insisted that to claim Britain's traditional belligerent rights would have united the world against her, 'and most
properly so – because we should have been maintaining a law which was contrary to the public opinion of the world, which was hostile to commerce, and
as unfavourable as possible to a mitigation of the evils of war'.[67] That put it on
a high plane of idealism, but the British policy was not innocent of calculation.
The Declaration was a deft mechanism to isolate any country (meaning America) which refused to abandon privateering, but could not claim the substantial benefit offered by the Declaration unless it did. By her refusal the United
States was deprived of her only serious naval strategy, and left with the support
of Spain, Mexico and Venezuela alone. France's brilliant diplomatic coup
gained a right for which she had fought for centuries, with British support for
the creation of a new international legal regime.[68]

In other respects, too, the Russian War altered the diplomatic and political
landscape. The British public rediscovered an interest in the armed services
and fell out of love with Cobdenite pacifism. As Cobden gloomily concluded,
'the aristocracy have gained immensely since the people took to soldiering'.[69]
The experience of fighting as allies of Napoleon III rather strengthened than

weakened British misgivings about him, especially as French naval expenditure on ships more suitable to fight Britain than Russia continued to rise
during the war.[70] Then the British and French found themselves fighting
together once more, this time in China, where fresh trouble broke out in October 1856. This second China (or 'Arrow') War repeated many features of the
first, with the complication that both France (in association with Britain) and
the United States (independently) were involved. The British government
sought the fulfilment of the terms of the 1842 Treaty of Nanking by the opening of Canton to foreign trade. The Imperial government did not take these
extorted concessions very seriously and faced a much graver threat from the
Taeping rebels, open enemies to Manchu rule who had overrun much of China.
Commissioner Yeh Ming-Chen, sent to Canton to negotiate with the British,
found himself trapped between the rebels outside the city, and local leaders
within, loyal to the dynasty but hostile to any concession to the hated foreigners. He wriggled out of that by inventing a fictitious imperial decree cancelling
the treaty, so that his flimsy position depended on deceiving his own government for as long as possible. Meanwhile Harry Parkes, the British consul, and
Sir John Bowring, the Governor of Hong Kong, were busy deceiving both the
British government and Sir Michael Seymour, the local naval commander-in-
chief. Since Parkes was one of the few British officials who knew Chinese, and
the Chinese themselves refused on principle to learn Western languages, he
had a considerable control over negotiations. Bowring was a doctrinaire, not
to say monomaniac, Cobdenite for whom any deception or aggression was
legitimate which opened China to free trade. Parkes possibly fabricated and
certainly exploited the incident concerning the allegedly British vessel *Arrow*,
arrested for opium smuggling, which triggered fighting in October 1856. As a
result, Seymour's ships pushed up the Pearl River and bombarded Canton on
3 November. British forces briefly occupied the city but were too few to hold
it and soon retreated to Hong Kong.[71]

In Britain public opinion was by no means entirely deceived by Parkes
and Bowring. On the contrary, their aggression aroused widespread disgust,
Bowring was denounced in the House of Lords, and an unlikely combination
of the Cobdenites and the Conservative opposition with parts of the government carried a motion of censure. Palmerston then called a general election
and won heavily. The 'Chinese election' changed the landscape of British politics: the 'peace party' of Cobden, Bright and their friends was almost extinguished; the Peelites were shattered and their leading members took refuge
either with the Liberals or the Tories; Palmerston's bold and bullying foreign
policy was vindicated.[72] The government now sent out the Earl of Elgin with

military reinforcements and instructions to impose a satisfactory settlement on the Chinese – to the private distress of Elgin, who stood for a sense of reason and moderation which impressed neither Whitehall nor Peking. On his way east, Elgin learned the news of widespread mutiny in the British Indian Army. As a result, all his reinforcements were diverted to India and the intended China campaign was reduced to a river war with ships alone. On 1 June 1857 men from the British warships fought a boat action against Chinese war-junks in Fatshan Creek near Canton. This was a narrow and costly victory which taught British officers that Chinese discipline and training had greatly improved. 'Great judgement was shown in selecting the position for the fleet,' Seymour reported, 'and the Chinese, particularly the last division attacked by Commodore Keppel, defended their ships with skill, courage and effect.'[73] Elgin and some of his troops finally arrived in China in September, and the British and French mounted a joint attack on Canton, which fell after a feeble resistance on 30 December. The allies then moved north. British and French ships easily forced their way past the forts at the mouth of the Peiho River. At Tientsin, half-way up to Peking, they met the imperial diplomats, and on 26 June 1858 a treaty was signed which conceded to all British demands.[74]

According to Western diplomatic rules, the matter was now settled, but the Chinese government was still much more fearful of the Taepings than of the remote and ineffectual Europeans. In June 1859 Elgin's brother the Hon. Frederick Bruce arrived as a plenipotentiary to exchange ratifications of the treaty only to find the Peiho forts, guarding the way to Peking, barred against him. A new naval commander-in-chief, Rear-Admiral James Hope, without his predecessor's experience of the China coast, ordered an immediate attack. By this time British overseas squadrons made extensive use of the small steam gunboats built for the Baltic campaign of 1856. Three of them were sunk in this disastrous attack, plus three others badly damaged; the admiral was gravely wounded, and the British part of the Anglo-French force suffered 30 per cent casualties. Elgin was sent back the following year with more ships and 20,000 British and French troops, which this time landed and took the Taku forts in the rear. The Chinese were no more impressed than before, an advance diplomatic party were tortured and murdered, and in the end the allied force occupied Peking on 13 October 1860 and burnt the suburban Summer Palace. After this the treaty was finally ratified and kept the peace for forty years; the British preserved at least some of their military reputation, and the Chinese Empire did not (as they feared) collapse.[75]

So at the end of a decade of almost unbroken wars against great land empires, British arms could claim some modest and partial successes, but British public opinion had moved a long way in an unexpected direction. The Manchester School and the 'Peace Party' were now in retreat, though still influential among the Liberals. Imperial expansion was still a minority cause, but public opinion was now engaged with the outside world, concerned at the condition of the armed forces, and ready to contemplate using them overseas.

FOUR

Steam and Iron

Ships and Weapons 1815–1860

In the first age of photography, warships were popular subjects, partly because anchored ships stayed still for the long exposures then necessary. There are therefore many photographs of warships from the 1840s and 1850s, which to the casual observer seem scarcely to have changed since the previous century. It is only when by chance these ships are seen lying beside survivors of thirty or forty years before that it becomes clear that a massive increase in size had taken place in a generation. This has its origins in the emergency measures adopted during the Napoleonic Wars to extend the lives of old ships of the line, which inspired Sir Robert Seppings, Surveyor of the Navy from 1813 to 1832, to design ships with added diagonal timbering to brace the longitudinals and verticals of the traditional hull structure. This allowed wooden ships to be built of greater length, and carrying heavier loads, without loss of rigidity, and to combine a heavy armament with finer lines fore and aft, providing fast three-deckers able to keep up with a cruising squadron. It also made possible the new 'round' bows and stern, formed of heavy scantlings carried to the upper deck, giving greatly increased protection against raking fire compared with the light transoms aft, and the weak athwartship beakhead bulkhead forward, of the old construction. In the 1820s, when both the American and French navies were building some very large and powerful ships of the line, Seppings made it possible for Britain to keep up, and indeed to surpass them. The greater cost of these big ships was one reason why the 1815 plan to keep one hundred ships of the line was never achieved. By 1822 the number available was down to sixty-eight, and in 1835 to fifty-eight. Foreign numbers were falling just as fast, but many of the British ships were the smaller and older Third Rates, so that admirals like Sir Robert Stopford in 1840 were liable to find their ships outclassed. In 1848 Lord Auckland and Sir William Parker agreed that a fleet of fifty of the new First and Second Rates would be sufficient to maintain naval supremacy, with fifteen more complete on the stocks, and timber ready-converted for a further fifteen.[1]

The greater size of the new warships also made possible the move towards a uniform calibre of armament. Again, this was a response to French and American moves, which highlighted the disadvantages of a mixture of guns of different sizes and calibre. In 1824 the French Navy adopted a standard 30-pounder calibre (equivalent to 33pdr in British measure), and both the British and American navies adopted 32pdr as their standard. This meant that in each fleet different patterns of guns for different ranges and situations could share common ammunition. The new standard was now almost as large as the heaviest guns had formerly been, so the weight of armament which ships carried, and the weight of broadside they fired, increased markedly. In practice, however, the change came gradually, for it involved a costly and lengthy programme of casting new guns, and there remained many older ships in service which had to be strengthened to support the weight of the new armaments. The Royal Navy officially adopted the standard 32pdr in 1827, but the change was barely complete before new calibres were introduced in the 1850s.[2]

Throughout the eighteenth century warship design had been a subject of controversy, which was certainly not stilled by the new designs of the 1820s. Seppings was a close ally of Sir Thomas Byam Martin, and for the Whig opposition the epitome of Tory naval architecture. It was integral to the Whig outlook that enlightened government decisions could only come from the right people with the right principles – meaning themselves, and gentlemen like them. For them 'experts' were essentially craftsmen and tradesmen who spoke for inherited attitudes and entrenched interests; allowing such a person as Seppings, who had started his career as a shipwright apprentice, to take decisions was an obvious sign of corruption. Abolishing the Navy Board in 1832 got rid of the wrong people as well as the wrong system and allowed Sir James Graham, the First Lord, to take progressive decisions untrammelled by pretended experts. For the same reason he closed the School of Naval Architecture, established at Portsmouth in 1811 to train future warship designers in a more formal and systematic way than had been possible by the old system of 'premium apprentices'.[3]

What Graham needed to replace Seppings was a gentleman amateur of impeccable Whig connections, and happily, the perfect candidate was available. Captain William Symonds was a talented yachtsman and amateur yacht designer with many friends among the social elite in the Royal Yacht Squadron, including George Vernon, the Marquis of Anglesea, Lord Lauderdale, Lord Yarborough and the Duke of Portland, who introduced him to the Duke of Clarence in 1827. In 1831 the Whig government ordered the frigate *Vernon* to Symonds' design, and the following year he was named Surveyor of the Navy in place of Seppings. Symonds had no training as a shipwright or naval architect: he drew the lines of his ships, but he knew little about ship structure and his designs had to be worked out for him by his assistant John Edye. As a yacht designer, however, he had real talent. Instead of the usual deep and ballasted hull-forms, his yachts were light and broad-beamed with a steep rise of floor. Unhappy in a head sea, they were weatherly, stiff and very fast in expert hands and in yacht-racing weather, and for his aristocratic supporters, his ability to win races proved he was the right man for the job. The 'Symondite' warships he designed were then raced against other designs in grown-up yacht races called 'trials of sailing'. The results of these trials depended greatly on the weather, the state of the ships' rigging and stowage, the skill of the officers and other matters open to interpretation – and the interpretations were usually political.

Among naval officers, better able to weigh the merits and defects of his designs, Symonds had some Tory supporters, and some Whig opponents, but for the civilian politicians of the 1830s and 1840s, naval technology was reduced to the simple question of who was first round the buoy, and for the Whigs it was self-evident that the gentleman amateur always wins. The alleged triumph of Symondite warship designs in turn 'proved' that the abolition of the Navy Board and the entire Whig programme of 1832 had been right. The merits of Symonds' ships, and his position as Surveyor, therefore became a purely political matter. Those able to consider his designs dispassionately weighed their undoubted speed against their poor performance in heavy weather, the deep roll which made them bad gun platforms, and their light armament relative to their great size and cost. Aboard the Symondite frigate *Pique* in 1835, 'The ship is at this moment lurching so heavily that I can hardly manage to write; everything is tumbling about, decks leaking, clothes all damp, hammocks dirty as well as ship, our rigging quite slack, and consequently the masts not quite as safe as they might be, with many other disagreeables caused by an incessant gale and heavy sea.'[4] Most serious of all, by the end of the 1840s the coming of the screw propeller opened the possibility of adding steam engines to ships of the line – but not to Symonds' hulls with their steeply rising floors. It is a caricature to say that Symonds was opposed to steam altogether; he designed some successful paddle sloops, but his model was the 1840s system of a sailing line-of-battleship manoeuvred into action by a paddle steamer secured alongside on the disengaged side. He opposed steam-powered ships of the line as premature, for they spelled the end of the big fast sailers with which he had made his name. If anything, the Symondite controversy was worse under the Tory government of 1841 to 1846, with Sir George Cockburn as Senior Naval Lord. He appointed a 'Committee on Naval Architecture', composed of graduates of the former School of Naval Architecture, to review Symonds' work. By the time the Whigs returned to power in 1846, they too were beginning to have misgivings. Whatever Symonds' talents as a designer, he had no interest in the Surveyor's duties of managing a programme of shipbuilding. The policy vacuum created by Graham's reform of the Admiralty left Symonds free to do what he liked, and what he liked did not include administration, compromise or conciliation. In 1847 a 'Committee of Reference' under the junior Naval Lord Captain Lord John Hay was appointed to review Symonds' work, and soon after, aged sixty-five and ill, he was eased into retirement.[5] 'Except on matters of religion,' Graham told the House of Commons, 'he did not know that any difference of opinion had been attended with so much bitterness – so much anger – so much resentment, as the merits of Sir W. Symonds and the virtue of his ships.'[6]

In his place Lord Auckland appointed Captain Baldwin Wake Walker, explicitly to provide 'more of judgement and general superintendence and much less of minute interference in construction'. 'In selecting you as successor to Sir William Symonds,' the Admiralty informed him, 'they have, consequently, looked more to sound practical knowledge and ability as a seaman, than to your qualifications as a shipbuilder. They wish you to bring a free and unbiassed judgement to bear upon the plans of others.'[7] In other words Walker was to manage the department: his assistants John Edye and Isaac Watts were the naval architects. This was an important recognition, by a Whig government, that professional expertise had an essential authority in technical matters which not even a gentleman could replace. Next year, 1848, Auckland re-established a training scheme for future naval architects at the Central School of Mathematics at Portsmouth. Unfortunately, Auckland's level-headed managerial competence was not universal. Five years later Sir James Graham returned as First Lord of the Admiralty in Aberdeen's government, and promptly closed the Central School.[8]

In 1815 Simon Goodrich, 'Mechanist to the Navy Board', was already actively experimenting with steam engines. By 1820 they were powerful enough for the Admiralty to order a steam tug. In 1824 Neale's expedition against Algiers included the steamer *Lightning*, and in 1826 the *African* steamed to Sierra Leone and back – much further than merchant steamers had yet ventured. By 1830 the Mediterranean steam packets were running to Alexandria in three stages: Falmouth to Gibraltar (1,010 miles), Gibraltar to Malta (970 miles) and Malta to Alexandria (860 miles). All these ships were small paddle steamers, nearly all with side-lever engines; shallow-draught and highly manoeuvrable, they were ideal for rivers and inshore waters, but an unsatisfactory compromise for sea passages. Their low-pressure boilers were fed with salt water and had to be frequently 'blown-down' and refilled with cold water to keep the salinity within safe limits, giving a fuel efficiency of no more than 10 per cent, and a short range under steam. Sail was essential for any long passage, but the engines and boilers forced the masts to be stepped in the wrong places, the paddles dragged badly even if declutched, and the windage of the paddle-boxes drove the steamers to leeward. On a wind, as a steamer heeled to her canvas, the lee paddle floats dug in and the ship yawed to leeward. The paddles required a broad, shallow hull which handled badly in a seaway, and steamers' beam over the paddle sponsons made it difficult to fit them into existing dry docks (for which reason naval steamers were often built with recessed sponsons). In spite of all this, nobody in the Navy doubted that steamers were already essential and would soon be much more so. At a dinner to mark Queen Victoria's coronation in 1837, Lord Minto the First Lord of the Admiralty, and Sir Thomas Byam Martin the former Controller, agreed that in the next war the best steam fleet would win.[9]

Steamers were now indispensable as tugs, packets and transports, but they were lightly armed, and scarcely qualified as warships except in the formal sense that in 1828 the first three appeared on the *Navy List*, with lieutenants in command. Their shallow hulls carried engines and boilers well above the waterline and exposed to damage in action, while the paddles were regarded as especially vulnerable (though experience was to show that even badly damaged wheels and floats worked surprisingly well so long as the engines were still turning). The paddle-boxes took up most of the broadside where guns were usually mounted. The first well-armed steamers were ordered in 1831 by the new Whig Admiralty Board led by Sir James Graham and Sir Thomas Hardy: four 800-ton ships with engines of 220 horsepower, armed with two 10-inch shell guns on deck, one forward and one aft, on revolving pivot mountings. These still-experimental heavy guns were designed to keep warships at a safe distance from the vulnerable steamers. From them derived a succession of larger paddle warships culminating in the four-funnelled steam frigate *Terrible* of 1845; with engines of over 2,000 HP, able to tow a three-decker at eight knots, but herself larger than an old seventy-four-gun ship of the line, costing twice as much, and still carrying only sixteen guns. The glaring problem remained: steam was indispensable, and by 1841 over a fifth of the Navy consisted of steamers, yet even the most costly steam warships had little fighting value. Attempts were made to develop tactics for a combined steam and sail fleet, with the steamers towing or manoeuvring the ships of the line, but it was scarcely a satisfactory solution.[10]

Paddle warships were responsible for two interesting innovations: one long forgotten, the other now universal. Ships often involved in transporting men and troops inshore needed good boats, but the paddle-boxes made it difficult to hoist them inboard, and there was limited space to hang them in davits. The 'paddle-box boat' was an ingenious solution proposed by Captain George Smith in 1838. These large boats were stowed upside-down above the paddle-wheels, forming the top of the paddle-boxes – they are prominent in many photographs of the larger naval paddle steamers. As the wheel revolved it threw up spray which constantly wetted the inside of the boat, keeping the planking tight with none of the difficulty usually experienced in keeping wooden boats watertight when out of the water for long. An ingenious reversing cradle allowed the heavy boat to be swung out for lowering.[11] The other innovation derived from paddle steamers is the bridge. Paddle-boxes blocked the view from the quarter-deck and made it impossible to con a steamer from the traditional standpoint beside the wheel, so officers soon learned to climb on top of a paddle-box to see where they were going, from which it was a short step to throw a light bridge across from one side to the other, and later to equip it with a wheel and engine-room telegraphs. Paddle-boxes are almost forgotten, but every ship is still navigated from a bridge.[12]

In the late 1830s iron was already coming into use as a shipbuilding material with tensile strength superior to timber, but the quality of wrought-iron plates was still uncertain, and the impossibility of using a magnetic compass seemed to rule out iron hulls for seagoing vessels. In 1839 Sir George Airy, the Astronomer-Royal, published (prematurely, as it transpired) a proposed solution to the compass problem. The same year John Laird of Birkenhead built the iron steamers *Nemesis* and *Phlegethon* for the East India Company, followed in 1842 by the *Guadalupe* and *Montezuma* for Mexico, the largest iron ships yet built. By this date Laird alone had built forty-four iron vessels, and the Admiralty was subject to growing Parliamentary pressure to do the same. The *Nemesis* returned from the China War in 1843 and Commander William Hall's reports, plus those of Commander Charlewood of the *Guadalupe*, persuaded the Admiralty to order a number of iron warships culminating in four remarkable iron frigates of over two thousand tons, laid down between September 1845 and March 1846.[13] At this date, under Peel's government, the First Lord was the colourless Earl of Haddington, the senior naval lord the forceful Tory Sir George Cockburn, and the Surveyor still Sir William Symonds. Cockburn and Symonds, being of opposite politics and policies, were on the worst of terms, and it is not entirely clear who was responsible for ordering the new iron ships.[14]

What was soon clear, or seemed to be, was that it had been a very expensive mistake. Hall and Charlewood reported that iron hulls were resistant to shot damage and easily repaired, but unusually secret firing trials begun at Woolwich Arsenal in August 1845, and reported to the Admiralty in September 1846 (after the new ships had been ordered), appeared to show the opposite. So did further firing that summer against the flimsy and corroded iron harbour craft *Ruby*. Sentiment in Parliament and elsewhere had now swung firmly against iron hulls, and the new Whig Admiralty Board decided to convert the expensive iron frigates to troopships and build no more warships of iron. 'The late Board of Admiralty have left us a bad legacy of numerous iron vessels,' Auckland wrote sadly in December 1846,

> many of which are yet unfinished, though we are bound by contract to accept them. We regard them as utterly unfit for the close collision of European war, and we must endeavour to apply them to the conveyance of troops and stores and other such services.[15]

Further firing trials between 1849 and 1851 and again in 1861 reached similar conclusions, and so did French trials in 1844.[16]

There is a puzzle here, for it is nowadays certain that wrought-iron plates of good quality do not shatter into deadly splinters when struck by solid shot. The experimental results, if correctly reported, were entirely misleading. Some, but not all, of the tests were conducted in freezing weather, which was not then known to affect the strength of iron. Possibly some of the plates were of poor quality, but surely not all. The 1849 to 1851 trials, however, were thorough, carefully conducted and carefully reported, and it is difficult to fault their conclusion that the iron plates they had available shattered when struck by shot. As a result, iron hulls were abandoned by all navies. The only way of taking advantage of its enormous strength and potential seemed to be to protect the iron hull with armour.[17]

Iron, moreover, had other disadvantages. It was liable to corrode, and it was extremely susceptible to fouling. The established answer to fouling was copper sheathing, but putting copper and iron in contact in salt water set up electrolytic corrosion which was capable of eating through an iron hull at an alarming rate. Moreover, copper itself had fallen out of favour because of the rate at which the expensive metal dissolved in use even on wooden hulls. In 1822 the Navy Board consulted Britain's most eminent chemist, Sir Humphrey Davy, President of the Royal Society, who recommended soldering iron or zinc 'protectors' to the copper. That worked, in a way. The copper ceased to dissolve, but it also ceased to work as an anti-fouling measure: 'barnacles of an immense size had attached themselves in clusters to the copper sheathing in the vicinity of the protectors'.[18] As we now know, copper remained bright in salt water only because it was constantly dissolving, and in the process giving off copper salts which poisoned weeds and barnacles (for which reason coppering is nowadays frowned upon as environmentally destructive). This debacle did some damage to the reputation of the Royal Society and science generally. It left the Admiralty less reverential towards scientists, and the scientists themselves more cautious in advancing their theories. It also left no obvious way of stopping iron hulls fouling except by frequent docking, and made it difficult to operate iron ships in the tropics, where hulls fouled three times as fast, and docks were rare.[19]

Iron hulls were closely connected to another important technical development, the screw propeller. This ancient idea was given new life by the steam engine, and attracted many inventors, led by the Swedish-American engineer John Ericsson, and the Englishman Francis Pettit Smith, whose rival designs were offered to the Admiralty in the late 1830s. Ericsson was the better engineer of the two; Smith the better businessman and manager, whose firm was adequately capitalized and capable of demonstrating a working example rather than just a good idea. At the Admiralty Sir Edward Parry and the Steam Department were immediately in favour, but Sir William Symonds the Surveyor was not. Parry unwisely involved Isambard Kingdom Brunel as a consultant, whose attempts to make money out of the position annoyed both Pettit Smith and Thomas Lloyd, Chief Engineer of the Woolwich Steam Factory. (The life of Brunel later published by his son makes no mention of his financial sharp practice and presents him as the victim of a reactionary Admiralty determined to block the new technology; an interpretation typical of the period.) Nevertheless the big picture was soon clear: in the language of the day, the 'screw' had rendered the 'steamer' (i.e. paddle steamer) instantly obsolete. 'I am led to believe,' Auckland wrote in August 1846, 'that very shortly the screw will in great measure supersede the paddle, that steamers of very large dimensions will not be found useful in proportion to their expense, and that we shall not again be persuaded to build an iron vessel.'[20] Everything about the paddle steamer, which could neither fight nor make long sea passages, was incompatible with a warship. The screw, however, could be fitted in existing or future sailing warships, with the engine and boiler in the hold and no sacrifice of armament. The only obvious exceptions were the 'Symondite' ships, whose hull form was ill-adapted to installing an engine and boiler. The advantages of screw propulsion were so great and so obvious that it hardly mattered if it were (as at first it seemed) mechanically less efficient than the paddle. However, there was yet no theoretical understanding of how the screw worked, and a long series of trials in the early 1840s were needed to work out empirically what was the best design. These trials showed that a short two-bladed screw with a coarse pitch offered satisfactory performance at the slow running speed of the engines of the day. Stopped in the vertical position, aligned with the sternpost, it gave reduced drag for sailing, and very soon the new 'banjo-frame' sternpost allowed the screw to be disconnected from the tailshaft and hoisted out of the water into a well in the stern. Combined with a telescopic funnel, this quickly converted the screw steamer into a perfect sailing warship, with no drag under water, no extra windage aloft, and no unsightly evidence of the industrial age visible at all. The only real disadvantage was that the hold was full of machinery, leaving little stowage for long voyages, and even this was mitigated by conversions of existing ships which were cut in two and lengthened by the insertion of a new central section to carry the engine and boiler. In practice steam ships of the line by the 1850s roughly divided into two classes: 1st and 2nd Rates, either newly built or radically converted by lengthening the hull, received powerful engines giving a speed of 10 or 11 knots (13 knots in the extreme case of the French *Napoléon* of 1852). Smaller and older ships were cheaply converted into what were called 'blockships', with a minimum machinery plant giving a speed of about six knots, sufficient for short passages, to fight under steam and to get in and out of port. When the French and British fleets mobilized for the Russian War, with fleets composed partly of steam ships of the line, it soon became clear that even the underpowered blockships were so much more versatile for all sorts of operations, and so much safer in confined waters, that the remaining sailing warships were usually left behind, or towed.[21]

As Surveyor, Byam Martin had a clear sense of the wisdom of making haste slowly in adopting new technology, allowing time for the best solution to become clear. The Whigs, identifying themselves as the party of progress, tended to be less critical enthusiasts. For Peel's Tory government to spend large amounts of public money on the new screw technology was politically risky, especially as the paddle steamer had already captured the image of modernity, while the screw looked like – in a sense was – a reactionary move, restoring the sailing warship to its primacy. It behoved the Admiralty to give thought to 'public relations' (to use a phrase then unknown). This was the prime motive for the well-known trials of the screw sloop *Rattler* and the paddle sloop *Alecto* in 1845, which culminated in a tug-of-war, before a large and distinguished audience, in which the *Rattler* triumphed. The public was not told that her engines were considerably more powerful than the *Alecto*'s (their 'nominal horsepower', the misleading figure then usually cited, was the same), nor that the Admiralty had already made its choice and ordered the first screw block-ships. The trial captured the public imagination and justified decisions which had already been taken on other grounds.[22]

In order to build screw steamers of any size it was necessary to overcome two significant technical problems. The engine in the hold was connected to the screw by an iron shaft running a third or more of the length of the ship. Forging such a shaft was a considerable feat. It had to be supported over its length by the new roller bearings, and to pass through the deadwood of the stern by a watertight joint. Eventually in 1854 John Penn devised a satisfactory 'stern-gland' which was packed with *lignum vitae*, a naturally oily, self-lubricating, tropical hardwood, but before that there were a number of accidents. The steam line-of-battleship *Royal Albert*, on her way home from the Black Sea in January 1856, suffered a complete failure of her stern gland, flooded fast, and had to be beached on the island of Kea, near Athens, to save the ship. Large wooden steamers were particularly liable to such disasters because the rigid iron shaft could not accommodate the natural flexing of a wooden hull, and the same flexing made internal watertight bulkheads more or less impossible. Here were more reasons to adopt iron construction.[23]

Yet another reason was the slow introduction of guns designed to fire explosive shells rather than solid shot, which can be dated from the publication of *La Nouvelle Force Maritime* by the French artillerist Henri-Joseph Paixhans in 1821. By making it possible for the first time to fire an explosive shell from a conventional gun with a high muzzle-velocity and a flat trajectory, without it exploding in the barrel, Paixhans opened the way to providing ships' guns with different ammunition for different targets. In practice, however, shells were lighter than shot of the same calibre, of considerably shorter range and ballistically less stable. The tendency was for ships to mount a limited number of large shell guns, often on the upper deck in pivot mountings, to supplement a conventional broadside. Paddle steamers, with limited space to mount any sort of guns, tended to adopt shell guns to deter warships from coming too close. This deterrence value rested on the shell's reputation (strongly promoted by Paixhans and his fellow artillerist Napoleon III) for terrible destruction of wooden hulls. Firing trials in both France and Britain, and early shell-firing steamers such as the East India Company's *Diana* in the Burma War of 1824–5 and the Greek *Karteria* during the War of Independence, aroused fears for British naval supremacy. Actual experience in action, notably the bombardment of Sebastopol, suggested that the destructive effect of shells on wooden ships had been much exaggerated. The sinking of the Danish line-of-battleship *Christian VIII* by Prussian batteries in Eckernförde in April 1849, often claimed as the effect of shell-fire, was actually due to the older technology of red-hot shot. The most dangerous of all the new artillery weapons to a wooden warship was the British Martin shell, filled with molten iron by a cupola furnace. Usually employed by shore batteries, it was taken to sea by some of the first ironclad battleships. Experiments suggested that Martin shells started fires which were impossible to extinguish.[24]

The obvious response to shell-fire was to build ships of iron, or to protect wooden ships with iron armour. Then it was discovered that iron hulls were fatally vulnerable, which seemed to suggest that all future warships, whether wooden or iron-hulled, would need armour. The sudden crisis of the Russian War, and exaggerated reports of the Battle of Sinope, pushed both Britain and France into action. During 1854 a common programme was worked out of simple armoured floating batteries – boxlike vessels of very limited seaworthiness, intended to engage coastal batteries. The first three, the French *Dévastation, Lave* and *Tonnante*, attacked the Kinburn forts at the mouth of the Dnieper River in October 1855, and amply proved the concept.[25]

Alongside the floating batteries came a large British 'mass-production' scheme to build gunboats and (slightly larger) gun-vessels; small and simple steam vessels (with auxiliary sail) intended to carry into action one or two heavy guns. The idea was that a fleet of them would deploy against a fortress as many guns as a ship of the line, but small vessels continually on the move under steam would be much less vulnerable. Against Sveaborg and Kinburn the new gunboats proved very successful, and at the Spithead naval review of 23 April 1856 which celebrated the end of the war, a large number of them were present to join in a mock attack on Southsea Castle; Henry VIII's old seaside battery serving as a discreet reminder to the invited diplomats of Britain's ability to attack their forts and harbours.[26]

FIVE

Men of Interest and Fortune

Social History: Officers 1815–1860

There were three stages to a commissioned officer's career in the eighteenth-century Navy, each run under different rules. First, boys went to sea hoping to rise to the first commissioned rank of lieutenant. Their promotions were made on merit, as judged mainly by their captains, regulated at the crucial stage of lieutenant's rank by that rarest of eighteenth-century mechanisms, a formal qualifying examination. The Admiralty had almost no control over these careers. It had no means of knowing who were the young gentlemen aspiring to commissioned rank, nor how many of them there were. When and how they joined the Navy, how their careers advanced thereafter, and what they learned (or did not learn) in the process were matters entirely outside its knowledge. In 1794 the Admiralty had signalled its distaste for the levelling principles of the French Revolution by creating the new rating of 'Boy 1st class, called Volunteer', exclusively for 'young gentlemen intended for the sea service', but as yet it left the choice, and the grounds of choice, entirely up to individual captains. Only when they presented themselves for their lieutenant's examination, after at least six years at sea, did the young gentlemen officially come to the Admiralty's attention, and even then it did not directly control the examination, which was conducted *viva voce* by the Navy Board at home, and by panels of captains on foreign stations. The Admiralty was obliged to accept whatever officers the system threw up, knowing scarcely anything about them. Once officers received their first commissions as lieutenants, however, the Admiralty gained a large degree of control over their careers, since appointments to particular ships, and promotions to Commander and Captain, were made directly by the Board in home waters, and subject to its confirmation even overseas. From post rank (i.e. Captain's rank)[1] the system again changed, and the Admiralty lost much of its control, not this time because it was ignorant of what was happening but because, by ironclad convention, captains rose in strict order of seniority, and admirals were chosen only from the top of the captains' list. The Admiralty still chose which captains to employ in command of which ships, but it could neither advance the promotion of deserving candidates nor delay that of the undeserving. Its choice of candidates for flag rank at any one moment was limited to the small number of captains at the top of the list, regardless of how many or how few possessed the talent, experience and physical fitness necessary for high command. The temporary rank of commodore, in effect an acting rear-admiral, allowed some flexibility, but was in practice only usable for senior captains who were already near to flag rank. Only the rank of 'rear admiral without distinction of squadron' (colloquially 'Yellow Admiral') had been established in 1747 to provide an avenue of notional promotion to what was really a form of retirement, but many officers with influence avoided this humiliation and continued in active rank (though not necessarily active employment). During the Revolutionary and Napoleonic Wars, in an age of high officer unemployment when there were plenty of spare captains, the Admiralty found the working admirals it needed by promoting large numbers of captains to flag rank, selecting the best of them for employment and ignoring the rest. Such was the oversupply of captains, in spite of a rapidly falling rate of promotion from commander, that there was no risk of running out of experienced candidates. The first rear-admirals of the French Revolutionary War, made in 1793, were captains of 1762, and the last of the Napoleonic War, made in 1814, were captains of 1795, so that in more than twenty years of war the time taken to rise to the top of the captains' list fell only from thirty-one to nineteen years, thanks to the creation of no fewer than 328 admirals, many of them superfluous and unemployable.[2]

Similar processes were taking effect below Captain's rank. By 1810 only 41 per cent of captains on the *Navy List* were actually serving, 44 per cent of commanders, and 60 per cent of lieutenants: all the rest were on half pay. Some of these were undoubtedly too old or ill to serve and effectively retired, but many were eager, indeed desperate, for employment. The coming of peace changed everything, and yet nothing. Commissioned and warrant officers had a permanent standing in the Service whether or not they were employed, and for commissioned officers in particular, whose commissions gave them the rank of gentlemen, it was disgraceful to suggest that they might be forced out of the Navy by any consideration, including age. A small number of the very elderly might be 'superannuated', but anything in the nature of retirement, even the use of any word implying such an idea, was considered extremely sensitive.[3] Successive Cabinets and Boards of Admiralty nibbled timidly at the edge of this problem, and hoped it would go away. A Navy which in 1813 had 4,873 commissioned officers – about twice as many as it needed for 147,000 men and 685 ships and vessels – then in 1814–15 added to their number by extensive promotions, including over a thousand more lieutenants. By 1817 the size of the active Service had fallen below 23,000 men manning 131 ships and vessels, but the numbers of lieutenants and command-ers were still growing, and nine out of ten of the 5,840 commissioned officers were unemployed. Ten years later the Navy had expanded to 33,000 men, with eight ships of the line in commission – for which it had 187 flag offi-cers, 830 captains, 868 commanders and 3,710 lieutenants. On 20 October 1827, the day of the battle of Navarino, the Navy had in commission fifty-two captain's commands and sixty-four commander's commands to employ all these officers.[4]

There was no possibility that a peacetime – or even a wartime – Navy could provide jobs for them all. Young officers were still needed, and young men still pressed to join, but soon it became clear to them that even if they could reach commissioned rank, it had little to offer them but status and unemployment. 'Our passed midshipmen are all disgusted,' wrote Napier in 1840,

> our youngsters see this, hear the grumbling, and become so also. I have two who have quitted the service; and their reason is, that when they see midshipmen who have passed eight or ten years, it is useless their continu-ing in such a profession. If we do not change our system, a catastrophe will befall us sooner or later.[5]

Meanwhile the existing officers grew steadily older and feebler, forgetting their skills and blocking the prospects of their juniors. In 1832 only 24 per cent of the lieutenants, 13 per cent of the commanders and less than 10 per cent of the captains were employed; ten years later those figures were 35 per cent, 19 per cent and 9 per cent. By the 1840s commanders spent half their time in that rank ashore and lieutenants three-quarters of their time. In 1841 there was a commander of forty-seven years' seniority on the list, and a lieutenant of sixty years. Half the captains in the Navy had never served afloat in that rank, and many of those who were serving had long passed their youth and vigour. When in 1834 the twenty-nine-year-old Commander Henry Keppel was appointed to command the brig *Childers* ('which my brother-in-law, Harry Stephenson, had obtained for me through his friend the Hon. George Dundas, a Sea Lord'), he found that there were five captains in the Mediterranean whose seniority in that rank dated from before he was born. By 1850 captains of 1814 were hoisting their flags for the first time after thirty-six years on the captains' list.[6] Thoughtful admirals like Sir William Parker contemplated the situation with something like anguish:

> I am a strong advocate for bringing forward *young* and *active* officers, in responsible situations, it is the only course by which we can hope to have an efficient Navy in case of European hostilities; all possible attention and protection is due to the *old* officers who have devoted their services to the country, but it is to the *younger* and not the infirm and declining portion of the profession that we must look, when the struggle comes on, and it is as absurd as it will prove futile to keep old gentlemen in training, who have nothing to *learn* and too feeble to stand the brunt of hard duty, however willing the spirit may be to set an example of activity and sound system.[7]

Up to post rank it was possible for the lucky and able like Keppel to be promoted fast – over the heads of the unlucky majority of their contemporaries – but the captains' list remained a slow but certain mill to grind keen young junior officers into exhausted old admirals, getting older as the century advanced. The commanders-in-chief of the Navy's main (and usually only) fleet, in the Mediterranean, between 1811 and 1828, had an average age of fifty-five. Between 1829 and 1837 it had risen to sixty-two, and between 1838 and 1853, to sixty-eight. Stopford was relieved in 1841 at the age of seventy-three, and his four successors in the Mediterranean command were appointed at sixty-seven, seventy-four, sixty-five and sixty-seven respectively. Meanwhile the French admirals they might have to fight were ten to twenty years younger; in the extreme case of Joinville (who as a member of the royal family had enjoyed very fast promotion), in 1846 he was thirty-seven years younger than Sir William Parker (who himself had been made post at nineteen by his uncle Lord St Vincent, and reached flag rank before he was fifty). It is fair to add that these British admirals – Parker above all – impressed their younger French contemporaries as fit, tough and vastly experienced.[8] From the 1840s, the growing difficulty of finding fit and suitable candidates for high rank from any party tended to dilute political influence. In 1846 Peel's First Lord, Lord Ellenborough, appointed the Whig Parker to command the Evolutionary Squadron because 'we really do not know where to go for any other man in whom we could place confidence'. He was only sixty-five, and the other possible candidates were all in their seventies.[9]

In 1831 Sir James Graham's Admiralty Board took the bold step of instituting a new category in the *Navy List*: 'Rear-Admirals on the Retired Half-Pay'.

Naturally the hated word aroused great opposition, and in 1840 the Admiralty surrendered and restored both the 'retired' and the 'superannuated' to the active list (abolishing the old 'Yellow Admiral' in the process), at the seniority they would have attained if nothing had happened. They were no younger, of course, and no more likely to be offered employment, but they had the dignity and steadily increasing half-pay of 'active' flag rank, and they continued to block the promotion of their juniors. A long series of efforts were made to tempt officers of various ranks into retirement with offers of notional promotion, but few accepted, the Admiralty had no power of compulsion, and nothing could be done to prevent the same problem recurring in a few years as the captains continued to grow older just as fast as before. To solve its difficulties the Admiralty really needed to combine the advancement of younger officers with the retirement of the older, but no one would retire if a promotion were in prospect, so the Admiralty had to promise to promote nobody in the hope of tempting some to retire – which of course made the situation even worse. Only in 1850 did the Admiralty actually force the most aged senior officers to accept 'reserved half pay', which was retirement in all but name, limiting the active flag list to 99 and captains to 350, but this still left too many officers on the list, far too late. 'Of one thing I am certain,' Parker wrote in 1850,

> namely, that in the present state of our senior officers, it cannot be for the interests of the country to employ old men as Captains, for they will be found disinclined to acquire a knowledge of modern system [sic], and too infirm to teach the young officers the valuable lessons which they have been schooled in in days gone by . . .[10]

The Navy was now changing fast as innovative technology was adopted, but aged senior officers were forgetting the old ways without learning the new.[11]

The consequences became painfully clear at the outbreak of the Russian War. The worst case of all was in the Pacific. At sixty-three Rear-Admiral David Price was the youngest British flag officer afloat, with a gallant record as a young officer in the French Wars, but he had spent almost all the past forty years ashore, and the life of a country gentleman in Wales had ill-prepared him for the responsibility of an isolated command. It took months to assemble his squadron, rendezvous with the French and cross the Pacific under sail to attack the Russian establishment of Petropavlovsk in Kamchatka. He was long past the physical and mental resilience of youth, the unaccustomed strain of command preyed on his mind, and the day before the planned attack he shot himself.[12] Perhaps this shameful episode had some good effect in bringing home the risks of the situation. In 1860 Sir John Pakington the recent First Lord told the Commons that 'successive Boards of Admiralty have from time to time been content to adopt mere stopgaps to meet the emergency of the moment, and have never had the courage to deal with the subject upon broad and permanent principles', adding later, 'I am convinced that the navy never will be satisfied, and never ought to be satisfied, until this miserable hand-to-mouth system is abandoned.'[13] But he could speak freely because he was already out of office; naval retirement was still an explosive subject which few Cabinets were anxious to touch. The problem cannot be said to have been finally solved, by the forces of nature rather than by government or Admiralty, until 13 February 1892, the day when Admiral of the Fleet Sir Provo Wallis, the last officer to have commanded a ship during the Great Wars, at length quitted the active list at the age of 100 after a naval career of eighty-eight years, most of them spent on half pay.[14]

The history of commissioned officers' promotion and retirement in the first half of the nineteenth century is a history of failure. What needed to be done was clear enough by the 1830s at the latest, but successive governments lacked the resolution to take painful decisions, and a bad situation slid steadily towards catastrophe. The subject of patronage and the machinery of selecting officers for promotion offers a different perspective, in which the Navy can be seen as a litmus paper revealing changing attitudes to influence, and changing definitions of merit. Here a key theme is the Admiralty's efforts to take over the powers of patronage and promotion, so many of which had until the nineteenth century belonged to captains and admirals. Its reason for doing so was clearly that patronage was power, and it wanted the power both to strengthen its control of the Navy, and to improve the social tone of the wardroom. In 1814 the Admiralty conducted a survey of the age and social status of all midshipmen afloat, and the following year it required captains to gain its prior approval before entering, disrating or discharging any mates, midshipmen or volunteers (these being the ratings in which most 'young gentlemen' served their first years afloat). From 1818 'Admiralty Midshipmen', under the Board's direct patronage, took precedence over the captains' protégés, and filled the most numerous vacancies, those created by illness. They also had the precious privilege of continuous service, without breaks between commissions. By these moves Lord Melville's Admiralty Board seized much of the captains' most valuable patronage, but some captains seem to have approved of what they saw as a mechanism to raise the social tone of the midshipmen's berth, and hence in time of the wardroom. The Royal Naval College at Portsmouth, expanded and reformed in 1806, was an important part of the machinery. Between 1814 and

1820 it sent into the Service 203 young gentlemen, about 6 per cent of the Navy's then seagoing officer strength. This was a small proportion of the requirement, but an influential one, and no less than one-third of the new lieutenants promoted in the exceptional year of 1830–31 had been educated at the College. The fees were £72 a year, with reductions for a limited number of officers' sons, but from 1817 some 65 per cent were paying the full fee. From 1830 the parents of young gentlemen not in the College had to undertake to support them with £40 to £50 a year until they reached commissioned rank, and one officer's widow left with seven children was curtly informed that 'as she cannot comply . . . her son cannot be admitted into H.M. Service'.[15] All these measures express the priorities of the Melville Admiralty, and it is obvious that its power to nominate 'Admiralty Midshipmen', the growing emphasis on naval education, and the fees associated with it, all worked together to make the Navy more socially exclusive.[16]

In the 1820s the Admiralty's choices for lieutenant were for the most part not the politically well-connected, but young men who had fought well in the Great Wars and had patrons in the Navy, the same sort whom the captains favoured. In February 1830, however, by which time the supply of wartime veterans of this age had already dried up, the Admiralty claimed control of volunteers' whole careers, not just their first entries as before. For a year its choices fell on a cohort of young men whose fathers were politically close to Melville and the ministry, but socially quite diverse – they included two brewers, two newspaper proprietors and a dockmaster. It is hard to know which of the three innovations – central government patronage, Tory politics or fathers in trade – would have been most distasteful to the Whigs, and it is no surprise that Sir James Graham abolished the system as soon as he arrived in office.[17]

What followed was a system of nomination for naval cadetship. The details changed frequently, but the trend was for a growing proportion of nominations to be reserved to the members of the Admiralty Board. By 1848 one hundred nominations were available each year, thirty-six of them to the First Lord in person, another thirty-six to the remaining Board members in turn, and the remainder to commanders-in-chief or senior captains. Whichever party was in power, most of these nominations went to the sons of gentlemen of rank and fortune, supported by eminent senior officers, and preferably by members of the government. Under Sir John Pakington, First Lord in Derby's ministry of 1858–9, 57 per cent of successful candidates were backed by (and in many cases were kinsmen of) peers, MPs, baronets or knights of his party, and a further 20 per cent by naval officers, mostly well connected with the Tories. Under the Duke of Somerset in Palmerston's ministry of 1859–66, the proportion of those favoured by Liberal peers, MPs, baronets or knights rose to 69 per cent. Even the most eminent naval families could not compete without political support. In spite of his very distinguished service in the Baltic during the Russian War, Bartholomew Sulivan very nearly failed to get his son into the Service, even though he could show that both the boy's grandfathers and all four of his great-grandfathers had reached flag rank.[18]

From 1830 to well into the 1860s Whig or Peelite governments were in office with only brief intermissions, and naval promotion tended to follow a typical Whig pattern, in which political connections operated through personal and family links, and family or friendship often trumped politics. When the Whigs took office in 1830, Tory admirals like Sir George Cockburn at the Admiralty and Sir Thomas Byam Martin at the Navy Board naturally left – but their political opponents were ejecting them from political office, not from the Navy, and recognized their claims to compensation. Cockburn went to be commander-in-chief in North America, and returned to the Admiralty under Peel's administration from 1841 to 1846, while in 1833 Byam Martin was offered but declined the Mediterranean command.[19] Sir Edward Codrington, commanding the 'Evolutionary Squadron' assembled in 1831 for tactical trials, took his son Henry as flag-lieutenant, and was able to make him commander on the 'haul-down vacancy' when he left the command. His fellow Whig Sir James Graham gave Henry a command in 1834, and two years later Lord Minto made him post.[20] The Tory Alexander Milne was six years unemployed under Whig administrations, until he was given a ship by Minto – a political opponent, but a fellow Lowland Scot. Minto, whose Admiralty Board included his brother Rear-Admiral George Elliot, was well known for putting family first – meaning the Elliots first, and other Whig families next.[21] In 1838 he promoted Henry Giffard to commander 'as a just compliment to poor Carter's memory': the young man deployed a dense web of Whig connections linking him to Minto and other members of his Board, and his grandfather Sir John Carter had been a noted Whig mayor of Portsmouth forty years before.[22] The Peelite Lord Ellenborough, briefly First Lord in 1846, was notoriously hostile to political appointments, but accepted 'that it is also allowable and right to have regard for the social position of the Families of such officers, the whole Profession being interested in inducing young men of high Station in Society to enter the Navy . . .'[23] It was not a big difference when social and political connections were often hard to distinguish.

There were some young men of high station whose claims were in any case too strong to be denied. As Sir William Parker wrote to Haddington in May

1844, 'It cannot but be gratifying to your Lordship to know, that although Commander Wellesley's connection to the greatest man in our country must naturally ensure his promotion, yet, come when it may, it will be conferred on a young man of great merits and high principle, who will do honour to it.'[24] It would have been unthinkable to overlook the Duke of Wellington's nephew, but evidently both Parker and the First Lord were more comfortable with a clear conscience. Two years later a similar question arose over a prime minister's grandson. 'I have naturally a wish to do whatever can be *properly* done for the grandson of my father's old friend,' the scrupulous Ellenborough wrote to Parker in May 1846,

> but I am apprehensive as to the health of the young gentleman, and of the fitness I know nothing . . . I think it, on principle, useful to the Navy to number amongst its officers men of family, and I know these will not be induced to enter the service without some prospect of receiving a certain degree of favour in the matter of promotion, and this I think fair to give them; but then this must be given without prejudice to the service, by appointing an unfit man.[25]

Parker was able to tell Ellenborough what he wanted to hear:

> I have very sincere pleasure in being able to make a satisfactory report of Mr Addington, who is a very correct, attentive, and honourable young man, and in perfect health. I am delighted to find that you are favourably disposed towards him, and entirely concur with your Lordship as to the advantage and expediency of introducing a fair proportion of young men of family into the Navy, where, when animated by proper zeal, they are certainly among our brightest ornaments; but unless they are inclined to follow up their profession, they are of course better out of it. I had the gratification of placing Mr Addington in the Navy at the request of his grandfather, Lord Sidmouth, with whom I was well acquainted, and the young man has more than realised my expectations. I can assure your Lordship, without flattery, that you are winning golden opinions throughout the Navy by the encouraging and upright manner in which your patronage is dispensed, and it cannot fail to have the best effect.[26]

A young officer might be directly rewarded with promotion for good service, but an especially useful reward was to establish a connection with an influential patron. The skill and leadership shown by Midshipman William Mends in the wreck of the *Thetis* in 1831 so impressed the court martial which investigated the shipwreck that several of its members offered to take him in their ships. He chose Captain the Hon. Frederick Grey, for a son of Earl Grey the Prime Minister could not fail to be an effectual patron. In 1835 Frederick Grey became the First Lord's private secretary (hence manager of his patronage), and 'needless to say his [Mends'] prospects of promotion became brighter'. Eighteen years later as a newly promoted Captain, Mends offered himself to Sir Edmund Lyons, whom he had never met, to be his flag-captain, and Lyons accepted him over 132 other applicants on the strength of his reputation in the Navy, opening the way for Mends to distinguish himself during the Russian War. Thus, one officer advanced his career through a combination of luck and talent. Politics came into the mix indirectly, but Mends was a naval officer's son with no political interest of his own.[27] Lyons illustrates a more unusual career pattern: he had been given his first command as a compensation to the family for the loss of his brother, killed at Navarino in 1827, and later left the sea to become a diplomat for nineteen years, while his seniority went on climbing up the captains' list. He was British minister in Stockholm, a newly widowed rear-admiral, when he accepted the call to go to the Black Sea in 1853:[28]

> 'As to the power of faith in the spiritual life,' a contemporary observed, 'there existed an analogue in the naval – namely, interest, which could remove mountains. In the course of my professional career I observed that, though it was advantageous and desirable for an officer to have seniority, ability, experience, services, there was a more excellent way, that of interest, the most useful form, perhaps of which was the Avuncular – especially the Scoto-avuncular. Oh! it was a very blessed thing indeed to have an uncle in high places, particularly if he happened to be an admiral with his flag flying.'[29]

This was not an exaggeration. Commanders-in-chief possessed much of the patronage not yet appropriated by the Admiralty Board, and used it to found the naval dynasties which were so prominent in the Victorian *Navy List*. In 1815 Rear-Admiral John Harvey went out as Commander-in-Chief Leeward Islands with his son John as flag-lieutenant, two of his Boteler nephews as lieutenants of the flagship, and a third a midshipman.[30] Such 'family ships' were a recognized phenomenon, which the Admiralty tried in vain to discourage.[31] In the early 1850s Rear-Admiral Fairfax Moresby was commander-in-chief in the Pacific with his son flag-lieutenant, two other sons in the squadron plus a son-in-law and various other connections.[32] In October 1847 Sir William Parker wrote from Malta to Mrs Edmund Palmer, lamenting the death of an old friend, but taking consolation from the opening it gave him to offer a commander's vacancy to her son, and to recall 'the affectionate kindness shown to myself by your warm-hearted father fifty-one years ago, when . . . I became his Lieutenant in the active and enviable little frigate *Magicienne*'.[33]

These cases make the conventions of the day fairly clear. In disposing of patronage, personal obligations mattered. A high standard was required of young officers seeking promotion, but there was no pretence of impartiality. Talented young men with well-placed friends and relatives had 'interest' and were likely be noticed; lucky young men who shone in action or in a crisis (and survived) might deserve attention. (This was the attraction of Arctic exploration. It was scarcely a career, but it offered at least full pay, and some chance of fame, until the disaster that beset Sir John Franklin's expedition, and the subsequent expeditions sent to find him and his men, put a stop to such exploration for a generation.)[34] For the great majority without specialist skills, luck or friends, there was not much to hope for. 'Men of interest and fortune passed them by, and great numbers became useless, discontented and too often vicious.'[35]

'What comes next? They become careless of themselves; most of them take to drink, more or less, for that is a habit almost impossible to wholly abstain from, while leading that kind of monotonous life; from that they become despised by their seniors in the service . . .'[36]

'Drinking to excess was common, and the Midshipmen sent below in the middle watch to mix the tumbler of spirits and water (gin being then the favourite beverage) of the officers in charge of the watch, used to bet who would put in most spirit and least water. In my first year's service two of our officers died from alcoholism.'[37] The diary of a seaman in the *Leander* in the Pacific in 1863–5 notes seven officers court-martialled for drinking, not counting the chief engineer who died of it.[38]

There was another factor of weight in a patronage-based career structure, which was money. In 1822 Captain Thomas White of the *Creole* on the South America station was almost sixty and looking to retire. Commander the Hon. Frederick Spencer and Lieutenant Thomas Porter were the heads of their respective Admiralty lists for promotion, and 'want promotion very bad . . . [therefore] they together made up £5000, which of course has made Captain White very ill and so he is going home'. White was invalided into a comfortable retirement, Spencer was made post into the *Creole*, and Porter relieved him in command of the *Alacrity*. At the end of a chain of consequential promotions, Midshipman Horatio Austin, follower of the commander-in-chief Sir Thomas Hardy, became a lieutenant. Spencer and Porter could put up the huge sum of £5,000 to hasten Captain White home because this was one of the

few stations with large exports of bullion and undeveloped international banking, where it was still necessary for warships to convey specie. At this date the
captain could charge 2 per cent for his trouble, of which ½ per cent went to
the commander-in-chief and another ½ per cent to Greenwich Hospital. Next
year the *Alacrity* was ordered home carrying a 'freight' of £200,000 deposited
by local British merchants, 1 per cent of which would have recouped Commander Porter's investment straightaway.[39]

Naval officers were not insensible to the attractions of freight. 'The Gulf of
Mexico is for dollars what the bank of Newfoundland is for fish,' Keppel noted,
and the fishing could be very agreeable.[40] A commander-in-chief on the South
American or Pacific stations might make £10,000 in three years; Hardy made
£15,000–£20,000 between 1819 and 1822. Commanders and captains earning
£300 to £500 a year might collect ten years' pay with a lucky voyage. In 1820
Captain Thomas Searle of the *Hyperion* conveyed more than $1,500,000 of
cargo from Callao in Peru, earning about £2,300. In 1848 Captain Henry Byam
Martin (son of Sir Thomas) of the *Grampus* shipped $2,628,900 – more than
half a million sterling – to Britain probably from the Pacific coast of Mexico,
earning him £5,351 1s 6d. Three years later Henry Keppel came home from
Chile with a freight of $900,000.[41]

These huge sums were legitimate earnings within the regulations, but also
powerful temptations to dishonesty. Commanders-in-chief reserved the juici-
est morsels for the well-connected, and expected something in return. Captains abandoned their stations without orders to go after freights, or ordered
their juniors off the lucrative coast to take their places. One captain stretched
the definition of bullion to ship a cargo of cochineal worth £40,000 from Vera
Cruz in eastern Mexico, in addition to two and a half million dollars in silver.
Most captains smuggled silver out of Mexico without paying the 6 per cent
export duty, sometimes in uncoined form which was doubly illegal. In 1846
the Earl of Aberdeen, the Foreign Secretary, issued a circular warning naval
officers to avoid impropriety. They understood him perfectly: in the middle of
the Oregon crisis the previous year, the frigate *America*, ordered to the mouth
of the Columbia River to represent British claims, instead abandoned her
station to pick up a freight at Mazatlán, 2,000 miles south on the Mexican
coast. Captain the Hon. John Gordon was severely reprimanded by a court
martial and resigned his command, but he had no more to fear than a well-
funded retirement, and continued to rise up the ranks until he died a full
admiral. Captain Gordon was Lord Aberdeen's brother.[42]

Besides freights, some prize money during the Russian War and head
money for pirates, there was one other useful earner for the Navy, the head

money for captured slaves. The rates were changed several times, but under the 1838 Act a laden slaver paid £5 for each slave living, £2 10s for each who had died, and 30s a ton for the ship. Between 1807 and 1846 over a million pounds was paid out in head money alone, but very inequitably divided, with a few fast ships taking the largest share, and much of the arduous and deadly work of patrol yielding nothing. Unlike freights, however, which profited the captain and admiral only, slave bounties were paid in the same way as prize money, on a sliding scale descending with rank so that all the ship's company gained something. When the steam sloop *Hecate* took the slaver *Nelampago* in July 1846, Commander Joseph West and his ship's company earned £5 a head for 468 living slaves (and half that for thirty-six already dead), tonnage of £220 10s, and £84 16s 7d for the sale of the hull. Less agency and expenses it came to £2,334 3s 8d, of which West's share was £291 15s 5½d, and every able seaman got £5 15s 8½d.[43]

Looking back on the early Victorian age, the next generation tended to shudder self-righteously at the corrupting operation of patronage, but even they admitted it had some advantages in an age of stagnant promotion:

> Although the grossest injustice was involved in the old system, whereby many feeble vessels, many youthful, inexperienced and commonplace young officers, were suddenly pitch-forked above their seniors of standing, services and experience, still the system had its bright side, as it ensured a fair amount of young blood in the higher ranks . . . in addition, now and then, a really first-class man was accidentally secured in this way, when he was still young, bright, zealous and energetic.[44]

An example was Geoffrey Phipps Hornby, who rose in a Whig age both because and in spite of his connection with the Tory Earl of Derby. He got his lieutenancy in 1844 on a death vacancy because the commander-in-chief's son was too young; he made commander in 1850, one day before his twenty-fifth birthday, on another death vacancy given by his father, Rear-Admiral Phipps Hornby. Then his father joined the Admiralty Board under the Derby government, and on leaving office in December 1852 was able to make his son a Captain. The young Hornby had to sit out the Russian War, when the Aberdeen and Palmerston administrations ignored him, but when Derby returned to office in 1858 he was given a plum command and the chance to demonstrate that he was indeed a first-class man, still young and zealous.[45]

The way 'first-class men' of the mid-century demonstrated their talents was more and more likely to be by mastery of the new skills and technologies of the age, and by the education and training associated with them. Education, however, has to be understood in a social context. It had something to do with imparting instruction, but for many contemporaries that was the least significant part of it. Dr James Inman, headmaster of the Royal Naval College, was a distinguished mathematician and author, but he was not a good teacher. He and his colleagues followed the standard method of the day, namely rote learning, and taught 'cramming' courses well over the heads of boys most of whom had no more than an elementary education. In their final year, aged fourteen or fifteen, the boys followed this curriculum:

> Fifth half-year: Fortifications, doctrine of projectiles and its application to gunnery: principles of flexions and application to the measurements of surfaces and solids: generation of various curves, resistance of moving bodies: mechanics, hydro-statics, optics, naval history and nautical discoveries.
>
> Sixth half-year: More difficult problems in Astronomy, motions of heavenly bodies, tides, lunar irregularities: the 'Principia' and other parts of Newton's Philosophy to those sufficiently advanced.[46]

Only a handful of the bright and well-prepared were sufficiently advanced to prosper intellectually at the College.[47] This need not surprise us, for the unreformed public schools of the day were much the same. Their pupils memorized large quantities of Latin verse, which allowed them to quote classical authors with the ease of a gentleman, but only a minority acquired any real command of the language. They were not at school primarily for education: 'For many, a great public school is not so much a place where book learning is to be acquired, as a sphere for the formation and development of the habits, character and physique of an English gentleman.'[48]

Most naval officers would have agreed that education was primarily about character rather than intellect, which may be why in 1837 Lord Minto's Admiralty Board decided to close the College to young gentlemen, all of whom now proceeded straight to sea on entering the Navy. Not much money can have been saved, since the College continued in use offering revision classes for older half-pay officers, still taught in the same dry style as before. 'In no part of this abstract course did we learn to apply our knowledge to practice, nor had we time. It was a course for three years instead of one and required superlative teaching. Main, of course, was very clever, but he did not profess to teach us . . .'.[49] To qualify for entry into the Navy nothing was now required of young gentlemen but to be not younger than twelve, 'able to write English correctly from dictation . . . acquainted with the first four rules of arithmetic, reduction and the rule of three'.[50] The real difficulty, of course, was to obtain a nomination, but this simple educational test established a precedent, and in 1839 an examination for the rating of midshipman was introduced. In 1851 the entry standard was slightly raised, and the regulations for the first time contemplated the possibility that a boy might fail.[51]

For twenty years, from 1837 to 1857, the 'naval cadets', as the volunteers were renamed in 1843, were supposed to receive on shipboard the same education which had formerly been offered to those who went to the College. This was to be provided by the warrant officer formerly called the schoolmaster, now 'naval instructor', whose pay and status were raised. In the first eighteen months of the 1837 scheme, however, only six of them joined the Navy, of whom only two were university graduates as intended. By September 1840 there were twenty-six on the *Navy List*, fewer than a third of them graduates. In 1842 it was therefore decreed that chaplains, most of whom were graduates, could act as naval instructors in addition to their religious duties, retaining three-quarters of the extra pay. This attracted chaplains, but discouraged naval instructors, so the numbers remained inadequate. As late as 1860 there were still twenty-six ships, including four flagships, with no instructor of any kind. Where there was no one to teach the syllabus afloat, it was not taught. Even when it was taught, it was the same desiccated material as before, most of it over the heads of the boys who were supposed to memorize it. At sea it was difficult for either instructors or pupils to find time and space for schoolwork, which many captains resented, and five or six hours a week was a real achievement.[52]

It is not surprising that there was a sharp and immediate fall in the results of the navigation examination required to pass for lieutenant, followed in the 1860s by several embarrassing cases of negligent grounding or shipwreck. About a third of the cadets entered between 1847 and 1857 had to be discharged, and many of the remainder proved unable to pass for lieutenant:[53]

> We learnt nothing of nautical astronomy, movements of the heavenly bodies, eclipses, winds, tides, currents, chart-work and so forth. I was never taught anything whatever about elementary chart-work till I taught myself after I became a lieutenant.[54]

Candidates were appearing who 'do not know the purpose of a sextant . . . some have never seen a chart . . . most of them have never seen a theodolite'.[55] All these young officers were already in uniform and in pay, so their failed careers represented a danger to the Service as well as a dead loss to the taxpayer, their families and themselves. Moreover, their education, even had it worked as intended, would have given them only a narrow and theoretical foundation for their work. Thinking admirals like Parker and Milne wanted thinking young officers and could see already that cramming with pure mathematics alone was not producing lieutenants safe to take charge of a watch, let alone broadening the minds or developing the powers of informed judgement of future senior officers.[56]

The question of naval education was closely linked with the rise of the new technologies. By the 1840s it was conventional wisdom that ambitious officers had to understand steam. 'I have come to the determination that the only way to get on in the service by one's own exertions, in these times of peace, is to join a steamer and to follow it up,' wrote Lieutenant Astley Cooper Key in 1844. Three years later Parker described him as 'a very intelligent and amiable young officer, and I believe has had the gratifying reward of promotion for his merits and scientific acquirements, which he bears with very becoming diffidence, displaying only a most praiseworthy zeal for his profession.' He was a post-captain at twenty-seven, but his was not only a steam-powered career; he was also an early gunnery officer, he was promoted commander for gallantry in action on the Rio Paraná, and as the son of Prince Albert's personal surgeon, he was not without well-placed connections.[57] At first officers learning about steam used some of their half-pay time to study as private pupils in the works of one of the big engine-building firms like Maudslay's or Napier's which supplied the Navy; 'they must commence in a proper manner, by pulling off their coat, and tucking up their shirt sleeves, fully determined to go through the whole course . . .'[58] From 1841 the College at Portsmouth offered a characteristically theoretical course, but many preferred the practical training available in the Woolwich Steam Factory, or at Malta where William Mends learnt his engineering. From 1849 it was necessary for an officer to pass a steam examination to serve aboard a steamer, and two years later Milne was pressing for it to become a general requirement. Not everyone saw the necessity, given that all steamers had engineers to take charge of the engine room, and the intellectual demands of gunnery were much higher: there was an underlying question of the relationship between command and technical expertise, to which more than one answer was possible.[59]

This brings us to the development of gunnery. Guns and ammunition had for centuries been the charge of a warrant officer, the gunner, but the new 'scientific' gunnery was entrusted from the first not to the gunners but to commissioned officers and to ratings. The eighteenth-century Navy had a formidable reputation for destructive close-range gunnery, but only fighting the American Navy in the war of 1812 had forced it to rediscover long-range gunnery – or as long as was possible with smooth-bore muzzle-loaders. In this war the Admiralty began to issue orders requiring the whole Navy to engage in gunnery drills – its first interference in a captain's responsibility for the fighting efficiency of his ship. By the 1830s the new 32-pounders offered greater range and accuracy, and the threat of shell guns made those qualities more critical. The shells of the day were simply hollow shot filled with powder. Their fuses were unreliable and their range and accuracy were considerably less than those of solid shot, so good long-range gunnery was the answer to the shell threat. The best range of the British 8-inch shell gun was 800 yards, whereas trials in 1838 showed that with expert shooting 45 per cent of 32pdr rounds would hit their target even at 2,000 yards. Conversely, the vulnerable steamers needed to develop accurate long-range shell-fire to keep powerful regular warships at a safe distance.[60]

Reports from Navarino, suggesting that British gun crews could not hit their target at long range and were not to be trusted with shells, persuaded both the Duke of Clarence and Lord Melville of the need for action, and in 1830 the old battleship *Excellent* in Portsmouth Harbour was established as a gunnery training ship, initially only for seamen gunners, but soon for officers as well. Sir James Graham did not abolish it, but added experimental functions, creating the prototype of many later British naval establishments which combined training and research. In her first twenty years the *Excellent* trained over 3,500 seamen gunners. Their performance in the bombardment of Acre silenced all critics.[61] At the same time the officers' gunnery course set other precedents. Unsurprisingly for a Portsmouth course heavily influenced by the Royal Naval College, it was taught to a very high standard, equivalent to a Cambridge mathematics degree and well beyond the capacity of most officers, but it established the small number who could pass as an intellectual elite. It did not take long for gunnery to be understood as a favoured route to promotion. The implication was that a future generation of senior officers would be chosen less from the well-connected, the gallant and the lucky, and more from the ranks of clever men who had passed difficult exams by memorizing enormous amounts of complex formulae. Sea officers had long been identified by their mastery of complex professional expertise, but formal training and formal assessment in a more abstract skill like gunnery was new.[62]

The relationship of command with social status and professional expertise bore directly on the changing position of the warrant officers. The eighteenth-century Navy had employed three distinct groups of warrant officers, who had little in common except for the historical accident that they held office by a warrant issued by one of the subordinate naval boards, rather than the more prestigious commission issued by the Admiralty. The boatswain, gunner and carpenter were the most ancient of the warrant officers, responsible respectively for the rigging and ground tackle, the guns, and the hull of the ship. They had come up from the lower deck and were unequivocally of lower middle-class standing, with no chance of further advancement. The surgeon and purser had something of the character of middle-class civilian professionals afloat, and from 1807 they were accepted as being of 'wardroom rank', with a uniform and a sword, which gave them social equality with the commissioned officers. The master, responsible for navigation and pilotage, had always been in a class of his own as the social and professional equal of the lieutenants. Finally, the chaplains fell into an ill-defined and uneasy space between commissioned and warrant rank.[63]

The haphazard structure of officers' ranks, and the poor 'fit' between social and naval rank, were uncomfortable to the nineteenth-century mind. The same forces which slowly generated a series of rates and ranks reserved to young gentlemen intended for lieutenant's rank (including in 1840 the new junior commissioned rank of 'mate', renamed sub-lieutenant in 1860), gradually sifted the warrant officers into gentlemen with commissioned rank and promotees from the lower deck with warrants. This, however, threw up another difficulty. General command aboard ship had always belonged to the commissioned officers – captains, commanders and lieutenants – and there was no intention of changing that, but if other officers received commissions without general command, new definitions were called for. Hence a distinction was created in the 1840s between 'military' and 'civil' officers. Military commissioned officers were the captains, commanders and lieutenants, those who had always had commissions and general command authority. Surgeons, pursers and chaplains were civil officers who received commissions in 1843 but had no general command authority beyond their immediate subordinates. The senior engineers joined them in 1847, and naval instructors in 1861. Military warrant officers were the boatswains, gunners and (to 1878) carpenters. In spite of their military status their standing in the Navy was falling, relatively and perhaps absolutely. Their pay scarcely covered the expense of their uniforms, in 1830 they lost their entitlement to a widow's pension, and in 1844 they were made subordinate even to naval cadets, who were not officers in any sense. Finally, engineers were civil warrant officers from 1837 to 1847, and carpenters became so in 1878. This complicated rank structure served its purpose in marking the social rank of a gentleman by a commission, and the power of general command by military rank.[64]

Of the new civil commissioned officers, the surgeons of the early nine-teenth century had changed the least. Although called 'surgeons' (as they still are), the naval doctors were early representatives of the modern 'general prac-titioner', mingling medicine and surgery, and an Act of 1815 exempting them from any requirement to be certificated by the civilian medical or surgical authorities made naval or military service an attractive start to a medical career ashore. In the immediate post-war years the over-supply of surgeons was as bad as that of other officers: in 1832 some 215 naval surgeons were employed out of 720 on the list. In addition, the Admiralty had the nomination of sur-geons of convict ships, which provided some further employment. But pay and promotion were better in the army, and the standard of naval surgeons left the Physician-General (Medical Director-General from 1844) in an unsatisfactory situation. Drink, desertion, fraudulent accounting, venereal disease and arrest for debt created too many vacancies. On the other hand, naval service gave surgeons unusual opportunities to distinguish themselves. From polar expe-ditions to anti-slaving patrols, they encountered extremes of environment and disease unknown to other medical men. They confronted some of the severest outbreaks of cholera and yellow fever. Their numerous scientific publications covered not only their medical work but a wide variety of scientific subjects including climate, agriculture, zoology, botany, ornithology, meteorology, eth-nography and archaeology. They made an important contribution to the devel-opment of 'medical arithmetic', meaning statistics, which were published annually in the Parliamentary Papers.[65]

The purser of 1815 was still both a ship's officer responsible for victualling and other consumable stores, and a private contractor responsible for supply-ing them at his own expense on fixed prices and conditions which might, if he were careful and lucky, allow him to make a profit. He took his own money to sea in order to buy supplies abroad, but he did not handle any public money until 1825, when ratings were allowed to draw 4s a month in cash from their wages from the purser. In 1842 his new situation was recognized with the new title of Purser and Paymaster, and next year he became one of the new civil commissioned officers. Finally in 1852 his evolution was complete with the title of Paymaster; a naval officer with a salary but no poundage, handling much public money but investing none of his own. From 1855 there was a regular hierarchy rising from Assistant Paymaster (equivalent to Sub-Lieutenant) to Paymaster 1st Class (equivalent to Commander), and a senior paymaster might serve as an admiral's secretary.[66]

Chaplains remained warrant officers 'of wardroom rank' until they received commissions in 1843, though those who were also naval instructors were not commissioned in that capacity until 1861. This was one of the many anomalies in the status of chaplains, who were paid and, in most respects, treated as officers, but claimed no particular rank and never wore uniform. The intention was to put no obstacle between chaplains and their congregations, but in an age when there was invariably a large social gulf between clergymen of the Church of England and working-class members of their congregations, ashore and afloat, the naval chaplains do not seem to have found their spiritual role easy:[67]

> The best eight years of a man's life are wasted when serving on board ship; and the period of time he passes there is a wearying, wearying, profitless business, to his own soul at least, and oftentimes to the souls of others. He is not placed, to begin with, in a position suitable to his character and education. He is allowed an income barely sufficient to support him; and opportunities are all but denied him of performing his duty . . . At sea, there is hope of doing a little good sometimes, if not directly, yet indirectly . . .[68]

The Russian War revived interest in naval chaplaincy, and raised the numbers serving to over seventy, but many of the more noteworthy examples of naval parochial ministry in the period were undertaken by Evangelical officers rather than chaplains.[69] Montagu Burrows, who was allowed by a 'magnanimous' chaplain to instruct the boys of his ship for Confirmation, describes himself as 'much in the position of a go-ahead curate in charge', though he was actually a watch-keeping lieutenant.[70]

The most revealing index of contemporary attitudes were the completely new ranks of engineers, but unfortunately their history has largely been written by twentieth-century naval engineers who reveal much more about their own professional anxieties than the realities of the nineteenth century. The very earliest naval steamers, mostly yard craft, were supplied with engineers by the engine-builders, following contemporary mercantile practice, but it was soon clear that the Navy required its own engineers, and it needed to establish a satisfactory position for them in the naval hierarchy, and naval society.[71] As early as 1830 Joshua Field, one of the partners of the engine-builders Maudslays, explained part of the problem to Sir Thomas Byam Martin:

> With reference to some of the Steam Vessels in His Majesty's Service, the machinery could not be better managed . . . but in some of the commissioned vessels the case is far otherwise, and I think it can be accounted for

chiefly from the want of a better understanding between the Officers and the Engineers, this arises very much from the education and previous habits of the only men qualified to manage these engines being quite at variance with the education and discipline of the Navy; having enjoyed in manufactories and workshop a loose kind of independence they do not readily fall in with that respectful and submissive demeanour necessary in the discipline of a King's Ship. On the other hand the officers do not make allowances for men so differently brought up from those men they have been accustomed to deal with, frequently treating them with harshness, and without understanding the subject, interfering with them in the execution of their duty . . .[72]

The Navy of the day was largely manned and officered from the southern counties of England, a predominantly rural, impoverished and conservative world. Many men came from naval families, and most seem to have been accustomed to a traditional deference. Engineers, by contrast, tended to come from the industrial districts of London, the Midlands and Scotland; their attitudes were often marked by Nonconformity and craft trades unionism. 'Socially and culturally their roots were in the labour aristocracy; they were not from naval or even maritime families; and they brought a different set of values with them – self-improvement, individualism and professional ambition.'[73] There was material here for a clash of cultures.

The first naval engineers' ranks were established in 1837 as warrant officers in three classes. Their social and professional position, as highly skilled manual craftsmen, was very similar to that of the carpenters, and warrant rank in itself seems to have been accepted as appropriate. But everything about engines was advancing very rapidly in importance, and in only ten years a new and original career structure was put in place. Now Assistant Engineers could advance to the commissioned rank of Chief Engineer (1st, 2nd and 3rd Class), and then in turn to Inspector of Machinery Afloat (equivalent to Captain), which seems to have stilled any complaints at lack of respect. The new engineer officers' ranks offered a full career structure founded on a thorough professional training well in advance of anything available elsewhere in the Navy at that date. It did not know the concept of half-pay: engineers were either employed at sea on sea-pay, or in harbour on the somewhat lower harbour-pay. The first training establishment for naval officers was the naval engineers' training ship *Devonshire*, established in 1857. By treating them as naval officers, with the same commitment as other officers, the Navy expected the same standards. The new voice-pipe and engine-room telegraph implicitly recognized the semi-detached status of the engine room and the responsibility of the engineer officer to manage it. The large engine-room crews of warships obliged the engineers to take charge of men as well as machines, in other words to act like officers and not just technicians. In 1842 the rate of leading stoker was introduced, and the shortage of junior engineers led to 'intelligent stokers' being allowed to stand engine-room watches in 1855. All this tended to make the engine room a miniature naval hierarchy of its own.[74]

The new scheme generated immediate tension with the old, informally trained and often ill-educated engineers. It also reflected and took some account of social tensions between engineers and other officers. In particular the fact that engineers began in a status similar to warrant rank and were then, well on in their careers, promoted to commissioned rank and the wardroom, forced them to bridge what had already become the major social division of the ship. In the world of the mid-nineteenth century, it required a real effort on both sides for an engineer, coming from the hard-drinking and ungenteel culture of the engine room, to settle in the wardroom. Some chief engineers preferred to stay in the engineers' mess even after promotion, for the social ease and lower mess bills, and to accommodate them the Admiralty created the status of assistant engineer 'qualified for charge', i.e. with the job and pay of a chief engineer.[75]

There is little evidence, however, that any of these social problems were serious or long-lasting. Engineer officers do not seem to have had more difficulties in getting on with their shipmates than any others, in spite of their rather different social background. The real threat to the naval engineers had not yet clearly emerged and has tended to be overlooked by historians: there were two different kinds of engineering expertise now available, developed in different ways and 'owned' by different sorts of officers. The engineer officers themselves were trained in their own self-contained professional culture which went back to the early days of the Industrial Revolution, and still preserved much of the craft-based, semi-manual traditions of early engineering. But many of the best and brightest of the commissioned officers had embraced steam and made themselves expert in it, often on the basis of the advanced 'scientific' courses at the Royal Naval College in Portsmouth which were well above the educational level of most officers, engineers not excepted. They knew less about the practical handling of engines, and were content to leave the engineers to manage the engine room, but in important respects they had more 'scientific' qualifications to manage engineering than the engineers did. Implicitly their presence posed the question of whether the Navy needed engineers, when perhaps engines, like guns (or hydrography, another of the new scientific officers' specialities), might similarly be entrusted to a small cadre of advanced experts backed by highly trained ratings. No one was asking this question in the 1850s, but it was there to be asked. Other navies such as the French, and later the American, did make do without seagoing professional engineer officers, and the time might come when the Royal Navy would confront that choice.

SIX

Continuous Service
Social History: Men 1815–1914

The Navy of 1815, and even more the Navy of 1845, had too many officers because an officer's commission connected him with the Service
for life, and extreme political difficulties stood in the way of severing
the connection. With ratings the situation was almost the opposite. Formally
speaking, there was no way a rating could make a career in the Navy: he joined
a ship for a commission of three years or so, and at the end he was paid off,
from his ship and consequently from the King's service. At the peace of 1814–
15, the total manpower of the Navy sank from 147,000 to just under 23,000 in
four years as ships were 'paid off' (decommissioned).[1] What happened to all
these men, what other living if any they managed to find ashore or afloat, were
matters of no concern to Parliament, but naval officers lamented the injustice
and impolity of discarding skilled men who had deserved well of their country, and would doubtless be needed again sooner or later. Throughout the first
half of the century, much thought and some action were devoted (as they had
been in the eighteenth century) to establishing reserve structures by which
men could be connected with the Navy in such a way as to make their services
available in wartime. Almost invariably it was assumed that these men would
be British merchant seamen, who would already possess the seamanlike skills
which were the Navy's prime requirement. Very few officers imagined that they
would be able to avoid the use of impressment altogether, and they therefore
worked to ensure that the Navy's legal powers of compulsion were not undermined, but they were acutely aware of the moral and political cost of even
mentioning it, and they longed to find some better and more equitable method
of wartime manning.[2] 'No one can attempt to defend impressment upon any
ground but that of state *Necessity* or, in other words, national *safety*,' wrote Sir
Thomas Byam Martin, 'because of the utter *impossibility* of accomplishing the
same object by other means . . .'[3]

The first attempt at improvement was the 1835 Merchant Seaman's Act promoted by Sir James Graham, which established a voluntary register of seamen and a five-year term of naval service. Some pains were taken not to draw seamen's attention to the fact that the Registrar, J. H. Brown, was a lieutenant on half pay, and that the register was a first step towards a scheme of compulsory wartime service. It never worked as intended, and the legal and practical difficulties of relying on merchant shipping for wartime manpower were growing. Brown's own claims for the register's value were tentative, and he admitted that it had never been tested in wartime: 'Conceiving that the merchant service is the source and resource of our naval power, and the element of a large Navy, I imagine that the machinery of this office . . . has a very great effect in bettering the condition of the source from which the Navy is manned.'[4] Impressment had existed because it had been impossible to persuade eighteenth-century Parliaments to impose state control on merchant shipping. It would undoubtedly be even harder in the age of Cobden and Bright, and the repeal of the Navigation Laws between 1849 and 1854 not only lifted any legal obligation to employ British seamen or ship British goods in British ships, but made a very public declaration that the state was no longer concerned to regulate merchant shipping. After centuries of identifying the merchant fleet with national security, the government had cast it adrift. The 1854 Merchant Shipping Act made the Board of Trade rather than the Admiralty the responsible government department, and transferred the merchant seamen's register, which came close to publicly abandoning impressment.[5]

Behind this lay not only the worship of free trade so characteristic of the age, but also the slow realization that merchant ships and fishing boats were no longer the natural recruiting ground for the Navy. Increasingly they represented other kinds of seafarers from other parts of the country, possessing skills more and more distant from naval requirements as the Navy adopted steam and new technologies while merchantmen ceased to carry guns but remained, for the most part, under sail into the 1860s. In the second half of the century the rise of specialized naval training and discipline, shore establishments and barracks, all served to mark out the Navy as a career distinct from seafaring in general.[6] In 1848 the Naval Lord responsible for manning admitted that men from the coasting trades were as good seamen as any, but declared the Navy did not want them, 'because they are not accustomed to any discipline, and they are accustomed to a good deal of filth'.[7] The naval reserves which existed were small and miscellaneous. The Coast Guard numbered 4,208 men in 1852, of whom only 1,522 were former naval men liable to be recalled for service. From the Baltic in 1854 it was reported that 'Our coastguardmen

90 · CONTINUOUS SERVICE

in this fleet generally are very respectable men, but they are very slow in their movements, and have no notion of being at all hurried in anything . . . it is evident to me and to others, that the coastguard must be thoroughly re-modelled if we wish it to be an efficient auxiliary to the navy in this service of emergency.'[8] The reserve of dockyard riggers (almost all ex-naval seamen) set up in 1848 had an establishment in 1852 of 475 men but an actual strength of 357. The Royal Naval Coast Volunteers set up in 1852 – 10,000 men to be recruited from fishermen – were not liable to serve more than 600 miles from Britain and were therefore useless for any general war. It was no surprise that a French parliamentary commission of 1851 concluded that Britain's inability to man the Navy in an emergency would be a considerable advantage to her enemies.[9]

Meanwhile it was not difficult to man the relatively small number of ships in commission in peacetime. The naval wage compared well with general wages in the depressed southern counties where the Navy recruited. To judge from ships' muster books, a high proportion of the men had been born in or near the dockyard towns and probably knew the Navy before they joined. There were outside prejudices against the alleged harshness of naval discipline, actively encouraged by Radicals in Parliament for whom flogging was the perfect rhetorical symbol of the 'aristocratic' mismanagement of the armed forces, but these prejudices seem to have found an audience mainly in parts of the country such as the North-East and Scotland where the Navy recruited very little. (As late as 1883 an attempt to recruit in the Orkneys met with complete failure because the Navy was unknown, but the press-gang was remembered.) Elsewhere warships had few difficulties in attracting men from British merchant ships when they needed to, and there was a conventional signal (a blue shirt on the fore-lift) for would-be volunteers to indicate their presence aboard a merchantman.[10] But discipline, and flogging in particular, were politically sensitive everywhere, and a quick way for a captain to attract hostile notice in the newspapers and service journals which the Admiralty Board would read. From 1846 admirals and the Admiralty were receiving individual punishment returns for each ship.[11] 'I am shocked at the report of the punishments on board of the *Amazon*,' wrote Lord Auckland in that year,

> and have come to the resolution of superseding Captain [James Stopford] in the command of her, and will send out another captain by the next mail. I rather repent the not having done so some days sooner, but I had hoped that your first reproof would have done good. I am satisfied that a captain who cannot maintain discipline without such frequent and severe punishments has not the qualities which are essential to command.[12]

Three years later Commander John Pitman of the *Childers* was dismissed from the Service for cruelty and oppression, of his officers as well as his men. Conversely when Commander Baillie Hamilton paid off the *Frolic* in 1847, the newspapers reported the outstanding good order of his ship: in a commission of four and a half years he had flogged just one man and lost only two to desertion. Up to the mid-century, few officers thought flogging could be completely abandoned, but it was a mark of the good officer to rely on it as little as possible. In 1827 the Duke of Clarence forbade the flogging of petty officers and required captains to put in their quarterly returns their reasons for disrating a petty officer. In 1830 a captain's power to flog was limited to forty-eight lashes, and in 1846 flogging in home ports required the written approval of the senior officer present.[13] All this meant that captains' powers were being restricted at the same time as the expectations laid on them were rising. The good officer's qualities, it was said, should include forbearance, command of temper, conciliation, firmness, tact, system, consistency, discretion, perseverance, activity, enterprise, zeal, knowledge of human nature, justice, confidence and self-possession. That, rather than property or genealogy, was what contemporaries meant when they insisted that an officer must be a gentleman: 'His being born and educated as such, in modern times, is essential to the well-being of the navy.'[14] All agreed that drink was the prime cause of most disciplinary trouble (it featured in a third of all courts-martial charges). The spirit issue was halved in 1824 to a quarter of a pint a day, though the introduction of imperial measures the following year then increased it by a fifth. In 1850 it was halved again. These reductions did much to improve naval discipline and to diminish the Navy's hard-drinking culture.[15] As early as 1839 one memoir claimed (in tones suggesting some fear of disbelief) that 'it is not uncommon to see Jack on shore, and come off, perfectly sober. I will not say it is universally so, but in a great measure . . .'[16]

In 1834 the Navy Estimates allowed for a thousand boys in place of five hundred men, and the following year the number was doubled. Most boys of this generation were literate when the older seamen were not. As a boy of thirteen in the *Asia* in 1836 William Ashcroft remembered:

> Whenever the mail left for England I had some thirty or forty letters to write, and to read when the mail arrived . . . Men would often bring off books from the shore, such as Captain Marryat's novels (we had a son of his in the ship), and I had to sit on the capstan reading while they sat around listening. If I said I could not read as I had some clothes to make and mend, there were always volunteers to do it for me . . . The Captain of

the Foretop, Harry Tongue, used to keep me in order and called himself my 'sea daddy'. I took him in hand to teach him to read and write and as soon as he could do so he changed his rating to Boatswain's mate. About twelve years later I saw him again in the Pacific when he was Boatswain of the *Thetis* frigate.[17]

Lord Auckland was particularly keen on boy training, and in January 1847 he commissioned Alexander Milne, then captain of the port flagship *St Vincent* at Plymouth, to establish a boys' training scheme: 'I shall be much gratified if under your good care the *St Vincent* should become one of our model schools for the example of others.' Now styled 'naval apprentices', the boys, aged between fourteen and sixteen, entered for seven years, with six weeks leave a year and their choice of ship on recommissioning. By the early 1850s about two thousand boys entered every year, and there were about five thousand in service at any one time. They were all taught to swim, which shows that the Navy had largely forgotten its old fear of desertion.[18]

In everything to do with manning, discipline and training, the key people were the petty officers, and much effort was devoted to improving their position and establishing them in a permanent naval career. The critical moment for a rating's career was the day his ship paid off, for that was when his connection with the Service, and therefore his accumulated 'social capital' of rating and reputation, were liable to be lost. The Admiralty tried as far as possible always to have a ship commission at a dockyard port soon after the last had paid off there, so that men anxious to continue a naval career would have that opportunity. Ships' muster books from the 1820s, which record previous service, often show men who had recently been paid off at the same port. For a petty officer this was a delicate moment, for until 1827 a man's rating was not permanent but lay entirely in the captain's gift. A prudent petty officer would try to follow an officer who knew him to a new ship, and 'if it was otherwise', John Bechervaise wrote, 'I got a recommendation from one captain to the other'.[19] On one occasion he was crossing Portsmouth Hard on his way to the paying-off of his ship when he met an officer he knew walking with another, the first lieutenant of the *Asia*, who at once asked Bechervaise if he wanted a ship. 'I answered yes, sir, if I could get my rate' (meaning keep his rating of quartermaster), which he was offered at once. His new captain then sent him ashore, 'telling me that as I was well known to the men just paid, he wished me to go on shore, and enter as many as I could recommend'. Bechervaise returned with thirteen good men, was given a sovereign as a reward and three weeks victualled ashore to carry on the good work, and in the end recruited no fewer than sixty-seven men for the *Asia*.[20] This anecdote reveals just how much the officers as well as the petty officers had to gain from the movement towards semi-continuous service. In 1827 petty officers' rates were made 'substantive', meaning permanent, like an officer's rank, and they were given the right to sign on to the port flagship and take leave between commissions.[21]

The new gunnery training ship *Excellent* set some important precedents for skilled ratings. Most of the new seamen gunners were former boys from the training ships, for it seems that the *Excellent*'s intense drills were rather too much for an older cohort of sailors. It cost £300 to train a seaman gunner, which would be wasted if the man then left the Navy, so in return for extra pay the seamen gunners were obliged to engage for five years' service (longer than a commission), with a free passage home for those whose time expired abroad; it was this five-year engagement which was offered to all ratings in 1835. From 1831 any man with twenty-one years' service could claim a Greenwich Hospital out-pension (a notable privilege in an age when any sort of retirement pension was still a great rarity). From 1846 all those eligible for a petty officer's rate received six weeks' paid leave (eight weeks from 1850) on turning over to a new ship, and in 1849 the first scheme of long-service badges was copied from the army, initially for five-, ten- or fifteen-years' good conduct, each carrying an increment of pay. A 'three-badge' able seaman, qualified as a seaman gunner, was now earning almost 50 per cent more than a plain able seaman. In 1850 and 1851 naval pay was raised, and paid monthly, with the possibility of making monthly 'allotments' to family or friends. In 1853 the new ratings of leading seaman (following from the leading stoker of 1840) and chief petty officer were introduced. All these incentives to make a career in the Navy helped to create a population of 'man-of-warsmen' who identified with the Service and made up a growing proportion of its crews. In 1834–35 some 30 per cent of recruits had previous naval service; between 1839 and 1847 the figure rose to 54 per cent (and 62 per cent of able seamen). By the early 1850s half the men re-engaged on paying off, and Alexander Milne could call it 'to a certain extent a standing Navy'.[22]

The manning system was now both effective and selective, taking its time to attract and retain the best men, but the time factor remained a worry. With a new Napoleon restless on his new throne across the Channel, and the French parliament identifying speed of mobilization as its key advantage, it seemed no moment for complacency. In 1852 the Derby government appointed an Admiralty committee under Sir William Parker on manning the Navy, which led to the first scheme of 'continuous service'. This was disrupted by the outbreak of the Russian War and had to be re-launched again after the war. Back in office in 1858, Derby then established a royal commission on manning the

Navy under the Earl of Hardwicke. In effect this was all one movement of reform, interrupted by the war, and scarcely any of it was new. Over twenty years admirals, officials and Admiralty Boards had been experimenting with better ways to man the Navy, and the measures introduced in the 1850s collected the most successful initiatives and formed them into a system. Its main architects were Milne and Sir Maurice Berkeley as long-serving Lords of the Admiralty, Parker as chairman of the 1852 Manning Committee, and the Admiralty clerk Charles Pennell as its secretary. Under the new system ratings were encouraged, though not yet compelled, to enter for ten years' 'Continuous Service', and those who re-engaged for a further ten years became eligible for a pension. At the same time the recruitment and training of boys were increased, with the intention that the Navy would soon draw all its seamen from boys it had already trained. At eighteen they (or rather their parents, since the age of legal majority was twenty-one) would sign up for their first ten years, and those who re-engaged would leave the Navy around the age of thirty-eight, or forty-three for a minority who continued for a 'fifth five'. In time the effect of this system would not only ensure the Navy a steady and sufficient supply of young men of its own upbringing, but a large reserve of 'retired' man-of-warsmen, still of military age and available to be recalled in wartime. The abolition in 1853 of the old rating of landsman, and the creation of the new rates of leading seaman and chief petty officer, marked the coming of a new Navy in which everybody would be a skilled man, or in training to become one. Between 1847 and 1859 Mrs Louisa Wafer of the 'Hole in the Wall' outside Portsmouth Dockyard, the best-known of the Navy's own 'bringers of men', had been responsible for recruiting 26,572 men, but in the 1860s this sort of casual 'external' recruitment was in rapid decline. By 1865 some 90 per cent of seamen were already on continuous service, and by 1871 almost all the younger men had come up from the boys' training ships, though it took at least twenty years for the products of the new system to populate the Navy completely, and longer still to build up a body of retired ratings to draw on in an emergency.[23]

The Hardwicke Commission filled in some of the gaps in the new system. It proposed a new Royal Naval Reserve (RNR) of merchant seamen and officers, unlike the Coast Volunteers qualified and liable for foreign service, who undertook (and were paid for) periodic naval training. After a slow start the RNR reached a strength of around 15,000 in the 1860s. At the Commission's recommendation a 'First Class for Conduct' was instituted, available to all ratings with a satisfactory record, which carried exemption from flogging except by a sentence of court martial.[24] In 1859 men on continuous service received a free issue of bedding and clothes – meaning the new uniform. In fact the uniform was no newer than the other measures; *Instructions to Pursers* of 1824 listed a standard range of clothing to be provided in every ship, seamen's 'uniform' already featured in published fashion plates, and in 1838 a new entrant to *Excellent* wrote home that he had had to buy 'a few clothes as we must all dress alike when we are mustered, which is every morning, and must not dress in white in the winter'.[25] The Admiralty Board's choice was partly based on studying Franz Winterhalter's 1846 portrait of the four-year-old Prince Albert Edward (the future King Edward VII) dressed in the seaman's uniform made for him aboard the royal yacht; and the Admiralty's mild 'desire . . . [that] these regulated articles of dress be worn' marks an important moment in the creation of a naval identity and *esprit de corps*.[26] In retrospect it can be seen that the manning system sponsored by the Parker Committee and the Hardwicke Commission finally solved the manning problem which had tormented the Navy for centuries. It provided sufficient men with sufficient training to man the Navy in both peace and war, and with some adaptation it met the supreme test of the two world wars. Not the least satisfactory aspect of it was that the French had great difficulty in setting up a long-service professional navy to match it.[27]

The new manning system was largely one for recruiting and training seamen, which as sail became less important increasingly meant all-purpose ratings, many of them with specialist skills indicated by non-substantive ratings and supplementary pay. 'Branches' like gunnery and (from 1876) torpedo formed part of the body of seamen, and their officers were specialists within the body of 'military' (later 'executive') officers. Professionally and socially, there was an important distinction between these seamen branches and the self-contained world of engine-room officers and ratings, who were recruited and trained separately and whose career paths did not intersect with those of seamen. They in turn were divided between engine-room ratings and the stokers in the boiler rooms. By 1858 no fewer than a quarter of the engine-room personnel were officers, and the demand for engineer officers was such that (as we have seen) stoker petty officers were taking on supervisory roles for which they were untrained – to the alarm of an age painfully familiar with the danger of boiler explosions. In 1868 both tendencies were sharply reversed: the rating of chief stoker was abolished, and the following year entries started of a new chief petty officer's rating of Engine Room Artificer (ERA), initially recruited from men in their twenties who had served a regular apprenticeship in an engineering trade (and therefore in the world of craft trades-unionism). They took the place of both the chief stokers and of many junior engineer officers, creating a distinctive 'middle class' in the engine room which scarcely existed elsewhere in the ship. By 1898 the engineer branch had grown almost sixfold in forty years, but the commissioned engineer officers were actually fewer than before, and the ERAs were now a quarter of the total. From the beginning ERAs messed apart with their own servant and insisted on an officer-style 'fore and aft' uniform with a collar and tie; when other petty officers gained the same privilege ten years later the ERAs made sure their uniforms alone carried no branch badges. They became and remained a distinctive class of highly skilled quasi-officers, the first generation of them directly recruited as adults, which had few parallels in British service – though they would have fitted comfortably into the *maistrance* of the French Navy.[28]

Stokers were recruited as adults from a variety of unskilled jobs, including the army, and received only an elementary six-month training. Little was expected of them but physical strength, though stoking was actually a skilled as well as arduous business, for efficient steaming with minimum smoke depended on each man maintaining an even spread of burning coal of the right depth over the whole ten-foot length of his furnace. 'It's a skilled job needing the firebed spread evenly and all the hollow spots filled and flaming to white heat. We wore blue tinted glasses to save our eyes from the white glare while we were looking where to spread the coal.'[29] The newest stokers worked in pairs as trimmers, repeatedly loading a box or 'skid' weighing 2–3cwt with another 2cwt of coal from the bunker and dragging it to the stokehold, where each pair supplied two furnaces or eight furnace doors. Every stoker was expected to shovel 2.4 tons of coal in a four-hour watch. In principle naval complements allowed continuous steaming at medium speed in three watches over at least forty-eight hours, but there were repeated complaints that in practice the stokers were too few or too weak to keep up that pace. As ships increased in size and speed the demand for and on stokers increased mercilessly. The battleship *Collingwood*, launched in 1882, had 98 stokers and 192 seamen (petty officers included in both cases) out of a complement of 441, with engines of 9,600 IHP giving 16.8 knots at full speed. Twenty-five years later the armoured cruiser (later 'battle-cruiser') *Invincible* developed 41,000 SHP for 25½ knots with a complement of 784, including 163 seamen and 244 stokers. Stokers had increased from 22 per cent to 31 per cent of the ship's company, but each had to generate almost twice as much horsepower as before (and considerably more than merchant ships expected of their firemen); experience was to show that even extreme efforts could not sustain full speed for more than a few hours. 'The engine and boiler rooms are hell, at sea; one cannot realise the life of the stokers and other "saints who toil below" until one actually experiences it.

SOCIAL HISTORY: MEN 1815-1914 · 97

These men's work can vie with any, trenches or deserts not excluded; their whole life in wartime is a vivid succession of discomforts and hardships, unparalleled in severity and monotony.'[30]

Stokers had a reputation in the Navy as troublemakers, which is not borne out by the statistics, but perhaps reflects their non-naval origins, making them seem somewhat 'foreign' to seamen and officers. Stokers were nevertheless paid considerably more than seaman ratings, and had better promotion prospects. One stoker in four was a leading hand, and by the early twentieth century more than 6 per cent reached petty officer (compared with 1.8 per cent of seamen). By 1910 there were more stokers in the Navy than seamen.[31]

In the second half of the nineteenth century the growing complexity, both of warships and of naval society, was reflected in the growing number of specialist rating branches, both within the seamen or 'military' part of the ship's company, and among the 'civil' branches outside. Many of these were moving up or down in status and shifting from one part of the ship to another. Signalmen were chosen from literate young seamen; at first they were barely distinguished from other seamen below the petty officer's rate of Yeoman of Signals, but they had become a distinct specialization by 1902 when the warrant rank of Signal Boatswain was created.[32] Artificers, craftsmen of warrant rank, had a higher status than petty officer artisans like blacksmiths, plumbers, painters or armourers, many of whom had analogues in the dockyards. Carpenters had declined to this status by 1878, only to be revived in another form as the Warrant Shipwright of 1918.[33] The Chief Armourer (ex-Torpedo Artificer) of 1894 was the beginning of an Armourers' Branch, which however was absorbed in 1919 into the new Ordnance Branch. The new technology of wireless was served by the Telegraphists' Branch of 1907, leading almost at once to warrant rank.[34]

Cooks, once important warrant officers, suffered a long decline in importance until the establishment of the first cookery school in 1873. Formal training meant qualifications and rising status; in 1910 the warrant rank of Instructor in Cookery (known on the lower deck as the 'Custard Boatswain') was established to command the three naval cookery schools, one in each manning port. The new 'general messing' system involved cooked meals being issued from a central galley to each mess, instead of the messes preparing their own food and bringing it in to be cooked. As a result ship's cooks had to learn cookery, and the first Warrant Instructor, Mr Alphonso Jago, wrote the first naval cookery manual.[35] These ship's cooks are not to be confused with the many domestics' ratings, which included Captain's Cook, Wardroom Cook, Gun Room Cook and Engineers' Cook. Domestics were the main group of ratings who did not adopt continuous service and still signed on for the voyage, often from places like Malta or Hong Kong.[36] The Sick Berth Attendants, with their petty officer's rate of Sick Berth Steward, were established in 1833, but until 1884 had neither pay nor training enough to attract good candidates.[37]

Naval nursing is worth attention not only for its intrinsic interest, but because of what it reveals about changing attitudes to class, and to women. In the first part of the century the naval hospitals recruited women as well as men as nurses, but they were no more than lower servants, and medical training was neither expected nor provided. Of Lucy Staines, matron of the Malta naval hospital, it was said in 1855 that 'I do not know that the Crown has a more devoted servant', but her nurses were all men, and naval nurses were more often mentioned in the context of drunkenness, by themselves or the patients, than of medical care. When the hospital ship *Minden* sailed for China in 1842 her nurses were all landmen, though she had three washerwomen aboard. At the same time things were changing, both in society and in the medical world. In the late 1840s surgery under general anaesthetic became possible, initially using 'ethereal vapour' (ether), later chloroform. This opened the way to curing many hitherto untreatable conditions and called for more intensive nursing.[38] In society at this time there was a growing number of educated middle-class women, unmarried and needing to earn a living, for whom nursing the sick was a socially respectable occupation. In the Russian War women nurses made headlines. Florence Nightingale's efforts to bring order into the chaos of the army medical service are well known, but her forgotten naval contemporary Eliza Mackenzie deserves to be remembered. Comparisons between them are odious: the naval casualties were relatively few and well looked after, so that Mrs Mackenzie's task in the naval hospital at Therapia, a suburb of Istanbul, was much easier than in a military hospital, but it is still worth quoting one who visited both the naval and military hospitals. At Therapia,

> Nothing could exceed the cleanliness, comfort and order which appeared to prevail . . . the patients are as happy as sailors ever are when sick and in bed . . . none of that confusion and resort to temporary expedients which so prevailed at Scutari . . . in its management and general economy, the one English thing I saw properly conducted in the East.[39]

Noteworthy is the tact with which Mrs Mackenzie maintained good relations with the naval surgeons, even being elected an honorary member of the officers' mess. An early practical problem arose over washing the hospital linen: 'Next week Dr Davidson wants my Nurses to do it and I know they neither can nor are willing. They are rather upper sort of people at home.' According to Mackenzie's deputy Mary Erskine,

[Davidson] I'm sure <u>dislikes any independent</u> power in his hospital, would rather have everyone strictly under martial law, with no right to an opinion of their own . . . [T]his is the almost universal feeling among doctors I believe and the cause of their jealousy . . . They hate interference in any shape and ladies of course are to a certain extent beyond their control.[40]

Mrs Mackenzie solved the difficulty by paying some Maltese women to do the washing, and appealed to her convalescent patients to help with the ironing. 'The men were so helpful to us at ironing and folding and would have done anything for us, which I explained to the [medical] gentlemen to be because we never spoke to them as if they were dogs! – a hint which I did not feel to be undesirable.'[41]

Almost thirty years later, the Navy was ready to adopt women nurses permanently. In June 1881 the Medical Director-General minuted, with precise social observation,

I see no reason why, as highly respectable female Nurses are employed in our Civil Hospitals, our Sailors should any longer be denied the invaluable benefit of good nursing in our Naval Hospitals. The nursing of the sick has of late years become a sphere of useful work for ladies of character and culture, assisted by a staff of respectable under Nurses, whose ranks are filled by servants of the upper class, such as upper housemaids from good families.[42]

Two years later a committee recommended 'a limited number of trained Sisters of the position of gentlewomen under the superintendence in each Hospital of a Head Sister'. They were civil servants not under naval discipline and officially without powers of command, but they were also 'officers of the hospitals, taking a position immediately after the surgeons'. From 1885 they appeared in the *Navy List* like other officers, they had their own cabins and were addressed as 'Madam'. This meant that ratings like Sick Berth Attendants (SBAs) were expected to obey their 'requests' as though they were orders. Being ladies, they could not treat 'afflictions of the middle third of the body' (as Fleet Surgeon Henry Norbury of Stonehouse put it in 1885). This was only one reason why the surgeons did not greet the women with enthusiasm; still less the SBAs, who found themselves both outranked and outclassed in skill. Initially the women did not go to sea, but in 1898 the hospital ship *Malacca* embarked two nursing sisters for the Benin expedition.[43]

Up to 1867 there were only two rating branches which offered the possibility of advancement to warrant rank (from seaman to boatswain or gunner, and from artificer to carpenter). By 1945 there were no fewer than twenty-four rating branches, plus others confined to the RNR and the Coast Guard, each with its own hierarchy rising through leading hands, petty officers, chief petty officers, warrant and commissioned warrant officers. All these ratings and ranks conformed to the traditional naval form: they expressed both the rising skills of the man, and rising rank or authority. There was an inherent tension here, for the requirements of a technical Navy led to many more petty officers (and indeed commissioned officers) than were needed for discipline and command, and the two meanings of 'rate' (technical skill and disciplinary authority) did not always match. From the creation of the torpedo-gunner and torpedo-gunner's mate of 1880 it was possible for a man's non-substantive, technical rate to be senior to his substantive rate. There were also financial complications, when naval pay consisted of a basic figure for the substantive rate to which might be added numerous allowances for special skills and responsibilities. Since many of these were liable to be lost on advancement, it was not uncommon for men to refuse promotion to a higher rate which would actually cost them money. Moreover, many were advanced in recognition of their skills who were not natural leaders. Leadership among ratings was often found less among the petty officers than among their juniors the leading hands, many of whom were leading hands of a mess, charged with keeping good order and harmony among twenty or thirty men living and eating together on an intensely crowded mess-deck. Leading hands of messes were often the mess caterer also, and a well-run junior ratings' mess might feed better than the midshipmen or even the wardroom officers. Coxswains of boats, on whose seamanship many lives might depend, were able or leading seamen. The delicate business of handling a boatload of drunken and combative libertymen coming aboard their ship at night was best left to one of them, partly because striking an officer or petty officer was a court-martial offence. Technical petty officers might complain that their seniority ought to give them command of a boat, but there were clear functional reasons why the command went to the rating with the right skills. This in fact was and still is a common naval principle, which could easily result in the command attaching to an officer or rating who was not the most senior present. It allowed many of the anomalies inherent in the double character of a rating to be avoided, at the price of a complex social structure requiring some flexibility and experience. On a similar principle the command of a ship at sea descended directly from the captain to the officer of the watch (usually a lieutenant), bypassing all other officers of intermediate seniority who were not seamen or not on watch.[44]

The weakness of petty officers, from a disciplinary point of view, led to the creation of the 'regulating branch' or 'ship's police' (the 'crushers'), headed by the Master-at-Arms, who had nothing else to do than enforce the rapidly grow-ing number of petty regulations. The late-Victorian and Edwardian Navy imposed exact and detailed regulations on matters such as uniform and every-day routine which had formerly been much more relaxed. These often vex-atious and childish rules justified the existence of the ship's police, and provided many opportunities for corruption, especially in barracks ashore. Most officers seem to have been comfortable with this sort of discipline, but some disap-proved, and in 1913, at the request of the new First Lord Winston Churchill, Captain Reginald Hall of the battle-cruiser *Queen Mary* went so far as to abol-ish his ship's police and throw all the authority onto the other petty officers. A major reason why the new torpedo boats and destroyers (and even more the new submarines) were popular, in spite of hard work and hard lying, was that there were no 'crushers' and discipline was relaxed and functional.[45]

In other ways the new disciplinary system codified by the 1860 and 1866 Naval Discipline Acts was more stable, orderly and humane. Although too many courts martial were held which common sense and tact might have avoided, summary punishments fell steadily from their peak in 1865. The late 1850s and early 1860s, before the new manning system had bedded down, were a bad time for naval discipline, with much desertion, several riots and small mutinies. The turning point was the 1866 system dividing men into three classes for leave, which gave the well-behaved majority an expectation of leave (though not a formal entitlement until 1890), and made stoppage of leave an effective punish-ment for the (usually drunken) minority. This was 'the cause of a great advance in general behaviour of men'.[46] Living for long periods in the extremely crowded environment of a ship at sea required a high degree of discipline and self-discipline, from young men to whom it did not necessarily come easily. Leave was a precious opportunity for them to breathe freely, to find space to relax. The release of tension on a 'run ashore' expressed itself in high spirits, and often in escapades which challenged the surrogate authority of civilian society ashore. In social terms these were a kind of safety valve which relieved the pressures of shipboard life, and wise officers took no more notice of them than they had to.[47]

The changing character of naval discipline was possibly the single most important factor in shaping the experience of naval life for both officers and ratings. Crudely speaking it may be said that up to the 1870s ratings were held responsible for their actions and flogged if they misbehaved. From 1879, when flogging in peacetime was suspended, men were subjected to an increasingly intricate web of detailed regulations which reduced their scope to think and act as adults. Much the same was true of the officers. As flogging, once an unremarkable commonplace, grew rarer and came to arouse public horror, officers were deprived of many of their powers to punish. Instead, they fell back on more numerous courts martial which awarded severe sentences for relatively trivial offences. Many ratings thought that a prison sentence was worse than a flogging, and many officers felt degraded by a system which no longer respected their independence or judgement. The bureaucratic formality of the new discipline increased the distance between officers and men, made petitioning rare and difficult, and undermined what remained of the old 'divisional system' by which officers had taken personal responsibility for the welfare of 'divisions' of ratings.[48] 'This has gone Entirely out of fashion and the officers take no interest in the men whatever,' as Sir Alexander Milne complained in 1861. 'They don't Even know them. It is the great blot of the Service and the one thing to be corrected . . .'[49]

There remained, however, some important social conventions which softened or frankly subverted the social distance between quarter deck and lower deck. The tradition of amateur theatricals survived from the eighteenth-century Navy and was revived aboard ships wintering in the Arctic. These efforts were not necessarily very sophisticated: in 1878 'A concert and Penny Readings was held on the Quarter Deck consisting of singing and dancing and recitations etc', to mark the second anniversary of the commissioning of HMS *Danae*. But in 1870 the ship's company of the *Racoon* played to packed houses for two nights in the Temperance Hall at Halifax, Nova Scotia, with excerpts from *Hamlet* and *Othello* besides songs and dances.[50] Ship's newspapers, music and dancing, theatricals and variety shows all expressed popular culture in socially acceptable ways, and involved officers and ratings working together. Pantomimes and comic songs made a safe space for mildly subversive comments. Officers might sing or act parts in shows put on by the lower deck. On these occasions all ranks and ratings sat in the audience, though not together, often joined in port by guests, including ladies. Officers and men sometimes played cricket on the same sides, not necessarily captained by an officer, and pulled or sailed together in regattas against other ships. On Christmas Day the captain made his 'rounds' to inspect the decorated messes in a cheerful procession headed by the youngest boy wearing the captain's uniform, accompanied by an unofficial band with clowns (the 'funny party'), and fuelled by unofficial alcohol. 'Crossing the Line', 'King Neptune' and his entourage captured anyone, officer or man, who had not crossed the Equator before, to be ducked and subjected to rough horseplay. This was when officers found out if they were really popular or not. Such status-reversals acted as a safety valve which reinforced the established order. Officers tolerated them because they knew that the show was discreetly controlled by senior ratings who would make sure it did not get out of hand.[51]

The new, rapidly growing, technically complex Navy of continuous-service ratings needed more and more shore establishments for training and accommodation. Port flagships had to be supplemented with numerous old hulks, picturesque but inconvenient and unhealthy. By the late 1880s the situation was becoming unworkable. In 1888 ships in reserve were divided into three groups, belonging to Portsmouth, Plymouth or Chatham (including Sheerness). In 1893 the whole manning system was divided to correspond, so that each man belonged to one of the three manning ports, and ships usually drew their whole company from one of them. A large naval barracks was built for each, which accommodated the manning 'pool', and provided basic training. The barracks, unlike the ships, were not over-provided with officers, and were run day-to-day by senior ratings without much interference. One result, as we have seen, was a good deal of lucrative petty corruption, notably involving the issuing of uniforms, and in the canteens which supplemented the unsatisfactory official rations. These abuses were not seriously tackled until 1907, when Commodore Spencer Login of Portsmouth Barracks investigated with Admiralty support. The result was a great improvement in the conditions of the men – at the price of a reduction in the autonomy of lower-deck life. Senior petty officers made much money from their little empires, making harsh and impossible regulations bearable for a price, but they had a strict moral code nevertheless, which they enforced by their own means without reference to the officers. They rewarded hard work and loyalty to shipmates; they protected the boys and other vulnerable groups. Lower-deck thieves or tyrants were liable to suffer inexplicable accidents which the 'Chiefs' (chief petty officers) somehow never noticed. Much of this lower-deck culture was still powerful in the 1940s, when the acute wartime shortage of experienced officers again threw much authority into the hands of an older generation of pensioner petty officers recalled to run the wartime training establishments. In both world wars the Navy's deep-rooted cohesion, its pride and self-confidence, rested heavily on this inherited lower-deck naval culture which owed little or nothing to the officers.[52]

This culture emerged rather suddenly into the public eye in the 1880s. The sentimental, comic, stock figure of the sailor had always been present on the stage, but real sailors enjoyed little public esteem. In the 1870s men in the new naval uniform were liable to be insulted in public and thrown out of theatres. By the 1890s they were popular and respected figures, their smart and distinctive uniforms accepted as symbols of an ideal national type, appropriate dress for middle-class boys and girls. Sailors understood that their uniforms turned heads – young women's heads in particular. Identified with cleanliness and self-discipline (to say nothing of a highly respectable career with a pension at the end of it), they were used to advertise all sorts of products. The Admiralty sent popular writers like Rudyard Kipling, Frank Bullen and Archibald Hurd to sea to extol the Service and its men. They were an antidote to the fears of national degeneracy exposed by the army's misfortunes in the South African War. The Navy could expect the highest standards from its recruits, most of whom came from the semi-skilled or skilled working class, shading into the lower middle class. It required not only basic literacy and numeracy but a character reference from a clergyman or policeman.[53]

This made for friction with the Evangelical temperance campaigner Miss Agnes Weston, who was strongly supported on religious grounds by a group of senior officers but did not arouse unequivocal enthusiasm on the lower deck. Her 'Sailors' Rests' at Devonport and Portsmouth were popular for their cheap and decent lodgings (if not for their cheerless teetotal atmosphere), but her fund-raising appeals caused great offence with their images of sailors as infantilized drunks needing redemption by 'Mother Weston'. By the end of the century this was out of date as an observation of fact, and unhelpful to campaigners for naval expansion and lower-deck reform alike.[54]

The Nonconformist churches with their hostility to alcohol were at the heart of the Liberal Party's electoral support, so drink was also a sensitive political issue, and as a Liberal First Lord of the Admiralty, Winston Churchill was under continual pressure to reduce or abolish the rum ration. He was ready to move cautiously in that direction, but he was aware of the traps. Genuine teetotallers were in a distinct minority, and financial incentives to ratings who declared themselves 'total abstainers' were easily converted into neat spirits on the next run ashore.[55]

The South African War revealed scandals in naval victualling, and the abortive Russian revolution of 1905 reminded people of the reasons for reform. The official-issue victuals were inadequate in quality and quantity, much food was rejected and destroyed, and men were forced to spend their own money in the naval canteens – which themselves were subject to a good deal of manipulation and corruption at the men's expense. As outside agitation and internal inquiries began to bring these facts out, the Admiralty became more concerned. The senior Admiralty clerk Oswyn Murray, Assistant Director of Victualling, opened discreet communication with the lower-deck campaigner Lionel Yexley, and encouraged him to keep up the pressure for change. In 1905 a committee investigated naval cookery, and in 1906 another regulated the canteens, taking evidence from elected ratings' representatives.[56]

All this was radical, for the scope for campaigning in a rigidly disciplined service was extremely limited. The early years of the twentieth century saw the emergence in most advanced countries of the first mass trades unions, strongly influenced by Marxism and leaning to varying degrees in the direction of revolutionary socialism. Not everybody in the Admiralty was well enough informed to distinguish this sort of trades unionism from the much older and more deeply rooted tradition of craft trades unions, typically small bodies of skilled men in particular specialist trades, concerned to defend their social and professional status against the unskilled workers below them. This sort of trades unionism, which owed more to John Wesley than Karl Marx, was typical of the world from which many skilled senior ratings came, ERAs in particular. Its characteristic form of social organization was the friendly society, the collective organization of self-employed skilled men. The naval form was the 'lower-deck societies', which from the 1880s began to present petitions to the Admiralty and 'earnest appeals' to the public requesting improved conditions. ERAs and artisans who were still trades union members were also able to approach MPs to bring up naval grievances in Parliament.

The tone of these approaches was studiously moderate and respectable, and the Admiralty must have been aware that the proportion of ratings they represented was tiny: perhaps two or three thousand out of more than 100,000 in the Navy. The leading figures in this movement were the warrant officers Harry Pursey and Henry Capper, and the retired petty officer James Wood, who wrote as 'Lionel Yexley'. Capper's campaign for 'commissioned warrant' rank was discreetly encouraged by Sir Evan Magregor, the Secretary of the Admiralty: 'Act, speak and write temperately, and you won't be interfered with. Then the Admiralty will be able to learn at first-hand what the men of the Navy really think and really need, and you will be benefiting both the men and the Board.'[57] Likewise Yexley's strength was not the appeal of his newspapers *The Bluejacket*, and later *The Fleet*, whose small circulation seems to have reached very few bluejackets, but the fact that he was obviously well informed about things which intelligent people in the Admiralty, like Oswyn Murray, realized they needed to know. *The Fleet* was owned by the printer and publisher Gerard Meynell, whose wife the naval historian Esther Hallam Moorhouse was a friend of Admiral Sir John Fisher, First Sea Lord from 1904 to 1910. Fisher met Yexley and was with difficulty convinced of the scale of corruption in the barracks. In 1909 Reginald McKenna the First Lord asked Yexley to propose reforms, which introduced the Admiralty Board to many of the real grievances of the lower deck. In 1911 Yexley's campaign against harsh and arbitrary summary punishments was backed by the now-retired Fisher, and attracted the new left-wing Liberal First Lord, Winston Churchill, fresh from reforming the prisons as Home Secretary.[58] Against the background of widespread strikes ashore, provoked by the 15 per cent rise in prices between 1900 and 1912, the 1912 'Loyal Appeal' of the lower-deck societies asked for a 20 per cent increase in naval pay. Churchill presented the Cabinet with Yexley's scheme:

> There is a deep and widespread sense of injustice and discontent through-out all ranks and ratings of the Navy. This discontent and the grievances which produce it are fanned and advertised in Parliament and the press. It is rendered more dangerous by every successful strike for higher wages which takes place on shore . . . The sailors have hitherto been restrained by their sense of discipline and loyalty, but we have no right to trade on this indefinitely.[59]

The increased 1912 pay rates which resulted – the first real increase in naval pay since 1853 – cost £561,350 added to the Navy Estimates, but still failed to address long-standing grievances. Unlike soldiers, sailors were charged the cost of their uniforms, their pay was stopped if they went into hospital, and their widows had no pensions. Already in 1914 the situation was beginning to slide again. Something like mass trades unionism was stirring, and arbitrary discipline in ships and barracks provoked near-mutinies, notably in March 1914 in the battleship *Zelandia*, commanded by the aggressive Captain Walter Cowan, whose career was punctuated by a long series of mutinies. He brought courts-martial charges against random scapegoats, which the Admiralty annulled on a technicality. Much of the Service press raged that the Admiralty, under a left-wing Liberal First Lord, was infected by Yexley's 'Socialist subver-sion'. This was at the height of the Irish Home Rule crisis, when the behaviour of the army in Ireland taught the lower deck that mutiny was all right for offi-cers. Thus, in the summer of 1914 the discipline of the Navy, like the unity of the United Kingdom, was under considerable strain.[60]

SEVEN

The Truth about the Navy
Policy and Operations 1860–1890

At the end of the 1850s Britain and France had lately been allies in a war against Russia, and were still allies in a war against China, but they remained as suspicious of one another as ever. Their competitive building of steam ships-of-the-line looked very like a naval arms race, and in July 1858 Sir Baldwin Walker, the Surveyor of the Navy, concluded that the French were almost ahead. They had already begun building the *Gloire*, the world's first seagoing ironclad. Formerly the Navy had trusted in its professional superiority over the French, but now as W. G. Romaine, the Secretary of the Admiralty, wrote in June 1859, 'their ships are as good as ours – their officers as well taught – better skilled in evolutions – and their men more generally instructed in gunnery, if not in seamanship.'[1] Napoleon III might be friendly, as he insisted, but his navy seemed clearly designed to back coercive diplomacy and French expansion; 'for the purpose of keeping us in check and overawing us upon some occasion', as Palmerston told Lord John Russell in September 1859.[2]

To understand how British public and professional opinion reacted to this threat it may help to sketch the state of naval professional thinking. There were now few officers left who remembered the French Wars, and very few who took a broad, strategic view of naval war. For most contemporaries, officers and well-informed civilians, the duties of the Navy could be divided into two parts. In peacetime its small and in many cases obsolete ships were dispersed about the world engaged in local defence and what was often called 'police-work'. In a war with France – few officers had yet noticed any other possible enemy capable of mounting a serious threat – the 'fighting ships' of the two powers would immediately meet in the Channel in a great battle which would decide the war. How and why the fleets would come together were seldom considered; it was widely believed that the war would break out instantaneously, with no cause and no warning, and would consist only of one single, decisive battle. This left no room for naval strategy, only tactics. There was very little for the Cabinet and the Admiralty to discuss: naval policy was reduced to the government's duty to provide an adequate force of 'fighting ships', and the admirals' duty to train their ships in steam tactics; complex manoeuvres designed to gain an advantage by gunnery (at very close range) or ramming, the new fashion of the steam age. The contemporary term 'fighting ship' partly reflects an era of rapid change in which technology had outpaced terminology and not yet developed the modern word 'battleship', but it also indicates the underlying assumption that battle was the only form of naval war. This assumption was widely shared, but it was especially comfortable to Liberals and Cobdenites, for it reassured them that providing a sufficient fleet of 'fighting ships' was all they needed to do to safeguard British naval supremacy. The rest could be left to the admirals, and there would be no need to spend money dispersing cruisers all over the world 'to multiply causes of quarrel and dispute', as Gladstone put it.[3] Since the battle must happen in the Channel, and France had to be the aggressor, the situation of British dockyards, and above all Portsmouth, was critical. Many wanted to spend heavily, converting the dockyards into fortresses capable of withstanding a prolonged siege in case the French succeeded in disembarking their army, if only to liberate the fleet from fear for its base when it sailed out to fight the great battle. In 1859 Palmerston set up a royal commission to recommend accordingly, and the chains of forts which resulted are still prominent around Portsmouth, Chatham, Plymouth and other places.[4]

Scarcely a year after the commission reported, however, events supervened which tended to suggest that other enemies than France, and other forms of naval warfare than a single battle, might exist after all. The secession of South Carolina from the United States of America in December 1860 led to open fighting the following spring. Britain was not involved, but in November 1861 the USS *San Jacinto* provoked a crisis by forcibly removing Confederate emissaries from the British steamer *Trent* in international waters. On this occasion war was narrowly averted, but both sides in the American Civil War expected, desired, and did what they could to ensure that Britain would take part. The Confederate States, for whom Britain was a natural and necessary ally, restricted the export of the raw cotton on which Britain's largest industry depended, meaning to coerce Britain into supporting their cause. Many on the Federal side wanted to make Britain an enemy rather than a friend, seeing a perfect opportunity to complete the Wars of Independence and 1812 with what a newspaper called 'the third revolutionary war upon which we have entered with the

English aristocracy'.[5] Victory could be taken for granted, bringing with it the conquest of Canada, if not all the territory 'between the Orinoco and the North Pole,' and undoubtedly the British working classes were thirsting for an American-inspired revolution just as those of France had been in 1789.[6]

Meanwhile the United States concentrated on imposing a blockade on southern ports. International and US law accepted that such a blockade could be enforced on foreign merchant ships only in a public war between sovereign states, and only then if the blockade were real and effective – meaning that the Federal government in practice conceded what it publicly denied, that the Confederacy had seceded from the Union and become a sovereign state; and that it adopted an even more extensive definition of belligerent rights than the British claims it had always denounced, though without abandoning its traditional rhetoric of 'freedom of the seas'. British statesmen, including Sir Alexander Milne, who was now Commander-in-Chief North America, were quietly satisfied to see the Americans establishing precedents which would no doubt be useful in the future, and Britain eventually recognized the Federal blockade, though it was never fully effective.[7] Both sides in the civil war realized that the fate of the Union blockade (and the extensive inland campaigns along the great rivers) turned on which side developed effective ironclads first, and both were keenly aware of the new ironclads being built in Europe. The French ironclad *Normandie* crossed the Atlantic to Mexican waters in 1862, and British ironclads would undoubtedly appear in American waters if Britain joined the war. Then came the sensational actions in Hampton Roads, at the mouth of Chesapeake Bay, on 8 and 9 March 1862. On the first day the improvised Confederate ironclad *Virginia* attacked the Union blockading force, sank two warships and drove the rest away. Next day the USS *Monitor*, the first of a revolutionary new type of ironclad, appeared and fought the *Virginia* without either ship being able to inflict any serious damage on the other. We shall return to the *Monitor* and her design, but here it is necessary to note that it was – and to an extent still is – unclear whether she had been designed to fight the stone and earthwork fortifications of Confederate ports, the improvised Confederate coastal ironclads, or the European seagoing ironclads which were imminently expected. Experience was to show that the *Monitor* and her derivatives were almost useless against forts, and only moderately effective against Confederate ironclads on the rare occasions they met. How they would have performed against the new British broadside ironclads remains an open question, so that both British and American partisans could (and still can) claim that their type of ironclad had been vindicated.[8]

In practice the American Civil War was not won at sea: the military and economic strength of the Union eventually crushed the South, without ever completely cutting it off from the outside world. The most effective naval action by either side was not the Union blockade but the handful of cruisers sent out by the Confederacy to attack Union merchant shipping, of which the most famous was the CSS *Alabama*. This small steam and sail warship, only moderately armed, appeared, almost by herself, to have destroyed the second-largest merchant fleet in the world, not so much by the capture and destruction of sixty-five American merchantmen worth over $7 million, as by inducing an insurance panic which caused American owners to transfer 750 ships to foreign flags (715 to British registry alone). In 1860 two-thirds of the trade of the port of New York had been carried by US ships; by 1863 three-quarters were in foreign hands. The Union economy and war effort did not suffer directly, since the Confederate Navy behaved as if it had subscribed to the Declaration of Paris and did not molest neutral ships carrying enemy goods, but the American merchant fleet has never recovered. Contemporaries blamed this all on the *Alabama*, but in retrospect it seems to have been mainly because US shipowners failed to make the transition from wooden sailing ships to iron steamers. At the end of the civil war in 1865, 33 per cent of American foreign trade was still under the US flag, but the proportion fell steadily thereafter until by 1910 it was below 9 per cent, and in 1914 the United States owned only 2 per cent of world deep-sea merchant shipping.[9]

The USA remained intensely hostile to Britain, which it regarded as the Confederacy's principal supporter, and the war still generated transatlantic tension long after it had ended. The *Alabama*, which was launched by the Laird Brothers' yard in Birkenhead in July 1862 and later commissioned into the Confederate Navy in a foreign port, had been secretly and illegally ordered by Confederate agents in defiance of Britain's declared neutrality; failure to prevent them was made the centrepiece of US claims on Britain which eventually extended to the whole cost of the war effort and the lost merchant fleet. Only in 1871 was a settlement reached by international arbitration valuing the losses due to the *Alabama* at $15.5 million, or £3.2 million. After this the diplomatic tension eased – but naval warfare could never be the same again. The demonstration of what a small cruiser could do against unprotected shipping posed a very obvious and uncomfortable challenge to the largest merchant fleet in the world, and forced British naval men to think again about the subject of trade defence which they had almost completely forgotten. Moreover, the Confederate government had also ordered two seagoing ironclad turret ships from Lairds, ostensibly for Egypt but actually intended to break the

Union naval blockade and turn the tide of the war at sea – which they might well have achieved, had not the now-alert British government blocked their completion and eventually bought the ships for British service in 1864. The Royal Navy had no obvious use for the 'Laird Rams', but £210,000 was a cheap price to avert war with the United States.[10]

After the repeal of the Corn Laws in 1846 people had foreseen a rise in agricultural imports into Britain, but initially they expected grain from the Russian Empire shipped from the Black Sea or the Baltic. As shipping costs fell, more distant producers entered the market, until by the 1870s imports from the United States, Canada and even Australia were becoming competitive. If shipping had to be protected from attack across the great oceans, it presented a new and formidable naval problem. But it was not clear that direct defence would be necessary. Many contemporaries, both naval officers and civilians, placed their faith in international law, and specifically the Declaration of Paris of 1856, which in the recent war had been observed even by countries which had not subscribed to it. That seemed to mean that in any future war Britain could lay up her merchant ships or transfer them to foreign flags, relying on neutral shipping to carry her trade unmolested by the belligerents. Some naval men welcomed the prospect of a strictly honourable naval war against officers and gentlemen, untainted by association with trade and tradesmen, but others were reluctant to give up the war against enemy shipping which had always been one of Britain's main strategic weapons (to say nothing of the main source of prize money for naval officers). All this was closely connected with blockade. In principle an effective blockade could keep enemy cruisers, enemy and neutral merchant ships in port, crippling enemy trade and protecting British trade, without any sacrifice of British belligerent rights – but blockade was almost as gross an interference with free trade as the capture of private property was, and for it to work the Royal Navy would have to be able to impose a more effective blockade against fast steamers than the US Navy had achieved.[11]

Connected with the protection of trade was the equally controversial and uncertain question of imperial defence. The imperial fortresses of Malta, Gibraltar and Bermuda were accepted as the responsibilities of the home government, to be garrisoned and fortified at the British taxpayers' expense. But the white-settler colonies of Canada, New Zealand and Australia were moving towards full self-government, which Whitehall assumed meant full responsibility for their own defence. The Colonial Naval Defence Act of 1865 empowered British colonies to create their own navies, which three of the Australian colonies did; Victoria's ironclad *Cerberus* was for a time the most powerful warship in the southern hemisphere.[12] In 1868 the British government withdrew imperial forces from New Zealand in the middle of a Maori War (a war of aggression against the Maoris, as it was viewed from Whitehall), and then presented the colonial government with the bill. This aroused outrage and threats to 'leave the empire', but British politicians of the 1860s did not believe in colonial patriotism, and were sure that the colonials would never volunteer to help the mother country (though they had done in the Russian War). After Confederation in 1867 all the British troops were withdrawn from Canada except for the two naval bases of Halifax and Esquimalt. As yet, however, few people had noted that there might be a naval dimension to imperial defence.[13]

In the 1870s there was a slow and feeble stirring of interest in the defence of trade among a few naval men, and even fewer civilians. The most important of them was Sir Alexander Milne, who became Senior Naval Lord on his return from the North American Station in 1866, then after an interval commanding in the Mediterranean, returned to the Admiralty to serve under both Liberals and Conservatives from 1872 to 1876. With his experience of organizing the transport for the Russian War, Milne was the first person in the Admiralty to point out, in 1859, that any future war would require an extensive coaling system which could not be improvised. The Admiralty was not even allowed to think about such things without Cabinet approval, as he was well aware:

> The *movement of ships* is regulated by the *Cabinet*, and is entirely unknown to myself as a Member of the Board, or to the Storekeeper General; therefore it is impossible to make arrangements for coal, for such movements . . . The question is a momentous one, and for the serious consideration of the Government; and it all centres in this; Is the Admiralty to keep up a supply of coal on all Foreign Stations, equal to the contingencies of a War? If not, then when War may be declared, our Fleets will be crippled for want of coals.[14]

If the coaling stations he called for were left undefended, the coal would just supply the enemy, so naval defence of shipping implied a large increase in the requirement for colonial defences. In 1873 Milne set the junior Naval Lord, Captain Arthur Hood, to study the defence of British trade, which, Hood concluded, would require thirty-seven unarmoured cruisers of three or four thousand tons and a speed of 15 knots. There were at most three such ships in the Navy. Building on this, Milne pushed for a cruiser 'establishment' of thirty frigates, fifty-five to sixty corvettes, forty-five sloops, sixty gun-vessels and as many gunboats – without which Britain risked another *Alabama* disaster. Not content with numbers, Milne sketched a strategy for the distribution of the cruisers, listing eighteen key areas each of which would need two or three cruisers to cover them, plus reliefs and other ships to guard colliers and coaling stations.[15]

In the mid-1870s, however, it would have been extremely difficult to find many public men, indeed many admirals, ready to take these expansive and expensive ideas seriously. Perhaps British shipping was theoretically vulnerable, but where was the threat? Tension with the United States eased after the settlement of the *Alabama* claims, and by 1873 the US Navy's notional forty-eight ironclads were down to two fit for service.[16] France had been catastrophically defeated by Prussia in 1870, losing her eastern provinces to the new German Reich. Napoleon III was overthrown, and a popular uprising was suppressed with great bloodshed and the destruction of most of the centre of Paris. The French Navy, already obsolescent, had been powerless to defend France, and much of its budget was then taken to reconstruct the army.[17] In Britain even the timidest were no longer lying awake worrying about French invasion, while the new Germany was a friendly power with no navy to speak of. They worried more about the insatiable demands for British naval help or naval intervention on every occasion, however trivial, from every corner of the world which had a sea coast, and many which had none. 'It is fortunate the world is not larger,' wearily declared the Duke of Somerset (First Lord 1859–66), 'for there is no other limit to the service of the fleets.'[18] 'From Vancouver's isle to the River Plate, from the West Indies to China,' he wrote, 'the Admiralty is called upon by secretaries of state to send ships of war.'[19] 'The body called the African Association of Liverpool,' Somerset warned the Foreign Secretary in 1864,

> are continually urging your department to enter upon hostile operations in the rivers of Africa for the purpose of enforcing claims on the part of British traders against the natives . . . When a squabble begins, acts of violence follow, and these applicants for naval force always assume that the white man is in the right, though any knowledge of the class of persons sent to the west coast [of Africa] on trading speculations would throw doubt on such a conclusion.[20]

Pirates and wreckers, missionaries and archaeologists, fishermen and explorers, head-hunters and filibusters, builders of lighthouses and telegraph stations, diggers of gold or guano, all demanded attention and aroused concern in the House of Commons. A major inland expedition into West Africa, the Ashanti War, had to be organized in 1873 to repel attacks on a coastal tribe under

British protection.[21] 'Blackbirding', slave-trading in the South Pacific, alleged by zealous officers who were too ready to apply their experience on the coasts of Africa to a quite different context, caused extensive difficulties.[22] Both Gladstone and Disraeli agreed that the only answer to these incessant demands was to reduce the number of warships overseas, starting with the large proportion which were of small military value, and instead rely on better steaming and better communications to bring force where and when it was needed. Between 1869 and 1874 Gladstone reduced the number of men on foreign stations from 17,000 to 11,500.[23]

If ever there was a time when Britain's overall strategic situation justified complacency, it was the 1870s, when Lord Derby's foreign policy was criticized as being 'to float lazily downstream, occasionally putting out a diplomatic boat-hook to avoid collisions'.[24] But of course it did not last. The 'Eastern Question', meaning the weakness and instability of the Ottoman Empire, was a constant focus of concern. Gladstone aroused the British public on behalf of persecuted Bulgarian Christians, and in April 1877 the Russians declared war in the same cause. Twenty-five years earlier a similar situation had stirred British anxiety, and there was more reason for it now. The opening of the Suez Canal in 1869 had made it even more important than before for Britain to keep the Russians well away from the Eastern Mediterranean. In May 1877 Britain formally warned St Petersburg accordingly, but the message was not heeded. By February 1878 the Russian army was on the outskirts of Constantinople, and at the sultan's request the British Mediterranean Fleet under Sir Geoffrey Phipps Hornby was lying off the city to protect it, having forced its way up the Dardanelles in the teeth of a midwinter snowstorm. Very little was needed to start a shooting war, and in the short term the ships could not have saved the city. Meanwhile the preliminary peace treaty (of San Stefano) between Russia and Turkey recognized the independence of Romania, Serbia, Montenegro and a greater Bulgaria with an Aegean sea coast – all of which new states were liable to be Russian satellites. All and more that Russia had lost and Turkey gained in the Russian War had now been reversed. Alarmed by the situation, the Western powers called a diplomatic congress at Berlin in 1878. At the Congress Russia was forced to give up some of its gains, in particular to restore the Ottoman territory which cut off Bulgaria from the Aegean, and therefore kept the Russian Black Sea squadron from easy access to the Mediterranean. Britain gained the Ottoman island of Cyprus, strategically placed to guard the way to the Suez Canal, but unfortunately useless without an adequate harbour. The Congress of Berlin was a diplomatic triumph for Disraeli, but it was obvious to thoughtful observers that Russia's opportunities to endanger the British position were only slightly reduced. The Ottoman Empire was no stronger than before. In central Asia, Russia continued to advance eastward, and by 1876 the desert oases of Bokhara and Khiva (in what is now Uzbekistan) were Russian protectorates. The Russians were still 600 miles away from India across some of the highest mountains in the world, but that was near enough to give light sleepers in England something else to worry about.[25]

A handful of public men, led by the Conservative MP and former Royal Marine J. C. R. Colomb, and seconded by Milne after his retirement in 1876, still strove to keep the question of imperial and trade defence in the public eye. The War Office paid more attention to them than the Admiralty did. The Russian war scare caused it to recommend spending £2 million on defending coaling stations, and in September 1879 Disraeli's government, following the classic method for burying an embarrassment, established a royal commission on the 'Defence of British Possessions and Commerce Abroad' under the presidency of the former Colonial Secretary the Earl of Carnarvon, with Milne as chairman. This commission built on the War Office's work, and adopted its method of weighing the value of a colonial station according to the value of the seaborne trade it handled. It calculated that a total of £406 million a year in seaborne trade and shipping worth £26 million had to be protected. It established reliable figures for the number of British steamers of different sizes and speeds. It plotted the principal trade routes and laid out a scheme for their protection. It questioned senior officials, starting with the Senior Naval Lord, Sir Astley Cooper Key, whose vague and rambling answers and 'alarming poverty of thought' aroused their misgivings. When Gladstone returned to power in April 1880 the Carnarvon Commission was allowed to continue its work discreetly, but its reports were unpublished and unpublicized; even Queen Victoria, in whose name the commission had been established, saw only a smuggled private copy.[26]

By the early 1880s, Britain and France were not only the joint owners of the Suez Canal, but in every way interested in Egypt itself, whose bankrupt government owed large sums to British and French bond-holders. Taxing the poor Egyptians to pay foreign capitalists roused nationalist anger against foreigners (encouraged by Colonel Arabi, the Egyptian Minister of War), ships were sent to protect foreign residents, and in June 1882 there was a riot in which about fifty Europeans were killed. Gladstone's ministers were unsure how to react, but Admiral Sir Beauchamp Seymour decided for them with a demand that the Alexandria Harbour forts which threatened his ships should be surrendered, which Colonel Arabi refused. The French withdrew, but on 11 and

12 July Seymour's ships bombarded the forts and set fire to the city. Then they occupied the city to restore order and 'protect the Canal', followed in August by a full-scale invasion of Egypt which installed the British in power, acting in the name of the Egyptian ruler the Khedive. Gladstone was genuinely determined to leave Egypt as soon as possible, but the risks of doing so grew rapidly. The Khedive was still on his throne, but the British had in effect destroyed his government; the Suez Canal was now a vital British interest, and the Muslim leader the Mahdi with his jihadist army in the Sudan stood ready to exploit any vacuum. So the British stayed in Egypt, in what might politely be called an anomalous situation. They paid the price of long-term political embarrassment, but they controlled the Canal and gained a third Mediterranean naval base which made Cyprus more superfluous than ever.[27]

Two years later, the British government and public were still preoccupied with Egypt and the Sudan. In the Commons Mr W. H. Smith, the former Conservative First Lord, collected material to mount a Parliamentary attack on the Liberal government for neglect and mismanagement of the Navy, but the public was far more interested in General Gordon's expedition to the Sudan, and Smith lost hope of distracting them. Then, in September 1884, the government was hit by a storm out of a clear sky. W. T. Stead, editor of the *Pall Mall Gazette*, was well known for his sensationalist campaigns: in 1883 against slum housing ('The Bitter Cry of Outcast London'); in January 1884 to send Gordon to the Sudan; the following year against child prostitution ('The Maiden Tribute of Modern Babylon'). Now he printed the first of a series of highly detailed articles entitled 'What is the Truth about the Navy? by One Who Knows the Facts'. Readers were given to understand that 'One Who Knows' was someone highly placed in the Admiralty, and that the mass of detail Stead printed was authentic. The story he told was of a Navy suffering from supine neglect in the face of rapid French and Russian re-armament. Smith was happy to take up the theme in Parliament, and as the campaign gathered momentum it embarrassed the Liberal government considerably. In the absence in Egypt of Lord Northbrook the First Lord, the government was driven in December to announce an emergency programme of £2.8 million to build ironclads which he had only recently declared were unnecessary.[28]

It is usually said that 'One Who Knows' was Captain John Fisher, then commanding the gunnery training ship *Excellent* at Portsmouth. Both he and Stead hinted as much long afterwards, but there are reasons for scepticism. Many of the 'revelations' in the articles were neither true nor secret, and did not come from any authority. Fisher was not in the Admiralty and not well placed to supply Stead with what he wanted. Although he loved to talk big and very much loved intrigue, Fisher usually acted prudently, and making a fool of his patron, the Senior Naval Lord Sir Astley Cooper Key, was not a prudent act for an ambitious young captain. Though other names have been suggested, it seems most likely that the real author of the articles was Stead himself, assembling information from diverse sources as journalists do. He did know Fisher, he talked to various admirals, including Cooper Key, and almost certainly to the leading Conservative admiral of the day, Sir Geoffrey Phipps Hornby, with his extensive following of officers ill-disposed to Mr Gladstone. Also useful was Stead's friend Reginald Brett, private secretary to Lord Hartington, the Secretary for War, across whose desk passed many relevant documents, including those of the Carnarvon Commission.[29]

Undoubtedly Stead was lucky in his timing, for in March 1885 a Russian column crossed the frontier into Afghanistan, provoking another alarm of war. Phipps Hornby took command of a British fleet assembled for the Baltic, while in the Far East the China Squadron occupied an island off the Korean coast to act as an advance base for operations against Vladivostok. In the face of these preparations the Russians withdrew, but the Conservative opposition in Britain did not. A large meeting representing City shipping and insurance interests took up the protection of trade, demanding a public guarantee of war risks insurance to prevent the sort of panic which had destroyed the US merchant fleet in 1863. The City was dominated by Liberals, but its spokesmen conspicuously failed to come to Gladstone's defence. The government now established an interdepartmental Colonial Defence Committee. It was still guided by the War Office, the only department to take the subject seriously, but it was difficult for the Cabinet to withstand interdepartmental consensus, and it led to £976,700 being spent on the defences of Aden, Trincomalee, Colombo, Singapore, Hong Kong, the Cape of Good Hope, Mauritius, Jamaica and St Lucia. Whitehall was now beginning to pay attention to the defence of trade, even if the Admiralty was not.[30]

At the same time, there were other important developments bearing on the defence of trade. Improvements in marine engineering (to be explained later) meant that by the mid-1880s many of the newer cargo and passenger steamers had a greater range and higher speed than the warships which would have to protect them in wartime. This suggested to many commentators that merchant ships themselves might be armed and commissioned for the protection of trade. Liberal spokesmen were particularly delighted by the idea that the unseen hand of free trade had created an efficient defence at no cost to the taxpayer – and none were more pleased than that unreconstructed Cobdenite Sir Nathaniel Barnaby, the Director of Naval Construction. Already in 1876 the Admiralty had established a register of suitable merchant ships with adequate watertight bulkheads. By 1885 it listed 155 ships of 12 knots or faster, plus another 255 slower ships. In 1883 and again in 1885 sixteen of them were chartered for experimental conversion – at a cost of £535,000 and £600,000 respectively, or about 5 per cent of the usual Navy Estimates, which rather deflated Liberal hopes of free defence. In 1887 mail contracts began to offer subsidies for steamers with strengthened decks ready to receive gun mountings.[31] Unfortunately for the British, the same technologies would serve just as well to attack merchant shipping as to defend it. France had a similar programme of earmarking potential merchant cruisers. The Russians organized a 'Volunteer Fleet' of fast merchant ships officered by naval officers and intended for instant conversion into raiding cruisers. Armed merchant cruisers were therefore no magic solution to British problems, but another component of a situation of growing complexity.[32]

Another complication arrived across the Channel in January 1886, when Vice-Admiral Hyacinthe Aube became Minister of Marine in the seventeen-month Republican government of Charles de Freycinet. Ever since the French Revolution, French society had been (and to an extent still is) divided into two camps: the one conservative and Catholic; the other republican, often anti-clerical, leaning more or less to the left and accommodating to Socialists, Protestants, Jews and Liberals. The French Navy was firmly in the hands of the right; in Republican eyes a battleship fleet was 'Versailles afloat', the symbol of the ironclad political and social establishment which they detested.[33] Aube (though himself a devout Catholic) was the leader of a radical naval movement known as the *Jeune École* ('Young School'), which proposed replacing the iron-clads with fast raiding cruisers for the open sea, and even faster steam torpedo boats for the narrow seas. Aube relished the prospect, not only of sinking the clumsy ironclads, but of sending passenger liners to the bottom with all their people. In France the meaning of the *Jeune École* was as much political and social as naval, and Aube had little time in office to bring about major change, but he did enough to make naval men think hard, in Britain and indeed all over the world. His favoured torpedo boats proved to be unseaworthy, but for many contemporaries his ideas still held water, and they threatened British naval supremacy in more ways than one.[34]

When the 1885 Russian war scare faded, Phipps Hornby did not at once disperse his 'Baltic fleet', but obtained permission to try something which the Navy had not undertaken in living memory: 'manoeuvres'. Taking his ships to the deep inlet of Berehaven on the west coast of Ireland, he practised blockad-ing and breaking a blockade. Besides yielding useful lessons, this exercise also garnered a good deal of publicity, as perhaps Phipps Hornby had foreseen. Journalists and artists working for the new illustrated papers hastened to Ireland to report what the Navy was doing, fuelling public interest. The following year, 1886, the Liberals returned briefly to power. For them public enthusiasm for the Navy was unwelcome, and no manoeuvres were held, but in 1887 the admirals had the chance to try out ideas for trade protection after the naval review for the Queen's golden jubilee. Once more the press followed the manoeuvres, and the public was keenly interested. Next year a specific problem was set: to test whether a close blockade could be mounted in modern conditions, and for the first time the journalists were invited to go afloat. Rear-Admiral George Tryon, 'the Achill Admiral' as he was officially dubbed (to avoid the untoward political implications of an 'Irish admiral' facing an 'English fleet'), was blockaded in Berehaven. He escaped with ease and proceeded on a sensational cruise around the British Isles, 'bombarding' and 'ransoming' Liverpool and other coastal towns, 'sinking' ninety-five merchant ships (without rescuing the crews), while the 'British' fleet abandoned the pursuit. The blockade part of the exercise actually provided useful lessons; the subsequent cruise cast grave doubt on Britain's traditional all-purpose strategy of blockade, and yielded brilliant public relations for naval expansion. Extracts of the umpires' report were immediately published, emphasizing the inadequacy of the Navy Estimates. The following year the 'Three Admirals' Report' on the 1888 manoeuvres, which called for a 'two-power standard' of naval strength, was even more nakedly political. Before it reached the Admiralty in November, W. H. White the recently appointed Director of Naval Construction had a new shipbuilding programme ready to meet it.[35]

W. T. Stead had startled the British political world by discovering a public ready to be concerned over 'the Truth about the Navy'. Behind this we can see the slow evolution of politics through the broadening of the franchise. The second Reform Act of 1867 had already brought most of the middle classes into the political nation, and at the very moment Stead published his articles, the third Reform Act extended the vote to about two-thirds of the adult male population, all who passed a very low property qualification. This breached the ancient principle that only taxpayers could legitimately participate in political decisions. Party leaders initially knew little about what the newly enfranchised thought, and were slow to appreciate that obscure matters like naval policy, which had hitherto belonged to the political elite, might be escaping into the unpoliced world of public opinion. By the time of the 1888 Manoeuvres it was clear beyond doubt that large parts of the public were not merely interested but excited and out of official control.[36]

The Marquess of Salisbury, the Conservative Prime Minister, was a statesman of the school of Gladstone and Disraeli for whom British naval supremacy was a fixed star in the political firmament which would stay up without any immoderate public spending. Although not indifferent to the needs of the Navy, he viewed admirals as no better than other experts:

> No lesson seems to be so deeply inculcated by the experience of life as that you never should trust experts. If you believe the doctors, nothing is wholesome: if you believe the theologians, nothing is innocent: if you believe the soldiers, nothing is safe. They all require to have their strong wine diluted by a very large admixture of insipid common sense.[37]

The remedy was to keep the admirals under control:

> The fault is in the constitution of the Admiralty. The experts – the pedants – have too much power. They ought to be advisers and subordinates. They are checks and colleagues . . . The result is that everything which is done by the First Lord of his own initiative has to be carried out in the teeth of a stiff, silent resistance, which is offered to every detail by persons who know much better than he can the points at which resistance is likely to be effective. The only remedy is to convert the First Lord into a Secretary of State.[38]

That would eliminate the Admiralty Board and its naval members, leaving authority in the hands of civilian statesmen who would not be tempted to waste money on warships. Salisbury's attitude to public enthusiasm for the Navy and to 'those hallucinations of which admirals are the victims'[39] was always cool, but his political instincts were acute, and he was quicker than Lord George Hamilton the First Lord to appreciate that public enthusiasm could be turned to political advantage. In the summer of 1888 he agreed that the Admiralty might present to the Cabinet requirements for 'certain eventualities' – meaning war. This was radical: no government in living memory had offered to build a fleet adequate for a major war, defined by a professional estimate of need rather than a political estimate of acceptability. Against Hamilton's misgivings he explicitly asked for 'a statement as to the strength necessary to enable us to fight France and Russia in combination'.[40] During the autumn and winter the Admiralty developed a war plan and a fleet to meet them, which were presented to the Cabinet on 1 December 1888. This was the origin of the Naval Defence Act, laid before Parliament the following March.[41]

The act was unprecedented in several respects. It was driven by public opinion, steered but scarcely controlled by the government. It presented a five-year naval building programme which in addition to increasing the annual Estimates by £600,000 a year, proposed to borrow £10 million to £11.5 million over seven years backed by a special tax, the whole amounting to £20 million of earmarked expenditure, which nearly doubled normal naval spending. This trampled on the most sacred principles of British public finance: that specific funds were never 'hypothecated' to specific purposes; and that money was borrowed only for capital investment, never to meet current expenditure. Gladstone's horror was redoubled by the realization that the act was calculated to divide the Liberal Party and tie the hands of a future government – very likely his own. The Act offered a standard of naval strength, the 'Two-Power Standard', which had the appearance of a rational and objective test to which governments could be held, while being in fact infinitely flexible, because all depended on secret information of other countries' shipbuilding, and professional judgement as to which old ships were or were not still effective. It was never made clear whether the standard was of sufficient strength to equal the next two powers, or a sufficient margin of superiority to defeat them. The public believed that the two were France and Russia, generally though wrongly thought to have a naval alliance against Britain, but the next two navies in point of strength were actually France and (friendly) Italy, so that the difference in size between the Italian and Russian navies provided another hidden margin. The total programme of the act was ten new battleships, thirty-eight cruisers of various sizes, eighteen torpedo boats and four fast gunboats. The last British naval building programme of comparable size had been the thirty ships of the line of 1677.[42]

The Naval Defence Act was an extraordinary triumph for the advocates of naval expansion, who had aroused public excitement for a subject which, even ten years before, had seemed the most obscure and tedious corner of public policy. The newly enfranchised public had been invited to participate in discussions which had hitherto been reserved to the experts, behind closed doors. It was no coincidence that three important naval pressure groups, the London Chamber of Commerce, the Navy League and the Navy Records Society, were all founded in the early 1890s.[43]

What it all meant in the long run is another question. The French were attempting to replace a large number of decaying and obsolete wooden-hulled ironclads left over from Napoleon III's reign, but all their efforts were clogged by erratic policy and inefficient dockyards. It took up to ten years to build French battleships, by which time they were obsolescent, and the Russian situation was no better. In the cold light of hindsight Stead's Franco-Russian 'threat' appears illusory, and the Admiralty's 'complacency' fully justified. Moreover, it soon became clear that the British had started an international naval race which gathered momentum right up to the First World War, creating major new navies like the German, Japanese and American, financed by multi-year 'naval laws', and inspiring similar programmes large and small all over the world. Certainly Britain was the best equipped, financially and industrially, to win this race, and on the obvious measures did win it, but we may still ask how much extra defence the Naval Defence Act really bought. On the other hand we can see too that an age of intense international competition was beginning in which British pre-eminence was to be challenged by newly industrialized rivals in different ways in different parts of the world. It is inconceivable that this challenge would not have been expressed at sea sooner or later, and probably sooner. The Naval Defence Act gained Britain an early lead in a race which was almost bound to have started before long. Moreover, the Act was not solely concerned with battleships but also with building a new fleet of cruisers for trade defence. It marked the return of a sophisticated understanding of war at sea forgotten for two generations, and a balanced fleet of different types and sizes of ships ready to undertake it. A tell-tale of the new understanding was the functional classifications of 'battleships' and 'cruisers', first adopted in the 1887 *Navy List*. 'The Truth about the Navy' may not have been true at all, but it helped to bring into focus the truth about naval warfare.[44]

EIGHT

The Phantom of the Old Board

Government and Administration 1860–1890

In their own eyes, the mid-Victorians were distinguished from previous ages and other countries by their commitment to reform, but their efforts encountered many obstacles founded on their own preconceptions and prejudices. Their Benthamite devotion to the responsibility of the individual was essentially a moral concept: considered as a practical driver of administrative change, it worked best in small organizations which really could be understood and controlled by a single individual. The Benthamites' conviction that the gentleman amateur, possessor of real knowledge derived from practical experience, was always superior to the expert theoretician, frequently prevented them from understanding a world of ever-growing complexity. When Benthamites encountered difficulties, they tended to blame the sins of the individual rather than the faults of the system, just as those in the seventeenth and eighteenth centuries had done.

Another way to understand the developments of this period is to study the administration of the Navy as an organism reacting to stimuli. Until the mid-1880s the stimuli came mainly from within Britain, from domestic politics and currents of opinion pressing upon government and Parliament. External stimuli existed – the call for naval action in different parts of the world, even in rare and remote cases the threat of naval attack – but they were far away both geographically and psychologically. What was expected of naval administration was chiefly that it should function according to the ethical standards which the public expected. The object was not simply to save money, but economical spending was a reliable indicator of administrative health and virtue. Much of the mid-Victorian public indeed, led by the newspapers and reviews, was convinced that all government industrial activity was inevitably and invariably corrupt and wasteful, captured by greedy private interests determined to exploit the taxpayer. The only solution was to abolish it and hand over its functions to private industry. There were always voices, especially but not only in the Liberal Party, calling for the drastic reduction or outright closure of dockyards and naval establishments.[1]

Gladstone was the best known, most talented and most determined of these voices, but his ideas were largely common to all parties. It was Disraeli as Chancellor of the Exchequer in the Earl of Derby's Conservative government in 1866 who denounced the naval Lords of the Admiralty as 'criminals' on discovering that the dockyards carried larger stocks of materials than private shipyards.[2] Very likely he did not know that the work of the dockyards was unlike that of a shipyard: there was no reason why a statesman should have been acquainted with such obscurities, or valued the information if he had happened to discover it. Disraeli's difficulty was to counter what on another occasion he called the 'wild suggestions of these ignorant & narrow minded Admirals'.[3] That charge was reasonable: few admirals were well-educated or familiar with the wider world, and perhaps the politicians who appointed them to the Admiralty Board were content that they were not. During the Russian War, Sir James Graham and Admiral Berkeley as Senior Naval Lord issued orders in the Admiralty's name through the Secretary without sharing any secrets with the junior naval lords.[4] Ten years later it was much the same. Only a handful of admirals (notably Milne and Phipps Hornby) were worth consulting on questions of policy, which were normally no business of the Admiralty's.[5] In 1867 Henry Lowry-Corry the First Lord told the Commons that the movement of Her Majesty's ships,

> depended upon considerations with which even the Lords of the Admiralty themselves were sometimes unacquainted, and which were kept within the bosom of the Cabinet. The Admiralty implicitly obeyed the instructions they received from the Cabinet on this point.[6]

Yet the Admiralty's arcane knowledge made it difficult to override. 'The Admiralty is beyond the control of a Chancellor of the Exchequer or any other subordinate Minister,' Disraeli complained to Derby in February 1867:

> It is the Prime Minister that can alone deal with that department . . . It is useless to attempt to reason with them: you must command. The whole system of administration is palsied by their mutinous spirit.[7]

It was not only a mutinous spirit which paralysed the Admiralty. Sir James Graham's abolition of the Navy Board, and imposition of individual responsibility in place of a functioning Admiralty Board, had left each Admiralty Lord to cope alone with a rapidly rising tide of paperwork. There were almost no naval officers in Whitehall to help the naval lords with professional questions, they had no time to talk to each other, and the Board meetings (249 in 1866), though they still took place and took time, were no longer the occasion for either discussion or decision. The ever-rising demands of routine administration stifled any temptations the naval lords might experience to think about naval policy. Meanwhile 'individual responsibility' had deprived the yard officers of any initiative and obliged them to submit even the most trivial questions to higher authority.[8] When responsibilities met or overlapped, as for example those of the dockyard superintendent and the local flag officer for ships in reserve, the doctrine made it difficult for them to discuss between themselves and reach common-sense solutions.[9] According to a report of 1862, if a captain proposed some alteration to his ship:

> The Captain writes a letter containing the suggestion to his Commander-in-Chief who forwards it to the Secretary of the Admiralty, who sends it to the Lord in whose department the matter is supposed to be, who orders the Controller to report, who sends it back to the Dock Yard Officers for the necessary explanations and reports, who send it back to the Controller, who sends the report with any observations he may think requisite to the Secretary of the Admiralty, who places it in the hands of the Lord to whose department it relates, who gives the requisite authority, which is communicated to the Controller.[10]

The Deputy Inspector in charge of Haslar Hospital across the harbour from Portsmouth, could not send a nurse to accompany a blind man to the railway station without seeking permission from the Admiralty – which never responded.[11] Admiralty regulations were issued and amended by different offices, but until Milne complained in 1860 no complete record was kept or issued of what was in force, so that nobody could agree what the regulations actually were.[12] By 1861 Graham himself thought the Admiralty he had reformed 'so far from being an example to be followed . . . might, on the whole, be regarded as an example to be avoided'.[13] Throughout the 1860s Parliamentary discontent with the Admiralty continued to grow. The gloomy Duke of Somerset complained in 1866 that 'the human memory cannot recall the period when the department of the Admiralty was not the subject of accusation and complaint'.[14] All complaints could be summed up as overspending, and the Conservatives lost the 1868 general election partly on the spending issue.[15]

Gladstone the new Prime Minister was determined not to make the same mistake. His First Lord of the Admiralty was Hugh Childers, a close associate who fully shared his views, and knew the Admiralty well, having served as

Civil Lord from 1864 to 1866. As Financial Secretary of the Treasury he was the author of the 1866 Exchequer and Audit Act that combined estimates, appropriation, expenditure and audit in a single system, which he now applied to the Admiralty. He pushed through a series of structural changes in the Admiralty and the dockyards, merging the dockyards and steam factories, closing Woolwich and Deptford Dockyards, moving out of Somerset House, breaking up large departments, eliminating duplication and promoting individual initiative. A higher class of civil servants was recruited by examination, and a new technology (the letter-press) spared the juniors much laborious copying of papers by hand.[16] The Admiralty Board had almost ceased to meet, and all lines of responsibility now met in the person of the First Lord. The ten subjects which his predecessor had handled personally, Childers increased to forty-two.[17]

Childers was well-prepared for office, but he did not know the Admiralty well enough to design all this unaided: he depended on an ally who supplied him with a complete scheme of reforms. Vice-Admiral Sir Robert Spencer Robinson had held the key office of Controller (formerly Surveyor) since 1861, which put him in charge of shipbuilding and the dockyards, by far the most important and expensive fraction of the Admiralty's responsibilities. He was able, ambitious, intimately familiar with the dockyards and their work – and best of all, a committed Gladstonian Liberal. He readily agreed to work with Childers, who made him Second Naval Lord. In this position, backed by the staff of the Controller's Department, which included most of the few naval officers in the Admiralty, Robinson was better than a rival to Sir Sydney Dacres the Senior Naval Lord, and Childers thought he could easily play them off against each other. He had underestimated Robinson. An outstanding if difficult subordinate had been transformed into an ungovernable colleague who was ready to grasp at the authority, not just of Dacres, but of the First Lord himself.[18]

By 1870 Robinson's relations with Childers had become strained, and those with both Dacres and Edward Reed, the Chief Constructor, had reached breaking point. One among the many subjects of dispute was the new turret ironclad *Captain*, ordered by the previous Board from a private shipyard to an unofficial design by an amateur naval architect. This combination would have appealed to almost any politician of that generation, and certainly did to Childers, who dismissed the misgivings of Robinson and Reed as professional jealousy and ordered the ship to sea. Reed resigned in July 1870, but Robinson was still in office when, on the night of 7 September, the *Captain* capsized and sank off Cape Finisterre with the loss of almost all her company, including

Childers' own son. This disaster raised many urgent questions, but at least Childers had answered one of them beyond doubt by taking the formal responsibility on himself. He used it to issue a Board Minute, printed in the newspapers on 1 December 'by command of their Lordships' (none of whom except Childers had previously seen it), which exonerated the First Lord himself and laid the entire blame for the tragedy on Reed and Robinson. This reduced the Admiralty to uproar, in the course of which Gladstone personally dismissed Robinson, and in March 1871 Childers followed him, broken in health and spirits and unlamented by all who had worked with him.[19] Three months later the troopship *Megaera*, one of the converted iron frigates of 1845, was beached in a sinking condition on the remote island of St Paul in the Indian Ocean. Investigation revealed that reports from naval and dockyard officers drawing attention to her dangerous condition had been mislaid in the Admiralty. This led to a Royal Commission which uncovered yet more damaging evidence.[20] 'I am called Secretary of the Board of Admiralty,' Vernon Lushington told it, 'but the Board of Admiralty does not exist, and the business of the Admiralty is all transacted here and there in various compartments, as I may say.' What Lushington called 'the phantom of the old Board' had come back to haunt Mr Gladstone.[21]

Childers' successor was George Goschen, President of the Poor Law Board. There was some sarcasm at the choice of one with no knowledge or experience of the Admiralty, but in the circumstances there was much to be said for a level-headed administrator and financial expert who inspired calm and confidence. Goschen made relatively few changes to Childers' reforms, but the new Controller, the efficient but unabrasive Rear-Admiral William Houston Stewart, was not offered a seat on the Admiralty Board. Another naval lord was added to take his place, and Board meetings were revived to improve the exchange of information. Most important of all, in November 1872 Goschen persuaded Sir Alexander Milne to return to the Admiralty for a second time as Senior Naval Lord. Not only did his great standing in the Navy help to restore confidence, but the fact of a Liberal ministry naming an admiral who had previously been First Naval Lord under the Conservative government of 1866 to 1868 sent a powerful signal that the aggressive partisanship of Childers and Robinson would not be revived. Milne's appointment marked the moment when the principle of non-party naval Lords of the Admiralty, which he had himself inaugurated as junior naval lord in 1847, became acceptable practice for the whole Board.[22]

'You will find it so very different from what it was, and such a pleasant change,' one of the Admiralty clerks wrote to Milne on learning that he was to return, 'I should think there never was a better Board as regards matter or manner.'[23] The manner was certainly different, but Goschen had only slightly changed Childers' structures. The naval members of the Board were still grossly overloaded, and the Senior Naval Lord was in the worst situation of all. 'You and I ought to be to a considerable extent relieved, or aided, by competent and qualified persons,' Milne wrote to another naval lord. 'This is not work, but it is incessant daily labour, which cannot last and everything thrown on my head to think of, and to keep in recollection . . .'[24] To Goschen he complained in September 1873 that

> there is no cohesion between the Naval Element in the Board. Admirals Tarleton & Seymour are nominally ignorant of what is done by the Senior N. Lord, great questions may be decided without their knowing what is being done . . . The Senior N. Lord in his Room . . . with a mass of papers of all descriptions to be read, considered, and minuted. He takes one after the other to get thro' them, some paper of more importance than another turns up, He makes a minute in the hurry . . . and it goes away – He has no one to consult with and the minute which has left his room may be executed without any check and unknown to any other Naval Member . . . the question really is how to work the present arrangement, how to relieve the Senior N. Lord, and how to get work done to prevent a mistake; also whether Naval Members of the Board should or should not act in some manner together on naval matters that is assist each other in the decision of purely Naval questions, also how the Secretary or Secretaries are to act in reference to the consideration of General Questions . . .[25]

An administrative system designed to minimize the influence of experts was now faced with a rising load of highly technical business. Behind Milne's fear that harassed naval lords without professional assistance would commit serious mistakes, lay a hint, which might well have given a civilian minister qualms, that they ought to have the opportunity to form a collective naval view.[26]

Five months later, in March 1874, the Conservatives under Disraeli were re-elected and retained Milne in office, reinforcing the Senior Naval Lord's new non-political status. With some difficulty George Ward Hunt the new First Lord persuaded Geoffrey Phipps Hornby, who shared Milne's opinion on the urgency of strengthening the naval element in the Admiralty, to join him on the Board in spite of his hatred of office work. By 1876, the year Milne turned seventy, it was obvious that he must soon retire, and Hornby was confident that the next Senior Naval Lord must be one of three admirals: Frederick

Beauchamp Seymour, Sir Astley Cooper Key, or himself. He therefore wrote
to the other two, proposing that they should form a compact, each undertaking to refuse office unless they were granted at least the beginnings of a naval
staff. That summer Milne did retire; Hornby was offered his seat and refused
it unless he could have additional staff. He took the Mediterranean squadron,
Beauchamp Seymour had recently taken command of the Channel squadron,
and Key was commanding in North America. Ward Hunt had no other candidate for the Admiralty but Sir Hastings Yelverton, who was sixty-eight and
almost totally deaf.[27] Both of them were dead within a year. The new First Lord,
Mr W. H. Smith, named George Wellesley as Senior Naval Lord, and when he
resigned in 1879 the position had to be filled for the third time in three years.
Of the three members of the 1876 'compact', Key alone was available, and he
eagerly accepted the offer. Recently re-married, with a large family and a
demanding young bride, Key needed the salary urgently. Moreover, he was one
of nature's bureaucrats, who 'could not bear to be without a full supply of "current business" to occupy his mind . . . a man who had gradually become an
administrator, disinclined to trust his mind beyond the solution of the medi-
ate'.[28] As a gunnery officer he had made significant contributions during his
career, but in six years at the Admiralty he was chiefly occupied in hiding
behind his paperwork and avoiding big questions.[29]

These six years, 1879–85, were exactly the period in which concern about
the state of the Navy began to make itself felt both inside and outside the
Admiralty. The Eastern crisis of 1878 had revealed an almost complete lack of
information in the Admiralty. Key was appointed to command a Baltic fleet
but could not discover anything about the situation there. The Russians sent a
cruiser squadron to sea from the Baltic, but the Admiralty was unaware of it
until the newspapers reported its arrival in New York. In February 1879 a committee recommended an intelligence department, but as soon as Key became
Senior Naval Lord he sat firmly on the proposal. Only in 1882 did the arguments of the Carnarvon Commission and the skilful advocacy of Captain
George Tryon, the new Secretary of the Admiralty, overcome Key's reluctance.
The bombardment of Alexandria in July of that year was conducted with the
benefit of intelligence from the War Office alone.[30] The situation was only
slightly better in the Russian war scare of 1885, when 'a lamentable want of precision and organization & a general unreadiness prevailed at the Admiralty',
and the test mobilization was a fiasco. The reserve ironclads took between
forty-nine and seventy-seven days to commission; some never succeeded
at all.[31]

The 1885 Russian crisis came on top of the 'Truth about the Navy' affair in the previous year, when Lord Northbrook's Admiralty was voted £2.8 million to spend on the ships which he had declared he did not need. Northbrook was one of several eminent financial experts in Gladstone's government; that was why he was in Egypt, examining other people's finances, when the storm broke in England. He was overwhelmed by the work Childers had bequeathed him, and to the government's intense embarrassment the Admiralty overspent its emergency vote by £800,000. As a result a standing Admiralty Financial Committee, with Treasury representation, was set up to oversee financial planning.[32] Next year the advisory Foreign Intelligence Committee set up in 1882 became the Foreign Intelligence Department, staffed by naval officers, with sections for intelligence and mobilization, though still no explicit planning responsibilities. The Financial and Intelligence Committees, though small in themselves, were significant indicators of change, bringing outside expertise into the Admiralty. The Gladstonian system Childers had installed was breaking down under the pressure of external events and the manifest inability of the Admiralty Board to do its job without expert assistance. Moreover the public was now beginning to pay attention.[33]

Key's successor in July 1885 was Sir Arthur Hood, like him a gunnery officer familiar with new technologies, and like him an enthusiastic administrator ill at ease with new thinking. It was Hood's misfortune to take office just as opinion outside the Admiralty was evolving fast, and questions were being urgently asked which had hitherto been unasked and even unaskable.[34] For example, the 1888 Commons Select Committee on the Navy Estimates pressed Hood to explain who fixed the strength of the Navy, and on what basis. He replied that the Cabinet alone was responsible, or alternatively the Admiralty Board, but certainly not himself; he did not know if the Admiralty had ever proffered a statement of the Navy's needs. He personally would like six more cruisers, but he did not know why. A complete war plan 'has been considered, and I think arranged for, so far as my personal knowledge goes'. Under pressure, he recollected that he himself had prepared it, though it would be 'dragging in a good deal' to say that the Admiralty Board had considered 'the possible eventuality of war'.[35] Within a month he had drawn up a war plan against France and Russia.[36] Hood was far from unique in his generation. After eight years at the Admiralty Board, Vice-Admiral Sir Anthony Hoskins had no idea how the strength of the Navy compared to foreign powers, and did not know whether politicians or naval officers were responsible for it. Asked about war plans, he could only suggest that 'I imagine that what your fleet would have to do in time of war would depend very much on what your enemy did'.[37] The reaction of the Permanent Secretary, Evan MacGregor, to probing questions from the same committee displayed a forgetfulness verging on senility.[38]

Behind these reactions we can see a fundamental shift in attitudes taking place. The Admiralty representatives spoke for conventions which had been unchallenged for two generations. They had no views on matters of policy which they had never been asked or permitted to consider. But in the outside world naval officers, Parliamentarians, journalists and members of the public in growing numbers were taking a serious interest in naval policy and strategy. The Admiralty's unwillingness to address, and inability to answer, the kind of questions the 1888 Select Committee put to them, caused growing alarm out of doors. The new Naval Intelligence Department, and the junior Naval Lord responsible for it, Captain Lord Charles Beresford, came to symbolize their concerns. Intelligence was controversial: to collect it implied thinking about the future and verged on planning for war. The Navy was beginning to nibble at strategy and even policy, to the alarm of both politicians and civil servants. All this was exposed to the public by Beresford's indiscretions. Lord George Hamilton preferred safe men, in or out of uniform, to form his Admiralty Board, but was unable to oppose the suggestion, from both Salisbury and the Prince of Wales, that Beresford, the gallant young hero of the bombardment of Alexandria and the subsequent Nile expedition, would add lustre to the administration. Instead, he principally contributed embarrassment. A fine practical seaman with no aptitude for administration, or discretion, Beresford rapidly made his position in the Admiralty untenable and was out of office within two years.[39]

At the level of the Cabinet, the Admiralty Board and the management of the dockyards, the years 1860 to 1890 present a history of weakness and instability. 'I have, I regret it deeply, served for sixteen years in connection with the dockyards,' declared the Controller Houston Stewart in 1881. 'I am now in the last year of my service and looking back I do not remember six months during which changes of some sort were not introduced into the management of the dockyards; the most radical . . . were in 1869.' This was the Childers system, which he pronounced 'a most complete failure'.[40] Discredited by the *Megaera* affair but only slightly changed by George Goschen, it continued throughout the 1870s. It was still rigidly centralized and bureaucratic. Expenditure was tightly controlled, but the accounts were too weak to give any clear idea of what the money was being spent on, and the Treasury was no help.[41] When Goschen became Chancellor of the Exchequer in 1887 he was 'struck by the uniform and almost constant attitude of positive hostility in language taken up by various Officers of the Treasury towards Naval and Military Officers generally'.[42] The

yard officers, risen through the ranks in most cases from shipwright apprentices, had no training in naval architecture adequate to supervise shipbuilding.
Because of the weakness of management, the dockyards built ships slowly, and
ships were further delayed by piecemeal alterations intended to keep them up
to date, without extra votes to pay for them. The results were demoralizing to
yard officers and naval officers alike.[43]

Nevertheless, there were obscure but significant improvements. The dockyard schools, founded in 1843 to educate illiterate apprentices, were improving
fast by the 1860s. They were an early example of the modern 'sandwich course';
meaning that the dockyards, unlike private employers in the age of the twelve-
hour day, gave the young men time off to attend classes. Three years' school-
ing was compulsory, with a fourth year for the ablest, and a fifth after the
abolition of the Central School of Mathematics in 1859. By 1945 the whole
course was officially rated equivalent to a university degree. The dockyard
schools were extremely competitive, and in turn the primary schools in the
dockyard towns competed to send their best pupils there. From the dockyard
schools emerged a new generation of foremen and supervisors with a professional education greatly superior to that of their predecessors, or their contemporaries in private shipyards. Moreover, the very best of the dockyard
schools' pupils were eligible to proceed to the new Royal School of Naval Architecture, established in South Kensington in 1864 before moving in 1873 to
Greenwich. Although it was open to private pupils, they were usually outclassed by the products of the dockyard schools, who went on to become the
leading naval constructors. In social terms it is remarkable that the twentieth-
century Directors of Naval Construction, by some way the most highly paid
civil servants in Britain, were drawn from working-class and lower middle-
class households in provincial industrial towns: with one exception the products of private schools were altogether absent.[44] In 1883 the constructors in
Admiralty employment were formally constituted into the Royal Corps of
Naval Constructors, from whom were drawn not only the warship designers
in the Admiralty, but the senior managers of the dockyards. This plan, which
owed a good deal to the French *Génie Maritime*, provided the dockyards with
expert senior management. Although the mass of dockyard employees were
no more highly trained than those of private shipyards, and the Admiralty was
only slightly more enlightened than private builders in its attitude towards
working-class education, the dockyard officers contrasted markedly with the
often-inept management of private shipyards.[45]

The new Royal Corps with its resounding title presented a powerful claim
to the authority of technical expertise for those ready to accept it, but it was

not clear how this related to the political authority of the Cabinet or the professional authority of naval officers. Sir Edward Reed, Chief Constructor from 1863 to 1870, then MP and unsparing public critic of the Admiralty for the next thirty years, always insisted that the Navy should accept whatever types of ship the designer chose to give it. Sir William Symonds and Captain Cowper Coles, designer of the *Captain*, had claimed the naval officer's authority. In practice the distribution of authority in the Admiralty of the 1880s was obscure.[46] When Lord George Hamilton took office as First Lord in July 1885 he found a class of armoured cruisers under construction which were seriously overweight because of piecemeal additions to the design during construction, for which nobody accepted responsibility. 'A Board of Admiralty,' Hamilton minuted,

> is for naval purposes a most effective system of administration, provided there is thorough cooperation between its different members, and the departments they respectively supervise. If no such co-operation with its attendant responsibility exists, the Board in its corporate capacity is simply a system for the avoidance of personal responsibility.[47]

Hamilton and William White, the new Director of Naval Construction, produced an elegant and sensible solution in August 1888, when they convened a meeting of senior naval officers which agreed outline requirements for a modern battleship. White then worked up alternative sketch designs, and in November the same committee chose one of them to build. Political authority having decided to build the battleships under the Naval Defence Act, the naval men agreed on their priorities guided by the naval architect's advice on what was possible, and the constructor then designed the class to meet those requirements as well as possible. In essence this remained the design process thereafter.[48]

Another significant development in the dockyards began in the early 1860s, almost by accident. The first iron-hulled ironclads were built in private shipyards, which alone possessed the expertise, but in 1861 the first dockyard-built iron hull, the *Achilles*, was laid down at Chatham. One hundred ironworkers were brought in to build her. The dockyard shipwrights could see clearly that their ancient craft was gravely threatened. In the summer of 1862 Admiral Robinson, the Controller, began to move shipwrights to the *Achilles* to retrain in iron, at which the ironworkers went on strike to preserve their monopoly of the lucrative new technology. Probably Robinson had anticipated this, and the dockyard reacted fast. The captain superintendent and the master shipwright gave the strikers fifteen minutes to return to work, and when all but two refused they were expelled from the yard. The two remaining, plus the dockyard smiths, now began to teach the shipwrights to work in iron. By October there were five hundred of them working on the *Achilles*. The spectacle attracted intense public curiosity, but to the general public it was largely invisible behind the high dockyard wall – invisible, but not inaudible. It inspired one of Charles Dickens' famous journalistic set-pieces, which evokes the soundscape of the high industrial age through the building of the *Achilles*:

> Ding, Clash, Dong, Bang, Boom, Rattle, Clash, Bang, Clink, Bang, Dong, Bang, Clatter, bang bang BANG! What on earth is this! This is, or soon will be, the *Achilles*, iron armour–plated ship. Twelve hundred men are working at her now; twelve hundred men working on stages over her sides, over her bows, over her stern, under her keel, between her decks, down in her hold, within her and without, crawling and creeping into the finest curves of her lines wherever it is possible for men to twist. Twelve hundred hammerers, measurers, caulkers, armourers, forgers, smiths, shipwrights; twelve hundred dingers, clashers, dongers, rattlers, clinkers, bangers bang-ers bangers! Yet all this stupendous uproar around the rising *Achilles* is as nothing to the reverberations with which the perfected *Achilles* shall resound upon the dreadful day when the full work is in hand for which this is but note of preparation – the day when the scuppers that are now fitting like great dry thirsty conduit-pipes, shall run red. All these busy fig-ures between decks, dimly seen bending at their work in smoke and fire, are as nothing to the figures that shall do work here of another kind in smoke and fire, that day. These steam-worked engines alongside, helping the ship by travelling to and fro, and wafting tons of iron plates about, as though they were so many leaves of trees, would be rent limb from limb if they stood by her for a minute then. To think that this *Achilles*, monstrous compound of iron tank and oaken chest, can ever swim or roll! To think that any force of wind and wave could ever break her! To think that wher-ever I see a glowing red-hot iron point thrust out of her side from within – as I do now, there, and there, and there! – and two watching men on a stage without, with bared arms and sledge-hammers, strike at it fiercely, and repeat their blows until it is black and flat, I see a rivet being driven home, of which there are many in every iron plate, and thousands upon thousands in the ship! . . .[49]

By embracing the new technology, the shipwrights saved their livelihood, and preserved the dockyards' tradition of all-purpose skilled men able to make anything. The boilermakers' union with its repeated demarcation disputes with other trades continued to damage the efficiency of private shipyards, but was shut out of the dockyards for forty years. The dockyard was now significantly more flexible and efficient than private shipyards, and when the *Achilles* turned out to cost less than the earlier contract-built ironclads, the shipwrights of Chatham (soon followed by the other dockyards) had won their fight to participate in iron shipbuilding. Far into the twentieth century the shipwrights, representatives of an ancient craft hastening to extinction in private yards, remained the proud aristocracy of the dockyards, supplying most of the yard officers.[50] 'All that pertaining to the construction of ships whether in wood, iron or steel we do, being our own, which we have done and shall continue to do to the satisfaction of their Lordships and the public . . . It is ourselves, the shipwrights, who build the nation's ships.'[51] Independent and self-confident, the dockyard men preserved something of the medieval craft tradition. Their petitions to the yard officers were not merely concerned with pay and conditions but were contributions to the management of the yards. Arthur Forwood, the Liverpool politician and shipowner who served on the Admiralty Board from 1886 to 1892, was struck by their 'free, frank and friendly' style. 'Us men is not odd men,' as one of them declared, 'we have been brought up to the work from boys. Ever since they started iron shipbuilding here I have been.'[52] By the 1880s, however, the falling shipbuilding costs associated with recession and the shift to steel construction had left the yards vulnerable again. Between 1885 and 1888 no battleships were laid down in the dockyards as private builders tendered at cheap rates, and many men were dismissed. The Naval Defence Act brought back full employment in the yards, but not the old trust. In 1892 a Liberal government which included trades unionist MPs allowed unions into the dockyards, where they slowly took over the representation of the workforce.[53]

The demands of the new technologies of steam and iron, and the rapid growth in the size of ships which they made possible, rendered most of the Navy's existing docks and basins obsolete. There were thirty-three dry docks in 1861, but almost all were too small for the new ironclads. Portsmouth could only dock the *Warrior* in that year by combining two docks. Nearly all the yards required extensive dredging to accommodate the ironclads, and there was a serious shortage of deep-water berths and moorings (especially at Portsmouth, where the *Excellent*'s gunnery range blocked access to Portchester Lake). The docks at Chatham were too shallow to accommodate big ships even on spring tides, except the new No. 3, finished in 1821 with a floor four feet below mean low water (the first big dock to require steam pumps to drain it). In 1815 Chatham had four dry docks, Portsmouth six and Plymouth five (counting the double dock as two). By 1914 the figures were eight, fifteen (including one floating dock) and eleven respectively. Between them these three yards had eleven basins with a total area of 163 acres, with another 56 acres in the new dockyard at Rosyth nearly ready.[54] Docks and basins were only the largest of the many works and buildings required by the Navy of the industrial age. There was extensive investment in naval hospitals, coaling stations, ordnance and victualling yards at home and abroad. Naval and Marine barracks were built adjoining the major dockyards. Railways to and within the yards saved much time and money in transporting materials. Gas lighting, which reached Portsmouth in 1862, made it possible for the yards to work all hours in emergencies.[55]

All of these constructions were, and many still are, highly impressive to the eye, but perhaps the most significant of all material innovations of the nineteenth century was virtually invisible. It took twenty-five years of investment and some heavy losses, but the completion of the first reliable transatlantic telegraph cable in 1866 may be taken to mark the moment when intercontinental communication times fell instantaneously from months to hours. Contemporaries talked enthusiastically of the 'practical annihilation of time and space',[56] and for an imperial and naval power with more time and space to handle than anyone else, the submarine cable was truly revolutionary. This difficult and expensive technology offered secure communications almost invulnerable to interference (except in shallow water). Britain possessed most of the world's capacity to manufacture underwater cables, had an effective monopoly of gutta percha, the only good insulator, trained the majority of the world's cable operators, owned (in 1904) more than twice as many cable-laying ships as the rest of the world put together, and alone had mastered the difficult art of recovering and repairing cables in deep water. The high fixed costs, advanced technology and very long life (seventy-five years on average) of undersea cables made it extremely difficult for foreigners to break into this monopoly.[57] The bold and aggressive Sir John Pender controlled two companies, Eastern and Western Telegraph, which between them owned 45 per cent of all privately owned cables in the world, including most of those running east to Australia and China, or west to the Americas, but with the discreet support of the British government he found the means to prevent any competitor from filling the obvious gap across the Pacific until 1902. As a result, by that year more than half of all international telegrams passed daily through Eastern Telegraph's headquarters in London. Telegrams were very costly, but Eastern Telegraph gave heavily discounted rates to the British government and to colonial newspapers, which silenced public criticism of Pender's lucrative monopoly. Foreign governments and businessmen suspected the danger of passing all their foreign communications through London, but they had no alternatives. They did not know that every day a messenger from Eastern Telegraph's office delivered a sack of telegrams to the Admiralty to be read and returned in twenty-four hours.[58] Much of this control of world secret communications lasted until and beyond the Second World War.

NINE

Steam Antics

Ships and Weapons 1860–1890

At the end of the Russian War it was obvious to all that the ironclad warship had come to stay, but in what form or forms was still unclear. The cautious Sir Baldwin Walker, the Surveyor of the Navy, was content as usual to watch the situation and allow other navies to make the first mistakes. This meant the French, convinced as they easily were that superior genius and technical education would make up for industrial weakness and allow them to overtake British naval supremacy. Stanislaus Dupuy de Lôme, *Directeur du matériel* and the most talented naval architect of the period, led the way with the design of the first armoured battleship in the world, the *Gloire*, laid down at Toulon in March 1858. He had already made himself an expert in iron construction by extensive visits to Britain, and was fully aware of the enormous advantage of an iron hull to support the strain of the engines and the weight of the guns and armour. Unfortunately, French industry could not supply the iron nor French dockyards work it, so he was forced to build in timber with some iron stiffening, which constrained him to a short, deep hull resembling an armoured two-decker ship of the line (though only one deck was fully armed). In the next fifteen months, before the *Gloire* had even been launched, five more French ironclads were laid down, one of them with an iron hull. By the time the *Gloire* ran her trials in the summer of 1860, it looked as though the French, having already achieved equality in steam ships of the line, were handsomely winning the ironclad naval race as well.[1]

The British watched these developments with anxiety, but their response was delayed by both technical and political uncertainties. Not until January 1859 did the Admiralty invite major private shipbuilders and the master shipwrights of the dockyards to propose designs for a 'frigate of 36 guns cased with wrought iron plates'. The Admiralty's own design by Isaac Watts was preferred over all the others, and in spite of the hostility of Benjamin Disraeli, then

Chancellor of the Exchequer, the new ironclad was ordered from the Thames Ironworks in May 1859. The *Warrior*, as she was named, did not commission until October 1861, more than a year after the *Gloire*. Still afloat and restored to her original appearance, this famous ship is one of the last survivors of the ironclad era. The *Warrior* is so well known that it needs to be stressed her design was not typical but unusual, even odd. She was indeed a 'frigate', not merely in the technical sense of mounting all her guns on the main deck, but in being a fast, long-range cruising warship. By building in iron, Watts had been able to adopt a long hull with fine lines, powerful engines and a powerful rig. The *Warrior* could steam over 14 knots, making her the fastest warship in the world, and in the right conditions she was almost as fast under sail. But only the central two-thirds of her length was armoured, with the steering gear exposed, and her great length made her very unwieldy. The French were building an armoured battlefleet, but the *Warrior* would have been somewhat vulnerable in a close action with it. Drawing an analogy from a later generation, we might call her a 'battle-cruiser' rather than a battleship, with a heavy armament and the speed to force or refuse action, but seeming more like a supplement than a replacement for the existing steam ships of the line – or perhaps a replacement for the big steam frigates *Mersey* and *Orlando* of 1858, which had stretched wooden construction rather further than it could safely go. The requirement for such a very costly and powerful frigate was not clearly set out, and there seems to have been some confusion between battleships and cruisers in the minds of ministers, whose muddled policy and preference for cheap but inadequate designs drove Sir Baldwin Walker to resign in 1861.[2]

The Anglo-French building race continued up to France's catastrophic defeat in the 1870 Franco-Prussian War, but by 1868 Britain already had nineteen ironclads against the French fifteen. The *Warrior* was followed by her sister the *Black Prince* and four more ironclad 'frigates', some of them over 400 feet long and five-masted, but this line of development was abandoned in a few years in favour of ships nearer to the contemporary idea of 'fighting ships'. By the mid-1860s tactical ideas emphasized fighting in close order with an emphasis on ramming, which called for short and manoeuvrable ships with as much 'end-on fire' as possible. Guns were growing rapidly in size and falling in numbers. Armour was getting thicker, and the area it was possible to cover with armour was shrinking. In response Edward Reed, the new Chief Constructor, developed the 'central battery' ironclad in the late 1860s, mounting a limited number of heavy guns in an armoured 'redoubt' amidships, arranged to give some possibilities of fire end-on, or nearly so. The waterline was protected by an armoured belt, but the rest of the hull was largely unarmoured.[3]

In addition, the British armoured fleet included a variety of other types. The biggest external influence on it in the late 1860s was not France, the obvious rival, but another potential enemy, the United States, and specifically John Ericsson's highly original design of the USS *Monitor*. This small ship (987 tons) consisted of a wooden raft body with a one-inch layer of iron armour on the deck, having a freeboard of 14 inches, so that the sea washed freely over the ship in all but the calmest weather. The raft body projected beyond the hull proper, which was entirely under water, unlit by natural light, poorly ventilated and exceedingly hot. The only substantial structure on deck was the single armoured turret containing two 11-inch SBMLs (smooth-bore muzzle-loaders). This turret normally rested on the deck but could be slightly raised and turned by a steam engine to train the guns. There was very little for an enemy to shoot at except the heavily armoured turret, since the deck could only be hit at a very oblique angle, but the *Monitor*'s own guns could not be trained precisely enough to hit anything except by accident. Her real weapon was the raft bow which was designed as a ram, and functioned as such in sinking two Union warships in the Hampton Roads action of 1862.[4]

Ericsson was a difficult and unscrupulous character whose relationship with the US Navy was fractious. He employed political pressure, and the hysterical relief generated by Hampton Roads, to get a lucrative monopoly of building 'monitors' (which soon became the standard term for any small turret ironclad), shutting out the rival official designs which were in some respects better. The *Monitor* herself foundered at sea when she was less than a year old, and the later monitors spent their lives in harbours and rivers. The biggest and best of them, the 3,400-ton *Miantonomoh* Class (an official, not an Ericsson, design), were marginally seaworthy, and the *Miantonomoh* herself crossed the Atlantic in 1866 (partly under tow) and visited Spithead, where her appearance aroused intense interest. Ericsson's triumph committed the US Navy to an ironclad type dangerous more to the British than the Confederates, and the monitors created a sensation in Britain because many people were willing to take at face value American claims that they were capable of teaching Britain a lesson.[5] 'Yankee ingenuity' was praised as much, or rather more, in London than in New York. Ericsson was not exactly a gentleman amateur, but he was presented as a neglected genius, and much of the Victorian public was ready to believe that his small, cheap ironclads were superior to the costly *Warrior* and her successors, whose armour their 15-inch muzzle-loaders could penetrate at short range.[6]

The feature that commentators concentrated on was the *Monitor*'s turret, and Ericsson was not the only enthusiast for mounting guns in a revolving armoured turret. In Britain the well-connected Captain Cowper Coles was a strong advocate of ironclads mounting guns in turrets, and he designed a turret revolving on a roller path which was much superior to Ericsson's. The advocates of turret ironclads, however, faced two serious difficulties, only one of which was yet evident. The obvious problem was that masts and rigging would interfere with the arcs of fire of turret guns, but in the then state of steam engineering a seagoing warship could not do without. The much less obvious problem was that heavy guns had to be mounted low in the ship for reasons of stability, and since turrets had to be on deck to get all-round arcs of fire, the early turret ships all had a low freeboard. This, as we now know, presented a major danger to stability, but at the time the word 'stability' was used in different senses, the theory of stability was poorly understood, and the stability of a design could not be calculated before construction.[7]

With the warm support of the Prince Consort, always a friend of modernity, Coles was able to get his turret submitted to firing trials in September 1861, from which it emerged with great credit. The first result was the sixteenth British ironclad, the *Prince Albert*, laid down in April 1862. She carried four 9-inch RMLs (rifled muzzle-loaders), each in its own centre-line turret, with no sailing rig to block their arcs of fire. At the same time the steam line-of-battleship *Royal Sovereign* was cut down and converted on similar lines. These ships were successful on their own terms, but with low freeboard and no sail they could not pretend to be fully seagoing. Coles and his supporters insisted that only a fully rigged turret ship would adequately prove his idea. In response the young Chief Constructor, Edward Reed (appointed in 1863 at the age of thirty-three), designed the ironclad *Monarch*, laid down in 1866 and completed in 1869. She had two twin turrets mounting four 12-inch RMLs with good arcs of fire on either beam, she was even faster than the *Warrior* under steam, had a full rig and adequate freeboard for stability and seakeeping. Coles was very critical, and with powerful public support demanded the opportunity to show how much better a naval officer could do than the civilian theoreticians of the Admiralty. The Liberal and Conservative ministries in turn yielded to pressure, and Coles' ironclad the *Captain* was laid down in January 1867 at Laird Brothers' shipyard in Birkenhead, designed by Lairds themselves to Coles' specification. Robinson and Reed insisted that the Admiralty was not responsible for her design, but Coles then fell ill and the question of responsibility was fudged. Designed for 8½-ft freeboard (which Robinson thought insufficient), the *Captain* completed badly overweight with only 6-ft freeboard. Nobody realized how dangerous this was, but an inclining experiment was ordered for information. This very new procedure consisted of a practical test of the ship's stability by observing her angle of heel as weights (a number of men) were moved from side to side. Many days of laborious advanced mathematics could calculate from this the maximum safe angle of heel – though no one yet knew quite what angle would be safe in practical circumstances. People were used to sailing ships with very high freeboard and high dynamic stability to stand up to their canvas, which could be safely pushed to at least 40° of heel. The experiment was conducted at Portsmouth on 29 July 1870, and the Admiralty constructor responsible reported his results on 23 August, after the *Captain* had sailed. They showed her 'maximum righting moment' was 20°: if she heeled beyond that point the forces acting to return her to the upright would decrease until at 40° they vanished. It was not as obvious then as it soon became that this was a perilously poor result: once the deck edge went underwater (at about 14° of heel) the ship was already in grave danger.[8]

The loss of the *Captain* threw warship design into a state of confusion. The authority of naval officers and naval architects alike seemed to be fatally undermined; the turret changed overnight from a symbol of modernity to one of disaster. The mastless ironclad *Devastation* of Reed's design, launched in July 1871, had a low hull with four 12-inch RMLs in two turrets, forward and aft of a central superstructure. In many eyes the lack of masts and the presence of turrets were equally fatal, and for some time *Devastation* was kept close to land in case she turned over. Lord Dufferin's 'Committee on the Designs of Ships of War' assembled by the Admiralty to investigate the *Captain* disaster and evaluate other recent designs, favoured the *Devastation* as the best available ironclad design, and to modern eyes she resembles the germ of the modern battleship, but her stability was barely sufficient, so her superstructure was extended to her side to give higher freeboard over her central section.[9]

To understand the confusing variety of ironclads it is necessary to consider the rapid development of guns and armour. The first ironclads appeared at the same time as the first rifled breech-loading guns, which promised large gains in range, accuracy and ease of loading. In the British case these guns were of the Armstrong pattern, in which a sliding breech-block was secured by a screw clamp. In small sizes the Armstrong gun worked well, but it soon became clear that the screw clamp of the big 110pdr could not reliably contain the explosion of the propellant, which was liable to blow out the breech-block. As a result the British abandoned heavy breech-loaders in 1863 and reverted to muzzle-loading, at the same time adopting the Palliser system of converting smoothbore guns to rifling. The French (and Germans) had a different breech mechanism but suffered similar problems. They retained breech-loaders, but until the invention of the de Bange obturator in 1872 their breeches were not reliably gas-tight and the guns could only be fired with reduced charges, there-fore with reduced range and accuracy. As a result the British rifled muzzle-loaders were superior to the French rifled breech-loaders in muzzle velocity, range and penetrative power until the late 1870s.[10]

The choice of muzzle- or breech-loading guns was more than a technical decision; it was, and often still is, loaded with much social significance. Breech-loading was new and a symbol of modernity. Many contemporary British critics – always led by *The Times* – were convinced that the military were of their nature backward and obscurantist, so keeping muzzle-loaders twenty years after the French had abandoned them was for the journalists obvious evidence of an obvious truth. Many modern historians have been of the same mind. Two related issues were the rivalry of state and private manu-facturers, and the uncertain legal status of intellectual property. Britain had a state gun designer and manufacturer, the Royal Gun Factory (RGF) at Woolwich Arsenal, part of the Ordnance establishment until the Ordnance Board was blamed for the army's failures in the Russian War and abolished in 1855; thereafter the RGF was attached to the War Office. It claimed a mon-opoly, but neither the army nor the Navy was satisfied with its products. As soon as the Crimean campaign cast a bright light on the inadequacy of Brit-ish siege guns, private inventors rushed to offer their designs. Two rivals led the field: the Manchester machine-tool manufacturer Joseph Whitworth, and the Newcastle engineer William Armstrong, who had made a fortune in hydraulic machinery for coal mines. The experts from Woolwich adjudicated between these and other gun designs, at the same time freely plundering ideas with which to improve their own guns. This in turn fed into the controversy over what patent system was appropriate for the industrial age. This eventu-ally led to the 1883 Patent Act, which obliged the government to pay royalties on patented designs but allowed it to claim the assignment of patents valu-able for military purposes, and to keep them secret. When Armstrong's rifled breech-loaders won the competition in 1859, and both his factory at Elswick on Tyne and the RGF began to manufacture the guns, Armstrong assigned his patents to the Crown in return for a ten-year contract and a guarantee on £50,000 of new capital. Now a national hero, he was knighted and became Engineer of Rifled Ordnance (subsequently Superintendent of the Royal Gun Factory) on an official salary of £2,000 a year. By the early 1860s the Elswick Ordnance Company was making over £400,000 a year, and Sir William Arm-strong was both an officer of the Crown designing guns for the Services, and a private manufacturer supplying the guns to his own designs. The phrase 'conflict of interest' was not yet current, but the problem was becoming evident – even before it became evident that the heavy Armstrong breech-loaders were seriously flawed.[11]

Armstrong's firm survived the failure of its early design because it was already the technical leader in heavy-gun manufacture, well ahead of Woolwich. Its guns dominated the era of the rifled muzzle-loader (say 1863–80). As they grew rapidly in size, these short, fat guns and their massive projectiles could be handled only by hydraulic machinery, manufactured by Armstrong, whose firm by 1885 had a near monopoly of heavy-gun mountings and their associated machinery. By this time a satisfactory breech mechanism was available, based on the French interrupted screw breech and the de Bange obturator. The first British ironclads armed with breech-loading guns appeared in 1882, but Armstrong was well ahead in breech-loading technology too, and the Woolwich authorities had no scruples about defending their interests by stealing proprietary secrets, deceiving the Secretary for War, and falsifying Parliamentary accounts to show that their costs were lower than those of private industry. All these tactics were exposed by a series of Parliamentary inquiries in the later 1880s, and as a result in 1886 the Treasury approved of the Admiralty buying guns from private firms – meaning breech-loaders from Armstrong. In 1888 an independent, joint-service Ordnance Department was established, as the Admiralty desired, which marks the point at which the Navy gained partial control of its own guns.[12]

What ended the era of the rifled muzzle-loader was the development in the 1870s of slow-burning 'prismatic' powder in place of fast-burning black powder. Slow-burning powder was in every way better, especially for rifled guns. It allowed the shell to be progressively accelerated and spun up a long but relatively light barrel, yielding higher muzzle velocity and greater range and accuracy with lower strains on the gun. This, however, implied big changes in both ship design and tactics. Long breech-loaders called for entirely different mountings and loading systems from short muzzle-loaders, and the tactics appropriate for fighting at a range of 2,000 yards or one mile (the maximum recommended by the captain of the *Excellent* in 1861) would not do if ranges extended, potentially, to several times that distance. Once the British had invested in the rifled muzzle-loader, it was practically and psychologically difficult to make the radical change to breech-loading – especially for men like Astley Cooper Key and Sir Arthur Hood, who had made their careers as experts in the older system. When the Navy did opt for breech-loaders again, the obstruction of the Woolwich authorities caused further delay.[13]

The age of the big muzzle-loader was an age of low accuracy and very low rates of fire. The new ironclad *Inflexible* at the bombardment of Alexandria in

1882 fired 208 rounds in ten and a half hours from her four 16-inch 81-ton guns, each of which needed more than twelve minutes to load and fire its 1,684lb shell, capable (at least on the gunnery range) of penetrating 23 inches of wrought-iron armour.[14] If two approaching fleets armed with such guns opened fire at 2,000 yards and closed at 12 knots, they would be alongside long before they could reload. This encouraged the fashion for the ram, initiated by the *Monitor* at Hampton Roads in 1862 and reinforced by the battle of Lissa in 1866, when the (already disabled) Italian flagship *Re d'Italia* was rammed and sunk by the Austrian flagship *Erzherzog Ferdinand Max*. Although it proved distressingly easy for ironclads in company to sink one another by accidental collision, deliberate ramming of an enemy still under way and under command turned out to be extremely difficult, and the fashion faded in the late 1880s as increasing gun ranges forced opposing fleets further apart.[15] The low rates of fire and uncertain accuracy of big muzzle-loaders were equally unsatisfactory for attacking fortifications, which called for a high volume of fire to overwhelm the defences. In the late 1860s and early 1870s this was foreseen as a duty of the new ironclads – it was apparently the primary function of the monitor *Glatton* of 1871 – but they could no longer develop the high volume of fire which had been effective against forts a generation before, and were surely lucky never to have had to fight more dangerous opponents than the Egyptians.[16] Short ranges meant that fleets had to be trained in very precise manoeuvring to bring their guns to bear with a minimum risk of accidental collisions. Phipps Hornby took the lead in the development of 'equal speed' manoeuvres which allowed ships of different design to be handled in close company. The resulting steam tactics ('steam antics' as they were called on the lower deck) were intensively practised and took their toll in collisions – notably that which sank the *Victoria*, flagship of the Mediterranean Fleet in 1893, with the loss of Admiral Sir George Tryon.[17]

The *Ajax* and *Agamemnon*, completed in 1883, were the last rigged ironclads, and the last to be armed with muzzle-loading guns. Their immediate successors were mastless turret ships developed from the *Devastation* of 1871. The great weight of the turrets meant that they had to be kept low, producing low-freeboard ships which were uncomfortable if not actively dangerous in a seaway. The naval manoeuvres exposed these weaknesses, especially in 1888, when the old *Warrior* and *Black Prince* comfortably maintained 10 knots in seas which stopped and even imperilled modern ships twenty years younger. By this time ironclads were already being built with an alternative system of mounting heavy guns on a turntable which revolved within a fixed, open, armoured breastwork called a barbette. This was lighter than a turret and allowed the guns to be mounted higher; it also offered space for the longer barrels of breech-loaders to be trained without engaging with the superstructure. The guns themselves just showed over the rim of the barbette, but the crew, the mounting and the loading machinery were all behind the armoured breastwork.[18]

At the same time as the barbette ironclads were coming into service, the new threat of torpedo boats was being countered by heavy Gatling, Gardner, Maxim or Nordenfelt machine guns, usually mounted high and sometimes in fighting-tops half-way up the masts – they in fact caused these 'mastless' ironclads to be re-rigged with heavier 'military masts' than before. At fighting ranges of under a mile, these machine guns were within range of enemy ironclads, and guns' crews working in open barbettes were at risk. As a result, barbettes from around 1890 were fitted with light armoured hoods, revolving with the guns, to protect the crews from machine-gun fire and splinters. The gunhouses of twentieth-century warships, revolving on top of a fixed armoured housing called a barbette which enclosed the training and loading machinery, were descended from these armoured hoods. Although often called turrets, they were in origin quite different from the gun turrets of the 1860s and 1870s.[19]

In his annual report for 1863, Gideon Welles, Secretary of the US Navy, announced that 'we need and should have steamers of high speed, constructed of wood, with which to sweep the ocean, and hunt down the ships of the enemy'.[20] The enemy he had in mind was obviously Britain, and the model he intended to imitate was the *Alabama*. The new American class of big, well-armed and fast cruisers, the *Wampanoag* Class, presented a threat which the Admiralty took very seriously. By 1865 the US plans were known in Whitehall, in February 1868 the *Wampanoag* ran her trials, and by the early 1870s it was known that this class was an almost complete failure. For about five years Spencer Robinson as Controller, and Edward Reed as Chief Constructor, confronted what seemed to be a grave threat to British shipping. Their answer was the big iron steam frigate *Inconstant*, completed in October 1869. She carried a powerful armament of ten 9-inch and four 7-inch RMLs, was the fastest ship in the world under steam at 16.2 knots and very fast under sail as well (which mattered, as she could not cross the Atlantic under steam alone). Length for speed, and strength to support powerful engines, made an iron hull essential, but it was still believed that unarmoured iron plating was a menace. Reed therefore sheathed the hull with a double thickness of plank, nine inches in total, which it was hoped would allow the hull to be penetrated cleanly if at all. Being watertight, the sheathing also allowed the hull to be coppered so that the *Inconstant* could cruise anywhere in the world. All this made an effective but very costly ship to deal with the American cruisers and provide cover for the many smaller British sloops and corvettes. One more like her was built before the evident failure of the *Wampanoag* Class allowed the First Lord, Hugh Childers, to opt for smaller and cheaper designs.[21]

Spencer Robinson was unusual for an admiral of his generation in having a clear sense that different types of warship corresponded to distinct strategic functions:

> All the time I was at the Admiralty I never heard it [strategy] referred to or examined in a large or comprehensive spirit – it always appeared to be too vast and too difficult to be seriously grappled with. Nevertheless, I am confident that there ought to be, in the Records of the Admiralty, a well-considered general outline of how a maritime war should be carried on. This would require a thorough study of the <u>nature</u> and <u>number</u> of ships we ought to have, and the disposition of the fleet with reference to hostilities.[22]

For most of his contemporaries, in or out of uniform, 'fighting ships' meant ironclads, and unarmoured ships were of little or no military value. 'Unprotected vessels, therefore, are of subordinate importance', declared Thomas Brassey, Liberal MP and Civil Lord of the Admiralty between 1880 and 1885:

> They are required for the police of the seas, and the protection of commerce; but I should consider it unwise on the part of the Admiralty to build a greater number of vessels of this class than are absolutely necessary in order to meet the demands of the Foreign Office for the protection of British interests abroad . . . costly as they are, we are told by high authorities that we may not reckon on our unarmoured ships as forming an essential part of our armed strength for war.

They were built, Brassey continued, 'for the training of seamen, for the purpose of exhibiting the British flag in foreign ports, and especially in the harbours of semi-barbarous Powers . . . for the repression of piracy and slavery, and for the punishment of offending savage tribes . . .'[23]

The unwisdom of investing much money in unarmoured ships seemed to increase with the growing number of ironclads to be found all over the world. In 1877 the *Inconstant*'s near-sister *Shah* fought the small Laird-built turret ironclad *Huascar* (which had fallen into the hands of some failed revolutionaries turned pirates) off the coast of Peru. At a range of around 2,000 yards the *Huascar* could not hit the *Shah*, and the *Shah* dared not close the range sufficiently to penetrate her armour.[24] An obvious conclusion was that colonial squadrons needed at least an ironclad flagship. Most French colonial squadrons had one already. Beginning with the *Kniaz Pozharskii* in 1873, the Russian Navy too had developed a series of big, fully rigged cruising ironclads of speed and long range, based at Vladivostok, far away from the main fleets of any nation but with unhindered access to the open oceans and the merchant shipping of the world. The first British response was the 'belted cruiser' *Shannon*, which entered service in 1878. Nathaniel Barnaby, her designer, was a proponent of the Cobdenite school, for whom an ironclad was solely a 'fighting ship', to fight other ironclads, with her guns arranged to fire ahead as much as possible and not much sacrificed to speed or range. As a result the *Shannon* was scarcely able to pursue the Russian cruisers, and spent most of her career in home waters. She was followed by the *Nelson* and *Northampton*, laid down in 1874, bigger ships endowed with better speed and range thanks to advances in engineering, adequate to fight the slower French colonial ironclads, but still no answer to the Russian ships. Further 'belted cruisers' followed in the early 1880s, all vainly attempting to combine the functions of 'fighting ship' and cruiser, culminating in the *Orlando* Class ordered in 1885 in response to the 'Truth about the Navy' campaign.[25]

These ships incorporated a number of important technical developments. The pioneering experiments of William Froude, using models to test ship stability, rolling and resistance, were taken up by Edward Reed about 1870. Similar attempts dated back to the eighteenth century, but Froude was the first to develop formulae which allowed model results to be reliably scaled up to full size to aid the ship designer. In 1870 the Admiralty paid for the world's first ship testing-tank to be built beside Froude's house at Torquay. The Admiralty Experiment Works, as it became known later, remained there after his death until it moved in 1886 to a site on Portsmouth Harbour beside Haslar Hospital. The work of William Froude and his son Edmund made it possible for British warship designers to produce better hull forms, faster and safer than those of other nations. Even when the basic science of hydrodynamics became widely known and other countries built ship-testing tanks (as Italy, Russia, Germany, the United States and France all did between 1888 and 1905), the long experience, deep theoretical understanding and extensive library of hull and propeller forms available to Admiralty constructors gave them an important advantage over foreign designers far into the twentieth century.[26]

Another development of this period was the adoption of steel. In 1874 Barnaby and his assistant William White visited the building yard of Lorient in Brittany and were impressed by the French use of steel. Most of the steel available in Britain at that time was produced by the Bessemer process, giving a high carbon content and a brittle temper, but the Landore works near Swansea used the French Siemens–Martin 'open hearth' process which produced carbon-free 'mild' (i.e. ductile) steel. The following year the small cruisers *Iris* and *Mercury*, in whose design White had a large share, incorporated much Landore steel, and soon the superior strength and ductility of steel (and its falling cost relative to iron) led to its widespread adoption, in gunfounding as well as shipbuilding. The ironclads *Colossus* and *Edinburgh* laid down in 1879 had steel hulls and armour.[27] Steel boilers were one of the components making possible the rising steam pressures of the 1870s; this also required perfecting the surface condenser to provide pure feed-water without corrosive side effects. By the late 1870s steam pressures of 60 to 70 lbs/sq.in were available, sufficient for compound engines, which expanded the steam through a high-pressure and then a low-pressure cylinder in succession. This markedly improved the thermal efficiency and fuel economy of the engine. Between 1870 and 1881 the average coal consumption of British warships per horsepower-hour fell by 29 per cent, and from 1881 to 1892 by another 36 per cent as steam pressures passed 150 lbs/sq.in and the compound engine in turn gave place to the triple-expansion engine. The introduction of closed-stokehold forced draught from around 1880, supplying the furnaces with air under pressure, yielded more steam but imposed a strain on both boilers and stokers which could not be sustained for long. A single watch of stokers and natural draught would suffice for about 80 per cent of full power, which was usually enough.[28]

All these developments meant increasing work and complexity for naval engineers. So likewise did the growing range of auxiliary machinery. In 1861 the *Warrior* had eight auxiliary engines with a total of 350 horsepower. The *Devastation* in 1872 had sixteen; the *Inflexible* of 1881 had eighty-two, including a steering engine, two fire pumps, a capstan engine, two bilge pumps, four auxiliary boiler feed pumps, four fan engines, two circulating pumps, two reversing engines, four steam/hydraulic pumps for turret machinery, four ash hoists, two pumps, two shot hoists, and two winch engines for hoisting boats. Air compressors for torpedoes and dynamos for electricity were soon added.[29] The first use of electricity was to power searchlights to detect night attack by torpedo boats, but the domestic lighting of ships followed soon after. The *Inflexible* was the first to have both, run off an 800-volt DC system which not surprisingly proved to be easily fatal to its operators. The Navy then adopted 80 volts DC as a standard, and by 1885 there were about one hundred ships with searchlights and ten with internal lighting. In 1900 the Navy adopted 100 volts DC, moving in 1908 to 220-volt DC ring mains. This was what was called 'high-power electricity', meaning current for power and lighting, which was generated and supplied by the ship's engineers. 'Low-power electricity' referred to what would nowadays be called electronics; electric signals used for firing circuits and the remote control of weapons and equipment. This was first introduced in the 1870s for mines and explosive charges, and remained the responsibility of the Torpedo Branch established in 1876.[30]

In 1857 Sir Alexander Milne calculated that ships going out to the Cape of Good Hope and on to Singapore or Hong Kong were little if at all faster under steam than sail. Twenty-five years later the compound engine had put most ocean passages within easy reach of modern steamers, warships or merchantmen. It was this which justified mastless ironclads, and the growing number of coaling stations around the world made it possible to apply the same logic to cruisers, but the Admiralty under Northbrook and Cooper Key remained firmly wedded to the idea that cruisers cruised under sail. As we have seen, it was mainly outside the Admiralty that people were worrying about threats to trade, and the design of the Navy's cruising warships reflected different priorities. In 1885 it was officially estimated that only five cruisers in the Navy could take a 10-knot convoy across the Atlantic in good weather. The corvettes of the *Comus* Class, the latest medium cruisers of the day, could steam to the Cape, and thence to Australia, at their most economical speed of 5½ knots, only if they were lucky with wind and weather. Usually they made such passages under sail, following, of necessity, a quite different track from the steamers. Even their full speed of 13 knots was slower than many of the steamers they might have to protect in wartime – partly because their full rig cost them at least 1½ knots in wind resistance. Yet for the purposes of imperial police-work they were all that could be desired; heavily armed and fully equipped for every variety of land and sea operations, capable of cruising independently for very long periods.[31]

These ships embodied at sea the same sort of professional thinking as the 1888 Select Committee heard from its witnesses, and the contrast between what the Navy was, and what many people now thought it ought to be, was all the sharper at sea where the alternatives were already present. In 1878 Sir William Armstrong decided to move into shipbuilding, and began constructing a new shipyard at Elswick on the Tyne. It was managed by Armstrong's partner George Rendel, and when he joined the Northbrook Admiralty Board in 1882, Armstrong recruited William White from the Admiralty to replace him (giving him £2,000 a year in place of £600, plus 2s a ton on every ship he designed). In July 1884 Armstrong's first cruiser, the Chilean *Esmeralda*, ran her trials and created an instant sensation. She was widely compared with the *Comus* Class, of roughly the same size: the *Esmeralda* was more than five knots faster, with double the range and a much heavier armament of breech-loading guns. She was one of the first 'protected cruisers', with an arched internal steel armour deck covering engines, boilers and magazines, and running the whole length of the ship. Such a deck (not unlike the *Monitor*'s twenty years before) could only be struck at an oblique angle and provided practically impenetrable protection for the ship's vital parts, though leaving her upperworks exposed. The *Comus* was an older design, and had a partial armour deck, but all the public saw in the comparison between the two ships was the gross incompetence of the Admiralty designers. This was unfair. The next British cruisers, the *Leander* Class completed in 1884, were unrigged ships not inferior to the *Esmeralda*, because W. H. Smith the First Lord had overruled Cooper Key's preference for a full rig. The difference between Elswick and the Admiralty was of strategic concept, not competence in naval architecture. William White, who had taken over the yard just as Rendel's *Esmeralda* was ready to launch, fully endorsed the 'Elswick cruiser' concept and himself designed some notable examples. Barely two years later, when Lord George Hamilton eased Barnaby into retirement, White was brought back to the Admiralty as Director of Naval Construction, and proceeded to build a fleet of Elswick-style protected cruisers under the Naval Defence Act.[32]

Besides breech-loading guns, another important innovation in warship weaponry in this period was the Whitehead torpedo (to be distinguished from the several other underwater weapons of the mid-century years which were also called 'torpedoes'). This, the modern torpedo, was developed by Robert Whitehead, an English engineer working in the Hungarian Adriatic port of Fiume (Rijeka).[33] After reports from the Mediterranean Fleet, the Admiralty agreed in 1871 to pay £15,000 for access to the 'Whitehead secret', the hydrostatic valve which kept the torpedo at a constant depth, and all other major naval powers soon followed suit. The weapon was still at this stage almost useless: slow, inaccurate and of very short range. Seven knots for 800 yards or 9½ knots for 250 yards were its limits. Navies were nevertheless willing to pay heavily for it because they could see its potential, and they spent the next thirty years investing in the new weapon before it began to live up to its promise. This meant that torpedo tactics, in France, Britain and elsewhere, advanced rapidly on a basis of optimism rather than hard experience. The torpedo's first real success was the sinking of the ironclad *Blanco Encalada* in 1891 during the Chilean civil war.[34]

The torpedo, like all underwater weapons, exploited the incompressibility of water, which makes an underwater explosion much more destructive than one in air. Torpedoes therefore seemed a natural 'giant-killer', able to attack the vulnerable bottom of the ironclad, and navies sought a vessel to deliver the torpedo with this in mind. The torpedo tube, once it was perfected in the 1880s, could be fitted in almost any sort of ship from ironclads downward, but there was a tendency for navies to concentrate on the small fast steam launches known as torpedo boats. These were mainly built by specialist yards whose skill in designing and constructing very fast and lightweight ships the dockyards could not equal. In Britain the leaders were Thornycroft (a Thames boat-yard which moved to Southampton in 1905), Yarrow (a Thames yard which moved to the Clyde in 1906), and J. Samuel White of Cowes in the Isle of Wight. In the Russian war scare of 1885 the Admiralty ordered more than fifty torpedo boats, almost all from these three builders. Like the French, the British soon found that these boats' advertised full speed of 20 knots or so was obtainable only in a flat calm. The larger and more seaworthy torpedo gunboats, of which eighteen were built under the Naval Defence Act, were miniature cruisers intended as counters to torpedo boats.[35]

TEN

The War of Steel and Gold

Policy and Operations 1890–1914

The new British ships built under the Naval Defence Act entered service in the early 1890s as the international situation evolved in ways uncomfortable to British governments. During that decade several newly industrialized powers were building modern navies which presented at least possible threats to British naval supremacy. Two of these new navies – those of Japan and the United States – were especially worrying because they were based far from European waters. For centuries all major naval powers had been in Europe, and British naval supremacy had been assured by a single main fleet in or near home waters, where it could both defend the country and indirectly control the waters of the whole world. Naval enemies outside European waters threatened to make this impossible, or possible only at the expense either of a much bigger navy, or of strategic alliances with other powers. This in turn was looking more difficult as both economic and colonial competition multiplied causes of dispute with different countries around the world. Britain presented the most dispersed of all the colonial empires, with widespread vulnerabilities. In North America, Canada would have to defend itself in the event of US aggression. In Asia the eastward advance of the Russian Empire threatened the frontiers of India. In several parts of Africa, French explorers, soldiers and colonial officials clashed with their British neighbours, while in 1891 the French Navy began (though it never finished) a building programme even larger than the Naval Defence Act. There was little that the British Navy could do about most of these threats, but any of them might precipitate a clash at sea as well as on land.[1] Surveying the situation in 1901, Lord Selborne the First Lord thought it wise to avoid any quarrel with Russia:

> Just the same, only differently and much more so, I would not quarrel with the United States if I could possibly avoid it . . . if the Americans

chose to pay for what they can easily afford, they can gradually build up
a Navy, firstly as large and then larger than ours and I am not sure they
will not do it.[2]

Nobody could be sure what form a major war might take. Some were confident that Britain would remain the great neutral power, as she had been during
the European and American wars of the mid-century, in which case much
would turn on the uncertain protection offered by international law to neutral
merchant shipping. Others feared foreign aggression, and especially the presumed alliance of France and Russia, with or without the support of the United
States. If this led to war, it was sure to be a naval war, involving either a clash
of battlefleets or a prolonged campaign for the defence of Britain's immense
seaborne trade, or both. A war against great continental military powers
aroused fears of invasion, and provoked disputes between proponents of naval
or military defence. The traditional British answer to these threats had been
naval blockade of the enemy's ports, but there was widespread disagreement
about what if any sort of blockade was still practicable. Uncertainty was – and
still is – multiplied by the different meanings of the word 'blockade' as used
by strategists, lawyers and economists.[3]

All these difficulties fell on British governments which were not well
equipped to handle them. As we shall see, as late as 1914 neither the Cabinet
nor the Admiralty had adequate means to form policy and strategy. What planning for war was being undertaken was often the work of informal and semi-
secret groups, and they were assembled by particular statesmen or senior
officers, having as much to do with their own rival ambitions as with forming
a coherent long-term government policy. They left scattered and muddled
archives which have led modern historians in different directions and provoked some lively clashes of interpretation. All this was taking place in the
context of rapidly changing naval technology, so that historians of technology,
strategy, diplomacy, administration, politics and (not least) personalities,
approaching different evidence from different directions, have painted strik-
ingly varied pictures. Endeavouring to present a coherent account of British
naval policy, historians (including this one) find it helpful to distinguish the
different lines of policy and strategy, but the artificial tidiness of dividing what
in reality was often mixed up together imposes its own distortions. A truly
authentic account of British naval policy would contain significant elements
of muddle and confusion. Finally, readers should be alert to a predominant
bias: it is common for British historians to adopt an exclusively British point
of view (all too often from sources only in English), and to assume implicitly

that Britain was, or ought to have been, in control of events. If things went wrong, it was all the fault of someone in Britain (usually someone in White-hall): if things went right, it was the natural result of ineffable British super-iority. In the real world, however, other countries could think and act for themselves. British statesmen and admirals were more often reacting to unex-pected events than developing deep-laid stratagems.

During the 1890s, the Admiralty expected to assemble the main Channel Squadron at Gibraltar on the outbreak of a naval war, with the intention of fighting the Franco-Russian forces in the Mediterranean, where the main French fleet was based, and where the Russian ships from the Black Sea could join them (it was assumed) by forcing the Turkish straits. The visit of a Rus-sian squadron to Toulon in 1893 drew public attention to this threat, while at the Admiralty the strong team of Lord Spencer and Admiral Sir Frederick Richards pressed for another building programme to supplement the Naval Defence Act. Like that Act, this was a political as much as a strategic move, and it was successful in both dimensions. The Navy got its new ships and the Liberal Cabinet split on the issue; Gladstone was forced into retirement in 1894 and replaced by the pro-naval 'Liberal Imperialist' Lord Rosebery.[4] Next year the Liberals fell from power and Salisbury returned as Prime Minister. With the main fleets in the Mediterranean, the British plan was for the English Chan-nel to be held against any French invasion attempt by torpedo boats, torpedo gunboats and the new torpedo-boat destroyers. This stimulated a big increase in spending on torpedo craft, while the intention to base a fleet at Gibraltar called for building new dry docks there, and moles to protect the port against attack from French torpedo craft.[5] That the government adopted these expen-sive projects reflected not only Richards' great strength of character, but the strong political position of the Admiralty when backed by the new mass elect-orate. That applied to operational as much as financial decisions. In the Arme-nian crisis of 1895, when the Cabinet proposed to send the Mediterranean Fleet up the Dardanelles to put pressure on Turkey, Richards flatly refused to risk the fleet being trapped between the Russians and the French and walked out of a Cabinet meeting to quash further discussion. Any politician of the 1880s would have been staggered to see a Senior Naval Lord dictating strategy to his political masters like this.[6]

A large proportion of the new British warships of the 1890s were cruisers, whose primary, though not sole, function was the protection of trade. This was agreed by all, but how they were to perform the duty was less clear. In the early 1890s the debate was mainly a professional one among naval officers, many of whom favoured the traditional method of convoy. 'Will you endeavour to hold a long line of communication by many weak detachments which are liable to an attack by an enemy at any point of the line,' argued one reserve officer who was himself the master of a merchant ship,

> or will you not rather, the means of transport being no object, keep a move-able column together which is capable of absolute defence against any force likely to be brought against it? I must confess that it scarcely appears to admit of argument.[7]

Many officers were convinced, but by the mid-1890s interest in convoy was fading. The naval manoeuvres directed attention to blockade as an all-purpose method of keeping enemy warships in port and out of mischief. The rapid spread of telegraph cables offered swift and accurate information about the movements of enemy cruisers which might be 'dogged' by British cruisers and eliminated without any disruption to merchant shipping. Cruisers with the very long range needed to protect or attack shipping in the open ocean were necessarily large and costly: in the 1890s the French and Russians together had only a handful, and the Admiralty could assign an equally powerful pursuer to track each of them. Even if international law did not safeguard private property at sea, as many expected it would, the 1903 Royal Commission on the Supply of Food accepted that the Royal Navy could.[8] The only large-scale attempt to test arrangements for trade defence, in the 1906 Manoeuvres, yielded unclear and unhelpful results.[9]

Trade defence mattered even more than it had in previous ages because of the rapid rise of food imports. Free trade hurt British agriculture, and over time permanently damaged the financial and political power of the landed classes, but it gave the working classes cheap food, including such luxuries as meat and butter, imported by refrigerated ships from distant parts of the world. The prosperity and contentment of the new mass electorate bought political support for the free trade on which Britain's trading position depended, but it also exposed a new strategic vulnerability. The late 1890s were a period of rising anxiety in which many in Britain were obsessed by foreign competition and national decline, economic, physical and moral.

'Social Darwinism' (a theory fathered on Darwin but actually derived from the biologist Herbert Spencer) proclaimed that only the fittest of nations would survive the healthy and inevitable process of struggle and war. One response was the eugenic movement's call for selective breeding to promote racial purity. Militarist and autocratic powers like Germany and Japan seemed to be the strongest and best adapted to survive; liberal Parliamentary democracies like Britain seemed to be the weakest.[10] In the words of the journalist Arnold White,

The strong and hungry will eat the weak, fat & defenceless whenever they can get a chance . . . No matter what the sentiments of the sheep are, mutton to wolves will continue to be an agreeable form of diet . . . We have all we want and now only wish to be left alone; but that desire is not shared by the great military nations on the Continent. If we want to keep what we have, we must defend it.[11]

All over the world the British Empire seemed to be under threat. By 1898 the Japanese were already reckoned to hold the local balance of power in the Far East. In the same year the unexpected victory of the United States over Spain marked the arrival of another new navy, remote from the centres of British naval power and invulnerable to its pressure, while the Russian government borrowed £27,560,000 to build a new Pacific Fleet.[12] More encouraging was the outcome of the Fashoda incident of that year, when Lord Salisbury was able to take a hard line with France and force the withdrawal of a French column from the Upper Nile. The following year the Scott–Muraviev agreement, delimiting British and Russian spheres of influence in China, lessened another area of tension.[13]

In the 1850s the Afrikaaners or Boers, Dutch-speaking settlers unhappy with British rule in the Cape of Good Hope, had established two independent republics, the Transvaal and the Orange Free State, in the interior of South Africa. The discovery of diamonds and gold led to an influx of English-speakers into their territory which provoked a war in the autumn of 1899. Eventually the British won a semi-victory of exhaustion in this 'South African' (or 'Boer') War, but the spectacle of the mighty British Empire deploying almost half a million men and taking three years to reduce enemies whose whole population, including women and children, was only about 100,000, displaying in the process a combination of incompetence and inhumanity, did great damage to Britain's reputation abroad, and induced gloom and introspection at home. By 1901 the war was costing twice as much as the Crimean War had done, and arousing new enemies. The following year the Cabinet accepted Selborne's argument that 'we must have a force which is reasonably calculated to beat France and Russia and we must have something in hand against Germany. We cannot afford a three Power Standard but we must have a real margin over the two Power Standard.'[14] Selborne feared that 'we shall be liable to be blackmailed by our "friends" if we give ourselves no margin'[15] – the 'friends' in question being Germany, Japan and the United States. His father-in-law Lord Salisbury, anguished at the inexorable rise of naval spending, took this occasion to retire; after Gladstone, Salisbury was the second eminent late-Victorian statesman to be shouldered aside by the growth of the Navy. In 1903 Selborne told the Cabinet (but not Parliament) that he now reckoned on the Two-Power Standard only against France and Russia.[16]

The fighting in South Africa was entirely inland, but the Navy was involved in two ways. The Boer forces were equipped with the latest weaponry, including long-range artillery which the British army could not match, so cruisers at the Cape landed heavy guns and sent them up-country on improvised carriages. More relevant to future naval warfare were British attempts to blockade the Portuguese port of Delagoa Bay (Maputo) in Mozambique, from which the railway to Johannesburg provided the Boers' only link to the outside world.[17] Neutral ships, notably the German steamer *Bundesrath*, laden with food but not weapons, were seized on flimsy grounds, the Cabinet rebelled against the abuse of international law, and the government was forced into a humiliating retreat. The episode (reinforced later by the experiences of the Russo-Japanese War) taught it that neutral shipping in wartime had to be treated with delicacy, and that traditional belligerent rights were scarcely enforceable in modern conditions.[18] What proved to be eminently enforceable, however, was a power conferred by new technology. To cut off the Boers from their foreign supporters, the British government refused from November 1899 to accept cypher telegrams over British cables running east of Aden, and subsequently required all messages to be submitted not just in plain language, but in plain English, so that British officials could more conveniently read them. The French, Germans, Dutch and Portuguese among others were obliged to expose their diplomatic and colonial business to British inspection. This made the British power of controlling international communications brutally clear.[19]

Before, during and after the South African War, as Britain's strategic situation seemed to get steadily weaker, naval planning concentrated on meeting the obvious enemies, France and Russia. The essential place to meet them was the Mediterranean, where France kept her main fleet, where Britain needed safe communications through the Suez Canal towards India, and where the Russian Black Sea fleet was prevented from intervention only by the decaying forces of the Ottoman Empire. This strategic situation was more or less constant, but new technology constantly altered the responses to it. If a British fleet were to steam through the Western Mediterranean from Gibraltar to Malta, it must pass close to French torpedo-boat bases in Algeria and Tunisia. Sir John Fisher as commander-in-chief in the Mediterranean during the South African War, and his second-in-command Lord Charles Beresford, proposed to deploy a large force of destroyers in the novel role of screening the fleet from torpedo attack. Fisher also wanted to use destroyers to keep the Russians away

from the Suez Canal until the main fleet could fight its way into the Eastern
Mediterranean. Lord Selborne the First Lord, and Lord Walter Kerr the Senior
Naval Lord, well informed of French and Russian weaknesses, were unimpressed by these arguments, and needed the destroyers in the Channel, where
the French were growing stronger. Fisher therefore planned to attack before
the French fleet in Toulon and the Russians in the Black Sea could combine
forces. To achieve this, he trained his fleet to maintain relatively high speeds
for long periods, and worked to develop long-range gunnery. Discovering that
Franco-Russian communications were passing over British cables through
Malta (to avoid Germany), he arranged for them to be intercepted and decyphered, and set up a plotting room in Malta to keep track of the enemy fleets.[20]

Towards the end of the 1890s Britain was unmistakably engaged in two
naval races simultaneously, in battleships and large cruisers, chiefly but not
only against France and Russia. The cruisers were bigger than the battleships,
only slightly less expensive, and needed larger crews. The Navy Estimates rose
inexorably, and the naval manning system was stretched to its limits to find
trained men. From the naval point of view the support of the electorate was a
priceless asset, and for many admirals it would have been enough to say that
it was every government's duty to support the Navy's claims, and the electorate's duty to vote for them. Those with more acute political instincts realized
that the naval race could not go on for ever: sooner or later the electors and
the politicians would demand naval supremacy at a cheaper price. No admiral
in the Navy had more sensitive political antennae and more extensive political
contacts than Sir John Fisher, who in 1899 was Commander-in-Chief North
America and West Indies, usually a retirement position. Yet in July this widely
distrusted officer, distinguished chiefly as a shore-based administrator, was
appointed to the Mediterranean, the most important and prestigious sea command in the Navy and an obvious stepping-stone to the Admiralty Board. This
sudden change of fortune has never been explained, but he was naturally in
regular touch with the First Lord George Goschen, and it is not difficult to
imagine that Fisher hinted at schemes which might secure British naval
supremacy and reduce the Navy Estimates at the same time. In February 1902
Goschen's successor Lord Selborne offered Fisher the position of Second Sea
Lord, 'because I believe there is a great deal to be done in connection with the
personnel'.[21] It is usually inferred that his career had been saved by some sort
of bargain. When Fisher finally achieved his ambition and became First Sea
Lord in October 1904, in spite of his age (nearly sixty-four) and Lord Walter
Kerr's forceful opposition, it was on the explicit condition that he save money,
and it appears that he was the only candidate who was prepared to accept it.[22]

By scrapping older cruisers and abolishing overseas squadrons, Fisher saved 11,000 men to form nucleus crews for the new Reserve Fleet organization. He closed overseas dockyards and dismissed 6,000 dockyard workers, reducing the 1905–06 Navy Estimates by £3.5 million, and another £1.5 million next year. When the new Liberal government of December 1905 demanded economies in shipbuilding, he complied. By paying off ships into reserve, he saved money on manpower – and emasculated Beresford's Channel Fleet. In Conservative eyes, at least, Fisher was now an active Liberal politician, sacrificing the Navy to advance his career.[23]

Among the European powers Germany, united in 1871 under Prussian leadership, was Britain's most natural friend, linked by centuries of alliance, by a common religion and culture, by intermarried royal families and intertwined economies, and above all by a common threat from France and Russia. So long as Wilhelm I reigned and Prince Otto von Bismarck was his chief minister, Germany was careful to avoid any action which might upset that relationship, but in 1888 the old emperor died, followed three months later by his liberal and Anglophile son Friedrich I, which put the unstable and aggressive young Wilhelm II on a throne constitutionally endowed with almost unfettered control of the armed forces. Two years later he dismissed Bismarck, but foreign observers who did not know Germany well were slow to appreciate how fast its policies were changing. While the number of Britain's potential enemies grew before and during the South African War, it was still natural for British ministers to look to Germany as a counterweight. They were shocked to discover German public opinion expressing undisguised loathing for the British, and German ministers adopting anti-British policies which seemed completely contrary to their own national interests. In September 1901 Selborne was still confident that Germany 'will never help us for love of us but she will refrain from assisting to injure us from instinct of self-preservation'.[24] Six months later he was more worried, but his friend and Cabinet colleague Arthur Balfour was incredulous:

> I find it extremely difficult to believe that we have, as you seem to suppose, much to fear from Germany – in the immediate future at all events. It seems to me so clear that, broadly speaking, her interests and ours are identical. But I have sorrowfully to admit that the world, unfortunately, is not always governed by enlightened self-interest.[25]

As yet, however, even the most pessimistic British ministers feared Germany only as a mischief-maker, ready to profit from Britain's war with France and Russia which everybody expected sooner or later. German policy did not represent a grave threat to Britain in itself, but it blocked the obvious escape route from Britain's difficulties: an Anglo-German alliance, which in November 1900 Selborne had considered 'the only alternative to an ever-increasing Navy and ever-increasing Navy estimates'.[26]

The end of the South African War in May 1902 left Britain in a mood of introspective gloom. Worse than the very high financial cost of victory over the Boer Republics, the war seemed to have revealed profound national weakness at home and gathered an invincible coalition of enemies abroad. One reaction was the movement for 'Imperial Preference' or 'tariff reform' led by the Liberal (later Liberal Unionist) politician Joseph Chamberlain, who in 1903 advocated a protected market for British and Empire agriculture, exchanging high food prices for security of supply. This, however, split the Liberal Unionists and lost them the 1906 election to the Liberal Party, so that in the end both Liberals and Unionists remained committed to free trade and the strategic vulnerability it implied.[27] But British diplomacy reacted to dangerous isolation with considerable agility. In 1901 the Hay–Pauncefote Treaty allowed the United States to build a Panama canal (in effect conceding the Caribbean as an American sphere of influence), and in 1903 the settlement of the Alaskan boundary dispute defused another cause of Anglo-American friction (at Canadian expense).[28] A naval understanding with Italy improved the strategic balance in the Mediterranean. The Japanese, who had had their own experience of isolation and humiliation in the aftermath of the 1895 Sino-Japanese War, were willing to enter an alliance which promised to neutralize much of the risk of the new Russian Pacific Fleet.[29] The attraction of the Japanese alliance for Britain was obvious, but the danger was that it might draw Britain into war with Russia, and hence France. The French diplomatic overtures of 1903 were warmly received in London because both powers had to fear the same thing; being dragged into a destructive war by Russian aggression. The resulting *Entente Cordiale* not only compromised a range of dangerous colonial disputes but split the opposing alliance and drew the French towards Britain.[30]

The diplomatic revolution of 1902–04 greatly improved Britain's situation, but it did not eliminate the threat from Russia. 'We all . . . must be impressed,' Selborne wrote in April 1904, 'with the great weakness which accrues to the British Empire from the fact that, whereas Russia can strike at us when she pleases through Afghanistan, we apparently can hit back at her nowhere.'[31] The Admiralty was aware that diplomatic arrangements could easily fall apart. The *Entente Cordiale* was exactly that: not a treaty but a 'friendly understanding', which bound nobody to anything. In the Far East, Russia and Japan vied for dominance of Korea and Manchuria, and in February 1904 war between them began with a surprise destroyer attack by the Japanese on the Russian squadron in Port Arthur (Lüshun) at the head of the Yellow Sea. The Japanese army landed at Chemulpo (Inchon) in Korea and advanced northward. After prolonged and very bloody fighting the Japanese took Port Arthur on 1 January 1905. Well before this, a Russian naval relief expedition had been despatched from the Baltic. On 21 October 1904 (Trafalgar Day), in a typical North Sea fog, these Russian warships fired on a group of Hull fishermen under the bizarre impression that they were Japanese torpedo boats, an incident which brought war very close. Only a few days before, the First Naval Lord, Lord Walter Kerr, had warned that 'One cannot shut one's eyes to the possibility of a Russo-German combination some day',[32] and the British suspected that the Germans had worked up the Russians to expect a surprise attack. They certainly gave the Russians material assistance without which they could never have made the long voyage to the Pacific. On paper the Russian force was more than twice as strong as the Japanese fleet, but its fighting efficiency was lamentable, and on 29 May 1905, off Tsushima in the Korea Strait, the Japanese won a total victory in which almost every Russian ship was sunk or captured.[33]

This astonishing and wholly unexpected Japanese triumph transformed Britain's strategic situation overnight. The Japanese ships had been built in Britain, and the world quite wrongly supposed the Japanese victory was due to covert British help. The (French-designed) Russian fleet was completely eliminated (except the Black Sea squadron, which had mutinied), and there was no risk that a now-isolated France would abandon her new friendship with Britain. Instead of straining to maintain the Two-Power Standard, Britain found herself with a comfortable margin over a Three-Power Standard. This was a happy transformation indeed, but it came at an awkward moment, just as Arthur Balfour's struggling Conservative government committed itself to a range of radical reforms in naval administration and warship design. When Lord Tweedmouth became First Lord in the new Liberal government under Sir Henry Campbell-Bannerman in December 1905, he inherited a naval policy in the process of wrenching changes to meet a danger which had just ceased to exist, but faced now with an unexpected challenge from a quite different direction.[34]

The new challenger was Germany, and it is from this year – not earlier – that the German Navy could be regarded as the principal threat to British naval supremacy. It is therefore necessary to give a brief sketch of the situation of Germany and its navy. In cultural and linguistic terms, Germany was ancient, but as a unified state it dated only from the victories of the Prussian army in the wars of 1866 and 1870. Bismarck's constitution of 1871 had created a new German Empire, or Reich, with Wilhelm I of Prussia as its emperor, which uneasily combined the agrarian, militarist constitution of Prussia with elements of a Parliamentary democracy.[35] Each of the constituent states of the Reich (Prussia being by far the largest of them with over 60 per cent of its territory and population) preserved its own government, parliament, royal family and army, supported by its own direct taxation: the Reich government levied only indirect taxes and supported the navy, which was the sole national armed service. The national Parliament, the *Reichstag*, was elected in constituencies which heavily overvalued rural voters on the great landed estates of the East, and under-represented the working classes of the rapidly industrializing cities of the Ruhr and the Rhineland. It could not initiate legislation and its main strength lay in the power to grant or withhold money. To further safeguard the primacy of the Prussian aristocracy and army, Bismarck reserved all national military affairs to the Kaiser (emperor) in person: neither the Reichstag nor the civilian ministers of the Reich government had any right to interfere, or even to be informed about them. The most senior generals possessed the *Immediatstellung*, the right to demand a private audience with the Kaiser at any time to present their requirements. Most of this was equally true of the navy, with the significant difference that the Reichstag had to be persuaded to vote the funds to support it, which was difficult without telling the parliamentarians why the money was needed. In 1889 Wilhelm II, keenly interested in his navy and in his own view the greatest living expert on it, divided the German Admiralty into three separate offices: the Naval High Command (*Oberkommando der Marine*, OKM), which included the naval staff; the Imperial Naval Office (*Reichsmarineamt*, RMA), a political department which handled relations with the Reichstag; and a Naval Cabinet (*Marinekabinett*), which was part of the Kaiser's personal military 'household' and controlled the appointments of naval officers. From 1897 to 1916 the head of the RMA was Rear-Admiral (eventually 'Grand Admiral', or Admiral of the Fleet) Alfred Tirpitz,[36] who supplied the political and administrative skills essential to the rise of the navy. The need for them was all the greater from 1899, when Wilhelm II abolished the OKM, leaving the staff and the senior admirals to deal with him in person. Lazy, erratic and immature, the Kaiser was incapable of real leadership, still less of replacing a substantial department single-handed, but Tirpitz, the master of bureaucratic guile, skilfully manoeuvred in the power vacuum at the heart of naval policy. By fracturing the leadership of the navy, Tirpitz had cut off the Kaiser (and the *Führer* in the next generation) from real understanding of naval affairs, leaving no machinery to generate strategic policy or link naval and military plans.[37]

Tirpitz's most essential task was to persuade the Reichstag to support the navy, and his instrument was the Naval Law (*Flottengesetz*) passed in 1898, which proposed to build nineteen battleships over a period of seven years. Almost at once Tirpitz took advantage of the anti-British feeling aroused by the South African War to bring in a second Naval Law in 1900, which doubled the planned fleet to thirty-eight battleships, to be completed by 1920. Amendments (*Novellen*) passed in 1906, 1908 and 1912 further increased the size of the fleet and the speed of its construction. Besides their ostensible function of committing the Reichstag to finance a massive expansion of the fleet, the Naval Laws served by suppressing alternative schemes to restrain the Kaiser's imagination within the bounds of reality, and to repress Tirpitz's opponents within the navy. There were many of them, because his plans had many glaring faults, and he wrecked the careers of anyone who pointed them out. In his obsession with battleships, he refused to spend money on anything else except torpedo boats, so that the German Navy lacked adequate dockyards, skilled manpower (especially engineers), training and many other essentials. It had few cruisers and very few submarines. Tirpitz did not conceal in private, and could not conceal in public, that his new fleet was intended to challenge British naval superiority. He proposed to build a fleet eventually totalling sixty battleships so discreetly that the supine British would not notice. In the event German public hostility, and the Kaiser's aggressive posturing during the South African War, drew ample attention to what was going on straight away. Tirpitz was sure that Britain was permanently isolated and could never escape the enmity of France and Russia – until it did. He was sure British forces could not be concentrated in home waters – until they were. He argued simultaneously that German naval strength would deter the British from attacking, and that they must necessarily attack with a reckless imprudence which would offer Germany a chance of victory. In an age when public statistics of national wealth and production were scarce, he was convinced Britain could never match German shipbuilding and financial resources, although Britain was the financial capital of the world, British firms controlled two-thirds of the world market for naval arms, and British shipbuilders could build more warships than all the other naval powers put together. The old Germany of 'blood and iron' was outclassed in the new 'war of steel and gold' which Tirpitz unleashed.[38] The strangest aspect of it all is that Tirpitz was better qualified than almost anyone in Germany to understand the truth. He was a clever man who knew Britain quite well, spoke good English, and sent his daughters to Cheltenham Ladies'

College. Yet all his plans were based on an imaginary Britain which bore scant relation to reality.[39]

The collapse of the Franco-Russian threat (completed in 1907 by an Anglo-Russian agreement on spheres of influence in central Asia),[40] and its abrupt replacement by the new German fleet, naturally transformed the British strategic situation, for the better in almost all respects. With few cruisers and only one overseas base of significance (Tsingtao/Qingdao in North China, otherwise Kiaochow/Jiaozhou), Germany presented a limited threat to British trade, and trade warfare was anyway one of the alternative policies which Tirpitz ruthlessly suppressed.[41] The two leading commercial ports of Germany, Hamburg on the Elbe and Bremen on the Weser, lay close to each other near the naval base of Wilhelmshaven in the German (or Heligoland) Bight, the southeastern corner of the North Sea. Even more than she had been in the Dutch Wars, England was perfectly situated by geography to impose a blockade on all of them. The main German advantage lay in the alternative connection between the North Sea and the Baltic via the Danish straits and the Kattegat, which conferred valuable strategic flexibility at the price of navigational and diplomatic obstacles. The straits also opened the British a way into the Baltic, where Germany was vulnerable to naval attack. The Mecklenburger and Pomeranian coasts, unlike the German North Sea coast, offer extensive beaches only ninety miles from Berlin, while the Baltic was the means by which Germany imported the Swedish iron ores essential to her steel industry. These imports did not come in through the small German Baltic ports with their indifferent railway connections but were borne by barge up the Rhine from Antwerp and Rotterdam, which were Germany's largest ports in terms of tonnage handled. Of the three Baltic straits, the Little Belt (between Jutland and Fyn) and the Great Belt (between Fyn and Zealand/Sjælland) lay entirely in Danish territorial waters, and the Sound (between Zealand and Scania/Skåne) mainly in Swedish waters. Only the Great Belt was deep enough to take battleships. The opening in 1895 of the Kaiser Wilhelm Canal from the Baltic naval station of Kiel to Brunsbüttel on the Elbe provided a swift means for German warships (and iron-ore imports) to pass between the Baltic and the North Sea through German territory, but by 1905 the latest battleships of the *Braunschweig* Class were already having serious difficulty negotiating the canal's tight curves.[42]

The Danish Straits offered an entry to the Baltic from the North Sea, outside German control. Sir John Fisher was quick to note the possibilities. Responding to the Kaiser's interference in Morocco in the summer of 1905, the Channel Fleet made a cruise into the Baltic, and Fisher took care to stir up memories of the two British attacks on Copenhagen in 1801 and 1807.[43] In thick fog, without taking pilots, Sir Arthur Wilson took his ships through the Belts in close formation – to the consternation of Danish admirals. At Swinemünde (Świnoujście) large crowds had gathered to watch the Kaiser review his fleet, but when the fog lifted, the wrong fleet lay at anchor before them: Wilson had arrived first and taken the inshore berth. This was more than a piece of bold and brilliant naval theatre; it was a shocking demonstration of Germany's vulnerability to naval attack. The cruise gave a severe fright to Wilhelm II and his admirals, the effects of which had not vanished even ten years later.[44] But the British too had concerns, and one aspect of the new situation weighed heavily on them: the most formidable army in the world, less than 400 miles away. It seemed to British planners inconceivable that in the event of war Germany would not try to invade across the North Sea. Nobody thought the British army could resist them for long, so it was imperative that the Navy should be able to.[45]

These factors were not being calmly evaluated in Britain, because the atmosphere was anything but calm, and because the machinery for such analysis scarcely existed. The Cabinet Committee of Imperial Defence, established by Balfour in 1904, was intended to study joint-service defence policy with non-Cabinet members, including admirals and generals, but its role was strictly advisory, and it could do little without the approval of its chairman the Prime Minister, who controlled both membership and agenda. Although intended to promote inter-service co-operation, it became in practice a theatre of inter-service rivalry, whose most useful work was done by technical subcommittees.[46] The Liberals took power in December 1905 because Balfour resigned, meaning to expose the deep divisions of the Liberal Party by forcing it into office – but he had miscalculated. In January 1906 the new Liberal government called a general election on a programme of social reform to be paid for by defence cuts, and it won heavily: in the new Parliament there were only 157 Conservative MPs against 376 Liberals (mostly Radicals), plus 83 Irish Nationalists and 54 of the new Labour Party who could be relied upon to vote with them against the Navy. But Tweedmouth was a Liberal Imperialist, closer on naval policy to the Conservative opposition than to his left-wing party colleagues. Sir John Fisher, promoted Admiral of the Fleet by the previous government so that he could serve to the age of seventy, remained in office as First Sea Lord. He had to reduce the Navy Estimates to satisfy the Liberals but was supported by Balfour from the Opposition front bench as being less dangerous than the alternatives. An unofficial cross-party alliance was now making naval policy, led, not by the colourless Tweedmouth, certainly not by the Prime

Minister Sir Henry Campbell-Bannerman and the government majority whose focus was on domestic policy, but by the two leading naval experts: Fisher in the Admiralty, acting almost as a Liberal minister, and Balfour from the Opposition benches of the Commons, together attacked from the back benches by the majority of both Liberals (demanding more money) and Conservatives (demanding more battleships). The Fisher–Balfour alliance wanted to continue a steady rate of naval construction, notwithstanding Britain's dominant position left by the collapse of France and Russia. Herbert Asquith, the Chancellor of the Exchequer, supported by most of his party, wanted to spend the money on social legislation such as old-age pensions. Fisher privately intended to disappoint both parties by getting the money but spending it on armoured cruisers instead of battleships.[47]

The political situation needs to be understood. The Radicals and their friends, in and out of Parliament, opposed 'bloated armaments' – excessive military spending – but they were not enemies of British naval supremacy, which commanded strong public support. The Radicals' arguments were based on the huge margin of British superiority, and they were well founded. As Fisher privately admitted to King Edward VII in October 1907, 'the English Navy is *now* four times stronger than the German Navy . . . we don't want to lay down any new ships at all – *we are so strong*. It is quite true.'[48] It would remain true so long as German shipbuilding did not outpace British. The Navy Law prescribed three battleships a year, and the Admiralty was allowed the same for the 1906–07 and 1907–08 financial years.[49]

Given the enormous Liberal majority, and the large margin of British naval supremacy, a reduction in the rate of British shipbuilding sooner or later must have been very likely. With moderation and patience Tirpitz's long-term goal of German naval supremacy could have been brought steadily nearer. The only thing able to upset his plans would be a powerful alarm of naval danger in British politics, one so powerful as to disarm Radical objections to 'bloated armaments'. This alarm Tirpitz obligingly provided with the *Novelle* of 1908. It was published on 17 November 1907, the same day that Wilhelm II left Windsor Castle after another visit to his British cousins, and one week after Fisher, in a speech at the Mansion House, had assured the City financiers that British naval supremacy was safe and 'they could sleep quiet in their beds'. The *Novelle* woke them up sharply. By reducing the standard battleship lifespan to twenty years, laying down four for 1908–09, and (as it seemed) another four for the following year with no Reichstag vote to pay for them, Germany seemed to vault over both industrial and constitutional barriers to a sudden increase in building. Now the British Opposition could credibly present the Cabinet (and

Fisher) as simpletons deceived by fair words. The British public was as wedded as ever to naval supremacy, expressed in numbers of battleships ('we want eight and we won't wait', as the Opposition chanted) and no government, however large its majority, could afford to ignore public alarm. Even the Radicals were reluctantly forced to accept that the German challenge was real.[50]

In April 1908 Asquith replaced the dying Campbell-Bannerman as Prime Minister, and the financial expert Reginald McKenna was made First Lord of the Admiralty. The veiled struggle between the naval alliance and the Radical enemies of naval expenditure continued. Asquith was supposed to be the leader of the pro-naval Liberal Imperialists, therefore an implicit ally of Balfour, but in reality he was moving leftwards to keep his party together. Asquith was a clever political tactician rather than a strategist: his supreme talent lay in avoiding decisions which might tend to split the Liberal Party – as many decisions did. While the Admiralty strove to pacify the Liberals by saving money, naval distrust of Fisher for playing the Radicals' game increased. In the Cabinet and the CID Fisher's dishonest and partisan handling of evidence, his prevarication and exaggeration, damaged the standing of the Admiralty and ruined the chances of joint-service planning. The super-patriots of the Imperial Maritime League (the 'Navier League' as it was called) split from the Navy League, accusing Fisher of treason. Balfour and the Conservative front bench consistently supported the Admiralty, but their back-benchers and supporters in the Navy were not so restrained.[51]

Then came another shock. F. A. Krupp's factory at Essen was the only German manufacturer of heavy guns and mountings for battleships, and its capacity was the bottleneck which limited the overall building programme. In July 1908 secret information reached the Admiralty that Krupp's plant had been extended to double its current output to eight or nine battleships a year. Moreover, two had already been laid down eight months before the Reichstag could vote the money for them. Once again, it seemed, Germany had found the means to brush aside both industrial and legal obstacles to overtake British strength. Although the source was dubious, this intelligence was genuine, and the interpretation was plausible, but in fact mistaken.[52]

With the evidence before it apparently establishing that Germany could now build eight battleships a year, the Cabinet split, with the Radicals accusing McKenna of believing false information. Eventually Asquith constructed a skilful compromise, offering four ships at once, and four later if necessary – and assuring both parties that he was on their side. In the end eight capital ships were ordered, plus two for the dominions, and six every year thereafter up to 1914, while Germany was unable to keep up even four a year.[53] Thus

Tirpitz achieved the worst of all worlds; convincing the British that the German naval challenge was real and deadly – which was true – and that German industry and finance were capable of carrying it rapidly into effect – which was not. Over time the realization brought about a permanent alteration in Liberal politics, converting the Radical Chancellor of the Exchequer David Lloyd George into a firm supporter of naval spending. As Asquith told the Foreign Secretary Sir Edward Grey, 'nobody here understands why Germany would need or how she can use 21 Dreadnoughts, unless for aggressive purposes, and primarily against ourselves'.[54] By surmounting both political and technical obstacles to a graduated income tax, Lloyd George's 'People's Budget', as he called it, increased government revenue by 30 per cent between 1908–09 and 1913–14 and paid for the first old-age pensions, while at the same time pushing up naval spending by more than 50 per cent.[55]

In March 1909 Admiral Lord Charles Beresford, lately commander-in-chief of the Channel Fleet, retired from the Navy after a period of strained relations with the Admiralty for which Fisher was not blameless. Beresford is almost invariably contrasted with his near contemporary Fisher, always to Fisher's advantage. Both were representatives of an uneducated generation of officers, who had made their way by force of character because they had little to contribute to the new technological professionalism of the younger officers. Beresford the gallant hero, a marquess's son and for much of his career an MP, prominent in society long before the public had heard of Fisher, used his social position to agitate for a stronger Navy. He had neither the need nor the taste for Fisher's characteristic methods of intrigue. Although not an original thinker, Beresford was the patron of cleverer men and a rallying-point for change within the Navy. He was a popular commander-in-chief, who took his captains into his confidence and encouraged professional debate. He was often (more often than Fisher) the advocate of intelligent innovations with wide naval support, particularly in the years 1900 to 1909, when he was almost continuously commanding fleets. He pushed for a naval staff at the Admiralty and insisted that battleships and cruisers had different functions and ought not to be confused. He appreciated the significance of mines well before other British admirals took them into account. He rightly complained that Fisher's division of his command into Home Fleet and Channel Fleet (reversed as soon as Beresford resigned) was dangerous. Now ashore, a popular figure who had recently inherited a fortune, and from 1910 MP for Portsmouth, he returned to the right wing of the Conservative Party where he had spent so much of his career and joined in its denunciations of Fisher's 'treason'. Each admiral had a large following of officers who imitated their leaders' bad behaviour and split the Navy into political and personal factions. A stronger First Lord than Tweedmouth would have nipped their feud in the bud five years before. If Fisher, like Beresford, had been obliged to retire at sixty-five (in 1906) according to the regulations, and both had gone together, they would have done their country much less damage. They illustrate with awful clarity why naval discipline, in its most basic form as self-discipline, really matters.[56]

Beresford's charges embarrassed the government and obliged Asquith to stage an official inquiry in the spring of 1909. In this Asquith's priorities were as usual political: vindicating either Fisher or Beresford would not help him reduce the Navy Estimates, so he produced a characteristic piece of casuistry which tended to undermine the Admiralty while ostensibly backing it.[57] The real problem was how to reunite a divided Service, and for Fisher, how to preserve his naval reforms on his retirement in 1911 when the 1910 election must probably produce either a Liberal majority, allowing Asquith to replace McKenna with a hostile Radical, or a Conservative majority and a hostile Beresfordite First Lord. The solution was for Fisher to retire a year early, in January 1910, to be succeeded by the surprising (and reluctant) choice of Sir Arthur Wilson; an outstanding sea commander devoid of human or political gifts, obstinate, secretive and inarticulate, who was three years retired and already out of touch. He had only one negative quality which outweighed all these positive defects: no known politics, and no involvement in the Fisher–Beresford feud. In the short time left to him (he was only one year younger than Fisher and would have to retire in 1912) Wilson's function was to safeguard Fisher's inheritance.[58]

McKenna and Wilson were in office at the time of the Agadir crisis in the summer of 1911, when both France and Germany interfered in Moroccan affairs and the British felt obliged to back the French. With war apparently imminent, the Navy was scattered and partly immobilized by a Cardiff coal strike, Wilson was away shooting, and few people who mattered could be found in the Admiralty. This gave ammunition to the Admiralty's enemies in the Cabinet and the War Office, ostensibly demanding the creation of a naval staff, in reality aiming for the adoption of a 'continental commitment' to send the British army to fight alongside the French. Unknown to the majority of Cabinet ministers, who would have been appalled, secret Anglo-French military talks going back to 1906 had already come close to committing Britain to exactly that.[59] At this moment Britain was in the midst of a grave constitutional crisis which had been developing over the previous three years. Stretching its customary authority, the House of Lords had rejected Lloyd George's 'People's Budget' in November 1909. In January and again in December 1910 Asquith won elections which, with the backing of King George V, established the constitutional superiority of the Commons, and on 10 August 1911 the Lords finally yielded. This settled one crisis, but the Liberals were now dependent on Irish Nationalist votes, and in 1912 introduced a bill devolving 'home rule' (self-government) to Ireland, which aroused fierce opposition in Ulster, in the Conservative Party and in the army. By the summer of 1914 when the Act finally passed, civil war seemed to be imminent, with many Anglo-Irish army officers, and some naval officers, talking of using force to keep Ireland British.[60]

It was therefore in a fevered atmosphere, as well as a railway strike and an intense heatwave, that the Committee of Imperial Defence met on 23 August 1911 to hear Sir Arthur Wilson for the Admiralty, and General Henry Wilson for the War Office, present their services' war plans. In General Wilson's words, 'the Navy's view was put so badly and incompetently by Arthur Wilson that it obscured the weaknesses in the army plans'.[61] The general was indeed the more effective speaker by far, and the result is usually described as a triumph for the soldiers' ambitions to fight in a European war, but it fell well short of a clear decision. Asquith had 'packed' the meeting by failing to invite those members likely to oppose a continental involvement, but the weaknesses of Henry Wilson's case were not invisible, and with or without its full membership the committee was purely advisory. No decisions could be or were taken there, and the Cabinet – mindful that continental warfare meant conscription which was electoral suicide – subsequently refused to endorse any unauthorized undertakings made by the General Staff.[62]

The immediate effect of this meeting was to raise the prestige of military planning and lower that of the Navy. More importantly, it marks an important stage in the progressive failure of joint-service planning in Britain. Many senior army officers longed to escape from the colonial playpen and join the big boys in a real European war, but as many or more accepted that the future of both services lay in working together, and in the years following the army's embarrassment in the South African War the way was clear for the Navy to take the lead. Unfortunately, Fisher's idea of taking the lead was remote from cordial co-operation. He meant to manoeuvre the army into a position of humiliating subservience. 'They will be *forced* to be ready, *forced* to get on, *forced* to co-operate and finally *forced* to be efficient!'[63] He wanted to make the army into 'a projectile fired by the Navy', and aimed by the Admiralty.[64] Soon enough Fisher's obstructive and dishonest tactics poisoned the chances of co-operation, and by 1911 the army was more than ready for revenge. This was not all Fisher's fault. The General Staff was riven by personal quarrels, and the Liberal government did not take its responsibility for defence seriously – but nevertheless

Fisher, and the civilian ministers who left him unsupervised, bear a large share of blame for the British government's failure to form realistic plans against the risk of war, and for the culture of deceit and revenge which permeated White-hall in 1914.[65]

The immediate consequence of the 1911 crisis was that McKenna was replaced as First Lord of the Admiralty by the leading Radical Winston Church-ill, who moved from the Home Office on 25 October, with a mandate to install a naval staff in the Admiralty. Like all Radicals, indeed virtually all Liberals, Churchill did not regard battleships as desirable in themselves and wanted to build as few as was consistent with British security. It was obvious to him and his party that the rational course would be for Germany and Britain to come to an understanding which would avoid the ruinous and fruitless naval arms race. Unfortunately, Wilhelm II regarded any such proposal as an insult to his honour, and Tirpitz greeted every overture as a craven surrender. The Germans were only prepared to talk if Britain first agreed to unconditional neutrality in any continental conflict, which clearly implied abandoning such treaty obliga-tions as her guarantee of Belgium's independence.[66] 'You must be brought to understand in England,' the Kaiser threatened the British admiral Prince Louis of Battenberg in May 1911, 'that Germany is the sole arbiter of peace or war on the Continent. If we wish to fight, we will do so with or without your leave.'[67] Nevertheless Churchill offered a naval building 'holiday' in January 1912. Ger-many's response was another *Novelle* which proposed to increase the manning strength of the fleet by more than 50 per cent, and the number of battleships from twenty-five to twenty-nine. Coming on top of the new Austro-Hungarian battleship squadron, this extinguished any hope of checking the naval arms race, and drove Churchill to a public commitment to maintain the new 160 per cent standard (which replaced the Two-Power Standard in 1912, to reflect the fact that there was now only one plausible enemy), and build two battle-ships for every one additional German battleship.[68]

By this time the German Navy's situation was worsening rapidly. For the first time the army was demanding funds from the Reichstag, and claiming a priority which could not be denied. Even Wilhelm II was losing interest in his 'mechanical toy',[69] and Tirpitz could no longer find the money to build the ships required by the Naval Law, let alone the additions called for by the 1912 *Novelle*. In Britain the budget was still balanced, social expenditure was grow-ing even faster than naval expenditure, and there was no sign that the limits of British wealth or resolve to maintain naval supremacy had been tested. The German threat had firmly welded the British agreements with France and Russia. Constitutionally, financially and industrially, Britain had shown the strength and flexibility which Germany lacked.[70] In February 1914 Tirpitz publicly abandoned the naval race and announced in the Reichstag that Churchill's eight to five ratio of Dreadnoughts was acceptable to Germany.[71] Yet even as German financial and industrial difficulties grew more acute, even as the British consistently outspent and outmanoeuvred them, Wilhelm II and his entourage continued to believe that Germany's greatness and power were both the only cause of Anglo-German friction, and the only cure for it. 'Reason, envy,' as the Kaiser exclaimed in December 1912; 'fear that we are becoming too great'.[72] There were observers, in the German Foreign Ministry and the RMA, who had a firmer grasp on reality, but the German constitution ensured that their voices were not heard.[73] What Wilhelm II did achieve was to make it harder and harder for Britain to adhere to her normal, almost automatic, foreign policy of neutrality in continental quarrels and reliance on free trade and naval power. Horrified as the Liberal Cabinet was to discover how far Britain had been secretly committed to campaigning in France, the aggressive intentions of Germany and the impossibility of negotiation became so clear that in the end the staff talks were not repudiated. With the Cabinet's attention fixed on the Irish crisis, and Asquith as usual skilfully avoiding uncomfortable questions, Britain was sliding sideways towards a European war.[74]

ELEVEN

The Biography of Great Men

Government and Administration 1890–1914

The Victorians admired Carlyle's dictum that 'the history of the world is but the biography of great men,'[1] and until surprisingly recently many British naval historians believed that the history of their world was but the biography of Sir John Fisher. The result was a great weight of adulatory writings which still distort our understanding – and yet do not include the modern biography which we so much need. It is therefore necessary to say enough to identify the real Fisher and sketch his influence.[2] His social origins were, by the Navy's standards, obscure and scarcely reputable; he abandoned his embarrassing parents as a boy and got into the Navy with a nomination from his godmother's neighbour, exploiting a flaw in a system designed to protect the social exclusivity of the officer corps. He was a product of the mid-century years when the Navy more or less abandoned the formal education of future officers. All his life he retained an uncritical enthusiasm for the latest technological marvels, but his understanding of science and engineering was seldom better than superficial, and few of his wild prophecies came true. As he grew older and more erratic, his imaginary super-weapons increasingly resembled the schoolboy designs that Wilhelm II tried to force on the German Navy.[3] As a young officer Fisher advanced his career by attending the Royal Engineers' training course in electricity and turning it into the Navy's first handbook on the subject, by which means he rose in 1874 to be the first commanding officer of the torpedo school-ship *Vernon* at Portsmouth, but once he attained Captain's rank he had no more need of electricity and dropped the subject. He must have been aware that a younger generation of officers were emerging from the *Britannia* and the new training establishments with a knowledge of science and technology well in advance of his.[4] During his career Fisher undertook as much sea-time as was necessary for promotion, but preferred to serve ashore, within easy reach of the political world. Everywhere his buoyant charm and his extravagant, exaggerated language made a great impression, but they worked best on those who did not know too much about the Navy. They were especially effective on journalists, whom he freely supplied with secret information tending to undermine his rivals. His boundless energy and enthusiasm, his ability to get things done and his self-image as a reformer, advanced his career and won the admiration of civilians (especially in the Liberal Party), but his standing in the Navy was undermined by his 'cynical egotism' and demand of 'absolute subserviency',[5] sliding in his later years into obsession and revenge. He was capable of driving through imaginative changes at ruthless speed, but he was temperamentally ill at ease with careful thought or extensive consultation. 'I never came across anyone with such pronounced personality, nor with such extraordinary driving power,' wrote one who worked with him during the First World War:

> His method was that of the mailed fist rather than the gloved hand, and in carrying out his schemes he made many enemies and hurt many people's feelings. When different schemes came before him he spent very little time in determining which should be chosen, and in his choice he seemed to be guided by instinct rather than by reason.[6]

He knew how to delegate and he could take advice, but he was incapable of compromise or moderation, and his only management style was personal dictatorship. Volatile and erratic, he frequently shifted his opinions on subjects and people (usually to extremes), and his love of intrigue did not teach him discretion. He adopted commonplace social prejudices such as anti-Catholicism and expressed them with indecent violence. Desperate to succeed Lord Walter Kerr, the only Catholic admiral in the Navy, as First Sea Lord, he spread accusations that Kerr was 'a slave to the Roman Catholic hierarchy', and the instrument of a Jesuit plot to undermine the Navy.[7] In other people's opinion Kerr was 'the embodiment of accuracy, moderation and reliability' – terms seldom applied to Fisher.[8]

Several shrewd and experienced First Lords of the Admiralty recognized both his strengths and weaknesses. 'Strong, ambitious and go-ahead . . .' wrote Lord George Hamilton,

> he made a rare splash in naval and other circles. Right throughout his career he showed instincts of genius, but, like most men so gifted, he was changeable and inconsistent. He was an extraordinary hustler and a marvellous showman. When controlled, he was an invaluable public servant; when uncontrolled, he was apt to be dangerous from his love of the

limelight and the ease with which he became obsessed with the fad of the moment.[9]

Fisher's real strengths lay not with technology, of which he had no deep understanding, nor with strategy, in which he took limited interest, but with practical administration, and with people. Lord Selborne brought him to the Admiralty in 1902 as Second Sea Lord, in charge of naval personnel, to tackle the manning crisis and oversee the new scheme of recruiting and educating future naval officers.[10] As we shall see, the 'Selborne Scheme' was not a success, but in dealing with the lower deck, Fisher's imaginative sympathy and impatience with convention were at their best. Force of character, not force of intellect, was his greatest reliance. 'Whatever success I have had is more attributable to the action of imagination than to the dictates of cold reason,' he declared: '*Emotion* rules the world! The *heart*, not the *brain*!'[11]

The quarter-century which elapsed between the Naval Defence Act of 1889 and the outbreak of the First World War in 1914 was a period of rapid naval growth never experienced in peacetime before or since, which threw an exceptional strain on the structure and administration of the Navy, even though Britain was not involved in any major naval campaign. Between the financial years 1889–90 and 1913–14 the Navy Estimates increased more than threefold, from £15.6 million a year to £51.6 million, and the numbers of officers and men in the Navy more than doubled, from 65,400 to 152,412.[12] For those who desired a strong Navy to confront foreign aggressors, these were good changes, but they were not easy to manage, especially combined with the abrupt change in strategic outlook in 1904–06 as Germany replaced France and Russia as Britain's most plausible enemy.

A key point frequently made by would-be reformers was the necessity for a 'naval staff', but the phrase was, and is, more often used to evoke an idea of modernity than to identify a specific organization, and it is necessary to unpack its several meanings. The naval reformers of the 1880s, as we have seen, were simply referring to professional assistance for the overworked Naval Lords in Whitehall. By the end of the century, commentators tended to be thinking of the 'Great General Staff' of the Prussian army, whose talents the British army in South Africa had so clearly lacked. From there it was a short step to proposing something similar for the Navy. Admirals often objected that the Navy had no use for a military staff. They had some reason, because most of the work of a Prussian-style general staff had to do with the complexities of moving armies; with roads and railways, fords and passes, billets, forage, water, and all the multitude of details which had to be arranged to move large bodies of troops.

A fleet carried its own supplies and within the limits of navigation could move freely wherever the admiral chose with virtually no preparation. Over the length of a campaign, however, the need of supply could not be ignored. Already in 1859, as we have noted, the question of a wartime coaling organization had forced Sir Alexander Milne to think about planning future campaigns. Captain W. H. Hall, the first head of the Naval Intelligence Department (NID), adopted a model of forecasting requirements which was in effect validated in 1888 when Lord Salisbury called for an estimate of the fleet necessary to fight France and Russia. By the 1890s the NID had shown that there was a lot of preparatory work to be done in assembling information and planning naval operations, and there was increasing acceptance that the NID itself was the basis of this sort of naval staff. What admirals found hard to believe was that it could have any role in actually conducting operations, as an army general staff did. In war they themselves would issue the needful orders from their flagships, with the help of the traditional admiral's staff of secretary and flag-lieutenant. There was no need and no opportunity for anyone in the Admiralty to do more than collect information in advance and lay down strategic guidelines.[13]

All that was about to change. In the late 1880s the German physicist Heinrich Hertz mapped the electromagnetic radiation which James Clark Maxwell had already proposed in theory. In 1890 a torpedo officer, Commander Henry Jackson, whose father-in-law was a mathematician and expert in Maxwell's work, identified 'Hertzian waves' as a possible method of detecting torpedo boats at night. By 1896, now a captain commanding the training ship *Defiance* at Devonport, Jackson was well advanced on wireless signalling. In that year he met the Italian-Irish inventor Guglielmo Marconi and discovered that they were both working on 'electrical signalling without conducting wires'. They agreed to collaborate.[14] At this point Marconi's wireless was the more technically advanced, but Jackson's was better suited to practical use at sea; indeed, Marconi had not realized that wireless had applications afloat. The Navy appreciated it at once. By 1899 Jackson was in charge of large-scale wireless experiments at sea and had attracted Fisher's notice; by 1900 the Navy had thirty-two Marconi and nineteen Jackson wireless sets in operation, which by the following year had risen to 105 seagoing sets and eight shore stations. The Italian and Japanese navies each had a handful of sets, and no other navy had any. In 1905 Jackson became Controller of the Navy.[15] As commander-in-chief in the Mediterranean, Fisher had set up a plotting room to track French and Russian naval movements from information coming in by telegraph, and when he went to the Admiralty he took his plot with him and installed it in the 'War Room'.

During and after the South African War the threat of French and Russian cruisers had led to the development of a Trade Defence Section of the NID which maintained a plot of British merchant shipping all over the world, relying heavily on the reporting organization built up by Sir Henry Hozier, the Secretary of Lloyd's of London. In 1904–05 the 'War Room' tracked the Russian fleet on its voyage to the Far East; by 1908 when the plots were updated every hour, it seemed that they would allow the Navy all over the world to be controlled from the Admiralty, using information coming in by cable which was available only at the centre. This meant that the Admiralty was equipping itself to become an operational command on a completely unprecedented scale. It also implied that a great deal of the autonomy of the admiral at sea was about to be sucked away. Naturally commanders-in-chief felt queasy, especially when the First Sea Lord was Fisher, a ruthless autocrat with a well-founded reputation for the abuse of private and secret information. Lord Charles Beresford in the Channel was one of the first to complain, and all the louder when his cruisers and destroyers were taken from him to be controlled centrally by the Admiralty, leaving him with twenty-one ships to command where his predecessor had had more than two hundred.[16] 'The advance of wireless telegraphy,' wrote the Director of Naval Intelligence in 1908,

> has been so great and so rapid that an entirely new development of strategic organization becomes imperative. With the present installation it is possible to receive information and to transmit orders over a large area from the Admiralty with certainty . . . The result of this enormous advance is that the Admiralty are compelled to assume the responsibility for the strategic movements of the fleet in a far more complete manner than was ever formerly practicable.[17]

This had enormous implications. If the central collection of information really compelled the Admiralty to take over the operational control of the whole Navy, it would need a real military-style staff on a large scale, not just an intelligence bureau. It would need actual war plans specified in advance, not just the traditional strategic guidelines to be developed at the discretion of the commanders-in-chief. But the biggest questions were whether central operational control could be made to work at all, and whether it was desirable even if possible. The annual Manoeuvres from 1908 to the outbreak of the war were partly devoted to trying to answer these questions.

By the turn of the century, it was becoming clear that the rise of torpedo craft had made the traditional close blockade too dangerous for big ships. Plans and manoeuvres concentrated on various forms of 'observational blockade', with the main fleet held at a safe distance from the enemy port while light forces kept watch close in. This called for greater endurance and seakeeping than destroyers could deliver, even against Cherbourg and Brest, and much more so against German ports 300 miles away on the other side of the North Sea. By 1907, therefore, the Navy was planning to establish advance anchorages in international waters among the shoals off the Danish North Sea coast, where destroyers on observational blockade could be supplied with fuel. Movements on this scale, spread over hundreds of miles, could only be controlled by wireless. Each destroyer flotilla was now to be led by one of the new light cruisers, ships big enough to step the tall masts needed for long-range wireless signalling.[18] After the 1908 manoeuvres the overall plan was 'First the trade warfare patrol lines at the access routes to and from the North Sea, second the Admiralty War Room radio control, third the trap concept of operations, fourth the observation blockade line to monitor the German bases and fifth the notion of offensive operations against the enemy coast to bait the German Navy into accepting the early decisive battle that the slow-working trade blockade was unlikely to provoke.'[19]

As the range of German destroyers increased, the positions in which the British battleships would be anchored tended to be set further back from German ports. The geography of the North Sea left the British room to do this, but as the battleships' planned anchorages retreated northward (and westward down the Channel), they left the advanced light forces more and more exposed. If they in turn were withdrawn, that would create opportunities for the Germans to raid or land on the British coast before the distant battleships could intervene. Serious invasion seemed to be unlikely, but the British feared a quick raid or a Japanese-style surprise torpedo attack on a fleet at anchor.[20] The essential defence would be a reliable and timely warning of what sailed from enemy ports and when. Already in 1905 it occurred to Balfour that the new submarines might provide it, but as yet the opposite shore of the North Sea was out of their range, and they could not carry long-range wireless. These considerations pushed the Navy back to close blockade, with destroyers backed by cruisers and they in turn by battleships, but then the new German submarines seemed to make that policy too dangerous. In 1912 and 1913 two fleets were planned, a northern one based in the Firth of Forth and a southern at Portland or Plymouth, but experiments with mid-North Sea patrol lines to locate the Germans and draw them into a trap between the two fleets failed because patrol lines in the open sea were much too porous. By 1913 the southern fleet of older battleships was looking too weak, and the northern too distant, to play their part in springing a trap; in the manoeuvres that summer Rear-Admiral John

Jellicoe commanding the 'enemy' fleet successfully landed 60,000 troops in the Humber before the defenders could react. In 1914 the best available policy seemed to be intermittent 'sweeps' across the North Sea by the main fleet, often enough (the Admiralty hoped) to make big German raids too dangerous, seldom enough to provide few targets for enemy submarines. Nobody was satisfied with it.[21]

In the years since the South African War, however, there had been important technical developments in an obscure aspect of naval war, little known to most naval officers and scarcely at all to the general public, but very relevant to blockade. Sea mines had been known since the Crimean War and American Civil War, usually in the form of 'blockade' or 'controlled' minefields, electrically operated from the shore. In Britain they were the responsibility of the Royal Engineers and regarded as part of the fixed defences of the dockyard ports. In the Russo-Japanese War, however, both sides laid sea mines in navigable waters offshore, primed to explode automatically on contact with any ship. The results were both materially and psychologically devastating. The Japanese lost two battleships including their flagship *Hatsuse*, while Admiral Stepan Makarov was blown up with his flagship *Petropavlovsk*. The world was horrified by the barbarity of this new unmanned and uncontrolled weapon, especially as the technology of minelaying in the open sea was so unfamiliar that many people thought that 'floating mines' had been left to drift at random, rather than moored in channels used by the enemy. Most naval and all public opinion expected minelaying in international waters to be forbidden by international agreement. British officers had particular reasons to reject a weapon which seemed to deny the very principle of the freedom of the seas, and threaten the battleships which assured it. As Beresford pointed out, 'under water warfare [is] a danger we have been in the habit of underrating, both in the Navy and in the country'.[22] He and the few other British officers who knew and thought about mines shared that revulsion, but they could see that mines offered advantages which would make it difficult to get them banned by international agreement. They could also see that Britain herself might be a major beneficiary, since mines laid off an enemy port might be exactly the weapon needed to enforce a blockade in the absence of a blockading squadron. The first step was to develop a suitable mine – in great secrecy and at minimal expense – which was undertaken by converting the now redundant controlled mines. By the end of 1905 the Navy was ready to adopt a form of warfare which the new Liberal government seemed certain to condemn.[23]

In 1908, after the Second Hague Peace Conference which had first mentioned submarine mines to international law, the Admiralty, still in great secrecy, ordered a stock of 10,000 mines, and the conversion of seven small cruisers to lay them. In February 1913 it adopted a new policy written by Captain George Ballard, Director of the Operations Division of the Naval Staff, of laying (or pretending to lay) 'declared' minefields with the intention of frightening merchant shipping out of much of the southern North Sea. This would reinforce the blockade, possibly without actually sinking any neutrals. It was certainly illegal as international law then stood, but it was calculated to gain the strategic point at the least political cost. By 14 August 1914 the Cabinet was already contemplating minelaying 'to blow up some neutral ships to deter others'. By the beginning of October, German U-boat attacks had largely overcome both the politicians' moral revulsion at minelaying, and the admirals' cultural revulsion. Neither group yet realized that the converted mines did not work.[24]

Since experiment suggested that submerged submarines could neither be detected nor attacked, the only effective defence against them for a fleet at sea was to keep the surfaced submarines too far away to get into a position to fire a torpedo, which had to be on the bow of the target, not more than a mile away at most. In principle this was not very difficult, because submerged submarines were so slow (say 5 knots for short periods, compared with a fleet speed of 18 or 19 knots), and the effective range of a submarine torpedo so short, that it was necessary to get into position on the surface and dive only at the last minute. A screen two miles or so ahead of the fleet and on either side should therefore provide sufficient protection. The screen would call for fast warships with a good gun armament, able to keep up at least 20 knots for long periods. Only modern oil-fired destroyers could achieve that, and a single flotilla of twenty-four was barely enough. This presented both a tactical and a strategic dilemma. Tactically, there were now at least three tasks for destroyers in company with the fleet: an attack on the enemy battleships with torpedoes, which called for concentration on the enemy's bow; defence against similar attack, which implied concentrating on the enemy flotilla; and defence against submarine attack, which called for a screen of destroyers dispersed around a perimeter. One flotilla could accomplish all three tasks, but not all at once. Strategically the problem was where to locate the destroyers. Until about 1910 they had normally cruised independently, along the coasts to defend against enemy landings, or off the enemy's coast in blockade. Now there was pressure to allocate at least part of the destroyer force to the main fleet to create what was called 'the Grand Fleet of Battle', combining battleships, cruisers and destroyers in a single enormous force. Under Sir George Callaghan (commander-in-chief 1911–14), the tactics and handling of this 'Grand Fleet' were constantly practised. The 1912 war plans gave the fleet one destroyer flotilla, with three more based at Harwich or Sheerness for 'reconnaissance towards the German coast'. Callaghan wanted more, considering the submarine 'a far greater menace to ships than the fleet generally gave them credit for'.[25] By 1914 each force had two flotillas, and the Admiralty promised to send the two Harwich flotillas to join the Grand Fleet if the German fleet put to sea. The creation of the Grand Fleet had the important effect of limiting the fleet's operational endurance to that of the destroyers, which was about three days' steaming at wartime speeds.[26]

Distinct from fleet action, but closely connected with it, were two other types of operation which the British planned and practised: defence against invasion, and British landing operations on enemy soil. Invariably the British assumed that the German army could and would allocate enough troops to overwhelm the British army if only they could be got ashore. They would have been incredulous had they known that there was almost no co-operation between the German army and navy, and that the German General Staff regarded seaborne expeditions as a frivolous diversion from the serious business of fighting the French and Russians.[27] Since no navy of this era built landing ships except the Russians in the Black Sea, troops would have to be transported in merchant ships (highly vulnerable to torpedo craft) and landed by ships' boats, which severely limited how many could be disembarked and how fast. The further back the British fleets were held, however, the more would depend on timely location and interception of the enemy – precisely what the 1912 and 1913 manoeuvres showed would be so difficult. These considerations raised delicate questions of inter-service politics; the Navy became more willing to admit the risk of enemy raids of up to 10,000 men, just as the army became reluctant to keep troops at home whom they hoped to deploy on the Continent. The Admiralty won a Cabinet commitment against stiff War Office resistance to keep two of the army's six divisions at home to guard against enemy landings.[28]

More controversial, then and now, were British naval plans for landings on German coasts. The capture of Heligoland or one of the Friesian islands to support a close blockade, or a direct assault on the locks of the Kaiser Wilhelm Canal, offered the prospect of crushing victory in themselves, and were highly likely to bring on a fleet action as well, but it was always doubtful if these heavily fortified targets lay anywhere near the realm of the possible, and it is still unclear how seriously the plans were taken even by their authors. The 1904 landing exercise at Clacton was a discouraging fiasco.[29] Another possibility was to force entry to the Baltic to stop Germany's access to Swedish iron ore, and to land British or Russian troops on the Pomeranian coast. As we have seen, the Germans were frightened by this threat, and in 1914 pressured the Danish government into mining the Great Belt to block it – an astonishing act of self-harm, which made it impossible for German battleships to reach the North Sea through the Kattegat and severely limited Germany's strategic options for the rest of the war. The Danes were careful to leave secret channels through the minefields by which their own small battleships could come and go regardless, and the northern side of the Sound, in Swedish territorial waters which the Swedes refused to obstruct, was still available for ships drawing no more than 22 feet to enter or leave the Baltic.[30]

In trying to test these various plans, the British found that central control by wireless threw up innumerable practical difficulties. In effect it reproduced on a very large scale the centralized control of a fleet in company with the flag-ship. In the early 1890s Admiral Sir George Tryon in the Mediterranean had trained his captains to follow his intentions without expecting every change of course to be signalled from the flagship: 'An Admiral must make his general plans clear to all his Captains and must trust chiefly to their loyalty and initiative in carrying out those plans during the course of an action.' Many of them found loyalty more comfortable than initiative, and after Tryon's death in the disastrous 1893 collision of the *Victoria*, caused precisely by captains failing to think for themselves, the Navy thankfully reverted to a model which assumed that the admiral could see everything and decide everything himself.[31] This worked, much of the time, for well-drilled small fleets within visual signalling distance in good weather. It was soon clear that it did not work for large forces spread across the notoriously foggy North Sea. Officers who had been taught that the senior officer always knew best, and most, continued to assume that he had the full picture even from scores of miles away. The Admiralty in London, which alone was keeping a plot, was reluctant to delegate to admirals at sea, while admirals at sea, who had no plots, were reluctant to delegate to their captains. Sir Arthur Wilson's practice was to signal exact courses to ships hundreds of miles away whose precise position and situation he could not know, removing all responsibility from the flag officers. 'They pay me to be an admiral,' one of them complained, 'they don't pay me to think.'[32] Wireless signals took time to cypher and decypher, they frequently failed to get through because of difficulties of tuning and interference, and too often they were obscurely worded and ambiguous. Many sighting reports failed to give the reporting ship's position, or the enemy's, or both. Central control by wireless conspicuously failed in the 1912 and 1913 manoeuvres, and most observers concluded that there was no practical alternative to admirals and captains using their initiative. But to whom, at what level of command, was the initiative to be allowed? Did the commander-in-chief's freedom to handle his own fleet mean that he alone could and would control more than a hundred ships spread across many square miles of sea? In practice the rise of the Grand Fleet tended to draw responsibility away from the Admiralty to the fleet at sea without doing much to encourage individual captains to think for themselves.[33]

The replacement of France and Russia by Germany as Britain's most likely enemy had the effect of concentrating much war planning on the North Sea, but the Admiralty could not and did not ignore the rest of the world. The South African War had reminded people that the status of neutral merchant shipping in wartime was undecided. In Britain, as we have noted, opinion was divided between those who assumed that Britain would once again be the great neutral power, as she had been in most of the major wars of the nineteenth century, and those who considered what she ought to aim for as a belligerent. They in turn spread across a spectrum, from those (predominantly on the right in politics) who sought the maximum freedom for a dominant sea power to exercise her belligerent rights, to those (mainly on the left) who advocated partial or even total immunity of private property from wartime capture. Those who wanted the dominant navy to flex its muscles had to face the uncomfortable fact that it had not worked in the South African War, when the neutral powers, in their traditional capacity as the court of appeal of international law, had in effect ruled against Britain. Those who hoped to limit belligerent rights had to face the scepticism of those who thought belligerents (and one in particular, namely Britain) would not and should not consent. There was also major doubt as to what mechanism might express belligerent rights. 'Blockade' was the traditional application of sea power against neutral shipping, but in the precise usage of lawyers (as distinct from the very loose usage of naval officers and historians) blockade was only 'effective' and legal if the blockaders lay sufficiently close to the blockaded port to offer a high risk of intercepting ships trying to enter or leave. Distant, notional or 'paper' blockades had no validity and neutral ports were exempt, so the end of close blockade meant the end of all legal blockade. There was, however, an alternative mechanism known to international law. It had always been agreed that belligerents were entitled to capture or even sink cargoes of 'contraband' – weapons and war materials destined for their enemies – wherever they might be encountered. A broad definition of contraband might make up to the dominant naval power much of what was lost by the failure of blockade.[34]

All these questions were discussed at the Second Hague Conference of 1907, which adopted a proposal for an International Prize Court, to which the decisions of national prize courts could be appealed – the first ever international court. This in turn required an agreed international law for it to apply, to settle which the leading maritime powers met in London in 1908–09. The range of international positions was very great, and the disagreements within the British delegation were almost as wide, but to the astonishment of many observers, the conference reached consensus on a new statement of the law of war at sea: the 'Declaration of London'. This allowed a blockade of an enemy port to be notified extending to the limit of the blockader's (self-defined) 'radius of action' and reckoned as effective if it offered a 'real threat' of capture. These definitions were broad and loose enough to cover most British requirements, and the consent of the USA and other powers traditionally strong for the freedom of wartime trade was a precious gain for Admiralty planners. What they had gained was ostensibly a mechanism for effective economic warfare, but behind that their real ambition was to force the German fleet to come out and fight. That would be a victory worth having: quick, decisive and psychologically satisfying. Britain and most other powers now regarded the Declaration as established international law and began to incorporate it into their domestic law and rules of engagement, while the diplomats undertook the slow process of collecting formal ratifications from all the participants. Then in 1914 the House of Lords, furious at its successive humiliations at the hands of the Liberal government, seized an opportunity of revenge by rejecting the Declaration. It was generally assumed that the Lords, having expressed their wounded pride, would succumb in the end, but the war intervened, leaving the Navy with a less than clear-cut legal position. Moreover, it soon became obvious that the Declaration of London had not addressed the legal questions which were to be most critical to the coming war at sea.[35]

While the Hague and London Conferences were meeting, public and official attention in Britain and elsewhere was increasingly distracted by experiments with airships and aeroplanes, which had obvious implications for national defence. In January 1909 a 'technical sub-committee' of the Committee of Imperial Defence, under the chairmanship of Lord Esher, considered how Britain should react to the development of aviation in France and Germany. A powerful searchlight was thrown on the subject by the Turco-Italian war of 1911–12, in which the Italians used both airships and aeroplanes, immediately followed by the Balkan Wars of 1912–13 in which Greek and Bulgarian aircraft were active. Already the Admiralty was intensely interested in aviation, especially after Winston Churchill became First Lord in October 1911. In April 1912 the joint-service Royal Flying Corps was established, and in November the Admiralty issued a list of the functions of the 'Naval Wing' of the RFC, including distant scouting for the fleet at sea, reconnaissance of enemy coasts, assisting destroyers to detect and destroy submarines, detecting minelaying and mines, reporting hostile craft in British coastal channels, assisting British submarines to locate targets to attack, screening ships and harbours from enemy air observation, and preventing air attack on dockyards, magazines and oil tanks. In the same year the US Navy, closely followed by the British, made the first successful aircraft flights taking off from ships, and from the water. In July 1914 Squadron-Commander Arthur Longmore, RNAS, dropped the first torpedo from an aircraft. All this is eloquent of the energy and imagination being applied to naval aviation. The official term 'the Naval Wing of the Royal Flying Corps' soon fell out of use, and on 1 June 1914 the Admiralty unilaterally established the Royal Naval Air Service as a quasi-independent service with its own structure of ranks and ratings, closely involved with the Navy but distinct from it.[36]

All questions of planning and organization for war bore hard on an Admiralty which had no staff capable of evaluating them. The NID was overworked and strongly identified with the use of history as an analytical tool, which Fisher despised and associated with Beresford's party. In 1909 Fisher abolished the Trade Division out of hand on discovering that its head was a follower of Beresford. Instead, he often drew on the War Course, later War College, established at Greenwich in 1902 then moved to Portsmouth in 1907. This offered courses for senior officers designed to introduce them to staff methods, and the teaching staff included some of the best minds associated with the Navy, notably Captain George Ballard and the civilian historian Julian Corbett. Ballard's 1906 committee drafted one of the most influential sets of war plans, and fulfilled Fisher's requirements in being a small informal planning unit under his immediate control.[37] Later planning groups were set up *ad hoc* by Fisher, Wilson and Churchill, but all of them were drafting outline war plans in the traditional style, leaving all the detail to the commander-in-chief. If central control by wireless was ever to work, the centre would need a very large and capable staff structure.[38]

The War Staff that Churchill set up in 1912, however, was no bigger than the old NID which it absorbed – twenty-seven officers and eighteen civil servants – and its functions were strictly advisory. It was equipped to act as a research department but was incapable of interfering in operations even if it had been allowed to. Churchill meant to do all the interfering himself, using the Chief of War Staff as an alternative source of professional advice to set against the First Sea Lord. The junior naval lords, who might have been a valuable source of professional judgement, were shut out of Churchill's 'War

Group' and given little to do. Instead of the civil servants who had been trained to run the War Room, it was manned by retired naval officers who might have been better employed on planning. The result was that all power was gathered at the centre, which was chronically undermanned and overworked, while the Admiralty as a whole was less rather than more able to control operations at sea.[39]

Taken in isolation, this judgement may seem to support the condemnations, fashionable until quite recently, of Britain's multiple weaknesses in the face of the rising power of Germany. In reality none of the great powers were anywhere near either the organization or the attitudes necessary to conduct a modern war. In Paris there was no Admiralty and no naval staff, though Admiral Augustin Boué de Lapeyrère commanding the main fleet had a personal staff afloat. The 'Quai d'Orsay' (the French Foreign Ministry) declined to share its diplomatic plans with the War Ministry, and the War Ministry did not speak to civilian politicians. The 1902 Franco-Italian convention intended to defuse tension on their common frontier was not disclosed to the French army until 1909. The Quai d'Orsay was successful in breaking some German codes, but in 1914 the commander-in-chief General Joseph Joffre refused to believe them.[40]

The German constitution, especially with Wilhelm II on the throne, was grossly incompetent to decide great issues of peace and war, and committed Germany to a war which was almost certainly unwinnable even with a more efficient structure of government. In 1911 the finance and naval ministers explained to the Kaiser the financial impossibility of his proposed naval expansion against Britain, but he simply ruled them out of order: 'the question of money plays no role in this,' he insisted, and in another conversation he declared, 'There is enough money available. The Reich's Treasury does not know what to do with all that money . . .'[41] After the abolition of the Naval High Command in 1899, the German Navy was run by uncoordinated rival commanders-in-chief without strategic direction. Only after the outbreak of war did the naval staff, the *Admiralstab*, gradually take on some central authority by assuming the Kaiser's powers without consulting him. In the United States neither army nor navy was informed about the administration's diplomacy, and could only guess what duties might be laid upon them in the event of war. The idea of sending an expedition to Europe in 1917 came as a complete shock.[42]

The usual reason for stressing Britain's weakness in 1914, however, rests on a view of economics rather than government. It is not possible to discuss Britain's economic situation in 1914 without exorcizing a ghost which still haunts

some corners of the historical imagination: the spectre of national decline. The
conviction that Britain ought to have been powerful but was actually growing
weaker, still has so strong a hold that not a few authors have been drawn into
writing what has memorably been described as 'anti-history': the invention of
bogus explanations for events which do not need to be explained, because they
never happened.[43] We shall encounter 'anti-naval history' more than once in
the twentieth century, and the same idea lurks everywhere behind popular
ideas of economic history. Readers should be clear from the outset, therefore,
that the British economy did not decline in the nineteenth century, nor in the
twentieth, though it undoubtedly changed. In adopting free trade, British
statesmen had intended from the beginning to spread the blessings of prosperity and good government to other nations, and in many, though not all
respects, they succeeded. The experience of the nineteenth century, like that
of the later twentieth century, showed that poor countries with large reserves
of underemployed people and resources were capable of rapid economic
growth, given basic stability, freedom to trade, and access to imported capital
and skills. In time many such countries became prosperous and attained the
level of more or less full employment and full exploitation of resources which
Britain had already reached; a level where internal economic growth was
limited to the long-term growth in productivity. In terms of income per head
the United States had already passed Britain by 1913, and Belgium, Germany
and Switzerland were not far behind. This convergence of living standards, as
poor people and poor countries caught up with the rich, was driven by free
trade, and particularly by the steep decline in long-distance shipping costs,
which halved between 1870 and 1913.[44]

British governments were pleased to see these changes, because they knew
it was both just and wise that Britain should share her prosperity and use her
sea power unselfishly. In an influential memorandum of 1907, Sir Eyre Crowe
of the Foreign Office explained:

> It would . . . be but natural that the power of a State supreme at sea should
> inspire universal jealousy and fear, and be ever exposed to the danger of
> being overthrown by a general combination of the world. Against such a
> combination no single nation could in the long run stand, least of all a
> small island kingdom not possessed of the military strength of a people
> trained to arms, and dependent for its food supply on overseas commerce.
> The danger can in practice only be averted – and history shows that it has
> been so averted – on condition that the national policy of the insular and
> naval State is so directed as to harmonize with the general desires and ideas

common to all mankind, and more particularly that it is closely identified with the primary and vital interests of a majority, or as many as possible, of the other nations.[45]

Events proved Crowe right. Germany's naked aggression united every great power against her save Austria-Hungary, while Britain, the great possessor power with so much to lose and so much to be envied, was able to draw essential support even from a traditional enemy like the United States. 'We are not a young people with an innocent record and a scanty inheritance,' Winston Churchill warned the Cabinet in January 1914:

> We have engrossed to ourselves . . . an altogether disproportionate share of the wealth and traffic of the world. We have got all we want in territory, and our claim to be left in unmolested enjoyment of vast and splendid possessions, mainly acquired by violence, largely maintained by force, often seems less reasonable to others than to us.[46]

But in the final reckoning, British naval and commercial strength offered many advantages and few threats to other major powers compared with the German alternative. British warships protected the shipping of all countries and discreetly covered the sea coasts of those with no adequate navies of their own – not least the United States, whose 'Monroe Doctrine' of excluding European powers from the Americas was in effect underwritten by the Royal Navy for most of the nineteenth century.[47]

Free trade went along with the abandonment of agricultural protectionism and the rise of imported food, which in time transformed the condition of the poor that had so worried the early Victorians. By 1914 the diet of the working class (four-fifths of the population) was largely imported: 80 per cent of the wheat consumed, 80 per cent of the lard, 75 per cent of the cheese, 66 per cent of the bacon, 50 per cent of condensed milk, most of what meat they could afford (and half of the cattle feed) came from abroad. Overall Britain produced 35 per cent of her foodstuffs, which compares with 80 per cent in Germany. Britain imported wheat from Russia, Turkey and Romania (35 per cent), North America (30 per cent), India (14 per cent), South America (13 per cent), Australia and New Zealand (8 per cent). The state shrank and was paid for mainly by income tax (laid on the rich), rather than indirect consumption taxes laid on the people at large. In most other major economies, such as France, Germany and the United States, landowners had too much political power for such changes to be tolerated; prices and tariffs remained high and the rich paid little direct taxation.[48]

As the British economy became richer and more sophisticated in the last quarter of the nineteenth century, capital and skills shifted from basic industries to more sophisticated manufactures, banking and finance where much higher profits were available. A generation of historians for whom crude steel was an index of national virility saw this as a sign of moral decay, but it powerfully reinforced Britain's economic strength. Political stability and the gold standard drew cheap capital to London from every land, made sterling the trading currency of the world, and Britain the centre of world commodity and re-export markets. British banks' deep pools of credit financed much of world trade, and British shipping carried much of it; major export economies such as Germany and the United States depended heavily on both. Lloyd's of London insured the German merchant fleet, and by 1913–14 some 60 per cent of the 'bills on London' issued by British banks financed transactions entirely between foreigners. By the early twentieth century, British investors owned, managed or controlled the vast majority of the world's railways outside Europe and the USA, and 40 per cent of all deep-sea cables. Three-fifths of the world's steam shipping was built in Britain and two-fifths owned there. Britain's dominant position in world communications translated into dominance of international information flows and all the business they brought. 'Invisible' earnings from banking, broking, insurance and services, which grew from £80 million a year to £170 million between 1870 and 1913, kept the balance of payments in credit and refreshed the stream of outward investment. Britain's share of world trade fell from 25 per cent in 1860 to 17 per cent in 1913 as more and more other countries joined in, but these new trading competitors were also new markets, and British exports rose rapidly, both in absolute terms and as a proportion of national production. In 1856 they represented 14.6 per cent of gross domestic product; by 1913 they were no less than 25 per cent. Between 1900 and 1913 British steamship tonnage rose by 55 per cent, invisible earnings increased by 54 per cent, British exports went up 80 per cent, British investments overseas and the income from them both nearly doubled, and the surplus on the balance of payments multiplied more than sixfold. In 1913 Britain, with a population of 46 million, had a greater gross domestic product than all other nations except the USA with 97 million people and Germany with 67 million – and adding overseas earnings to get gross national product overtook Germany's lead. This was 'decline' only in a rather specialized sense of the word.[49]

The real danger to British economic strength on the eve of the war did not lie in competition with foreign powers, but in complementarity. With 44 per cent of world foreign investments, 30 per cent of world manufactured exports, nine times US earnings from shipping and services and four times the German steam fleet, Britain was vastly more heavily invested in international trade than any other major power. It was the key to her economic success, but it was also her greatest vulnerability. She had more to lose than any other power from serious disruption of the international trading system, and her security all depended directly or indirectly on naval power. The fundamental reason for the great change in British political sentiment towards the Navy in the late 1880s was a realization, by political leaders and by the expanding electorate, that national life and prosperity were now inextricably bound up with the freedom of seaborne trade.[50] But naval power was not exorbitantly expensive. The real cost of defence as a proportion of national income was lower in Britain than in any other major power except the USA. 'The weary Titan staggers under the too vast orb of its fate,' Joseph Chamberlain told the Imperial Conference in 1902, but even in 1906–12, the years of the naval race with Germany, the titan was not heavily burdened. There was nothing stopping Britain from spending more on defence apart from a reluctance to increase the still very low rates of taxation. Notwithstanding the huge growth in both naval and social spending under the Liberal government of 1905–15, the economy was growing faster; government spending as a proportion of gross domestic product fell from 13.3 per cent to 11.9 per cent between 1900 and 1913, and defence spending as a proportion remained the same. The big change was that in the nine years leading up to the First World War the naval share of defence spending rose from 49.2 per cent to 61.2 per cent.[51]

———•◆•———

TWELVE

The Navy Belongs to Us
Social History: Officers 1860–1914

By the end of the Russian War in 1856 it was obvious that the experiment of training future commissioned officers entirely at sea had failed badly. The examination standard of the naval cadets was low and falling, lieutenants emerged from the new system lacking basic professional competence, while the boy seamen coming out of Greenwich Hospital School and the new training ships were visibly better educated than their future officers. In 1856 Captain Robert Harris of the training ship *Illustrious* put his own son through his ship alongside the boys, and recommended to Alexander Milne, the responsible Admiralty Lord, that a training ship would do as well for the naval cadets. Next year the first batch of cadets joined the *Illustrious*, and two years later they moved to the bigger *Britannia*.[1] This rather surprising choice was known as the unhealthiest ship in the Navy; three years before she had lost 139 men to a cholera epidemic in the Black Sea. She was still unhealthy in Portsmouth Harbour, and equally so in the bleak and windswept anchorage of Portland, so in September 1863 (in the midst of a scarlet fever epidemic), she was towed to Dartmouth, on a sheltered river remote from the moral dangers of large towns. In 1869 the screw First-Rate *Prince of Wales* of 1860, a newer (but almost equally sickly) ship, took her place and her name.[2]

The *Britannia* (first and second) at Dartmouth was for forty years the Navy's prime means of forming future officers, but the process was always controversial and subject to repeated inquiries and revisions. An American report of 1880 described it as 'a combination of makeshifts, resulting from a series of tentative and spasmodic efforts in almost every form which naval education is capable of taking'.[3] Both in the Navy and in society at large, there was deep disagreement about the nature and purpose of education. The Navy never seems to have been clear on the difference between education and training, and which of the two the *Britannia* was meant to provide. Both cadets in

Britannia and midshipmen afterwards were treated sometimes as schoolboys and sometimes as officers. In the world at large the rising prestige of professional training and status implied that the qualifications for authority could be taught and learned, whereas the Navy's rhetoric insisted on the hereditary qualities of the gentleman, which were intangible, unexaminable and scarcely definable; the naval term 'officer-like qualities' evoked (and still evokes) the Navy's confidence that it knew what it wanted even if it could not explain what it was.[4] If the idea was that the cadets should learn how to be gentlemen, it was not obvious whom they could learn from. Almost all the teaching aboard the *Britannia* was done by petty officers or civilian schoolmasters; until 1890 discipline was entirely in the hands of petty officers, and the ship's officers were scarcely present. Although the official discipline was not severe by the standards of the day, there was a great deal of neglect, bullying and corruption.[5]

As the professional ideal became more influential, educational tests both to enter the *Britannia* and to advance thereafter became more numerous and difficult. From 1874 there were two nominations, and from 1885 three nominations for every place, and an examination selected the best of each intake, which clearly had an effect in pushing up the educational standard of entry. In 1868 only half the cadets reached sub-lieutenant, of whom 73 per cent were commissioned as lieutenants, taking an average of four years to get there. By 1900 some 86 per cent reached sub-lieutenant and 92 per cent of them became lieutenants, in an average of 2.2 years. These results were obtained with the help of some cheating, however, and the teaching was still largely by rote, so the boys were 'crammed' to get into the Navy and then crammed again with the overloaded and heavily mathematical syllabus.[6] One cadet had the misfortune to have been taught by a private tutor to reason things out for himself. 'This method of learning . . . proved in after years to be a considerable handicap, as it prevented me from ever acquiring the habit of rapidly assimilating information, the accepted substitute for education, during the whole of my naval career.' In the *Britannia*, 'there was far too much theory and far too little practice. There were also far too many lectures and far too much theoretical mathematics.'[7] To a later schoolmaster it seemed that a cadet's education 'stopped, to all intents and purposes, the moment he entered the *Britannia*'.[8] Naval critics objected that the emphasis on rote-learning gave the advantage to candidates who had been prepared at expensive 'crammers', while the overloaded syllabus of the *Britannia* left the cadets exhausted.[9] Left-wing critics in Parliament objected that fees of £70 a year recovered only a fraction of the cost of running the ship, which was therefore providing a 'charity education' to candidates chosen by nomination – a system of political corruption favouring the protégés of the party in power. Between 1863 and 1881 the ship cost a total of £578,569 to run, of which only £120,832 was recovered from parents, an average of £71 each. These critics vainly demanded that the fees be raised as high as necessary to recover true costs from the beneficiaries, which on these figures would have been £342 for a year's training. Eton, the most expensive school in England, cost about £200 a year.[10]

This bears on another function of the *Britannia*, which was not explained to the public. The nominations, fees and conditions of entry were designed to remedy one of the glaring faults of the 1837 system by filtering out socially undesirable candidates as early and discreetly as possible. 'We want the sons of gentlemen,' declared Vice-Admiral Alfred Ryder, who as the Duke of Somerset's private secretary had had much to do with setting up the *Britannia*. 'We want the sons of men I say who are not pauper gentlemen. We want, and it is better for us to have, the sons of men of some little independence.'[11] The sort of 'pauper gentleman' he might have had in mind was the failed colonial coffee planter Captain William Fisher, John's father.[12] In the new system established in 1857 almost all nominations were reserved to members of the Admiralty Board, though commanders-in-chief were still allowed two on hoisting their flags, and captains one in their whole career. The 'claims' of successful candidates recorded in the First Lords' Nomination Books consisted almost wholly of strong social connections with the upper classes, and political connections to government MPs or peers. Not many candidates came from the upper classes themselves; they were overwhelmingly from well-to-do professional families, but a respectable income at that level was an unspoken condition for acceptance, and the *Britannia*'s fees were designed to enforce it. The professions of the fathers of boys entering between 1860 and 1880 were: army 29.8 per cent, Church 18.2 per cent, Navy 16.3 per cent, independent (including landowners) 15.1 per cent and commerce 6.1 per cent.[13]

As the system stood in 1863, cadets entered at about age fourteen (fifteen from 1896), to spend a year in the *Britannia* followed by four or more in the fleet, still studying, as cadets, midshipmen and finally sub-lieutenants. Study in ships at sea was only marginally less unsatisfactory than before, and the boys quickly forgot what they had memorized without understanding. To pass for lieutenant they had to pass in gunnery aboard the *Excellent*, and in navigation and steam at the Royal Naval College Portsmouth, before actual promotion when a vacancy occurred. In 1870 Hugh Childers established an inquiry into officers' 'higher education'. As a graduate of Cambridge and the founder of the University of Melbourne, he presumably understood what higher education was, but the officers of eminent scientific qualifications who made up the committee clearly did not, and proposed only a range of narrowly technical courses to be taught at the Royal Naval College at Portsmouth. Meanwhile Childers was also trying to save money by closing the largely empty Greenwich Hospital. The remaining in-pensioners were moved on, but a new use for the vast range of buildings was hard to find, and the fact that Greenwich was the Prime Minister's constituency lent urgency to the search. It was George Goschen who hit on the solution in 1872. In twenty-four hours, before the Admiralty had realized what was happening, he and Gladstone had decided to turn the Hospital into a naval college. It was far too big for the Navy and cost nearly seven times as much to run as the college at Portsmouth where the admirals actually wanted their teaching, but they were given no choice, and in 1873 the sub-lieutenants' courses migrated to Greenwich. Far from being higher education in any sense, they consisted in re-cramming the mathematics which the young men had learnt at Dartmouth five years before and immediately forgotten; many of them could not manage even that without the help of private tutors. 'Though the average age of my class was about twenty-four, the methods of tuition were those of the secondary school rather than the university.'[14] The curriculum remained overcrowded, over-advanced and over-abstract for the abilities of both lecturers and students, and the results of the navigation examination were consistently poor.[15]

Observers outside the Navy, and some within it, were unhappy at this. In 1877 a committee of civil servants and university academics surveying the teaching at Greenwich argued that 'there is no acquirement which is more likely to be of practical use to a naval officer than a knowledge of modern languages, modern history, political geography and the outlines of international law' – subjects few or none of which were taught at the college.[16] Several critics wanted the boys to get a complete education on shore, at their parents' expense, before joining the Navy at seventeen or eighteen. This was the view of Admiral Ryder, and of the 1885 Luard Committee, both aiming to eliminate cramming and produce better officers at less cost.[17] For at least a generation thoughtful naval men had been seeking to escape from the narrow and repressive curriculum of Dartmouth to something which would develop future officers' powers of independent judgement. 'Owing to the early age at which our officers go to sea,' Milne complained in 1862, 'and from their continued service until they are made Commanders, they have few if any opportunities of becoming acquainted or being able to study the many branches of general science which are now taught as part of general education.' As a young officer on half-pay Milne himself had followed courses at Edinburgh University, and wanted the Navy to offer something similar: 'Very great was the advantage I gained from the *personal attendance* at the public lectures, Natural Philosophy in all its branches, Chemistry, Geology, Astronomy and Languages . . . Practical and interesting knowledge, which by expanding their minds would render them more efficient officers in the Service.'[18] Those like Ryder and the Luard Committee who called for future officers to receive a complete education before they joined the Service had similar ideas.

More influential, however, was the call for science, whose social and intellectual claims seemed to be so strong, and for specialization, evidently so essential to master the high technology of the new Navy. So, the Navy embraced a different kind of higher education in developing the specialist executive officers of the gunnery, torpedo, navigating and other branches, whose skills were based on mastery of complex technologies and advanced formulae. These skills were really needed, but the way they were chosen and nurtured had social implications. Gunnery officers were not just experts in gunnery, ballistics and related sciences; they were also the guardians of such military practices as drill and marching, hitherto scarcely known in the Navy and still, in the 1880s, regarded as strange and unseamanlike. It was they who taught the Navy to salute with a hand raised to the hat brim (formally adopted in 1890, though it was not till the 1920s that sailors were persuaded to use the same hand each time). Where Dartmouth moulded the plastic minds of the cadets by cramming them with mathematics, HMS *Excellent* did the same to adults by means of parade-ground drill. In the 1880s the establishment moved ashore from the old hulk to the reclaimed mudbank of Whale Island in Portsmouth Harbour, where there was room for the essential parade grounds. Gunnery, therefore, whether considered as the key to victory or as the royal road to promotion, was strictly identified with discipline and orthodoxy.[19] Torpedoes and electricity were even more technically advanced but had different social connotations. Where gunnery officers drilled large crews, torpedo officers were more likely to work with small teams of experts. Their reputation was as 'exceedingly, painfully and boringly scientific': original and independent, but socially inept and incapable of conversation, they were the 'computer nerds' of their day. By 1933 the First Sea Lord was fearful that they were becoming so specialized as 'to be growing less suitable relative to other branches for promotion to the higher ranks'.[20]

Most people in the Navy, and Sir John Fisher in particular, were wedded to choosing future officers young, when they were 'docile and plastic', ready to adopt the Navy as a 'vocation in life'.[21] 'Vocation' was the right word, though cadets of fourteen were too young to appreciate the almost monastic degree of dedication and self-sacrifice which the Navy expected. Officers accepted limited pay and limited education for an arduous and dangerous life. Only about one in three would reach the rank of commander, the level at which it became professionally and financially possible to marry. But at a time when the landed classes were facing financial crisis, the Navy offered status and honour to upper middle-class young men at less cost than any comparable profession. The high social status of the naval officer, the illusion of gentleman-like independence and the association with royalty, mattered a great deal to families few of whom could have aimed so high without the Navy's help. In effect naval officers were being paid partly in honour and partly in money, and many of their discontents arose from Admiralty moves which seemed to undermine the honour without adding to the money.[22]

Several factors forced change on the Admiralty. The system of generating officers established in 1857 was slow, costly and inflexible, taking at least seven years to produce a trained lieutenant, and another twelve to seventeen years for the lucky minority to make commander. This discouraged applicants and produced shortages, made worse by rapid growth as a Navy of 834 lieutenants in 1883 expanded to one with 2,227 in 1914. The result was a series of crises of supply, starting in 1890 when one hundred new lieutenants were needed, and Lord George Hamilton refused the warrant officers' petition to be allowed to fill the vacancies. Instead, he transferred one hundred lieutenants from the RNR. The 'Hungry Hundred' were followed in 1895 by the 'Famishing Fifty', and they by further drafts from the RNR in 1898 and 1913. Campaigners for the promotion of ratings or warrant officers were unhappy, but the ex-reserve lieutenants – merchant navy officers already well on in their careers – had the advantage of being too old to have any promotion prospects, and therefore damaged nobody else's.[23] Another small but influential contribution to officer entry was made by the 1903 Direct Entry scheme, which offered cadetships to candidates from the training ships *Conway* and *Worcester*, and the Nautical Training College at Pangbourne, which educated young men to be merchant navy officers. Unlike the Dartmouth cadets who were exposed to a naval ethos but did not in reality either join the Navy or see much of the sea until after they left the College, the merchant navy cadets arrived already knowing a good deal of seamanship.[24]

At the same time the situation of the naval engineers was generating other pressures. The Admiralty had long been anxious to raise both their social status and their professional standards, which it understood were bound to be linked. A committee under Astley Cooper Key which reported in 1876 put its finger on the problem:

Notwithstanding the high education to be given, and the position in which the Engineer Officers will be placed on board Ship as Commissioned Officers, a large portion of the Candidates for entry as Engineer Students are sons of artificers of various grades in the dockyards, of seamen and marines, or of others belonging to the same class of society. As it is undoubtedly desirable that Officers should be highly educated to perform the duties of Naval Engineers, and hold the rank of commissioned officers, it is equally desirable that they should be in all respects fitted to take their place with Officers of corresponding rank in wardroom or gunroom messes. This evidently cannot be the case with the majority of the Students lately entered . . . We have received evidence that the indiscriminate admission of lads from the lower ranks of society deters Officers, and other professional men from allowing their sons to compete for these appointments . . .[25]

By the 1880s there was increasing concern that neither the number nor the quality of engineer officers was adequate to the Navy's needs. Their training at the Royal Naval Engineering College at Keyham (next to Devonport Dockyard) was still based on manual workshop skills, and their professional standards appeared to be falling rather than rising. The troubled and nearly disastrous introduction of water-tube boilers in the 1890s, though partly the fault of the characteristic haste of Fisher as Controller of the Navy (1892–97), also revealed that British stokers and engineer officers could not master a technology copied from the French without much difficulty and extra training. Both socially and professionally the engineer officers were not the equals of their messmates in the wardroom. The new gunnery and torpedo officers (instituted 1876 and 1885 respectively), with their advanced scientific and mathematical training, were not impressed.[26]

The obvious remedy was to find engineer officers in the same way, selecting them from among the ablest sub-lieutenants and putting them through intense courses based on higher mathematics which would qualify them to take charge of an engine room. Under them the existing ERAs and the new warrant rank of artificer engineer would see to the practical management of the machinery. The new-style engineer officers would be specialists within the general body of military (the new term was 'executive') officers, and might expect to follow a similar career pattern to gunnery or torpedo officers, with the middle years of their careers spent in a succession of specialist positions ashore or afloat, and the ablest rising to command ships as commanders and captains. Lord Selborne was already exploring this possibility in 1901, and it was evidently one of the personnel reforms which Fisher was brought to the Admiralty to tackle.[27]

Fisher approached the Selborne Scheme with his characteristic enthusiasm, and in his hands it rapidly grew in scope and ambition. The expanded scheme was designed to meet a number of objectives, satisfying different constituencies with promises not all of which were candid, or mutually compatible. For the Admiralty Board, Fisher undertook to find a new breed of engineer from among the executive officers, solving both technical and social problems at a stroke. He also intended to produce dual-purpose or convertible officers who would at some unspecified but not distant date go to fill the shortage of lieutenants. Fisher was especially keen on this 'interchangeability' because he had convinced himself that engines – above all his then passion, 'oil' (i.e. diesel) engines, which he expected to replace steam at any moment – were becoming so reliable that engineers would very soon be redundant. 'The fact is that we are coming to chauffeurs! & any d—d fool will be good enough almost for the engine room!'[28] (He thought paymasters and Royal Marine officers were redundant already.) In the meantime, in 1903 Fisher strengthened the technical support available to engineer officers by recruiting 'Boy Artificers' as future ERAs, and creating the warrant rank of Mechanician for stokers. Perhaps for this reason he seems not to have been worried that the new scheme brought entry of future engineer officers to an almost complete halt from 1905 to 1913. However interested in engineering, young officers would not volunteer for a career whose future prospects were so obscure. 'Many of the smartest lads at Osborne have raised this point with me – "we love engineering and would rather be Engineers than anything else, but we do want to command our own ships and our own fleets." '[29] Unfortunately the technological miracle Fisher relied on never took place. Engines continued to need skilled management, and the Navy's shortage of engineers grew ever more acute. Meanwhile the new scheme attracted almost no one to the Marines, and altogether ignored paymasters, chaplains, instructors and surgeons.[30] The new Royal Naval College then building at Dartmouth to replace the insanitary old *Britannia* was too small to accommodate the new scheme, and the cadets of the first two years went to a new College installed in temporary buildings on the site of the stables of Queen Victoria's favourite residence of Osborne, in the Isle of Wight. They proved to be at least as unhealthy as the old hulks.[31]

Selborne's career specializations (with or without interchange between them) were quite different from the US Navy's new organization, sometimes said to have been Fisher's model, of generalist 'line officers' supported by expert petty and warrant officers who were excluded from commissioned rank.[32] His scheme trained all junior officers together, initially including the Royal Marines, so that all would be interchangeable, but how and at what level these interchanges might take place were not worked out, and in practice they were never made possible beyond sub-lieutenant's rank. The Selborne Scheme, as officially announced in December 1902, made a sub-lieutenant's choice of engineering 'definitive and final'. 'Every endeavour will be made to provide ... opportunities equal to those of the executive branch, including the same opportunity of rising to Flag Rank',[33] but even the Scheme's firmest supporters (who included both Battenberg and Beresford) doubted if engineers could possibly learn and practise their profession at the same time as gaining the bridge experience necessary to command ships or squadrons. In 1903 engineer officers received higher pay, automatic promotion as far as commander's rank, and new titles, so that for example Chief Engineers became Engineer Lieutenants, and Fleet Engineers, Engineer Commanders – but it did not take much cynicism to recognize these concessions as compensation for the higher ranks which were already moving out of their reach. In 1905 Selborne's successor Lord Cawdor proposed a modified scheme of non-permanent specialization, but it offered less than two years' engineering training in place of the five given to the old-style engineer officers, and it was soon clear that this would not be adequate.[34]

To Lord Selborne, Fisher offered a solution to a pressing political problem. The engineering lobby, led by the Institute of Marine Engineers, had significant support in Parliament for its arguments that naval engineers were unjustly neglected and denied the authority to which they were entitled, because of social prejudice. The language used by the IME implied, as Selborne understood, that the campaign was rather aimed at power for the Institute than justice for the engineers, who provided a convenient stalking horse. What the Admiralty had to fear was a quasi-trades union controlling a separate corps of engineer officers. For that reason, the admirals were especially allergic to engineer officers' claims to take undivided responsibility for the discipline of engine-room crews. Fisher offered emollient promises of opening opportunities to engineers, not explaining that he meant the new-style engineer-specialist executive officers whom he intended to create. The old engineer officers on whom the IME's hopes rested were going to be abolished, not promoted.[35] The IME and its supporters were easily deceived because they more than half believed their own propaganda, that engineers' social prospects were frustrated by an upper-class clique resistant to progress. In reality the naval officers were middle-class experts with a high opinion of engineering – so high that they had every intention of taking control of it themselves, raising its standards and using it to cement their authority. The executive and engineer officers, like the Admiralty and the IME, were disputing power: they all agreed on the importance of engineering as a key to it.[36]

Another objective of the Selborne Scheme was to reform the intellectual formation of future officers. The Admiralty recruited J. A. Ewing, Professor of Applied Mechanics at Cambridge, as Director of Education to preside over a grand experiment in 'modern' education – meaning one based on history, languages and natural sciences rather than the classics, similar to the 'modern sides' offered by many public schools.[37] In practice the Navy very soon suppressed Ewing's ideals. The officers of the new college at Dartmouth undermined the headmaster and revived the curriculum of the old *Britannia*, which was

> monstrously mechanical and included a great deal of practical and theoretical engineering . . . The humanities were hardly recognized. One of the results of this kind of mechanized education was to produce a brand of naval officer incapable of expressing himself either in speech or on paper and without any conception of the strategical and tactical problems of defence.[38]

This was a common theme of naval critics:

> Instead of studying engineering, mathematics, theory of gunnery and learning the work of signalmen, artificers and warrant officers, we want to study organisation, staff work, strategy and tactics. We want theory but it must be the right kind; the practice of expressing thoughts in carefully chosen words, is, for example, a necessary form of training, for the lack of it spells confusion in war. Even in peacetime, there is something pathetic in the toilful speechlessness of the Navy where much work is wasted or misdirected owing to inability to discuss or criticise it intelligibly.[39]

The cadets were intelligent, and their educational level had risen considerably in half a century, but they were still taught largely by rote, the course was still heavily overloaded with theoretical mathematics, and Fisher's hasty scheme had reduced their future careers to something approaching chaos. It increased the time taken to make a lieutenant from seven to nine years, retaining the same 'graduating' age by starting two years earlier, at twelve and a half. This pushed the total cost to parents up to at least £560 (say £700–£750 including uniforms), making entry to the Navy significantly more selective than before – which was the reverse of Fisher's intention – and excluding the social class from which engineer officers had hitherto been recruited. The scheme also took boys a year younger than before, ensuring that preparatory schools were reluctant to co-operate.[40] An Admiralty memorandum of 1906 pointed out the obvious consequences:

The officers of the Navy will be drawn exclusively from the well-to-do classes, or, as some critics will put it, from the aristocratic classes . . . Neither brains, nor character, nor manners are the exclusive endowment of those whose parents can afford to spend £1,000 on their education . . . it would be better for the efficiency of the Service that the officers of the Navy should be selected from a population of 41½ millions instead of from a population of 1½ millions . . . Whether we like it or not, this reform will *have* to come sooner or later. Personally, I believe that nothing but good would come from identifying the nation with Navy.[41]

Earlier entry, higher cost and longer training worsened the shortage of officers and disrupted nearly all aspects of officer training. The new scheme had not been running for long before it became obvious that it was not attracting either the numbers or the quality of applicants the Navy needed. Out of about 170 applicants a year in the years up to 1914, 70 cadets were being accepted, including many whom the interviewers wished to reject. Churchill wanted to lower the cost of a Dartmouth education and widen the catchment area for both naval and political reasons. 'The complaint is often made,' he reminded his Cabinet colleagues, 'that the Navy is a rich man's Navy, and that the classes from which we draw for the supply of officers to the Fleet are the prosperous middle classes . . . It is said that a Liberal Government that has been in power for nearly nine years, has done little or nothing towards assisting the children of poor parents to enter what is perhaps the finest service in the state.'[42] The Liberal ministers readily agreed, but not so readily as to spend much money, and Churchill pondered an alternative line of advance.

In the years after the South African War, while the Selborne Scheme was being worked out, changing social attitudes generated political pressure to broaden the range of candidates eligible to become naval officers. Several different campaigns pressed the Admiralty to favour different constituencies. Chief warrant officers, the highest warrant rank since 1865, took rank with but after sub-lieutenants, and from 1887 were allowed the honorary rank of lieutenant on retirement, so when lieutenants were scarce, it was easy for campaigners like Henry Capper to urge the claims of warrant officers, many of whom were visibly more experienced and competent than commissioned officers just their seniors. Against that stood the social reality that the warrant officers were likely to be at least fifteen years older and set in a different social and professional mould which it would be painful to break. For them promotion to lieutenant would involve a sacrifice of pay, and would be difficult for anyone who was already married. Moreover, it was not in the Navy's interest to turn experienced senior warrant officers, who were scarce and precious, into sub-lieutenants who were neither. Warrant officers were called officers, and to an extent employed as such, but in social terms they were treated as higher petty officers. Capper, who himself came from a middle-class family and had near relatives among the commissioned officers, records the experience of being turned away from the leading officers' naval tailor, Gieves, and excluded from social occasions to which midshipmen were invited. 'I regard you, Mr Capper,' his captain said, 'as one of my most responsible professional officers, but in social matters you must *not* consider yourself an officer.'[43] Most sensitive of all, warrant officers were trying to compete for commissions, but the monopoly of commissioned rank was a precious bulwark of the vulnerable upper middle class – feeling all the more vulnerable as social and economic pressure was added to the political pressure of the 1911 crisis. Capper was candidly warned off by the mother of a sub-lieutenant, one of his shipmates: 'I have the greatest sympathy with you personally in your desire to rise, but you have chosen the wrong service. The Navy belongs to us, and if you were to win the commissions you ask for it would be at the expense of our sons and nephews whose birthright it is.'[44] From 1903 a limited number of senior warrant officers did win commissions, but usually to fill specific positions ashore, and only at the end of their careers when they posed no threat to anyone's promotion prospects. These 'commissioned warrant officers' remained in all respects part of the body of warrant officers, which had been extended upwards (eventually as far as the rank of commander in some branches) without offering any means of transferring across to the commissioned officers' career path.[45]

Lionel Yexley's campaign for direct promotion of young ratings was an alternative and rival to Capper's. He hoped to catch promising candidates when they were younger and more flexible, better able to make the social and professional leap to commissioned rank, and with better career prospects if they succeeded. The 1910 proposal by Reginald McKenna, the then First Lord, to offer scholarships to Osborne addressed a similar objective, for the benefit of younger boys of a higher social class. This aroused predictable hostility, both among naval officers, and among those Radical critics who regarded the college as much too cheap already. Moreover, McKenna's position had already been weakened by a scandal at Osborne. Cadet George Archer-Shee, who entered the college in 1908 from a Catholic school, was presently expelled on a false charge of theft, leading to a sensational court case which showed the Admiralty in a poor light, and uncomfortably exposed the college's function of filtering out undesirables.[46] It was left to Churchill to take up Yexley's plan in the form of the 1913 'Mate Scheme', which was backed by both sides in the

House of Commons, but opposed and partly sabotaged by the Admiralty Board under Battenberg. The distinctive rank of 'Mate' singled out the ex-lower deck officers, candidates effectively had to be single and teetotal, and their promotion came too late for them to blend in with the sub-lieutenants. Nevertheless, wartime demand for junior officers allowed 371 seamen, 161 ERAs and 12 Marines to reach commissioned rank by this route by 1918.[47]

All new routes of advancement changed the structure of the Navy and opened new social opportunities for its personnel. The same was true of the naval reserves, which were developing at the same time and in related ways; Selborne as First Lord took a particular interest in them. In 1901 the position of ratings who had served their time for pension was formalized by the creation of a Royal Fleet Reserve of former ratings discharged within the previous seven years. Two years later the Admiralty responded to the initiative of civilians who wanted a volunteer naval reserve, not confined to professional seamen like the RNR. The members of the Royal Naval Volunteer Reserve, established in 1903, undertook regular naval training and in the event of emergency committed themselves to serve under naval discipline, anywhere in the world. The Marquis of Montrose was prominent among its founders, and a quarter of the RNVR's strength was in Scotland. The RN regarded it with some disdain and could not think of anything that non-seamen amateurs could usefully do, but those who met the new reservists in person were impressed by their intelligence and keenness. 'My opinion of them,' wrote the captain of the cruiser *Bacchante* in 1905, 'is that they are more desirable for us in a war than the R.N.R.; they are more intelligent, and you can teach them more in a week than you can the R.N.R. in a month . . . [but] they take themselves seriously, and must be taken seriously or the whole scheme will collapse.'[48] Their obligation was to undertake forty 'drills' (evening or weekend training sessions) a year, but in the early years the average was 90–100 each. There was a common misapprehension, in the Navy and elsewhere, that the RNVR recruited from yachtsmen. In fact, yachtsmen had other things to do with their weekends, and the RNVR officers were mostly middle-class professionals not sufficiently well-off to keep a yacht.[49] Another significant addition to the naval reserves was the RNR Trawler Section, established in 1910 at Beresford's suggestion to enlist fishing vessels and their crews together, initially for minesweeping but in the event also for anti-submarine patrol.[50]

The arrival of Churchill in 1912, with an established record as a social reformer and a strong political mandate to force change on a reluctant Admiralty, made it possible to tackle some of the chaos left by the Selborne Scheme. Like his predecessors, Churchill hoped to reduce the social and financial barriers to becoming a naval officer, and he was more aware than they had been that the existing entry fell well short of the Navy's needs in both quantity and quality. 'I was unfavourably impressed with the last batches of cadets I saw . . ' he remarked soon after his arrival; 'they looked a most undistinguished and mediocre lot'.[51] Moreover he was sceptical of the intellectual value of the education they were about to receive. 'I cannot feel convinced that the Osborne and Dartmouth courses . . . constitute an educational system which is as trustworthy or as solid as the long 4 years' course given to maturer minds at Annapolis University, or the rigorous professional instruction imparted to the already highly educated German cadets of 17 or 18.'[52]

Churchill's most radical move was to copy from the new Royal Marine officer scheme the 'special entry' of future officers at seventeen or eighteen by means of a public examination, run by the Civil Service Commission rather than the Admiralty, and in principle open to boys from any sort of school (though no poor family could have afforded to keep a son in school for three years beyond the school-leaving age of fourteen). There were still social qualifications to be passed: like the twelve-year-old cadets they had to be white British subjects, and had to pass an Admiralty Interview Board of senior officers who were attentive to their gentlemanlike behaviour, but the new scheme clearly weakened the social defences of commissioned rank. Though the special entry was colloquially called the 'public school entry', in practice only a small proportion came from the great public schools. The majority had been educated by minor public schools (cheaper than Dartmouth), and from the first entry in 1913 a significant minority came from grammar and state secondary schools for which their parents had paid low fees or none at all. Perhaps it was only the very acute shortage of junior officers which quelled the admirals' resistance to a scheme which for all its distasteful social features, at least offered to train lieutenants in five years instead of nine.[53]

The principles on which the special entry was based directly contradicted much of what Dartmouth and the Selborne Scheme professed to stand for. Instead of catching the boys young when their minds were plastic and moulding them to the Service, the special entry halved the cost and time of training by choosing able young men from a relatively wide social range who had been brought up outside the Navy. It was too late for the favoured naval technique of cramming with pure mathematics: they had been educated already. The Interview Board was not only a social filter: from the beginning it was looking for character and powers of leadership in young men old enough to have developed them. Instead of selecting small boys from the right families in the confidence that they must grow up to become good officers, it looked for young men who already displayed at least some of the qualities the Navy needed. The first 'special entry' was in 1913, and the new scheme was not making a significant contribution to the Navy until after the First World War, but in a long perspective it pointed the way to the future. In 1924 it was effectively merged with the existing Direct Entry scheme from the merchant navy colleges.[54]

To evaluate the Royal Navy's efforts to reform the selection and professional training of naval officers it is helpful to compare with the efforts of other navies. It is also helpful to distinguish (more clearly than contemporaries did) between strictly professional judgements and political or emotional factors. In Germany in the early 1890s Alfred Tirpitz was developing a practical, empirical approach to naval tactics developed from Prussian military traditions and connected in many respects with the thinking of contemporary strategists like the American Mahan, the British Colomb or the French Aube. At the same time, however, Mahan was teaching his readers, both German and American, to treat the navy as the essential leader of peacetime economic and colonial expansion. On both sides of the Atlantic a frankly political layer had been added to naval strategy, supported by emotion more than reason. The political Tirpitz set aside his own rational strategic arguments to follow the ideological Mahan, and to adopt the emotional language calculated to excite Wilhelm II. The result was 'the gradual displacement of naval strategy by the ideology of sea power'.[55] Realistic enemies such as France and Russia were abandoned in favour of Mahan's navalist propaganda for a world-class fleet. When Tirpitz became State Secretary (*Staatssekretär*) of the *Reichsmarineamt* in the summer of 1897 he exchanged a rational power strategy for an emotional engagement with *Seegeltung* (naval status or reputation); commanding respect rather than commanding the sea. Instead of considering how much Germany needed the support of a neutral Britain, he forced her to become a reluctant enemy.[56] He refused to offer a reasoned argument why Germany had to fight Britain: 'We have to concentrate our united strength on building a fleet against England, because that alone can give us naval power. In other words, the battle has to be fought and won before we can consider how to exploit it.'[57] In the words of Michael Stürmer, 'Tirpitz was like King Croesus of Lydia, who was warned by the Delphic Oracle that if he crossed the River Halys a great empire would fall. Tirpitz tried it, and it turned out to be the German Reich which was doomed.'[58]

———◦◦◦———

THIRTEEN

Man-Eating Vessels

Ships and Weapons 1890–1914

The quarter-century which elapsed from the Naval Defence Act to the outbreak of the First World War was marked by a rapid and intense development of warships and their weapons. The naval arms race which opposed Britain to France and Russia, then later to Germany, was a competition of both number and quality. The number of ships was relatively easy for contemporaries to reckon; their qualities were harder to estimate without the test of battle. The effective service life of a modern warship during this period was somewhere between twenty and thirty years, so that ships which were still in good material condition and apparently fit for years of further service, might in fact be dangerously obsolete in the face of the latest weapons. The factors which made ships and weapons effective were becoming less visible, and less intelligible to the inexpert judge. A generation before, warships could be classified by eye with fair accuracy by the number and size of their guns: as gun ranges increased in the early years of the new century, more and more depended on the advanced and secret instruments of fire control, and the most powerful ships were in many cases those with the fewest guns visible. Longer-range weapons, faster ships and bigger squadrons changed the dynamics of tactics, forcing admirals to take decisions more quickly, and demanding swifter and clearer signals. More and more the human eye, human judgement and human reactions needed to be aided if not replaced by instruments and machinery.[1]

It is in this period that for the first time one can clearly discern the influence on naval warfare of the 'equipment cycle', which became a ubiquitous factor in all forms of twentieth-century warfare. A warship or weapon system would typically take ten or fifteen years to conceive, design, build and put into service. It might remain in service for anything up to half a century. Its whole service life described a curve of effectiveness, reaching its peak sometime after first entering service when the initial problems had been solved and the best way to use the weapon had been worked out, then gradually declining over long years of active service with successive additions and modifications delaying the inevitable process of obsolescence. Some particularly successful and versatile designs enjoyed second or even third careers in roles which had not originally been foreseen. The equipment cycle had enormous strategic implications. In an ideal world a navy, or any armed force, would go to war at the best possible point of the equipment cycle, with every weapon nearly new and at maximum efficiency. In reality this was never possible, for nobody could predict when the next war would start, and no country had the financial and industrial resources to renew all its weapon systems at once. In 1914, when all the major belligerents had been engaged for years in a prolonged naval arms race, their fleets were as near as physically possible composed of homogeneous squadrons of modern warships, but there was still a gradient everywhere from modern to obsolete designs. Moreover, the very rapid development of new weapons and the scarcity of recent war experience had left everybody unsure of how the next war would be fought, with plenty of room for unpleasant shocks when it actually began.

During the great 'naval race' of 1890 to 1914 all the participants built ships in homogeneous classes, and as fast as they could. Around 1900 the best ship-yards in Britain and Germany could build a battleship in about three years; French yards needed about three and a half years, American yards rather more, and the worst, in Russia, took about five years. Warships were the most complex, difficult and profitable ships to build, and the flood of new orders following the Naval Defence Act stimulated heavy investment in British ship-yards and ancillary industries such as engine-building, heavy guns and armour plate.[2] The Admiralty's usual practice was to order the first ship of a class from one of the royal dockyards, where the work could be carefully costed and initial problems dealt with by the Admiralty's own constructors, who retained the intellectual leadership of the building process. Other orders then went to private British yards entered on the 'Admiralty List' as technically and financially qualified to build to the Navy's standards. This in turn put them in a strong position to bid for foreign orders. To be struck off the Admiralty List, as Cammell Laird was in 1906 for falsifying test results, was a very serious matter: the entire board and much of the senior management were replaced, and the firm paid no dividend for four years. Practically the whole world was anxious to have the best modern warships, but only a few countries had the industrial capacity to build them, and none could compete with British yards on quality or price. Between 1860 and 1904 fifty-three battleships were built in

British dockyards and thirty-three in private yards for the Royal Navy, plus a further twenty-three ordered for foreign buyers. Between 1906 and 1914 thirteen more battleships were ordered for foreign navies, all but four of them from either Armstrong on the Tyne or Vickers at Barrow-in-Furness. By 1904 the rapid increase in battleship size had outclassed all the royal dockyards except Portsmouth and Devonport, though Pembroke was still producing cruisers, and Chatham came to specialize in submarines which could be built in shelter and secrecy on the old covered slips. The Admiralty kept a tight control on costs and battleship-building was only modestly profitable, but the returns on armour and ordnance, which the Admiralty could not manufacture for itself, were much higher. This encouraged mergers: Armstrong bought Whitworth in 1897, the Glasgow steel firm of John Brown bought a shipyard downriver at Clydebank in 1899, and in 1903 the Sheffield steel firm of Charles Cammell merged with Lairds' shipyard on the Mersey. Completely new battleship-building yards were constructed by Cammell Laird nearby at Tranmere, William Beardmore at Dalmuir on the Clyde, and Armstrong at High Walker on the Tyne.[3]

In place of the erratic process from which British warship designs of the 1870s and 1880s had emerged, the passing of the Naval Defence Act, the return of Sir William White as Director of Naval Construction and the adoption of Lord George Hamilton's committee process of establishing requirements marked the start of a fifteen-year period of stability and steady progress in naval architecture. Its first fruits were the seven battleships of the *Royal Sovereign* Class, laid down from 1889 to 1891. They were armed with four heavy (13.5-inch) breech-loading guns in two twin barbette mountings, one at each end of the central superstructure, plus ten of the new 6-inch 'quick-firing' guns. With one more deck than the previous class, the battleships had eighteen feet of freeboard fore and aft and were much better seaboats. Their triple-expansion engines gave them a maximum speed (with forced draught) of 16½ knots. Handsome, comfortable ships, visibly superior to their foreign contemporaries, they established the type of what much later came to be called the 'pre-Dreadnought' battleship, which was steadily improved without fundamental change through successive classes down to the *King Edward VII* Class laid down in 1902–04.[4] These designs were shaped by contemporary guns and gunnery, and especially by the development in the late 1880s of 'quick-firing' guns with 'fixed ammunition' (meaning that the shell was fixed to a brass case containing the propellant, like a large rifle cartridge which could be loaded as a unit). Up to a maximum of 6-inch, fixed ammunition could be loaded by hand; a single movement of a lever closed the breech for firing, and another opened it and ejected the spent shell case. Combined with the new pedestal mounting which pivoted the gun about its point of balance and allowed one or two men to lay and train it, this raised the possible rate of fire fivefold in five years. The new 4.7-inch QF gun of 1887 could fire fifteen aimed rounds a minute, almost ten times faster than the existing 5-inch gun. Within ten years 6-inch QF guns with trained crews could achieve 75 per cent hits from a ship under way at ranges of 1,600 to 2,200 yards, and the 'smokeless' powder of the mid-1890s made it possible to keep up such rates of fire without blinding the guns' crews with smoke.[5] Each QF gun was laid individually by its own gunlayer, and competitive prize firings (up till 1904 conducted at a stationary target at a range of 1,400 to 1,600 yards) made heroes of the best gunlayers and the best-shooting ships. In the late 1890s Captain Percy Scott developed simple but effective equipment for training gunlayers in continuous aim which rapidly improved the general standard of shooting. These methods only worked, however, with guns light enough to be worked by hand, within the range of a telescopic sight (about 2,000 yards). In 1899 the Navy adopted Barr and Stroud's 4½-foot range-finder, which would take ranges up to 4,000 yards, then just beyond torpedo range.[6]

The battleships' heavy guns (12-inch from the *Majestic* Class of 1893–4) scarcely outranged the light QF guns, and it seemed that every part of a battleship's upperworks not protected by armour was liable to be rapidly destroyed by a hail of light shells filled with the powerful new high explosives. The QF gun therefore provided a strong incentive to increase the range and rate of fire of heavy guns. The *Majestic* Class had eight rounds of 'ready-use' shell by the guns, but thereafter had to return the guns to the centre-line to load more. Not until the *Formidable* and *Implacable*, completed in 1901, was the hydraulic machinery of the mountings sufficiently refined to load the heavy guns at any angle of train or elevation, allowing the gun one aimed round a minute, and the ship one two-gun salvo every 30 seconds. This was just fast enough in principle to keep the guns roughly on their target and to correct the aim of the next salvo by the results of the last, but the instruments to do so did not yet exist. The simplest firing solutions assumed a column of enemy ships on the beam steering a roughly parallel course, so that a single line ahead was the only safe and easily handled formation. In this case the major component of ship movement affecting gunnery was usually roll, and there were two ways to deal with it. The earlier, and simpler, was to train the guns for line, set a suitable elevation and allow the ship to roll the sights on, using some instrument to fire at the correct moment, which occurred twice in each roll cycle, or about once a minute in an average sea. A later and better solution was to keep the guns permanently laid on the target as the ship rolled beneath them ('continuous aim'), but this required sophisticated stabilization and precise hydraulic control. By 1909 the 12-inch main armament of the newer battleships had an elevating speed of 3° a second, and the new 13.5-inch guns could manage 5° a second, sufficient for continuous aim in a moderate sea. By 1912 good gunlayers could hunt a 16°–18° roll, out to out, enough for accurate shooting in quite a heavy sea.[7]

Meanwhile the range of the torpedo was increasing faster than the range of the gun. By the mid-1890s the British 18-inch torpedo could run 800 yards at almost 30 knots, and the addition of the Obry gyroscope in 1896 doubled its accurate range. By 1910 the 21-inch torpedo could reach 6,000 yards, the typical limit of North Sea visibility. Before the First World War 'wet heater' torpedoes, which supplemented the energy of compressed air with a fuel-air burner (the 'heater') and water injection, could achieve either 45 knots or 10,000 yards' range; contemporary aircraft could scarcely fly faster or further. A major reason to adopt the 'Grand Fleet' concept with destroyers accompanying the battleships was the likelihood of torpedo attack beyond battleship gunnery range. Assuming that the only feasible formation to deploy the gunfire of a large number of battleships was a long single line in close order engaging an enemy on the beam, then the torpedo target was in effect a single line many miles long, of which about one-third was ship and the rest gaps: an unmissable target for a 'browning shot' (i.e. not aimed at an individual target) even five miles away. It was widely assumed that a single torpedo hit might be fatal to a battleship, and a mass torpedo attack could scarcely fail to get at least one-third hits. There seemed to be a dangerous vulnerability here, and it was easy to assume that the enemy would exploit it (although in reality the German Navy disapproved of wasting expensive torpedoes on 'browning shots' and insisted on aimed fire at good targets). But the growing torpedo threat made it urgently necessary to develop means of accurate gunnery which could keep an enemy outside torpedo as well as QF gun range. Another highly desirable capability was 'helm-free gunnery'; means of keeping the guns continuously trained on the target while the ship manoeuvred to avoid incoming torpedoes.[8]

It soon became clear that accurate long-range gunnery would be very difficult if each gun, or each pair of guns, was aimed separately. What was needed was to link all the heavy guns of a ship so that their fire could be concentrated on a single target by a single gunlayer with sights carried as high as possible, to provide a long range of vision clear of smoke and spray. Percy Scott was the first British officer to understand the necessity for such 'directors' (though the

Russians had had them since the 1880s), which in practice meant not single gunlayers but teams manning a number of instruments. To co-ordinate different gun mountings so that they could be controlled as one forced both hydraulic and electronic technology to new limits. The first director trials in 1910 were not a success, and the system was not officially adopted until 1913, when it could be combined with continuous aim to allow the higher rate of fire of 'rapid independent' shooting, each gun firing as fast as possible as soon as the target was found, instead of having to wait until the sights rolled on to fire a full broadside or a salvo (a half-broadside), then observing the fall of shot and correcting the aim before firing again. Although it took a long time to perfect director firing, it was clear early in the process that it offered the best hope of fast accurate shooting at long range. The necessity of long-range gunnery to keep out of reach of torpedoes pointed to a major redesign of battleships, because it was impossible to control guns of different calibre with a single director, but the later 'pre-Dreadnought' British battleships of the *King Edward VII* and *Lord Nelson* Classes (laid down 1902–05) had a mixed heavy armament of 12-inch and 9.2-inch guns.[9]

Similar considerations applied to cruisers. Sir William White as Director of Naval Construction from 1885 to 1901 was strongly identified with the protected cruiser, of which he built more than a hundred, and the 6-inch quick-firing gun, with which most of them were armed. Only in the smallest and largest sizes did he vary the formula. The huge *Powerful* and *Terrible*, laid down in 1894 to match the big Russian cruisers *Rurik* and *Rossiya*, carried two 9.2-inch guns, with a speed of 22 knots and enough coal for a range of 7,000 miles at 14 knots. Such ships could pursue their quarry across the world, exploiting the information delivered by the cable network. No other navy could match them, if only because in 1895 none outside Europe had a 500-foot dry dock, but their water-tube boilers gave much trouble, and they were so costly in money and manpower that they were never repeated. However, the introduction of Harvey face-hardened armour in the early 1890s, followed by the Krupp Cemented process in 1896, made it possible to cover the large exposed sides of the big cruisers with light armour capable of keeping out 6-inch shells, nullifying the threat of the quick-firer. From the turn of the century, therefore, the Royal Navy began building armoured cruisers again. Twenty-six were laid down between 1898 and 1902, mostly armed with two or four heavy guns plus numerous 6-inch quick-firers; nine more with 7.5-inch or 9.2-inch guns followed in 1903–05. These were the 'man-eating vessels', larger than a battleship and almost as costly, of which Sir Frederick Richards complained.[10] In design and armament they resembled fast light battleships, and it was generally believed that they could fight as battleships in favourable circumstances. In the Russo-Japanese War the Japanese started with six battleships (of which two were lost early to Russian mines) and six armoured cruisers, and at Tsushima in May 1905 the cruisers fought in the line of battle with great credit.[11]

The British expected large protected or armoured cruisers to be deployed to attack their foreign trade, and it was widely assumed that fast merchant ships could readily be armed to attack or defend trade. British and foreign governments paid subsidies to fast liners partly manned by naval reservists and fitted to mount guns. The first generation of British armoured cruisers were intended in part to counter the threat of such 'armed merchant cruisers'. In practice, however, during the Russo-Japanese War and again the First World War, armed liners proved to be a very expensive and rather vulnerable way to carry guns into action. Most of them were more useful as armed or unarmed transports, troopships, and other naval auxiliaries.[12]

It has been explained that two simultaneous naval races, in battleships and armoured cruisers, led to the financial and political crisis which helped Sir John Fisher to become First Sea Lord in 1904. To secure his position he had to reduce naval spending, and he was already thinking of economizing by moving towards a fast battleship type which would combine the functions of battleship and armoured cruiser. He wanted sustained high speed as an instrument of strategic as well as tactical flexibility, and he was happy with the idea of moving these fast capital ships around the world under wireless control to counter enemy cruisers, rather than keep them concentrated in home waters attracting torpedo attack. He favoured heavy guns for long-range shooting but seems to have had almost no understanding of the problems of fire-control. Like all Fisher's projects, this started as a series of pithy slogans and moved only part of the way towards a developed strategic plan.[13]

In January and February 1905 the Admiralty's 'Design Committee' met to consider the Navy's next generation of big ships. This was before Tsushima, but they had available reports of the first action of the Russo-Japanese War, fought on 10 August 1904 at the astonishingly long range of over 12,000 yards. Although the committee is often treated simply as a vehicle for Fisher's ideas, much of its thinking pre-dated his arrival, and Selborne insisted that it consult widely and follow the direction of the Admiralty Board. Its conclusion that a homogeneous battery of heavy guns was essential for long-range shooting followed clearly from recent experience. It was equally clear that demanding sustained high speed from triple-expansion engines was asking for trouble. By way of proof, in November 1905 Rear-Admiral Battenberg took a squadron of six armoured cruisers across the Atlantic from New York to Gibraltar at a mean speed of 18½ knots. Only three of them arrived, and they all needed major repairs afterwards.[14] Nevertheless the decision to adopt Charles Parsons' turbine engines was a brave one. Sir William White and Sir John Durston, the Engineer-in-Chief of the Navy, had inspected Parsons' small 'demonstrator' vessel the *Turbinia* in 1896, and the following year she was allowed to show off her astonishing speed of 34½ knots at the Jubilee Review at Spithead, but the turbine's subsequent development was troubled; several of the early turbine destroyers were shaken to pieces and sunk by vibration, and the biggest successful turbine-powered ship in 1905 was a small passenger steamer. The bold decision to adopt the turbine nevertheless was an outstanding success, saving about a thousand tons and providing a capacity for sustained high-speed steaming which had never been seen before in any large warship. The new battleship could comfortably sustain her full speed of 21 knots for as long as the stokers could, and on her trials early in 1907 she steamed to the West Indies and back at an average speed of 17 knots with no trouble at all.[15] For a midshipman who moved in November 1914 from a 23-year-old protected cruiser to a new battle-cruiser, the transition was a revelation: 'instead of the bump and thump and noise of the *Sappho*'s reciprocating engines, the *New Zealand* seemed to glide through the waters, and at ordinary manoeuvring speeds between decks it was impossible to determine that the ship was actually under way'.[16]

In early 1905 the Design Committee was taking technical decisions without knowing whether they would apply to battleships, or armoured cruisers, or both. This was not the only 'loose end' in the design process. A heavy battery of heavy guns left little or no possibility of mounting the usual quick-firers, but the immature technology of fire control was not ready to support an 'all big-gun' armament. The turbine engine had not yet proved itself, and if it did prove capable of sustained high speed the coal-fired boilers and stokers would be called upon to produce a volume of steam which was likely to be beyond their capacity. Oil firing, still ten years ahead, was what the new design really needed. Fisher forced through an untidy assortment of new technologies with his customary haste, when there were, and are, reasons to think that it would have been wiser to advance more deliberately and prove each innovation in turn before combining them. The need for haste sprang, not from strategic or technical pressure, but from the government's and Fisher's need to save money while ostentatiously protecting naval supremacy – meaning that politics and public relations played a large part in the decision. Armoured cruisers were more urgently needed than battleships; Fisher believed in their ability to take the place of battleships, and would have been happy to order four of them, but others in the Admiralty, starting with Selborne, were not convinced. 'I always said that the battleship held the field, that the battleship counted for more than anything else, and that no number of cruisers could be substitutes for them.'[17] For many officers the point of the big cruisers was not to fight battleships but to hunt down fast raiding cruisers. The final decision was for three cruisers and a single battleship, to be built first as the trials ship of the programme. With his customary genius for politics and publicity Fisher made a brilliant show of building her. The *Dreadnought*, as she was named, was built at Portsmouth Dockyard, ostensibly in a year and a day, but actually in about eighteen months or half the usual time, a feat achieved by extensive prefabrication, the use of electric lighting to allow long working hours, and a massive concentration of labour which brought much of the rest of the dockyard to a standstill.[18]

The *Dreadnought* made so powerful a public impact that she was very soon seen to have established a completely new class of battleship, and fleets were rapidly divided into 'Dreadnoughts' and (now obsolescent) 'Pre-Dreadnoughts'. Her appearance threw the building policies of other navies into confusion, and brought the German programme to a complete halt. Tirpitz assumed that had been the intention, though there is no evidence that Fisher had even noticed the opportunity. Tirpitz's whole strategy for handling the Reichstag depended on a promise of fixed building costs which left no room for technological surprises, but he was now obliged to adopt a battleship design costing 46 per cent more than the previous class, besides replacing the 28cm (11-inch) heavy gun which had only just been adopted, lengthening building slips in the shipyards, and completely reconstructing the Kaiser Wilhelm Canal. At first there was no question of German industry being able to build turbines, and the new *Nassau* Class battleships were two knots slower than the *Dreadnought*.[19]

The Admiralty Board's decision to build three armoured cruisers and one battleship of the new type had the effect of prolonging the separate development of battleships and armoured cruisers instead of the 'fusion' type of fast battleship, 'armoured vessel' or 'capital ship' (all terms used by the Admiralty around 1905) which Fisher briefly advocated, Lord Cawdor proposed to adopt in 1905, and the light of hindsight suggests was the most fruitful line of development. As a result of this decision and the events of the First World War, much of the history of large warships in the era of the two World Wars has come to be written in terms of a binary contrast between battleships and 'battle-cruisers' (to use the later term), which is substantially misleading. It would be more realistic to think of battleships or 'large armoured ships' as contemporaries did, as a single type with heavier and slower or faster and lighter variants, with naval opinion fluctuating between them, but Fisher always favouring speed over armour.[20]

Part of his reasoning was that around 1905 it seemed that the new 'capped' armour-piercing shells could penetrate all known armour at the expected fighting ranges of 4,000–6,000 yards, though as ranges increased later the value of heavy armour was restored. Almost all contemporaries assumed that shell damage would be cumulative; the torpedo was the only weapon with the power to sink a big ship suddenly, and the armoured cruisers' speed was a good defence against it. The experience of the Russo-Japanese War was that cordite, the standard British 'smokeless' propellant adopted in 1901, might burn but would not explode, while unfused shells would require a direct hit to detonate them. For all these reasons the three 'Dreadnought' armoured cruisers of the *Invincible* Class, laid down in 1906, were perceived as impressively powerful, carrying eight 12-inch guns (double the long-range armament of most battleships), and capable of crossing the Atlantic non-stop at 25½ knots. The Germans were especially impressed, as they had just committed themselves to an inferior armoured cruiser design (the future *Blücher*) and did not discover the details of the new British ships until it was too late to change. The only cogent criticism seemed to be that pursuing commerce raiders or scouting ahead of the battle fleet did not call for the expense of 12-inch guns, for which reason the 1908–09 building programme originally included two armoured cruisers armed only with 9.2-inch guns. Then it was reported that the Germans had adopted battleship-calibre guns for their big cruisers, so the British reverted to 12-inch.[21]

An important step up in fighting power came with the four battleships of the *Orion* Class, laid down in 1910 with 13.5-inch guns. The heavier shell combined greater destructive power with better ballistic performance and accuracy at long ranges, while with 20° elevation (5° more than previous classes) the guns could easily range to 24,000 yards, or twelve miles. The *Lion* of the same programme was the first to drop the designation 'armoured cruiser' in favour of the new phrase 'battle-cruiser', which was then retrospectively applied to the older Dreadnought armoured cruisers. This marks the continued influence of the now-retired Fisher on the new First Lord Winston Churchill, pushing towards the concept of the fast battleship whose principal function was to act as a fast wing of the battle fleet – though even the new *Lion* was still very lightly armoured to fight battleships, and the earlier ships were yet weaker. At the same time the pressure to gather naval strength in the North Sea to face the growing German 'High Seas Fleet' led to a process of concentrating many, and eventually all, of the 'battle-cruisers' in home waters, effectively abandoning the functions of protecting trade and commanding distant seas which had dominated the original armoured-cruiser concept. Now they were treated as the most powerful cruisers of the fleet scouting force. Even the *Australia*, ordered by the newly united Australian Commonwealth in 1910 as the flagship of the new Royal Australian Navy, was eventually to spend most of the First World War with the Grand Fleet.[22]

The rise of the torpedo naturally meant the rise of the torpedo boat. The British had been interested since the days of the *Jeune École*, and the French 'torpilleurs de haute mer' of 1888 inspired first the torpedo gunboats of 1888–93, then the faster 'torpedo-boat destroyers' from 1893. The 'T.B.D.' was simply an enlarged torpedo boat with two 18-inch torpedo tubes and some small guns: thirty-six '27-knotters' were built to variant designs by specialist builders from 1895 onwards, followed from 1896 by sixty '30-knotters'. Contemporaries were staggered by these speeds, and those who had experienced them vied with one another in hyperbole:

> It was like a nightmare. The vibration shook not only your body but your intestines and finally seemed to settle on your heart. The breeze along the deck made it difficult to walk . . . All we could do was get under the lee of the conning-tower and hang on while the devil's darning-needle tore up and down the coast . . . The wake ran out behind us like white hot iron; the engine-room was one lather of oil and water; the engines were running 400 to the minute; the gauges, the main steam pipes and everything that wasn't actually built in to her were quivering and jumping; there was half an inch of oil and water on the floors and you couldn't see the cranks in the crankpit.[23]

In practice such speeds were largely hyperbole, obtainable only for short periods in a flat calm. The boats did not have enough stokers to keep up full steam for long, and at piston speeds of up to 1,300 feet per minute their light-weight hulls and engines were shaken to pieces by vibration. A report of 1900 credits the '27-knotters' with a service speed of 19–22 knots in calm water, and the '30-knotters' with 26–27 knots. In seven-foot waves (say Force 5 on the Beaufort Scale; ordinary Channel weather) 8–10 knots was a prudent speed, and the old torpedo gunboats were superior.[24] The first turbine destroyers at the turn of the century escaped most of the vibration problem, but they were no faster in a seaway, and the turbines revolved much too fast for the screws, which suffered severe cavitation. In 1901 it was reported:

A destroyer could not steam more than 50 miles at more than 10 or 12 knots with a fairly heavy sea right ahead and expect to be fit for service at the end of it . . . On 10th and 11th October 1901, *Crane* was the sole survivor of eight TBDs after steaming 10 knots for 200 miles against a moderately heavy sea, and she had to seek shelter for repairs to damage caused by trying to increase to 15 kts with the sea right ahead.[25]

The solution was found with the River Class destroyers of 1902–04 which had a raised forecastle in imitation of the large torpedo boats of the German *S-90* Class (equivalent to British destroyers, though the German Navy had not yet adopted the term). Their full speed was only 25½ knots, but they could maintain something like that in a seaway, and with a small bridge and charthouse were much better fitted for sea passages than the 30-knotters. This basic 'raised forecastle' destroyer design remained the Admiralty's favourite for almost half a century.[26]

This did not mean that everyone agreed on the function of a destroyer. Defensive or offensive, armed primarily with the gun or the torpedo, accompanying the battle fleet or cruising independently, all remained disputed questions. Wherever they were, the advent of wireless made it essential that flotillas should be within signalling range of the Admiralty and the admirals, meaning that a 'Captain D' had to command his flotilla from a ship big enough to carry a small staff, fast enough to keep up with destroyers, with tall masts to support the aerials and sufficient electric power for a wireless range of several hundred miles. This requirement led to a range of small fast cruisers, variously called 'scouts' and 'light cruisers', some meant to lead destroyer flotillas, some to defend against them, and some to scout for the battle fleet.[27]

Destroyers and torpedo craft were the test-bed of the water-tube boilers which the Royal Navy adopted with such difficulty at the end of the 1890s. Unlike the 'fire-tubes' of older patterns of naval boiler, the water-tube boiler led water through many small-bore steel tubes (the bicycle industry's particular contribution to the Dreadnought age) fitted in the furnace, which 'flashed up' steam very fast, in a compact space, but needed careful management to avoid explosions.[28] The necessity of raising a lot of steam fast, in a cramped hull with insufficient stokers, meant that destroyer designers were the first to confront the uncomfortable qualities of coal. Welsh steam coal was the finest in the world and represented an enormous advantage for British warships and merchantmen everywhere. When she first arrived in the Pacific the *Australia* lost five knots of speed by burning New South Wales coal, before adopting Westport coal from New Zealand, which was almost as good as Welsh. Other navies envied and used Welsh coal, and envied even more the British commercial network of coal merchants and colliers which distributed it around the world. Navies without access to British coal, such as the Russian expedition going out to the Far East in 1905, or the US 'Great White Fleet' on its voyage round the world between 1907 and 1909, found their movements severely hampered. German warships ran their trials with what was euphemistically called 'torpedo-boat coal', and never attained their designed speeds in wartime without it. According to the German official history, 'only the utmost exertions of the stokehold personnel' made it possible for the battle-cruisers to maintain 22 knots in 1915, though they were designed for 27 to 30 knots.[29] The Austro-Hungarian Navy fought the entire First World War on a stock of Welsh coal which had not quite run out in 1918. But against all this had to be set the inescapable disadvantages of coal, which were worst of all in small ships. In wartime, ships had to be coaled every few days; an immensely laborious and dangerous process taking much of a day, coating the whole ship, crew and delicate equipment in filthy abrasive dust. When US officers came aboard the ships of the Grand Fleet in 1917, they were appalled by their condition: 'very dirty; coal dust ground in and salt water everywhere. Rust all over; mess-decks kept as well as possible and fairly clean . . . under conditions of practically continuous coaling and going to sea in bad weather with no chance to clean up.'[30] Between 1910 and 1912 sixteen men were killed and twenty-three badly injured while coaling British ships. In social terms coaling was a leveller and a unifier, 'the only time that everybody could swear at each other',[31] with virtually all ranks and ratings labouring together in old clothes or fancy dress. Fast coaling was a reliable indicator of high morale, but it was an immense tax on fighting efficiency. Turbine engines, with their capacity for sustained high speed, brutally exposed the impossibility of most coal-burning warships carrying enough stokers to attain it.[32]

The alternative was oil, and as early as 1902 the Admiralty Fuel Experimental Station at Haslar was set up to develop equipment for oil-fired boilers. Although twice as expensive, oil had 40 per cent greater calorific value than coal and stowed to 95 per cent of bunker capacity. All sorts of awkward spaces could stow oil but not coal. Corrosion, maintenance and trimming all became much easier. The saving in stokers went a good way to solving the manning and accommodation crises. The coal-fired *Beagle* Class destroyers of 1909–10 and the oil-fired *Acorn* Class of the following year were designed for the same speed and endurance: the *Acorns* displaced 20 per cent less than the *Beagles*, cost 16 per cent less, needed 72 officers and men instead of 96, carried a heavier armament and were 1½ knots faster. Without the need for coaling they could be available for at least 20 per cent more days, they could raise steam faster, they made much less smoke, and their speed was no longer limited by human endurance. In five years, oil firing doubled the power-to-machinery weight ratio of British destroyers. The contrast was just as glaring in big ships. The coal-fired battle-cruiser *Lion* needed 608 men in engine and boiler rooms to develop 70,000 SHP: eight years later the oil-fired *Hood* produced more than twice the horsepower with barely half the men. The real and serious strategic dangers of depending on a fuel imported from a distant and unstable part of the world (the Persian Gulf) could not stand in the way of such advantages.[33]

Of all the new warships of this period, perhaps the most radical was the submarine. 'New' was not literally true; inventors had been experimenting with submarines since the eighteenth century, and the French Navy had been attracted by the idea since the mid-nineteenth, but the first design effective enough to interest the Royal Navy was produced by the Irish-American inventor John Holland. Five of this design were ordered in 1900. The submarine was allegedly damned as 'a low class of weapon, underhand, unfair and damned un-English', according to Captain Reginald Bacon, the first Inspecting Captain of Submarines, but it is not clear who if anyone actually used those words, and the British showed absolutely no reluctance to adopt the new type themselves, though willing enough to discourage others.[34] From the Holland boats were developed a series of classes leading up to the fifty-six boats of the E Class of 1912–16 which were the first really effective British cruising submarines. At a cost of over £100,000 each (more than a destroyer), they carried four or five 18-inch torpedo tubes with reloads (plus a deck gun for some of the class), with a speed of 15 knots surfaced on diesel engines, or 9 knots on electric motors submerged. Their surface range of 3,000 miles at 10 knots was sufficient for extended patrols, and during the war boats of this class penetrated both the Baltic and the Sea of Marmara. The success of this design was based on the successful Vickers submarine diesel engine (later adopted by the US builder Electric Boat of Groton, Connecticut). Other, less successful British submarines of this period were the result of efforts to meet various special requirements, notably the K Class of fast steam submarines, designed in 1913 though not built until 1915–16, which were intended to get ahead of the enemy fleet and ambush the battleships. Despite the difficulty of closing down a steam plant to dive, they were technically quite successful, but their intended mission required operating on the surface at high speed at night in close proximity to big ships, which led to a disastrous series of collisions on exercises, while their submerged speed of less than 10 knots disbarred them from underwater participation in a fleet action.[35]

This illustrates a basic problem with the early submarines: the difficulty of working out what they would be good for. The results of exercises greatly depended on the exercise rules, which were mere arbitrary assumptions in the absence of experience. It was obvious to most admirals that the submarine would be a menace to big warships, especially in coastal waters. In 1904 Sir William May, the then Controller, predicted 'in a few years when we come to sea-going [submarine] vessels, there will be a real revolution in naval warfare'. By 1913 Sir George Callaghan was convinced that 'the value of the submarine as a weapon, both of offence and defence, is enormous'.[36] Experts like Arthur Balfour who remembered the *Jeune École* understood that submarines could attack merchant ships, and did not allow moral revulsion to cloud their judgement.[37] Churchill in 1914 dismissed such ideas as 'frankly unthinkable propositions', but they were being thought both inside and outside the Navy.[38] Balfour foresaw the possible consequences:

> We might conceivably find ourselves surrounded by seas in which no enemy's battleship could live, and which no enemy's troops could cross, but which would yet be as little under our control, for military or commercial purposes, as if we were the inferior maritime power. If there were any chance of such an extreme hypothesis being realised, we should not only be useless allies to any friendly power on the Continent, but we should have the utmost difficulty in keeping ourselves alive.[39]

The technical success of the submarine was heavily dependent on the new technology of the internal combustion engine, of which the 'oil' or diesel engine proved to be the most suitable type. In Britain, the United States, France and Germany in particular, much work was being undertaken in the years before the outbreak of war to develop powerful and reliable submarine engines. Petrol engines, as used in the Royal Navy's first, American-designed submarines, proved to be very dangerous, but a reliable diesel design was not available until the E Class. The German Navy adopted diesels for its first submarines soon afterwards. Other navies were still struggling with submarine diesel technology (and even more, with larger diesels for surface ships) well after the First World War.[40]

An even newer and more radical technology than the submarine was the aircraft, which was eagerly explored by both Navy and army partly because it had an obvious and essential function, reconnaissance. The first British naval pilots started training in 1911; in December of that year Lieutenant Arthur Longmore made the first landing on water. By January 1912 British aircraft had flown from a ship at anchor, and by May from a ship under way. That month the joint-service Royal Flying Corps (RFC) was constituted, with personnel lent by both Navy and army, and in August 1912 the brilliant and ambitious Captain Murray Sueter became Director of the Admiralty Air Department. Next year aircraft took part in the annual naval manoeuvres, and by 1914 the Navy had about 140 in service. Winston Churchill was an enthusiast for aeroplanes and flying who took a close interest in the new Royal Naval Air Service. The infant RNAS might be named Churchill's – or Sueter's – private air force, but it was not a seagoing naval air force. It included 'seaplanes' (a term Churchill coined), but scarcely any shipborne aircraft. It was, however, intensely committed to technical development. Whereas the army wanted a slow and stable machine for reconnaissance, the Navy already foresaw the need for fast fighters and long-range bombers, and appreciated the crucial importance of air navigation. In a prescient paper of 1911, the airman and submariner Lieutenant Hugh Williamson considered the value of aircraft against submarines. By 1914 the RNAS was developing anti-aircraft guns and bombsights.[41]

In the last years before the outbreak of the First World War, the possibilities of long-range gunnery attracted intense interest in the British fleet. What ranges and what tactics were possible or desirable were questions disputed among experts then, and among historians now. The newer British ships could range to 24,000 yards and beyond, but whether anyone could see to hit at that distance in the North Sea was very doubtful. It was a matter of observation that German Dreadnought battleships still carried a medium battery of 5.9-inch (15cm) guns suitable for a medium-range battle, and in fact it was only the experience of this war which forced the Germans to abandon the idea of fighting at that range. Callaghan wanted to open fire at 15,000–16,000 yards in 1913, and in August 1914 the Grand Fleet Battle Orders prescribed a minimum range of 9,000 yards.[42] British ships had available a constantly developing range of different fire-control instruments roughly divisible into two 'families', grouped around the 'Argo Clock' produced by Arthur Pollen's Argo Company, and its 'Service' rival the Dreyer Fire Control Table, designed by Lieutenant Frederic Dreyer. Dreyer's Table was relatively simple mechanically and conceptually: a large paper strip unrolled continually across a table with traces recording range-finder ranges, observed fall of shot and other information. Ranges and range rates were recorded, and to some extent predicted, as lines or curves on the paper, and the naked eye could take in the main elements of the gunnery situation. It was suitable for an action on more or less parallel courses (and hence maximum vulnerability to torpedoes) but was ill-adapted to high range rates or rapid alterations of course. The Argo Clock, by contrast, was a 'black box' containing a sophisticated mechanical integrator – in effect an early computer – which cost at least three times as much but offered greater tactical flexibility and the opportunity to read off the target's range and bearing rates. Dreyer and his supporters argued that the extra expense was pointless, when the necessary command and control of a big fleet rendered tactical flexibility undesirable if not impossible. They also disliked dealing with a private businessman whom they accused of overcharging and sharp practice, and the unsavoury associations of Pollen's name undoubtedly damaged his case. His father was one of the Oxford dons who had 'perverted to Rome' in the wake of Cardinal John Henry Newman, and his brother was a noted Jesuit controversialist. Such links did not endear an outsider to the Navy of the day, though only Fisher was crass enough to speak openly of Catholic plots.[43] What was worse he associated Pollen with Beresford. Sir John Jellicoe, as commander-in-chief of the Grand Fleet from August 1914 to November 1916, ruled in favour of Dreyer and most British capital ships during the war were fitted with Dreyer Tables, but in the longer run a close connection with Jellicoe and the unsatisfactory British gunnery at the battle of Jutland did Dreyer's reputation no good, and after the war the key elements of Pollen's gear were incorporated in the very successful Admiralty Fire Control Table.[44]

In an ideal world fire-control instruments would observe and predict the movements of the target so accurately as to obtain hits almost as soon as fire was opened, and hold the target thereafter. In practice no system in use during the First World War could achieve such a performance, and all of them depended in part on correcting errors by observing shell splashes. Gunnery, and indeed navigation, was seriously affected by the smoke produced by coal-fired ships at speed. 'It is not easy to remember the vast quantities of smoke which a coal-fired ship steaming at full power could make, particularly battle cruisers whose three large funnels seemed hardly big enough to allow all the smoke to escape. It came out of the funnels almost like toothpaste out of a tube and then started to spread, the cloud getting wider and wider as the distance from the funnel increased, obscuring more and more of the horizon.'[45]

Spotting the fall of shot at long range was difficult even in good visibility, and even if the shells of a salvo were tightly grouped (which was itself hard to achieve). Shells which were out for line would fall to left or right of the target, out of the field of view of the observer peering through his telescope; 'overs' tended to be hidden behind the target, and only 'shorts' were easy to spot. The whole correction process took time, during which of course the enemy was moving (and shooting back). The shells' time of flight was 31 seconds at 18,500 yards range, in which time a ship steaming 25 knots had moved over 40 yards. There was great value in starting with as accurate a range-finder range as possible and having an accurate estimate of the enemy's course and speed in order to hold the range, but neither was easy. The mean error of the Barr & Stroud 9-foot range-finder was at least plus or minus 400 yards at 15,000 yards range. The 12-inch guns of the older British Dreadnoughts had a salvo spread of at least 400 yards at 12,000 yards range, though the heavier shells of the later 13.5-inch guns reduced the spread to 300 yards, and the 15-inch guns of the *Queen Elizabeth* Class to only 200 yards. These were only two of the many components of the 'pool of errors' which affected gunnery accuracy. In practical wartime operational conditions it was difficult to get either spotting corrections or range-finder ranges fast enough to feed either fire-control system with the information it needed to hold a target through high range or bearing rates, and the errors of the fire-control tables were trivial compared to the errors generated by the instruments, especially the range-finders.[46] The primitive German fire-control gave better initial results at the battle of Jutland, it seems partly because stereoscopic range-finders coped better in poor light, and partly because of better training for the high range rates which the Germans had anticipated would be generated by two fleets approaching one another head-on. The superiority of German range-finders and the inability of British industry to manufacture optical glass, formerly favourite explanations, appear to be completely mythical. The German manufacturer Carl Zeiss of Jena was forced before the war to adopt the generally unsatisfactory stereoscopic range-finder, whose performance fell off rapidly in action, because the Glasgow firm of Barr & Stroud controlled all the patents on the coincidence type and shut them out of world markets.[47]

Fire control is probably the single most dramatic example of naval warfare as the domain of very advanced technology. The Argo Clock was in effect a mechanical computer which had an important influence on the mathematical theory of computation. The rise of modern fire control also had a significant and at first sight improbable effect on everyday life afloat. The fire-control tables and other instruments were as far as possible centralized in a compartment called the 'transmitting station' safely located below the armoured deck, from which the firing solutions were transmitted to the guns. The crews of the transmitting stations were made up of Royal Marine bandsmen, in the belief that skill in handling delicate instruments was transferable. The result was a proliferation of bands, whose music accompanied work such as coaling, and recreation such as dances aboard all the larger British warships of the Dreadnought era.[48]

FOURTEEN

What to Do with the Fleet

Policy and Operations 1914–1915

Modern writers and readers find it easy to smile at the simplicity of the people of 1914, who were convinced that the war would be over by Christmas – but their conviction did not spring from simplicity. On the contrary, the statesmen – and many of the admirals and generals – had a sophisticated understanding of the complexity and fragility of the world economic and financial systems, which bound together all advanced economies in an interlocking web of mutual dependency, centred on London. 'Thank heavens it's summer months and before the dark nights of winter are on us it ought to be all over,' Vice-Admiral Beatty of the Battle-Cruiser Squadron wrote to his wife on 5 August. 'There is not sufficient money in the world to permit such a gigantic struggle to be continued for any great length of time.'[1] A war between the major powers would wreck their economic system and plunge them into chaos. No advanced society could long survive the collapse of the mechanisms by which its people were paid and fed. Governments feared mass unemployment and riots, while socialists and trades unionists talked of a general strike against a capitalist war. It followed, therefore, that a long war would be impossible. It seemed to follow also that modern war must culminate almost at once in a great battle, for there would be no time for any slower route to a decision. For the British Cabinet, discussing whether to take a marginal part in a continental struggle or none at all, a central fact was that British banks financed a large part of international trade and British ships carried it. Whether as a belligerent or a neutral, Britain could not escape involvement in a general war, and arguably had more to gain and no more to risk as a participant than as a bystander.[2] As Sir Edward Grey, the Foreign Secretary, told the Commons on 3 August, 'For us, with a powerful fleet, which we believe able to protect our commerce, to protect our shores, and to protect our interests, if we are engaged in war, we shall suffer but little more than we shall suffer even if we stand aside.'[3]

While the Balkan crisis developed during July 1914, however, and the great continental armies began to mobilize, the British Cabinet had been too pre-occupied with Ireland to pay much attention, and there was no one else in the country to do so. It was a settled constitutional principle that great national decisions in peace or war were taken in Cabinet, usually by consensus. Admirals or generals might occasionally be present by invitation, but had no voice in decisions. The armed services had neither the authority nor the organization to form strategy for themselves. But the Cabinet of 1914 represented the discordant fractions of the Liberal Party, who agreed only in being reluctant to engage with the unpleasant behaviour of foreigners, and profoundly unwilling to take a share in their quarrels. This suited well with the common attitude that the overwhelming, brief, brutality of a major war must perforce be left to the military men. Civilian ministers should stand aside and leave the soldiers to their trade. In Germany this was the formal constitutional principle; even in Britain with its robust Parliamentary tradition, there was a widespread feeling that civilian politicians had little to contribute when the guns began to fire. This feeling was expressed by the appointment on 6 August 1914 of Field Marshal Earl Kitchener as Secretary for War, putting Britain's best-known military hero into the Cabinet to manage the army and the War Office without civilian interference. Sir Edward Grey at the Foreign Office regarded war as the province of the generals alone and abdicated from policy. Although the Liberals were completely committed to the principle of Parliamentary and Cabinet supremacy, their reluctance to take responsibility for the war, and Asquith's habitual skill in avoiding confrontation, tended in practice to allow the great decisions of 1914–15 to be taken by Kitchener, Asquith and Churchill with little reference to the Cabinet, still less to the Admiralty or the War Office.[4] Sir Henry Oliver, Chief of the Admiralty War Staff, claimed on 14 January 1915,

> that his time is wholly taken up with trying to manage 'two stupid old men & one raving lunatic' – meaning Fisher, A. K. Wilson and Churchill. He says 'I play them off against one another' – & his efforts to prevent any of their stupid or wild schemes to be put into execution really occupies him to the exclusion of anything else. It doesn't sound an ideal system to be running a great war on . . .[5]

The first crisis of 1914, however, was financial and not military, and this the Cabinet resolved swiftly and effectively. In the week beginning 27 July all the major stock exchanges were forced to close. Banks tottered, the bond markets collapsed, and international trade finance dried up. By Friday 31 July a total failure of the world financial system was imminent, and on Sunday 2 August the next week was declared a British bank holiday. During that week the Cabinet took big decisions fast to keep the financial system working, pumping liquidity into the banks by discounting all pre-war bills, protecting debtors, and setting up a government-backed 'War Risks' marine insurance scheme.[6]

On Monday 3 August, Germany declared war on France and invaded Belgium, which united all the British Cabinet save the ultra-Radicals behind a declaration of war the very next day, but without any agreement on how to fight it, or for what aims. After three days of hesitation four infantry divisions (and one cavalry) of the British army were despatched as the 'British Expeditionary Force' to support Belgian resistance and guard the exposed northern flank of the French army, leaving two divisions to preserve internal order at home. Nothing was decided beyond that, and the Cabinet evidently assumed that the war would be over before more could be demanded. On 5 September, Germany's three opponents, Britain, France and Russia, concluded a formal alliance, but its terms left a massive, unexplored, gap between what France and Russia might expect of Britain, and what she was willing to provide.[7]

By land and sea, the fluid situation in the opening weeks of the war, and the weakness of effective central planning by any of the leading belligerents, left scope for a variety of unplanned and imaginative operations. Several of them concerned the territory along the Channel coast of Flanders and Picardy which was not yet of much interest to the French and German armies massing inland, but mattered a great deal to the British as they tried to bring the British Expeditionary Force in, at first through Ostend, then Dunkirk, Calais, Boulogne and Le Havre. The German Navy for its part was anxious to occupy the Belgian and French coast at least as far down the Channel as Boulogne, and established the Flanders Naval Division, later Corps (*Marinekorps Flandern*) under Admiral Ludwig von Schröder. Marines and naval reservists made up his infantry and manned heavy coastal artillery, to which was later added a growing force of torpedo boats, small submarines and naval aircraft, to compose an original and effective 'all-arms' coastal formation. The British, French and Belgians succeeded in stopping the German advance down the coast on a line just within Belgian territory east of Dunkirk.[8]

In both British and German navies, in home waters and abroad, operations were disjointed by the absence of an operational naval staff. The *Admiralstab*, as we have seen, had no authority over the numerous rival naval commanders-in-chief, all of whom had the *Immediatvortrag* and could deal personally with the Kaiser, whereas the 'Admiralty War Staff' in Whitehall was a research organization not authorized to interfere in operations at all. The Chief of the War Staff and the First Sea Lord advised the First Lord separately; they represented parallel but not converging organizations, and the War Staff was not in the chain of command. Nor were the various retired senior officers who occupied ill-defined roles around the Admiralty. The war was directed by the 'Admiralty War Group' (First Lord, First Sea Lord, Chief of War Staff and Secretary of the Admiralty) without much support. Wireless had already given the Admiralty both the opportunity and the habit of interfering in operations all over the world, but as yet it largely lacked the organization and the people needed to control its vast and scattered responsibilities.[9]

The first consequences were felt in the Mediterranean. There the naval strength of the Triple Alliance (Austria-Hungary, Germany and Italy) almost balanced that of France and Britain, and a great battle between the two warring camps was widely anticipated, but instead the Italians abruptly declared neutrality and subsequently changed sides, leaving the Austro-Hungarian fleet isolated in the Adriatic, while the German Mediterranean Division, consisting of the battle-cruiser *Goeben* and the light cruiser *Breslau*, was pursued by British ships, but gave them the slip just before the declaration of war was known. For the next week Rear-Admiral Wilhelm Souchon dodged Sir Archibald Milne around the Aegean, including a lengthy stop to coal from a German steamer in the Cyclades. Souchon's movements were known to the Foreign Office, the Admiralty and Rear-Admiral Mark Kerr, the British officer commanding the Greek Navy, but neither clear information nor unambiguous orders reached Milne. Meanwhile a political struggle between pro-German and pro-Western factions at the Ottoman court was resolved in the Germans' favour, and the German ships arrived in Istanbul on 10 August to cement the new alliance. This muddle cost an easy victory for the Allies, and had grave strategic consequences.[10]

A fortnight later an action in the Heligoland Bight demonstrated that the Admiralty was just as capable of injecting confusion into an operation much closer to home, in which the British held the initiative. The plan was a joint operation against German patrols by British submarines (commanded by Captain Roger Keyes) and destroyers from Harwich (under Commodore Reginald Tyrwhitt), with Beatty's battle-cruisers in support. None of these three was fully informed of the others' presence, the staff made a gross error in plotting their movements, and it was only thanks to quick reactions that there were no casualties to friendly fire as unknown ships loomed at speed out of the fog. Fortunately for the British, German staff-work was even worse. In spite of planning for at least ten years to meet a British attack precisely there in the Heligoland Bight, the Germans were taken completely by surprise, and lost three light cruisers in confused fighting. Their main fleet, lying as usual in Jade Bay outside Wilhelmshaven, was unable to intervene because the big ships could only cross the bar near high water, a fact whose practical consequences had apparently been overlooked. The British for their part thought to check the depth on the bar only when the operation was well under way, and then could not find the information, which was printed in the *North Sea Pilot*, available in every ship's chart room.[11]

A fundamental problem for both navies was that no amount of pre-war exercises had psychologically prepared them – or perhaps ever could have prepared them – for the reality of modern war. One new technology (already introduced) had a radical impact: submarines. Admiral Tirpitz had always been an enemy of the submarine, as of everything else which threatened to divert spending from his precious battleships, but a small German submarine force had lately been formed, based on the island of Heligoland for the defence of the German Bight. For this most of the boats were armed with four 18-inch torpedo tubes and six torpedoes. In 1914 only Lieutenant-Commander Otto Weddigen of *U-9* had ever practised firing both bow tubes, or reloading tubes underwater. The U-boats were not expected to go more than thirty miles from Heligoland, and at first did not carry chronometers for navigation in the open sea, but the operational endurance of the new, diesel-engined, boats was greater than the British realized; in the 1911 manoeuvres some of them stayed eleven days at sea.[12]

It has been explained that submerged submarines were so slow that any ship keeping up a speed of, say, 15 knots was largely invulnerable except in confined waters. There were only a few warships, however, whose engines and stokers were capable of sustaining such a speed for long, and a normal pre-war cruising speed would have been 10 knots or less. The small cruiser *Pathfinder* was sunk by *U-21* in the Firth of Forth on 5 September while steaming at five knots. This caused the Admiralty to fix a minimum patrol speed of 15 knots, but for most ships that was impossible. On the Broad Fourteens (an area of shoals off the Dutch coast) a cruiser patrol was maintained to detect the High Seas Fleet, imminently expected to push down Channel – to the alarm of people in the Admiralty, including Churchill, who feared that the old, slow, *Bacchante* Class armoured cruisers, patrolling at 9–12 knots, were vulnerable to all sorts of attack. Sir Doveton Sturdee, the Chief of the War Staff, refused to remove them until some of the new, fast light cruisers were available to relieve them. The Germans did not know of the patrol, but on 22 September *U-9* met three cruisers off the Hook of Holland steaming on a steady course at 10 knots and torpedoed the *Aboukir*. Her captain believed he was out of range of German submarines and must have been mined. The *Hogue* stopped to lower her boats and was hit by two torpedoes before she had closed her watertight doors. Finally, the *Cressy*, attempting to keep under way at slow speed without abandoning the men in the water, was hit and sunk in her turn. In four deliberate attacks at close range Weddigen had fired his entire outfit of six torpedoes and achieved four hits. The old armoured cruisers were vulnerable to underwater damage, and it took more than an Admiralty signal to make captains 'submarine-minded'. More than 1,400 men died, two-thirds of the three ships' companies. Prince Louis of Battenberg, the First Sea Lord, tried to put pressure on the subsequent court martial not to blame the Admiralty, but Churchill (who must have known how much he himself would be damaged) forbade Battenberg to interfere.[13] After this disaster British (and German) officers swiftly became submarine-minded, or at least submarine-obsessed. In Germany, where the Fleet's failure to win a great victory had already induced a mood of black despair, submarines were suddenly the subject of hysterical and even blasphemous adulation; one newspaper declared that even God could not fight against a U-boat.[14] At sea phantom periscopes generated repeated panics. Until Scapa Flow and the Firth of Forth could be protected by anti-submarine nets the Grand Fleet fled to various anchorages on the West Coast of Scotland and Ireland. On 30 October Jellicoe informed the Admiralty that in any future encounter with the High Seas Fleet he would assume that he was being lured into a submarine trap and refuse to pursue. This came close to renouncing the quest for decisive victory, but the Admiralty formally approved.[15] By the end of 1914 British cruisers' average cruising speeds had increased more than four knots since the outbreak of war. Other navies were slower to take account of the submarine danger. In April 1915 in the Adriatic, Lieutenant Georg Ritter von Trapp commanding the Austro-Hungarian submarine *U-5* met the French armoured cruiser *Léon Gambetta* steaming at six knots and sank her.[16]

Japan, eyeing Germany's Pacific colonies with interest, joined the war in August, and the German East Asiatic Squadron of two armoured and three light cruisers under Rear-Admiral Maximilian Graf von Spee kept away from his vulnerable base of Tsingtao and headed eastward across the Pacific towards South America – keeping well clear of Australian waters and the battle-cruiser *Australia*, which was clearly superior to his armoured cruisers the *Scharnhorst* and *Gneisenau*. Rear-Admiral Sir Christopher Cradock commanding the South American Station had two smaller and weaker reservist-manned armoured cruisers, the *Good Hope* and *Monmouth*, and one modern light cruiser, the *Glasgow*, plus the old battleship *Canopus*, whose four 12-inch guns were intended to outmatch and outrange the Germans. Without the battleship's guns he would be in great danger, and his orders were categorical not to leave her behind, but false reports of grave machinery trouble, originated by an engineer officer in the midst of a nervous breakdown, persuaded Cradock to do exactly that. He was convinced that von Spee would have headed north for the new Panama Canal as the quickest way home, and took it as confirmation that only one German warship was using wireless nearby. Von Spee was passing all his long-range signals through one ship precisely for this reason, and the famously gallant and impetuous Cradock fell straight into the trap. On 1 November, off Coronel on the Chilean coast, the faster German squadron surprised and outmanoeuvred the British, sinking the *Good Hope* and *Monmouth* and killing the admiral and almost all his men at no cost save the expenditure of more than half their ammunition. The Admiralty's Pacific dispositions had been muddled and its signals ambiguous, but it had tried to warn Cradock, and was not primarily to blame for his disaster. At home, however, the defeat (in what for some reason was called Britain's first naval battle since Trafalgar) aroused powerful public disgust, which damaged, and sometimes still damages, Churchill's reputation.[17]

An energetic young First Lord who never hesitated to involve himself in operations was the obvious public scapegoat for any disappointment, but in the Cabinet and the Admiralty the focus of discontent was on Battenberg the First Sea Lord, who seemed exhausted and ineffectual, and the pompous and inflexible Sturdee. On 30 October Churchill replaced Battenberg by recalling Lord Fisher (as he had now become). Churchill was confident that he could control the old troublemaker, but the king was appalled, and many others had misgivings. 'Two very strong and clever men,' commented Vice-Admiral Beatty, 'one old, wily and of vast experience, one young, self-assertive with great self-satisfaction but unstable. They cannot work together; they cannot both run the show.'[18] Sturdee, a prominent follower of Beresford, was instantly removed from the War Staff and sent to the South Atlantic commanding a powerful cruiser force led by the *Invincible* and *Inflexible*. His job was to make up for the disaster of Coronel for which he himself was widely blamed.[19] Now it was von Spee's turn to fall into the same trap as he had set for Rear-Admiral Kit Cradock by mounting a risky and unnecessary attack on the Falkland Islands, supposing from the limited British wireless traffic that they would be undefended. Instead, he met Sturdee's force just arrived, and a long day of good weather (8 December) allowed the battle-cruisers to deploy their superior speed and armament at leisure. Four of the German ships were sunk; only the light cruiser *Dresden* (which alone had turbine engines) escaped for a while. At the same time the battle-cruisers *Australia* and *Princess Royal* were sent to guard the Pacific and Caribbean ends of the Panama Canal. This successful campaign was the only use of the early battle-cruisers in the role for which they had originally been designed; hunting down cruisers in the distant oceans.[20]

Coronel and the Falklands, together with the brief but spectacular raiding career in the Indian Ocean of the light cruiser *Emden* (sunk by the Australian cruiser *Sydney* in November), were the high points and almost the total of the German threat to British trade in distant waters.[21] These minor actions of limited strategic significance dominated the headlines because they were unaccountably empty of the event which should have occupied them. The Grand Fleet and the High Seas Fleet had not fought the great battle in the North Sea which was universally expected to settle the command of the seas, if not the outcome of the whole war, within a few days of its start. This fact was a cause of growing distress to both navies, whose officers had bound up all their identity and sense of purpose in their self-image as men of honour anxious to risk their lives in a fight against any odds. Before the war they had convinced themselves that they must have their battle and their victory, because the enemy would be compelled to fight soon, and in the most disadvantageous possible manner. The British believed that the German fleet would have to come out into the central North Sea to seek battle on British terms; the Germans, in contrast, were confident that the Grand Fleet would take the first opportunity to entangle itself among the shoals of the Heligoland Bight, within easy reach of German torpedo craft. Not until just before the outbreak of war did Tirpitz ask the commander-in-chief of the High Seas Fleet, Admiral Friedrich von Ingenohl, 'what will you do with the fleet if the English do not appear in the German Bight at all?'[22] Ingenohl and his successors spent the next four years trying to find a convincing answer. On both sides the admirals were forced to confront devastating doubts as to the purpose and value of the battle fleets, even (in Germany's case) of the whole navy. These fears coloured every reaction to the naval war, even as early as 1914, but with growing force as the war continued. Most of the operations of both British and German fleets can be construed as attempted answers to those who asked why they had not fought and won the war long since, as they had so often and so loudly promised to do.[23]

It was very soon known that the Grand Fleet had gone north on the outbreak of war (though not at once that its new base was the vast anchorage of Scapa Flow in the Orkneys), and that British troops were crossing the Channel, covered only by the old pre-Dreadnought battleships still based at the Nore. The Straits of Dover are about three hundred miles from the High Seas

Fleet at Wilhelmshaven and six hundred from the Grand Fleet at Scapa Flow, so that a bold German attack offered a good chance of inflicting grave loss on the British army and a heavy defeat on the Navy – this was why a cruiser patrol off the Dutch coast was essential to provide some warning. The Germans had to fear, of course, that the Grand Fleet would arrive from the north in time enough for revenge, but this too offered prospects of setting up a shallow-water submarine or mine trap – precisely Jellicoe's nightmare, though the Germans did not know it. Nor did they discover until too late that after Coronel four battle-cruisers were detached to pursue von Spee, that the new battleship *Audacious* had been sunk off Ireland by a mine on 27 October, and that several other new Dreadnoughts were absent with engine trouble or collision damage. As a result the two fleets were virtually equal in strength for several months; the Germans never again had an opportunity to bring on a battle on such favourable terms.[24]

After the Heligoland Bight action, however, Wilhelm II forbade his navy to undertake any offensive without his permission, and only one German admiral (Franz von Hipper, commanding the battle-cruisers) was minded to run any risks. None of them took seriously the idea of helping the army by disrupting the deployment of the British Expeditionary Force on the Continent, still less was either the army or navy thinking of a landing in Britain, as the War Office feared.[25] Instead the German battle-cruisers covered a minelaying operation off Yarmouth on 3 November. Hipper found it very difficult to co-ordinate his forces, or even to navigate with sufficient accuracy, British ships found it just as difficult to fix their positions, and the War Staff of the Admiralty proved to be far too slow to cope with incoming information. It was satisfactory that the local British patrols reacted quickly and effectively, and the Germans achieved almost nothing, but it was evidently thanks to luck as much as judgement.[26]

Six weeks later, partly in reaction to the news of von Spee's disaster, they tried again. This time the plan was for the battle-cruisers to bombard Hartlepool, Whitby and Scarborough (significantly further north than before), then fall back on the main High Seas Fleet waiting off the Dogger Bank in the central North Sea. The Admiralty knew only of the battle-cruisers' operation (from signals intelligence), and judged it sufficient, over Jellicoe's misgivings, to send the six battleships of Sir George Warrender's Second Battle Squadron to back Beatty's battle-cruisers. Warrender's rendezvous for dawn on 16 December was only thirty miles from von Ingenohl's for the whole High Seas Fleet. Instead of catching Hipper's battle-cruisers as they withdrew, there was a high risk that Warrender and Beatty would themselves be caught by overwhelming force and suffer exactly the disaster which the Germans needed to reverse the odds in their favour. Just before dawn, British and German destroyers met in a series of confused actions. Frightened that he was about to meet the whole Grand Fleet, von Ingenohl withdrew south-eastward, only ten miles (about a quarter of an hour) before he would have made contact with Warrender and Beatty. Returning from the coast, Hipper's cruisers and destroyers encountered Beatty's, but heavy weather added to the usual confusion generated by incompetent reporting and ships well out of their reckoning, and it was only afterwards, too late, that the situation became clear.[27] There was a good deal of recrimination when each side realized how narrowly they had avoided triumph or disaster. In the British fleet, people were beginning to understand that the pre-war stress on using wireless as little as possible had been carried too far. Those signals which were sent were not always clear (though some of them were *en clair*, unencrypted) and too often omitted the transmitting ship's position, making it impossible for the admiral to make sense of the situation even if the signal reached him. Captains of ships of every size, and even admirals, showed a lamentable failure to think and act for themselves – and, what was worse, to think for others, to put themselves in the position of their colleagues and superiors to understand what they needed to know. In the Admiralty neither numbers nor organization was adequate to keep up with a complex situation at sea, and much of the information which should have been signalled to and from ships at sea was sent too late or not at all. Nevertheless, the Admiralty's first reaction to this episode was to tell Jellicoe that the War Room, having the best means of understanding the overall situation, would now control forces at sea up to the moment of encountering the enemy. At the same time Beatty's battle-cruisers were moved 200 miles south to the Firth of Forth, giving them a better chance of intercepting a German raid, though at a greater risk of being separated from the Grand Fleet in Scapa Flow.[28]

The intense psychological pressure on both fleets to do something – anything – to justify their existence did not diminish. On 23 January 1915, with much of the High Seas Fleet out of action with engine trouble, Hipper got permission to take his battle-cruisers to sweep the central North Sea for wireless-equipped fishing vessels which the Germans supposed were reporting their movements. His own wireless signals gave away to the British that he was coming. Believing that the British battle-cruisers were still in the Orkneys, Hipper was unaware of his danger until he met Beatty's force at dawn on 24 January off the Dogger Bank. The odds were five British battle-cruisers against four German, one of them the weak *Blücher*, and Hipper immediately fled for home at full speed. On paper the oldest and slowest British battle-cruisers were about a knot faster than the best speed of the German squadron, and on the day the Germans were burning German coal and (Hipper reckoned) were at least three knots slower than the British. There was every prospect of a crushing British victory, but incompetent signalling allowed the Germans to escape with the loss only of the *Blücher*. Both flagships, Beatty's *Lion* and Hipper's *Seydlitz*, were badly damaged, in *Seydlitz*'s case by an ammunition fire which burned out her two after turrets.[29]

By early 1915 it was becoming clear to all the belligerents that their pre-war strategic assumptions had been badly wrong. The BEF was ashore and had contributed significantly to the battle of the Marne in September 1914 which checked the German advance on Paris, but there had been nothing like a decisive victory for either army. Lord Kitchener, virtually the only senior British figure who had always expected a long war, was committed to raising a new and vastly bigger British army which he intended to hold back for the moment when the Germans and French armies were both exhausted and Britain could dictate the terms of peace. But the consequences of French collapse would be so grave for Britain that the French could and did demand unlimited British help to avert it. Because of French military weakness, and British commitment to the French alliance, British grand strategy was beginning to be controlled from Paris by a sort of implicit blackmail, as it continued to be until near the end of the war. Kitchener's new armies were to be thrown away piecemeal in a series of hopeless and ruinous offensives to meet French requirements. By 1915 the Cabinet was growing desperate for an alternative, and only the Navy could provide it. The question was where and how.[30]

The choice seemed to lie between an attack on Germany in the Baltic, or on Turkey in the Levant. Other schemes having been rejected on political or practical grounds, the Mediterranean option resolved itself into a plan to force the Dardanelles, knock Turkey out of the war, and open access to the Black Sea. Russia was gravely threatened by the Turks in the Caucasus; her inability to export her grain surplus from Black Sea ports as usual threatened to ruin her war economy and starve much of Western Europe, including Britain, where food prices were rising fast. No one who had observed the performance of the Ottoman Empire in the Balkan Wars of 1912–13, in which it had been heavily defeated by Italy, Greece and Bulgaria among others, would expect it to resist a British assault for long, and its latest offensive against the Suez Canal was repulsed on 3 February 1915. Fisher was keen on the Baltic and pushed the building of a fleet of shallow-draft warships to force the Sound, but until they could be completed, he was ready to go along with a Dardanelles plan so long as only old ships were risked, and sufficient troops were available to seize the shore batteries. Kitchener, the dominant voice in Cabinet on all military questions, was open to the idea so long as only ships were risked, and no British troops were called for. Churchill favoured a purely naval assault, which could easily be abandoned if it went wrong, so long as no troops were diverted from 'the decisive theatre and the most formidable antagonist to win cheaper laurels in easier fields'.[31] It seems that no one consulted the 1906 General Staff study of an attack on the Dardanelles, but all the Cabinet could agree that the scheme, whichever scheme it was, had to succeed and would succeed, and Asquith was the last man to upset a consensus based on wishful thinking.[32]

The British battleships opened their bombardment of the Dardanelles forts on 19 February 1915, and had silenced them by 3 March. Only slowly did it become clear that the forts' guns were not permanently damaged. The straits had been heavily mined, but the available minesweepers were converted fishing craft which lacked the power to tow sweeps against a strong current and were defenceless in the face of mobile howitzer batteries on both shores which the big ships could not see or counter. On 18 March a major naval assault by the full Anglo-French fleet of sixteen pre-Dreadnought battleships was heavily defeated, with three battleships sunk by mines and three more badly damaged. Admiral De Robeck, the new commander-in-chief, now reported that it would be necessary to occupy the whole Gallipoli peninsula – a rocky ridge fifty miles long – before the ships could try again. The Cabinet War Council hesitated, and decided to despatch troops as far as the island of Lemnos but no further until the Navy had forced the straits. The troops were shipped in confusion and had to be unloaded and re-arranged at Alexandria. By the time they had arrived the Navy had failed, and the Cabinet had decided, against Churchill's furious resistance, that they would have to be landed. The troops – British, French, Australians and New Zealanders – were a mixed bag, few of them fully fit and none of them trained or equipped for amphibious operations. General Sir Ian Hamilton was despatched to take command with little in the way of staff or plans, and he never saw the very full military and naval intelligence available in London. It had been clear for weeks what was coming, the possible landing beaches were few and obvious, and the Turks had worked hard to fortify them. The landings, on 25 April, succeeded in gaining initial footholds at extremely high cost, but were never able to get much further. By 10 May De Robeck judged that the campaign had failed: 'from the vigour of the enemy's resistance it is improbable that the passage of the Fleet in the Marmora will be decisive and therefore it is equally probable that the Straits will be closed behind the Fleet'.[33] It took another seven months before the Cabinet faced up to the consequences. A further landing on 6 August disintegrated into a costly rout. The only example of careful and thorough planning in the entire campaign, and the only unqualified 'success', was the withdrawal of all 17,000 men in December 1915 and January 1916, which was achieved without a single casualty. It was high time, for German submarines now threatened the whole operation, and Bulgaria's entry into the war on 14 October 1915 opened direct railway links by which Turkey's allies despatched the heavy artillery and other munitions that the Turks had hitherto lacked.[34]

After the Dardanelles campaign no one could say that naval, or at least amphibious, warfare did not yield decisive results – but from the British point of view they were entirely the wrong results. The Turkish army's triumph under Colonel Mustafa Kemal Bey launched his military and later political rise to become the future Atatürk, founder of the Turkish Republic. In the short term it was the sultan's victory, and a serious peril to the sovereign who ruled more Muslim subjects than any other: George V. British India now seemed immediately threatened by the Ottoman Empire, without much diminishing the long-term danger from Britain's permanent enemy, and temporary ally, Russia. In March 1915 the Russians were promised control of the Turkish Straits at the peace settlement, which removed any possibility of a negotiated settlement with Turkey and presented precisely the danger to the Middle East and India that Britain had repeatedly fought to prevent throughout the nineteenth century. For many British statesmen the real, long-term war was being fought in the East, and it was going very badly. As the Gallipoli campaign slid towards defeat, the Cabinet put pressure on General Charles Townshend, commanding the Indian Army garrison in Iraq, to advance on Baghdad. Townshend thought this was foolhardy, and he was right. After his initial success the Turkish army counter-attacked, the British force was surrounded, besieged in the small town of Kut el Amara, and forced to surrender on 29 April 1916. In military terms the British position in Mesopotamia could be and later was retrieved, but the political damage to British prestige in the Muslim world, and therefore to the stability of India, was much more serious.[35]

From the beginning of the war, the British applied an economic blockade of Germany as one of their weapons. This was not – or not yet – the 'hunger blockade' of German propaganda, for British planners had no mind to target civilians and believed that Germany was largely self-sufficient in food anyway. Its target was the industrial raw materials which Germany imported by sea. The intention was not to strangle German industry so much as to humiliate the German Navy and force it out to fight and be defeated. As Sir Henry Jackson explained to Churchill, 'The War Plans are directed against Germany's mercantile marine, with the hopes that sufficient pressure can be brought, through dislocating her trade, for the German Fleet to seek action with ours, and so end the struggle.'[36] Until the Navy could enter the Baltic, what was exposed to British naval action was Germany's deep-sea shipping, almost all owned in Bremen or Hamburg, and its seaborne imports from the world beyond Europe.[37] Much and eventually all of the British blockade depended on action ashore and abroad by lawyers, diplomats and bankers, but initially the Admiralty took it for granted that naval patrols would be needed to arrest German ships and German-owned cargoes, for which purpose the 10th Cruiser Squadron was deployed to the waters north of the British Isles. It was very soon clear that these ageing protected cruisers, built twenty years before to patrol the trade routes of empire, were unfit to keep the northern seas in winter. Indeed, the whole Navy was shocked by what for most officers was their first prolonged experience of the North Atlantic (and even the North Sea) in hard weather. As quickly as possible the warships were replaced by 'armed merchant cruisers', mostly middle-sized passenger-cargo liners given an improvised armament and commissioned into the Navy. These bigger ships had the range and sea-keeping ability needed for the 'Northern Patrol'.[38]

On 21 November 1914 Admiral Tirpitz gave an indiscreet interview to an American journalist in which he revealed some significant military secrets and damaged his own reputation. One of his themes was the formidable threat of the submarine: 'England wants to starve us, but we can play the same game.'[39] Less than four months of frustrated waiting was already turning German naval thinking away from the battle-fleet and towards the possibility of using U-boats to impose a German counter-blockade. The first official proposal for a U-boat campaign against British merchant shipping was put forward early in October 1914 by Commander Herman Bauer, senior officer of the submarines belonging to the High Seas Fleet, and already by the end of the year it had attracted much support.[40]

Before exploring the consequences, it is necessary to sketch some background. Like other German warships, U-boats were divided between different commands which were independent of one another and subject to no co-ordination unless the Kaiser himself chose to impose any. There was therefore no single German submarine policy, and at various stages during the war U-boats in different parts of the world were obeying, or disobeying, quite different orders. The largest single U-boat unit was Bauer's command attached to the High Seas Fleet and based in the North Sea, which included almost all the large boats with sufficient range to operate all round the British Isles. When German statesmen and senior officers referred to U-boats, it was usually the High Seas Fleet boats which they meant. Next in importance came the small coastal submarines belonging to the Flanders Naval Corps. In February 1915 there were twenty-seven U-boats in commission, twenty in the North Sea and seven in the Baltic. By the end of that year the figures were fourteen in Flanders, ten in the North Sea, eight in the Adriatic, seven in the Baltic, and five in Constantinople – of which about one-third might be on patrol at any one time.[41]

It was during 1915, and mostly by the Germans, that the basic elements of a submarine campaign against merchant shipping were worked out, and at the cost of some anachronism, it may be helpful to sketch them in advance. By far the most common and effective method of submarine attack was on the surface. German U-boats were fast enough on the surface to catch most merchant ships, their hulls were designed principally for surface operations, and from 1915 all but the smallest were armed with a gun on deck. The U-boats attacked only in daylight, usually not far from the coast, in weather good enough to allow an officer to board a prize and ascertain her cargo and nationality. Ships which appeared to belong to the enemy were sunk by scuttling charges or by firing a few shells (occasionally a torpedo) into the engine room. The crews would take refuge in their boats (at that period virtually all rigged with mast and sail) and be given a course or a tow for the nearest land. For the U-boat, this method was simple, effective and almost risk-free. Hardly any ordinary cargo ships were armed or carried wireless. If by chance a warship were sighted, the U-boat was almost certain to see her in good time to dive, and once submerged became invulnerable.[42]

The second form of submarine attack was minelaying. Indiscriminate of its nature and illegal in international waters, minelaying in areas likely to be frequented by enemy shipping was a productive method of attack. The mine which sank the *Audacious*, for example, was part of a field laid just north of Tory Island, off the north-west corner of Ireland. British ships going to and from Scapa Flow were very likely to round it, and often conducted firing practice in the vicinity. These mines were laid by a surface ship, but U-boats were so much less vulnerable that they soon took over almost all 'offensive' minelaying (i.e. in enemy waters, as distinct from defensive minefields laid to protect one's own channels and bases). In the narrows of the Channel, where most shipping was enemy and much of it military, the coastal submarines of the Flanders Naval Corps found minelaying extremely effective. Mines could be swept, but submarine-laid mines in particular were seldom detected except by ships running onto them, and minesweeping itself imposed a heavy burden on the enemy.[43]

The third way in which a submarine might attack a warship or merchant ship was a submerged attack with torpedoes, already the most familiar to the public and the generality of naval men, but in reality by far the rarest and most difficult. Against warships, which could not be safely approached on the surface, there was no alternative to torpedoes, but they were expensive, scarce, unreliable, and seldom hit at ranges of over a thousand yards (half a mile). Until late in the war a target's speed, inclination and distance had to be judged by eye, and only a minority of submarine officers had the 'periscope eye'. Even the latest U-boats in 1915 had a maximum speed on batteries underwater of less than 10 knots, or an endurance of about eighty miles at five knots – hence the description sometimes applied to them of 'locomotive mines', chiefly dangerous to ships which blundered into them unawares. Only ships stopped or at anchor were really vulnerable to submerged attack; but ships steaming very slowly on a steady course, ships in confined waters and unable to alter course, ships making a predictable landfall, and ships operating in the same area for several days together, might offer the U-boat opportunities. Only a lucky chance would place a U-boat in position to attack any other ship.[44]

The larger and faster merchantmen, typically passenger or cargo liners with service speeds of 12–14 knots and upwards, were not easy to board from a small boat and could outrun a U-boat on the surface, so they could only be attacked by torpedo, but this raised a major legal and moral difficulty. We shall return to the uncertainties of international law, but outside Germany it was generally agreed that sinking merchant ships without warning was well outside any accepted definition of civilized or lawful behaviour. Armed merchant cruisers were warships and could be attacked as such; naval auxiliaries and troopships probably the same; ships laden with contraband could be sunk after the crew had been put in a place of safety. Neutral and passenger shipping and hospital ships should have been immune from attack (though not necessarily capture) in almost all circumstances. Unfortunately, the same merchant ships might serve in any of these different roles, and it was often impossible to tell the categories apart without boarding and searching. A quick look through the periscope might reveal obvious tell-tale signs such as guns mounted, but it would not distinguish troops from civilian passengers nor reveal anything about the cargo. Even the nationality of a target was often hard to tell at a distance, and the flying of false flags when not in action was a traditional and legitimate form of deception. It was therefore impossible in most circumstances to make a submerged attack on any of the larger and more valuable merchantmen without risking a grave breach of legality and humanity. The war was less than three months old when *U-24* torpedoed the French steamer *Amiral Ganteaume*, identified as a troopship but actually carrying Belgian refugees. This may have been a genuine mistake, but without boarding and searching, mistakes were unavoidable.[45]

It should have been impossible to undertake any campaign against merchant shipping without the most careful consideration of the legal, moral and political factors, but in fact the submarine offensive announced on 4 February 1915 by the new commander-in-chief of the High Seas Fleet, Vice-Admiral Hugo von Pohl, was adopted casually, with very little thought or preparation and only verbal approval from the Kaiser and the Chancellor. German leaders were aware that what they proposed might be regarded in some quarters as illegal, but they were not troubled by it. The German service view was that there were no such things as 'laws of war' (in the sense of *jus in bello*, law governing the conduct of war): war was inherently law-free, no legal or moral restrictions could apply to the German army or navy, and 'military necessity' justified any action which contributed to victory. It was the duty of civilians of every nation to submit to the demands of the German armed forces or suffer the consequences. So far from avoiding passenger ships, the U-boats were ordered to make them a special target, as an example to others of the penalty for defying Germany. Tirpitz was confident that it would be enough to sink a few to frighten them all into port.[46]

The Declaration of London of 1909, which had codified the modern law of war at sea, ignored the existence of submarines almost totally. The Declaration prescribed 'cruiser rules' for surface ships attacking enemy merchant shipping, rules that were based on a simplified and somewhat utopian version of the practice of the Napoleonic Wars. Prizes were to be sent in for adjudication by a prize court, their crews landed safely. In the few circumstances in which a prize might legitimately be destroyed, the crew were to be held in safety aboard the cruiser. Submarines were too small to carry prize crews or take prisoners, so they could not literally apply the cruiser rules. In practice, however, merchant seamen put into their boats, in fair weather and in coastal waters, were not likely to come to harm. Although the German 'prize rules' stretched the letter of the Declaration, they more or less conformed to its spirit, and the cost in civilian lives was low so long as passenger ships were not attacked.[47]

The bulk of the first German U-boat campaign of February to September 1915 was virtually invisible to German and American statesmen and senior officers, and easily overlooked even by British officers, because it was simply an effective but undramatic economic blockade in which nobody of social or political importance was killed. For German admirals, such action was remote from war and victory as they understood them. The 'unrestricted' (or rather 'unlimited', *uneingeschränkt*) submarine warfare which Germany now declared referred in practice to submerged torpedo attack without warning, especially on passenger ships. This was the least useful contribution to economic blockade but had the greatest possible political and moral impact. Admirals and civilian leaders in Germany, Britain and in neutral countries reacted very differently to such attacks, but all of them, when they considered submarine warfare, thought first of submerged torpedo attack because they were chiefly or entirely concerned with the politics rather than the economics of war.[48]

The single dominant political event of the first U-boat campaign was the sinking of the Cunard transatlantic liner *Lusitania* by *U-20* off the Old Head of Kinsale on 7 May 1915. More than 1,200 people lost their lives, including 79 children and 128 American citizens. Although apologists for Germany have laboured ever since to excuse it as an accident, it is beyond doubt that this was a deliberate ambush. Eastbound ships from New York to Liverpool had to make a landfall in the south-west of Ireland, and the Fastnet Rock, Galley Head or the Old Head (in that order, coming from the west) were the obvious choices. The German Embassy in Washington had issued public warnings that Cunard liners would be attacked, and *U-20* had been waiting for several days before she sighted the *Lusitania* coming from Galley Head to round the Old Head. The Admiralty knew of *U-20*'s whereabouts, had warned the liner of the danger, and suggested going the longer way round by the North Channel as a safer alternative, but good timekeeping was commercially vital to Cunard, and Captain William Turner, the *Lusitania*'s master, must have reckoned that a ship steaming at least 20 knots was an impossibly difficult target.[49]

The result of the sinking was a furious chorus of condemnation from almost all over the world, even including Germany's allies, which did grave damage to its diplomatic position. Only German officers were satisfied. 'For me the heavy loss of life is just as important as the material destruction,' commented one. 'Terror is what counts in submarine warfare.'[50] When the Chancellor Theobald von Bethmann Hollweg persuaded Wilhelm II to forbid attacks on passenger liners, Tirpitz and his friend Vice-Admiral Gustav Bachmann, the chief of the *Admiralstab*, resigned in disgust, lamenting that 'German world prestige will be badly hurt' by such feebleness.[51] Here was a clash of values which ran right through the U-boat campaigns of the Great War. The admirals demanded the ruthless willpower of 'unlimited' submarine attack, an authentically German way of war which they expected would stun enemies and neutrals into submission. They regarded the prize rules as womanish weakness – but the submariners preferred them, because they worked.[52] Eight of the most successful U-boat captains of 1915 sank between them ninety-eight British and fifteen neutral ships by the 'prize rules', and only eight ships without warning.

The most successful of all, Lieutenant-Commander Max Valentiner of *U-38*, expended six torpedoes, 410 88mm shells and ten scuttling charges (almost his full outfit) to sink thirty ships in one patrol in August 1915, every one by the prize rules.[53] This was the most destructive U-boat patrol in British waters. By choosing to keep to the prize rules despite their orders, the German submariners sank a steadily rising tonnage of British ships. British merchant shipping losses from all causes (but mainly submarines and mines) rose from a monthly average of 46,000 tons (GRT) up to February 1915, to 85,000 tons over the next seven months, with a peak of 149,000 tons in August 1915. In seven months 787,000 tons of shipping was sunk, not all of it British and some of it carrying cargoes for Germany. This was scarcely sufficient to defeat the British Empire, which had over 21 million tons of shipping available; even at the August peak, losses did not exceed new building. But the High Seas Fleet had begun the campaign with only fifteen long-range U-boats, of which no more than six were usually at sea at any time. There were never more than twenty-five U-boats available in all the commands together. Fifteen U-boats were sunk, and the seventeen ordered over the summer of 1915 would take eighteen months to build.[54]

By the autumn of 1915 U-boat attacks had generated such international uproar that in September the High Seas Fleet boats were ordered to abandon submerged attacks and keep to the prize rules. Many of them needed a refit anyway, and the remainder went to the Mediterranean, where the numerous unavoidable straits and headlands offered good torpedo prospects, and there were few American travellers to make political complications. Allied supplies for the campaigns in Egypt, Salonika, Gallipoli and elsewhere were all vulnerable, and bad feeling between the naval allies Britain, France and Italy weakened an already ineffectual anti-submarine effort.[55]

British anti-submarine measures were limited by the absence of any means of detecting or attacking submerged submarines, but U-boats spent so much of their time on the surface that this was more an excuse than a reason. In the clear light of hindsight, the main cause of failure was that British methods unintentionally but inevitably exposed merchant shipping to the maximum danger and kept the warships as far away from the enemy as possible. Minefields and nets offered limited protection to fixed channels in shallow water only. Merchant ships were advised to follow secret routes, patrolled by warships – whose presence simply advertised the routes. From 1915 the British mounted a major effort to arm as many merchant ships as possible with a gun, with the intention of making it too dangerous for U-boats to stop and search prizes. In this sense the British tried to promote 'unrestricted submarine warfare', to force submarines to attack submerged with torpedoes, because they knew how inefficient and difficult a method it really was. Unfortunately, the U-boats refused to rise (or rather dive) to this bait. As the number of armed merchantmen increased, the submarines were simply armed with bigger guns of longer range. Instead of risking a boarding officer's life, the U-boats now risked enemy merchant seamen's lives by opening fire first and forcing them to abandon ship. This was also an effective counter to the other British anti-submarine innovation, the 'Q-ships'. These were merchant ships with a disguised naval crew and a concealed armament, ready to open fire suddenly on a U-boat which approached to board. They had some initial success, but soon the Germans were alert to the danger, and when in any doubt they simply shelled the target at long range or torpedoed her on the surface. Q-ships caught the British naval imagination and inspired a big effort, but after the first few weeks their only effect was to increase the danger to merchant seamen.[56]

The new Royal Naval Air Service went into action in 1914 with scarcely any formal plans. Its leading characters, and its patron Winston Churchill, were opportunists of energy and initiative who took every opportunity to exploit the new technology and extend the Navy's range in every dimension. In 1914 aircraft (in the modern sense of the word) were only one of several new air technologies. Visually and psychologically, military flying was dominated by the huge rigid airships designed by Count Ferdinand von Zeppelin for the German army and later navy. Their speed, range and ceiling greatly exceeded those of heavier-than-air machines, and until late in the First World War most conventional naval wisdom (exemplified by Jellicoe) rated airships well above other aircraft. Trials held in September 1911 revealed that the first British naval airship, though nicknamed the *Mayfly*, did not, and Churchill preferred winged aircraft because they were quicker and cheaper to build.[57] Since the BEF had taken all the army's aircraft with it to France, the RNAS assumed responsibility for the defence of Britain against the only existing air threat, the German army's Zeppelins. For this purpose the RNVR Anti-Aircraft Corps was established in October 1914. At Dunkirk, Commander Charles Samson set up an air station to counter the Zeppelins, which could only be done by attacking their bases. As early as 22 September Samson mounted an air raid on the Zeppelin base at Düsseldorf, 190 miles away in the Rhineland. This was ineffective, but a second attack on 8 October destroyed a Zeppelin. At the same time the naval aircraft scouted over the still open country between German and British positions in Flanders, and a force of improvised armoured cars was established to rescue crashed airmen from the German cavalry. In November Samson's aircraft flew from an airfield in eastern France to attack Friedrichshafen on Lake Constance, where the Zeppelins were built.[58] German naval Zeppelin bases were out of range of any land-based attack, but the Admiralty was now converting Channel and other short-sea passenger ferries into seaplane carriers, with their after-passenger saloons replaced by a hanger, and derricks to hoist the aircraft into the water. The first of them, the *Engadine*, *Riviera* and *Empress*, attacked the naval Zeppelin sheds at Nordholz near Cuxhaven on Christmas Day 1914; the first ever naval air attack from the sea. It was largely a failure; few of the flimsy aircraft found the target and their feeble weapons did no damage, but both sides were impressed by the possibilities. The seaplane carriers had spent four hours off the German coast unmolested, and the German counter-attack by seaplanes and Zeppelins convinced British officers that ships under way at sea had little to fear from air attack.[59]

Beyond the North Sea, more or less improvised naval air units appeared in many parts of the world, and in a considerable range of operations. In the Eastern Mediterranean the captured German merchant ship *Aenne Rickmers* served as a seaplane carrier under the management of the Egyptian Ports and Lights Service, with British Merchant Navy officers, a mainly Greek crew with some naval ratings and Marines, aircraft and aircrew lent by the French Navy, and the whole commanded by an officer of the Dublin Fusiliers. This motley crew performed essential service reporting the advance of the Turkish army across Sinai and ensuring their defeat in February 1915. Naval aircraft spotted for warships bombarding Turkish forts in the Dardanelles and made early torpedo attacks. In June 1915 naval aircraft bombed a German Zeppelin on the ground near Brussels, and the same month Flight Sub-Lieutenant Reginald Warneford RNAS achieved a notable first in destroying the German naval airship *LZ 37* by bombing her in flight, after which the Brussels airship base was abandoned. In East Africa in June and July 1915 RNAS aircraft spotting for the guns of the monitors *Severn* and *Mersey* allowed them to sink the German cruiser *Königsberg*, which had taken refuge up the Rufiji River.[60]

FIFTEEN

Losing the Plot

Policy and Operations 1916–1918

By the end of 1915 it seemed increasingly clear that neither battle-fleet in the North Sea needed, or even truly desired, to run big risks to bring on an action. The Germans were frightened of being caught again by British Dreadnoughts, and Jellicoe was frightened of German destroyers and submarines. In January 1916 a new and aggressive commander-in-chief of the High Seas Fleet, Vice-Admiral Reinhard Scheer, succeeded the sickly Hugo von Pohl. Scheer was determined to revive the German policy, abandoned after the Dogger Bank action, of trying to isolate a detachment of the Grand Fleet – not so much in the hope of victory, more for political reasons, 'to justify its [the fleet's] existence and the vast sums exacted from the resources of our people for its maintenance'.[1] For outright victory he looked to 'unrestricted' submarine attacks. Scheer's initial plan for another raid on the English coast was frustrated by weather unfavourable for Zeppelin reconnaissance, and changed to a cruise up the eastern side of the North Sea into Norwegian waters. In spite of repeated near-interceptions, the Germans still did not suspect that their signals could be read, and Admiral Hipper's battle-cruisers were surprised to encounter the British battle-cruisers off the coast of Denmark on 31 May 1916.[2]

Thus began the battle of Jutland. The Germans at once turned south to fall back on the High Seas Fleet, and Vice-Admiral Beatty pursued in disorder, throwing away the vital first few minutes the gunnery officers needed to designate targets, plot ranges, range-rates and deflection, before opening fire. The substantial errors in range-taking by the flagship *Lion* then brought the British ships well within German gun range before they started firing. This allowed the Germans to gain an early gunnery advantage, and Beatty's headlong pursuit left behind the 5th Battle Squadron – the new fast battleships of the *Queen Elizabeth* Class – which had been attached to his command for just such an eventuality.[3] 'The Battle Cruisers' name up here is mud,' noted an officer of Beatty's force visiting Scapa Flow, 'owing to the inefficiency of their gunnery and the general casualness and lack of concentration with which they appear to treat the war.'[4] This perception was justified, though how fully justified has only recently become clear. In pursuit of an obsession with rate of fire which dated to the Dogger Bank action and before, the battle-cruisers had dismantled many of the anti-flash shutters designed to prevent a fire in a turret from spreading down the ammunition hoists to the magazines, and had adopted the suicidal practice of removing bags of propellant from their protective cases, so that any serious damage to the gun turret risked a cordite 'deflagration', an intense fire which could readily reach the magazines and destroy the ship. It is now certain that this was the reason the battle-cruisers *Indefatigable*, *Queen Mary* and *Invincible* blew up during the battle of Jutland; divers have found bare charges still scattered about the wreck of the *Queen Mary* on the bottom of the North Sea.[5]

The flagship *Lion* narrowly escaped the same fate. Not long before Jutland, her chief gunner (the warrant officer responsible for the magazines) was dismissed by court martial, and his relief, Alexander Grant, tackled the frightening chaos he had inherited with a rare combination of tact, professional skill and strength of character, enforcing safe practice in ammunition handling without reducing the ship's rate of fire, or exposing his superiors, the flag-captain and the gunnery lieutenant, to the blame they richly deserved. The result was that *Lion*'s magazines did not explode when one of her turrets was hit and burnt out.[6]

In spite of knowing that the High Seas Fleet was coming north towards him, Beatty mishandled the encounter and left the 5th Battle Squadron in an exposed position at the rear of his line as the two battle-cruiser forces reversed course and chased north. Fortunately, the *Queen Elizabeths* were heavily armoured and withstood the concentrated fire of the leading German battle-ships. It was now Beatty's task to deliver the German fleet to Jellicoe in the position and disposition which would favour British victory, but it was very difficult in the thick weather of the North Sea to know with sufficient accuracy the relative positions of the Grand Fleet and the Battle Cruiser Fleet. The Grand Fleet cruised in a compact rectangular formation of six columns abreast, easily handled and screened, capable of being deployed into a single line of battle facing in any direction – given about fifteen minutes' notice and accurate knowledge of the enemy's position. The High Seas Fleet cruised in the same unwieldy, nine-mile-long single line in which it fought; it had no need to deploy, but ran a serious risk of running head-on into trouble in the weakest possible formation. For this reason (as the British knew), its gunnery officers were trained to handle the very high range rates which would be generated by two fleets approaching head-on, and its captains practised the 'battle about-turn', a method of abruptly reversing course which it was very soon to have need of.[7] Jellicoe received only vague and scanty reports from Beatty and had to guess when and how to deploy, which he did faultlessly in spite of what turned out to be a twelve-mile cumulative error in the two squadrons' positions. Notwithstanding the obvious reasons for the Germans to expect the Grand Fleet to be at sea, and to suspect that Beatty was leading them to it, only Hipper had a sense of danger, remarking as he peered into the murk ahead, 'Something lurks in that soup. We would do well not to thrust into it too deeply.'[8] Scheer was taken completely by surprise when he found himself steaming head-on into a line of British battleships stretched across his path, heavily outnumbered and with half his guns unable to bear. The battle-cruisers at the head of his line were the most exposed, and suffered the worst, but the visibility was so poor that most of the British battleships caught only glimpses of the enemy, and the Germans were able to reverse course and escape by the 'battle about-turn'.[9]

This was the moment for Jellicoe to claim his victory by a close pursuit, but he was still obsessed by the thought of destroyer or submarine traps, though he knew the Germans had been caught by surprise, and it was rationally impossible for them to have set up such a thing in the past few hours of hard steaming. He also assumed, without any evidence, that the only reason for the High Seas Fleet to be at sea was to cover an invasion force, which must be crossing the southern North Sea at that moment, and so concluded that his duty was to hold himself in readiness to sink it rather than be lured away by the self-indulgent search for victory (a line of reasoning familiar to eighteenth-century French admirals). For the same reason the Admiralty forbade Commodore Tyrwhitt and the Harwich destroyer force to join the battle.[10] This might have been the end of the affair, had not Scheer reversed his course by another 'about-turn' and steamed straight back into the trap he had so narrowly escaped. This time the weather was clearer, the German ships were lit up against the evening light and suffered heavy damage, while the British line to the eastward was hidden in darkness. In desperation Scheer ordered the four remaining battle-cruisers (Hipper's flagship the *Lützow* had already fallen out of line) to 'charge' the enemy, using an order which survived in the German signal-book from the days of ramming tactics. Under cover of this movement and a destroyer attack, Scheer once more turned his battleships and retreated in disorder.[11]

Subsequently he offered some very flimsy explanations for his apparently lunatic second attack, though once after a good dinner he admitted: 'My idea? I had no idea . . . the thing just happened.'[12] In retrospect it looks as though Scheer had completely lost 'situational awareness'; after several hours of steaming and firing in bad visibility he was unable to form a mental picture of the relative positions of his own ships and the enemy's and was blundering about at random. It is doubtful if many officers could have done better without artificial aids, and there seems to have been only one officer present at Jutland who had one: Jellicoe. The British fleet flagship the *Iron Duke* had an automatic dead-reckoning plotter with log and gyro feeds, generating a record of her movements, to which the best available information of the whereabouts of friends and foes could be added. Despite all the numerous failures of British ships to report themselves and the enemy, the flagship's plot put Jellicoe in a better position to control the battle than anyone else – at least in daylight.[13]

It was a settled British doctrine that night fighting was unpredictable and dangerous, especially in the presence of enemy torpedo craft, so Jellicoe did not attempt to follow the German ships as they disappeared into the dusk. Since the British blocked the Germans' way home, there was every reason to wait for the dawn to bring another glorious First of June. Scheer seems to have had no clear idea of the Grand Fleet's whereabouts when he set course for the Horns Reef Lightship off the Danish coast, marking the entrance to the northern swept channel through the minefields of the Heligoland Bight. During the night the German fleet crossed close astern of the Grand Fleet, repeatedly clashing with its cruisers and destroyers and several times sighted by the battleships, but Jellicoe was unable to understand what was happening from the few sighting reports he received, many of them giving erroneous positions. The Admiralty knew from intercepted signals that Scheer was steering for the Horns Reef but did not pass on the information. The result was that the Germans escaped behind the minefields in the early morning.[14]

The British reacted to their almost-victory with anguished disappointment. It was obvious that failures of British training, organization and equipment had allowed the High Seas Fleet to escape from imminent destruction. One reaction was a huge effort to remedy these defects, which began straight after the battle and was not completed at the end of the war two years later. Another consequence, perhaps inevitable in the Navy trained by Fisher and Beresford, was recriminations and rivalries. The Battle-Cruiser Force, loyal to their charismatic leader Beatty who had led them in the thick of the fighting, blamed the Grand Fleet's failure to close the trap on the rigid centralization, defensiveness and lack of initiative imposed by Jellicoe's standing orders. Jellicoe himself was aware of the problem. The officers of the Grand Fleet, confident in their high professional standards and thorough training, pointed the finger at the arrogant and slipshod practices of the officers of the Battle-Cruisers, many of whom believed that 'we are *it*, and we can learn nothing from anyone'.[15] There was justice on both sides, but the result was once more to divide the Navy into warring factions whose quarrels were not entirely stilled even two generations later.[16]

The worst of all British failures, with the least excuse and the gravest consequences, was the collapse of magazine discipline in the battle-cruisers. Investigation after the battle revealed at once what had gone wrong, but Beatty took the lead in suppressing the facts and denying the blame. Instead, he insisted that the battle-cruisers' gunnery had been superb but British shells were defective (by implication blaming Jellicoe as Director of Naval Ordnance 1904–07), and that the ships were inadequately armoured, for which he faulted the naval constructors in the Admiralty. The echoes of these falsehoods have scarcely died yet. The truth was suppressed 'to preserve morale' – perhaps especially the morale of those senior officers whose careers were at risk – but the lessons were discreetly learnt and applied, and one officer at least got what he deserved. A week after the battle Mr Grant, the Chief Gunner of the *Lion*, who knew enough to blow up dozens of careers, was specially promoted lieutenant by Order in Council and given command of a destroyer. He eventually retired as a full captain and wrote his memoirs, but discreet to the last, he never published them.[17]

Thanks to sinking the three battle-cruisers the Germans could justly claim to have suffered fewer losses than they had inflicted, and an heroic myth of decisive victory was erected which made it impossible to criticize Tirpitz or Scheer – then or long after their deaths, since the German Navy was commanded until 1943 by former officers of the High Seas Fleet who were determined to preserve its legacy. Their story was that the Grand Fleet had been intercepted and frustrated in a plan to push down the Kattegat towards the Baltic, for which reason the action was named in German the 'battle of the Skagerrak', though it had been fought entirely in the North Sea. Privately, however, Scheer and his captains knew very well how close they had come to catastrophe, and the Kaiser was bluntly told that 'even the most successful result from a high seas battle will not compel England to make peace'.[18] The battleships had run their course; now it was up to the U-boats.[19]

At the beginning of 1916 there were sixty-three U-boats in service, of which forty-two were operational *Frontboote*, half of them coastal submarines of the UB and UC classes. There were only seventeen large modern seagoing boats, of which the ten belonging to the High Seas Fleet carried the burden of the trade war. Tirpitz claimed that they would bring Britain to her knees in six months of unrestricted warfare, but most German leaders were sceptical. The *Admiralstab*'s February 1916 plan for unrestricted submarine war called for almost eight times as many U-boats as were then available: 270 large and 96 small torpedo-armed submarines, plus 74 large and 46 small minelayers. On the basis of extravagantly optimistic estimates, the plan forecast that five months of unrestricted attack would reduce the British merchant fleet to 39 per cent of its existing strength. As before, however, it is a mistake to assess German plans as a rational exercise in economic warfare; they were essentially presented in political and psychological terms. Trapped in the bloody Verdun campaign, the army was desperate for help and the navy had committed its prestige to its new form of ruthless war and decisive battle. In February 1916 the German government announced a second 'unrestricted' submarine campaign. Civilians who questioned the logic simply identified themselves to the admirals as weak and un-German, but the submariners were as reluctant as ever to abandon the prize rules. In February and March U-boats sank sixty-eight merchantmen in the Irish Sea and the western Channel, only eight of them without warning.[20]

Then on 24 March 1916, *UB-24* torpedoed the French Channel ferry *Sussex*, killing about eighty passengers, four of them Americans. However incoherent President Wilson's view of international law, he never wavered in his conviction that its highest purpose was to safeguard American travellers, so this attack generated an immediate crisis. Under intense pressure, the German government ordered U-boats outside the Mediterranean to revert to the prize rules. In reality at least three-quarters of the sinkings so far had been under the prize rules, but no one in authority knew that, in Germany or the United States. Admiral Scheer, under whose command most of the affected submarines came, reacted on 25 April with what can only be described as a tantrum:[21]

> Previous experience shows that it is impracticable to prosecute a submarine trade war by the prize rules, and the boats would be exposed to destruction to no purpose, so I have ordered them all into port. The submarine campaign against England will cease forthwith.[22]

In defiance of the Kaiser's orders, and to the fury of the U-boat men, Scheer abandoned Germany's most effective naval weapon for over six months, saving about a million tons of Allied shipping. Initially the *UB* (torpedo and gun-armed) boats of the Flanders flotilla came into port as well, leaving only the minelayers (*UC* class) operational. From August 1916 the *UB* boats were allowed back on patrol, strictly according to prize rules. Commander Karl Bartenbach their senior officer was disgusted, but the submariners were not daunted. In one week in September three boats sank thirty ships according to the prize rules in the 200-mile stretch of the English Channel between Beachy Head and the Eddystone. There the three U-boats were hunted by forty-nine destroyers, forty-eight torpedo boats, seven Q-ships and more than four hundred other patrol vessels, but keeping a strict wireless discipline (very unlike other German ships) they were extremely difficult to locate. In attack they ran scarcely any risk: in the thirteen months from October 1915 to October 1916 just one U-boat was lost attacking according to the prize rules, and two more up to the end of January 1917. Only military transports sailing under escort were beyond their reach. The Dover barrage of minefields and anti-submarine nets provided no effective obstacle to the Flanders U-boats, which passed freely up and down the Channel.[23]

The German and Austrian Mediterranean U-boats were based in the Adriatic, but the attempt to keep them in by an anti-submarine barrage across the Straits of Otranto (fifty miles across and 300 to 500 fathoms deep) was a complete (and completely predictable) failure. Here too the U-boats much preferred to operate on the surface.[24] In August 1916 Lieutenant-Commander Lothar von Arnauld de la Perière of U-35 sank no fewer than fifty-four ships, every one by the prize rules. It was, and still is, the single most destructive submarine patrol in history (reckoned by number of ships sunk), but he himself described it as 'pretty tame and boring . . . We had scarcely had any real adventure; it was all rather humdrum. We stopped the ships, the crew took to their boats, we checked the ship's papers, gave the men a course to the nearest land and then sank the prize.'[25]

By August 1916 the U-boat campaign was taking over from the battle-fleets as the main theatre of naval war. The demands of anti-submarine work had reduced the Grand Fleet to a screen of only seventy destroyers, and both Jellicoe and Beatty agreed that with such scanty protection it was not wise to go south of the Dogger Bank. The U-boat force of the High Seas Fleet had been diverted against trade and was no longer available to try to ambush the Grand Fleet, while twenty-four of its destroyers were sent to support the Flanders U-boats. On 26 October 1916 they mounted a destructive raid on the Dover Straits which persuaded Jellicoe that Britain would lose the war unless the Germans were driven out of Flanders. From this dated the naval pressure that led next year to the British army offensive of Passchendaele, which cost so much and gained so little.[26]

In Germany the critical situation on the Eastern Front, where Romania and Italy became enemies in August 1916 and the Austro-Hungarian forces were in retreat, convinced the army that victory on land was impossible. A public campaign in favour of unrestricted submarine war was now organized by generals and admirals together. Only a handful of the admirals, and none of the generals, had any idea that U-boat warfare was more effective in its 'restricted' form, on the surface. In the U-boat campaigns of February to September 1915 and February to May 1916, 85 per cent of merchant ships were sunk by the prize rules; in the third campaign, from October 1916 to January 1917, the figure went up to 98.5 per cent. Scheer, Bauer, and his successor in command of the High Seas Fleet U-boats, Captain Andreas Michelsen, all managed to ignore and suppress the fact. From 1917 U-boats were ordered to attack submerged or at night if possible, and otherwise to fire without warning as though they were submerged, to achieve the maximum shock and loss of life even at the price of reduced sinkings.[27]

From the resumption of U-boat attacks in October 1916 the level of sinkings rose steadily, because the Flanders flotilla was now equipped with larger coastal submarines of the *UB.II* class, which could operate down the Channel and along the west coast of France. The pressure for 'unrestricted' U-boat attacks continued to increase, and at a conference at Pless (Pszczynie) in Silesia in January 1917 the decision was taken to start on 1 February, in the expectation of bringing Britain to surrender by 1 August. For this purpose, 105 U-boats were available on 1 February: 46 belonging to the High Seas Fleet, 23 in the Flanders flotilla, 23 in the Mediterranean, and the remainder in the Baltic or at Constantinople. In February they sank over half a million tons of shipping, and by April the monthly total had reached a peak of 860,334 tons. In three months more than two million tons of shipping had been sunk, 1.25 million of them British, for the cost of only nine submarines. The rate of loss was 23 per cent per annum of the Allies' total ocean-going merchant fleet, rising to over 50 per cent at the end of April. Using the Germans' favourite measure of tonnage sunk per U-boat day at sea, the figure was 484.49 tons in the three months November 1916 to January 1917, and 538.93 tons from February to June 1917. In the face of such losses many neutral ships refused to sail, further reducing the effective shipping pool. The British contemplated the necessity of making peace not later than November 1917; Jellicoe and the Admiralty Board openly despaired.[28] There was a high risk of virtual bankruptcy well before the summer. At the beginning of 1916 Britain had introduced conscription, risking economic collapse by taking men from industry on the gamble that Germany would collapse first. That gamble failed on the Somme. At the end of November, the US Federal Reserve Board advised bankers to extend no more credit to Britain, meaning that the war could only be continued on American sufferance if at all. When David Lloyd George formed a new coalition government in December 1916, it was an open question how long Britain could stay in the war.[29]

Counter-measures to the U-boat threat still consisted chiefly in 'offensive patrols' and 'patrolled routes', which in practice amounted to aimless steaming about. Merchant shipping was controlled on principles which ensured the U-boats a frequent supply of undefended individual steamers, and warships made sure to avoid the prescribed routes. 'I never send men of war on the transport routes,' declared Rear-Admiral Mark Kerr in the Mediterranean, 'they are all marked by submarines and very unhealthy places.'[30] Warships seldom arrived at the scene of a sinking in time to disturb the submarine, and had no means of anticipating where they would attack. The new depth charges offered a means of attacking a submerged submarine, but it still could not be located under water. Much effort was devoted to hydrophones (underwater microphones), which however chiefly detected the noise of the ship operating them. More effective was minelaying, including offensive minefields laid in the swept channels in and out of the Heligoland Bight, which caused rising casualties to U-boats and surface patrols until by June 1918 the High Seas Fleet had virtually abandoned the Bight.[31]

There was of course a very well-known and long-practised method of ensuring that all merchant ships were defended, namely convoy, which concentrated the escorts in the one place where they were essentially needed. For naval officers, steaming slowly in company with slow merchantmen did not feel satisfyingly aggressive, but it forced the enemy to attack where the defenders were waiting for him, whereas 'offensive patrols' in hard reality differed little from running away. What was more, though few naval officers appreciated it, the effect of concentrating merchant ships in one place was to prevent them from being anywhere else at the same time: a convoy emptied the ocean of targets and was itself only a little easier to find than an individual ship. All this would have been well known to the handful of naval men who had studied the unfashionable subject of trade defence. It was also well known – or at least, easily knowable – to the larger number who had actual experience of current convoys, starting with the Grand Fleet itself, which from the viewpoint of a U-boat was in effect a big convoy with a strong destroyer escort. The same was true of troop ships and military transports, which were escorted from the beginning of the war.[32]

As the submarine crisis developed, an increasing number of people began to think about convoy. The objections to it were ostensibly practical. It was assumed (on the basis, it seems, of Grand Fleet experience) that only destroyers could escort a convoy, in the ratio of one or more for every ship escorted, though experience was to show that a few slow armed trawlers were just as effective. It was also assumed that existing patrols, however useless, could not be abandoned, so that the adoption of convoy would require building a new fleet of many hundreds of destroyers – fast, expensive, sophisticated small warships produced only by specialist builders. By elementary statistical errors, the number of ships requiring protection was grossly overestimated: 120–140 ships entering port each week and the same number sailing were inflated to 5,000 shipping movements. It was objected that merchant seamen were incapable of steaming in company without collision, though troopships and transports had no difficulty. It was objected that the disruptive effect of many ships arriving at once would overwhelm the ports, without taking account of the existing delays, amounting to 30 or 40 per cent in some trades, imposed by keeping ships in port for days or weeks when U-boats were reported offshore. It was objected that the Declaration of London clearly assumed that only military shipping would be convoyed, so that convoys by definition became legitimate targets – but Germany's 'unrestricted' submarine campaign, declaring all shipping including hospital ships as targets, evidently dissolved that objection.[33]

Behind all these arguments lay unacknowledged but powerful emotional commitments. In the minds of officers, convoy was a defensive form of war (as indeed it is, at a tactical level), and the defensive was strongly identified with moral failure and even cowardice. 'Offensive measures' (which often meant high-speed steaming to nowhere in particular) were expressions of courage and national resolve, even if they achieved nothing. Convoys therefore occupied much the same psychological space for senior British officers as the prize rules did for Germans: they might *work*, but they were repugnant to deeply held values. The difference was that the British so badly wanted to win that logic and experience did slowly make headway against atavistic prejudice. The Anti-Submarine Division of the Naval Staff, created by Jellicoe when he came to the Admiralty in December 1916, helped by providing a forum where experience could be collected and analysed.[34] For German senior officers, the attraction of 'unrestricted' submarine warfare was precisely that it epitomized German aggression and contradicted unacceptable facts; it represented the triumph of attitude over reality. 'The spirit which drives the submarine war,' declared Scheer's chief of staff, Captain Adolf von Trotha, has the strongest effect on enemy and neutral alike . . . The nearer we come to the end of the war, the greater the importance of sheer willpower; at the end of the day strength of commitment will be decisive.[35]

In the words of a modern German historian, 'Here we encounter once more a German strategy built on the assumption that victory must be possible, because it was essential.'[36] There was also a domestic political objective behind the new German submarine campaign. Forcing Wilhelm II, Bethmann Hollweg and the now centre-left majority of the Reichstag to accept the 'unrestricted' submarine war which all three opposed was a big step towards imposing a right-wing dictatorship, led by Tirpitz as co-founder of the 'Fatherland Party', with the object of gaining Germany's original war aims and stopping the slide towards democracy and a compromise peace. This failed because the Kaiser himself, uncharacteristically decisive, blocked Tirpitz's path to power.[37]

Although Jellicoe and the Admiralty Board were wrapped in despair, at the level below the Board ideas were evolving both in the Admiralty and at sea. From July 1916 destroyers and aircraft from Harwich convoyed Dutch food exports from the Hook of Holland, mainly to prevent the threat of surface attack, and with almost total success. People noticed such experiments and wanted to imitate them. In October 1916 George Ballard, now Admiral Superintendent of Malta Dockyard, proposed a trial of convoy in the Mediterranean. Two months later Rear-Admiral Sir Rosslyn Wemyss commanding in the Eastern Mediterranean made the same suggestion. Captain Reginald Drax, Beatty's chief of staff in the *Lion*, argued with exceptionally clear logic that even unescorted convoys would be better than unescorted single ships, and Norwegian shipowners demanded convoy for the Scandinavian trade. The French, whose coalfields were mostly in German hands, depended on British coal, and could not endure the effective 30–40 per cent blockade caused by sailings suspended on submarine alarms. The French naval staff analysed the data and presented the Admiralty with a meticulously argued convoy scheme, which was adopted in February 1917:

> You yourself will be forced to form convoys and to escort them in order to continue to trade. We forced you to do this twice in the past, with our privateers [pirates]. You will be forced to do it once more. This organisation of the French coal trade that I am requesting will be a trial run for you.[38]

These convoys were partly under sail and escorted only by a handful of trawlers, but losses fell at once to 0.13 per cent. In the Baltic, the Swedish and later German navies operated convoys against the attacks of British and Russian submarines. After it was clear that convoys worked, many people claimed to have thought of them first. In fact, there seems to have been no single inventor or single decision, but rather a general movement of ideas and experiments over roughly the six months from December 1916 which progressively dissolved the objections to convoy and led to its general adoption from May 1917. The final push was the possibility of American destroyers to add to the escort force after the United States declared war on Germany in April, though in the event their number and efficiency turned out to have been much exaggerated. Although it is easy, and in many ways fully justifiable, to criticize the Admiralty for its illogical opposition to convoy, it is fair to note that from the re-introduction of 'unrestricted' U-boat attacks in February 1917 it took only three months for the solution to be identified.[39]

Contemporaries believed, and some historians still believe, that the crisis of the U-boat war dated from the renewal of 'unrestricted' submarine attacks on 1 February 1917 to the introduction of convoy from May onwards. In fact, the significance of both dates is exaggerated. By withdrawing his U-boats for much of 1916 Scheer made the 'restricted' submarine campaign under the prize rules appear much less effective than it naturally was. 'Unrestricted' submarine attacks, as we have seen, were less rather than more dangerous than the prize rules, and even from February to May 1917 some 40 per cent of sinkings were still made according to the prize rules, in defiance of orders. Using the German measure, the rate of sinkings per submarine rose 11 per cent in February, but the increase in sinkings overall was entirely due to an increase in the level of submarine effort, from 581 submarine-days at sea in January to 860 in February. A total of 108 U-boats (of all classes together) were completed in 1916 and eighty-seven in 1917 (but only thirty-two in each year of the larger seagoing boats). Counting just the operational *Frontboote*, the High Seas Fleet had forty-nine in February 1917, fifty-nine next month and sixty-one in April, which was nearly the highest figure it ever attained. From the April 1917 peak, U-boat sinkings declined rapidly by all measures. By August – when the convoy system was only just beginning to be effective – they had fallen below the February figure. Between April and October, 85 per cent of submarine sinkings were of ships sailing independently, out of convoy. Their rate of loss was 6 per cent; the convoys lost 0.3 per cent.[40] The British survived the crisis months of February to August, before convoy, partly by tackling port congestion, reducing inessential imports, and drawing the essentials from nearer rather than more distant suppliers (North America rather than Australia, for instance), all of which used shipping more efficiently. There had already been a big increase in domestic agricultural production, which saved 6.7 million tons of imports between 1913 and 1918. In the summer, depth charges became available in quantity for the first time, allowing escorts to attack submerged U-boats effectively just as they were obliged to close convoys in order to attack. Most often, however, they did not attack, because they could not find the convoys. Of 219 Atlantic convoys which sailed in the last quarter of 1917, only thirty-nine were sighted by a U-boat, and only eighteen were successfully attacked. By September the Germans realized that the U-boats' rate of sinking was falling, and neutral shipowners were not being frightened away from carrying lucrative British cargoes. Although the Germans had hoped to sink 40 per cent of grain cargoes to Britain, the actual figure only once (in March 1917) exceeded 10 per cent, and in the first six months of the submarine campaign Britain's grain reserves more than doubled.[41] In the Mediterranean poor relations with, and even more between, the allies France and Italy delayed the introduction of convoy, to which the French contributed few escorts and the Italians none at all. In British opinion, the most efficient allies were the Greeks, and a flotilla of Japanese destroyers.[42]

On the German side there was an almost wilful refusal to invest in the U-boat arm. The U-boat force reached its maximum of almost one hundred operational boats in 1916, and its strength declined thereafter. Battleship-building was halted, but proposals for a mass submarine-building programme were several times refused on the grounds that the war would soon be over. No torpedo-armed submarine (as distinct from the small minelayers) was laid down between April 1915 and May 1916, and the shipyards, hampered by shortages of all kinds, were so slow that the fastest full-size U-boat ever built took eleven months over 1915–16, and no boat ordered after Jutland was completed before the end of the war, thirty-one months later. The August 1918 'Scheer Programme' promised 450 U-boats, but this was a mere fantasy. Only the Flanders Naval Corps was continually innovative, especially in 1917 when destroyers, aircraft, minesweepers and submarines were skilfully integrated.[43]

In February 1917, mutinies in the Russian army led to the abdication of the Tsar and the creation of a Provisional Government. Two months later the French army was paralysed by serious mutinies. The British offensive of Passchendaele (July–November) failed completely to clear the Flanders coast, the Italian army was crushed by the Austro-Hungarians (with German help) at Caporetto in November, and the same month the new Russian regime was overthrown by the Bolsheviks, who immediately sought peace with Germany. All Germany's enemies were now badly weakened or totally defeated, except the United States, which entered the war in April, infuriated by the U-boat campaign. This restored Britain's financial credit but left the fighting otherwise unaffected, since the USA was as yet quite unequipped to fight, and President Wilson had forbidden any preparation for war. A destroyer squadron crossed the Atlantic to participate in the anti-submarine campaign, and later four battleships were added to the Grand Fleet's already overwhelming superiority, but the Americans (like Kitchener before them) declined to send troops until they could raise and train an entire army, capable of winning the war and dominating Europe. In effect the British now found themselves employed by the US Treasury to hold the ring until their new masters were ready to take over. 'When the war is over,' President Wilson told his main foreign-policy adviser, 'Colonel' Edward House, 'we can force them to our way of thinking, because by that time they will . . . be financially in our hands.'[44] Great resources were expended in building a new US merchant fleet to capture the world carrying trade. Wilson also threatened to dismantle the British Empire, though in July he suspended the US Navy's massive battle-fleet programme. By the autumn of 1917 it was clear that convoys worked, and the U-boat campaign was failing, but it was not at all clear who was going to win the wider war.[45]

The entry of the United States into the war offered its naval officers their eagerly awaited opportunity to demonstrate the superiority of American boldness and ingenuity, but it was not so easy to identify how and where they might be deployed. The US enthusiastically took on an ambitious scheme to seal the northern exit of the North Sea by a gigantic mine barrage from Scotland to Norway, but the defects of the available mines, the great depth of the water along the Norwegian coast, Norway's refusal to mine her own territorial waters until just before the war ended, and the sheer scale of the project, prevented it having much useful effect. $21 million was spent to lay 70,117 deep mines, which possibly sank three U-boats in total out of the forty-two a month which passed the barrage.[46]

In November and December 1917, a British deep minefield (designed to catch submerged submarines without affecting ships on the surface) was laid in the Dover Strait using mines of a new design copied from the Germans. Surface patrols deploying powerful magnesium flares forced U-boats to dive into the minefields, inflicting losses which reduced the threat of the Flanders U-boats down-Channel. Then on 22 April 1918 a British naval landing force attacked the heavily defended port of Zeebrugge. The Flanders submarines and destroyers were mostly based in the inland port of Bruges and reached the sea by canals to Zeebrugge and Ostend. The object of the British attack was to block the canal by scuttling some old cruisers. This attack met with only brief success, and another on the alternative canal port of Ostend the following month was even less successful, but they were pressed with great gallantry and heavy casualties which touched the popular imagination and raised naval morale. Just as the morale of the High Seas Fleet was collapsing, the Zeebrugge raid did a lot to restore the Royal Navy's public esteem, and self-esteem. Meanwhile the Dover barrage was becoming more effective, the new (and still unsuspected) British magnetic mines were causing growing U-boat losses, and in June 1918 an air raid damaged the locks at Bruges and imprisoned the U-boats for a month. In September 1918, as the German army finally retreated, the U-boats began to abandon their bases in Flanders.[47]

As convoys made it increasingly difficult for U-boats to find targets, the U-boats tended in 1918 to move into coastal waters where much coastal shipping, and deep-sea shipping dispersed from ocean convoys on arrival at the major ports, was still unescorted. The obvious counter was a system of coastal convoys. Although the routes were fixed and concealment was scarcely possible, convoy worked just as well in coastal waters as in the open ocean. Coastal convoys prompted some U-boats to attack on the surface at night for the first time, though without success. The Admiralty expected them to concentrate for massed attacks, but U-boat captains preferred their freedom and ignored the possibilities of co-operation.[48]

The defeat of Russia made the war much wider than before. By the Treaty of Brest-Litovsk of March 1918, Russia not only withdrew from the war but ceded the Baltic states to Germany and parts of the Caucasus to the Ottoman Empire. The Russian Empire was already divided by civil wars from which an independent Poland emerged. The German armies formerly fighting Russia were now available to reinforce the Western Front, to occupy the Baltic lands, or to push into the Caucasus and back Ottoman expansion south and east towards Persia, the Middle East and India. All three possibilities caused grave anxieties for the British government. A fortnight after the signing of Brest-Litovsk a German offensive in the West shattered the BEF and drove it headlong towards the Channel coast. By early June, German shells were falling on Paris. The victorious alliance of Germany, Austria-Hungary, Bulgaria and Turkey seemed poised to master Europe and central Asia, while the USA helped itself to British trade and the Japanese gained the Far East. If Britain and the British Empire were to survive, it was vital to hold both the Channel ports and the Middle East, and this in turn demanded that British worldwide seaborne trade and communications should continue to function.[49]

In fact, the Central Powers had passed the extreme limit of their strength. The victorious German army in its apparent hour of triumph was stopped and driven back (mainly by the British) on the Western Front. In three months, August to October 1918, Germany, Austria-Hungary, Bulgaria and the Ottoman

Empire all sued for peace. On 1 November, British battleships anchored before Constantinople, two days later the High Seas Fleet mutinied, and on the 9th Wilhelm II abdicated. Two now-forgotten campaigns of 1917–18 played a significant part in British survival. One was Sir Edmund Allenby's advance northward from Egypt through Palestine, in which his armies captured Jerusalem in December 1917, won a decisive victory at Megiddo in September 1918, and took Damascus and Aleppo the following month. The other was the British operations around and on the Caspian Sea in 1918, including an improvised naval squadron with two seaplane carriers, which gained naval command of the Caspian and blocked either Germans or Bolsheviks from moving eastward towards Persia and India. These two campaigns laid the essential foundations of empire by securing the British position in the Middle East, though the threats they countered turned out to be less grave than had been feared.[50]

The Great War was the first in which aircraft were widely employed in naval warfare, and among the belligerents the British took the lead in most aspects except the use of rigid airships, the German speciality. To understand what happened in British naval aviation during the war it is essential to distinguish naval aviation from the activities of the Royal Naval Air Service, not all of which had to do with the Navy, or even aircraft. Several of the RNAS's early leaders were omnivorous 'empire-builders', such as Captain Murray Sueter and Wing Commander Charles Samson, but in May 1915 the strenuous, imaginative and mildly chaotic spirit of Churchill's leadership gave way to Balfour's more logical and orthodox integration of the Royal Naval Air Service with the Navy, so that Naval Air Stations reported to their local naval commander-in-chief rather than inventing activities for themselves.

When Churchill left the Admiralty in May 1915, Samson had to hand over to the War Office fifteen armoured-car squadrons, three armoured trains, several kite-balloon squadrons and a 1,500-man anti-aircraft force (though the development of tanks remained the responsibility of the 'Admiralty Landships Committee' set up by the Director of Naval Construction). This sort of buccaneering approach was calculated to annoy other services, and indeed the regular Navy. In February 1916 the RNAS was forced to hand over the air and anti-aircraft defence of Britain to the army, retaining only over-water flying.[51] In a further concession to conventional wisdom, a British rigid airship programme was revived at the same time.[52]

Shortly before, in January 1916, Rear-Admiral Rosslyn Wemyss, Commander-in-Chief East Indies, had formed the East Indies and Egypt Seaplane Squadron, which has some claim to be called the world's first 'carrier squadron'.[53] What chiefly interested the Admiralty Air Department and the

RNAS leadership in 1916, however, was not naval flying but strategic bombing as the answer to Zeppelins and U-boats alike. In this they found allies in the French, who were keen to attack German industry, and had an advanced aero-engine industry to contribute. In May 1916, No. 3 Wing RNAS formed in secrecy at Luxeuil in eastern France, under French command, to participate in a French strategic bombing campaign which the Royal Flying Corps (RFC) strongly resented when it found out. In October, No. 3 Wing moved to an airfield near Nancy to be nearer its targets in the Saar. Its bombing was guided by a sophisticated analysis by Lieutenant-Commander Viscount Tiverton, which identified as a key target the synthetic nitrate plants on which the German explosives industry depended: BASF at Ludwigshafen; Meister, Lucius & Brüning at Höchst; and Bayer of Cologne. On days when these distant targets were inaccessible, the nearby Saar steelworks made useful substitutes.[54]

In May 1916, the same month as No. 3 Wing RNAS was formed, an Air Board was established to co-ordinate the manifestly uncoordinated aviation policies of the Navy and army. The discovery that the RNAS had secretly established a private strategic bomber force in France without telling the War Office provided a case in point. Lord Curzon, the Air Board's first chairman, loathed Balfour and was as far from neutrality between the Admiralty and the War Office as it was possible to be. He encouraged the press to attack the Admiralty for neglecting aviation, and was openly joined by Captain Sueter, the former Director of the Admiralty Air Department, whose ambition was to become the head of an independent air service. Public disquiet over Zeppelin bombing raids – trivial as the damage they inflicted appeared to be to a later generation – added more fuel to the fire, and the fact that the RFC desperately needed fighter aircraft and the RNAS had all the best of them further envenomed inter-service relations.[55]

Meanwhile the seagoing Navy in general, and the Grand Fleet in particular, resented the diversion of naval air effort from naval needs. In air matters as in others Jellicoe was convinced that the enemy was vastly better provided than he was himself, and attributed Scheer's escape after Jutland to Zeppelin reconnaissance. In reality the German airships suffered from North Sea visibility as badly as the ships, and their navigation was even worse, so that on the rare occasions when they sighted British ships and correctly identified them, their reported positions were usually too far adrift to be useful. A British seaplane from the *Engadine* briefly participated in Jutland, but a flimsy, underpowered aircraft with a defective wireless set could make no effective contribution to naval reconnaissance. It was not the RNAS but the innovative Austro-Hungarian naval air force, fully integrated with fleet operations, which achieved a notable 'first' in September 1916 when two flying-boats not only sank the French submarine *Foucault* in the Adriatic, but captured her entire crew.[56]

Jellicoe was a convinced supporter of naval flying whose arrival at the Admiralty did a great deal to change the atmosphere there, but he represented the Grand Fleet's interest in seaborne aircraft integrated into naval operations, whereas the press had largely adopted the RNAS as the forerunner of a land-based independent air service. Between July and September 1917 the three reports of Major-General Jan Smuts' committee on air defence proposed just such a service as the answer to the raids on London by German Gotha bombers, and the Cabinet was already moving that way.[57] Only Sir Hugh Trenchard, commander of the RFC in France, took the opposite line that a unified 'air force' was a German plot to wreck the Royal Flying Corps, but Lloyd George had already made up his mind. The new Royal Air Force, dominated by the RFC, came into existence on 1 April 1918. It took the RNAS long-range bomber force and used it for tactical purposes. Only when it had lost its cherished bombers did the Admiralty Air Division start to take a serious interest in torpedo bombing, anti-submarine aircraft and other naval flying, and by the end of the war it was already clear that there was no chance that the new Air Staff would agree. The Navy's political defeat was not the result of lack of enthusiasm for aircraft, but lack of clear thinking on how to employ them. First Churchill set up a semi-detached private force, then Balfour allowed it to drift further away from naval requirements. By the time the dangers became clear, the Admiralty had lost control of land-based naval aviation, and had limited influence over the supply of aircraft to the Navy.[58]

But in the final year (1917–18) of the RNAS its *naval* aircraft enjoyed a final flourish, notably at Felixstowe Naval Air Station, where a series of powerful and well-armed flying-boats were built, designed by Wing-Commander John Porte. The Felixstowe flying-boats set up a 'spider's web' pattern of regular anti-submarine patrols in the southern North Sea, centred on the Noord Hinder Lightship and exploiting wireless intelligence of the movements of U-boats. The aircraft as yet had few means of damaging or destroying submarines, but by locating them and forcing them to dive they effectively neutralized them, and it seems likely that several U-boats whose fate was never established were actually sunk by aircraft. Most of the anti-submarine air effort, however, involved much simpler but more reliable aircraft; kite balloons and non-rigid 'blimp' airships. Kite balloons, adopted from the army, were simply aerodynamically shaped balloons towed by a ship, with an observer in a basket linked to the ship by telephone. First used to spot for gunfire at Gallipoli in 1915–16, they soon proved very effective against submarines. Warships found kite balloons could be towed at up to 22 knots, an observer at 3,000 feet could see sixty miles in clear weather, and a convoy could easily fly one or several, providing complete warning of surfaced submarines in daylight. As a bonus, minefields could often be observed from the air and the coastal convoy system sharply reduced losses to mines. More than 150 ships were fitted with kite balloons. Alternatively, many coastal convoys were covered by self-propelled 'blimps'; small, simple non-rigid airships, ideal for slow-speed patrolling, though (like the German Zeppelins) more liable than winged aircraft to be grounded by bad weather. In addition, unarmed obsolete aircraft flew 'scarecrow patrols' over convoys to frighten U-boats into submerging. By April 1918 all naval airships and more than 80 per cent of RNAS two-seater aircraft were fitted with wireless to report what they could observe and direct ships to attack surfaced U-boats. In the course of 1918 some 4,869 convoys in home waters were escorted by seaplanes or landplanes, 2,141 by airships and 131 by kite balloons; of which just two, one and three respectively were attacked. In the whole war only five ships were ever sunk from convoys with air cover. By the end of the war the former RNAS operated a daily average of 190 aeroplanes, 300 seaplanes and flying-boats, and 75 airships, together flying 14,000 hours a month on average, with 28 U-boats sighted and 19 attacked. These figures were not matched in the Second World War until mid-1943.[59]

The army's hostility to the RNAS strategic bombing programme finally succeeded in getting No. 3 Wing disbanded in April 1917 – but in June and July Britain herself came under air attack from German Gotha G.IV aircraft based in Belgium. With an endurance of four hours in the air, a ceiling of 21,000 feet and a bomb load of a thousand pounds, the Gotha was a real strategic bomber. Its wingspan of 78 feet was greater than that of any German aircraft over Britain in the Second World War (though its contemporary the Zeppelin-Staaken R-VI *Riesenflugzeug*, or 'Giant', was even bigger, with a wingspan of 138 feet). On 13 June 1917 a Gotha air raid on London killed 162 people around Liverpool Street Station, and another on 7 July caused further casualties. The public divided its anger equally between the Germans and the RFC, now responsible for home air defence. There seemed to be no easy answer to bombing except retaliation, so suddenly the RFC wanted the strategic bombers which only the RNAS possessed.[60]

The Grand Fleet, meanwhile, empowered by Lloyd George's War Cabinet appointing Jellicoe as First Sea Lord and Beatty to command the Grand Fleet in December 1916, was developing a naval air strategy of its own using shipborne aircraft. In August 1917 Captain Herbert Richmond of the battleship

Conqueror and Flight-Commander Frederick Rutland RNAS (he who had flown the *Engadine*'s seaplane at Jutland) proposed a force of 120 of the new Sopwith Cuckoo torpedo-bombers aboard eight aircraft carriers to attack the High Seas Fleet in Jade Bay. The same month the Zeppelin *L-23* was shot down off the Danish coast by a Sopwith Pup fighter flown off an improvised platform on the light cruiser *Yarmouth*. This led to a programme of fitting short flying-off platforms over cruisers' forward guns, from which light naval fighters could take off with the ship steaming into the wind. From this Rutland developed longer and heavier platforms mounted on battleships' gun turrets which could be turned into the wind to fly-off two-seater reconnaissance aircraft without the ship having to alter course. By the end of the war ships of the Grand Fleet carried more than a hundred aircraft without counting the 'Flying Squadron of the Grand Fleet', originally formed in July 1917 with five seaplane carriers, which in November 1917 became a flag-officer's command under Rear-Admiral Richard Phillimore as 'Admiral Commanding Aircraft'. By this date Beatty knew that the Navy was about to lose its aircraft to the new Royal Air Force, but at least Phillimore's authority over aircraft afloat could not be challenged. On 1 December 1918 the Flying Squadron had 54 aircraft, including 18 torpedo-bombers, crewed by 80 pilots, 46 observers and 498 airmen. The rest of the Grand Fleet and its associated air stations added 124 pilots, 44 observers, 1,054 airmen and 161 Wrens. The planned mass torpedo-bomber attack on the High Seas Fleet was still beyond the reach of the possible, but not far beyond, and Beatty eagerly embraced the scheme. In July 1918 seven Sopwith Camels from the *Furious* attacked the Zeppelin sheds at Tondern (Tønder) in Jutland and destroyed two airships. This was the world's first air attack by wheeled aircraft taking off from a ship's flight deck, though it was not yet possible to land back onto *Furious* and the returning aircraft had to 'ditch' in the sea. The war ended before the planned mass torpedo attack could be mounted on the German fleet, but in 1919 it was run as an exercise on British warships in Portland Harbour.[61]

SIXTEEN

The Rise of the Warfare State
Government and Administration 1914–1918

T he failure of the battle-fleets to deliver victory directed naval attention towards alternative forms of victory, starting with economic warfare, but in this as in other aspects of the war, different ministries were left to pursue their own war aims with only weak co-ordination. The Admiralty from the first applied what it called 'blockade', meaning measures to stop Germany's foreign trade and block her access to essential imports. In the first week of the war 245 German merchant ships were captured and 1,059 laid up in neutral ports, leaving 221 in the Baltic and virtually none free to trade anywhere else in the world. The word 'blockade', generally used then and now, was strictly improper, for the only legal form of blockade would have been a close blockade, which was operationally impossible off German ports, and legally impossible off the neutral ports which actually shipped most German imports and exports. By seizing Belgium, Germany had moved Antwerp from the neutral to the enemy category, but that still left Rotterdam, Amsterdam and Copenhagen besides many smaller Dutch and Scandinavian ports handling the bulk of German foreign trade. In legal terms Britain's right to arrest neutral shipping was at best uncertain. The principle of the 'continuous voyage', first laid down in the eighteenth century by the High Court of Admiralty, held that a single shipment might make part or all of its journey under neutral flags, and be trans-shipped from one to another, but could still be seized if it was ultimately coming from or going to the enemy. The Declaration of London reaffirmed this principle only for absolute, not conditional, contraband. Thus, a cargo of, say, cotton, shipped from a neutral US port to neutral Copenhagen in a neutral ship, could be condemned only on clear proof that the ultimate destination was Germany, and the ultimate purpose to make guncotton, since explosives were absolute contraband liable to seizure in all circumstances. Most raw materials were absolutely free, and food was conditional contraband, which could be condemned only on proof that it was intended to feed the enemy forces. The authors of the Declaration of London had assumed that merchant ships still carried authentic documents naming the owners and consignees of their cargoes, as they had in the eighteenth century. In reality, by the early twentieth century most cargoes were shipped by anonymous agents and often changed hands during the voyage. The documents travelled separately, and it was rare for a ship's manifest to reveal the true owners or ultimate destination of her cargo. Consequently, it was hard to get even the most suspicious cargo condemned in the Prize Court, and economic warfare at sea became all but impossible. This had been the intention of the drafters of the Declaration of London, who anticipated that Britain would once again be the greatest neutral trader in wartime.[1]

In the summer of 1914 British priorities began to change. On 29 October an Order in Council radically extended belligerent rights by assuming the power to declare a neutral state a 'base of supplies for the enemy', so that neutral ports might become enemy ports by proxy, and the neutral shipper would have to prove his innocence, if he could. Circumstantial evidence was now quite enough for the British prize court. Lard, for instance, was a raw material for nitroglycerine: if US lard exports to Scandinavia in October and November 1914 were sixty times greater than in the same period of the previous year, that was enough to prove that the Scandinavians were buying on behalf of German explosives manufacturers. If copper imports into European neutral countries suddenly increased sevenfold, 'the presumption is very strong that the bulk of the copper consigned to these countries has recently been intended not for their own use but for that of a belligerent who cannot import it directly'.[2] In acting thus the British easily convinced themselves that commonsense presumption was as good as formal proof and that they were the true upholders of international law. The neutral traders who profited so greatly from clandestine dealings with Germany naturally preferred a more rigid insistence on documentary evidence.[3]

The British government, however, was as divided on blockade as on all other aspects of its strategy and applied the powers it had assumed with extreme hesitation and inconsistency. The Board of Trade, that citadel of free-trade Liberalism, was not even pretending to back the blockade. It stood for business as usual, in order to pay for the war, so City banks continued to finance international trade, Germany's included. The War Office had broken all its promises not to recruit skilled men from industry, so exports were collapsing, imperilling the balance of payments and the finance of the war. Lloyd George at the Exchequer wanted total war, to win quickly while he still could.

The Admiralty (and the French) wanted a ruthless application of sea power against Germany and those who traded with her, but the Foreign Office, which oversaw the blockade, was alert to the consequences of ruining the US economy by blocking cotton exports. Slowly it became aware that British firms were just as deeply involved as the neutrals in indirect trade with the enemy. Danish factories, for instance, packed imported US meat for the German army in tins made of British tinplate. Both Britain and France exempted key industries from controls, so that German airships were built with French aluminium frames and covered with British cotton fabric.[4]

The British army of 1914 was essentially unmechanized; Kitchener said that equipping it 'was not much more difficult than buying a straw hat at Harrods'.[5] He aimed to mobilize as many men as possible as quickly as possible to win the war on the Western Front single-handed, and was shocked to discover that the British munitions industry was not capable of supplying unlimited quantities of artillery and ammunition at no notice, especially when a quarter of its workforce had been killed in action in the first six months of the war. Instead of obstructing war, as many had expected, the workers craved it. In the first two months 750,000 men (10 per cent of the British industrial workforce) volunteered; 1.2 million between August and December 1914. It was this which gave Kitchener his mass army, and a Cabinet incapable of leadership then allowed him to take over the conduct of the war. As a military man in wartime, he expected obedience: it was the duty of all other departments to yield to the War Office's demands, and he had no idea of negotiation or discussion within government. He vetoed the Board of Trade's proposal for national manpower planning, and conscription was still politically unimaginable to a Liberal Cabinet. Kitchener wanted an army of seventy divisions, which was fifteen more than the Treasury and the Board of Trade thought the money and manpower of the country could sustain, but he dismissed their objections:[6]

> This is not a Government's war on limited liability principles, but the Nation's war, and we shall not win it except by a supreme national effort such as our enemies are making . . . We should remember that, if we do not win, no soundness of finance will avail us. We shall be bled white.[7]

Kitchener's dominance of the Cabinet sidelined the Committee of Imperial Defence and the General Staff, eliminating staff work and co-ordination between services. Kitchener himself took a significant step towards limiting his power in 1916 by accepting the Chief of the Imperial General Staff, Sir William Robertson, as the professional head of the army and his principal service adviser – which clearly implied that Kitchener himself had shed his uniform to 'take rank' as Secretary of State for War and a Cabinet minister, rather than as a field marshal and a military hero. However, the decision to adopt conscription in April 1916 effectively handed over the conduct of the war to the War Office, leaving strategy, industry and agriculture out of account. Kitchener himself was eliminated in June 1916 (to the private relief of his Cabinet colleagues) when the ship taking him on a military mission to Russia, HMS *Hampshire*, was mined and sunk west of the Orkney Islands.[8]

In May 1915 Asquith had to reconstruct his weakened government as a coalition, and the Conservative backbenchers – still strongly Beresfordite – insisted on a clean sweep at the Admiralty as their price for joining the Liberals. Fisher resigned and Churchill was forced out, replaced by the leading Conservative naval expert, Arthur Balfour.[9] By now the Foreign Office, the Board of Trade and the Admiralty were completely at loggerheads, but the Cabinet ministers who could agree on so little all agreed to blame the disappointments of the Gallipoli operation on Churchill – almost the only one of them who had opposed the landings from the start – rather than on Kitchener, who had dominated the major decisions. The French and the public were becoming aware that Britain's half-hearted muddle was half supporting the German war effort. Asquith formed a new version of the War Council named the Dardanelles Committee (later War Committee), but decisions were lost even more effectively than before in his thicket of ad hoc committees without agendas or minutes. Balfour the urbane philosopher was possibly the most learned First Lord of the Admiralty in history, but he had neither the temperament nor (as a Conservative minister in a still mainly Liberal government) the political authority to inject urgency and leadership:

> He 'did his work at the Admiralty I believe quite admirably, but in Cabinet all the faults which he had shown as P.M. in the 1900 [Parliament] were accentuated. He yearned for decisions just as heartily as [Asquith] loathed them; yet he never did anything to obtain them . . . He had the vision which the P.M. lacked, but it led to nothing. Philosophy is the worst possible training for politics.[10]

By the end of 1915 Britain was sliding into a major political and financial crisis, with the government all but paralysed. Jellicoe, who had established his own economic intelligence staff in the Grand Fleet, was playing a growing part in informing and inspiring Parliamentary pressure on the government.[11]

In February 1916 Asquith was forced to concede the creation of a Ministry of Blockade with the power to override other departments. In the same month the creation of a 'black list' of firms trading with the enemy in effect outlawed neutrality and finally abandoned the pre-war world economy. In June 1916 an allied conference at Paris established a unified system of economic war. 'Blockade' had now largely ceased to be a physical barrier to trade and become a worldwide system of contraband control, based on detailed information about individual traders and cargoes collected by cable and postal censorship, and denying credit, insurance and coal to those who supplied the enemy. A rationing policy based on good knowledge of the real consumption of neutral countries allowed them sufficient imports for their own use but no surplus to re-export to Germany. The British government made agreements with American industrial lobbies such as the Rubber Agreement and the Textile Alliance, which were granted import privileges in return for stopping 'leakage' of exports to Germany. Although the United States was still neutral, it was at her suggestion that an inspection regime was established in American and other neutral ports, which issued 'navicerts' to merchant ships of all nations carrying cargoes acceptable to Britain and her allies. The 'navicert' was the bureaucratic answer to the U-boat; it did not sink ships or kill seafarers, it simply stopped cargoes from sailing which would supply the enemy.[12]

The central organization that made all this possible was the Trade Clearing House, later War Trade Intelligence Department, which collected, indexed, classified and circulated information about firms and individuals who had, or might have, dealings with the enemy. At its busiest period over the winter of 1916–17 the department read about a thousand telegrams and twenty-three letters a day; by the end of the war it had read about 80 million telegrams in many languages, and its 'Traders' Index' listed about one million names. Every month it issued new editions of the *General Black List* and *Who's Who in War Trade*, besides detailed analyses of numerous individual cases. This informal, civilian (and nearly half female) organization came to be so completely trusted in Whitehall for the accuracy and impartiality of its research that even military departments like the Admiralty handed over their own economic intelligence units and relied entirely on the WTID. At the end of the war the department was closed, but the massive card-indexes which formed its institutional memory were carefully guarded in case Britain might once again find herself engaged in economic warfare. Indeed, the WTID's significance went beyond economics; it provided an admirable template for a joint civilian-military interdepartmental intelligence organization as a 'force-multiplier' in modern warfare.[13]

In an information war like this, neutral and belligerent rights were the subject of constant bargaining and compromise even more than they had been in former eras. Norwegian fishermen, for instance, depended on coal and other supplies from Britain, and therefore sold 85 per cent of their catch in Britain. When German U-boats sank Norwegian ships in reprisal, Sweden and Denmark came to Norway's support and forced Germany to retreat. Dutch trawlers got their coal from Germany and were less susceptible to British pressure, but allowed the British to outbid the Germans for a proportion of their catch. Norway exported copper ore to Germany, until the British stopped coal supplies and in effect forced the Norwegian merchant fleet to trade on British rather than German account. The Dutch government banned British armed merchantmen from its ports, but interned U-boats which grounded on its coast, angering each side about equally. Knowing that Rotterdam, Amsterdam and Dordrecht functioned practically as German ports under the 1831 Rhine Convention, the Dutch realized that the British had a strong case against them for un-neutral behaviour. They therefore consented to the creation of a discreet and unofficial arrangement between the leading Dutch trading and shipping companies, the 'Netherlands Overseas Trust' ('NOT'),[14] which undertook to police Dutch foreign trade and guarantee no re-exports to Germany (except coffee and tobacco which the British agreed to). The Dutch government, which had no legal power to act in this way, remained invisible, and the British worked through the NOT. In 1916, with evidence that Dutch food exports to Germany had massively increased during the war, the British applied heavy pressure, and the Dutch consented to reduce German purchases, though not to eliminate them altogether. At times the Dutch seemed on the verge of being sucked into the war, but ultimately both belligerents preferred them to be neutral.[15]

As in previous wars, powerful belligerents changed the rules to suit themselves – but as in previous wars, the neutral powers in effect acted as a court of appeal for international law, reacting against obvious abuses. Belligerents could not afford to provoke neutrals into active enmity or even war. Britain above all could not afford to provoke the United States into hostility, and continually adapted its policy to retain at least a minimum of neutral goodwill. Instead of following suit, Germany stuck rigidly to its position that war dissolved the whole edifice of international law, leaving Germany free to do whatever she wished. Neutrals that did not accept this – which of course none of them did – were gradually driven into the British camp despite all their frustrations with British policy, while Britain herself was able to justify otherwise unjustifiable actions as reprisals for German illegalities. It is not wholly cynical to sum up the First World War as a contest between Britain and Germany to see who could be the first and worst abuser of belligerent rights to provoke the United States to war. By heroic feats of brutality and aggression, Germany won this contest – and lost the war.[16]

It would have been natural to expect the Americans, as the greatest of the neutral powers, to gather the others in a new 'League of Armed Neutrality', capable of applying irresistible pressure on the belligerents.[17] This did not happen because US policy, while freely invoking the name of international law, actually followed an erratic line of its own which departed from accepted legal principles in many respects, and made no pretence of treating other neutral powers as equals. President Woodrow Wilson was an historian who drew parallels between himself and James Madison (the only previous President from Princeton University) and was determined to avoid Madison's mistake of committing the United States to fight for Napoleon in 1812. Neither Wilson nor his advisers knew much about international law, and his concept of neutrality was based on moral superiority rather than impartiality. As the prophet ordained to lead the nations into the promised land of peace, he had the right and duty to arbitrate between them. Keeping his eyes firmly fixed on the distant horizon, he preferred to overlook tiresome practicalities. In private he became increasingly convinced (by the U-boat campaign in particular) that Germany did not deserve support, but in public he maintained a pretence of neutrality by erratic swerves from one view to another; one of his greatest strengths was his ability to remain utterly convinced of his own consistency while repeatedly reversing his position. In all this Britain quite falsely proclaimed that it was following the precedents established by American policy during the civil war, and the US privately agreed to take the same line, sacrificing the rights of other neutral traders in return for the exemption of her cotton exports from British controls. Even the Admiralty was astonished at Washington's supine abandonment of neutral rights, but after the sinking of the *Lusitania* in 1915, no country would identify with a pro-German position. Not for the last time, Germany chose means rather than ends: extreme, gratuitous military violence which destroyed political goals and undermined military effectiveness. Hitherto a firm opponent of US naval expansion, Wilson suddenly in 1916 backed a huge building programme of ten battleships, six battle-cruisers, ten light cruisers, fifty destroyers and sixty-seven submarines. Congress voted $500 million over three years, allowing four battleships and four battle-cruisers to be ordered at once. The first year's vote of $312 million was seven times Britain's annual naval spending from 1904 to 1914, and thirty times Germany's between 1909 and 1914. It is unclear what Wilson or Congress meant to do with this fleet, but the leadership of the US Navy looked forward to a fantasy war against an Anglo-Japanese coalition, and in the 1915 and 1916 naval manoeuvres rehearsed the defeat of a British invasion.[18]

The United States finally entered the war in April 1917 as a 'co-belligerent' rather than an ally, but in practice she fully joined in the enforcement of the blockade, which became very much more dangerous to Germany. By now it was bearing heavily on the civilian population. German farmers had already lost three-fifths of their men and horses to the army, while fertilizer production was converted to explosives, but the government refused to raise agricultural prices to encourage output, and much of what was produced went to the black market rather than the meagre official rations. Through the 'turnip winter' of 1916–17 and beyond, Germans in the countryside were well fed, army and naval officers and their families were very well fed, but ordinary soldiers and sailors, the urban working classes and all who could not afford black-market prices suffered, while neutrals whose own imports were 'rationed' by the blockade were prevented from making up the difference.[19]

During 1916 Asquith's now-coalition government continued to weaken. The Admiralty's inability to find any answer to U-boat attacks, and the War Office's futile and bloody frontal attacks on entrenched German positions, aroused a rising sense of anger and desperation, but the public and Parliament were still fully committed to the war, and the difficulty was to identify a politician who could construct a better government with better policies, and without a general election. The fractious British Cabinet was desperate to do something but could not generate sufficient unity to face hard decisions. With France and Russia apparently on the verge of military collapse, and Britain of bankruptcy, American offers to broker a 'decent peace' seemed very attractive to the Liberals – but not to Andrew Bonar Law and the Conservatives, with a majority in the Commons, and in all probability a majority in a general election, who still demanded victory, mistrusted President Wilson's devious manoeuvres in the wake of the sinking of the *Lusitania*, and after the 1916 Naval Act regarded the US as a potential enemy more than an honest arbitrator.[20]

The major political change came in December 1916, when David Lloyd George became Prime Minister of a new coalition, with the Ulster Unionist leader Sir Edward Carson as First Lord of the Admiralty, Jellicoe as First Sea Lord, and Beatty succeeding to the command of the Grand Fleet. Lloyd George as wartime Prime Minister was the greatest possible contrast to Asquith: 'very clever, with vision, prevision, driving power and courage in wonderful combination', as Selborne put it, but 'he would leave anyone in the lurch'.[21] Vigorous, eloquent, imaginative, supple and devious, he drove through radical changes and appointed others who did the same. To win the war he changed the social and constitutional landscape of Britain, creating a semi-centralized welfare and warfare state much of which has never been dismantled. He turned the premiership into something like an American presidency, with the new

Cabinet Office as the central secretariat which extended its control into all areas of government, and a personal secretariat in Downing Street. His War Cabinet consisted of just five Liberal and Unionist leaders, 'a dictatorship in commission', in the words of the new Cabinet Secretary Maurice Hankey; many of the working ministers outside Cabinet were not politicians but business-men.[22] In practice the new War Cabinet functioned as a series of standing committees which co-ordinated policy and strategy between departments, while the Cabinet itself arbitrated in disputes between them. The establishment in November 1917 of the inter-allied Supreme War Council at Versailles gave Lloyd George an external influence to counterbalance the Imperial General Staff, which allowed the Cabinet more freedom of manoeuvre.[23]

Lloyd George's 1917 War Cabinet was the first British government of the war with a capacity to form and execute policy equal to the needs of the moment. The Admiralty likewise evolved under pressure, especially the pressure to act as an operational headquarters empowered by wireless to exercise direct control over ships at sea. At the beginning of the war, as we have seen, it was already acting in this way, but the whole duty fell on a handful of grossly overworked senior officers. Even when the staff were increasingly drawn into supporting decision-makers, they were still too few to control the range and complexity of operations at sea. The inability of admirals at sea to comprehend and control everything that was going on in their commands allowed, and compelled, the Admiralty to act as a super-headquarters, but without sufficient capacity to do it properly. The Admiralty could do enough to inject a great deal of muddle into action at sea, but until well after Jutland it still lacked the structure and manpower to exercise effective mastery of the situation at sea. In October 1917 the First Sea Lord was given formal authority by Order in Council to issue operational orders, and in January 1918 the Cabinet was sufficiently confident in the Naval Staff to extend the power to his subordinates. At the same time the Admiralty was being drawn into filling the vacuum left by the Cabinet's inability to formulate grand strategy. In the new machinery of wartime government, the naval and military staffs had expanded enormously to take on the responsibilities which the civilian government was unable or unwilling to handle. As a result, the First Sea Lord was increasingly present in Cabinet as a quasi-minister, supported by a uniformed and civilian staff. Jellicoe brought many officers with recent sea experience from the Grand Fleet, and was a major employer of civilians, including women and (wartime entry) RNVR officers. By 1917 the power of the Admiralty had expanded both upwards, into the sphere of policy which had hitherto belonged to ministers alone, and outwards, to usurp much of the authority of the commanders-in-chief. According to pre-war convention, neither naval offi-cers nor Admiralty clerks could legitimately make policy, but the new Plans Division of the Naval Staff, created in July 1917, was in practice a policy and co-ordinating department, and acted as the First Sea Lord's private office. By 1918 it was acceptable for both officers and senior civil servants of the Naval Staff to acknowledge that in formulating 'staff requirements' they were at least sharing in policy-making. Where naval staff were still gravely deficient even in 1918 was in operational commands facing the enemy, like Dover, where the commanders-in-chief did not have the research and planning capacity to sup-port the operations they were expected to undertake.[24]

The reorganization of the Naval Staff in May 1917, when it was completely and formally merged with the operational side of the Admiralty, was not so much a radical change as the explicit recognition of developments over many months past. Jellicoe as First Sea Lord now took on the title of Chief of the Naval Staff as well. He, with the Deputy and Assistant Chiefs of Staff, all admi-rals, ran the operational side of the Admiralty, while civilian Lords Commis-sioners dealt with the administration of the Navy, and the Admiralty Board was formally divided into two committees correspondingly. These changes addressed the major remaining faults in Admiralty organization, but they did not change the people: a philosopher First Lord like Balfour, who pondered big questions of policy but provided very little active leadership; a Deputy, later Chief of the Naval Staff like Sir Henry Oliver (1915-18), whose voracious appe-tite for detail and total inability to delegate left no time at all to glance at big issues; a dry, precise, inflexible bachelor Secretary of the Admiralty like Sir William Graham Greene (1911-17), master of administrative forms – they might all have been regarded as normal or even ideal holders of their positions a few years before, but all fell short of the demands of wartime.[25] Oliver was still obsessively hoarding administrative trivia and would not surrender even his typing, while to the growing alarm of ministers Jellicoe sank steadily further into gloom, refusing to change, to delegate, or to let go of obviously incompe-tent friends.[26]

In July 1917 the lightweight Carson was replaced by Sir Eric Geddes, a typ-ical Lloyd George minister, being a Scottish railway traffic manager who had made his reputation organizing the railway network supporting the Western Front. Geddes did not find this background won him easy authority over the Admiralty, and the abrupt manner with which he dismissed Jellicoe on Christ-mas Eve 1917 lost him much of what support he had. The new First Sea Lord, Sir Rosslyn Wemyss, was initially an unpopular and distrusted figure, and moreover a very unconventional choice to be the professional head of the

Navy. He was not a gunnery officer or a technical specialist of any kind, and he had spent the war in the Mediterranean rather than the Grand Fleet. Remarkably, for a British admiral of his generation, he had a natural talent for choosing the right people and leaving them to get on with their jobs. He throve on responsibility, but administration bored him, and he delegated it with relief: 'In the same proportion as I have been able to shed details,' he told Geddes in February 1918, 'so has my work become increasingly interesting, and I am able to give my mind to policy and bigger matters much more easily.'[27] A sophisticated, statesmanlike figure with an easy command of French, Wemyss was ideally suited to lead the Navy in a coalition war. Geddes and Wemyss between them understood what the Naval Staff had to do, assigned it the number and quality of people it needed, and left it to get on with its job. A new Secretary of the Admiralty, Sir Oswyn Murray, brought a new energy and harmony to Admiralty administration. 'Since Sir Rosslyn Wemyss became First Sea Lord,' Geddes told Lloyd George, 'the tone of the staff working in the Navy has changed from indecision, vacillation, secrecy and over-work, combined with caution even amounting to timidity, to keen co-operation with a broad offensive outlook and the best possible chance being given to the younger men.'[28] Different divisions of the Naval Staff were integrated, unlike before, and intelligence was shared. A notable example was the new Anti-Submarine Division Chart Room, where convoy movements and U-boat intelligence were plotted together so that the convoys could be diverted away from the submarines.[29]

Behind these changes lay a new clarity of thought and language. At the beginning of the war the prevailing idea of strategy in Britain was close to what is now called the 'operational level', dealing with details below the level of grand strategy, and therefore the business of the General Staff rather than the Cabinet. Much the same was true in Germany, where intelligent observers of 'the most stupid of all wars' (to quote Crown Prince Rupert of Bavaria) complained that it seemed to have no political objectives at all, and in France where the essentially tactical concept of the 'spirit of the offensive' led to the domination of trench warfare. But by 1917 the new British Cabinet had reached a broader understanding of strategy, which was to be passed on to the generation which fought the Second World War.[30]

For the British government as a whole, learning to manage a modern war meant ministries learning to work together, and this was possible only to a limited extent until the Cabinet itself learnt to work together under Lloyd George. Until then ministries were rivals, and the Admiralty was at a great advantage because, as the heir of the Navy Board, it had been dealing with industry since the sixteenth century. Its stock of heavy guns, machinery and advanced technology vastly exceeded the army's. Before the War Office had awoken to the demands of modern war, the Admiralty had put in its orders, protected its workers from conscription and claimed a large share of national steel production. Of the 480,000 protected industrial workers in July 1915, 400,000 belonged to the Admiralty, which controlled three-quarters of the maritime industrial labour force and virtually all its skilled men. The Ministry of Munitions never succeeded in laying claim to any of them and had to rely heavily on unskilled women throughout the war:

> In a period when a general view and a just proportion were the master-keys, they [the Admiralty] vigorously asserted their claim to be a realm within a realm – efficient, colossal, indispensable, well-disposed, but independent.[31]

This generated much resentment among less fortunate, or less provident, ministries and ministers.[32]

Another area of naval administration which suffered from lack of clear thinking and consistent policy was scientific research. The Navy had long been involved in applied research, the practical development of weapons and equipment whose basic form was already identified, but it had little familiarity with fundamental research; no clear sense of what it was nor how to do it. The more the public saw reason to be dissatisfied with the conduct of the war, the more numerous the interest groups which claimed to have the secret of victory. Scientists were prominent among them and argued loudly in the press that science had been neglected, and that the war effort demanded a single department to co-ordinate all scientific research. When Arthur Balfour became First Lord in May 1915, he was both sympathetic to the idea, and alert to the political expediency of yielding to public pressure. This was the origin of the Board of Invention and Research, set up under the Admiralty at the beginning of July. From the beginning its founding idea ('research is a good thing and will somehow lead to valuable discoveries') was fatally compromised by another, unspoken objective ('something must be found to keep Lord Fisher out of mischief'). Fisher's emotional, unschooled enthusiasms had always been the polar opposite of the careful investigation needed for any sort of scientific research, and by this stage in his life, aged seventy-four, he had largely lost whatever instincts of restraint and moderation he had ever possessed. As Chairman of the 'Board of Intrigue and Revenge' (as it was soon named) his abusive and vindictive behaviour soon reduced the new organization to uproar. Naval establishments already engaged in research fought to keep their work out of

Fisher's hands, but he had a destructive effect on anti-submarine research in particular.[33]

In 1914 the Navy bought a quarter or more of the output of British ship-builders; by 1916 the proportion was three-quarters, and merchant shipbuild-ing had fallen to one-third of its pre-war level. That had to change as the U-boat crisis mounted. The Admiralty was put in charge of the whole shipbuilding and ship-repair industry because it alone controlled the steel, labour and man-agerial capacity which were needed. It was able to bring about a huge increase in merchant shipbuilding accompanied by a lesser but still formidable increase in warship building. Against this, the maintenance of the Navy in wartime did not keep pace with arduous wartime service, and much of the fleet was worn out by 1918. Fisher's sharp reduction in dockyard capacity in 1906 had a destructive effect ten years later, only partly made up by the new dockyard at Rosyth on the Firth of Forth which started working in 1916.[34] As a consumer, the Navy used 2.28 million tons of coal and 1.9 million tons of oil at Scapa Flow alone during the war, and worldwide it burnt between 5½ and 7½ million tons of coal. By 1915 it employed 365 colliers, which had risen to 651 by April 1916. During the war it lost 253 colliers, most of them to submarine attack, to avoid which as much coal as possible was carried north by the single-track Highland Railway. When the Grand Fleet moved south to the Firth of Forth in 1918 it saved much scarce shipping capacity.[35]

The same long experience in handling contracts and contractors in advanced military technologies which gave the Admiralty so many advantages over the War Office, applied equally to the new technology of aircraft, but almost all aspects of naval aviation had as much to do with inter-departmental politics and relations with contractors as with fighting the enemy. The fact that the experts and the public alike grossly over-estimated what aeroplanes could do only increased their political significance. From the beginning, the army thought tactically about aeroplanes, and the RNAS thought strategically. The army looked for the offensive spirit; the Navy developed the best technology, generating a competitive market for aircraft and aero-engines which led to rapid improvements in performance and a ninety-two-fold increase in engine production in four years. The soldiers asked for low-performance, stable, all-purpose aerial platforms for scouting and artillery spotting: the naval airmen wanted high performance and were already thinking of long-range strategic bombing. 'Air power' (the phrase they coined) would do what sea power was meant to, deciding the issue of the war with a great battle. Increasingly the RNAS saw itself as the new battle-fleet, the Navy's answer to the bloody immo-bility of the Western Front. For the senior officers of the RFC, this was a mischievous fantasy, distracting attention from the urgent needs of the hour with airy visions of a remote future. Independent observers agreed:

> The military wing is a success largely because it has been developed and trained as a branch of the army and with military objects strictly in view. The naval wing is a failure because it has not been designed for naval objects with the result that it has degenerated into a crowd of highly-skilled but ill-disciplined privateersmen. What is wanted is to make the naval wing more 'naval', not more 'aerial'.[36]

The RFC abandoned bombing when it found it could hit nothing; its commanding officer, Brigadier-General Hugh Trenchard, was flatly opposed to it, and hated Colonel Frederick Sykes, the RFC's leading advocate of bombing.[37]

In all naval operations navigation was the most basic requirement and the most frequent failure. The North Sea was notoriously foggy and all ships relied heavily on dead-reckoning, but were frequently put out by variable currents and tidal streams. Even battleships, with the best instruments, soon got out of their reckoning: five miles out after eight hours' steaming was typical, and destroyers were often ten or fifteen miles adrift. Only the newest ships had gyro compasses, and even gyros were affected by heavy seas. Magnetic compasses were worse: although navigators in principle used the standard 360° compass, courses were usually estimated by eye and signalled in compass points (of 11¼°), with a one-point margin of error either way. The Royal Navy of 1914 had no standard format to report the position of a distant contact, though the need had already been noted. The German standard gridded chart was a more practical design, but the squares were too big for North Sea visibility at its best, let alone as reduced by the funnel smoke of many coal-fired ships in company. Even big ships at sea had too few navigators, signalmen and telegraphists to maintain continuous watches and keep account of complex and constantly changing information; it was much worse for destroyers. Only one big British warship was wrecked during the war (the armoured cruiser *Argyll*, on the Bell Rock off Arbroath in October 1915), but eight destroyers were. The Germans lost three, and the French five destroyers sunk in collisions. Between 1916 and 1918 the Harwich Force alone suffered sixty-three collisions and eighteen groundings. Minefields, laid or reported by ships with only a hazy idea of where they were, were a menace to their own side as well as the enemy.[38]

It remains to consider the effect of wireless on every aspect of command and control. It was not exactly new in 1914, but its impact on wartime operations was still hard to assess. Existing sets transmitted on long or medium wave with still-imprecise tuning, which meant that a few stations absorbed much of the available waveband. Poorly tuned systems generated massive interference and demanded tight wireless discipline with a minimum of signals, habits which stuck with the Royal Navy even after tuned sets became general. At these wavelengths signals followed the curvature of the earth, and high-powered shore stations with tall masts could achieve ranges of thousands of miles, but ships were limited to hundreds of miles, and submarines had to erect temporary masts to reach a few score. The Telefunken 'quenched spark' arc transmitter had unusually precise tuning, and the Germans took pride in its 'high, clear' signals, resistant to jamming. They were slow to realize how far away the signals were audible. At this date all signals were 'broadcasts' which radiated in all directions, so transmitters identified themselves by call-signs. The study of call-signs and other characteristics of signals ('traffic analysis'), supplemented later by direction-finding, allowed experienced operators to discover a great deal of what was going on at sea even without understanding the signals themselves. Conscious of the enormous advantage the British derived from controlling most of the world telegraph cable network, the Germans invested heavily in a chain of high-powered wireless stations intended to allow worldwide communications between German territories and forces. The Admiralty set up a rather different system, with local medium-range transmitters to keep contact with ships in different parts of the world, connected by cable for secure long-range communication. By 1910 the Admiralty could talk to any British ship between Greenland and Aden, but neither the British nor the German network was complete in 1914. The German overseas transmitters were silenced in the early months of the war, except those in the United States, which were allowed to continue transmitting in plain language only.[39]

Many, though not all, wireless signals were coded, encyphered, or both. The two terms need to be distinguished. Code books were printed vocabularies of words and phrases each indicated by a group of letters or numbers, such as navies had used for flag signals for over a century. They were universally adopted commercially to reduce the high cost of telegrams, and secret code books were used by diplomats and the military, both for telegrams and wireless signals. Such code books, however, being widely distributed and infrequently replaced, offered only a low level of secrecy, so security-conscious organizations usually added some sort of cypher for additional protection – though many of these super-encyphers were simple enough. On pre-war manoeuvres, British ships had frequently attacked each other's cyphers, which were within the capacity of the average wardroom. This gave naval officers some sense of the vulnerability of their signals, and the importance of keeping them to a minimum. Even before the war, the growing volume of traffic to be encyphered had inspired the search for a cypher machine.[40]

The German Navy had three main code books in 1914: the older *Signalbuch der Kaiserlichen Marine* (*SKM*), used by major units, the *Verkehrsbuch* (*VB*), for flag officers, and the *Handelsverkehrsbuch* (*HVB*), used by merchant ships, U-boats and Zeppelins.[41] A well-known set of stories relates how copies of all three fell into British hands between August and November 1914: the *SKM* passed on by the Russian Navy, which had found it aboard the grounded and abandoned German cruiser *Magdeburg*; the *HVB* seized by the Royal Australian Navy from the German steamer *Hobart* off Melbourne; and the *VB* dredged up by a British trawler off the Dutch coast, supposedly from the sunken destroyer *T-119*. According to the established version, the codes were put in the hands of a new, unconventional and partly civilian-manned Admiralty organization called 'Room 40', established on the outbreak of the war by Alfred Ewing, the Cambridge engineering professor who had been recruited in 1902 as Director of Education. This proceeded to 'break German wireless codes', putting a priceless asset into the hands of the Naval Staff – which squandered it.[42]

These stories combine a number of cherished tropes which will be familiar to readers of modern British history. Their moral is that civilians, and especially academics, have to teach the blundering military men how to wage war; and that amateur skill and luck always trump hard work and boring expertise in the solution of difficult technical problems. Attractive stories, and familiar themes for English readers – but there are several reasons to doubt them in addition to their obvious implausibility. All three of the captured codes were used in super-encyphered form, meaning that the code books alone, though certainly valuable, would not have betrayed any message unless the (admittedly simple) cyphers had first been decrypted. For this reason the Germans were relaxed about the compromise of the *SKM*, which they suspected. Although the *Magdeburg* and the *Hobart* were certainly captured, and the *T-119* was indeed sunk, it is not certain what was taken from the cruiser, nor is it self-evident that a small destroyer could have been carrying a 'flag-officer only' code book. The German naval Cypher Service (*Entzifferungsdienst*), which heard the story later and investigated, thought it was a fiction designed to cover something else.[43] The strongest reason for agreeing is that it seems all three code books were being read in the Admiralty *before* they had been captured. Fleet Paymaster Charles Rotter of the Naval Intelligence Division had been studying German medium-wave naval signals since 1911, and it was to him that the captured code books were delivered. Rotter quickly broke the flimsy super-encypher of the *SKM*, and he was evidently already experienced at such work. The implication might be that the captures, real or otherwise, provided a suitable cover for earlier cryptography.[44]

Ewing's 'Room 40' seems to have been established shortly before the war to work on high-power long-wave traffic from the major German land stations. That task soon ended as the German colonies were overrun and the stations closed down, when Room 40 turned to monitoring German cable traffic. It might have been logical to combine Ewing's group with Rotter's, but Ewing was too senior to be subordinated to the NID, and he did not get on with Rear-Admiral Sir Reginald Hall, the Director of Naval Intelligence, so Room 40 remained separate until after Ewing left the Admiralty in October 1916 to become Principal of the University of Edinburgh. It seems that Ewing had previous experience with cryptography, and with early cypher machines. As an engineer he was a specialist in underwater telegraph cables, a fact that may have been relevant to his first appointment to the Admiralty, which happened just as Fisher was setting up his original 'War Room' in Malta to handle intercepted Russian telegrams.[45]

At the outbreak of the war both British and German navies were naive and incompetent in signals security. In November 1914 the *Admiralstab* circulated 200 copies of a bulletin announcing the capture of the French Navy's main operational cypher: not the best way to preserve a valuable secret. A British signal of December 1914 quoted a decyphered German one verbatim, a gross blunder which at a stroke risked exposing the British cypher, British cryptography, and the capture of the squared chart used by the German Navy to indicate positions. A German signal did the same thing as late as 1917. Most of what the German Navy knew about British naval cyphers was learnt from a Bavarian army wireless unit at Roubaix near Lille. The Russians and Austro-Hungarians were also well ahead in cryptography, while British and British Indian Military Intelligence were possibly better than Naval Intelligence, and certainly more discreet. At sea, however, the British were more alert to the insecurity of open-broadcast wireless systems, and learnt faster than the Germans. The High Seas Fleet generated many needless signals, often in port, where there was no need of wireless, which provided British cryptographers with a good 'depth' of material to analyse. It continued code books in service for months or years after they were known to have been compromised, relying on frequent changes of cypher, but each new cypher key was usually signalled to ships at sea in the old key, which nullified the whole process.

The German naval 'Reporting Service' (*Beobachtungsdienst*, a cover name concealing the Cypher Service) was set up in February 1916 inland at

Neumünster, some way from the *Admiralstab* in Berlin or any of the operational commands; its decyphers were distributed by wireless and immediately read by both British and Russians. Alert to the danger of cryptography, the British signalled as little as possible, and tried to keep the limited channels for flag officers only. Flagships in port had telegraph and later telephone lines laid to their buoys to provide secure overland communications. Winston Churchill had a more sophisticated understanding of wireless intelligence than most of the admirals on either side; he understood the value of analysing routine traffic, and forbade the retransmission of decrypts.[46]

The main reason why British ships so frequently failed to report what their admiral needed to know was evidently that they had learnt the security lesson too well. The same obsession with secrecy which forbade Admiralty departments and Naval Staff divisions in Whitehall to share intelligence with one another was multiplied at sea by the danger of interception and the shortage of waveband.[47] In retrospect it is easy to see how the mistakes were made, but it bears stressing that there is no ideal solution to the insecurity of communications. The greater the volume of traffic, over any communication system, the greater the opportunities of leakage. Even the most secure (and cumbersome) cyphers only buy time, and in many operational contexts a high degree of secrecy is neither possible nor necessary. The only absolute security is never to communicate anything: all signalling involves security risks, and the only rational policy is to strike a balance between risk and reward.

SEVENTEEN

The Uttermost Parts of the Sea

Social History 1914–1918

The First World War broke out while the Navy was struggling with a crisis of officer recruitment and supply. It badly needed more and better engineer officers, but the Selborne Scheme, forced through with Fisher's characteristic haste, had markedly reduced the supply of all sorts of officers and almost completely stopped the entry of engineer officers for the eight years 1905 to 1913. An incomplete and inconsistent project had been promoted with a combination of muddle and dishonesty which gave many officers reasons to doubt the Admiralty's good faith. Engineer officers especially had been allowed to gain the impression that the scheme offered them promotion, even to flag rank, which was never made possible, and perhaps never seriously intended. After most of a lifetime in command, admirals should have been good at handling people: they should have needed no reminding of the importance of plain dealing if young men were to entrust their lives and careers to the Navy. Instead, the early twentieth-century Admiralty managed its officers with incompetence and dishonesty. It did not think clearly about its objectives, and it showed marked reluctance to take responsibility for its decisions. One of the many consequences of the First World War was to expose naval decision-making to the outside world. What the world saw was not merely gross errors, especially in the anti-submarine war, but weakness of leadership and lack of moral courage.[1]

For senior officers of this period (and long afterwards), reacting against the politicized faction-fighting of Fisher and Beresford, the greatest naval virtue was 'loyalty'. At its best this meant comradely mutual support without destructive carping; at its worst it meant slavish worship of senior officers and a craven avoidance of responsibility. But there were not a few clever and strong-minded critics who were prepared to defy convention by asking irritating questions about the conduct of the war, and who found admirals broad-minded enough to protect them. They included Herbert Richmond, Reginald Plunkett (later Drax),[2] Reginald Henderson, Kenneth Dewar and Percy Scott. All of them had notable professional reputations: Richmond and Drax as torpedo specialists; Henderson, Dewar and Scott as gunnery officers. Richmond was already writing important works of naval history which are still valuable a century later. Richmond, Plunkett and Dewar were among the founders in 1912 of the *Naval Review*, a private journal (still flourishing) intended to stimulate professional thinking among officers. 'What I hope to develop is the mental habit of reasoning things out, getting to the bottom of things, evolving principles & spreading interest in the higher side of our work,' Richmond wrote. 'I wonder what the authorities will say when it reaches their ears!'[3] All of them ran professional risks in thinking and publishing for themselves, but senior officers, including Beatty and Wemyss (but not Jellicoe), understood the value of what they were doing, and the Navy displayed considerable tolerance for these unconventional minds and not always emollient personalities. All five of these critics became admirals, and Richmond, Drax and Henderson reached full admiral on the active list.[4]

They were among the leaders of opinion in the Navy, but it would be wrong to present them as an embattled minority struggling against inertia and complacency. On the contrary, the situation of the Navy, the weakness of the Admiralty, the boredom and seeming futility of much war service, provoked varying degrees of regret, shame and anguish among even the least reflective officers. 'At times our inactivity frets me to such an extent that I can hardly bear it,' wrote Beatty to his wife in June 1915:

> The greatest war of all time is proceeding, the finest deeds of heroism are being performed daily, the dreams of the past, of glory & achievement are being uprooted & proved impossible of accomplishment. The country is in such need, the spirit is so willing, and yet we are doomed to do nothing, achieve nothing & sit day after day working out schemes that will never be carried out . . .[5]

What made it worse was that naval officers were achieving nothing in relative comfort:

> The Navy goes to war in a luxurious way compared to our gallant Army. Contrast their hours in the trenches, rain, lying on the ground, marches etc. with us. We have long hours at sea, but we have to come in for coal, and that usually means 24 hrs. rest and clean up. Our food is as good as in peace, we have a piano, a comfortable and well lit and warmed mess, with books, magazines, papers, a cabin, slightly denuded true, but a cabin with a bunk.[6]

Many officers longed to share the danger of the trenches, and younger ones tried to transfer to submarines, coastal motor-boats or the RNAS. Naval reservists who saw the RN officers at first hand were unimpressed, even contemptuous. 'All the same, you know, the Navy's rotten . . .' one RNVR officer wrote in 1918. 'It has good stuff in it but it wants, not reform, but revolution. The chief thing that is wrong is the fear of responsibility; everyone is afraid of his immediate superior and exerts himself chiefly in clearing his own yard-arm.'[7] The worst period was the first half of 1917, with the Admiralty incapable of meeting the U-boat threat and Jellicoe openly despairing. 'The state of stagnation amongst the big ships has reached an appalling stage', wrote Midshipman Geoffrey Harper of the battle-cruiser *Courageous*. 'A big ship only goes to sea an average of 24 hours a month . . . Only the destroyers and small craft are doing anything at all.'[8] The surrender of the High Seas Fleet in 1918 was a day of mourning for the victorious battle that never was, as much as of rejoicing at peace and victory. Opinions differed on what had gone wrong, but all agreed that there was urgent work to be done to ensure it never happened again. It was soon obvious, moreover, that the Navy had forfeited the extraordinary luxury of uncritical public support which it had enjoyed before the war.[9]

Boredom and demoralization had predictable consequences, especially aboard the big ships swinging round their moorings at Scapa Flow. There was too much drinking in port (though not at sea). A lieutenant, allowed a wine bill of up to £5 a month with gin at about five shillings a bottle, could legally drink two-thirds of a bottle a day – though the captain had means of knowing how much his officers were drinking in the wardroom, and they were forbidden to buy one another drinks. The sub-lieutenants who kept order in the gun-rooms (with little or no supervision) used the cane so freely as to alarm senior officers and provoke inquiry into bullying:

> There was here a danger . . . that these methods instilled into officers at a very early age too high a regard for, and obedience to, authority: a too strongly developed sense of the importance of rank and seniority resulting in the reluctance of junior officers to express their own opinions, and a too ready and unquestioning acceptance of those of their seniors. I think it tended to stifle initiative and fresh ideas and to create a tradition of rigid conformity.[10]

The worst sufferers seem to have been the ex-Dartmouth boys: the 'special entry' – and even more the colonials – were older and better able to stand up for themselves.[11]

The High Seas Fleet suffered from similar but worse problems of idleness and demoralization. Although the humiliating submission of engineer officers, excluded from the wardroom and junior to sub-lieutenants, was very slightly relieved during the war, nothing at all was done for the indispensable warrant officers. The transfer of many able commissioned officers to U-boats, the glaring contrast between officers' living conditions (many of them lodging in comfort ashore) and the increasingly hungry men on the lower deck progressively weakened the bonds of discipline, but the engineer and warrant officers so much resented their own bad treatment that they stood aside and left the commissioned officers unsupported to face unrest, mutiny and eventually revolution.[12]

The Royal Naval Engineering College at Keyham admitted its last entry in 1905 and closed in 1910. In 1913 it re-opened to deliver a one-year engineering course to those of the new Selborne Scheme lieutenants who opted for this career. There were far too few of them for the Navy's needs, and it was soon clear that the theoretical knowledge gained in two terms at Greenwich and one year's specialist training at Keyham (plus workshop experience as boys at Dartmouth) came nowhere near replacing the five years' practical training of the old-style engineer officers. What made it worse was the sharp and public social distinction made between them. The old Engineer Lieutenant was not an executive officer and lacked the 'executive curl' in the upper ring of gold lace on his sleeve. The new Lieutenant (E) was an executive officer with the curl, with the right to sit on courts martial and with powers of command in the engine room. His status and prospects were greater, but his practical efficiency was less:

> At this time [1914] you had two distinct types – the Engineers and the monied people who had taken up engineering. They weren't really very practical engineers and they relied on us very greatly. The old Engineers were the ones you respected, for their knowledge of engineering, and often they were hard nuts to crack. The other ones were easier to get on with, but often they relied on you for quite a lot of practical knowledge. I would say in the earlier stages they weren't fully capable of taking charge, though they are now, when machinery has got very technical. Then, when machinery was simpler, they had to rely on us for the practical side of it.[13]

In 1915 all engineer officers joined the executive branch, with the appropriate curl on their sleeves and (for commanders and above) oak leaves on their caps, but their titles of rank still plainly distinguished the two generations, and betrayed Fisher's original intention to integrate only the new Lieutenants (E) into the body of commissioned officers.[14]

At the outbreak of the war, when it was still expected to last only a short time, the naval cadets from Dartmouth were sent straight to sea. Some of them were killed, but most of them did well. Like their ancestors a century before, they learnt faster and better from real wartime sea service than they would have done in the classroom, and many of them were promoted early to midshipmen. 'We were professional seamen, we had learnt from our forefathers and our traditions; what we had to realise was that not only must we be professional seamen, but also professionals at sea warfare, which was not the same thing.'[15] As soon as possible the wartime Navy reverted to its usual methods of training future officers, but the disadvantages were now more obvious than ever:

> Temporary service officers of the R.N.R. & R.N.V.R. have been employed in destroyers & other smaller craft, where they obtained experience as fighting men and seamen under the finest conditions – the conditions of active service. Midshipmen, R.N., of the same age, intended for permanent service, have been locked up on board battleships in order to be under instruction. They acquired neither sea – nor fighting – experience. The reason for this was that if they went to small vessels, they would not be able to pass their examinations, this being rated of greater importance than practical war experience.[16]

The experience of the war went a long way to dissipate the Navy's infatuation with cramming pure mathematics as a means of education. In 1915 a committee recommended that cadets who were intending to become engineers should spend their sea-time in the engine room. At the same time midshipmen who had decided against engineering had the engineering part of their syllabus reduced from one-third to one-eighth of the whole. Although this was only a temporary wartime expedient, it marked the first important breach in the Selborne principle of 'interchangeability'. By 1915 in fact it was becoming clear that the whole Selborne Scheme was seriously flawed, if not completely unworkable. The new Special Entry scheme could produce officers in half the time and at less than half the cost, to the Navy and to their parents. By the end of the war, it was already helping to make up the shortage of lieutenants which Fisher and the Selborne Scheme had created.[17]

The performance of naval officers in the First World War generated a good deal of criticism. Since their upbringing and education had been exclusively naval from an early age, it was inevitable that much of this criticism pointed directly at Dartmouth. Mental exhaustion, lack of initiative and inability to think and write clearly were directly traced to relentless cramming with abstract mathematics.[18] 'Warrior aptitudes' were neglected in favour of 'narrow seamanship, housekeeping and show-piece talents'.[19] Where French officers were equipped 'to think about the naval problems of the day, to express these ideas on paper, and encouraged to submit their memoranda to those above them',[20] 'in the British Navy . . . capacity to think was a handicap and an independent or critical mind was a definite disability'.[21] 'Enterprise, initiative, enthusiasm, inventiveness, departure from the official mould, and a host of valuable attributes were all discouraged if not regarded almost as objectionable; even individuality or a too-enquiring mind were out of place.'[22] Made by contemporaries, such remarks were usually anti-Fisher; they criticized the harsh repression of dissenting views which marked Fisher's style of leadership. These tended to be the opinions of those whose careers had suffered for their independence, opinions which could be dismissed as sour grapes. 'In such cases, serious thinking may be more dangerous than secret drinking.'[23]

Evidently these post-war comments were also meant to attribute (or deflect) blame. They imply that lost victories could have been won if officers had been better educated or taught to think, if initiative and independence of mind had been encouraged, if senior officers had trusted their subordinates.[24] One of the most cogent and astringent naval voices making these points during and after the war was Admiral Sir Herbert Richmond, prominent in post-war reforms of naval staff training and in retirement an eminent naval historian. In 1933 he wrote a long letter to a naval friend:

> I firmly believe that the alterations which I have so long desired in naval training are essential. I have thought it all over in the years since 1915 & 1916 when we used to talk of it. The experience of the war confirmed, I think, my beliefs. I never thought we should fail in courage. I feared we should fail in the conduct of war, & that the cause of failure would lie in our want of real education – the power to think out problems. SNOs [Senior Naval Officers] tell me that that was what happened. We showed no sign of any strategical insight in the war. We worked by catchword . . . We stuffed knowledge of a superficial kind into boys: we never taught them to think out things themselves. Not only that: we deprecated individual thought or originality. The great idea was – & is, alas – conformity. No one, today even, realises how gravely the Navy failed in the war: and any attempts to exhume its shortcomings are treated as personal attacks upon the unfortunate Flag Officers who had never been prepared by their training to undertake the great & responsible duties of direction & command in war. They were technicians, pure & simple – artillerists, torpedoists,

electricians, navigators: not fighting commanders. They had the greatest chance in the history of the world at Jutland. Never in all our naval history had we gone into a great battle with such a superiority over our enemy, never had we come out with such disproportionate losses and more indecisive result.[25]

Against such criticisms several points can be made. Firstly, obviously, Richmond would have persuaded more and offended fewer of his naval contemporaries if he could have moderated his aggressive tone. Beyond that there are underlying structural factors to consider. The crisis in officer supply generated by the rapid growth of the Navy, and made much worse by the Selborne Scheme, meant that all sorts of training suffered badly in the years immediately before the First World War. Courses were repeatedly curtailed or abandoned, the new Naval Staff was set up with very little staff training, and the accelerated promotion available from 1903 made it possible for good candidates to be commanders at thirty, captains at thirty-five and rear-admirals by forty-five, putting officers of limited experience in command of ships and squadrons. The serious shortage of officers translated into abnormal promotion prospects. Out of the July 1881 term of cadets, twenty-five became lieutenants, of whom two died, and all the rest made captain. The January 1885 term had thirty-six lieutenants, of whom six died or were invalided out of the Service, and of the remaining thirty, twenty-seven became commanders and twenty, captains. The Autumn 1889 term yielded forty-three lieutenants, of whom nine died or were invalided, twenty-five became commanders and eighteen, captains. No fewer than 12 per cent of the cadets entering in 1878 and 1888 reached flag rank. These figures must have meant that many commonplace officers were reaching captain's or admiral's rank; mediocre talents to whom prudent admirals would be reluctant to delegate. Jellicoe's candid opinion of his vice-admirals in the Grand Fleet was extremely unflattering. All this would have had a bad effect on operational efficiency even in a more liberal and flexible intellectual atmosphere.[26]

Beyond this there is a broader point to be made. It is an historical commonplace that the Navy in the Second World War displayed all the flexibility and initiative which had been so lacking in the First – but only twenty years elapsed between the two. Many commanders and all captains and above in the second war had been trained before the Great War. It is uncommon for adults to change completely the ideas and attitudes with which they have been brought up; making every allowance for lessons learnt, one would scarcely expect the senior naval officers of the Second World War to have cast off the faults of their upbringing so completely. This suggests that much should be attributed to the very different circumstances in which the two wars were fought. In the Great War many ships and officers served with the big fleets, the Grand Fleet in particular. The limits of contemporary signalling technology meant that these huge formations could only be handled in a rigid and centralized manner. Twenty years later campaigns were fought between smaller formations, at higher speeds and over greater distances, with command and signalling methods which had been deliberately developed to promote flexibility and initiative. Now officers had incentive and opportunity to do what had been difficult or impossible before. It is also worth drawing attention to the conference of senior officers which was planned to follow the 1914 test mobilization, to discuss recent manoeuvres and current professional challenges. In the event the war overtook the conference, but not before a good deal of preparation had been undertaken, with papers and proposals circulated in advance which give a good sense of the intellectual temperature of the Navy in 1914. These senior officers were clearly not at all resistant to change and debate; they were keen to promote initiative and tactical flexibility, and were full of imaginative ideas.[27]

It has been explained in Chapter 6 that inflation, trades unionism and external political crises were putting naval discipline under some strain in the years leading up to the First World War. In wartime conditions were harsher, and inflation badly eroded the naval wage. Many wartime recruits were trades unionists, shocked to discover that strikes were illegal in the Navy, and some retired officers recalled for war service were not models of tact in handling their men. There was material for trouble here, and the events of the Russian Revolution in 1917, and the (nearly successful) German Revolution the following year, reminded officers that they stood on shaky ground. In retrospect it seems that these fears (or hopes) were exaggerated. Long-serving ratings regarded themselves as skilled professionals, took pride in being in the Navy and were cool towards mass trades unionism with its taint of socialism and disloyalty. Explicitly or implicitly, their first demand was always to be treated with respect (just as it had been in the eighteenth century).[28] Even stokers were now the owners of essential skills, especially in oil-fired ships, and illiteracy was fast disappearing. Officers, who were nearer to their men, understood this better than the Admiralty, which was influenced by its experience of trades unionism in the dockyards. In 1917 the lower-deck societies revived and circulated a 'loyal address' asking for a 50 per cent increase in pay and better promotion, pensions and victualling allowances. Consulted by the Admiralty, Beatty and other admirals replied that officers were popular, but the Admiralty was not; its failure to respond to grievances was encouraging trades unionism. Unrest 'would probably disappear were the men convinced that their point of view would be fully understood and sympathetically treated at the Admiralty, for which [opinion] there is some justification.'[29] This was not completely fair: by 1918 some 38 per cent of ratings were married (up from 10 per cent in 1912), Treasury figures showed a family's cost of living had gone up 74 per cent during the war, and many families were hungry. What they wanted was money more than sympathy, and the Admiralty could give only what the Cabinet allowed. Where the Admiralty could have made a real difference at small cost was in adjusting the complex details of allowances and differentials between branches and rates, which generated many unintended and unnecessary grievances, over status as much as money. But except in a few cases of extraordinarily bad leadership, the enduring strength of the relationship between officers and men protected the Navy from political troubles outside. Officers could and did support well-founded complaints. The Admiralty was aware that petitions, benefit societies and lower-deck newspapers, even if technically against regulations, were important safety valves and valuable indicators of lower-deck sentiment. 'Grousing' was universal and served the same purposes. So did censorship: the officers who read their ship's company's letters home to check for breaches of security took note of their men's feelings at the same time, and the men understood that this was a quick way to get a message to authority. The Navy may have been stratified and class-ridden, but in that it faithfully reflected British society: paternalist officers and deferential men satisfied one another's expectations.[30]

Between 1914 and 1918 some 2,323 men (0.4 per cent of the Navy's 1918 strength of 640,000) were tried by court martial. A total of 1,104 were convicted of any sort of mutiny, disobedience, desertion, insubordination, neglect of duty and the like, with a peak in 1917. One man was found guilty of murder but declared insane. In the whole period from 1913 to 1946 only two death sentences were passed by a British naval court martial. These figures do not give the impression of a serious breakdown in discipline. Nor do the handful of mutinies which occurred during the war years. The worst case was in the old cruiser *Leviathan*, alongside at Birkenhead in 1918. The officers overworked the men, allowed them no opportunity for rest or leave, then lost control of them altogether: 150 men walked out of the ship, taking the piano. The Admiralty quietly reclassified the affair as an 'outbreak' and laid the whole blame on the captain and commander.[31]

Just as they had been under sail a century before, most of the worst hardships of naval life were generated – or at least made much worse – by overcrowding. There was no privacy and no space to spare. The 'heads' (latrines) were inadequate for the numbers. Only ERAs and stokers had bathrooms; hot water was hard to obtain, and messes had only one wooden tub each to wash clothes, men and mess-traps. Meals were the central point of mess-deck life. The leading hand (usually also the mess caterer), as 'father' of the mess, presided at table and was expected to serve food out with exact fairness.[32]

Much of the domestic economy of a ship was based on 'firms' of two or more men providing goods and services. Some of this was clandestine, but most of it was tolerated or even regulated by the Master-at-Arms (who was not necessarily incorruptible). Barbers, inevitably nicknamed 'Sweeney Todd', provided one essential service. 'Bacca' firms rolled the official-issue leaf tobacco. 'Jewing' (tailoring) firms made whole or part uniforms: strictly 'pusser' for kit inspections, 'tiddlyvated' for 'occasions' ashore. Such firms needed a member in each watch to be always on hand for urgent orders. Many sailors could ply a needle, but other trades were more specialized, or needed special equipment. Stokers were best placed to run dhobey (washing) firms, having privileged access to hot water and drying space in the boiler rooms. The blacksmith and plumber did 'snobbing' (cobbling), the painter and shipwright various small crafts. Sick Berth ratings ran photography firms or 'goffers' (iced-lemonade stalls). Taking on a 'firm' was hard work, but it was possible for a married man to make a real difference to his family: one two-man dhobey firm in the cruiser *Carlisle* on a commission in the Far East in 1919–20 made £150 to £200 each, enough to buy the freeholds of their houses.[33] Even more lucrative was illegal gambling, especially 'Crown and Anchor' (sometimes with loaded dice), but aside from the risk, some of the profits would have to be spent paying lookouts, and paying-off suspicious petty officers.[34]

For everyone afloat, officers as well as men, wartime service meant long periods confined to the ship, and everywhere officers worked to keep up morale by providing opportunities for relaxation and diversion. In the Grand Fleet at Scapa Flow, where 'we in the *Dreadnought* never saw a tree, a train or a woman',[35] bad weather often made it impossible to go ashore for days at a time, and there was little to do ashore anyway except (for officers) walking and fishing. The unexciting little town of Kirkwall was a long boat trip and two hours' walk from the fleet anchorage, and the ships were normally at no more than four hours' notice for sea. Ships might organize cross-country marches for their men, with the opportunity (under a sympathetic officer) of a smoke and a chat, but in winter it was dark by three o'clock, and the climate in the Orkneys, in Beatty's words, was 'bitter cold and damp, never less than half a gale of wind, but it is healthy so they say. I suppose it must be, otherwise we could never stand the monotony of grey skies, heavy seas and wind, nothing but wind, cold and penetrating.'[36] 'The fact is that I am "weary, in the uttermost parts of the sea", wrote Lieutenant-Commander Oswald Frewen of the light cruiser *Comus* in his diary in January 1917, 'War-weary, Scapa-weary, weary of seeing the same old damned agony of grey, grey, grey, grey sky, grey sea, grey ship. I could do with a drop of Mediterranean . . .'[37] Those who had the Mediterranean were not necessarily much better off. In the destroyer *Chelmer* off the Dardanelles, 'The whole winter [of 1914–15] was too terrible for words, blowing gales nearly every day and the cold was appalling, especially in a destroyer with none of the usual comforts of life. We used to get flooded out, wardroom, cabins and everywhere, about two or three times a week . . .'[38] The best excitement Scapa Flow could offer officers was a golf course at Stromness and another (built during the war) on the island of Flotta, near the main fleet anchorage. Here too some officers kept allotments, and here were rugby, football and boxing for the men, strongly encouraged as a means of keeping them fit and happy, and of bringing officers and men together. (This was why Dartmouth cadets learnt to play soccer, the lower deck's game, as well as rugby like other public schoolboys.) In 1917 four professional boxing coaches were specially entered as chief petty officers RNVR and sent to Scapa to train naval boxers; Beatty claimed that the fleet boxing carnival in July 1917 attracted 18,000 spectators. In the fleet regatta that summer the commander-in-chief himself rowed stroke in the flagship's 'veterans' boat'.[39]

Most ships had some sort of library. Scottish daily papers (and the Manchester edition of the *Daily Mail*) reached the Grand Fleet late on the day of publication, though London papers came twenty-four hours late. There were bands and gramophones, so the men could dance on deck in good weather. Jellicoe made sure that every big ship in the Grand Fleet had a film projector; in nineteen months, 1917–19, the Fleet Cinema Committee spent more than £14,000 on projectors and films. Even more popular were the entertainments the ships made for themselves. Much energy was put into organizing 'concert parties', a term which embraced all sorts of amateur acting and music-making. These were an antidote to boredom, the focus of much effort and organization by officers and men working together. The transport *Ghourko* was fitted out as a theatre seating more than a hundred, and ships competed to book her for their productions.[40] In February 1916 the battleship *Warspite* put on a successful pantomime which played to 800 officers and then to lower-deck houses. 'This was even a better audience to play the ass to, as their laughter is spontaneous and unrestrained,' noted Sub-Lieutenant Herbert Packer. 'Of course they laughed where the officers didn't and vice versa.'[41]

The Cromarty Firth, where some of the cruisers were based, was less exposed than Scapa Flow and offered prettier country but was only slightly less remote. The battle-cruisers lay in the Firth of Forth from 1915, within sight of the big city of Edinburgh and two hundred miles nearer the enemy (though not so much nearer in terms of time because the Forth was awkward to clear in a hurry). For officers it was easy to get permission to go into the city, checking hourly that their ship had not been ordered to sea. Married officers who could afford it might install their wives in lodgings nearby, but only with formal leave was it possible to sleep ashore. The Forth could be almost as cold and windy as Scapa Flow, but lying off a capital city the sense of isolation and abandonment was absent. This was the battle-cruisers' privilege for three years, until anti-submarine nets were rigged to protect a larger anchorage, allowing the whole fleet to come south in April 1918.[42]

Many officers and men, of course, had little to do with the main fleets and had a quite different experience of the war. In destroyers, where a mess of fourteen men had slinging berths for perhaps six hammocks, wartime service was 'hard lying' indeed, but men and officers were close and there were few disciplinary problems. 'There was a tremendous camaraderie on board,' a midshipman remembered; 'you knew everyone; it was to a certain extent a picked ship's company. You were doing a man's work and you were treated as a man.'[43] To join a destroyer, 'you had to be a mature sailor. No boys, ordinary seamen or stokers 2nd class were admitted. Anyone who got V.D. got an immediate draft to a big ship.'[44] Service in submarines was even more dangerous and arduous. There was little possibility of washing at sea, so 'that bath and all the others I had [aboard the depot ship] after returning from fourteen days' patrol were the finest things I ever enjoyed in my life. Black from oil fumes, greasy, uncomfortable and tired, to flop into a hot bath and lie in plenty of changes of water and soak till all the dirt and tiredness had oozed out was only a degree removed from sheer heaven.'[45] Until the 'E' Class (launched 1912-17) the heads were impossible to use except on the surface at night, so submariners tended to suffer from chronic constipation. But they were an elite, and knew it, effectively a private navy combining very thorough training with relaxed and functional discipline and a high sense of responsibility. Social segregation between officers and men was impossible. Submarine pay virtually doubled a rating's income; most submariners could afford to marry, and they were allowed much night leave in port.[46]

Submarine service and the Naval Air Service had many characteristics in common. Both were arduous and dangerous, both depended on mastery of advanced technology, in both, officers and men fought together and depended on one another's professional skill, and both offered young officers the opportunity of responsibility and command at an early age. Both laid a strong emphasis on technical training and publications and have been identified as pioneers of what was later called operational research. They strongly attracted the ablest and boldest young officers of their generation, and it is striking how many of them qualified in both submarines and aircraft. Any shortlist of the most influential pioneers of naval flying would have to include Reginald Bacon, Murray Sueter, Arthur Longmore, John Porte the flying-boat designer and Hugh Williamson the aircraft-carrier pioneer, all of whom were submariners.[47]

The wartime British army was built up on a core of pre-war regulars by massive recruitment (from 1916 conscription) of officers and men for 'hostilities only', who formed the overwhelming majority by the end of the war. About 4½ million men served in the army, which was at least nine times the total for the Navy. In some respects, the war made the British a nation of infantrymen, replacing the pre-war population's sentimental attachment to the Navy with a real experience of wartime soldiering. The effects are detectable even a century later in the general familiarity with military terminology, contrasted with a complete ignorance of naval language.[48] The Navy, being made up of long-serving professionals with a high level of expertise, foresaw little use for expanded wartime recruitment. The war would doubtless be over long before new men could be trained: what the Navy needed was reserves to provide ready-trained men quickly. Between 1914 and 1917 the total strength of the Navy grew from 146,047 to 420,301 (288 per cent), but most of this increase came from mobilizing the reserves and recruiting others to join them for hostilities only. The 46,732 reservists of 1914 increased in number by 250 per cent to 116,693 in 1917, but the number of regular Navy and Marines expanded by only 18 per cent (compared to 5 per cent growth from 1889 to 1914).[49]

These figures conceal some problems generated by hasty decisions taken in 1914 when the war was not expected to last more than a few months. Between August and October 1914 the Navy – and Churchill in person – was heavily involved in checking the German advance down the coast of Flanders, for which purpose most of the available Royal Marines were landed to defend Antwerp. To reinforce them Churchill turned to the only uncommitted manpower under his control, the RNVR – at more or less the same time as Admiral von Schröder was converting German naval reservists into the infantrymen of the *Marinekorps Flandern*. The RNVR infantrymen were then sent to the Mediterranean and onwards, landing at Gallipoli, and on their return to

Britain in 1916 were incorporated into the army as the Royal Naval Division. For the pre-war volunteers who had committed their time to training for the Navy, this was a bitter betrayal, and the Navy realized too late how badly it needed them to man the numerous small craft demanded by the anti-submarine war. What was worse, the Navy then recruited 5,000 officers and 120,000 ratings into the RNVR for wartime service, giving them the opportunity to serve afloat which had been denied to the original pre-war volunteers. These serious blunders arose from short-term thinking in an emergency, but they were all of a piece with the Navy's consistent mismanagement of its own long-term personnel. Naval officers were surprised to find that the professional seamen of the RNR were actually good for something, and averted their gaze from the uncomfortable fact that they were better than the regular Navy at seamanlike tasks such as boatwork and inshore navigation. (It was significant that submarine navigating officers, with by far the trickiest pilotage task of all, were heavily drawn from the RNR.) The amateurs of the RNVR (or not-so amateur, for many were former seafarers) were regarded with disdain and largely excluded from regular warships.[50]

One reason for this was the difficulty of integrating regular naval personnel with reservists whose wartime promotion could be extremely fast. 'The Service in general resents the manner in which youths are allowed to obtain the rank of Chief Petty Officer practically on entry, and obtain privileges . . . which the majority of active service ratings only obtain by years of service,'[51] stated a report of December 1917. It was unfair and divisive if newly entered reservists were treated as equal in experience and authority to those with many more years of service than theirs, but it was impossible to develop new services in a few years without rapid advancement to fill the senior rates and ranks. The extreme example of this problem, and the most radical solution to it, was presented by the RNAS, which grew from nothing in 1912 to have more than 5,000 officers in 1918. Whereas the great majority of wartime army officers had been directly recruited from civilian life and it was not difficult to train a proportion of them as airmen, naval officers were career professionals in very short supply. It was out of the question to transfer a large number of them to flying duties, and only a handful of the senior ranks of the RNAS held rank in the Navy or Marines as well. In the whole RNAS, only 397 officers, 217 ratings and 604 boys out of more than 50,000 personnel actually belonged to the Navy: all the rest were directly recruited from civilian life or other services. The officers had little naval training and held only 'grades', rising from Flight Sub-Lieutenant to Wing Captain, which resembled naval ranks but were not equivalent. This made it possible to grow the new service very fast, but

impossible to integrate it into the Navy. Since in its early years the RNAS was
almost entirely land-based, and led by officers who wanted it to be as independent as possible, this was agreeable to them. The Admiralty was slow to
awake to the implications for the future of its naval air force. On the creation
of the Royal Air Force in 1918, nearly all the naval airmen who chose to stay in
uniform joined it, because they had no naval experience or naval career to
revert to.[52]

There was another new naval service which was even more sharply distinguished from the seagoing Navy, the Women's Royal Naval Service, created in
1917. By this stage of the war very large numbers of women were contributing
to the war effort in all sorts of non-combatant roles, and in one sense all the
Admiralty did was to put into uniform women employees who worked closely
with the Navy. In legal terms the WRNS remained a species of civilians in
uniform, not subject to the Naval Discipline Act, but this greatly understates
the political and psychological significance of the new women's services. In a
period when the campaign for women's suffrage frequently occupied the headlines, making it possible for women to work with the Navy – to participate
with men even on the margins of that most masculine of all activities, making
war – had radical connotations, and a number of the officers of the new service (including its future head Elvira Laughton) had been active before the war
in the Women's Social and Political Union (WSPU) – the radical (and marginally illegal) 'suffragette' movement. They would scarcely have been tolerated
with Carson and Jellicoe at the Admiralty, but Sir Eric Geddes was more remote
from the Establishment, and he had expert advice to hand from his sister Dr
Mona Chalmers Watson, Chief Controller of the Women's Auxiliary Army
Corps, and another veteran of the WSPU. The new Director of the WRNS,
Dame Katharine Furse, had resigned from the Red Cross because she was not
allowed the authority she felt she needed. The Admiralty gave her a free hand
to organize the new service without male supervision, to devise its own scheme
of ranks and ratings, and to design its uniforms. At her first meeting with
Geddes, 'I asked him whether I might choose my own staff and he said certainly and that no one would interfere and that he hoped I might bring with
me a lot of Devonshire House [i.e. Red Cross] staff which I said I would do
with great pleasure.'[53] The Second Sea Lord told Furse that she had 'equivalent
rank to a Rear-Admiral for certain purposes', and from October 1918 WRNS
officers were listed in the *Navy List*.[54] Many 'Wrens' (the obvious term was soon
adopted officially) served in the sort of domestic and clerical jobs which
women already did in peacetime, but many more really were 'freeing a man
for the fleet', as WRNS recruiting posters urged (provoking some discreet

sabotage from men not keen to be freed from a comfortable berth ashore). When the 438 officers and 5,054 ratings of the new service were disbanded on 1 October 1919, after less than two years in existence, they were intensely reluctant to return to civilian life, and the officers formed the Association of Wrens specifically as a foundation for the future reconstitution of the service.[55]

EIGHTEEN

Leaders and Followers

Ships and Weapons 1914–1940

The pre-1914 naval arms race had the effect of speeding up the equipment cycle, as a rapid succession of warships introduced new designs and weapons virtually every year – often before their predecessors had even been completed and evaluated. The war did as much to slow as to speed the pace of change. Shipyards which had formerly had the first priority for everything now found that ships were delayed by shortages of labour and materials. A rising number of damaged ships awaiting repair competed with new construction. Instead of battleships coming first, the U-boat threat caused smaller warships and even merchantmen to be regarded as more urgent. As a result, at the end of four and a quarter years of war, relatively few large warships – of cruiser size and upwards – had been completed whose designs took even limited account of the experience of the war. 'Post-Jutland' designs, incorporating the lessons of recent fighting (not only the battle of Jutland itself) and the study of surrendered German ships, did not appear until well after the war, when (as we shall see) post-war circumstances caused the delay or cancellation of many of them. The result was that during the Second World War the major naval powers still depended heavily on warships, especially battleships, originally designed during and even before the First World War. New weapons, equipment and engines to improve existing ships took on great importance when treaty restrictions or lack of money forbade the replacement of the ships themselves. During the First World War much of the most obvious innovation and ingenuity in warship design was expended on the smaller classes, which could be designed and built quickly to face the new threats of mines and submarines or to deploy the new weapon of naval aircraft. The period of the Great War and after was therefore an extended transition between pre-war warship designs, whose weaknesses were quickly exposed, and 'post-Jutland' designs, which took a long time to appear.

The first gunnery actions of the war were a shock to all the participants. Firing at unexpectedly long ranges with sharp alterations of course presented almost insuperable problems for the simple fire-control of the early battle-cruisers at the Falklands, neither of which had directors or fire-control tables. The German ships zig-zagged to throw off their enemy's aim, in the process throwing their own shooting off even more effectively. Spray, smoke and vibration defeated most attempts to take ranges, and spotting corrections could not make up the difference.[1] At the Dogger Bank, the British and Germans were amazed that the action began at a range of 21,000 yards, and *Lion* scored a hit at 19,000. Gunsights, range-finders and other instruments had to be hastily recalibrated. The *Tiger*, the only British ship in this action with a director, was the only one able to keep shooting in conditions of spray and smoke, which forced the other battle-cruisers to check fire repeatedly. After the battle the Germans, shaken by how near the *Seydlitz* had come to blowing up, installed anti-flash barriers and safety interlocks on the hoists which carried propellant from the magazines to the guns. The German ships had shot better than the British, but afterwards the British officers concentrated on increasing their rate of fire rather than their accuracy. Historians, more interested in moral than technical lessons, have tended to blame Beatty in person for mishandling his squadron, and his flag-lieutenant Ralph Seymour for mishandling his signals. There is reason for both criticisms, but it is more instructive to look at structural problems before blaming individuals. The speed of ships and the effective range of their guns were already much greater than had been anticipated less than a year before; the 'battle-space' was now too large, and changing too fast, for any admiral to be able to keep a realistic mental picture of the movements of scores of ships, friends and enemies, many or all of which would be out of his sight, while ships with little idea of their own positions could hardly plot or report other ships' whereabouts with any accuracy. The volume and precision of the signals and navigational data required to integrate large formations suddenly exceeded both human and technological capacity. 'Signals went through like clockwork . . .', as Seymour claimed. 'When I say they went like clockwork I mean until the clock stopped, which it did at the critical moment when we really wanted to signal.'[2] In the short term the available systems, human and technical, could not keep up with the requirements of a modern action, and would not have been able to do so even if no officer had ever made a mistake.[3]

Jutland, as the only full-scale fleet gunnery action of the Dreadnought era, yielded more controversy than any other. The 'lessons' of the battle, as promulgated by both Jellicoe and Beatty and their respective followers, had as much to do with forgetting as learning. After the battle the Navy's magazine safety was thoroughly overhauled, in great secrecy. This could be done quite quickly, but it took longer to reformulate the cordite propellant to make it more stable. Cordite was one of the new 'smokeless' propellants adopted late in the nineteenth century, with the object of reducing gun smoke sufficiently to make fire-control possible, and therefore long-range shooting. Unfortunately, the propellants were based on high-explosives (nitroglycerine, in the case of cordite) which tended to instability, and led to a series of disastrous magazine explosions before and during the war, at the time attributed to mysterious saboteurs. The victims included the French battleships *Iéna* and *Liberté*, the British *Vanguard*, the Italian *Leonardo da Vinci*, the Russian *Imperatritsa Maria* and the Japanese *Kawachi* and *Mutsu*. The British overrated the stability of cordite, and only very careful research after the war uncovered the minute impurities which caused the trouble. The German Navy survived careless magazine practices and flimsy anti-flash precautions mainly because its TNT-based propellant was extremely stable.[4]

Related to the weaknesses of propellants were the weaknesses of British shells. Beatty's claim that his battle-cruisers' gunnery had been excellent and should have sunk the German battle-cruisers, depended on his assertion that British shells had hit but failed to penetrate German armour. Post-war analysis makes it sufficiently clear that it was only the battle-cruisers which appeared to suffer this problem: British battleships with the same guns hit frequently in the conditions which favoured the Dreyer Table (adequate visibility, low range and bearing rates), and British shells (or at least the heavy 13.5-inch and 15-inch shells) often penetrated German armour. Nevertheless there were legitimate concerns about the quality of British armour-piercing shell, and the major effort to address them which Jellicoe and Beatty set in train was not just a smokescreen. It was inherently hard to design and test armour-piercing shell because of the acute difficulty of reproducing, and observing on the firing range, the performance of shells fired at long ranges in action, when they were likely to strike at unpredictable and oblique angles. It was especially hard to produce a fuse which would reliably burst the shell a fraction of a second after it had struck and penetrated the armour (or, yet more difficult, if it had not struck armour at all but only some lighter structure). For this and other reasons the armour-piercing shells of all navies suffered a considerable proportion of failures to explode. The extensive tests set in train after Jutland revealed that British AP shell suffered from three faults: the Lyddite bursting charge was too sensitive and liable to explode on impact instead of just after; the shell steel was too brittle and liable to shatter on oblique impacts; and the fuse (a

German design, ironically, which the German Navy itself had recently abandoned) was not reliable. Even so, it is not clear that British shell was overall really worse than that of other navies, and German armour was certainly not better, but the British effort to improve shell design produced powerful and reliable shells for the next war.[5]

The Admiralty's enthusiasm for battle-cruisers cooled after Fisher retired in 1910, and even the fast but well-armoured battleships of the *Queen Elizabeth* Class, designed to match the effective sea speed of German battle-cruisers, were not repeated. On the eve of the war the Admiralty was planning to use the *Queen Elizabeths* as the fast wing of the fleet and treat the battle-cruisers as cruisers again, distributed among the cruiser squadrons to strengthen the fleet's scouting capacity (and lessen the battle-cruisers' exposure to battleship gunfire). Instead of more fast battleships, five slow but heavily armoured battleships of the *Royal Sovereign* Class were laid down in 1913–14. Their armour scheme carried the main armour deck higher in the hull than that of their predecessors, giving a greater armoured volume, a higher centre of gravity and a reduced metacentric height. This made them easy rollers and steady gun-platforms, at the price of reduced stability reserves. This was a risk, but most of the class were later fitted with anti-torpedo bulges which made them stiffer again in their undamaged condition. Three more of this class were planned, but when Fisher returned to the Admiralty in 1914 he succeeded in getting them changed into the two very large, very fast (32 knots), and very lightly armoured battle-cruisers *Renown* and *Repulse*. When they joined the Grand Fleet soon after Jutland, in which battle three battle-cruisers had been destroyed (as the fleet believed) by plunging shell-fire penetrating their inadequate deck armour, the new ships' lack of protection made a very poor impression, and in the immediate post-war years both were reconstructed with as much additional armour as could easily be worked in, leaving them as 30-knot battle-cruisers. Fisher was also responsible for the 'large light cruisers' – really ultra-light battle-cruisers – *Glorious, Courageous* and *Furious* (unkindly nicknamed 'Curious', 'Outrageous' and 'Spurious'), designed with shallow draught for his intended Baltic expedition. As usual with Fisher's projects, they were built in a hurry with many aspects of the design not properly worked out. It is not clear how they could have corrected the fire of four (in *Furious*'s case only two) very heavy guns, nor what kind of naval action in the Baltic was envisaged – but in the event they finished up being converted into something entirely different anyway.[6]

Some of the most successful British wartime designs were of light cruisers and destroyers, in both cases because a satisfactory basic type had been established before the war which could be developed without radical change. The wartime light cruisers performed well in action, and proved to be tough and resistant to damage in spite of their slight protection, though at only 4,000–5,000 tons (less than a modern destroyer) they were vulnerable to torpedoes. The designs were careful but 'tight', with little spare space or topweight for wartime expansion, but they had long and successful careers, most of them serving through the Second World War. One of them, the *Caroline*, is still afloat (in 2024), the last survivor of Jutland. An important engineering innovation, first tried in light cruisers and destroyers and generally adopted during the war, was geared turbine drive. This made it possible to combine the most efficient turbine speed with the most efficient screw speed, which was much slower, yielding a slight increase in ship speed and a great improvement in fuel economy.[7]

Wartime destroyers were built in large numbers (no fewer than 373 were ordered) in a series of basic classes referred to as 'Admiralty' designs. Their builders were allowed latitude in machinery arrangements so long as they met the contract speed, but most of them had three boilers and three funnels. The specialist destroyer builders like Thornycroft (in Southampton) and Yarrow (on the Clyde near Glasgow) were allowed to build their own designs in competition with the Admiralty. All of these little ships of around a thousand tons (like submarines, still 'boats' in contemporary naval parlance) conformed to the 'raised forecastle' design, with three or four 4-inch guns, two single, twin and later triple torpedo tubes, and a full speed of something above 30 knots. Wartime experience in the North Sea – especially the Grand Fleet's experience of entering Scapa Flow through the very rough seas of the Pentland Firth – showed that destroyer bridges mounted well forward on the forecastle were liable to be damaged or even destroyed by green seas coming inboard, and subjected the bridge crews to very violent motions in a head sea. This encouraged designers to clear deck space by trunking the two forward boiler uptakes into a single large funnel so that the bridge could be shifted further aft, where the apparent motion of a ship pitching into a head sea was reduced. The displaced amidships gun was moved to the forecastle to give two forward guns, one superfiring above the other, yielding more firepower in chase, and some protection for the bridge from incoming head seas. To replace light cruisers in command of destroyer flotillas, 'destroyer leaders' of around 1,500 tons were developed, and this 300-foot destroyer-leader hull was the basis of the outstanding destroyers of the 'V' and 'W' Classes of 1917–19 which incorporated all the experience of the war, with triple 21-inch torpedo tubes and 4.7-inch guns. Most of this class were built with galvanized steel plating and framing, an expensive investment in longevity which paid a large dividend twenty years later. The only significant weakness of British destroyers, widely recognized at the time, was their limited endurance, notionally around 2,000 miles at 15 knots plus 500 at full speed, but in practice less, which effectively limited the Grand Fleet to three or four days at sea. There was no magic recipe for greater range; it simply called for bigger and more expensive ships carrying more fuel, but wartime, with money available, was the moment to establish a new standard of longer range. One may suspect that the Naval Staff had not fully escaped from the habits of thought of the coal-fired age, in which speed and range were limited by human stamina rather than fuel capacity.[8]

A minesweeping organization had already been set up in 1911 as the RNR Trawler Section, but it soon became clear that converted fishing vessels would not be enough, and late in 1914 the Admiralty designed a new class of 'minesweeping sloops' named after flowers. They were followed by a series of generally similar classes. These were simple ships constructed to (simpler and heavier) merchant-ship standards by small yards which never normally worked for the Navy. Although as large as a destroyer (and better seaboats), the sloops had a speed of only 16 or 17 knots, and could defend themselves with two 4-inch or 4.7-inch guns. Almost from the start it was clear that they could serve equally well as anti-submarine escorts. By late 1916 about 1,400 steam trawlers out of 1,900 in the British fleet had been requisitioned for naval service and trawler owners were reluctant to build any more which would simply be taken up by the Navy. This forced the Admiralty to build 540 trawlers itself, to a design easily convertible to fishing at the end of the war. The success of requisitioned excursion steamers as shallow-draught minesweepers led to the building of a class of paddle minesweepers – the first class of paddle warships since the 1850s.[9]

Another new warship type grew from the coastal campaign in Flanders, for which naval heavy gunfire support was urgently wanted. In November 1914 the Admiralty bought from the US company Bethlehem Steel four twin 14-inch gun turrets ordered for the Greek battle-cruiser *Salamis*, which was being built in Germany. A simple barge-like shallow-draught hull was designed, capable of supporting the weight and firing stresses of a heavy gun turret, and fitted with Tennyson d'Eyncourt's new anti-torpedo bulges. The old name 'monitor' was revived for these four ships, which went out to take part in the Dardanelles campaign, and they were followed by a variety of monitors designed to employ spare or cast-off heavy gun turrets. The talented young constructor Charles Lillicrap was responsible for thirty-five ships of six different designs in four months. These slow and unglamorous vessels did good service in coastal campaigns, and the bulges provided effective protection against torpedoes. In 1918 the monitor *General Wolfe*, armed with an 18-inch gun from the *Furious*, engaged targets inland in Flanders at 36,000 yards (roughly 18 miles), the longest range at which any British warship had ever fired a gun.[10]

Perhaps the greatest challenge for warship designers was the development of ships to carry aircraft. As we have seen, the first and simplest answer was seaplane carriers, but seaplanes could only fly on fairly calm days, and the weight of their floats made them sluggish performers. The Admiralty's productive relations with talented aircraft designers like Thomas Sopwith produced a series of wheeled fighters with light wing loading, which could take off from short flying-off platforms and climb fast to the high altitudes (in extreme cases up to 20,000 feet) that Zeppelins could attain. Several seaplane carriers acquired flying-off platforms to launch wheeled aircraft. The biggest of them was the Cunard liner *Campania* of 1883, bought from the scrapyard in 1914 and fitted with a 200-foot forward runway: on good days her old engines could still make 18 knots, just sufficient to keep up with the Grand Fleet and launch aircraft. But what the Grand Fleet wanted was an effective counter to German Zeppelins, and reconnaissance aircraft to give early warning of enemy submarines ahead of the fleet; flying-off answered only half the problem, even if aircraft fitted with floatation bags could sometimes be recovered from the sea. What was needed was a big, fast ship able to land aircraft as well as fly them off – and Beatty's plan to attack the High Seas Fleet at anchor required not one but eight of them.[11]

The first choice was the incomplete Italian liner *Conte Rosso* being built on the Clyde, bought from the builders in August 1916, and redesigned by the naval constructor John Narbeth with a single flight deck running from end to end, with a large hangar beneath, 330 feet long, 48 feet wide, with 20 foot clear height (enough for aircraft to be moved by gantry cranes above those parked below). A 30-foot by 36-foot lift carried aircraft between flight deck and hangar. Modern readers may find these details banal and obvious, but in 1917 no 'flat-top' aircraft carrier at all like this had ever been built. Indeed, no carrier with such a spacious hangar was built again for a generation: even in the Second World War the *Argus*, as she became, was rare in being able to strike down modern fighters with non-folding wings. The loss of the seaplane carrier *Ben-my-Chree* in January 1917, hit and set on fire by Turkish artillery while lying in Castellorizo harbour in the Eastern Mediterranean, taught British constructors to treat petrol and petrol fumes with great respect. *Argus*'s hangar was isolated from the rest of the ship by air locks, subdivided by fire curtains and provided with powerful ventilation to disperse fumes, while the petrol stowage was arranged with great care. The ship had no funnel, but smoke was discharged through two large ducts under the after end of the flight deck. Commander Hugh Williamson urged an 'island' superstructure on one edge of the flight deck. Tests in a wind tunnel, followed by actual trials with a mockup on the deck of the completed *Argus*, showed that islands on both sides generated unacceptable turbulence, but a single island to starboard (because rotary-engined aircraft with clockwise-turning airscrews could more easily climb away to port) presented no difficulties, indeed was helpful to pilots in judging their landings. The *Argus* never had a permanent island, but her trials were decisive in fixing the basic aircraft carrier design which has lasted ever since.[12]

At the end of the war *Argus* was complete and working up her air group for the attack on the High Seas Fleet. Meanwhile another hull suitable for conversion presented itself early in 1917, the *Furious*. The credibility of Fisher's 'light battle-cruiser' was now completely exploded; nobody thought a very long, very light hull could stand the firing of 18-inch guns for long, but it was a promising basis for an aircraft carrier, so before she was even complete her forward 18-inch turret was removed and replaced with a flying-off deck. Flying-off was now a well-established procedure, but in August 1917 trials of landing on this deck conclusively demonstrated its impossibility, and cost the life of Squadron-Commander Edwin Dunning. The next stage was to remove the after-gun turret as well and replace it with a spacious landing deck, leaving the funnel, bridge and mast standing amidships. There was now plenty of space to land, but experience soon showed that it was as dangerous aft as forward, because aircraft approaching from astern flew into the hot funnel gasses and turbulence generated by the superstructure. In this condition, with two separate flight decks and two hangars stowing a total of sixteen aircraft, which she could fly off but not land on, the *Furious* mounted the Tondern raid in July 1918. A similar conversion of the smaller cruiser *Vindictive*, completed at the war's end in October 1918, suffered from the identical limitation. By 1918 experts such as the airmen Frederick Rutland and Hugh Williamson and the naval architect John Narbeth were converging on the flush-deck form as the best solution to operating aircraft at sea, and the first landing trials on the *Argus* in September 1918 confirmed it. She was followed by the *Eagle* (21,630 tons, 22½ knots; the former Chilean battleship *Almirante Cochrane* bought on the slip in 1918), which had a full starboard-side island.[13]

At a time when many naval officers (Americans in particular) wanted to divide their treaty-permitted tonnage into as many small carriers as possible, in order to eke out the tonnage and reduce the risk of losing these vulnerable ships all at once, the accident of the Washington Treaty settlement (explained in the next chapter) instead gave the leading navies a small number of big ships. The Royal Navy had the three former battle-cruisers *Furious*, *Courageous* and *Glorious* to convert into large, fast aircraft carriers (of 22,500 tons and 30 knots speed), plus the slower conversions *Argus* and *Eagle*. The same process gave the US Navy the even bigger carriers *Lexington* and *Saratoga* (37,680 tons but declared as 33,000; 33¼ knots), while the Japanese Navy gained the former battleships *Akagi* and *Kaga* (30,000 tons but declared as 26,900; 31 knots and 27½ knots speed respectively). Most navies expected great things from aircraft, but which great things would be possible, and how, was quite unclear everywhere. In particular no one agreed how aircraft were to be organized for military purposes, and by whom. The simplest administrative solution was to change nothing, creating an army air force to support military operations, and a naval air force for the Navy. This was the Japanese approach, but it was inherently unstable, creating an unregulated competition between two rival but unequal air forces, the naval air force being by some way the larger and more technically advanced. By the mid-1930s the majority of Japanese naval aircraft were deployed well inland, because the Imperial Army Air Force had in effect 'lost the contract' for the China War, especially for long-range bombing.[14]

In the United States over-water flying was disputed in a similar way, but the disputes were within rival services as well as between them. Everywhere airmen dreamt of setting up as a separate service, exploiting the British precedent, so the control of naval aircraft was a sensitive point, and there was no agreement on the definition of a 'naval aircraft'. Was it limited to aeroplanes which landed on water or flew from a ship – or could it also include wheeled land-based aircraft which flew over water? Did a naval air force have a natural monopoly on operations over water? The US Army Air Corps invested in long-range bombers partly in order to capture the US Navy's official task of offshore national defence. This was an inter-service rivalry with intra-service implications, for within the USN airmen were keenly interested in aeroplanes as the decisive weapon which would presently supersede battleships – not for a moment forgetting that they themselves might then claim to replace the 'battleship admirals' in command. US legislation of 1921, sponsored by friends of the Army Air Corps, required the admiral commanding the US Navy's new Bureau of Aeronautics to be an airman. This was intended to block the development of US naval aviation, since the senior serving naval airman (J. H. Towers) was then only a commander, but Rear-Admiral William A. Moffett, first head of the Bureau of Aeronautics, was able to step into the position by acquiring a nominal qualification as an observer. In 1925 a Congressional inquiry (the 'Morrow Board') recommended that air stations and aircraft carriers should be commanded by airmen. None with sufficient seniority and experience were yet in existence, but a nominal observer's course was set up for senior officers, and others obtained private pilot's licences. Together these improved the career prospects of some non-airmen, and opened at least limited possibilities for airmen to reach flag rank, at the price of instituting another rival 'tribe' to divide the body of naval officers.[15]

Unfortunately for their ambitions the only airborne weapon capable of sinking a large armoured warship was the torpedo, a difficult technology with which the USN had always struggled. By the late 1930s it was close to abandoning aerial torpedoes altogether to concentrate on the new technique of dive-bombing, which threatened aircraft carriers but not battleships (whose heavy armoured decks were not penetrable by bombs dropped in this manner). Admiral Moffett was a gifted politician with powerful friends in Congress, an opponent of a separate naval air force which would threaten the battleships and divide the naval camp, and an ardent advocate of fighter-carrying airships – until he was killed in the crash of the *Akron* in 1933. In 1931 the USN abandoned its claim to operate land-based aircraft over water to the Army Air Corps, partly to save money and pacify Congress, but mainly because it was developing the Consolidated Catalina, a long-range flying-boat bomber (lightly disguised as a 'patrol plane') to command the air over the sea. When war came in 1941 the US Army and Navy were still disputing control of operations over water, with rival patrol, bombing and anti-submarine forces.[16]

In the 1920s, while the Royal Navy concentrated on its new carriers, other major navies devoted money and attention to the reconstruction of existing battleships which the Washington Treaty forbade them to replace. By 1933 the US Navy had spent £16 million on rebuilding battleships (equivalent to £6–8 million at British shipbuilding prices), and the Japanese Navy £9 million. This bought, in most cases, new engines and boilers for greater speed and endurance, and new gun mountings with increased trunnion height for greater elevation and therefore range. It was not possible to make radical changes to existing armour schemes without pulling old ships to pieces completely, but additional deck armour against long-range plunging shells could be added. All this increased weight, and much of it reduced stability, but adding anti-torpedo bulges offset these ill effects at the price of a knot or two of speed. The British did not spend heavily on reconstruction except in the period between 1930, when the extension of the Washington limits blocked hope of building new battleships, and 1936, when new construction was again possible. The battleships *Warspite*, *Queen Elizabeth* and *Valiant* and the battle-cruiser *Renown* were all fully modernized, and the *Hood*, which had already received additional armour while being built, was to have been next. The *Queen Elizabeth* illustrates the advances which had been made in marine engineering over twenty years. As built she had twenty-four boilers, producing saturated steam at 235psi. Rebuilt in 1938 with geared turbines, she had eight boilers giving superheated steam at 400psi and 700°F. Her machinery weight had been halved, it occupied 30 per cent less space than before, steam consumption was down 25 per cent, and the ship's endurance at 10 knots was increased threefold.[17]

The two new battleships allowed to Britain by the Washington Treaty, the *Nelson* and *Rodney*, were launched in 1925. They were slow (23-knot) versions of a cancelled 32-knot battle-cruiser design, with their whole main armament of nine 16-inch guns in three triple turrets placed forward of the bridge, an arrangement which permitted machinery and magazines to be enclosed in a shorter armoured citadel than the conventional placing of heavy gun turrets fore and aft. The Washington Treaty allowed over-age battleships to be replaced from 1931, postponed to 1936 by the London Treaty. From 1928 the Admiralty was working on new designs, assuming that the existing limit of 35,000 tons and 14-inch guns would be the minimum acceptable to other powers. The Second London Naval Treaty of 1936 contained an escalator clause permitting the signatories to increase their battleship limits to 45,000 tons and 16-inch guns in 1938 if by then Japan had not signed, and in March 1938 they claimed this right. It already seemed unlikely in 1936 that Japan would conform to the 14-inch limit, but not until after the war was it discovered that the new Japanese battleships were in fact of 63,000 tons, with 18-inch guns. The British dilemma was that they badly needed to start building new battleships at once in the face of a rapidly worsening international situation and could not afford to wait two years for confirmation that bigger ships and guns would be acceptable. As a result, the five new *King George V* Class battleships (laid down in 1937) were armed with 14-inch guns, but very heavily armoured for their size, to stand up to 16-inch gunfire if necessary. This was rational, but there was also an emotional factor behind the decision. Sir Ernle Chatfield, the First Sea Lord who made the final choice, had been Beatty's flag-captain at Jutland. He never forgot the explosion of the three battle-cruisers, and always insisted on the heaviest possible battleship armour:

> [Henderson] put Chatfield case very politely and said it was the psychological shock of what he saw at Jutland. I pointed out that *Queen Mary* and

co went up through cordite fires and Controller said 'Yes; Chatfield knows and I know. Nevertheless the effect on Chatfield is such that he feels under no circumstances will he be responsible for a ship that has the faintest chance of blowing up.'[18]

In this and most respects the ingenious but cramped *King George V* design performed well. Her armour was as good as or better than that of any contemporary battleship, though the very complex quadruple 14-inch gun turrets gave trouble.[19]

Twelve years elapsed between the launch of the *Nelson* and *Rodney* and the five *King George V* Class, but the designers were kept busy with other classes, starting with the heavy cruisers of the County Classes which dominated British construction in the late 1920s. Seventeen (including two Australian) were launched between 1926 and 1929.[20] By the early 1930s, however, experience with the costly heavy cruisers, and especially the slow rate of fire of their 8-inch guns, was turning the Admiralty back to the greater volume of fire possible with a 6-inch armament. Then the cruiser age limits in the 1930 London Treaty in effect blocked Britain from building new heavy cruisers, and the cruisers built by all the naval powers in the years before the outbreak of war were mostly armed with 6-inch guns, reliable and with a high rate of fire. Strict fire discipline had to be imposed in the Mediterranean Fleet in June 1941 to prevent the cruisers firing off all their 6-inch ammunition. Even lighter calibres were used against aircraft. Between 1935 and 1939 four old 'C' Class light cruisers (launched 1916–18) were converted into anti-aircraft cruisers, with their 6-inch guns replaced with 4-inch ones on high-angle mountings with the best available fire control for engaging aircraft. Nevertheless, the British were ahead of other navies in anti-aircraft gunnery. In 1940–41 the light cruiser *Delhi* (launched in 1919) was re-armed as an AA Cruiser at Norfolk Navy Yard with American 5-inch guns and fire control, to give the USN some vicarious experience before it undertook similar conversions, though in the event the US plan was overtaken by the war and the USN never acquired any anti-aircraft cruisers.[21]

The Royal Navy was amply provided with destroyers in 1918 and had no need to resume building them for ten years after the war. In 1926 Yarrow and Thornycroft each built one destroyer to a common specification but to their own designs, and in 1929 a new 'A' Class of eight destroyers and one larger leader was laid down, to be followed by another class every year. Allowing twelve years for the life of a destroyer, this implied a post-war fleet of 108, in addition to which the Royal Canadian Navy took two more 'A' Class in 1930 and the whole 'C' Class of 1931. By the 1930s the Admiralty calculated its war requirement as sixteen flotillas, 144 boats, including leaders, and with the completion of the 'I' Class in 1937 it actually had 162 without counting contributions from the Dominions. All of these were closely based on the proven 'V' and 'W' Classes, with four 4.7-inch guns (leaders had five) and two quadruple banks of 21-inch torpedo tubes. Their trial speed of 35 knots was calculated as equal to 31¾ knots on a full load of fuel and ammunition. They carried depth charges (and could embark a deck-load of mines by temporarily landing two of their guns); they were fitted with 'Asdic' equipment to detect submerged submarines, a fire-control clock, a gyro compass driving an automated tactical plotter with tactical range-finders to feed it, as well as a gunnery range-finder for fire-control. These were sophisticated small warships with a wide and growing range of capabilities extending well beyond torpedo attack on an enemy battle-fleet: 'literally a small cruiser with a powerful armament, expensive fire control, great speed and endurance, high-angle guns and comfortable accommodation', in the words of Sir Ernle Chatfield (then Controller) in 1927.[22] This in fact is, and already was by the end of the 1930s, grounds for criticism: an excellent basic design had been repeated with incremental improvements but without re-examining the concept as it drifted gradually towards overload and obsolescence.[23]

The criticisms came from several directions. The twenty destroyers of the Japanese *Fubuki* Class, launched between 1927 and 1931, carried six 5-inch guns in enclosed twin gunhouses, and nine 24-inch torpedo tubes. They were followed by German, French and Italian 'super-destroyers' which all outmatched the British boats in speed and armament, and seemed to call for a substantially bigger and faster basic destroyer in response. Some critics also objected to the scanty British anti-aircraft armament, but those interwar air forces which paid attention to ships concentrated on high-level formation bombing of serious targets (meaning battleships, which repeated experience demonstrated that they could not hit), so agile destroyers did not seem to be much at risk. More cogent was the continued problem of the limited steaming range of destroyers, which had caused so much trouble during the war, and threatened to nullify British plans for a fleet based on Singapore to advance towards Japan. The only way to address it was to build bigger ships carrying more fuel (which would inevitably mean fewer and more costly destroyers), or to design much more economical machinery. The way to fuel economy had already been explored for bigger ships and the basic direction was clear: higher pressure and temperature steam. This was easy to express, and as far as the boilers were concerned relatively easy to produce, but the turbines and many other parts of the machinery had to be redesigned to exploit

high-pressure and high-temperature steam. *Amazon*, the Thornycroft prototype of 1926, had steam conditions of 150° superheat at 260psi, giving a range
of 3,400 miles at 15 knots, but the Engineer-in-Chief wanted 5,000 miles at
12 knots.[24]

The next experiment was with the 'A' Class destroyer *Acheron* of 1927, fitted
with Thornycroft boilers at 500psi and 750°F (which compared with the new
Admiralty standard three-drum boiler at 300psi and 600°F). The ship was
engined by Parsons, who were the primary turbine designers for both the RN
and the USN. Neither navy was satisfied with Parsons, but in a severe slump
a virtual monopolist had no incentive to invest heavily in new engine designs.
The Admiralty had its own boiler research establishment, the Admiralty Fuel
Experimental Station, and in 1917 it established the Admiralty Engineering
Laboratory to work on large diesels for submarines, but it still relied on the
marine engine-builders to do their own turbine research and development.
The Engineer-in-Chief had hoped for a 7 per cent saving in fuel consumption,
but problems with *Acheron*'s turbines soon persuaded him that the move to
advanced steam conditions was premature, and the Admiralty abandoned its
trials and sent her to rejoin her flotilla in the Mediterranean after what seems
to have been only a token effort. This is surprising: the problem of destroyer
endurance was serious and long-standing, and no experienced engineer could
have expected to solve it without prolonged efforts. The tone of bland complacency with which senior Royal Navy engineers remembered the period, and
their warm nostalgia for coal-firing, reminds us that all these officers belonged
to the older generation of naval engineers who had been associated with mechanical problems since the 1880s.[25]

All this can be put in context by comparing British efforts with those of
other navies. An officer well qualified to compare British and German destroyers of the 1930s was Commander Rolf Johannesson, captain of the big German
destroyer *Erich Steinbrinck* in the 1940 Norwegian campaign, during which
she suffered from repeated engine trouble and defective torpedoes. In sixty-
five months of war service between 1939 and 1945, this ship was in dockyard
hands for forty-one months, mostly for machinery repairs, plus four collisions
and a grounding. Only one of her fifteen sister ships had a satisfactory record
of reliability, and in January 1941 half the class was taken out of service to be
re-engined. But in August 1942 Johannesson was given command of the
Hermes, the only German destroyer in the Mediterranean. This was the former
Greek destroyer *Vassileus Georgios*, bombed and sunk in port in April 1941 and
then refloated by the Germans. She had been built on the Clyde by Yarrow,
and in every respect except her guns was a unit of the British 'G' Class of 1938.

Although the *Hermes* was smaller and less heavily armed than his former command, Johannesson was delighted by the contrast: 'The *Hermes* was a real "working destroyer". She did not break down and was seldom in dockyard hands; when I needed to get to sea in a hurry I would have changed nothing about her . . .'[26]

The US Navy, like the British, was dependent on Parsons and on shipbuilders who were averse to expensive experiments. During the First World War it had attempted to escape from Parsons' geared turbines by fitting its new battleships with a General Electric turbo-electric plant, which proved to be an overweight and expensive dead end. Rear-Admiral Samuel M. Robinson, appointed head of the US Navy's Bureau of Engineering in 1931, was determined to adopt high-pressure steam and double-reduction geared turbines in the face of considerable opposition from Parsons and other marine engine builders. It took almost ten years' effort, and a large share of the $281 million which President Roosevelt diverted to warship-building from Congressional votes under the National Industrial Recovery Act. With this money Robinson persuaded firms like General Electric and Westinghouse, which built turbines for power stations, to enter the marine market and design high-pressure, high-temperature boiler and turbine plant as an integrated whole, with careful attention to details like steam-tight joints which were a source of endless trouble in British ships. The first fruits were the *Mahan* Class destroyers of 1935–6, whose cramped engine rooms gave the new machinery a poor reputation, but later destroyers and further developments up to 1940 vindicated Robinson's programme. When war came the US Navy's newest destroyers (about ninety were completed between the *Somers* Class of 1937 and December 1941, with many more following) possessed powerful, reliable and economical machinery which was a generation ahead of that in British ships. The same contrast applied to the new US fast battleships *North Carolina* and *Washington* (launched in 1940) compared with the older *King George V* Class.[27]

In the interwar years there seemed to be almost no way for a ship to detect an approaching air attack outside visual range, which would give at best a couple of minutes' warning in clear weather – much too little for defensive fighters to take off from a carrier and gain height. It was equally impossible to keep up standing fighter patrols of aircraft with very limited endurance. These considerations guided the design of the British armoured fleet carriers in the 1930s, which combined a heavy anti-aircraft armament with an ingenious protective system often referred to as an armoured deck, but more accurately described as an internal armoured box whose top surface formed the flight deck. This was designed to protect the ship's aircraft from either air attack or cruiser shellfire, while also using the armour to provide much of the structural strength of the hull. The armoured carriers were a very clever and advanced design (inspired by Sir Reginald Henderson as Flag Officer Aircraft Carriers 1931–4 and Controller of the Navy 1934–9), but in retrospect we can say that they were too clever, and depended on too many immature technologies. The heaviest armour which could be provided on their displacement proved to be insufficient to protect them against the heaviest German bombs, and their air group (with 12–15 fighters) was small enough to be swamped, whereas the unarmoured *Ark Royal* with twenty-four fighters was never damaged by air attack.[28]

The German Navy's first post-war big ships were the three *Panzerschiffe* or 'armoured ships' of the *Deutschland* Class, laid down 1929 to 1932. They were officially classed using the vocabulary of the Versailles Treaty, but privately referred to as 'small battle-cruisers', and aptly christened 'pocket battleships' by the British press. Their design exploited the fact that Germany alone was limited by the Versailles and not the Washington settlement, and could build replacements for the old Pre-Dreadnought battleships armed with 11-inch guns, easily superior to the 8-inch guns of Washington-Treaty heavy cruisers. Although they were somewhat slower than British cruisers, their diesel engines were intended to give them long range for commerce-raiding operations, which both British and German navies agreed would be the most serious threat to British shipping. Unfortunately, the big diesels proved to be very unreliable and so the next German armoured ships reverted to steam. Although often referred to in English as 'battle-cruisers', the *Scharnhorst* and *Gneisenau*, laid down in 1934, were more like small battleships, heavily armoured but armed with the same 11-inch guns in triple turrets as the *Panzerschiffe*.[29]

The transatlantic liners *Bremen* and *Europa* of 1928 adopted steam at 340psi and 700°F, following power-station practice, and the German Navy followed suit. A new gunnery training ship and a class of coastal escorts were intended to test the new high-pressure, high-temperature steam plant before it was installed in the Type 34 destroyers laid down in late 1934, but in the event the destroyers were built first and it was too late to change anything by the time it became clear that their engines and boilers were a disaster. They used steam at over 1,000psi – four times the pressure of any previous German destroyer. The machinery was extremely complex, the engine rooms so cramped that access and maintenance were scarcely possible, the German Navy was critically short of engineer officers, and neither ship's staff nor dockyard personnel could understand the technology. Breakdowns were so frequent that destroyer officers became reluctant to risk their ships at sea (besides that this class were very poor seaboats).[30]

In 1933 the Admiralty began planning for the shipbuilding regime which would arrive with the expiry of the London Naval Treaty at the end of 1935. The expected limits on overall tonnage and the size of individual destroyer types would be very difficult to reconcile with British requirements without risking defeat at the hands of the cruisers and 'super-destroyers' already built or anticipated from foreign navies. The Navy was building the very light (only 5,200-ton) 6-inch cruisers of the Arethusa Class, which seemed to be the absolute minimum feasible cruiser. Japan's withdrawal from the Washington Treaty structure in 1935 abolished national tonnage limits, but categories of warship were still restricted by the 1930 London Treaty, which limited destroyers to 1,500 tons, yet allowed a limited number of destroyer leaders up to 1,850 tons. From this emerged the Admiralty concept of the 'V Leader', which was not a conventional destroyer leader but a destroyer-like ship not larger than 1,850 tons, to be built from 1936 and intended to fill the gap between destroyer flotillas and light cruisers. They were launched in 1937 as the 'Tribal' Class of sixteen ships (to which three Australian and eight Canadian ships were later added). They were armed with six 4.7-inch guns in three twin gunhouses with a limited AA capacity, plus one quadruple bank of 21-inch torpedoes, and lighter AA guns. These handsome and powerful ships made a great impression and were always in the front line in the Second World War, in which all but four of the original sixteen were sunk. They set a new standard for British destroyers: after the 'Tribals' the interwar standard destroyer design was no longer acceptable, and overall destroyer tonnage was no longer limited, so the 'J', 'K' and 'L' Classes of 1938–40 carried the same six 4.7-inch gun armament as the Tribals, with ten 21-inch torpedo tubes, on a standard displacement approaching 2,000 tons.[31]

By the 1930s the Royal Navy had a large destroyer force, of which a significant part was over-age by treaty and could be replaced from 1936 with annual classes of nine boats each. The Admiralty would have preferred to build more destroyers than the treaty limits allowed. An alternative was to build ships of destroyer quality but no faster than 20 knots, which put them outside the treaty definition of destroyers. This was the origin of the sloops built from 1933, which were anti-aircraft escorts with a main armament of six four-inch guns in twin mountings, with as sophisticated a fire-control fit as was then possible in small ships. Their function was to cover wartime convoys to and from London passing through the North Sea or English Channel within range of enemy aircraft. In the event they entered service after the fall of France and spent most of their careers escorting convoys in the Atlantic, but they proved to be excellent anti-submarine as well as anti-aircraft escorts which played a distinguished part in the Atlantic convoy campaigns (though their range was low for transatlantic voyages).[32]

In the interwar years naval construction, especially of the bigger classes, was heavily constrained by arms limitation treaties as well as the usual factors of money, time, dock size and shipbuilding capacity. There were, however, less obvious ways in which warships' power and effectiveness could be increased. Putting aside sharp practice or plain cheating in tonnage measurement, which helped Germany, Italy and the United States to cut some awkward corners, there was a legitimate and widespread tendency to gain advantage with new equipment which was not treaty-limited. The British and Germans developed new armour with about 25 per cent greater resistance than before, but the USN fell behind.[33] Battleship gun size was restricted by treaty, but gun range was not, leading to a concealed 'arms race' in advanced fire-control for long-range shooting. The most sophisticated such equipment was the Admiralty Fire Control Table fitted in the new and rebuilt British battleships. Although it was too big to be accommodated in the older, unreconstructed ships, there were enough at sea by 1939 for every three-ship division of battleships to have one 'master ship' for concentration firing.[34] Torpedo range and technology was another dimension of intense, and intensely secret, competition by which navies sought to gain unsuspected advantages. In this dimension the Japanese succeeded, where both British and Americans failed, in developing a heavy (24-inch) 'heater' torpedo for cruisers and later destroyers, powered by compressed oxygen rather than compressed air. This Type 93 torpedo (often referred to in Western sources by the completely bogus Oriental name of 'Long Lance') could be set for speeds from 36 to 50 knots and ranges up to 43,700 yards; figures far greater than were suspected or believed in Western navies until after the war in spite of the heavy losses that the torpedo inflicted.[35]

NINETEEN

The Peace to End War

Policy and Operations 1919–1930

I t is not difficult to divide the winners from the losers of the First World War by the conventional military and territorial criteria. Germany had to return the western provinces of Alsace and Lorraine which she had taken from France in 1871, and the much vaster extent of eastern territories seized from Russia in 1917 – Finland, the Baltic provinces, Poland, the Ukraine, most of Byelorussia and the Caucasus, amounting to a third of the cultivated land, half the industry and 80 per cent of the coal of the Russian Empire. Austria-Hungary was divided and dismembered into Austria, Hungary, and a number of newly independent states carved out of them on principles resembling American-style racial segregation, with language standing proxy for race – though in much of the Dual Monarchy the association of language with national sentiment was recent at best, and many of the different populations lived so intimately mixed together that it was impossible to divide them into nationally homogeneous states and provinces. The Ottoman Empire was likewise broken up to the profit of the Western Powers and local princes who had chosen their side. France gained Syria and the Lebanon from the Ottomans. Russia, already dismembered by the Treaty of Brest-Litovsk in 1917 and convulsed by the overthrow of the monarchy soon afterwards, was befriended by the victorious Allies, who hoped but failed to restore her former state. Having joined the victors, Italy was rewarded for numerous defeats with large tracts of formerly Austrian territory in the Alps and the Veneto, many of whose populations spoke German. Britain gained effective control or predominant influence over most of the Middle East except those parts ceded to France. This would have been an untidy and illogical series of radical changes even if the decisions of the peace conferences had been carried out as the victors agreed, but in practice the diplomats' work was overtaken before it could be completed by local wars in the former Austro-Hungarian and Ottoman empires.[1]

The peace settlement was not at all a peaceable process but a continuation of international rivalry by other means, with wartime friendships and enmities re-arranged as imperial and naval disputes, submerged during the war, re-emerged to divide the former allies. Economic warfare, which had played so large a part in the war, played an even larger part in the peace. Anxious to demobilize their armies without relaxing the pressure on Germany to sign a peace, Britain and her allies kept up the economic blockade of Germany, while Germany continued her wartime policy of feeding the army and navy at the expense of the civilian population. The result was widespread malnutrition among German civilians, which discredited Allied policies and was exploited to transform the image of German aggressors into one of German victims.[2]

The fate of the former German fleet, interned at Scapa Flow under the armistice terms, keenly interested those (like the French and the Americans) who wanted the ships for themselves, and those (like the British) who merely wanted to prevent any rivals gaining them. In the end the Allies almost agreed to scuttle the German ships in deep water, but before it could be done the Germans themselves sank their fleet in Scapa Flow in June 1919. This was presented as a heroic gesture of defiance, but it was so obviously in Britain's interest that many foreigners suspected collusion. The only direct sufferer was Germany herself, which was punished for her treachery by losing the remaining modern cruisers and destroyers which might have formed the nucleus of a revived navy, plus merchant shipping, floating cranes, floating docks and other infrastructure. The remaining cruisers and destroyers went to France and Italy; all the German Navy was left with was six pre-Dreadnought battleships and a handful of obsolete torpedo boats.[3]

The several peace negotiations, notionally separate and held in different places, overlapped in time and subject. The Versailles Conference (January to December 1919) not only attempted to settle the consequences of the war with Germany and Austria-Hungary, but at the same time set up the embryonic world political organization of the League of Nations. The conference opened with American and British admirals striking aggressive attitudes towards each other, while the US government played the part, less of a victorious belligerent than of a white knight, unsullied by the guilt of war and bearing the torch of enlightened humanitarianism. The US Navy believed, and the British feared, that British debts to American banks would now be rapidly translated into US naval dominance. Even the American admirals, who should have understood their political system, failed to appreciate that sentiment in Congress was moving against them, while behind the scenes President Wilson and Lloyd George were discreetly sketching a settlement.[4]

Unfortunately, this was not all that happened behind the scenes. In the autumn of 1919 Wilson suffered one or more strokes, kept secret at the time, which effectively paralysed him and his government until the inauguration of President Warren G. Harding in March 1921. Without strong presidential leadership there was no chance of carrying measures through an increasingly restive Congress. To the disgust of the British, who refused to believe that an American government could lack a majority in its own parliament to carry out its declared policy, the Senate rejected the Treaty of Versailles and the League of Nations. The League, which had been assigned a central role in upholding the peace settlement, was crippled from the start. Having forced through a post-war settlement to its own specification, it seemed the United States had cynically abandoned it and left others to carry the burden of peace. After this nobody trusted American diplomacy for a generation.[5]

British statesmen had not forgotten their pre-war commitment to British sea power. They were well aware that the country's financial strength had been badly damaged by the war and sought to replace a naval arms race with diplomacy where possible, but they did not shrink from the necessity to rebuild the fleet. Although the scuttling of the High Seas Fleet had left Britain with more battleships than the rest of the world put together, most of them were obsolescent and worn out. The United States Navy was publicly committed to overtaking Britain as quickly as possible, and the 1916 legislation, which financed ten new American battleships and six battle-cruisers, newer and much bigger than any British rivals, gave them the means to get most of the way there. In December 1920 the Committee of Imperial Defence agreed on a new British building programme of eight battleships if no agreement could be reached with the United States, but Lord Lee, named First Lord of the Admiralty in February 1921, was quite clear what outcome he preferred:

> Apart from the financial and economic impossibility of our engaging, with any hope of success, in an armament race with America, I feel it would matter little which country emerged victorious (in a military sense) from such an insane encounter – for both nations would be irretrievably ruined and, meanwhile, civilization would have perished.[6]

If the British began new shipbuilding, there would be no chance of avoiding another naval arms race, so to keep the door open to a diplomatic settlement

Lloyd George insisted on the imposition of a secret planning assumption blocking new capital ship orders for ten years from 1919. This was the origin of the 'Ten Year Rule', which in the demonology of popular British naval history still sometimes features as a sinister Treasury plot to expose Britain to foreign aggressors. In reality the Treasury was not involved, the only plausible foreign aggressor was the United States and the object of the rule was not primarily to save money.[7]

The public opinion and the political leaders of the world, contemplating the bloody catastrophe of a war which had left few nations untouched, naturally demanded to know whom or what to blame. One obvious answer was the stock target of the pre-war left, 'bloated armaments', and no armaments were more bloated and more conspicuous than the Dreadnought battle-fleets. Many were prepared to believe that the naval arms race had itself promoted or even caused the war – from which it seemed to follow that shipbuilders and arms manufacturers were the 'guilty men', and limiting or reducing battle-fleets would make future war less likely. Disgust at battle-fleets for somehow causing the war was added to disgust at them for failing to win it. By 1921 the pre-war sport of naval arms-racing was deeply unpopular, and battleships were the ideal target for arms limitation, because they were so expensive and so easily identifiable. The major naval powers whose representatives assembled in Washington in November 1921 at the invitation of the new US government knew this, and expected to negotiate about naval strength, but none of them (least of all the American admirals) anticipated the dramatic opening speech of Charles E. Hughes, the new US Secretary of State. Instead of a conventional welcome to the delegates, Hughes set out a highly detailed plan to limit the American, British and Japanese battle-fleets by tonnage in the ratio of 5:5:3 (with smaller quotas for France and Italy). He listed by name no fewer than seventy capital ships (battleships or battle-cruisers) to be scrapped forthwith: thirty American (including all sixteen ships of the 1916 programme which was already under way), twenty-three British and seventeen Japanese. This would be followed by a ten-year 'holiday' in capital-ship construction, after which new ships could be built within the original national tonnage allowances to replace those over twenty years old, no individual ship to displace more than 35,000 tons. All the powers would have to abandon their new ships, planned or already being built. On every side the admirals were appalled, but Hughes' bold proposal had attractions for all the major naval powers, beyond the obvious one of saving money. Hughes knew that he was only abandoning US naval ambitions which Congress was unlikely to pay for, in return for real sacrifices by others. The US

Navy, however, stood to gain the prestige of notional equality with the Royal Navy, even if the ships to realize it were never built, while Britain's real position as the leading naval power was safeguarded at no cost for at least ten years. The British were able to scrap a lot of worn-out and obsolete battleships to set against other powers' new construction, preserving the value of the wartime *Queen Elizabeth* and 'R' Class battleships for years after they would otherwise have been outclassed, while building the new cruisers and aircraft carriers which they needed more urgently. Having gone to Washington expecting to have to spend heavily to gain parity with the US Navy and a 50 per cent margin over the Japanese Navy, the British came away with free parity with the USN, a 67 per cent margin over the Japanese Navy, a better than two-power standard in Europe and a considerable saving on their planned construction budget. In defiance of all traditions of consensus (and threats of assassination), the Japanese Navy Minister Admiral Katō Tomosaburō abandoned Japan's 1920 plan to build sixteen capital ships and saved his country from isolation and bankruptcy. He also preserved the Japanese fleet at a relative strength it had never reached before, and probably would not have retained for long without the artificial support of the treaty. By renouncing the possibility of building bases in the western Pacific (anywhere between Singapore, Hawaii and Japan), the US and Japan kept their respective fleets out of range of each other and calmed their mutual paranoia about surprise attacks. For all naval powers the building holiday made a new battleship race impossible and imposed a sort of stability; Hughes' bold proposal was therefore accepted with only slight modification. The Japanese were allowed to keep the just-completed battleship *Mutsu*, built by public subscription, the British to build two new battleships, and the US to keep two of the 1916 programme. Each of the participants was permitted to convert some incomplete battle-cruiser hulls into aircraft carriers. Only the French regarded the Washington Treaty as a humiliation. Instead of arbitrating between Britain and the United States, as they had intended, they found themselves reduced to equal status with Italy, though their real position was better than it seemed. Hardly anyone noticed that the treaty, by restricting navies but not armies, might favour some future continental aggressor against a naval power.[8]

The Washington (or 'Five-Power') naval treaty was only part of a wider settlement. Neither Congress nor President Harding was sympathetic to the US Navy's ambitions. What the new American administration really wanted was the dissolution of the Anglo-Japanese alliance, which (for reasons not easy to understand) it regarded as a mortal threat. Since this alliance had originally been intended to block Russian expansion in the Far East, and Russia had now disintegrated into civil war, the British were open to persuasion on the subject. It was obvious to them that the United States was both a more valuable friend and a more dangerous enemy than Japan, if they had to choose between the two. 'Embarrassing, to say the least of it, as our position in the Far East would be in the event of hostilities with Japan, it is unquestionable that if we had to break with one or the other, it must be Japan and not the United States.'[9] Moreover the connection with Japan was unpopular in Australia and Canada for reasons both of strategy and racial prejudice. Winston Churchill, the Chancellor of the Exchequer, argued forcefully that if Japanese aggression was to be feared in the future, the alliance would be of no use to restrain it.[10] The result was the 'Four-Power Treaty' between Britain, the US, Japan and France, which replaced the Anglo-Japanese alliance with mutual guarantees of each other's possessions; followed by the 'Nine-Power Treaty', which added Italy, the Netherlands, Belgium, Portugal and China to guarantee China's independence and adopt the favourite American 'Open Door' policy, repudiating the exclusive trading privileges of Western Powers in China. In this way the treaties not only limited armaments but tried to still the quarrels which might call them into action.[11]

In addressing the causes as well as the instruments of war, the Washington settlement was remarkably successful in its day, and Britain was its major beneficiary. By freezing the status quo, it preserved Britain as the leading naval and imperial power of the world, though it also increased her liabilities as guarantor of the post-war settlement. It kept the battleship as the standard of naval power and confined submarines and aircraft carriers to the position of auxiliaries to the battle-fleets. It offered Britain and Japan a graceful way to escape an alliance which no longer fitted their circumstances, and an opportunity to make friends with the United States. It gave Britain a 'one-power standard' against the US, which no one in London intended to fight, equivalent to a two-power standard against Japan in combination with any one European power, and better than the two-power standard of the 1890s. But no treaty could have pleased every participant. American admirals, many of whom longed for the means and opportunity to fight Britain, were disgusted that the well-meaning simpletons of the US State Department had yet again been outwitted by the subtle and devious British negotiators. Warmer Anglo-American relations were balanced by French suspicion and resentment of both. The suppression of the anti-racialist declaration promised for the League of Nations charter, followed by the overtly anti-Japanese legislation passed in Australia and the US in the 1920s, fuelled resentment and hatred in Japan.[12] Changing politics, diplomacy and technology placed the Washington settlement under growing strain in the 1930s. Looking further into the future, as the Admiralty noted in 1922, a US fleet too far away to threaten Japan 'rules obligations out, so far as effective interference with Japan in the western basin of the Pacific Ocean is concerned, and leaves the British Empire the sole Power to counter, with Naval Forces, any aggressive tendencies on the part of Japan'.[13]

It must not be supposed that from 1919 to 1922 the world waited in peaceful expectation for the diplomats to settle the post-war world order. In fact most of the former Russian Empire and large parts of the Ottoman Empire rapidly disintegrated into local wars as different groups tried to establish 'facts on the ground', and British warships were drawn in as far as geography allowed. At the Armistice, Rear-Admiral Edwin Alexander-Sinclair was sent with a light cruiser squadron to the Baltic 'to show the British flag and support British policy as circumstances dictate'. With some help from Balfour the Foreign Secretary, the Admiralty translated this gnomic guidance into orders that 'a Bolshevik man-of-war operating off the coast of the Baltic provinces must be assumed to be doing so with hostile intent and should be treated accordingly'.[14] The British squadron was now fighting for the independence of Estonia and Finland against the Bolsheviks. Further south, much of Latvia was in the hands of German *Freikorps* led by General Rüdiger von der Goltz, aiming to establish a new German Empire in the homeland of the old (German-speaking) Baltic nobility, and opposed to, occasionally allied to, at times even disguised as, the forces of the Russian Provisional Government (the 'Whites'), the Bolsheviks (the 'Reds'), Western interventionists, Latvian and Polish nationalists. The Bolshevik fleet in Kronstadt, whose 'activated squadron' included two modern battleships besides other warships, vastly outmatched all the other warships in the Baltic, at least on paper. At the head of the Gulf of Finland near Petrograd (St Petersburg), a British naval officer attached to the Secret Intelligence Service, Lieutenant Augustus Agar, established a secret base for two coastal motor boats which ran night-time missions into the city in support of the British agent Paul Dukes. Meanwhile, in another part of the wood, ships and troops (including a considerable force of Royal Marines) advanced south from the White Sea along the Dvina River to support the White Russians against the Reds. Alexander-Sinclair and his successor Rear-Admiral Sir Walter Cowan had to contend with considerable discontent and several small mutinies among sailors and Marines who had engaged for 'hostilities only' and knew that the rest of the Services were being demobilized. They also had to operate in waters thickly sown with ill-charted minefields. In the face of these difficulties, with few orders and little clear guidance from London, the British ships were effective in saving the independence of Estonia and (with French help) of Latvia, in spite of the enormous superiority of the Red fleet. Taking a break from secret service, Lieutenant Agar torpedoed and sank the Bolshevik cruiser *Oleg* in June 1919, and in August led an attack by CMBs and aircraft on Kronstadt which sank the battleships *Andrei Pervozvannyi* and *Petropavlovsk* at their moorings, after which the Russian fleet gave no trouble. But naval intervention was in every sense marginal to the outcome of the Russian Civil War. Away from the Baltic coast, the British were unable to help any of the Red Army's enemies, and the only inland nation which succeeded in making good her independence from the Russian Empire – Poland – did so largely by her own efforts.[15]

In the Mediterranean the uncertain situation while a peace settlement was under negotiation resembled that in the Baltic. Most of the British fleet moved up to the Black Sea, but there were also cruiser squadrons in the Aegean and the Adriatic, plus flotillas on the Danube and the Caspian Sea. The British and French had to support the White Russians against the Reds, and deal with a German army still occupying the Crimea, but mutiny in the French fleet ended the hope of holding Sebastopol against the Reds. Lloyd George, whose involvement in foreign policy went well beyond what would be normal for a Prime Minister, was a warm supporter of Greek ambitions to restore Greek rule to western Asia Minor, where Greek populations were still present even 468 years after the fall of Byzantium. In support of these plans, British, Greek and Italian troops occupied Smyrna in May 1919. The Greeks at once advanced inland despite Allied misgivings, and Colonel Mustapha Kemal, the hero of Gallipoli, took the lead in Turkish resistance – ignoring the sultan's government in Istanbul, which soon ceased to have any influence in Anatolia. The paralysis of the Allies as this new crisis rapidly developed owed something to the paralysis of the US government due to President Wilson's stroke. The Supreme War Council soon showed itself determined to impose a peace on Greek terms, ignoring the warnings of those on the spot that this would play into the hands of Kemal and the Turkish nationalists. In August 1920 the humiliating peace treaty of Sèvres did exactly that. The Greeks still showed no sign of moderation or prudence, and by the end of 1920 the Allies were ready to repudiate them. In the course of 1921, the Greeks were repeatedly defeated by Kemal's forces, and in September 1922 the Turks entered Smyrna. The city was burnt, some of the 250,000 Greeks and Armenians in it were massacred, and Allied ships with great

difficulty evacuated the remainder. Thanks largely to Lloyd George's mischievous intervention, the British government was now alienated from
France and on the verge of war with Turkey. Only Kemal's restraint, and deft
diplomacy by the British officers on the spot (mainly General Sir Charles
Harington), whose warnings had so often been ignored, averted the worst
consequences of London's folly and opened the way to a peaceful settlement
of the 'Chanak Crisis'. In November 1923, by which time the sultan was overthrown and Kemal was the President of a secular Turkish republic, the British battleships were at last free to leave Istanbul.[16]

The ideas and attitudes which shaped public life and international relations
changed less between 1914 and 1919 than is often imagined. In all the leading
powers naval strength was still regarded as the ultimate expression of real power,
and in Britain all parties were committed to naval supremacy. Great powers
have always traded on their reputation, and warships – above all, battleships –
were the physical embodiment of reputation. This rested on their known ability to fight, but a naval power which had to fight had already lost a major part
of the battle, because real war was (and is) heavily influenced by chance, and
may easily embarrass even the most powerful fleet. It was in peacetime that
the experts had leisure to measure the strength of the fleets, and then that the
most powerful of them deployed the full weight of their notional firepower in
international diplomacy. What naval strength was essential, or possible, and
how to measure it, were fundamental questions in British public life in the
years after the First World War. The traditional test of 'naval supremacy', or the
more recent naval 'standards' measured against one or more foreign fleets,
remained in use, but alternative, more realistic, calculations were available
based on the real force necessary to protect specific vital interests against actual
threats.[17]

Another major element of uncertainty had been injected into naval strategy by the coming of aircraft to naval warfare. At the end of the war everyone
understood that aircraft were going to be important, but the real capabilities
and achievements of existing machines were so restricted that the debate
tended to be conducted in terms of what future aircraft might be able to do
in imagined circumstances. Ideas and attitudes took the place of facts and
experience, while science fiction had as much influence as naval strategy. To
the public, air warfare seemed exciting and modern for aesthetic and social
rather than military reasons. Many military airmen in Britain and abroad
were fascinated by the possibilities of bombing as a weapon to strike the moral
fragility of civil society. Contemporary military doctrine stressed the triumph
of superior willpower, the moral force deployed by the best trained and the

best bred, and airmen eagerly appropriated these quasi-fascist ideas. This meant bombing unprotected civilians, but the newly formed RAF, allergic to future planning and speculative thought, avoided uncomfortable public debates.[18]

For naval men, however, it was clear that there were essential military functions which aircraft could already perform, with others in prospect. Reconnaissance aircraft could greatly increase the sea area effectively controlled by the battle-fleet (at least in daylight), they could promote interception and avert dangerous surprises, and they could increase the fighting range of big ships by spotting for gunfire beyond the range of the ships' instruments. Other aircraft had already proved that they could play an indispensable role in anti-submarine warfare.[19] There were four important forms, all familiar by 1918, in which aircraft could be employed in naval war, and for a realistic understanding of naval aviation it is necessary to keep all four in mind. Carrier aircraft – wheeled aircraft flying from ships with a flight deck – are the general favourite of modern writers, though their ability to operate in the open sea was bought at a high price and their numbers were always severely limited. Most aircraft participating in naval warfare were wheeled machines flying from shore airfields, and naturally not available out of flying range of a friendly coast. Many (in the early years most) shipborne aircraft were seaplanes carried by battleships, cruisers and other ships, put in the water by crane or launched from a catapult or flying-off platform, and recovered after landing on the water. This was only possible in fine weather. Finally, there were the flying-boats, obsolete today and frequently forgotten by historians, but filling a crucial gap in the ecology of naval aviation in the era of the world wars. The limited power of the available aero-engines meant that heavy lift or long range could only be provided by multi-engined – and therefore heavy – aircraft which normally needed permanent concrete runways to reach flying speed. Flying-boats alone were not so limited: their waterborne hulls allowed them to fly with no preparation from any suitable area of fairly sheltered water, and (if supported by a tender) they could remove fast to another base. This allowed them to make essential contributions to naval warfare in the many areas of the world where heavy bombers and paved runways were unavailable.[20]

Perhaps the gravest distortion of reality in the naval history of the twentieth century comes from the obvious but uncomfortable fact that a high proportion of historians are not so much impartial seekers after truth as partisan loyalists of particular services or branches. This fault is most clearly visible in the treatment of naval aviation, because in all the major belligerents it was divided between services, and in most of them inter-service co-operation was poor or non-existent. Loyalist historians continue to write books in which the contribution of rival services is undervalued or ignored, sometimes with the ill-concealed intention of influencing current policy. In Britain air force historians often take their cue from the official histories of the two world wars sponsored by the Air Ministry, which largely omit the RNAS from the first, and entirely omit Coastal Command from the second.[21] Nevertheless, as we shall see, the actual relations of the Royal Navy and the Royal Air Force, before and during the Second World War, were warm and fruitful compared with those between the air forces of the Imperial Japanese Navy and Army, and those between the US Navy and the US Army Air Corps.

The biggest problem in Britain was that the RAF was set up in 1918 in a way calculated (perhaps deliberately) to promote and profit from inter-service discord. As a result a whole range of administrative, strategic and technical questions tended to be reduced to matters of inter-service politics, negotiated between departments or adjudicated by a non-specialist Cabinet on political rather than technical grounds. This made for bad blood and bad decisions. Virtually everything of value which the airmen could offer in the interwar years had to do with military or naval operations, so the RAF's situation and strategy required inter-service co-operation, which its politics forbade. All three services suffered as a result, but the RAF suffered the most. What was worse was the RAF's anti-intellectual internal culture, amateurish and hostile to free inquiry. The service spent heavily on speculative research into weapons like guided missiles and airships, which were unconnected with rival services but did not work, while actively suppressing the practical solutions to operational problems such as bomb-aiming, aerial navigation and defence against fighters which it had inherited from the RNAS. RAF exercises were designed to confirm preconceived ideas and ignored if they did not. The RAF's very small force of flying-boats was employed in 'proving' that aircraft could replace cruisers, instead of developing their complementary roles.[22]

At the end of the war the British were the possessors – monopolists in many cases – of valuable war experience which they were about to translate into new ships and weapons. The naval ideal would have been to scrap much of their recent tonnage, not yet old but already obsolescent and worn-out by hard war service, replacing it with new designs and the latest equipment. Financially and politically, this was out of the question. The country had won what the public had learnt to call 'the war to end all wars', a war which an important sector of public opinion blamed on the pre-war arms race. It would not do to celebrate the victory by starting a new arms race. Moreover, as we shall see, Britain and other naval powers soon accepted treaty limitations on the size and number of warships which they could build. These limitations increasingly distorted the fleet structure of the participating navies, which were artificially fixed in their 1918 form. The new treaties preserved battleships as the unquestioned arbiters of the naval battle, while the potential of aircraft and submarines was restrained. This favoured the defenders of orthodoxy, and the 'possessor powers' (Britain above all) which already had powerful battle-fleets.[23]

But in most naval powers, and especially in Britain and the United States, the defenders of battleships were also the leading proponents of aircraft. The experience of the war had convinced all naval officers that a modern fleet needed aircraft for many essential functions, especially for reconnaissance, and to spot for long-range gunfire which many officers saw as the key to future victory. In 1920 Sir Charles Madden, then commanding the Atlantic Fleet (and a future First Sea Lord), 'told me it was his considered opinion that the results of a naval battle in the future depended on the air and the side that had aerial supremacy would win a naval fight provided the ships were anywhere near equal . . . He also added that, given air supremacy, he would be quite willing with a British fleet to take twice the strength of any other fleet.'[24]

The RNAS at the moment of its abolition had two thousand aircraft; by the winter of 1920 there were only about fifty left to work with the fleet, and only a hundred or so at the end of the 1920s. In 1930 the RAF's 'Coastal Area' had only twenty-six aircraft. The new Fleet Air Arm or FAA (meaning the fleet arm of the RAF rather than the air arm of the fleet, but the ambiguous grammar suited all) had lost most of its aircraft but retained much of its naval character. The terms of the 1923 Balfour Report which established the FAA gave naval commanders full tactical control of its aircraft at sea. Some 70 per cent of the pilots and all the observers were naval officers, and in 1924 naval pilots' courses resumed. In 1928 the Air Section of the Naval Staff became a full Division, and in 1929 the expansion of the FAA to man the new carriers *Courageous* and *Glorious* was completed. With five large carriers and one small in service by 1930, the Royal Navy could and sometimes did take virtually the whole Fleet Air Arm to sea. This made it something like a pure carrier force, unlike the other two naval air forces which possessed carriers, Japan and the United States. In 1926 the US Navy had 890 aircraft but only one carrier (the converted collier *Langley*), the Japanese Naval Air Force had 540 aircraft but only the small carrier *Hosho*, and the Fleet Air Arm had no more than 150 aircraft, but twice as many afloat as either of the others, while precisely eleven shore-based aircraft were assigned by the RAF to naval co-operation. The new carriers played a central role in fleet exercises; for example, Sir Roger Keyes, Commander-in-Chief Mediterranean in 1925–8, repeatedly exercised the relief of 'Singapore' against a 'Japanese' fleet with carriers. The FAA was still small, but it was the favoured protégé of the Admiralty, which in prestige and political weight greatly outmatched the Air Ministry, and unlike the RAF the FAA was visibly committed to critical aspects of national defence. The real weakness of British naval aviation was that the Navy had no control over the design and supply of its own aircraft, which were entirely in the hands of the Air Ministry. The Air Ministry attempted to forbid all communication between RAF Coastal Area and the Admiralty, while the Naval Staff, which shrank from 336 members to 87 between 1918 and 1920, suffered acutely in forming naval air policy from the complete loss of its Air Division in 1918.[25]

The Washington Treaty had 'frozen' battleship construction save for one Japanese and two American ships, all virtually complete, and two British ships, not yet designed and built, which became the *Nelson* and *Rodney*. What the treaty could not freeze was the underlying rivalry and insecurity which drove competitive shipbuilding. The treaty limited cruisers to a maximum of 10,000 tons and 8-inch guns, though most modern cruisers were smaller than this, and its immediate effect was to generate a miniature arms race in the new 'heavy' or 'treaty' cruisers, built up to the new limits. The Admiralty interpreted the 'Ten Year Rule' as an instruction to be ready for war in 1929, and warned the Cabinet that any backsliding in naval shipbuilding in the meantime would be interpreted by the public as an abandonment of the 'one-power standard' adopted by the Cabinet in 1925. A one-power standard was acceptable to the Admiralty, because the British had no intention of fighting the United States, but a fleet which was notionally a match for the Americans was also equal to the leading fleets in Europe and the East (France and Japan) together. At the same time the government committed itself to build a major naval base at Singapore to which the fleet could be deployed if it were needed in the Far East. It was well understood that the resignation of the Admiralty Board would probably bring down the government, and Beatty was never afraid to bully the politicians, but the internal debates were not a crude confrontation. As Chancellor of the Exchequer from 1924 to 1929, Winston Churchill was his own man, taking up a position midway between the Admiralty and his own advisers in the Treasury. He insisted that the Singapore base had to be built to safeguard Australia and New Zealand, but only on a defensive scale: he would not take seriously the idea of a naval offensive either against or by Japan, 2,900 miles to the north:[26]

> A war with Japan! But why should there be a war with Japan? I do not believe there is the slightest chance of it in our lifetime . . . Japan is at the

other end of the world. She cannot menace our vital security in any way . . . The only war it would be worth our while to fight would be to prevent an invasion of Australia, and that I am certain will never happen in any period, even the most remote, which we or our children need foresee. I am therefore convinced that war with Japan is not a possibility any reasonable Government need take into account.[27]

The success of the Washington Treaty encouraged the idea that the same approach, of limits to the size and number of permitted warships, might be applied to cruisers, and in 1927 a conference with this objective assembled in Geneva at the invitation of the new US President Calvin Coolidge. This time the tight discipline and careful planning which the Harding administration had applied at Washington were lacking. Coolidge and Congress wanted to limit naval expenditure, but the US delegation was dominated by Rear-Admiral Hilary P. Jones, President of the General Board of the US Navy, for whom the object was to dethrone British naval supremacy at any expense whatever. The initial US proposal was to limit heavy cruisers in the familiar 5:5:3 ratio, but the Japanese regarded the new cruisers as miniature battleships and would not accept less than 70 per cent of British strength. Although the design of the big heavy cruisers reflected American requirements for very long range, the US Navy was the slowest to build them. Between 1922 and 1926 Congress authorized eight heavy cruisers but voted money for only one; the US Navy's entire construction during that period was one cruiser, one submarine and six river gunboats. Seven more cruisers followed in the brief revival after the failure of the Geneva conference before Congress lost interest again. Admiral Jones's proposal that every other navy should cut their numbers back to the level which the US Navy could afford was calculated to infuriate everyone, and the conference broke up in discord. The overall result was that between 1922 and 1928 the Royal Navy laid down 60,000 tons of warships a year, above the pre-war (1888–1914) average, and almost as much as the United States and Japan combined. The British tonnage included fifteen of the new heavy cruisers, compared with twelve Japanese, eight American, five French and three Italian in the same period.[28]

The failure of the Geneva conference could be regarded as a victory for British naval strength, but it owed more to the incoherence of American diplomacy than the strength of the Admiralty's position. Stanley Baldwin the Prime Minister, and Austen Chamberlain the Foreign Secretary, allowed the conference to collapse in defence of a target of seventy cruisers as the essential minimum to defend British trade, though the logic behind the figure was unclear, the Royal Navy had not in reality had so many cruisers in service since the war, and in 1929 had only fifty-three actually afloat. There was bound to be a reaction. Alarmed by the cost of building a fleet of seventy cruisers when the Royal Navy already had more than the US and Japan together, aware that the Ten Year Rule was about to expire, Churchill got the Cabinet to agree in 1928 that the ten-year period would roll forward until cancelled. In the United States opinion was so outraged at the British coup that in December 1928 Congress voted to build fifteen new heavy cruisers (though under US Congressional procedure, this did not imply any commitment to pay for the construction). Then in March 1929 the Quaker-educated Herbert Hoover became US President, and in June 1929 the Labour Party won the British General Election, installing two governments committed to naval disarmament.[29]

In the Western democracies, the public remained as strongly convinced as ever that disarmament was the best hope of peace. The new British and US governments made informal contact to discuss the principles of another naval disarmament conference, intending to extend the ten-year Washington battleship-building 'holiday' by another five years (i.e. to 1936), and to fix some formula by which cruisers of different tonnage and armament could be measured against each other. The US Navy preferred the big heavy cruisers not only, as it claimed, because it needed long range for the Pacific, but also because it suspected that the British wanted numerous smaller cruisers to establish a blockade, in order to win the next war in the same way it claimed to have won the last. Many US officers were determined to be on the right side next time, fighting against the British, and intended to use their heavy cruisers to smash through that blockade. Almost the only thing the two governments had agreed on by the time the conference actually assembled in London in January 1930 was the desirability of excluding naval officers from the discussions, but with hindsight it seems that one of the real gains of the early negotiation was greater trust between American and British representatives (and between US officers and their President), for both of which the US Admiral William V. Pratt deserves much of the credit. In the conference itself the United States pushed hard to reduce Britain's 'cruiser allowance' to fifty ships. The Admiralty was more concerned to get steady replacement of the ships it had than commitment to a total which was distant and effectively theoretical, so it was prepared to swap paper heavy cruisers for real light cruisers – but only until 1936, by which time it hoped to be able to expand. The conference created the new category of 6-inch gunned 'light cruisers' which the Admiralty really wanted and gave Britain the largest share of them. Ramsay Mac-Donald was alarmed that the Admiralty was 'increasing the fighting efficiency of the Navy' instead of reducing it, and the Treasury was alarmed at the cost. Then MacDonald without warning abandoned his support for new battleships and proposed another five-year 'holiday' (with serious consequences for shipbuilding capacity). It has been argued that this was the moment when Britain finally abandoned naval supremacy, but in the depths of the financial crisis it is very unlikely that the government could have found the money for a new class of battleship, and the Admiralty chose to work with MacDonald rather than against him. He for his part made big political sacrifices but managed to gain agreement with the United States while keeping his party, his government and the Admiralty together, when another Geneva failure would have been very easy.[30]

Japan was with great difficulty persuaded to sign the London Treaty with what was called the 'Reed–Matsudaira Compromise' between the United States and Japan, skilfully brokered by Robert Craigie of the Foreign Office, which was secretly reading both Japanese and American telegrams and knew their negotiating positions. The 'Compromise' was a late success of the pro-Western 'treaty faction' of the Imperial Japanese Navy, but the anger it aroused there helped to fuel the final triumph of the anti-Western 'fleet faction' which subsequently drove Japan to war.[31] France and Italy refused to participate in the conference at all. These were ominous signs for the future, but on the key axis of Anglo-American relations, the London Treaty rescued Britain from the dangerous isolation created by the failure at Geneva, which would in any case have made a future British naval blockade impossible. Although Britain appeared to have made all the concessions, the Admiralty secured a revival of cruiser building. Sir Esmé Howard, the British ambassador in Washington, had advised MacDonald to disarm American anglophobia by accepting nominal naval parity, confident that Congress would never pay for the actual ships, and he was right. By 1939 the British had twice as many cruisers as the US, and the two navies were becoming discreet friends.[32]

The world applauded the London Treaty as another step on the road to disarmament and peace. Those who looked more closely were concerned that only Britain and the United States of the naval powers still seemed to be committed to disarmament. What was not yet clear to contemporaries was that the London Treaty marked the end of an era. Ever since the war the United States, and its navy, had dominated British foreign policy. As Robert Craigie wrote in 1928:

> Britain is faced in the United States of America with a phenomenon for which there is no parallel in our modern history – a state twenty-five times

as large, five times as wealthy, three times as populous, twice as ambitious, almost invulnerable, and at least our equal in prosperity, vital energy, technical equipment and industrial science. This State has risen to its present stage of development at a time when Great Britain is still staggering from the effects of the superhuman effort made during the War, is loaded with a great burden of debt and is crippled by the evil of unemployment.[33]

During the 1930s this picture changed fast as the US Navy declined, the US economy collapsed, and the US government progressively withdrew from world affairs. In their place new and much graver threats arose as a series of foreign governments fell into the hands of aggressive militarists.[34]

TWENTY

Dreaming in Continents

Policy and Operations 1931–1939

I n October 1929 the disastrous fall of the New York Stock Exchange began a world economic crisis marked by a sharp contraction of the money supply, generating a deep depression. Orthodox economics with its insistence on sound money had no answer to this collapse of economic activity save mass unemployment. Only Fascists, Communists and the Japanese were ready to print money to revive the economy. In June 1930 the US Smoot–Hawley Act sharply raised tariffs on external trade, wrecking what remained of world prosperity, abandoning the Japanese leaders who had put their faith in it, and making it impossible for Germany to earn enough foreign exchange to pay war reparations. In September 1931 the Japanese army (against Cabinet orders) invaded Manchuria, the most economically advanced region of China, aiming to make up for the lost world trade by creating a self-sufficient empire across the Sea of Japan. The following January the Japanese Navy attacked Shanghai. From these events the Sino-Japanese War spread and became general all over North and Central China after the 'Marco Polo Bridge incident' of July 1937. The military now dominated the Japanese Cabinet, and they killed civilian ministers who opposed them. Two successive prime ministers were murdered in 1931 and 1932 respectively. The 'Young Officers' Revolt' of February 1936 led to the killing of several ministers (including the Finance Minister Takahashi Korekiyo, whose bold reflationary policies had lifted Japan out of the 1929 slump) before Emperor Hirohito suppressed it. The official religion of 'State Shinto' was now filling the political and social space occupied in Europe by fascism and national socialism. The League of Nations could not restrain Japan, since none of its members was able or willing to fight the aggressor, and the United States limited itself to words. The long-prepared League of Nations Disarmament Conference collapsed soon after it assembled in 1932; in January 1933 Adolf Hitler was elected Chancellor of Germany, and the following year was declared *Führer* ('Leader'), with sole executive powers.[1]

In just over three years, the optimism which had driven successive disarmament conferences had been shattered by the rise of extremism and aggression. Western statesmen did not completely abandon diplomacy, but they sharply reduced their hopes of how much it could achieve. A major war was already in progress in the Far East, and the chances of war in Europe were obviously rising, but public opinion in the Western democracies was deeply reluctant to confront the danger. The challenge for policy-makers, in Britain, the United States, France and elsewhere, was how to rearm against the new aggressors without enough time, money or public support. In Britain two successive Conservative prime ministers – Stanley Baldwin (in his third term in office, 1935–7) and Neville Chamberlain (1937–40) – chose to keep most of their fears to themselves and rearm only as fast as could be done without frightening the public. The only prominent British politician who openly warned of the danger of war was Winston Churchill, whose forewarnings were readily dismissed in political circles as the voice of unscrupulous ambition, but were beginning to make an impression on the public. The Admiralty's nightmare of a simultaneous naval threat in Europe and the Far East now seemed to be approaching at speed, just as the naval strength forgone to successive disarmament treaties made it impossible to meet both threats at once.[2]

In this situation Britain had some practical advantages over the United States. First and most obviously, the British political nation had a world outlook. Even the uneducated knew that the country's prosperity was bound up with its world trading and financial system. They knew that what happened in Africa, in South America, in the Far East or the South Pacific mattered to them. They did not, however, have any detailed knowledge of foreign policy or grand strategy. Parliament expected to debate and pass the Service Estimates proposed by the government, which could rely on its majority to pass them *en bloc* unless it had badly misjudged the political situation, and usually revealed its strategic assumptions only in general terms. Detailed policy-making took place behind closed doors, among ministers, senior officers and civil servants who were neither ignorant nor complacent. Within the narrow but slowly widening limits imposed by the financial and political situation, it was possible for them to make discreet plans and preparations for war without alarming the public. Thus, in March 1932 the Chiefs of Staff persuaded the Cabinet to drop the (still secret) Ten Year Rule, whose bad effects included 'a complacent optimism in public opinion . . . which increases the difficulty of taking the necessary steps to ameliorate the situation'.[3] At the same time work resumed on the suspended Singapore naval base. In November 1933 the Cabinet Defence Requirements Sub-Committee (DRC)[4] produced a realistic survey of the strategic situation, identifying the most urgent defence needs. In America, where there were no central bodies equivalent to the Cabinet Office or the Chiefs of Staff, where legislation was debated item by item in public, and where a majority of politicians and people believed that the misfortunes of the outside world were no concern of theirs, a weak government and an isolationist Congress averted their eyes from the dangers which threatened them in the 1930s. Rival policies and services competed to attract public attention – which was almost wholly concentrated on domestic affairs – while from 1933 President Franklin D. Roosevelt, the man who said 'yes' to everyone, presided over a chaos of competing agencies with his distinctive combination of charm and duplicity.[5]

The darkening clouds of the early 1930s form the background to the Anglo-German Naval Agreement of June 1935, by which the British government agreed to Germany breaking the terms of the Treaty of Versailles and building a new fleet up to 35 per cent of the tonnage allowed to Britain by the Washington Treaty. Historians used to interpret this in the light of their obsession with 'appeasement', as a pusillanimous surrender to the dictator. The reality was rather different. British ministers appreciated at once that the new Nazi regime could not be prevented from re-arming, and would present a grave danger to Britain if it did. The Admiralty knew that the German Navy had been cheating on the terms of the Treaty of Versailles for years and did not expect it to be any more honest in future. It knew about the clandestine U-boats which the Nazi regime had begun building in 1933, and was alert to the serious risk that Germany would build a big submarine fleet and repeat the almost-fatal offensive of 1917. It was aware of the danger that Germany's new 'armoured ships' would present as commerce raiders.[6]

Nevertheless Britain held a few good cards, starting with excellent intelligence from a range of sources, including a long-term MI6 agent, Dr Karl Krüger, a naval architect in the U-boat design office.[7] Most importantly, the Admiralty understood that the head of the German Navy, Admiral Erich Raeder, and those around him, were followers of Tirpitz, still dedicated to his historic mission of creating a mighty battle-fleet to reassert Germany's true status among the great powers. They resented U-boats, which they accused of losing them the First World War, and regarded the 'armoured ships' as no better than a stop-gap. The Admiralty correctly assessed the German ambition to build a conventional battleship-centred fleet up to 35 per cent of British strength by 1942. The object of the agreement for the British was to tempt the Germans by offering them exactly that, on condition of adopting a Washington-style fleet with no more 'armoured ships', and as few U-boats as possible. In the long term, of course, Germany might build another High Seas Fleet (which was why Churchill opposed the agreement), but given the parlous state of the German shipbuilding industry and national finances, even 35 per cent of British strength had to be many years ahead. In February 1934 Japan renounced the Washington and London treaties and announced her intention of building up to parity with both Britain and the United States. The Japanese threat seemed certain to come to a head sooner than the German, and the British balanced fleet would just suffice to deal with both threats, one after the other.[8]

This was a risky strategy, but it was finely calculated on accurate intelligence to make the best use of Britain's straitened naval resources by avoiding an asymmetric threat, and in the short term, up to 1939, it worked exactly as intended. The planned U-boat force was cut back from seventy-two boats to fifty-four and replaced by juvenile plans for fleets of super-battleships which captured much of Germany's steel, copper and other scarce materials (leaving the army seriously short of ammunition in 1939 as a result), while remaining far beyond the navy's capacity to complete. The German Navy's 'Z Plan', in its relatively modest January 1939 form, envisaged building a fleet of ten super-battleships, eight aircraft carriers, 15 'armoured ships', five heavy and 24 light cruisers, 68 destroyers and 249 U-boats. In the fantasy version adopted in the summer of 1940 the plan was expanded to 80 battleships, 15 to 20 carriers, 100 cruisers, 500 submarines and so on. Meanwhile in the real world neither steel nor manpower existed to realize even the 1939 scheme. The new light battleships *Scharnhorst* and *Gneisenau* were eighteen months behind schedule, the *Scharnhorst* had to be fitted with Swiss engines because no German firm could take on the work, and the first German aircraft carrier, laid down in 1937, was suffering from machinery problems which in the end proved to be incurable. The 1939 plan required six million tons of fuel oil and two million of diesel, though Germany's total consumption of all mineral oils was only just over six million tons a year, less than half of it from domestic production.[9] 'These people dream in continents,' commented General Franz Halder, the head of the Army High Command.[10]

While the Anglo-German negotiations were under way, in October 1935, the Italian invasion of Ethiopia provided a brutally clear example of real appeasement – of Mussolini, not Hitler – and its consequences. The French gave Mussolini a free hand from the start and the United States tacitly supported him, leaving Britain the choice of vindicating the League of Nations single-handedly, or abandoning it. Italy relied on imported oil, and had almost

2½ million men in East Africa entirely dependent on the Suez Canal, which gave Britain two hands on her throat – neither of which it used, because the Foreign Office feared an oil embargo would arouse US hostility, and Chamberlain the Prime Minister saw Italy as a possible ally against Germany (though he was reading Italian telegrams which made that very improbable). Instead, Britain applied 'light' (meaning nominal) sanctions, and agreed with France (in the 'Hoare–Laval pact') to impose on Ethiopia a settlement just short of total surrender. The public was outraged, and the pact was disowned, but nothing effective was done to help the Ethiopians. Armed with excellent intelligence (from an agent in the British Embassy in Rome among other sources), Mussolini easily called the British bluff. He gained a huge triumph and became an open enemy of Britain. The world now knew that the League of Nations was a sham, and that none of the democracies would take a stand against aggression. Sir William Fisher commanding the Mediterranean Fleet had been ready to fight and confident of winning despite serious deficiencies (of anti-aircraft ammunition, among other things), but the Naval Staff feared that the price of victory would be losses which would make it difficult or impossible to face the Japanese afterwards. Sir Ernle Chatfield, the First Sea Lord since 1933, favoured entangling Italy in East Africa, where her forces would be a hostage to British naval power. But the fact remained that Britain's conduct in the Ethiopian crisis had massively forfeited both fear and respect, as the Germans and Japanese were the first to note. The basic problem of British defence policy was now established for the next six years: instead of two there were now three likely enemies, widely dispersed and no longer afraid of her. Britain might just be able to fight two of them, but not all three at once.[11]

The following year, in July 1936, a revolt by the Spanish army against the new republican government led to civil war in which both Italy and Germany intervened on the side of the rebels. Britain aspired only to preserve neutrality and evacuate refugees, in the face of indiscriminate air attacks by both sides. Public opinion and the muddled ignorance of the Foreign Secretary, Anthony Eden, pushed the Royal Navy into an obviously illegal position in relation to the 'Nationalist' (i.e. rebel) naval blockade, and the Italian Navy retaliated with attacks by 'unidentified' submarines. In August 1937 the *Iride* (commanded by the noted Fascist Lieutenant Junio Valerio Borghese) fired a torpedo at the destroyer *Havock*, but (to the Admiralty's regret) escaped the subsequent hunt. Only in February 1938 were British warships allowed to attack any unidentified submarines in Spanish waters, whereupon they disappeared. The whole exhausting campaign had saved many civilian lives but done little or nothing to deter aggression, and in 1939 the Nationalist victory in the civil war installed

General Francisco Franco as another hostile dictator in a position very dangerous to Britain.[12]

By extending the Washington settlement for a further five years, the 1930 Treaty of London had set the timetable for another naval conference, which assembled at the end of 1935. The Japanese refused to participate unless they were granted parity with Britain and the United States beforehand, so the negotiations were between Britain, the US, and France only. The Admiralty and Foreign Office agreed that the Washington Treaty hierarchy of national tonnage allowances had in practice encouraged rather than hindered a shipbuilding race. Shrunken by the Depression, the British shipbuilding industry was no longer well placed to win such a race, so the British promoted a new treaty structure, abandoning national tonnage limits in favour of limits on the size of individual ships of each major type. In the next two years Germany, Russia and Italy signed equivalent treaties. Since the second London Naval Treaty did not restrict overall fleet size, it did not stand in the way of rearmament. The treaty was signed on 25 March 1936, and one month later a supplementary Navy Estimate was laid before Parliament including two battleships, a carrier and twenty-four other warships. Five battleships and four fleet carriers in all were laid down in 1937, part of a total of a million tons of British warships built between 1928 and 1941 (which compares with 700,000 tons built by the US and 600,000 tons by Japan over the same period).[13] By this time British naval expansion was well under way, and these figures put interwar naval 'disarmament' in perspective: 'Ultimately, a navy that was outbuilding its potential friends and foes alike and rigging the system of global naval arms control for its own strategic purposes cannot be described as being in a state of decline.'[14]

Policy-makers in Britain who confronted the likelihood of war had to make critical and agonizing choices of strategy and priority. The first question was which threat was the more urgent: East or West, Japan or Germany? In 1933 the DRC reckoned Japan was the immediate threat and Germany the 'ultimate potential enemy', but not a present danger for at least five years. Only Sir Warren Fisher, the Secretary of the Treasury, thought Japan could be appeased, but the Admiralty hoped a stronger Navy would deter Japanese aggression, while Britain and France together would neutralize German ambitions in the West.[15] To fight in East and West simultaneously would be a desperate extremity. In January 1937 Chatfield declared it

> exceedingly doubtful, even if we increase our Naval and air strength to the utmost possible limit under voluntary conditions of service, whether we can maintain the Empire if engaged simultaneously east and west. To fight

two such wars would be something greater than we have ever done before, and it is something which we should not contemplate.[16]

The DRC adopted the Admiralty's arguments almost completely. It stopped short of supporting the proposed 'New Standard Fleet' (of twenty battleships, fifteen carriers and one hundred cruisers), capable of fighting both Germany and Japan, only because the target seemed to be too distant for present planning purposes. Instead, the DRC endorsed a better than one-power standard of fifteen battleships, five carriers and seventy cruisers, officially supposed to take seven years to achieve. In practice the Admiralty had more shipbuilding capacity than it admitted and built faster than the plan allowed. 'I am bound to say that I cannot avoid a suspicion that the Admiralty have not been altogether frank with us in this matter,' noted Edward Bridges of the Treasury in January 1937,[17] but Warren Fisher 'played the game' and pretended not to notice. By February 1938 the Admiralty had built almost all of the seven-year plan in three years and was able to push on towards the New Standard Fleet as fast as possible.[18]

Shipbuilding and financial capacity were technical matters which were settled below the level of the Cabinet. Much more political was the question of inter-service priority. Here a major influence was the public's obsession with apocalyptic visions of whole cities wiped out by air attack in an afternoon. The RAF, which had done much to generate these fantasies, had no answer to them, since it maintained that fighter defence was impossible. The politicians, however, were not prepared to tell their constituents that they were all doomed, and demanded effective air defence. In 1934 the Cabinet agreed to rob the other services (mainly the army) to build a home defence force of eighty squadrons of fighters – to the disgust of the Air Staff, which wanted bombers instead. By 1937 ministers and the public had worked themselves into a panic, convinced that the *Luftwaffe* enjoyed vast superiority over the RAF, and predicting 150,000 civilian casualties a week from German air attack (the same civilian deaths from air attack as Britain actually suffered in the entire Second World War). In reality the Luftwaffe was half the size that Air Intelligence supposed, and had no aircraft capable of bombing Britain from airfields in Germany. It was a light-weight, tactical, 'shock' air force, designed to provide close support to a fast-moving land offensive. It could not attack Britain unless the Netherlands and Belgium had first been conquered, and its hopes of developing a long-range strategic bombing capacity had made little progress by 1939.[19]

Stanley Baldwin, the Conservative leader in the coalition government of 1931–5, was the minister responsible for one particular item of secret air defence research, not mentioned in Cabinet until 1935, and entirely unknown to the public. His well-known 1932 remark that 'the bomber will always get through' was based on the impossibility of providing early warning of attack, which was the critical weakness of the existing air defence organization, first developed against the German bombers of 1917–18. By 1934 he appreciated that the new instrument later known as 'radar' might provide the answer.[20] Under his leadership the Treasury generously funded this research, and at the same time decisions were taken at a very high level which steered the BBC's new television service into choices of equipment and wavelength that neatly matched the requirements of air-warning radar.[21]

In Europe the shadow of the Great War dominated all military planning, dictating what national leaders wanted to do, had to do, and were determined not to do. It was now an established orthodoxy in Britain that naval blockade had forced Germany to terms in 1918. For the Navy this meant that sea power had really won the war, albeit without the much-desired victorious battle. For the politicians and the people this meant that there was a route to victory which did not lead back through the mud and blood of the trenches. The British government had long been determined not to raise another mass army to fight on the Continent. Economic warfare had become the British secret weapon. British naval strategy for a war against Germany was dominated by blockade, which had worked before and was all the more likely to work again by 1938, with the German 'rearmament economy' critically short of foreign exchange and essential imports. British planners assumed that Germany would have to win fast by a 'knock-out blow', and Britain could anticipate three offensives against merchant shipping: from U-boats, major surface warships, and aircraft, mainly in the approaches to the port of London, the only shipping route within flying range of German airfields. The Admiralty had prepared against all three threats by building anti-aircraft and anti-submarine escorts, and planning to adopt a general convoy system immediately a submarine threat appeared, strengthened against surface attack by capital ships and aircraft carriers. It had exact knowledge of the German naval threat in September 1939: the *Scharnhorst* and *Gneisenau*, the three 'armoured ships', two heavy cruisers (the *Admiral Hipper* and *Blücher*), six light cruisers and twenty-seven operational seagoing submarines.[22]

The Admiralty believed that the Luftwaffe was too distant and ill-equipped to do much damage at sea. It took the U-boats seriously, but it knew that convoy was the answer to them, and it was clear that the German heavy ships were the most serious threat. The German naval command, the *Seekriegsleitung* (SKL), agreed. Captain Werner Fürbringer, the leading German submarine expert, advised that the British underwater detection apparatus 'Asdic' (whose nature was secret but whose artfully mysterious name had been deliberately leaked to Germany) meant that 'every English convoy . . . will be secured by defensive forces, fully capable of destroying with certainty any attacking U-boat, even under the surface'.[23] In 1936 Germany in good faith signed the London Protocol, an international agreement that submarines would not attack merchant ships without warning (much like the 'prize rules' of the First World War). As the Admiralty knew, all German studies agreed that only sur-face ships would be effective against merchant shipping.[24] The last German officer of rank who still defended the U-boat was Captain Karl Dönitz, appointed in 1935 to command the first revived U-boat flotilla, and in 1939 promoted to Rear-Admiral and Flag Officer, Submarines (*Befehlshaber der Unterseeboote*; *BdU*). Dönitz was a big-ship officer who had briefly com-manded a U-boat in 1916–17, and lost her in embarrassing circumstances. Since then he had avoided submarines, and was quite ignorant about them when, and indeed after, he was unexpectedly promoted. It is sufficiently clear that he was chosen, over the heads of experts like Fürbringer, as a devoted Nazi and a harsh disciplinarian, to ensure the Party's control of the submarine arm. He continued this mission, ever more ardent and fanatical to the end, as commander-in-chief of the navy and finally as Hitler's chosen successor and the last Führer of the Third Reich.[25]

Meanwhile the march of the aggressors continued. In March 1936 the German army overthrew a key element of the 1919 peace settlement by re-occupying the Rhineland and advancing to the French border. Two years later the *Anschluss* ('connection') added Austria to Germany, and in September 1938 Hitler used the presence of German-speaking populations in parts of Bohemia as an excuse to demand a partition of Czechoslovakia to the profit of Germany. Neville Chamberlain flew to Munich to present himself as an 'impartial arbi-ter' in the name of peace by imposing Hitler's solution. Hitler professed to offer a European settlement jointly guaranteed by Germany and Britain, but less than six months later in March 1939 he cynically cast aside his undertakings and occupied the remainder of Czechoslovakia. The German absorption of France's ally Czechoslovakia eliminated a well-equipped army of 1,250,000 men in thirty-five divisions which would have formed the core of resistance to Germany in central Europe. Germany seized military equipment sufficient for twenty new divisions, including three armoured divisions equipped with the new Czech T35 and T38 tanks. The British government bore a major share of the responsibility for this moral, political and military disaster, and was in no position to refuse French demands for *un effort de sang*, 'a commitment in blood' to make up part of what had been lost to French security. In something like panic, Britain re-introduced conscription and undertook to increase the five regular divisions of the British army to thirty-two to fight alongside France – and not only on the Western Front, for at the same time Britain issued guarantees of support to Poland, Romania, Greece and even Turkey. Much of the Royal Navy would now have to stay in the Mediterranean to protect them, even if it were needed in the Far East at the same time. Every strategic lesson learnt from the Great War had been thrown away. The 'war to end all wars' had simply paved the way for another, to be fought over the same ground but in far worse circumstances. The Treasury warned that the country was in no condition to finance a major war alone. The US Johnson Act of 1934 made it impossible for Britain to raise American loans, and the 1937 Neutrality Act shut off American arms exports. On 23 August 1939 came the final shock: the astonishing Molotov–Ribbentrop Pact, by which the mortal enemies Germany and Soviet Russia reached an accommodation. At the time this seemed inexplicable, though we now know that it was driven by Stalin's obsessive conviction that his capitalist enemies, Britain, France and Germany, were planning a joint assault on the Soviet Union which it could not hope to survive. A week later the new alliance went to war: first Germany invaded Poland from the west on 1 September, and on 17 September the Russians attacked from the east. Having just guaranteed Poland's borders, the British were bound in honour to declare war on Germany:

> So with immense reluctance, and in full realisation of the unfavourable odds, the British government decided once again to confront German power with armed force as they had in 1914, and to overthrow the regime wielding it. But the odds were now not only unfavourable; they were impossible . . . The war for the mastery of Europe that had begun in 1914 was over, and the Germans had won it.[26]

Moreover, though it took some weeks for Whitehall to absorb the reality, Britain now had no naval strategy against Germany. Blockade was meaningless, for Germany with a friendly Soviet Empire at her back could want for nothing. All that remained was to return to the trenches. Over the winter of 1939–40 Britain moved 400,000 men, 69,000 vehicles and 724,000 tons of supplies to France to constitute the most completely equipped and mechanized small army in the world. In the spring it was ready to go to war alongside the French, and of course under French command.[27]

There are still some histories which accuse British planners of complacent neglect of the defence of the Far East, relying on a single, static plan, 'main fleet to Singapore', which turned out to be obsolete and unworkable when it was needed in 1942. In fact the Navy thought hard and realistically about war against Japan. There was no single plan but many plans and studies covering all sorts of possible scenarios, and continually under revision as the situation developed. By the late 1930s the Navy assumed a defensive campaign in increasingly bleak circumstances, as the naval threat of Germany overshadowed the prospects of reinforcement from Europe. In April 1936 the Admiralty considered that Britain could face the Germans in the North Sea and still spare seven battleships and three carriers for the Far East; only slightly less than the Japanese main fleet.

Adding Italy to the list of likely enemies made the situation much grimmer. In November 1937 the Committee of Imperial Defence reported that 'we cannot foresee the time' when Britain could fight Germany, Italy and Japan at once. The Italian Air Force, the *Regia Aeronautica*, was assessed in 1938 as having six times as many aircraft as Britain could deploy to the Mediterranean, of equal or better quality. If Italy entered the war, it seemed unlikely that Malta could be held, or at least used, meaning that traffic through the Mediterranean would become impossible, and there would be no British dry dock to receive a damaged capital ship between Gibraltar and Singapore. Malta was not written off: in 1939 it was the first overseas base to get radar, in May 1940 (after the German breakthrough in the Ardennes) a fifth battalion of infantry was added to the garrison, and next month it received eighteen more anti-aircraft guns. Nevertheless, the likelihood was that Malta would be isolated and besieged, and in fact the Italian naval staff was even then debating whether it would be essential to capture the island, or whether it would suffice to 'neutralize' it by air attack instead. Admiral Domenico Cavagnari, the Chief of Staff, favoured handing the problem over to the *Regia Aeronautica*.

Either way the French would have to hold the Western Mediterranean while the British defended the Middle East, the Indian Ocean and Malaya with only a precarious line of supply round the Cape of Good Hope. In 1939 there were fifteen large modern British submarines in the South China Sea to hold off a Japanese fleet coming south (and twelve Dutch boats in the Java Sea presumed to have the same mission, though the Dutch refused even the most secret staff contacts for fear of compromising their neutrality). It was very doubtful how long the submarines could hold the ring unsupported. In July 1939 the Committee of Imperial Defence proposed allowing ninety days for the main fleet to reach Singapore; on the outbreak of the European war in September this estimate doubled to six months.[28]

One further factor which offered some hope to British planners was the possibility of direct or indirect support for Singapore and Malaya from the United States, whose own possessions in the Philippines lay nearby. Work began in 1933 on a new US base at Pearl Harbor on Oahu Island in the central Pacific, with a similar strategic function to Singapore: to permit the main fleet to advance to a position near enough to Japan to deter aggression, and if necessary to support a counter-attack. For this reason, Chamberlain requested and Roosevelt agreed to move the US Fleet from San Francisco to Pearl Harbor in April 1940. The weakness of Pearl Harbor in British eyes was that it was too far from the enemy: 3,400 miles from Tokyo, and 4,850 miles from Manila. It seemed all too likely that the Japanese could overrun the Philippines or Malaya before the elderly and slow US battleships could react. For Admiral James O. Richardson commanding the US Fleet, the weakness of Pearl Harbor was that it was still not much more than an anchorage, lightly defended and lacking facilities for the training that his fleet badly needed. With increasing urgency, he pestered Roosevelt for permission to return to California, only to be dismissed in February 1941 when he openly told the President that his admirals did not trust him.[29]

The ultimate British ambition was to persuade the United States to station their fleet at Singapore. This was strategically the best place to block a Japanese advance, but politically and logistically the project was quite impossible, and it is strange that the Admiralty was so slow to realize it. Secret naval discussions between the two countries took place in Washington between January and March 1941, but the US would not commit herself to fight, or indicate in what circumstances she might. The only unequivocal US warning was that 'it would be a serious mistake for the United Kingdom, in making their strategical dispositions to withstand a Japanese attack against Singapore, to count upon prompt military support by the United States'. Admiral Husband E. Kimmel, who had succeeded to the Pacific part of Richardson's command, thought action against the Japanese would be too dangerous, but was confident that the mere existence of his fleet would suffice to restrain them.[30] Moreover, the British did not speak to the Americans with a single voice. The Foreign Office and the Admiralty agreed that the friendship of the Americans was vital, but the Treasury preferred to conciliate Japan, and Neville Chamberlain the Prime Minister despised the US: 'She will give us plenty of assurances of goodwill especially if we will promise to do all the fighting but the moment she is asked to contribute something she invariably takes refuge behind Congress.'[31] Further fuel was put on this fire by the anglophobe US ambassador in London, Joseph P. Kennedy, who urged Roosevelt on no account to support the British Empire against Japan.[32] Chamberlain chose to regard Italy and Germany as friends in spite of growing evidence to the contrary. In February 1938 Anthony Eden resigned as Foreign Secretary when Chamberlain preferred the assurances of the Italian ambassador over the secret evidence of Mussolini's hostility provided by British cryptography.[33]

The public image (and very much the self-image) of Neville Chamberlain was of a strong leader of his party, and from May 1937 of the government. He did not tolerate dissent and was working through Conservative Central Office to get Winston Churchill 'deselected' as MP for Epping. This only failed when Hitler seized the remainder of Czechoslovakia in March 1939, and Mussolini invaded Albania the following month, cruelly exposing the naivety of those who still accepted them as honourable statesmen, and underlining Churchill's public warnings. An opinion poll of May 1939 recorded 56 per cent in favour of Churchill returning to the Cabinet, though even then Chamberlain and his supporters were in full control of the government and had no intention of complying. When Germany invaded Poland in September 1939, Churchill's claims could no longer be ignored and he became First Lord of the Admiralty once more, but part of Chamberlain's reason for offering that office was that it would confine Churchill to a limited area of the war effort and isolate him from potential allies elsewhere. Churchill had an unequalled experience of war and government from his youth, whereas Chamberlain's political upbringing had been largely in Birmingham municipal politics. His instinct was to divide and rule. This is how we must understand Churchill's title of 'chairman of the Military Coordination Committee' announced on 3 April. He received no formal power to co-ordinate the other Services, but the title alone was certain to generate friction, and to draw on his head a large share of the blame for whatever went wrong with the war.[34]

Two great wars were now beginning, in Europe and the Far East, and at the start neither was a naval war. Both were continental military campaigns fought chiefly by mass armies (and their air forces), and the first question to be answered by this study is how, and how far, the Second World War ever became a naval war. We must be clear that in some respects it never did. The post-war American occupiers of Japan forbade the Japanese to use their standard, and quite accurate, term 'Greater East Asian War', and insisted on naming it the 'Pacific War', the name which has since become general in most Western languages. The effect was to ignore and conceal both the early years of the China War before the United States became involved in 1942, and the latter years after Japan was defeated in 1945 but the Chinese Civil War continued. The mass Chinese and Japanese armies which had done most of the fighting over thirteen years of unbroken struggle, were relegated to the margins of history, as written in English. Even the US and Australian armies which had taken a large share of the fighting in the South Pacific from 1942 to 1945 were cast into the shade, as the US Navy claimed rhetorical ownership of the eastern war as a US naval victory – though the US fought for fewer than four years (1942–5) out of the thirteen years of the China War (1937–49), and it was in those years alone that fighting at sea was important to what was otherwise a long series of inland, continental campaigns. The new name was a brilliant stroke of public relations and a total distortion of reality, which leaves the naval historian to explain how far, by whom and in what ways the Second World War really was fought at sea.[35]

The European fighting was driven by the dictators – Stalin and Hitler above all, but also Mussolini, Franco and others – who sought to dominate Europe and dictate its future. Although war was spreading in both East and West in 1939, the two conflicts remained separate, and there were good reasons to expect them to remain so. The Japanese were fighting to control China, and naturally did not want to draw in any foreign power which might oppose them. That meant Russia, their old foe, and the Fascist powers, Germany and Italy, which were close to the Nationalist Chinese government. The essential for Japan was to keep Soviet Russia and the United States out of the China War, and since both were isolationist powers content to watch their rivals destroy one another, Japan had good chances of success. By embracing Japan's most dangerous enemy in the Molotov–Ribbentrop Pact the Germans had betrayed the German-Japanese alliance and outraged the Japanese government, which declared strict neutrality in the European war. Above all it was essential for Japan to avoid drawing the United States into the war, since the Japanese war economy was totally dependent on American imports, which included (among other things) almost half her requirement of iron, three-quarters of her oil, more than half her machine tools, and all her manganese and molybdenum. Of thirty-two commodities essential for war, Japan's own resources sufficiently supplied only two (graphite and sulphur), and most of the rest came from the US. Happily for Japanese military planners, isolationist sentiment was strong in Congress, and especially hostile to any idea of defending other people's colonial empires: the French in Indo-China, the Dutch in the East Indies, or the British in Malaya and India. This left the Japanese a clear way to expand southwards so long as they avoided the US Empire in the Philippines. Of the European powers, only Britain, France and the Netherlands were seriously committed to the East, and from 1939 all three were too busy in Europe to risk trouble elsewhere. The Italian Navy had a worldwide outlook, and dreamed of an oceanic fleet, but in actual practice it was largely confined to the

Mediterranean and the Red Sea in 1940. As for the Germans, their mental horizon did not extend far beyond Europe, and only the navy had some conception of practical connections between east and west. When the unexpected news reached Berlin in December 1941 that the Japanese Naval Air Force had attacked the US Navy at 'Pearl Harbor', no one on Hitler's staff could find the place on the map.[36]

Admiral Erich Raeder, commander-in-chief of the German Navy in 1939, believed Hitler's assurances that he would have at least until 1944 to build up a new German battle-fleet, and was depressed by the unexpected outbreak of war when his surface forces were still too weak to do more than 'lay the foundations for future reconstruction by dying with honour'.[37] On the outbreak of war it was uncertain whether the Germans would observe the London Protocol. The U-boats had orders to do so, but on 3 September Lieutenant Fritz-Julius Lemp commanding U-30 sank the passenger liner *Athenia* 'by mistake', correctly calculating that his superiors would not repudiate him. This action precipitated unrestricted submarine warfare, as it was meant to do, and the Admiralty at once began the process of implementing convoys.[38] At first the great majority of merchant ships were still unescorted and vulnerable, but the convoys worked as efficiently as expected as soon as they could be organized (initially as far as 15° West, 250 miles west of Ireland). At the end of May 1940, after nine months of war, a total of 503 British merchant ships had been sunk by enemy action in the whole world, but only thirty-six of them had been in convoy.[39] The ten big Type IX U-boats alone had the range to operate beyond the eastern Atlantic from bases in Germany, and by June 1940 six of them had been sunk. Attempts were made to organize U-boat groups at sea in October and November 1939, and again in February 1940, none of them with much success.[40] The submarines were hampered by a mine barrage in the Dover Straits which sank three U-boats, and by numerous operational problems. Attempts to dive below 50 metres generated more defects than the dockyards could cope with. The *SKL* (Naval High Command) and the *BdU* (Submarine Command) quarrelled over which of them had tactical control of the U-boats and sent them rival orders using different terminology. The main U-boat success of the early months was the successful penetration by U-47 of Scapa Flow on 14 October 1939 to torpedo the old battleship *Royal Oak* at anchor (though Lieutenant Günther Prien had to attack twice after his first torpedoes failed to run properly). Overall, however, the U-boat force was declining. By April 1940 twenty-three had been lost since the outbreak of war and only thirteen replacements had been launched.[41]

France and Britain could discover no means of aiding Poland during her one-month fight for survival in September 1939 against German and Russian invasions (though they might have done, had they realized that almost the entire German army had gone East, leaving no watch on the Rhine).[42] In November 1939 the Germans began laying magnetic mines from aircraft, damaging the battleship *Nelson*, the cruiser *Belfast* and many merchant ships. Without knowledge of the mines' firing circuits no counter-measures were possible, but almost at once one was recovered intact from the mudflats off Shoeburyness on the Essex coast. This allowed the deployment of 'degaussing' measures which protected ships by masking their magnetic polarity, and the electric 'LL sweep' which allowed minesweepers to detonate magnetic mines. Having begun their campaign with a stock of only 1,500 mines, the Germans soon found that what had initially been a very dangerous weapon had been effectively neutralized.[43]

The experts on both sides had expected the gravest threat to British shipping to come not from submarines but big warships, able to deal with the armed merchant cruisers which were the usual ocean escorts of convoys. In November 1939 the *Scharnhorst* sank the AMC *Rawalpindi* which was patrolling off the Faroe Islands, but for various reasons starting with chronic engine trouble, the German heavy ships did not mount a sustained threat to the Atlantic convoys until late 1940.[44] The only big German warship outside home waters on the outbreak of war, the 'armoured ship' *Admiral Graf Spee*, entered the River Plate estuary in December 1939 to attack the plentiful British shipping to be found there. On the 13th she met a British squadron of one heavy and two light cruisers under Commodore Henry Harwood. The German ship with her heavy armour and 11-inch guns was comfortably superior to any of them, but British ships had now largely abandoned the 'single line' tactics of twenty years before, and Harwood divided his squadron to attack from separate bearings, each ship manoeuvring independently. Captain Hans Langsdorff was able to damage the heavy cruiser *Exeter* badly, but while he fired at her, his own ship suffered from the 6-inch shells of the light cruisers. In particular, the shipboard refinery plant which allowed her big diesel engines to run on bunker oil (diesel fuel being still a novelty not available in many ports) was smashed beyond immediate repair, leaving her little prospect of escaping home before British reinforcements arrived. Determined not to throw away the lives of his men to no purpose in a fight against hopeless odds (as von Spee himself had done twenty-five years before), Langsdorff sent them ashore, scuttled his ship and shot himself, leaving the British a small but heartening victory.[45]

In the air neither Bomber Command nor Coastal Command could locate enemy ships; Coastal Command had no long-range aircraft and almost no weapons against either surface ships or submarines. Three RAF bombing attacks on German ports in December 1939 suffered unacceptable losses, and it was soon obvious that the Wellington bombers could neither defend themselves by day, nor locate targets by night – but the Luftwaffe's contributions to the naval war were almost equally ineffectual. An attack on the Home Fleet and on a convoy off Cromer in October both failed with heavy losses, and in February 1940 two German destroyers, mistaken for British, were driven into a minefield and sunk.[46] The British air defence system of anti-aircraft guns and radar-directed fighters was extended to cover Scapa Flow in March 1940, just in time to inflict a heavy defeat on German air raids in April, after which the Home Fleet's base was left in peace.[47]

TWENTY-ONE

No One Like a Naval Man

Social History 1919–1940

The Great War interrupted several important reforms of naval officers' career structure, such as the Selborne Scheme and the Special Entry, and witnessed the birth or growth of other new forms of naval service such as the RNVR. These incomplete innovations, added to the experience of the war generally, provided much incentive and material for change, but in the immediate post-war years the Admiralty gave an impression of being exhausted and reluctant to confront difficult social problems. Pre-war the Navy had anticipated that a serious shortage of officers would develop by 1920, but in the event too many wartime entries and not many casualties had the opposite effect. The Royal Naval College Osborne was still taking in terms of over a hundred boys until January 1919, two months after the war had ended. The parents of all these boys had to undertake, on their entry at twelve years old, that they would make the Navy 'their profession in life' until the age of forty-five at least. If they left before that age, they forfeited all pension rights. They were effectively indentured labour, committed to the Navy for over thirty years, but the Admiralty did not make any equivalent commitment to them. This they found out in 1921 when the former First Lord, Sir Eric Geddes, was appointed to chair a committee 'to review national expenditure', which led to the abrupt dismissal of a third of all captains and 350 lieutenants and above, in addition to 200 who left voluntarily. The Treasury supported reasonable severance terms for the dismissed officers, but there was no serious attempt to offer them alternative employment. Fairly or not, the 'Geddes Axe' was received, and is still remembered, as the brutal repudiation of a debt of honour. King George V sent each officer a personal message of regret: the Admiralty sent nothing.[1]

Unfortunately, this turned out to be only the first of many episodes which illustrated the Admiralty's failure to understand or to apply decent standards of management. In the Navy this was received as a moral failure, a betrayal of standards, but behind it lay a failure of administrative competence. In its public announcements the Admiralty repeatedly used evasive, misleading language, and adopted contradictory or illogical measures. It encouraged the ablest young officers to quit the Navy, and then refused less distinguished officers who applied to leave. In some cases, it forbade those guilty of crimes or misconduct to resign – thus treating the Service as a penal institution. A significant reason for this strange behaviour was that the Admiralty's service records were too primitive to provide the information necessary for intelligent management, and some of the information which was collected was not kept in one place in the Admiralty in Whitehall but elsewhere, such as Dartmouth, where it could not easily be consulted. The system was full of anomalies which could be 'gamed'. Nine young men forced out as naval cadets by the 'Geddes Axe' then re-entered by the Special Entry scheme and went on to successful careers. The key decisions affecting young officers' futures were not taken by senior officers, in most cases, but by Admiralty civil servants who had no personal knowledge of the candidates. Although naval cadets believed that their future careers depended on getting first-class certificates in the five subjects of their final examinations, in reality little notice was taken of the results. Later analyses which tried to compare the quality and promotion rates of officers who had entered the Navy from Dartmouth or by the (much smaller) 'Special Entry' tended to conclude that the differences between the two groups were narrow.[2]

An important factor in naval officers' careers was the branch structure. Young officers reaching lieutenant's rank could elect to train as a member of one of the professional 'branches' within the body of executive or seaman officers. These were Gunnery, Torpedo, Navigation, Signals, Submarines, Hydrography, Physical Training, Pilot, Observer and (from 1923) Anti-Submarine. Of these, Gunnery was universally believed to be the most prestigious and difficult to enter – though in reality almost all those who applied for it were accepted. The Gunnery course lasted nearly one year, to a level considered comparable to a first-year degree course, though the content was entirely chosen by gunnery officers themselves rather than the Naval Staff and a good deal of it consisted of arcane detail of little practical importance. The Admiralty seems in practice to have taken as many officers of reasonable competence as applied for each branch, without having worked out a requirement for any given number. Occasionally an appeal was made for a short-handed branch such as Air Observers. Immediately after the First World War about half of each year's intake of midshipmen became specialists (61 out of the 118 midshipmen of 1921, for example), and the remainder stayed as non-specialist

seaman officers – 'salt horse' lieutenants, as the expression was – and the proportion who joined a branch was rising. By 1935, 88 per cent of lieutenants
were specialists of one sort or another.[3]

Those who joined branches such as Gunnery, Torpedo, Signals or Navigation would become experts in their chosen subject, alternating positions ashore
in training and research establishments with seagoing appointments as a head
of department of a ship or a squadron. After a successful career such a specialist could hope to become commander (i.e. executive officer) of a big warship
(cruiser or larger) in the rank of commander,[4] and the ablest would rise to be
captains of big ships, and then perhaps admirals. Specialist branches, some of
them very influential in the Naval Staff, were known to take a paternal interest in the careers of officers of their branch, which added to the sense that these
were the best choices for the ambitious. Submariners and hydrographers, by
contrast, joined something more like a private navy of small ships which did
not belong to a fleet but normally operated alone, each branch having its own
admiral (Flag Officer Submarines and the Hydrographer of the Navy respectively). Both, especially submarines, offered the chance of independent command early in a career, but only submarines offered a fair prospect of reaching
flag rank. Anti-Submarine, initially a small and unfashionable branch (with
only eleven out of 1,029 lieutenants, and sixteen out of 972 commanders in
1935), had something of the same character. Pilots and Observers naturally
served in and belonged to ships carrying aircraft; not only carriers, but capital
ships and cruisers with catapult-launched reconnaissance aircraft.[5] Meanwhile
those who chose 'general service', the non-specialist seamen officers, lacked
branch patronage, but had the chance to command a smaller warship such as
a destroyer earlier in their careers, usually at lieutenant-commander's rank, in
wartime as early as lieutenant. (Lieutenant-commander, the rank created in
1914, was essentially only a new name for a lieutenant of eight years' seniority.)
They might expect several successive commands, but would probably retire as
a commander. Nevertheless, many young officers were happy to take the
chance of an active life commanding at sea, rather than a quasi-academic specialization in advanced technology with a small chance of reaching flag rank
in the end.

The development of the officers' branch structure was closely connected
with the reform of officers' professional formation. Those who knew the Navy
knew the Dartmouth type:

> A definite breed of fit, tough, daring, highly trained but sketchily educated
> professionals, ready for instant duty, for parades or tea parties, for

catastrophes, for peace or war; confident leaders, alert seamen, fair administrators, poor delegators; officers of wide interests and narrow vision, strong on tactics, weak on strategy; an able, active, cheerful, monosyllabic elite.[6]

By the end of the war the urgent need to reconstruct the training both of engineers and non-engineers was widely recognized. Wartime operations, especially staff-work, had revealed ever more clearly the need for officers who could think logically and express themselves clearly. Vice-Admiral Beatty was backed by Herbert Richmond as Director of the new Training and Staff Duties Division of the Naval Staff in 1918, Reginald Drax (Director of the Naval Staff College) and Kenneth Dewar (Director of the Plans Division) in pushing initiative, common doctrine and clarity of expression. Neither Richmond nor his ideas were universally popular, but they were part of an influential current of opinion calling for a better education, a knowledge of the world, and a more intellectual and reflective cast of mind, which the Navy had hitherto looked for, if at all, only among paymasters and hydrographers.[7] The only naval education which came anywhere near to satisfying this requirement was the two-term Cambridge University lieutenants' course which ran from 1919 to 1922, and included some elements of a general humane education. It was intended to counteract officers' alleged lack of 'the imagination, versatility, breadth of vision and independence of thought which a wider field of training would serve to develop', and their 'deficiency in power of expression and general literary ability'.[8] However, it was justified to the Treasury as making up for what young officers had missed during the war by passing almost directly from midshipmen to lieutenants. The Cambridge course was therefore abolished when the wartime generation had passed through (to the relief of the university and colleges, which had found it a considerable imposition). In its place, however, a new sub-lieutenants' course of similar content was instituted at RNC Greenwich, which from 1929 included an 'Introductory War Course' studying the lessons of the recent war. There appears to have been only one interwar seaman officer who actually had a university degree: Captain Francis Sandford, a Torpedo officer who took an Oxford BA in Modern History in 1921 but died of blood poisoning at the age of thirty-eight in 1926, on the verge of being considered for flag rank.[9]

Many aspects of the naval officers' career structure may appear curious, and some of them would have perplexed the officers themselves if they had fully understood them. Admirals were chosen for preference from those who had the least experience commanding at sea, whereas those with the most were forced to retire young. Captains of big ships were often appointed who knew a good deal about organization and man-management, but little or nothing about seamanship and ship-handling. Although regarded as future leaders, they had almost no training in leadership, or experience in independent command. An exception which illustrates the rule is the career of Andrew Cunningham, a quintessential 'salt-horse' destroyer officer whose outstanding service in command of destroyers during the First World War made him a much-decorated captain. From the age of twenty-five until he reached flag rank at forty-eight in 1932 he had commanded every ship in which he served, developing unmatched resources of judgement and self-confidence. He might never have had the chance to deploy them as an admiral if the First World War had not overtaken him at the right moment in his career. Even among his contemporaries who had also had wartime opportunities, very few enjoyed comparable careers.[10]

The careers of non-seaman commissioned officers like engineers, paymasters, surgeons and Royal Marines were all severely disrupted by the Selborne Scheme, and the shortage of engineer officers was the most critical and urgent consequence. During the war the scheme continued in force, but it became ever clearer that it was never going to yield the number or quality of engineers the Navy needed. In 1920 only twenty-five midshipmen opted to sit the engineers' qualifying examination, of whom six failed and none gained a First Class pass. In that year engineers were constituted a distinct class of executive officers, with substantially higher pay and better promotion prospects than the rest up to the rank of captain, and in 1922 the Royal Naval Engineering College at Keyham resumed training of Engineer Midshipmen. The Selborne Scheme had now irretrievably broken down (insofar as it had ever worked at all), and in 1925 the fact was finally recognized by general command status being confined to executive officers, though the engineers remained military officers and in full command of engine-room ratings. Naval officers (commissioned and warrant) were now divided into twelve categories: Executive, Engineer, Medical, Dental, Accountant, Instructor, Chaplains, Shipwrights, Ordnance, Electrical, Schoolmasters and Wardmasters. Of these branches the last five existed only as warrant ranks, and naval chaplains had no particular rank at all, only a pay scale rising with seniority, and a convention that they should be regarded as equal in rank to whomever they happened to be speaking with. The 'Great Betrayal', as it was named by some engineers, announced by a characteristically tactless circular, essentially recognized the failure of an ill-managed and misconceived experiment.[11]

Betrayed or not, the engineers quickly recovered their morale and *esprit de corps* under the new system. They now trained together from midshipmen, and from the beginning their teaching and learning were carried to at least university standard. The Navy was very soon aware that the new generation of young engineer officers were considerably more competent than the pre-1914 entries. There was also an observable social difference, because from 1918 the great majority of the young engineers had come in by the 'Special Entry' or 'Public School' scheme (colloquially known as the 'Pubs'), whose rules allowed the Admiralty to offer as many places for each branch as it needed, at whatever entry standard it cared to impose. Unlike the 'Darts', therefore, the 'Pubs' could be precisely targeted to fill vacancies – of which the most numerous and urgent were for engineers. They were drawn from similar (but somewhat less well-to-do) family backgrounds to the 'Darts', only they had not been thrown into a cold bath of naval tradition in boyhood but had made their own choice of career as young adults after an upbringing in civil society ashore. One further, not unimportant, factor raised the status of naval engineering. Like other naval officers' establishments, the Royal Naval Engineering College played rugby, but with four years to train and grow, the engineers produced much stronger players who regularly defeated all comers and represented the Navy against the sporting world.[12]

The Geddes Axe very soon turned out not to have stabilized the officers' career structure. By 1924 the Navy had more lieutenant-commanders than in 1918, and the total was still rising. It did not peak until 1931, by which time more than one-fifth were being passed over for promotion to commander. In 1933 there were 354 passed-over lieutenant-commanders still serving, unable to retire before forty-five even if they wanted to. Ships had too many middle-ranking officers, all striving to distinguish themselves in some way in the handling of everyday routine which was well within the competence of their juniors, or dully serving out their time for pension with nothing more to hope for. Ships and fleets were minutely over-managed and over-centralized. Forced redundancies were imposed again in 1926, 1929 and 1931, further damaging officers' morale, and clearly demonstrating that the Admiralty was incapable of manpower planning.[13]

All this was in the context of repeated pay cuts. In 1919 the Navy received a substantial increase over the 1917 pay rates in recognition of wartime inflation, but it did not last long. In 1924 officers' pay was cut by 5½ per cent because of a 'fall in the cost of living', at the same time as the civil service (including the Lords of the Admiralty) received a 'cost of living increase' (calculated over a slightly different period). Naval officers' pay was then cut again in 1927, 1929, 1930, and twice in 1931. All these measures were justified by the falling cost of living which followed from the government's severely deflationary economic policy, which also generated mass unemployment, and dissuaded officers and ratings, however unhappy, from trying to leave the Service. One imposition was unique to naval officers. Unlike ratings, unlike army and air force officers, unlike the Dominion navies, British naval officers received no marriage allowance until 1938, on the grounds that the 1919 naval pay award had included a 'marriage element'. Many therefore endured enforced celibacy, or married poverty, further depressing morale. Discontent with the Navy, added to the economic losses of the Depression, sharply reduced the number of families able and willing to pay Dartmouth fees. In 1936 only twenty-six boys passed the entrance examination, so the pass mark was lowered to admit seventeen more – which was still not enough to make up a term of forty-five. At the joint Passing Out parades every six months, the 'Darts' made a poor show in comparison with the 'Pubs' (though the 'Pubs' had the advantage of being a year older). In March 1939 the Special Entry took sixteen out of seventeen First Class passes, and seventeen out of eighteen prizes. In July the 'Pubs' took all the prizes.[14]

In 1919 the government was acutely conscious that naval pay had fallen well behind civilian earnings, and that trades unions and even revolutionary movements were now advancing in many parts of the industrial world. The Russian Revolution of 1917, and the almost-successful German Revolution of 1918–19 (in both of which naval personnel had taken a leading part), seemed for some time to herald a general collapse of the old political order, and fuelled the generous 1919 naval pay settlement. The Admiralty was now sensitive to its delicate political position. It was one thing to buy off trouble with money, but quite another to leave an opening for the lower-deck societies to develop into a naval trades union. First the 1919–23 Welfare Committees were abandoned, then in 1922 both the new system of Welfare Conferences and the existing lower-deck societies were strictly limited to welfare questions. Ratings' access to MPs, and even their voting rights, were restricted, and men lecturing at Speakers' Corner in Hyde Park risked arrest. In 1929 one man received a month's imprisonment for writing to his MP.[15]

The 1919 rates of naval pay survived the 'Geddes Axe' of 1922 when so many officers were dismissed, and the 1923 Anderson Committee, which reported that the lower deck were now overpaid. The Admiralty tended to agree: 'Undoubtedly the lower deck are very well off. Some of the higher ratings keep motor bicycles and can afford to take the more expensive seats at local entertainments and their meals at places which officers patronise. In some cases they are able to buy their houses . . .'[16] Conditions afloat were improving in some respects, including new messing arrangements and a sharp fall in the number of courts martial and summary punishments, but promotion was stagnant. Worst of all, from 1925 new entrants were paid a basic rate of 3s a day whereas existing ratings were allowed to retain the 1919 rate of 4s. This was divisive and unsettling, and it was hard or impossible to maintain a family on the 1925 scale. By no possible logic could both scales be fair simultaneously, and all that defended the higher 1919 scale was the repeated promises of successive governments and Boards of Admiralty. The years 1922 and 1923 were of full employment when recruitment was difficult, but thereafter unemployment rose fast, and was never less than 10 per cent up to 1940. As a result rates of re-engagement to continue a naval career rose likewise. By 1925, 64 per cent of seamen, 72 per cent of stokers and 98 per cent of ERAs signed on for a second term of service (compared with about half of seamen and stokers before the war). The Services were extensively deployed as strike-breakers in the 1919 railway strike, the 1921 South Wales miners' strike, and the General Strike of 1926. The Navy was loyal, but it did not follow that it was happy.[17]

On 4 January 1931 there was a mutiny in the old submarine depot ship *Lucia* at Plymouth among men who refused to work on Sunday. Various ratings were punished, but the court of inquiry was severely critical of her captain and commander, who were put on half pay 'with an expression of the Board's serious displeasure'. At this date a Labour government under James Ramsay MacDonald was in office, and the First Lord A. V. Alexander was under pressure from both Labour and Communist parties demanding trades union rights for naval ratings. In May 1931 a Confidential Admiralty Fleet Order reminding commanding officers of the correct procedure for stating grievances included the phrase 'punishment of anyone for making a frivolous or vexatious complaint is no longer allowed, provided that the complainant . . . complies with the regulations'. This was no more than a restatement of the existing position, but in naval wardrooms these events were widely understood to reveal that the hard left was taking over, and that officers who attempted to enforce naval discipline would receive no more support from the Admiralty. Officers' already poor morale received a further blow.[18]

These were local incidents in the context of the world economic crisis which followed the US stock market crash of October 1929. Only the United States could have stopped the slump, but the government in Washington had little control over economic policy and was the enemy of the financial establishment in New York. In August 1931 orthodox economists and bankers on both sides of the Atlantic demanded that the British government cut expenditure – unemployment benefit in particular.[19] On the 24th the Labour government fell, and MacDonald split his party by agreeing to remain Prime Minister of a coalition 'National Government' mainly composed of Liberals and Conservatives. The new government excluded the Service ministers from the Cabinet.[20] Sir Austen Chamberlain, the First Lord of the Admiralty, had hoped to return to the Foreign Office and regarded the Admiralty as a 'menial' job requiring no more than an hour's work a day. The new Admiralty Board seems to have made little effort to win him over, or even to brief him. On 8 September, the day the ships of the Atlantic Fleet sailed from their home ports to resume exercises at Invergordon, the Board informed the Cabinet that it was ready to impose the lower 1925 pay scale immediately on those still receiving the 1919 rate, though it would be 'regarded by the whole Navy as a breach of faith' – which it obviously was. The Admiralty was advised that this would be an unequivocal breach of contract which could only be upheld in court by pleading Crown privilege. At this point both Sir Frederick Field, the First Sea Lord, and Sir Michael Hodges, commander-in-chief of the Atlantic Fleet, were off sick, several other members of the Admiralty Board were on leave, and Chamberlain did not consult any of those still available. Responsibility in the Atlantic Fleet devolved to Rear-Admiral Wilfred Tomkinson, but the Admiralty Registry (responsible for communications) seems to have forgotten about him, and the key correspondence was sent to the fleet flagship to await Hodges' return, or not sent at all. The next senior flag officer, Rear-Admiral E. A. Astley-Ruston, one day junior to Tomkinson and on poor terms with him, received the Admiralty letter but did not pass it on. With Field and Hodges in hospital, and Tomkinson still in the dark, both the Fleet and the Admiralty were effectively leaderless as the crisis developed. After days of ominous rumours, the Admiralty's official announcement of the reduced pay scale was issued on Thursday 10 September, when the fleet was still at sea. Not until Sunday the 13th were the men able to get ashore to buy newspapers which confirmed their suspicions. Hodges who should have issued the announcement to the fleet was still in hospital, and Tomkinson found out about the reduced pay scale by accident only on Sunday evening. Many older ratings who had married on the assurance of the 1919 pay scale had reason to fear that their families would be made homeless if it were cut, but senior officers who should have cared a great deal about their men's welfare were themselves unaware of the Admiralty's intentions and showed a marked lack of the initiative and moral courage the crisis demanded. The men read the newspapers and listened to the wireless with keen attention; they seem to have realized what was happening faster than their officers did. Moreover, from their arrival on Saturday the 12th they all had access to a 'wet' canteen ashore at

Invergordon which acted as a perfect focus for exchanging information and ideas between ships.[21]

By this time the men of the Atlantic Fleet understood that the silent Admiralty was going to betray them, and that their own officers were sympathetic but powerless. They would have to take action for themselves, but they were extremely careful to avoid mutiny, the essence of which is the deliberate refusal to obey an order. Instead, the men were polite to their officers, but elusive when orders were expected. The officers for their part carefully phrased their wishes in the form of requests, the refusal of which could not be construed as mutiny. In a legal sense, therefore, the full extent of the Invergordon 'Mutiny' was a failure to weigh anchor, and nobody was ever charged with it. The 'mutineers' never contemplated violence, and the officers never expected it. This non-mutiny was led by long-serving 'three-badge' able seamen, the main victims of the pay cut. Petty officers were conspicuously absent, and junior ratings already on the 1925 scale were not allowed to participate. Nobody explained to the men (and few of the officers seemed to have understood) that a reduction of basic pay from 4s to 3s was less than 25 per cent when various allowances were added in: it was still considerably more than the 11 per cent cut imposed on the officers (albeit this was the sixth cut in officers' pay since 1919).[22]

Tomkinson gave the order to weigh anchor on Tuesday morning only when the Admiralty did not react to his warning that it was likely to be disobeyed. When he gave the Admiralty a full report of the situation, they seem to have ignored it in the hope that it would go away; indeed, Tomkinson himself was ignored throughout. Only on Wednesday the 16th did the Admiralty accept Admiral Field's plan to order the fleet back to home ports for a thorough investigation of the men's grievances – by which time the men had construed the Admiralty's silence as another rejection. Harry Pursey, the pre-war campaigner for commissioned warrant rank, was now a lieutenant-commander in the fleet flagship *Hood*, where he defused the situation by proposing a 'make and mend'. He was convinced that if the Admiralty had ordered a return to home ports on Tuesday morning, the 'mutiny' would have been over in two hours.[23] Pursey reports a revealing conversation:

Hood: Master-at-Arms reported to Commander: 'Stoker X wishes to see you, sir.' Stoker: 'We've had a meeting on the foc'sle and we've decided: if other ships don't go . . . we won't go. If other ships go . . . we will go . . . We won't stay here alone . . . Can you please tell us whether the other ships will go?' Commander: 'Quite honestly . . . I don't know. When I do . . . I will let you know.'[24]

Nobody in the fleet knew what was happening, and from the most senior to the most junior they felt abandoned. With some exceptions, demoralized officers up to and including the Admiralty Board failed to take responsibility and allowed an unnecessary crisis to develop. The 'mutineers' were drawn into filling a vacuum of leadership, acting on behalf of their officers rather than against them – as they said at the time, 'We are doing this for you as well as for ourselves.'[25] Within the Navy this was widely understood. The admirals blamed each other, but the Navy blamed the Admiralty. Admiral Tyrwhitt, now Commander-in-Chief, The Nore, said it openly; King George V agreed, and so did Sir John Kelly, the new commander-in-chief of the Atlantic Fleet, a popular and outspoken character who was believed to have been brought out of retirement at the king's insistence.[26] Only one of the eight captains in the Atlantic Fleet rose to the situation: Captain Arthur Power of the cruiser *Dorsetshire* (the only one of the eight who later reached flag rank). His routine was that if he appeared on deck without his cap on, he was there informally, and men were not expected to stop work and salute. In the crisis of the 'mutiny', he came on deck capless to speak to his men, promising to stand by them if they would turn to work:

> Then he quietly said, 'I am going aft. I have work to do. I hope you will do the same.' To a man, we followed him aft to our muster stations. It was a remarkably moving moment and one that I will remember for ever.[27]

The news of the 'mutiny' of the Atlantic Fleet caused widespread panic among journalists and politicians. On 17 and 18 September £28 million in gold was withdrawn from the Bank of England, forcing Britain off the gold standard. It is clear that the 'mutiny' was the immediate (though not the long-term) cause. On the 21st the Cabinet was informed that a general mutiny of the Navy was planned for the following day. MI5 reported a vast imaginary Communist conspiracy, while the real Communist Party, taken entirely by surprise, made ineffectual noises.

British newspapers reported cautiously, but in New York and Paris the press confidently announced a Communist revolution. All this was the work of overstimulated imaginations, as presently became clear.[28] As the fleet steamed southward on 16 and 17 September, captains and commanders began collecting statements of income and expenditure from their men to illustrate the hardships which were to be imposed on them:

> It is not exaggeration to say that, in many cases, it is not hardship they are facing but the ruin of their carefully and thriftily built-up homes. These

men literally budget their commitments in pence. What little margin they have disappears entirely under the new scale.[29]

Men who were just keeping a small home going, paying off instalments on furniture, insurance or mortgages, would have lost everything; others with larger families could not have sent enough home to feed them . . .[30]

On 21 September, while this process was still going on, Ramsay MacDonald announced that no pay (except senior officers') would be reduced by more than 10 per cent. The 'mutiny' was now over. In better-commanded fleets it had never begun. The Mediterranean Fleet was scattered and on the advice of the Fleet Wireless Officer (Lord Louis Mountbatten) communications between ships were monitored, suppressing any trouble.[31]

There were, and sometimes still are, other 'Invergordon Mutinies' known to historians if not to history: they include the overthrow of higher authority, the revolt of the working class, the rise of trades unionism, and the collapse of deference. All of these stories were either imaginary or irrelevant to the Navy. The shock cleared people's heads, and in the Navy opinion soon agreed that the disaster could never have happened if officers, especially senior officers, had done their duty. It had always been an article of naval faith that:

To allow causes of complaint, whether real or imaginary, to be put forward in such a manner [i.e. collectively] is, in the opinion of their Lordships, not only entirely foreign to the best traditions and discipline of the Navy, but must inevitably tend to alienate the Men from their Officers, upon whom they should, and rightly, rely for sympathetic and energetic support of any legitimate grievance whensoever it may arise.[32]

A century and a half earlier Cuthbert Collingwood had exclaimed 'What! mutiny in my ship? then it must be my fault, or the fault of my officers . . .'[33] In the same spirit, the officers of the 1930s largely blamed themselves for Invergordon, and set to work to restore discipline, in the broad sense of healthy social relations. Admiral Kelly made it a virtual condition of accepting the command of the Atlantic Fleet that the Admiralty Board should be completely replaced, and with one very significant exception it was.[34]

The exception was Sir Frederick Field, the First Sea Lord, appointed in July 1930. His is a name not much remembered by historians; it is often said that he had only risen so far because the leading candidate, Sir Roger Keyes, had spoiled his reputation, and it is sometimes implied that Field's only historical importance was to be on hand to take the blame for Invergordon. He would have been the obvious scapegoat, especially as his health was uncertain, but he was not blamed. Instead, he was retained in office to complete the important personnel reforms he had begun the year before, which addressed the faults of the Selborne Scheme and others, many of which went well back into the nineteenth century. An Admiralty Fleet Order (AFO) of September 1932 set out a clear and logical progression of young officers' formation, for the first time distinguishing between education and training. Dartmouth was to provide the cadets with education (only professional education for the Special Entry, who spent a few months there between leaving school and joining their first ships). Midshipmen were to spend their sea-time not in the classroom, but at work alongside the men, and as much as possible in boats, learning in the process leadership, seamanship and officer-like qualities. Lieutenants, the AFO insisted, needed a formation on three levels: a general education (not limited to science and mathematics), professional knowledge (to be gained on their sub-lieutenant's courses) and officer-like qualities (to be learnt from opportunity, responsibility and sea experience):

> There has been a tendency for these three points, which form the most important training of all, to be neglected for the sake of technical instruction at sea. It cannot be too strongly emphasized that although professional knowledge is an important factor in the power of command, it is in itself insufficient, and must not be allowed to prejudice the training in officer-like qualities . . . It is their Lordships' view that while weapon skill can be achieved by an intensive period of drill, the development of qualities of leadership and initiative requires years of application of a system designed with that end in view.[35]

As the First Lord explained in the House of Commons in 1932, officers needed skill and morale. 'Morale as here used, includes all those personal qualities such as initiative, resource, leadership, enthusiasm and discipline which are essential for the efficient use of men.'[36] The training cruiser, abolished in 1924, was restored in 1932, combining midshipmen of the two entries, giving them the chance to work alongside ratings, and to take it in turns to take charge of working parties. From 1932 new commanding officers were issued with a pamphlet 'Notes on Dealing with Insubordination', which emphasized the captain's duty to forestall trouble by satisfying legitimate grievances. The same year new 'Schemes of Complement' were designed to throw more authority onto the petty officers, and in 1935 the secret Binney Report on peace and war complements aimed to reduce the peacetime proportion of officers as far as possible to accustom all ranks to greater responsibility. In 1935 a standing Review of Service Conditions took the place of the defunct Welfare

Conferences, and a Director of Personal Services was appointed, directly under the Second Sea Lord. In the 1930s it became fashionable for noted officers like Admiral Drax and Captain Rory O'Conor to think and write about leadership – even on occasion to use that still strange and un-English word.[37] 'Your endeavour,' wrote Captain Francis Pridham of the *Hood* in 1937, 'should be to inspire in your men a feeling of respect for you and confidence in your sympathetic interest and understanding of their problems, as well as in your professional ability. This is the sure basis of discipline and leadership.'[38]

This is not to say that all the evils thrown into relief by Invergordon were cured at once. There were too many midshipmen for all to have a good chance of learning seamanship and leadership in boats. Commanders who well knew that ships were judged by the appearance and handling of their boats would want to give that responsibility to the best midshipmen, when it was the weaker candidates who had the most to learn. Field had eliminated the endless cramming with pure mathematics, but there was still no history, tactics or strategy in the naval curriculum to form the minds or hone the judgement of future leaders.[39] Thoughtful officers could see the weaknesses as well as the strengths of their training:

> [The naval officer] is a man of action and never at a loss. He must make up his mind on every occasion instantaneously and without hesitation, and he must be prepared to take on *any* job at a moment's notice. Now just in these characteristics lie his strength and his weakness. They make him the finest ship's officer in the world, but they render him unsuitable for work that requires administrative, organizing (if it implies more than 'telling off' parties to work) or reflective capacity, and what is more they *prevent him from realizing that there is any kind of work that he cannot do.*[40]

After Invergordon there was no more complacency. Opinions varied over what needed to be done most urgently, but virtually all officers (and indeed ratings) agreed that change was badly needed. A new 'National' (but Conservative-dominated) coalition government under Ramsay MacDonald took office in November 1931, with a new Admiralty Board headed by the former Conservative Chief Whip (and retired Commander RN), the charming and popular Sir Bolton Eyres Monsell. Field, still heavily involved in his personnel reforms, remained First Sea Lord until succeeded by Beatty's protégé Sir Ernle Chatfield in 1933. Unlike the more self-effacing Field, Chatfield was a forceful figure with a notable public presence (though like so many gunnery officers he was half-deaf, and his social touch with civilian politicians was not infallible). He and Monsell provided the political and professional leadership the Admiralty urgently needed. One of their first decisions was that the Admiralty Board would now go on visits of inspection wearing uniform rather than top hat and frock coat, to show whose side they were on. (The civilian members were clothed in a sort of 'yachting rig'.) The Admiralty, hitherto indifferent to it, now revived the old divisional system which divided the ship's company into small groups, each under the personal supervision of an officer. A reform of 1933 replacing the ineffective 'Mate Scheme' with a new system of selecting 'upper yardmen' for promotion directly from young ratings to junior officers, owed much to Monsell's skilful negotiations with the Treasury. It was followed in 1936 by a new twelve-year 'short service' rating enlistment (seven years in the fleet and five in the reserves), and by the creation of the Royal Naval Volunteer (Supplementary) Reserve, a list of potential officers with skills valuable to the Navy who undertook to serve the country in an emergency, but (until March 1939) did no regular peacetime training. It was the RNVSR rather than the RNVR which introduced some experienced yachtsmen to the wartime Navy – but since their uniforms were the same, with the same distinctive wavy rank stripes on their sleeves, they tended to be lumped together as the 'Wavy Navy'.[41]

Among the ratings morale and recruitment remained depressed into the mid-1930s, primarily because of low pay. A skilled tradesman ashore could earn £4 6s a week, but an able seaman, supposedly a skilled man, earned no more than £2 14s – less than a farm labourer, a junior postman or a government typist aged below twenty-one. Among those who did volunteer there was a marked shortage of men educated above elementary level, suitable for technical ratings.[42] By the mid-1930s lower-deck morale was beginning to recover, partly because the underlying causes – above all low pay – were at last being addressed, partly because it was increasingly obvious that war was coming as the Navy moved towards a war footing. In 1934 half the 1931 pay cut for ratings was restored, and the following year the 1919 scale was restored in full to pre-1925 recruits. In 1936 a marriage allowance was given to ratings aged over twenty-five. The only obvious failure of these years was Field's abortive scheme for promotion from the lower deck to officer's rank, which Chatfield did not favour, and which offered to increase the supply of middle-ranking commissioned officers, of whom there were already too many.[43] Another mistake which is apparent with hindsight was not to have set up a regular channel of advancement from able seaman to leading seaman and petty officer. The acute shortage of these higher ratings which had developed by 1943 was the consequence.[44]

This however was part of a long-standing problem inherent in the double

character of a petty officer, who was both a skilled man advanced for his professional skill, and (in theory) a junior officer able to command bodies of men.
In practice many technical petty officers, artificers, mechanicians and artisans
lacked either the talent or the opportunity to become effective leaders in the
way able rates and leading hands, the long-serving ratings who set the tone of
wartime ships' companies, had to do to gain advancement. Technical petty
officers were promoted for their skill, and ordinary seamen made up to able
seaman when they had passed an exam, but other leading hands and petty officers could only be promoted to fill vacancies. Mixed up with status and authority were practical and symbolic questions such as uniform and messing. From
1923 all petty officers past their first year wore an officer-style 'fore and aft' uniform with a collar and tie, and from 1925 all chief petty officers wore brass
sleeve buttons. This showed the ratings who carried disciplinary authority, or
should have done, but it did not magically endow them with powers of leadership. Moreover in many ships, especially small ones, petty officers had to
mess with junior rates. In big ships another component of social authority was
generated by invisible status hierarchies which put rating branches like writers, sick-berth stewards, telegraphists and signalmen (better dressed, better
educated, working more with officers) at the head of an unofficial scale which
ran down to engine-room rates and stokers.[45] Adding all these together made
a complex and fluid shipboard society, a stage on which ratings might play
many parts at once:

> H. was one of the finest and yet one of the worst men I have ever met. I
> admired him very much, and his faults were greatly outweighed by his vir-
> tues. He had absolutely no morals, drank like a fish, would steal anything
> from stores or dockyard (never from a pal); a confirmed gambler who lived
> with another man's wife and literally found a wife in every port. On the
> other hand he would do anything to help a shipmate and was kindness
> itself to any youngster who got into trouble. When he gambled he played
> fair; when he borrowed money – and he would borrow from anyone – it
> was always returned at the end of the month and he would ask the loan of
> it for another month if necessary. A splendid seaman, he would do the
> most dangerous job with a laugh. I have seen him go up the mast on a
> rough day to help a boy who was nervous.[46]

The hinge of the social life of the Navy, the critical axis on which all discipline
and social life turned, was the relationship between officers and men. Invergordon frightened the Navy and the country because for a time there seemed
a real possibility that the hinge might fail. But in retrospect the historian must

be impressed by the deep and strong roots of naval society revealed by research among retired ratings. Of course they did not all like all their officers, but there are consistent reports that officers got better during the first half of the twentieth century. Ratings hated petty tyrants, selfish officers who made life more difficult than it needed to be, officers who were 'not gentlemen'. They were very liable to identify these last among commissioned warrant officers, and especially among former 'upper yardmen' promoted young from the lower deck. It is difficult to judge to what extent these complaints were justified. The lower deck was socially conservative and deeply attached to tradition, especially the tradition of good officers who cared for their men. There was a discontented minority of ratings, often of left-wing politics, who felt alienated from their messmates as much or more than from their officers. A commissioned warrant officer was really a senior petty officer and could not pretend to be the same person as a lieutenant or a lieutenant-commander just because he had later risen to the same rank. An upper-yardman, by contrast, was selected and advanced young precisely in the hope that he could blend in among the sub-lieutenants, taking on the mannerisms and protective colouring of the former cadets. Many succeeded so well that ships' companies forgot or never realized where they had come from and accepted them as 'proper' officers. Wartime officers, as we shall see, came to be selected and advanced on an almost classless basis, which tended to obscure social divisions:[47]

> In practice the bonds that drew Royal Navy officers and ratings together were substantially stronger than the differences that tended to separate them. An effective ship's company, the leaders and the led, was united by cause, bound by tradition, camaraderie and, at times, dangers of cheek-by-jowl life in a man-of-war at sea and, in the last resort, upheld by that distinctive British trait, a cheerful, dogged mock-sardonic capacity for endurance in adversity.[48]

People's reasons for joining the Navy varied according to taste and opportunity. Some were escaping poverty and unemployment; some were attracted by travel and adventure:

> I was taught discipline, a trade, and a pride in achievement. I enjoyed comradeship to a degree I believe unavailable in any other walk of life. I was fed, clothed and housed, and travelled to many parts of the world that I otherwise would never have been able to visit . . .[49]

The distinctive uniform was important, especially 'tiddlyvated' to attract the girls, with unauthorized alternatives like high heels, wide bell-bottoms, tight flannels with unofficial embroidery and scrubbed collars ironed to shine. Authority fought a constant losing battle against such 'tiddly suits'.[50] Strongest of all was the emotional bond which united shipmates. 'The sailor fought for more than just his life, for that was cheap enough, to be sure. When a sailor "belonged" to a ship his main loyalty was to his ship and his mates. If they endured enough together, his family came second.'[51] 'There is no one like a naval man. I mix with no other than that even today. And I know them before they speak.'[52]

In the late 1930s the Association of Wrens set up in 1919 was still full of life, and so was Dame Katharine Furse the former Director of the WRNS. However, the death in July 1936 of the great Sir Oswyn Murray, Secretary of the Admiralty since 1917, left a void in the higher administration of the Navy which the transfer of Sir Archibald Carter from the India Office did not repair. The Admiralty showed little of the energy and imagination it had deployed under Murray and dragged reluctantly behind the RAF and the army in the revival of the women's services. Late in 1938 Carter and the head of the Civil Establishments Branch (responsible for Admiralty civil servants) decided to revive the old name WRNS while avoiding as far as possible its dangerous connections with political radicalism and the Navy. Early in 1939 a Ministry of Labour pamphlet implying that all three armed services were acting in step provoked 15,000 applications to join the WRNS, forcing the Admiralty to do something to respond. 'I cannot help feeling,' dryly observed the former Wren officer Vera Laughton (now Mrs Mathews), 'that knowledge of the unanswered letters was a spur in urging very busy men to action . . . What they were looking for,' she believed, 'was someone on whom they could dump the whole thing and leave her to get on with it.'[53] When Mathews was appointed Director of the WRNS in April 1939 'under the Second Sea Lord', she did not realize that Sir Archibald Carter and the Civil Establishments Branch of the Admiralty were in the process of taking over her old Service. 'I had no idea at the time what a handicap this would be; I merely knew it was a wrong status.'[54] She soon found that Carter had no sympathy for the Wrens' ambitions to work with the Navy as they had done before, and she was treated simply as a civil servant. Carter and the Civil Establishments Branch sneered at the idea of Wren officers having ranks comparable with the Navy and blocked the issue of a naval-style uniform, or any uniform at all. For the first two years of its new existence the WRNS was caught in a bureaucratic struggle between Carter and the Admiralty civil servants on one side, and on the other Admiral Sir Charles Little, the Second Sea Lord, and the majority of the naval commanders-in-chief of the home stations, who remembered the former Wrens with admiration, and wanted them back as they had been twenty years before, an auxiliary closely integrated with the Navy.[55] In this struggle Vera Mathews was a more dangerous opponent than Carter realized. As she told the Labour leader Clement Attlee, 'When, at the age of twenty, you have stood in the gutter selling the *Suffragette* while passers-by spat on you, at the age of fifty you can face anything!'[56] Moreover, her deputy, Angela Goodenough, had previously been the senior woman civil servant in the Admiralty and was an expert pilot through the corridors of power. The fact that Carter and his people were not paying attention and did not take the women seriously allowed Mathews the freedom to work without interference by delegating widely to subordinates who were encouraged to approach the local naval authorities and offer their services. The effect was to promote local initiatives which in many cases were rooted and flourishing before the Admiralty noticed. The first Wren plotters were appointed by Admiral Ramsay at Dover during the Dunkirk evacuation. The Harwich sub-command was the first to have female Duty Staff Officers. Western Approaches claimed to have been the first command to train Wren mechanics. Other commands quickly copied, and it was very soon too late for Civil Establishments to interfere. Early schemes set up by various naval commands included Wren telegraphists (wireless operators), cypher operators, plotters, motorcycle despatch riders, degaussing recorders and parachute packers.[57] Ordnance Wrens serviced the anti-aircraft guns of small craft, and Wren boat's crews learnt to fire them in their own defence.[58] In November 1939, following the insistence of the Medical Women's Federation on equal pay for women, Dr Genevieve Rewcastle was appointed Medical Superintendent of the WRNS on the same pay as a Surgeon Lieutenant, which was done simply by giving her a commission as such in the RNVR. She was for some time the only female RN officer in the *Navy List*, though later other women doctors and dentists were appointed in the same way.[59] Not every senior naval officer had the imagination to look beyond the obvious clerical and domestic jobs for women, but many did. 'Progressive bases' were training their own Wren signallers and telegraphists well before the regular schools were set up in August 1941. In October 1941 Sir Charles Forbes, Commander-in-Chief Plymouth, started using Wren boat's crews. It was proverbial in the Navy that 'a ship is known by her boats': Wren boat's crews were very soon an outstanding advertisement for their service. One Wren coxswain wrote home describing her experience of bringing a boatload of eighty drunken libertymen aboard their ship, late on a blowing night when several of them fell overboard and had to be fished out by Wrens with boat-hooks. 'It was a terrific experience and I think I must be pretty hard boiled as it didn't worry me at all. None of them ever get fighting drunk. You have just got to treat them all like a lot of small boys.'[60] In 1941, at the suggestion of Admiral Drax, Commander-in-Chief, The Nore, the Navy officially abandoned any restriction to 'duties conventionally applicable to women' except work which called for sea experience or great physical strength.[61] In April 1941 the WRNS were formally transferred back from Civil Establishments to the Second Sea Lord. This was the same moment that Ernest Bevin, the Trades Union leader who had become Minister of Labour, brought in the registration of women as well as men for national service – precisely what the WRNS stood for and Carter opposed.[62]

TWENTY-TWO

The Naval Fabric

Government and Administration 1919–1940

For Britain as for other participants in the First World War, it was a grave national trial which enforced many changes in the constitution and structure of government. Some of these happened during the war itself, but many consequential changes followed (mostly without publicity) during the twenty years of peace which followed. The dominant theme of these changes was co-ordination between government departments which in pre-war years had been allowed to organize their responsibilities with only limited reference to each other. The clearest and sharpest lessons of experience grew from the relations of the Admiralty and the War Office, the Navy and the army – to which had now been added a third armed service, the Air Force. No lesson of the war seemed more obvious than that the service departments must learn to work together – but all the difficulty lay in translating that platitude into practical machinery which would avoid the disastrous errors of the war years. The worst obstacles sprang not so much from inter-service relations, as from the widespread failure to define and regulate the boundaries of civil and military responsibilities, between ministers and senior servicemen. No one wanted to revive Kitchener's domineering control over the General Staff and the Cabinet, nor his neutering of the Committee of Imperial Defence. In November 1919 the CID was revived, but in practice most of its work was done by a smaller Defence Sub-Committee combining the chiefs of staff and the Prime Minister. This worked well during the 1922 alarm of war with Turkey (an early episode in which signals intelligence played an essential part), and in 1923 it became a permanent Chiefs of Staff Committee. Now the defence departments were run on a day-to-day basis by their professional heads rather than their ministers, who combined to make joint-service policy between them. The total subordination of military to civilian control which had marked the Victorian era in Britain was no more. Even in peacetime the men in uniform ran not only the armed services and the defence departments, but much of the inter-departmental machinery which had grown up to co-ordinate a national war effort. They still depended heavily on the administrative skills of their civil servants, and their ministers still appeared in Parliament to defend their departments, especially their Estimates, but civilians were no longer the sole or even predominant authors of defence policy.[1]

The rising importance and influence of the chiefs of staff might at first appear to be a discreet, slow-motion seizure of power by the military, but this was neither the intention nor the effect. The experience of the Great War had taught thoughtful contemporaries that a rational wartime government had to take military expertise seriously. To respond to the demands of total war, decision-making structures had to be developed at the centre which integrated the military into civil society. The Admiralty was better equipped to face this challenge than any other department, because for more than a century it had been in charge of the Navy in both civilian and military dimensions: it stood at the head of a great civil-military administrative and industrial structure, but it was also an operational headquarters and central staff which now (thanks to telegraphs and wireless) was able to exercise ultimate command over the whole Navy worldwide. The War Office had never functioned in either dimension (except as the inheritor of the civilian administration of the Ordnance Board). But it was in the nature of the new situation that the relative efficiency of the Admiralty did not solve the gravest problems; in certain respects it made them worse. What was needed – as many contemporaries could see – was cordial co-operation and equality of esteem between the senior officers of the three armed services, but none of the three could supply it alone, and the inter-service structures set up in 1919 seemed almost to be designed to generate discord. Serious attempts to absorb the lessons of the war, such as Admiral Phillimore's 1919 Post-War Questions Committee, or Bonar Law's December 1920 Naval Shipbuilding Sub-Committee (of the CID), tended to be diverted into defence of the Admiralty against partisan political attacks. It was already becoming clear that naval aviation had been left in a muddle by decisions based on short-term expediency, the worst of them being the divide between designers and users of naval aircraft. 'Failure to fight this matter to the finish,' wrote Phillimore, who had been 'Admiral commanding Aircraft' from 1918 to 1919, 'and to acquiesce in the present indefensible and illogical policy because a too hasty surrender was made last year – presumably under political pressure – will, I am convinced be fraught with great danger to the efficiency of His Majesty's Navy.'[2] The Naval Staff, under heavy attack after the war by MPs for whom a sea officer ashore was the epitome of useless bureaucracy, soon felt severely the loss of its Air Division. It was revived as a section in 1920 under Commander Richard Bell Davies, a naval airman who had won a VC at the Dardanelles, but in the 1920s the available staff officers were too few and too junior to have a big influence on naval air planning. By 1930 the want of leadership and technical support was obvious, and the new position of Rear-Admiral Aircraft Carriers was filled by the outstanding Reginald Henderson, recently captain of the *Furious*; 'a brilliant officer, full of imagination, resource and initiative' in Chatfield's words.[3] Henderson's position was analogous to that of Flag Officer Submarines, but he flew his flag at sea not only to take personal charge of building up the practical capabilities of the carrier force, but to insulate him from Air Ministry harassment. Under him Captain H. C. Rawlings, Director of the Naval Air Division of the Naval Staff from 1932 to 1934, played an important part in reconstructing the Admiralty's technical capacity in air matters. As a personal friend of the aircraft manufacturer Richard Fairey, he also had a lot to do with Fairey's new torpedo bomber the Swordfish.[4]

Equality of esteem was anyway bound to be difficult when the Services were transparently of different structure and very unequal effectiveness. Aircraft were obviously becoming integral to both fleets and armies: no modern armed force could do without them, but neither could it do with them as a source of disunity.[5] As Chatfield the First Sea Lord told an inquiry in 1933, 'The air side is an integral part of our naval operation . . . not something which is added on like the submarine, but something which is an integral part of the navy itself, closely woven into the naval fabric.'[6] Repeatedly Chatfield tried to insist that realistic defence policy could only be made by the three services and the Cabinet acting together: 'I have an important C.I.D. Meeting next week at which the Chiefs of Staff are pressing for a policy to work on,' he wrote in 1933. 'Are we to be ready or are we not? If so, when, and what for?'[7]

Much about the practical politics of inter-service co-operation flowed from the simple fact that there were now three armed services instead of two, and political authority in defence matters depended more and more on inter-departmental alliances. Any two service departments in alliance had an excellent chance of outmatching the third. Beatty's powerful personality and political talents favoured the Admiralty during the early 1920s, but they also aroused alarm and hostility among those who feared naval domination. 'You are the only First Sea Lord I have known in my 26 years,' Sir Maurice Hankey told him in 1927, 'who could really talk on even terms to the highest cabinet ministers and stand up to them in argument. Fisher is an exception, but Fisher was a crank, and even he didn't really state a case clearly.'[8] The creation of the Chiefs of Staff Committee gave Beatty a platform from which to advance the

Navy's arguments, usually in alliance with the army. In 1924 the Trenchard–Keyes agreement compromised several of the contentious issues in dispute between the Admiralty and the Air Ministry (helped by the fact that the two negotiators, Sir Hugh Trenchard, Chief of the Air Staff, and Sir Roger Keyes, Deputy Chief of the Naval Staff, were closely connected by marriage). The Navy now provided all the observers and 70 per cent of the pilots of the Fleet Air Arm, which was entirely under naval operational control when afloat, but partly administered and entirely equipped by the Air Force. Relations afloat between the two services were friendly, in spite of what look like attempts by the Air Ministry to divide them. It insisted that Air Force officers afloat were passengers who took no part in the work of the ship, and blocked the Admiralty's desire to train rating pilots on the grounds that only a gentleman could command an aircraft.[9]

The Trenchard–Keyes agreement worked on a day-to-day level, but it avoided rather than solved the basic question of control and authority over naval aviation. At a higher level the services made progress during the 1920s in developing joint-service policies, but the Air Staff's hostility to joint-service integration was always an obstacle; its ambition was to be accepted as a sort of allied power or co-belligerent capable of winning wars single-handed, or at best loosely co-operating with the other services, though the real work of the airmen was still almost entirely in close support of military or naval operations. From 1925 to 1927 Beatty presided as chairman of the Chiefs of Staff Committee in the absence of a minister, which was most of the time. In this position he pressed to improve the machinery for joint-service policy formation. He especially feared that the unwillingness of politicians to answer awkward questions would deprive the services of the political leadership they needed in wartime. In January 1921 he stated that the Admiralty needed to know

> what the political and military requirements are: that we have been unable to get for over a year, although we have asked for it, and until we do have some express directions from the government of the country, the Admiralty are quite incapable of producing any plan, right or wrong.[10]

Beatty was open to the idea of a ministry of defence, so long as the single-service ministers were suppressed and the chiefs of staff became fully responsible for the service departments. He strongly supported the new Imperial Defence College set up in 1926 to generate joint-service policy and training. This was all very relevant to the question of naval aviation, because the Air Staff feared joint-service thinking as a threat to its independence. The lack of it undermined all three services. Naval aviation suffered less than other types of military flying because it was backed by a powerful patron, convinced of the importance of aircraft and clear about why it needed them. The army suffered the worst: in 1939 Britain went to war with almost no aircraft, weapons or techniques for the air support of troops, against Germany, whose air force specialized in little else.[11]

The national and international context of defence policy was heavily conditioned by the financial situation. During the First World War all the belligerents increased the money supply and suffered inflation (a 110 per cent increase in consumer prices in Britain, less than in other belligerents) – which in effect was a hidden tax paying for part of the cost of the war. During the war up to April 1917 Britain had raised money privately from US banks, all of which debts were in due course repaid. Once the United States entered the war it began to lend directly to the British government, which acted both for itself and as an agent for France, Russia and other co-belligerents which lacked the sophisticated international banking system available in London. The US refused to deal in sterling, the main international currency, but insisted on cash repayment in dollars, so British banks supplied the dollars and took on the debts of America's allies. At the end of the war the US had lent a total of $10,327 million to its fellow belligerents, of which the $4,227 million owed by Britain was more than offset by the $6,753 million the Allies owed to Britain in return. But all the belligerents had suffered more or less serious economic damage from the war, and none of them were in a position to pay their wartime debts immediately, in cash, as the US bankers demanded. In New York, Britain was therefore held responsible for many of its former allies' debts.[12]

Between 1913 and 1919 the British national debt rose from just under £20 million to £270 million. During the 1920s interest on the debt amounted to over £300 million a year or about 40 per cent of government revenue, and it was still around 25 per cent in 1939. The price of preserving the pre-war sterling exchange rate was a tenfold increase in the national debt. German investors, by contrast, were wiped out by inflation, so that by 1928 the German national debt was 8.4 per cent of GNP, and the British, 178 per cent. The crisis of international finance came with the slump of 1929–31. Only the United States could have stopped it, but the American government had little control over economic policy, and an atomized banking system provided no defence against the collapse of demand, so that between 1929 and 1933 US GDP fell by one-third and unemployment rose to 25 per cent. In Germany, US loans under the 'Dawes Plan' initially financed the country's recovery from catastrophic inflation, but they tailed off in 1928. By 1932 unemployment had risen to 35 per cent and industrial production stood at 60 per cent of what it had been in 1929.[13]

During the Napoleonic Wars Britain had financed its allies' war effort very much as the United States did a hundred years later, but with the essential difference that the British had paid 'subsidies' to their allies, not loans. By 1815 the British national debt was 200 per cent of national income (worse than 1918), but by writing off the subsidies Britain cleared the immense cost of the war from the international financial system and allowed post-war reconstruction. The US government of 1919 was no friend of the financial establishment in New York ('the citadel of privilege . . . reactionary, sinister, unscrupulous, mercenary and sordid', in the revealing words of President Wilson's son-in-law and Treasury Secretary, William McAdoo).[14] The American government accepted no responsibility for the financial situation, and allowed the bankers to demand cash repayment which was effectively impossible. Combined with the demand for 'war reparations' from Germany, this inflexibility played a large part in paralysing the international financial system in the 1920s, damaged the reputation of the USA abroad, and crippled the post-war reconstruction of Europe. Whereas Britain in the nineteenth century had found its major investment opportunities overseas and exported capital all over the world, US bankers in the 1920s had ample opportunities to make big profits in the booming domestic economy and largely ignored the rest of the world. This allowed British firms to regain many overseas markets which had seemed lost to American competition during the war, but it prevented the circulation of American capital abroad. Nineteenth-century Britain had promoted free trade and world prosperity, but the interwar USA retreated into domestic protectionism which damaged world trade and indirectly promoted the rise of the dictators.[15] The heavy tariffs imposed by the 1930 Smoot–Hawley Act effectively made it impossible for Germany to pay the war reparations she owed, and pushed her to repudiating her foreign debts in 1933. In the same year the British government suspended repayments of war debt, and in response the 1934 Johnson Act took the United States a step further into isolation, forbidding foreign governments or individuals with unpaid US debts (Britain now included) from raising new US loans. The USA was now openly fearful of engaging with foreign investors and foreigners in general, and the Neutrality Acts of 1935–7 forbade US citizens to sell munitions to foreign belligerents or travel in foreign ships. US governments were largely prohibited from intervention in overseas affairs, but in 1937 Roosevelt was able to persuade Congress to permit non-arms exports to belligerents able to pay cash and transport the goods in their own ships – which could only mean Britain, for so long as she had cash.[16]

In Britain the Treasury's cautious management of huge wartime debts generated deflation and high unemployment but avoided inflation and social collapse. Unlike in the United States and Germany, the banks survived. Taxation remained heavy and progressive, and in the twenty years from 1918 to 1938 British public spending rose faster than in any other peacetime years of the twentieth century, from 12 per cent of GDP (including 4 per cent on defence) in 1913, to 26 per cent in 1937 (including 5 per cent on defence and 10½ per cent on social services). The turning point came with the Invergordon 'mutiny' in 1931. Being driven off the 'gold standard' (meaning the pre-war exchange rate of sterling against gold), which seemed to contemporaries to be a political and economic catastrophe, in fact opened the way for a cautious and skilful devaluation, leading to an expansion of money and credit which revived economic confidence. Deflationary economic policy had already led to falling interest rates, allowing the Treasury in 1932 to convert the 5 per cent War Loan to 3½ per cent, saving £72 million a year. British industrial output fell 20 per cent between 1929 and 1931, but in the 1930s there was a consumer boom, and by 1935 output had risen to 120 per cent of the 1929 figure. The new electrical distribution system, the 'National Grid', almost complete by the mid-1930s, halved the cost of electricity and boosted all sorts of light industry.[17]

In 1935, the year the DRC adopted the 'New Standard Fleet' later reckoned as requiring twenty battleships (instead of fifteen), the Treasury began to finance defence spending by loans as well as taxation, and next year it moved from annual Estimates to a rolling programme designed to encourage long-term contracts and investment, initially planned to fit a 'ration' of £1,500 million over five years. This is sometimes identified as the moment the British government first adopted 'Keynesian' economic principles (rather ahead of John Maynard Keynes himself, whose great work *The General Theory of Employment, Interest and Money* was not published until the following year). In the spring of 1938, the Treasury allowed the Admiralty a 'ration' of £410 million for 1939–42, which compared to an estimated cost of £395 million to build a one-power fleet, or £443 million for the New Standard Fleet. In practice the 'ration' gave the Admiralty enough to employ all its shipbuilding capacity up to 1942, with the notional possibility of an abrupt stop in orders after 1941 which it knew would be politically unacceptable in practice. By this time private firms with key contracts were in a strong position to ask for special help to avoid delays, and the Admiralty was ruthless in supporting its favourite contractors. In January 1937, for example, it pre-ordered twenty triple 6-inch gun turrets for the new *Fiji* Class light cruisers, 'forgetting' to obtain the approval of the Treasury Emergency Expenditure Committee. By the time the Treasury found out it was too late: 'We have to face the fact that the commitment is irrevocable and that there is nothing we can do.'[18] From 1938 there were almost no absolute financial limits, only different industries more or less well situated to spend money advantageously. With efficient internal cost accounting and determined leadership, the Admiralty did better at this than the War Office. As a result, a Director-General of Munitions Production was established in the War Office in 1936: Engineer Vice-Admiral Sir Harold Brown, the recently retired Engineer-in-Chief of the Navy. The Air Ministry did best of all, not because its cost controls were good, but because the Cabinet awarded it priority, and because it was building the new aircraft and aero-engine works of the 'shadow factories' scheme, owned by the Crown but managed under contract by private firms in related industries like car manufacture with access to their own pools of skilled labour. This provided a way of spending money in a non-inflationary way on new manufacturing capacity, flexible in purpose but available for armaments if necessary, thus preparing unobtrusively for re-armament with the least possible disruption of peacetime industry. It also tempted aircraft companies to expand by calming their fears of being bankrupted by a sudden cessation of government orders (as Sopwith had been in 1920). The Admiralty was well ahead of such a policy. Since 1925 it had been discreetly subsidizing key firms in naval shipbuilding and armaments, and by 1935 it had considerable spare capacity which it lacked skilled manpower to exploit. It could not solve its difficulties just by throwing money at the problem.[19]

Arguably the most effective joint-service policies were the least known, especially to the public. The Principal Supply Officers' Committee (PSOC) of 1924 was a notable example. This obscure but influential body, whose first chairman was the Scottish industrialist Lord Weir, gathered all parts of government which purchased supplies or equipment, and divided their spending among a flexible web of sub-committees collectively known as the Supply Board, in such a way that responsibility was shared and particular departments could no longer capture 'their' industries. This was achieved by private negotiation without compulsory powers, and avoided recreating the cumbersome industrial monolith of the wartime Ministry of Supply.[20] It also avoided drawing the attention of the public, still emotionally attracted to the idea that the 'merchants of death' had caused the Great War, to the extent to which the government was providing itself with the means to fight again. Only the Abyssinian crisis and the Defence White Paper of 1935 exposed the public to official alarm, and even that was expressed in cautious and general terms.[21]

One of the strategic supplies which most concerned the Supply Board was oil, which had become critically scarce during the submarine attacks of 1917.

In 1918 total Allied (not including US) oil consumption was 9.1 million tons, of which the Navy alone took 3.8 million tons. In 1912 Churchill as First Lord of the Admiralty had bought a controlling interest in the Anglo-Persian Oil Company in order to provide the Navy with fuel for the new oil-fired ships he was ordering, but the Persian Gulf was a very inconvenient area from which to draw oil except for campaigns in the Indian Ocean or the Far East, and the oil itself was too viscous to use unrefined outside hot climates. In 1921 a refinery entered service at Swansea which used the new 'cracking' process to break the Persian oil into its different fractions (from heavy fuel oil to light petrol), but the crude feedstock still had to be shipped from the Persian Gulf. In the post-war settlement Britain gained effective control of Iraq and its oilfields, which added supply but were no more accessible than Persian oil. If the Navy was to be free to operate anywhere, it had to have oil available wherever it went. In 1918 some 65 per cent of world oil supply came from the United States, 2 per cent from Persia, and 2 per cent from the British Empire. This represented a grave strategic vulnerability for the Navy, and the Admiralty wanted sufficient stocks to replicate at least some of the 'bunker control' it already exerted over coal-fired shipping. Hence in 1921 the Admiralty got Treasury approval for 3½ million tons of oil storage overseas, in addition to 4½ million tons at home already approved. This tankage was managed by the Oil Board, part of the Supply Board system.[22]

The PSOC and the Supply Board were discreet but official and legal. The secret Warship Builders' Committee set up in 1926 was an illegal cartel whose members shared bids and costs to maintain a price floor under Admiralty orders, which yielded them about 10 per cent profit even in the hardest years of the early 1930s. It was through their intervention that Cammell Laird was awarded the contract for the new carrier *Ark Royal*, although the firm was originally the highest bidder before the committee adjusted the figures. The Admiralty, and ultimately the taxpayer, were the victims of the cartel's activities, but the Admiralty fully shared the cartel's anxiety to keep as much warship-building capacity in existence as possible, and employed much the same methods itself, awarding non-competitive contracts to keep the expertise of key firms alive, and providing a variety of discreet subsidies to support specialist industrial skills. As the Director of Navy Contracts stated in March 1932, the Admiralty 'varie[s] the policy of inviting competitive tenders in the case of certain armament firms whose designing staff and productive capacity [it] is essential to maintain as a nucleus in an emergency. In such instances, it is customary to confine the orders to these firms on condition that fair prices are charged and that they can meet delivery requirements . . .' The few records of the Warship

Builders' Committee which have survived suggest that the Admiralty was at least partly aware of what was going on and preferred not to investigate.[23]

The National Shipbuilders' Security Scheme was set up in 1930, not directly by the government but by the Bank of England, to buy and 'sterilize' (i.e. destroy) shipyards. Between 1930 and 1939 it liquidated 212 berths with a capacity of 1¼ million tons, equivalent to 36 per cent of national shipbuilding capacity in 1930. This was legal and out in the open, but exceedingly controversial. Its object was to restore the profitability of shipbuilding by reducing excess shipbuilding capacity (warship-building included), and its moving spirit was Sir James Lithgow. Industrial relations on Clydeside were seldom amicable, but Lithgow was exceptionally hated among workmen who perfectly understood that 'sterilizing surplus capacity' was but a classical translation of 'throwing shipyard men out of work'. The Admiralty found itself on both sides in the bitter disputes between shipyards and trades unions. Lithgow was one of the ablest and most influential Scottish industrialists, a key ally of government in the era of the world wars, but his personal interest in reducing labour costs and increasing shipyard profitability ran counter to the naval and national interest in maintaining the maximum population of skilled shipyard labour, which was the essential determinant of shipbuilding output and productivity. Like other leaders of the Shipbuilding Employers' Federation, Lithgow was violently opposed to 'state aid or interference', but welcomed 'friendly support without strings attached'.[24] The distinction was a fine one, but perfectly clear on Clydeside: 'friendly support' was liable to leak straight into shipyard profits, whereas 'state aid' implied political control on the spending of public funds, and possibly even concern for the welfare of the shipyard workforce. Under the guidance of Lithgow and others, the Bank of England, acting through National Shipbuilders' Security (NSS), leant towards 'friendly support'. In July 1934, for example, it bought the Armstrong Walker yard on Tyneside for £125,000, not for 'sterilization' but 'care and maintenance'. At the same time the former Palmer's Yard at Hebburn was sold to Vickers. The net effect was that NSS lost £15,000 but Vickers disposed of a yard it did not want and gained another which it did covet, plus a profit of £40,000. Meanwhile the country preserved the core capacity of one of the leading warship-building yards, at a moment when only a few senior people in the Supply Board and NSS knew that the yard would shortly be in line to receive an order for the new battleship *King George V* and other warships. As a key member of the PSOC and the Warshipbuilders' Committee, Lithgow was now working in secret against a major objective of National Shipbuilders' Security, of which he himself was chairman and founder. He was spending the Bank of England's funds on maintaining instead of destroying warship-building capacity, while still 'steri-lizing' yards which built tramp shipping. Even so the NSS was far from having eliminated over-capacity in British shipbuilding. There were still about a hun-dred empty shipbuilding berths available in 1935, representing 750,000 tons capacity (which compares with actual construction of 80,000 tons in the period 1933–5). Yet in February 1936 Lithgow used his own firm's money to buy the redundant (but modern) Beardmore shipyard on the Clyde when he alone knew of its essential role in planned naval expansion. By late 1936 re-armament was gathering speed, and the Scottish industrialists Lithgow, Lord Weir and Sir Arthur Balfour (shortly to become Lord Riverdale), who made up the PSOC's 'Advisory Panel of Industrialists' created in October 1933, were deeply and profitably engaged in business to which their unpaid service on key com-mittees had given them early access. But it would be equally true to say that only they – Lithgow in particular – had been ready to hazard their fortunes on politically toxic re-armament well before there was any significant public support for it, or any government had the courage to tell the public the truth about the risks of war. Lithgow's official work gave him inside information highly relevant to his private interests, and he evidently did not feel that he couldn't profit from it – but he took a serious risk in committing to re-armament, and saved vital shipbuilding capacity which would otherwise have been destroyed.[25]

Public discourse in the 1930s was still preoccupied with peace and disarma-ment. The Geneva Disarmament Conference of 1932–3, the US Nye Commis-sion of 1934, and the 1935–6 Royal Commission on the Manufacture and Trade in Armaments, all expressed and promoted the widespread popular belief that arms manufacturers encouraged wars. In November 1937 some 62 per cent of British men declared to a public opinion survey that they would not volunteer to fight, and 78 per cent of women would not urge their husbands to do so. Even after the Munich crisis next year, 75 per cent of the British population still approved of appeasement, 60 per cent were happy with Neville Chamber-lain as Prime Minister, and only 4 per cent preferred Churchill. British gov-ernment policy, by contrast, was increasingly centred on re-armament from the 1933 DRC report, and therefore involved discreet co-operation with the 'merchants of death'. Re-armament was managed by Treasury civil servants led by the Second Secretary Sir Richard Hopkins, whose aim until 1938 was to achieve maximum weapons production without impinging on the peacetime economy in ways the public would notice. From 1932 to 1935 defence spending remained steady at 3 per cent of GNP, while over the same period German defence spending rose from 1 per cent to 8 per cent of GNP. In 1934 the

Cabinet cut back the DRC's recommended spending on urgent deficiencies partly in order to honour its public promises to restore pre-1931 rates of naval pay. Then between 1936 and 1940 British defence spending rose from 4 per cent of GNP to 46 per cent, by which time it had substantially overtaken German defence expenditure at 38 per cent.[26]

The Treasury's function, as Warren Fisher the Permanent Secretary understood it, was to act as a 'candid friend' rather than an 'abominable no-man', sharpening proposals and allocating priorities by asking tough questions. He was overworked, neurotic, perhaps 'rather mad' as Hankey suggested, but under his leadership the Treasury was pushing re-armament faster than the Service departments found comfortable.[27] As the economy recovered from the slump of the early 1930s, the government was anxious not to 'crowd out' industry producing for the civilian market, nor to generate inflation by ordering more weapons than industry could supply, nor yet to strain the balance of payments (one sixth of re-armament costs being in foreign exchange) – but 'the feeling is imparted from the files that the Treasury wanted to be convinced by the Admiralty's arguments, within the borders of credulity and overall defence policy'.[28] It wanted rearmament and deterrence, but not at the price of a financial crash which would wreck both. Financial control was the key instrument of both policy and politics, the means by which Neville Chamberlain, as Chancellor of the Exchequer from 1931 to 1937, and then Prime Minister, dominated the government. Sir John Simon, Chamberlain's successor as Chancellor, was feeble and vacillating. Hopkins had to attend the Cabinet in 1939 to explain the finances of re-armament which his minister did not understand.[29]

By 1933 the relationship of the Air Force to the other services, and to government as a whole, was a running sore which broke out in a series of crises. The Air Staff was visibly determined to keep the Fleet Air Arm as small and obsolete as possible. In 1934 the Under-Secretary for Air wrote to the First Lord objecting to the Admiralty's intention to build a new aircraft carrier (the future *Ark Royal*) and claiming a right of veto over the Admiralty's decision. This was not a private disagreement between two senior officials, but an open assault on a prominent part of the government's defence policy, which had already been approved by the Cabinet. Sir Warren Fisher, as *ex officio* head of the Civil Service, abhorred inter-departmental rivalry and expected senior civil servants to co-operate cordially with one another in the national interest. He was not amused by the tone of the Air Ministry's correspondence:

> The style and type of letters identify Sir Christopher Bullock [the Permanent Secretary] with this business; he is a very clever young man, but most

argumentative and singularly gifted in rubbing people up the wrong way; he never knows when to stop nor the limits of his own or other people's affairs (I am very disappointed in the absence of any sign of his maturing or mellowing).[30]

Bullock was ambitious and pugnacious; he fed the Parliamentary Opposition with speeches and papers attacking the government he was supposed to serve and negotiated privately with Imperial Airways (a company effectively controlled by his ministry) to obtain honours and financial advantages for himself. He was warned of the consequences of such outrageous conduct and apologized in writing, but he did not change his ways. Finally in August 1936 he was summarily dismissed without pension by the Prime Minister; a unique fate for a British civil servant of his rank.[31]

Between 1934 and 1936, while the Bullock affair developed in the background, the Air Ministry and the Admiralty were involved in important decisions concerning national defence. It is clear in retrospect, and seems to have been clear enough at the time to those in the know, that the already blemished reputation of the Air Ministry was sliding fast. In April 1934 a Cabinet Sub-Committee (taking Hitler's boasts for truth) considered how to regain 'air parity' with Germany. Its members included the Colonial Secretary Sir Philip Cunliffe-Lister, now also chairman of the CID Committee on Air Defence and in effect air minister in waiting. Another member was the ubiquitous Lord Weir, who had been much involved with the foundation of the RAF and agreed to help on the explicit condition that the Fleet Air Arm question was not to be revived. Lord Londonderry, the official Secretary of State for Air from 1931 to 1935, was conspicuously omitted from the committee; by common consent he lacked the judgement needed for high office and was often left out of the most delicate policy discussions.[32] His department impressed even less. 'Since Hugh Trenchard [retired 1929] we have had no Chief of the Air Staff (except in name),' declared Warren Fisher in 1939.[33] Neville Chamberlain's private secretary complained that it was 'lamentable that we cannot have men of the highest calibre at the head of the Air Ministry and the Air Force', referring to Bullock and Sir Edward Ellington, the Chief of the Air Staff.[34] Ellington was an ineffectual and inarticulate leader who had never flown on operations, while his successor Sir Cyril Newall was condemned by his own officers as 'a weak link in the nation's defences'.[35]

In June 1935 Cunliffe-Lister took over as Air Minister, at the same time taking a peerage as Viscount Swinton. In March 1936 Baldwin took a half-step in the direction of a minister of defence by appointing the lawyer and MP Sir

Thomas Inskip as 'Minister for the Co-ordination of Defence'. Inskip was known as an efficient and discreet conciliator, but with no department of his own he had only his personal talents to back him. His first task was to chair a committee assessing the vulnerability of capital ships to air attack. On this occasion the Air Ministry refused the Admiralty's request to develop a dive-bombing sight, presumably lest their claims of the accuracy of bombing be put to the test.[36]

Presently the First Lord (now Lord Monsell) asked Inskip to look at the training of Fleet Air Arm pilots. His report in November 1936 hinted at broader disquiet and seemed to glance at the (officially closed) question of responsibility for naval aviation. Next month Inskip proposed a wider inquiry to Baldwin the Prime Minister, but Swinton was not told what was afoot. By this stage a majority of Cabinet ministers had evidently lost all patience with the chaotic and leaderless Air Ministry. In different but equally discreditable circumstances it shed its minister, its permanent secretary and two chiefs of staff in less than five years; now Swinton too was on the verge of a nervous breakdown, and the formidable First Sea Lord Chatfield was closing in. He told Baldwin that 'unless an immediate enquiry is held I shall lose the confidence of the service':[37] an undisguised threat of resignation, made in the knowledge that his possible reliefs Sir William Fisher and Sir Roger Backhouse (to say nothing of the press and the public) were behind him. Warren Fisher was now pressing for an immediate decision to hand over the Fleet Air Arm without waiting for detailed costing:

> The controversy . . . is a canker in the proper relationship of these two military Services, and had [Ellington] the present Chief of Air Staff been anything more than a routine officer, he would have recognised that the Navy have a case . . . [A] good relationship between the two Services is a national interest and generosity of attitude is . . . a greater contribution than petty parochialism.[38]

In February 1937, with Swinton on sick leave and still unaware of what was going on, Baldwin asked Inskip to reopen the Fleet Air Arm question. With a speed which strongly suggests that everything had been decided beforehand, without even pretending to wait for evidence from the Air Ministry, Inskip proceeded to recommend the transfer of the Fleet Air Arm to the Navy: 'a more natural order than the present system'. With difficulty Lord Weir was persuaded not to resign.[39]

The transfer of the Fleet Air Arm, announced in July 1937, was almost as great a shock to the Admiralty as to the Air Ministry. The pressure for change had come from the aircrew, not the admirals: the Naval Staff had never expected to regain control of its air service. Sir Archibald Carter, the new Secretary of the Admiralty, 'does not appear to have been a man of Murray's character and intellect', and nothing was prepared.[40] The reorganization of the Fleet Air Arm was a hasty improvisation with many responsibilities left in the Air Ministry's hands. Inskip did not adopt the Admiralty's proposal to take over the RAF's 'Coastal Area', reuniting sea and land-based naval aircraft, knowing that this would have taken much time and created conflict, and required legislation for the compulsory transfer of RAF personnel. The risk of war was rising fast, a workable system was urgently needed, and from the Admiralty's perspective the transfer of the Air Ministry's industrial responsibilities to the new Ministry of Aircraft Production in May 1940 at first seemed a promising development. In any case the Admiralty was clear that the basic essential was not a particular organization but a harmonious relationship with the Air Ministry, to gain which would be worth sacrificing a good deal. In the event the new Fleet Air Arm came three years too late to make an efficient contribution to the war effort, and the new Minister of Aircraft Production, Lord Beaverbrook, plunged the British aircraft industry into disorder just in time to disrupt the design and production of naval aircraft for the rest of the war. When the Fleet Arm was formally transferred in May 1939 it had only 885 aircraft (many of them useless) to meet a modest requirement of 1,400, and 2,600 personnel instead of 4,530. But against all reasonable hopes, the Fleet Air Arm became a scene of reconciliation between the Admiralty and the Air Ministry. The Air Staff must have realized how much damage their tactics had caused, to their own reputation and the national interest, and from 1937 they co-operated loyally with the process of transfer. Finally in October 1940 the appointment of Air Marshal Sir Charles Portal as Chief of the Air Staff gave the RAF, for the first time in its history, a leader of high intelligence and acute political instincts – and one whose brother Captain Reginald Portal was a senior naval airman, and later a member of the Admiralty Board as ACNS (Air) 1943–4.[41]

The Air Staff's disdain for the Fleet Air Arm and its duties applied at least equally to the RAF squadrons assigned to the 'Coastal Area' and responsible for over-water patrolling. The Air Staff repeatedly refused to develop aircraft or equipment for torpedo- or dive-bombing, or to use bomber aircraft for maritime patrol. In 1936 it was planning to fit Coastal Area's reconnaissance aircraft with engines unsuitable for the role without telling the Admiralty, which suggests that senior RAF officers contemplated a disloyal if not actually criminal act of sabotage. They certainly favoured manufacturers' profits over the national interest. A considerable list of different aircraft were actually introduced into service with Coastal Area (from 1936 Coastal Command) during the 1930s, which had failed on trials or were known to be useless before they were ordered. The standard maritime patrol aircraft from 1935 to 1942, the Avro Anson, had a radius of action (300 miles) and a payload (360lbs) markedly inferior to its 1918 predecessor the Blackburn Kangaroo. No Coastal Command aircraft could match the performance of the Kangaroo until the arrival of the American Lockheed Hudson in 1940. In the opening months of the war the gross inadequacy of shore-based reconnaissance and anti-submarine aircraft forced the Admiralty to risk deploying aircraft carriers in coastal waters, leading to the sinking of the *Courageous* in September 1939 by a German submarine.[42]

From 1934 to 1938 the Cabinet gave the RAF the first priority over the other two services but insisted that the money go to fighters and anti-aircraft guns, not the bombers the Air Staff preferred. This decision was informed by good technical advice, much of it coming from airmen not in thrall to the Air Staff line. Air Chief Marshal Sir Edgar Ludlow-Hewitt, who took command of Bomber Command in September 1937, bluntly declared it to be completely unprepared for war and unable to fly safely in peacetime. Even the Air Staff privately agreed: 'The Metropolitan Air Force in general, and the Bomber Command in particular, are at present almost totally unfitted for war.'[43] Without coherent strategy, tactics, doctrine or experience; with no planning, no operational research and scant intelligence, the Air Staff found it 'exceedingly difficult and profoundly distressing'[44] to prepare for war as the Cabinet and the other Services demanded. Cabinet ministers may not have been technical experts, but many of them were shrewd and experienced politicians with forensic skills learnt in Parliament and the courts. They recognized weak men and weak arguments when they met them. The consequence was that for much of the 1930s the Cabinet devoted the largest share of defence spending to a service whose contribution it regarded as vital, but in whose leadership it had no confidence whatever.[45]

The US declaration of war in April 1917 had been partly provoked by the exposure of a secret telegram from Arthur Zimmerman, the German Foreign Minister, tempting Mexico to declare war on the United States. Although the public did not then know it, the Zimmerman Telegram had been decyphered by 'Room 40', and after the war the indiscreet memoirs of Sir John Fisher and Winston Churchill among others made the world aware of an exciting dimension of cryptography which added to the existing public interest in secret agents. Wartime cryptography in Britain had been largely conducted by the Admiralty, but in 1919 'Room 40' (NID 25 to give it its new title as part of the

388 · THE NAVAL FABRIC

Naval Intelligence Division) was put under Foreign Office control on the grounds that it was now mainly concerned with diplomatic communications, though it remained physically in the Admiralty until 1921; until his death in 1939 its head was the former Director of Naval Intelligence, Rear-Admiral Hugh Sinclair. Known publicly as the 'Government Code & Cypher School' (GC&CS), it was a department of the (officially non-existent) Secret Intelligence Service, but its working head, Commander Alastair Denniston, and other senior figures had come from NID 25. This was a large organization, in the 1930s equal to a fifth or a quarter of the Foreign Office or the Treasury. It received daily sacks of telegrams from the cable companies, to be copied and returned in twenty-four hours. Thanks to its cryptographic resources British representatives at the interwar naval conferences benefited from reading the telegrams of many foreign countries, but this asset declined as careless security revealed too much. Until the first Labour government of 1924 much raw intelligence was circulated to the Cabinet, and in 1927 Baldwin betrayed an important source by reading to the House of Commons verbatim telegrams from the Russian Foreign Minister. By the 1930s only the sleepier foreign powers were unaware of the danger. Moreover, British cyphers were far from invulnerable, and the publicity given to cryptography distracted attention both from old-fashioned insecurities such as embassy servants (about whom the Foreign Office ignored repeated warnings), and from modern technologies such as aerial photography (which the RAF abandoned).[46]

Cryptography concerned both cables and wireless, and both technologies were developing fast in the interwar years. From 1923 the new 'loaded' cables with automatic repeaters could transmit much faster than manual transmission and reception, so the cable companies introduced multiplexing, with up to eight channels carried simultaneously on a single cable. The following year Marconi introduced short-wave wireless, using low-power high-frequency directional signals reflected off the ionosphere. Existing long-wave wireless depended on a small number of costly stations with tall masts, broadcasting high-power messages in Morse code. Now, suddenly, the new short-wave voice 'radio' put cheap worldwide communications within reach of a mass public. This was a social and military revolution. Soon every home could listen to news and music programmes from across the world, every schoolboy could learn to build a set, and even the smallest ships could receive and transmit long-range signals. Unlike the old naval world of fixed telegraph communications, naval warfare in the short-wave era was infinitely flexible and complex, rewarding initiative and demanding investment in signals intelligence. The new short-wave technology threatened to bankrupt the old wireless companies, starting with Marconi's own firm, faced with the competition of the Post Office short-wave radio stations. In this crisis Marconi called in his political debts and merged his firm with the Pender telegraph interests to form a new company called Cable & Wireless, combining medium-wave and short-wave wireless with Eastern Telegraph's international cable network in a system subsidized by the profitable short-wave stations. The Admiralty still had the Post Office 500 kilowatt long-wave wireless transmitter at Rugby in Warwickshire, capable of signalling to the whole Navy anywhere in the world, including submerged submarines in the Mediterranean and Eastern Atlantic. Although parts of the system were reduced to 'care and maintenance' in the 1930s, Britain had preserved the core of its worldwide communication systems. The US Navy tried to achieve something similar but moved too soon, before the significance of short-wave became clear, and failed to get access to the supplies of gutta percha necessary for a cable industry. As a result, Britain still possessed the only secure worldwide communication system at the outbreak of the Second World War – though events were to prove that it was not as secure as had been hoped.[47]

The Germans adopted the Enigma commercial cypher machine to serve a standard short-wave radio system connecting all three services and most departments of government, including the railways. The German Navy had the best training and cypher security of the German services, and the Luftwaffe the worst, but naval operations so frequently involved aircraft that Luftwaffe signals often yielded essential naval information. The *Beobachtungsdienst* (*B-Dienst*) or 'Reporting Service', the German Navy's wireless intelligence organization, had a staff of three in 1929, and over 500 ten years later. German military signalling attracted the attention of the Polish secret service, which created a secret cryptographic unit staffed by advanced mathematicians who developed basic decyphering machines referred to as 'bombes'.[48] All this was passed to France and Britain in 1939, giving GC&CS invaluable help in decyphering Enigma signals.[49]

Code and cypher machines went back to the beginning of the twentieth century, and by the 1930s products like the Enigma and the similar Swedish Hagelin machine were sold to governments, armed forces and private companies in many countries. The Hagelin machine in turn became the basis of standard equipment in both the United States and Japan. A GC&CS committee in 1929 investigated cypher machines but was not satisfied with their security and regarded 'long subtractor' book cyphers as safer for the low signal volumes then anticipated. The first important British cypher machine was a private venture by Wing Commander O. G. Lywood, RAF, approved by

GC&CS in 1935. Known as 'Typex',[50] the first model was an on-line cypher teleprinter adapted from Enigma technology. Later versions were portable off-line machines like the original Enigma. By 1939 the security of Typex was better than that of Enigma, and improving continually as the British learnt more about the weaknesses of the German design. Typex Mk.I provided the British with secure strategic communications, and all three services adopted Typex Mk.II for tactical signalling, but the only manufacturer of Typex machines had quite insufficient capacity to meet the demand. In October 1939 the Navy ordered 630 Typex Mk.II machines; more than the other services but still sufficient only for shore headquarters and some flagships. Even in May 1944, when total production amounted to 5,016 machines for all users, this was still 4,000 short of the desired number. Total Typex production during the war was about 12,000, compared with over 40,000 German Enigma machines. Typex was an excellent machine, fast and secure, but there were never enough of them to replace the older book cyphers afloat. British super-encypherment was steadily improved, but until the full adoption of 'stencil subtractor frames' in June 1943 significant vulnerabilities remained in medium- and low-level operational cyphers.[51]

British naval intelligence took an interest in the whole world, but naturally concentrated on likely enemies. Of these Japan tended to occupy a class apart because of the difficulty of the language. From the 1920s the Navy devoted significant efforts to signals intelligence in the Far East, partly because it was difficult to establish other intelligence sources in a country in which Westerners were few and conspicuous. In 1921 a South Pacific direction-finding network was founded, and the same year the Royal Australian Navy made a first attempt to train telegraphists to read Morse code in Japanese *kana* characters. Ships and units in the Far East collected intercepts of Japanese signals to pass to GC&CS, whose specialist in the subject was the borrowed RAN officer Paymaster Lieutenant-Commander Eric Nave. In the 1930s British submarines (secretly refuelled at sea by steamers of the Glen Line) paid clandestine visits to Japanese naval anchorages to observe and photograph. In 1935 a joint-service (but predominantly naval) intelligence organization, the Far East Combined Bureau, was established at Hong Kong and made rapid progress against Japanese naval cyphers. The Japanese were convinced that their language was impregnable to foreigners, and at this time their signals procedure was very careless. In 1926 the published official reports of the death of the Emperor Yoshihito and the succession of Hirohito were signalled verbatim to overseas ships and garrisons in every code currently in use, exposing each in turn to anyone who could read a Japanese newspaper. In 1934 GC&CS broke into the product of the new Japanese diplomatic cypher machine, and the following year the Metropolitan Police built them a decypher machine. In November 1938 John Tiltman of GC&CS broke the Japanese Navy's new General Operational Code.[52] All this material yielded unequivocal evidence of Japanese aggressive plans, and in August 1939 the Far East Combined Bureau moved from Hong Kong to the less-vulnerable (but less well-situated) Singapore.[53] Japanese signals also exposed some Japanese spies, notably the former RNAS and RAF officer Frederick Rutland, an expert in carrier design who took part in the RAF Sempill Mission to Japan in 1921–2 and reported regularly to Japan thereafter. In 1933 he established himself in the United States to set up a Japanese spy ring there. He was already under regular surveillance by MI6, and the US authorities were warned, but he was not arrested until he returned to Britain in 1941. 'The Master of Sempill' (later Lord Sempill) who led the RAF mission was one of a notable group of interwar Fascist sympathizers in or close to the RAF, and himself acted as a Japanese spy from 1922 to 1926.[54]

Other countries developed other methods of acquiring foreign codes. The United States robbed Japanese consulates. The Germans tapped international telephone lines. Italian military intelligence specialized in burgling embassy safes (British embassies being particularly insecure). The Italian Navy, however, concentrated on wireless cryptography with considerable success. As so often it was careless procedures rather than technical deficiencies which allowed enemies to break into coded signals, and the Italians had no monopoly on carelessness. During the Spanish Civil War patient British study had made good progress against the Italian fleet cypher SM16S (called 'ZIG' by GC&CS), when in 1937 the Russians exposed the 'unidentified' Fascist submarines by publishing their signals – so the now-useless cypher ZIG was replaced by the impenetrable ZOG. Further leaks led to another version (ZAG), which was replaced in January 1940 by yet another, named 'Gabriella' by the British, which in June was recovered by divers from the sunken submarine *Uebi Scebelli*. With it was the new fleet cypher SM 19 S ('Stella'), which helped the Mediterranean Fleet to intercept the Italian fleet at Punta Stilo on 9 July 1940. Less than a week later, however, the Italians decrypted a British signal containing an unparaphrased quotation from a Stella signal, which of course gave the game away. The Italians issued new super-encyphers at once, after which the British never again read the Italian main fleet cypher. As a result of this fiasco the Mediterranean Fleet was forced to hand over all serious cryptography to GC&CS and confine itself to low-grade tactical traffic. Early in August 1940, however, the submarines *Pandora* and *Proteus* succeeded in cutting the Italian cable from Syracuse to Tripoli, leaving signals to Italy's North

African Empire dependent on the limited capacity of the 1912 cable between Syracuse and Benghazi. This forced the Italian naval headquarters in Rome, the *Comando Supremo della Marina* (nicknamed the *Supermarina* from its telegraphic address), to buy Swedish Hagelin C38 cypher machines to signal much of their traffic by wireless.[55]

In peace as in war, the Admiralty was an operational headquarters as well as an administrative and policy-forming organization, so the Abyssinian crisis of 1935, closely followed by the outbreak of the Spanish Civil War the following year, drew attention to its operational functions. Vice-Admiral Sir William James, Deputy Chief of the Naval Staff from 1935 and formerly head of 'Room 40', pushed hard for a new and better organization to collect, analyse and distribute operational intelligence to the Navy. The germ of the Operational Intelligence Centre (OIC) was formed in 1937 under Paymaster Lieutenant-Commander Norman Denning with a staff composed of himself and three Admiralty clerks, who first practised tracking clandestine Italian submarines in the Mediterranean under James's close supervision. From the start the OIC combined naval intelligence from all sources, including GC&CS, and James established the essential principle that GC&CS submitted complete signals to the naval experts, decyphered, translated, but not paraphrased. The Operational Intelligence Centre, as part of NID, the senior division of the Naval Staff, was the interpretative authority. Although it was not itself an operational command and could not issue orders, during the Munich crisis of 1938 it was given permission to signal intelligence directly to ships and commands, which in practice made it an essential link in the command structure. In March 1939 the new Director of Naval Intelligence, Rear-Admiral John Godfrey, appointed Captain (retired Rear-Admiral) Jock Clayton, another survivor of Room 40, as Director of the OIC, giving it almost equivalent standing to a division of the Naval Staff. The Norwegian campaign tested the new structure. The loss of the carrier *Glorious* in particular shocked the Naval Staff, which had received a warning but failed to pass it to the Home Fleet. The Naval Staff immediately invited GC&CS's expert on German naval signals, the twenty-year-old Cambridge undergraduate F. H. Hinsley, to spend a month in the Admiralty with several visits to the Home Fleet at Scapa Flow to explain his work, and it installed scrambler telephones to maintain close contact between the cryptographers and the Naval Staff in future. The senior officers in the Naval Staff did not underrate their own professional skill, and bestowing so much trust on a young civilian with almost no naval knowledge was a mark of an astonishing change of heart. Hinsley (and therefore GC&CS) had been accepted as a trusted collaborator of the OIC. The OIC was an important influence on the development of GC&CS in the early years of the war, from a series of separate service units sharing a common site, into an integrated, joint-service intelligence organization.[56]

The British, who had been the first to profit from wireless intelligence at the beginning of the century, were still alert to its importance in the interwar years, but do not seem to have fully appreciated how completely short-wave was transforming the wireless world. In 1927 the services expected a total wartime requirement from all services to transmit up to 110,000 code groups a day to and from overseas stations. In reality the army wireless link to Cairo alone was carrying 62,000 groups a day by November 1942, the War Office and Air Ministry alone were each transmitting well over a million groups a day between 1943 and 1945, and as we shall see there were many opportunities for enemies to take advantage of them.[57]

TWENTY-THREE

A Certain Eventuality

Policy and Operations 1940

B y the early winter of 1939, the British and French on one side, and the Germans on the other, were faced with awkward choices of where and how to prosecute the war in which they found themselves. In the twenty years of peace the German Navy had given much thought to escaping the prison of the North Sea in which they had been trapped in the previous war. The German army dismissed the navy's hopes of pushing westwards to the Atlantic coast of France, but an alternative scheme, not calling for the defeat of the major military power of western Europe, was to strike northward to use Norway as a stepping-stone to the open ocean. From this idea developed a plan to seize Denmark and Norway in quick succession.[1] Such an action, under the nose of the Royal Navy, 'violates all principles of naval war', as Admiral Raeder admitted: it would obviously be necessary to move fast and accept big risks.[2] Norway had recovered her long-lost independence in 1905 after more than five hundred years of Danish and then Swedish rule. Her territory extends for over a thousand miles north to south, but in places only a few miles from west to east, almost bisected by deep fjords. Most of the population and the two major cities of Oslo and Bergen lie in the south; in 1940 there were few main roads or railways north of Bergen and almost none north of Trondheim; what overland connections to the north existed ran through Swedish territory, and most traffic went by sea. The bulk (or rather, length) of the country could only be conquered by seizing the west coast seaports from the seaward – a perilous proposition for the Germans, who reckoned that 'British superiority in all types [of ship] was so extraordinarily great that the entire navy might be lost in this one operation.'[3]

At the same time the British were becoming aware that blockade would not work automatically for them and making their own plans to act in Scandinavia. The Soviet Union, now a public ally of Germany, had joined in the invasion of Poland and was threatening Finland and the Baltic states with territorial demands which made it likely that British help would soon be required. On 30 November 1939, 450,000 Soviet troops with over 1,000 tanks attacked Finland. Massively outnumbered, the Finns fought back with great skill and determination. Churchill was alert to the significance of German reliance on the Kiruna–Gällivare iron mines in Swedish Lapland, whose ores were carried by railway, either to the Baltic port of Luleå and thence southward by sea, or in winter when the Gulf of Bothnia froze, westward to the Atlantic port of Narvik and so southward down the Norwegian coast through the inshore channels called the Leads. Stopping the ships carrying high-grade iron ore to German blast furnaces would be a very desirable by-product of action to support the Finns' resistance to Soviet aggression. The difficulty was to find a means of cutting off a trade which was economically essential to both Norway and Sweden without making enemies of them, and incidentally destroying any hope of conveying help to the beleaguered Finns.[4] While the British government pondered this dilemma, the German and Norwegian governments watched intently. Then in February 1940, the German naval oiler *Altmark* entered Norwegian waters, homeward-bound from the South Atlantic where she had supplied the *Graf Spee*, and (as the British suspected) carrying many British merchant seamen whose ships the *Graf Spee* had sunk. Under international law it was a neutral state's duty to set these civilian prisoners free, but the Norwegian government was desperate not to provoke German hostility, and pretended to be unaware of them. With the agreement of Lord Halifax the Foreign Secretary, Churchill ordered the *Altmark* to be stopped. On the night of 16 February, in Jøssing Fjord near the southern tip of Norway, she was boarded by the destroyer *Cossack* and three hundred prisoners were liberated. In Britain the incident was received as a popular triumph – but the Norwegians were right to be frightened of the consequences, for this penetration of Norwegian territorial waters, clearly ordered from London, was just the evidence which Raeder wanted to convince Hitler that Norway was effectively under British control, and blocked German access to the open Atlantic. German planning for an invasion had already begun; on 21 February a commanding general was named. Meanwhile the evidence that German warships were using Norwegian waters as their own encouraged British preparations to mine the Leads, while on 12 March the Finns were forced to sign an armistice.[5]

Both British and German governments were now preparing to intervene in Norway, and each was aware that the other was planning something. By early April British warships were ready to lay declared minefields (not all of them real) to block the Leads, and German troops were ready to embark for Norwegian west-coast ports. The British operations were set for 8 April, while the German

'Weser Day', the launch of Operation *Weserübung*, was 9 April. Two major, over-lapping operations were starting, covering much of the North Sea, involving many British warships and virtually the whole German Navy besides many troop transports. Moreover, a violent gale was now blowing up. The German plan was to seize Denmark overnight before the Danish government could react, which worked exactly as intended. With a capital city only a few hours' drive from an open frontier, the Danes had no time even to declare war. The next stage of the operation was to serve the Norwegians the same way, but here geography was not so favourable. The German Navy planned simultaneous seaborne attacks on Oslo, Kristiansand and Egersund in southern Norway, Bergen and Trondheim on the west coast, and Narvik in the north. At the same time the Luftwaffe would seize by airborne assault Fornebu airfield outside Oslo, and Sola airfield near Stavanger on the west coast. In order for all the assaults to go in at dawn on 9 April, ships had to sail from 3 April onwards. Every available German warship was needed, including some which were far from ready for war, and subsequent supplies and reinforcements would have to sail unescorted.[6]

Even before 'Weser Day', things began to go wrong. On 8 April the Polish submarine *Orzeł* sank the German transport *Rio de Janeiro* in the Skagerrak. Many survivors were landed in Norway, soldiers in German combat gear who admitted that they were on their way to attack Bergen, but the Norwegian government did not react publicly. Since 1937 Norwegian defence spending and readiness had increased quite rapidly, but no one in the government thought Norway could resist a German invasion alone, and the assumption was that Britain must swiftly be drawn in. Until then it was essential not to give the Germans an excuse to strike by any premature mobilization. Although most of the Norwegian ports had at least some seaward defences dating from the age of Swedish rule before 1905, many were unmanned, and their command-ing officers had received no warnings or orders. The Drøbak Narrows below Oslo were defended by three old 28-cm (11-inch) guns and a torpedo battery, commanded by the sixty-five-year-old Colonel Birger Eriksen. The Germans knew of the defences, but evidently did not take them seriously. The squadron was led up the fjord by the flagship, the new heavy cruiser *Blücher*, just com-missioned, not worked up, but crowded with embarked troops and passengers. Her magazines were full of practice shell with live ammunition stowed anyhow on top. She had not raised steam for full speed and was unable to escape when the heavy guns fired, followed immediately by two 50-cm (21-inch) torpedoes. There had been no exercise of fire-fighting, damage control or abandoning ship, all three of which were immediately needed. Stopped and burning uncon-trollably, the *Blücher* capsized and sank.[7]

Colonel Eriksen had fired without orders, but his initiative probably saved Norwegian independence, for the sinking of the *Blücher* delayed the German capture of Oslo just long enough to allow the king and government to escape northwards. All the other ports of southern and central Norway fell into German hands with little or no fighting. The naval battle for southern Norway was certainly hopeless once the Luftwaffe had captured Fornebu and Sola, especially as the unit concerned was *Fliegerkorps X*, commanded by the former naval officer Lieutenant-General Hans Geisler, which included the only German specialist anti-shipping squadrons. The British troops who had been held ready aboard cruisers during the minelaying operation to oppose a German counter-stroke, were landed on 7 April shortly before a different but more urgent need for a counter-attack presented itself. This decision is sometimes decried as a serious strategic error, and blamed on Churchill, though it appears to have been taken by Sir Dudley Pound the First Sea Lord, and probably made little difference.[8] Just possibly these troops might have been able to seize and hold the key port of Trondheim without air cover, but they would have been well within range of German aircraft at Sola and well out of range of any airfield in Britain. The British in any case did not attempt to capture Trondheim or Bergen from the Germans by direct assault, but instead landed at Namsos to the north of Trondheim, and Åndalsnes to the south, both on branch lines to Trondheim, up which the British troops intended to advance. The ill-equipped and ill-trained Territorial units did not make good progress (nor a good impression on the Norwegian army), and the arrival of fresh German troops from the south soon ended any prospect of taking Trondheim. At sea the collision of British and German ships generated considerable confusion. British officers were alert to the risk of German warships breaking out into the Atlantic to attack British shipping and were ready to interpret sighting reports of enemy warships in that sense. Although the Admiralty knew that the Germans were taking a close interest in Norway, it took much persuading that the German Navy was ready to run the enormous risk of a full-scale invasion with so little to gain. Confusion was deepened by Admiralty signals interfering without explanation in the responsibilities of flag officers at sea.[9]

Very early on the morning of 9 April, west of the Lofoten Islands, the *Scharnhorst* and *Gneisenau*, covering the German landings, met the old (but modernized) battle-cruiser *Renown*, covering the British minelaying, in a violent gale which caused all three ships real difficulty. The Germans were poor seaboats; *Scharnhorst* had both her forward turrets flooded by heavy seas, *Gneisenau* was hit twice, and they were glad to get clear of the *Renown*. Next day, 10 April, the morning weather over Bergen was fine and an air strike by Fleet Air Arm Skua dive-bombers from Hatston in the Orkneys sank the light cruiser *Königsberg* alongside her quay. This was the first ever sinking of any armoured ship by air attack, or by dive-bombing, and at 480 nautical miles there and back it was at extreme range for single-engined aircraft, but the circumstances were particularly favourable. There were no German fighters present, the target was stationary, her anti-aircraft guns were soon silenced by loss of electric power, and the attackers were able to bomb almost undisturbed.[10] Further successful Skua attacks followed in April and May. But for most of the Norwegian campaign the Germans had strong air superiority, with over 500 aircraft available by the end of April, the Norwegian Army Air Corps had only a few light aircraft, and almost the whole country except Bergen was out of range of British airfields. British carriers ferried some aircraft across the North Sea, but the RAF (the 'least mobile of all the services' as Churchill lamented)[11] normally required a month's notice and a railway siding to set up an airfield, and they were not operational for long. The French *Chasseurs Alpins*, supposedly expert in Arctic warfare, turned out to be baffled by the wrong kind of snow, and had left their ski bindings behind. Once the Germans, and in particular the Luftwaffe, were established ashore, it seems unlikely that they could have been dislodged, but the humiliating incompetence of the Anglo-French force was a cruel disappointment to the Norwegians.[12]

Only in the far north did the campaign go better for the Norwegians and their allies, at least for a time. The main German landing force, two thousand Austrian mountain troops, was embarked aboard nine destroyers under Commodore Friedrich Bonte, which entered the Ofotfjord leading up to Narvik in heavy snow early on the morning of 9 April. Both the elderly coast-defence ships guarding the harbour were sunk and the Germans were able to seize the port with little further opposition. After their voyage of almost a thousand miles from Germany they were very low on fuel, but only one of the tankers which were supposed to be waiting for them was there. All the field guns that the destroyers had embarked had been washed overboard during the gale. Bonte knew that British warships were nearby but took few precautions. The Admiralty knew that Vice-Admiral William Whitworth with the battle-cruisers *Renown* and *Repulse* was the senior officer on the spot, but they commandeered five of his destroyers and ordered them up the Ofotfjord without consultation. Captain Bernard Warburton-Lee had been warned by the Norwegian pilots that six German destroyers 'larger than yours' and a U-boat had already gone up the fjord, but did not feel able to query a direct order from the Admiralty. The result was a confused fight at short range in heavy snow, with two destroyers sunk on each side (plus a German ammunition ship which arrived in the middle of the fight). At the end of the action only two German destroyers were still seaworthy.[13]

On 13 April Admiral Whitworth, now flying his flag in the battleship *Warspite*, took her up the fjord not knowing that no fewer than five U-boats were waiting for him. Her Swordfish catapult aircraft scouted ahead, reporting several destroyers and submarines, and sinking the anchored *U-64* by dive-bombing. This second Narvik action was an unequivocal victory, leaving the way open for a landing to recapture the port as Whitworth and the Norwegians urged, but no landing force was available. Commander Erich Bey, who succeeded to the command of the German destroyers after Bonte was killed, and lost every one of them by his timid and hesitant leadership, was promoted as a hero, in the interests of morale – with unfortunate results later.[14] The German landing force still held Narvik, and defended it with great tenacity though their nearest support was now five hundred miles south around Trondheim. Pressed ever closer by the Norwegians and their allies and aided only by highly un-neutral support from Sweden, the Germans were eventually driven out of Narvik by a joint Polish-French-Norwegian landing from British ships on 27 April. Less than a month later the British government, for reasons to be explained, decided to withdraw all its forces from Norway.[15]

The Norwegian campaign, though brief and strategically peripheral, was watched with intense interest by armed forces everywhere, eager to learn how modern weapons would perform. One obvious lesson was the vulnerability of warships to air attack, notwithstanding that the Royal Navy was well known to have invested more than any other navy in modern anti-aircraft armament. Almost all pre-war attention had focused on the supposed vulnerability of battleships. This campaign, confirmed by later experience, suggested that large armoured warships were hard to sink. It was smaller warships like destroyers, ubiquitous and indispensable, which were seriously threatened by aircraft, and even then British losses were not overwhelming. In two months of intense operations, during much of which the Germans enjoyed undisputed command of the air, the Luftwaffe sank one British cruiser, six destroyers or sloops, and twenty-one merchant ships. Across the Atlantic, however, the news from Norway caused great alarm in the US Navy, many of whose ships had no modern anti-aircraft weapons at all. An emergency board under Rear-Admiral Ernest J. King was set up to identify and apply instant solutions. Of course there were no instant solutions, but King's ruthless leadership made his reputation with President Roosevelt.[16]

The greatest vulnerability of the British forces in Norway was not air attack but the insecurity of their signals. Instead of keeping wireless silence on operations as they had expected, British ships observing the Spanish Civil War and later fighting the Norwegian campaign generated a large volume of signals which gave a head start to the *Beobachtungsdienst*. It is clear now that the disasters and failures of the Norwegian campaign at sea were not primarily the fault of incompetent admirals or politicians, so often blamed by British historians, but reflect the extensive penetration of British naval signals by the *B-Dienst*.[17]

Another apparent lesson of the campaign was the complete failure of German submarines to have any success in ideal conditions. In this case the U-boats had clearly failed because their weapons had failed: a high proportion of their torpedoes (and many of those fired by the destroyers as well) had failed to run properly, or failed to explode on striking a target. The *Warspite* was harmlessly torpedoed four times, and various cruisers a total of sixteen times. Both Admiral Dönitz and the naval high command had known of the problem beforehand. In this respect the Germans were lucky to capture the damaged British minelaying submarine *Seal*, trapped in shallow water in the Skagerrak on 2 May. By copying her torpedo pistols the Germans solved the worst (though not the only) fault of their own design.[18]

British forces suffered conspicuous failures of equipment and expertise as well, many of them attributable to arrogance and distrust of Norwegian advice. Operating in unfamiliar conditions, the British urgently needed the help of those who knew the climate and the country, and too often rejected it with unhappy results. The Navy was not the worst offender, but there were some egregious naval blunders, including the wreck of the cruiser *Effingham* on 18 May near Bodø, caused by refusing a pilot and misreading a Norwegian chart.[19] The gravest disaster was the sinking of the carrier *Glorious* on 8 June during the final evacuation. With great skill RAF Hurricane fighters which were neither fitted nor trained for deck landings were landed back onto the carrier. The ship then set off home across the North Sea in calm, clear weather with no escort save two destroyers, no aircraft aloft or even ready, and no steam for full speed. In this condition she encountered the *Scharnhorst* and *Gneisenau*, which were in range almost as soon as they sighted her. Prewar exercises had amply demonstrated the risk to a carrier of being caught by enemy cruisers, but nobody had imagined that it could happen in good visibility. The few survivors were unable to explain such gross blunders, which remain a mystery, but there has been a tendency to blame the known poor relations between Captain Guy D'Oyly Hughes and his officers, especially of the Fleet Air Arm. Although he had made his first reputation as a submariner, he was an experienced carrier officer and airman: it is lack of sympathy and tact which has been alleged, not lack of knowledge. Perhaps that was blameworthy, but all that can be said with certainty is that (as we have already noted) the Naval Staff failed to pass on a warning of the German attack which they had received from MI6. The result was the loss of an elderly but valuable ship and 1,515 lives. Her two destroyers, the *Ardent* and *Acasta*, sacrificed themselves to cover the *Glorious*, but not altogether in vain, for *Acasta* torpedoed and badly damaged the *Scharnhorst*. Then on the return voyage the *Gneisenau* was torpedoed and damaged by the British submarine *Clyde*. Admiral Wilhelm Marschall, the German fleet commander, who had exceeded his orders, was blamed for the damage and dismissed, rather than congratulated for sinking the *Glorious*.[20] The brilliant victory of the Norwegian campaign as a whole cost the German Navy a heavy cruiser, two light cruisers, ten destroyers and six submarines sunk, besides more or less serious damage to many of its remaining ships. By the end of June its seagoing strength was reduced to one light cruiser, three destroyers and one submarine.[21] Furthermore, the remaining ships of the German Navy found their strategic situation not much improved. On 13 April the British seized the Faroe Islands, followed by Iceland in early May. Both were under Danish sovereignty, and because Denmark had not declared war on Germany but submitted to occupation, they could legitimately be treated as enemy territory. They gave the British ports and airfields which were much more useful for the North Atlantic than Norway could ever be.[22]

Once the Germans had rebuilt their ammunition stocks and made up the considerable deficiencies revealed by the Polish campaign, they could attack in the West, but they were most anxious not to refight the First World War by attacking the powerful system of fortifications, the 'Maginot Line', which the French had built along the Rhine frontier. Only on the Belgian frontier in the North, where the Maginot Line did not extend, was there limited room to manoeuvre, but here the French and British had excellent chances to block an advancing German army, and here the Germans foresaw that they would be blocked. There seemed even less chance of a breakthrough after a complete copy of the German plan fell into French hands in a crashed aircraft in January 1940. Only Lieutenant-General Erich von Manstein had an alternative scheme – already rejected as impossibly reckless – to drive south-west behind the Allied armies, along a single narrow road through the wooded Ardennes mountains and across the deep gorge of the Meuse to reach the sea near Abbeville. Its chances of success were assessed at scarcely 10 per cent, but for want of any alternative the plan was adopted. The French for their part chose in the spring of 1940 to abandon their pedestrian but solid defensive strategy and shift the best of their army to the far left wing, meaning to sweep along the coast and around the rear of the German army to link up with the Dutch. The two plans, French and German, were now almost mirror images of one another, each intending to outflank the enemy on the left wing and hook right around his rear. The big difference was that if the German attack failed there would still be room to retreat eastward and southward into Germany, but behind the French and British armies lay an impassable barrier against which they could be driven: the sea. Each side had adopted a high-risk approach, depending on speed, tactical flexibility and initiative: known strengths of the German army, and known weaknesses of the French, who preferred a *bataille conduite* ('methodical battle') under centralized control. The German assault was launched on 10 May, and with extreme daring, brilliant improvisation and intense air support it narrowly succeeded – although throughout the campaign the Germans were outnumbered in men, tanks and aircraft, and the unmechanized bulk of their army hardly caught up with the fighting at all. The result was a comprehensive disaster for the Western powers. The German offensive reached the sea on 20 May. The best French troops, the whole Belgian army and most of the British Expeditionary Force (BEF) – 1,700,000 men – were cut off from France and trapped against the coast. Subsequently this unplanned and very lucky victory was dressed up as the destined product of Hitler's military genius and German racial superiority, immortalized with a suitable German word (*Blitzkrieg*; 'lightning war') invented by an English journalist.[23]

For many senior British participants, the obvious cause of defeat in the Norwegian campaign was the disorganization of the British government and its unfitness for efficient and rational wartime decision-making. Some modern historians are much attached to this explanation, which they are eager to blame on the faults of character they discern in Churchill as the First Lord of the Admiralty. Contemporaries in Parliament and government in 1940 who knew him personally and observed him at work came to exactly the opposite conclusion. Already on 26 September 1939 his first great speech in the House of Commons, though perfectly loyal to the government, made a sharp contrast with Chamberlain's dull and spiritless performance. 'Old Parliamentary hands confessed that never in their experience had they seen a single speech so change the temper of the House.'[24] Although Churchill was still politically isolated and had many opponents, and although he was the obvious scapegoat for defeat in Norway and Chamberlain certainly intended that he should be blamed, the Norwegian campaign generated a powerful and eventually overwhelming

Parliamentary demand that Churchill should replace Chamberlain as Prime Minister, which he did on 10 May, in the midst of the crisis generated by the German advance into the Low Countries.[25]

In forming his government Churchill followed the precedent of Lloyd George's War Cabinet, building on a core of senior political figures: the Labour leaders Clement Attlee and Arthur Greenwood, the Establishment's favourite candidate Lord Halifax the Foreign Secretary, and Chamberlain, who still commanded the majority of the Conservative Party and agreed to serve as Lord President of the Council. Again following Lloyd George, several of Churchill's other ministers were businessmen or other non-politicians. His most radical and important innovation was to make himself Minister of Defence as well as Prime Minister, unequivocally taking personal leadership of the war effort. 'It took Armageddon to make me Prime Minister', he told a friend, 'but now I am determined that power shall be in no other hands but my own. There will be no more Kitcheners, Fishers or Haigs'[26] – and (he might have added) no more of Chamberlain's instinct to divide and rule. Attlee, now Deputy Prime Minister, like Churchill a veteran of the Western Front who had read and thought much about the conduct of war, completely agreed with the decision. The effects were powerful and immediate. 'He put a bomb under Whitehall. From then until the end of the war he was constantly urging, driving, probing, restless in his search for new ways for getting at the enemy, and you had to be continually on your toes, always searching into your own mind for the means of improving the job you were set to do.'[27] 'Previously we had seen this dynamo threshing around unharnessed and uncentred, dislocating and disrupting, even destroying from time to time', wrote Colonel Ian Jacob, the Military Assistant Secretary of the War Cabinet. 'Now, with the dynamo in the right place, it was a different story . . . It is impossible to put into words the change that we felt. His power seemed to be turned on all the time.'[28] 'Anybody who served anywhere near him was devoted to him. It is hard to say why. He was not kind or considerate. He bothered nothing about us. He knew the names only of those very close to him and would hardly let anyone else come into his presence. He was free with abuse and complaint. He was exacting beyond reason and ruthlessly critical. Not only did he get away with it but nobody wanted him otherwise. He was unusual, unpredictable, exciting, original, stimulating, provocative, outrageous, uniquely experienced, abundantly talented, humorous, entertaining . . . a great man.'[29]

The individual Service ministers still existed, and spoke for their departments in the Commons, but their position was unequivocally subordinate to Churchill as Minister of Defence, and it was not they but the Chiefs of Staff who were members of the Cabinet Defence Committee (Operations), which took the important military decisions.[30]

Most of the BEF took refuge behind improvised defences around the small railway port of Dunkirk (Dunkerque), before which the Germans halted for twenty-four hours before resuming their drive down the coast to Abbeville, where they caught up with their leading tanks. This pause was ordered by Hitler personally, not with any idea of letting the British escape, but because it was so obvious that they could not escape, and to teach the German generals who was master. At the equivalent moment in 1914 the German offensive had been stopped by a counter-attack which had spoiled the chance of a crushing victory, and to avoid the same danger it was now necessary to allow the infantry time to catch up. Resupplied and reordered, the German advance resumed on 27 May, with the same prime objective as before: to overrun the French defences before they could recover their balance. The Germans did not stop until the French called for an armistice at the beginning of July.[31]

On the evening of 26 May, when it was clear that no French counter-attack was going to materialize, the evacuation was ordered of as many men of the BEF as could be saved from Dunkirk: up to 45,000 were hoped for in the short time estimated to be available. 'When I arrived with my party of twelve officers and one hundred and fifty men,' recorded Captain W. G. Tennant, newly appointed 'Senior Naval Officer Dunkirk' on 27 May, 'I asked the generals how long we should expect to have for the evacuation before the enemy broke through and they replied "Twenty four hours, perhaps thirty six!"'[32] Although Dunkirk is only thirty-nine miles from Dover by the usual route, it was far from being an ideal evacuation port for Operation 'Dynamo'. It was only just within range of air cover from Britain. The coast of West Flanders shoals very gently, revealing extensive sands at low water which keep seagoing ships half a mile offshore or more. On the initial assumption that the port would soon be rendered unusable (as most of it was), everyone would have to be lifted off the open beaches in ships' boats, an exceedingly slow process if the weather permitted it at all. Vice-Admiral Bertram Ramsay at Dover had under his command thirty-nine destroyers (one-fifth of the Royal Navy's total), thirty-eight minesweepers and thirty-six (civilian-manned) ferries besides smaller craft, also some French, Belgian and Dutch ships present but not under his command. The normal ferry route from Dover crosses almost to Calais and then runs inside the sandbanks close along the French shore to Dunkirk. This had to be abandoned at once because it was already within range of German artillery. There was a long northerly route (87 miles) outside the Flanders Banks, and later an intricate central route (55 miles) through the sands was found, which the Germans did not detect for several days. What completely transformed the operation was Captain Tennant's discovery that it was possible to berth deep-draught ships against the outside of the eastern mole or breakwater protecting the harbour entrance, permitting destroyers and passenger ferries to embark troops directly and quickly. The narrow mole was a difficult target to bomb or shell, especially as the port was shrouded in thick black smoke from burning oil tanks, and by extreme good fortune it was never hit. Moreover, the weather throughout remained extraordinarily calm and fine, and by 31 May the small numbers being lifted off the open beaches were boosted by a considerable number of motor-boats and other powered craft, many of them civilian-manned and crossing from England on their own initiative, which took men out to ships offshore, and some of which even made the return passage. Dunkirk was not finally evacuated until 4 June, by which time no fewer than 366,000 Allied troops had made their escape, including almost all the British present besides many French and Belgians. A lively popular mythology gives the entire credit to private boat-owners, but in fact only a few thousand men were carried across the Channel that way (though almost 100,000 were taken off the beaches to ships offshore). A total of 56 destroyer crossings carried 102,843 men; 87,810 came aboard passenger ferries; the minesweepers carried 48,472; 230 trawlers and drifters transported 28,709 men; and forty-five Dutch *schuiten* (small coasters) brought 22,698. The great majority were got away solely because the East Mole remained usable. More than sixty ships, large or small, were sunk during the eight days and nights of the operation, but the overall casualty rate was remarkably small. The BEF lost most of its weapons and equipment, but the trained men survived to fight another day. Moreover, later evacuations using westward ports from Le Havre to St-Jean-de-Luz saved a further 140,000 British troops and 47,000 Allies, including many Poles and Czechs:

> This was perhaps the greatest deliverance the country has ever had, for nearly all her army were got back again. It was no victory. It was no miracle worked by the Navy and the hundreds of other craft. They did a good job. But it was all brought about by the mercy of God and the stupidity of the enemy . . .

Had the army been lost it is probable that the government would have fallen, and its successor would have sought whatever terms Hitler was willing to offer.[33]

In Britain and indeed throughout the world, most people took it for granted that the German army, whose brilliant staff-work had once again been on display, had planned an immediate invasion of England. A large fraction of the Navy's destroyers in home waters were now withdrawn from the Home Fleet and the convoys and concentrated on 'anti-invasion patrols', within easy reach of the English Channel. In fact, the German generals were as astonished at their success as everyone else, and their first reaction was to begin demobilization. With the collapse of France, the war was obviously over, and presently the British would wake up to their defeat.[34] The Luftwaffe was keen to gain credit for a decisive intervention, and in August it began to mount air raids on Southern England, but the other German services had already abandoned the idea of an invasion as impossible, and only went through the motions of planning one thereafter in case the Führer took the idea up seriously for another year. For the moment there were hardly any warships fit for service, the navy had been given no warning of the army's plans, while the army had no landing craft at all, and no knowledge of amphibious warfare. Arriving on the coast, the German generals were alarmed to discover the existence of tides; the naval officers doubted if they were capable of crossing the Channel even without opposition. In any case Hitler was reluctant to invade, and conscious of the usefulness of the British Empire in blocking US and Japanese expansion. He only wanted what he thought Chamberlain had already offered him: a complaisant British government presenting no obstacle to German and Italian aggression. But to the mounting puzzlement and fury of Hitler and his staff, the British refused to play by the rules and acknowledge their defeat, so it was up to the airmen to teach them a lesson. At the end of June the Luftwaffe deployed a plan to grind down the British air defences and aircraft industry, which they expected would take four days. This was wildly optimistic: as the attackers, fighting over enemy territory, the Germans naturally suffered the heavier losses (twice as many pilots), and they did not understand that British aircraft production was considerably higher than German.[35] Although the Luftwaffe had devoted some efforts to discovering if the British possessed radar, the Germans were searching on the wrong wavelengths (the ones they used themselves). It was an unpleasant surprise to discover that the British had a sophisticated air-defence system based on radar location of the enemy, and fighters directed by high-frequency radio. By December 1940 the Luftwaffe had dropped thousands of bombs on British soil and killed many civilians, but only seventeen bombs had hit anything of significant value to war production.[36]

On the outbreak of war the Italian services were planning for a major war not earlier than 1943, and were extremely reluctant to be drawn in, but Mussolini was eager to participate and profit from victory. In February 1940 he declared that 'we cannot possibly remain absent from this drama, which will re-write the history of entire continents'.[37] As France collapsed, he could contain himself no longer, and on 10 June Italy declared war on France and Britain. The Italian fleet now had six battleships, but the new and powerful *Littorio* and *Vittorio Veneto*, launched in 1937, were not ready for service until the summer of 1940. The older battleships *Andrea Doria* and *Caio Duilio*, originally launched in 1913, were due to complete their reconstruction about the same time. Only the *Conte di Cavour* and *Giulio Cesare*, launched in 1911 and rebuilt in the 1930s, were ready for action the day Italy declared war, to face a notional total of five British and five French battleships in the Mediterranean (though they were distributed into several different squadrons, and all of them save the French *Dunkerque* and *Strasbourg* were of the pre-Washington Treaty era). Add to these odds a real scarcity of modern destroyers, and oil for less than six months' wartime consumption, and the Italian admirals' difficulties were not imaginary.[38]

The strategic situation, however, was very much in Italy's favour, and becoming more so every day as the German army advanced into France. The main Italian field army in Libya, facing the British in Egypt, was in effect campaigning on a desert island, with real desert on one side, sea on the other, and a single coast road connecting the seaports of Tripoli and Benghazi to the front line. Libya was totally dependent on seaborne imports for every necessity of war and life, but the sea passages were short, for example 550 miles from Naples to Tripoli by the Sicilian Channel, or thirty-six hours at fifteen knots, almost all of it under friendly air cover. Italian convoys were small, mainly because both Libyan and Italian ports were small and ill-equipped, and the convoys fitted into the already dense traffic of coastal shipping on which much of mainland as well as island Italy depended. Tripoli could handle five cargo ships and four troopships at once, Naples could take fourteen ships at a time, but smaller ports like Bari and Brindisi could accommodate only five. For the whole war from June 1940 to January 1943 the average of 993 Italian convoys was 1.9 ships defended by 2.2 escorts. From June 1940 to January 1941 the *Regia Marina* escorted 86 outward convoys to Libya (total 173 ships) and 73 return convoys (total 158 ships), losing only four ships out of 331 voyages. Although all these ships passed no more than 150 miles away from the British in Malta, 97.6 per cent of the cargoes were safely delivered. Over the same period 1,480 ships sailed to supply Italian garrisons in Albania, Greece and the Aegean, losing 0.8 per cent of them.[39]

The British army in Egypt was equally dependent on seaborne supply, but the distances were rather different. When the Admiralty suspended regular through-Mediterranean convoys on 16 May 1940, it added 20,000 miles overnight to the voyage from British ports round Africa to Suez, which absorbed almost a quarter of the British-controlled merchant fleet and created an instant worldwide crisis of shipping capacity and trade protection, often ascribed to U-boats, but in fact entirely the consequence of losing control of the Mediterranean on the fall of France. There were initially no fighters to defend Malta or Gibraltar, so to get out of range of the *Regia Aeronautica* the Mediterranean Fleet withdrew its base from Malta to Alexandria in May (following the floating dock which had already been towed from Portsmouth in the summer of 1939). To sustain the garrison of Malta over the next two and a half years required a series of convoys from Alexandria, Gibraltar or both, almost all of which became major fleet operations conducted within easy range of Italian airfields in Sicily and Libya, and the Italian main fleet in Taranto.[40]

The immediate Mediterranean crisis arose from the astonishing (and in British eyes, disgraceful) collapse of France, which seemed to have made less resistance to the Nazis than Poland or Norway, though a powerful modern navy and large garrisons in North and West Africa were available and, in most cases, willing to continue the struggle. Even today this is an exceedingly painful subject for French historians, but it has to be said that the information then reaching the British government from France was broadly correct. It indicated a swift decline from determination towards pliability and collaboration, and strongly implicated the anglophobe Admiral François Darlan, commander-in-chief of the French Navy in 1940, later Minister of Marine under Marshal Pétain's collaborationist government, effectively head of state from February 1941 to April 1942, and thereafter head of the armed forces and the Marshal's designated successor. With Darlan in control the British government had to fear a double catastrophe: that the powerful and modern French fleet would supply Hitler with the naval strength he needed to carry the war overseas; and that the United States, which was terrified of that very event, would never forgive Britain for surrendering the outward defences of America. On 25 May 1940 the first discussion among the Chiefs of Staff of 'British Strategy in a Certain Eventuality' – the eventuality of French collapse – assumed 'full economic and financial support' from the United States, 'without which we do not think we could continue this war with any chance of success'.[41] To win that support in the teeth of American suspicion and hostility it was urgently necessary to demonstrate to Washington a ruthless determination to fight, and above all to keep the French warships out of German hands. This was the reality behind the British demands that French warships be surrendered, disabled or removed out of German reach. When Admiral Marcel Gensoul, commanding the principal French Mediterranean squadron at Mers-el-Kébir on the Algerian coast (whose signals the Admiralty could read), appeared to be trying to evade those demands and organize resistance (in other words to fight in the German interest), the British ships were ordered to open fire on 3 July. Some 1,300 French sailors died as a result, mainly in the sinking of the battleship *Bretagne*. Sir James Somerville, to whom it fell to carry out the detestable order, considered it 'the biggest political blunder of modern times' – but we know now that it convinced Roosevelt that Britain would fight, and was worth American support.[42] Only at Alexandria was Admiral Sir Andrew Cunningham able to negotiate a peaceful agreement with Vice-Admiral Robert Godfroy to disarm the French warships there, by adroitly appealing over the admiral's head to his captains and ships' companies.[43]

A small number of individual officers and men and (mostly small) French warships rallied to the 'Free French' movement set up by General Charles de Gaulle, but in the Mediterranean the British now faced the Italians without assistance. Cunningham and the Mediterranean Fleet were based at Alexandria, with three battleships and the old carrier *Eagle*, while Somerville commanded 'Force H' at Gibraltar. This small but powerful squadron, usually consisting of the new carrier *Ark Royal* with one or two battle-cruisers or fast battleships, operated under direct Admiralty control in the Mediterranean or Atlantic as necessary. This was a new concept in naval operations, which had been developed in pre-war exercises to exploit the flexibility of both warships and carrier aircraft to act over a wide area. The intention was for a small but fast and powerful force to use speed, initiative and freedom to move east or west to keep the enemy off balance and make up for the loss of the French battleships. The first clash between the navies in the Mediterranean occurred off the coast of Calabria on 9 July, between Cunningham's fleet, covering ships conveying dockyard workers and equipment from Malta to Alexandria, and the Italian fleet under Vice-Admiral Inigo Campioni, who was returning to Taranto having covered convoys to Libya. Both admirals were aided to understand the situation by reading some enemy signals, but Campioni was under strict orders not to run risks or use his initiative. With the help of reconnaissance by an RAF flying-boat and air searches by his own aircraft from *Eagle*, Cunningham was able to intercept Campioni's two battleships and fourteen cruisers and bring on an action at long range, in which the modernized flagship *Warspite* hit the *Giulio Cesare* at 26,000 yards (13 miles) – a spectacular vindication of the Admiralty Fire Control Table, even if in most respects the action was (in Cunningham's words) 'irritating and disappointing' for both sides.[44] For the first but by no means the last time the ill-trained Fleet Air Arm torpedo bombers were unable to hit moving targets. Neither air attacks nor battleship gunnery slowed down the faster Italian battleships, and neither fleet was able to interfere with the other's convoy. Cunningham suspected from decyphered signals that Campioni was trying to draw him into a submarine ambush and therefore declined to pursue him too closely. No fewer than 435 Italian aircraft spent all afternoon bombing both fleets in turn from 12,000 feet, impressing Cunningham but hitting nothing.[45] As a senior Italian airman commented sourly, 'This ought to be regarded as a practical demonstration of the delusion of high-level bombing, a delusion which was later to receive a great many blows on every front and from all the belligerents.'[46] Vice-Admiral Eberhard Weichold, head of the German military mission in Rome, told the Italians next day that their navy had 'missed its decisive moment': the British were about to discover that they had lost their access to Italian fleet signals for ever.[47]

That summer both the British and the Germans were hoping to enlist the support of France, in particular of the powerful and modern French fleet, the only one of the French armed services not demobilized under the terms of the Franco-German armistice. Admiral Raeder and the German naval staff promoted a strategy aimed at gaining the support of France and Spain, then capturing Suez, Gibraltar, the Azores and the Canaries, to open the way to a worldwide naval campaign against the naval enemy, Britain. Hitler and his general staff, the *Oberkommando der Wehrmacht* (OKW), were sceptical. The 'gigantic fraud' of bribing three potential allies (France, Spain and Italy) with the same African territories did not seem promising. Hitler did not trust Marshal Pétain's government and assumed that Britain was only going through the motions of making war to obtain a better peace. She could no longer be a serious enemy, and the OKW was already planning Germany's next major effort against Russia. This inevitable victory would then open the way for a final world campaign against Britain and the United States, at which point (but not before) Hitler was prepared to talk naval strategy.[48] The British government had now adopted General de Gaulle as their French leader, hoping that he could attract at least some of his countrymen to continue the struggle, and needed to show both the French and the Americans an unbending determination to fight. They also needed to neutralize the new fast battleship *Richelieu*, which had narrowly escaped, still not quite complete, as the German army entered Brest, and taken refuge at Dakar in French West Africa. From there she could easily move to a German-controlled port if the French were minded (as seemed not unlikely) to seek revenge for the British bombardment of Mers-el-Kébir. These considerations led to plans awkwardly combining a Gaullist appeal to the garrison of Senegal with a British naval attack on the *Richelieu*.

The available forces could not sustain a major assault, which would in any case have been a political disaster. The plan therefore depended on complete surprise and poor French morale, neither of which the British Chiefs of Staff thought likely, but both de Gaulle and the British had pressing political reasons to do something. The naval attack came first, on 8 July, when aircraft from the carrier *Hermes* badly damaged the battleship. Then the intended landing, Operation 'Menace' on 23 September, was an almost complete failure. De Gaulle's appeal aroused no response, and the French forces defended Dakar with vigour. There were, however, some inconspicuous but real gains from these operations. The British Navy and army co-operated with an efficiency which made a pleasing contrast with the recent amphibious operations in Norway, though de Gaulle and his staff (in a different ship at his insistence) were incompetent and troublesome. The *Richelieu* blew up two of her main armament guns trying to open fire with defective ammunition, further disabling her for the foreseeable future. At the same time a Free French victory at Libreville in Gabon, further south in the Bight of Benin, had the important consequence of opening a trans-African air route which was to become an essential means of sending air reinforcements to the Middle East and beyond. Despite the understandable public bitterness between Paris and London, both governments took pains to prevent their respective colonies going to war against each other, which would have made things even worse.[49]

In September 1940 Roosevelt promoted the 'destroyers for bases' agreement, by which fifty superannuated American fleet destroyers built at the end of the First World War were swapped for ninety-nine-year leases to establish US naval bases in the West Indies and other British territories in the Western Hemisphere. The public was told, and Churchill may have partly believed, that these destroyers would be a precious reinforcement to British convoy escorts, but the reality was that they had been designed for maximum possible speed in a flat calm, in anticipation of a great fleet battle to be fought in the Caribbean. This was a fantasy in 1915 and a nightmare by 1941. The destroyers were entirely unsuitable for their new function: marginally stable, barely seaworthy in Atlantic conditions and in poor repair, they needed a great deal of work in already overloaded British dockyards before they were good for anything.[50] Their real functions were less operational than political, and their value to Churchill and the British was as tangible proofs of US commitment to British victory. They were an unequivocal statement of hostility which would have fully justified a German declaration of war on the United States – which, however, Hitler was anxious to avoid. They also had an implicit but real political significance to Roosevelt. The locations of the bases were Newfoundland,

Bermuda, the Bahamas, Jamaica, St Lucia, Trinidad, Antigua and British Guiana. All but the last were part of eighteenth-century British America, and therefore a natural part of the independent United States in the eyes of the original American rebels, which undoubtedly Roosevelt had not forgotten. Britain's extremity was America's opportunity to complete the work of the Founding Fathers, quickly, before the Germans arrived, and Roosevelt's language in private, with its extravagant comparisons with the Louisiana Purchase, implied that leased bases were not the limit of his ambition. Nor did he rely on negotiation alone: by May 1940 the US government was prepared to seize British, French, Dutch and Danish possessions in the Western Hemisphere by force.[51]

In Operation 'Hats' at the end of August 1940, Cunningham and Somerville successfully covered the passage of supplies to Malta and reinforcements to the Mediterranean Fleet, including the new carrier *Illustrious* and the reconstructed battleship *Valiant* – but without signals intelligence they never realized that the Italian fleet, now with four battleships and thirteen cruisers, was hunting for them. Nor did they learn until later of failed attacks on Gibraltar and Alexandria by Italian frogmen.[52] As some compensation for the loss of signals intelligence, in September the RAF at Malta received three American Glenn Martin Maryland aircraft, originally ordered by France, whose high speed and high operational ceiling made them ideal for photo reconnaissance. This was timely, because the British had revived a plan for an aerial torpedo attack on the Italian fleet which went back at least five years, and ultimately derived from Admiral Beatty's 1918 scheme to attack the German fleet. This called for aerial reconnaissance of the Italian fleet at its moorings in the Mar Grande, the outer anchorage of Taranto. Pre-war exercises had persuaded Cunningham that it would be very difficult to fight a slow convoy through the Mediterranean in the face of the Italian fleet. Now, when Malta needed frequent re-supply and the Italians were soon to have available not four but six modern or modernized battleships, it was urgently necessary to reduce their force somehow, and carrier air attack was the obvious method. Air Chief Marshal Sir Arthur Longmore, commanding the RAF in the Mediterranean, who as a Squadron Commander RNAS had himself dropped the first ever aerial torpedo from a British aircraft in July 1914, embraced the plan with enthusiasm. The attack on the *Richelieu* at Dakar on 8 July had taught the Fleet Air Arm the best speed and depth settings for their aerial torpedoes when attacking a target moored in shallow water – such as the Italian battleships, which drew over 30 feet and lay in about 40 feet of water in the Mar Grande.[53]

In the final plan the attack on the Italian fleet on 11 November was only one element in a complex scheme which included four British convoys (one each

to and from the Aegean and Malta), reinforcements the length of the Mediterranean from Gibraltar to Alexandria, and others to the new advanced base at
Suda Bay in Crete. To cover all these movements Force H bombarded the port
of Cagliari on Sardinia while some of Cunningham's ships attacked an Italian
convoy in the Strait of Otranto, and Rear-Admiral Lyster with the carrier group
formed around the *Illustrious* struck the Italian fleet anchorage at a moment
dictated exactly by the rising of the moon, so that the Swordfish torpedo bombers glided in in darkness with their engines throttled back, but their targets
were silhouetted while the defenders were distracted by dive-bombing in the
inner anchorage (the Mar Piccolo) and by flares dropped by other aircraft.
Eleven torpedoes were dropped, of which three hit the new *Littorio*, and one
each the *Conte di Cavour* and the *Caio Duilio*. All three battleships sank at their
shallow moorings with their upperworks still above water. The Italians had
been aware of the danger of air attack, but their defences were passive and disorganized. Only one-third of the planned torpedo nets had been laid, and the
British torpedoes were set to run at the precise depth to be most effective: just
below the bottom of the nets, just under the keels of the battleships where the
'Duplex' (combined contact and magnetic) pistols would explode the warheads
at the most destructive point.[54]

Because the Italian battleships sank in shallow water and bottomed upright,
all three could be salvaged. The *Littorio* was back in service in four months
and the *Caio Duilio* in six months, but the old *Conte di Cavour*, though
refloated, was never recommissioned. In the meantime the fleet took refuge in
northern ports from Naples to La Spezia, only re-assembling in the spring of
1941. Taranto was a great victory for the Mediterranean Fleet, and especially
for the Fleet Air Arm (which still celebrates it with a dinner every year), but
it was not 'decisive' in the classic sense. Its effect lasted only six months, and
we shall see that the Italians found means of striking back. Only a fortnight
later, on 27 November, Admiral Campioni with his remaining battleships *Vittorio Veneto* and *Giulio Cesare* fought a running battle with Somerville south
of Sardinia around the usual east–west British convoy movements. (This is the
action variously referred to as 'Cape Spartivento', 'Capo Teulada' and Operation 'Collar'.) Once again, the Italian bombers missed from high altitude, and
the British torpedo bombers missed from low altitude. Like the others this
action was not decisive, and the Italian admirals were once again disgusted
with their heavy gunnery, the big ships consistently getting the range but dispersing their salvoes all around the target (though the cruiser *Berwick* was hit
twice by 8-inch shells). It is only recently that a modern gunnery expert has
convincingly diagnosed the problem, which affected all the *Regia Marina*'s big

guns, whose tight rifling 'overspun' (and therefore overstabilized) the shells, forcing them to fly in a rigid straight line rather than follow their natural ballistic curve to the target. The reputations of both admirals suffered from this action, and Campioni was relieved by his second, the gunnery expert Vice-Admiral Angelo Iachino.[55]

Until the fall of France the main threats to British oceanic shipping could be ranked in descending order, starting with surface attack from warships or disguised armed merchantmen (commonly referred to in English as 'raiders'). Next came U-boats in the Western Approaches, then minelaying by ships or aircraft in the approaches to London and other major ports, and fourthly air attack on coastal convoys. After June 1940 big warships and raiders were still the gravest threat in the open sea, and the remaining dangers in descending order were mines, coastal air attack, German motor torpedo boats in the Channel and North Sea, and lastly U-boats. German raiders cruised over much of the central and South Atlantic, the Indian Ocean and parts of the South Pacific, where British trade was not yet in convoy. Raiders signalled little, and the first intelligence of their movements was often the disappearance of British merchantmen which failed to arrive weeks later. In the North Atlantic convoy escorts were badly depleted to make up anti-invasion patrols, German U-boats were now settling into bases in France which gave them shorter passages and longer time on patrol, while the *Beobachtungsdienst* provided excellent signals intelligence on the Royal Navy's movements. In September and October 1940, the German submariners' first 'Happy Time', three lightly escorted eastbound convoys (HX 72, SC 7 and HX 79) lost thirty-one merchantmen out of 130 between them. This was a real German victory, but it was in every way untypical, since few convoys suffered heavy losses, most losses to U-boats were out of convoy, and the gravest threat was from surface warships, not submarines.[56] In November 1940 the armoured ship *Admiral Scheer* sank the Armed Merchant Cruiser *Jervis Bay* and five of the thirty-seven ships of her convoy, HX 84, eastbound from Halifax, Nova Scotia. Next month the heavy cruiser *Admiral Hipper* was driven off an important and heavily escorted convoy of troopships bound for the Middle East. After this alarm the British began to strengthen convoy escorts with old battleships.[57]

TWENTY-FOUR

Most of the World Already

Government and Administration 1941

T he autumn of 1940, marking the beginning of a new, oceanic phase of the war, is a suitable moment to survey the leading naval powers and assess their plans and capabilities. This is often done simply by counting ships and comparing rival weapons and technologies, but such a method by itself does not penetrate far into the subject. It was the thinking of navies, their different experiences of the past and different ideas of the future, which did most to shape their strengths and weaknesses. Before the First World War the naval world in general had expected a great battle to be fought in the North Sea (and another the Mediterranean), at or very soon after the outbreak of war. It was still assumed, as it had been for half a century and more, that these battles would happen swiftly, naturally and inevitably, that they would always yield a clear victory, leading automatically to command of the sea and victory in the war. Everything therefore depended on tactics for the decisive battle, which became a gambler's throw that would settle the fate of nations in a few hours. Policy and strategy were scarcely called for, and civilian government had little to say. Thanks in part to the popular American naval writer Alfred T. Mahan, these ideas became deeply embedded in the naval consciousness. Everywhere morale, the triumph of the will, was taken to be both the instrument of victory and the expression of racial superiority. Willpower is a functional virtue for the fighting man who has to screw up his courage in the face of death, and in all the military and naval powers willpower tended to distort if not displace reason as a driver of decisions, and not only in military affairs. For most military men, and many civilians, it was axiomatic that the noblest national virtues were expressed by the will rather than the mind.[1]

The real gulf between naval culture in Britain and elsewhere opened after the First World War, as the British (and to some extent the French) learnt the lessons of experience which other navies had not had or did not care to study. The British had always preferred practical experience to abstract theory. Navies without history had to found colleges to manufacture it, but until the late nineteenth century it was assumed that British admirals would know what to do without needing to be told. But even before the Great War had ended, they looked at their collective experiences with a new eye and realized that battle was not the only possible route to victory. Now the admirals began to understand that Britain was the possessor of a great empire, dependent on a worldwide trading system and merchant fleet. It had vital interests to defend all over the world, and few unsatisfied ambitions. As Sir Ernle Chatfield wrote in 1934, 'We are in the remarkable position of not wanting to quarrel with anybody because we have got most of the world already, or the best parts of it, and we only want to keep what we have got and prevent others from taking it away from us.'[2] The Navy's strategic posture, therefore, had to be defensive, however aggressively it might attack at a tactical level. Battles were very desirable because they yielded quick results, but blockade and attrition would do as well if necessary. The interwar naval conferences forced British officers to think more clearly about what they really needed, and why. The study of Jutland and other actions of the Great War encouraged them to develop bold and aggressive tactics to seize fleeting opportunities of victory – but they now knew they would in all probability be attacking in a defensive strategic context. Although British admirals still longed for the opportunity of battle, they were no longer naive about its likelihood or its purpose.[3]

This opened a significant gap between British and American attitudes. US senior officers, admirals and generals, were heavily influenced by German staff college doctrines, and believed devoutly in concentrating their forces to engage the main body of the enemy in the *Entscheidungsschlacht*, the 'decisive battle'. Other forms of naval war, such as protecting merchant shipping – whose importance the British had relearnt by painful experience – were liable to be condemned by Americans (and Japanese) as betraying a lack of 'offensive spirit', distractions from the pursuit of victory, at best of lesser importance, at worst cowardly and dishonourable. The British fully shared the US sense of the importance of winning battles whenever opportunity offered and aimed to keep their main fleets concentrated and ready to fight, but they knew from centuries of history as well as the experience of the last war that such opportunities were rare. In the meantime the war went on, much of it in the form of attritional campaigns such as the attack and defence of convoys, which made an essential contribution to victory or defeat. In practice, all sorts of warship right up to the older battleships were sometimes used in the protection of trade, but admirals and the Admiralty were alert to re-forming the battle-fleet if the enemy main fleet approached.[4]

One other fundamental aspect of naval culture was true in different ways in each of the naval powers. Navies expressed their purposes in professional terms, but everywhere the language they used betrayed emotional as much as rational commitment, and pointed to domestic social and political ambitions as well as military objectives. In Germany, the navy Tirpitz created had always understood itself primarily in political and symbolic terms. As the military situation began to collapse late in the Great War, naval officers engaged more and more openly in the politics of the extreme right. When they were defeated in the end, it only proved to them that the civilians had stabbed them in the back, that they had not lost at sea, but 'through the spiritual collapse of the home front'.[5] The German naval officer-corps survived into the peace with its composition and attitudes unchanged, and from the beginning worked illegally to subvert the new Weimar republic. Public opinion in the political world had been decisively changed by the war, but the navy had become only more radical and fanatical. It still saw itself as 'a pure expression of the national feeling of the German people'; its function to safeguard the sacred flame of seapower by any means (murder not excepted) until Germany could be healed of the 'sickness' of a republic.[6] It is not true that the German navy learnt nothing from the First World War, for its strategic thinking was certainly marked by experience, but its political and social outlook preserved and even enhanced the authentic Wilhelmine preference for internal culture over external reality. Hitler's coming to power provided it with the perfect opportunity to escape into an agreeable fantasy world, shielded from unpleasant facts by its characteristic 'autistic thinking'.[7]

Of all the naval belligerents in the Great War, the British and the Germans had the most fighting experience. The US and Japanese navies emerged in 1918 with their nineteenth-century ideas intact and unblemished, like an uncirculated medal; it has been claimed that on the eve of Pearl Harbor in 1941 the US Navy had fought for only fifty-six hours in its entire history.[8] The Pacific navies still believed devoutly in the inevitable, decisive battle, and devoted all their efforts to building the great battle-fleets which would win the war in an afternoon. They both (the Japanese especially) placed enormous faith in their racial and moral superiority. In both navies, a high proportion of their interwar training effort was devoted to fleet action according to the tactical principles of 1916. Both expected their battleships to fight in a single line ahead, and therefore stressed mass torpedo attack. Both built large submarine fleets, but only to contribute to the fleet action. Although both invested heavily in carriers and naval aircraft, the leaders of the two navies agreed entirely that their role was auxiliary, to gain and keep command of the air over the battle-space in order to protect the aircraft spotting for the battleships' long-range gunfire. They regarded carriers as extremely vulnerable and unlikely to survive long in the vicinity of the enemy, but if they lasted long enough to ensure the battleships' victory, they would have served their purpose. Indifferent to other people's experience, neither navy applied much thought to trade protection or anti-submarine warfare. To a remarkable extent, the Pacific navies prepared for a second world war as though the first had never happened.[9]

To understand the US Navy's plans it is essential to understand its political situation. The professional head of the service, the Chief of Naval Operations, answered directly to the President. So did the commander-in-chief of the fleet (meaning the single battle-fleet), who was the CNO's junior, but not under his command. The commander-in-chief had a staff afloat, but there was no general staff or operational headquarters ashore. Naval administration was divided into a number of autonomous 'Bureaus' run by the uniformed but shore-based 'staff officers', who had nothing to do with 'staff-work' in the modern sense but were technicians and administrators who answered to the Secretary of the Navy – that is to say they were 'staff officers' in much the same sense as the Royal Navy had used the phrase in the nineteenth century. American naval officers greatly admired the supremacy of the military in Wilhelmine Germany and longed for an all-powerful naval head of their service, supported by a naval general staff of seagoing officers, with Congress and the civilian political world supplying only uncritical admiration and limitless amounts of money. Congress blocked these dangerous ambitions. The naval officers' biggest success was the abolition of seagoing engineer officers in 1899, as a first step to eliminating civilian bureaucracy and political control from the Navy. There were still graduate engineers among the 'staff officers' ashore, but from now on US engine rooms at sea were (and still are except in nuclear-powered ships) commanded by non-specialist 'line officers' (executive or seaman officers, in British parlance), with engineer petty and warrant officers under their command to supply technical expertise. The General Board of 1909 was not the general staff the US line officers had hoped for but an advisory panel of senior officers with no legal status; the Chief of Naval Operations created in 1915 was not equivalent to a British First Sea Lord but a harmless figurehead with little control over naval operations and even less over policy or administration. Neither could achieve much until the President formed strategic policy, and no President of the interwar period – least of all Franklin Roosevelt – had any mind to do that. Even in 1930 the US Navy's 'war plan' dealt essentially with defence against the least likely possible threat: a Canadian invasion. Only in 1940 did the two Services gain the right to report directly to the President without passing through the State Department, which went a good way to isolate civilian government from the war.[10]

To improve its situation the US Navy needed political support, but few Senators or Congressmen were interested in the navy for its own sake, and many were instinctively hostile to it as a costly instrument of militarism, imperialism and other evils of the old world. Political support could be bought in the conventional American manner by pouring public money into the districts of selected Congressmen, for which reason the USN had at least twice as many dockyards as it needed (but too few men to man its ships). Unfortunately, most states and districts had no seacoast and were out of the navy's reach. This was a major reason for its enthusiasm for naval aviation, which allowed the USN to scatter the map of the inland United States with numerous naval airfields. They were wasteful from the military standpoint, and drained money from the rest of the navy, but they bought valuable political support. This did not make the navy an uncritical enthusiast for shipborne aviation. On the contrary, the USN was infatuated with battleships, which made up a quarter of all its ships in 1911, and still more than one-third of its total displacement in 1922. Its senior officers were virtually all battleship men. Some naval airmen developed heretical thoughts about sinking battleships, but in public it was politic to keep to their official mission of serving the 'battle line' by reconnaissance and spotting. In any case the USN's chronic inability to build working aerial torpedoes forced it to specialize in dive-bombing, a deadly threat to carriers but not to heavily armoured ships.[11]

Since the beginning of the twentieth century, the US Navy had concentrated its planning on 'War Plan Red' and 'War Plan Orange', against Britain and Japan respectively, or the two in combination. These 'war plans' were essentially political projects, designed to win the battle where it really mattered, on Capitol Hill, by persuading Congress that naval war against one or both was a real risk. With no general staff and no policy guidelines from President Roosevelt, the USN could not make realistic operational plans, while the administration's strategy by the late 1930s was not to fight at all but to squeeze Japan by imposing an ever-tighter economic blockade. This confronted the Japanese with a clear threat and a timetable for action. In July 1939 the US gave six months' notice of cancelling the 1911 Treaty of Commerce and Navigation, and from July 1940 it began to block selected exports, starting with aviation fuel. By the Lend-Lease Act of March 1941 the US abandoned neutrality and extended military aid to Britain, Russia and China. In June and July, the US, shortly followed by Britain and the Netherlands, froze German, Italian and Japanese assets. In August 1941, while Roosevelt was away meeting Churchill off Newfoundland, the Deputy Secretary of State Sumner Welles imposed a total oil embargo on Japan – apparently misunderstanding Roosevelt's intentions (always a risk with a President who seldom expressed himself clearly and discouraged written records of his meetings). Finally on 26 November 1941 Cordell Hull, the Secretary of State, demanded that Japan withdraw from Indo-China (Vietnam) and all parts of China, including Manchuria. Japan now had no alternative but to abandon the China War or fight the United States, but the US administration refused to believe that Japan could attack, and Congress authorized no preparations for war.[12]

The two obvious reasons to assume that Japan could not and would not embark on another war were China and Russia. Ten years of war in China had already cost Japan 600,000 casualties by December 1941. The imperial army had repeatedly demonstrated that it could defeat Chinese armies and conquer vast areas of territory, but overall victory seemed more remote than ever, as Japan's insatiable aggressions and atrocities repelled its natural friends, and united such unlikely bedfellows as Russian Communists, Chinese Nationalists and Chinese Communists. By tradition the Japanese army had always regarded Russia as its principal foe, but the China War inclined it to keep the peace on the northern frontier. In May and June 1939 Japanese troops were sharply defeated by the Soviet army in a brief but fierce undeclared war at Nomonhan in Inner Mongolia, which quenched the imperial army's remaining enthusiasm for a Russian campaign. Two months later, in August 1939, came the shocking news of the Molotov–Ribbentrop Pact, an alliance between the apparently irreconcilable enemies, Germany and Soviet Russia. In Europe it sounded the doom of Poland and the Baltic republics; in Asia it betrayed the German-Japanese alliance sealed by the 'Anti-Comintern Pact' of 1936, and brought down the Japanese government. There was little likelihood now of Japan assisting Germany against Russia or anyone else, so the European and Eastern wars remained firmly disconnected.[13]

There remained the imperial navy's plans for a 'southern advance', notionally to support the army's campaign in China, really to secure for the navy a dominant position in imperial strategy. Observation of the Imperial Japanese Navy in action along the China coast, in particular its successful landing in bad weather at Hangchow (Hangzhou) in November 1937, gave the Royal Navy a high opinion of Japanese skill in amphibious warfare. The Japanese had demonstrated that they could land on the exposed beaches of the winter monsoon as well as in the summer, which seemed to double the threat to Malaya.

General William Dobbie, commanding the defences of Malaya and Singapore, now persuaded Whitehall that they could not be held against a serious Japanese attack without major reinforcements. By advancing southward along the coast of China, the IJN progressively cut off the Chinese armies in the interior from outside help, a process completed with the occupation of northern Indochina (Vietnam) in September 1940. China's only connection with the outside world was now the British-controlled 'Burma Road', the precarious overland route from Burma through the mountains to Yunnan. In February 1939 the Japanese had already occupied Hainan Island, followed immediately by the Spratly Islands in the South China Sea. Hainan was peripheral to the China War and the Spratlys completely irrelevant, but the Japanese had now surrounded Hong Kong and gained an anchorage only 650 miles from Singapore. In July 1941 the Vichy French government allowed them to occupy southern Indo-China, putting Japanese naval aircraft at Saigon only 564 miles from Singapore.[14]

Having both travelled in secrecy by warship, Roosevelt and Churchill met at the 'Riviera' conference at Argentia (Placentia Bay) on the coast of Newfoundland in August 1941 to discuss the practicalities of the growing US participation in the Atlantic campaign. Without revealing much detail or entering into any written commitments, they issued what came to be called the 'Atlantic Charter', hostile to Nazi Germany in tone but some way short of a US declaration of war. Roosevelt wished to make the 'Charter' condemn empires and colonies, but for obvious reasons Churchill declined to be drawn so far. By a declaration on 1 January 1942, however, the 'United Nations', as they now styled themselves, committed themselves to a list of general but not meaningless principles: no territorial aggrandizement, territorial changes only with the consent of the inhabitants, restoration of self-government to those deprived of it, global economic co-operation, 'freedom from fear and want', freedom of the seas, and disarmament of the aggressor nations.[15]

At the Argentia meeting Britain and Canada, eager to draw the United States further into the naval war, agreed to put anti-submarine operations in the western Atlantic under Rear-Admiral Arthur L. Bristol, USN, whose 'requests' were to be treated as orders even though America was not at war. In July 1941 the USA took over the garrison of Iceland, and US supply convoys to Iceland were fitted into the existing British transatlantic convoy system. This was obviously a bait to tempt German U-boats to attack US ships, which the U-boats were strictly ordered not to do. As a temporary arrangement the Royal Canadian Navy took responsibility for slow convoys, mainly escorted by corvettes, and the US Navy escorted fast convoys with destroyers. There were major weaknesses in this arrangement. The USN concept of anti-submarine warfare in 1941 was very like the Royal Navy's in 1915: it was all about hunting U-boats, and little about protecting merchantmen. Wartime mobilization had expanded the manpower strength of the Royal Navy about eight-fold, the US Navy about twenty-fold, and the RCN fifty-fold. The RCN desperately needed anti-submarine training and equipment but was now effectively cut off from Western Approaches Command, where anti-submarine techniques and technology were advancing with some speed, and attached to a foreign navy where they were neglected. To add further confusion, Congress intervened in the long-standing disputes between the air forces of the USN and the US Army by forbidding the USN to fly wheeled aircraft from shore bases – but the USAAF aircraft flying patrols over the Atlantic from Newfoundland refused to have anything to do with the US Navy. Just as the RN and the RAF were approaching a working compromise over the control of Coastal Command, relations between the rival US air forces broke down completely. The result of this shambles was some serious convoy disasters, which US senior officers blamed on everyone but themselves.[16]

The command of the sea, as all navies understood to a greater or lesser degree, conferred the freedom to trade and transport around the larger part of the world. For Britain the most important sea was the Atlantic, which gave access to the products of the US economy, and to precious raw materials from all over the world. Likewise, it would allow US forces to intervene in Europe and Africa, if they could be induced to fight – which was still very unsure in the autumn of 1940. For the British and German navies, the Atlantic, especially the North Atlantic, was critical to their war effort. This is often reduced in popular histories to endless battles between U-boats and convoys, which certainly occurred, but were much rarer than the casual reader might imagine. All the belligerents were taken completely by surprise by the collapse of France, and had to improvise methods of fighting a long-range, oceanic campaign with ships and submarines designed for medium-range operations around the coasts of Europe. The use of French bases in the Bay of Biscay now allowed even the smaller Type VII U-boats (the majority of the German force) to cruise about 450 miles further west, well into the central Atlantic, and the patrols of Coastal Command aircraft, slowly increasing in range and number, provided an incentive to the U-boats to operate further to the west to avoid air attack. The British naturally reacted by providing convoy further westward. Atlantic convoy organization was the overall responsibility of the Trade Division of the Naval Staff, and in detail of the Commander-in-Chief Western Approaches; initially at Plymouth, then moving to Liverpool in February 1941 since with the Germans in France it was no longer safe to run large convoys south of Ireland and up the English Channel. From 15 February, Coastal Command, though still part of the RAF, was put under Admiralty operational control, and Admiral Sir Percy Noble shared his headquarters in Liverpool with Air Vice-Marshal James Robb to control the Atlantic convoys. Under an admiral well known for his charm and tact this proved to be a striking success, avoiding the appearance of the Admiralty giving orders to the Air Staff, but achieving a high degree of effective joint-service co-operation at the command level. What this did not solve was the long-running difficulty of extracting aircraft suitable for naval requirements from an Air Ministry-dominated production system which was indifferent or hostile to them.[17]

The Admiralty was anxious to apply the principles pioneered at Liverpool to naval-air co-operation in the Mediterranean. So long as Sir Arthur Longmore remained Air Officer Commanding Middle East, naval-air relations were amicable, but the Air Staff sought to block naval influence over local air operations, and Longmore's relief, Air Marshal Arthur Tedder, who arrived in June 1941, did not get on so well with Admiral Sir Andrew Cunningham. At the same time circumstances were forcing the RAF and the Fleet Air Arm to work together. After the damaged *Formidable* was sent to the United States for repairs in July 1941 there was no British carrier stationed in the Eastern Mediterranean for thirty-eight months, and the surviving naval aircraft were based ashore under RAF command, where they provided a significant addition to the RAF's numbers and skills.[18] 'The German reconnaissance and bombing performances are infinitely better than ours out here,' Cunningham complained in September 1941, 'neither does our reconnaissance approach the Italian in efficiency.'[19] Naval observers therefore taught the RAF, which still had almost no trained navigators, how to fix their position over sea or desert. At sea the naval airmen showed the RAF how to avoid the heavy losses it had suffered in low-level bombing of enemy convoys, by dive-bombing or attacking with torpedoes and rockets instead. As Cunningham wrote to Admiral Pound in September 1941, 'The RAF have at last discovered that the much despised Swordfish and Albacores are the most accurate bombers we have got because they dive bomb and also because they go so slowly they invariably find their targets.'[20] Finally, in November, Cunningham was able to report 'We won, to a great extent, our battle for a Coastal Command. 201 is now 201, Naval Co-operation Group. The Air Ministry fought like tigers not to have anything naval in the name but DP [Pound] and I stood firm. A very good fellow Slatter who has done a lot of carrier work is now the AOC and matters are much improved.'[21]

The majority of the British escort vessels available in 1941 lacked the range to cross the Atlantic, but from April 1941 they could refuel in Iceland, which formed a natural mid-point of the convoy system, and allowed convoys to be escorted to 35°W, well to the west of Iceland. From May 1941 convoys began to make non-stop transatlantic passages under continuous escort (refuelling the escorts at sea or sending them in to Iceland to refuel in passing), and at the same time Coastal Command, which now had about 200 mostly modern aircraft, began to base some of them in Iceland. In daylight, and when the weather permitted, most of the transatlantic convoy routes could now be covered at least intermittently by aircraft from Northern Ireland, Iceland or Newfoundland, but there remained a 300-mile 'air-gap' south-east of Greenland.[22]

It is impossible to mention Coastal Command and its aircraft without introducing the Ministry of Aircraft Production, created in May 1940 to take over the Air Ministry's oversight of the aircraft industry. Its first minister was the Canadian politician and newspaper proprietor Lord Beaverbook. Arriving in an atmosphere of crisis with invasion apparently imminent, he revelled in the exciting confusion. Having inherited an efficient department set up by Air Chief Marshal Sir Wilfrid Freeman and the former railway manager Sir Ernest Lemon, the architects of the 'Shadow Factories' scheme, in less than a year he had managed to reduce it to confusion and uproar. He imposed production targets that he knew to be unrealistic, meaning to inspire the factories to achieve the impossible, which only demoralized and disorganized them. Contemptuous of 'the air marshals', whom he regarded as the epitome of obstructionism, Beaverbrook proclaimed his slogans that 'committees take the punch out of war', and 'organisation is the enemy of improvisation'.[23] Improvisation was his favourite working method, so he left the structure of his ministry as fluid as possible, with many positions undefined and even unnamed. He hated meetings and minutes and preferred to do business by telephone, frequently ringing up manufacturers with orders to drop whatever they were doing to take up his latest enthusiasm. Departments and companies whose work was abandoned naturally objected, so Beaverbrook's interventions generated an inter-departmental war of competing priorities and caused an abrupt collapse of aircraft production. He cancelled many new aircraft and the new engine under development for the Swordfish's successor, the Fairey Barracuda. The most polite verdict on Beaverbrook as a minister is Air Marshal Tedder's; that he was 'a short-term solution and a long-term catastrophe'.[24]

Churchill undoubtedly bears a large share of responsibility for that catastrophe, but his reasons for bringing Beaverbrook into the Cabinet looked well beyond the fortunes of the British aircraft industry. His supreme priority in

1940 was to draw the United States into the war, and an enthusiastic North American like Beaverbrook was a valuable ally. Churchill, Beaverbrook and the British ambassador to Washington, Lord Lothian, worked closely together to reassure and enlist Roosevelt and General H. H. Arnold, Chief of Staff of the US Army Air Force. In November 1940 the new British Air Commission separated from the British Purchasing Commission in Washington and settled in the commercial capital of New York. It needed impressive representatives of the British aircraft industry to deal with US aircraft manufacturers, and few were more impressive than its new Director-General, Sir Charles Fairey. 'Tiny' Fairey was a big man in every sense: founder and majority owner of one of Britain's most successful aircraft companies, a powerful speaker, and 6 feet 5 inches tall. He supervised an organization with over 500 British personnel by the summer of 1942. Fairey, General Arnold and Rear-Admiral John Towers formed the Joint Aircraft Committee in Washington which distributed US-manufactured aircraft to Lend-Lease recipients. As far as possible Fairey suppressed the quarrels of the RAF and USAAF. He deployed his extensive links in right-wing politics and the aircraft industry on both sides of the Atlantic. But it was equally valuable, indeed essential if American industrialists were to be enlisted, that though he was politically conservative, Fairey was untainted by anti-Semitism and steered clear of the connections, so fashionable in British aviation circles, with friends of Hitler like Lord Sempill, Lord Rothermere and Lord Londonderry.[25]

Fairey's presence in the United States contributed greatly to the Allied war effort, but his company was now bereft of the strong leadership it was used to, and in October 1939 he suffered the first of a series of heart attacks. Sir Stafford Cripps, the new Minister of Aircraft Production as of November 1942, put in G. E. Marden, an accountant with no industrial experience, to run Fairey's factories. He divided the management into warring factions and aroused growing complaints to both the ministry and the Admiralty. Also in November, Admiral Sir Noel Laurence, 'Chief Naval Representative' in the Ministry of Aircraft Production, reported that the company's workers had been complaining about inept management to anyone who would listen; nobody of ability was willing to work under the existing directors.[26] 'I have seen the red light as regards production of these aircraft for a long time now and the very grave position in which we find ourselves is, in my opinion, entirely due to inefficiency.'[27] In April 1943 the First Lord told Churchill that 'The basic cause of the late delivery of Barracudas . . . has been the lack of forethought, drive and energy on the part of the Fairey management.'[28] Evidently he was anxious to deflect the blame away from the Admiralty, and Fairey's local difficulties were not trivial, but the fundamental problems arose from the imbalance of power between the Admiralty, the Air Staff and the Ministry of Aircraft Production. It is clear enough in retrospect, and had been clear to admirals like Phillimore and Henderson since 1918, that the Admiralty could not take full responsibility for the naval air service if it was denied authority over the design and manufacture of aircraft.[29]

In peacetime Britain's most important seaport by far was London, where inbound cargoes were distributed and outbound collected, by coastal shipping or by railway. On the south and east coasts coastwise shipping was now exposed to attack by aircraft, by 'E-boats' (the British official term for German or Italian motor torpedo boats), by heavy artillery in the Dover Strait, and by destroyer minelaying. There was no alternative distribution system which might avoid these dangers, for the railway network lacked the capacity to take over bulk cargoes, and the main lines ran north and south rather than east and west. For heavy industry, agriculture and (not least) electricity, much of which was generated by coal-fired power stations supplied by sea, it was essential to establish a complete system of coastal convoys, which by 1941 provided most English and Scottish ports with one clockwise and one anticlockwise sailing every day, and which of course had to be defended against a nearby enemy. London alone required more than 10 million tons of coal a year to maintain gas, electricity, water, sewerage and transport. A major effort was made to shift as much deep-sea trade as possible from London to West Coast ports, but this was not easy. Many of the smaller ships trading into London were accustomed to lie at river moorings using their own derricks to discharge cargo over the side into lighters which were then towed to wharfs with suitable cranes, warehouses and railway sidings. Bigger cargo-liners serving more distant ports tended to use the enclosed docks with a maintained water level which were entered from the Thames through locks. Other ports, such as Liverpool, with a tidal range of more than 30 feet at springs, and Bristol, with a range over 40 feet, depended entirely on enclosed basins which ships had to lock into or out of on the top of the tides. The Clyde offered an immense expanse of sheltered water, never bombed except in the spring of 1941, but the available commercial wharfs were scattered and tended to specialize in particular trades. Most of the Clyde is too deep for ships to anchor, so large convoys had to assemble further up the coast in various West Highland sea lochs. Many ships which normally traded to London had the wrong cargo-handling gear and the wrong skills to shift to other ports, while the West Coast could not easily find the cranes, dockers or railway connections needed to take over London's trade. Other changes were forced by wartime developments. Instead of importing iron ore to make steel, for example, it made sense for Britain to save shipping capacity by importing finished steel, but to distribute these increased steel imports required a twenty-two-fold increase in the number of special railway wagons. The cumulative effect of port congestion over the winter of 1940–41 was equivalent to the loss of 5 per cent of the cargo shipped on the North Atlantic. A massive effort over many months by the new Ministry of War Transport, formed in May 1941 by amalgamating the Ministries of Transport and Shipping, plus the appointment of Regional Port Directors with near-dictatorial powers for Liverpool, Bristol and the Clyde, was needed to break the back of this problem.[30]

Convoy was obviously a method of defending merchant ships against attack, chiefly from submarines or aircraft. Much of the effectiveness of the convoy system, however, came from evasion rather than defence. Gathering merchantmen into convoys emptied the ocean of targets, which the U-boats had no easy means of locating. From the low bridge of a Type VII U-boat the horizon was about five miles away in good weather, though the masts or smoke of a ship still hull-down might be sighted at fifteen or twenty miles on a clear day. Hundreds if not thousands of these small submarines would have been needed to maintain all-weather patrol lines across all the convoy routes, but by April 1940 twenty-three of the initial twenty-seven operational U-boats had been lost, and only thirteen replacements launched.[31] In February 1941 the operational U-boat force fell to twenty-one boats, its lowest number ever. What the navy's *BdU* needed was long-range reconnaissance aircraft equipped to signal directly to the submarines. This was technically feasible, as any reader of the German Navy's official journal the *Marine Rundschau* would have known, since a 1936 article by a Dutch naval officer had described the integrated system of submarine patrols and long-range flying boats which the Dutch were setting up (using German aircraft and equipment) to defend the Java Sea. Unfortunately, the Luftwaffe had only a small force of converted airliners (the Focke-Wulf 200 'Kondor') with the range to make even limited patrols over the Atlantic, its head Field-Marshal Hermann Göring was hostile to co-operating with the navy, only indirect communication was possible between aircraft and submarines, and the airmen's navigational skills were too poor to provide accurate information when they did sight targets. Lieutenant-Colonel Martin Harlinghausen, the former naval officer who in 1940–41 commanded the Kondor squadron *KG 40* at Mérignac near Bordeaux, did his best, but at higher levels German naval-air co-operation was poor.[32]

Both sides badly needed intelligence of the enemy's whereabouts, and neither possessed the many long-range aircraft they required for effective searches.

In the nine months from July 1940 to March 1941 the British escort force in the North Atlantic doubled to 350 ships, of which about three-quarters were usually ready for operations at any one time. This worked out as about eight escorts to every U-boat, or around four for every convoy. From February 1941 Admiral Noble began to organize his escorts into permanent escort groups, accustomed to working together. But between January and March 1941 the *Scharnhorst* and *Gneisenau* (repaired since the Norwegian campaign) were cruising in the North Atlantic and the armoured ship *Admiral Scheer* in the South Atlantic and Indian Ocean. The Admiralty Operational Intelligence Centre lacked the information to track them in the open sea, the *Beobachtungsdienst* was able to read many Admiralty signals re-routing convoys fast enough to be tactically useful, and the convoys were horribly vulnerable to meeting German heavy ships.[33]

The Government Code & Cypher School (GC&CS) learnt much about German signals procedure from the Poles in 1940, and was reading the Luftwaffe's Enigma currently from May 1940. However, its first significant success against the German Navy's version of Enigma, which had an additional cypher rotor and presented many special difficulties, came during the Norwegian campaign in April, from the destroyer *Griffin*, which captured the disguised German trawler *Polares* with cypher materials, allowing six days' traffic in the 'Dolphin' or *Heimisch* ('Home Waters', including the North Atlantic) cypher to be read, and giving a first insight into Enigma's vulnerabilities.[34] Then the Admiralty adopted an operation proposed by F. H. (Harry) Hinsley of GC&CS, which succeeded in capturing the German Atlantic weather-ship *München* on 7 May, just after she had put to sea for two months, with complete Enigma materials for the whole of May and June, plus the weather-reporting code which was heavily used by the Luftwaffe and provided many 'cribs' giving initial access to daily Enigma settings. By pure coincidence, the previous day Commander Joe Baker-Cresswell of the destroyer *Bulldog*, commanding the escort of the westbound convoy OB 318, had blown *U-110* to the surface, killed her captain (Fritz-Julius Lemp, who had sunk the *Athenia* in 1939) with shellfire and captured the boat, complete with her Enigma machine set up to transmit secret 'officer-only' signals, and a mass of equipment and cypher materials. This allowed naval Enigma to be read for the first half of June, and on 28 June another weather-ship, the *Lauenburg*, yielded the settings for July. After this the Dolphin/*Heimisch* (later called *Hydra*) cypher was read more or less daily for the rest of the war. Best of all, *Bulldog*'s prize sank after a few hours, none of the U-boat's survivors knew she had been in British hands and Admiral Dönitz remained unaware of the intelligence disaster he had suffered. The

British could now fix the position of the abbreviated 'short signals' (*Kurzsignale*) which the Germans thought impossible, allowing sighting reports to be easily picked out and convoys diverted from danger at the last moment. Baker-Cresswell was awarded the DSO, and at the investiture the king told him that it had been 'the most important single event in the whole war at sea'. It was scarcely an exaggeration.[35]

Young Harry Hinsley, who played so notable a part in these actions when still only an undergraduate, grew up to become a post-war Vice-Chancellor of Cambridge University, and the principal editor of the official history of *British Intelligence in the Second World War*, which does not neglect the contribution of GC&CS to the anti-submarine war, and may have unwittingly exaggerated it in some respects. Successful convoy diversion was a particularly important factor in the second half of 1941, and Hinsley claims the whole credit for cryptography, but this was only one of several influences at work. Hitler's diversion of U-boats to the Mediterranean, Norway and North Russia during this period sharply reduced the weight of attack against the North Atlantic convoys, and so did the restoration of the 15-knot convoy speed limit.[36] This is a well-known example of Churchill's personal interference in the conduct of the war at sea, which annoyed senior naval officers at the time, and has been denounced by historians since. It is worth a brief comment. Churchill was always searching for ways of attacking the enemy more effectively, and he put pressure on the Naval Staff to reduce the minimum convoy speed from 15 knots to 13 in order to allow 14- and 15-knot merchantmen to sail independently, in the hope that additional losses of 'independents' would be more than made up by more efficient use of the faster ships. The Naval Staff was sceptical, in the event the statistics proved them right, and the 15-knot limit was restored in June. Another Churchill convoy scheme, this one against the Kondor bombers rather than the U-boats, was the 'Catapult-Armed Merchantmen' (CAMs). As their name indicates, thirty-five merchant ships were fitted with an old Hurricane fighter mounted on a catapult, as a one-shot deterrent. Between them they made 170 transatlantic crossings and launched Hurricanes eight times. Two German aircraft were shot down, two damaged and three driven away. In practice the majority of Atlantic convoys were only briefly within range of the Kondors, neither the threat of air attack nor the deterrent was very effective, and it soon appeared that a boost to merchant seamen's morale did not justify the rare occasions when CAMs were able to launch a fighter, so this scheme too was dropped. Both episodes illustrate Churchill's imaginative drive to improve the effectiveness of the war effort; they also show that he was ready to abandon his favourite projects when the evidence was clearly against them. His Battle of the Atlantic Committee of March 1941 mainly busied itself with improving port efficiency and repairing damaged merchant ships.[37]

There was another way to supply air defence to an ocean convoy, which had been considered in interwar plans, and which both the Royal Navy and the US Navy were exploring in 1941; what came to be called the escort carrier. HMS *Audacity* (converted from a captured German cargo-liner) and the USS *Long Island* (converted from an incomplete US merchant ship) were similar small, simple, diesel-powered ships (therefore not needing a full funnel as steamers did) which commissioned at almost the same time in June 1941. *Audacity*'s first task was to provide fighter cover for convoys to and from Gibraltar, which as they crossed the Bay of Biscay came within easy range of the Kondors based at Mérignac. In this role she initially carried six US-built Grumman Martlets, the British version of a USN carrier fighter. In her short career she amply proved the concept, and as a bonus provided very effective anti-submarine cover even without anti-submarine weapons, simply by sighting nearby U-boats and directing escorts against them. In December she played a leading part in the successful defence of convoy HG 76 by one of the new permanent escort groups, EG 36, commanded by Commander F. J. Walker. In this action the escorts sank five U-boats, but the *Audacity* herself was sunk too. Both Dönitz and the Admiralty were impressed by her, and the Admiralty at once set about obtaining suitable hulls for conversion, the first of which, a US merchant ship, was completed in November as HMS *Archer*.[38]

Westbound Atlantic convoys took up their deep-sea formation on clearing the North Channel or the Inner Hebrides, while the escorts joined from their base at Londonderry. At sea the merchant ships were controlled, and if necessary manoeuvred, by the Convoy Commodore, usually a retired admiral or captain RN serving in the rank of Commodore RNR and sailing in a big ship with extra signalmen. The warship escort was in overall command, though the senior officer of the escort was not often over the rank of commander. In the open sea the convoy formed in a number of parallel columns; in 1941 typically six to nine with up to five ships in each column at intervals of two cables (400 yards), the columns being three cables apart by day, opening out to five cables by night. In this 'broad front' formation only the two outer columns could easily be torpedoed by a submarine firing from outside the escort screen. The majority of convoy escorts were small, with little speed in hand to chase a surfaced U-boat (the Type VII could make 17 knots when sea conditions allowed; the larger Type IX, mainly used in distant waters, was slightly faster). These slow escorts normally formed a screen around the convoy, ideally (if there were enough of them) at intervals of a mile or so, allowing their Asdic sets (with a range in normal conditions of about 1,500 yards) to provide overlapping arcs of search to detect U-boats approaching submerged – though in practice Asdic was mainly effective not in making a first detection, but in hunting U-boats which had already attacked or been sighted and forced to dive. The escort commander's ship and one or two others of the escort were faster (usually old destroyers), giving a limited capacity to sally out from the screen to intercept U-boats detected on the surface before they could attack. In September 1940 the U-boat command decided to concentrate on surfaced night attack, when the U-boats could use their speed without (as they believed) being detectable by Asdic. The German Navy knew about radar, but the medium frequencies (and therefore large aerials) which they used themselves could not be deployed by warships smaller than a cruiser and did not seem to offer much threat to surfaced U-boats.[39]

The first British radar effective against U-boats came at the beginning of 1941 with Coastal Command's ASV ('Air to Surface Vessel') fitted to its new Lockheed Hudson patrol aircraft (with a radius of action of 350 miles) and the big Short Sunderland flying-boats (600-mile radius). Carried by Swordfish and Wellingtons flying from Malta by night, ASV allowed Italian convoys to be detected and illuminated by flares. ASV-fitted Swordfish at Gibraltar tracked U-boats trying to get through the Straits by night, with deadly effect. The shipboard version of ASV Mk.I was known as Type 286. With a fixed aerial working on a wavelength of 1.5m, it could not pick out the low silhouette of a U-boat amid the 'clutter' of echoes from waves, but it could see bigger ships, and was extremely useful for convoy station-keeping at night. By March 1941 ninety escorts had Type 286, though the weight of the aerial aloft was dangerous to stability, and that summer a lighter, revolving aerial entered service. This Mk.II ASV could detect a big ship from 60 miles away, or a destroyer at 20 miles.[40]

Radar became available to convoy escorts not long after the U-boats had adopted the policy of attacking on the surface. Radar's first victim was *U-100*, rammed by the destroyer *Vanoc* in March 1941. Very soon U-boat men developed something of an obsession with radar as the most dangerous British anti-submarine device. Dönitz ran his Atlantic U-boat campaign from a seaside villa at Kernevel, near Lorient in Brittany, with a minuscule staff of fewer than thirty (cooks and typists included). His command style was extremely centralized, with U-boats expected to report daily by wireless. At a day-to-day level this campaign was directed by six staff officers in three watches of two. Grossly overworked, they had almost no capacity to analyse technical questions, and were far away from the main naval staff in Berlin, which itself lacked technical departments. Radar was genuinely a very important advance, and in time Dönitz became convinced that it was the secret of every British success, and the excuse for not exploring other possibilities.[41]

Most though not all signals were sent to and from the U-boats by short-wave (high-frequency) wireless, relying on the impossibility of any enemy intercepting signals which followed, not the curvature of the earth but a 'line of sight' up into the sky, to be reflected off the ionosphere and down to earth hundreds of miles away. Even if by chance the signal were detected by an enemy, German experts assured Dönitz that it would be impossible to take a bearing on it. As early as January 1941 the B-Dienst reported that British ships appeared to be taking bearings on high-frequency signals, the Germans already knew that the French could do it, and Admiral Darlan personally warned Dönitz about British capabilities. However, BdU preferred to trust the German wireless experts who dismissed the report as impossible, and no clear warning was published to the German Navy as a whole until June 1944 – long after the U-boat campaign had been comprehensively defeated. This was more than simply a case of technical incompetence; a more fundamental factor was the navy's centralized and authoritarian management style, combined with the ingrained conviction of the German armed forces that it was the business of military men to direct the work of civilian experts. The British, and the Admiralty in particular, took security seriously but were more relaxed about formal status, having learnt in the First World War to build teams combining civilian with military talents, and men with women.[42]

One civilian expert who made essential technical contributions to the anti-submarine war was Wacław Struszyński, evacuated from Poland in 1939 and taken in by the Admiralty Signal Establishment. One of his key discoveries was that a short-wave transmitter pointed upwards to reflect off the ionosphere also emitted a secondary local 'ground wave', detectable on the surface within twenty or thirty miles, which allowed a ship with an 'Adcock aerial' to take the bearing of a nearby short-wave transmission. This high-frequency direction-finding (HF/DF or 'huff-duff') mattered because the centralized German command style, reinforced by BdU's acute difficulty in locating enemy convoys in the open sea without adequate aerial reconnaissance, pushed the Germans to rely very heavily on the security of short-wave signals. The excellent work of the B-Dienst extracted a good deal of information from British signals, but the Admiralty was careful not to signal exact positions in an intelligible form, and much of it was in the form of alterations of course or changes of plan which only made sense if the convoy in question had already been located and identified. As Dönitz slowly built up the size of his U-boat fleet, he began in 1941 to experiment with 'herd tactics' (*Rudeltaktik*: the popular translation 'wolf pack' expresses British fears better than German practice), in order to spread the boats of a group in a line of search, and then if they sighted a convoy, to close them up for a group attack. Using most of the U-boat force for reconnaissance, even when it worked, consumed much time and fuel, and required many signals, always including a contact report from the first U-boat to make a sighting, immediately followed by voluminous signals from *BdU* as he took over tactical control of the operation. The form of a sighting report was easy to identify, and by the summer of 1941 every convoy had at least one escort, usually several, fitted with an Adcock aerial which would give a bearing on the 'ground wave' of a nearby U-boat transmitting a signal – hence the rising number of U-boats reporting that they had been interrupted in making a sighting report by a fast escort bearing down on them. For the Germans, not suspecting the possibility of HF/DF, these narrow escapes were proof of the quasi-magical powers of the British radar which had reached the convoy escorts at about the same time. Moreover, the British were already working on methods of adding new magic by taking a bearing at long range off the 'sky wave'.[43]

Since the late 1930s the Signal School had been searching for means of generating shorter wavelengths than could be obtained from radio valves. In September 1939 Birmingham University was given an Admiralty contract to work on microwaves, which led to the first cavity magnetron and the first prototype 'centimetric' radar (on 10cm wavelength) in February 1941. This gave such promising results that the Director of the RN Signal School immediately ordered parts for 150 sets on his own authority. In May 1941 the corvette *Orchis* ran sea-trials of the first production set of the new Type 271 radar; twenty-five escorts were fitted with it by July, and fifty by December. In its early form, Type 271 came as a prefabricated unit combining the radar office with the scanner on its roof, the whole to be mounted high enough to allow all-round search. Many escorts, especially the sloops and old destroyers with their narrow hulls, could not safely accept the topweight, and the new radar was initially fitted only to the broader-beamed corvettes. The prominent 'lantern' of Type 271 radar mounted behind a corvette's bridge was easily spotted by a U-boat even at night, whereas the inconspicuous 'birdcage' of the Adcock aerial at the mainmast head was identifiable only at close range in daylight. Because the faster escorts and the escort group commanders did not have the precious radar information in front of them, to put it to use effectively required highly integrated escort groups sharing information by the VHF voice radio with which Western Approaches anti-submarine escorts were now fitted. In August 1941 the new 'strapped magnetron' increased the power output of Type 271 radar from 5kW to 70kW and doubled its effective range. Its first notable success in action came in April 1942 when the sloop *Stork* sank *U-587* using radar information passed by the corvette *Vetch*. Type 271 in turn became the parent of a large family of naval and air centimetric radar sets which conferred a critical operational advantage to ships and aircraft, not only through its own performance, but even more by its accidental capacity to distract the Germans from their vulnerability to HF/DF.[44]

The Italian 'Royal Navy' (*Regia Marina*) of the nineteenth century, the age of 'Liberal Italy', had been a reliable friend of Britain and rival of France,[45] but from the 1920s the *Regia Marina* came increasingly under the influence of the Fascist Party, which was more impressed by large squadrons and big ships, without asking what the technology was good for and whether it worked. The Fascist regime built a large submarine fleet, but much of its equipment was defective, and the training of officers and men was quite inadequate for a serious war. Italy was the only major naval power with no training school for submariners, nor until 1925 even for submarine officers.[46] As a matter of principle, the Fascists regarded technical experts as subordinate to politicians: 'The technician is a person of routine, and of action to the low level expected of the non-combatant; the fighting man is distinguished above all by a calm readiness to take decisions in the face of danger.'[47] This dismissive attitude to technical skills had the obvious effect, especially on the submarines. From 1926 the technical branches in Italian submarines were effectively desk-bound, with no powers of command afloat, and by the 1930s recruits were very scarce. Volunteers and skilled men cost more than conscripts and old technology, and the Fascists favoured cosy oligopolies, some of them (notably Ansaldo, the Ligurian firm with strong Fascist connections which supplied the navy's defective heavy guns) notoriously dishonest.[48] Only in the design and manufacture of torpedoes were the Italians (with the benefit of the engineering traditions of the original Whitehead Company) generally as good as any naval power except perhaps Japan, and considerably better than Germany or the United States.[49] Under Mussolini and his devoted follower Admiral Domenico Cavagnari, Chief of Staff of the Navy from 1934 to 1940 and then wartime commander-in-chief, all decisions came from the centre and initiative was a very dirty word. Ships at sea had to communicate with each other via Rome, and the navy and air force likewise. The navy had little experience of anti-submarine operations or convoy organization, was quite unaccustomed to operating in the dark and before the war had refused to support the development of radar, for which it did not foresee any use. The British Naval Attaché in Rome reported that the

1925 Italian manoeuvres were 'if possible an even greater fiasco than those of 1924 . . . The whole plan demonstrates an extraordinary ignorance of reality.'[50] In the 1930s many training courses were suspended to save money, and during the disastrous partial mobilization of March 1938 a great deal of damage was done to modern equipment by untrained operators.[51] Considering how weak and backward were Italy's economy and society by European standards, none of this is surprising, but it is worth noting how much the Italian forces learnt in four years of war, inflicting substantial losses on Britain at sea and in North Africa, and developing competent naval air and anti-submarine forces among others.

There are points of comparison between Fascist Italy and Japan, whose Meiji Constitution of 1890 drew largely on Bismarck's German Reich of 1871, but has to be understood in a very different social context. From the 1920s Japanese government was increasingly dominated by the official religion of 'State Shinto', which discounted 'science, technology, weapons systems, rationality, institutions, and material factors in warfare . . . The emperor-centric nation-state required the complete subordination of the individual to a strategy of aggressive territorial expansion in pursuit of the collective goal of a Japanese global order, a Pax Japonica.'[52] Business leaders and civilian politicians who dared to oppose the domination of the military were now at risk of assassination by naval officers. Within the Japanese Navy the 'Treaty Faction' which had negotiated the naval treaties of 1922 and 1930 was suppressed by the aggressive 'Fleet Faction' which forced Japan's exit from the 1935 London Naval Conference. The 'Manchurian Incident' (meaning the Japanese invasion of Manchuria, starting in September 1931) was a remarkable military and economic success, the foundation of Japan's highly productive war (and post-war) economy, but it was a political disaster. Chiang Kai-shek, the Chinese leader, would have been a natural ally of Japan and Germany against Soviet Russia, which could scarcely have survived the combination, but the Japanese army always forced its enemies to unite. The soldiers attributed their victories over China (1894–5) and Russia (1904–5) to superior willpower, which they were confident would always work, rather than to the incompetence of their enemies. Following the German precedent, the Meiji constitution had set up parallel civilian and military governments, but at first the powerful influence of the *genro*, the elder statesmen of the imperial court, held government together. From the 1930s the 'Command Group' led by Admiral Katō Kanji dominated the Navy Ministry and expelled their moderate opponents. The last of the *genro* was Prince Saionji Kinmochi, who died in 1940. The weak Admiral Nagano Osami, who became head of the Naval General Staff in April 1941, was unable to impose authority on his juniors. The Command Group's reliance on 'spiritual superiority' is sometimes read in English as a superstitious reference to religious authority, but really reflects the influence of nineteenth-century European military writers (read in translation, of course) with their stress on the dominant effect of superior morale: the reference is to *esprit de corps* rather than the Holy Spirit.[53]

Western writers often explain Japanese politics of the 1930s by invoking the spirit of *Bushidō*, presented as the core of Japanese national character and the inheritance of the samurai:

> In its popular interpretation, the tenets ascribed to *bushidō* include courage, benevolence, politeness, selflessness, sincerity, honour, loyalty, self-control, and a strong sense of justice – virtues also found in texts romanticizing the European chivalric ideal. This similarity is not coincidental, as the first significant discussions of modern *bushidō* were directly inspired by English discourse on the roots of the gentleman in medieval knighthood.[54]

The word *bushidō* itself is an anachronistic portmanteau term invented in the late nineteenth century to cover a range of obsolete language and mostly foreign ideas. As an artificial ideology with no solid historical roots, it served the militarist regime of the 1930s as a flexible instrument of propaganda, but it is an obfuscation rather than an explanation of Japanese thinking.[55]

Less well known in the West, but much more useful to explain Japanese politics and decision-making (before, during and after the Second World War), is the crucial distinction in Japanese culture between *honne*, a personal inner conviction of the truth, and *tatemae*, the conventional wisdom one feels obliged to adopt in public as a loyal member of a community or an organization. *Amae* expresses a relationship of dependence on a person in a parental position who may discern and act on unexpressed *honne* and has the authority to demand honest answers to straight questions. He judges after listening to his juniors and assessing what they really feel; he speaks with 'the voice of heaven' (*ten-no-koye*), and the emperor (*tenno*, 'king of heaven') is the ultimate patron. Japanese society still understands a strong public duty to maintain unity, so to act without paternal authority on an ethical conviction, even if correct, may still be condemned as an assault on the harmony of society. Konoye Fumimaro, Prime Minister in 1941, was expected by the army and navy to give his *honne* for peace so that they could speak out for it too, but he felt unable to contradict Admiral Nagano, the Chief of the Naval General Staff, who had already told Emperor Hirohito about the navy's choice for war. Both services were 'playing chicken', offering *tatemae* which they knew to be suicidal and relying on the emperor to perceive their *honne*. He, however, seems to have been influenced by what he had learnt on his tour of Europe in 1921 of the position of a constitutional monarch, and felt unable to go against both the government and the services. But Hirohito was capable of speaking with the voice of heaven. He had already done it in 1936 when he confronted the mutinous 'Young Officers' and compelled them to surrender and commit suicide. He was to do it again in 1945.[56]

TWENTY-FIVE

At Last, a Real War

Policy and Operations 1941

On the last day of November 1940 Churchill wrote a fifteen-page personal letter to Roosevelt, setting out his strategic ideas for the forthcoming year:

> The decision for 1941 lies upon the seas; unless we can establish our ability to feed this Island, to import munitions of all kinds which we need, unless we can move our armies to the various theatres where Hitler and his confederate Mussolini may be met, and maintain them there . . . we may fall by the way and the time needed by the United States to complete her defensive preparations may not therefore be forthcoming. It is therefore in shipping and in the power to transport across the ocean, particularly the Atlantic Ocean, that in 1941 the crunch of the whole war will be found . . . If you are convinced, Mr President, that defeat of the Nazi and Fascist tyranny is a matter of high consequence to the people of the United States and to the Western Hemisphere, you will regard this letter not as an appeal for aid, but as a statement of the minimum action necessary to achieve our common purpose.[1]

The phrasing is delicate but unambiguous. Churchill knew that Britain's financial ability to fight a world war alone was limited. He also knew that there were many other voices in Roosevelt's ear, some of them pleased to see British arms purchases helping to finance American re-armament, some of them not sorry to bankrupt Britain in the process, many of them simply incredulous that the wealthiest state in the world could possibly want for money. The British Treasury warned Churchill that Britain, now shut out of the US money markets by the Neutrality Acts, would exhaust her borrowing capacity rapidly, but the US Treasury assured the President that Britain and France had ample reserves to pay for imports in 1940. Chamberlain for his part was confident that

Germany's financial position was the weaker and there was no cause for urgency: 'I have always held that Hitler missed the bus in September 1938 . . . the opportunity will not recur.'[2]

Popular histories tend to give the impression that the convoy war in the open ocean was fought by small warships alone, but this is a misunderstanding. All navies understood that it was heavy ships (battleships and cruisers) which held or lost the command of the sea. So long as the British Home Fleet held the ultimate command of the sea, British convoys were protected from heavy attack and could concentrate on U-boats. The Home Fleet was normally kept at Scapa Flow to intercept the German heavy ships if they attempted to put to sea, while older battleships strengthened the escort of some convoys. In January 1941 the *Scharnhorst* and *Gneisenau* were driven off one convoy by the battleship *Ramillies*, and in March they were driven off another by the *Malaya*, but it was impossible to provide a battleship escort for every convoy, and this cruise was very effective in disrupting the convoy system besides sinking sixteen individual merchant ships.[3]

For the German Navy the precious strategic prize of the French Atlantic dockyards made it possible to support big ships close to their operational areas despite the chronic unreliability of German machinery. Although not fast workers, the French dockyard officers and workmen were loyal to their new masters, their workmanship was better than anything available in German yards, and German officers praised them enthusiastically as 'willing', 'hard-working', 'faultless' and 'especially good'.[4] Unfortunately for them, by 1941 Coastal Command had developed an effective torpedo-bomber force using the twin-engined Bristol Beaufort, developed from the Blenheim light bomber. Brittany was well within bombing range of Britain, and the German heavy ships attracted a weight of air attacks which reflected British alarm. In two months no fewer than 1,161 RAF aircraft attacked Brest. The heavy cruiser *Admiral Hipper* returned to Brest from an Atlantic cruise on 14 February 1941, but in entering dry dock she hit an unmarked wreck and damaged a propeller. A new propeller had to be ordered from Germany, putting her out of action for months. The *Scharnhorst* and *Gneisenau* returned to Brest on 22 March with bad boiler trouble, and the *Gneisenau* was docked, but when the dock was drained she was discovered to be sitting on a large unexploded bomb with a time fuse. She was hastily refloated and moved out to a buoy, where she was hit by an RAF aerial torpedo and to save her from sinking had to be returned to the same dock, still with its unexploded bomb, which was presently followed by further bombs. Then an unlucky bomb hit on the *Prinz Eugen* needed five months of repairs, and by the summer of 1941 all three big ships were badly damaged.[5]

It is common to read studies of the war in the Mediterranean which treat it as a single, self-contained theatre; it is rarer to meet authors who remind their readers that it remained the Middle Sea, as it had been since antiquity, the central theatre of war in and around which the neighbouring (and often the distant) nations met to campaign. A fundamental question which contemporaries had to address was whether the land still surrounded the sea, as it had done in the conception of the ancient world, or whether it was more realistic to take a world perspective on the sea enclosing the land. Britain was fighting in the Mediterranean because she had essential interests to defend in the Middle East as well as the central communications spine (by sea and by underwater cables) between its European and Asian possessions – and because North Africa was now the only area in which Britain could confront the German army. These seaborne communications meant that Mediterranean campaigns were not at all enclosed, but closely connected with both the Atlantic and the Indian Ocean (and potentially with the Black Sea as well). The warships and transports of those who controlled the Suez Canal and the Straits of Gibraltar could move quickly and easily into and out of the Mediterranean. Aircraft could do the same, particularly if they belonged to a service like the Luftwaffe which was trained and organized for rapid long-distance moves. Moreover, most of the fleets and armies in the Mediterranean basin were supplied from outside. At the beginning of 1941 Britain's only major land campaigns were against Italy in North and East Africa, but more than half the British army in North Africa was made up of Indian, Australian and New Zealand troops. To sustain them required seaborne supplies to be protected over enormous distances. A campaign fought largely on land in North Africa had naval ramifications which extended from the Atlantic to the Indian Ocean and the South Pacific. Moreover, Italy's attack on Greece in the autumn of 1940, sharply defeated by the Greek army, had opened a new front requiring British support, and therefore British supply convoys. It soon required German support as well, since the misadventures of the Italian army forced the Germans to reinforce the Mediterranean by sending General Geisler's *Fliegerkorps X* from Norway. In December 1940 the German air corps, with more than 300 aircraft, including dive-bombers and torpedo bombers, was installed on Sicilian and Calabrian airfields ideally situated to dominate the Central Mediterranean. Admiral Cunningham only heard of their arrival on 9 January (a significant intelligence failure), and the following day the carrier *Illustrious* was badly damaged by a skilful joint attack by Italian bombers (which first decoyed away the defending fighters) followed by German dive-bombers, and had to be sent to the United States for repairs.[6]

. The battle of Navarino in 1827, the last British naval action fought by ships of the line under ail. Allied (British, French and Russian) ships have run into Navarino Bay and anchored mong the Turkish/Egyptian fleet. A Turkish ship of the line is on fire on the left.

2. Sir James Graham, First Lord of the Admiralty, 1830–34 and 1853–5. Graham was raised to the office of First Lord of the Admiralty as a reward for his work in carrying the 1832 Reform Act through the Commons. He knew nothing about the Navy, and was convinced that all forms of technical expertise were highly undesirable in a minister. In his two terms as First Lord he did all he could to eliminate from the Admiralty all experts, and above all naval officers.

3. *Achilles* building in dock, Chatham 1863, at the time of Dickens' evocative description.

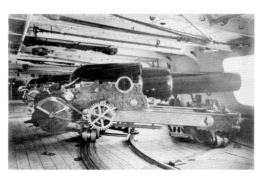

4. A 10-inch muzzle-loading rifled gun aboard HMS *Sultan*, 1870.

5. Later heavy guns were breech-loaders. Thi is the forward 9.2-inch gun of the armoured cruiser HMS *Warspite*, 1884.

6. HMS *Captain* in front of the covered slips at Chatham, 1869–70. A rare photograph of the short-lived battleship whose loss horrified the mid-Victorian public and gravely damaged the reputation of the Admiralty of the day. The dangerously low freeboard is visible.

7. A paraffin wax model of a new hull form is prepared for the test tank in the Admiralty Experimental Works, Haslar. The man in the deerstalker is almost certainly Robert Edmund Froude, who succeeded his father William Froude as Superintendent of the establishment in 1879 and moved with it to Haslar in 1886.

8. Sir Alexander Milne, First Naval Lord, 1866–8. Probably the most influential British naval officer of the 19th century.

10. Sir Geoffrey Phipps Hornby, the leading sea-going admiral of the 1870s.

9. Hugh Childers, First Lord of the Admiralty, 1868–71. Gladstone's favourite lieutenant, he overruled his admiralty colleagues to send the Captain to the sea and then tried to blame them when she sank.

11. The powerful ironclad HMS *Inflexible* drying sails in 1881. One of the last masted battleships in the Navy.

12. HMS *Ramillies* in 1893. The transition from sail to steam was now complete and her military masts supported machine guns, not sails.

13. The first all big-gun battleship, HMS *Dreadnought*, launched February 1906. Her powerful battery of heavy guns is visible: she carried more than twice the firepower of any other battleship, and at higher speed.

14. Admiral of the Fleet Sir John Fisher, First Sea Lord 1904–10, pictured in 1910 soon after he became 1st Baron Fisher of Kilverston. He returned as First Sea Lord 1914–15. 'Whatever success I have had is more attributable to the action of imagination than to the dictates of cold reason,' he declared: 'Emotion rules the world! The heart, not the brain!'

15. Winston Churchill as Home Secretary shortly before he became First Lord of the Admiralty in 1911. Having made his reputation as a prison reformer as well as a war reporter and an author, Churchill was moved to the Admiralty to clear up the chaos and inter-service rivalry generated by Sir John Fisher and made worse by Germany's aggressive naval building. In three years Churchill forced Admiral Tirpitz to abandon his naval race, but was too late to restore British joint-service war planning.

27. A 'Hedgehog' anti-submarine mortar on the forecastle of HMS *Westcott*. This was an early ahead-throwing anti-submarine weapon.

28. Depth charges exploding astern of the destroyer HMS *Vanoc*. The most widely used anti-submarine weapons, depth charges had the disadvantage of being dropped astern of the attacker, giving a short opportunity for the alert U-boat skipper to take avoiding action.

29. Commander F. J. ('Johnny') Walker, one of the first noted anti-submarine tacticians, on the bridge of HMS *Starling*.

30. A hospital ship carrying wounded soldiers away during the evacuation of Dunkirk, 27 May to 4 June 1940. Columns of smoke from burning oil tanks can be seen in the background.

31. British soldiers wade out to a waiting destroyer off Dunkirk. This painfully slow and dangerous procedure inspired an urgent search for motorboats to be sent to Dunkirk to lift troops off the beaches and out to ships waiting offshore.

32. Evacuated troops aboard a destroyer about to berth at Dover, 31 May 1940. In all, 366,000 allied troops were evacuated from Dunkirk between 27 May and 4 June 1940.

33. Western Approaches Command, Derby House, Liverpool; the joint naval and Air Force headquarters for the Battle of the Atlantic.

34. Hudson aircraft of Coastal Command overflying a convoy.

35. HMS *Hornet*, Coastal Forces base at Gosport. Motor torpedo boats and motor gunboats were widely used to protect coastal convoys and attack enemy vessels in the Channel.

36. A tanker sailing from the Caribbean torpedoed by a U-boat. For much of 1942, this essential traffic was unprotected because of the US Navy's refusal to adopt convoy.

37. The icicle-encrusted deck of a Canadian destroyer after escorting a convoy through a bitter storm. The ice endangered the stability of the vessel and made working conditions extremely hazardous.

38. The Commander-in-Chief, Western Approaches, Admiral Sir Max Horton, in his HQ at Derby House, July 1943. Behind him is part of the wall map showing the current convoy situation.

39. Commodore Gilbert Stephenson, subsequently Admiral Sir Gilbert Stephenson, on board his training ship *Western Isles* in Tobermory Bay, where between 1940 and 1945 he trained more than a thousand anti-submarine escorts for the North Atlantic.

52. Torpedo Wrens of the Women's Royal Naval Service (WRNS) pushing a submarine torpedo, Portsmouth.

53. Wren Air Mechanics.

54. Third Officer Eileen Wood, WRNS, operating a Typex Mark II cypher machine.

55. Mrs (later Dame) Vera Laughton Mathews, Director WRNS, pictured soon after her appointment in 1940.

56. Tank Landing Ships, mostly US-built, were essential to deliver all sorts of vehicles to the assault beaches. These LSTs are part of the assault force which landed at Anzio, south of Rome, in January 1944.

57. An aerial view of the Mulberry Harbour at Arromanches (Gold Beach), part of the Normandy landings, June 1944.

58. A Landing Craft Tank (LCT) unloading onto the beach as part of the D-Day landing operations.

59. An Able Seaman standing against the ice encrusted barbette of HMS *Belfast* while escorting an Arctic convoy, November 1943.

60. Escorts and merchant ships of the ill-fated convoy PQ17 assembling in Hvalfjord, Iceland, May 1942. Off the port bow of the photographer's ship is the destroyer *Icarus* and beyond her the Russian tanker *Azerbaijan*.

61. The view from the bridge of the cruiser HMS *Sheffield* in heavy seas while escorting convoy JW 53 to Russia, February 1943. The ship suffered serious structural damage during three days of storms and had to return to port for repairs.

62. Firefighters on the deck of HMS *Formidable* after a Japanese suicide plane crashed onto the flight deck while she was operating off the Sakishima Islands in support of the Okinawa landings, May 1945.

63. Three of the four carriers of the British Pacific Fleet, July 1945. On *Formidable*'s flight deck are Avenger and Corsair aircraft. Astern of her are *Victorious* and *Implacable*.

64. Admiral Chester W. Nimitz Commanding the US Pacific Fleet visiting Admiral Sir Bruce Fraser aboard his flagship HMS *Duke of York* at Guam, August 1945. Nimitz is inspecting a Royal Marine Guard of Honour.

A month later in the Western Mediterranean Admiral Somerville with Force H from Gibraltar attacked Genoa, La Spezia and Leghorn (Livorno) with a combination of naval bombardment and carrier air raids. Only limited damage was caused, but it was at least good for British morale to demonstrate that British ships could spend three days in Italian home waters on the Ligurian Riviera, while the Italian fleet and a large number of Italian aircraft searched for them in the wrong direction. The embarrassment of the *Regia Aeronautica* helped to pave the way for another encounter at the end of March. Under pressure from the Germans, who assured him that their aircraft had torpedoed two of Cunningham's battleships and driven away his remaining carrier the *Formidable*, Admiral Iachino planned a sweep south of Crete to intercept British convoys to Greece. He sailed on 27 March with his flagship the new battleship *Vittorio Veneto*, eight cruisers and fourteen destroyers, unaware that Cunningham already knew a good deal about the operation from decrypted Luftwaffe signals. Early next day Iachino met British cruisers south of Crete, and the presence of British carrier aircraft soon made it clear that *Formidable* had not left the scene, so he turned for home. Cunningham hoped to achieve what had so often been practised in pre-war exercises: air strikes to slow down a fleeing enemy and bring on a battle. In the mid-afternoon the *Vittorio Veneto* was hit by an aerial torpedo which reduced her to six knots for some time, and at dusk the heavy cruiser *Pola* was stopped by another. Persuaded by sketchy air reconnaissance that Cunningham's fleet was still distant, Iachino left Vice-Admiral Carlo Cattaneo with two other heavy cruisers to look after the damaged *Pola*. Lacking radar, lying stopped in the dark, the Italian cruisers did not detect the approach of the British battleships until they switched on searchlights and opened fire at 4,000 yards range. All three cruisers and two destroyers were sunk in a few minutes. Italian naval gunnery had not improved: in the whole day's fighting, the Italian heavy ships fired 542 8-inch and 94 15-inch shells without a single hit. Although the accuracy of the British torpedo aircraft had yet again been disappointing, the battle of Matapan at least proved the pre-war concept of using carrier air attack to slow down a fleeing enemy and force him to battle. It also taught the Italians not to trust German assurances; henceforth Italian admirals declined to operate outside the range of friendly (meaning Italian) fighter cover in the Central Mediterranean, defined as sixty nautical miles radius from Cape Passero, the southern tip of Sicily. The *Vittorio Veneto* survived the disaster, but was out of action until August 1941, and again from December to June 1942 after she was torpedoed by a British submarine.[7]

A week after Matapan, the German army invaded northern Greece and drove swiftly southward. Having just built up a British army to support Greece, the Navy had to improvise an evacuation to Crete without air cover at the end of April, followed by an evacuation of Crete itself at the end of May. The German assault on the island was led by paratroops, and decrypted Luftwaffe signals had provided complete details of their plans, but with overwhelming air superiority they still conquered Crete and inflicted the Royal Navy's heaviest defeat of the war to date. As Cunningham acknowledged to the Admiralty on 23 May,

> I am afraid that in coastal area we have to admit defeat and accept the fact that losses are too great to justify us in trying to prevent seaborne attacks on Crete. This is a melancholy conclusion but it must be faced. As I have always feared enemy command of air unchallenged by our own Air Force and in these restricted waters with Mediterranean weather is too great odds for us to take on . . . it is perhaps fortunate that H.M.S. *Formidable* was immobilised as I doubt if she would now be afloat.[8]

The Navy managed to evacuate about half the 32,000 defenders to Egypt, but at the cost of the battleships *Valiant* and *Warspite* damaged, three cruisers and six destroyers sunk, three cruisers and seven destroyers badly damaged. Only a quarter of the Mediterranean Fleet survived undamaged. These were the modern warships intended if necessary to form the core of a British Eastern Fleet, and the aircraft sent to reinforce the Middle East were the same ones which might otherwise have been available for the defence of Malaya. Simultaneous war in the Mediterranean and the Far East had been the nightmare of the pre-war Admiralty, and the situation in the Far East was ominous. The Luftwaffe had prepared a victory for the Japanese unwittingly, for there was no real strategic co-ordination between the notional allies of the Axis. From a German perspective, Crete was simply a barren prize won at intolerable cost. The parachutists suffered such heavy losses that the air assault force was disbanded and never used again – which probably extinguished any possibility of taking Malta, the essential preliminary to the capture of the Suez Canal. For the British Cabinet the defence of Greece had been a desperate measure from the start, but win or lose, it was politically essential to fight, to demonstrate to Australia and New Zealand, whose men were a large proportion of those saved from Crete, that the mother country would run all risks on their behalf. It was even more necessary to show the US Congress, just then debating the Lend-Lease Act, that Britain would not forsake Greece, her only remaining ally under arms.[9] 'Military defeat or miscalculation can be redeemed,' Churchill declared in a broadcast on 27 April. 'The fortunes of war are fickle and changing. But an act of shame would deprive us of the respect which we now enjoy throughout the world, and this would sap the vitals of our strength.'[10]

April and May 1941, six months before Japan entered the war, were the lowest point in Britain's military fortunes. Having devastated the Central Mediterranean, *Fliegerkorps X* was sent to support the attack on Yugoslavia and Greece; 125 Allied merchant ships were sunk or captured during the Greek campaign (March–May 1941). The Greek Prime Minister, Alexandros Koryzis, shot himself, and the senior RAF officer on Malta collapsed with a nervous breakdown. With the exception of the five merchantmen of the *Tarigo* convoy, sunk by British destroyers in April, Italian convoys ran with little interference. Profiting from the British army reinforcements diverted to Greece, General Rommel wiped out the 1940–41 victories of General Richard O'Connor and retook Cyrenaica in thirty days, putting German instead of British aircraft onto the Libyan airfields which commanded the Central Mediterranean, driving the Navy (submarines excepted) out of Malta and leaving the besieged fortress of Tobruk on the Egyptian frontier precariously dependent on coastal shipping. Cunningham's only remaining carrier, the *Formidable*, had to remain in harbour because she had just five fighters left; the *Regia Aeronautica* commanded the skies over the Mediterranean, and Cunningham feared that his sailors' morale was beginning to crack under the strain of incessant, unopposed bombing.[11] 'Just as you and I thought,' he wrote to Rear-Admiral Algernon Willis,

> so the Greek expedition turned out. Dunkirk was nothing to it except the scale. Our wretched soldiers never saw a British plane for 12 days before they evacuated and of course our ships and shipping had no fighter protection. I had only five Fulmars left . . . and so kept *Formidable* and battleships in harbour to release destroyers to take off the soldiers.[12]

'The Admiral,' Churchill wrote of Cunningham that month,

> has abandoned all hopes of blocking Tripoli and perhaps Benghazi also . . . Every single one of our plans has failed. The enemy has completely established himself in the Central Mediterranean. We are afraid of his dive bombers at every point. Our ships cannot enforce any blockade between Italy and Cyrenaica or Greece and Cyrenaica.[13]

But the British Cabinet still strove to send reinforcements to the Mediterranean theatre, including the 238 tanks sent (with considerable daring) straight through the Mediterranean to Alexandria in May, under cover of thick weather, and the 224 fighters flown into Malta from carriers in a series of operations between April and June, of which 109 remained on the island and the rest went on to Egypt.[14]

In Hitler's mind British troops and aircraft in central Greece threatened the rear of the planned assault on Russia, and the Romanian oilfields on which the German war effort heavily depended – but as the British looked eastward, the German advances in North Africa and the Balkans looked like the two jaws of a pincer closing on the Middle East, and the pro-German *coup d'état* in Baghdad on 2 April led by the Iraqi politician Rashid Ali al-Gaylani confirmed the picture. Stalin was equally convinced that the Germans had taken the Balkans on their way to Suez, and dismissed British warnings that Germany was preparing a Russian offensive as crude attempts to undermine his German alliance. Soviet military intelligence knew better, but after Stalin had shot most of the senior officers of the Soviet army for supposedly plotting against him, the survivors were not anxious to offer him unwelcome information. British warnings only reinforced his conviction that he was facing an Anglo-German plot, and he refused to believe in the German assault even after it had begun. Meanwhile neither the Germans nor the Vichy French forces in Syria were able to support Rashid Ali effectively, but the British reacted fast. A naval expedition was sent from the Eastern Fleet, bringing troops up the Shatt el-Arab to occupy the vital oilfields, Free French forces invaded Syria from Egypt and on 11 July the Vichy government's only serious campaign against Britain collapsed.[15]

All this was happening as the naval war against Germany reached its climax in the North Atlantic, where British shipping was threatened by German heavy ships, already at sea or likely to be soon. Above all the big new battleship *Bismarck*, now working up in the Baltic, was reckoned to be at least a match for any British capital ship, and her sister the *Tirpitz* was expected to complete shortly. The Admiralty anticipated that the Germans would wait until their four battleships (*Scharnhorst, Gneisenau, Bismarck* and *Tirpitz*) were ready to sail together in overwhelming force, but in Berlin Admiral Raeder was anxious to win glory for the navy while he still had enough oil to fuel the battleships, while the British were still heavily committed to the Mediterranean, and before the army could capture all the headlines by conquering Russia.[16] As so often happened with German warships, *Scharnhorst* and *Gneisenau* returned from their Atlantic cruise at the end of March with serious engine trouble, so to the dismay of Admiral Günther Lütjens, the 'fleet commander', he was forced to go to sea in May with a 'fleet' consisting of only two ships, the *Bismarck* and the heavy cruiser *Prinz Eugen*. Even after eight months repairing defects the *Bismarck* only got to sea by cannibalizing other ships, and her anti-aircraft fire-control was not fully operational. Lütjens believed no British battleships were at sea, and it must have been a shock to be intercepted by the *Hood* and *Prince of Wales* in the Denmark Strait on 24 May.[17] The famous *Hood* was no longer new and there were known flaws in both her armour and her Dreyer Fire Control Table; *Prince of Wales* was newly commissioned and not yet fully worked up, but overall the two British ships had double the weight of the German broadsides and excellent prospects of victory. Instead, the *Hood* was destroyed by a magazine explosion, and the damaged *Prince of Wales* broke off the action. This shocking catastrophe could not and cannot be explained for certain, but the latest analysis makes a strong case that the *Hood* was unlucky to be hit at an awkward angle permitting the handling space of her after 4-inch anti-aircraft guns to be penetrated, generating a cordite fire which spread to a main armament magazine. The *Bismarck's* shooting was otherwise indifferent and the odds against this accident were long – but war is the domain of chance, and there is no fighting without risk.[18]

The Admiralty reacted fast. In three days it had deployed five battleships, two battle-cruisers, two carriers, thirteen cruisers, thirty-three destroyers, eight submarines and numerous aircraft in search of the *Bismarck*. The *Ark Royal* of Force H came straight from flying off fighters to reinforce Malta. Yet soon after the action, the *Bismarck* evaded the British cruisers, and for two days it seemed she might escape all pursuit. An air attack from the carrier *Victorious* on the evening of 25 May caused only minor damage, but late on the 26th another air attack from the *Ark Royal* achieved two torpedo hits, one of which jammed *Bismarck's* rudders and made it impossible to hold a straight course, delivering her to the pursuit. On the morning of the 27th the battleships *Rodney* and *King George V* quickly disabled the *Bismarck*, though it took almost two hours of shelling and several cruiser torpedoes before she sank. She left her sister-ship the *Tirpitz* a powerful psychological legacy. Although the British already knew much about the *Bismarck* and learnt more later, what they remembered was not her old-fashioned design and surprising vulnerability to long-range shellfire, not the repeated demonstration that aircraft could locate and cripple even the most powerful battleship, but the great size and apparently almost magical strength which had destroyed the *Hood*. For the next three years the *Tirpitz*, scarcely going to sea, yet exercised a remorseless pressure on British naval strategy merely by existing, and by her existence evoking the traumatic loss of the *Hood*. 'A fleet in being', the phrase coined in 1690 by Lord Torrington to explain the strategic influence even of an inferior fleet so long as it avoided defeat, recurred to the minds of British (and Italian) admirals 250 years later.[19]

While the RAF made repeated and costly attacks on German heavy ships lying in the Breton ports, six German disguised merchant 'raiders' enjoyed their most successful period in the first half of 1941, operating mainly against unescorted merchantmen in the South Atlantic and Indian Ocean, and supported by an efficient system of supply ships. Thirty-nine merchant ships were sunk or captured for the loss of only one German and one Italian raider. Two of the raiders returned home safely. In the second half of the year the progressive spread of the convoy system reduced the raiders' opportunities; the four raiders still at sea sank only six merchantmen, plus one made prize. Two of the raiders returned home safely and two were sunk. This includes the dramatic case of the *Kormoran*, intercepted on 19 November off Western Australia by the Australian light cruiser *Sydney*, which rashly approached very close before challenging and was fatally damaged when the raider opened fire. Both ships sank, the *Sydney* with no survivors.[20]

The RAF had now begun to learn how to attack ships effectively with torpedoes and bombs, and German ships in Brest were subject to such heavy British air attacks that in April 1941 Raeder forbade the port to be used except in an emergency. The armoured ship *Lützow* (formerly *Deutschland*), the last German heavy ship in the North Atlantic, was intercepted on the Norwegian coast with the help of signals intelligence and torpedoed by the RAF in June 1941, putting her in dock until January 1942. Next month the *Scharnhorst* was badly bombed near La Rochelle and put out of action for eight months.[21]

For more than ten years the Admiralty had regarded Japan as its most dangerous adversary. Pre-war Admiralty planning assumed that British trade and territory in the East must be defended by an adequate fleet with a secure base, and as Hong Kong was too advanced and exposed, it had been determined that Singapore was the only feasible location. In 1938 the Singapore base had been completed as far as the initial 'Red Scheme', with one dry dock capable of receiving a modern battleship, and sufficient resources to maintain one division of four capital ships, or a scant one-third of the fleet which it would be necessary to base there to meet the Japanese main fleet. From the beginning the gap between planned requirement and actual capacity was spanned by wishful thinking, and the fall of France made the strategic situation much worse. In September 1940 Britain candidly informed the Australian government that it could not send a fleet to the East until Germany and Italy had been defeated, though Churchill promised to send aid in the event of a 'large-scale invasion' of Australia. As Britain became more involved in fighting Italy and Germany in 1941, the Japanese threat became yet more serious, but the Eastern Fleet grew weaker as its most modern warships were taken to reinforce the

Mediterranean. In March, Air Vice-Marshal Sir Robert Brooke-Popham, Commander-in-Chief Far East, summed up the situation for the Cabinet:

> Primarily of course the defence of Singapore depends upon the Navy but as we haven't got any ships, it's been laid down quite rightly that we must reply mainly upon the air. But as we are so short of aeroplanes we have to face the fact that landings are at least possible and so we come back to dependence largely upon the Army.[22]

At least the inadequacy of the Singapore 'Red Scheme' was of no immediate concern, when the chances of gathering any sort of battle-fleet to use the base were receding fast.[23]

Delayed six weeks by the Greek campaign, Operation 'Barbarossa', the German invasion of Russia, began on 22 June. General Hans Jeschonnek, chief of staff of the Luftwaffe, exclaimed in delight, 'At last, a real war!'[24] Like most foreign observers he expected that the Soviet army would collapse at least as fast as the French had done the previous year. The Germans depended on it, and were quite unprepared for the campaign to drag on into the winter.[25] An immediate effect of the Russian campaign was to divert most of the German aircraft from the Mediterranean, permitting the air strength of Malta to be rebuilt. From May 1941 radar-equipped British torpedo bombers, co-ordinated with reconnaissance aircraft, operated at night against Italian convoys which themselves had no radar and no air cover by night. Over six months, from June to November, the convoys lost 9.6 per cent of their shipping, 12.8 per cent of the personnel who embarked for Libya, 22.7 per cent of the material, and (most serious of all for the German-Italian army), 30.1 per cent of the fuel loaded. Further losses were caused by attacks on coastwise shipping bringing supplies which had been unloaded at Tripoli, up to Benghazi, the nearest port to the front line. By August, when the 10th Submarine Flotilla returned, the strength of Malta's garrison was 22,000 men, with 230 heavy anti-aircraft guns, 103 coast-defence guns, and supplies for eight to fifteen months. In September the submarine *Upholder* sank two liners laden with German troops in one night. On the night of 9 November 'Force K', a Malta striking force of two light cruisers and two destroyers, sank without loss an entire (radar-less) Italian convoy carrying 34,473 tons of munitions and 17,821 tons of fuel. A month later, under heavy German pressure to improve the supply position, the *Supermarina* despatched two light cruisers with a deck cargo of petrol, but the British (without sending any explicit order which might have betrayed their signals intelligence) were able to steer a group of destroyers on a course to intercept the cruisers off Cape Bon, where both were sunk. The attacks of Force K and the torpedo bombers, plus RAF bombing of Benghazi, sank 62 per cent of the supplies shipped to Libya in November, turned the British army's 'Crusader' offensive into a narrow victory, and forced General Rommel repeatedly to postpone his planned attack on Tobruk.[26]

Heavy pressure was applied on the Italians to make more effort, and on the Germans to deploy their most effective weapons: aircraft and submarines. Raeder was forced to divert twenty-four U-boats to the Mediterranean, more or less abandoning the North Atlantic campaign, and *Fliegerkorps II* of the Luftwaffe was ordered south in December.[27] By the spring of 1942 about one-fifth of the Luftwaffe's entire strength had been diverted from the Russian front to the Central Mediterranean. These were two of the causes of an abrupt reversal of British naval fortunes, but there were others. In September the fighting around the British Malta convoy code-named 'Halberd' demonstrated the growing effectiveness of the *Regia Aeronautica*'s new torpedo-bomber force, established the previous year, which pushed home their attacks to close range (earning the admiring comment 'a really gallant lot' from Admiral Sir James Somerville) and damaged the battleship *Nelson*. Worse befell the *Ark Royal*, torpedoed by *U-81* off Gibraltar on 14 November. Although she was hit by only a single torpedo, the damage control was mismanaged and she sank under tow. This sinking, Sir Stanley Goodall the Director of Naval Construction acknowledged, 'had shaken us to the core'.[28] Less than a fortnight later, on 25 November, the battleship *Barham* zigzagged right onto *U-331*, was hit at very close range by four torpedoes and blew up as she turned over. Cunningham's fleet was now reduced to two battleships, which he hoped would still be enough, but 'I must keep them rather in cotton wool as it wouldn't do to get another put out of action.'[29]

In December 1941 Malta's grave shortage of fuel justified the risk of sending the tanker *Breconshire* from Alexandria escorted by light cruisers only. This little convoy crossed with the Italian southbound convoy M.42, covered by the main Italian fleet of four battleships, two heavy cruisers and thirty smaller ships. Despite the gross disparity of force, Rear-Admiral Philip Vian was able to get his tanker into Malta on 18 December thanks to boldness, good fortune and erroneous Italian air reconnaissance which deceived Admiral Iachino into thinking he faced a battleship force. This distant skirmish, sometimes dignified with the title of 'the first Battle of Sirte', was fought in a full gale, and owes some of its fame to dramatic photographs of ships fighting in heavy seas. In strategic terms both sides could claim success, but the big Italian convoy, escorted by forces which the Royal Navy could not possibly match in these waters, delivered the supplies that made possible Rommel's January 1942 offensive.[30]

Rear-Admiral Vian replenished Malta's fuel, but he exhausted its luck. The Italians had already observed that British ships navigating the intricate passages through the islands and reefs between Sicily and Africa were using Asdic as an echo-sounder to follow the hundred-fathom line. This was too deep for normal minelaying, and should have been safe, but the *Regia Marina* had been able to obtain some deep-water mines from the Germans with which to set an ambush. They were laid by three Italian light cruisers on 1 May. More than seven months later, on the night of 18–19 December, Force K ran onto these mines, losing the cruiser *Neptune* (with only one survivor) and the destroyer *Kandahar*, plus the cruiser *Aurora* badly damaged.[31]

After the successful delivery of convoy M.42, Cunningham warned the Admiralty that 'The enemy has experienced freedom of movement and must enjoy the taste . . . he will become more venturesome.'[32] He did. Thirty-six minutes after the sinking of Force K, the *Queen Elizabeth* and *Valiant*, the Mediterranean Fleet's last battleships which Cunningham had resolved to 'keep in cotton wool', were sunk in Alexandria Harbour by explosive charges laid by Italian divers steering underwater powered sleds officially named SLC (for *Siluri Lenta Corsa*, 'Slow-Running Torpedoes'), but known to the divers as *maiali* ('swine'). In a skilful and daring operation, long-prepared in great secrecy, the *maiali* had been released by a submarine off the port, and crept in through the anti-submarine nets by following an inbound warship. Although the Italian Navy had been using various *mezzi insidiosi* ('stealth weapons') since the previous war, and the *maiali* had been deployed in several attacks already, this blow was quite unexpected. The Taranto raid had been avenged – though the British battleships, like the Italian, were sunk in shallow water and could eventually be salved and returned to service, *Valiant* in August 1942 and *Queen Elizabeth* in January 1944. But that was all in the future: in the grim present of December 1941, without heavy ships to command the Central Mediterranean, the British could do only a little to prevent Italian convoys bringing supplies to the German-Italian army in Libya; 92 per cent of sailings arrived safely between 17 December and the end of March 1942.[33]

It is perhaps not surprising that British naval historians have tended to pass over this great Italian victory, but it needs to be explained why Italian historians are still more embarrassed by it, and the Italian Navy is certainly not holding an annual dinner to commemorate it. These *mezzi insidiosi* had been developed by a secret unit known as the *Decima Flottiglia MAS* ('10th MTB Flotilla'), which was the darling of the Fascist Party. After Italy ejected the Fascists from power in 1943, withdrew from the war and joined the Allies, part of this unit remained loyal to Mussolini's rump 'Italian Social Republic' in northern Italy, carrying on the war until 1945 on the German side, and in the German tradition functioning as a naval 'death squad' under the command of the 'Black Prince' himself, Commander Junio Valerio Borghese. After the war he became a leading figure on the extreme right of Italian politics, who first led and then abandoned the abortive Fascist *coup d'état* of 1970. Most post-war Italian historians and naval officers had rather bury such a man than praise him, and consequently the name and achievements of the *Decima Flottiglia MAS* have been largely suppressed.[34]

The crisis of the Mediterranean naval war came together with the long-feared crisis of Japanese aggression in the East. At the 'Riviera' Conference held in mid-August 1941 aboard ship off the coast of Newfoundland, Churchill and Roosevelt agreed that the US Navy would take over the escort of British convoys in the Western Atlantic, using aggressive tactics designed to provoke open war with Germany, or at least to take the pressure off the Home Fleet. This would allow the British to reinforce the grandly titled 'Eastern Fleet', which at that point consisted only of some old light cruisers and destroyers to cover the whole of the pre-war East Indies and China stations, the Indian Ocean and the South China Sea. The surviving four slow and largely unmodernized 'R' Class battleships of 1915–16, the *Ramillies, Resolution, Revenge* and *Royal Sovereign* (which the Admiralty with good reason had hitherto regarded as too weak to face modern warships), were to be stationed at Cape Town as some distant protection to the Indian Ocean, while a new Eastern Fleet was to be assembled by transferring Force H from Gibraltar, and adding the battleship *Rodney*, a carrier, and the old battlecruisers *Repulse* and *Renown*. On 10 October the Admiralty informed other commands that the *Rodney* and the 'R' Class would go to the East Indies at once, 'and probably further east as soon as possible'. Immediately Churchill intervened: 'This major Fleet movement has not been approved by me or the Defence Committee. No action must be taken pending decision.'[35] For some years historians have combined to accuse Churchill of neglecting the defences of the Eastern Empire, and rashly exposing the capital ships *Prince of Wales* and *Repulse* to destruction, but the most recent and complete studies[36] produce powerful evidence that this was almost the opposite of the truth. It was the hitherto realistic Admiralty which moved from late 1941 towards a forward strategy based on careless optimism, while the Prime Minister asked awkward questions and imposed caution. Indeed, it is this campaign which offers the earliest indication that Admiral Pound's professional judgement may already have been affected by the brain tumour which killed him in October 1943.[37]

The same Admiralty which had previously demanded a balanced fleet with adequate air cover, now in early November sent the two battleships to the East by themselves. It seems to have been influenced by recent experience in the Mediterranean. The 'Halberd' convoy from Gibraltar to Malta in late September 1941 was attacked by twenty-nine torpedo bombers, twenty-four high-level bombers, nine dive-bombers and sixty fighters. The Italian pilots by now were skilled and dangerous, flying aircraft of similar performance to the Japanese Navy's, but a balanced modern fleet of three battleships, one carrier, five cruisers, eighteen destroyers and eighteen long-range fighters from Malta, with radar direction of the defending fighters and an effective AA gunnery barrage, got eight out of nine transports safely into Malta. This experience showed that a convoy could be fought through heavy air attack; it also showed the scale and quality of defence which would be needed if a Japanese air attack were to be as heavy and as dangerous as an Italian one. The Admiralty was also influenced by the success of 'Force H', the pioneer 'carrier task force' (to use the later US naval term) in both the Mediterranean and the Atlantic. This seemed to indicate that a small force of fast and powerful modern warships, with sufficient support from sea- or land-based aircraft, could apply pressure on a much larger fleet.[38]

It is important here to note something often overlooked, both among policy-makers at the time and historians since: there were two distinct strategic schemes under discussion. The Admiralty was concentrating on creating a force to protect Singapore and Malaya against Japanese attack coming through the South China Sea, north of the Malacca Strait and the East Indies island barrier, but close to the Philippines and the possibility of US air power. Churchill, however, was particularly concerned with a force to protect British shipping in the Indian Ocean, south of the East Indies, against the raiders which the Germans had already deployed there, and the Japanese very well might (and in the event did). Here, where the Japanese main fleet threat was more distant, and there were British aircraft based on Ceylon, the analogy with Force H made better sense. Both of these schemes, however, belonged in a deterrent strategy which by late November seemed more and more likely to be too late, for both required adequate modern forces which were far from ready.[39]

A significant factor in the Admiralty's decision to send the two ships was American pressure on Britain to deploy an effective fleet to protect Malaya – without which, it was implied, the United States would not feel obliged to offer any naval help. What Roosevelt did offer was to strengthen the air defences of the Philippines. In October the US Army Air Force was planning by March 1942 to have 136 B-17 bombers stationed there, plus 57 dive-bombers, 130 fighters, and a 'significant force' of the big new B-24 bomber, claimed to be capable of bombing Japan from the Philippines. The USAAF leaders (General George C. Marshall, Chief of Staff of the Army, General Hap Arnold of the Army Air Force, and Henry L. Stimson the Secretary of War) were confident that this would be enough to deter the Japanese, and the Admiralty hoped that the same aircraft would cover the big ships they meant to deploy to the same area. The British had not yet learnt how large a discount had to be applied to Roosevelt's assurances, but it is still surprising that they were not more sceptical towards the USAAF's grand scheme, with its vague timetable and casual assumptions, and in particular not more alert to the danger that these preparations would tempt the Japanese to a pre-emptive strike.[40] The US forces (and even more Congress and the government) refused to take seriously the idea that they themselves might be attacked, and were chronically liable to overrate the effectiveness of new American technology, in this case bombers. Rather in the style of the RAF, they preferred to look ahead six months or so to a hopeful future dominated by heavy bombers, passing quickly over the uncomfortable present when they were not yet in place.[41] Both Britain and the US credited the Japanese with a prudent and cautious outlook, and believed that they could be deterred by a show of firmness. The British had broken into the Japanese diplomatic machine cypher in 1934 and the Americans penetrated its 1939 successor (which they called 'Purple'), but the Japanese military did not confide all their plans to diplomats. Western observers failed to allow for the degree to which the decision to go to war was taken out of the hands of civilian politicians after the resignation of Prime Minister Konoe Fumimaro in October 1941. Thereafter the decisions which led to war fell to the Japanese military – the Naval General Staff in particular – with its nineteenth-century faith in the moral supremacy of the bold attack. What they knew about the German triumph in Norway confirmed this conclusion. (Unlike the Italians, who also studied this campaign, they did not know much about the contribution of wireless intelligence.)[42]

What nobody in Britain or the United States seems to have appreciated was that there were two centres of Japanese naval decision-making: the cautious Naval General Staff in Tokyo, dominated by orthodox battleship admirals, and the Combined Fleet staff aboard Admiral Yamamoto Isoroku's flagship, which was developing radical ideas of a decisive victory gained by surprise air attack. These ideas were adopted but not originated by Yamamoto; they owed much to Commander Genda Minoru, one of the few airmen officers in the Japanese Navy (most of whose aircrew were ratings). Genda had been air attaché in London in 1940, but it is not true (as is sometimes suggested) that the Japanese plans were inspired by the British attack on Taranto. The Japanese Naval Air Force had been founded after the First World War by ex-RNAS officers like Frederick Rutland, so both British and Japanese naval airmen shared a common professional tradition inherited from the RNAS of 1918, and neither had forgotten its planned air attack on the High Seas Fleet.[43]

At the Imperial Conference of 6 September 1941, the two Japanese services presented their war plans for the emperor's approval. Admiral Nagano Osami, Chief of the Naval General Staff (a Harvard man who had spent years in the US and spoke good English), explained candidly that Japan needed to win fast, before the US oil embargo could bite. If the enemy (here Nagano was evidently thinking of the British) 'should aim for a quick war leading to an early decision . . . this would be the very thing we hope for'. The danger which the admiral foresaw was that the United States would prefer a long war, in which case 'our Empire does not have the means to take the offensive, overcome the enemy, and make them give up the will to fight'.[44] Yamamoto's radical response was to leave the Naval General Staff to manage the 'southern advance' while he took the six big carriers, now designated the *Kidō Butai* ('mobile force') on a sort of 'private venture' offensive to attack the US fleet, not in the Marshall Islands where it expected to fight, but 2,500 miles further eastward, with a surprise attack on its advanced base of Pearl Harbor.[45] This would remove the risk of US battleships arriving in time to defeat the 'southern advance' and save the Philippines. The final decision to adopt this plan was taken on 3 November, leaving a very short time to overcome several major technical difficulties. The carriers could not attack a place 3,700 miles from home without refuelling, so the Japanese had to improvise methods of refuelling at sea, which they had never tried. They had to develop new 'air tails' to drop torpedoes in shallow water (in this case they were encouraged by knowing that the Fleet Air Arm had succeeded in doing the same at Taranto). They could not hope to sink the US battleships by aerial torpedoes alone, however, since the battleships moored in Pearl Harbor in pairs along the shore and only the outboard ship of each pair was vulnerable. The airmen therefore improvised armour-piercing bombs out of adapted shells and trained to bomb from 3,000 metres (a little under 10,000 feet), a height calculated to give just enough velocity for the bombs to penetrate battleship armour, just low enough to give some chance of hitting the targets. To provide the 'southern advance' with air cover in the absence of the carriers the Japanese had to stretch the range of their naval fighters far enough to cover the invasion of the Philippines from airfields in Formosa (Taiwan). This attack would have to be made in daylight, five and a half hours later than the Pearl Harbor attack, when the defences would be fully alert. All the preparations had to be made in deep secrecy and wireless silence, cloaked by elaborate deceptions.[46]

Despite all these precautions, it was obvious to both Washington and London that a crisis was approaching. On 27 November senior American naval officers in the Pacific were warned that 'an aggressive move by Japan is expected within the next few days', with a suggestion that likely targets would be the Philippines, Thailand, Borneo or Malaya.[47] Neither the US Army Air Force or the US Navy, jointly responsible for the air defence of Hawaii, took seriously the idea that they themselves might be the target, because for both services it was obvious that a Japanese attack was impossible, irrational – in the last analysis unthinkable. Pre-war exercises had repeatedly shown that a naval air attack on Hawaii, which might come from any point of the compass, could only be reliably detected by keeping at least 150 reconnaissance aircraft in the air at once. This was far more than the two US air forces had between them, and their aircrew were in any case exhausted by their training programme. US intelligence, however, confidently located the Japanese carriers far away in home waters, and the US Navy had convinced itself that torpedo attack was impossible in the shallow water of Pearl Harbor (partly because they thought that Taranto was twice as deep). The Dutch sent warning that the Japanese main fleet was heading east, but US authorities paid no attention. The radical innovation of the First Air Fleet, created on 1 April 1941 and re-equipped with a new doctrine and the latest aircraft, seems to have been unknown to any Western intelligence service, and the significant changes to Japanese wireless call-signs and cyphers introduced at the beginning of December aroused no alarm.[48]

The Japanese attack on Pearl Harbor was timed for 8.30 on Sunday morning 7 December, half an hour after the Japanese declaration of war should have been delivered in Washington, though in the event it was very late. No attention was paid to the experimental radar system (which detected the Japanese aircraft), there were no defending aircraft in the air, and initially no anti-aircraft fire. The Japanese attack was, as usual, planned in great detail, but, rather unusually, delivered in considerable disorder. Against a totally unprepared enemy it made no difference. The midget submarine attacks which formed an important component of the Japanese plan, failed completely, but in every other respect the attack delivered almost everything which had been intended or expected. Of the eight US battleships, two were total losses (including the *Arizona*, whose forward magazines were detonated by an improvised dive-bomb), three were beached or sunk but eventually refloated, and three more were only lightly damaged. The three carriers were all away from port, as the Japanese knew. The US air forces between them lost 188 aircraft of all types destroyed and 159 badly damaged, leaving only 43 still airworthy. The dockyard repair shops and the enormous fuel reserve, both of which Genda had wished to attack, were left untouched, which greatly assisted the US Navy to recover.[49]

Meanwhile 'Force Z', the modern battleship *Prince of Wales* and the unmodernized battle-cruiser *Repulse* under the command of Acting Vice-Admiral Sir Tom Phillips, had to go straight to Singapore for urgent repairs to the battleship's boilers. She arrived on 2 December and was barely out of dock when the Japanese landed in northern Malaya on the 7th. It was too late to do anything save to seek out the enemy and fight him, but Phillips, who had spent much of his recent career ashore in the Admiralty, did not report that he was under air attack until it was too late to send fighter cover (which was available, and might possibly have arrived in time to make a difference). The British had access to excellent intelligence from the Far East Combined Bureau, but when Phillips arrived at Singapore he took little time to study it, and he may have sailed on his last voyage under the serious misapprehension that the air threat he faced came from bombers of the Imperial Japanese Army Air Force, rather than the much more dangerous torpedo bombers of the Naval Air Force.[50] Experienced fighting admirals like Somerville had deep misgivings about Phillips' lack of 'sea sense': 'I shudder to think of the Pocket Napoleon and his party', Somerville wrote to Cunningham in October. 'All the tricks to learn and no solid sea experience to fall back on.' After the event Somerville wrote to another colleague, 'Alas our forecasts about Tom P were only too true. I felt in my bones all the time that he would have to pay sooner or later for his lack of practical war experience & his lack of sea sense but I did not imagine that it would have to be at such a price . . . Battleships by themselves are quite useless whilst co-operation with shore based aircraft requires a lot of practice *and* experience.'[51] The Japanese naval aircraft, flying from French airfields near Saigon, displayed outstanding professional skill in locating the British ships at a range of nearly 600 miles and skilfully co-ordinating their attacks (the more so as they were short of torpedoes and had only one each). The old *Repulse* with her negligible anti-aircraft armament was brilliantly handled by Captain Tennant and almost survived, but the modern *Prince of Wales*, with her advanced anti-torpedo protection supposedly proof against 1,000lb explosive charges, was completely disabled by the first torpedo hit (330lb warhead) on the port outer shaft bracket as the ship was turning under full helm and full power. The shaft broke up, causing massive underwater damage which disabled all internal communications and nearly all her anti-aircraft armament. This should never have happened: it has been suggested that the shaft may have suffered undetected damage from a near-miss bomb which fell alongside while the ship was fitting out in Birkenhead in August 1940, but on any interpretation the sinking of the *Prince of Wales* reflects badly on British naval constructors as well as brilliantly on Japanese naval airmen. For Sir Stanley Goodall, the DNC, the sinking of the new battleship was 'the worst blow conceivable'.[52]

The sinking of the *Prince of Wales* and *Repulse* was a famous naval disaster, and historians obsessed by the theme of decline have freely adopted it as a symbol of the downfall of the British Empire, and the obsolescence of the battleship. Much of this is over-coloured, not to say histrionic. If any event announced the fall of the British Empire it was the surrender of Malaya on 15 February 1942 by a defending garrison which outnumbered their Japanese attackers three to one. Warships are built to fight, and even the biggest of them are liable to be sunk. Aircraft had been a factor of growing weight in naval warfare for half a century, and no naval officers were surprised to find that they could sink battleships in the right circumstances, though the *Prince of Wales* was the first to be sunk when under way in the open sea. Long before the war the Naval Staff had decided that all major naval operations required adequate cover from land- or sea-based aircraft, and without it the disaster was highly predictable. If anybody imagined that this action proved the obsolescence of the battleship, they only needed to contemplate the desperate position of the British in the Eastern Mediterranean at that moment, attempting to supply their own army and intercept the supplies going to the enemy with nothing left to command the sea but aircraft and small warships.[53] The worst British mistake was to believe, despite numerous warning signs, that American forces could and would resist Japanese aggression. The complete failure of the US fleet, virtually undefended at Pearl Harbor; of the USAAF bombers, totally undefended on their Philippine airfields more than eight hours after hearing the news of Pearl Harbor; and of the US Asiatic Fleet (especially the submarines with their elderly officers and dysfunctional weapons), would have fatally exposed even a much more resolute defence of Malaya.[54]

The strategic chessboard of the naval war had now been completely overturned. In the space of less than a fortnight, between the Pearl Harbor attack on 7 December, the sinking of the *Prince of Wales* and the *Repulse* on 10 December, and the sinking of the Mediterranean Fleet on 19 December, the principal fleets of Britain and the United States had been eliminated. Both retained substantial naval strength in home waters, with many powerful new ships under construction and some powerful old ones under repair, but in the unforgiving light of the present moment, there was now little left afloat to oppose the

Italian fleet in the Mediterranean, or the Japanese fleet in the Pacific. But this was not all that changed in the first half of December. By their quixotic decision to declare war on the USA on the 11th, Germany and Italy united the European and China Wars for the first time. Had Roosevelt chosen, on 7 December or during the five days which followed, to step back from his ambiguous declarations against Germany and Italy to concentrate on fighting Japanese aggression, it seems very likely, in the enraged state of US public opinion, that Congress would have followed his lead. This was Churchill's greatest fear. Britain and Russia might have been left behind in growing isolation as discarded allies carrying the burden of an unpopular European war with less and less American help. However, Britain's visible determination to fight persuaded both her Axis enemies and her American quasi-ally, so Hitler and Mussolini forged what now became the Western Alliance and pushed it into taking the decision to liberate Europe first. At last, it really was a world war.[55]

TWENTY-SIX

Great Liberty

Policy and Operations 1942

In the Far East the consequences of the naval disasters of December 1941 unfolded over the next six months. Singapore surrendered on 15 February, and the Dutch-led Allied fleet and air force which fought the Japanese in the Java Sea on 27 February only briefly checked the Japanese advance. The defenders (the Dutch in particular) enjoyed good intelligence and substantial air power. They knew how thinly the Japanese invasion forces were stretched, and how narrow their margin of victory was, but in the end it was a total victory nevertheless, greater than any in naval history. In five months the Japanese gained 250,000 prisoners and sank 105 ships for the loss of 21,000 casualties, 562 aircraft and 27 small ships. By early March virtually the whole arc of the East Indies from Malaya to New Guinea was in Japanese hands. The US battle-fleet was already sunk; the US Army, which as a military power had ranked seventeenth in the world in 1939 (it was nearly as powerful as Portugal), surrendered 35,000 men, its only field army, to the Japanese on the Bataan Peninsula near Manila on 9 April, and lost the island fortress of Corregidor a month later.[1]

By now the Japanese had overrun the oilfields of the East Indies, and the Germans seemed to be on the verge of seizing the Middle East, with the oil of Persia and Iraq. The Allied strategy of 'Germany first', first agreed at the 'Arcadia' conference in Washington over Christmas 1941, assumed that Japan could be contained in the meanwhile, but by early 1942 the Japanese had broken all possible bounds. The way was wide open for the Imperial Navy to move into the South Pacific or advance right to the Californian coast to cut the links between Australia and the United States, to enter the Indian Ocean to land in Ceylon or Western Australia, and to cut the shipping route up the East African coast and through the Red Sea which supplied the British army in North Africa. The Imperial Army could invade India overland through Burma. Any of these moves could be combined with steps to cut off supplies shipped to Russia through Persia, and to China via India. For the British it seemed virtually impossible to spread their inadequate forces to cover so great a range of threats. There has never been a campaign which better illustrates Francis Bacon's aphorism: 'He that commands the sea is at great liberty, and may take as much and as little of the war as he will.'[2] Perhaps it illustrates the dangers as well as the advantages of having so wide a range of tempting choices. Certainly, the necessity of taking decisions brought out the vicious inter-service disputes which afflicted all the participants in the Pacific War: between the Japanese Navy and Army and their respective air forces, between the US Navy, Army and Marine Corps and *their* respective airmen, between Britons, Americans and Australians. Opinions were also divided within the Japanese Navy. The Naval General Staff in Tokyo favoured a southern or south-eastern advance to cut communications between the USA and Australia, but Admiral Yamamoto and his staff afloat in the Combined Fleet, still wedded to the nineteenth-century concept of the 'decisive battle' which decides everything, and determined to repeat the triumph of Tsushima in the Russo-Japanese War of 1904–5, wanted to bring on fleet actions to win the war against the British and the Americans, in that order.[3]

After Pearl Harbor the three US battleships which survived with only light damage (*Maryland*, *Pennsylvania* and *Tennessee*) were sent to California for repairs, and a new Pacific battle-fleet was not reconstituted at Pearl Harbor with new ships and transfers from the Atlantic until August 1942, so that for eight months the way was wide open for the Japanese main fleet to seize the Hawaiian Islands and threaten California – or would have been, if the Japanese army had been willing to play. Even when the Pacific Fleet, the US Navy's 'Task Force One', was re-assembled, the old battleships were too slow and thirsty to be practically usable against a modern enemy over the great distances of the Pacific, and Admiral Chester W. Nimitz the new fleet commander was anyway reluctant to risk his capital ships within reach of Japanese torpedoes until the moment came for the big battle. The United States was the only significant belligerent not short of oil, but the seven refuelling oilers available in the Pacific were barely sufficient to support the carriers *Yorktown*, *Enterprise* and *Lexington* (the three which remained operational in those waters after the *Saratoga* was torpedoed by a Japanese submarine in January and sent to Bremerton for repairs). So the battleships stayed in port, leaving the strategic initiative to the Japanese, while the carriers operated individually in accordance with US naval doctrine, moving fast and avoiding high risk by mounting occasional 'tip and run' raids on Japanese airfields, mainly on the scattered islands lying in the wide tract of the central Pacific between Hawaii and the Philippines, the waters where both navies still thought it most likely that they would fight their great fleet action. Besides several cancelled operations, in the first three months of 1942 the *Enterprise* and *Yorktown* raided Japanese airfields in the Marshall Islands on 1 February, the *Enterprise* raided Wake Island on 24 February and Marcus Island (Minamitorishima) on 4 March, and on 10 March the *Lexington* and *Yorktown* sent their aircraft from the Coral Sea over the Owen Stanley Mountains of central New Guinea (more than 13,000 feet high) to attack Lae and Salamaua on the north coast, where Japanese and Australian landing forces were already fighting. These raids exposed many technical deficiencies of the US aircraft and weapons, including guns which jammed and bomb-sights which fogged up when diving, and the urgent need of incendiary bullets, delayed-action bomb fuses, IFF, and above all escort fighters to protect torpedo bombers.[4]

Meanwhile the Japanese main fleet under Admiral Nagumo Chūichi concentrated on the British threat from the new Eastern Fleet then assembling in the Indian Ocean under Admiral Sir James Somerville, who arrived to take command at the end of March. Both admirals were starved of intelligence. Nagumo overestimated the British fleet, which was largely made up of obsolete ships, and Somerville underestimated his opponent's strength. Far East Combined Bureau, the Royal Naval intelligence organization, had been evacuated from Hong Kong, Singapore and Colombo in succession to come to rest at Kilindini in East Africa, where it was safe from the enemy but remote from the naval war, with poor wireless reception and hardly any connection to what survived of the British cable network. Somerville's best source of intelligence on Japanese fleet movements should have been the US Navy, but this channel was largely blocked by inter-service rivalry. From March 1942, US forces in the Indian Ocean formed part of the new South-West Pacific Command under General Douglas MacArthur, who was happy to take American, Australian and British warships to support his own campaigns, but treated Admiral Nimitz's Central Pacific Command as a professional rival, verging on a public enemy. MacArthur knew that the British and Australians talked to each other, and to his US competitors, with whom he had no desire to share information. On the collapse of the Allied defence in the East Indies most of the RAN and USN intelligence resources had finished up in Australia but under US command as part of 'FRUMEL' ('Fleet Radio Unit Melbourne'), whose commanding officer understood that his most urgent priority was to prevent any secret information leaking to the British. The best naval intelligence on the Japanese main fleet came from Nimitz's headquarters in Pearl Harbor, but Somerville had no access to it.[5]

In the first week of April, almost as soon as Somerville arrived in his new command, and before he had had any time to improve its training and efficiency, Nagumo entered the Indian Ocean with the Japanese carrier force, intending to attack Ceylon and destroy the British Eastern Fleet. Nagumo's fleet included four fast battleships and five fleet carriers with about 275 aircraft; Somerville had two carriers and five battleships, but four of the five were the old 'R' Class and the carrier force urgently needed modern aircraft. A fleet action by day was likely to be a disaster and Somerville's orders were to run no grave risks, but he still hoped for a chance to use his radar-equipped Albacore torpedo bombers for a night attack which might, with much luck, catch the Japanese at their only vulnerable moment. In the event on 5 April Somerville almost succeeded in catching two of the Japanese carriers detached from the main body and unaware of their danger, but at the critical moment he was unable to fix their position accurately enough for a night attack with aircraft whose radar range (with ASV Mk.2) was barely thirty miles. Somerville was running big risks to get as close as he did and was undoubtedly lucky to avoid disaster, but the Japanese might have earned some luck for themselves by devoting more attention to reconnaissance; instead of which they ignored the presence of the Eastern Fleet in the vicinity despite sighting at least one British carrier aircraft, and never located its secret refuelling anchorage at Addu Atoll in the Maldives, even with the help of the *B-Dienst*. With characteristic rigidity the Japanese stuck to an elaborate plan while the situation changed rapidly around them, but as they returned to home waters in April, they could at least congratulate themselves on sinking two cruisers and the small carrier *Hermes*. At long odds, however, Somerville had preserved his 'fleet in being' and frustrated Nagumo's plans.[6]

At almost the same time there sailed from various British ports the ships of a bold amphibious operation which had been hastily assembled to attack a port 9,000 miles away in the Indian Ocean: the French naval base of Diego Suarez (Antsiranana) at the northern end of Madagascar. The sinking of the *Prince of Wales* and *Repulse* had been made possible by the hospitality of the Vichy French authorities, the supplies of the British army in North Africa were acutely vulnerable to the Japanese submarines already operating in the Mozambique Channel, and it was urgently necessary to forestall another French-supported Japanese incursion. The assault force was carried in fourteen merchant ships and an experimental landing ship, covered by two carriers, the old battleship *Ramillies* (borrowed from the Eastern Fleet), two tankers, and some cruisers and destroyers. The initial landing was made on 5 May, and the campaign lasted three days. The French garrison held a strong position and initially fought with determination, but their resistance collapsed when a destroyer forced her way into the port and landed a party of Royal Marines to seize the French headquarters. Successful operations with moderate casualties are fated to be forgotten, but this deserves to be remembered as a skilful and successful exercise in strategic foresight, the forerunner of many subsequent seaborne expeditions (though there was never another over such a long range), one which cut off an opportunity that the Japanese were not quick enough to exploit.[7]

So central did the campaign against German U-boats become to the outcome of the war in the West that today it requires an effort to remember that in 1941 and 1942 the war at sea in most parts of the world was still being fought primarily by large surface ships. The *Scharnhorst* and *Gneisenau* returned to Brest in March 1941, and were joined in June (after the sinking of the *Bismarck*) by the heavy cruiser *Prinz Eugen*. As usual after two months at sea their machinery was in a deplorable condition, and Brest dockyard laboured to repair them while the RAF subjected them to repeated air attacks in the teeth of heavy fighter and anti-aircraft defences. Göring grew increasingly reluctant to sacrifice his fighters to protect warships which seldom went to sea, while Hitler was now convinced that northern Norway was the *Schicksalzone*, the 'fateful area' on which the Allies' attention was fixed, where the issue of the war would be settled. Admiral Raeder argued that Germany's heavy ships in Brest might still win the war in the North Atlantic, but he was overruled. By the end of the year there were signs that the German heavy ships were preparing to leave Brest and move east. In December Rear-Admiral Lumley Lyster, Flag Officer Aircraft Carriers, privately warned Air Marshal Philip Joubert de la Ferté of Coastal Command that his striking forces were dangerously weak:

> I do not think we can afford to reduce any more at home, whatever the requirements abroad may be. The day to day work is so vital and a 'break-out', which is not intercepted and destroyed would take some laughing-off, especially if it were done by any of the Brest party.[8]

Two months later it happened. Joubert issued an 'imminent alert' on 3 February 1942, but when the 'Brest party' (the *Scharnhorst*, *Gneisenau* and *Prinz Eugen*) sailed on the 11th his command was not alert. Both Naval and Air Staff were persuaded of the 'strong probability' that if the German heavy ships came up the Channel, they would sail from Brest in daylight to pass the Straits of Dover in darkness. Perhaps sensing their opportunity, the Germans did the opposite. The three heavy ships and their escorting destroyers sailed from Brest just before midnight to begin what British journalists labelled the 'Channel

Dash'. They should have been detected before long by a series of radar-equipped patrol aircraft, but assorted blunders and equipment failures allowed the ships to steam undetected up the Channel until they were finally reported off Le Touquet, opposite Dungeness, at 10.30 in the morning. There was no time to organize a co-ordinated attack, which might have been effective, but various scratch groups of RAF and Fleet Air Arm aircraft, motor torpedo boats, coastal batteries, and destroyers were thrown into action piecemeal and suffered heavy losses to no effect. The whole fiasco reflected badly on most of the British services involved, and demonstrated what should have been well understood already: the unwisdom of improvised attacks on a powerful enemy by ill-trained personnel, and the folly of the Air Staff doctrine that specialist weapons and training for maritime operations were unnecessary. From a wider perspective, as Raeder soberly observed, the German tactical triumph was really a strategic setback, which removed the big ships from the only waters where they might yet have won a major victory. Moreover, the operation did not end as well for the Germans as it began. The Admiralty had time to mine the channels off the Dutch coast ahead of the German ships, inflicting damage from which the *Gneisenau* never recovered, and which kept the *Scharnhorst* out of action until September 1943. The *Prinz Eugen* reached German waters unscathed but was then torpedoed and badly damaged off Trondheim by the submarine *Trident* in February 1942.[9]

One month later a British raiding force entered the Loire estuary to attack the large graving dock which had been built at St Nazaire in 1932 to accommodate the transatlantic liner *Normandie*. The *Tirpitz* was known to be preparing for sea, presumably to operate in the Atlantic. Recent precedent strongly suggested that she would soon be returning in need of repairs, and the Normandie Dock was the only one on the Atlantic coast big enough to receive her. The object of the raid was to make that impossible by putting the dock out of action. HMS *Campbeltown*, one of the old US destroyers transferred in 1940, was rammed into the caisson of the dock at 1.30 on the morning of 28 March. By noon that day the surviving raiders had withdrawn, the ship was crowded with German officers who for some inexplicable reason neglected to search her and were only made aware of the three-ton explosive charge concealed in her forecastle when it blew up, killing them all and wrecking the caisson beyond repair. The raid cost heavy British casualties, and we know now that the Germans had not yet thought about using the dock, but it was undoubtedly an ingenious conception which made it impossible for the Germans to operate the *Tirpitz* in the way most dangerous to Britain.[10]

In January 1942 the *Tirpitz*, *Admiral Scheer* and the damaged *Prinz Eugen*

assembled at Trondheim to form a new northern squadron, including a fifth
of the total U-boat strength, and new long-range bombers. The next twelve
months (March 1942 to February 1943) were critical for the Arctic convoys
(PQ series eastbound, returning as QP), which still carried 90 per cent of the
Western military supplies to Russia. Each convoy needed three layers of
escort: close anti-submarine, then the nearby cruisers, and finally the more
distant covering force of battleships and carriers from the Home Fleet, which
had barely enough strength to provide them even with the help of some borrowed American ships. Of all the ships and crews in convoy and escorts, only
the anti-submarine trawlers, which in peacetime fished the 'distant waters' of
the Barents Sea, were familiar with Arctic conditions. The convoy route was
only twelve hours' steaming at high speed from the new German advance
anchorage of Altafjord (Altenfjord), and Luftwaffe signals could not be
decrypted fast enough to warn of attacks from nearby airfields, though 'Headache' (intercept operators listening to German airmen's voice chatter) might
provide up to twenty minutes' warning. On 7 March PQ 12, QP 8, the Home
Fleet and the *Tirpitz* were all searching for one another in thick weather within
a hundred miles. Two days later *Victorious* was able to mount an air attack on
the *Tirpitz* off the Lofoten Islands, but the ill-trained pilots failed, as the
Report of Proceedings bluntly acknowledged, from 'an accumulation of elementary mistakes in the conduct of the attack' (though the incident did alarm
the Germans, whose ineffectual anti-aircraft fire had contributed little to the
British failure).[11] Three days later Sir John Tovey, commanding the operation
from the battleship *King George V*, found it so difficult to maintain an accurate plot of his scattered cruisers and destroyers in frequent fog that he had to
ask the Admiralty to take over control rather than break wireless silence. One
encouraging surprise was that the numerous U-boats in the Arctic, though
well provided with the aerial reconnaissance which they so badly lacked in
the Atlantic, were largely ineffective. The Luftwaffe, however, was learning
how to attack shipping with both torpedo- and dive-bombers, which sank
seven ships out of thirty-six in PQ 16 at the end of May.[12] Rear-Admiral Stuart
Bonham-Carter, who had two flagships of his cruiser squadron (*Trinidad* and
Edinburgh) sunk under him in succession in the Barents Sea in May, reported
on his return,

> I am convinced that until the aerodromes in North Norway are neutralised
> and there are some hours of darkness that the continuation of these con-
> voys should be stopped. If they must continue for political reasons, very
> serious and heavy losses must be expected. The force of the German attacks

will increase, not diminish. We in the Navy are paid to do this sort of job, but it is beginning to ask too much of the men of the Merchant Navy. We may be able to avoid bombs and torpedoes with our speed, a six or eight knot ship has not this advantage.[13]

This set the scene for the crisis of convoy PQ 17 in July. Having refused Stalin the 'Second Front' which Roosevelt had rashly promised, the Allies had agreed to continue the North Russian convoys, even in the permanent daylight of the Arctic summer. Tovey echoed Bonham-Carter's judgement, thinking it impossible for the Home Fleet to cover an Arctic convoy against a German surface force of the *Tirpitz*, two 'armoured ships', a heavy cruiser and ten fleet destroyers.[14] The Luftwaffe had more than a hundred Ju-88 bombers, forty-two He-111 torpedo bombers, twenty dive-bombers, eight Kondor bombers and a large number of reconnaissance aircraft available – the equivalent of at least five British fleet carriers against Tovey's one. A timely shipment of 15,000 tons of oil made it possible for the German heavy ships to intervene. Since the convoy had to pass close to Altafjord (which has several possible exits), the Germans could delay their order to sail until the last moment, and once he knew that the German heavy ships had united, Admiral Pound (overruling Tovey and against the advice of his staff) decided that he had no choice but to scatter the convoy, making heavy losses inevitable. It was dispersed on 4 July, and twenty-two ships were sunk out of thirty-five. Pound was strongly criticized by British, Russians and Americans present in Arctic waters, echoed by modern historians, but it seems clear now that if the convoy had to be run, it needed a powerful air escort or an improbable degree of luck. There is also an essential intelligence dimension to this episode, which not all historians have taken into account, for Pound was not guessing that the German heavy ships were about to attack; he had reliable means of knowing the gist of their orders.[15] Captain Henry Denham, the British naval attaché in Stockholm, working with Norwegian diplomats, had developed productive contacts with Colonel Carl Björnstjerna, chief of combined intelligence on the Swedish General Staff. Fearful of sharing the fate of Norway, Sweden had already made grossly un-neutral concessions to German demands, including permission to communicate with German forces in northern Norway over Swedish telephone and teleprinter lines. By the end of 1942 Björnstjerna's extensive cryptographic operation was reading these German signals at the rate of 10,000 telegrams a year, transmitted by the misnamed Siemens & Halske *Geheimschreiber* cypher teleprinter. Aware from the general course of the war that it was high time to make friends with the British, Björnstjerna was now passing the substance of messages of interest to Denham in 'chance' lunch-time conversations in the woods of the Djurgården in Stockholm.[16]

The experience of PQ 17 persuaded Tovey that a powerful destroyer escort with air cover could defend a convoy better than risking a battleship within range of German torpedo bombers, and he himself could control the battle better from Scapa Flow than at sea. These ideas were tried with the next Arctic convoy PQ 18 in September, which was defended by sixteen fleet destroyers and the escort carrier *Avenger*. At the last moment the *Tirpitz* had bearing trouble and the German heavy ships stayed in port, but the convoy was heavily attacked by U-boats and torpedo bombers, which sank thirteen merchant ships for the loss of four U-boats and more than forty aircraft. Although better than the catastrophe of PQ 17, a 28 per cent loss was unacceptably high, but the Navy's heavy investment in defending PQ 18 went some way to restore its damaged reputation among merchant seamen. *Avenger*'s old Sea Hurricanes Mk.II provided effective air cover with the aid of air warning from a 'Headache' operator; an encouraging indication that even an escort carrier might be sufficient to protect against a heavy land-based air attack. *Luftflotte V*'s losses in torpedo bombers were never made good, and the German air threat to the Arctic convoys was past its peak.[17]

After PQ 18 the Arctic convoys were suspended in favour of Operation 'Pedestal' in the Mediterranean, and a new series started at the end of December with JW 51B. In the near-permanent darkness of the Arctic winter no attempt was made to provide it with air cover and the escort consisted of the cruisers *Jamaica* and *Sheffield* with five fleet destroyers borrowed from the Home Fleet. The Germans set in motion a pre-planned attack named *Regenbogen* ('Rainbow') by the heavy cruiser *Admiral Hipper* and the former 'armoured ship' *Lützow* (now reclassified as a heavy cruiser), each accompanied by three of the big German fleet destroyers. This should have been ample strength for victory, but Vice-Admiral Oskar Kummetz was fighting in near-darkness with radar ranging but no capacity for blind fire, whereas the British cruisers with efficient radar and flashless powder were able to take the *Lützow* by surprise and hit her hard. Kummetz in the usual German style had orders from three different flag officers who agreed only to forbid risks, with the natural consequence of muddle and indecision. The Germans' long-standing lack of oil meant lack of sea time and lack of tactical experience. Hitler had been promised a victory and was enraged to hear that the German ships had been driven off by the weaker British escort. With difficulty he was persuaded not to pay off all the big German warships forthwith, but in January 1943 Admiral Raeder resigned his command and was succeeded by Admiral Dönitz.[18]

At almost the same moment as the Diego Suarez landing, between 4 and 8 May 1942 but far to the eastward on the other side of Australia, the American and Japanese navies fought the air actions collectively known as the Battle of the Coral Sea. The Japanese were trying to capture Port Moresby to establish a permanent position between Australia and the Solomon Islands. Much of this plan the Americans had deduced from fragmentary intercepted signals, but it was US naval policy that carriers (in this case the *Yorktown* and *Lexington*) should keep well apart as separate admirals' commands, and for the first time in a naval battle the American and Japanese surface ships (none larger than a cruiser) never sighted one another. Both naval air forces suffered from poor voice radios, navigation and identification were weak on both sides, the US Navy had limited ability to control aircraft by radar, and the Japanese none, but the Japanese had better plotting and tactical control of their ships than the USN did. Some of the action occurred in the Solomon Islands, in MacArthur's command, who wanted to prevent Nimitz poaching on his preserves. The result of all this was a chaotic week during which the Japanese light carrier *Shoho* and the very large US carrier *Lexington* were both sunk, but the planned Japanese assault on Port Moresby was abandoned.[19]

Yamamoto believed that two US carriers had been sunk at the Coral Sea, and saw an opportunity to draw the survivors into a trap by attacking the advanced US airfield on Midway Atoll, 1,300 miles west north-west of Oahu. The US Navy deduced the target from fragmentary signal decrypts. Thus began the battle of Midway on 4 June. Both fleets went into action in extraordinary disorder. On the Japanese side key intelligence was not passed from Yamamoto's flagship to the carrier force under Admiral Nagumo, who wrongly believed he had achieved complete surprise. In the open ocean it was difficult to mount effective reconnaissance with no idea of the direction from which an attack might be expected, the USN had no settled techniques of air scouting, and its only common practice was that everyone was expected to use their initiative. As usual, the Japanese adopted a complex and rigid formal plan, and as usual there was little co-ordination between different US flag officers. The three American carriers present (including the *Yorktown*, hastily patched up after serious damage at the Coral Sea) came under the tactical command of the 'black shoe' (meaning battleship) officers Rear-Admirals Frank Fletcher and Raymond Spruance. Captain Marc A. Mitscher of the carrier *Hornet* was an airman who particularly resented finding himself under their command and refused to believe the intelligence on which they relied. As a result, he failed to get his airmen to keep together; rival squadron commanders quarrelled over who was in overall command, different carriers' aircraft tuned their radios to different frequencies, the aircraft split into separate groups and flew off on diverging courses at random. A high proportion of the US aircraft which took the 'flight to nowhere' were shot down or never seen again, but the main group of dive-bombers kept together and by extreme good fortune approached the Japanese carriers from two different bearings, just as they were preparing to launch their air attack. The Douglas Dauntless was an outstanding dive-bomber, stable even in a vertical dive, and the Japanese carriers were highly vulnerable to fire. So were the US carriers, but only the *Yorktown* was sunk against four big Japanese carriers, the *Akagi*, *Kaga*, *Soryu* and *Hiryu*.[20] 'This should be kept in mind as a lesson showing that war is not predictable,' noted Yamamoto's chief of staff in his diary.[21]

The Battle of Midway is sometimes presented as the US Navy's Trafalgar, and in some respects this is a helpful comparison. Neither victory won the war, but both defeated dangerous enemy offensives, and significantly changed the nature of naval warfare in the following years. But Midway did not reflect much credit on US naval organization nor introduce the era of carrier warfare: in fact it almost ended it for the next two years. The aged US battleships were not present, because there were barely enough oilers to keep just a handful of carriers steaming. The Japanese still had five fleet carriers (*Shokaku*, *Zuikaku*, *Junyo*, *Hiyo* and *Zuiho*), and at once began building new carriers to replace the lost ships, but mostly avoided fleet actions for the next two years until they were ready. The US Navy did the same. Omitting the unsatisfactory small carrier *Ranger*, much used as an aircraft ferry, it had four fleet carriers left in service after Midway, the *Saratoga*, *Enterprise*, *Hornet* and *Wasp*, of which the last two were sunk soon afterwards. That left two useful fleet carriers to hold the line with the British carrier *Victorious* for the next four months until the converted light cruisers of the *Independence* Class and the first of the new *Essex* Class fleet carriers began to enter service in 1943. In May 1943 the US Navy had four new carriers. By the end of that year, with seven of the *Essex* Class completed (and nineteen more to follow eventually), the USN was able to resume serious carrier warfare, but for eighteen months after Midway the US Navy in the Pacific, though still heavily committed to wheeled aircraft, had to fly most of them from islands. This pinned the main Pacific naval campaign of 1942 to a confined area in and around the Solomon Islands, providing good opportunities for submarines, which the Americans ignored but the Japanese exploited to sink the carrier *Wasp* and the cruiser *Juneau*, and to damage the big carrier *Saratoga* (which was lucky to survive when her turbo-electric drive short-circuited) and the new fast battleship *North Carolina*, both of which were out of action for three months. The only other US fast battleship in the Pacific, the *South Dakota*, grounded near Tonga on 6 September but was back in service in a month. There are some points of comparison between the 1942 Pacific campaign and the contemporary naval air battle in the Mediterranean, likewise a war of rival convoys striving to supply the armies through confined waters, though there the British and Italian convoys crossed at right angles and collided only rarely, whereas in the Solomons US and Japanese ships approached from opposite ends of the island chain to land troops and supplies by night close to the front line and to each other. Only twice did the surviving carrier forces clash in the open sea north of the Solomons; in the battle of the Eastern Solomons between 23 and 25 August (when the Japanese carrier *Ryujo* was sunk), and the battle of the Santa Cruz Islands from 25 to 27 October (when the USS *Hornet* was sunk). All this fighting occurred more or less exactly on the boundary between Nimitz's and MacArthur's commands, with their habitual inter-service quarrels.[22]

The Japanese supported their Solomons campaign from a new naval and air station at Rabaul on the island of New Britain. The Japanese drive southeastward had to be stopped if communications were to be kept open between Australia, New Zealand and the United States, and the US Marine Corps was the only US force with the needful skill in amphibious warfare. The Marine expedition sailed from Fiji on 31 July and landed on Guadalcanal and Florida Island in the Solomons a week later. The Japanese were there already, and their first reinforcements arrived on 19 August. This was the first American landing operation since Cuba in 1898, but the Marine Corps had devoted thought and experiment to amphibious warfare. (Indeed, in the general opinion of British officers who came into contact with them, the Marine Corps was consistently the most thoughtful of all the US services.) This was just as well, for the expedition was improvised in extreme haste, and the only practice landing was a disaster. Vice-Admiral Robert L. Ghormley, who was the senior flag officer in the area and supposed by Nimitz to be in personal command, made himself scarce. Rear-Admiral Frank Fletcher refused to wait off the landing beaches: he sailed with a thousand men and three-quarters of the Marine Corps stores still aboard and left the remaining Marine transports at anchor unprotected by ships or aircraft. This was strictly in line with the US Navy's carrier doctrine and its contempt for merchant shipping, but the Marines were very lucky not to be attacked by the nearby Japanese; nor did they react well when they discovered that the USN had abandoned them and that the expedition's supplies were all adrift. By 23 September there were eighty loaded transports at Nouméa in New Caledonia, and as many more nearby at Espiritu Santo, with no wharves, cranes or labour to unload them and no information as to what they carried.[23] Most of the responsibility for this chaos belongs to the new Chief of Naval Operations, Admiral Ernest King – who is supposed to have exclaimed 'I don't know what the hell this "logistics" is that [General] Marshall is always talking about' – but as the President's new favourite he was untouchable, so Ghormley was blamed.[24]

This was the beginning of an intense and hard-fought sixteen-month coastal campaign along the 470-mile chain of the Solomon Islands from Guadalcanal in the south-east, where in the initial phase the front line between Japanese soldiers and US Marines ran across the island, and almost bisected the vital airstrip of Henderson Field, up to the island of New Ireland in the north-west. From the battle of Savo Island on 8–9 August 1942 (the US Navy's worst defeat since 1812) to the battle of Tassafaronga on 30 November six major night actions were fought in New Georgia Sound (in American 'the Slot'), between Guadalcanal, Savo and Florida Islands. There were some Australian ships fighting with the USN, and one British admiral,[25] but no British ships, and it is a fair simplification to treat this as a Japanese-American struggle. It is nevertheless important for this study to offer some analysis of the style of naval fighting in the Solomons campaign, because the methods used on both sides were highly revealing of their respective strengths and weaknesses, they influenced other navies, and the results were strategically crucial. The USN's tactics were shaped by a number of basic assumptions. Fundamentally the Americans were certain that they were racially superior to the Japanese: bigger, stronger and whiter, with better eyesight and better brains. Technological superiority was everything for the US Navy, and American technology was obviously better than everyone else's: intelligence to the contrary could safely be dismissed. Even after they had discovered that some Japanese weapons really were better than American ones (the superiority of the Zero fighter was a 'terrific blow'),[26] US commentators still tended (and still tend) to take the supremacy of technology itself for granted and look there for the first causes of every success or failure. The Japanese, by contrast, had inherited many of their attitudes from the British. They valued superior technology and developed some of what they had learned (particularly about torpedoes) well beyond British levels, but their professional focus was always on organization. They trained continually and relentlessly at the highest possible speeds, seeking out the dangers of night and bad weather to make their exercises more realistic, accepting high risks and inevitable casualties. They pushed themselves and their equipment to the limit, and then stretched the limit further. They developed flashless powder and superior optics for night fighting. So far from being short-sighted, Japanese officers consistently sighted their enemies first

in night actions and reacted faster. Although American radar was more technically advanced and useful for ranging, it was not good enough for blind fire,
the Japanese arguably understood radar better, and their skill at plotting helped
them to keep intellectual control of complex situations. They trained in standard tactical procedures common to the whole Imperial Navy, so that any
random group of ships was always ready for unexpected encounters. The US
Navy, by contrast, did not even have unambiguous common signals in 1942,
and believed that every flag officer ought to train his ships in his own tactics,
meaning in practice that months could elapse before a new formation achieved
fighting efficiency, and the transfer of ships or officers between squadrons was
liable to plunge everything into confusion. US squadrons relied heavily on the
new technology of voice radio, but in action their radio discipline usually disintegrated into incoherent yelling. In the Guadalcanal campaign the consequence was a sequence of disasters. The American ships fought in a single line
ahead because they knew no other tactic, and blamed their heavy torpedo
losses on imagined Japanese 'submarine traps'. Their understanding of night
fighting had not advanced as far as the Great War. 'Somewhere in the Valhalla
of warriors,' a modern US naval tactician comments, 'Jellicoe must have looked
down on those dark nights punctured with the violence of the torpedo and
with a thin smile shaken his head at the Americans who took so long to learn
what he knew in 1914.'[27]

US senior officers of all services remained officially committed to
Roosevelt's 'Germany First' strategy, but in private they were convinced that
their naive President was being manipulated by the sinister British, who had
persuaded him to abandon their favourite plans of a frontal assault on German-
controlled Europe and a counter-attack against the Japanese in the Pacific,
deploying vast forces which the British knew were years ahead at best. The
British realized that they would have to find most of the troops for any overseas expedition, and calculated in the spring of 1942 that they could send a
maximum of six divisions to fight overseas. They did not share the American
yearning to revisit the Western Front, and aimed to fight with a minimum
expenditure of blood and a maximum reliance on naval and industrial superiority. If, as the Allies agreed, it was politically essential to demonstrate US
commitment to the joint war in 1942, the Mediterranean was the only feasible
option. For many US senior officers, this was intolerable. 'As the British won't
go through with what they agreed to,' General Marshall raged, 'we will turn
our backs on them and take up the war with Japan,'[28] but Roosevelt easily called
his bluff by asking for detailed plans, which did not exist. Marshall, King and
Harry L. Hopkins were sent to London with orders to reach an agreement in

a week on a strategy that would commit the US Army to fighting Germany in 1942 – which could only be in the Mediterranean, with British troops guided by British strategy.[29]

It was politically essential that the North African landings which the Allies planned, collectively named Operation 'Torch', should appear to be led by the United States, the only one of the Western Allies which had civil relations with Vichy France, though this did not prevent some serious fighting in Algeria followed by a five-month campaign to capture Tunisia. Operation 'Torch' required the assembly and escort of several large assault convoys from Britain or the US. These were vulnerable targets for U-boats, and a large fraction of the Allied anti-submarine forces were diverted from escorting merchant convoys to covering the invasion forces. By the end of December 1942 the Admiralty reckoned Allied shipping losses for the year at 360,000 tons, plus one million tons of shipping capacity diverted to support the landings, plus 875,000 tons of merchant shipping seized in French ports by the Germans. Against that the Allies themselves had seized one million tons of shipping in North African ports, and hoped to save more than a million tons a year by opening the Mediterranean to through traffic, making good all the shipping losses of 1941 – but in the short term the escorts diverted to protect the invasion convoys combined with exceptionally bad winter weather to generate a convoy crisis in the Atlantic.

In November 1942 the tough submariner Admiral Sir Max Horton was made Commander-in-Chief Western Approaches. Immediately he demanded that the RCN and USN raise the standards of their anti-submarine forces. In December, after the disastrous failure of the Canadian escorts of convoy ONS 154, the Canadian government consented to the withdrawal of all the Canadian Escort Groups for retraining.[30] Churchill revived the Cabinet Anti-U-Boat Committee and took the chair himself. Even in the US Navy, complacency was giving way to panic. Strong pressure was applied for the nine different American and Canadian naval commands in the Western Atlantic to be amalgamated under a Canadian admiral; King called a conference with the intention of blocking any common policy on Atlantic convoys, but failed.[31] Shipbuilding resources were hastily rearranged to reflect the new priority of anti-submarine warfare. Between February and December 1942 the US Army's share of US war expenditure fell from 35 per cent to 20 per cent. Planned US merchant shipbuilding increased from 19 to 28 million tons; towards the end of the year America was spending more on destroyer escorts than on battleships, cruisers and carriers together.[32]

The North Atlantic U-boat offensive against British convoys, which the

Germans had largely suspended in the first half of 1942 while they concentrated on sinking the undefended merchant shipping so plentiful in North American waters, resumed in the summer of 1942. The heavy losses of tankers in US waters now forced the convoys to economize on oil by abandoning evasion and sticking to predictable 'Great Circle' courses.[33] In the Mediterranean all thirty-seven merchantmen which sailed from Egypt to Malta in the sixteen months from August 1940 to December 1941 arrived safely, but after the loss of the Mediterranean Fleet battleships the British situation deteriorated fast. British Malta convoys from February to June 1942 were cancelled or driven back, and in the whole period from January to November 1942 only eight out of twenty-five cargo ships which sailed for Malta arrived safely. By contrast the Italian convoy K7 to North Africa in February 1942 was a complete success, with much smoother inter-Allied and inter-service co-operation than before. On 22 March a British attempt to pass a convoy from Alexandria to Malta led to another battle of Sirte, like the first fought in a heavy gale (in which two Italian destroyers foundered). Admiral Vian was able to keep the Italian battleship *Littorio* at a distance with smokescreens and destroyer torpedo attacks. He got his little convoy into Malta, but all four ships were then sunk in harbour by air attack, though a part of their cargoes was salved. In one respect, however, this almost complete failure bore significant fruit. The sight of an Italian battleship apparently driven off by British destroyers so infuriated the Germans that they refused to provide any more air cover or oil to the Italian fleet. As a result, the Italian battleships stayed in port during Operation 'Pedestal' in August, which in the event was their last and best chance to turn the tide of the Mediterranean campaign. At the end of March Cunningham hauled down his flag as Commander-in-Chief Mediterranean. Between March and April twice the tonnage of bombs was dropped on Malta as had fallen on London during the whole of the London Blitz. In the air Malta was defended only by obsolete Hurricane fighters, and the RAF's new Bristol Beaufort torpedo bombers which had arrived in January (twenty months after they entered service over the North Sea, a revealing index of Air Staff priorities) suffered heavily in the German air raids.[34]

In June the simultaneous Malta convoys 'Harpoon' (from the West) and 'Vigorous' (from the East) lost all but two of their seventeen merchantmen laden with stores, and no fuel at all got through. 'Events proved with painful clarity that our striking forces had nothing like the weight required to stop a fast and powerful enemy force, and in no way compensated for our lack of heavy ships.'[35] The remaining British submarines abandoned Malta soon afterwards (suffering an additional disaster when their depot ship *Medway* was

sunk by a U-boat, taking with her the entire British stock of submarine torpedoes and spare submarine engines in the Eastern Mediterranean), and in May
Fliegerkorps II returned to Russia having gained a complete victory in the
Mediterranean. This was General Rommel's hour of triumph, too: having
advanced 240 miles in six months, on 21 June he took the surrender of Tobruk,
and on the 25th he defeated the British army at Mersa Matruh, forcing it back
to its last defensible position at El Alamein, only sixty-five miles from Alexandria. On the 27th Hitler decided to abandon the planned assault on Malta
to throw all resources against the Alamein front, and next day the Mediterranean Fleet headquarters fled from Alexandria in some disorder.[36]

The whole British position in the Mediterranean and Indian Ocean now
hung in the balance, and Malta (collectively awarded the George Cross for
civilian bravery on 16 April) was the key to it. The civilian population of Malta
was now reduced to the near-starvation ration of 2,600 calories a day, but Lord
Gort the Governor was prepared to hold out until late September. Both sides
brought up fresh forces and new weapons. The British suspended the Arctic
convoys in order to send much of the Home Fleet to the Mediterranean, providing escort and covering forces which totalled two battleships, three carriers, seven cruisers and twenty-four destroyers. The Germans diverted 220
aircraft from the desert campaign. Churchill persuaded Roosevelt to lend the
USS *Wasp*, a carrier whose unusually large lifts were big enough to accept the
non-folding wings of a Supermarine Spitfire. In May she and the *Eagle* delivered sixty-two Spitfires Mk.V, the first of more than 300 which by August had
given the RAF command of the air over Malta. The Italians deployed their
new *motosiluranti*, 60-ton seagoing motor torpedo boats, modelled on German
S-boats. The summer convoy, code-named 'Pedestal', was planned in great
detail; the cargoes of the fourteen merchantmen were sorted in fields beside
the railway sidings of Didcot in Berkshire so that every ship carried a proportion of the whole, and no single sinking could lose the whole supply of any
essential. The exception was the big US tanker *Ohio*, laden with the fuel on
which everything depended. Although Roosevelt had authorized her participation, Admiral King forbade an American crew from taking part, so she was
re-registered under the British flag.[37]

As there was now little British naval strength left in the Eastern Mediterranean the convoy had to come through Gibraltar, where it would certainly be
reported by Italian and German agents across the bay in Algeciras. As expected,
it was subjected to very heavy air attacks, but to the surprise of both sides,
seventy-two mostly obsolete but radar-directed carrier fighters, supplemented
by heavy anti-aircraft fire from both warships and merchantmen, were able to

put up a very effective defence against eighty-seven long-range bombers, 101 dive-bombers, 152 torpedo bombers and 237 fighters. In the absence of Italian heavy ships, the most destructive attacks came from submarines and MTBs, but five merchantmen completed the voyage. The last and most essential to reach Malta was the *Ohio*, badly damaged but with her cargo of 12,000 tons of fuel intact. She entered Grand Harbour on the morning of 15 August, the feast of the Assumption of the Virgin Mary, patroness of Malta since the great siege of 1565, and no one in that devoutly Catholic island thought the ship's survival was an accident.[38]

The fuel the *Ohio* carried made it possible for aircraft and submarines to resume attacks on Italian convoys. From August to November ships and air-craft from Malta were responsible for 72 per cent of Italian shipping losses on the North African routes. Rommel's complaints of Italian incompetence went down well with Hitler, but Field Marshal Albert Kesselring, the overall German commander in the theatre, was not impressed, and cut back Rommel's demand for an extra 30,000 tons of fuel to 5,700 tons, which the Italians by great efforts managed to deliver. The real causes of Rommel's difficulties were his own unrealistic demands, the limitless appetite of the Russian front, and above all the failure to eliminate the threat of Malta. He opened his offensive on 30 August with fuel for four and a half days' fighting instead of fifteen, just as Malta's new fuel supply allowed it to resume full activity. In the three crucial September weeks of the Alam Halfa battle, attacks from Malta sank 43,662 tons of supplies. Vice-Admiral Eberhard Weichold, the senior German liaison offi-cer in Rome, was clear that the failure to capture Malta had doomed all Rom-mel's plans; Admiral Raeder and Marshal Ugo Cavallero, Chief of Staff of the Italian Army, agreed. On 6 September Cavallero wrote in his diary, 'if Malta is not neutralized we shall lose everything'. By mid-October the fuel shortage was paralysing the Italian-German army.[39]

The siege of Malta could not be said to have been lifted until November at the earliest, when the 'Stoneage' convoy delivered four ships from Alexandria, but by then the German-Italian army had been defeated at El Alamein and was in full retreat. On 4 November General Bernard Montgomery commanding the British Eighth Army dined with his opposite number and prisoner Wil-helm Ritter von Thoma. The narrow and costly victory of the 'Pedestal' convoy had turned the tide of the war in the Mediterranean, and already it was flow-ing strongly in favour of the Western Allies.[40] Four days later, on 8 November, the main assault forces of Operation 'Torch' landed: the British along the North African Mediterranean coasts, the Americans on the Atlantic coast of Morocco. Although these assault convoys had been assembling for months, and their presence could scarcely be concealed, the Germans found it surprisingly difficult to get a coherent intelligence picture. *BdU* sent twenty-five U-boats (half the submarine force in the North Atlantic) to the Atlantic coast of Morocco and achieved much less than could have been expected with the same numbers on the North Atlantic convoy routes. The US expertise in amphibious warfare was represented by the Marine Corps, still pinned down in the Solomon Islands, and the US Army had a lot to learn on the job. The French Navy, ignoring its secret orders from Marshal Pétain's government to avoid fighting the Americans, suffered heavy losses and scuttled most of its fleet to no profit at all.[41]

TWENTY-SEVEN

Unsordid Acts

Government and Administration 1942

Although formal structures of alliance faced many constitutional and practical obstacles which took a long time to surmount, from 1942 Britain and the United States were fighting on the same side, and for any historian (but especially one writing in English) a great part of the underlying history of the war concerns the relations of two societies on opposite sides of the Atlantic, 'having everything in common, except of course language' in Oscar Wilde's famous – and profoundly mistaken – phrase.[1] In reality the assumption that Britain and the USA had everything – or even a lot – in common was (and often still is) the source of dangerous misconceptions. Language was only the simplest, most superficial element of mutual confusion: less obvious and more dangerous were the very different and often incompatible structures of government. Beneath them in turn lay the unconscious, pervasive, cultural assumptions that led people to tackle problems in particular ways which seemed obvious on one side of the Atlantic, but sinister and irrational on the other. Similar though less acute difficulties lurked in other parts of the English-speaking world such as Canada and Australia. The problems of translating foreign tongues, for example those which divided allies such as the Germans and Italians (or parts of the British Empire such as Canada and South Africa), were by comparison simpler to understand, because nobody expected different languages and histories to generate a common culture without much effort, and the frontiers of language and culture more or less marched together. It is also important to be aware of the opposite phenomenon: common cultures which spanned language barriers, notably the (British-influenced but genuinely international) professional culture of naval officers, who not infrequently found that they could share more comfortably across a language barrier with other naval officers, than across a cultural barrier in their own language.

The historian of naval warfare is therefore called to provide at least a sketch of the personalities and structures of government which shaped decision-making. From the British perspective, the problems of understanding America started at the top, with the President. His office had much in common with an absolute monarchy surrounded by courtiers and favourites, and yet his powers seemed frustratingly limited, and his wishes obscure. It was not obvious even to Americans how influential were discreet individuals such as the retired admiral William D. Leahy, one of Roosevelt's few close friends, who returned to Washington in 1942 after two years as US ambassador to Vichy France. Leahy had an access to the President which neither the members of his Cabinet nor the Chiefs of Staff ever enjoyed; as the President's 'personal chief of staff' he interpreted Roosevelt's ambiguities and chose which presidential decisions to release to the Service heads. As the President's health failed, Leahy's influence rose, and even after Roosevelt died in April 1945 the admiral remained chairman of the US Chiefs of Staff until 1949.[2] Another key personality at Roosevelt's court, who held no formal office and was frequently off sick, was Harry L. Hopkins, who made up for the chronic weakness of the US diplomatic corps by acting as Roosevelt's personal representative, trusted by both Churchill and Stalin, and took a large share of the management of the Lend-Lease programme.[3]

When Churchill, Roosevelt and their military commanders met for the first time as *de facto* allies, at the 'Arcadia' Conference in Washington at the end of December 1941, the British team comprised the Prime Minister, the three Chiefs of Staff (Pound, Portal and Field Marshal Sir John Dill, the outgoing CIGS), and Lord Beaverbrook, the Minister of Supply. Roosevelt's party consisted of General George C. Marshall, Chief of Staff of the US Army, General 'Hap' Arnold for the Army Air Corps (Marshall's subordinate, but evidently included as Portal's 'opposite number'), Henry Stimson the Secretary of War, Frank Knox the Secretary of the Navy, and the ubiquitous Harry Hopkins as himself. The composition of the group roughly followed the British model, but as yet no American body equivalent to the British Chiefs of Staff had been established: Roosevelt had simply assembled them *ad hoc*. Not until the end of the conference were the US Joint Chiefs of Staff formally created as the counterpart of the British Chiefs of Staff.[4]

The US Army had no tradition or machinery of strategic planning. Its working assumption was that armies were expressions of the national will, generated by political leaders – in their case, the President. American generals and admirals of this generation were much influenced by the Oxford historian (Henry) Spenser Wilkinson, whose 1890 book *The Brain of an Army: A Popular Account of the German General Staff* introduced English-speaking senior officers on both sides of the Atlantic to the ideas of Carl von Clausewitz. 'War is political action,' Wilkinson taught them. 'It arises from political conditions, it ends in political conditions.'[5] Such maxims eased US generals into assuming that the American economy should and could deliver whatever the political leadership demanded, but they knew little about what commitments the President might have undertaken. Roosevelt for his part was looking for realistic estimates of costs and requirements based on workable plans, and it was some time before he could extract anything useful from the US armed services, which had limited experience of such an exercise. Only in December 1941 did the US Army produce an initial estimate that America could assemble armies fit to fight Germany in Europe by the spring of 1944. It followed that all their ideas of invading Europe in 1942 or 1943 were mere fantasy, but the US Army continued to demand far more, far faster, than could possibly be produced. Roosevelt's memorandum of May 1942 called for a major American offensive against Germany in 1942, and General Marshall did not discover until the eve of the Casablanca Conference in January 1943 that this idea of invading Europe that year was a pipe dream, notwithstanding the President's expressed wishes. Moreover, the US leaders were slow to confront the political implications of demanding an offensive in 1942, well before the US Army could mount one from its own resources. The British would have to provide the bulk of the forces, and Sir Alan Brooke the Chief of the Imperial General Staff had commanded the BEF in the retreat to Dunkirk. Unlike the Americans, who had blithely assured the Russians that they could expect a second front in 1942, he knew what the Germans could do, and he had a blocking veto over any British-led offensive. Post-war research calculated that the German Army consistently displayed 20–30 per cent higher combat efficiency than either British or US armies, and inflicted 50 per cent higher casualties man for man. By 1943 the US Army had found this out for themselves.[6]

Naturally but more than unfortunately, it soon became clear that the new 'Joint Chiefs' had brought with them the fratricidal quarrels which had always characterized relations within and between the American armed services. The US Navy and Army had no joint doctrine, no unity of operational command, and no tradition of cordial co-operation. The US Navy had long suffered (as Roosevelt very well knew) from the rivalry of the Chief of Naval Operations, the commander-in-chief and the Secretary of the Navy, all three of whom were present at this conference. Immediately before the Arcadia meeting Roosevelt had revived the title of commander-in-chief and bestowed it on Admiral Ernest J. King, whom he brought to Washington to set up the USN's first permanent operational headquarters. King's first act was to change the short form of his title from CINCUS (pronounced 'sink us') to COMINCH. Admiral Stark, still Chief of Naval Operations (and a close friend of Roosevelt), was shut out of King's headquarters and confined to planning and administrative matters under Frank Knox – in effect he was reduced to a 'staff officer', the ultimate humiliation. Presently Stark resigned (as he was undoubtedly meant to), and Roosevelt sent him to London as his personal representative, where he was treated as an extra member of the British Chiefs of Staff with almost total access to secret information. Field Marshal Dill became Stark's counterpart in Washington, where he stayed until his death in November 1944, making an outstanding contribution to allied unity. To complete his seizure of naval power, King now became CNO as well as commander-in-chief, with authority over both the US Navy at sea and the Bureaus 'under the Secretary of the Navy' – with whom he instantly clashed. The USN's administrative 'bureaus' and its new Washington headquarters now shared the Main Navy Building but little else. In the War Department Building next door Stimson and General Marshall had adjacent offices, but King never spoke to Knox and loathed the Secretary's deputy and eventual successor James V. Forrestal. King always preferred to do nothing rather than to share authority. He had unprecedented power to act or to block action, neither of which he used unless they served his ambitions. Too late Roosevelt realized that he had made the 'arrogant, aloof and suspicious' King into a naval Caesar with all but absolute power in the Navy Department.[7] In May 1942 King tried again to extract the 'Bureaus' from the control of the Secretary of the Navy, but Roosevelt had now awoken to what was going on and blocked King's ambitions. Presidential authority and Congressional oversight over the Navy were already heavily compromised. Making every allowance for the urgency of the moment and Roosevelt's habitual detachment from mere administration, it still seems extraordinary that an American statesman, long familiar with Washington and brought up to reverence the checks and balances of the US constitution, should have casually thrown them all overboard to favour the unconcealed ambition of the most hated man in the US Navy.[8]

The reason was evidently that Roosevelt, formerly Under-Secretary of the Navy during the Great War, was still perfectly at home with inter- and intra-service rivalry himself. He always talked of the US Navy as 'us', and the US Army as 'them'. He favoured King as his chosen leader in the battles against rival services. In the South Pacific these rivalries ensured that the USN and the Marine Corps displaced the army in the Guadalcanal campaign. General MacArthur was a potential Republican presidential candidate who had lost his aircraft in the Philippines; naturally Roosevelt preferred his man King to command. Within the USN flag officers had always expressed

their power of command by asserting their independence from other officers. They did not willingly copy doctrines and procedures from one another.
For an American admiral to adopt the methods of a foreign service (British
anti-submarine or amphibious techniques, for example) was seen as disloyal
and subversive.[9]

These conditions inflamed the always sensitive relations between US admirals and naval airmen. King himself was a 'carpetbagger' who had risen to flag
rank as Chief of the Bureau of Aeronautics from 1933 to 1936, with the help of
a nominal flying qualification. To the disgust of the real naval airmen, and in
particular of the senior airman, Captain John H. Towers, this allowed King to
take rank over them all. As commander-in-chief he built up the US Navy's
first central operational staff, but he got rid of Towers, who was forbidden to
go to sea, and made sure there were no other airmen on it who might challenge his authority. King's constant reorganizations of the Navy Department,
which so exasperated Roosevelt that he forbade any more changes in August
1943, were all about increasing his power. No US naval airman was promoted
to flag rank until March 1943, and it was glaringly obvious why. Shut out of sea
command and the corridors of power alike until after the war, US naval airmen
envied the Fleet Air Arm its one, and from 1943 two, airmen admirals on the
Admiralty Board.[10]

British officers then, and historians later, have been apt to attribute King's
aggressive and overbearing manner to simple anglophobia. In fact, King's
hatreds (the word is scarcely too strong) were always directed primarily against
other Americans, his professional enemies. His daughter described her father
as 'the most even-tempered man in the Navy . . . always in a rage',[11] but British
admirals were not his rivals, and he worked effectively with Pound among
others. What is hard to deny is that King seriously lacked the fundamental
quality of unselfish devotion to duty on which naval officers in every country
were and had to be judged. He enjoyed demonstrating his power to break rules
with impunity. In the era of Prohibition, he was often drunk in public. He readily abused his power to advance his own career and damage other officers
(especially airmen) against whom he held a grudge. Women, including the
wives of brother officers, were never safe in his vicinity. It is worth quoting a
very shrewd judge of character who met him in 1942:

> a facade, without much behind him. He was well informed, he knew how
> to make a decision and stick to it, and he could inspire fear in his subor-
> dinates. I got no impression of a really first rate mind. He was insanely vain
> and a megalomaniac.[12]

Eisenhower thought much the same: 'an arbitrary, stubborn type, with not too much brains and a tendency toward bullying his juniors'.[13] King's worst failing was jealousy: he was intensely aware that his own career, though it had given him much professional experience, had included scarcely any wartime command, and he could not stomach being seen to learn from officers who were known for leadership in war. Because the United States had entered both world wars so late, most of them were not Americans. King's career raises uncomfortable questions which US naval historians are still avoiding more than sixty years after his death. The fact that such a destructive character, with no extraordinary professional talents and almost no experience of wartime command, was raised to be head of the US Navy and empowered to do it so much damage, does not reflect well on his service or his country.[14]

One thing which can be offered as a sort of defence of Admiral King is that other US senior officers behaved as badly. In the Far East US strategy was paralysed by the bitter enmity of General Joseph W. Stilwell ('Vinegar Joe') and the Air Force general Claire L. Chennault, backed by Marshall and Roosevelt respectively. Chennault hoped for a great air victory in China, won by himself. Stilwell wanted a campaign for Burma, won by himself, but his real war aim was to get rid of the Chinese leader Chiang Kai-shek (Jiang Jieshi), whom he hated and hoped to kill. The result in that theatre of war was that nothing was achieved save enormous loss of life.[15]

The Lend-Lease Act of March 1941 allowed the President to transfer weapons and war materials to any nation which he deemed 'vital to the defense of the United States' as a loan rather than a gift.[16] This brilliant political stroke outflanked existing legislation designed to block the US from helping any belligerent, and avoided the rancour generated by the 'war debts' of the First World War. Although slow to get under way, 'Lend-Lease' eventually became an effective exchange scheme by which new ships and weapons were married with trained and experienced personnel, vastly improving the overall effectiveness of the Allied war effort. Whether it truly deserved Churchill's diplomatic praise as 'the most unsordid act in the whole of recorded history' is more doubtful.[17] The American terms to Britain were designed to ensure that she paid cash for everything until she was as near as possible bankrupt. From 1941, as we have seen, some damaged British warships were repaired in US Navy Yards on Lend-Lease terms, but Britain apparently received no new weapons which she had not already paid for before the autumn of 1942, and what US aid was promised was often cancelled or diverted without warning.[18] Canadian aid to Britain and British aid to the United States, each of similar size to American aid in proportion to the donors' GNP, and given without strings, have a better claim to be called 'unsordid'.[19]

From the beginning, well before the Lend-Lease Act, Anglo-American cooperation in arms manufacture was both more widespread and more complicated than the simple idea of US gifts to Britain conveys. Even before the Soviet Union was added to the US Lend-Lease legislation in November 1941, British supplies were being shipped to Russia via Murmansk and Archangel, and British convoys carried American as well as British manufactures. New evidence shows that at this critical stage, over the winter of 1941–2 when the survival of Moscow and Leningrad hung in the balance, British tanks made up about 9 per cent of Russian strength overall, and one-third of the heavy and medium tanks defending Moscow in December 1941. In the same period Britain shipped 1,323 fighters to Russia, both British-made Hawker Hurricanes and US-made Curtiss Tomahawks and Kittyhawks. In both cases these were inferior to the latest German aircraft but better than anything the Russians were then producing. Britain also supplied much aluminium and rubber, together with modern equipment such as Asdic sets, magnetic mines and depth charges.[20]

In 1939 Britain had net foreign assets remaining of about £5 billion, which the government had no option but to spend as recklessly as the Americans demanded. Some of this went on simple purchase of weapons and equipment. Much of it went on joint industrial projects such as the production of British aero engines in US factories; some of them to be shipped to Britain, others to transform the performance of under-powered US aircraft. Apart from aircraft, American industry could supply only limited amounts of war supplies until well into 1942. In 1941 only 11.5 per cent of British munitions came from the United States, including both British purchases and the first shipments under Lend-Lease. After Lend-Lease got going, Britain began to buy many semi-finished goods instead of manufactures from the USA, to save shipping space. By the end of 1941 Britain had received over 5,000 US aircraft, and in 1942, 7,775. By comparison the Luftwaffe received seventy-nine aircraft from French and Dutch manufacturers in 1941, and 743 in 1942 – but counting only aircraft underrates the fruits of conquest. Germany was able to use 30–40 per cent of the industrial production of France, the Netherlands, Norway and Bohemia-Moravia (the industrialized parts of Czechoslovakia). The sophisticated French economy alone provided Germany with many industrial products and as much food as the whole of the USSR.[21]

The largest Anglo-American industrial project of 1940–41 was the Admiralty's venture into American merchant shipbuilding in partnership with Todd Shipbuilding of Maine, and the building contractor Henry J. Kaiser, whose talent for publicity and keen financial nose were to earn him an undeserved but still not extinct reputation as the hero of prefabricated shipbuilding (much to the disgust of the experts in existing American shipyards, who had been doing it for years). Under the auspices of the PSOC, the Admiralty (as the responsible department for merchant as well as naval shipbuilding) had already invited shipyards which built tramp steamers to submit simple basic designs suitable for mass production. In 1940–41 its first large orders to US and Canadian yards were based on the design of the *Empire Liberty*, launched by J. L. Thompson of Sunderland in August 1941. In January 1942, with the United States now committed to the war, the Admiralty sold its two US shipyards to the US Maritime Commission, which adapted the *Empire Liberty* design to US building practices and named it the 'Liberty Ship'.[22]

Merchant shipbuilding was perhaps the single most important articulation of the Allied war effort, for on merchant shipping depended virtually all transport between the Western Allies, the feeding of civilian populations (starting but by no means finishing with Britain's own), all major military campaigns, the supply of raw materials to industries and the distribution of their products. Merchant shipping was at once the essential unifying instrument of the Allied war effort, the motor of Britain's economy, and the symbol of so much about Britain's past which Americans envied and hated. Historians are apt to seek rational explanations for the past, but the wartime alliances on both sides were in many respects driven by emotions as much as reasons.

Admiral Dönitz regarded his U-boats as the instrument to disintegrate and starve the British war effort, and Churchill was alert to the danger that he might succeed. This made the organization and defence of merchant convoys, especially across the North Atlantic, a critical vulnerability of British naval strategy, and merchant shipbuilding an essential instrument of survival. Churchill watched the U-boat situation carefully, especially at threatening times such as Spring 1941 and late 1942, 'but he did not frighten easily, and he did not frighten often'.[23] It is often argued that he should have been frightened sooner of the consequences of lack of air cover over Atlantic convoys. In 1941–2 Coastal Command operated a single squadron of American-built Consolidated Liberator 'Very Long Range' four-engined bombers with a range of 2,400 miles, sufficient to provide occasional patrols over almost all of the North Atlantic – but these Liberators Mk.I, already out of production by 1942, had only been handed over to Coastal Command because it had been discovered that their prominent engine flares made them vulnerable to German night-fighters. Later marks were more suitable for night-bombing of Germany, and the Air Staff knew that the USAAF was demanding that the British be refused American bombers if they were going to use them over the sea – undoubtedly because the USAAF feared that the precedent could be used against them by their ultimate enemy, the US Navy, which also wanted VLR aircraft but had been denied them by Congress. In these disputes Portal, Chief of the Air Staff, was a more effective advocate for maritime air power than Pound the First Sea Lord, who was already showing signs of failing health, while Churchill seems to have been most impressed by Sir Arthur Harris of Bomber Command, who denounced Coastal Command as 'an obstacle to victory'.[24] Air Marshal Sir Philip Joubert de la Ferté, commanding Coastal Command, favoured using long-range aircraft at a more favourable range as part of the RAF's 'Bay Offensive', using aircraft equipped with radar and the powerful Leigh Lights against U-boats crossing the Bay of Biscay on the surface at night. Then in the summer of 1942 KG40 at Mérignac re-equipped with the long-range Ju88C night-fighter, and both aircraft and U-boats adopted the Métox radar detector, which picked up ASV Mk.II, making the Bay of Biscay safe for U-boats on the surface at night, and dangerous to both escorts and British aircraft still using the older metric radar sets. It was urgent to convert ships and aircraft to the centimetric ASV Mk.III, in the teeth of opposition from Air Marshal Harris, who did not wish to share the technology with a rival command.[25]

The Admiralty for its part preferred the new escort carriers, expected to enter service in 1942, to VLR aircraft. Then in November 1942 the new American-built escort carrier HMS *Avenger* was torpedoed and blew up, and four months later her sister *Dasher* was sunk by a petrol explosion. These disasters revealed fatal design faults which the Admiralty insisted on addressing, delaying the next batch of Lend-Lease escort carriers, which never arrived in time to make a significant contribution to the Atlantic convoy war. The Air Staff behaved throughout as though only US manufacturers could build long-range aircraft. At no stage was Britain's most successful heavy bomber, the Avro Lancaster, seriously considered as a candidate for maritime patrol, though Portal was willing to lend some, and this aircraft subsequently excelled in the role after the war. Critics argued then, and argue still, that Churchill relied on US shipbuilding to make up U-boat losses, rather than force 'Bomber' Harris to obey orders and release a proportion of his heavy bomber force to provide air cover over the convoys.[26]

A major component of the mid-winter convoy crisis was the continued lack of very long-range aircraft to close the 'Greenland Air Gap'. As before, British long-range bombers were regarded as untouchable, and Admiral Pound approached this most sensitive of inter-service questions with extreme caution, although the planned 'irreducible minimum tonnage' of 27 million tons a year of imports into Britain was now drifting out of sight. In practice these contro-verted decisions were compromised. In June 1942 a report by Rear-Admiral Patrick Brind and Air Vice-Marshal John Slessor (respectively Vice-Chiefs of the Naval and Air Staff) recommended reinforcing Coastal Command with 126 aircraft, including thirty-six Lancasters. The Lancasters were refused, but Coastal Command received thirty-two Liberators Mk.III with a range of 1,680 miles, which made an important contribution to the anti-submarine war, even if that range did not completely close the Greenland air gap.[27]

What is beyond dispute is that the RAF clung to the long-range bomber on emotional rather than rational grounds: 'a faith wholly at variance with the known facts of the situation'.[28] In 1942 there was already good evidence, known to the Air Staff and the War Cabinet, that British night-bombers were incap-able of finding or hitting targets smaller than large cities, and that the impact of British bombing on U-boat production was negligible. The pre-war air power theories had been exploded – but upon them the RAF had hung its main justification for the existence of an independent air force. The war had amply demonstrated the value of aircraft in modern warfare – which no one had doubted since 1915 – but the actual aircraft the RAF had committed to, used in the only way it knew, stood condemned as a bloody catastrophe. It was trench warfare with wings, and the worst of it was not just the futile sacrifice of so many young lives, but the foreclosed opportunities of more hopeful alter-native routes to victory. The other services, both the Navy and army, demanded the air cover which they urgently needed to fulfil their missions. In August 1942 Sir John Tovey, commanding the Home Fleet, sent a formal despatch to the Admiralty:

> Whatever the results of the bombing of cities might be . . . it could not of itself win the war, whereas the failure of our sea communications would assuredly lose it . . . I informed Their Lordships that in my opinion the situation at sea was now so grave that the time had come for a stand to be made, even if this led to Their taking the extreme step of resignation.[29]

The public resignation of the Board of Admiralty in the midst of the worst mili-tary and political crisis of the war would probably have brought down the gov-ernment. By the last quarter of 1942 half British current consumption of raw materials was being drawn from stocks, and it looked as though Churchill had lost his calculated gamble that bombing could win the war before the U-boats did. It was also becoming clear that the US interpretation of the agreed Allied strategy of 'Germany first' involved diverting so much war material to the Pacific that by mid-1943 Britain might be starved by the Americans as well as the

Germans. Roosevelt's promise to ensure Britain's minimum requirements had been made without consultation and the US War Shipping Administration refused to honour it. During 1942 Britain's available merchant fleet declined by two million tons while America's rose by 2.7 million tons. King told the Casablanca Conference in January 1943 that the United States was devoting 15 per cent of its resources to the war against Japan. The true figure, which he knew perfectly well, was over 50 per cent.[30]

The allocation of shipping and landing craft was a crux of Anglo-American relations. British bankers and industrialists well remembered how the US government had tried to take over vital trade routes in 1918, and urged the government to defend British interests. Americans – still in 1942 with limited understanding of the enormous shipping needs of a transcontinental war – responded that they had not gone to war to defend the British Empire.[31] In February 1942 Sir Arthur Salter, head of the British Merchant Shipping Mission in Washington, circulated an estimate of the transatlantic shipping situation at the end of 1941. He acknowledged that U-boat sinkings in the second half of 1941 had been reduced to 120,000 tons a month, but the overall balance between new building and losses was barely even. 'If losses continue at this rate . . . we shall be no better able in 1943 than we are in 1942 to undertake substantial overseas operations; and indeed that the danger of starvation or of shutting down munitions factories in the UK will be very great.' In the event the British import requirement was reduced by a third, mainly by rationing, but much of what was saved was then wasted by inefficiencies, in particular the 'hoarding' of ships and cargoes by US senior officers in various parts of the world which wasted nine million tons a year. By 1942 British imports had fallen to 60 per cent of the 1939 level, and British production of consumer goods was 35 per cent below peacetime levels.[32]

Most US oil production was shipped from the Gulf of Mexico, and much of it then passed up the 'Eastern Sea Frontier' (Florida to Maine) on its way to northern US ports and on across the Atlantic. By Allied agreement these areas were an entirely American responsibility, and the British assumed that the US Navy would protect shipping by applying the now well-understood convoy system, with which Admiral King (the former Commander-in-Chief Atlantic) was familiar. The USN's force of anti-submarine escorts, still negligible at the beginning of 1941, was now growing; by June 1942 it had 527 ships, including 190 destroyers, with at least basic anti-submarine weapons (though not, in many cases, basic training). Most of them were in the Pacific, but the transfer of even a small proportion would have sufficed to escort shipping up the US East Coast, which fed the British population and industry, carried fuel for British and

American ships and aircraft in European waters, and supplied oil for domestic heating and industry in New England. This might be thought a sufficient incentive for action, but to the astonishment and anger of the British, King flatly refused to institute convoys in the US sector and almost ignored the rapidly rising losses of merchant ships along the coast and in the Caribbean. Nine-tenths of the victims were unescorted, and many of them were the precious tankers which were indispensable to the war effort everywhere. British and Canadian offers of help and advice were rejected.[33] Between January and March 1942 monthly sinkings in the North Atlantic almost doubled, from 420,000 tons to 834,000 tons. British-controlled shipping alone lost 650,000 tons in the first nine months of the year, and 708,000 tons in the last quarter. In addition, 220–30 ships of 1.25 million tons were sunk, and 200,000 tons damaged, in the Caribbean and the Gulf of Mexico. A quarter of all Allied merchant ships lost in the entire war were sunk by U-boats in the first eight months of 1942, nearly all in American waters. Between a third and a half of them were British ships or part of the British-controlled shipping pool, and all of them were part of the Allied merchant fleet on which rested the whole conduct of a worldwide war.[34]

It was clear enough that the crisis demanded that the US Navy had to co-operate with the US Army Air Force (which contributed the larger share of anti-submarine aircraft). According to a British report of March 1941, 'It is one of the most unfortunate aspects of Service policy in the United States that the Army and Navy really seem to hate each other more than they do the Germans.'[35] To work with the Army Air Force was an intense humiliation for King, but even worse would be the adoption of convoys, which would be nothing less than a public acknowledgement that the British had been right. Cunningham, who was in Washington in the first half of 1942, remarked that the US Navy Department was determined not to learn from other people's experience of anti-submarine warfare; 'in fact rather than benefiting by our experience they prefer to have a disaster of their own to learn by . . . But as most of the aircraft engaged in A/S work belong to the army and as the jealousy between the two services is extreme, rather worse than our own relations with the RAF, it is difficult to get them to make progress, but they are coming along.'[36] Neither US air force wanted to be involved in trade protection, but each insisted on taking a share the better to block their hated rivals. The Army Air Force, however, hoped one day to be able to imitate the RAF and become independent (as in the end it did in 1947), and was more friendly to the RAF than to the US Navy. The USN was consistently the service most hostile to any co-operation with anybody.[37]

In spite of warnings from the Admiralty, pleas from American officers, and

the loan of British escorts, Admiral King flatly refused to take effective measures to protect merchant shipping on the East Coast of the United States. This
was the U-boats' second 'Happy Time'. There were no convoys, navigation
lights were left burning as usual, and so were the bright lights of coastal towns
which silhouetted shipping moving along the coast. US warships communicated freely on voice radio in plain language, which told listening U-boats
everything they needed to know. Between January and June 1942 U-boats sank
100 ships (588,000 tons) along the 'Eastern Sea Frontier' (the US East Coast
from Maine to Florida). Between February and September 1942, they sank over
180 more ships (almost a million tons) in the Caribbean and Gulf of Mexico.
In the Caribbean the first convoys were not organized until July 1942. From
mid-December 1941 to the end of August 1942 German U-boats sank more
than three million tons of Allied shipping, more than 90 per cent of them unescorted and in US waters. This was 25 per cent above the loss rate of the previous year, and one-quarter of the total losses to U-boat attack over the whole
war. In the first quarter of 1942 sinkings in the North Atlantic (mainly in US
coastal waters) almost doubled, from 419,907 tons to 834,164 tons. Only in
April 1942, under heavy pressure from the Admiralty and the US Army, did
the US Navy begin to organize convoys, but even then many escorts lacked
the most basic training and equipment. In the worst months of May and June,
85 per cent of Allied shipping losses in the whole world were in US waters:
nineteen U-boats sank over a million tons of shipping with the negligible loss
of one submarine for every thirty-nine merchantmen. As a result, in the first
half of the year Allied tanker capacity fell 7 per cent, just as more tankers were
needed to make up for the loss of the oilfields of Burma and the East Indies.
This great catastrophe, a much greater blow to the war effort than any land
battle, was in no sense a failure of the convoy system, for almost all the lost
ships were 'independents', abandoned unprotected to their fate. Only in August
1942 did the USN reluctantly begin to take a share of the anti-submarine campaign, but King still obstructed the convoy system as much as he could.
Although both British and Germans both well understood that convoys were
the key to victory in the North Atlantic, and even a one-knot increase in a convoy's speed greatly reduced the risk of losses, King refused to take the trouble
to sort ships into different speeds. The U-boats also caused a sharp fall in US
aircraft production by sinking 22 per cent of the ships which freighted bauxite
from British Guiana and Surinam to be refined into aluminium with Canadian
hydroelectricity.[38]

This was one of the heaviest and most shameful naval defeats suffered by
the Western Allies during the entire war. The sinking of so many essential

tankers was a far graver loss to the war effort than the five aged battleships sunk at Pearl Harbor. It is hard to avoid the conclusion that the largest share of the responsibility falls on Ernest King, who from December 1941 was commander-in-chief of the entire US Navy, with greater powers than any Chief of Naval Operations had ever held. Friends of the US Navy (who are numerous) and friends of the admiral (who are rarer) have laboured to excuse him ever since without discovering any persuasive arguments. He relished his reputation for ruthless aggression and stressed the importance of flexibility and initiative, but in this case he displayed only inertia, and conspicuously failed to confront clear and urgent decisions. He hated joint commands and even liaison officers, and refused to respond to the secret intelligence (including the Cabinet War Room Record and the First Lord's Daily Report) which the British shared with him from June 1942. Even Professor (and Honorary Rear-Admiral) Samuel E. Morison of Harvard, official historian and generous friend of the US Navy, condemned it as 'woefully unprepared, materially and mentally, for the U-boat blitz on the Atlantic Coast that began in January 1942 . . . this unpreparedness was largely the Navy's own fault . . . it had no plans ready for a reasonable protection to shipping . . . and was unable to improvise them for several months'.[39]

The only factor which averted an even greater disaster was the inefficiency of the German U-boat arm. When Hitler declared war on the United States, U-boats were the only German instruments of war which could hurt the USA, so *BdU* immediately organized a submarine offensive under the cover name *Paukenschlag* ('Drumroll') to attack US shipping on the East Coast. Hitler insisted on keeping up to half the U-boats in Norway or the Mediterranean, and the offensive in US waters was largely carried out by the big Type IX U-boats, originally designed to operate in the Mediterranean from bases in Germany, which alone had the range to cross the Atlantic and conduct an operational patrol before returning. The more numerous Type VII boats could just manage a short patrol off Newfoundland but could reach no further west. Although about sixty of the Type IX were notionally available, no more than six of them were actually at sea at the beginning of the operation. In January 1942 there were 249 U-boats in commission of all classes, but only ninety-one were *Frontboote*, ready for operations; the rest were training or refitting. Of the ninety-one, only fifty-five were in the Atlantic, of which thirty-three were undergoing maintenance, leaving twenty-two at sea, half on passage and half on patrol. This meant that fewer than 5 per cent of the submarines were anywhere near fighting the enemy. Then from March 1942 the first of the new Type XIV submarine tankers (nicknamed *Milchkühe*, 'milch cows') began to come into service, each capable of providing fuel and torpedo reloads to several Type VIIs. As a result, the average U-boat Atlantic patrol went up from forty-one days to sixty-two, or even eighty-two with a second replenishment at sea. In the twelve months from June 1942 the submarine tankers refuelled 390 U-boats at sea without once being interrupted. These submarine tankers were what the Germans needed to make use of their existing U-boat fleet at transatlantic range, but happily for the Allies only six were available in 1942 and four more later; too few and much too late to turn the issue of the campaign.[40]

In 1942 Britain had few opportunities to take the offensive in any kind of warfare, but in October 1942 Captain (presently Acting Vice-Admiral) Lord Louis Mountbatten was appointed to command the new 'Combined Operations' organization with Churchill's personal exhortation 'You are to give no thought for the defensive. Your whole attention is to be concentrated on the offensive.'[41] What Churchill envisaged in the short term was small-scale coastal raids, but his distant vision was firmly set on the reconquest of Europe. That was plainly impossible in 1942, but young Mountbatten (at forty-two very young for a Captain, ridiculously young for a Vice-Admiral, and twenty-eight years younger than Admiral of the Fleet Lord Keyes, the hero of Zeebrugge whom he was relieving) was to apply his considerable talents to building up the necessary organization. Besides a good deal of training and research, Combined Operations recruited specialist assault units named 'Commandos' with which it undertook more than fifty large or small raids along the enemy-occupied coast of Europe from France to Norway between 1940 and 1943, with mixed fortunes. The largest in 1941 were attacks on the Lofoten Islands and Vågsøy island in March and December respectively, both of which inflicted significant casualties on the Germans and returned with prisoners, Norwegian volunteers, and important cypher materials. Then followed the St Nazaire raid in March 1942 and the biggest of these operations, the Dieppe raid on 19 August 1942, which was a costly failure, losing 2,000 prisoners and nearly 1,000 dead. It was clear in retrospect that it had been a mistake to mount a 'reconnaissance in force' with inadequate force and training to take a strongly held port, but the orthodox military view was that there was no way to invade Europe without capturing a major port, and no way of learning how to do it but by trying. Many of the senior officers and organizations involved pressed urgently for the chance to fight and learn, even if the risks were high and there was no conventional victory on offer. The Canadian army contributed much of the pressure and incurred most of the casualties. The only really well-prepared and well-trained unit at Dieppe, Lord Lovat's Commando, successfully captured and destroyed a German battery on the western cliffs at Varengeville. The long and intense planning which went into the Mediterranean landings of 1943 and the Normandy landings of 1944 show that lessons were learnt from Dieppe among other operations. Meanwhile the brutal evidence of the Dieppe disaster was of real service to the British in persuading both Americans and Russians that amphibious operations were difficult and dangerous.[42]

At the beginning of 1942 British naval intelligence still enjoyed extensive access to German naval signals encrypted in the Dolphin/*Heimisch* cypher, but on 1 February the German Navy adopted a new cypher with four Enigma rotors instead of three, known to the Germans as *Triton*, and to the British as 'Shark'. Fortunately the old three-rotor 'Dolphin' cypher remained in use by surface ships, and in home waters, including Norway and the Baltic, the principal naval training areas, which provided good advance warning of ships and U-boats preparing to go to sea, besides furnishing many 'cribs' and clues to 'Shark'. New four-rotor 'bombes' to decrypt 'Shark' were ordered, but both the design and manufacture threw up many difficulties, and the four-rotor bombes were not available until the spring of 1943. For fourteen months from 1 February 1942 naval intelligence now had to forgo the precious cypher materials which had transformed convoy operations in the North Atlantic. Until the summer of 1942 the worst consequence of this was to blind the British to the signs that the German cryptographers of the *B-Dienst* were making excellent progress with British Naval Cypher No. 3. In current operational circumstances British cyphers were scarcely relevant to the disasters on the US East Coast, an American responsibility where nobody was even attempting to organize convoys, and those U-boats which were able to get across the Atlantic easily found undefended targets everywhere. Operating individually rather than in groups they had limited need to signal, while on shore the US Navy's divided commands did not talk to one another, and the US Office of Naval Intelligence had no connection with operations.[43]

It was the Norwegian campaign which first alerted the Admiralty to the weaknesses of its operational cyphers and helped GC&CS to understand some of its own limitations. The Code & Cypher School, as it was in 1940 and 1941, preferred glamorous code-breaking and star cryptographers to dull administration. It was not well managed, and it was slow to adjust to the new era of cypher machines which called for advanced mathematics and new equipment. Its most successful cryptographic unit was 'Dilly's Girls', the mainly female team led by Dillwyn Knox, who attacked Italian naval cyphers and earned a large share of the credit for the victory of Matapan. Knox was an old-school cryptographer from Room 40, by profession a scholar of ancient Greek papyri, but one of the few of his generation who successfully made the transfer to breaking machine cyphers. In October 1941 he broke the *Abwehr* (German counter-intelligence) Enigma cypher, which in time made it possible for Britain to control the most important German espionage organization and use it to feed the enemy with false information. By 1942 Knox was dying of cancer, and GC&CS was moving away from small groups of eccentric scholars and growing rapidly in size and efficiency as large teams worked sophisticated machines in continuous watches, night and day. Many of these machines were built by the telephone engineers of the General Post Office, or by British Tabulating Machines, a licensee of the American firm IBM, whose licence allowed it to research and manufacture independently, and which soon left its American parent behind. The Tabulating Machine Section of GC&CS had a staff of 150 and used 1.4 million punched cards a week.[44] By 1941 an organization which had grown up with manual cryptography and then moved to 'bombes' confronted the new challenge of 'Fish', which much later was identified as the Lorenz SZ 40/42 cypher teleprinter. Hollerith machines using relays to sort punched cards, and later (as they slowly became available) 'bombes' which worked through possible solutions electronically at unprecedented speeds, could generate working solutions to Enigma messages, but were not fast enough to cope with 'Fish', which had never been seen by GC&CS and could only be reconstructed in theory. Max Newman, the Cambridge mathematician who led his research group (the 'Newmanry') on 'Fish', and Tommy Flowers, the Post Office engineer and expert on wireless valves (vacuum tubes), attacked the 'Fish' problem from different directions and helped to build up a layered solution around the prototype analytical computer called 'Colossus'. To succeed they had to overcome obstacles which were as much financial and administrative as technical. They needed a massive increase in the size and resources of GC&CS. Colonel Stewart Menzies, who succeeded as head of MI6 and GC&CS on the death of Admiral Sinclair in November 1939, exploiting the fact that the Secret Service accounts were not audited by the Treasury, approached BTM with the offer of £100,000 (roughly equal to GC&CS's annual budget, or the entire capital value of the company) to build the prototype 'Colossus'. But lack of people, not money, was the worst problem. On Sinclair's death GC&CS employed about 200. Already by 1941 it was acutely short of able staff, and the new machines would need large crews working continuous shifts. Bletchley was a small town already stressed by the rapid growth of the secret cuckoo in its nest. The institution could not persuade officials of its needs when they could not be told of its work, or even its existence. Nor could it pay for the people it was trying to recruit, for in the wartime economy the intelligent young women it sought could earn better wages than the civil service rates GC&CS could pay. Desperate situations call for desperate measures. Churchill had recently visited GC&CS and met its chiefs. On Trafalgar Day, 21 October 1941, the four leaders in mechanical cryptanalysis (Hugh Alexander, Stuart Milner-Barry, Alan Turing and Gordon Welchman), without telling Menzies, wrote a personal letter to Churchill explaining what they needed and why. His response was immediate: 'Make sure they have all they want on extreme priority and report to me that this has been done.'[45] Even this did not immediately unblock the situation. Only at the end of December did the Chiefs of Staff order an investigation which led to a reorganization putting all signals intelligence under Paymaster Commander Edward Travis, who succeeded Alastair Denniston as working head of GC&CS in February 1942. It is at this point that GC&CS (still in organizational terms a department of the Secret Service) became fully and officially a joint-service organization. The personnel problem was solved by appealing to the WRNS, which created the rate of 'Special Duties X' for GC&CS and populated it with women of good intelligence and education. The first eight Wrens to work on 'bombes' had been assigned in March 1941 'as an experiment, as it was doubted if girls could do the work'.[46] By 1942 there was no doubt at all that they could. The WRNS were under discipline and relished responsibility without expecting to be paid extra to contribute to the war effort. Although the Civil Service unions managed to keep the WRNS out of the Admiralty, they had no foothold at Bletchley, where GC&CS came to depend heavily on the Wrens' intelligence and dedication. In time they made up about one-fifth of the over 9,000 people working at GC&CS and its outstations.[47]

By 1942 it was clear that military organizations like the Admiralty Operational Intelligence Centre had to be more closely linked to GC&CS. High-speed automatic teleprinter circuits connected Bletchley Park with Whitehall, but overseas communications still depended on cables. Concerned that telegraph cables might be vulnerable to interception in shallow water (as some had been in 1914–18), the Navy conducted experiments in 1941 which reassured it that cutting underwater cables would be difficult in wartime conditions, though not impossible.[48] This was overconfident. Immediately after Italy entered the war on 10 June 1940, Italian cable ships succeeded in locating and cutting Eastern Telegraph's through-Mediterranean cables where they crossed the Skerki Bank south-west of Sicily. This strategic disaster blacked-out secure communications between Whitehall and the whole overseas empire east of Gibraltar, excepting only the ports served by the unreliable old cable round the Cape and up the coast of East Africa. Communication with the Mediterranean, the Middle East and the Far East now depended on wireless, and bulky documents had to be sent 'by hand of British Master', meaning by merchant ship. The weakness of British cyphers was becoming clearer every day by 1942. The cumbersome system of sending material derived from Enigma decrypts and classified 'Ultra' (i.e. more than 'Most Secret') from GC&CS to the Mediterranean imposed an average delay of five hours, whereas Admiral Iachino had a cryptographic section aboard his flagship which could sometimes break British operational signals in a few minutes. Typex was getting better the more the British mastered Enigma, and small volumes of very sensitive material could be encyphered by the unbreakable 'one-time pad' (in effect a unique cypher used once and then discarded), but that still left exposed an enormous volume of signals of medium security, collectively (and often individually) of high importance.[49]

One security breach in particular came close to causing fatal damage. As part of his campaign to draw America into the war, Churchill arranged for a US military attaché, Colonel Bonner Fellers, to be attached to the British headquarters in Cairo, where he was given full access to all three British services up to but not including the 'Ultra secret'. Every day Fellers sent a comprehensive report of current activity to General Marshall in Washington. For want of the cable, it had to go by wireless, using the State Department's 'Black Code'. Fellers had misgivings about its security, and would have had more had he read the telegrams that Churchill was sending Roosevelt, plainly but vainly hinting that the British had the strongest possible reason to know the weakness of State Department cyphers. In this case Italian military intelligence had stolen the code from the US Embassy in Rome and made an undetected copy. For the first six months of 1942 everything that Fellers knew – all the plans of the British Army and most of those of the Navy and Air Force as well – arrived every morning on General Rommel's table with his breakfast egg. No wonder his staff referred to Fellers as 'the good source' (*die gute Quelle*). This is how Erwin Rommel won the reputation of a military genius which he has never entirely lost in the English-speaking world (and never gained in his own service, where senior generals regarded him as an over-promoted court favourite). This was a major cause of the failure of successive British Malta convoys; this was how Rommel's Italian-German army was able to drive relentlessly onward until in June 1942 he stood poised to overrun the Nile delta. Fellers' final report on 11 June was largely responsible for the failure of the 'Harpoon' and 'Vigorous' convoys. But British intelligence in both Cairo and Bletchley had been urgently investigating the obvious security breach for months, and by May they were closing in. In June Churchill personally presented the facts to Roosevelt, and Fellers was immediately recalled to Washington. For Roosevelt the evidence

that American incompetence had come close to inflicting a strategic catastrophe on Britain was acutely embarrassing. Churchill's hand was very much
strengthened in dealing with the US government, while Roosevelt transferred
a quantity of tanks and guns to make up for British losses. At the last possible
moment Rommel himself fell headlong into the same trap and was fed with
false intelligence by the British which turned his retreat into a rout. Captain
Alfred Seebohm's tactical wireless intelligence company, which provided
another important component of Rommel's information, was thrown piecemeal into the collapsing front and captured. Meanwhile the Italians, who had
long had a poor opinion of German signals security, stopped using Enigma
machines at once. Unfortunately for them they too were dependent on wireless because their cables had been cut, and they did not realize that their Hagelin cypher machines were as vulnerable as Enigma.[50]

The British had long urged the US services to co-operate with one another,
and met stiff resistance, especially from the US Navy. After the Fellers affair,
and the first American visits to GC&CS which followed, US officers could no
longer deny how far behind their intelligence services had fallen. The British
urged, indeed demanded, that Americans learn to work with each other and
their allies, which in practice meant adopting British organization and methods, with the more or less explicit threat that the United States could not expect
access to British secrets unless it improved its security. The US government
was in no position to refuse, but the US Navy remained determined to resist
the menace of co-operation by every possible means. In April Commander
Rodger Winn, the (partly American-educated) RNVR barrister who presided
over the Submarine Tracking Room in the Admiralty, visited Washington and
managed to persuade Admiral King's Operational Staff OP-20-G to share work
on German naval Enigma. In the Indian Ocean, however, where the American position was strong, Admiral Somerville continued to receive scanty assistance. In September 1942 the Holden agreement handed over British Enigma
information in return for an American undertaking to share 'relevant' Japanese
intelligence, which turned out to mean very little. Later, however, the reviving
Far East Combined Bureau at Kilindini in Kenya broke several important Japanese cyphers, and (removed to Ceylon and renamed as HMS *Anderson*) re-
emerged in 1943 as a serious contributor to British naval intelligence and a
cryptographic ally the Americans could not afford to ignore.[51]

TWENTY-EIGHT

———•◆•———

A Right to Good Officers
Social History 1941–1942

L ike the other armed services, the Navy was a permanent organization
of long-serving professionals, which also had to be capable of rapid
expansion at short notice to an unknown maximum size. This called
for an awkward combination of complex organization and supple improvisation, all in the context of a new national recruitment system which was
intended to avoid the chaos and waste of the disorganized volunteering of
1914–15. Under the National Service Act of September 1939 all male British
subjects aged between eighteen and forty-one and resident in the United
Kingdom were liable for service unless they were medically unfit or already
employed in a 'reserved occupation'.[1] Volunteers were not sought and barely
even permitted: all were to be registered for national service and called up by
age, starting with twenty- to twenty-two-year-olds in December 1939, and
nineteen- to twenty-seven-year-olds next month. By the spring of 1942 all
men up to forty-seven and women up to thirty-one were obliged to register
for service. Women were not eligible for combat, mothers with children
younger than fourteen were never called up (though many volunteered), and
men over forty were put in 'static and sedentary duties'. The whole country
was liable to serve in some civil or military capacity but had to wait to be
called up. In this sense there were no real volunteers entering the fighting services after the outbreak of war except for boys younger than eighteen and men
over forty-seven (later fifty), but there remained substantial voluntary elements in the whole recruitment process. New recruits could indicate a choice
of service, and about three times as many opted for the Navy as it could accept,
so in that sense it was an all-volunteer service, able to pick the best one-third
out of a mass of would-be naval personnel, though from 1942 it had to accept
a proportion who were 'Medical Grade II' (less than fully fit). Otherwise the
standards of health and eyesight remained high; only artificers, sick-berth

attendants, writers, cooks, stewards and supply ratings were allowed to wear glasses. By April 1940 the Navy's manpower strength was 310,000 men, of which 130,000 were peacetime regulars, 60,000 were reservists recalled to service, and 120,000 were new entrants. These last were classed as 'Hostilities Only', conscripted for the length of the war.[2]

The school-leaving age was fourteen, and only about one child in seven entered the academically selective grammar schools which taught to Lower or Higher School Certificate at sixteen or eighteen. Most boys leaving school faced a boring wait of three or four years before they were called up for the infantry, but the sea offered several more attractive openings. Boy seamen could enter the Navy for 'Continuous Service' (i.e. the career, regular Navy) at fifteen, their parents signing them up for twelve years from age eighteen, and apprentices in engineering and technical branches of the Navy started their training at fifteen or sixteen. At about the same age merchant ships took boys to train as seamen, or 'apprentices' to train as officers. For all of them, going to sea promised travel and excitement, and merchant ships paid better than the Navy. (They were also believed to offer easier discipline, though one RNR Midshipman, called up in 1940, found the officers of a destroyer much friendlier and less formal than he was used to in a merchant ship.) For all these reasons British merchant ships continued to find as many volunteers as they needed despite the dangers of wartime voyages under submarine attack.[3]

The effects of the outbreak of war on an individual warship's company varied. Regular warships of destroyer-size and upwards, many of them already in commission before the outbreak of war, had a high proportion of long-service professionals among both officers and (even more important) senior ratings. As the war developed the proportion of new recruits rose steadily but not abruptly, and a great deal of training could be provided on the job in the traditional manner. At the other end of the scale, the small anti-submarine escorts of the 'Flower' Class (classed as 'corvettes'), designed to protect coastal convoys in the Channel or North Sea, were deliberately left until late in the pre-war expansion plan because they could be built fast. The first were ordered at the end of July 1939, and by the end of that year 115 were building. Six months later the fall of France meant that these newly commissioned coastal warships had to be used to protect transatlantic convoys, which called for voyaging and fighting on a scale they had never been designed for, and more than doubled their originally planned complement of twenty-nine officers and men, generating an instant manning crisis. The little ships were now grossly overcrowded, with a bad incidence of tuberculosis, and only the barest minimum of

experienced officers and petty officers were available to man them. The majority of the first generation of corvettes (sixty-seven of the eighty-one in commission by June 1941) were commanded by RNR Lieutenants – peacetime
Merchant Navy officers accustomed to the sea – but the supply of suitable candidates was limited, and merchant shipowners needed them too, so in wartime
new officers were only accepted into the RNR if they were already master
mariners (i.e. holders of a foreign-going master's certificate). The pre-war,
'regular' RNVR was a small force (limited to 5,500 officers and men till 1938),
which trained together but had few opportunities to serve at sea. In the initial
stage of mobilization in 1939 new RNVSR officers (officially, though not in
every case really, with sea, or at least yachting, experience already) were being
taken in with no more than ten days' training while their new uniforms were
being made: 'The standard to be reached by a Sub-Lieutenant R.N.V.R. in September 1939 was the possession of a full uniform. An additional pair of trousers would almost certainly have led to accelerated promotion.'[4] For the benefit
of the RNVSR, the Board of Trade had set up in 1938 a Coastal Yachtmaster's
Certificate as an introduction to small-ship command, so the Admiralty began
cautiously to choose new captains of corvettes from among those so qualified.
When Lieutenant Denys Rayner commissioned the corvette *Verbena* at the
end of 1940 (the first entirely RNVR-officered ship in the Navy), his officers
were two Sub-Lieutenants and a Midshipman, and Rayner himself was the
only one with a naval watch-keeping certificate. By peacetime standards this
looked like a desperate expedient, but it was more in the nature of a calculated
experiment. Rayner was an experienced yachtsman with some naval training,
and his ship was going to serve in company with other ships escorting convoys, where more senior and experienced officers would usually be within signalling distance. If he could mould a happy and reasonably efficient ship's
company, he could take his place in a convoy escort. His success opened the
way for a minority of outstanding RNVR (ex-RNVSR) officers to be given
commands, but the limited supply of reservists was quickly exhausted by the
emergency.[5]

By 1940 it was already clear that the Navy needed a system to mass-produce
small-ship officers out of landsmen with little or no experience of seafaring or
command. In September 1939 RNVSR officers began to be trained at HMS
King Alfred, a new establishment installed in the almost-complete Hove Municipal Swimming Pool, though it soon spilled over into schools and other buildings in the vicinity. In January 1940 *King Alfred* began to run ten-week courses
for officer candidates from the lower deck under what was known as the 'White
Paper Scheme'. On 29 May some of them were sent to Dunkirk to help with

the evacuation. From 1941 the RNVR ceased to enter new ratings and became the usual destination for 'Hostilities Only' (HO) officer candidates, who might be promoted fast if they had talent, precisely because they were in the Navy for hostilities only and would not stay in the peacetime Service to spoil the regulars' career prospects. The remaining 'old' RNVR still serving on peacetime regulations had reason to resent the HO's more rapid promotion, but the urgent search for potential officers soon gathered up most of those with some previous naval training. By 1942 the selection of what were called 'CW candidates'[6] from new HO recruits serving their initial sea-time, was an established routine. In principle they were chosen from men of good education, but already in 1942 higher education was scarce, and the selectors learnt to look for intelligence and character instead. Many older candidates, already part-way through a very diverse range of careers, had professional experience which went a good way to make up for deficiencies in formal education.[7] Lieutenant-Commander John Mosse, who commissioned the sloop *Mermaid* in 1944, surveyed her ship's company:

> Dixon, a first class navigator, was a businessman. Danskin was an accountant, wardroom clown and piano player. Of the two Sub Lieutenants, Oakley the Gunnery Control Officer was a chemist, whilst the all important Anti-Submarine Control Officer was one Caughey Gauntlett, a practising Salvationist . . . The Sailors numbered one hundred and eighty, of whom eighty percent were Hostilities Only.[8]

Before they could be commissioned, CW candidates had to serve at least three months on the lower deck, wearing caps which distinguished them as officer candidates – a socially awkward situation, requiring tact and tolerance all round, and another abrupt break with the pre-war practice of training officers and ratings separately. Sea-time on the lower deck allowed unsuitable candidates to be identified and diverted elsewhere; the remainder entered *King Alfred* as a division of 160 to 200 'Probationary Temporary Acting Sub-Lieutenants' every week. The function of the establishment, in the words of Captain John Pelly who commanded it throughout the war, was 'to instil in every man the alertness, enthusiasm, broadmindedness, sense of responsibility, conscience and good humour (as well as a basic knowledge of technical subjects) which centuries of Service experience have shown to be necessary if a naval officer is to carry out his normal duties'. One of Pelly's principles was that 'the ratings have few rights, but they definitely have got a right to good officers'.[9] If they impressed the trainers, these '60-day wonders' might gain their first commissions on the basis of three months at sea on the lower deck and three months training ashore (compared to seven years in peacetime to pass through Dartmouth and midshipmen's sea-time).[10]

Something had to be sacrificed to train new officers in one-fourteenth of the time hitherto considered necessary. The real difference (apart from age) between adult reservist officers and teenage candidates for the regular RN was that RN officers (once they had reached Lieutenant's rank and acquired a watch-keeping certificate) were in principle qualified to do all sorts of naval work, and promotable as far as their talent and experience could carry them. By 1941 virtually all wartime entry HO officers were commissioned into the RNVR, but before 1943 only a minority rose above the rank of Lieutenant, most of them served in small ships, and almost all of them became specialists in one kind of naval service only, notably anti-submarine warfare, coastal forces (motor torpedo boats and the like), combined operations (landing craft), minesweeping, naval flying in the Fleet Air Arm, and some submariners. These junior officers would pass much or all their wartime careers in a single branch of the Navy, and never be very far away from experienced seniors. They needed, and were given, thorough training, they were expected to be able to use their initiative, but they did not have to know much about the Navy outside their branch. RNVR officers were only reckoned as fully equivalent to RN officers of the same rank if they were qualified to command – which the majority never were – and at this stage even those who did rise to command ships usually stayed in the same branch of the Navy.[11] When the newly promoted Lieutenant-Commander Nicholas Monsarrat, RNVR (one of the early RNVSR yachtsmen), took command of the new frigate *Ettrick* in December 1943, he reflected that this was 'the only sort of Navy I knew anything about; the ship I was going to command would be the biggest one I had ever boarded, and her job, convoy escort, had been my life for as long as I could remember'.[12]

In 1942 the Navy adopted a long-term manning plan looking ahead beyond victory to the reconstruction of a peacetime Service, without generating the surplus of officers which had caused such difficulties in the 1920s and 1930s. At this point the Navy took control of the Sea Cadet Corps, which enrolled boys of twelve to seventeen, and resumed the suspended recruitment of Boy Seamen of fifteen who would grow up to 'Continuous Service', meaning a full career on the lower deck. Both Dartmouth and the 'Special Entry' continued to take in future officers, at thirteen and eighteen respectively. In 1941 a scholarship scheme was introduced for Dartmouth boys, offering means-tested places ranging from full fees (£65 a term) for those whose parents earned over £700 a year, down to no fees for those earning less than £300. (That still left the requirement to keep a boy in school at least three years beyond the school-leaving age, plus a range of incidental expenses, all of which kept the College out of reach of most of the working classes.) Some 297 boys from state schools competed for ten places, and sixty-five applied from private schools, though in subsequent years the number of applicants from state schools declined (possibly because the 'Special Entry' was more attractive). Dartmouth usually took forty-five cadets each (biennial) term; from 1936 the 'Special Entry' took 100 for the Executive Branch, thirty-six engineers, thirty-two for the Supply Branch and forty Royal Marines. It remained a matter of debate which system produced the better officers, but to generate the range and number of candidates required it was necessary that both should function.[13]

All schemes for entering and training commissioned officers invited comparison with warrant officers, who were typically long-serving career ratings who had risen from petty officer. A Commissioned Warrant Officer ranked with a sub-lieutenant, but a typical sub-lieutenant would be ten or twenty years younger, with a better education behind him and a better future ahead. Those who wanted to open officer careers to the lower deck – Winston Churchill and the wartime First Lord of the Admiralty A. V. Alexander, to look no further – were apt to regard warrant officers as wasted talent. The difficulty was that the national education system in the 1940s educated only a small proportion of the population to officer level, and even the brightest and best warrant officers were likely to be too old to rise far as commissioned officers. They were also liable to be stranded on the return of peace, unable to step back and resume their previous naval careers as ratings, but unqualified for further promotion. Some of the same problems applied to 'upper yardmen', bright young ratings selected young for promotion to commissioned rank. The 1933 scheme functioned effectively during the war, but even the best candidates faced great difficulties in rising as naval officers with what was in most cases only an elementary education. One uniquely successful case was Richard Trowbridge, a Hampshire farmer's son who entered (from a grammar school) as a Boy Seaman of fifteen in 1935, was promoted Sub-Lieutenant in 1940, and rose after the war to be a Rear-Admiral and a knight.[14]

In January 1939 the Navy (not including Royal Marines) had 9,762 commissioned officers; by June 1943 it had 57,682, almost six times as many, and yet it was often noted that the quality had if anything improved. In the early years of the war the Navy was usually training about 3,000 officers, or up to 30 per cent of its strength, at any given time, which occupied a substantial fraction of the most experienced officers and ratings, and meant that almost from the beginning the actual fighting in small ships was largely left to men new to the Navy and the sea. To train a new Navy at the same time as fighting a major war the Navy had to draw deeply on its long traditions and profound self-confidence, largely transmitted by retired officers and ratings recalled for service. These were the ones who passed on the naval ethos to their trainees, by example as much as by formal instruction. Through them the trainees learnt 'officer-like' appearance and behaviour as a symbol of standards and self-confidence. They learnt to delegate work and pass on information as an expression of trust as well as a means of integration. The naval ideal of service was 'steady efficiency and devotion to duty, rather than gallantry'.[15] Heroism was associated with helping shipmates, for example in a sinking ship, rather than with killing the enemy. A good ship's company served and fought together as a team, supported by an unwritten contract of mutual support. An ambitious captain who seemed to be risking everyone's lives in the search for promotion threatened that contract – for which reason the Admiralty was equivocal about awarding officers medals for personal gallantry, and much preferred to reward initiative and commitment.[16] The crew of the submarine *United* who had suffered under a medal-hunting captain were alarmed to find that his relief was only twenty-three, but drew some comfort from discovering that he was married and 'might want to live'.[17]

In many conscious and explicit ways the Navy was deeply bound by tradition – and yet to fight a major war while expanding very fast called for an imaginative ruthlessness with social and naval conventions which marks a real change of attitude from the First World War. The Navy handled even such sensitive subjects as rank and seniority with remarkable flexibility. As a matter of course retired officers recalled for service were employed at least one step below their previous rank in order not to block the promotion prospects of a younger generation, and those still serving over sixty were usually transferred to the RNVR.[18] We can say on the authority of the Jewish admiral Max Horton that the Navy was almost innocent of anti-Semitism (one of the many differences between the RN and the USN).[19]

Another way in which the Navy responded to wartime demand was the proliferation of specialized 'manning pools'. For example, the RNVR Special Branch (not to be confused with the Supplementary Reserve) started as a small body of 'gentlemen of considerable organising and administrative experience' (an oblique reference to matters of special secrecy), recruited by advertisement from those aged between thirty and forty. Most of them worked ashore in staff and intelligence work, though later an important contingent were added to serve afloat in another secret trade as RDF (i.e. radar) officers. The Special Branch were identified by a green stripe among the gold on their sleeves.[20]

A bigger 'manning pool' was the Fleet Air Arm (FAA), which in 1939 became the Navy's fourth manning port (after Chatham, Portsmouth and Devonport). Like most British wartime aircrew, the naval airmen were taught to fly in Canada under the Empire Air Scheme. In September 1939 the FAA had 360 pilots and 332 under training, and by the end of 1940 the output was fifty pilots a month, but standards and output fell as casualties increased. In July 1941 the FAA had 940 pilots, but new pilots were joining their squadrons with only 120 hours' flying time – which goes far to explain the disappointing performance of British naval aircraft in 1941–2. Then in the summer of 1941 (before the USA had entered the war) Rear-Admiral John Towers USN, then Chief of the Bureau of Aeronautics, gave the FAA privileged access to the US Navy's air-training school at Pensacola, Florida, and by 1944 the 'Towers Scheme' was training 44 per cent of the FAA's intake. This training was naturally on US aircraft and flight decks, which eased the adoption of US aircraft into the Royal Navy but caused the FAA some difficulties with the incompatible British carrier catapults. Besides this most valuable practical aid, the Towers Scheme had long-term social and even political consequences in creating a body of British 'Pensacola Veterans' who in the post-war years kept up a warm inter-service friendship, cherished on both sides. Crossing a different ocean, young men from Australia and New Zealand, eager to fight and fly, sought to join their countries' air forces in much greater numbers than were needed, so many of them volunteered for the Fleet Air Arm instead, giving it a pronounced Antipodean accent, and raising both numbers and training standards. By July 1942 the FAA had 1,632 aircrew, and new airmen were joining their squadrons with 180 to 200 hours' flying time and ten weeks' operational training. Most of these wartime recruits joined the FAA as ratings and were made up to Midshipmen or Sub-Lieutenants (Air) as soon as they gained their pilot's or observer's wings. Promotion was fast, and by the end of the war most naval fighter squadrons were commanded by Lieutenant-Commanders of the 1941–2 entry.[21]

Wartime flying was dangerous, but not as dangerous as submarines. (Over the whole war the whole Royal Navy lost 7.6 per cent of its personnel killed, but British submarines lost 38 per cent of their men.)[22] From 1940, for the first time, a proportion of British submariners were not volunteers. Lieutenant Arthur Hezlet was one of them:

> There are two great advantages of serving in a submarine. One was that your pay almost doubled. As a lieutenant you were paid 13s 6d a day. You got six shillings extra for submarines and three shillings for every night you slept in them, so you were very substantially better off than anyone in

general service. The other was that you got a very early command, generally at about the age of twenty-eight. So after a little while in submarines I
said 'kindly transfer my name onto the volunteers. I will stay now I'm
here.'[23]

In both world wars the British submarine service lost approximately one-third
of its boats and the equivalent of 100 per cent of its initial manpower. 'It was
still a "private Navy", inordinately proud of its tradition, jealous of its privileges, and, if slightly inclined to be piratical, the most enthusiastic, loyal and
happy branch of the Service.'[24] Max Horton, the distinguished First World War
submariner, was Flag Officer Submarines from 1940 to 1942 and kept up the
training standards of the service. 'It is essential to keep the standard high,' he
told his officers,

> nothing can be neglected – it is not a kindness to overlook slackness or
> mistakes, it is really a great cruelty to do so – cruelty to wives and relatives
> of the man you let off, and his shipmates and to yourself. There is no margin
> for mistakes in submarines; you are either alive or dead.[25]

In a submerged attack everything depended on the judgement of the submarine CO at the periscope, for he alone could see what was happening, and
anyone whose nerve seemed to be failing was relieved at once. The age of promotion to first command fell steadily as the war progressed. In British boats
lieutenants qualified for command at five and a half to six and a half years'
seniority in 1940, which had fallen to one to two years by 1943. The figures were
similar in German U-boats; by 1943 the average U-boat skipper was twenty-
three, and one boat in three returned from patrol. The British submarine service never made the mistake of the US Navy, which for the first half of the war
awarded submarine command to safe, middle-aged officers strictly ordered to
run no risks, with the result that US submarines were largely ineffectual until
late 1944 and spent much of the war on air-sea rescue duty. The story was similar in the Italian Navy, and for similar reasons. Submarines were extremely
crowded even by comparison with corvettes, with bunks for two out of three,
a high sickness rate, and poor ventilation even on the surface. Submariners ate
well (ratings and officers alike), with luxuries like Marmite (but not much fresh
food), and had more comfortable working clothes than German submariners
in their rubber 'U-boat suit'. Of all the wartime navies, only the Italians forbade smoking in submerged submarines – though they were indifferent to
night vision, which every other submarine service regarded as extremely
important.[26]

Another manning pool which in 1939 existed only in embryo was electrical engineering, still officially the responsibility of the Torpedo Branch, which was increasingly overloaded by the rapid increase in the quantity and range of electrical equipment afloat. By 1943 the Torpedo Schools were teaching no fewer than 131 different courses. As an immediate response, RNVR Electrical Officers were recruited from graduates. This did not help with the very urgent problem of small-ship radar, especially the more or less hand-built early sets of Type 271, critically important to the anti-submarine war but requiring expert nursing to keep them working in North Atlantic conditions. Since radar had been too secret for universities to know about before the war, graduates had never heard of it, so the RN Signal School had to train 'RDF Officers', many of them undergraduates called up after their first university year (the standard wartime practice for male university students) from courses in physics, electrical engineering or mathematics. When they went to sea they initially reported personally to the captain, who alone was (in theory if not always in practice) in the 'radar secret' – an arrangement which gave the young radar officers powerful patrons. Dr Charles Wright, Director of Scientific Research at the Admiralty, was a Canadian, aware that some Canadian universities were already teaching the new subject of 'radio physics'. In 1941 he was instrumental in recruiting some twenty Canadian radio physics graduates (followed by more later) into the RCNVR (Special Branch) to become naval radar officers. Many of them served with the Royal Navy, where they made an important contribution in building up its radar expertise.[27]

This was advanced science, but a much larger group of RNVR officers and HO ratings served in the mainly low-technology manning pool of amphibious warfare. Gavin Douglas commanded the tank landing craft LCT 397 in 1944:

> The crew of my own craft were all little more than boys: the eldest was twenty-five, and only three out of the ten hands carried were entitled to draw a rum issue, which means that only three were older than twenty. My Motor Mechanic, in charge of the craft's machinery with two assistants, was a fair-haired, boyishly smooth-faced expert of nineteen, and the First Lieutenant was a happy-go-lucky New Zealander of twenty-one. At the age of forty-five, I felt the complete horny-handed old sea dog in such company. One or two of the hands had been at sea before. The Coxswain had seen most of the Mediterranean landings in minor landing craft and was a fair seaman, but none of the others was much advanced from the landsman he had been not many months before.[28]

The Royal Marines, as a distinct but not totally independent service belonging to the Navy, was another element of the naval recruiting and training situation. The Royal Marine officer-training model has already been cited as one of the inspirations of the 1913 Special Entry scheme for naval officers. In 1939 it was supplemented by a Royal Marine Temporary Officers' Scheme which took young men with no particular training directly into service. This was not a success and was soon replaced by army-style Officer Cadet Training Units. Before the war the Royal Marines were still heavily committed to bands and fire control, but they were also drawn on as part of the Mobile Naval Base Defence Organization, whose function was to defend (but not to capture) the temporary advanced bases which were expected to be required. The first was the Mediterranean Fleet's advanced base of Suda Bay, and more than half its defenders were captured when the Germans overran Crete in May 1941. From 1942 the Marines became increasingly involved in the 'Commando' raiding parties of Combined Operations, but they also manned some heavy-gun batteries (notably at Dover), the defensive gun armament of some merchant ships, and formed units of Royal Marine Engineers which functioned to establish temporary bases in a similar fashion (but on a smaller scale) to the US Navy's Construction Battalions ('Seabees'). This did not exhaust the Marines' versatility; there were even some Royal Marine pilots in the Fleet Air Arm.[29]

The extravagant requirement for naval training was possibly the single greatest organizational challenge which the Navy faced in the Second World War. It had been anticipated, but like most other demands of the war, it was made much heavier and more urgent by the fall of France. By fortunate coincidence a 1938 Act of Parliament encouraging employers to give their workers a week's annual holiday had stimulated the building of seaside holiday camps, a number of which were just finished when the war broke out and were quickly requisitioned for naval training. Other naval establishments moved from exposed positions on the Channel coast to the Clyde or the West Highlands, where there was plenty of sheltered deep water and few enemy aircraft. The anti-submarine warfare school, HMS *Osprey*, migrated from Portland to Dunoon, with a satellite (HMS *Nimrod*) down the Clyde at Campbeltown. Amphibious warfare training settled nearby, with a headquarters at Inveraray on Loch Fyne and another large base on the other side of the Clyde at Largs. The Fleet Air Arm did a great deal of its training in the Northern Isles, close to the Home Fleet's base at Scapa Flow, where there was plenty of uncrowded sea and air space (and unlimited supplies of wind and fog). Deck landing was practised in the Clyde with the old *Argus*, which was stationed there for part of the war, and the new escort carriers, which worked up there. As the naval air service expanded in 1943–4 to man the new carriers for the Pacific, it took over many existing RAF stations in Scotland and the isles. Elsewhere in Scotland motor torpedo boats, motor gunboats and the like trained in the West Highlands at Fort William and at Ardrishaig on Loch Fyne. On the East Coast minesweepers practised in the shallower waters of the Firth of Forth. At the beginning of the war this was still the business of the trawler branch of the RNR, which had its own structure of ranks and ratings using fishermen's terminology, with 'Skippers RNR' as warrant officers in command. The trawler skipper was a fine seaman, accustomed to handling warps and trawls, but typically had trouble adapting to the precise navigation needed to sweep magnetic and other ground mines:

> The necessity for meticulous station keeping, navigational accuracy and constant vigilance ran counter to his ingrained habits. The temporary reserve officer of the other classes, usually better educated, more amenable to training and bringing to the task a fresh, enthusiastic and unbiased mind, proved far more efficient and reliable.[30]

So it was decided that the fishermen made their best contribution to the war effort by feeding the people, and by the end of the war two-thirds of the minesweeper officers came from the RNVR.[31]

Of all the naval training establishments to settle in Scotland, the best-known was probably HMS *Western Isles* (a real ship unlike so many naval bases). A 1937 Naval Staff study of 'Provision and Training of Anti-Submarine Personnel' led to plans to establish a joint Anglo-French anti-submarine school at Lorient in Brittany – but these plans like so many others had to be hastily adjusted in the summer of 1940, and the now-British establishment settled aboard a former passenger ferry moored in Tobermory Bay on the Isle of Mull. Newly commissioned anti-submarine escorts from trawlers and corvettes up to sloops and frigates went there to 'work up' to full efficiency. In a week or two the *Western Isles* had to make a coherent team out of a gathering of strangers: a few experts, many men with basic training, some who had never spent a night at sea. In command was Commodore (Vice-Admiral retired) Gilbert Stephenson, a veteran of the anti-submarine campaign in the Great War, who had finished his first naval career in 1929 as an outstanding Commodore of Portsmouth Barracks. At the age of sixty-two in 1940, he was a famous naval character: unconventional, forceful, often alarming, with a mischievous sense of humour: the hero of numerous anecdotes (some of them true), he well knew how to use his personality to impress and inspire. The intense training the *Western Isles* provided in every one of the ship's functions and every part of her organization (not forgetting such humble but essential duties as cooking and cleaning) was frequently interrupted by unannounced emergencies designed to test nerve and initiative.[32] 'My number one priority was *Spirit*,' Stephenson wrote:

> This was the first essential – determination to win. Next came *Discipline*: it's no good being the finest men in the world if you are not going to obey orders. Third – *Administration*: making sure the work of the ship was evenly divided: that meals were in the right place at the right time; that the whole organisation of the ship was both stable and elastic. Then, lastly – and this may surprise you – lastly, *Technique* – how to use the equipment. That would have been quite useless unless the spirit was right in the first place.[33]

Entirely without authority, the Commodore assumed the power to dismiss officers (captains not excepted) if he thought they were not equal to their jobs. 'I had a rule never to ask *permission* to do anything, never to *ask* for anything – take it and tell them to pay for it, do it and tell them I'd done it!'[34] Stephenson earned his terrifying reputation, but in fact he devoted most of his effort to supporting and encouraging inexperienced officers, and only removed a small minority of the dangerously incompetent. So effective was Stephenson's working-up that other commands wanted to share in it. In February 1943 he complained that even destroyers were trying to squeeze in, aware that they were 'in many cases pathetically in need of fundamental assistance in both their A/S and gunnery organisation'. To cope with the demand a satellite working-up base was established at Stornoway in the Outer Hebrides. By October 1944 Stephenson's organization had worked up over a thousand newly commissioned escorts (some of them more than once), leading to a jocular exchange of signals with Admiral Horton comparing him to Helen of Troy.[35]

The length of the working-up syllabus varied with the size of the ship. In January 1941 when most of the ships coming to Tobermory were corvettes, it took a fortnight. The big new frigates of 1943 were allowed twenty days.[36] During 1941 and 1942 there was a steady evolution of training methods. Working-up was only the start: once operational, escorts required continual refresher training and courses in new tactics and equipment. Some of this could be done at sea on passage, for (contrary to the impression one can get from popular histories) most convoy days at sea were uneventful – but precisely for that reason escort groups needed more intensive training than could be provided by infrequent contact with the enemy. By January 1943 each Western Approaches escort group followed a 100-day operational cycle which

included seven sea days' training, when the 'Training Captain' in the armed
yacht *Philante* took the escorts to practise all sorts of anti-submarine tactics,
and fourteen days in port with one watch on leave while the others worked on
training, boiler cleaning and maintenance. Horton brought in a fellow submariner, Captain George Simpson, who had commanded the Malta flotilla
through the hardest years of the siege, and made him Commodore commanding a new escort base at Londonderry, where he had the services of several
'clockwork mice', as the Navy called them – practice submarines for the escorts
to hunt. Some of these were old boats belonging to the Royal Navy or Allied
navies, but effective training called for modern submarines with realistic speed
and diving depth, so from September 1943 it became routine for newly commissioned British submarines to work up and polish their technique with a
few weeks playing clockwork mice before they went on war patrol.[37]

Anti-submarine tactics had scarcely existed in 1940, when escorts knew
little more than how to form a screen around the convoy. Looking back from
the later stages of the war officers judged that 'the rather haphazard escort
methods of the early days – tremendously hard work, long endurance, moderate skill, and little science – had no place now, in a job which had been organ-
ised and sharpened into a lethal routine'.[38] This 'lethal routine' sprang from
intense training. By 1941 there were a number of notably successful escort
group commanders, including Commander F. J. ('Johnny') Walker, Captain
Joe Baker-Cresswell and Lieutenant-Commander Peter Gretton – but each had
their own methods, and there were no standard anti-submarine tactics. Walker
alone had devised a tactic (named 'Buttercup') for a convoy attacked at night
by U-boats on the surface. All the escorts turned outwards and fired starshell
for twenty minutes, illuminating surfaced U-boats, and back-lighting any
caught between the escorts and the falling starshell. If the U-boats dived to
escape illumination, they exposed themselves to Asdic search at an effective
range. 'Buttercup' sank two U-boats in the battle for convoy HG 76 in December 1941, which was an encouraging start – but 'Buttercup' assumed that the
attack had come from surfaced U-boats outside the screen. At this time U-boat
numbers and sinkings were once more rising alarmingly, and Churchill was
taking a close interest in the anti-submarine campaign. It has been suggested
that Churchill personally intervened in December 1941, advised by the retired
Vice-Admiral Cecil Usborne and the Second Sea Lord, Admiral Sir Charles
Little. This cannot be entirely correct. The Second Sea Lord dealt with personnel, not operations, and Little was no longer at the Admiralty but had joined
the British Joint Staff Mission in Washington in June 1941. Usborne did advise
Churchill, and Admiral Pound must have been involved, because the scheme

now adopted looked very like political interference in the responsibilities of a commander-in-chief (Sir Percy Noble of Western Approaches), an exceedingly delicate manoeuvre which the Churchill of 1915 might have risked, but the Churchill of 1942 would never have undertaken without the First Sea Lord's backing. No admiral would welcome outsiders teaching him how to run his command, and in this case the outsider sent by the Admiralty to set up an anti-submarine tactical school was Commander Gilbert Roberts, not an expert in the subject but a destroyer gunnery officer who had been invalided out of the Navy with tuberculosis in 1938 – though he had relevant staff college experience of using board games to explore tactical problems in the style of the German *Kriegsspiele*.[39]

Noble received him coolly, but he was allocated some rooms and a small staff: two lieutenant-commanders, a chief yeoman of signals with experience of the Tactical School at Portsmouth, four Wren officers and four Wren ratings. Roberts began by interviewing as many escort commanders as he could, asking them about the tactics they adopted to defeat a U-boat attack. He found that very few apart from Walker had worked out a tactic in advance, and he was not convinced that Walker's 'Buttercup' was sound. Studying the reports, Roberts began to suspect that U-boats were getting inside the screen to fire at close range. Seeking expert advice, he telephoned the staff of Flag Officer Submarines, and to his surprise was answered by Sir Max Horton himself. Horton advised him that a U-boat could, indeed must, get inside the escort screen and among the convoy, because the screen was normally stationed about 5,000 yards out from the convoy, and the range of the new German electric torpedo was only 5,400 yards. Hitherto the German U-boats had fired 'heater' torpedoes like those used by British submarines, which gave a powerful drive with a range of over 15,000 yards on the 30-knot setting, but noisy and detectable by hydrophones or Asdic in time to take avoiding action. The new German G7e electric torpedo was quiet (and cheap to manufacture), but its short range made it difficult to fire from outside the escort screen. The noted submariner Commander Otto Kretschmer of *U-99* therefore developed a tactic for getting inside the screen and attacking at close range on the surface.[40]

Meanwhile Roberts had laid out his 'tactical floor', divided into 10-inch squares, each representing a square mile, the whole floor twenty miles square. On this he reconstructed the successful defence of convoy HG 76, and satisfied himself that the reports he had been studying had to mean that U-boats were firing from inside the escort screen. When he was ready, he invited the admiral to see a demonstration. The Wrens plotted the movement of HG 76 across the tactical floor, while Roberts explained his interpretation of the

German attack, and proposed a counter tactic. Admiral Noble was completely converted, and in a signal to the Admiralty generously acknowledged the discovery of a 'cardinal error in our anti-submarine thinking'. Roberts was promoted to Acting Captain on the spot and told 'I want to see you often in the Operations Room downstairs.'[41] Gretton is a witness to the impact of Roberts and his 'Western Approaches Tactical Unit':

> Much has been written about Captain Gilbert Roberts who ran the place and it should be enough here to say that he was the ideal man for the job. He did invaluable work by careful analysis of records, he detected new enemy methods of attack, he invented new search schemes for finding U-boats and he helped weld groups together. But above all he made a number of really stupid officers really THINK, sometimes for the first time in their lives . . .
>
> Gilbert Roberts succeeded in improving everyone who came to do his course, and this was his greatest achievement. I went whenever I could find a week to spare and, later on, took the Captains of the ships of my group with me, for he combined a vivid imagination with a good tactical and technical knowledge and a theatrical flair for getting his points across.[42]

Western Approaches Tactical Unit (WATU) became a leading example of new naval training methods:

> What was fundamental to the effectiveness of these systems was coherent doctrine and at a higher level than had been achieved prior to the war. It was the 'industrialisation' of tactical development, the introduction of operational research and the creation of an effective chain of analysis, innovation, test and publication that finally allowed the enforcement of systematic, navy-wide procedures. This in turn made both shore and sea training on the large scale practicable, since it provided formulae and processes with which to work (and which did work) and valid standards to aim at.[43]

In conception these training methods were sophisticated and imaginative, but the actual equipment of WATU was simple: chalk and string to mark up the tactical floor, bedsheets to screen the individual tables at which sat the officers attending a course, with only a restricted view of a nearby part of the tactical floor to represent the escort's limited range of view. The Wrens moved the symbols, marked up the floor, and acted as messengers to and from the participating officers, bearing notes to convey signals and orders. Having little naval training and no sea experience, the Wrens could not officially act as instructors themselves, but they quickly learnt the tactical principles and became expert and enthusiastic participants in the courses, well able to offer discreet suggestions to officers in difficulties, and on occasion to play the parts of escort captains themselves. When Admiral Horton took over Western Approaches Command in November 1942 and first participated in a WATU course, he was invited (as a famous submariner) to play the role of a shadowing U-boat in a trial of the new 'Beta Search' tactic, designed to eliminate a shadower before he could home in on other U-boats. One of the escort COs was played by the eighteen-year-old Wren Janet Okell – who to his annoyance promptly sank him several times running. This was not a unique event by 1942, when Wrens were playing a rapidly growing role in naval training, and in many other naval activities which would previously have been regarded as improper for women and impossible for those without sea experience. As a powerful expression of official admiration for WATU's work, on the day Noble left Western Approaches and Horton took over, King George VI, the Queen and the Director WRNS visited the unit and watched a demonstration of its methods.[44]

The first overseas draft of Wren Telegraphists sailed for Singapore in January 1941. The next overseas party were meant for Gibraltar but were all killed when their ship was torpedoed in August 1941. This must have been a shock, but volunteers came forward at once to take their places. The tragedy led the Admiralty to order that in future Wrens going overseas should if possible be given passage in HM Ships. In October eight Wren cypher officers sailed for Gibraltar aboard the battleship *Malaya*. Once afloat, they made themselves useful by joining in the work of the ship, providing another discreetly eloquent demonstration of how far the WRNS could integrate with the Navy. Three years later, in 1944, when Wrens afloat were not quite such a novelty, the cruiser *Aurora* carried a large draft of Wrens from North Africa to Italy and caused a sensation by entering Naples with the Wrens lining the forecastle.[45]

The WRNS were not merely learning from the Navy, but in significant respects teaching it. Vera Mathews was determined from the start to set up a classless recruitment and promotion system. From March 1941, as soon as she was in full command of her service, there was no direct recruitment of Wren officers; all new recruits to the WRNS joined as probationer ratings for a fortnight's initial training under a deliberately tough regime. Those who passed were rewarded with their first uniform and were allocated to a branch after an interview with a senior Wren officer. Some of the early Wren officers were the daughters of naval families, but as soon as possible Mathews chose officers only from Wren ratings who had demonstrated leadership, regardless of family or social status. This appears to have been before the RNVR began taking HO officer candidates from the lower deck, and it was certainly in advance of the other women's services, which continued to look for the right families rather than the right qualities.[46] In September 1941 Wren officers' ranks were 'equated' with naval ranks, and in 1942 an Admiralty Fleet Order established the authority of Wren officers and petty officers over male naval ratings. In the same year the naval nurses (Queen Alexandra's Royal Naval Nursing Service, QARNNS), together with the other service nurses, were given 'equivalent rank', so a Nursing Sister equalled a Lieutenant, and the Matron-in-Chief took rank with a Commodore. There were no nurse ratings, but the joint-service Voluntary Aid Detachments provided untrained female assistance in naval hospitals under the nurses' supervision.[47]

The distinctive character and high reputation of the WRNS, their smart and feminine image, owed a good deal to a paradoxical relationship with the Navy. The women worked very closely with the Navy, but belonged to a separate service which was in many respects autonomous; male officers had no authority over their internal affairs. They ran their own establishments, wrote their own regulations, and in disciplinary matters answered to their own officers, though they often worked together under naval command. Wrens were expected to show initiative and intelligence well beyond what would be normal in men of equivalent rates – which by the middle years of the war was a realistic reflection of the lower standards of intelligence and education among male recruits as the manpower situation became ever tighter. The contrast with the other women's services was clear to contemporaries. The Navy was proud of the WRNS, and their presence was invariably good for morale.[48] Observers noted the sailors' 'special affection' for Wrens, who were 'looked on, not as fair game but as part of the Service, and thus to be protected and preserved from outsiders'.[49] One Wren served under a tough old CPO who called Wrens 'Flighty young things, can't expect them to do a man's job properly' – but then he was overheard in a storeroom telling another Chief, 'Don't you criticise them girls. Better than your lads in many ways. Do their jobs well, they do.' 'So we knew he was an old softie really.'[50]

Some overseas commanders-in-chief had misgivings about accepting the WRNS, but by 1941 the Admiralty had no doubts. Sir William Whitworth, the new Second Sea Lord, wrote to Admiral Cunningham in the Mediterranean in November 1941, 'I was glad to see that you have agreed to accept Wrens, and a large number of them . . . I am very much impressed by their work and their keenness. They take their service very seriously and join up to play their part in the war, rather than to have a good time; although they don't mind having a good time in non-working hours, which is as it should be . . .'[51]

The WRNS uniforms were the same for officers and ratings except for badges and caps. The officer-like uniform (designed by the well-known couturier Edward Molyneux and including that precious wartime luxury, a pair of silk stockings) was a real attraction, and others appreciated the seamen's 'bell-bottoms', first issued to Wrens for boat-work in February 1941 – this in a generation when a woman wearing trousers might still be regarded as somewhat 'fast'. The unpopular early 'pudding-basin' hat worn by Wren ratings was replaced in August 1942 by a soft version of the sailor's cap.[52]

By 1942 jobs entrusted to the WRNS included Bomb Range Markers, Meteorologists, Vision Testers, Parachute Packers, Experimental Gunnery, Torpedo Attack Assessors, painters, welders, turners, drivers of tractors and cranes, 'tailoresses' and mine-watchers. 'Suggestions for widening the scope of Wrens' employment always came from the Navy, and every new category in which they triumphed opened men's eyes to the possibility of their undertaking something else.'[53] A rating of 'RDF [radar] Operator' was established in September 1940, followed in May 1941 by Radio Mechanic.[54] Many commanders-in-chief allowed Wrens to go to sea for the day on trials, and at least one is reported to have sailed in a submarine on patrol. By April 1942 the operators of the Submarine Attack Teachers, the 'simulators' which trained submarine captains, were entirely Wrens. At Portsmouth:

> The simulator was housed in a building on the *Dolphin* quay and had two floors: the lower one known as the control room had a rotating conning tower with a periscope and various instruments including a gramophone playing underwater noises. The most important instrument was the 'fruit machine' which was a mechanical analogue computer; this was fed with target information, submarine depth &c, and worked out the torpedo firing conditions. The upper floor had mechanisms to control the movement of the model targets along a rail track some fifty yards long. In addition, in this room there was a large plotting table on which the torpedo tracks were recorded for critical analysis. The models were all very tiny but accurate replicas of enemy shipping, and were kept up to date throughout the war and of course, were subject to tight security. The whole complex was Top Secret and had to be manned at night by two Wrens which meant I slept on board every third night . . . The officers' training lasted six weeks, three with us and the other three at sea. During the three weeks before the next course arrived, we carried out all the maintenance: the cleaning, polishing and scrubbing necessary to satisfy our very critical commander. This work was carried out by the six Wrens, as no other personnel were allowed into the

facility. One course were invited to a dance in the Wrennery at Alverstoke: 'During the evening we chided them, saying that we Wrens, having been through dozens of attacks, could achieve more hits on enemy targets than they could. They answered jokingly, "Why don't you come out to sea and show us ?"' So it was arranged, with the consent of the admiral and the senior Wren Officer, that the Attack Teacher's crew could go to sea for a day to practise submerged attacks with dummy torpedoes in the Channel.

The narrator of this reminiscence, the then Leading Wren Hazel Hough, hit the target ship with her second torpedo.[55] Wren cypher officers accompanied Churchill on his wartime voyages to overseas conferences. Others served afloat in the 'Monsters' (fast liners serving as troopships). The Wrens' success in skilled technical rates such as Torpedo Wrens, Radio Mechanics and Air Mechanics delighted the Navy. Wren Air Mechanics were authorized to sign a certificate of airworthiness, a serious responsibility usually limited to officers. 'Reports from Naval Air Stations show that these girls are producing astonishing results. Their energy and intelligence put the men to shame, as does the fact that on average they "qualify to sign" in a month, while the average man takes three months. Naval Air Stations are clamouring for more . . .'[56] The Wren Radio Mechanics needed School Certificate in mathematics or physics before passing a thirty-week course. They were described by the Director WRNS as 'thoroughly superior people and had every air of knowing it . . . magnificent girls, well set up, clever and confident . . .'[57] Unlike the WAAF, there was no question of the WRNS forbidding women to handle explosives and ammunition. The secret Operation 'Outward' involved Wrens launching balloons carrying explosives to drift across the Channel. In December 1941 the National Service Act formally declared the women's services to be part of the 'armed services'.[58]

TWENTY-NINE

Aircraft in Co-operation with the Navy

Aircraft 1920–1942

By far the most important and influential of the new military technologies of the twentieth century was flying, which by 1918 was integral to most aspects of war at sea. The Admiralty had applied its long experience of nurturing new technology to aircraft with great success, and at the end of the war a range of different types for different functions were in production or development for the RNAS, including fighters, bombers, anti-submarine and reconnaissance aircraft. Peace abruptly slowed the pace of innovation, but it did not stop. The introduction of the Fairey Flycatcher in 1924 gave the Fleet Air Arm a versatile little fighter which could fly off carrier decks or battleship and cruiser flying-off platforms, and even straight out of the open forward end of a carrier's hangar. It could be fitted with wheels, floats or both, and was the first British naval aircraft to be stressed for vertical dives, which made possible the first British experiments with dive-bombing. At this date the capabilities of RAF and FAA single-engined aircraft largely overlapped. The Fairey IIIF spotter-reconnaissance aircraft and light bomber was in naval service from 1926 to 1936, fitted with wheels or floats, but almost the same aircraft (with a crew of two instead of three) was in RAF service too.[1]

Nevertheless, the two services had quite different ideas of military aviation. The Air Staff believed in general-purpose aircraft, fighters or light bombers, flown by non-specialist, interchangeable pilots fortified by moral rather than technical qualities. There was no room in this vision for specialist skills such as navigation, bombing accuracy or fighter defence. This doctrine crippled the development of all sorts of military aviation, and could only be maintained by suppressing planning, critical thought and intelligence on foreign air forces. Entry to and graduation from the RAF Staff College depended on 'correct' answers, and exercises were interpreted in the light of what should have happened rather than what had. The limited intellect and muddled thinking of Sir

Hugh Trenchard, the RAF's first Chief of Staff, stamped the RAF's 'cavalry culture', which placed a higher value on horsemanship than technology. In the first, 1928, edition of the RAF *War Manual,* the chapter on 'Aircraft in Co-Operation with the Navy' was left entirely blank – which was an accurate expression of the Air Ministry's thinking on that subject. Yet there was no excuse for ignorance; only ten years earlier, the Naval Staff Air Division had printed a comprehensive series of naval air handbooks and reports, all of which were easily available in the Air Ministry. In the 1920s when its future seemed to be in doubt, the RAF survived by offering a cheap method of controlling distant tribes by bombing their villages, but in the 1930s the growing possibility of war against serious military powers was beginning to expose the RAF's deficiencies, and provoked a series of clashes between the Cabinet and the Air Ministry.[2]

The Air Ministry effectively controlled both military and civil aviation and acted as the patron of the British aircraft manufacturing industry, which therefore tended to fall behind its more technically ambitious foreign competitors. Although arguably stronger than in Germany or the United States, aircraft manufacturing in Britain as in other countries was a craft industry chiefly composed of small, recently founded companies. Three British firms served the small naval aircraft market: Fairey, Blackburn and Supermarine, the ultra-specialist builder of miniature flying boats and racing seaplanes. In considering these companies and their products, readers need to be alert to the unsophisticated prejudices of those (rather too numerous) historians who prefer a cultural interpretation of an imagined past to a real understanding of the history of technology. Biplanes are not best understood as a symbolic expression of reactionary policies or technological weakness: this was simply the obvious wing form for all sorts of aircraft in a period of low flying speeds. By the mid-1930s, however, engines were developing fast, and higher power outputs prompted designers to create monoplane wings able to withstand the stresses of high speed. New engines like the 1,000 HP Rolls-Royce Merlin gave outstanding performance to a small, light fighter like the Supermarine Spitfire, but bigger and heavier naval aircraft with longer range and multiple functions needed engines of 2,000 HP and upwards, which did not appear until the 1940s. Carrier aircraft had a particular problem, because carrier landing and take-off demanded excellent low-speed manoeuvrability and stability, but there seemed then to be no possible wing design suitable for both low and high speed. Flying boats and seaplanes, on the other hand, had a unique opportunity, for on water they could land and take off at considerably higher speeds than land planes (especially land planes using grass airstrips), which offered better solutions to many of the problems of wing design. For this reason, research into small fast aircraft in the early 1930s was chiefly centred on racing seaplanes, of which Supermarine was the leading British builder.[3]

All these themes can be illustrated by looking at some notable British naval aircraft of this period. In the 1920s British warships of cruiser size and upwards still carried wheeled spotter and reconnaissance aircraft (mostly Flycatchers) on flying-off platforms on top of their gun turrets, but with the growing size of wheeled aircraft and the impossibility of recovering them from the sea, this was clearly a technique with no future, and by the 1930s most capital ships and cruisers were fitted with catapults to launch seaplanes. At first the Admiralty, frustrated by the numerous devices deployed by the Air Ministry to block naval aviation, took seriously the possibility that it might have to make up a fleet striking force from catapult aircraft alone. For this reason (and also to allow carrier airmen to fly for practice when their ships were in port) the new naval torpedo bomber, the Fairey Swordfish, was designed to land on floats instead of wheels if necessary, and to be launchable from a catapult, fully armed with a laden weight of 6,000lbs, at a take-off speed not over 60 knots – though by the time the aircraft entered service in 1936 the new fleet carrier *Ark Royal* was under construction and there was no question of the Navy being reduced to mounting torpedo strikes with catapult aircraft alone. The Swordfish's origin as a catapult aircraft is one key to its extraordinarily stable and tractable slow-speed handling, combined with an agility which belied its size (it was described as 'nearly as manoeuvrable as a man on a bicycle'), plus the capacity to carry more than its own weight in a range of weapons, equipment and unofficial cargo underneath the aircraft, under the wings or lashed to the fuselage, 'with negligible effect on an already negligible performance' – hence its affectionate nickname the 'Stringbag', which could always be stretched to carry some more shopping. It was unique in the world in having fully folding wings stressed both for torpedo-bombing and vertical dive-bombing.[4]

This allowed the Fleet Air Arm to develop expertise in both methods of attack, which few other air forces could match. Moreover, during the 1930s the service developed a unique attack technique which combined the two. Torpedo bombers, which had to carry a weapon weighing about three-quarters of a ton and drop it from a very low altitude, were forced to adopt a low, slow approach which left them highly vulnerable to fighter attack and anti-aircraft gunnery in daylight. But the Swordfish with an experienced pilot could approach its target at medium height, giving no clue as to its intentions, then just as it came into AA range plunge straight into a vertical dive at 200 knots and pull out at the last moment to drop its torpedo too close and too late for the target to evade.[5] This technique relied on the aircraft's extraordinary agility, and exploited developments in air torpedoes which the British had borrowed from a country sometimes overlooked in the context of naval aviation: Norway. In the 1930s Captain A. J. Bull of the Norwegian naval air station at Horten in the Oslofjord developed torpedo 'air rudders' which locked onto the torpedo hydrovanes, so that the torpedo gyroscope could fly it into the sea at speeds up to 150 knots, striking the water exactly at the correct angle, when the wooden 'air tail' fell off and the torpedo resumed its hydrodynamic character. Bull's team also developed the 1938 Drum Control Gear, which dropped the torpedo on wires 18 feet long, so that it initially took up the correct (slightly nose-down) attitude, falling without yaw or roll until the wires had run off.[6]

The Swordfish's contemporary, the Supermarine Walrus, was primarily a catapult-mounted reconnaissance and spotting aircraft for cruisers and capital ships. Most such aircraft in other navies were seaplanes, but the Walrus was a biplane amphibian flying-boat, with a good claim to be the most seaworthy small aircraft in the world. Its single engine was mounted under the upper plane facing aft, well clear of the spray to which radial-engined seaplanes were vulnerable, while the crew of three enjoyed (for the first time in British naval service) a spacious enclosed cockpit. Stately rather than nimble, the Walrus cruised at 85 knots: 'she wallows in the trough of the rough airs as a heifer knee deep in a boggy meadow'.[7] But the ability to land and take off in rough seas (as well as on runways and flight decks) made the Walrus uniquely valuable to patrolling cruisers and gave it an important secondary role in air-sea rescue. One of the slowest military aircraft in the world, it was designed by Supermarine's chief designer R. J. Mitchell at almost the same time as he was working on one of the fastest, the Spitfire, and while he was dying of cancer.[8]

For the designers of carriers and carrier aircraft, one of the basic problems was that the number of naval aircraft functions indicated a much greater range of different aircraft than there was room for in the cramped hangars. This pushed designers towards multi-role aircraft, such as the Blackburn Skua (fighter dive-bomber), or the Fairey Swordfish (torpedo-spotter-reconnaissance), which tended to have inferior performance to specialist land aircraft. Small orders going to small firms with limited development resources had the same effect. Short-range single-seat land aircraft were usually faster and more agile than naval machines carrying a navigator as well as a pilot, with sufficient fuel for a longer cruising range. The interwar Air Staff assured the Admiralty that the Fleet Air Arm would seldom encounter high-performance modern aircraft, but experience in the Norwegian and Mediterranean campaigns soon disproved that easy assumption. The Americans and Japanese in the Pacific likewise learnt that land-based aircraft frequently participated in naval air fighting. All air forces discovered that more powerful engines and higher speeds pushed them towards monoplanes with narrow, low drag but highly loaded wings. This meant higher performance but reduced agility, higher stalling speeds than were easily compatible with deck landings and narrow track undercarriages which were liable to capsize on a moving flight deck. British studies between 1929 and 1931 suggested that the main fleet would need at least 400 aircraft, and Reginald Henderson, in 1931 the first Rear-Admiral Aircraft Carriers since Richard Phillimore in 1917–18, was working on multi-carrier tactics for massed strikes, but the five available carriers could deploy only 250 aircraft between them.[9]

The Admiralty was already more interested in fighters than the Air Ministry, and insisted on the development of a reflector sight for good deflection shooting. In February 1940 it issued a new Fleet Air Arm fighter policy, which listed four objectives for naval fighters: shooting down shadowers and attackers, destroying enemy aircraft spotting for heavy guns, protecting British spotters (all of which could be done by a single-seater aircraft), and lastly escorting British strike aircraft to their (possibly distant) targets, which would require a navigator. The Norwegian campaign presently demonstrated that British naval aircraft were liable to meet the Junkers 88 light bomber (with a speed of 285mph) and the Messerschmitt Bf 110 heavy fighter (350mph in the latest version), though less often the even faster Messerschmitt Bf 109 single-seat fighter, whose very short range meant that it was seldom encountered over the open sea. To meet these fast aircraft the Fleet Air Arm flew two two-seater fighters: the Blackburn Skua Mk.2 of 1938 with a maximum speed of 196 knots (225mph) and the Fairey Fulmar Mk.2 of 1940 with a maximum speed of 230 knots (265mph), together with the single-seater Gloster Sea Gladiator (last of the biplane fighters), with a speed of 220 knots (253mph) but barely one hour's endurance. The Fulmar, a stop-gap conversion of a light bomber design, was too slow but offered at least long range and a good armament to fulfil its intended role as a 'reconnaissance fighter', able to force its way through opposing fighters to locate the enemy fleet. Its production was brought to an abrupt halt in May 1940 by the Cabinet's decision to give RAF aircraft absolute priority and cancel all others, leaving the FAA no fighters except the few remaining Skuas. In the Norwegian campaign the Fleet Air Arm was left to face the Luftwaffe, as Sir Charles Forbes the Commander-in-Chief Home Fleet complained, with the slowest aircraft in the world, which in addition to their designed carrier roles had to take on the fighter defence of naval air stations that the RAF abruptly abandoned at the moment of crisis. Thanks to the fortuitous existence of an unsinkable aircraft carrier in the northern part of the North Sea (Hatston airfield, near Kirkwall in the Orkneys), this was possible, to the limited extent that a 230-knot Fulmar could chase a 260-knot Ju.88. The 196-knot Skua fighter dive-bomber was, as Forbes remarked, 'in a class by itself, and it is a great pity that it has no modern counterpart'.[10] By the autumn of 1941 the FAA was desperate for modern fighters, but could only look forward to receiving fixed-wing 'Sea Hurricanes' converted from obsolete Hawker Hurricanes Mk.1 discarded by the RAF, some of them previously crashed. The Hurricane's big wing gave it the good slow-speed handling qualities a carrier aircraft needed, and its maximum speed of 268 knots (at altitude) was respectable, but without folding wings the aircraft had to live permanently on deck with their tails rigged over the side on outriggers to make space for other aircraft to land and take off – in which position the Hurricane's fabric-covered aluminium construction was very exposed to salt-water corrosion. Churchill was astonished when he visited the carrier *Indomitable* in September 1941 to be told what the FAA had to fly:[11] 'I trust it may be arranged that only the finest aeroplanes that can do the work go into all aircraft-carriers. All this year it has been apparent that the power to launch the highest class fighters from aircraft-carriers may re-open to the Fleet great strategic doors which have been closed against them.'[12]

In March 1940 the decision was taken to design a single-seat day-fighter for the Fleet Air Arm, but it was two or three years too late to design and build a British aircraft to meet the current crisis. The only alternative source of modern aircraft was the United States, from which the Royal Navy was able to buy 181 of the new Grumman F4F fighter, named by the British the 'Martlet'. This was a sturdy, reliable and agile single-seat carrier fighter with a maximum speed of 265 knots, suitable for short flight decks, and available because the US Navy had rejected it on account of faults which the manufacturer was eventually able to cure. Although the early deliveries (up to March 1941) had non-folding wings and could not be struck down by any surviving British fleet carrier except *Furious*, in most respects the Martlet was a very lucky find, and the British were able to take over an originally French order for a version of the F4F with armour to protect the pilot, which the USN did not receive until the spring of 1942.[13] Also at the end of 1941 the prototype naval fighter the Fairey Firefly appeared, though it was not in full production and carrier service until 1943. This was a successor to the Fulmar in the role of two-seater long-range reconnaissance and escort fighter. With four 20mm canon and eight 60lb rockets or two 1,000lb bombs under the wings it was exceptionally well armed, while its Youngman flaps gave it remarkable agility and easy deck landing. A

variant was fitted with radar as a night-fighter, and the aircraft had a successful post-war career well into the 1950s.[14]

The essential key to understanding the variety of naval aircraft which were
or were not available from British and American aircraft manufacturers in 1940
was the different expectations with which the different navies had gone to war.
Although both British and Americans had built carriers to deploy naval aircraft, they foresaw different styles of naval air warfare. In the air as on the sea
the US Navy expected to fight a brief but intense war which would be decided
by one great battle, or at most a few. US carriers were therefore designed with
long flight decks to pack in the maximum possible number of aircraft on deck,
to be flown off all at once for a massive attack against the enemy carriers, which
were assumed to be not far away and easily located. Even in peacetime US carriers lost numerous aircraft to accidents, and it was implicitly assumed that
many of their aircraft would never return from a wartime strike, easing the
problem of landing large numbers of aircraft all at once.[15]

British admirals thought a lot about aircraft in a fleet action, but they also
expected to fly off aircraft at frequent intervals to provide reconnaissance, anti-
submarine patrols, fighter defence, air strikes against near or distant enemies
and other duties, which would generate a constant traffic of different types of
aircraft landing and taking off. Much or all of the flight deck would have to be
kept clear for them, and therefore refuelling and re-arming would have to be
done in the hangar below. Hence British carrier procedure involved heavy use
of the lifts, which themselves blocked the flight deck, and made US-style mass
strikes possible only with long preparation. A 1929 exercise by aircraft from
Courageous in which thirty-two aircraft were flown off in twenty-one minutes,
but then took ninety minutes to land on, seemed to show that strikes of over
thirty aircraft would scarcely be feasible.[16]

The Japanese Naval Air Force expected to engage in the 'dog-fighting' tactics of the previous war, with individual pilots duelling like samurai. It therefore highly valued speed and agility, but Japanese industry could not produce
the high-tensile steel needed to match the bigger and more powerful engines
which in the 1930s were emerging in Britain and the United States. This pushed
Japanese aircraft designers towards very light aircraft which achieved prodi-
gies of speed and range with small engines. The most famous was the Mitsubishi 'Type Zero' carrier fighter of 1940 designed by Horikoshi Jirō to meet naval
requirements of a speed of 270kts at 13,000ft, a landing speed below 58kts, a
take-off run less than 230ft, armed with two 20mm cannon and two 7.7mm
machine guns, and at least as manoeuvrable as the previous Mitsubishi carrier
fighter (also by Horikoshi). The rival naval aircraft builder Nakajima thought

it impossible to combine all these qualities and declined to enter the competition. With a full speed of 288 knots (332mph) at 15,000ft, the Zero was faster than a Spitfire or a Messerschmitt Bf 109, much nimbler than both and with thrice the range (1,900 miles with drop tanks). The US Navy and the RAF had some intelligence about the Zero, but refused to believe it.[17] Horikoshi's fighter was a brilliant design, but its extraordinary performance was achieved by extraordinary risks and sacrifices. It was an 'origami' aircraft, so to speak, with very light wing-loading and flimsy structure, driven by a small engine. With neither armour to protect the pilot nor self-sealing fuel tanks it was very vulnerable, especially to fire. The rifle-calibre machine guns were barely effective, and the cannon had only sixty rounds a gun – seven seconds' firing at a low rate of fire.[18] The Zero was only the most famous of a generation of Japanese naval aircraft which shared many of its virtues and weaknesses. The Mitsubishi Type 96 bomber of 1936 was faster than all naval fighters in the world and superior to all other bombers except the prototype of the US B-17. The Aichi Type 99 dive-bomber of 1940 was at least as good as the Junkers 87 'Stuka', and the Nakajima Type 97 of 1938 was easily the best torpedo bomber in the world (and also the first Japanese naval aircraft with folding wings). But all of them were lightly built and vulnerable, especially to fire. The outstanding exception which proved that Japanese designers were capable of building robust aircraft when they chose was the big Kawanishi Type 2 flying boat of 1941, well armed and armoured with a range of 3,900 miles.[19]

Much of the Zero's extraordinary performance was not even driven by naval requirements but by the very long-range bombing missions from Formosa (Taiwan) and Kyushu against Chinese targets 400–500 miles inland which the Naval Air Force undertook from 1937 to 1940. This taught the naval airmen (and foreign observers) that Japanese bombers were vulnerable and needed long-range fighter escorts. It was satisfying to the Imperial Navy to discover how much better the Imperial Japanese Naval Air Force was than the Army Air Force, but it might have been even better if the rival forces had learnt to co-operate. The Japanese bombers caused great damage to inland cities like Chungking (Chongqing) without much affecting the course of the war on the ground, but the naval airmen did not reflect on the limitations of air power. Nor did their experience of a grinding war of attrition over China shake their confidence that the war at sea to which they returned in 1941 would be nothing but a brief burst of glory.[20] Justly proud of their superlative training, they took too little account of their technical deficiencies. The voice radio installed in the early stages of the Pacific War (in shipborne aircraft only) was of poor quality. The island air bases in the Pacific were too far apart for even Japanese aircraft to fly from one to another, and there was no efficient organization to build airfields. With no air-sea rescue service, no ferry system for replacement aircraft, and no training for fresh aircrew beyond posting newly qualified airmen straight to operational squadrons, the naval air force simply used up its precious skilled men without thought for the future.[21] The Japanese aircraft industry was an island of modernity surrounded by old-fashioned if not archaic practices – a situation neatly symbolized by the fact that the first proto-type of the Zero was delivered from the factory at Nagoya to Kakamigahara airfield twenty miles away, by oxcart. In spite of the rapid growth of the Japa-nese aircraft industry, its pool of technical and scientific expertise was shallow, and the increase of government control in the late 1930s stifled competition and innovation. The rivalry of the two air forces was crippling, and was taken so far as to force Nakajima, a rare manufacturer which served both services, to build a wall dividing its factory in two to keep them apart.[22]

The Swordfish was still quite new when the European war broke out in 1939, but the decision had already been taken to cease production that autumn and replace it with the Fairey Albacore, a lightly modernized version of the Swordfish with a more powerful engine and an enclosed cockpit, giving a max-imum speed of 138 knots and an endurance of up to six hours. The conserva-tive biplane design was chosen to produce an effective torpedo bomber with minimal delay and technical risk. Amiable and reliable but sluggish, as late as July 1940 the Albacore was reckoned no worse (and only slightly slower) than the new US monoplane torpedo bomber the Douglas Devastator. However, the Albacore never replaced the agile Swordfish as a Fleet Air Arm favourite, and in October 1939 it was decided to order 400 more Swordfish instead of Albacores because they were simpler to build and could be ready four months sooner.[23]

The intended successor to the Albacore, the Fairey Barracuda, was a modern monoplane designed for both torpedo- and dive-bombing. The secret of its remarkable versatility (and bizarre appearance) was the use of Young-man flaps, an early form of variable-geometry wing which Fairey pioneered. The flaps could be deployed for excellent slow-speed handling when landing or taking off from carriers; in a vertical dive they acted as air brakes and made both dive-bombing and diving torpedo drops possible, while for high-speed level flight they stowed below the trailing edge of the wing. But most of these outstanding features were nullified by Beaverbrook's cancellation of the power-ful Rolls-Royce Exe engine for which the aircraft had been designed. Delayed almost two years by this, the Barracuda Mk.I did not appear until May 1942, with a 1,260 HP Merlin 30 engine which proved to be quite inadequate. The

Mk.II with a 1,640 HP Merlin 32 engine followed in the autumn of 1942, but was still underpowered, especially for tropical conditions. As a result, the Barracuda was scarcely used as a torpedo bomber, and achieved its greatest success as a dive-bomber in the Arctic, attacking the *Tirpitz* at anchor in Kaafjord in April 1944.[24]

The torpedo was still the air weapon of choice against heavy ships, and as late as February 1942 the Naval Staff still expected to rely heavily on the Swordfish, but it was clearly too slow to be risked within range of modern fighters in daylight, and the Admiralty's faith in Fairey's was fading. In March 1943 Sir Percy Noble, now head of the British Admiralty Delegation in Washington, compared the available British torpedo bombers:

> The Barracuda is already nearly 2 years late and is that much out of date. In performance, range, offensive load and defensive fire it compares unfavourably with current U.S. types and very unfavourably with new types in the 'mock-up' stage or better. The Barracuda is superior to any comparable American type navigationally. The Swordfish was obsolete in 1939 and will be ineffective as an operational aircraft in 1945. Apart from its complete lack of performance, armour and defensive fire, its range is so limited that it cannot be employed from first-line carriers.[25]

The blame for this grave situation must be laid on a chain of extraordinarily poor decisions made variously by the Cabinet, the Admiralty and the Ministry of Aircraft Production. The destructive consequences of putting the new Ministry under Lord Beaverbrook in 1940 we have already observed. In July 1942 Rear-Admiral Lumley Lyster, the Fifth Sea Lord (in charge of the Naval Air Service), was moved to the operational command of Rear-Admiral, Home Fleet Aircraft Carriers, and his administrative responsibilities were passed to the retired Admiral Sir Frederic Dreyer as 'Chief of Naval Air Services'. Dreyer was a long-standing follower of Admiral Jellicoe and a noted gunnery expert of the previous generation, the original author of the fire-control table which bore his name, whose rise towards the top of the Service had been abruptly halted in 1931 by the Invergordon 'Mutiny', for which as the current Deputy Chief of the Naval Staff he bore considerable blame. In 1942 he was sixty-four, much too old to remedy his entire ignorance of naval aviation, and people in the Admiralty had lost patience with his favourite monologue on 'Myself, and how I did it'. Pound was responsible for this 'controversial' and 'unsatisfactory' appointment; yet another reason to question his failing judgement. It is easier to understand why Churchill insisted on Dreyer's removal only six months later, in January 1943.[26]

In June 1943 Commodore Matthew Slattery, 'Chief Naval Representative' in the Ministry of Aircraft Production, was interviewed by the distinguished Cambridge medievalist Professor Michael Postan, then serving as an official historian. It was already obvious to them both that there was much wrong with the production of British naval aircraft. Slattery said that the Admiralty had never really understood Fleet Air Arm requirements and possibilities till recently. 'They realised that it was a new factor, but did not really understand the possibilities because they did not know anything about the technical side and were unable to state their case at the Cabinet or Chiefs of Staff meetings.' The Air Ministry dominated the Ministry of Aircraft Production and refused to lend anybody to help the Admiralty. 'On the other hand, the Admiralty was very much to blame for the lack of planning during the latter part of 1941 and the summer of 1942 during which period there was no proper direction of the Fleet Air Arm at all . . . [Slattery] thought 1942 was the real black period but it continued up to January 1943.' (This undoubtedly refers to Dreyer's time in control, though Postan's minute tactfully does not name him.) Slattery 'thinks the Navy has been badly served by this Ministry and continues to be so, though it is much better than it was. The reason is because the FAA is such small fry compared with the RAF that its problems inevitably get overlooked.' Postan's guarded minute avoids stirring up trouble, but it is obvious that he and Slattery understood that the Admiralty could not take real responsibility for the Naval Air Service without authority over the design and manufacture of naval aircraft.[27]

Looking for a substitute for the Barracuda, the Admiralty's eyes had already turned to the Grumman Avenger, which entered US Navy service early in 1942, and thanks to Lend-Lease reached the Fleet Air Arm (aboard the USS *Saratoga* in the Pacific) early the following year. The Avenger had the characteristic tubby appearance of Grumman aircraft and was designed to carry a torpedo in an internal bomb bay, though in British service it was used in bombing, minelaying and anti-submarine roles. It was faster and more comfortable than a Swordfish and gave good service in many forms of day attack. It was an exceptionally tough aircraft, well armed and armoured, safe and easy to crash on land or water, and justly popular with its crews, many of whom owed their lives to it. But it was not stressed for steep dives, which ruled out both dive-bombing and the Fleet Air Arm's torpedo-bombing technique (which from late 1941 the USN was learning to use). This drastically reduced the Avenger's offensive value at sea and emasculated the British fleet carriers in the Indian Ocean and Pacific campaigns of 1943–4. Its American contemporary the Grumman Helldiver was designed for dive-bombing, but was in many respects inferior to the Barracuda.[28]

Another US aircraft which came into the hands of the Fleet Air Arm partly because no one else would receive it was the Vought Corsair, a fast and powerful but brutally dangerous single-seat fighter (fighter dive-bomber from Mk.II) adopted in 1941, which the US Navy initially passed to the Marine Corps to fly from airstrips ashore because it was too dangerous to fly from a carrier. On the deck the Corsair pilot had almost no visibility in any direction except vertically upward, in the air the aircraft stalled without warning, and its deck-landing characteristics were unwelcoming, to say the least. A test-pilot's verdict was that the Corsair 'could be landed on a deck without undue difficulty by an experienced pilot in ideal conditions'. The prospects of average pilots in ordinary conditions could be inferred.[29] The first British carrier squadrons were formed in the summer of 1943, before the US Navy's, and as the Corsair's gull wing folded vertically upwards it was necessary to crop the wingtips to fit into British carrier hangars.[30] These Lend-Lease US aircraft were an extremely welcome remedy for the failures of British production, but in most cases except the Martlet, US requirements were met before British, and they reached British hands sometime after they were desperately needed. There was also a warning from experience, well understood by 1943: 'not only do American aircraft frequently fail to achieve the performance claimed for them but also . . . there is a constant danger of those earmarked for Great Britain being diverted to American use'.[31]

For the US Navy with its still largely nineteenth-century concept of warfare, naval battles fought by battleships were the essential instrument of victory. Carriers were important primarily to gain command of the air over the battle-space, protecting the spotting aircraft which gave the battleships the power to engage at long range, and frustrating the enemy's attempts to do the same. Carriers were vulnerable and not likely to last long, but once the great naval victory had been won their essential work would be done. These ideas were developed between the wars through exercises ('fleet problems' in USN terminology) which were usually conducted in the Caribbean or off the Pacific coast of Central America, in fine daylight weather and over short ranges which suited single-seat aircraft without navigators.[32]

Behind these ideas lay the already intense rivalry between naval airmen and the battleship officers who dominated their service. Without effective torpedoes the US airmen could not offer a serious threat to battleships, but they were always on the look-out for opportunities to assert themselves over the 'black-shoe' (battleship) officers. Their chosen form of attack was dive-bombing, originally adopted by the US Marines from RNAS bombing practice, then developed with heavier bombs in the 1930s to threaten carriers. A key factor in these different forms of attack was that both torpedo- and dive-bombing imposed severe but different strains on the wings. Many light bombers could not safely undertake either, and few if any aircraft could do both except the Swordfish and the later Fairey Barracuda. In 1929 the FAA tried the RAF's favoured tactic of level bombing from altitude, and soon concluded that over 8,000 feet (the minimum height necessary for a falling bomb to penetrate a battleship's horizontal armour) the percentage of hits was nil. The Royal Navy was still keen to combine bomb and torpedo attack, and a 1931 report of the US Navy's early experiments (given wide publicity by the Hollywood film *Hell Divers*) encouraged the Fleet Air Arm to learn dive-bombing. In time it became clear that neither AA guns nor defensive fighters were effective against dive-bombers, though the inability of the British 'Queen Bee' drone target (essentially a wireless-controlled version of the Tiger Moth light aircraft) to imitate a dive-bomber may have delayed the discovery. The arrival of the Skua in 1938 was a big step forward, though a suitable dive-bombing sight was not yet available.[33]

Another key technology was anti-aircraft gunnery. This had made a good deal of progress during the First World War on land and sea with QF guns on high-angle mountings firing shrapnel shells fused to explode at a predicted altitude. These were dangerous to airships, and capable of keeping aircraft high enough to frustrate accurate bombing. The 1931 Anti-Aircraft Gunnery Committee analysed the situation as it then stood with sophisticated mathematical modelling based on hypothetical situations which closely corresponded to the 'Channel Dash' of the *Scharnhorst* and *Gneisenau,* and the last voyage of the *Prince of Wales* and *Repulse* (both in 1941) and can be tested against their experience. The committee compared the British naval High Angle Control System, based on a range-finder range plus an estimated course and speed of the target aircraft, with the tachymetric systems adopted by the US Navy and the Germans in which the range, bearing and elevation of the target were measured by observation rather than guessed. This it believed would give much lower errors, which was certainly correct in principle. In practice, however, with the technology available in the 1930s when aircraft speed and agility were advancing rapidly, most of the difference between the two approaches was obliterated by fuse variation, shot dispersal and instrument error, and only a heavy barrage at fairly close range was effective. Dive-bombing, which might have changed the committee's views, was rejected on RAF advice that it was impossible to fit an aircraft with dive brakes, and in 1941 the proximity fuse was still in the future.[34]

At the beginning of 1941 the air defence of warships seemed to be a problem well on the way to solution by the application of a technology hitherto unknown at sea: air-warning radar. Between August and October 1940 the battle of Britain revealed to the airmen of the world what was now possible in a defensive air battle in which the defenders possessed air-warning radar and could control their fighters with short-wave voice radio. The combination of the 'Chain Home' radar and the Royal Observer Corps with the Filter Rooms in which their reports were plotted together, and from which orders to defending aircraft were transmitted, constituted the 'brain' of the air-defence system, which vectored defending fighters to intercept incoming air attacks. The radar was quite primitive and the most advanced technology in the system was the VHF voice radio which connected the pilots with their ground controllers; much of the communications depended simply on telephone lines, and the essential character of the system was not a machine but a 'picture-centric' human organization, which descended directly from the RNAS London Air Defence Area of 1915. This puzzled later visitors, especially Americans, who expected to marvel at advanced technology and were shown only telephones, radios and maps.[35]

Even before the war began, however, there was an essential technical element present in the early British radar systems known as IFF, for 'Identify Friend or Foe'. This was a device fitted to an aircraft or a ship which recognized a friendly radar signal and responded by identifying itself. Soon after the United States entered the war Britain and the US agreed to adopt the British IFF Mk.3 as an Allied standard. It was obvious from the beginning that accurate IFF, which could be relied upon to identify friends without alerting foes, would be indispensable to any air operations over sea or land, and especially to any system of fighter direction. What was easy to state, however, was anything but easy to put into practice, and for much of the war the British were the only belligerents who were able to deploy reliable IFF. The Germans never succeeded in adopting equipment compatible with the radar and weapons of all their services, though they had considerable success in exploiting the insecurity of RAF airborne radar to home night-fighters onto British bombers.[36] The Japanese made good early progress with radar but soon fell behind, partly because of their inveterate interservice rivalry. All the belligerents initially imposed excessive secrecy which severely hampered their research and innovation, but the British and Americans were the first to understand the value of sharing information.[37]

Air-warning radar made it possible for short-range defending fighters to remain on the ground as the enemy approached, and then to climb straight to the right position and altitude to intercept. This was precisely what aircraft carriers needed, as naval men realized at once. From the moment radar-equipped ships went to war in the Norwegian campaign of 1940, and very soon afterwards in the Mediterranean, attempts were being made to inform defending aircraft of the whereabouts of attackers. The *Illustrious* commissioned in April 1940 with the first Type 79 air-warning radar and went out to the Western Mediterranean. During 1941 she and *Ark Royal* learnt to apply at sea the techniques of radar direction which had served the RAF during the Battle of Britain, and in July 1941 the first British naval Fighter Direction Centre was set up at RNAS Yeovilton to disseminate the new techniques. They proved to be just as effective in establishing local air superiority at sea. With sufficient warning, defending fighters were regularly able to break up attacks and disperse even much faster attackers. Then the arrival of *Fliegerkorps X* at the end of 1941 drove off *Illustrious* and *Formidable* in turn and seemed to mark a decisive defeat for the Fleet Air Arm in the Mediterranean.[38] In December 1941 *Illustrious*, *Formidable* and *Indomitable* were together for a few days in Norfolk, Virginia, which allowed fruitful discussion of standard procedures between their Fighter Controllers. During 1942 both British and Americans worked on fighter direction and learned from each other, sharing techniques and equipment. After the chaos of the battle of Midway in June and the effective air defence of the 'Pedestal' convoy two months later the US Navy adopted RAF-style plotting techniques, but poor VHF tuning, undisciplined voice chatter and the lack of common procedures still bedevilled American communications and led to the loss of the *Hornet* at the battle of the Santa Cruz Islands in October 1942. The lack of American IFF was the root cause of many these problems, generating a great deal of voice traffic to interrogate unidentified radar contacts.[39]

THIRTY

A Young and Vigorous Nation
Policy and Operations 1943

The Western allies met at Casablanca in January 1943 to agree their grand strategy for the coming year in an atmosphere of uncertainty if not crisis. After two years demanding the impossible, the US Army's planners had just conceded that there was no possibility of invading Europe before 1944. This was not because they were convinced by the elegance of British staff-work, but because the hard experience of Operation 'Torch' had taught them that major amphibious operations were not as easy as they had imagined. For the US Joint Chiefs of Staff the most urgent task was to allocate priorities and resources among the different US services and their senior officers. But any decision on these most sensitive subjects was certain to arouse inter-service and inter-Allied friction, and Roosevelt's instincts were typically to postpone difficult decisions. This is how we must understand the President's invocation of the famous phrase 'unconditional surrender', first used in 1862 by General Ulysses Grant during the American Civil War. It effectively refused to articulate war aims or policy and handed over the initiative to the military men. Roosevelt was content to wait on the events they would bring about and choose his moment to discreetly steer them his way.[1]

A key point of Anglo-American friction was the allocation of landing craft and transports to amphibious operations. There was a variety of possible objectives, in the Mediterranean, the Indian Ocean, the Pacific and elsewhere, and the practical difficulty of long-distance amphibious operations was matched by the political and emotional friction the planning process generated. The Americans were strongly committed to the strategic goal of supporting China, which they regarded as a major ally if not also a great power, and proposed to reach from India with the aid of a massive airlift over the Himalayas. The British thought this was probably impossible and certainly a low priority compared with the defeat of Germany and Japan, but they had learnt by experience to avoid needless quarrels and wait for Washington to encounter unavoidable military realities in its own time – a scepticism which the Americans sensed and attributed to selfish imperialism. Stimson told Roosevelt that the British position was 'the result of a fatigued and defeatist government which had lost its initiative, blocking the help of a young and vigorous nation whose strength had not yet been tapped by either war'.[2] But among many US senior officers, especially army officers, the dominant sentiment was resentment and anger that the ancient enemy had somehow wormed his way into the confidence of their President and planted hesitations and obstacles to trip them on the path to victory.[3]

This inter-allied friction was worsened by bad news from the North Atlantic, coming on top of the worst winter of the war. On 3 January 1943 a westbound U-boat accidentally sighted and reported the lightly escorted convoy TM 1, consisting of nine laden tankers on passage from Trinidad to the Mediterranean. Ignoring the Admiralty's order to alter course, this convoy ran into a concentration of U-boats which sank seven of the tankers. This seemed to be a grave omen for the Atlantic convoys. Then in February the big westbound convoy ON 166 lost 14 out of 49 ships to a U-boat group, and in March the slow eastbound convoy SC 118 lost ten ships out of 61. More than a third of the 61 North Atlantic convoys which sailed between February and May suffered losses. The performance of the *B-Dienst* cryptographers over the same period seemed to match or even exceed that of GC&CS; the Admiralty was aware that the Germans were regularly reading the daily U-boat situation reports signalled from London. March seemed at the time to be particularly disastrous: between 16 and 20 March allied signals intelligence struggled to read German traffic in the new *Triton*/Shark cypher just as the *B-Dienst* was able to locate the fast eastbound convoy HX 229 and the slow eastbound SC 122 nearby as they passed through the Greenland air gap, and vector against them a total of 40 U-boats in three groups. In a week of fog and gales aircraft were only briefly in touch, and in four days 22 merchant ships were sunk in return for a single U-boat. Worldwide, in the first twenty days of March more than half a million tons of merchant shipping was sunk, two-thirds of them in convoy. For the first time the Admiralty admitted to fear that the convoy system might no longer be effective. Late in March Admiral Pound told the Cabinet Anti-Submarine Committee that 'we can no longer rely on evading the U-boat packs and, hence, we shall have to fight the convoys through them.'[4]

Yet it was a myth that the U-boats were winning the North Atlantic campaign, as even the imperfect statistics available to the Admiralty should have indicated. In retrospect it is clear that Dönitz was already losing his 'tonnage war' before the end of 1942, and throughout the following year the defensive strength of the convoys was steadily being reinforced. At the same time as HX 229 and SC 122 were suffering, there were fourteen other allied convoys at sea in the North Atlantic, only one of which had been located by *BdU*. The Washington Convoy conference in March 1943 changed the command structure of the North Atlantic from the end of April, with Western Approaches Command extended as far west as the Grand Banks of Newfoundland in 47° W, a Canadian admiral in charge from there down to New York, and the USN responsible only for transatlantic convoys crossing directly between the Caribbean and the Mediterranean. At the same time Admiral King established a 'paper fleet', the 10th Fleet, which had no actual ships but took on general authority over the US naval anti-submarine effort, while the conference set up an Allied Anti-Submarine Survey Board to impose common methods and standards on the British, Canadian and US commands. Having discovered just how few long-range aircraft were available over the convoy routes, Roosevelt insisted on the USAAF handing over more of them. At the same time the Admiralty Operational Research unit produced a rigorous mathematical analysis which clearly established that aircraft were most effective against submarines in the vicinity of convoys, where the U-boats gathered to attack. Air Marshal Portal was convinced, and ordered all new Liberators which came to the RAF to be allocated to Coastal Command. From March British aircraft now re-equipping with ASV Mk.III centimetric radar (undetectable by Métox) once again made night crossing of the Bay of Biscay perilous to U-boats. In the same month Admiral Horton, C-in-C Western Approaches, insisted on the return of the anti-submarine escorts which he had lent to Operation 'Torch' the previous year, and in addition was able to borrow some Home Fleet destroyers himself to make up support groups to reinforce threatened convoys. In this period of alarm and crisis, only the most optimistic observers believed the convoy battles of March and April 1943 would be a turning point in the North Atlantic campaign – but hindsight and post-war analysis show that new shipbuilding had overtaken losses six months before, in the previous autumn.[5]

By midwinter 1942–3 the German-Italian army in North Africa was retreating eastward before the advancing US Army, and westward before the advancing British. In February the Germans were able to inflict a sharp check on the US Army at the Kasserine Pass in Tunisia, but the effects were only temporary. Instead of seizing the brief opportunity to evacuate as many men as possible, Hitler decided on the advice of Admiral Raeder that Tunisia was a good defensive position and ordered the North African garrison to be reinforced.

But allied air and naval strength in the central Mediterranean was now increasing fast, with supplies reaching the British round Africa and through the Suez Canal, and coming to the Americans straight across the Atlantic to Oran and Algiers. By early March the British had advanced a thousand miles since the battle of El Alamein and the Axis armies had lost almost all their bridgehead in North Africa except Tunisia. By mid-April 1943 there were about 3,250 allied aircraft in the central Mediterranean, facing around 900 German and the same number of Italian aircraft. In February Cunningham returned to Malta to hoist his flag as C-in-C Mediterranean, though now as allied naval commander-in-chief for the whole Mediterranean rather than a seagoing tactical commander. His main seagoing fleet was 'Force H' with two carriers and four battleships under Sir Algernon Willis. On 12 May the Axis forces in North Africa which Hitler had forbidden to be evacuated, surrendered instead, with the loss of 40,000 killed or wounded and 265,000 prisoners of war; more Germans surrendered at Tunis than at Stalingrad four months earlier, and the victory was won at a much lower cost.[6]

The Western alliance's big strategic decision had already been taken at the Casablanca conference in January, where the British had successfully argued that the next allied target should be Sicily, which could conveniently be isolated and attacked with the forces already assembled in the central Mediterranean for the Tunisian campaign, and which promised the huge strategic prize of reopening the Mediterranean to through shipping. In fact the first eastbound through convoys passed along the newly swept 'Tunisian War Channel' in May 1943, when nearby Sicily was still in enemy hands. By the summer over 400 ships a month were taking the new passage, saving six weeks over the voyage round the Cape of Good Hope.[7]

At the same time it was beginning to become clear to the US generals that their hopes of invading Europe and defeating the Germans in the summer of 1943 (Operation 'Roundup') demanded more and better troops, and many more landing craft, than were yet available. Roosevelt was more aware than his generals that the army of a democratic nation had to earn the support of the people, which meant that while the US Marines struggled for survival in the Solomon Islands and the Red Army fought the German tanks, the US Army had to do more to justify its existence than just make plans. If the invasion of Europe was not yet possible, there were rival courses of action available, less palatable to the US soldiers. The US Navy proposed a Pacific campaign of successive amphibious landings, led of course by the admirals, which would dominate the national war effort. More than strength, it would demand common plans and doctrine within and between the two US services, the lack of which in the recent campaigns had been embarrassingly obvious. Faced with rival services each demanding to take the lead, the US Joint Chiefs of Staff fell back (not for the last time) on an opportunistic compromise strategy of piecemeal advances. At the level of inter-allied grand strategy, where the Americans wanted to commit to the Pacific and the British to the Mediterranean, the same process of incremental compromise offered an acceptable means of putting off awkward decisions as long as possible.[8]

The major naval campaigns of 1943 had become increasingly a war of logistics, with few big ships present on either side. The great fleet action, once so ardently desired and expected by the Pacific navies, had never seemed further away. Instead, the naval war turned on trade and supply. In the Indian Ocean six U-boats based on Penang and others off the Cape of Good Hope waged a destructive campaign against the British convoys supplying the Middle East. The Germans urged their Japanese ally to join in, but the Japanese had never taken attack on trade very seriously, neither ally was honest with the other, and no determined attempt was made to combine their strategies. In the South Pacific the hapless and divided US submarine force came under a new flag officer in January 1943, Rear-Admiral Charles Lockwood. More than a year after the US had entered the war, he was the first American admiral to take seriously his captains' incessant complaints of defective torpedoes, although solutions to the weapon's defects were still far off.[9] In the Solomons, the US forces held only those parts of Bougainville Island which they needed for airfields and landing places, and did not even notice the brilliant operation in early February by which Rear-Admiral Tanaka Raizo in one night evacuated the entire garrison of Guadalcanal, 10,652 men. The three armies involved in the New Guinea campaign (Japanese, Australian and US) fought in roadless and mountainous jungle ashore but depended almost completely on seaborne supply and reinforcement. The so-called 'battle of the Bismarck Sea' in March 1943 was essentially a series of RAAF and USAAF air attacks on Japanese destroyers and transports attempting to land reinforcements in New Guinea, of whom only 1,200 men arrived out of 6,900 embarked.[10] That same month, far away to the north in the Aleutian Islands, was fought a vanishingly rare example of the sort of operation the US and Japanese navies had spent so many peacetime hours practising but so seldom used in anger: a long-range daylight gunnery action. The Japanese heavy cruisers *Nachi* and *Maya* spent all day fighting the USS *Salt Lake City*, shot away almost all their ammunition to little effect, and allowed the damaged US cruiser to escape in the end.[11]

All the different theatres of war at sea were connected, and the Western alliance slowly began to draw ahead as the allied nations, and the US services, gradually and reluctantly learned to share resources and information with one another. But the politicized and wasteful Anglo-US system still tended to avoid difficult decisions and defer to the dominant egos of senior officers, which generated needless danger and delay. At the end of March the US Joint Chiefs of Staff, with Leahy in the chair, agreed to divide the Central and South-Western Pacific commands, giving the US Navy in the Central Pacific its chance to fight a fleet action against the Japanese. All it lacked in early 1943 was ships, and above all carriers, of which only the *Saratoga* was left in the Pacific. At this time the US Navy was thinking seriously of what might become possible with the new carriers coming forward later in the year, equipped with four-channel VHF radio, radar with PPI displays, working IFF and other equipment hitherto little known in the US Navy, which offered the possibility of controlling the aircraft of a group of carriers together. This would represent a controversial change in US carrier policy, but it seemed to be the most promising method of fighting Japanese carriers which themselves were already accustomed to operate as a group with a common screen. The arrival of HMS *Victorious* to reinforce the Pacific in March 1943 brought two different 'carrier systems' into direct contact for the first time and allowed US officers to gain practical experience with the new equipment. The joint Anglo-American Pacific force was still too weak to undertake any offensive except for the unopposed occupation of New Georgia in the Solomon Islands in June and July, but they had time to develop a hybrid carrier air force. Having much superior fighter direction, *Victorious* operated the joint fighter force, while *Saratoga* embarked the strike aircraft. Both navies learnt a lot from working together, but *Victorious* returned home to refit in August, and as there was almost no air fighting, historians have largely ignored the episode. The real fruit of this period was the new US naval publication PAC-10, 'Pacific Fleet Tactical Orders and Doctrine', of June 1943, which for the first time laid down common tactical procedures for the entire Pacific Fleet, allowing admirals to exchange forces and plan joint operations over great distances. This would not have surprised British or Japanese naval officers, but for the US Navy it was radical, and the beginning of a sustained improvement in tactical competence which eventually spread beyond the Pacific Fleet.[12]

There still remained much work for the US Navy to do. In the South Pacific the US destroyers claimed repeated successes in night actions which they attributed to their superior radar. The technical superiority was real, but many of the victories were imaginary. The Japanese habitually sighted their enemy first and opened fired first, while the US ships concentrated on shooting at the biggest radar echo nearby and left the Japanese destroyers free to deploy their heavy torpedoes at ranges which the USN still regarded as impossible. In a single week in July the Japanese torpedoed four allied cruisers (three US and one New Zealander). Only in August at Vella Gulf a US destroyer squadron using a radar plot really ambushed Japanese destroyers for the first time. Not until October could the USN claim a victory in a night action against a roughly equal Japanese squadron which was taken by surprise off Cape Esperance, though experience was to prove that the US Navy was still far from a match for the Japanese at night. In the autumn the US Pacific Fleet abandoned its practice of screening each carrier individually in favour of the British (and Japanese) common screen for a carrier group, which was economical in ships, threw up more concentrated AA fire, and simplified fighter direction.[13]

The US attacks on Marcus Island on 31 August, and on Wake Island in early October, were trials of the new doctrines and new equipment. The Wake Island raids in particular involved attacking a target 537 miles from the Japanese airfield on Eniwetok, 594 miles from Kwajalein, 640 miles from Wotje – but two thousand miles from Pearl Harbor. The USN was still intensely aware of the longer range of Japanese naval aircraft, and the planned attack on Wake Island had to be conducted by carriers alone, well out of range of land-based support and well within range of Japanese retaliation. Though some things went wrong, as they always do in wartime, the overall results were encouraging.[14]

In the North Atlantic the German U-boat force, which had frightened the allies over the winter, launched its largest offensive in the spring of 1943. In the whole month of March U-boats worldwide sank 71 ships out of convoy (including some stragglers). But at the end of that month the tide turned abruptly. As the Russians were now receiving much of their supplies through Persia or by sea across the North Pacific to Vladivostok, the allied Arctic convoys were suspended from March to October 1943, freeing modern destroyers to be formed into Support Groups to reinforce threatened Atlantic convoys. March was also when at long last Coastal Command received a significant reinforcement of long-range Liberator and Flying Fortress aircraft. Early in April 1943 Admiral King was embarrassed by a pointed report from the Allied Anti-Submarine Survey Board into releasing more very long-range aircraft. Under pressure from Roosevelt and Henry Stimson, the Secretary of War, the USAAF also was forced to hand over more Liberators to the RCAF. 'Shark' was now yielding to the efforts of the cryptographers, and U-boat signals began to reveal unmistakable signs of failing morale.[15]

The results of these developments were both clear and immediate. In early May the slow westbound convoy ONS 5 was attacked in the Greenland Air Gap, initially by sixteen U-boats and eventually by more than forty, precipitating a week of intense fighting in a heavy gale succeeded by icebergs and dense fog. The Escort Group B7 (i.e. 7th British Escort Group), commanded by Commander Peter Gretton in the destroyer *Duncan*, consisted of two destroyers, one new frigate, four corvettes and two trawlers, immediately reinforced by the 3rd Escort Group of five fleet destroyers sent by Western Approaches Command, and later by the five sloops and frigates of the 1st Escort Group. But the weather was too bad for the destroyers to refuel at sea and several, including Gretton's *Duncan*, had to part company in search of oil, so in the middle of the action the command of the group devolved to the next-senior captain, Lieutenant-Commander Robert Sherwood RNR of the frigate *Tay*. It was now standard practice that the 'home team' (in this case Gretton's group) remained in charge even if reinforced, so for the larger part of the action Sherwood (in peacetime the master of an Irish Sea ferry), commanded a mixed force including the 1st Escort Group (five sloops and frigates under a Commander RN) and the 3rd Escort Group (five fleet destroyers under Captain J. A. McCoy RN). Pre-war Royal Navy captains would have been staggered at the idea of fighting a major action with nineteen warships all under the command of a merchant navy reservist junior to themselves, but Captain McCoy's comment in his Report of Proceedings was simply that the arrangement was 'remarkably justified by action and there is no doubt in my mind that the "Command" has been correctly placed'.[16] This was not the only moral to be drawn from an engagement which both sides immediately recognized as a clear British victory. It is still not absolutely certain what happened to all the ships and submarines which vanished during a week of intense fighting, but probably nine U-boats were sunk and four or five more badly damaged for the loss of thirteen merchantmen: a ruinous 'exchange rate' for the Germans. As usual Admiral Dönitz blamed everything on a mythical super-radar capable of locating entire patrol lines, with rather more reason than usual, for in fog as well as darkness radar was really critical, and without it the U-boats were gravely disadvantaged against escorts fitted with centimetric radar.[17]

Nevertheless, lack of radar was only one element of the now overwhelming technical vulnerability of German submarines. Both British and US escort carriers were now available to add to the land-based VLR aircraft providing air support to Atlantic convoys, and many of the aircraft were armed with the 'Mark 24 mine' or 'Fido': not a mine at all but the cover-name of a US weapon unsuspected by the Germans, an air-dropped homing torpedo designed to pursue a diving submarine. The US escort carriers operated around the Azores where the remaining U-boat tankers met their 'clients', and the weather favoured intensive flying. Between June and December ten of the remaining thirteen German submarine tankers in the Atlantic were sunk. Further north, on the convoy routes, British Swordfish aircraft were now armed with armour-piercing rockets capable of penetrating a surfaced U-boat's pressure hull. Before the end of May the balance of forces had tipped so fast that Western Approaches Command, confident in the superiority of its weapons and training, was deliberately routing convoys on 'great circle' courses (the most economical in distance and fuel) regardless of concentrations of U-boats which might be in the way. During May seventy-two U-boats in twelve groups were deployed against seven Atlantic convoys and together sank only seven out of 276 ships, for the loss of fourteen U-boats sunk and four damaged. In this single month a third of the *Frontboote* were sunk worldwide, forty-one U-boats in all.[18] At the end of the month Dönitz withdrew his U-boats from the Atlantic – temporarily, as he assured his men (and perhaps himself), pending the arrival of new weapons: 'Then we shall win; my faith in our weapons and in you tells me so.'[19]

Operation 'Husky', the Allied landing in southern Sicily on 10 July 1943, was much larger than any previous Allied amphibious operation. The strategic objective of the Sicily expedition was to force Italy out of the war, open the Mediterranean completely and free a million tons of merchant shipping. Thanks largely to the skilful and meticulous planning of Admiral Sir Bertram Ramsay, and the significant technical contribution of Mountbatten's Combined Operations organization, all these objectives were achieved. Although some of the assault forces were able to cross by landing craft directly from Tunisia, the main convoys sailed from more distant North African ports stretching from Alexandria to Algiers, from the Clyde, and even across the Atlantic from Norfolk, Virginia. Many landing ships (designed only for short passages) crossed the Atlantic in groups. The first wave of the landings delivered 160,000 British, US and Canadian troops, with 600 tanks, 1,800 guns and 14,000 vehicles, carried by more than 600 transports and landing ships. As the whole operation was exposed to the nearby and still-formidable Italian fleet (which in the event never put to sea), it was covered by six British battleships and two fleet carriers, ten British and five US cruisers and twenty-three British submarines, besides large numbers of smaller warships.[20]

By the end of July it was clear to the defenders of Sicily that the island could not be held much longer against the overwhelming force of the Anglo-American assault. With great skill the Germans achieved what they had failed to do in Tunisia: a successful evacuation, in this case across the Messina Strait in August, which removed over 100,000 German and Italian troops with much of their weapons and equipment, secretly and with few losses. Nevertheless, the Allied campaign as a whole was an outstanding success, swift and economical. British troops crossed the Strait of Messina on 3 September, and on the 9th the Allies landed on the mainland at Salerno, south of Naples (the most northerly beaches within range of air cover from Sicily). Axis forces abandoned Sardinia and Corsica immediately (an evacuation organized at the same time as the German army evacuated the Crimea across the Kerch Strait), while on 25 July the Fascist Grand Council restored King Victor Emmanuel III and dismissed Mussolini from office. On 8 September Italy concluded an armistice with the Western Allies, but to disengage from fighting alongside the German Army required swift political and military action, and was botched in both dimensions. The army was told nothing of what was afoot and the navy little, giving the Germans time to disarm much of the Italian Army. The fleet under Admiral Carlo Bergamini did not surrender at Malta as agreed but initially headed north to the Strait of Bonifacio where the Luftwaffe caught them on 9 September and sank the new flagship *Roma* with an FX-1400 glider bomb, killing Bergamini and most of the crew, and eliminating any remaining Italian naval loyalty to the Axis cause. The other Italian heavy ships reached Malta to surrender on 11 September.[21]

The conquest of Sicily and the landings in southern Italy opened possibilities further East which the British Middle East Headquarters in Cairo tried to exploit with an amphibious operation to seize the Dodecanese Islands. Even with limited forces there seemed a fair hope of bringing Turkey into the war and bombing the Romanian oilfields on which the *Wehrmacht* depended, but the German reaction was swift and effective, and the recapture of Rhodes and its airfields doomed the offensive. Eisenhower had no authority to send reinforcements outside his command and the senior British commanders in the area (Cunningham, Tedder and Alexander) fully agreed that the Italian campaign called for all the force they had.[22]

In May 1943 Mountbatten was appointed Allied Supreme Commander for South-East Asia. He was now the leading expert in amphibious operations, which were expected to play an essential part in Allied plans in the Indian Ocean. The Americans looked to him to reopen the 'Burma Road' to supply their favourite Chinese ally, though for most of the year Admiral Somerville had been unable to operate at all in the Bay of Bengal (the eastern part of the Indian Ocean) for want of adequate air power, and now faced a growing shipping crisis which threatened famine in Bengal. In the event hardly any of the

Allied plans proved to be possible, which may have been fortunate, for they had been designed to meet political rather than operational priorities. The Burma plan envisaged General Stilwell taking orders from Mountbatten and Marshal Chiang, both of whom he treated with outspoken contempt, while Somerville's fleet was under Admiralty control and only came under Mountbatten's command for amphibious operations. At the 'Sextant' Conference, held in Cairo on 22–6 November 1943, the Allies at last agreed to adopt the US Navy's Central Pacific strategy and give it priority over MacArthur's South-West Pacific Command, which was at least a step in the direction of an overall scheme of strategic priorities.[23] In the Central Pacific in November 1943 the amphibious landings on Bougainville in the Solomon Islands and Tarawa in the Gilbert Islands were successes won at high cost – on Tarawa the US Marines lost more than a thousand killed (17 per cent of their assault force) in three days.[24]

On 10 June 1943 the new British Naval Cypher 5 was finally brought into service after a massive administrative operation of secure worldwide distribution of cypher materials, abruptly ending German access to British signals. From October Portugal allowed Allied aircraft to use airfields in the Azores, stopping up the last major Atlantic 'air gap' in which the surviving U-boat tankers had sheltered. The new German *Wanze* radar detector proved to be ineffective against Allied radars on 10-cm wavelength such as the Type 271 family. In September 1943 Dönitz attempted to revive his submarine campaign, though the U-boats' prospects were if anything even bleaker than they had been four months before.[25] As usual Dönitz believed the most optimistic U-boat reports, and found ways to dismiss inescapable bad news. The first use of the *Zaunkönig* homing torpedo in September was credited with sinking twelve destroyers plus three probables and nine merchant ships; 'undoubtedly a splendid achievement' in the words of *BdU*,[26] but in reality largely wishful thinking. The real score was three escorts sunk and one damaged, and effective counter-measures against the *Zaunkönig* were already on their way. In October SC 143 with a strengthened escort was deliberately routed through a U-boat group to protect other and weaker convoys. Whenever *BdU* suspected a security leak, 'Italian traitors' was the ever-popular explanation; even when *BdU* acknowledged to itself in November that 'the enemy can see our hand and we cannot glimpse his',[27] it still took refuge in its standard explanations for every problem: ubiquitous aircraft and 'magic radar' which could read signals. In November convoy attacks the Germans lost ten U-boats and sank one warship and one merchantman.[28]

Most remarkably of all, it was not until December 1943 that U-boat headquarters finally acknowledged that submarine operations in the open sea depended critically on effective air reconnaissance – which had been true since about 1917, and had been well known to experts like Werner Fürbringer in the 1930s. If he rather than an ideologue like Dönitz had been appointed to revive the U-boat service (and if the Luftwaffe had made an effective contribution to the war in the Atlantic), the U-boats might not have been reduced in December 1943 to a long-range reconnaissance force of two or three Ju 290 a day to sweep the whole North Atlantic. By then signalling had become so dangerous that *BdU* had almost no news from U-boats at sea. That month Dönitz told Hitler that 'Surfaced U-boat operations are finished'.[29]

Only in the far North did the Germans still have surface warships powerful enough to exercise a genuine strategic pressure, covering the coastal shipping which supplied their troops fighting in northern Russia, and threatening the Allied convoys to Russia when they resumed in November. But most of the Luftwaffe's anti-shipping strike force (ninety-nine bombers and sixty torpedo bombers) was sent to the Mediterranean to counter Operation 'Torch' in November 1942 and never returned. The biggest remaining threat was the battleship *Tirpitz*, damaged by an attack by midget submarines in September 1943, repaired where she lay in the Kaafjord with the aid of coffer dams, but out of action for six months and never fully operational again (though this was not known to the Admiralty at the time).[30] The smaller battleship *Scharnhorst* nearby was the German Navy's only remaining effective heavy ship, and Dönitz was very aware of the political necessity of using her to win a victory. The relief flag-officer Rear-Admiral Erich Bey was unhappy about attacking a British convoy in winter darkness, with inferior radar and no air reconnaissance, but under heavy pressure to do something persuaded himself that the enemy would 'reveal a weakness or commit some gross blunder'.[31] So the *Scharnhorst* sailed on Christmas Day to attack the Murmansk convoy JW 55B, not having received any definite information of a battleship covering the convoy, though that was standard British practice. In a first action with two cruisers the *Scharnhorst*'s fixed forward radar set was knocked out, leaving her blind ahead. With better radar the British cruisers and destroyers led the *Scharnhorst* away from the convoy and towards the battleship *Duke of York*, which was able to open blind fire at seven miles' range and hit with her first broadside. The faster German ship still had a chance to escape, but she was taken completely by surprise well inside the battleship's gun range, and then hit by destroyer torpedoes, which finished her. It was the last battleship action in British naval history.[32]

THIRTY-ONE

Give Them the Third Best

Government and Administration 1943

A dmiral Dönitz was absolutely right to point out in September 1943 that for the Western Allies 'shipping is the foundation and practical expression of their strategic freedom'.[1] (He scarcely needed to add his opinion that the U-boat was Germany's most effective answer.) The huge economic and strategic benefit of cheap worldwide sea transport had been the foundation of British economic success since at latest the eighteenth century, and in wartime it remained the fundamental enabler of victory and economic survival. It was cheaper to ship a ton of coal 3,620 miles from Cardiff to Port Said at the eastern end of the Mediterranean than to send it by train 150 miles to London. The sea gave access to the best and cheapest sources of food and raw materials all over the world (not only from British colonies or in British ships). British official statistics concentrated on British ships and the long-distance cargoes they carried, rather overlooking the 'home' (meaning European) trades which in peacetime provided a considerable share of British imports but were dominated by foreign shipping. Many wartime statistics also omitted munitions, which by 1944 constituted over half of all inbound cargoes. The British dry-cargo fleet in September 1939 had a deadweight tonnage (i.e. cargo capacity) of 18.7 million tons. By 1943 the British-controlled merchant fleet amounted to 20 million tons, only about half of which were actually British ships, with many of the remainder flying the flags of European governments in exile. As the manpower shortage grew more serious during the war, many British merchant ships transferred to the Norwegian flag because the Norwegians still had crews available. The wartime trend for British shipping was to replace imports of bulky food and raw materials with light manufactures, a change which cost foreign exchange but saved shipping capacity. British food imports were reduced to half the peacetime average and total imports (not counting munitions) fell by 30 per cent, but oil imports rose. The sharp reduction in food imports did not directly affect the population, because most of the imported food which was sacrificed was animal feeds, replaced (at higher cost but lower volume) by imported meat and cheese for human consumption. Imported fruit and vegetables, most of which had formerly come from now enemy-controlled parts of Europe anyway, were replaced by home-grown crops; oranges and bananas gave way to apples. The flow of shipping was never seriously threatened; the merchant navy, which lost a higher proportion of its crews than any other service except Bomber Command, paid the price of the U-boat campaign, but the British population prospered. Wartime imports forgone amounted to 32 per cent of the peacetime requirement, of which at most 9 per cent represented actual losses at sea and the rest came from reduced consumption – but the British population was not really feeling the pinch. Only one-third of the British wartime food supply (measured in calories) was subject to rationing at all. At least until 1945, the overall effect of food rationing was not to reduce personal consumption, but to prevent high war-time earnings being spent on imported luxuries. The wartime diet was dull but sufficient and healthy; factory workers, servicemen and children received extra, and public health improved.[2]

The U-boat campaign in the North Atlantic never seriously threatened the British food supply, but might have been a more successful strategic instrument had it aimed specifically at the shipping needed for overseas expeditions. Ocean liners, of which Britain owned or controlled a large proportion, were essential to move troops over long distances; they were big and valuable targets, many of which were sunk and very few built during the war years. To take an example of the practical implications, the Australian 9th Division was withdrawn from the Eighth Army in early 1943, after more than two years of hard fighting in North Africa. Operation 'Pamphlet' to bring the 31,000 men home down the Red Sea and across the Indian Ocean, within range of Japanese ships and aircraft, involved considerable risk and required the whole of Admiral Somerville's Eastern Fleet to cover the movement of the four overcrowded liners *Queen Mary*, *Aquitania*, *Île de France* and *Nieuw Amsterdam*.[3] At the Casablanca Conference in January 1943 the Allies had adopted an ambitious Mediterranean strategy without reckoning where the shipping was to come from, but Dönitz never chose to exploit this vulnerability by concentrating on high-value cargoes and ships. He always insisted on a crude 'tonnage war', which in effect concentrated on the slowest and most vulnerable ships, the easiest to sink but also the oldest and least valuable to the Western Allies.[4]

In 1943 there remained large holes in Allied planning, notably about shipping capacity. To judge from the sources, some of those responsible for wartime decision-making in Britain and the United States were (and not a few of those who write about them nowadays still are) thoroughly muddled about the different meanings of the word 'ton', which in measuring ships is usually a unit of volume rather than weight.[5] To illustrate how important it is to choose the right unit of measure, and make the choice clear, readers may note that a 'Liberty Ship' measured 7,176 tons 'gross register', 4,300 tons 'net register', about 14,300 tons standard displacement, or about 10,800 tons deadweight – gross and net tonnage being exact measures of volume fixed by the dimensions of the ship, but deadweight and displacement varying with the density of water and the weight of the cargo. The T2 tanker, another wartime standard design, measured about 10,000 tons gross or 16,000 tons deadweight. Choosing the wrong measure, or mixing them up, had (and sometimes still has) very bad effects on clarity of thinking and planning.[6] Britain's minimum import require-ments were 25 million tons for 1942 and 27 million for 1943. President Roosevelt had agreed these figures without telling his staff, and undoubtedly without exploring the meanings of the word 'ton'. The US Army came away from the Casablanca Conference committed, it believed, to supply 2.5 million tons dead-weight of British imports, but the US War Shipping Administration under Roosevelt's instructions had agreed 7.2 million tons. This organization's name implied a unified American organization, but in reality the US Army and Navy were running rival transport fleets and using incompatible statistics. By March 1943 the discrepancies were becoming obvious, and the Allies blamed each other.[7] For an American general like George S. Patton, the culprits were not hard to find:

> The British are running the show in the sea, on the land and in the air. They are running it to their advantage and are playing us for suckers, not only in a military sense, but politically also . . . This war is being fought for the benefit of the British Empire and for post-war considerations. No one gives a damn about winning it for itself now.[8]

This was the US Army's authentic world view, and more often than not the US Navy's as well: in their minds the United States was the eternal victim of a sinister world conspiracy – not by the Communists, who were fellow pro-gressives and natural allies, but by the hereditary enemy, Britain, which had once again seduced a weak President as she had done twenty-five years before. In General Stilwell's inimitable phrase, 'The Limeys have his ear, while we have the hind tit'; or in the more decorous prose of the US Joint War Plans Committee,

She dominates her empire by controlling the economic destiny of her dominions and crown colonies. She maintains her position in the European area by preserving the balance of power on the Continent. She exploits the resources and people of other nations to insure her position of dominance.[9]

Back in the real world, however, by 1943 the isolationist voices were fading even in Washington. Soon younger US Army officers were beginning to favour the British Empire as a force for order and stability, and questioning whether the Soviet Union was really America's natural ally. But as late as December 1944 the Greek Communist revolt against the royalist government which the Allies had just installed in Athens aroused instant American enthusiasm, and Admiral King tried to prevent US shipping from bringing supplies to support the Greek government, meaning in real terms that he intervened on the German side.[10]

The Casablanca Conference had confirmed the existing 'Germany First' strategy in principle, but in practice did little to check the steady drift away from the focus on victory in Europe. A major factor was the enormous naval construction programme to which the United States was now committed. Between 1940 and 1942 six new relatively fast (28-knot) battleships of the *North Carolina* and *South Dakota* Classes were launched, followed by six more 33-knot ships of the *Iowa* Class, launched from 1942 to 1944 (two of which were cancelled incomplete). Yet another class of six battleships was cancelled in July 1943, together with half the six-ship *Alaska* Class of light battleships with 12-inch guns, inspired by the *Scharnhorst* design and launched between 1943 and 1945, leaving the US Navy with only thirteen new fast capital ships to add to the thirteen older and slower survivors of the battle-line of 1911–21. Whatever principle had driven this building programme, it could scarcely have been 'Germany First' after 1942 at the very latest. Still less could fear of the German Navy, which never succeeded in completing a single aircraft carrier, have justified the twenty-six new fleet carriers of the *Essex* Class launched between 1942 and 1945. The size and number of these ships, and of the numerous cruisers and destroyers which accompanied them, meant that the Pacific was the only plausible, or even possible, theatre of war in which the bulk of them could be deployed. In one sense they were the expression in steel of Roosevelt's style of decision-making: avoiding commitment and long-term planning, putting as little as possible in writing, saying 'yes' to everyone – but always to the USN first. This left the big strategic and political choices open for as long as possible. To choose the South Pacific and the Philippines was to opt for General MacArthur and the US Army; to prefer the central Pacific was to go for Admirals King and Nimitz and the US Navy. A series of American and Allied conferences, held at Washington in March, May and June 1943, at Quebec in August, and at Cairo in November, nibbled delicately at the margins of these intensely sensitive decisions without risking any irrevocable commitments.[11]

A major part of the remedy for a shortage of ships was of course shipbuilding. The Admiralty had long been accustomed to assume that Britain had plenty of shipbuilding capacity, but by 1943 shipyard manpower, and above all specialist skills, had become extremely scarce. American shipyards at their wartime peak employed about 1.6 million workers (six times as many shipyard workers as in Britain), and built faster than British yards, but never achieved more than about half British levels of productivity. From 1940 to 1945 US yards built 4.7 million tons displacement of warships, and British yards 2.4 million tons. For merchant ships US yards built 38 million tons gross against 6 million tons in Britain, which reflects the high output of new yards laid out on open sites to build simple standard designs like the Liberty ship. The peak output of merchant ships from British yards was about one-third higher than it had been in the First World War, from fewer yards and fewer workers, but by 1943 the manpower situation was the main limiting factor everywhere. British shipbuilding employment reached its peak of 272,500 in September 1943, when the Second Sea Lord wished to call up 190,000 men just for naval service for 1944, but the total manpower available for all the services and the whole British war economy combined was only 180,000. By December the Navy calculated that it would require 247,000 men and 41,500 women, but it knew it could expect to receive only 50,000 men and some tens of thousands of women, plus a prospect of 17,000 men for the Fleet Air Arm from an unspecified source (later revealed as New Zealand). This intake would barely cover wastage, and there was no question of major expansion.[12]

Apart from manpower the sharpest supply constraint on Allied projects was neither warships nor merchant ships but landing craft, a high proportion of which were absorbed by the campaign in the Pacific which the US Navy was determined should be all-American, and if possible all-naval. It was this more than any strategic logic which fuelled the US determination not to be sucked into a prolonged Italian campaign once Sicily was taken and the Mediterranean once more open to through traffic. At a superficial diplomatic level this was a cultural clash between British understatement and boisterous American self-confidence, but the underlying cause was a real difference of political priorities. The only Mediterranean commitment which the US Joint Chiefs of Staff favoured was a landing in the south of France (Operation 'Anvil') designed to strike the rear of the German army just as the main Allied expeditionary force (Operation 'Overlord') landed on the Channel coast. The default assumption of US senior officers was still to interpret alternative British proposals as a sinister plot to rebuild the British Empire and rule the world. All Americans could agree, indeed had to agree, on this interpretation, because that alone lightly masked the eternal rivalry of the US Army and Navy which still absorbed so high a proportion of the emotional energy of the US services. Only the US Joint Chiefs of Staff could arbitrate between the Central Pacific command under Admiral Nimitz and the South-West Pacific under General MacArthur, who used the title of 'Supreme Commander' but had much the smaller share of real military strength. The 'Joint Chiefs' were content to leave the problem unresolved for as long as possible and the general himself far away in Australia. Nobody wanted MacArthur back in Washington, where his immense popularity might easily be translated into political power as a Minister of Defense, or a Republican presidential candidate in the 1944 election.[13]

On 5 October 1943 the dying Admiral Pound was succeeded as First Sea Lord by Sir Andrew Cunningham. Churchill was not completely happy with a naval leader of ironclad willpower and immense personal prestige and had invited Sir Bruce Fraser of the Home Fleet to become First Sea Lord, but with great magnanimity Fraser insisted that Cunningham had the stronger claim. A major reason was his high standing with the Americans. Senior US figures had come to know and respect Cunningham in the spring and summer of 1942 when he was head of the British Admiralty Delegation in Washington, they had supported him as Allied Naval Commander in the Mediterranean through the North African, Sicily and Italian landings, and he had built a strong relationship of mutual confidence with General Eisenhower as Supreme Allied Commander in the Mediterranean. US admirals, for their part, especially appreciated the appointment of an Allied naval commander whom even Ernest King could not bully.[14]

The first strategic decision facing the Allies was whether to invest in the Mediterranean area to clear the German army out of Italy, as the British urged, or to concentrate on an offensive against Germany, which the Americans preferred. The Americans had no great difficulty in winning this debate, not only because their strategic case was probably the stronger, but because by late 1943 they were backed by a dominant superiority in manpower and supply. In 1943 British shipbuilding added about 630,000 tons displacement of new warships to the war effort, yards elsewhere in the Empire built 52,500 tons, and US shipyards built 804,000 tons for Britain under Lend-Lease – just over half the

British total. Naturally these figures lent weight to the American position in any dispute between the Allies and taught the British to avoid disagreement unless their case was exceptionally strong. But only a limited range of disputes, at a high strategic level, set the British and Americans seriously at odds. In practice a much higher proportion of disagreements were between Americans, and usually between different US Services.[15]

At least six different rival parties can be identified among the US Services in the Pacific alone: the US Navy's battleships and main fleet, the US carrier force and the naval aircraft, the US Marine Corps and its aircraft, the US submarines, the US Army and its dominant character General Douglas MacArthur, and the US Army Air Force and its Chief of Staff General H. H. ('Hap') Arnold. These parties can be identified both among the senior officers present at the time, and among the historians writing about the war thereafter, a high proportion of whom have been participants in these campaigns, or their kinsmen and supporters. Moreover, the post-war US Navy was, and to a considerable extent still is, divided into the rival 'tribes' of surface ships, submarines, airmen and Marines, and much of its post-war history has been written by the members or supporters of one of these 'tribes', in many cases with the ill-concealed intention of claiming most of the credit for victory and ignoring or disparaging all the other participants. It is impossible to write anything intelligent about the naval war without saying something about these rival claims, the more so since the British also had some involvement, both in fighting these campaigns and in writing their histories.

The US Army Air Corps, as it was from 1926 to June 1941, was then renamed the US Army Air Forces until September 1947, when it finally achieved its ambition of becoming an independent service as the US Air Force. Throughout the Second World War it was heavily committed to inter-service rivalry, and reluctant to undertake warlike operations which did not serve its political purposes. General Arnold was determined to keep the bulk of his aircraft for campaigns in Europe, and came close to blaming the US Navy's losses in the Solomon Islands campaign on cowardice; in his words a lack of 'leaders who know and understand modern warfare; men who are aggressive and not afraid to fight their ships'.[16] He refused to send to the Pacific any of the P-38 Lightnings, the only long-range US fighter, and the B-17 heavy bombers which were deployed there proved to be completely unable to hit moving ships. In 1943 when the USAAF (by day) and the RAF (by night) were able to undertake their air offensive against German targets from bases in England, neither bomber force made good their grandiose claims. In January and February 1943 RAF bombers devastated Lorient and St Nazaire on the Atlantic coast but barely inconvenienced the U-boats in their massive concrete shelters. The over-all capacity of the two ports was reduced, but so many of the U-boats formerly based there had been sunk in the Atlantic that spring that the reduction in port capacity hardly mattered. Fortunately for the British, the French authorities had foreseen what was going to happen and evacuated the civilian populations of the towns, avoiding what would otherwise have been a massacre of the inno-cents and a political disaster. The 'Gomorrah' raids on Hamburg in July 1943 killed 30,000–50,000 German civilians but caused only slight production losses. But both British and American bombers suffered unacceptable losses and were forced to abandon their campaigns as it became clear that they had greatly exaggerated the effectiveness of their weapons. The disaster of the second US Schweinfurt raid of 14 October 1943, which cost 198 out of 291 heavy bombers lost or damaged, came as USAAF morale was already failing. By the Cairo Conference of December 1943, the Allied air forces had to confront the fact that they had suffered a serious defeat in the air war over Germany, which threatened the plan to invade Europe in 1944.[17]

Another US force whose effectiveness was (and often still is) inflated is the USN submarine force. Nowadays submarines occupy a prominent share of the US Navy's order of battle, and their numerous supporters tend to gloss over the mediocre performance of US submarines from 1941 to 1944 – a failure the more conspicuous since the submarines themselves were with one critical excep-tion an excellent design of long range, well armed and equipped. The exception was the disastrous record of US torpedo design and production, which was a monopoly of the US Navy's Torpedo Station at Newport, Rhode Island. The Tor-pedo Station developed a dual-purpose magnetic/mechanical torpedo pistol, deemed too secret to undergo more than cursory testing, and protected against subsequent complaints by the local Congressmen and the Bureau of Ordnance – with very bad effects on the achievement and morale of US submariners. In 1942 US submarines' performance was markedly inferior to Japanese submar-ines, and they sank only one-tenth of the tonnage sunk by German U-boats. This is a contrast all the more striking since the Germans suffered from torpedo faults as serious as the American ones, and very similar in nature. The follow-ing year was only slightly better, and it was not until late 1944 that US submar-ines had reliable weapons which ran straight and exploded on contact. But blaming everything on technical faults is simply the mirror-image of the char-acteristic American conviction that technology cures all problems. The US des-troyer force fired the same unreliable torpedoes as the submarines, but, having a better fighting record, had less to explain away and made less of their defects. The real weakness of the US submarine service was a peacetime system of choosing elderly commanding officers, enforcing extreme caution, and relieving any who were observed to be running risks. The result was a submarine force which in the Solomon Islands campaign proved to be good only for air-sea rescue. Early war experience taught the Japanese Navy that US submarines were a negligible danger – which was true then, until at length in the course of 1943 a new generation of US submarine captains brought a new spirit of aggression to the Pacific submarine war. The US Navy was able to feed the US submarines with reliable intelligence by applying its existing cryptographic access to Japanese naval signals, plus the Imperial Army's 'Water Transport Code', which was broken in March 1943 by the Indian Army's Wireless Experimental Centre at Delhi. Now the US submarines, fed with copious signals intelligence and equipped with VHF voice radio for tactical communication, could and did organize themselves into 'wolf packs' which worked together in night surface attacks, and deserved the wolfish comparison much more than the German U-boats – which, unlike real wolves, had great difficulty in finding their prey. This in turn drove the Japanese Navy to organize its first anti-submarine force and its first convoys, and in 1944 sinkings on both sides rose rapidly.[18]

In November 1943 General Alfred Jodl, Chief of Staff of the OKW, declared that 'we shall win because we must win, or the history of the world will make no sense'.[19] What really made no sense was German naval policy. For the first four years of the European war the OKM clung resolutely to Dönitz's preference for small U-boats, suitable for confined waters and (as U-boat engineers complained) fitted to 1918 standards. As late as 1942 he was still proclaiming that 'the German submarine in its conception, construction and engineering has achieved the perfection of this type, both for surfaced and submerged operations'.[20] Only when Dönitz replaced Admiral Raeder at the end of January 1943 (on the same day the 6th Army surrendered at Stalingrad) did the German leadership begin to confront their situation, and even then it evoked more brutal and even hysterical rhetoric than rational analysis.[21]

Meanwhile an immense effort was wasted trying to leapfrog several engineering revolutions to develop Hellmuth Walter's hydrogen-peroxide fuelled gas-turbine submarine engine. Hydrogen peroxide (H_2O_2) is a powerful rocket fuel – in its concentrated form ('high-test peroxide') in effect a liquid explosive which detonates on contact with any organic compound (oil, for instance), and must be handled in containers of glass or stainless steel. Walter believed that it would fuel a turbine which would drive a submerged submarine at high speed, and other countries including Britain, Russia and Sweden at various dates have taken its potential seriously as a propellant of submarines or torpedoes – generally with fatal results.[22]

The time wasted between the obsolete Type VII U-boats on the one hand, and Walter's utopian dreams on the other, ensured that the Germans did not make a serious attempt to design a modern U-boat for Atlantic operations, using proven technology, until the new Armaments Minister Albert Speer gained control of naval armaments in June 1943. These new 'electro boats', the Type XXI and the smaller Type XXIII, were originally intended to be propelled by Walter turbines at high underwater speeds, then redesigned with conventional propulsion but retaining the new highly streamlined hull form combined with extra battery power.[23] But modern design needed to be matched by modern building practice. Until mid-1943 U-boats were still being built by experienced shipbuilders supervised by Rudolf Blohm (of the leading Hamburg shipbuilders Blohm & Voss) using traditional methods, at traditional speed. A total of 238 U-boats were completed in 1942, costing 77 million man-hours and taking nearly two years each on average. Unfortunately, the new submarine-building programme was less a radical innovation than a political propaganda show: Speer and his thrusting young managers, alive with the Nazi spirit and 'working towards the Führer', would show the stuffy old shipbuilders how to do it. He convinced Hitler, and perhaps he even convinced himself, but in the real world his bogus prefabrication scheme and falsified production statistics wrecked the submarine programme comprehensively. Speer (himself an architect and town planner rather than an engineer, who had risen in Hitler's favour as an ardent Nazi) had read about prefabrication in America, and planned to build the new submarines in sections in inland machine shops, away from bombing, transporting the completed sections by canal to shipyards at Bremen, Hamburg and Danzig for final assembly. He did not realize that the fine tolerances required to assemble a deep-diving submarine pressure hull from sections would be well beyond the competence of provincial engineering firms – until the first of the new boats sank on launching. Nor did he take account of the lack of any remaining battery-manufacturing plant in Germany to supply the new submarine programme. Eventually a few of the new boats were brought to seagoing condition after an immense effort, but the first two of the Type XXI put to sea on their first war patrols almost a year after their planned completion date, and two days before Germany surrendered.[24]

At the same time as the new U-boat programme, it was decided to adopt a range of new weapons, including the T5 *Zaunkönig* homing torpedo, and the Hs 293 and Fritz X radio-controlled glider bombs. It was much too late to introduce these weapons, which contained very little really new technology and could have been begun well before the outbreak of war. Hitler signed a programme of 11,134 warships, including 2,400 U-boats, all to be built by 1948. To realize this fantasy Dönitz demanded 141,800 shipyard workers, later increased to 262,000, including 86,300 forced workers, effectively slaves. Hitler buttressed his hopes with the idea that by some madness Japan would declare war on Russia, which would seek an armistice with Germany, allowing Germany in turn to defeat Britain and the United States. Meanwhile the absurd production targets were submerged by chaotic bureaucracy and vanished into a fantasy world in which everything was promised, and nothing achieved. Dönitz assured Hitler that a last-minute reversal of fortunes was still possible, but he must have known it was not.[25]

It is instructive to contrast Speer with Patrick Blackett, Professor of Physics at the University of Manchester, former naval officer and future Nobel prizewinner, who in 1941 became head of the 'Operational Research' Section of Coastal Command, and next year moved to the Admiralty, where he soon rose to be a senior member of the Naval Staff as Director of Naval Operational Research. 'Operational Research', which Blackett largely invented, was and is the application of sophisticated mathematics to analyse plans and projects – instead of relying on what he called 'gusts of emotion'.[26] It is an important example of the rational approach to war which the Axis powers seldom matched; as a factor in victory it has been reckoned as important as cryptography, though much less well known.[27] A valuable early success in 1941 was Blackett's demonstration that air-dropped depth charges were being set to explode too deep, and therefore too late. From 100 feet the setting was progressively reduced to 25 feet in the summer of 1942, a major cause of the increased 'lethality' of Coastal Command's attacks on U-boats from 1 per cent in 1941 to 25 per cent by the end of the war. Blackett thought that if operational research had been adopted earlier in the war it could have saved a million tons of shipping. In 1942 he proved that Bomber Command was not merely ineffective but counter-productive: the shipping effort required to sustain the USAAF and RAF bomber forces flying from British airfields in their campaign against Germany vastly exceeded the military benefit of the bombing, so that to remove three-quarters of the bomber force would save a million tons of shipping a year. Unfortunately, the Cabinet was not yet ready to embrace logic as a path to victory. [27A]

Blackett had more success with his demonstration that slow convoys lost 50 per cent more ships than fast ones, but that the number of ships sunk per attacking U-boat was unrelated to convoy size. Doubling the size of the convoy with the same number of escorts halved the percentage of losses; doubling the number of escorts as well halved the proportion of losses again. In the spring of 1943, the Admiralty adopted Blackett's policy of giant convoys, which rose from forty ships to as many as 200. It was fundamental to his thinking that the search for 'dream weapons' was simply escapism: what was needed was to get better performance from existing weapons of known imperfection. 'Relatively too much scientific effort has been expended hitherto in the production of new devices and too little on the proper use of what we have got.'[28] It was the same attitude which inspired the dictum of the radar pioneer Robert Watson-Watt: 'Give them the third best to go on with; the second best comes too late and the best never comes.'[29]

Happily, the Germans made few attempts to analyse their operations with comparable rigour, but the Naval Scientific Operations Staff which Dönitz set up at the end of 1943 showed what could have been achieved. Starting with a directional antenna for the new *Naxos* 10cm radar warning set, these scientists then developed countermeasures to radar on 3cm wavelength, which they foresaw would be the next sensor in the Allied armoury. This was first detected in February 1944 – one of the few occasions in more than two years that the German Navy gained the scientific initiative even for a short time.[30] This would have been the way to regain technical superiority in the war at sea, and it was well that the Germans made only spasmodic efforts to develop strategies guided by logical analysis.

THIRTY-TWO

Armament and Re-armament

Ships and Aircraft 1941–1944

V iewed through the prism of armament and re-armament, the European War began with a series of false starts. In the 1930s as the
Admiralty worked towards the New Standard Fleet, naval expenditure concentrated on new battleships, carriers, cruisers and destroyers
intended for the main fleets. The Admiralty had accepted the Washington
Treaty 5:3 ratio of British to Japanese battleship strength because Japan was
then the only plausible battleship-armed enemy. In the 1930s the Germans
and Italians began building modern battleships again and took up increasingly hostile foreign policies, so that as the interwar treaty limitations
expired, the ageing ships of the British battle-fleet were more and more
exposed. The five new battleships of the *King George V* Class, laid down in
1939–40 and completed in 1940–42, were to have been followed by the four
45,000-ton, 16-inch battleships of the *Lion* Class (as permitted by the second
London Naval Treaty), of which the first two were laid down in the summer
of 1939. Almost immediately they were suspended in favour of ships more
urgently needed; first convoy escorts, later landing craft. By the mid-1940s,
at the crux of the war, experience seemed to confirm that battleships and
carriers were equally indispensable to the future of naval warfare. Unknown
to the Admiralty, Japan, Russia and Germany were already planning much
bigger battleships, of which two (the Japanese *Yamato* and *Musashi* of 64,000
tons with nine 18-inch guns) were launched in 1940 and entered service in
1942. Had the *Lions* been built, they would have been badly outclassed by the
Yamatos, but in the event only one more British battleship was built, the *Vanguard*, launched in November 1944. She was a version of the cancelled *Lion*
Class which saved time by making use of four old-fashioned but serviceable
twin 15-inch gun turrets left over from the conversion of *Courageous* and
Glorious in the 1920s – but not enough time was saved, for the ship was finally

completed in August 1946, after the war was over and both the Japanese ships had been sunk.[1]

In January 1944 Sir Stanley Goodall 'stepped upstairs' to become Assistant Controller, opening the way for his brilliant deputy Charles Lillicrap to succeed as DNC. A few days later Goodall lunched with Sir Andrew Cunningham the First Sea Lord, and afterwards summed up their conversation in his diary, 'He said "there won't be an aircraft carrier afloat in 20 years' time, they will all be islands." I said I thought battleships were dead! We are poles asunder.'[2] It was a reasonable disagreement, in the midst of a war which had provided evidence that capital ships old and new were both vulnerable and indispensable. In Cunningham's (mainly Mediterranean) experience, shore-based aircraft had driven carriers away for long periods, and the famous *Ark Royal* had been sunk by a submarine; in the Pacific the distances were such that shore-based aircraft were not present in many areas where only carriers could provide air cover. Related to this was a basic difference between American and British carrier design. US carriers' main hull structure extended from the keel up to the hangar deck; the hangars themselves and the flight decks were not structural but light and flexible, with expansion joints in the decks and wide openings in the sides which allowed aircraft to warm up their engines before they were brought up on deck to fly. The long flight decks (and the relatively friendly climate of the Pacific) allowed the carriers to keep most of their aircraft permanently on deck, ready to fly off the largest possible first strike – but this design was quite unsuitable for continuous flying operations. Moreover, the shallow hull girder was heavily stressed, and the hangars provided little protection to fuelling and arming. Beginning with the three *Illustrious* Class (launched 1939) the British fleet carriers adopted a radically different scheme with the hangars enclosed within the hull, fuel and ammunition handled with great care according to magazine regulations, and the armoured flight deck as the upper strength deck. This provided a deep hull girder with a strong but light structure, incorporating the internal armoured bulkheads of the hangars, but the added armour absorbed much space and topweight, and limited the number of aircraft which could be carried. The lift wells at each end of the hangars were the weak point of the armour scheme. The British ships were designed to rely on a heavy anti-aircraft battery and to strike the aircraft below decks if air attack threatened; a plan which turned out to be neither effective nor necessary. The US Navy for its part intended to fly off all its strike aircraft before the enemy could appear, and tended to gloss over the question of how, or whether, it would get them back. For both navies the solution to their problems was to come from the unexpected invention of radar, making it possible for a carrier to intercept attackers and direct defenders.[3]

With the completion of the *Ark Royal* in 1938 the Royal Navy had four fleet carriers in service (the others being the converted battlecruisers *Furious, Courageous* and *Glorious*), with four more under construction (*Illustrious, Victorious, Formidable* and *Indomitable*, all completed in 1941), plus the older and slower conversions *Argus* and *Eagle* and the smaller *Hermes*. None of these ships, nor any of the aircraft carriers of the American and Japanese navies, had been designed with the benefit of wartime experience, for there had been no naval war since they had been built. The three navies had different but equally theoretical ideas of how aircraft and carriers would be used. Wartime experience disabused them of many of these ideas, but it was too late to change the ships they had built and were building. Aircraft entered service during the war which reflected recent fighting experience, but big ships took much longer to design and build. The most modern British carriers to serve in the Second World War were the *Implacable* and *Indefatigable*, laid down in 1939 as a further development of the *Illustrious* and *Indomitable* Classes; the first large British carriers to incorporate the lessons of the war were the second *Eagle* and *Ark Royal*, completed in the 1950s.[4]

The situation of the US Navy was comparable. The twenty-six big carriers of the *Essex* Class completed between 1943 and 1950 were an enlarged version of the *Yorktown* Class of 1934. To fill the gap before the *Essex* Class appeared, there were nine smaller carriers of the *Independence* Class launched in 1942–3 (improvised conversions of incomplete light cruiser hulls), and the four *Sangamon* Class (converted oilers completed in 1942). The three armoured carriers of the *Midway* Class, the only big US carriers designed as such with the benefit of war experience, were completed too late to play any part in the war. What could be changed in the light of recent experience and new equipment was the composition of the ships' air groups and the tactics of air defence, but not the ships. The same was true of their enemies: none of the Japanese carriers completed during the war represented any significant development of pre-war thinking. As far as large warships were concerned, therefore, the major navies fought the Second World War largely with the ships and ideas which they had developed in peacetime.[5]

Because the US Navy was frightened that enemy scouts would locate American carriers and sink them one by one, its doctrine was that carriers should keep as far as possible out of touch with one another. This was why the US carriers *Enterprise* and *Hornet* made no attempt to support the *Yorktown* at the battle of Midway, though she was sunk only 20 miles away from them.

By contrast both British and Japanese carriers habitually operated together within a shared screen of ships and aircraft, a practice not copied by the USN until June 1943. But ideas were copied across the Pacific in both directions; by the 1930s the Admiralty was thinking of adopting American flight-deck procedure, with many of the strike aircraft parked permanently on deck, but in Whitehall the admirals were careful to disguise ideas which implied a big increase in the number of carrier aircraft. The RAF was intensely sensitive about this subject, and the Admiralty strove with some success to avoid for as long as possible provoking another inter-service dispute.[6]

The British armoured-carrier designs relied heavily on anti-aircraft defence, but the experience of the Norwegian and Mediterranean campaigns soon showed how much that had been overrated by all navies. During 1941 British thinking turned to a fighter-carrier for fleet defence. To relieve the overloaded DNC's department the design project was passed to Vickers-Armstrong at the end of 1941. J. S. Redshaw, Vickers' chief naval architect, produced the simple and efficient design of the *Colossus* Class 'light fleet carriers', the first four of which were ordered in March 1942. Twelve were launched by the end of 1944 and eight more later; they were too late to contribute much to the war, but all had long and successful post-war careers in various navies.

All sorts of aircraft carriers were compound weapon systems whose effectiveness was shaped by the interaction of ship and aircraft design in the circumstances (many of them unforeseen) of wartime. In the case of escort carriers, many of which were built in the US to American designs, the differences between US and British carrier practice, and the Royal Navy's already serious manpower shortages, caused further complications. Admiral King complained in August 1943 that the British were too slow to man escort carriers allocated to them under Lend-Lease; perhaps suspecting that King was bluffing, the British offered to return seven escort carriers, whereupon it emerged that the US Navy could not man them either. The Fleet Air Arm aircraft aboard British escort carriers had a lower operating tempo than American aircraft, because British aircraft could not be launched from US catapults, because the British could not afford the manpower to man their flight decks on an American scale, and because the US aircraft were faster and of longer range. Against that, the British depth charge was twice as effective as the American, the American Grumman Avenger, unlike the Fairey Swordfish, could not be fitted with the ASV Mk.XI centimetric radar which greatly improved the success rate of attacks on surfaced U-boats by night, and, most importantly, the Swordfish had an unequalled capacity to fly in weather too bad for more modern aircraft. Like a modern helicopter, it attacked low and slow, combining accuracy with surprise.[7] 'I fancied,' as one naval pilot remembered,

> the 'Stringbag' would never reach oblivion, there would be no limbo deep enough from which that extraordinary biplane would not return in its slow persistent glory, staggering along at 80 knots with a bicycle strapped to its fuselage and a dog in the back cockpit. Less fancifully it is worth recording that the Swordfish was the ideal anti-submarine aircraft for Russian convoys; it could fly by day and night in weather conditions which . . . left the Avengers helpless.[8]

As their name indicates, escort carriers were originally intended to provide air cover to merchant convoys, but in practice they proved to be useful, indeed essential, for so many other purposes that convoy escort was often crowded out. They provided close air support for all the major amphibious operations. In August 1944, to take an example at random, seven British and two American escort carriers were providing air cover for the Allied landings in the South of France. In all the theatres of the war at sea they were heavily used as aircraft ferries to deliver fresh aircraft to carriers and airfields on the front line. To keep 250 aircraft operational aboard the four fleet carriers of the British Pacific Fleet in 1944–5 required more than 2,000 in transit from the other side of the world, and sixteen escort carriers to ferry them (though some of these were supplying US as well as British fleet carriers).[9]

The largest and best-equipped British escort carriers were the converted cargo liners *Activity*, *Vindex*, *Nairana*, *Campania* and *Pretoria Castle*, which entered service in 1942 and 1943. The biggest of them, the *Pretoria Castle*, had a hangar for fifteen aircraft, and was mainly used for training carrier pilots. From September 1942 the *Campania*, *Vindex* and *Nairana*, which had an aircraft direction and radar outfit sufficient to handle aircraft in 'white-out' conditions when the flight deck was sometimes invisible from the bridge, spent most of their operational careers in the Arctic. In October and November 1944 convoy escorts, including three escort carriers led by Rear-Admiral Frederick Dalrymple-Hamilton flying his flag in *Vindex*, mounted one of the last big air anti-submarine operations, but U-boats continued to attack Arctic convoys to the very end of the war in May 1945.[10]

These 'grown-up' escort carriers were too good and too scarce for routine Atlantic convoys, which still needed air cover as much as ever, and in 1943 one of the original escort-carrier ideas was revived as the 'Merchant Aircraft Carrier'. The basic plan was to provide a convoy with its own air cover by fitting a flight deck to diesel-powered tankers and grain carriers, which did not need a funnel to make steam, and could load and discharge cargo by flexible hoses without needing derricks or hatches. The grain-carrier version carried four Swordfish aircraft in a small hangar; the tankers had only three aircraft, which lived permanently on deck, but their flight deck was longer. Everything depended on the Swordfish's unique ability to take off at 60 knots with a full load of weapons. The 'MAC-ships' also sidestepped the already acute shortage of naval manpower since they were merchant ships under the Red Ensign and entirely civilian-manned except for the aircrew and flight-deck personnel. Following the precedent established by the Catapult-Armed Merchantmen, the master of the ship became the launching authority, and the naval party signed articles as members of the crew under his orders. The first of them, the *Empire MacAlpine*, sailed in May 1943, and there were eventually nineteen, including two Dutch tankers with Dutch naval airmen. They escorted a total of 217 convoys, of which only one was ever successfully attacked. They made it possible for convoys to take the southern 'Great Circle' route, which saved a good deal of mileage but removed the ships from the reach of land-based air cover. Besides providing air cover and carrying their normal cargo, the MAC-ships carried unfused spare depth charges for the escorts, triced up under the edge of the flight deck, and the tankers doubled as refuelling oilers. By 1944, when the U-boat threat had almost disappeared from the open Atlantic, some eastbound voyages acted as aircraft ferries. They also gave a real boost to Merchant Navy morale. 'Merchant sailors usually found the Royal Navy snobby, bossy and over-organized, while the Royal Navy usually saw merchant sailors as uncouth, loutish and ill-disciplined.' The naval airmen, however,

> showed every respect towards their new shipmates, proudly wearing the silver 'MN' badge in their lapels, and greatly enjoying the rage that this entirely legitimate act caused in more hide-bound naval officers ashore; and before long they hit upon another very visible method of showing their regard . . . The Stringbags used in the MAC-ships were painted pure white, being the best camouflage for day-flying over the sea, and were otherwise entirely standard Fleet Air Arm planes – except that in many flights, so great was the MN loyalty, the aircrew would paint out the words ROYAL NAVY on the fuselage of their planes and substitute MERCHANT NAVY.[11]

In the 1920s while the Admiralty concentrated on building the new category (created by the Washington Treaty) of 'heavy cruisers' with 8-inch guns, there was no urgent need to add to the existing stock of smaller 'fleet' cruisers intended to span the gap between battleships and destroyers. By the 1930s it was evidently time to revive the idea of light cruisers, which now came in two distinct sizes. First the five ships of the *Leander* Class were completed in 1933–4, shortly followed by three more, which were transferred to Australia. These were very light cruisers, mounting eight 6-inch guns on a standard displacement between 7,000 and 7,500 tons. There followed the four even smaller ships of the *Arethusa* Class completed between 1935 and 1937, armed with only six 6-inch guns.[12] Meanwhile the Japanese were building much larger cruisers like the *Mogami* Class, 'light' in that their guns were only 6-inch, but with fifteen guns in five triple turrets (and in 1939–40 re-armed with ten 8-inch, though the Admiralty did not find that out until much later). They were declared as displacing 8,500 tons, though in reality their displacement had risen to 13,000–15,000 tons by the time they had been re-armed and their more serious defects of stability and structural strength had been addressed. In response the eight ships of the British *Southampton* Class mounted twelve 6-inch in triple turrets on a tonnage of 9,000–10,000 tons, and were originally fitted with three catapult-mounted Swordfish torpedo bombers on floats, to hunt and sink enemy raiders in the open sea. Then, after Japan withdrew from the 1936 London Naval Treaty, Britain and the United States agreed to abandon all limits on overall tonnage of different classes, but to impose a limit of 8,000 tons for individual cruisers. The designers of the *Fiji* (Colony) Class which followed (launched 1939–41) managed to retain the same main battery as the *Southampton* Class, but the design was now very tight, and all this class eventually had to sacrifice one triple turret to save weight and space for new radar and anti-aircraft guns. The *Dido* Class cruisers, contemporaries of the *Fiji* Class, were armed with the same twin 5.25-inch mountings as formed the secondary armament of the *King George V* Class battleships. Because these were dual-purpose (high or low angle) mounts the *Didos* were and often still are referred to as anti-aircraft cruisers, but in fact their primary function was as 'fleet cruisers' for surface action, and the 5.25-inch mounting lacked the rate of fire for an effective anti-aircraft weapon. They were followed by the *Minotaur* Class (launched 1943–5), which followed the three-turret version of the *Fiji* Class, but only three were completed as designed. The later four ships of the class were completed post-war to a modified design.[13]

One further variety of cruiser ought to be mentioned: the 'armed merchant cruisers' (AMC) created by fitting an armament (usually old 6-inch guns with a primitive fire control) to requisitioned cargo-liners. These were first taken up as 'ocean escorts' to the first convoys, in which position they were vulnerable to torpedo attack, but an effective passive defence was achieved by filling their holds with sealed empty oil drums, which preserved damaged stability and allowed several of them to steam home in spite of torpedo damage. Most of these AMC were later replaced on convoy duty by new escorts, and were re-converted to troopships, landing ships or naval auxiliaries.[14]

Only in November 1938, as the likelihood of a German war increased, did the Admiralty turn its attention to a large programme of small warships which became the oddly classed 'corvettes' of the Flower Class, designed to provide anti-submarine escorts to coastal convoys around the British Isles. The design was based on a successful whale-catcher built by Smith's Dock of North Shields in Northumberland. The details were worked out over the winter of 1938–9, and the first 115 ships were ordered between July and December 1939 – not long before the fall of France ruined Britain's strategic situation and largely eliminated the corvettes' intended functions. It would no longer be possible to run big convoys up the Channel or through the North Sea, and the requirement now was for oceanic, in particular transatlantic, escorts, for which the corvettes were much too small. Their original planned complement was twenty-nine officers and men, which had gone up to forty-seven in the autumn of 1940 for transatlantic service, and over sixty by the time they began to go to sea in early 1941, to provide for new equipment and continuous watchkeeping. With more than double their originally intended crew, they were grossly overcrowded, with poor ventilation and a bad incidence of tuberculosis. Their endurance, notionally 4,400 miles, was in practice nearer 2,750 miles, and less in bad weather – quite insufficient for a non-stop transatlantic passage. This was not their only failing; reports from corvettes soon spoke of the impossibility of effective work aboard ships which rolled so heavily; 'It is not that the men lack courage or resolution; merely that the physical strain is insupportable.' Sir Bruce Fraser, the Controller, bluntly condemned the corvettes as 'useless'.[15] More soberly, modern studies suggest that in the open Atlantic ship motion disabled the corvettes as functional warships for at least one day in four. Yet the Navy now had no choice but to use them to protect ocean convoys. During 1941 the 'Flowers' were modified to correct their defects as far as possible, with deep bilge keels to check the worst rolling, and a forecastle extended aft for two-thirds of the ship's length to add accommodation and provide safe covered passageways for men to move fore and aft. Nothing could be done to stop these short ships pitching heavily into the long Atlantic rollers, which many officers on the bridge found was a worse trial than rolling. After June 1940 only fifteen more were ordered from British yards, though the Canadians continued to build corvettes to the modified design into 1944, using shipyards on the Great Lakes which were constrained to a maximum length of 270 feet by the size of the locks giving access to the St Lawrence River.[16]

Contemporary with the 'Flowers' and almost exactly the same size (just under 1,000 tons) were the Hunt Class 'Escort destroyers'; junior versions of fleet destroyers intended to provide coastal convoys with 25–6 knot anti-aircraft escorts mounting six 4-inch high-angle guns in twin mountings. By the time they were ordered the Director of Naval Construction's department, already short-handed before the war, was under intense strain: in Goodall the DNC's words, 'a corps of old men & youngsters with far too few between the ages of 30 & 45. The old men are feeling the strain, most of the youngsters are doing well but inexperience is against them.'[17] Naval architecture in the 1940s already depended greatly on sophisticated mathematical analysis, but in the pre-computer age ship designers often had to rely on approximate calculations using formulae and slide rules. The Admiralty's senior professional staff, the Constructors, could delegate routine work to their draughtsmen, but it was regarded as essential that stability calculations be made twice, by two senior constructors working independently. In the case of the Hunt Class the calculation was evidently made only once, and it contained a small but fatal error: in calculating the ships' metacentric height, the height of the upper deck above the keel was read off the draught as seven feet instead of seventeen. The fault was not discovered until February 1940 when the first of them, the *Atherstone*, was submitted to the standard 'inclining experiment' to check her stability, which proved to be completely inadequate. The first twenty-three of the class were already afloat, and almost nothing could be done but to sacrifice half their armament to save topweight. A further thirty-three ships still on the building ways were 'kippered' by being cut in half lengthwise and opened up to increase their beam, with later ships of the class laid down to these revised dimensions. 'My first big mistake which was overcome without spilling much gravy,' Goodall commented in his diary. In truth a great deal of gravy was spilled, in the form of time and money wasted when every escort was precious. His resignation was declined, but the head of the 'Destroyer Group' was taken off design work. Goodall was privately critical of several other designs from his own department, including the *Southampton* Class light cruisers ('very disappointing mainly due to badly designed details').[18] In April 1943 there was another significant stability error in calculating the metacentric height of the new 'light fleet carriers', though this was a Vickers rather than an Admiralty design, and the mistake was caught before it could do serious harm. Behind these blunders lay the acute wartime strain on senior staff of the Admiralty, which can be illustrated by the fact that two successive Controllers of the Navy (Sir Reginald Henderson in 1939 and Sir Frederick Wake-Walker in 1945) both died of overwork aged fifty-seven. So did the Engineer-in-Chief in 1946, aged sixty-two, and his intended successor collapsed soon afterwards. Sir Henry Markham, the experienced Admiralty clerk who replaced Archibald Carter as Secretary of the Admiralty in 1940, died in 1946 aged only forty-nine.[19]

The fall of France, and the inadequacy of the corvettes to escort the transatlantic convoys which were now needed, set the Admiralty constructors to work in November 1940 on what was initially called a 'twin-screw corvette', a clumsy phrase later dropped for the Canadian coinage of 'frigate'. To save time, it was decided to use two of the same standard four-cylinder triple-expansion engines as the Flower Class, driving a bigger and longer hull (just over 300 feet long, 1,370 tons, compared with 208 feet and 980 tons of the modified 'Flower' Class) at a maximum speed of 20 knots. Higher speed would have been better, but these limits allowed many small yards to switch with minimal delay to building the new River Class frigates. Although they had the same triple-expansion engines as the corvettes, the new frigates had water-tube boilers without superheaters, producing better acceleration for chasing U-boats, with saturated or 'wet' steam which helped to lubricate the exposed cylinders. The design was approved in March 1941, and the first of the new class, the *Exe*, was completed in April 1942. They were armed with two 4-inch guns and a heavy battery of depth-charge throwers. Ten 20mm Oerlikon light AA guns were planned but were initially in short supply. With 470 tons of oil, they had an endurance of 5,000 miles at 15 knots, increased after the first twenty-four ships to 650 tons and 7,500 miles by sacrificing their little-used minesweeping capacity. Fifty-seven were built in Britain and sixty-seven in Canada, divided between the RCN, RN and USN; twelve more were built in Australia. An American version of the River Class was built by Kaiser-Walsh at Providence, Rhode Island, for the Royal Navy, which named them after minor colonies. There were twenty-one ships, built faster than their sister ships in British yards, but the building quality was unsatisfactory and the building cost extremely high. To use shipyards with building ways too short for a 300-foot hull, a modern version of a single-screw corvette, the Castle Class, was approved in May 1943, of which twenty-four were built. Although substantially bigger than the Flower Class, with the same engine, they were half a knot faster with double the range thanks to a longer hull and better form.[20]

Meanwhile the US Navy, which had initially foreseen no requirement at all for anti-submarine escorts, in December 1942 began building a very large class of 'destroyer escorts', of a similar basic design to British frigates but divided into different versions by variations in their armament and machinery. More than a thousand were ordered, but the building programme did not begin until more than three years after the likelihood of a major anti-submarine campaign should have been visible, and only eighteen months before the collapse of the German U-boat campaign in the autumn of 1943. As a result, only 563 destroyer escorts were completed, of which seventy-eight were turned over to the Royal Navy under Lend-Lease as the 'Captain Class', bearing the names of British sea officers of the Napoleonic Wars. Designed for heavy 5-inch guns which in the event were not available and had to be replaced with 3-inch, this class were much too stiff, and rolled so violently that handling depth charges in a seaway was difficult and dangerous. Larger bilge-keels and added top-weight (in the form of depth charges stowed on deck) went a good way to curing the problem, however, and the ships' luxurious accommodation delighted British sailors.[21]

The handsome and efficient River Class frigates were still being launched from Canadian shipyards well into 1944, but the Admiralty had already moved on to a more technically ambitious design, the Loch Class, similar in appearance but partly prefabricated and armed with new anti-submarine weapons. To gain the advantages of something like mass production, the design was sealed for two years in January 1943, prohibiting further alterations, though *Loch Fada*, the first of the class, was not laid down until June and completed at the end of March 1944. Thirty ships followed, almost all in 1944, followed by twenty-five of the 'Bay' Class, with the same hull but a mixed anti-submarine and anti-aircraft armament intended for the Pacific. The prefabrication of the Loch Class was a skilful adaptation to British circumstances. There was no question of copying the best American practice by laying out a new yard on a flat, unobstructed virgin site, for there were no such sites left in the British Isles. Instead the hull design (jointly produced by the Admiralty and the Clyde shipyard of John Brown) had simple lines with as few curves as possible and was divided into two-and-a-half-ton units, small enough to be lifted by standard shipyard cranes and moved by railway, which were subcontracted to bridge-builders and other steel fabricators, then assembled and launched by six different yards. Adopting another Canadian innovation, the ships were then fitted-out in two big basins, at Dalmuir on the Clyde and Hendon Dock on the Wear, which between them served the whole programme. This semi-prefabrication process cost about 50 per cent more than conventional building but saved a good deal of time. Unlike the Germans trying to assemble the first Type XXI U-boats at the same time, the British yards took pains to ensure that their frigate sections fitted together to make a fair ship, and the class had long and successful careers in the post-war years.[22]

The Loch Class frigates were designed from the start to carry an integrated range of weapons and sensors. In 1943 the standard anti-submarine weapon was still the depth charge, but it had been significantly improved during the war. The rate of sinking, initially only 7 feet a second, had risen to 16 feet a second with the heavier Mk.VII at the end of 1940. An arrangement of depth-charge throwers created a pattern of ten charges covering a larger lethal area. By 1943 better training and depth-finding Asdic had raised the chances of a successful depth-charge attack from 1 per cent to about 5 per cent. By this time the British had discovered the one quality of German U-boats which had markedly improved since 1918: greater diving depth. An attacking frigate would lose Asdic contact 20–25 seconds before passing over the submerged U-boat's position, and the charges needed another 35 seconds to sink to 250 feet. Their lethal range was calculated (perhaps optimistically) at 30 feet. At a submerged speed of four knots the U-boat could move 300 feet in any direction in the one minute between the escort losing contact and the depth charge exploding, giving a cool-headed and experienced U-boat commander excellent chances of evasion. These chances were a function of the basic geometry of the escort's attack, using information from a sensor (Asdic) which searched ahead, but dropping a weapon over the stern that then sank relatively slowly. The obvious solution was an ahead-throwing anti-submarine weapon which could be fired when the attacking escort was still in contact with the U-boat.[23]

The first attempt was the 'Hedgehog', adopted in 1942, consisting of a frame on the forecastle mounting twenty-four single spigot mortars firing contact-fused bombs, each big enough to do fatal damage if it struck a submarine's pressure hull, as well as setting off other bombs nearby. The bombs were aimed to cover a circle of 120-foot diameter ahead of the ship, but the weapon proved to be less successful and less popular than had been hoped. If no bomb made contact there was no explosion and no morale effect, neither frightening the U-boat crew nor cheering the attackers. Whereas U-boats fatally damaged by depth charges tried to struggle to the surface to abandon ship, Hedgehog's victims left no clear evidence of their loss and tended to be recorded only as 'possibles'. Whereas everybody knew how to handle a depth charge, the new weapon was complex and needed special training, which was not at first understood. Not until 1944 did a research project establish that the Hedgehog was only really effective in shoal water; during the Normandy landings when U-boats were operating in the shallow waters of the English Channel, better than 40 per cent of Hedgehog attacks were successful.[24] By this time the Admiralty had discovered how deep the latest U-boats could dive; there was a confirmed report of a U-boat diving to 700 feet in June 1943 which lent urgency to the search for another ahead-throwing weapon. What was needed was a deep-water weapon plus an Asdic which could measure not only the bearing of the target but also its depth or slant range. The new weapon was the 'Squid' triple-barrelled anti-submarine mortar, which fired three 400-lb projectiles sinking at high speed (42 feet per second) to form a triangle 120 feet on a side, at a mean range 275 yards ahead of the ship. This was slaved to the new depth-finding Type 147 Asdic, which could fire the mortars automatically when they came into range, yielding upwards of 60 per cent successful attacks.[25] In the last year of the war U-boats equipped with snorkels were able to lie undetected on the bottom for long periods, absorbing a considerable anti-submarine effort with scanty results – so long as they were too timid to reveal their presence by attacking anything. The Admiralty was worried by the imminent arrival of the new high-speed U-boats, but trials with the 'high-speed target' *Seraph*, a submarine converted to imitate the performance of the new U-boats, suggested that the new weapons and sensors would have offered an adequate response.[26]

Besides warships in the strict sense of the word, navies had to provide a range of auxiliaries which grew ever more numerous and diverse as the naval campaigns spread further away from the fixed resources of ports and dock-yards. Tankers and oilers accompanied transatlantic and Arctic convoys to refuel escorts; at sea if the weather permitted, but sometimes in sheltered anchorages on the Arctic or Iceland coasts. Every convoy had one or two 'rescue ships', usually smaller passenger vessels belonging to coastal shipping lines, with medical care and suitable accommodation to receive survivors of sunken ships, ideally of shallow draught in the hope that torpedoes set to sink laden cargo ships might pass beneath them. Deep-sea salvage tugs were attached to convoys to tow damaged merchantmen. In the Indian Ocean, where the loss of Singapore in 1942 had left quite inadequate dockyard resources, repair ships had to be fitted out with suitable stores and workshops, and accommodation ships had to be found to house the workers. Depot ships were needed for destroyers and submarines. The worst problem in the Far East was the acute shortage of dry docks, which were extremely costly in time and materials to build, and almost impossible to improvise. In principle, floating docks could be towed into position, but were cumbersome and vulnerable at best, and were seldom moved even in peacetime.[27]

The material elements of naval power comprised not only ships and air-craft, but their weapons and equipment, which grew ever more diverse and complicated in the twentieth century. The self-image of modern navies is very strongly bound up with technical mastery, which by the 1940s was tending to overtake, or at least to subsume, the ancient pride in seamanship that for centuries had identified naval men. Merchant seamen still took as much professional pride in seamanship as ever, and in private reckoned themselves better seamen than the Navy; there was a degree of professional rivalry between the two which was not lessened by the conditions of wartime in which warships often exercised authority over merchant ships. War made seafaring ever more technical, and the more advanced technology belonged particularly to the navies, but naval operations involved merchant ships almost as much as warships, a considerable proportion of smaller warships were commanded by RNR (i.e. Merchant Navy) officers, and among all the participants in the naval war, many different nationalities were represented.

Of all the new technologies of the Second World War the first to make an impact was what came to be called 'radar'. In the British popular imagination this is always thought of as a British innovation, but at sea in 1939–40 it was the Germans who took the lead. The *Graf Spee* received the first '*Seetakt*' set in January 1938, and may have been shooting with radar ranges during the River Plate action in December 1939. Seven months later the *Scharnhorst* opened fire on the *Glorious* using a radar range of 14 miles, and in January 1941 *Scharnhorst* and *Gneisenau* evaded a Home Fleet ambush south of Iceland thanks to a better radar range. It is the more surprising that the Germans allowed their technical lead to fade so quickly. The *Scharnhorst* was sunk in December 1943 still relying on a *Seetakt* radar which failed in action from the concussion of heavy gunfire – as it had often done before.[28]

The new weapons Dönitz promised in 1943 were not imaginary, but they did not amount to more than marginal improvements. The first operational use of the T5 *Zaunkönig* ('wren') acoustic homing torpedo in September 1943 sank three escorts and six merchantmen for the loss of three U-boats, a modest success which did not justify the exaggerated claims that Dönitz swallowed uncritically. Unfortunately for him signals and other intelligence sources had forewarned the British, who had both tactical and technical counter-measures almost ready.[29] The new Hs.293 glider bomb sank several smaller warships, but was vulnerable to jamming and AA gunfire. The heavier FX-1400 likewise depended on guidance from an accompanying aircraft but badly damaged several big ships, including the old battleship *Warspite*, and achieved one spectacular success in sinking the new Italian battleship *Roma* on her passage to surrender. Both weapons were far too few and too late to turn the course of the naval war. Dönitz's decision to fit the U-boats with a stronger anti-aircraft battery and order them to fight on the surface played into Allied hands; when bad weather reduced Allied air activity, *BdU*, with its characteristic inclination to self-deception, chose to interpret it as proof of the effectiveness of German AA fire.[30]

The Germans also had other weapons under development, but what seems remarkable is the refusal of Dönitz and his staff to look beyond the search for *eine kleine elektrische Erfindung* ('some little electrical gadget')[31] which would solve all their problems. They never seriously re-examined their rooted assumptions, especially their faith in *Rudeltaktik* (which was of little use without intelligence or reconnaissance to locate the convoys), and their obsession with radar as a sort of magic able to master all sorts of difficulties (although German scientists understood electromagnetic radiation and, had they been consulted, could surely have guided the admirals towards a more rational analysis). Although the Germans had captured British Asdic sets on the fall of France, U-Boat Command lacked any operational research unit and never developed effective counter-measures. The Germans did not realize the existence of H/F D/F – the most fatal of all weaknesses of the U-boats – until the last year of the war.[32]

THIRTY-THREE

Life Is What You Make It In the Navy

Social History 1943–1945

By November 1942 Britain's overall manpower situation was already under severe strain. The army and the RAF received only half as many men as they needed, and even the privileged Navy was allowed only 85 per cent of its demand. In 1943 the Navy was again favoured; between April and December it received 190,000 men and women, the RAF had 100,000, and the army 145,000. Recruits' preferences still mattered, and the RAF, which had been three times as popular as the Navy in 1940, was already falling behind the Navy by 1942. But that only meant the Navy's manpower shortage was somewhat less acute than the other services' in terms of crude numbers. What made it worse was the Navy's high appetite for the scarce recruits whose education would qualify them for technical ratings. By September 1943 the initial training schools which taught new recruits the basic elements of naval life were expected to provide 240 men a month suitable to train as 'submarine detectors' (i.e. Asdic operators), 250 a month to become torpedomen, 650 to train as gunnery ratings, and more than 1,000 as radar operators. Asdic operators were particularly essential, and the latest sets with automatic steering left the operator conning the ship during an attack, throwing additional responsibility on the 'submarine detector'.[1]

It already seemed impossible to man the training establishments without paying off a number of ships. As one reaction to the manning crisis, efforts were made to make the recruitment process more intelligent and flexible. In 1941 the post of Senior Psychologist was created, with eight (later thirteen) industrial psychologists under him to assess the abilities of naval recruits with greater sophistication than retired petty officers could command. These were not clinical psychologists, still less psychiatrists, which the army used. The Admiralty was not much worried about mental illness or defect, which should have been screened out in the early stages of recruitment. The function of

these industrial psychologists was to assess recruits' experience and aptitudes using questionnaires and tests, in order to assign them to appropriate
branches of the Service. Very soon Wrens drawn from such professions as
teachers, social workers and employment officers proved to be highly suitable
for this work. They trained at the London School of Economics and were initially rated petty officers; eventually there were about 300 of them, including
fifty officers.[2] Their careful assessment was an important factor in the Navy's
success in the mass-training of new recruits. A 1942 inquiry into engineering
training praised the Navy for the efficiency with which it identified recruits
with some engineering knowledge and distributed them into appropriate
ranks, ratings and branches. (It also criticized the army for failing to do the
same.) There was a bewildering variety of engineering rates available. At the
top the Engine Room Artificer (ERA) was on a par with a junior engineer
officer in a merchant ship. He would start in the Navy as an artificer apprentice on passing a stiff entry examination at fifteen or sixteen. After four and
a half years' training he became a petty officer, and a CPO soon afterwards.
By 1944 600 ERAs were trained annually, half of them air artificers, the rest
divided between fitters, turners, engine smiths, coppersmiths, moulders and
other engineering trades. The first air artificers' course started in 1938 and
lasted three years, meaning that for much of the war the Fleet Air Arm was
heavily dependent on volunteers transferring from the RAF. Electrical and
Ordnance Artificers followed a four-and-a-half-year training parallel to the
ERA, and they too were accompanied by 'dilutee' (i.e. less skilled) rates of
Electrical and Ordnance Mechanic. Artisans such as shipwrights, blacksmiths,
plumbers and painters were craftsmen of the same naval status as artificers,
but who also worked ashore in the dockyards. Unlike other CPOs, they had
few or no opportunities to rise to warrant rank. Stokers were recruited as
adults (eighteen to twenty-five) with a lower educational level and social status
than engineer ratings but better prospects of reaching petty officer, which
made this a 'second chance' entry route for ambitious recruits who had failed
to distinguish themselves at school. Mechanicians were selected from good
leading stokers who could rise to artificer (CPO rate) with only eighteen
months' training. This too proved to be an attractive route of advancement,
but it had the disadvantage of removing too many intelligent men from the
boiler room where they were still wanted. Mechanics (Engine Room, Electrical or Ordnance) were another new category of 'dilutee' engineering rating
created in 1941 to work in shore establishments only. Motor mechanics (leading hands) were trained or retrained to handle the petrol or diesel engines of
coastal forces and small craft. By 1943 there was capacity and demand for

6,000 a year, but fewer than half as many could be found from the diminishing numbers available to the Navy.[3]

Early in the war it was clear that the Torpedo Branch was overloaded with most of the responsibility for electrical and electronic equipment in addition to underwater weapons. Eventually the solution was to be sought in a major reconstruction of branch responsibilities, but the middle of the war did not seem the right moment for major disruption, so for most of the war the Navy had to manage with a series of *ad hoc* expedients. The RNVR Electrical Officers we have already met, and the RDF (later Radar) Officers who joined them. Skilled ratings to support these technical officers had to be sought from the Electrical Artificers introduced in 1912 to work with electric motors and electrical machinery, whose skills scarcely stretched to electronics. The new rate of Electrical Artificer (Radio), later divided into 'electrical' and 'radio electrical', was intended to meet the requirement, but the apprentices needed between nine and eighteen months' training, and it was late in the war before the training schools could satisfy the Navy's demand. Below the artificers came the Wireless Mechanics, renamed Radio Mechanics in 1942 when radar was added to their responsibilities. Recruits (including a growing proportion of Wrens) spent twenty weeks at a technical college on the basic technical knowledge, four weeks at HMS *Scotia* on the Clyde, finishing with ten weeks at the RN Signal School (HMS *Mercury*) near Portsmouth, where they learnt to manage naval radio and radar sets.[4] For many women, the opportunity to learn advanced military technologies and to make a visibly important contribution to the war effort was a transformative experience. One young Wren, a former beautician, vigorously rejected the idea of returning to her old job at the end of the war: 'I love it! I never want to go back to my own job, I want to be a radio mech. for always.'[5] 'Whether they can put it into words or not,' wrote Vera Mathews after the war, 'this was the tremendous gain: the sense of having taken part in something of enormous importance, of having justified their existence.'[6]

Very soon the process of 'diluting' the skilled manpower of the peacetime Navy had to extend much further than the RNVR-dominated small-ship Navy created in 1940-41. Early in 1942 the Admiralty announced that it was

> essential to extend the existing arrangements for the replacement of R.N. Officers by Reserve officers to all major war vessels not already affected . . . the Fleet must be manned by Reserve officers with a leavening of Active Service officers, and not manned by R.N. Officers diluted with Reserve officers.[7]

574 · LIFE IS WHAT YOU MAKE IT IN THE NAVY

This meant that RNVR officers were no longer confined to the 'small-ship Navy' but increasingly distributed throughout the Fleet. Peacetime regular officers and long-service ratings alike were increasingly scarce in almost all ships. Already in 1942 Captain Harry Oram of the cruiser *Hawkins* reckoned that two-thirds of his men were 'immature sailors' who had been at sea for less than two years, but he was encouraged by their keenness to adopt the traditions of the Navy, so that 'we were able to run our complicated machines on a very weak mixture of RN spirit'. By 1942 the lower deck of the cruiser *Newfoundland* was made up of 30 per cent long-service ratings, 66 per cent Hostilities Only, and 4 per cent Royal Fleet Reserve or other naval pensioners.[8]

By this time the 'CW' method of selecting RNVR candidates from HO recruits to the lower deck was giving concern, because it was too slow and 'hit and miss' in its selection methods. The captains who were supposed to identify and recommend candidates for commissions were liable to be too busy commanding a ship in wartime to devote proper attention to the CW candidates. Another problem was that after their three months at sea on the lower deck, it was difficult to retrieve candidates whose ships might by then be on the other side of the world. Moreover, it was painfully clear that the Navy's shortage of petty officers and leading hands was at least as acute as its need for officers, so that taking the best men for commissions only made the shortage of petty officers worse. What was needed was a system which identified the best candidates for different ranks and responsibilities at the point of recruitment, without previous naval service to draw on, and did so more quickly and accurately than the CW system. In September 1942 Captain Oram had become Director of Training and Staff Duties at the Admiralty and read an article in the popular magazine *Picture Post* outlining the War Office's new methods of selecting army officers by a three-day course of tests carefully designed by industrial psychologists, which was claimed to be almost 100 per cent successful in identifying good candidates. By March 1943 the Admiralty had a naval equivalent course running, which identified good officer candidates and then trained them aboard three training ships moored in the Firth of Forth. This new scheme identified officer candidates much faster and more accurately than the previous methods and made it possible to 'dilute' the regular RN officers more than ever. By force of circumstances – certainly with no desire to be socially revolutionary – the Navy had now taken a big step in the direction of choosing officers on a classless basis, or at least without paying the attention which in the past had always been applied in peacetime to suitable accent, upbringing and education.[9]

By the end of the war there were about three times as many RNVR as RN officers in the Navy, and even such intensely specialized branches as submarines were affected. Reserve officers 'qualified for command' ranked with regular RN officers according to their rank and seniority. Twenty destroyers and more than fifty frigates and corvettes were commanded by RNVR officers. More than half of the British submarine officers now belonged to the RNVR; twelve boats had RNVR captains, plus another seven in the Dominion navies. In November 1945 the escort carrier *Hunter* was commanded by a Captain RNVR, and had another escort carrier under her orders commanded by a junior RN captain. Other RNVR officers commanded important bases, staff departments and escort groups. The least dilution of skill was found among the officers of the biggest ships. The battleship *Duke of York* in April 1945 still had regular RN officers as captain, commander, first lieutenant, gunnery, torpedo and navigating officers and all ten engineer officers – but she also had twenty-three RNVR officers in various ranks up to Lieutenant-Commander. The Fleet Air Arm by the closing year of the war was almost an RNVR monopoly. The COs of fighter squadrons were typically Lieutenant-Commanders of the 1941-2 entries.[10] Many RNVR officers made distinguished contributions to other aspects of the war effort – none more distinctive than the feat of Lieutenant David James, captured in February 1943 when MGB 79 was sunk in a fight off the Hook of Holland, who subsequently escaped from the German naval prisoner-of-war camp at Westertimke near Bremen, wearing his own uniform with its wavy stripes (unfamiliar to German officials), and carrying forged papers identifying him as a Lieutenant Bugerov of the Bulgarian Navy.[11]

Petty officers were at the centre of many of the Navy's manning difficulties, for the Navy expected of them a combination of qualities which could not be generated anything like as fast as raw numbers of men could be recruited. As the Admiralty observed before the war,

> Petty officers are not advanced to that rating solely as a result of seniority and on passing examinations. They must possess personality and tact, and be ready to accept the responsibility of their position. They should work at all times for the well-being and efficiency of the service as a whole. They should set an example of loyalty and discipline.[12]

Petty officers were especially scarce in the new rating branches like Radar and Asdic, for the branches grew much faster than the ratings could gain the experience to be advanced to petty officer. The US Navy (which had no non-substantive rates) promoted petty officers much more freely, and thought the Royal Navy should do the same, but US observers also noticed with some surprise that British naval officers in wartime, so many of whom were

4

inexperienced, were able to lean a good deal on the skill and knowledge of their petty officers:

> For example the signalmen not only read but interpret the signals. They always tell the OOD[13] the meaning of the signal but not the signal itself. They also know the tactical publications very thoroughly. The officers were not concerned with such matters, except the captain who knew the meaning of all the signals . . . [Most of the officers] did not have even a working knowledge of the equipment with which they worked. They did not seem interested in such matters. This is no doubt due to the great reliance placed on their petty officers.[14]

The US Navy faced even worse shortages of experience, but its response was the rote learning of standard solutions to common difficulties. In the first year of the war it was common for destroyer escorts, and sometimes even larger ships, to commission with no qualified watchkeepers. The escort carrier USS *Nassau*, to take an extreme example, commissioned in August 1942 with nobody but the captain qualified to stand a watch, and no officer who had ever fired a gun.[15]

For the Royal Navy the most precious petty officer was the coxswain, the senior chief petty officer of a warship up to destroyer size. The minimum formal qualification was at least three years qualified for petty officer, and at least five years served in the rates of leading hand and petty officer, which meant that in a small ship in which most of the lower deck were Hostilities Only, the coxswain would be one of the few peacetime regulars, possibly the only one. Normally he combined the roles of Master-at-Arms and Supply CPO, in charge of lower-deck discipline and food. In action and at critical moments (though not usually as a routine), he actually steered the ship, as his title of 'coxswain' implied. Always the coxswain was the captain's confidential adviser on the morale and feelings of his men:

> The Coxswain in particular has an especial position in the ship's company. There is no reason why he should not be a Second Officer of the Watch at sea. He should be a constant link between the Captain and the messdeck. He should know of any bad feeling in any mess; of any leading hand who is running his mess badly. If he can have an office of his own, his position is greatly enhanced. He must have the respect, but also the confidence of the ratings. He must be capable of reprimanding the other Petty Officers. He must have the welfare of the ship's company consistently at heart. If the junior ratings call him 'Sir', so much the better, and he should see that the

other Petty Officers when on duty are addressed in a manner befitting their state.[16]

To quote another American who served in the wartime RNVR, the coxswain was 'the key man below-decks, a man to lean on, the very pivot on which good discipline depends. This strong faithful arm . . . a tower of strength, pointing the way for a ship's company.'[17] A tactless and hated officer of the destroyer *Laforey* was discreetly removed after the coxswain and two other CPOs had had a quiet word with the captain.[18]

At the same time as the regular officers and ratings were being diluted by newly trained 'Hostilities Only' personnel, the ships' complements were growing to man new weapons and equipment. From 1940 to 1945 the complements of the *King George V* Class battleships increased by 23 per cent, the *Dido* Class cruisers by 19 per cent and the *Javelin* Class destroyers by 18 per cent – and these were among the most modern warships in the Navy, designed with the latest weapons and equipment in view. The carriers were the worst case. The *Victorious* was launched in 1939 to carry thirty-three aircraft and by 1945 she carried sixty. In that period her full ship's company, including the air group, rose 67 per cent, from 1,236 to 2,065.[19]

Overcrowded ships multiplied the stresses on aircrew, who often operated from spartan airfields when they were ashore – which they could not help contrasting with the luxurious accommodation of peacetime RAF stations. In 1940 naval surgeons were alarmed by the excessive nervous stress imposed by naval flying, and the impossibility of adopting the RAF's solution to it (generous leave). Much of this anxiety arose from addressing a problem which was new to the Navy. About 5 per cent of carrier pilots experienced some sort of nervous breakdown, which by naval standards was an alarmingly high figure, the cause of which was not immediately clear. Fleet Air Arm morale was high and the intense strain of an RAF tour of duty was absent; naval airmen's experience was dominated not so much by casualties in action as by boredom, tiredness and loneliness, the cold and exhaustion of open cockpits and the high accident rate of carrier flying. Conditions were poor aboard the armoured carriers, where aircrew berthed in heat and poor ventilation below the waterline, while the escort carriers were 'no better than a slum environment'. Aboard *Nairana* in the Arctic,

I had time to be aware of great weariness: the perpetual pitch and roll of the ship, bitter cold, sleeplessness, dim smelly passageways, ladders to climb to the deck with the frozen metals of the handholds and the dragging pull of the safety lines, the squall of wind and snow sweeping across the forward well-deck on the way to the Operations Flat, the discomfort of oilskins and life-belts, the dimness and sudden brightness of lights, the dread of keen icy wind on the flight deck at dawn, the noise and vibration of aircraft engines and, above all else, a hatred and fear of the sea.[20]

Unfortunately, it was difficult to vary airmen's lives by allotting them a share of ship's duties, of which they knew too little to be useful:

There was no escape from it all. Your Corsair was in the hangar, one deck up. The flight-deck, that torrid arena in the grim game of life and death, was only two short ladders beyond that. Life was lived, utterly and completely, within a space of something like 10,000 square yards. Within that area we ate, slept, drank, chatted with our friends, attended church, watched films, took our exercise – and flew, landed or crashed our aircraft. Friendships became, if anything, too close, and the hurt [of losing friends] was all the more painful for that very reason.[21]

Doctors drawing on RAF experience tended to diagnose nervous stress as the consequence of constant danger, for which their prescription was regular leave on a fixed scale. Carrier airmen at sea had few chances to go on leave, and rather blamed leave for breaking up the morale and cohesion of the squadron. Naval practice developed of awarding flexible leave according to opportunity and need.[22]

'The Branch', as the Fleet Air Arm called itself, tended to keep a certain distance from the regular Navy:

In their training [airmen] were not taught much about ships' routine, and the 'fish-heads' (nickname for non-flying officers) certainly discouraged them gently from finding out. Each side preserved its own mystique.[23]

Visiting a big ship,

We found the atmosphere of a battleship's wardroom hospitable if a trifle formal. They, in turn, must have eyed critically our scruffy uniforms with their occasional foreign buttons (top buttons were frequently left undone to denote fighter pilots), string instead of shoelaces, paper collars, shapeless caps and half-Wellington boots.[24]

Engineering, as has been noted already, was a British weakness which was brought into high relief by the very long-range sustained steaming needed by the British Pacific Fleet. The talented engineer officer Commander Louis Le Bailly wrote a very influential report for Sir Bruce Fraser in which he analysed the difficulties which could be traced back to the eight-year training gap imposed by the Selborne Scheme. He identified five distinct problems: furnace brickwork damaged by contaminated fuel and prolonged high-speed steaming; leaking superheaters; leaking steam joints and glands; perpetual water shortages as the evaporators were unable to supply the demand of the boilers and ship's company; and primitive main machinery design with excessive fuel consumption. To these should be added poor ventilation and overloaded sanitation. Unlike many commentators, then and since, Le Bailly did not simply report that everything American was better. On the contrary, he praised the high abilities of the few (shore-based) specialist US engineers but acknowledged the poor quality of USN engineering ratings, who were unsupported at sea.[25] He might have added that the very poor engineering performance of wartime German surface ships makes other nations' achievements look much better.

The submarine service, which had long been a small private Navy with extremely high morale and performance (maximum wartime strength was just over 9,000 officers and men), preserved these standards through the Second World War in spite of the fact that it was no longer an all-volunteer force and suffered 38 per cent killed in action. By September 1942 only 69 per cent of regular RN officers had volunteered for submarines, and in 1941 there were cases of 'refusal of duty' among HO ratings drafted into submarines. By 1943 the proportion of reservist submarine officers (almost all RNVR) had risen to 60 per cent – but the wartime standards of the submarine captains' course (the 'Perisher') were not relaxed at all. Successful candidates faced with dangerous situations when exhausted and hung-over had to display quick and calm judgement. Wartime experience confirmed that only young officers were worth considering: Lieutenant-Commanders over five years' seniority were 'unlikely to inflict damage on the enemy, and should not be appointed to command operational submarines in time of war'.[26] These were the qualities of the best candidates:

> All accepted responsibility eagerly and were self-confident. They were strong willed, tenacious and determined; they were brave; and they possessed great physical and mental stamina. They all cared passionately for their ships' companies, had a strong sense of humour and many were surprisingly modest. Their professional experience and training had developed quick calculating brains, the ability to delegate, presence, and 'a good periscope eye'.[27]

The 'periscope eye' means natural three-dimensional vision and the capacity to size up the submarine's situation and understand how it develops. This is the verdict of a post-war 'pressed' submarine officer who, like Arthur Hezlet, never regretted the choice which had been forced on him:

> All these years later, it emerges as nothing short of an inspired appoint-ment for me, because in a submarine, you are required to become a respon-sible citizen from Day One. You have to grow up, quickly. The Submarine Service is nothing like being on board surface ships, which by and large tend not to sink, and anyway, if they do, are inclined to do so rather slowly, providing a very sporting chance to its company of surviving the event. In submarines, which are apt to sink rather suddenly, you are expected to understand and to be able to work every bit of equipment on board. I was thus required to become not only a semi-engineer, but also to learn in turn to be the Gunnery Officer, the Navigation Officer, the Communications Officer, the Electrical Officer, the Torpedo Officer, the Sonar Officer, before I could hope for front-line command in about six years' time. Suddenly I was to be permitted, in a position of responsibility, to undertake the very kind of work I had always liked most. It was exactly right for me – though I did not of course know it at the time.[28]

Perhaps the hardest test for the historian is to evoke in a few paragraphs the reality of life at sea in wartime in all its diversity. Popular histories sometimes paint a lurid picture of incessant deadly danger, but it would be more realistic to concentrate on permanent discomforts, overcrowding, and (in many seas) the constant awareness of the possibility of sudden attack – even though experienced people would have had some sense that the *probability* of attack was not very high. Even in the North Atlantic, where escorting convoys was as arduous and dangerous as anywhere, actual fighting was an ever-present possibility rather than a common reality. The captain of the destroyer *Ilex* cal-culated that in the last three months of 1942 his ship had been at sea in the Atlantic for seventy-three out of ninety-seven days and steamed 19,668 miles with no actual fighting at all.[29]

Statistics like this convey a dimension of reality, but they cannot convey what it felt like and smelled like to be there. This is Ordinary Seaman K. Stott writing to his wife from the ex-US destroyer *Rockingham* in December 1941:

> Lying in my bunk last night I tried to catalogue some of the things I shall remember about destroyer life. I think they would fall into three catego-ries, smells, noises and sights, in that order. I don't think I shall ever forget the hot reek of fuel oil; the alcoholic gush of sweetness, vaguely distasteful, when damp demerara sugar is opened up; the noise of crockery rattling in

the cages during the night as the ship rolls and heaves; the sound of the boatswain's pipe, his 'wakey wakey'; the sight, from the bridge, of the stern wallowing as the seas smash over her; the skyline swinging violently to port, and the funnels crazy against the sky, already seeming braced for the inevitable lurch to starboard that follows. I could go on: the hot, horrid smell of cigarette smoke coming up through the voice pipes when you are queasy, and haven't had a cigarette yourself for days; the peculiar shake she gives just before you know she is going to stop a heavy sea; the queer taste of a 'duff' made with flour that has gone slightly mouldy . . .[30]

Another slice of life at sea on convoy duty comes from a letter home written in January 1942 by Lieutenant-Commander Tobias Scott of the destroyer *Wishart*:

Although this job is much better than sitting in the Admiralty there are times one must admit when it rains and it is dark and it is blowing a gale and everything gets capsized and the galley fire gets swamped and you've run out of bread, fresh meat and vegetables, and you've lost your convoy and the chart is wet and you're rolling like hell with the sea on the quarter and the wind astern and funnel smoke coming over the bridge and the hours go slow and you know that when you do get in to harbour there won't be any eggs, milk or potatoes and that anyway you'll go straight to sea again as soon as you've oiled so why go in anyway and the glass is still falling so there's no hope of the blow letting up, and your steward brings you a cold dinner on a dirty plate . . .

But come the dawn and the sunlight and you see your convoy and you swell with pride and satisfaction and your heart gives a whoop and you say 'Look at 'em! We're bringing Home the Goods! What a wonderful chap I am! Now I'm doing a job worth doing!' And you exult as you let go the Banging Depth Charges on what you hope is a U-boat and you think Hooray! I, Tobias, am winning this war! Life is good and sweet and strong. Then a dollop of spray hits you in the back of the neck to put you in your place and the Midshipman's sight turns out to be right and he shows you the mistake in yours and you realize you're just a worm after all.[31]

All sorts of ships were badly overcrowded in wartime, cramped and dirty. By 1942 V&W Class destroyers, designed twenty-five years before for a complement of 115, were berthing 170. The corvettes were still more crowded for the reasons we have noted, but even the new River Class frigates commissioned with up to 150 per cent of their designed complement to man the new weapons and equipment which were constantly being added while they were building. To accommodate so many men more space was needed for ventilation ducts and fans, which could only be taken from accommodation. In the Tropics there was a high rate of prickly heat, boils, colds and dysentery, and men ashore were healthier than afloat. Those who could find space to sling their hammocks were allowed only 21 inches width a man. Even in a bigger ship like the old cruiser *Emerald* 'passageways are obstructed by lockers and men asleep for whom there is not sufficient room in the mess decks', and in the East Indies many found it more comfortable to sleep on deck.[32] Closed up in heavy weather British ships were badly ventilated, and lower-deck culture did not much favour fresh air even when it was available. Discomfort was multiplied when dressed for action wearing anti-flash gear. With the constant fear of a torpedo, men slept badly in mess-decks with poor escape routes. The Royal Navy favoured open bridges (and converted the US Navy to its view), calculating that 30–50 per cent of first contacts were made by eye even when most ships had radar, and that officers (who had responsibility) tended to spot danger before lookouts. Heavy rolling and constant seasickness exhausted even those accustomed to the sea, degrading judgement and performance. The prewar Navy assumed that real men could cope with cold and hardship, and only late in the war did it undertake operational research which revealed how far their abilities were affected by seasickness, exhaustion and cold. US-built ships were lavishly manned by British standards and even more overcrowded, ruthlessly stripped of everything inflammable or alcoholic but generously equipped with heads and showers – besides water-fountains, laundries and other luxuries which were regarded with suspicion by British admirals and sailors alike. A more surprising contrast was with the exiled Dutch Navy, which in spite of having no access to its home dockyards was reported as keeping its ships (both Dutch and British-built) cleaner and with better damage control than the Royal Navy's.[33]

Even a bigger and newer ship like the light cruiser *Ajax* (launched 1934) suffered from much of the overcrowding of the old destroyers. Her mess-decks had too few slinging billets for the number of hammocks, and too few kit lockers and racks for caps and ditty boxes. The 'bathrooms' had no baths, only basins and a few showers. Clothes one washed in a bucket, though there were some drying spaces. *Ajax* did have a NAAFI canteen and served meals by 'general messing' ('Jago's System'), in which the ship's cooks did all the cooking and messes collected their meals in large trays to carry back to their mess-decks to eat, whereas the older ships were fed by 'canteen messing', in which messes had to prepare their own meals and carry them to the galley to be cooked:[34]

After the meal, all the irritations of overcrowding seemed to be intensified. Every mess was 'washing up' at the same time; men carrying cans of hot water bumped into one another and into the ironwork; scraps of food mingled with fugitive potato peelings on the deck . . . On these occasions, when mugs and spoons and books were likely to be flung to and fro by the ship's crazy movement, when the narrow air between jumbled bodies and ammunition hoists was filled with steam and tobacco smoke, when shouts churned the thickening atmosphere; on these occasions a poor effete old gentleman in his late twenties may be forgiven for wandering off to sit on a depth-charge.[35]

But a better-placed rating like a writer might escape many of these vexations:

When one became established in any kind of craft, large or small, various dodges and perquisites were soon exploited. For instance, being in the pay section, I never slept in our mess – the office was much better – usually four of us slung our hammocks there. This was a great advantage; we had our card schools, chess matches, wrote our letters in more or less privacy and if we ever wanted a snack or a brew we always had the wherewithal to make one. Our office was next to the Gun Room pantry and we always kept the messman happy with his pay for services rendered in the form of cups of coffee and savoury snacks. Life is what you make it in the Navy.[36]

Naval rations were better than those of the army or the RAF, but badly cooked and often served on dirty dishes. Ratings wanted standard English food even in the tropics, and did not take well to foreign novelties like rice. Emergency-action messing in the Arctic was soup and hot pies – and the pies were an innovation. Rats were everywhere. Tinned food was popular, but an attempt to issue dried soup in submarines was unsuccessful. In the cruiser *Belfast* off the Normandy beaches in 1944 many men suffered from boils for want of fresh vegetables. In the tropics efforts were made to increase supplies of drinking water and issue salt and lime juice. British officers admired the well-equipped galleys of US-built ships, but rejected segregated American messes on principle, as destructive of mess-deck solidarity, and found American food too rich and sweet. The experience of British ships in the Pacific (and of visiting US ships with cafeteria messing) encouraged radical thoughts which were difficult to put into practice on the spot but which bore fruit aboard later British ships in the 1950s and 1960s.[37]

In the closing year of the war the chronic shortage of manpower in general, and particularly of skilled men trained to handle new weapons and equipment, was especially acute in the Indian Ocean and the Pacific, the far-thest waters from the home establishments where most naval training took place. The traditional naval master–apprentice system of training could not handle the need for mass-produced expertise and complex new training sys-tems had to be devised. For anti-submarine training alone the Royal Navy needed fifty submarines by early 1945, and many (now Allied) French and Ital-ian submarines were pressed into service as 'clockwork mice'.[38]

In May 1945 the Japanese heavy cruiser *Haguro* was sent from Singapore (now the base of the remaining few big Japanese ships still operational) to evacuate the garrison of the Andaman Islands. The British East Indies Fleet was warned by signals intelligence and the *Haguro* was sighted by aircraft from the escort carrier *Shah*, functioning (as was now normal) as a miniature fleet carrier, providing air cover for ships operating far away from the main fleets and fleet carriers. Five destroyers were sent to sweep up the Malacca Strait to intercept the *Haguro*. It was typical monsoon weather, with heavy rain squalls blotting out the radar echo at intervals. Ordinary Seaman Norman Poole, keep-ing the radar watch aboard one of the destroyers, reported sighting a dark shape in a squall thirty-four miles away, which he identified as a big ship. This was well beyond the range of Type 293 radar and there was no possible point of land there, so the officers on the bridge were sceptical. The leading radar operator and the radio mechanic adjusted the set, but Poole re-adjusted it and regained the contact. For an hour Poole demonstrated persistence 'almost to the point of insubordination' as they closed the contact which he alone had seen, but in the end he persuaded both his captain and the 'Captain D' of the destroyer flotilla that there really was something hiding in the rain cloud, so they mounted a classic night torpedo attack and sank the cruiser. The rate of 'ordinary seaman' indicated a new recruit who had completed his basic train-ing but not yet acquired any specialist skills. Poole could be expected to have learnt to march, to identify and salute an officer, to know port from starboard – but not to contradict the leading hand of a technical branch and several offi-cers. For this demonstration of competence and strength of character leading to a successful engagement Poole was awarded the Distinguished Service Medal.[39] The episode was a triumph, but it also illustrates some of the continu-ing difficulties springing from the rushed start of the RDF (Radar) branch in 1942 and the pressure on an inadequate number of trained operators. This was one of the factors pushing the Admiralty to establish a new Electrical Branch, which was instituted in January 1946.[40]

The morale of British ships' companies depended greatly on a rich tissue of traditional social activities. Cards and games like 'uckers' (a sort of ludo),

ship's pets, concert parties and fancy dress, fishing and sewing were all popular, and often involved officers and men together with the unofficial or official
consumption of alcohol. Naval language and customs such as 'Crossing the
Line' ceremonies or the sale of dead men's effects (a form of charitable collection for widows and orphans), fascinating to those new to the sea who were
carefully instructed in them, bonded recruits to their new way of life. The rum
issue was a daily high point of a ship's ceremonial life, though those younger
than twenty could not share it, and a significant minority preferred to declare
themselves 'total abstainers' and pocket the savings. In reality rum was an
almost universal currency afloat, involved in all sorts of commercial and social
life and attractive to the officially teetotal as much as to their shipmates. More
high-minded leisure activities revolved around ship's libraries, lectures by officers and discussion groups on current affairs. Anglican religious ceremonies
were required by law, though not universally popular. Catholic bishops insisted
that their faithful be allowed to go ashore to Mass when in port, but the Established Church preserved its monopoly at sea.[41]

The fact that the men of the Merchant Navy were better paid than the Royal
Navy was an obvious point of friction ashore, and sometimes afloat. There was
a legal mechanism which permitted merchant ships complete with their crews
to be taken up for naval service on what were called 'T124 Articles' (from the
Board of Trade form of that number), which obliged the men to observe naval
discipline and serve under martial law but allowed them to keep their Merchant Navy pay rates. Convoy rescue ships and rescue tugs were usually
manned on the T124 system, which amounted to double naval pay. Some escort
carriers were partly T124-manned, though the air groups were always Fleet Air
Arm. Most merchant ships had an old gun mounted aft as a defensive armament to discourage U-boats from surface attack, and many of the gun's crews
were borrowed from the army, which formed a Maritime Regiment of Artillery. By 1942 many merchant ships also had a serious light anti-aircraft armament, but usually manned by their own seamen. The mixture of pay and
conditions of service generated by these improvised wartime arrangements
was an obvious source of discontent, but in general it seems to have been
accepted as one among many wartime sacrifices. Seamen must have been aware
that though the Navy lost more than 8 per cent of its men killed in action, the
heaviest casualties of any of the armed services, the merchant fleet lost about
28,000 dead, roughly half of those whose ships were sunk.[42]

By 1944 the Admiralty foresaw a potentially serious morale problem. Until
that stage in the war British naval morale had been consistently high, but loom-
ing ahead was the prospect of a Japanese war which dragged on, possibly for

586 · LIFE IS WHAT YOU MAKE IT IN THE NAVY

years, after victory in Europe had allowed the other Services to demobilize at least their Hostilities Only personnel. The Admiralty calculated that one sailor would be released for every twenty soldiers. Fortunately, the sudden collapse of Japanese resistance before any large number of army or air force personnel had been sent East allowed the Navy to avoid the anticipated crisis.[43] In November 1944 Rear-Admiral R. K. Dickson was appointed to the new position of Chief of Naval Information, with a mission to 'sell' the Navy to the British public, to the American public and to itself. This was propelled by a rather alarmist report which played up the superiority of the RAF in handling the media. In fact the interwar and wartime Navy had an effective publicity policy and produced some classic films, notably Noël Coward's *In Which We Serve* in 1942. The new 1944 publicity policy, including the naval magazine *Ditty Box*, was a response to a new situation and an anticipated problem which never in the event arrived because of the sudden and unexpected Japanese surrender. In May 1945 Admiral Dickson gave a lecture to the Royal United Services Institute in which he coined the fine slogan that in the Navy 'All that is not Warfare is Welfare'.[44]

THIRTY-FOUR

Cape Deception
Policy and Operations 1944–1945

Any reader who has followed this book so far will not need to be persuaded that the Second World War was really a world war, in which the different theatres were all more or less connected with one another. If they are treated separately, however, as they so often are, it is less obvious that the culminating points, the decisive campaigns, occurred at different times in different places by sea and land. In the North Atlantic the U-boat campaign which started in 1940 tipped suddenly and dramatically in the spring of 1943 and (except in the Arctic) had almost collapsed by the summer. In the Mediterranean campaign of 1940–43 the distances were for the most part shorter than in the Atlantic (though the lines of supply and reinforcement were very long indeed), but both the British on one side and the Germans and Italians on the other had to mount major amphibious operations to deploy their armies, the tides of victory ebbed and flowed repeatedly, and the participants changed as important navies were driven out of the Mediterranean war (France), came to join it (the USA) or changed sides (Italy). In the Pacific there was very little fighting until the dramatic Japanese offensive of December 1941 started six months of almost unbroken conquests, after which most of the ocean was more or less at peace again for almost two years after the battle of Midway in June 1942. There was intense local fighting in the South Pacific and briefly in the South China Sea and Indian Ocean, but the major fleets of Japan, the United States and Britain were too far apart and too busy rebuilding their strength to restart major campaigns until the beginning of 1944. For the most part the peaks of the naval war in different parts of the world did not coincide, indeed could not, because in so many cases the same ships were doing the fighting in different seas in succession. The Japanese in particular, and the British for much of the time, could not deploy more than one major fleet each, and could only act at widely scattered points across the globe with the help of a great deal of long-range steaming. The United States alone had the resources to build up major new fleets stationed in both Eastern and Western Hemispheres at the same time, but not before 1943–5 when her belated re-armament programmes had borne fruit, and the hostile fleets of Italy and Germany had been reduced or eliminated.

One significant psychological factor is worth noting which by this stage in the war weighed on both US and British admirals. By 1943 the Royal Navy had lost to submarine attack the battleships *Barham* and *Royal Oak*, the carriers *Courageous*, *Ark Royal* and *Eagle*, to heavy gunfire the battleship *Hood* and the carrier *Glorious*, to Italian frogmen the *Queen Elizabeth* and the *Valiant*, and to air attack the *Prince of Wales* and the *Repulse*. German air attack in the Mediterranean had shown that three inches of deck armour was by no means sufficient to protect the new carriers from dive-bombers. These losses were not just a severe reduction in British naval strength, but the sinking of the *Hood*, the *Ark Royal* and the *Prince of Wales* were real shocks to the self-confidence of even the toughest senior officers. In the middle years of the war, they forced the Royal Navy into defensive strategies in the Mediterranean and the Indian Ocean, and for some time they obliged it to abandon the China Seas and the Pacific altogether. Even when they were able to take up the offensive again, hard experience had taught them caution. Much the same was true of the impact of war losses on the US Navy. Pearl Harbor above all persuaded a generation of American admirals that Japanese naval airmen were supermen, and Japanese naval aircraft vastly superior to their own. The sinking of the *Lexington*, *Yorktown*, *Wasp* and *Hornet* – leaving only the *Saratoga* and *Enterprise* surviving of the pre-war carriers – reinforced the idea.[1] The disastrous South Pacific battles of 1943 then taught the USN never to fight the Japanese by night. The effects of these lessons likewise were slow to fade, and in 1944–5 US admirals approached Japanese waters with trepidation long after the real balance of forces, as we can assess it with the benefit of hindsight, had ceased to justify so much caution.

From 1943 the Western Allies were able to deploy growing naval and shipping resources against progressively weaker enemies. From this stage in the war the growing Allied control of the seas exploited the power of distance to concentrate strength and evade or disperse enemy resistance. This command of the sea ultimately rested on powerful warships, but at an everyday level the most important practical instrument of control of the sea was the mass production of simple cargo ships – 'Liberty Ships' and others – to transport goods, supplies and troops around the world, which was as critical an advantage in the strategic as in the economic dimension. Next in importance came landing ships and craft, which were needed for nearly all the major campaigns, and never available in sufficient numbers. Although the United States and Britain cancelled enormous fleets of warships when it became clear that the naval war was almost over in 1944, the atomic bomb ended the war ashore much faster than anyone had anticipated, and they still had a great many warships under construction when the war at sea ended in 1945. From 1943 the strategic situation was changing at bewildering speed as the possibilities and uncertainties increased. This threw a mass of critical decisions on the Allies, who were now able to reach for objectives which had been impossible, but still had only crude and improvised mechanisms for collective planning. Hitherto the Allies' stock response to delicate decisions had been to avoid them as long as possible, and tackle them as slowly as possible. Now it was urgent to confront the decisions on which victory in the war and power in the post-war world would probably turn. Admirals, generals and politicians who were in principle on the same side but were also entrenched rivals, now approached the long-anticipated decisive moments which would shape the fortunes of their countries, their services, and themselves.

By the Trident and Quadrant conferences (May and August 1943 respectively) the Western alliance was largely united behind the decision to invade German-occupied Western Europe in the early summer of 1944, but in the Pacific different branches of the US forces still promoted rival strategies. The US Navy planned to capture the Gilbert Islands (Kiribati) as a stepping-stone to the Marshall Islands in the central Pacific and hoped by this advance to bring on the long-desired fleet action with the Japanese. It was also likely to provoke the first serious test of the new fleet tactics laid out in PAC-10. The first stage was Operation 'Galvanic', the attack on the Gilbert Islands in November 1943, concentrating on Tarawa, which had the only airfield in the group. This costly victory (the US Marines lost more than a thousand killed in three days) provided important lessons for the next advance, Operation 'Flintlock' in January and February 1944, in which the US forces invaded the Marshall Islands and occupied the atolls of Eniwetok, Kwajalein (where the Japanese were in the process of building an airfield), and Majuro (which was suitable as a fleet anchorage). The next target in the US Navy's advance was the big atoll of Truk to the westward, which has the best anchorage in the central Pacific and had become the main Japanese fleet base. The geography of Truk was unfavourable to direct assault, so the US hoped to destroy the airfields and shipping with carrier air strikes. Operation 'Hailstone', carried out on 17–18 February, was an outstanding success, except that the Japanese had foreseen the attack and most of their ships had already left Truk – a disappointment for those who still believed that victory in a fleet action was the only real victory, but a vindication for the new techniques of long-range seaborne air attack which were now a serious possibility. By February eight of the new *Essex* Class fleet carriers had reached the Pacific Fleet, giving it the air-striking strength which it had lacked for two years past.

In the spring of 1944 both sides were preparing what they intended to be decisive offensives. The Japanese Army launched a major southward advance code-named 'Ichigo' which by February 1945 had overrun most of central and southern China. The Japanese Navy re-organized the bulk of its warships into the First Mobile Fleet (somewhat in the style of an American Task Force), and based it at Singapore, where it could draw oil from Sumatra nearby, and was ready for the fleet action expected to occur somewhere to the east of the Philippines. At about the same time the US Navy adopted British-style fighter direction with carriers sharing a common screen.[2]

General MacArthur, the self-styled 'Supreme Commander' in the South-West Pacific, demanded that he and his American-Australian army should lead the offensive against Japan from New Guinea through the Philippines to Hong Kong and China, with the US 7th Fleet under Admiral Thomas Kincaid acting as his private navy. This would please American public opinion by beginning the liberation of China, offer the USAAF Chinese airfields from which their new B-29 bombers could reach Japan, and above all satisfy MacArthur's vanity by allowing him to reconquer the islands he had lost in 1942. As the US Navy soon realized, this was a long and winding trail to gratify a monstrous ego, and there were better alternatives coming into view. Japan had hitherto been out of range of the US Navy's Central Pacific command under Admiral Nimitz at Pearl Harbor, but the successful air raid on Truk in February 1944 opened the possibility of a thousand-mile leap northwards to capture Guam, Saipan and Tinian in the Mariana Islands. The Japanese were (correctly) reported to have new aircraft of exceptionally long range, and the prospect of attacking far out of range of any US airfields, relying entirely on carrier-borne aircraft, made US admirals nervous. Nevertheless, the decision was taken for Vice-Admiral Raymond Spruance's Fifth Fleet to attack the Marianas in June and July 1944, relying on air cover from the seven fleet and eight light carriers of Rear-Admiral Marc Mitscher's Fast Carrier Force. Spruance was a battleship admiral commanding the fast battleship force, by temperament precise and careful, and automatically regarded by airmen such as Mitscher as a hidebound formalist and an enemy to the aviators' ambitions to win the war by themselves. The Japanese fleet likewise was commanded by battleship men whose objective was to defeat the Americans in a great fleet action. As soon as the US forces landed on Saipan on 15 June, the First Mobile Fleet sailed from the Philippines to meet it.[3]

The two fleets never met, because the cautious Spruance (true to type in the airmen's opinion) kept his ships well clear of the dangers of a night battle, and the Battle of the Philippine Sea (as it is usually called in English) consisted largely of heavy American air attacks on a Japanese fleet still strong in ships and aircraft, skilfully handled by Vice-Admiral Ozawa Jizaburō, but crippled by a shortage of experienced airmen. Although the very long-range Japanese aircraft as usual located their enemy first, the superior American fighter direction and radar-laid anti-aircraft guns shot down most of the attackers. The Japanese lost three carriers and several hundred aircrew; the Americans lost no ships and only about twenty airmen – but many US airmen still bewailed Spruance's caution, which, they claimed, had cost them their 'decisive victory'. Late on 20 June, when he was sure the Japanese were in full retreat, Spruance released Mitscher, who mounted an evening strike at extreme range. The US Navy still had only a limited ability to fly by night and many of these aircraft never found their way back to their carriers, but the sea was calm, and 143 of the 177 missing airmen were rescued from their rubber dinghies by destroyers the following day. By the end of August the Marianas were in US hands and new airfields were under construction.[4]

At roughly the same time as the US Navy in the Pacific was demonstrating the new techniques of naval air attack, on the other side of the world Air Marshal Arthur Harris of Bomber Command was demonstrating how not to use heavy bombers by a series of night attacks on Berlin, at extreme range, in the face of strong anti-aircraft and fighter defences. Sir Charles Portal and much of his Air Staff were by now sceptical of or openly hostile to 'Bomber' Harris, but he still had strong political support. The result was a chain of heavy losses culminating in the disastrous Nuremberg raid of 30–31 March 1944 in which 11.8 per cent of the British heavy bombers were destroyed in one night for virtually no effect. At the same time the USAAF's daylight raids also suffered serious losses, but at least caused heavy damage in Germany. After this even Harris admitted defeat and sought long-range night-fighter escorts.[5]

In the same period (January–March 1944) the Allied air forces were learning to operate with growing effectiveness over the sea. The adoption of ASV Mk.III radar on 10cm wavelength did not at first sink many U-boats (partly because the USAAF lacked an equivalent to the British Leigh Light), but it had a destructive effect on U-boat morale as the Germans soon realized that they were being tracked again. To the further damage of morale, U-boat command was deceived into believing that the older metre-wave Métox radar-warning sets were somehow betraying the U-boats and ordered them to be removed – at a period when they were still effective in detecting the majority of Allied airborne radar. From February 1944 the Admiralty was adopting large Arctic convoys, with new escorts and stronger anti-aircraft armament for the merchant ships. In March the eastbound convoy J W 58, with two escort carriers, was fought through several U-boat groups with no losses at all out of the convoy, but four U-boats and six German aircraft destroyed. Then the return convoy RA 59 sank three more U-boats for the loss of one merchantman. Overall, the British escorts covering Arctic convoys in the first five months of 1944 sank thirteen U-boats. *BdU* comforted itself with claims of sunken escorts which were mostly wishful thinking, but in April the Luftwaffe withdrew from the Arctic convoy operations after heavy losses. At the same period R A F aircraft detached from the 'bomber stream' going eastward towards Berlin resumed high-altitude radar-guided minelaying of the southern Baltic, which caused severe disruption to U-boats under training and to iron-ore shipments from Sweden. In contrast to the costly failure of the bombing of Berlin, this was a model of the effective use of heavy bombers with minimal casualties. By this time Swedish iron-ore exports to Germany, though as profitable as ever, were a growing embarrassment to Sweden as it became ever more obvious that Germany was losing the war. In March the Swedes refused to accept any more iron-ore cargoes for Rotterdam, putting the railways under huge strain. Then in May 1944 British Mosquito light bombers mined the Kiel Canal.[6]

The sinking of the *Scharnhorst* in December 1943 showed that a radar-equipped enemy could fight as well by night as by day, which shocked the German naval command. Until German ships could get adequate radar fire-control it was obvious what would happen to the *Tirpitz* if she were caught at sea. Only Dönitz was still unconvinced, but Hitler realistically assessed the battleship as of little more use until she could be provided with air cover. In April 1944 a successful Fleet Air Arm carrier dive-bomber attack knocked her out for a further three months. In September she was fatally damaged by 12,000lb 'Tallboy' bombs from R A F Lancaster heavy bombers, and finally destroyed by a further attack in November 1944. In retrospect both British and German naval staffs quite reasonably calculated that although she had only once ever fired her guns in anger, her silent presence as a 'fleet in being' had exercised real pressure on naval strategy as far away as Japan.[7]

After the *Tirpitz* was crippled in September 1944 the Allied Arctic convoys resumed, though at the same time the Germans were able to evacuate their troops from the Polar coast with minimal losses. The very poor Asdic conditions in the Arctic helped the U-boats; by the autumn of 1944 their losses were down to the 1942 level and morale was good. But at the same period attacks on other German shipping grew rapidly. In August Sweden withdrew insurance for ships trading to Germany, which increased German shipping costs by 25 per cent. Then in September Finland's armistice with the Soviet Union shut her ports to German ships and Sweden finally closed her Baltic ports to Axis shipping, so that German iron-ore imports could only be shipped from Narvik, and only in German ships.[8]

By early 1944 Allied attention and reinforcements in European waters were concentrated on the forthcoming landings in France.

The Allies had initiated long-range discussion of the reconquest of occupied Europe as early as the 'Argonaut' Conference in June 1942, and in April 1943 Lieutenant-General Frederick Morgan was appointed as 'Chief of Staff to the Supreme Allied Commander' to begin detailed planning. The Supreme Commander himself had not yet been named, and throughout the remainder of 1943 Morgan was forced to defer numerous major decisions until he appeared. Meanwhile Morgan was ordered to prepare an assault on a three-division front, though intelligence indicated that the Germans had fifty-nine divisions in France, forty-one of them north of the River Loire and within 150 miles at most of the Normandy coast. In the event, on 'D' Day itself in June, the Allies committed thirty-nine divisions to Operation 'Overlord' (twenty-three infantry, twelve armoured and four airborne) – approximately equal to German strength in or near Normandy, but only if the Allied armies could be landed more or less intact. As a rule of thumb, soldiers assumed that an attack required at least three times the strength of the defenders, but in this case the Germans appeared to command a large initial superiority, and Morgan by himself did not have the authority to address the problem. Not until December was Dwight Eisenhower named as the Allied Supreme Commander. Although almost devoid of fighting experience, Eisenhower had already shown outstanding qualities of leadership and diplomacy in the Mediterranean campaign, and Roosevelt had clearly identified that these were what was needed. His deputy Supreme Commander, Air Chief Marshal Sir Arthur Tedder, and his three service senior officers, Admiral Sir Bertram Ramsay, General Sir Bernard Montgomery and Air Marshal Sir Trafford Leigh-Mallory, were all highly experienced – and all British, which itself explains why the Supreme Commander had to be an American. Eisenhower's greatest achievement was to set up a genuinely international staff, harmonious and efficient. In a war marked by a number of very long-range amphibious operations, Operation 'Overlord' was conspicuously short range, as the two sides were divided only by the width of the English Channel. A key advantage this conferred on the Allied planners was the possibility of providing intense air support from British airfields within the operational radius of a Spitfire, which was about 150 miles. The other side of the same coin was the danger of German air attack from nearby airfields in France, which the planners took very seriously.[9]

Given that the Germans might easily outnumber the attackers, if not at the moment of the landing then soon after, a major dilemma for the planners was how and where to embark the massive reinforcements which would have to reach the invasion beaches before German counter-attacks could. As soon as Montgomery arrived in January 1944 he insisted with his characteristic asperity that a three-division front was not enough, and the plans were changed to accommodate a five-division landing plus glider-borne or parachute units. The actual landing date ('D-Day' in the terminology of the US Army) was deferred a month to 5 June 1944 to accumulate more landing craft, which left only seventeen weeks to rework the plans on virtually double the previous scale.[10]

Allied shipping movements along the English Channel were in many cases within radar and even visual range of the Germans, and with landing ships and craft spread all along the south coast of England and beyond by the spring of 1944, it was obvious to the Germans that a landing was coming somewhere along the length of the Channel. It was extremely important to the British to conceal as long as possible when and where the blow would fall. British generals knew how thinly their manpower was stretched, and had not forgotten the bloody failures of frontal assault on the Western Front twenty-five years before and at Dieppe two years before. They had the strongest incentive to deceive the enemy as to where and how the attack would come. British amphibious operations therefore tended to rely heavily on stealth. They sent in engineers by night to disarm beach obstacles, whereas American generals tended to prefer overwhelming force and crushing victory, and were apt to regard deception as a near relative of cowardice. This philosophical difference, born of varied experience, created sharp differences of opinion between the Allies. With the bulk of the assault forces assembling early in 1944, less than six months before the planned attack, there was too little time available to develop and impose on British, American, Canadian and Polish officers a common system of amphibious assault tactics.[11]

About 7,000 ships were assembled, including seven battleships, twenty-four cruisers, two monitors, thirty-five destroyers and 2,775 landing craft of sundry types, to land 132,715 troops in the initial waves. The critical strategic decision was where the assault should be concentrated, and the obvious choice would have been the narrowest point of the Channel, across the Dover Strait between Kent and the Pas-de-Calais. Here, however, the French coastline was mostly lined by cliffs and heavily fortified, so the Allied planners chose instead to land on a sixty-mile stretch of the coast of Normandy between the mouth of the Seine and the Cotentin Peninsula. This shore was less forbidding and there were a range of promising beaches more or less sheltered from the prevailing wind. The elaborate British deception plan was extraordinarily successful in fooling the Germans that the main Allied landing would be in the Pas-de-Calais. Four weeks *after* D-Day the Germans still regarded the Normandy landing as a feint and held twenty-two divisions in reserve to meet an entirely fictitious First US Army Group which they believed was waiting in East Anglia to open another front.[12]

A major problem for the Allied planners was the serious shortage of amphibious landing ships, most of them built and monopolized by the US Navy, which was conspicuously reluctant to support a largely British operation. This in turn bore on the scarcity of major ports along the south coast of England. The naval ports of Portsmouth and Plymouth would be intensively used by the Navy. The largest remaining port on the south coast was Southampton, in peacetime predominantly a passenger port handling transatlantic liners. Ports east of Southampton (the Isle of Wight, the Solent, Shoreham and Newhaven) were assigned to the eastern, British, beaches in Normandy (Gold, June, Sword), and those west of Southampton (Poole, Weymouth, Portland, Torbay, Salcombe and round to the Bristol Channel) belonged to the western, American, beaches (Utah and Omaha), with Southampton divided between the two. Two airborne divisions and five infantry divisions were to land at dawn on 'D-Day' morning, with convoys of follow-up shipping coming from the Thames and Plymouth timed to arrive on the following tide that afternoon. Thereafter reinforcements were planned to arrive at a rate of one and one-third divisions a day. Given moderate weather, medium landing craft such as the Landing Craft Tank (LCT) could easily cross the Channel on their own bottoms, but a major construction programme was needed to build slips and hards in creeks and harbours along the south coast where their vehicles could be embarked. Numerous moorings had to be laid where the landing craft could lie until the moment came to embark their troops and vehicles. An enormous training programme had to be rapidly put into effect to train landing-craft officers and men (not all belonging to the Navy, for many were drawn from the Royal Marines). There was a huge variety of specialist skills and functions needed afloat, and the British supply of skilled manpower was already stretched alarmingly thin. 'Manpower' was no longer the proper term, for this was the first major military operation in which women participated, notably the

WRNS officers who at the last moment came aboard landing ships and craft to deliver their secret orders. In many cases the definition of 'officer' had to be stretched to its limits. One 'Landing Barge Kitchen' (whose function was to provide hot meals to the crews of small craft working off the invasion beaches) had a crew of twenty-five commanded by a midshipman RNVR aged just nineteen.[13]

The landing craft and landing ships could not accommodate the assault forces they carried for long, so it was necessary that they should embark their men, vehicles and secret orders at the last moment and then move along the coast towards the 'Spout', as it was called. This was the meeting area off the Nab Tower south-east of the Isle of Wight where the coastal convoys were distributed into one of ten parallel swept channels across the Channel. These led through the German minefields and into the Bay of the Seine where the five landing beaches lay in an arc stretching from a point south of Saint-Vaast-la-Hougue at the western end, to the little port of Ouistreham at the mouth of the River Orne at the eastward end. This required very precise manoeuvres, and to handle hundreds of slow and clumsy landing craft in close company without collisions the planners adopted the system of 'Equal Speed' signals originally devised by the mid-Victorians to handle the early steam men-of-war.[14]

A major worry for Allied planners was their respective air forces. Both the RAF and the USAAF were ardently committed to strategic bombing, which over the winter of 1943–4 had handed the Luftwaffe a major victory, but neither was willing to contribute to 'Overlord'. Air Marshal Harris of Bomber Command eventually obeyed a direct order from Eisenhower to attack the French railway system, but as late as April 1944 many Allied airmen were still refusing to obey orders, and many senior officers were refusing to impose discipline on their men. But the British and American air forces did eventually achieve a real victory against their better judgement. After catastrophic losses and a collapse of morale, both bomber forces were forced to seek long-range fighter escorts, which not only protected the bombers but forced an air battle that inflicted crippling losses on the German fighter force by the time of the Allied landings in early June. Until thirty-six hours before the Normandy landings, however, both air forces had flatly refused to adopt forward air controllers, whose value in directing air attacks in direct support of troops on the ground had been amply proved in the Mediterranean campaigns. As a result, for the first month of the fighting in Normandy the Allied air forces were ineffectual where they were most urgently needed.[15]

The plans for Operation 'Neptune' (the naval component of 'Overlord') were largely fixed by careful calculations of moon and tide, and there was limited scope for delay to avoid bad weather. This was exactly the crisis which Eisenhower faced on 5 June when he received the weather forecast for the next twenty-four hours predicting a gale.

Specifically, the forecast spoke of a gale on the 5th, followed by a short lull and then another gale. It was possible to impose a delay of twenty-four hours, gambling that the lull would suffice to make a landing possible, but any longer wait would require the whole elaborate assault arrangements to be stood down, and probably reveal the plans to the Germans. Therefore, Eisenhower decided to postpone 'D-Day' for twenty-four hours only. It was later discovered that he had drafted a communiqué accepting full responsibility for defeat, but he never needed to use it. The Germans, who had received much the same weather forecast as Eisenhower had, relaxed on the assumption that there could be no amphibious operation for days if not weeks, and failed even to report a number of vessels which had missed the signal postponing 'D-Day' and appeared off the French coast on 5 June. No notice was taken of the BBC French Service reading a couplet of the poet Verlaine, which the Germans knew was a pre-arranged alert to the French Resistance for some big operation. Even when the assault forces came ashore on 6 June, the Germans were astonishingly slow to react. Parachutists, both real men and dummies, had been scattered at various points to spread confusion, which was gratifyingly successful. Four out of the five landing beaches were secured quickly with only moderate casualties. The only near disaster was Omaha Beach, where General Omar Bradley insisted on a frontal assault in daylight, the preliminary bombardment was well off-target, the amphibious tanks were almost all swamped and drowned, and the landing ships discharged their troops twelve miles out into a choppy sea. The result was chaos and heavy casualties, but the attackers substantially outnumbered the defenders, the Germans had no transport and could not move, and slowly men of the experienced 1st US Division began to seize some initiative and fight their way inland. Overall, 'Neptune' was remarkably successful, and by the end of the first day's fighting on 6 June, a total of 132,715 men had been landed. Even Omaha Beach, the unluckiest, suffered only about 3,000 casualties. The 'Overlord' campaign as a whole was easily the largest amphibious operation in history, involving 1,931,885 soldiers, 649,554 airmen and 285,000 naval personnel. There was still months of heavy fighting to follow, and the German army was far from collapse, but this was their last opportunity to win a victory which might, just might, have made it possible to discuss terms of peace short of absolute surrender. By mid-June the Allied armies had landed thirteen infantry, three airborne and three armoured divisions: half a million soldiers and 77,000 vehicles. By 5 July, twenty-nine days after the initial assault, there were a million men ashore in France.[16] On 25 July the War Diary of Admiral Theodor Krancke, the senior German naval officer in France, quoted a decyphered Allied signal listing the quantities of supplies and men recently unloaded. 'The amounts stated represent many times the reserves of material and men moved up to the front by us,' the admiral noted, 'and present a clear picture of the enemy's superiority, and of the advantages of seaborne supplies, given sea and air superiority.'[17]

By the formal end of the Normandy campaign in late August (Paris fell on the 25th), 830,000 British Empire troops and 1.2 million US troops had been landed with 440,000 vehicles and 3.1 million tons of stores.[18]

The skilful German defence of Western Europe prolonged the campaign and tied up many of the troops and landing craft which were urgently needed in the Far East. The Scheldt estuary was not finally cleared until 26 October 1944, opening access to the port of Antwerp, which itself had been captured sixty days before. Fortunately the final German offensive in the Ardennes in December failed to reach Antwerp, and thanks to the success of the Allied Mediterranean landings the ports of Marseilles and Toulon were also available to bring in reinforcements. Overall the 'short-sea' cross-Channel offensive within range of ample land-based air cover was extremely cost-effective compared with the much longer distances of the Mediterranean and the Middle East, and the even greater distances to be crossed in the Pacific. Between June and December 1944 the Western Front was supported by 17 per cent of the shipping tonnage which had been needed in the summer of 1942 to sustain the Middle East and India. Seven million tons deadweight had supplied twenty-seven divisions in the Mediterranean; only one million tons was needed to support ninety divisions in the West.[19]

By May 1944 Admiral Somerville in the Indian Ocean had a respectable modern fleet with four new or rebuilt battleships (*Queen Elizabeth*, *Renown*, *Valiant* and the French *Richelieu*), the carriers *Illustrious* and *Saratoga*, seven cruisers and sixteen modern destroyers. In May this force sailed from Ceylon to mount a strike against the dockyard and oil refinery of Surabaya on Java, refuelling at sea on the way in Exmouth Gulf on the north-west coast of Australia. This was a valuable and instructive opportunity to operate with a US carrier, but the *Saratoga* then returned to America for a refit. In July and August, now with three British carriers, Somerville was able to mount further air strikes against Japanese targets on Sumatra, which gave the Fleet Air Arm squadrons excellent practice and reduced the Japanese output of aviation fuel by two-thirds. At the same time stronger British and US submarine forces based in Australia pushed their patrols into the Malacca Straits and later the Java Sea. American and British aircraft flying from India laid mines in the Gulf of Siam and later the Malacca Straits.[20]

The original reason South-East Asia Command had been set up and given to Mountbatten, the specialist in combined operations, had been to mount amphibious operations in the Indian Ocean in support of the British recon-quest of Burma, and the American ambitions to link up with the Chinese, but in the event little of this was possible. All the available landing craft were eaten up by the Normandy landings, the Mediterranean or the Pacific, and in the end the reconquest of Burma could only be achieved by a lengthy and exhaust-ing overland campaign from India. The first attempt to mount air raids on Japan from Chinese airfields in June and July 1944 demonstrated the prohibi-tive logistic cost of even a minimal effort sustained by air transport over the Himalayas. The situation was frustrating for Mountbatten, especially by the spring of 1944 when Somerville's Eastern Fleet (operating mostly within South-East Asia Command's area, but almost entirely outside Mountbatten's control) was acquiring the means to take the offensive. The two admirals preserved civil relations, but neither was happy with the situation, and there were objective reasons for Admiral Cunningham, First Sea Lord since October 1943, to ponder alternatives. Somerville had been two and a half years in an arduous command, and Cunningham needed an admiral of his charm, fighting experience and toughness to stand up to Admiral King, so in August 1944 Somerville relieved Sir Percy Noble at the British Admiralty Delegation in Washington, and Sir Bruce Fraser transferred from the Home Fleet to take Somerville's place.[21]

Fraser had been Churchill's first choice to succeed Admiral Pound as First Sea Lord, and sending him to the Far East might at first sight seem to be a demotion, but the political and strategic significance of this most distant Brit-ish naval responsibility was rising rapidly. Two interconnected political and strategic questions had to be answered: how if at all the British could re-enter the China Seas and the South Pacific; and whether the United States would tolerate a British return to what had formerly been part of her empire. The British Chiefs of Staff and the Foreign Office were clear that it was essential that Britain should do her utmost to build on the wartime alliance and pre-serve the friendship of the USA after the war. They knew that there were still many isolationist Americans who believed that they had been lured into a war to restore the British Empire, and the only convincing argument against them would be a wholehearted effort to support the US war against Japan. Some American leaders such as the long-serving Secretary of State Cordell Hull understood that Britain had to be seen to take a full share in the war against

Japan to avoid post-war resentments such as had arisen over war debts in the 1920s. On the other hand, the huge distances involved, the now serious shortage of shipping, and the very urgent need to restore the British economy made it more than doubtful how much Britain was capable of doing. For the British Chiefs of Staff, the most embarrassing difficulty was that Churchill, who could usually be relied upon to appreciate the diplomatic and grand strategic aspects of any question, argued that Britain should limit her effort to the Indian Ocean. He was particularly keen on a plan to invade Sumatra, which might open the Malacca Strait, cut off the Japanese from their main source of oil and lead on towards Singapore – all which in American eyes would certainly look like using US aid to rebuild the British Empire just as the US invasion of the Marshall Islands was launched. Already in February 1944 Admiral Noble in Washington reported that the US Navy suspected that the British hoped to leave the Americans to do the serious fighting, and the Director of Plans in the Naval Staff minuted 'THIS MUST BE PUT RIGHT QUICKLY or untold harm will be done.'[22] It was clear to the Chiefs of Staff that they had to make some effective contribution soon to the common war effort in the Pacific if they hoped to preserve the alliance with the United States and get their recaptured colonies back. As Cunningham noted in his diary on 14 July:

> They are obviously afraid of the Americans laying down the law as to what is to happen when Japan is defeated to the various islands, ports and other territories. This appears to be quite likely if the Americans are left to fight the Japanese by themselves. But they will not lift a finger to get a force into the Pacific; they prefer to hang about outside and recapture our own rubber trees.[23]

The US victory in the Philippine Sea battle opened the way for a naval offensive northwards into the Pacific, and reopened the intense debate among the British Chiefs of Staff over whether Britain could and should take part in it. The majority opinion was that Britain urgently needed to commit to supporting the US Navy's prospective Pacific offensive, and in August the Chiefs of Staff gained Churchill's reluctant consent to offer the British Eastern Fleet as a component of it. At the 'Octagon' conference in Quebec in September 1944 the British offered to join a Pacific advance, Roosevelt accepted at once, and Admiral King embarrassed the other US representatives by a furious outburst of hostility. 'We had a great deal of trouble with King who lost his temper entirely and was opposed by the whole of his own [Joint Chiefs of Staff] Committee,' Field Marshal Brooke recorded. 'He was determined, if he could, not to admit British naval forces into Nimitz's command in the Central Pacific.'[24]

Ostensibly he objected on the practical grounds that the British were unfamiliar with long-range operations based on refuelling at sea, and lacked the time and shipping to learn. This was not an imaginary problem:

> Entirely apart from the subject of command, I believe the strongest argument arguing against joint operations, at least for the present, is the fact that the British Fleet is not sufficiently trained to keep up with the standard of performance maintained in our fleet, either in combat operations or refuelling at sea . . . the truth of the matter is that the British are years behind us in the organization and administration of a fleet train . . . the distances from their sources of supply . . . will be staggering.[25]

There was much truth in this, as the British were acutely aware, but it was as obvious to them as it was to the Americans that King's outburst was driven by jealousy and could not be allowed to wreck the alliance. It was urgently necessary to demonstrate to the world and the American public that the British were fully engaged in the common cause (and to demonstrate to the other US services which were King's real enemies that he did not dictate US strategy). British senior officers understood that the US Navy had developed 'the most modern type of naval warfare yet evolved', and were eager to learn by experience. King was obliged to accept with an ill grace but did all he could to undermine the decision in practice. In November the Eastern Fleet was renamed the British Pacific Fleet, and in December the major part of it sailed for its future base of Sydney. At the end of December Fraser flew to Pearl Harbor and reached an amicable agreement with Nimitz that the British would operate as a second Fast Carrier Force under either Admiral William Halsey or Vice-Admiral Raymond Spruance (who alternated in tactical command of the same fleet, styled Third Fleet when under Halsey and Fifth Fleet under Spruance). Following Nimitz's example, Fraser would remain in overall command ashore but leave tactical command at sea to Vice-Admiral Sir Bernard Rawlings, who did not outrank Halsey or Spruance.[26]

The Third Fleet under Halsey and the Fifth under Spruance were the same force with the same status, but the erratic and unseamanlike Halsey was a complete contrast to the methodical Spruance. Halsey was a severe trial to his fleet, and his slovenly and careless second-in-command Vice-Admiral John S. McCain was little better. In December 1944 the fleet steamed into a typhoon, which neither Halsey nor McCain took seriously until it was too late. Many ships were damaged and three destroyers foundered with almost all hands. McCain was relieved of his command but Halsey was back in command in June 1945 when he drove his fleet into another typhoon. Two

602 · CAPE DECEPTION

carriers lost parts of their flight decks and the cruiser *Pittsburgh* had her bows torn off with heavy loss of life. This time Halsey only escaped dismissal through political influence.[27]

By the summer of 1944 it was becoming clear that from the Marianas the new B-29 bombers could bomb Japan with no need of airfields in China, nor therefore of a Philippine campaign to gratify MacArthur. For Admiral King the possibility of seizing the leadership of the Pacific campaign from the US Army was delightful; for MacArthur it was intolerable. Throwing aside all pretence of loyalty, he bluntly threatened President Roosevelt that if he were denied his chance of glory, he would resign his command and stand for the presidency in the forthcoming election of November 1944. He was already a popular hero with an established group of Republican supporters, and the threat was credible. The President yielded – or appeared to yield. Roosevelt hated public disputes; 'the unexcelled master of political manipulation liked making things happen without leaving fingerprints'. His health was already failing, and it was sufficient for his purposes that MacArthur had shown his hand and gravely damaged his reputation among the small group of senior people who were aware of his behaviour.[28]

Nevertheless, MacArthur got his Philippine invasion, because the only available alternative campaign, an assault on Formosa (Taiwan), would require a large army which could not be assembled until German resistance had been overcome in North-West Europe – which was clearly not imminent. The naval side of the Philippine expedition would have to draw on Vice-Admiral Thomas Kincaid's 7th Fleet from the South-West Pacific Command, which was responsible in various respects to MacArthur, to General Marshall and Henry Stimson, the Secretary of War in Washington, and to John Curtin, the Prime Minister of Australia – but was not part of the US naval chain of command through Admiral Nimitz in Pearl Harbor to Admiral King in Washington. MacArthur forbade Kincaid to communicate with Nimitz and ordered all signals between the two fleets to pass through his advance headquarters at Ulithi, not via Pearl Harbor. Moreover, 'Bull' Halsey, commanding the Third Fleet (consisting mainly of Task Force 38, the Fast Carrier Force under Admiral Mitscher), was attached to Kincaid's fleet for the Philippine operation but remained under Nimitz's orders, and persuaded Nimitz (without telling MacArthur) to change his (Halsey's) primary objective from covering the landings to destroying the enemy's main fleet – in other words to remedy Spruance's failure to fight a fleet action two months before. As a result the US Navy went into the Philippine invasion in October 1944 divided between two forces with different admirals, different chains of command, contradictory orders and minimal communication between them. This was not quite the ideal of unified tactical doctrine which had been set out the previous year in PAC-10.[29]

The US landings were concentrated in Leyte Gulf on the Pacific coast of the Philippines, covered by Kincaid with six battleships, sixteen escort carriers and many other warships, while Halsey's Third Fleet with seventeen carriers and another six battleships was nearby. In a characteristically complex operational plan the Japanese deployed their forces in several groups the largest of which (Admiral Kurita Takeo with five battleships and twelve cruisers) came through the islands from the west and emerged by the San Bernardino Strait to the north of Leyte Gulf, while Vice-Admiral Nishimura Shōji and Rear-Admiral Shima Kiyohide with another group of two battleships and four cruisers came from the south-west through the Surigao Strait. Meanwhile Vice-Admiral Ozawa Jizaburō with four carriers and two battleships from Japanese ports approached Leyte from the north-east. These moves set the scene for three major and several lesser naval battles, all fought on 25 October and known collectively as the battle of Leyte Gulf. Ozawa's carriers had few aircraft left and were intended as decoys to lure away the US carriers and expose the landing force to destruction. This part of the Japanese plan succeeded admirably at first. Halsey at once set off north-eastward in search of the longed-for fleet victory, ignoring numerous warnings that the real Japanese fleet was coming through the San Bernardino Strait behind him, and sending only a brief and fatally ambiguous signal to tell Kincaid what he was doing. Halsey spent a busy forenoon mounting air strikes against almost defenceless Japanese carriers, of which he sank four without asking himself what had happened to the battleships and the main body of the Japanese fleet. Not until late morning did Halsey react to anguished pleas for support by returning with his battleships to support the landing forces, but too late to confront the Japanese fleet. Admiral Mitscher and the carriers did not return to Leyte Gulf until the following day. There they learnt that Admiral Kurita in the super-battleship *Yamato* had attacked the landing forces at dawn on 25 October when they were defended only by escort carriers and destroyer escorts. In this crisis the Pacific Fleet's new common doctrine, overlooked by Halsey, was applied with skill and gallantry by junior officers to improvise an effective response to a surprise attack by a much more powerful enemy – helped by the fact that the Japanese fleet was itself badly over-extended with a foolhardy plan, that Admirals Nishimura and Shima coming up from the south were on very poor terms with each other and never joined forces as they had been ordered to, while Kurita seems to have been too ill with dengue fever to think straight. Nevertheless, a muddled and politicized American command system and a sickly President were saved from a near-disaster only by enormously superior strength. The US Navy missed its chance of a 'decisive battle' as American admirals had been taught at the US Naval War College to define it; namely US battleships sinking the enemy battleships, but won an indisputable and overwhelming victory nevertheless – which, with a nice historical irony, takes its name from the northern point of Luzon, named by the early Spanish explorers Cabo Engaño, 'Cape Deception'.[30]

By the end of 1944 British naval intelligence was worried by its information on the rapid growth of the German U-boat fleet. It forecast that early in the new year the *Kriegsmarine* would have in service twenty-five of the new Type XXI and XXIII U-boats to add to seventy to ninety older boats now fitted with the snorkel. The first sinkings by snorkel-fitted U-boats in British coastal waters in September 1944, and the difficulty of detecting them, caused the Admiralty some alarm. In January 1945 U-boats were operating in the Irish Sea for the first time since 1939. By this time German submariners were aware of the vulnerability of their communications and signalled rarely, leaving both the Admiralty and the *Seekriegsleitung* (*SKL*) ignorant of their activities. But post-war analysis shows that in the last phase of the war at sea, from June 1944 to May 1945, the German *Wirkungsgrad* ('performance indicator') of tonnage sunk per U-boat day at sea fell to only 36 tons, at the same time as they were losing two U-boats sunk for every merchant ship. The only outstanding performance of the snorkel-equipped boats was their ability to remain submerged, inactive and undetected for long periods on the bottom in coastal waters. With almost no signals and no aerial reconnaissance they had hardly any means of locating targets, and any activity they did undertake was liable to reveal their position. It was only the final surrender which opened the eyes of the *SKL* to the severity of their losses: 'The real situation, as now revealed, was infinitely worse than we had feared . . .'[31]

Admiral Dönitz's answer to every setback was not fresh thinking but racial purity and fanatical loyalty to the Führer in a fight to the death with no concessions to reason or humanity. He demanded from his submariners 'fanatical dedication', the 'harshest will to win', 'unconditional obedience' and 'commitment to the last breath' – phrases taken from decrypted signals which gave Allied intelligence a vivid sense of the atmosphere of hysterical anti-Semitism which surrounded him.[32] He insisted to his staff that only a total identification with the Nazi *Führerstaat* could save them, and hailed Hitler's survival of the July assassination plot as a new guarantee of German victory. ('Yet another of Dönitz's repeated escapes into the illusory world of those under Hitler's spell and unable or unwilling to think for themselves.')[33] Nine thousand men were transferred from submarine building to infantry, though there were no weapons for them and the U-boats which had been abandoned were still at least marginally effective.[34]

Apart from U-boats, the only significant German naval force still operational by the latter half of 1944 was the *S-Boote* (motor torpedo boats), which were already very short of torpedoes and running out of spare engines, but made an impressive effort with coastal minelaying. Commodore Rudolf Petersen, who commanded the *S-Boote*, is worth noting as a senior officer who kept his distance from the Nazi Party, ignored orders for near-suicide operations, and evaded Dönitz's order not to rescue enemy survivors from the water.[35]

In the closing weeks of the war the major effort of the *Kriegsmarine* in European waters had almost nothing to do with U-boats, but was the evacuation of more than a million retreating troops and civilian refugees trapped along the eastern shore of the Baltic in Estonia, Lithuania and East Prussia by the advancing Russian army. In spite of the disastrous sinking of the liner *Wilhelm Gustloff* by a Russian submarine (with the loss of all but 1,200 of the 8,000–10,000 refugees aboard; probably the worst maritime loss of life in history), of the *General Steuben* with 4,000 wounded soldiers (of whom only 700 were saved), and of the *Goya* with just 334 saved out of 7,000 refugees embarked, the navy managed to save 345,477 wounded men, 181,775 unwounded troops and 1,206,377 civilian refugees, with 'only' about 30,000 (2.5 per cent) lost. This helped to establish its high post-war reputation in Germany. The main British involvement in these final Baltic operations was aerial minelaying and the reinforced escort force held in readiness for what was expected to be a dangerous offensive by the new U-boats in the new year. The Arctic convoys, which were the only route available to reinforce Russia until after the fall of Stalingrad in February 1943, carried in total just less than a quarter of all supplies from the Western Allies. Most of the rest came late in the war through the Persian Gulf and thence overland through Persia, or across the North Pacific to Vladivostok in Russian ships. The last Arctic convoy, J W 66 to Murmansk, sailed in April 1945. In the Atlantic submarine campaign as a whole the Germans began in 1939 with fifty-seven U-boats of all classes, built 1,110 more and captured fifteen Allied submarines; a total of 1,182 U-boats, of which 859 became operational *Frontboote*, which together performed over 3,000 war patrols, sank 2,610 merchant ships of about 13 million tons gross plus 178 warships, and killed about 40,000 crewmen. Some 648 *Frontboote* were lost at sea and 109 in port, of which 215 were sunk on their first patrol, and 429 with all hands. About 30,000 U-boatmen perished, more than 60 per cent of the operational crews.[36]

In the Far East, the campaigns grew in intensity towards the end of 1944. There was still no immediate prospect of troops from Europe to assault Formosa, and the Japanese Army was energetically driving the Chinese out of the airfields in central China which the USAAF had hoped to use, so the Americans were limited to long-range bombing and Marine landings to capture island airfields, while MacArthur's troops slowly reconquered the Philippines. From November 1944 B-29 bombers of the USAAF began to bomb Tokyo from Saipan in the Marianas; a 3,000-mile round trip, with US submarines stationed along the route to rescue crashed airmen. Unfortunately, the big bombers were no more accurate over the Pacific than they had been in Europe (especially bombing through winter cloud cover), so General Arnold proposed to provide a long-range fighter escort, which in turn required an expedition to capture the island of Iwo Jima, midway between the Marianas and Japan. The initial landing took place on 19 February 1945, but the island was heavily fortified and took six weeks of intense fighting to capture, while the airfield which had cost so many lives turned out to make little difference to the campaign.[37]

At the end of October 1944 occurred a sudden, dramatic development in the campaign: the first attacks by Japanese suicide bombers, officially styled *tokkōtai* ('special attack') units, though nowadays usually called *kamikaze*.[38] Given that Japan still had many modern aircraft but an acute shortage of skilled pilots, there was a certain brutal logic to encouraging (in many cases ordering) trainee pilots to volunteer as self-guided missiles to sink Allied ships. Over the six months it lasted the suicide offensive was a severe ordeal for the crews of Allied ships. Although Japanese reports exaggerated the successes of the suicide attacks, the US and Allied losses were serious. In January 1945 suicide attacks were heavily and effectively used against the invaders of Luzon. On the 6th, Bruce Fraser narrowly escaped death when a Japanese aircraft crashed on the bridge of the US battleship *New Mexico* while he was aboard for a conference with General MacArthur. In February suicide bombers off Iwo Jima sank the escort carrier *Bismarck Sea* and badly damaged the big carrier *Saratoga*. On 19 March off Okinawa the US carrier *Franklin* was nearly sunk by a single undetected dive-bomber with two bombs while she was refuelling aircraft, which set her on fire, killing 724 men and wounding 265. In the same attack the *Wasp* lost a further two hundred dead, after which the fast carriers withdrew for a period. Between 26 March and 22 June the Japanese lost 2,200 aircraft in conventional attacks to sink two US ships and damage sixty-one. In the same period 1,900 suicide attacks sank 26 ships and damaged 176. It was obvious which was the more effective form of attack.[39]

On 1 April the United States began Operation 'Iceberg' to capture the large island of Okinawa, in the Ryukyu Islands midway between Japan and Formosa, with airfields which were essential to air movement between Japan and the Japanese Army in China. For the first time the British fleet was invited to participate, which 'gave great and universal satisfaction' to the British crews.[40] The British Fleet was thirty-two days continually at sea and managed two days of strikes for every two days replenishing: still not as efficient as the US Navy but much better than before. In some respects, moreover, the British were clearly ahead of the Americans. British radar guided fighters to intercept attacking aircraft which US radar could not see. *Indefatigable* was hit by a suicide bomber on 1 April but was flying again in an hour. On 4 May *Formidable* was damaged by a suicide attack which started several fires. Returning from refuelling, the carrier was hit by another suicide attack on 9 May, which did the ship little damage but destroyed eighteen aircraft. In the same attack Admiral Mitscher's flagship the carrier *Bunker Hill* lost 660 killed or wounded and the *Enterprise* was also obliged to withdraw to the USA for repairs. During the Okinawa fighting the US Navy lost thirty-eight ships sunk and 350 damaged by suicide attacks.[41]

By the time the Allies met for the Potsdam Conference in late July 1945 to agree the treatment of surrendered Germany, the bitter fighting on and over Iwo Jima and Okinawa and the very slow progress in clearing well-prepared Japanese defences were seriously worrying the US admirals and generals. In August the Japanese garrison of the southern island of Kyushu alone was estimated at fourteen divisions, and the US Army predicted 46,000 US dead in an invasion of Japan (subsequently amended to one million to justify the use of atomic bombs). Instead of regarding the British offers to participate as a political and administrative annoyance, it began to occur to some US leaders that they might need as much help as they could get. The admirals were alarmed in particular by their vulnerability when fighting out of range of shore-based air support, and for six months they suppressed public knowledge of their losses off Okinawa. Although the British carriers' armour was by no means proof against suicide attacks, and *Illustrious* had to return to Britain to repair the damage sustained in April, the contrast with their own losses of thirty ships and 4,900 men in twelve weeks made a powerful impression on US admirals. They were particularly struck by the British armour, and did not appreciate that what made the difference was more the British enclosed hangars and rigorous precautions against fire, which could be traced directly back to the loss of the *Ben-my-Chree* in 1917. The US Navy had intended to defeat Japan by blockade while the USAAF placed its hope on bombing, but the unpleasant possibility now presented itself that even combined they might not suffice to force Japan's surrender. In the approaches to Okinawa the US had four fleet carriers knocked out and an escort carrier sunk. On 6 April the US carriers off Okinawa suffered so badly from a mass attack by over 700 suicide aircraft that the whole operation seemed to be in doubt. But on the Japanese side the situation was so desperate that the Imperial Army and Navy air forces actually co-operated, whereas on the American side senior officers could still indulge their prejudices. Most of the Japanese aircraft came from Formosa, but MacArthur, who had aircraft on Luzon within range, refused to help the navy, so Spruance (in his own words 'with his fingers crossed') ordered Task Force 57 (the British Pacific Fleet) to neutralize the two main airfields in the north of Formosa. This succeeded in drawing most of the Japanese attack away from the US ships, and Vice-Admiral Rawlings volunteered to stay on station to cover the hard-pressed US carriers for two more days, an offer which was gratefully received.[42] Behind the scenes, Admiral King was still working to exclude the British ships from Operation 'Iceberg', and General MacArthur was still trying to detach the British Pacific Fleet from Nimitz's command and add it to his own, but after the Okinawa operation both Nimitz and Spruance recommended that the British carriers should be integrated into the US fast carrier force.[43]

While Operation 'Iceberg' was under way, on 6 April, Mitscher's carrier force was threatened by a suicide squadron of a different sort: the super-battleship *Yamato* sailed from the Inland Sea with a handful of escorts. Only a few aircraft were available to accompany her, and there was insufficient fuel to give the battleship even a theoretical prospect of return. There was no rational prospect of inflicting significant loss on the enemy; the only motive for the operation was to refute criticism of naval passivity. Although Mitscher's airmen were out of practice in torpedo attacks, which they had not used for some time, it took them only ninety minutes to sink the world's largest battleship with ten torpedo and three bomb hits. With her were lost a light cruiser and four destroyers, together with 3,500 to 4,000 Japanese seamen. The US Navy lost ten aircraft and twelve aircrew.[44]

By a minor irony of history, it was the British ships left behind in the Indian Ocean and not the US Navy in the Pacific which were able to inflict the last defeat on the Japanese Navy in a traditional surface action. As we have seen, the heavy cruiser *Haguro* (which had taken a large share in the Japanese victory in the battle of the Java Sea, three years before and not far away) was sunk in the Malacca Strait in May 1945 by a classic night destroyer attack. Next month the heavy cruiser *Ashigara* was sunk in the Bangka Strait by the submarine *Trenchant* (commanded by Arthur Hezlet), and one of the last Japanese heavy cruisers, the *Takao*, was crippled in Singapore Roads by British midget submarines. All three of these successes were made possible by intercepted Japanese signals.[45]

In July 1945, when the British ships returned to the Pacific after refuelling, it was Admiral Halsey's turn in command and he was reluctant to accept them because he had understood that he was not allowed to give the British orders or treat them as an integral part of his fleet. Once he realized that that was precisely what the British wanted, Halsey was content, but then, cruising off Honshu with no Japanese ships or aircraft operating, Halsey was ordered to exclude British participation in air attacks on the Japanese naval base of Kure in case the British got some credit – thus putting publicity for the US Navy ahead of the national interest, and all to promote pointless token attacks on immobilized and useless ships. For the British, however, further opportunities to train alongside US ships and demonstrate their commitment to Allied victory fully justified the effort.[46]

THIRTY-FIVE

Warfare and Welfare

Government and Administration 1944–1945

During the Second World War the Wehrmacht in the East, and the navy under Admiral Dönitz's command, deliberately abandoned the established laws of war and explicitly approved all sorts of criminality, which promoted indiscipline and demoralization. Although Germany was the most modern of nations in its own self-image, Nazi ideology mingled a fascination with new technology with an ambivalence towards modernity and rationality, and a deep-seated reluctance to share military secrets with civilians. Engineers in the Luftwaffe and the other German services were semi-civilians with no powers of command or operational experience. The Luftwaffe research department was ignored, and dissolved in 1942. Many scientists were called up to serve as infantrymen, until the loss of the battle of the Atlantic spurred Hitler to allow scientists to be recalled from the front. Everywhere in the Wehrmacht research had a low priority and was cut off from staff-work, which in the German services dealt with operations, but not necessarily with logistics or technology. Engineers took no interest in manufacture, so the Luftwaffe was still fighting with pre-war aircraft designs in 1944. Much of this was equally true of the navy, which kept technology and engineering well clear of operations. Efforts to harmonize service technical departments just led to power struggles. Many German war industries, notably aero engines, were not only inferior to their contemporaries abroad but relatively weaker than they had been in the previous war. It was a similar story with a related technology, high-speed diesel engines for S-boats. The new Mercedes-Benz 518 failed completely, but the production of the previous engine had already stopped, so when the stock of engines ran out in November 1944 the German navy lost one of its few remaining effective weapons. Albert Speer's claimed peak of armaments production in July 1944 was based on falsified figures. In reality Allied air attacks were already systematically wrecking German industry, coal and oil supplies. From September 1944 they concentrated on the railways, critical for coal and power supplies, and the addition to the Allied order of battle of long-range fighters which destroyed the Luftwaffe's defensive strength brought Germany to catastrophe. In September 1944 the German navy abandoned the building of oil-fired minesweepers in favour of a thirty-year-old coal-fired version, because there was at least some coal still available.[1]

German handling of signals intelligence, which had been one of the Wehrmacht's great strengths in 1940 and had contributed so much to the triumphant campaigns in Norway and France, by 1944 had been perverted to buttress German self-satisfaction. The *SKL* remained convinced that its short-wave signals were immune to direction-finding and its cyphers impenetrable, even when it was reading Allied 'U-Boat Situation Reports' with frequent references to 'D/F'. The *SKL* failed to take elementary security precautions such as rephrasing decrypts, which allowed the Allies to be sure by May 1943 that their cyphers had been broken. Warned by a message from a German prisoner-of-war early in 1945 that *U-505* had been captured (off West Africa by the US Navy in June 1944), the *SKL* attributed all subsequent intelligence problems to this incident, and ignored all other evidence of enemy penetration, even the reports of a German spy in the US Naval administration in Washington, and the US attacks on U-boats' refuelling rendezvous off the Azores, which could only have been revealed by decrypts. From November 1944 U-boats began using private Enigma keys (*Sonderschlüssel*), equivalent to One-Time Pads, but by then there were scarcely any U-boats still at sea to make use of them.[2]

The wartime organization and inter-allied co-operation of the Axis were in most cases weaker than those of the Western powers, for all their faults. In Germany Albert Speer's achievements – or pretended achievements – in increasing production of German armaments promoted the exciting idea that anything was possible and all dreams could be revived. 'The fact that the engineers understood nothing about strategy and the generals nothing about technology, and that any cooperation between the two groups was at best rudimentary, no doubt played a part in this.'[3] Hitler was aware from the start that 'we have so much to answer for that we must win'.[4] In December 1944 Dönitz adopted a fantasy programme for rebuilding the German Navy, though he had good intelligence of the size of the fleets now assembling to overrun Germany. It was a sample of his thinking throughout the war, 'another of Dönitz's repeated escapes into deceptive illusions, following the example of Hitler, who neither would nor could change his thinking'.[5] Indeed, this preference for agreeable fantasy over harsh reality can be directly traced back to Tirpitz in the 1890s. As the situation grew worse in 1944, Dönitz's language became ever more detached from reality. As late as February 1945, with the Russians already across the Oder and approaching the outskirts of Berlin, he told Rear-Admiral Eberhard Godt, his successor as *BdU*, 'I must again assert my innermost conviction that the Führer has always been right. All his plans and projects have succeeded in spite of the opposition of the generals, who cannot see beyond their petty affairs . . .'[6] In the same month he assured Hitler that the *Kriegsmarine* had 551 operational U-boats, and that the new Type XXI could make a submerged voyage from Germany to Japan without surfacing. The reality was that the first Type XXI sailed on her first patrol on 30 April 1945, a week before Germany's final surrender, and never sank anything.[7]

Readers who have followed this narrative as far as 1944 will certainly appreciate that the story of Britain's war at sea is a story of government and society afloat as much as a history of the Navy – or rather, a story which involves the governments and societies of all the different countries that took part in the naval war. It is impossible to write a realistic account of the war as it affected Britain without bringing in the many other peoples and nations which took a larger or smaller part in the war as enemies, allies, or other participants. To take a simple example, the British convoy system was run by the British Admiralty, but employed many Allied ships and accepted and protected merchant ships of every nation not overtly enemy. A typical convoy would include some genuine neutrals, and some ships belonging to ports or owners in countries occupied by the enemy but still physically free to trade on their owner's account between foreign ports. This included several of the largest merchant fleets in the world, notably those of Denmark (a country entirely under enemy control but with many merchant ships managed abroad and effectively part of the Allies' shipping pool), and Norway (also under enemy occupation but an active belligerent and ally with a legitimate government in exile and its own armed forces in addition to a large merchant fleet, part of whose earnings supported the national war effort). The British Dominions (Canada, Australia, South Africa and New Zealand), whose legal status caused Americans a surprising amount of confusion, were in most respects entirely sovereign states, only sharing a head of state (King George VI), and fighting alongside Britain by decision of their own sovereign governments and parliaments. Canada and Australia in particular had important navies and armies which were closely connected to both British and US forces. The smallest Dominion, New Zealand, formed a 'Naval Division' of the Royal Navy from 1921 until the establishment of the Royal New Zealand Navy in October 1941. Another significant category was made up of the neutral countries which were gradually drawn into the war. Japan, which had been a leading participant in the China War since July 1937 at the latest, did not go to war against the European powers until 1941. A later belligerent was Brazil, with a significant navy and merchant fleet, which entered the war against Germany and Italy in August 1942 and participated in the anti-submarine campaigns in both North and South Atlantic.

In a coalition war, diplomacy and politics are bound to matter as much as strategy, and from its inception the British Pacific Fleet had many important political duties in addition to fighting the Japanese. Admirals Fraser and Rawlings were keenly aware of the importance of keeping the promises to the other Allies which Britain had made at Quebec in September 1944. As Rawlings stressed, 'If we give any part of the Americans any opportunity to say "The British have quit" or "can't take it" – then something must be lost that could never perhaps be regained.'[8] Moreover, for Fraser and his officers, serving alongside the US Navy in the Pacific was not only a matter of fulfilling British obligations, but a precious opportunity to learn new ways of war, and to strengthen friendships for the future:

> From a national point of view, it was of the utmost importance that the British Fleet should engage in the most modern type of naval warfare yet evolved, and to do so by fighting in company with its originators and prime exponents. In no other way could we have learned the technical lessons which this type of warfare teaches . . . The Navy has already obtained combat lessons of incalculable worth in the large scale strategic deployment of big naval forces at long distances from their home bases, and in the tactical operation of these forces at previously unheard of distances from their most advanced bases . . . Finally, from a point of view of national prestige, it has been of the utmost importance that our Dominions should see the British navy engaged, if not in equal numbers, at least on an equal footing, with the American forces in the Pacific, and it would have been disastrous from this point of view if the British Pacific Fleet, after being sent to the Pacific, had been relegated, as the Australians consider their own forces to have been relegated to a 'back area'.[9]

The 'modern type of naval warfare' to which Fraser referred was a campaign not based on permanent naval ports and dockyards, but on a mobile base known as a 'fleet train', capable of accompanying, or at least following, the fleet, and supplying the fuel, ammunition, stores, repairs and equipment it needed for sustained operations.[10] Before the war both the US and British navies had foreseen the need for such an organization, and the Admiralty's first plans dated from 1936, but during the battle of the Atlantic there had been neither opportunity nor spare shipping to realize them. The loss of Singapore on the outbreak of the Japanese war abruptly brought the fleet train to the top of a new agenda. A nucleus was ready in mid-1943, and the effort was speeded up after the 'Octagon' Conference at Quebec in September 1944 at which the decision was taken to establish the British Pacific Fleet. At this stage the Admiralty reckoned the requirement to include at least a number of repair ships, floating docks, depot ships for destroyers and submarines, together with maintenance ships for escorts, coastal forces, minesweepers, armaments, instruments and radar, airframes and engines. Tankers would be needed to supply oil, aviation fuel and water; store issuing ships to supply naval, victualling, armament and air stores, and aircraft transports to sustain the operations of the carriers. There would be a call for headquarters ships, hospital ships, amenity ships, tugs, lighters and harbour craft, and accommodation ships for the large workforce of the fleet train. Boom and net layers would protect the fleet anchorages. Water tankers, it was later reported,

> just, and only just, kept us going, and we eagerly awaited the first distilling ship. She arrived during the second series of operations, but our hopes were dimmed when it was found that, with the high sea-water temperature and some recurring defects in the plant, she could only supply a very small proportion of our needs. She used coal at an alarming rate when distilling (being the only coal burner in the Fleet Train), so our only collier was berthed alongside her, and a small party of sailors was employed fairly continuously on transferring coal from one to the other. But the collier (oil-fired) used a prodigious amount of fresh water as her boiler leaked badly, so the result was that these two ships spent most of their time furiously maintaining each other. The incident was not amusing at the time.[11]

The fleet train had to be set up to cover immense distances, with quite inadequate shipping resources and quite insufficient time. The BPF's rear base at Sydney was more than 12,000 miles from the UK, ill-equipped to support a fleet of this size and afflicted by notoriously poor labour relations. A weak Australian Cabinet with a dying Prime Minister was little help.[12] Eventually the British fleet train included over one hundred ships. One of the most interesting of them was the cargo-liner *Menestheus*, converted into an 'amenity ship', which evidently drew on the Admiralty's corporate memory of how the morale of the Grand Fleet at Scapa Flow had been maintained in the previous war. The ship was 'provided with a stage (complete with concert party) and cinema, buffets and recreation space, barbers, tailors, and shoe repair shops, a library, and last but not least, a brewery whose endeavour was to brew the best of British beers from distilled water'.[13] Although she arrived just too late to participate in the final campaign off Okinawa, the *Menestheus* with her brewery capable of producing 70,000 pints a week, caused a sensation in the US Navy (still officially 'dry'), which made fruitless attempts to buy her.[14]

Another key necessity for the fleet was docks. Singapore was now in enemy hands. At the time of the fleet's arrival the biggest graving dock in Sydney was the Sutherland Dock on Cockatoo Island, which could take nothing larger than a cruiser. Fortunately, the new Captain Cook Dock down the harbour on Garden Island opened in March 1945, with dimensions of 1,139 feet long, 147 feet beam and 45 feet draught over the sill, so that there was at least one dry dock in the South Pacific capable of receiving any British or US carrier. Even three weeks before the dock was officially open, it took in the carrier *Illustrious* for emergency repairs on 2 March. Further away in the Indian Ocean was Bombay Dockyard (described by Admiral Somerville in August 1943 as 'this most inefficient establishment'), and Trincomalee with the new floating dock AFD 23 with a 50,000-ton lift, built by Braithwaite Burn & Jessop of Bombay. In August 1944 this essential new dock (the only British dock in the Indian Ocean capable of taking a battleship) was wrecked by an inexperienced dockmaster who was left unsupervised to lift the battleship *Valiant*, a delicate job right at the limit of the dock's capacity and (as the event proved) well beyond the limit of the dockmaster's competence. The ship was badly damaged and never returned to service; the dock broke up and sank, leaving no dock in the Indian Ocean to support the BPF. In this respect at least it was fortunate that the operating areas of the British fleet turned out to be far from the Indian Ocean. Manus Island, which the British took over from the US Navy as a forward base in November 1944, was in the Pacific north of New Guinea (1,800 miles north of Sydney), and from there the fleet's line of advance was northwards towards the Philippines.[15]

In an ideal world the fleet train would have been assembled and trained before it was needed for operations, but in the actual situation of December 1944 the former Eastern Fleet, now renamed the British Pacific Fleet, had to go to war before most of its planned fleet train had assembled, let alone 'worked up' to efficiency. Both fleet and train had to learn new ways of war in the midst of actual operations, with little advance preparation. In this process the priority was to master American skills even at the price of neglecting what the Fleet Air Arm already knew. British naval aircraft had developed considerable skills in night flying before the war and demonstrated them in the Mediterranean, but now there was no time to train a new generation of aircrew in night operations, nor to fit the carriers with blind-landing gear. It was more urgent to relearn the basics of daylight flight-deck procedure with American equipment, American aircraft and American methods. Captain Edward C. Ewen, the experienced US carrier captain who was attached to Rawlings as liaison officer, had many constructive criticisms of British procedure to offer: for example, that the flight deck and maintenance crews needed to be reinforced, that the unpainted steel decks were slippery and dangerous (US carriers' flight decks had a wooden non-slip surface), that the inadequate 'avgas' (aircraft fuel) supply to the flight deck slowed refuelling, and that the British catapults (mounted proud of the armoured deck) made it difficult to fit drop tanks to extend aircraft range. Ewen contrasted the popular Rawlings' easy tact with the less effective leadership of his 'rude' and 'neurotic' second-in-command Rear-Admiral Philip Vian (a contrast which was no news to British officers).[16]

At the end of 1944 only one-third of the shipping tonnage needed for a 'fleet train' for the Pacific was available, and many of the ships allocated to it were worn out by hard service and in no fit condition for a new campaign. Lord Leathers, the Minister for Shipping, was responsible for distributing merchant shipping between competing departments, but the equivalent US organization, the War Shipping Administration, was effectively a satellite of the US Navy and controlled by Admiral King, who had no intention of diverting anything from his own service to the British. What strength the dying Roosevelt could spare in the autumn of 1944 was committed to his fourth and final presidential campaign (which itself contributed to chilling the atmosphere of Anglo-American relations), and in any case overt interference was never his style.[17] But the very existence of the British Pacific Fleet, which Admiral King so obviously loathed, was a conspicuous marker that his wings had been clipped. Other US services were beginning to ask why the USN had to have so large a share of US resources. The British contribution might justify curbing the USN's voracious appetite for shipbuilding (much of it not for present use but for two or more years ahead). Ernest King himself was cordially hated by many US senior naval officers, who took pleasure in helping the British in every way which did not have to be reported to Washington. The Nimitz–Fraser agreement of December 1944 was notably generous to the British. A 'broader interpretation' of King's order that the British must be completely self-supporting allowed the two navies to pool their fuel stocks in the Pacific, to the considerable advantage of the British.[18] A request to borrow three Avenger aircraft (which would have to go through Washington) was refused with a hint to resubmit it later, and 'Sure enough, when we got up to

Manus, the American CO there said, "I'm sorry, but we don't issue less than six – and if you've got a bottle of whisky you can have a dozen!" ' 'I have found that the American logistical authorities in the Pacific have interpreted self sufficiency in a very liberal sense,' Fraser commented, and Vian agreed: 'Indeed, the Australian base never was able to supply and maintain us properly. Without the generous help of United States bases, fuelling facilities and spare parts, the Fleet would have been hard set to keep going.'[19] It is hardly possible to doubt that this generous assistance of the British was a tacit expression of the disgust which many senior US naval officers felt at the behaviour of their commander-in-chief.

Moreover, in the Pacific even more than the rest of the world, the British faced a growing manpower crisis in 1944 which would have made it impossible to accept large additions to the fleet even if a good fairy had presented them. Britain and the empire had suffered half a million casualties since 1939. Out of a British workforce of 23.5 million, 5.2 million men were under arms, 7.8 million were in the armaments industries, and 10.4 million were still in the civilian economy. The Royal Navy had priority over all the other services and was the only one still able to grow; in the twelve months to September 1943 it expanded from 529,000 to 710,00 officers and men, and from 60,400 to 74,000 women (WRNS and nurses). At its peak in 1944 the RN counted nearly 900,000 personnel – but this was nothing like as many as it needed. For want of key ratings many available ships could not be commissioned, so the old and damaged were laid up and many new ships were transferred to Dominion and Allied navies which were better able to man them.[20]

The spearhead of the US Navy in the Pacific was the Fast Carrier Force (Task Force 50, later 58) which was developed over the six months or so from September 1943 to March 1944 as the new *Essex* Class carriers joined the fleet. In its final form it was composed of four Task Groups, each with three carriers, three new fast battleships, a light cruiser and seven destroyers. Each Task Group was bigger than the US fleet at Midway in 1942, or the British Mediterranean Fleet at the same date.[21] At first stationary 'Service Squadrons' of tankers and supply ships were anchored at atolls within reach of the areas where the carriers were expected to operate. The first of these temporary bases was Funafuti Atoll in the Ellice Islands (Tuvalu) in October 1943, which supported the assault on Tarawa in November. In February 1944 Service Squadron 10 anchored at Majuro Atoll in the Marshall Islands to supply the different task groups of Spruance's Fifth Fleet in Operation 'Flintlock', the seizure of the main islands of that group. This time Service Squadron 8 provided a shuttle service of fuel and supplies from Majuro to the Task Groups of the Fifth Fleet at sea.

Although the USN had conducted some peacetime exercises of refuelling at sea – at slow speed and in fine weather – and by the end of 1943 was accustomed to setting up temporary bases in sheltered anchorages, 'Flintlock' was the first major operation which depended on replenishment under way at sea. Its success marked the launch of a new 'combined arms' concept of mobile naval operations, integrating battleships, carriers, cruisers, destroyers and supply ships in a dispersed and flexible but closely co-ordinated fleet structure. The Fast Carriers were the core of the new fleet, but its novelty was not the replacement of battleships by carriers (which was still some way in the future), it was the integration of all sorts of ships and forces into a mobile fleet operating far from fixed bases. This was what the British Pacific Fleet had come to study and learn.[22]

A key factor in the supply of US carrier operations, now largely directed against stationary land targets, was that US carriers were capable of a substantially higher intensity of attacks than British. American carriers, which normally kept all their aircraft on deck, and conceived of their operations as a single mass 'strike' to win the battle at a stroke, were capable of launching seventy-two aircraft in thirty-five minutes. British flight-deck procedure, developed for continuous operations in Atlantic weather, struck the aircraft down to the hangar to refuel, and the numbers permitted by deck parking were beyond the capacity of the flight-deck crews to refuel without much bigger crews than the British ships could accommodate or find.[23]

Ulithi Atoll in the Caroline Islands, 700 miles east of the Philippines, was occupied without a fight in late September 1944 in preparation for the carrier attacks planned in October against Japanese air bases in the northern Philippines, Formosa (Taiwan) and the Ryukyu Islands. Here a fleet of obsolete tankers was anchored with 400,000 barrels of oil and 'avgas'. Initially, operational forces visited the Service Squadrons to refuel at anchor, but in October 1944 a new At Sea Logistics Service Group (TG 30.8) was created to supply the fast carriers and their immediate escorts under way at sea. It consisted of thirty-three oilers, eleven escort carriers carrying replacement aircraft, and twelve ammunition ships, all escorted by eighteen destroyers and twenty-six destroyer escorts. They drew their stocks from Ulithi and met the operational task groups at sea to transfer fuel and supplies in positions chosen to fit the operations in hand.[24]

It is worth asking why the British had not developed something like this system in four years of escorting convoys across the Atlantic. Several factors were probably involved, starting with the obvious difference that the convoy war required quite small numbers of smaller warships to be refuelled at intervals to cover the 3,000–4,000-mile width of the Atlantic, whereas the US landing operations in the Pacific involved much larger forces than any one convoy, but in most cases shorter operational ranges and shorter campaigns. Another factor was the endurance, indeed revival, of pre-war anglophobia. The US Navy now had available a rapidly growing fleet of new tankers and cargo ships suitable for service as fleet auxiliaries, but less than two years after the Casablanca Conference many of the jealousies of American politicians and senior officers were still on display, and it was politically unacceptable to pass any of these new ships to the British under 'Lend-Lease'. Neither Congress nor Admiral King would tolerate the transfer to Britain of hulls which might conceivably serve a commercial purpose, though the British were able to acquire some of the Canadian-built Liberty Ships of the 'Fort' Class for the fleet train. The scarcity of merchant shipping available to Britain was not only the consequence of war losses, but of the lavish provision demanded by the US authorities for their troops overseas, which led to a steep fall in the level of emergency stocks in Britain. By January 1945 the margin was down to two months' supply for the civilian population (and even two months the Americans claimed was a needless luxury). They also refused to feed the starving population of newly liberated Europe, which the British took on instead. By 1945 adult malnourishment was appearing among the British population, but the US forces were never stinted, and the United States never imposed any effective oversight over shipping resources.[25]

Navigational factors affected the adoption of replenishment at sea. In the Western Pacific, where the fetch of the sea is moderated by numerous reefs and islands, the weather was often friendly to refuelling or transferring stores between ships steaming on parallel courses abreast, typically 100 to 150 feet apart at speeds of no more than 10 or 12 knots, when the 'canal effect' which tends to suck together ships steaming close abreast would be manageable. This would have been much more difficult in the deep rollers of the open Atlantic, over unbroken depths of 2,000 fathoms and more, particularly before the development of modern automatic helm gear, so during the war up to 1944 British convoy escorts more often refuelled at sea from astern of the oiler, which was slower than the new US technique of abeam refuelling but easier and safer. Moreover, the slow-speed refuelling customary in the Pacific would have been impossible in the Atlantic in the presence of an active U-boat threat, but the Japanese submarine service never developed any interest in attacking merchant shipping (though their Armed Merchant Cruisers several times attempted it). The submarine threat in the Pacific was so low that approaching the (still enemy-occupied) Philippines from the eastward across the Pacific, the US Navy normally did not bother to convoy shipping until within about 750 miles of Guam.[26]

A significant organizational development which affected the structure and strategy of the Fast Carrier Force happened at the end of February 1944, when the airman Vice-Admiral John H. Towers was promoted to be Deputy Commander-in-Chief under Admiral Nimitz, and the unadventurous Charles A. Pownall was replaced in command of the carrier group by Admiral Mitscher. Although Towers was still only an administrative 'type commander' with no operational responsibilities, for the airmen this was a significant step towards their ambition of fleet command. A key ally in their campaign was the Under-Secretary of the Navy, James V. Forrestal, who shared Towers' hatred of Ernest King. Two months later in April 1944 Frank Knox died of a heart attack and Forrestal replaced him as Secretary of the Navy. King remained in office as Chief of Naval Operations until he was relieved by Nimitz in December 1945, but from the moment Roosevelt forced him to accept the British Pacific Fleet in September 1944 his political power was visibly waning, and he no longer had unlimited scope to block the rise of the airmen. From the early months of 1944 the US Navy was in the process of evolving from a 'battleship Navy' into a 'carrier Navy'. The change was initially a matter of attitudes and only gradually of force structure and organization, but Forrestal's promotion marks a significant stage in the process.[27]

One of the most important, but also the most delicate dimensions of Allied co-operation in the Pacific was intelligence sharing. The difficulties which we have already noted in the Indian Ocean were still present at the end of 1943. HMS *Anderson*, the new naval intelligence station at Colombo in Ceylon (Sri Lanka), enjoyed excellent signal reception but took in much more material than it had the capacity to process. In January 1944, however, Harry Hinsley (still only twenty-five) was able to negotiate the BRUSA agreement between GC&CS and OP-20-G, the US Navy's cryptographic department in Washington, to which were later added links to the US Navy's stations in Honolulu, Melbourne and Colombo, and the 'Radio Analysis Group' at Guam. The BRUSA partners communicated using a version of the USN Combined Cypher Machine which did not interconnect with other US signals, so much of the information flow was one-way. As a rule, the US services were more ready to share with the British than with each other, but the US Navy's rigid refusal to share access to its Electronic Cypher Machine was so damaging that it almost broke up the Anglo-American intelligence-sharing regime. BRUSA was a considerable advance on previous non-cooperation, but GC&CS still resented its status as a poor relation of OP-20-G, which had been so generously treated by the British over JN25 and Enigma. Behind this was perhaps King's establishment in 1943 of the 'Combat Intelligence Division' of the (notional) Tenth Fleet, a mechanism by which King was able to retain a degree of personal control over the US Navy's anti-submarine operations everywhere in the world behind the backs of the local naval commanders-in-chief. In October 1944 OP-20-G belatedly realized that the rest of the world was learning to co-operate under British leadership, while they were on the brink of losing access to the growing volume of important materials coming from *Anderson*, from the Indian Army's Wireless Experimental Centre in Delhi, and from the Indian branch of the Combined Services Detailed Interrogation Centre in the Red Fort in Delhi, whose friendly treatment of captured Japanese signals specialists was especially fruitful. In the Pacific, Nimitz promised Fraser the same ULTRA access as Spruance had, but the real obstacles were in Washington, and in Australia, where the USN's long-standing refusal to share intelligence with MacArthur's headquarters in Brisbane must have cost many lives, most of them American. No fundamental change was possible until finally in 1944 George Marshall, US Army Chief of Staff, began to overhaul the chaotic central administration of the army. In December 1944 the US Army departments responsible for interception, cryptanalysis and interpretation of enemy signals were finally connected to one another, opening a flood of new material to consumers (but straining relations with the Chinese and French, whose abysmal signals security was exposed). In February the President began for the first time to see some of the high-level Japanese traffic sent in the diplomatic cypher code-named MAGIC. The same month Marshall and King agreed to set up an Army-Navy Communications Intelligence Board, but as the title plainly revealed, the object was not to promote intelligence-sharing but to shut the USAAF out. Two months later, on 12 April, Roosevelt died, and Vice-President Harry S. Truman succeeded to the presidency. He appears to have received no previous security briefing and had never heard of Ultra or the atom bomb.[28]

In Tokyo it was already clear to the emperor and his senior officers by 1943 that Japan could not win. By that time the military police, the *Kempetei*, had become a sort of Gestapo which kept ministers and courtiers under constant surveillance to keep the soldiers in power, but it was important that the Japanese constitution, unlike the German, had been corrupted but never overthrown, and was still officially in force. In July 1944, after the fall of Saipan, the military regime of General Tōjō Hideki was constitutionally replaced by the Koiso–Yonai administration, a joint military and naval government which was widely understood as a step towards ending the war. Although in grave danger of a military coup, the emperor was able to use his authority to open secret negotiations with the United States, exploiting the shocks generated both by the atomic bomb dropped on Hiroshima on 6 August 1945, and (perhaps rather more) by the Russian declaration of war and invasion of Manchuria the same day.[29]

Any date in history may serve as the beginning or end of a study. In the case of this volume, the third of a series, the starting date was fixed by the outside dates of Volume 2, 1649 to 1815. A finishing date was not so simple to choose. An obvious possibility would have been 1945, giving a volume covering 130 years to succeed one which covered 166 years – not an unreasonable disproportion. But in other respects 1945 seems to be unsatisfactory. Although often cited as the end of the Second World War, it really marks the end only of the European part of the war. The war in the East, often but misleadingly called the Pacific War, was essentially a war for the control of China in which the Japanese were the prime aggressors. It can be dated from various episodes in the 1930s but it certainly did not end in August 1945 when the atomic bombs were dropped on Hiroshima and Nagasaki. Instead it continued in the form of the Chinese Civil War, which was finally fought to a victory by the Chinese Communists in December 1949 when the last of the defeated Nationalist forces escaped to Formosa (Taiwan).[1]

Britain and the United States became allies in the aftermath of the Pearl Harbor attack (December 1941), and up to 1945 both governments worked to cement the alliance and strengthen the bonds uniting the two populations. For Churchill's government this was relatively easy, because the British people were already well disposed towards the United States, and largely unaware of the extent to which dislike of Great Britain was a core element of American patriotism. While the war lasted, the Englishman in the street had little sense of the degree to which American assistance had sustained the common war-effort on terms that deliberately undermined the British economy. During the war British exports fell from £471 million to £258 million, imports grew from £858 million to £1,299 million, Britain's overseas debts increased fivefold and (most serious of all) the forced sale of overseas assets halved the overseas income which for over a century had allowed Britain to run a comfortable surplus on the balance of payments. The Lend-Lease agreement which was central to British economic survival during the war was abruptly terminated without warning on 9 August 1945 by an American demand for the repayment of $650 million, precipitating a financial crisis which was only deferred by a US loan of \$3.75 billion to be repaid on harsh terms over fifty years. 'It is aggravating,' commented *The Economist*, 'to find that the reward for losing a quarter of our national wealth in the common cause is to pay tribute for half a century to those who have been enriched by the war.'[2] The British government deficit now rose fast. Bread and potatoes were rationed for the first time, and over the winter of 1945–6 the adult population of Britain, which during the war had enjoyed a dull but fully adequate diet, was exhibiting increasing signs of malnutrition. Then the winter of 1946–7 was exceptionally hard, with snow blocking many roads and railway lines, leading to a shortage of coal and therefore electricity, which badly damaged industrial output and forced unemployment up to 1.8 million people. In the summer of 1947 sterling became fully convertible, which was a condition of the 1945 loan, but this soon led to a run on the pound and a forced devaluation. The loss of its pre-war financial reserves had left the British economy in a vulnerable condition which was now fully exposed to both governments for the first time. At the same time events in the world called for more rather than fewer actions by Britain in general, and the Royal Navy in particular.[3]

By 1946, when Stalin's ambitions to control Europe were becoming very clear and France seemed at imminent risk of falling to Communist rule, the new American President Harry S. Truman realized that he could not simply demobilize the US armed forces and leave the world to manage without American participation. A key moment came over the winter of 1946–7 when Britain confessed that it lacked the strength to sustain the Greek and Turkish governments against Communist subversion. At risk was the control of the oilfields of the Middle East and the airfields which would be essential in any war against the Soviet Union. This inspired the president to proclaim the 'Truman Doctrine' in March 1947, promising support for democratic governments facing totalitarian subversion. This was followed by the Marshall Plan enacted in April 1948, created by the Secretary of State (and former General) George C. Marshall, which offered economic assistance to rebuild the devastated economies of postwar Europe. Its success provoked Communist coups in Hungary in 1947 and Czechoslovakia the following year. Finland narrowly escaped the same fate in March 1948, then in June 1948 the western zones of Berlin occupied by Britain, France and the United States were blockaded by the Russian army, which surrounded them. For almost a year the Allied garrisons and civilian population of West Berlin were sustained only by air supplies, until in May 1949 the Soviets abandoned their attempt to force the Western garrisons out. The Berlin crisis forced the rapid establishment of an effective American-European alliance, formalized by the North Atlantic Treaty of April 1949.[4]

A key factor in the Anglo-American connection was nuclear fission, which had been the subject of research in the 1930s by physicists in Britain, Germany and the United States among other countries. Unusual among politicians of his generation, Winston Churchill had a good knowledge of nuclear physics and was alive to its opportunities and dangers. Even before Pearl Harbor he had discussed it with President Roosevelt. Initially Britain was in the lead, and continued to contribute an important share of the scientific research teams, but increasingly from 1942 Allied nuclear research migrated to America or Canada, where there was no bombing or blackout, and no shortage of electricity. The first, very secret and unwritten Anglo-American agreement on nuclear research was concluded in August 1942. The first written agreement was signed at Quebec in August 1943, and renewed at Roosevelt's country estate of Hyde Park in upstate New York in September 1944. This committed the signatories to continue their shared research after the defeat of Japan, but in the aftermath of Roosevelt's death on 12 April 1945 the only American copy was apparently mislaid, and those who had signed it took no action to inform the new President of its existence. This left Congress free to pass the Atomic Energy Act of 1946, known as the McMahon Act, which converted the tripartite 'Manhattan Project' that had built the first atomic bombs into an American national organization from which British and Canadian citizens were forthwith expelled. This betrayal of a key element of the wartime alliance made the new power balance brutally clear, and for a time seemed to mark the start of a new era of American isolationism. Although Britain had already allowed the US Air Force to base nuclear-armed bombers in Britain, in 1950 and 1951 the United States twice refused Britain access to its atomic test range.[5]

The atomic bombs fell on Hiroshima on 6 August 1945 and Nagasaki on the 9th, though the Nagasaki bomb badly missed its target and caused relatively little damage though quite considerable loss of life. On 8 August, Russia declared war on Japan, and next day invaded Manchuria, which seems to have hastened Japan to make peace even more effectively than the atomic bombs did. Japan announced its surrender by wireless on 15 August 1945, and on 2 September an official surrender ceremony was held aboard the battleship USS *Missouri* in Tokyo Bay. Sir Bruce Fraser signed for the United Kingdom, but there were few British ships present. Only a few weeks before, the Americans had begun preparations for an invasion of the Japanese home islands, which threatened to be a bloody and desperate campaign. Now Japanese resistance had abruptly collapsed, and the great (and almost entirely American) fleet gathered in Tokyo Bay symbolized for the United States Navy its own dominant share in the victory. US naval officers took it for granted that they had won the war, and the war had won the US Navy many friends in Washington. It was an acute shock for senior officers returning to their home ports that autumn to be greeted, however, not by cheering crowds but by the triumphant and triumphalist US Army Air Forces, claiming monopoly control of a new 'Air Age' dominated by atomic warfare. The US Navy now had a new and still expanding fleet, built around the *Essex* Class fleet carriers, but the first generation of atomic bombs weighed about five tons each and could only be carried by the largest four-engined bombers, specially adapted B-29s, which could not possibly fly off carriers. The USAAF proclaimed what many politicians believed, that atomic weapons were now the only instrument of warfare which mattered, and with current technology they really seemed to be a natural monopoly of the air forces.[6]

Behind this Air Force campaign lay a project for unification of the services which was backed by President Truman and General George Marshall. Inevitably this was understood by the US Navy and Marine Corps as a takeover, which was greeted with bitter resistance. Eventually in July 1947 a new 'National Military Establishment' (later renamed the Department of Defense) created three services under a Secretary of Defense, but inter-service disputes continued. The new US Air Force (formerly the Army Air Forces) was obsessed by the battle to reject military control and retain its independence. The US Navy was equally determined to resist the ambition of the Air Force to take over the Navy's aircraft. It was self-evident to senior officers everywhere that atomic weapons would be the key to victory in future wars. The US Navy would have no future unless it could claim at least a share in such campaigns.[7] In March 1948 a meeting of the US Joint Chiefs of Staff at Key West in Florida agreed that the Navy might claim a limited share in an atomic war – but no official record of the meeting was taken, and each service had a different recollection of what had been agreed. The Navy's hopes were bound up with its planned flush-deck super-carrier the USS *United States*, the first ship designed to carry nuclear bombers. In March 1949 James Forrestal was replaced as Secretary of Defense by Louis A. Johnson, whose career had been closely connected with the Army Air Force. In April the keel of the *United States* was laid, and immediately Johnson cancelled the ship. The public and the US Navy assumed that this meant the end of the US carrier force, and Johnson went out of his way to confirm the impression. 'Admiral,' he told Admiral Richard L. Conolly, commanding in the Eastern Atlantic and the Mediterranean:

> the Navy is on its way out. Now, take amphibious operations. There's no reason for having a Navy and a Marine Corps. General Bradley [chairman

of the Joint Chiefs] . . . tells me that amphibious operations are a thing of the past . . . We'll never have any more amphibious operations. That does away with the Marine Corps. And the Air Force can do anything that the Navy can do nowadays, so that does away with the Navy.[8]

Although the US Navy still had the three big *Midway* Class carriers and the *Essex* Class ships were still being built, it was evident that the Navy's footing on the margins of the atomic weapons programme was precarious. Admiral Louis E. Denfeld, Chief of Naval Operations from December 1947 until his dismissal on 1 November 1949, allowed himself to be enlisted to support what was called 'The Revolt of the Admirals', in which friends of the Navy falsely accused Secretary Johnson of corrupt practices and directly challenged President Truman's defence policy. In September 1949 the first Soviet atomic bomb was exploded, far in advance of any American forecasts, reinforcing the atmosphere of alarm in Washington.[9] So far the US Navy's strategic and political case had been handled with conspicuous incompetence. In Congressional hearings before the House Armed Services Committee the Air Force had been allowed to distract attention from the serious flaws in its arguments. For the next fiscal year 1951 Congress authorized nine naval Air Groups (compared to twenty-four for 1949), and the eleven carriers in commission were reduced to six. The future of US naval aviation looked dark, and the US naval airmen were in desperate need of friends.[10]

The situation changed literally overnight on 25 June 1950 when the North Korean army crossed the 38th parallel to invade the South. The United Nations condemned the aggression and called on its members to resist. There followed a complex and exceptionally bloody war which pitted the North Korean and later Chinese armies with Russian assistance against the South Korean army with American and other foreign detachments acting under the United Nations resolution. This war has never formally ended, but fighting stopped with an armistice in July 1953, leaving the front line very close to where it had started near the 38th parallel. The war was fought almost entirely on Korean soil and in the air overhead, but United Nations ships bombarded enemy positions along the coasts, and both US and British carrier aircraft supported the troops ashore. The political and strategic consequences extended over much of the world. The shock of the unexpected attack by Communist forces convinced Western governments that the third world war had begun and would very soon extend to Europe. Exhausted and largely demobilized fleets and armies braced themselves for further struggles. In Britain the new war raised defence spending to 10 per cent of GDP for 1952–3; this time the United States gave some material support but refused any financial help. By May 1952 British defence spending, as a proportion of national income, was higher than it had been in the late 1930s, and Attlee's Labour government proposed to raise it further to 14 per cent. Rising taxation helped to lose him the next general election and return Churchill and the Conservatives to power in October 1951. The Korean War mobilization lasted long enough to revive and renew the armed services, before it became clear that the British economy without American support was incapable of supporting full mobilization for long. Between 1952 and 1956 British defence spending declined from 11.3 per cent of GNP to 9.3 per cent.[11]

At sea the British ships in Eastern waters when the fighting started were immediately placed at the disposal of the US Vice-Admiral Charles Turner Joy. The two available carriers, HMS *Triumph* (which launched the first naval air strike of the war) and the USS *Valley Forge*, co-operated efficiently, the British taking the west coast and the Americans the east coast. In 1951 a British admiral was for a time in command of the Allied naval group. Not much of this made headlines, but it earned gratitude and reinforced links of friendship between navies which mattered all the more in a period when Anglo-American government relations were still fairly frosty. Intelligent observers took note of the fact that US jet aircraft based in Japan were almost completely out of range of Korea, where the United Nations forces depended heavily on the support of American and British carrier aircraft. The Korean War also gave the US Marines a timely opportunity to demonstrate both their professional skill in the bold and dangerous amphibious landing at Inchon near the South Korean capital of Seoul in September 1950, and their gallantry in forming the rearguard which covered the retreat of the United Nations forces from the Chosin Reservoir before the advancing Chinese army in November 1950. This made the Marines national heroes and gave their commandant a seat with the Joint Chiefs of Staff; there was no more talk of abolishing the Marine Corps.[12]

Behind these strategic and political factors, the carrier navies had to grapple with difficult technical questions. It has been explained that US carriers were built with long, narrow flight decks in the expectation that they would park their aircraft largely on deck and fly them off in mass strikes which were meant to win command of the air over the naval battle-space. War experience soon demonstrated that this had not been an altogether correct forecast of future naval aviation, but of course it was too late to alter the design of the US carriers, all of which (including the new *Essex* Class) had the same long, narrow flight decks. The USN was committed to its existing flight-deck procedure and aircraft technology. But in 1944 both the British and German air forces introduced the first jet aircraft, which were capable of much higher speeds than their predecessors. Already in 1950 in the early stages of the Korean War the North Korean air force was operating Russian-built Mig-15 jets with notably better performance than the British and American carrier fighters which opposed them. Jet engines developed greater power than piston-engines, but only when they had already reached high speeds; propeller-driven aircraft alone generated the superior initial power and acceleration needed to take off in the short run of a carrier's deck, whereas jets needed long concrete runways to reach their flying speed. To fly jets from carriers would need new technologies to provide a powerful acceleration to take off and a powerful deceleration to land. The limited performance of existing carrier aircraft meant that they were unlikely ever to be able to lift atomic weapons. Confident that its existing carriers and carrier aircraft were the finest in the world, the US Navy's Bureau of Aeronautics believed it had no need of any radical change, and it had no research establishment to investigate fundamental problems of aircraft design.[13]

The Fleet Air Arm, by contrast, was an 'unsatisfied power', keenly aware that it needed to do better, and it enjoyed the services of the Royal Aircraft Establishment at Farnborough. Seeking a more powerful catapult to launch bigger and faster aircraft, the USN Bureau of Aeronautics calculated in 1948 that a hydraulic catapult able to launch a 100,000-lb aircraft (the size of a nuclear bomber) would itself weigh 800 tons and require liquid explosive charges of 150-lbs a shot – two figures which alarmed the Americans seriously enough to consider the British alternative technology. Farnborough was already working on a steam catapult fed from the ship's boilers, and in January 1952 the light fleet carrier HMS *Perseus* arrived in Philadelphia to demonstrate a prototype. The Bureau of Aeronautics did not welcome the foreign technology, but the trials aboard the *Perseus* allowed the British naval test pilot Eric Brown to demonstrate beyond doubt that the steam catapult was capable of launching the largest naval aircraft yet in service. He did so in the most spectacular and alarming fashion by launching his aircraft when the *Perseus* was not at sea, steaming into the wind, but alongside a quay with the wind coming from astern.[14]

Moreover, in the course of the trials the British put forward an equally revolutionary idea, the angled deck. By painting a landing path on the flight deck angled several degrees to port to clear the forward end of the flight deck where the catapults were fitted, it would be possible to accept jet aircraft landing at high speed but still clear to go around again for another attempt if they failed to pick up an arrester wire, without crashing into the aircraft ranged behind the catapults to be launched. This the British tried with a landing path angled 10 degrees to port on the flight deck of the carrier *Triumph*, with a success which convinced the US Navy to order the conversion of the carrier *Antietam*. She in turn visited Britain in May 1953 and persuaded the Admiralty to begin converting the new British fleet carriers in the same way.[15]

Finally the British proposed a solution to another technical problem: that jet aircraft landed at too high a speed for the pilots to see and react to the 'batsman's' signals correcting their height and angle of approach. The mirror landing sight consisted of a powerful light at the after end of the flight deck pointing forward into an adjustable concave mirror mounted on the after end of the island. The pilot coming in to land watched the reflected light and kept it lined up with the row of three green lights on each side of the mirror, while the angle of the mirror could be adjusted to suit the speed and angle of approach of whichever type of aircraft was coming in. This simple and practical device, combined with heavier arrester gear, allowed carriers to land fast jets reliably and safely. Together the angled deck, the steam catapult and the mirror landing sight formed a complete system which ushered in the jet age afloat, and later, as atomic bombs were reduced in size, made it possible for both navies to arm their carrier aircraft with small atomic weapons. The new British inventions saved the US carrier fleet from immediate obsolescence and enabled the US Navy to claim a share of the nuclear deterrent. Although the public was hardly aware, naval men knew that the RN had powerful claims on American gratitude. The new British fleet carrier *Ark Royal* commissioned in February 1955 with a partial angled deck, steam catapults and a mirror landing sight which embodied the new system in British service. This combination of conceptually clever but physically simple equipment is reminiscent of the wartime submarine and anti-submarine 'attack teachers' which had been pioneered ten years before by the Western Approaches Tactical Unit.[16]

The surprising and very unusual willingness of the USN to adopt foreign equipment was a good omen for Anglo-American co-operation, but very soon afterwards it had to overcome the worst crisis of mutual hostility since the 1930s if not the nineteenth century. This was the Suez crisis of 1956, which at the time seemed to have comprehensively wrecked Anglo-American relations and generated a series of Middle Eastern wars which has not stopped almost seventy years later. The crisis was provoked by the Egyptian government's announcement of the 'seizure' of the Suez Canal in July 1956. The British and French governments represented this as unlawful confiscation, which was a significant misunderstanding. In fact the 1888 Suez Canal Convention clearly regarded the canal itself as the property of the Egyptian government; the Suez Canal Company was a predominantly French business with a concession to operate the canal, which the Egyptian President Gamal Abdel Nasser proposed to cancel. President Dwight Eisenhower and his Secretary of State John Foster Dulles, both exceptionally intelligent and well-informed statesmen, insisted that as long as the canal continued to function normally (which it did until it was attacked) this was simply a commercial dispute between the Egyptian government and the Suez company, which with a modicum of goodwill could be settled by diplomacy and law. There was no need for any of the parties to resort to force. Unfortunately the British Prime Minister Sir Anthony Eden, who very much identified himself as a leading opponent of appeasement in the 1930s, chose to cast Nasser in the role of another Hitler, to be fought with every possible weapon. Concealing his activities from the Americans, Eden joined with France and Israel in a secret plan to seize the canal by force. As a military operation this was in most respects a success, but it was a diplomatic disaster. It aroused furious opposition all over the Middle East, it gravely embarrassed American efforts to aid the new anti-Russian government of Hungary elected in October, and it very soon plunged Britain and France into a financial crisis from which the Americans absolutely refused to rescue them until their forces conformed to the UN resolution and withdrew from the Canal Zone. The canal was closed for months by Egyptian blockships, and Eden's political career was sunk for ever. In the end Britain was left humiliated, exposed as untrustworthy and gravely weakened, while Dulles's promising scheme to bring peace to the Middle East was wrecked.[17]

Yet remarkably enough, the years after the Suez crisis – perhaps in part as a reaction to it – turned into a golden age of Anglo-American naval and military co-operation. Even before the crisis the 1954 Atomic Energy Act had allowed the US government to share essential nuclear information with its NATO allies. The British assault on Port Said on 6 November 1956, picking up an idea from the US Marines, was achieved with the world's first helicopter assault landing. Directly after Suez, overcoming the hostility of Congress and the brutally aggressive Rear-Admiral Hyman G. Rickover who controlled the US nuclear submarine programme, Mountbatten (First Sea Lord in 1955) with Eisenhower's discreet encouragement was able to develop a fruitful Anglo-American nuclear submarine co-operation. In October 1957 at Washington, Eisenhower and the new British Prime Minister, Harold Macmillan, issued a 'Declaration of Common Purpose'. In July 1958 the 'shameful' McMahon Act was completely reversed, revealing to the Americans that in some areas of nuclear technology the British were now ahead. Whereas Britain had never been treated as an equal in the Truman era, and was seldom consulted in advance on matters which concerned her, there was now extensive co-operation, especially between the armed forces of NATO, which culminated in the December 1962 Nassau conference at which President Kennedy offered Britain the Polaris submarine missile.[18]

The crisis of Anglo-American relations was unquestionably the Suez affair, when Eden's folly came very close to wrecking the new Western alliance. Eisenhower had every reason to resent Eden's behaviour, and it is a mark of his greatness as a statesman that he put aside his private feelings and consistently laboured to rebuild US alliances as soon as possible. He was encouraged by a voice from the past, for it was at this moment, in the aftermath of Suez, that Winston Churchill, now old and out of office, without the knowledge of the British government wrote a personal letter to Eisenhower:

> I do believe, with unfaltering conviction, that the theme of the Anglo-American alliance is more important today than at any time since the war. You and I had some part in raising it to the plane on which it has stood . . . it will now be an act of folly, on which our whole civilization may founder, to let events in the Middle East come between us. There seems to be a growing misunderstanding and frustration on both sides of the Atlantic. If they be allowed to develop, the skies will darken and it is the Soviet Union that will ride the storm . . . If we do not take immediate action in harmony, it is no exaggeration that we must expect to see the Middle East and the North African coastline under Soviet control and Western Europe placed at the mercy of the Russians . . . I write this letter because I know where your heart lies. You are now the only one who can influence events both in UNO and the free world to ensure that the great essentials are not lost in bickerings and pettiness among the nations. Yours is indeed a heavy responsibility and there is no greater believer in your capacity to bear it or well-wisher to your task than your old friend WSC.[19]

From the 1950s, British naval policy and activity increasingly fell into a pattern in which the country was pulled one way by financial weakness, and the other way by political and military obligations. The Korean War turned out not to be the Third World War, but it ushered in the Cold War, which provoked a succession of hot but limited wars in various parts of the world. The 'Malayan Emergency' (1948–60) was a twelve-year struggle against a Chinese-backed communist guerrilla movement. It was followed by the 'Indonesian Confrontation' (1963–6), in which Indonesian forces operated mainly along the jungle frontier between the British colonies of North Borneo (Sabah) and Sarawak and the Indonesian province of Kalimantan. Indonesia meant to frustrate the merger of the Malay States with North Borneo and Sarawak to form the new state of Malaysia. After the overthrow of the Indonesian leader Sukarno this attempt was abandoned. In both campaigns, but especially in Borneo, where movement through the jungle depended heavily on river traffic and helicopters, small warships and naval helicopters were involved, with aircraft flying both from jungle airstrips and from carriers. In both campaigns the different British services co-operated effectively, often with other Commonwealth forces from Australia and elsewhere. These wars are forgotten today because they were successful: Malaysia and Singapore are peaceful and democratic states. The obvious contrast is with the Vietnam War (1955–75), though there the Communist guerrillas enjoyed the geographical advantage of easier contact with their foreign sponsors. At roughly the same time, in the summer of 1961, a British naval task force landed troops which rescued Kuwait from Iraqi aggression, while in January 1964 a mutiny in the Tanganyika Rifles was suppressed by Royal Marines landed at Dar es Salaam.[20]

Operational success, however, went along with the financial strain which operations in distant waters always imposed on the balance of payments. When the Labour Party narrowly won the 1964 election it was firmly committed to the Indian Ocean and Harold Wilson the new Prime Minister (meaning to support India in the face of Chinese aggression) declared that Britain's frontier lay on the Himalayas, but that did not long survive the weakness of the pound. The Ministry of Defence spent £250 million a year overseas, mostly 'East of Suez', which could be presented as a direct threat to the strength of the economy. In February 1966 the new fleet carrier, the still-unnamed 'CVA-01', whose intended functions had been bound up with 'East of Suez', was cancelled. In November 1967 a currency crisis led to a 14 per cent devaluation of sterling; in January 1968 the Defence Secretary Denis Healey announced that Britain would withdraw completely from everywhere east of Suez except Hong Kong, and the Ministry of Defence sold off its entire stock of desert uniforms. In 1976 another sterling crisis forced Britain to borrow $3.9 billion from the International Monetary Fund. In 1979 the Navy's last fleet carrier, the *Ark Royal*, was paid off, and in 1981 a new Defence Secretary, the former banker John Nott, issued a Defence White Paper which sketched something like a withdrawal of the Royal Navy to the North Atlantic. All this had a very bad effect on British naval morale, and abroad was widely seen as a sign of moral collapse – certainly in Argentina, where the military regime seized the opportunity to invade the Falkland Islands in March and April 1982. Both in Buenos Aires and in Washington, it was assumed that Britain would not fight and could not win. Not a few people in Whitehall thought the same. On the evening of 31 March, with invasion clearly imminent, Sir Henry Leach the First Sea Lord

attended a meeting in the House of Commons and chanced to meet Mrs
Thatcher the Prime Minister, whom he found depressed by the defeatist advice
she had received from the Ministry of Defence. The admiral encouraged her
with assurances that a suitable force could be quickly assembled. 'He also haz-
arded the political view that, if an Argentine invasion did occur, the Navy not
only could but should respond.'[21] Only once before in British history, against
Diego Suarez in 1942, had a British amphibious expedition been launched at
almost as great a range. There is no need to rehearse the events of this daring
campaign, which ended with the surrender of the Argentine troops at Port
Stanley in June, but the course of the war glaringly highlighted the need of the
old *Ark Royal*'s capacities, especially airborne radar. It did not lead to any
immediate change in British policy, but it undoubtedly worked a powerful
change in public attitudes towards Britain's place in the world, and the Navy's
significance to Britain.[22]

'East of Suez' had long been much more than just a line out of Rudyard
Kipling's verse.[23] To the strategist it evoked the critical importance of the Suez
Canal as an artery of seaborne trade from Britain to India, Australia and the
Far East. It symbolized both the value and the cost of post-imperial defence
obligations. For many observers in Whitehall by the 1970s, 'East of Suez' stood
for imperial nostalgia and profitless expense. The future lay in joining the
Common Market, as Britain did in January 1973. Mr Nott before he left office
presided over a substantial programme of naval shipbuilding to make up the
losses of the Falklands War, and renewed the British nuclear deterrent by
adopting the Trident missile and new submarines to carry it, but he did not
publicly change his policy of retreating to the Eastern Atlantic. Yet though in
theory Britain had now completely withdrawn from 'East of Suez', in January
and February 1991 a substantial British squadron (and an entire armoured division) formed part of the US-led coalition which fought the Gulf War to eject
Iraq from its conquest of Kuwait. In 1997 the incoming Blair government's
defence review concluded that the future was uncertain, that Britain was deeply
immersed in the world economic system, and that 'if Britain did not go to the
crisis, the crisis would come to them'. There was now a large, semi-permanent
British naval presence in the Persian Gulf: 'The British concluded that they
simply could not disengage completely from the area, because it contained too
many interests deemed crucial to Britain's prosperity and security.'[24] In the
1990s the decisions were taken to build six landing ships of two different classes
and two 65,000-ton fleet carriers, now in service as the *Queen Elizabeth* and
Prince of Wales – by some way the largest ships ever built for the Royal Navy.
In 2021 the AUKUS partnership linked Australia, Britain and the US in a joint

project to equip the Royal Australian Navy with nuclear-powered (but conventionally armed) submarines. Whether these bold decisions were the right ones, and whether they were taken in time to deter aggression, only experience will tell, but it is absolutely clear that Britain as a naval power is inextricably committed to allies and trading partners in the rest of the world, and 'East of Suez' in the Indian Ocean and Pacific in particular. It is equally clear that the world is a dangerous place, and that Britain, her allies and other countries which attempt to uphold the rule of law at sea are subject to a growing incidence of threats and attacks. At the time of writing (2024), Russia is fully committed to a war of conquest against Ukraine, accompanied by repeated threats against countries (Britain among them) which help Ukraine's defence. In the Red Sea, British and other merchant ships are subject to attacks by Houthi tribesmen from the Yemen, armed and encouraged by Iran. In the China Seas, China bullies the weaker powers nearby (especially the Philippines) and frequently threatens to attack Taiwan, Japan and other neighbours which offer to defend their rights under international law. The question is sometimes asked whether Britain is still a naval power. It seems more and more likely that our only real question will be whether to fight for ourselves and our friends, or to yield.

CHRONOLOGY

1815
Jan 8: Battle of New Orleans.
Mar 1: Napoleon returns to France.
Jun 18: Battle of Waterloo.
Jul 7: Allied armies enter Paris.
Jul 14: Napoleon surrenders to the Royal Navy.
Aug 7: Napoleon sails for St Helena.

1816
Aug 27: Bombardment of Algiers.

1819
Feb 6: East India Company establishes a settlement at Singapore.

1821
May 5: Death of Napoleon on St Helena.

1822
Jan 15: Establishment of HM Coastguard.
Jan 27: Greece declares independence.
Oct 12: Brazil proclaims independence from Portugal.

1823
Dec 2: Monroe Doctrine.

1826
May 22: HMS *Adventure* and *Beagle* set off to survey Patagonia and Tierra
del Fuego.

1827
Jul 26: Britain, France and Russia agree to intervene in the Greek War of
Independence.
Oct 20: Combined British, French and Russian squadron destroys the Turkish
and Egyptian fleet at the Battle of Navarino.

1828
Apr 26: Russia declares war on the Ottoman Empire.
May 18: Start of the Portuguese Civil War.
Jul 15: Board of Longitude is dissolved.

1829

Sep 14: Treaty of Adrianople opens the Dardanelles to all commercial shipping.

1830

Feb 3: Greece declared independent at London Conference.
Jul 5: French take Algiers.
Oct 4: Belgian Declaration of Independence.

1831

Dec 25: Start of the Jamaican Slave Revolt.
Dec 27: HMS *Beagle* leaves on her second voyage with Charles Darwin on board.

1832

Jun 1: Navy and Victualling Boards are merged with the Board of Admiralty.
Nov 7: Squadron under Sir Pulteny Malcolm begins blockade of Dutch ports.
Dec 23: Fall of Antwerp brings the blockade of Dutch ports to an end.

1833

Jan 3: Captain Onslow in HMS *Clio* claims the Falkland Islands for Britain.
Jul 5: Captain Charles Napier leads Dom Pedro's fleet to victory in the Battle of Cape St Vincent.
Aug 21: Charter Act passed removing the remaining monopolies of the British East India Company.

1834

Jul 9: Don Carlos claims the Spanish throne triggering the First Carlist War.
Aug 1: Slavery is banned in most British Dominions.
Sep 19: 'Notices to Mariners' are formally introduced.

1838

Oct 1: Start of the First Afghan War.

1839

Jan 19: Capture of Aden by HMS *Volage*.
Mar: Start of the First Opium War (to Aug 1842).
Aug 23: British forces occupy Hong Kong.

1840

Feb 6: Treaty of Waitangi signed between Britain and the Maoris.
Jul 15: Britain, Austria, Russia and Prussia agree to back Turkey against Mehmet Ali of Egypt.
Aug 16: Captain James Clark Ross sets sail from Australia with HMS *Erebus* and *Terror* to chart Antarctica and find the magnetic South Pole.
Nov 3: Bombardment and capture of Acre.
Nov 27: Alexandria surrenders to Napier, ending the Syrian War.

1841

Jan 25: Captain Sir Edward Belcher, HMS *Sulphur*, claims Hong Kong for Britain.
Jul 13: Dardanelles closed to foreign warships.

1842

Mar: Mexican-American hostilities begin (end Feb 1848).
Mar 14: Admiralty Compass Department established.

1845

May 20: Franklin Expedition sails.
Jul 15: First cruise of the Experimental Squadron to settle differences in ship design.

1846

Jan 14: Launch of HMS *Amphion*, the Royal Navy's first screw frigate.
Jun 26: Repeal of the Corn Laws.

1847

Oct 12: Tea and sugar made available free in lieu of grog.

1848

Mar 20: 'Year of Revolutions': Ongoing revolts in Venice, Milan, Parma and
Berlin.
Apr 8: Sicily declares independence from Naples.
Jun 19: German Confederation decides to purchase a navy.
Sep 11: Naples and Sicily conclude an armistice aided by Vice-Admiral Sir
William Parker, commander-in-chief, Mediterranean Fleet.

1849

Jun 4: Battle of Heligoland: fleet of the German Confederation defeated by the
Danish Navy.

1850

Jan 15: RN Squadron blockades the Piraeus during the Don Pacifico Affair.
Mar 4: HMS *Medea* takes thirteen pirate junks in Mirs Bay, China.
Apr 19: Clayton–Bulwer Treaty signed, Britain and US agreeing that any
inter-oceanic canal created through Panama should be neutral.
May 16: France launches *Napoléon*, first steam ship of the line.
Aug 28: Anglo-French Telegraph Company lays first experimental cross-channel
telegraph cable.

1851

Dec 26: Capture of Lagos.

1852

Apr 2: German Confederation fleet is dissolved.
Apr 5: Second Burmese War (to Jan 1853).
Dec 2: French Republic dissolved with Napoleon III declaring himself Emperor.

1853

Jul 2: Russian forces invade the Ottoman Danubian Principalities.

Sep 23: British Fleet ordered to Constantinople.

Oct 4: Ottoman Empire declares war on Russia.

Nov 30: Russian Navy destroys a Turkish squadron at the Battle of Sinope.

1854

Jan 3: Anglo-French fleet enters the Black Sea.

Feb 23: Admiral Sir Charles Napier appointed to command the North Sea Fleet while Rear-Admiral Sir Richard Dundas is given command of the Mediterranean Fleet.

Mar 11: Napier sails from Spithead, commanding the first British steam fleet to go to war.

Mar 28: Britain and France declare war on Russia.

Aug: Capture of the Russian fortress of Bomarsund in the Åland Islands.

Oct 17: First bombardment of Sevastopol.

Oct 25: Battle of Balaclava.

Nov 5: Battle of Inkerman.

Dec: Napier is relieved by Dundas.

1855

Jan 30: Royal Marines divided into Artillery and Light Infantry.

Feb 1: Allied fleet begins the blockade of Russia's Black Sea ports.

Jun 21: Royal Navy begins its first minesweeping operation in the approaches to Kronstadt.

Aug 13: Sveaborg bombarded and captured.

Sep 9: Sevastopol falls.

Sep 19: Naval brigade in Crimea is disbanded.

Oct 9: Blockade of Archangel ends.

1856

Jan 29: Victoria Cross instituted.

Mar 30: Treaty of Paris ends war with Russia.

Apr 16: Declaration of Paris attempts to codify maritime law and outlaw privateering.

Oct 8: The *Arrow* Incident provokes the start of the Second China War.

Nov 1: Start of the Anglo-Persian War.

1857

May 10: Start of the Indian Mutiny.

June 1: Action of Fatshan Creek.

Dec 29: Anglo-French forces take Canton, China.

1858

Jun 26: Treaty of Tientsin ends the Second China War.

Aug 2: The Government of India Act passes control of India from the East India Company to the British government.

1859

Mar 1: End of the Indian Mutiny.

Apr–Jul: Franco-Austrian War in Northern Italy, confirming Austrian rule of Venice.

Aug 13: Royal Naval Reserve established.

Nov 24: France launches *Gloire*, the first ironclad battleship.

1860

Apr 8: War against China formally resumes (to Oct 24).

Dec 29: HMS *Warrior* launched, the first British iron-hulled, armour-plated warship.

1861

Feb 9: Formation of the Confederate States of America.

Mar 17: Victor Emmanuel proclaimed king of unified Italy.

Apr 12: Start of the American Civil War.

May 13: Britain issues a declaration of neutrality in the American Civil War.

1862

Mar 8–9: Battle of Hampton Roads, first engagement between ironclads.

Aug 24: Commission of the British-built Confederate cruiser *Alabama*.

1863

Feb 7: Flagship of the Australia Station, HMS *Orpheus*, wrecked on the Manukau Bar, New Zealand, killing the Commodore and 189 men.

Aug 15: Start of the Anglo-Satsuma War.

Sep 30: HMS *Britannia* arrives on the River Dart for use as a cadet training ship.

Oct: Two Laird turret ironclads ordered by the Confederate States from Laird Brothers, Birkenhead, are seized by the British government.

1864

Mar 29: Britain cede the Ionian Islands to Greece.

Aug 5: Royal Navy adopts the White Ensign.

1865

Jun 9: End of the American Civil War.

1866

Jun 20: Italy declares war on Austria (to 3 Oct).

Jul 3: Prussian Army defeats Austrians at Sadowa (Köninggrätz).

Jul 20: Austrian fleet defeats Italians at Lissa.

Jul 27: Cable ship *Great Eastern* finishes laying the first successful transatlantic cable.
Aug 23: Peace of Prague officially ends hostilities between Prussia and Austria.
Oct 3: Treaty of Vienna officially ends hostilities between Italy and Austria.

1867

Mar 29: British North America Act establishes the Dominion of Canada.
Mar 30: US purchases Alaska from Russia.
Apr 16: Formation of the North German Confederation.

1869

Jul: Imperial Japanese Navy established.
Nov 17: Suez Canal opened.

1870

Mar 22: Cable ships finish laying submarine cable from Bombay to Aden and Suez, directly linking India with Britain.
Jul 19: France declares war on Prussia.
Sep 1–2: Battle of Sedan and capture of Napoleon III.
Sep 4: France declares itself a republic.
Sep 7: Loss of HMS *Captain* off Cape Finisterre.

1871

Jan 10: German states unite as a single country under the Prussian Wilhelm I.
Jan 28: Paris falls and an armistice is signed.
May 10: Treaty of Frankfurt signed: France cedes Alsace-Lorraine to Germany.
Jul 12: HMS *Devastation* launched as the Royal Navy's first battleship without sails.

1872

Aug 14: *Alabama* dispute settled by arbitration by Britain paying $15,500,000.

1873

HMS *Challenger* discovers the Mid-Atlantic Ridge.
Feb 1: Royal Naval College, Greenwich, opened.
Apr 23: Start of the Ashanti War (to 4 Feb 1874).
Jun 5: Anti-slavery expedition against the Sultan of Zanzibar.
Oct 22: Alliance of the 'Three Emperors' between Germany, Russia and Austria.

1874

Jan 1: British East India Company officially dissolved.

1875

Mar 23: HMS *Challenger* takes soundings of the deepest known point of the world's oceans, the Mariana Trench.

May 20: *Alert* and *Discovery* set sail from Portsmouth on the British Arctic Expedition to reach the North Pole.
Nov 24: British government purchases the controlling interest in the Suez Canal.

1876
Jul 14: Explosion of a box boiler aboard HMS *Thunderer* killing forty-five.
Aug: Merchant Shipping Act passed.

1877
Apr 24: Start of the Russo-Turkish War.
Jul 21: British Cabinet resolves to enter the war on the side of Turkey if Constantinople is occupied.

1878
Jan 28: Turkey signs armistice with Russia.
Feb 2: Greece declares war on Turkey.
Feb 13: The Mediterranean Fleet under Vice-Admiral Geoffrey Phipps Hornby transits the Dardanelles to protect Constantinople from an advancing Russian army.
Jul 13: The Congress and Treaty of Berlin ends the Russo-Turkish War.
Nov 19: Naval Brigade from HMS *Active* lands at Durban to participate in the Zulu Wars.

1879
Jan 2: Major turret explosion aboard HMS *Thunderer* causes the Navy to abandon its use of muzzle-loading guns.
Jan 22: Battles of Isandlwana and Rorke's Drift.
Sep 1: Peace treaty signed with the Zulus.

1880
Jul 1: Royal Naval Engineering College founded at Keyham.
Dec 20: Start of the First Boer War (to Mar 1881).

1881
Mar 1: Royal Naval Medical School, Haslar, opened.

1882
May 19: Mediterranean Fleet under Seymour arrives off Alexandria.
May 20: Triple Alliance formed between Germany, Austria-Hungary and Italy.
Jul 13: Mediterranean Fleet bombards and captures Alexandria.
Dec: Foreign Intelligence Committee of the Admiralty established.

1884
Feb 18: Major-General Charles Gordon arrives in Khartoum, Sudan.
Feb 29: Naval Brigade participates in the Second Battle of El Teb, Sudan.

Mar 18: Mahdist forces lay siege to Khartoum.
Oct 7: Nile Expedition sets off from Alexandria.

1885
Jan 17: Naval Brigade under Captain Lord Charles Beresford participates in the Battle of Abu Klea, Sudan.
Jan 26: Khartoum falls to Mahdist forces and Gordon is killed.
Mar 30: Russian forces occupy Pendjeh.
Nov 7: Start of the Third Burma War.
Nov 28: British forces occupy Mandalay.

1886
Jan 1: Britain annexes upper Burma.
May 8: Mediterranean Fleet joins an international force in the blockade of Greece to prevent war with Turkey.

1887
Jan 21: Foreign Intelligence Committee renamed Naval Intelligence Department.
Feb 12: Anglo-Italian Agreement to maintain the status quo in the Mediterranean, which the Austrians join the following month.

1888
Oct 29: Convention of Constantinople signed guaranteeing to keep the Suez Canal open in both peace and war.

1889
May 31: Naval Defence Act establishes the 'two-power standard'.

1892
Jan 1: Start of the Gambia River expedition.

1893
Jan 17: Franco-Russian Alliance signed.

1894
Feb 22: Gambia expeditionary force landed from HMS *Raleigh*.

1895
Apr 17: Treaty of Shimonoseki ends the Sino-Japanese War.
Oct 17: Mediterranean Fleet deployed off the Dardanelles to apply pressure on Turkey during the Armenian crisis.

1896
Mar 18: Start of the Sudan campaign.

1897
Feb 15: Royal Marines land in Crete to assist in suppressing a revolt.
Feb 18: Naval Brigade participates in the capture of Benin.

Jun 26: Diamond Jubilee Fleet Review off Spithead.
Dec 16: Treaty of Constantinople officially ends the Greco-Turkish War.

1898
Mar 28: Germany enacts First Naval Law.
Apr 25: United States declares war on Spain.
Sep 18: Fashoda Incident.
Dec 10: Treaty of Paris ends the Spanish American War.

1899
Oct 12: Start of the South African War.
Scott–Muraviev Agreement delimits British and Russian spheres of influence in China.

1900
Jan 6: Naval Brigade participates in the defence of Ladysmith.
Feb 27: Naval Brigade participates in the capture of Paardeberg, South Africa.
Jun 12: Germany enacts Second Naval Law.
Aug 31: British forces take Johannesburg, Transvaal.
Nov 9: Russia occupies Manchuria.

1901
Jan 1: Commonwealth of Australia proclaimed.

1902
Jan 30: Signing of the Anglo-Japanese Alliance.
Feb 5: First dive by *Holland I*, the Royal Navy's first submarine.
May 31: End of the South African War.

1903
Aug 4: Royal Naval College Osborne opened.
Royal Naval Volunteer Reserve is formed.

1904
Jan 11: Committee of Imperial Defence established.
Feb 8: Start of the Russo-Japanese War.
Apr 8: Entente Cordiale signed between Britain and France.
May 4: US begins work on the Panama Canal.
Aug 10: Attempt by Russian Fleet to break out of Port Arthur, defeated in the Battle of the Yellow Sea.

1905
Jan 1: Japanese capture Port Arthur.
May 27–28: Battle of Tsushima.
Sep 5: Treaty of Portsmouth ends the Russo-Japanese War.
Oct 26: Sweden grants independence to Norway.

1906
June 5: Germany enacts Third Naval Law.

1907
Aug 31: Signing of the Anglo-Russian entente.

1908
Jun 14: Germany enacts Fourth Naval Law.
Dec 4: London Naval Conference opens.

1909
Mar 12: Governments of Australia and New Zealand offer to finance a battle-cruiser each for the RN.
Apr 29: Chancellor of the Exchequer David Lloyd George introduces budget with significant tax increase to cover large expansions in naval and social expenditure.

1910
May 4: Foundation of the Canadian Naval Service.

1911
Mar 22: Royal Fleet Auxiliary established.
Jul 1: Start of Agadir Crisis.
Sep 29: Italo-Turkish War (ends 18 Oct 1912)
Oct 11: Revolution begins in China.

1912
Jan 8: Establishment of the Naval War Staff.
Apr 13: Formation of the Royal Flying Corps with a military and a naval wing.

1914
Jul 1: Royal Naval Air Service divides from the RFC.
Jul 28: Austria declares war on Serbia starting the First World War.
Aug 4: Britain declares war on Germany.
Aug 10: German warships *Goeben* and *Breslau* pass through the Dardanelles to be handed to the Ottoman Empire.
Aug 15: Panama Canal opens.
Aug 28: Battle of Heligoland Bight.
Oct 30: Admiral of the Fleet Lord Fisher becomes First Sea Lord for a second time.
Nov 1: Battle of Coronel.
Nov 5: Britain declares war on the Ottoman Empire.
Dec 8: Battle of the Falklands.

1915
Jan 24: Battle of Dogger Bank.
Feb 3: Turkish attack on the Suez Canal fails.

Feb 19: Allied Fleet begins bombardment of the outer forts of the Dardanelles.

Apr 25: Allied forces land on the Gallipoli peninsula.

May 7: RMS *Lusitania* sunk by U-20 off Ireland.

May 15: Fisher resigns as First Sea Lord.

May 31: First German Zeppelin raids on London.

1916

Jan 8: Completion of the evacuation of Allied troops from the Gallipoli peninsula.

Apr 24: Irish rebellion in Dublin.

May 31: Battle of Jutland.

Aug 28: Italy declares war on Germany.

Nov 28: First German bombing raid on Britain using aeroplanes.

Dec 7: National Coalition Government formed under David Lloyd George.

1917

Feb 1: Germany declares its use of unrestricted submarine warfare for the second time.

Mar 8: Start of the Russian Revolution.

Mar 16: Tsar Nicholas II abdicates.

Apr 6: United States declares war on Germany.

May 14: Post of First Sea Lord is combined with that of Chief of the Naval Staff.

May 22: First convoy sails in the Mediterranean.

May 24: First convoy sails in the Atlantic.

Jun 14: Convoy system approved by the Admiralty.

Jun 24: Russian Black Sea Fleet mutinies at Sevastopol.

Jul 9: HMS *Vanguard* destroyed by magazine explosion at Scapa Flow.

Aug 17: Report of the Smuts Commission on aviation recommends the formation of a unified air force.

Nov 7: Bolshevik Revolution in Russia begins.

Nov 9: Rapallo Conference ends with agreement on the creation of a Supreme Allied War Council.

Nov 29: Formation of the Women's Royal Naval Service.

1918

Jan 10: Russian civil war begins.

Mar 3: Treaty of Brest-Litovsk signed, ending the war in the east.

Mar 7: Royal Navy commences operations against Murmansk and Archangel.

Apr 1: Creation of the Royal Air Force.

Apr 12: The Grand Fleet's main base moves from Scapa Flow to Rosyth.

Jul 17: Execution of Tsar Nicholas II and his family.

Oct 22: Spanish influenza reaches its peak in Britain.

Nov 11: Germany signs an Armistice with the Western Powers.
Nov 21: German High Seas Fleet surrenders.

1919
Apr 7: The Grand Fleet is broken up and the Atlantic and Mediterranean Fleets reconstituted.
Jun 21: German High Seas Fleet is scuttled by its crews in Scapa Flow.
Jun 28: Naval blockade of Germany is officially lifted with the signing of the Paris Peace Treaty.
Oct 1: WRNS disbanded.
Nov 1: Naval Intelligence Division 25 ('Room 40') merges with Military Intelligence Section 1b to form the government Code and Cypher School.
Nov 8: Britain announces its intention to withdraw from Russia.

1920
Jan 21: Naval operations against the 'Mad Mullah' of Somaliland.
Jan 21: Conclusion of the Paris Peace Conferences and inaugural General Assembly of the League of Nations.

1921
Jan 3: Herbert Smith of Sopwith arrives in Japan leading a team of aircraft designers to create Mitsubishi's aircraft division.
Mar 31: Coalminers' strike: Atlantic Fleet ships' companies supply men to protect essential services in the first use of the Emergency Powers Act.
Jun 20: Announcement to build naval base at Singapore.
Jun 20: New Zealand Naval Forces become New Zealand Division of the Royal Navy.
Aug: Sir Eric Geddes appointed head of a Committee on National Expenditure.
Nov: Mission under Sir William Forbes-Sempill arrives in Japan to share technology on naval aviation.
Nov 12: Washington Naval Conference opens (ends Feb 1922).

1922
Feb 6: Washington Naval Treaty is signed by Allies of WWI, agreeing to prevent an arms race by limiting naval construction.
Feb 21: Geddes report imposes financial and manpower cuts on the Armed Services ('Geddes Axe').
Sep 3: King George V confers title of 'Merchant Navy' on British Mercantile Marine.

1923
Feb 27: Start of the world cruise of the Special Service Squadron.
May 24: End of the Irish Civil War.
Jul 21: Report of the Balfour Committee framing Navy–RAF relations.

Jul 24: Treaty of Lausanne signed. Peace between Greece, Turkey and the Allies.
Aug 17: Anglo-Japanese Alliance ends.
Aug 31: Italian forces seize Corfu.

1924
Jul: Trenchard–Keyes Agreement signed setting out framework for relations between the Navy and the RAF.
Sep 30: Naval control of Germany abolished.
Nov 29: USS *Langley* joins the Pacific Fleet as the US Navy's first fully operational carrier.

1926
May 4: General Strike begins.
Sep 1: Formation of the Imperial Defence College.

1927
May 13: Black Friday, collapse of the German economy.
Jun 20: Second Washington Naval Conference.

1929
Oct 24: Wall Street Crash.

1930
France begins construction of the Maginot Line.
Jan 21: London Naval Conference opened.

1931
Jul 25: May Committee Report on British Government finances recommends drastic economies.
Sep 11: Government decision to reduce pay across the armed services appears in the press.
Sep 15: Atlantic Fleet mutinies at Invergordon.
Sep 16: Mutiny ends and the Atlantic Fleet sails to its home ports.
Sep 18: Manchurian Incident staged by the Japanese as a pretext for the Japanese invasion of Manchuria.
Sep 21: Britain abandons the Gold Standard.
Dec 11: Statute of Westminster formally establishes legislative equality for the Dominions.

1932
Mar: Atlantic Fleet renamed Home Fleet in the aftermath of Invergordon.
Mar 23: Cabinet decision to abandon the Ten Years Rule.

1933
Jan 30: Adolf Hitler becomes Chancellor of Germany.
Mar 23: Enabling Law passed giving Hitler dictatorial powers in Germany.

Mar 27: Japan withdraws from the League of Nations.
Apr 25: US and Canada abandon the Gold Standard.

1934
Mar 19: First report of the Defence Requirements Committee.
Mar 27: Vinson–Trammell Act passed in the United States.
Jun 11: Geneva Disarmament Conference fails.
Aug 2: Hitler declared Führer and Head of State in Germany.
Dec 19: London Naval Conference ends without resolution as Japan renounces all previous naval treaties.

1935
Mar 16: Germany renounces the disarmament clauses of the Versailles Treaty.
Jun 18: Anglo-German Naval Agreement signed.
Aug 31: US passes the Neutrality Act.
Sep 15: Germany enacts the Nuremberg Laws.
Oct 3: Italy invades Abyssinia.
Dec 9: Discussions open for a second London Naval Treaty.

1936
Jan 15: Japan withdraws from the London Naval Conference.
Mar 13: Sir Thomas Inskip appointed Minister for Co-ordination of Defence.
Mar 25: Second London Naval Treaty signed.
May 5: Italian forces capture Addis Ababa.
Jul 17: Start of the Spanish Civil War.
Jul 26: Germany and Italy agree to assist Nationalist forces in Spain.
Nov 1: Rome–Berlin Axis signed.
Nov 25: Anti-Comintern Pact signed between Nazi Germany and the Empire of Japan.
Dec 10: King Edward VIII abdicates.

1937
Mar 19: First Defence Loans Act passed.
Apr 26: Attack on Guernica by Nationalist forces and the German Luftwaffe.
May 1: Neutrality Act passed in the US.
Jul 7: Japan invades the remainder of China.
Jul 30: Inskip Report proposes putting the Fleet Air Arm under naval control.
Nov: Admiralty Operational Intelligence Centre established.

1938
Mar 11: German forces occupy Austria.
May 20: British partial mobilization.
Jul 11: Nomonhan Incident; fighting between Japan and the Soviet Union in Inner Mongolia.
Sep 27: The Royal Navy mobilizes.

Sep 30: Munich agreement signed.

Oct 2: Japan withdraws from the League of Nations.

Nov 9–10: *Kristallnacht* in Germany.

1939

Feb 27: Britain and France recognize General Franco's Nationalists as the Spanish government.

Mar 15: Germany invades the remainder of Czechoslovakia.

Mar 31: Britain and France guarantee support to Poland in the event of German aggression.

Apr 1: End of the Spanish Civil War.

Apr 12: WRNS reconstituted.

Apr 27: Germany officially renounces the Anglo-German Naval Treaty.

May 22: Germany and Italy sign the 'Pact of Steel' military alliance.

May 24: Handover of the Fleet Air Arm from the RAF to the Navy.

Aug 23: Molotov–Ribbentrop Pact signed, non-aggression pact between Nazi Germany and the Soviet Union.

Sep 1: Germany invades Poland.

Sep 3: Britain and France declare war on Germany.

Sep 4: President Franklin Roosevelt declares the neutrality of the US.

Sep 17: Soviet Union invades Poland and subsequently divides territory with Germany.

Sep 30: British Expeditionary Force deployed to France.

Nov: Convoy system for British merchant shipping fully operational.

Nov 4: US amends 1937 Neutrality Act to permit Britain and France to purchase military equipment from American companies.

Dec 13: Battle of the River Plate.

1940

Mar: Frisch–Peierls Memorandum from the University of Birmingham outlines the possibility of constructing an atomic bomb.

Apr 9: Germany invades Norway.

Apr 10: First Battle of Narvik.

Apr 13: Second Battle of Narvik.

May 10: National Coalition Government formed under Winston Churchill following the resignation of Neville Chamberlain.

May 25: Order issued for the Allied evacuation of Norway.

Jun 4: Completion of Operation 'Dynamo' evacuates 338,226 Allied troops from France.

Jun 8: HMS *Glorious* sunk off Norway by the German battle-cruisers *Scharnhorst* and *Gneisenau*.

Jun 10: Italy declares war on France and Britain.

Jun 14: Paris falls.

Jun 22: Franco-German Armistice signed at Versailles.

Jun 30: Force H forms at Gibraltar.
Jul 3: Royal Navy destroys elements of the French fleet in harbour at Mers-el-Kébir.
Sep 2: 'Destroyers for Bases' Deal signed between Britain and the US.
Oct 7: Germany seizes Romanian oilfields.
Nov 11–12: Fleet Air Arm sinks three Italian battleships in Taranto harbour.

1941
Feb 7: Western Approaches command shifted from Plymouth to Liverpool.
Feb 15: RAF Coastal Command is placed under the operational control of the Admiralty.
Mar 11: US Lend-Lease Act passed to allow USA to lend or lease war supplies to any nation deemed 'vital to the defense of the United States'.
Mar 27–9: Battle of Matapan.
Apr 13: Soviet Union signs a non-aggression pact with Japan.
Apr 23: Greece signs an armistice with Germany.
Apr 24: Operation 'Demon', Mediterranean Fleet under Cunningham commences evacuation of British forces from Greece.
May 24: HMS *Hood* sunk in the Denmark Strait by the German battleship *Bismarck*.
May 27: *Bismarck* sunk by the Home Fleet.
June 22: Germany invades the Soviet Union in Operation 'Barbarossa'.
Aug 21: First Arctic convoy sails for Archangel.
Sep 1: US Navy assumes responsibility for escorting transatlantic convoys as far as Iceland and commences a patrol in the Denmark Strait.
Sep 8: Start of the siege of Leningrad.
Oct 17: General Tōjō Hideki becomes Prime Minister of Japan, effectively marking military rule in the country.
Nov 14: HMS *Ark Royal* sunk by U81 off Gibraltar.
Dec 7: Japanese attack on Pearl Harbor.
Dec 8: Britain and the US declare war on Japan.
Dec 10: HMS *Prince of Wales* and HMS *Repulse* sunk by Japanese aircraft off the coast of Malaya.
Dec 10: Japanese forces take Guam.
Dec 19: HMS *Queen Elizabeth* and *Valiant* sunk at their moorings in Alexandria by Italian 'human torpedoes'.
Dec 22: First Washington Conference (code name 'Arcadia') between United Kingdom and USA, with discussion of a future United Nations.
Dec 23: Japanese forces take Wake Island.
Dec 25: Japanese forces take Hong Kong.

1942
Jan 11: Japan declares war on the Netherlands and begins landings on the Dutch East Indies.

Jan 11: Operation 'Drumroll', German U-boats begin operating off the coast of the US.

Jan 16: Japanese forces invade Burma.

Jan 20: Wannsee Conference.

Jan 21: German and Italian forces begin an offensive in North Africa.

Feb 6: Britain and the US establish the Combined Chiefs of Staff.

Feb 11: German battle-cruisers *Scharnhorst* and *Gneisenau* leave Brest to begin Operation 'Cerberus', the Channel Dash.

Feb 12: ANZAC Squadron is formed and integrated into the American Command Structure (later Task Force 44).

Feb 13: *Scharnhorst* and *Gneisenau* successfully reach Wilhelmshaven despite mine damage.

Feb 15: Fall of Singapore and capture of the oil refineries of the Dutch East indies by Japan.

Feb 27: Battle of the Java Sea.

Apr 5: Japanese carriers attack Ceylon.

Apr 18: Doolittle Raid, USAAF bomb Tokyo.

May 5: British capture of Diego Suarez.

May 6: US Army surrenders the Philippines to Japan.

Jun 4–7: Battle of Midway.

Jun 20: Britain and US agree to pool resources in the development of nuclear power and transfer all research and construction effort to the US (Manhattan Project).

Jun 21: German forces take Tobruk, forcing the Mediterranean Fleet to retreat through the Suez Canal into the Red Sea.

June 25: Second Washington Conference between Britain and the USA to discuss how best to aid the Soviet Union.

Jul 1: First Battle of El Alamein.

Jul 4: USAAF begins offensive operations over Europe.

July 4: Arctic Convoy PQ 17 ordered to scatter.

Aug 15: Operation 'Pedestal' relieves Malta.

Aug 23: Start of the Battle of Stalingrad.

Oct 11–12: Battle of Cape Esperance.

Nov 8–16: Operation 'Torch': Allied invasion of North Africa.

Dec 19: British and Indian forces begin an offensive into Burma.

Dec 31: Battle of the Barents Sea.

1943

Jan 14: Start of the 'Symbol' Conference at Casablanca.

Jan 31: Erich Raeder replaced as Head of the German Navy by Admiral Karl Dönitz.

Jan 31: German forces surrender Stalingrad.

Mar 2–4: Battle of the Bismarck Sea.

Mar 14–20: Defence of convoys HX 228, SC 121, HX 229 and SC 122 in the North Atlantic, with the loss of twenty-one ships.

May 4–6: Battle for Convoy ONS 5 begins 'Black May' for German U-boats in the North Atlantic.
May 12–25: Third Washington Conference ('Trident'), strategic meeting between United Kingdom and USA.
May 24: German U-boats ordered to withdraw from the North Atlantic.
Jul 9: Allied invasion of Sicily ('Husky').
Jul 25: Mussolini dismissed from office.
Aug 17–24: First Quebec Conference ('Quadrant') held between USA, Canada and Britain.
Sep 3: Italy surrenders to the Allies. Allied forces cross the Strait of Messina into Italy ('Baytown').
Sep 9: Invasion of Italy at Salerno and Taranto ('Avalanche' and 'Slapstick'). Italian Fleet surrenders at Malta.
Sep 22: Midget submarines attack the Tirpitz in Kaafjord, north Norway ('Source').
Sep 23: Italian Social Republic (Fascist-German puppet state) created in Northern Italy.
Oct 13: Italy declares war on Germany.
Nov 1: US forces land on Bougainville in the Solomon Islands.
Nov 22–6: Cairo Conference ('Sextant') held between United States, United Kingdom and China agreed Allied policy towards Japan and post-war Asia.
Nov 28–Dec 1: Tehran Conference ('Eureka') between Roosevelt, Churchill and Stalin commits to opening a second front against Germany.
Dec 26: Battle of North Cape (sinking of the *Scharnhorst*).

1944
Jan 22: Amphibious landing at Anzio ('Shingle').
Feb 17: US 5th Fleet launches air strikes against the Japanese naval base at Truk, Caroline Islands ('Hailstone').
Feb 22: US 5th Fleet begins air strikes against Japanese forces in the Marianas Islands.
Apr 3: Fleet Air Arm strikes damage *Tirpitz* in Kaafjord ('Tungsten').
Apr 19: Eastern Fleet with USS *Saratoga* launches air strikes on Japanese at Sumatra, Dutch East Indies ('Cockpit').
May 17: Eastern Fleet with USS *Saratoga* launches air strikes on Japanese at Surabaya, Java, Dutch East Indies ('Transom').
Jun 6: Allied landings in Normandy ('Overlord').
Jun 19–20: Battle of the Philippine Sea.
Jul 21: US landing on Guam ('Stevedore').
Jul 24: US forces land on Tinian, Mariana Islands.
July 25: Eastern Fleet air strikes on Sabang, Dutch East Indies ('Crimson').
Aug 9: Floating dry dock collapses at Trincomalee, damaging HMS *Valiant* beyond repair.
Aug 15: Allied landings on the Côte d'Azur ('Dragoon').

Aug 24: Home Fleet air strikes seriously damage Tirpitz in Kaafjord ('Goodwood III').

Aug 24: Eastern Fleet air strikes on Emmahaven and the Padang cement works on Sumatra, Dutch East Indies ('Banquet').

Sep 12–16: Second Quebec Conference ('Octagon') between United Kingdom and United States. Roosevelt accepts offer of a British Pacific Fleet.

Sep 17: Eastern Fleet launches air strikes on Sigli, Sumatra, Dutch East Indies ('Light').

Oct 10: US 3rd Fleet air strikes against Japanese forces on Okinawa and Formosa.

Oct 25: First kamikaze attack by Japanese on USN fleet.

Nov 12: Tirpitz sunk near Tromsø ('Catechism').

Nov 22: The Eastern Fleet is redesignated as the British Pacific Fleet.

Nov 24: USAAF makes its first bombing raid on Japan from the Mariana Islands.

1945

Jan 3: British amphibious assault on Akyab, Burma ('Lightning').

Jan 4: Eastern Fleet air strike on the Japanese-held oil refineries at Pangkalan Brandan, Sumatra ('Lentil').

Jan 6: USS *New Mexico* struck by a Japanese kamikaze off Luzon, Philippines, nearly killing Admiral Sir Bruce Fraser.

Jan 21: Dönitz orders the German Navy to begin operations to evacuate East Prussia ('Hannibal').

Jan 24: British air strike on the Japanese-held oil refineries at Palembang, Sumatra ('Meridian I').

Jan 29: Air strike on the Japanese-held oil refineries at Palembang, Sumatra ('Meridian II').

Feb 4–11: Yalta Conference ('Argonaut') on post-war reorganization between the USA, Britain and Russia.

Feb 10: British Pacific Fleet arrives at Sydney.

Feb 19: US landing on Iwo Jima ('Detachment').

Mar 18: British Pacific Fleet assigned to Admiral Nimitz's Pacific Ocean Area as TF 57.

Mar 26: British Pacific Fleet begins independent operations against Japanese airfields on the Sakishima Gunto and Formosa.

Apr 1: First Kamikaze attack on the British Pacific Fleet lightly damages HMS *Indefatigable*.

Apr 7: Japanese Battleship *Yamato* sunk in the East China Sea.

Apr 28: Benito Mussolini executed by Italian Communists.

May 8: Germany surrenders.

Jun 31: British midget submarines sink Japanese heavy cruiser *Takao* at Singapore and cut undersea cables off Saigon and Hong Kong.

Jul 17: British Pacific Fleet participates as the US 3rd Fleet resumes operations against the Japanese Home Islands with air strikes and shore bombardment.

17 Jul–2 Aug: USA, Britain and Soviet Union meet to plan post-war peace settlement (Potsdam Conference).

Aug 6: Atom bomb dropped on Hiroshima.

Aug 9: Atom bomb dropped on Nagasaki.

Aug 9: British Pacific Fleet participates as the US 3rd Fleet resumes operations against the Home Islands in Honshu and Hokkaido and then south to Tokyo.

Aug 15: British Pacific Fleet participates in the last air strike of WWII with the US 3rd Fleet against Tokyo.

Aug 24: End of the Lend-Lease Programme.

Aug 30: East Indies Fleet liberates Hong Kong.

Sep 2: Japanese surrender is signed on deck of USS *Missouri*. Admiral Sir Bruce Fraser signs on behalf of the British Empire.

Oct 15: British government takes emergency powers to deal with the balance of payments crisis following the end of Lend-Lease.

Dec 3: Lieutenant-Commander Eric Brown performs the RN's first deck landing of a jet aircraft aboard HMS *Ocean*.

Dec 6: Anglo-American Loan Agreement signed granting Britain $3.75 billion in return for, amongst other things, the convertibility of sterling.

Dec 27: World Bank and International Monetary Fund established following the signing of the Bretton Woods Agreement.

Dec: The British Pacific Fleet is disbanded and its forces are absorbed into the East Indies fleet.

1947

Jan 1: Ministry of Defence established.

Feb 7: British plan for the partition of Palestine is rejected by both Jews and Arabs.

Mar 12: President Harry Truman announces the Truman Doctrine.

Jun 5: US Secretary of State George Marshall announces a European Recovery Programme, later to be known as the Marshall Plan.

1948

Jun 24: Soviet Union blockades Berlin.

1949

Apr 4: Signing of the North Atlantic Treaty creates the North Atlantic Treaty Organization.

Oct 6: Mutual Defence Assistance Act passed in the US providing military aid to NATO countries.

1950

Jun 25: North Korean People's Army invades the Republic of Korea, starting the Korean War.

Jun 28: Seoul falls to the North Korean People's Army.

Sep 15: UN amphibious assault at Inchon.

Sep 15: British National Service is extended to two years.
Oct 19: UN forces take Pyongyang.
Dec 13: Marshall Aid to Britain ends.
Dec 31: Chinese forces enter Korea across the Yalu River.

1951
Jan 1: Chinese and North Korean forces cross the 38th Parallel and enter South Korea.
Jan 5: UN forces evacuated at Inchon.

1952
Oct 3: First British atomic weapon is detonated off Montebello Islands, off Western Australia ('Hurricane').

1953
Jul 27: Ceasefire is declared in the Korean War.

1954
May 24: HMS *Centaur* re-commissions as the RN's first aircraft carrier with an angled flight deck.

1955
Nov 1: Vietnam/Second Indochina War begins.
Nov 22: Soviet Union tests its first true thermonuclear weapon.

1956
Jul 26: Egyptian government 'nationalizes' the Suez Canal. Britain, France and the US respond by implementing financial restrictions on Egypt.
Oct 29: Israeli forces invade Egypt.
Oct 31: Anglo-French operation to seize the Suez Canal Zone ('Musketeer').
Nov 6: British government unilaterally declares a ceasefire.
Dec 22: Anglo-French forces withdraw from the Canal Zone to be replaced by UN forces.

1957
Mar 6: UN Emergency Force takes over the Gaza Strip from Israeli forces.

1960
Oct 21: HMS *Dreadnought*, the RN's first nuclear-powered submarine, is launched.

1961
Mar 3: USN Submarine Squadron 14 arrives at Holy Loch, the only US strategic deterrent submarine force to be stationed outside the US.
Jun 25: President Kassem of Iraq claims Kuwait as a part of Iraq.
Jul 1: First elements of a British Task Force arrive off Kuwait.
Aug 13: Construction of the Berlin Wall begins.
Oct 19: British forces withdraw from Kuwait.

1962
Oct 16–29: Cuban Missile Crisis.
Dec 18: Nassau Agreement signed by President Kennedy. The United States agrees to sell Polaris missiles to Britain.

1963
Jan 20: President Sukarno of Indonesia announces a policy of 'confrontation' with the Malaysian Federation.

1964
Jan 25: Royal Marines land at Dar es Salaam to suppress a mutiny in the Tanganyika Rifles.
Oct 16: China tests its first atomic weapon.

1965
Jun 27: US ground forces begin their first offensive operations in South Vietnam.

1966
Feb 14: Defence White Paper announces the end of the CVA-01 aircraft-carrier replacement programme.

1967
Sep 10: Referendum in Gibraltar votes by 12,138 to 44 to remain British.
Nov 18: Currency crisis: sterling devalued by 14 per cent.
Dec 19: France vetoes British entry into the EEC.

1968
Jan 16: British government announces large spending cuts and military withdrawal from everywhere east of Suez, barring Hong Kong.

1969
Jun 30: RN officially assumes responsibility for British nuclear deterrent from the RAF.

1970
Sep 21: Jordan appeals for intervention from Britain and US amid worsening situation in the country.

1971
Nov 4: 'Final withdrawal' of Royal Navy presence from the Persian Gulf.

1973
Jan 27: Paris Peace Accords signed ending the Vietnam War.

1975
Apr 30: Fall of Saigon.

1976
Jan 13: Argentina suspends diplomatic relations with Britain over possession of the Falkland Islands.
Sep 29: Britain begins negotiations with the IMF for a $3.9 billion loan.

1977
Nov 25: RN ships deployed to the Falkland Islands in response to Argentine landings on South Thule ('Journeyman').

1978
Dec 15: British naval base at Bahrain closes.

1979
Feb 14: HMS *Ark Royal*, the RN's last conventional aircraft carrier, is decommissioned for the last time.
Jun 18: Strategic Arms Limitation Treaty II signed between US and Soviet Union.
Dec 25: Soviet Union invades Afghanistan.

1980
Sep 22: Iraqi invasion of Iran: start of the Iran-Iraq War.
Oct 7: Royal Navy begins the Armilla Patrol in the Persian Gulf.

1981
Publication of Defence White Paper.

1982
Mar: Polaris Sales Agreement updated to obtain Trident II.
Mar 19: Argentina invades South Georgia.
Apr 3: Argentine forces invade the remainder of the Falklands.
Apr 4: British Task Force departs ('Corporate').
Apr 25: British forces retake South Georgia.
May 1: British forces begin operations against Argentine forces in the rest of the Falklands.
May 2: Argentine cruiser *General Belgrano* sunk by HMS *Conqueror*.
May 21: Landings at San Carlos Water.
Jun 14: Argentine troops surrender at Port Stanley.

1986
Jan 15: Evacuation of civilian refugees from South Yemen.

1988
Aug 20: End of the Iran-Iraq War.

1990
Aug 2: Iraq invades Kuwait.

1991
Jan 17: Start of reconquest of Kuwait from Iraq (Operation 'Desert Storm').
Feb 28: Ceasefire declared, ending 'Desert Storm'.

1993
Jan 1: Carrier Task Group containing HMS *Ark Royal* leaves Portsmouth for the Adriatic to support UN Operations in the former Yugoslavia.

1995
Jan 27: HMS *Marlborough* evacuates British nationals from civil war in Sierra Leone.
Feb 1: HMS *Exeter* covers withdrawal of UN forces from Somalia.

1997
Jul 1: Hong Kong handed over to China.

1998
Feb 11: HMS *Monmouth* despatched to Sierra Leone to provide humanitarian aid during civil war ('Resilient' and 'Basilica').
Jul: Strategic Defence Review published.
Dec 16–19: Operation 'Desert Fox' against Iraq.

1999
Jan 30: Carrier task force led by HMS *Invincible* arrives in the Persian Gulf to help enforce the 'no-fly zone' over southern Iraq.
Mar 24: Start of Operation 'Allied Force' in Kosovo (ends Jun).

2000
May 7: Start of Operation 'Palliser' in Sierra Leone.

2001
Sep 11: Terrorist attack on the World Trade Center Towers, New York.
Oct 7: RN submarines launch cruise missiles as part of US-led operations in Afghanistan ('Veritas' and 'Enduring Freedom').
Nov 13: Fall of Kabul.

2003
Feb 21: HMS *Iron Duke* deployed to Sierra Leone ('Keeling').
Mar 19: British forces join US-led invasion of Iraq ('Telic' and 'Iraqi Freedom').
Apr 6: British forces enter Basra.
Apr: Fall of Baghdad.

2017
Dec 7: HMS *Queen Elizabeth* is commissioned.
Dec 21: HMS *Prince of Wales* is launched.

2019
Dec 10: HMS *Prince of Wales* is commissioned.

2021
Sep 15: Trilateral AUKUS security pact signed between Australia, the United Kingdom and the USA.

2022
Feb 24: Russia invades Ukraine.

2023
Apr 4: Finland joins NATO.

2024
Jan 12: Following Houthi attacks on shipping in the Red Sea, Britain, the US and a joint force conduct missile attacks on Yemeni targets ('Poseidon Archer').
Mar 7: Sweden joins NATO.

APPENDIX II

SHIPS

The purpose of this appendix is to provide a brief summary of the naval strength of Britain and other leading naval powers. As this volume covers a period of great change in warship design, it has been necessary to divide it into three periods: 1820–1860, 1860–1905 and 1905–1955. In the first period the ships are classified as ships of the line (including some with auxiliary steam power), cruisers (frigates and corvettes), and steamers (mostly paddle steamers with a few screw steamers in the 1850s). From 1860 to 1905 the categories change to ships of the line, ironclads, frigates and smaller cruisers (mostly classed as corvettes, sloops or gunboats). By this time almost all seagoing warships had at least auxiliary steam power, 'steamers' were still numerous but increasingly elderly, and navies were moving towards an organization of a fleet of 'battleships' accompanied by 'cruisers' of various sizes. The British formally adopted this classification in the 1887 *Navy List*, and most other navies followed suit soon afterwards. In this appendix the 1860–1905 table distinguishes (obsolescent wooden) ships of the line, and ironclads which were in process of being reclassified as 'battleships'. Finally, the third table lists only battleships, aircraft carriers and cruisers of all sizes. The major navies for the purposes of this appendix are Britain, the United States, France, Russia/Soviet Union, Japan, Germany, Italy (from unification in 1860) and Austria-Hungary (to 1918). For most of this appendix the ships are listed at five-year intervals, but annually in the period of the two world wars. The ships are counted from 1 January following their completion or commissioning date until their loss or decommissioning.

Source: *Conway's All the World's Fighting Ships . . . 1860–1995*, ed. Robert Gardiner et al. (London, 1979–95, 4 vols). Russian figures for 1860 are for the steam fleet in 1861 (nearly all in the Baltic), taken from *Russian Warships in the Age of Sail 1696–1860: Design, Construction, Careers and Fates*, ed. John Tredrea and Eduard Sozaev (Barnsley, 2010), pp. 406–30. 'Cruisers' are in this case only screw or paddle frigates, not counting a considerable force of steam corvettes, 'clippers' and gunboats.

Ships of the Line

Year	Britain	France	Netherlands	Spain	Denmark	Russia	United States	Austria
1820	112	48	7	14	3	43	7	2
1825	96	43	6	5	3	47	7	0
1830	82	33	5	3	4	47	7	0
1835	80	27	5	3	6	42	7	0
1840	77	23	5	2	6	46	7	0
1845	77	23	4	1	6	45	6	0
1850	73	26	5	1	5	47	7	0
1855	81	43	5	2	6	27	10	0
1860	87	43	2	8	7	18	17	1

Cruisers

Year	Britain	France	Netherlands	Spain	Denmark	Russia	United States	Austria
1820	101	31	14	13	5	20	7	3
1825	86	33	16	8	7	24	9	5
1830	100	40	17	5	8	26	10	5
1835	90	35	16	3	7	33	10	4
1840	76	32	17	5	7	25	11	4
1845	68	30	17	6	8	26	12	3
1850	146	81	13	6	8	21	12	4
1855	166	82	31	6	7	14	22	8
1860	226	100	44	8	8	35	29	15

Steamers

Year	Britain	France	Netherlands	Spain	Denmark	Russia	United States	Austria
1820	0	0	0	0	0	0	1	0
1825	0	0	0	0	0	0	1	0
1830	0	5	1	0	0	1	0	0
1835	11	12	1	1	0	1	0	0
1840	25	27	4	1	0	6	1	0
1845	53	55	9	5	2	14	4	0
1850	59	64	11	15	3	15	8	4
1855	59	61	12	21	3	10	5	5
1860	56	53	9	19	3	10	6	4

Nation	Britain				United States			
Year	Ships of the Line	Ironclads	Frigates	Cruisers	Ships of the Line	Ironclads	Frigates	Cruisers
1861	70	0	50	0	2	0	20	0
1865	72	11	51	0	0	24	9	0
1870	60	30	37	0	0	31	15	0
1875	51	46	38	0	0	21	17	0
1880	45	52	29	4	0	16	12	0
1885	39	54	18	5	0	14	8	0
1890	34	52	14	26	0	14	4	4
1895	32	64	12	61	0	13	4	17
1900	29	69	12	85	0	14	4	20
1905	24	59	10	107	0	15	3	25

Nation	France				Russia			
Year	Ships of the Line	Ironclads	Frigates	Cruisers	Ships of the Line	Ironclads	Frigates	Cruisers
1861	40	0	59	0	9	0	5	0
1865	37	6	44	0	5	15	6	0
1870	24	16	34	17	5	23	8	0
1875	14	16	26	32	2	25	6	0
1880	8	20	12	42	2	27	5	2
1885	0	16	8	52	1	27	4	3
1890	0	20	2	53	1	29	4	9
1895	0	20	1	56	0	32	4	9
1900	0	26	0	58	0	41	0	12
1905	0	26	0	59	0	33	0	19

Nation	Japan			Prussia/Germany		
Year	Ironclads	Frigates	Cruisers	Ironclads	Frigates	Cruisers
1861	0	0	0	0	5	0
1865	0	0	0	0	8	0
1870	1	2	0	4	8	0
1875	2	5	0	4	8	0
1880	5	5	0	10	8	1
1885	5	5	0	12	4	3
1890	5	9	4	12	3	10
1895	5	8	13	21	2	19
1900	5	6	22	25	0	25
1905	6	5	27	34	0	38

Nation	Italy				Austria-Hungary			
Year	Ships of the Line	Ironclads	Frigates	Cruisers	Ships of the Line	Ironclads	Frigates	Cruisers
1861	0	0	0	0	1	0	6	0
1865	1	7	12	0	1	5	7	0
1870	1	14	10	0	0	7	4	0
1875	1	17	9	0	0	7	1	0
1880	0	14	3	0	0	11	1	0
1885	0	14	3	0	0	11	0	0
1890	0	17	3	13	0	11	0	3
1895	0	19	2	26	0	10	0	6
1900	0	18	2	29	0	11	0	7
1905	0	15	0	31	0	10	0	10

Nation	Britain			United States		
Year	Battleships	Aircraft Carriers	Cruisers	Battleships	Aircraft Carriers	Cruisers
1906	65	0	121	13	0	29
1910	60	0	126	26	0	40
1915	72	4	122	33	0	38
1917	66	10	120	37	0	37
1918	64	11	124	38	0	36
1919	58	11	121	39	0	34
1920	47	8	120	39	0	33
1925	22	6	50	17	1	31
1930	20	7	56	17	3	33
1935	15	7	52	14	4	27
1939	14	8	62	14	6	33
1940	14	7	65	14	6	38
1941	13	8	69	14	7	38
1942	13	10	68	14	9	38
1943	13	14	61	18	16	42
1944	13	43	65	20	54	50
1945	10	51	63	24	92	61
1946	10	47	64	24	111	75
1947	11	19	32	23	49	36
1948	11	19	32	23	51	36
1949	5	16	30	16	51	39
1950	5	15	29	16	51	41
1955	5	17	26	16	52	42

Nation	France			Russia/Soviet Union		
Year	Battleships	Aircraft Carriers	Cruisers	Battleships	Aircraft Carriers	Cruisers
1906	27	0	73	17	0	17
1910	30	0	65	10	0	19
1915	31	1	44	17	1	17
1917	30	4	40	18	8	18
1918	29	5	37	17	8	16
1919	29	5	35	7	4	15
1920	28	1	29	5	2	13
1925	9	0	18	3	0	3
1930	9	1	17	3	0	5
1935	9	2	19	3	0	5
1939	8	2	20	3	0	8
1940	8	2	19	3	0	9
1941	7	2	19	3	0	10
1942	7	2	19	2	0	8
1943	4	1	12	2	0	7
1944	4	1	12	2	0	8
1945	3	0	12	3	0	10
1946	2	1	12	3	0	10
1947	2	1	12	3	0	9
1948	2	1	12	3	0	9
1949	2	1	14	4	0	10
1950	3	1	14	3	0	12
1955	2	3	11	3	0	28

Nation	Japan			Germany/West Germany		
Year	Battleships	Aircraft Carriers	Cruisers	Battleships	Aircraft Carriers	Cruisers
1906	7	0	21	24	0	37
1910	14	0	26	24	0	50
1915	22	1	27	40	0	35
1917	22	1	25	33	0	31
1918	23	1	24	35	0	30
1919	23	1	24	35	0	32
1920	23	1	26	18	0	19
1925	10	2	28	8	0	8
1930	9	4	39	7	0	8
1935	9	6	40	3	0	9
1939	9	9	44	1	0	9
1940	10	11	44	4	0	10

Nation	Japan			Germany/West Germany		
Year	Battleships	Aircraft Carriers	Cruisers	Battleships	Aircraft Carriers	Cruisers
1941	10	12	45	5	0	8
1942	11	15	46	5	0	8
1943	10	14	39	4	0	8
1944	9	13	40	3	0	8
1945	5	6	17	1	0	8
1946	0	0	0	0	0	0
1947	0	0	0	0	0	0
1948	0	0	0	0	0	0
1949	0	0	0	0	0	0
1950	0	0	0	0	0	0
1955	0	0	0	0	0	0

Nation	Italy			Austria-Hungary		
Year	Battleships	Aircraft Carriers	Cruisers	Battleships	Aircraft Carriers	Cruisers
1906	14	0	33	8	0	10
1910	15	0	29	11	0	10
1915	16	0	29	16	0	11
1917	15	0	26	17	0	12
1918	14	0	26	16	0	12
1919	14	0	24			
1920	14	0	23			
1925	7	0	14			
1930	4	0	14			
1935	4	0	24			
1939	4	0	23			
1940	4	0	22			
1941	5	0	21			
1942	5	0	14			
1943	6	0	12			
1944	5	0	9			
1945	5	0	9			
1946	5	0	9			
1947	5	0	9			
1948	5	0	9			
1949	2	0	7			
1950	2	0	6			
1955	2	0	5			

FLEETS

Appendix II compares the notional strength of the major navies, but in reality a varying but significant proportion of the ships would always be unavailable because refitting, under repair or in reserve. These tables provide a series of 'snapshots' of the distribution of British ships in actual service at various dates, divided into fleets and stations with the commanders-in-chief briefly indicated. I have not attempted to provide the same information for the twentieth century, when the fluid patterns of naval warfare and the rapid movements of ships over long distances made it very difficult for even the Admiralty to compile accurate and up-to-date information of this nature.

20 October 1827, Battle of Navarino

Rates	1st	2nd	3rd	4th	5th	6th	Sloops
East Indies (Gage)				1		3	5
Cape of Good Hope (Christian)					1	2	3
South America (Otway)		1			3	3	3
West Indies (Fleming)				1	2	1	11
North America (Lyle)					1	1	2
Lakes of Canada (Barrie)							1
Mediterranean (Codrington)		1	2	1	4	2	15
Lisbon (Beauclerk)			3		1		2
Coast of Africa (Collier)					1	1	2
Cork (Champion)					1		4
Plymouth (Northesk)	1	1	1				4
Portsmouth (Stopford)	1		2				1
Chatham (Blackwood)	1		2				3
Particular Service					2	4	6

Source PRO: ADM 8/107.

10/11 September/October 1840, Bombardment and Capture of Beirut

Rates	1st	2nd	3rd	4th	5th	6th	Sloops	Steam Vessels
East Indies (Elliot)			3		2	4	10	
Brazils and Cape of Good Hope (King)				1	1	2	7	
Coast of Africa (?)							2	
Pacific (Ross)				1		3	3	
North America and West Indies (Harvey)				1	1	3	10	10
Lakes of Canada (Sandown)				1				3
Mediterranean (Stopford)	1	7	6		2	6	4	12
Lisbon (Coffin)							1	
Plymouth (Moore)								
Portsmouth (Codrington)								
Sheerness (Digby)								
Particular Service					1			

Source PRO: ADM 8/120.

June/July 1855, Attack on Sevastopol

Rates	1st	2nd	3rd	4th	5th	6th	Sloops	Steam Vessels
East Indies, China and Australia (Stirling)				2	1	3	11	
Cape of Good Hope (Trotter)					1		4	
West Coast of Africa (Adams)						1	7	3
South-East Coast of America (Hope Johnstone)				1			2	
West Coast of America (Bruce)		1		1	1	3	1	
North America and West Indies (Fanshaw)			1		1	2	8	
Mediterranean (Lyons)	2	8		1	6	9	8	9
Baltic (Dundas)	2	9	9	3	3	8	10	7
Plymouth (Parker)	1		1					
Portsmouth (Cochrane)	2							2
Sheerness (Gordon)	1	1	1					
Woolwich (Shepherd)						1		2
Cork (Carroll)						1		1
Particular Service					1	1	3	3

Source PRO: ADM 8/135.

September 1870, Franco-Prussian War

Rates	Armoured Ships	Turret Ships	1st	2nd	3rd	4th	5th	6th	Sloops	Steam Vessels
East Indies (Heath)						1		1	3	
China (Kellett)	1							1	3	1
Australia (Stirling)								2	2	
Cape of Good Hope and West Coast of Africa (Dowell)								2		1
South-East Coast of America (Bedingfeld)								1		
Pacific (Farquhar)	1							2	3	
North America and West Indies (Wellesley)	1							5	4	
Mediterranean (Milne)	7								1	
Channel (Yelverton)	5	2				1	1			1
Devonport (Codrington)										2
Portsmouth (Hope)										3
Sheerness (Elliot)										2
Woolwich (Inglis)										
Pembroke (Hall)										
Queenstown (Forbes)						1				
Particular Service						6		3		1

Source PRO: ADM 8/149.

February 1878, Russo-Turkish War

Rates	Armoured Ships	Turret Ships	1st	2nd	3rd	4th	5th	6th	Sloops	Steam Vessels
East Indies (Corbett)						1		1	3	
China (Hillyar)	1							3	1	
Australia (Hoskins)								3	1	
Cape of Good Hope and West Coast of Africa (Sullivan)							1			1
South-East Coast of America (Carter)							1			
Pacific (De Horsey)						1		2	4	
North America and West Indies (Cooper Key)	1						1	1	1	

Rates	Armoured Ships	Turret Ships	1st	2nd	3rd	4th	5th	6th	Sloops	Steam Vessels
Mediterranean (Phipps Hornby)	11					1		1	2	1
Channel (Hay)	3									
Devonport (Symonds)		1								2
Portsmouth (Elliot)		1								3
Sheerness (King-Hall)				1						1
Greenwich (Sharp)										
Pembroke (Parkin)										
Queenstown (Hillyar)					1					
Particular Service								1		1

Source PRO: ADM 8/157.

July–October 1893, Fashoda Incident

Rates	Battleships		Cruisers			Sloops	Others	
		Coast Defence	1st Class	2nd Class	3rd Class		Gun Boats	Torpedo Boats
East Indies (Kennedy)		1		1	3		3	4
China (Freemantle)			1	3	4	1	9	
Australia (Bowden-Smith)			1		7		3	1
Cape of Good Hope and West Coast of Africa (Bedford)		1		1	5	1	4	
South-East Coast of America (Lang)				1		3		
Pacific (Stephenson)			1		5		1	
North America and West Indies (Hopkins)			1		6		1	
Mediterranean (Culme-Seymour)	10		1	3	3	4	1	2
Channel (Fairfax)	3		3		1			1
Plymouth (Lyons)	2	1					7	6
Portsmouth (Clanwilliam)	1		1				12	6
Sheerness (Heneage)	1						3	2
Chatham								
Pembroke (Cochrane)	1							
Queenstown (St John)	1							
Particular Service							2	
Training Squadron				2	2			

Source PRO: ADM 8/172.

ADMIRALS AND OFFICIALS

For most of the period covered by this volume, the office of Lord High Admiral of England, later Great Britain, was in commission, executed by a board of Lords Commissioners (the 'Lords of the Admiralty') made up of senior sea officers and civilian politicians. The head of this board, the First Lord of the Admiralty, was a civilian politician usually of Cabinet rank who acted and spoke in Parliament as the Navy's responsible minister. The Senior or First Naval Lord (both terms were used) evolved in the course of the nineteenth century from a primarily political office, held by an admiral who (until Sir Maurice Berkeley in 1857) was also a member of Parliament, into the professional (and non-political) head of the Royal Navy, renamed by Sir John Fisher the First Sea Lord, and from 1917 holding concurrently the position of Chief of the Naval Staff. In 1964 the Sovereign assumed the office of Lord High Admiral, the Admiralty Board ceased to exist, and the title of 'First Sea Lord' remained as a colloquial synonym for the Chief of the Naval Staff. In June 2011, on his ninetieth birthday, HRH Prince Philip was granted the title of Lord High Admiral, which has been vacant since his death on 9 April 2021.

Lords High Admiral

1827, May	HRH The Duke of Clarence	2011, Jun	HRH Prince Philip
1964, Apr	HM Queen Elizabeth II		

First Lords of the Admiralty

1812, Mar	Robert Dundas, 2nd Viscount Melville	1841, Sep	Thomas Hamilton, 9th Earl of Haddington
1828, Sep	Robert Dundas, 2nd Viscount Melville	1846, Jan	Edward Law, 1st Earl of Ellenborough
1830, Nov	Sir James Graham, 2nd Baronet	1846, Jul	George Eden, 1st Earl of Auckland
1834, Jun	George Eden, 2nd Baron Auckland	1849, Jan	Sir Francis Baring, 3rd Baronet
1834, Dec	Thomas de Grey, 2nd Earl de Grey	1852, Jan	Sir James Graham, 2nd Baronet
1835, Apr	George Eden, 2nd Baron Auckland	1852, Mar	Algernon Percy, 4th Duke of Northumberland
1835, Sep	Gilbert Elliot-Murray-Kynynmound, 2nd Earl Minto	1855, Mar	Sir Charles Wood, 3rd Baronet

1858, Mar	Sir John Pakington, 1st Baronet of Westwood	1916, Dec	Sir Edward Carson
1859, Jun	Edward Seymour, 12th Duke of Somerset	1917, Jul	Sir Eric Geddes
		1919, Jan	Walter Long
1866, Jul	Sir John Pakington, 1st Baronet of Westwood	1921, Feb	Arthur Lee, 1st Baron of Fareham
1867, Mar	The Hon. Henry Lowry-Corry	1922, Oct	Leopold Amery
		1924, Jan	Frederic Thesiger, 1st Viscount Chelmsford
1868, Dec	Hugh Childers	1924, Nov	William Bridgeman
1871, Mar	George Goschen	1929, Jun	Albert (A.V.) Alexander
1874, Mar	George Ward Hunt	1931, Aug	Sir Austen Chamberlain
1877, Aug	William Henry Smith	1931, Nov	Sir Bolton Eyres-Monsell
1880, May	Thomas Baring, 1st Earl of Northbrook	1936, Jun	Sir Samuel Hoare, Bt
		1937, Oct	Alfred Duff Cooper
1885, Jul	Lord George Hamilton	1938, Oct	James, 7th Earl Stanhope
1886, Feb	George Robinson, 1st Marquess of Ripon	1939, Sep	Winston Churchill
		1940, May	Albert Alexander
1886, Aug	Lord George Hamilton	1945, May	Brendan Bracken
1892, Aug	John, Earl Spencer	1945, Aug	Albert Alexander
1895, Jul	George Goschen	1946, Oct	George Hall, later Viscount
1900, Nov	William Palmer, 2nd Earl of Selborne	1951, May	Francis, Lord Pakenham
		1951, Dec	James Thomas, later 1st Viscount Cilcennin
1905, Mar	Frederick Campbell, 3rd Earl Cawdor	1956, Oct	Quintin Hogg, 2nd Viscount Hailsham
1905, Dec	Edward Marjoribanks, 2nd Baron Tweedmouth	1957, Oct	George Douglas-Hamilton, 10th Earl of Selkirk
1908, Apr	Reginald McKenna	1959, Oct	Peter, 6th Baron Carrington
1911, Oct	Winston Churchill	1963, Oct	George, 2nd Earl Jellicoe
1915, May	Arthur Balfour		

First or Senior Naval Lords

1814, Aug	Vice-Admiral Sir Joseph Yorke	1820, Mar	Vice-Admiral Sir William Johnstone Hope
1818, Apr	Vice-Admiral Sir Graham Moore		

Senior Members of the Lord High Admiral's Council

1827, May	Sir William Johnstone Hope	1828, Mar	Vice-Admiral Sir George Cockburn, 10th Bt

First or Senior Naval Lords

1828, Sep	Sir George Cockburn	1834, Dec	Sir George Cockburn
1830, Nov	Rear-Admiral Sir Thomas Masterman Hardy, 1st Bt	1835, Apr	Sir Charles Adam
		1841, Sep	Sir George Cockburn
1834, Aug	Rear-Admiral the Hon. George Dundas	1846, Jul	Admiral Sir William Parker, 1st Bt
1834, Nov	Admiral Sir Charles Adam	1846, Jul	Sir Charles Adam

1847, Jul	Rear-Admiral Sir James Deans Dundas
1852, Feb	Vice-Admiral The Hon. Maurice Berkeley
1852, Mar	Vice-Admiral Hyde Parker
1854, Jun	The Hon. Maurice Berkeley
1857, Nov	Vice-Admiral The Hon. Sir Richard Saunders Dundas
1858, Mar	Vice-Admiral William Fanshawe Martin
1859, Jun	Vice-Admiral The Hon. Sir Richard Saunders Dundas
1861, Jun	Vice-Admiral The Hon. Sir Frederick Grey
1866, Jul	Vice-Admiral Sir Alexander Milne
1868, Dec	Admiral Sir Sydney Dacres
1872, Nov	Sir Alexander Milne
1876, Sep	Admiral Sir Hastings Yelverton
1877, Nov	Sir George Wellesley
1879, Sep	Admiral Sir Astley Cooper Key
1885, Jul	Vice-Admiral Sir Arthur Hood
1886, Feb	Admiral Lord John Hay
1886, Aug	Sir Arthur Hood
1889, Oct	Admiral Sir Richard Vesey Hamilton
1891, Sep	Admiral Sir Anthony Hoskins
1893, Nov	Admiral Sir Frederick Richards
1899, Aug	Admiral Lord Walter Kerr

First Sea Lords

1904, Oct	Admiral Sir John Fisher
1910, Jan	Admiral Sir Arthur Wilson
1911, Dec	Admiral Sir Francis Bridgeman
1912, Dec	Admiral Prince Louis of Battenberg
1914, Oct	John Fisher, 1st Baron of Kilverstone
1915, May	Admiral Sir Henry Jackson
1916, Dec	Admiral Sir John Jellicoe
1918, Jan	Admiral Sir Rosslyn Wemyss
1919, Nov	Admiral of the Fleet David, 1st Earl Beatty
1927, Jul	Admiral of the Fleet Sir Charles Madden, 1st Bt.
1930, Jul	Admiral Sir Frederick Field
1933, Jan	Admiral Sir Ernle Chatfield, later Admiral of the Fleet Baron Chatfield
1938, Sep	Admiral Sir Roger Backhouse
1939, Jun	Admiral of the Fleet Sir Dudley Pound
1943, Oct	Admiral of the Fleet Sir Andrew Cunningham, 1st Bt, later Viscount Cunningham of Hyndhope
1946, Jun	Admiral Sir John Cunningham
1948, Sep	Admiral of the Fleet Baron Fraser of North Cape
1951, Dec	Admiral Sir Rhoderick McGrigor
1955, Apr	Admiral, later Admiral of the Fleet Earl Mountbatten of Burma
1959, Oct	Admiral Sir Charles Lambe
1960, May	Admiral Sir Caspar John
1963, Aug	Admiral Sir David Luce

Sources:

The London Gazette

Oxford Dictionary of National Biography (Oxford, 2004, 60 vols., continually kept up to date online)

Rodger, N. A. M., *The Admiralty* (Lavenham, 1979)

Sainty, J. C., *Admiralty Officials, 1660–1870*

APPENDIX V

MANPOWER

Total Seamen and Marines

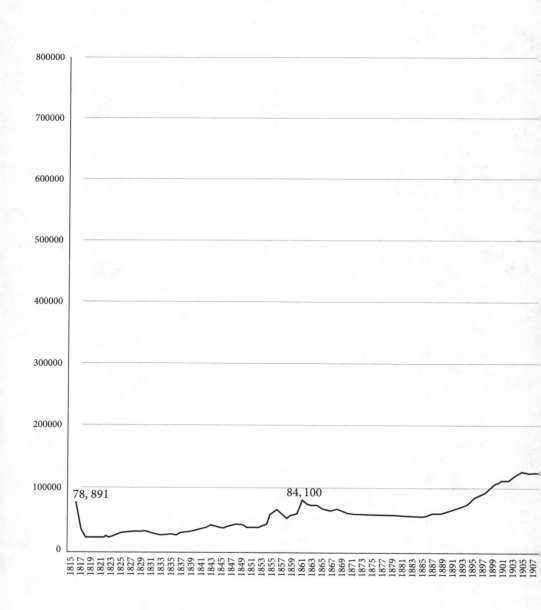

This graph represents the surviving statistics of British naval and Marine manpower from 1815 to 2009, which are available in detailed form only to 1855, thanks to the work of the 1859 Harwicke Commission (printed in HC 1859 Sess.I VI,362 and HC 1868–9 XXXV,1177–1179). Later statistics derive from the Navy Estimates (as reproduced in *Whitaker's Almanack*), which (as their name implies) were forecasts produced to gain Parliamentary approval for naval expenditure. The figures for 1939–45 come from the Central Statistical Office pamphlet *Fighting with Figures*.

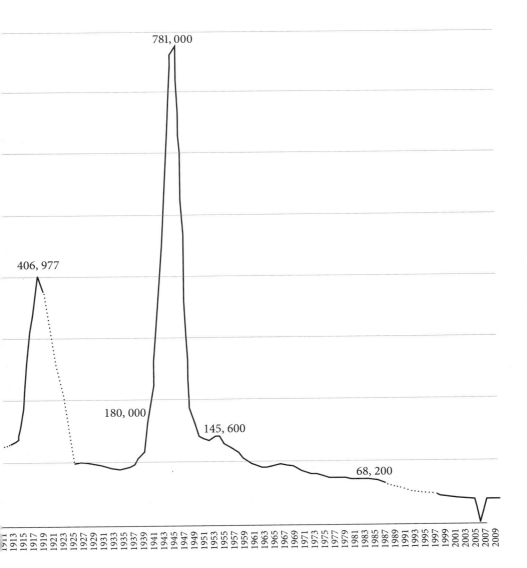

REFERENCES

Introduction

1 'The Song of the Dead' (1896).
2 'Some nations increase, others decline, and in a short while the generations of the living are changed, and like runners hand on the torch of life.' Titus Lucretius Carus, *De Rerum Natura*, Bk. II, l. 8.

Chapter 1

1 McCain and Hopkins, *British Imperialism*, p. 89. Mokyr, 'Industrial Revolution'. Engerman and O'Brien, 'Industrial Revolution'.
2 Barry M. Gough, 'The British Reoccupation and Colonization of the Falkland Islands, or Malvinas, 1832–1843', *Albion* XXII (1990), pp. 261–87, at p. 269.
3 Ronald Hyam, *Britain's Imperial Century, 1815–1914: A Study of Empire and Expansion* (London, 1976), p. 54.
4 Bartlett, 'Castlereagh'. Alfaro Zaforteza, 'Vienna Settlement', pp. 88–9.
5 Hilton, *Mad, Bad and Dangerous*, pp. 259–76 and 398–9. *CO*, pp. 473–4.
6 Harling, 'Old Corruption', pp. 231–2, summarizing the opinions of the Tory leader Sir Robert Peel.
7 Mitchell, *Whig World*, Mandler, *Aristocratic Government*, and Hilton, *Mad, Bad, and Dangerous*, are excellent guides to the political landscape. On the Manchester Party see McCord, 'Cobden and Bright', and Semmel, *Free Trade Imperialism*, pp. 161–208.
8 Mitchell, *Whig World*, p. 117. Hilton, *Age of Atonement*, is a brilliant study of the religious life of the age.
9 *ODNB* sv Sharp.
10 Williams, *Napier*, p. 222. *GBSP*, pp. 57–66. Bartlett, 'Statecraft, Power and Influence', pp. 175–177.
11 Lambert, 'Preparing for the Long Peace'; idem, *Last Sailing Battlefleet*, quoted p. 5.
12 MacMillan, 'British Naval Gunnery', p. 149, quoting Cochrane to Lord Melville, 24 Dec 1826, from PRO: ADM 7/712.
13 *GBSP*, pp. 69–74. Symonds, *Navalists*, pp. 199–235. Lambert, 'Winning without Fighting'.
14 Graham and Humphreys, *Navy and South America* (quoted p. 259). Vale, 'Lord Cochrane in Chile', and *Cochrane in the Pacific: Fortune and Freedom in Spanish America* (London, 2007).
15 Vale, *War betwixt Englishmen*. Ferns, *Britain and Argentina*, pp. 157–95.
16 Ryan, 'Price of Legitimacy', pp. 232–6. Panzac, *Les corsaires barbaresques*, pp. 228–44. G. S. van Krieken, 'Het Engels–Nederlandse bombardement van Algiers in 1816', *TvZ* VI (1987), pp. 138–50. Bartlett, *Great Britain and Sea Power*, pp. 61–4. Lambert, *Last Sailing Battlefleet*, p. 99. François Jacquin, 'La fin de la course barbaresque en 1830', *CHM* 51 (2003), pp. 12–33, at pp. 15–18. Caitlin M. Gale, 'Barbary's Slow Death: European Attempts to Eradicate North African Piracy in the Early Nineteenth Century', *JMR* XVIII (2016), pp. 139–54. Alfaro Zaforteza, 'Vienna Settlement', pp. 97–100.
17 Bourchier, *Codrington* I, 360; to Lady Spencer, 10 Jun 1827.
18 '. . . vous devez apporter un soin extrême à ce que les mesures que vous prendrez envers la marine ottomane ne dégènerent pas en hostilités': Douin, *Navarin*, p. 78, quoting agreed orders of 12 Jul 1827 to the three admirals.
19 Anderson, *Naval Wars in the Levant*, pp. 483–533. Jones, *Piracy in the Levant*. Fotakis, 'Modern Greek State'. Panzac, *La*

marine ottomane, pp. 273–85. Daly, *Russian Seapower*, pp. 2–8. Holland, *Blue-Water Empire*, p. 48. Bourchier, *Codrington* II, 63–75, prints much of his correspondence. Douin, *Navarin*, is still the most complete account of the campaign. Charles McPherson, *Life on board a Man-of-War: including a full account of the battle of Navarino* (Glasgow, 1829), pp. 125–74, gives an evocative lower-deck narrative of the battle seen from the *Genoa*, and Boteler, *Recollections*, pp. 185–94, another.

20 Webster, *Palmerston* I, 78–81. Battesti, *La Marine de Napoléon III*, I, 21.

21 *GBSP*, pp. 78–88. Webster, *Palmerston* I, 95–6 and 104–76. Parker, *Graham* I, 149. Lambert, 'Palmerston and Sea-Power', pp. 42–3.

22 *GBSP*, pp. 75–81. Lambert, 'Palmerston and Sea Power', 'Napier, Palmerston and Palmella', and *Admirals*, pp. 215–20. Webster, *Palmerston* I, 237–57. Phillimore, *Parker* II, 383–8.

23 *GBSP*, pp. 96–7. McLean, *Surgeons of the Fleet*, pp. 57–61.

24 Hunter, *Policing the Seas*, pp. 62–8. Rubin, *Law of Piracy*, pp. 219–20. Ryan, 'Price of Legitimacy'. Eltis, *Transatlantic Slave Trade*, pp. 23–31, 92–3 and 101–13. Lambert, 'Slavery, Free Trade', pp. 65–9. Law, 'International Law'. Alfaro Zaforteza, 'Vienna Settlement', pp. 97–100. Grindal, *Opposing the Slavers*, pp. 138–282.

25 Von Grafenstein, 'Corso y piratería'. Hunter, *Policing the Seas*, pp. 73–89. *GBSP*, pp. 69–71.

26 Kelly, *Britain and the Persian Gulf*, pp. 99–159 and 209–10, takes the traditional Anglo-Indian view; Al-Qāsimī, *Arab Piracy*, presents a vigorous and scholarly case for the defence; Davies, *Blood-Red Arab Flag*, steers a middle course.

27 Keppel, *Sailor's Life* I, 288–321 and II, 1–21; *idem*, *Expedition to Borneo* II, 143–62. Burrows, *Autobiography*, pp. 52–66. Graham, *Indian Ocean*, pp. 20 and 363–401. Rubin, *Law of Piracy*, pp. 222–63. Senior, *Naval History*, pp. 100–11. HC: 1851 LVI Pt. I.

28 Fox, *British Admirals and Chinese Pirates*, pp. 110–42 and 201–4.

29 Day, *Hydrographic Service*, pp. 39–53. Angster, *Erdbeeren und Piraten*, pp. 13–14. Cock, 'Beaufort'. James, 'Faraday', and 'Davy'. Lambert, 'Science and Sea Power', pp. 10–18. Cawood, 'Magnetic Crusade'. Waring, 'Board of Longitude'.

30 Reidy, *Tides of History*, *passim*. Samson, 'Empire of Science', pp. 256–78. *GBSP*, p. 153.

31 Herschel, *Scientific Enquiry*, pp. iii–iv and 29–31 (quoted p. iii). McLean, *Surgeons of the Fleet*, pp. 51–4. Cock, 'Scientific Servicemen'. Rodger, 'Naval Thought', pp. 145–6. Stafford, 'Scientific Exploration', pp. 294–6. Holger Hoock, *Empires of the Imagination: Politics, War, and the Arts in the British World, 1750–1850* (London, 2010), pp. 243–59. Patrick Louvier, 'Les officiers de marine britannique et la Méditerranée au XIXe siècle: un regard intime et singulier?', *RHM* XXII–XXIII (2017), pp. 277–302.

32 David Cannadine, *Ornamentalism: How the British Saw Their Empire* (London, 2001), p. 59.

33 Angster, *Erdbeeren und Piraten*, pp. 10–17, 63–6, 134, 141–5, 193, 204–5, 218–25, 231–45 and 284. Lynn, 'Policy, Trade and Informal Empire', pp. 101–5 (both quotations p. 102).

34 John Barrow, *A Chronological History of Voyages into the Arctic Regions* (London, 1818), pp. 378–9.

35 Richard Drayton, *Nature's Government: Science, Imperial Britain, and the 'Improvement' of the World* (Yale, 2000) p. 202, quoting Rear-Admiral George Richards.

36 Gough, *Peard Journal*, pp. 7–18. Angster, *Erdbeeren und Piraten*, pp. 171–7. Drayton, *Nature's Government*. Cawood, 'Magnetic Crusade', and 'Terrestrial Magnetism'. Cock, 'Scientific Servicemen'. Lambert, *Franklin*, pp. 72–82 and 167–8. Stafford, 'Scientific Exploration', pp. 294–8.

Chapter 2

1 Lambert, *Last Sailing Battlefleet*, pp. 13–16. Harling, 'Old Corruption', pp. 166–72. Harling and Mandler, 'From

"Fiscal-Military" State to Laissez-Faire State', pp. 47–54. Monod, *Imperial Island*, p. 324. *CO*, pp. 473–88, outlines administrative developments from 1793 to 1815.

2 Cock and Rodger, *Naval Records*, pp. 25–30, provides a brief guide to naval administrative history.

3 C. I. Hamilton, 'Croker', p. 75.

4 Monod, *Imperial Island*, p. 321. C. I. Hamilton, *Modern Admiralty*, pp. 36–51 and 80–106.

5 Knight, *William IV*, pp. 56–65. (See also Knight's important and long-unpublished paper 'The battle for control of the Royal Navy, 1801–1835', now available on-line at GlobalMaritimeHistory.com.) Lambert, 'Wellington and the Navy', pp. 189–208. Morriss, 'Military Men Fall Out' (quoted p. 130). Note that Cockburn, regarded by the king and everyone else as the leading member of the Council, was not its most senior naval member.

6 Ward, *Graham*, pp. 96–121. Hamilton, *Modern Admiralty*, pp. 63–9, 75 and 108–9. Knight, *William IV*, pp. 65–7 and 73–7. Lambert, *Last Sailing Battlefleet*, pp. 23–30; *idem*, 'Wellington and the Navy', pp. 212–21, and 'Naval Strategic Revolution', p. 152. MacDougall, *Chatham Dockyard*, pp. 322–4, 341 (quoted) and 353. Barrow, *Memoir*, pp. 404–15. Memoranda by Barrow in *BND*, pp. 650–52.

7 *CO*, pp. 476–82.

8 Ward, *Graham*, p. 128.

9 To Earl Grey, 6 Dec 1831: *BND*, No. 385, p. 647.

10 Morriss, *Naval Power and British Culture*, pp. 195–205. C. I. Hamilton, *Modern Admiralty*, pp. 56–63 and 130–31; *idem*, *Portsmouth Dockyard Papers*, p. xliv. Parker, *Graham* I, 155–68. Lambert, 'Wellington and the Navy', pp. 186–9 and 217–21. *GBSP*, pp. 10–13.

11 Knight, 'Battle for Control', is one of the few authors to take proper note of Parnell; *ODNB* sv Parnell is rather a disappointment.

12 Coad, *Support for the Fleet*, pp. 13–24 and 95–106. Crimmin, 'Supply of Timber', pp. 226–7. A. D. Lambert, *Last Sailing Battlefleet*, pp. 111–21.

13 Coad, *Support for the Fleet*, pp. 276–82 and 299–314. 'Weevil' was not an abusive nickname but the actual name of the site of Royal Clarence Yard.

14 Owen, 'Packet Service'. Howard Robinson, *Carrying British Mails Overseas* (London, 1964), pp. 110–35. Brown, *Paddle Warships*, pp. 82–7. Parry, *Parry*, pp. 197–217. The old myth that Melville deplored the adoption of steam has been killed many times but will not die: see Peter Hore, 'Lord Melville, the Admiralty and the Coming of Steam Navigation', *MM* LXXXVI (2000), pp. 157–72.

15 Coad, *Support for the Fleet*, pp. 27–41, 121–30 and 193–9. Evans, *Building the Steam Navy*, pp. 10–105 and 113–26. Laing, *Steam Wooden Warship Building*. *BND*, pp. 682–8. Brown, *Paddle Warships*, p. 70. C. I. Hamilton, *Portsmouth Dockyard Papers*, pp. xxvi–xxvii, xxxi–xxxii and xxxv. Plymouth Dockyard officially adopted the new name of Devonport in 1843; the Keyham Steam Factory is now incorporated in the North Yard at Devonport.

16 Buchanan and Doughty, 'Steam Engine Manufacturers'. Macleod et al., 'Invention and Innovation'. Arnold, *Iron Shipbuilding*, pp. 11–12. Banbury, *Shipbuilders*, map facing p. 159. Peebles, *Warshipbuilding*, pp. 10–12.

17 C. I. Hamilton, *Modern Admiralty*, pp. 64–9, 80–83 and 116–19; *idem*, *Anglo-French Naval Rivalry*, p. 255; 'Baltic Campaign', (quoted) p. 111. Barrow, *Memoir*, pp. 408–18. Memoranda by Barrow in *BND*, pp. 650–52. MacDougall, *Chatham Dockyard*, p. 350.

18 Capt. Alexander Milne to Rear-Admiral Sir Charles Napier, 16 Jan 1848, in Beeler, *Milne Papers* I, 220.

19 Leggett, *Shaping the Royal Navy*, pp. 40–41.

20 Hamilton, 'Baltic Campaign', pp. 105 and 111.

21 MacDougall, *Chatham Dockyard*, pp. 359–60, quoting Ellenborough from *Hansard* in 1854.

22 PRO: ADM 116/3453. Cf. Select Committee on the Board of Admiralty, HC 1861 (438) V, p. 138, Q.1008 and p. 162, Q.1185.

23 CO, pp. 103–4. Haas, *Management Odyssey*, pp. 67–8. MacDougall, *Chatham Dockyard*, pp. 274–80.

24 MacDougall, *Chatham Dockyard*, p. 276.

25 Capt. A. Milne to Duke of Northumberland, 20 Nov 1852, in Beeler, *Milne Papers* I, 335.

26 Haas, *Management Odyssey*, p. 121.

27 Haas, *Management Odyssey*, pp. 75–83 and 97–100. MacDougall, *Chatham Dockyard*, pp. 261–313. GBSP, pp. 299–300. Laing, *Steam Wooden Warship Building*, pp. 18–22. Hamilton, *Portsmouth Dockyard Papers*, pp. xxv–xxvi, xxxii, xl–xli and 110–11.

28 MacDougall, *Chatham Dockyard*, pp. 211–13, 234–9. Haas, *Management Odyssey*, pp. 69–74, 82–7, 96–108. MacDougall, 'A Demand Fulfilled'. Hamilton, *Portsmouth Dockyard Papers*, pp. xxvi, xxxviii, 165–70 and 177–8. Morriss, *Naval Power and British Culture*, pp. 221–2 and 230–35.

29 Morriss, *Naval Power and British Culture*, pp. 195–219. Haas, *Management Odyssey*, pp. 77 and 89–91. Hamilton, *Portsmouth Dockyard Papers*, pp. xliv and liv.

30 GBSP, pp. 12–19. Hamilton, 'Baltic Campaign'. Lambert, *Crimean War*, pp. xix–xx. Baumgart, *Englischen Akten* I, 239. Lambert, '"Good, while it lasts"', pp. 31–3. Hamilton, 'Policy-Makers and Financial Control', pp. 371–4.

31 Sir W. Parker to Ld John Russell, 13 Jan 1849: Phillimore, *Parker* III, 455.

32 GBSP, pp. 259–60. Beeler, *Milne Papers* I, xii–xv, 205–13 and 319. Phillimore, *Parker* II, 420.

33 Beeler, 'A Whig Private Secretary'. C. I. Hamilton, *Portsmouth Dockyard Papers*, pp. 177–8 and 331–2. A. D. Lambert, *Warrior*, pp. 16–17.

34 Beeler, *Milne Papers* I, 379–88 and 575–6. A. D. Lambert, *Battleships in Transition*, pp. 62–3. C. I. Hamilton, *Anglo-French Naval Rivalry*, pp. 68–9. Dunn, '"Cement of Mediocrity"'. Mends, *Mends*, pp. 336–7.

Chapter 3

1 GBSP, pp. 119–40. Graham, *Politics of Naval Supremacy*, pp. 73–9. Anderson, *Naval Wars in the Levant*, pp. 552–66. Brown, *Palmerston*, pp. 212–37. Kelly, *Britain and the Persian Gulf*, pp. 320–43. Daly, *Russian Seapower*, pp. 143–7. Lambert, 'Palmerston and Sea-Power', pp. 55–8. Napier, *Napier* II, 1–92. Matzke, *Deterrence through Strength*, pp. 155–82. Graham, *Indian Ocean*, pp. 274–304. Lambert, 'Syrian Campaign', pp. 79–84. Louvier, *La puissance navale*, pp. 40–47. Hattendorf, 'Bombardment of Acre', (quoted) p. 210.

2 Lambert, 'Palmerston and Sea-Power', p. 58.

3 To Minto, 17 Nov 1840: Hattendorf, 'Bombardment of Acre', p. 220. Lambert, 'Syrian Campaign', p. 92, quotes the same MS in slightly different wording.

4 GBSP, pp. 143–7. Darwin, *Empire Project*, p. 28. Daly, *Russian Seapower*, pp. 163–71. Lambert, 'Palmerston and Sea-Power', pp. 58–60. Battesti, *La Marine de Napoléon III* I, 27. Napier, *Napier* II, 93–118. Matzke, *Deterrence through Strength*, pp. 183–94. Louvier, *La puissance navale*, pp. 94–113. Hattendorf, 'Bombardment of Acre'. Lambert, 'Syrian Campaign', pp. 85–7. Burrows, *Autobiography*, pp. 126–30. Hore, *Habit of Victory*, pp. 250–52. Bourchier, *Letters of Sir Henry Codrington*, pp. 152–98. Yaacov Kahanov, Eliezer Stern, Deborah Cvikel and Yav Me-Bar, 'Between Shoal and Wall: The Naval Bombardment of Akko, 1840', *MM* C (2014), pp. 147–67. W. B. Rowbotham, 'Naval Operations on the Coast of Syria, 1840', *JRUSI* XCVII (1952), pp. 566–78.

5 Melbourne to Sir W. Parker, 3 Jul 1841: Phillimore, *Parker* II, 448. Lovell, *Opium War*, pp. 116–22.

6 Melancon, *China Policy*, p. 72.

7 Lynn, 'Policy, Trade, and Informal Empire', p. 104.

8 Fay, *Opium War*, pp. 6–12, 43–56, 67–89, 128–53 and 187–215. Melancon, *China Policy*, pp. 1–6, 17–79 and 99–129. Lovell, *Opium War*, pp. 1–8, 63–8 and 102–5.

Matzke, *Deterrence through Strength*, pp. 105–38. Graham, *China Station*, pp. 6–8 and 17–104.

9 21 April 1841: Fay, *Opium War*, p. 309.

10 Fay, *Opium War*, pp. 230–36, 261–4, 270–98. Melancon, *China Policy*, pp. 129–39. Matzke, *Deterrence through Strength*, pp. 139–41. Graham, *China Station*, pp. 134–5 and 141–77. Marshall, *Nemesis*, pp. 79–104. Lovell, *Opium War*, pp. 130–33 and 141–3.

11 Fay, *Opium War*, pp. 349–62. Matzke, *Deterrence through Strength*, pp. 142–9. Graham, *China Station*, pp. 193–226 and 254–63. The dollar in this case is the Spanish or Mexican silver dollar, at 6.38 to the pound or roughly 3s 2d; not the US dollar, in 1842 worth 4.76 to the pound or 4s 2d.

12 Fay, *Opium War*, p. 182. Melancon, *China Policy*, pp. 100–101. Hilton, *Mad, Bad and Dangerous*, pp. 570–72.

13 Ferns, *Britain and Argentina*, pp. 241–75. Avenel, *Rio de la Plata*, pp. 16–80. Sulivan, *Sulivan*, pp. 52–92. Vale, *War betixt Englishmen*, pp. 232–4. McLean, 'The British in the Paraná'. Colomb, *Key*, pp. 110–12.

14 Brown, *Before the Ironclad*, pp. 80–82. Paul Quinn, 'The Mexican Frigate Guadalupe', *MM* XCVI (2010), pp. 323–9. D. K. Brown, 'The Paddle Frigate Guadaloupe', *Warship* 11 (1979), pp. 211–12.

15 *GBSP*, p. 119. Bach, *Australia Station*, pp. 17–18 and 69–71.

16 Bach, *Australia Station*, p. 39.

17 C. I. Hamilton, *Anglo-French Naval Rivalry*, pp. 17–18. Bach, *Australia Station*, pp. 22–9. Gash, *Peel*, pp. 508–10. This Dupetit-Thouars is not to be confused with his uncle Captain Aristide Aubert, killed at the battle of the Nile in 1798, nor with his nephew Abel Nicolas Bergasse and great-nephew Aristide Bergasse, both admirals.

18 *GBSP*, pp. 149 and 175–6.

19 Partridge, *Military Planning*, p. 22.

20 *GBSP*, pp. 151–71. Gash, *Peel*, pp. 504–25. Hamilton, 'Joinville's Note'. Brisou, *L'énergie vapeur*, pp. 535–6. Gooch, 'Bolt from the Blue', pp. 2–3.

21 *GBSP*, p. 185.

22 Partridge, 'Russell Cabinet', p. 232.

23 Gooch, *Later Russell Correspondence* I, 242. The tag from the Roman poet Lucan means '[only] the shadow of a great name remains'.

24 Memorandum of 10 Apr 1847: Gooch, *Later Russell Correspondence* I, 259. By December 1847 he was talking of up to 100,000 troops landed without warning before noon of any day in the year: Wilbur D. Jones, *The American Problem in British Diplomacy, 1841–1861* (London, 1974), p. 57.

25 *GBSP*, pp. 163, 173–4, 181–247. I have corrected Bartlett's exchange rate for the franc (p. 181) from Denzel, *World Exchange Rates*, p. 287. Partridge, 'Russell Cabinet', pp. 237–43. Gooch, *Later Russell Correspondence* I, 247–8. Gash, *Peel*, pp. 514–25. Battesti, *La Marine de Napoléon III* I, 46–51. A. D. Lambert, *Battleships in Transition*, pp. 30–38. C. I. Hamilton, *Anglo-French Naval Rivalry*, pp. 36–57.

26 *GBSP*, p. 259.

27 *GBSP*, pp. 251–61. Jerome Devitt, 'The "Navalization" of Ireland: The Royal Navy and the Irish Insurrection in the 1840s', *MM* CI (2015), pp. 388–409. Napier, *Napier* II, 188–9. McCord, 'Cobden and Bright'. Partridge, 'Russell Cabinet', pp. 233–46. Partridge, *Military Planning*, pp. 8–17. Semmel, *Free Trade Imperialism*, pp. 159–62.

28 McCord, 'Cobden and Bright', p. 90.

29 Eltis, *Transatlantic Slave Trade*, pp. 23–31, 81–5, 102–8. Mbaeyi, *Military and Naval Forces*, pp. 73–6. Lambert, 'Slavery, Free Trade'. Drescher, 'British Abolitionism', pp. 133–41. Semmel, *Liberalism and Naval Strategy*, pp. 40–42. Ryan, 'Price of Legitimacy', pp. 231–9. Hunter, *Policing the Seas*, pp. 134–8. *GBSP*, p. 269. Mulligan, 'Anti-Slavery Policy'. Alfaro Zaforteza, 'Vienna Settlement', pp. 97–100.

30 Jones, *American Problem*, p. 217 n.22.

31 Lloyd, *Slave Trade*, p. 113.

32 Graham, *Indian Ocean*, pp. 98–129, 147–76 and 198–228. Kelly, *Britain and the Persian Gulf*, pp. 422–44 and 576–635. Howell, *Slave Trade*, pp. 1–50. Hunter,

Policing the Seas, pp. 134–8 and 160–62. Eltis, *Transatlantic Slave Trade*, pp. 120–22 and 213–16. Lambert, 'Slavery, Free Trade', pp. 71–6. Beachey, 'Anti-Slave Patrol'.

33 Eltis, *Transatlantic Slave Trade*, pp. 92–102. Hunter, *Policing the Seas*, pp. 163–7. Semmel, *Liberalism and Naval Strategy*, pp. 47–9. Ryan, 'Price of Legitimacy', pp. 243–54. Bethell, *Brazilian Slave Trade*, pp. 321–41. Law, 'International Law'. Grindal, *Opposing the Slavers*, App. A, prints a list of all slavers captured by British warships in the Atlantic, 1807–39.

34 Eltis, *Transatlantic Slave Trade*, pp. 92–7. Hunter, *Policing the Seas*, pp. 138–40. Mitcham, 'White Man's Grave', pp. 55–6. Oldfield, 'After Emancipation', p. 55. Grindal, *Opposing the Slavers*, App. G. The casualty figures are incomplete, and the true losses almost certainly higher.

35 Brown, *Poxed and Scurvied*, p. 117, quoting the ship's log.

36 Capt. A. P. Eardley-Wilmot, Commodore West Africa, to Admiralty, 19 Dec 1865, in *BND*, p. 638.

37 Mitcham, 'White Man's Grave'. Watt, 'Anti-Slavery Squadrons'. Harrison, 'West African Service'. Canney, *Africa Squadron*, pp. 52–8. Lloyd, *Slave Trade*, pp. 281–4. J. R. McNeill, *Mosquito Empires: Ecology and War in the Greater Caribbean, 1620–1914* (Cambridge, 2010), pp. 52–5.

38 Lambert, *Admirals*, pp. 233–41. Phillimore, *Parker* III, 33, 63–9, 137, 169–70, 180, 224, 234–5, 240, 242. Louvier, *La puissance navale*, pp. 43–7.

39 Arvel B. Erickson, *The Public Career of Sir James Graham* (Oxford, 1952), p. 350. A 'team' here means a team of coach horses.

40 Baumgart, *Englischen Akten* I, 239.

41 J. T. Ward, *Sir James Graham* (London, 1967), pp. 263–4. Lambert, *Crimean War*, pp. 58–60. Figes, *Crimea*, pp. xxii–xxiii. Curtiss, *Russia's Crimean War*, pp. 167–9. Goldfrank, *Crimean War*, pp. 1–5. Lambert, '"Good, while it lasts"', pp. 31–3. Piedmont-Sardinia was the northern part of not-yet-unified Italy.

42 Rath, *Crimean War*, p. xv.

43 Graham to Clarendon, 1 Mar 1854: Baumgart, *Englischen Akten* II, 255.

44 Battesti, *La Marine de Napoléon III* I, 72 and 79. Lambert, '"Good, while it lasts"', pp. 32 and 34. Figes, *Crimea*, pp. 194–6. Anderson, *Liberal State at War*, p. 36.

45 Badem, *Ottoman Crimean War*, pp. 110–26. Panzac, *La marine ottomane*, pp. 325–7. Figes, *Crimea*, p. 142. Curtiss, *Russia's Crimean War*, pp. 206–7. Baxter, *Ironclad Warship*, p. 70. Battesti, *La Marine de Napoléon III* I, 75, claims that Nakhimov had 200 Paixhans guns, but her authority is unclear and I have preferred the Russian sources cited by Badem (p. 120) and Lawrence Sondhaus, *Naval Warfare 1815–1914* (London, 2001), p. 58.

46 Lambert, *Crimean War*, pp. 58–62, 107, 112. Eardley-Wilmot, *Lyons*, pp. 126–9. Battesti, *La Marine de Napoléon III* I, 102–11.

47 Lambert, *Crimean War*, pp. 61–5, 113–20. Bonner-Smith and Dewar, *Russian War 1854*, pp. 207–20. Battesti, *La Marine de Napoléon III* I, 82–4. Rath, *Crimean War*, p. xv.

48 Captain W. Mends' diary-letter to his wife, 12 Aug 1854: Mends, *Mends*, p. 112.

49 Lambert, *Crimean War*, pp. 114–42. Heath, *Letters from the Black Sea*, p. 84. Mends, *Mends*, pp. 115–32, 166–9, 180–84 and 358–60. Lambert, '"Good, while it lasts"', pp. 37–8. Brown, *Before the Ironclad*, pp. 142–4. Figes, *Crimea*, pp. 239–40. Battesti, *La Marine de Napoléon III* I, 114–19.

50 Captain W. Mends' diary-letter to his wife, 31 Oct 1854: Mends, *Mends*, p. 187.

51 Lambert, *Crimean War*, pp. 148–9. Dewar, *Russian War 1855 – Black Sea*, pp. 3–5, 62–5 and 159–64. Dunn, '"Cement of Mediocrity"'.

52 Dewar, *Russian War 1855 – Black Sea*, pp. 164–96 and 346–51. Conacher, *Britain and the Crimea*, pp. 100 and 123. Battesti, *La Marine de Napoléon III* I, 139–52. Lambert, *Crimean War*, pp. 223–33 and 257–62.

53 *GBSP*, pp. 334–5. Parker, *Graham* II, 223. Goldfrank, *Crimean War*, pp. 250–51. Lambert, 'Britain and the Baltic', p. 306. Lambert, *Crimean War*, pp. 74–5.

54 Graham to Queen Victoria, 9 Feb 1854, in Parker, *Graham* II, 228. Phillimore, *Parker* I, xiv.

55 Graham to Napier, 2 Jul 1854: Bonner-Smith, *Russian War 1854*, p. 11.

56 Bonner-Smith, *Russian War 1854*, pp. 3–5 and 12–18. Phillimore, *Parker* III, 721. *ODNB* sv Napier. Lambert, *Crimean War*, pp. 176–82. Hamilton, 'Baltic Campaign', pp. 89–100 and 107–11. Lambert, 'Keppel's Account of Bomarsund'. Brown, *Before the Ironclad*, p. 140. Lambert, 'Britain and the Baltic', pp. 306–8. Keppel, *Sailor's Life* II, 233–5. Rath, *Crimean War*, pp. 58–68. Battesti, *La Marine de Napoléon III* I, 98–101. Greenhill and Giffard, *British Assault*, gives much detail on the campaign with good charts and illustrations.

57 Sulivan, *Sulivan*, p. 295. Otway, *Paget*, (quoted) pp. 96–7.

58 Hamilton, 'Baltic Campaign', pp. 97–111. Bonner-Smith, *Russian War 1854*, pp. 12–21. Hore, *Habit of Victory*, pp. 260–61. Brown, *Before the Ironclad*, pp. 145–50. Lambert, *Crimean War*, pp. 163–6 and 197–222. Sulivan, *Sulivan*, pp. 131–8 and 222–7. Battesti, *La Marine de Napoléon III* I, 89–94. Bourchier, *Letters of Sir Henry Codrington*, pp. 366–98. Greenhill and Giffard, *British Assault*, pp. 185–94. Lambert, 'Looking for Gunboats'. Rath, *Crimean War*, pp. 50–54.

59 Hamilton, 'Baltic Campaign', pp. 93–6. Lambert, *Crimean War*, pp. 163–4, 185–90, 270–77.

60 Briggs, *Naval Administrations*, p. 262. Perhaps Dundas was really worn out; he died of a heart attack at fifty-nine.

61 Sulivan, *Sulivan*, p. 303.

62 Conacher, *Britain and the Crimea*, pp. 1–9. Lambert, *Crimean War*, pp. 271–7. Sulivan, *Sulivan*, pp. 287–305. Don, *Reminiscences*, pp. 76–7. Brown, *Before the Ironclad*, pp. 152–3. Battesti, *La Marine de Napoléon III* I, 126–30.

63 Lambert, 'Under the Heel of Britannia'. Don, *Reminiscences*, pp. 93–102. Sulivan, *Sulivan*, pp. 318–36. Bonner-Smith, *Russian War 1855, Baltic*, pp. 184–97. Battesti, *La Marine de Napoléon III* I, 130–32. Lambert, *Crimean War*, pp. 281–7.

64 Lambert, *Crimean War*, pp. 293 and 304–11. Lambert, 'Under the Heel of Britannia', pp. 122–3. Lambert, 'Britain and the Baltic', pp. 309–10. Battesti, *La Marine de Napoléon III* I, 153–6. Anderson, 'Economic Warfare', p. 45. Brown, *Before the Ironclad*, p. 208. Fuller, *Empire, Technology and Seapower*, pp. 181–98. Rath, *Crimean War*, pp. 181–96.

65 John D. Grainger, *The First Pacific War: Britain and Russia, 1854–56* (Woodbridge, 2008). Akrigg and Akrigg, *Virago*, pp. 181–91. Battesti, *La Marine de Napoléon III* I, 101–2 and 133–4. Massimo Coltrinari, 'La guerra di Crimea in Artide', *Rassegna Storica del Risorgimento* LXXIII (1986), pp. 187–93. Hore, *Habit of Victory*, pp. 257–9. Lambert, 'The Royal Navy's White Sea Campaign of 1854', *Trafalgar Chronicle* XX (2010), pp. 164–87.

66 *BDOW* VIII, 204; to Palmerston, 6 Apr 1856.

67 Tracy, *Belligerent Rights*, p. 4.

68 Anderson, *Liberal State at War*, pp. 248–74. Anderson, 'Economic Warfare'. Hamilton, 'Declaration of Paris'. Hamilton, *Anglo-French Naval Rivalry*, pp. 301–9. Lambert, 'Crimean War Blockade'. Tracy, *Belligerent Rights*, pp. xviii–xx, 10–23 and 83–90. Tracy, *Attack on Maritime Trade*, pp. 83–7. Lemnitzer, 'Moral League of Nations'. Lemnitzer, *Power, Law and the End of Privateering*, pp. 173–9. Hobson, *Imperialism at Sea*, pp. 65–71. Frei, *International Law and Maritime Strategy*, pp. 17–19. Russell, *Prize Courts and U-boats*, p. 9, prints the text of the Declaration of Paris.

69 McCord, 'Cobden and Bright', pp. 107–14 (quoted p. 114).

70 Partridge, *Military Planning*, pp. 24–7. Hamilton, *Anglo-French Naval Rivalry*, pp. 290–92. Friedman, *British Cruisers* I, 306–7 n.69.

71 Wong, *Deadly Dreams*, pp. 3–152. Graham, *China Station*, pp. 299–309. Bonner-Smith and Lumby, *Second China War*, pp. 2–154. Battesti, *La Marine de Napoléon III* II, 813–24. Lovell, *Opium War*, pp. 244–5 and 252–66.

72 Parker, *Graham* II, 302–5. Wong, *Deadly Dreams*, pp. 84–108 and 298–300. Graham, *China Station*, pp. 318–21.

73 Bonner-Smith and Lumby, *Second China War*, p. 207.

74 Keppel, *Sailor's Life* III, 1–7. Rowbotham, *Naval Brigades*. Bonner-Smith and Lumby, *Second China War*, pp. 197–208. Graham, *China Station*, pp. 314–27.

75 Bonner-Smith and Lumby, *Second China War*, pp. 390–400. Graham, *China Station*, pp. 365–407. Battesti, *La Marine de Napoléon III* II, 827–57.

Chapter 4

1 *CO*, p. 422. *GBSP*, pp. 23–33. Brown, *Before the Ironclad*, pp. 3, 16–19, 29–37 and 204. Lambert, 'Science and Sea Power'. Wright, 'Young and Seppings'. Lambert, *Last Sailing Battlefleet*, pp. 59–67 and 124–30. Phillimore, *Parker* III, 322 and 330–31.

2 MacMillan, 'British Naval Gunnery', pp. 135–66. Thomas Adams, 'A Standard Caliber: The Genesis of the French 30-Pounder', in Freeman, *Les empires en guerre et paix*, pp. 195–203. Boudriot and Berti, *L'artillerie de mer*, pp. 17–22. Douglas, *Naval Gunnery*, pp. 583–4 and 601–7.

3 Brown, *Before the Ironclad*, pp. 20–24. Brown, *Century of Naval Construction*, pp. 26–7. Dickinson, *Educating the Royal Navy*, pp. 54–5. Hamilton, *Anglo-French Naval Rivalry*, pp. 221–4. Leggett, *Shaping the Royal Navy*, pp. 39–52; and 'Neptune's New Clothes', pp. 84–5.

4 Mends, *Mends*, pp. 40–41.

5 Sharp, *Symonds*, pp. 45–7, 68–9, 75, 86–7, 91 and 118–48. Lambert, *Last Sailing Battlefleet*, pp. 58–9, 67–86 and 161–2. Lambert, *Battleships in Transition*, pp. 15–17. Lambert, 'Naval Strategic Revolution', pp. 152–3. Lambert, 'Screw Propeller'. Leggett, *Shaping the Royal Navy*, pp. 27–58, 64–9 and 76–81. Phillimore, *Parker* II, 341, 402; III, 60. Mends, *Mends*, pp. 32–42. Friedman, *British Battleships* I, 20–21.

6 Lambert, *Last Sailing Battlefleet*, p. 86.

7 Leggett, *Shaping the Royal Navy*, pp. 81 and 82.

8 Leggett, *Shaping the Royal Navy*, pp. 82–3. Lambert, *Last Sailing Battlefleet*, pp. 83–6. Lambert, *Battleships in Transition*, pp. 25–9. Coles, 'Technical Education', pp. 213–17.

9 Greenhill and Giffard, *Steam, Politics*, pp. 30–52. Brown, *Before the Ironclad*, pp. 55–7. Brown, *Paddle Warships*, pp. 11–15. Griffiths, *Steam at Sea*, pp. 7–10, 35–6 and 56–60. *GBSP*, p. 212. Rippon, *Engineering* I, 29–30.

10 *GBSP*, pp. 207, 211, 216–17 and 226. Brown, *Paddle Warships*. Brown, *Before the Ironclad*, pp. 52–63 and 71–72. Lambert, 'Naval Strategic Revolution', p. 154. Matzke, *Deterrence through Strength*, pp. 39–43. Baxter, *Ironclad Warship*, p. 227. Griffiths, *Steam at Sea*, p. 73.

11 Greenhill and Giffard, *Steam, Politics*, p. 193. Brown, *Paddle Warships*, pp. 78–80. Laing, *Steam Wooden Warship Building*, p. 9.

12 Brown, *Paddle Warships*, p. 7, prints a photograph of a model of the *Lightning* of 1823 serving as a survey ship in the Baltic in 1854, which shows her bridge clearly.

13 Lambert, *Battleships in Transition*, pp. 25–33. Baxter, *Ironclad Warship*, pp. 33–4. Brown, *Before the Ironclad*, pp. 73–87. Brown, 'Iron Warships'. Brown, *Paddle Warships*, pp. 42–5 and 65. Brown, 'Nemesis'. Marshall, *Nemesis*, pp. 23–34. Quinn, 'Guadalupe', pp. 325–6. May, *Marine Navigation*, pp. 97–101. Charles H. Cotter, 'The Early History of Ship Magnetism: The Airy-Scoresby Controversy', *Annals of Science* XXXIV (1977), pp. 589–99. The most detailed descriptions of the early British iron steamers are in Stanislas Dupuy de Lôme's *Mémoire sur la construction des bâtiments en fer* (Paris, 1844), pp. 87–116.

14 Lambert, *Battleships in Transition*, p. 28, attributes the decision to 'progressive civilian Lords of the Admiralty', but apart from the First Lord there was only one, Hon. Henry Fitzroy, Civil Lord from February 1845 to July 1846, an obscure young MP in his first

ministerial office who can scarcely have had so much influence. More likely is Cockburn, who certainly favoured iron (Morriss, *Cockburn*, p. 255), or the 'Committee on Naval Architecture'.

15 To Sir W. Parker, 6 Dec 1846: Phillimore, *Parker* III, 107.

16 Brown, *Before the Ironclad*, pp. 88–94. Brown, 'Iron Warships'. Brown and Campbell, 'Attack and Defence'. Brisou, *L'énergie vapeur*, pp. 552–3. Baxter, *Ironclad Warship*, pp. 37–41.

17 Brown, *Before the Ironclad*, pp. 92–8. Rippon, *Engineering* I, 25. Brown and Campbell, 'Attack and Defence', pp. 17–18.

18 Commissioner Charles Cunningham to Navy Board, 18 May 1827: MacDougall, *Chatham Dockyard*, p. 18.

19 James, 'Davy', and 'Faraday'. D. K. Brown, 'Roughness and Fouling', *Warship* 12 (1979), pp. 283–6.

20 To Sir W. Parker, 24 Aug 1846: Phillimore, *Parker* III, 77.

21 Lambert, *Battleships in Transition*, pp. 22–61. Lambert, 'Screw Propeller' and 'John Ericsson', gives the fullest accounts of Pettit Smith, Ericsson and Brunel's convoluted dealings with the Admiralty. Brisou, *L'énergie vapeur*, pp. 535–40. Hamilton, *Anglo-French Naval Rivalry*, pp. 26–57. Brown, *Before the Ironclad*, pp. 99–112 and 161–7. Greenhill and Giffard, *Steam, Politics*, pp. 133–62. Battesti, *La Marine de Napoléon III* I, 52–7. Friedman, *British Battleships* I, 56–71.

22 Greenhill and Giffard, *Steam, Politics*, pp. 50–52. *GBSP*, pp. 327–9. Brown, *Before the Ironclad*, pp. 112–22. Brown, 'Screw Propeller', p. 61.

23 *GBSP*, p. 325. Arnold, *Iron Shipbuilding*, p. 11. Griffiths, *Steam at Sea*, p. 33. Mends, *Mends*, pp. 305–10.

24 Baxter, *Ironclad Warship*, pp. 18–26 and 68–70. Brown, *Before the Ironclad*, pp. 64–6, 132–3 and 159–60. MacMillan, 'British Naval Gunnery', pp. 167, 184–222, 230–32, 266–76 and 294–300. Douglas, *Naval Gunnery*, pp. 238–47 and 284–9. Hamilton, *Anglo-French Naval Rivalry*, pp. 23–5. Boudriot and Berti, *L'artillerie de mer*, pp. 116–29. D. K. Brown, 'Shells at Sevastopol', *Warship* 10 (1979), pp.

74–9. Beeler, *Milne Papers* I, 690. Hamilton, *Portsmouth Dockyard Papers*, pp. 286–7. A cupola furnace for Martin shells can still be inspected in the restored *Warrior* at Portsmouth.

25 Baxter, *Ironclad Warship*, pp. 57–87. Brown, *Before the Ironclad*, pp. 156–8. Battesti, *La Marine de Napoléon III* I, 145–52. Lambert, *Crimean War*, pp. 257–62. Dewar, *Russian War 1855 – Black Sea*, pp. 346–51. Hamilton, *Anglo-French Naval Rivalry*, pp. 74–6.

26 Brown, *Before the Ironclad*, pp. 145–50. Lambert, *Battleships in Transition*, pp. 44–5. Lambert, ' "Good, while it lasts" ', pp. 42–3 and 51.

Chapter 5

1 Since all commanding officers, and by custom all officers of the rank of commander, were styled 'Captain X', it was necessary to refer to a 'post-captain' to distinguish the rank from the title.

2 *CO*, p. 521. Rodger, 'Officers, Gentlemen' and 'Commissioned Officers' Careers'. Rodger, *Wooden World*. Clowes, *Royal Navy* IV, 192–5, and V, 39–43, prints the flag lists of 1793–1801 and 1804–14.

3 Until recently, retired RN officers were still borne on the 'Emergency List' and liable in principle to be recalled for service at any age.

4 *CO*, pp. 518–22. Rodger, 'Commissioned Officers' Careers'. Wilcox, 'These Peaceable Times', pp. 475–6. Phillimore, *Parker* I, 419. Lewis, *Navy in Transition*, pp. 66, 69, 72, 78, 84 and 87. Appendix III.

5 To Palmerston, 17 Jan 1840: Napier, *Napier* I, 400.

6 Lewis, *Navy in Transition*, pp. 78, 84 and 87. *GBSP*, p. 318. Clowes, *Royal Navy* VI, 205 and 538–49. Keppel, *Sailor's Life* I, 164 (quoted) and 169. Note that Keppel and Dundas were Tories, but the promotion came from a Whig Admiralty.

7 To Sir E. Lyons, 18 Oct 1847: Phillimore, *Parker* III, 261.

8 Louvier, *La puissance navale*, pp. 63–4, 69–74 and 144–5. Beeler, 'Fit for Service Abroad', p. 302.

9 *GBSP*, p. 231.

10 To Sir F. Baring, Christmas Day 1850: Phillimore, *Parker* III, 664.

11 Beeler, 'Fit for Service Abroad'. Dandeker, 'Patronage'. Lewis, *Navy in Transition*, pp. 73–6 and 117–21. Beeler, *Milne Papers* I, 288–9. Clowes, *Royal Navy*, VI, 206–7.

12 Lewis, *Navy in Transition*, pp. 73–6 and 79–81. Akrigg and Akrigg, *Virago*, pp. 183–91. Grainger, *First Pacific War*, Stone and Crampton, 'Franco-British Attack', and Rath, *Crimean War*, pp. 111–41, give accounts of the campaign. Ashcroft, 'Reminiscences' LIII, 275–7, was an eyewitness.

13 Beeler, 'Fit for Service Abroad', pp. 304 and 305.

14 *ODNB*. [William Arthur], *The Active List of Flag Officers and Captains . . .* (Portsmouth, 1883), p. 18. Beeler, ' "Fit for Service Abroad" '.

15 PRO: ADM 6/198, p. 28.

16 Cavell, *Midshipmen*, pp. 157–64 and 179–80 (modifying the conclusions of Lewis, *Navy in Transition*, pp. 19–32). Rodger, 'Officers, Gentlemen', pp. 141–4. *NRG*, pp. 19–20. Dickinson, *Educating the Navy*, pp. 46–50. HC 1821 XV, p. 277, and 1833 XXIV, p. 279.

17 Vale, 'Appointment, Promotion and "Interest" ', pp. 63–5. Vale, *Frigate of King George*, pp. 116–20. Cavell, *Midshipmen*, pp. 172–3. PRO: ADM 6/198 lists the 1830 nominations. Rodger, 'Officers, Gentlemen', p. 144.

18 *GBSP*, p. 317. Rodger, 'Officers, Gentlemen', pp. 145–6.

19 Louvier, *La puissance navale*, p. 49.

20 Bourchier, *Letters of Sir Henry Codrington*, pp. 49 and 65.

21 Beeler, *Milne* I, 53–4. Phillimore, *Parker* II, 419.

22 Greenhill and Giffard, *Steam, Politics*, pp. 103–7.

23 To W. A. Baillie Hamilton, 2nd Secretary, 6 Jul 1846: *GBSP*, p. 316.

24 Phillimore, *Parker* II, 649.

25 Phillimore, *Parker* III, 41–2.

26 Phillimore, *Parker* III, 54–5.

27 Mends, *Mends*, pp. 26, 43 (quoted) and 96–7.

28 Eardley-Wilmot, *Lyons*, pp. 37, 58–77, 119 and 126.

29 Norman, *At School and at Sea*, p. 65. The allusion is to 1 Corinthians 12:31 and 13:2.

30 Boteler, *Recollections*, p. 56.

31 *BND*, p. 707.

32 Akrigg and Akrigg, *Virago*, pp. 68–9.

33 Phillimore, *Parker* III, 263. Mrs Palmer's father was Captain W. H. Ricketts, Parker's cousin and a nephew of Earl St Vincent, who had himself married his own first cousin. This made for a complicated family tree: Parker was Lady St Vincent's nephew, Lord St Vincent's first cousin once removed, and Henrietta Palmer's second cousin.

34 Wilcox, 'These Peaceable Times', pp. 478–80.

35 Burrows, *Autobiography*, p. 7.

36 Broadhead, *Memoirs* II, 10.

37 Sir Evelyn Wood, *From Midshipman to Field Marshal* (London, 1906, 2 vols) I, 13 (referring to 1852).

38 H. W. F. Baynham, 'A Seaman in H.M.S. *Leander*, 1863–6', *MM* LI (1965), pp. 343–52, at p. 347.

39 Vale, 'Appointment, Promotion and "Interest" ', p. 67, quoting Midshipman Charles Drinkwater.

40 Keppel, *Sailor's Life* I, 57.

41 Lewis, *Navy in Transition*, pp. 212–13. A. M. Broadley and R. G. Bartelot, *Nelson's Hardy: His Life, Letters and Friends* (London, 1909), pp. 188 and 190. Gough, 'Specie Conveyance'. Keppel, *Sailor's Life* II, 199.

42 Mends, *Mends*, p. 4. Gough, *Peard Journal*, pp. 42–3 and 251. Keppel, *Sailor's Life* I, 62–5. Vale, *Frigate of King George*, pp. 22–3, 84 and 97. Fanshawe, *Fanshawe*, pp. 260–61. Akrigg and Akrigg, *Virago*, pp. 141–51 and 198. Gough, 'Specie Conveyance', pp. 424–6. Riley, *Blue-Jacket*, p. 117. Ashcroft, 'Reminiscences' LIII, 164–5.

43 Lloyd, *Slave Trade*, pp. 79–84. Anon, 'The Woodhead Prize Account Ledger 1842–65', *Three Banks Review* 76 (1967), pp. 36–47.

44 Norman, *At School and at Sea*, p. 66.

45 Lambert, *Admirals*, pp. 247–52. Egerton, *Hornby*, pp. 43–9.

46 Lewis, *England's Sea-Officers*, pp. 91–2.

47 E.g. Sulivan, *Sulivan*, pp. 9–11; Burrows, *Autobiography*, pp. 11–12; Colomb, *Key*, pp. 3–8.

48 Norman, *At School and at Sea*, pp. 13–17 (quoted p. 17).

49 Burrows, *Autobiography*, p. 140 (referring to 1841–2). The Rev. Thomas J. Main had been a Senior Wrangler at Cambridge.

50 HC 1849 XXXII, p. 241, 'Qualifications required for appointment as naval cadet'.

51 Dickinson, *Educating the Navy*, pp. 54–8 and 82–3. Rodger, 'Officers, Gentlemen', pp. 145–6. Lewis, *Navy in Transition*, pp. 108–9. Cavell, *Midshipmen*, pp. 206–7. Colomb, *Key*, p. 69. Christopher Lloyd, 'The Royal Naval Colleges at Portsmouth and Greenwich', *MM* LII (1966), pp. 145–56, at p. 148. F. B. Sullivan, 'The Naval Schoolmaster during the Eighteenth Century and the Early Nineteenth Century', *MM* LXII (1976), pp. 311–26, at pp. 323–4.

52 Dickinson, *Educating the Navy*, pp. 57–61 and 80–81. *NRG*, pp. 28–9. Beeler, *Milne Papers* I, pp. 606 and 625–70.

53 Dickinson, *Educating the Navy*, p. 62. Beeler, *Milne Papers* II, xxiv and 446. Hamilton, *Portsmouth Dockyard Papers*, p. 133.

54 Norman, *At School and at Sea*, p. 61.

55 Dickinson, *Educating the Navy*, p. 81.

56 Phillimore, *Parker* II, 406, 736–7 and 743–4. Dickinson, *Educating the Navy*, pp. 70–71. Mends, *Mends*, pp. 317–19. Beeler, *Milne Papers* I, 606.

57 Colomb, *Key*, p. 87. Phillimore, *Parker* III, 265. *GBSP*, p. 317 n.1.

58 Eardley-Wilmot, *The Midshipman's Friend*, pp. 147–8.

59 James Napier, *Life of Robert Napier of West Shandon* (Edinburgh, 1904), pp. 157–8. Mends, *Mends*, p. 75. Beeler, *Milne Papers* I, 300–303. Miller, 'Jack Tar to Bluejacket', p. 211. Greenhill and Giffard, *Steam, Politics*, pp. 89–91 and 168. Penn, *Up Funnel*, pp. 26–30 and 51–3.

60 MacMillan, 'British Naval Gunnery', pp. 43–4, 64–5, 84–106 and 226–32. Douglas,

Naval Gunnery, pp. 123–8. Matzke, *Deterrence*, pp. 38–9. Lambert, *Last Sailing Battlefleet*, pp. 101–7.

61 MacMillan, 'British Naval Gunnery', pp. 243–50. *BND*, pp. 704–6. Napier, *Napier* II, 114. *GBSP*, p. 42. Matzke, *Deterrence*, pp. 38–9 and 172. Burrows, *Autobiography*, pp. 126–8.

62 Douglas, *Naval Gunnery*, pp. 14–22. *GBSP*, pp. 319–23. Colomb, *Key*, pp. 65–72.

63 *CO*, pp. 383–4, 393–4 and 527.

64 *NRG*, pp. 6–8 and 17–20. Lavery, *Royal Tars*, p. 292. Lavery, *Able Seamen*, pp. 26–7. Beeler, *Milne Papers* I, 259.

65 Akroyd et al., *Advancing with the Army*, pp. 57 and 220–21. McLean, *Surgeons of the Fleet*, pp. 24–38, 51–4, 66–74, 150–67. Preston, 'Constructing Communities', pp. 208–20. Harrison, 'West African Service'. Sir James Watt, 'Naval and Civilian Influences in Eighteenth- and Nineteenth-Century Medical Practice', *MM* XCVII (2011), pp. 148–66. M. J. Cullen, *The Statistical Movement in Victorian England* (Hassocks, 1975), pp. 50–52.

66 Lewis, *England's Sea-Officers*, pp. 248–50. Warlow, *The Pusser and his Men*, p. 43. *NRG*, pp. 23–5.

67 Blake, *Religion in the British Navy*, pp. 109–14. Norman, *At School and at Sea*, pp. 152–4.

68 Mrs Tom Kelly, *From the Fleet in the Fifties: A History of the Crimean War* (London, 1902), p. 405, quoting a letter of January 1856 from the Rev. S. K. Stothert, Chaplain of the *Queen* in the Black Sea.

69 Blake, *Religion in the British Navy*, pp. 109–10 *passim*.

70 Burrows, *Autobiography*, pp. 188–91.

71 Hamblin, 'Marine Engineering', pp. 53–5.

72 Greenhill and Giffard, *Steam, Politics*, pp. 85–6.

73 Walton, 'Officers or Engineers?', p. 183 (quoted). Miller, *Dressed to Kill*, p. 81.

74 Walton, 'Officers or Engineers?'. Walton, 'Corporation and Community', pp. 42–9. Penn, *Up Funnel*, pp. 36–41 and 72–4. Miller, 'Jack Tar to Bluejacket', pp. 209–10. Chamberlain, 'Stokers', p. 30.

75 Walton, 'Officers or Engineers?', p. 194.
Akrigg and Akrigg, *Virago*, p. 47. Penn,
Up Funnel, p. 83.

Chapter 6

1 App. V.
2 Parker, *Graham* I, 160. Bromley,
Manning Pamphlets, pp. 173–88. Palmer,
Navigation Laws, pp. 65, 137 and 175.
3 Bromley, *Manning Pamphlets*, p. 175,
quoting an 1834 pamphlet by Martin.
4 Lords' Select Committee on the
Navigation Laws, 1848, 3rd Report: HC
1847–48 XX Pt. II (754), p. 692/708
Q.7499.
5 Lavery, *Royal Tars*, pp. 318–21. Walton,
'Recruiting Seamen', pp. 33 and 36.
Palmer, *Navigation Laws*, pp. 63, 65, 176–
7. Miller, 'Jack Tar to Bluejacket', pp. 239–
42 and 264–71.
6 Miller, 'Jack Tar to Bluejacket', pp. 198
and 266–7. Walton, 'Corporation and
Community', pp. 37–48 and 61–2.
7 Evidence of Capt. M. F. F. Berkeley to
Lords' Select Committee on the
Navigation Laws, 1848, 3rd Report: HC
1847–48 XX Pt. II (754), p. 822/838,
Q.8433.
8 Sir Henry Codrington to his wife, 16 Jun
1854, in Bourchier, *Letters of Sir Henry
Codrington*, p. 378.
9 Lavery, *Able Seamen*, pp. 23–4. Taylor,
'Manning'. Miller, 'Jack Tar to Bluejacket',
p. 225. Beeler, *Milne Papers* I, 248–9.
Huddie, 'Coast Volunteers'.
10 Walton, 'Recruiting Seamen', pp. 31–2.
Preston, 'Constructing Communities',
pp. 71 and 272. Norman, *At School and at
Sea*, p. 310. *BND*, p. 732. Lavery, *Shield of
Empire*, pp. 159–61. Much the fullest
information about where the Navy
found its officers and ratings is in the
as-yet-unpublished researches of Dr
David Sheppard, based on analysis of
census returns. I am most grateful to
him for sharing his findings.
11 Rasor, *Reform*, pp. 43–4 and 48–55.
Winton, *Life on the Lower-Deck*, pp. 174–
7. Lavery, *Royal Tars*, p. 325.
12 To Sir W. Parker, 7 Oct 1846, in
Phillimore, *Parker* III, 84 (where the

captain's name has been omitted).
Stopford was not superseded but court-
martialled and acquitted, cf. Preston,
'Constructing Communities', pp.
127–32.
13 Lambert, 'Modern Naval Rating', p. 37.
Winton, *Life on the Lower-Deck*, p. 68.
Miller, 'Jack Tar to Bluejacket', pp. 164–6.
14 Eardley-Wilmot, *The Midshipman's
Friend*, pp. 69 (quoted) and 73–80.
15 Preston, 'Constructing Communities',
pp. 132–4 and 195. Miller, 'Jack Tar to
Bluejacket', pp. 150–56.
16 Bechervaise, *Thirty-Six Years*, p. 272.
17 Ashcroft, 'Reminiscences' LII, 62.
18 Lavery, *Royal Tars*, pp. 335–7. Beeler,
Milne Papers I, 194–5. Miller, 'Jack Tar to
Bluejacket', pp. 224–5. Phillimore, *Parker*
III, 107. Walton, 'Recruiting Seamen', pp.
37–40.
19 Bechervaise, *A Farewell to my Old
Shipmates*, p. 16.
20 Bechervaise, *Thirty-Six Years*, p. 269.
21 Walton, 'Recruiting Seamen', p. 41.
22 Walton, 'Recruiting Seamen'. Miller, 'Jack
Tar to Bluejacket', p. 209. Lambert,
'Modern Naval Rating', pp. 33–7. Beeler,
Milne Papers I, 238 and 252–5. Lavery,
Royal Tars, pp. 330–37, and *Able Seamen*,
p. 25. Preston, 'Constructing
Communities', pp. 78–85 and 265–79.
23 Walton, 'Recruiting Seamen', p. 30.
Walton, 'Corporation and Community',
pp. 66–73 and 118–19. Taylor, 'Manning',
XLIV, 306–7, and XLV, 46–50. Beeler,
Milne Papers I, 350–53.
24 Rasor, *Reform*, pp. 32–3 and 113–15.
Lambert, 'Modern Naval Rating', pp. 39–
40. Lavery, *Able Seamen*, pp. 20–22, 25
and 41–57. Hamilton, *Anglo-French
Naval Rivalry*, pp. 157–60. *BND*, pp.
708–14 and 717–23. Bromley, *Manning
Pamphlets*, pp. 363–71. Beeler, *Milne
Papers* I, 212–13, 350–53 and 607–8.
Bowen, *Royal Naval Reserve*, pp. 11–25.
25 Winton, 'Life and Education', pp. 257–9.
26 Jarrett, *British Naval Dress*, pp. 91–2 and
99–100 (quoted p. 100). Miller, *Dressed
to Kill*, pp. 84–7. Lavery, *Able Seamen*, pp.
41–4. Lavery, *Royal Tars*, pp. 302–3.
Miller, 'Jack Tar to Bluejacket', p. 178.
Winterhalter's painting is still in the

Royal Collection and has often been reproduced.

27 Hamilton, *Anglo-French Naval Rivalry*, pp. 163–73. Battesti, *La Marine de Napoléon III* I, 437–88.

28 Walton, 'Corporation and Community', pp. 82, 94–9 and 107. Lavery, *Able Seamen*, pp. 73–7, 98 and 104. Chamberlain, 'Stokers', pp. 94–5. HC 1898 (288) LVI, p. 639. For the origin of the *maistrance* (still a distinctive feature of the French Navy today), see Battesti, *La Marine de Napoléon III* I, 475–88.

29 Arthur, *Lost Voices*, p. 12, quoting Leading Stoker Jack Cotterell of the cruiser *Gloucester* in 1915.

30 Scrimgeour, *Dartmouth to Jutland*, p. 356, referring to the coal-fired battle-cruiser *Invincible* in 1915.

31 Chamberlain, 'Stokers', pp. 30–37, 55–7, 68–71, 74–6, 79, 82, 86–8, 94–5, 264–5 and 287–9. Lavery, *Able Seamen*, pp. 127–8 and 364. Walton, 'Corporation and Community', p. 110 n.15 and 130–32.

32 *NRG*, p. 10. Lavery, *Able Seamen*, pp. 77–8. Ashcroft, 'Reminiscences' LII, 62.

33 *NRG*, p. 9. Lavery, *Able Seamen*, pp. 107–8. McKee, *Sober Men*, pp. 231–4.

34 *NRG*, pp. 10–11. *BND*, pp. 735–6 and 974–5. Lavery, *Able Seamen*, pp. 166–8. Blond, 'Technology and Tradition', pp. 152–6.

35 Akiyama, *Feeding the Nation*, pp. 150 and 160–63. Warlow, *The Pusser and his Men*, pp. 54–6.

36 Walton, 'Corporation and Community', p. 358, printing an 1860 Table of Complements. Lavery, *Able Seamen*, pp. 128–30.

37 Brown, *Poxed and Scurvied*, pp. 175–6. Brown, *Fittest of the Fit*, pp. 39–41. Keevil, Lloyd and Coulter, *Medicine and the Navy* IV, 62–6. Lavery, *Able Seamen*, pp. 107 and 130. S. G. Clark, 'Farewell to the SBA', *JRNMS* LXX (1984), pp. 3–8.

38 McLean, *Surgeons of the Fleet*, pp. 97–100 and 127–8; quoted p. 109. Robert E. Johnson, *Sir John Richardson: Arctic Explorer, Natural Historian, Naval Surgeon* (London, 1976), p. 69. Harland, *Naval Nursing Service*, p. 12.

39 Brown, *Poxed and Scurvied*, p. 171, quoting S. G. Osborne.

40 Stanley, *Women and the Navy*, p. 34.

41 Harland, *Naval Nursing Service*, p. 8. Cf. McLean, *Surgeons of the Fleet*, pp. 161–7, 172 and 211; Keevil, Lloyd and Coulter, *Medicine and the Navy* IV, 149–50; Stanley, *Women and the Navy*, p. 34. Akiyama, *Feeding the Nation*, pp. 154–63.

42 Harland, *Naval Nursing Service*, p. 15.

43 Harland, *Naval Nursing Service*, pp. 16–21 (quoted). Wells, *Social History*, p. 46. Kathleen M. Harland, 'A Short History of Queen Alexandra's Royal Naval Nursing Service', *JRNMS* LXX (1984), pp. 59–65, at p. 60. Stanley, *Women and the Navy*, pp. 35–41.

44 *NRG*, pp. 8–12. Lavery, *Able Seamen*, pp. 94–5. McKee, *Sober Men*, pp. 73–5, 94–8, 104–5 and 171–2. Moore, *Greenie*, p. 96. Goldrick, *After Jutland*, p. 20.

45 Wells, *Social History*, pp. 33, 49–51 and 86–7. Lavery, *Able Seamen*, pp. 70–73, 124–6, 138–40, 157–61, 168–70, 174–5 and 225. Yexley, *Inner Life of the Navy*, pp. 57–60, 126–34 and 153–65. Winton, *Life on the Lower-Deck*, p. 261. Knock, *Clear Lower Deck*, pp. 60–64 and 147–8. McKee, *Sober Men*, pp. 71–3 and 171–2. Baynham, *Men from the Dreadnoughts*, pp. 26–9 and 94–9. Carew, *Lower Deck*, pp. 27–30. Lambert, *Submarine Service*, p. xx. Capper, *Aft – from the Hawsehole*, p. 20.

46 Walton, 'New Kinds of Discipline', pp. 149–52. Lavery, *Able Seamen*, pp. 59–60. Kemp, *British Sailor*, pp. 205–6. Rasor, *Reform*, pp. 64–75. Hamilton, *Portsmouth Dockyard Papers*, pp. 320–52 and 365–6. H. W. F. Baynham, 'A Seaman in H.M.S. *Leander*, 1863–6', *MM* LI (1965), pp. 343–52, at p. 349. Walton, 'Corporation and Community', pp. 157–63 and 313–14 (quoting Capt. J. G. Goodenough in 1866, p. 314).

47 Walton, 'Corporation and Community', pp. 164–7.

48 Walton, 'New Kinds of Discipline'. Lavery, *Able Seamen*, pp. 66–8. Broadhead, *Memoirs* II, 77. Rasor, *Reform*, pp. 46–59. Walton, 'Corporation and Community', pp. 264–5 and 173–4.

Spector, *At War at Sea*, pp. 54–6.
Winton, *Life on the Lower-Deck*, pp.
174–82.

49 Milne to Sir Frederick Grey, 24 Jun 1861,
in Beeler, *Milne Papers* II, 313.

50 Walton, 'Corporation and Community',
pp. 152 and 181. Winton, *Life on the
Lower-Deck*, p. 99.

51 Walton, 'Corporation and Community',
pp. 182–3, 199–202 and 321–9. McKee,
Sober Men, pp. 160–64. 'The Journal of
George Thomas Mann, Recording the
Events of His Service in the Royal Navy
1871–1880', ed. Maurice Welsh and Avard
Mann (Faversham Papers No. 50,
Faversham, 1996), p. 19. Baynham, 'A
Seaman in H.M.S. *Leander*', p. 345.
Yexley, *Inner Life of the Navy*, pp. 199–
200. Ashcroft, 'Reminiscences' LII, 63,
and LIII, 359.

52 Lavery, *Able Seamen*, pp. 125–37. Spector,
At War at Sea, pp. 58–60. Carew, *Lower
Deck*, pp. 19–30. Conley, *Jack Tar to
Union Jack*, pp. 139–41. Knock, *Clear
Lower Deck*, pp. 63–4. Yexley, *Inner Life
of the Navy*, pp. 41–4, 118–34, 153–65 and
203–6. Wells, *Social History*, pp. 49–52.
McKee, *Sober Men*, pp. 200–204.
Baynham, *Men from the Dreadnoughts*,
pp. 26–9 and 94–7.

53 Winton, *Life on the Lower-Deck*, pp.
223–4. Conley, *Jack Tar to Union Jack*,
pp. 2–9 and 141–5. Lavery, *Able Seamen*,
pp. 96–8. Spector, *At War at Sea*, pp.
32–3. McKee, *Sober Men*, pp. 13–15, 33
and 67–70. Rüger, *Great Naval Game*,
pp. 58–64. Colville, 'Jack Tar and the
Gentleman Officer', pp. 107–10 and 119–
26. Clare Rose, 'The Meanings of the
Late Victorian Sailor Suit', *JMR* XI
(2009), pp. 24–50. The South African
War is described in Ch. 10.

54 Conley, *Jack Tar to Union Jack*, pp. 67–90
and 123–32. Knock, *Clear Lower Deck*,
pp. 227–42. Rowe, 'Discipline and
Morale', p. 79.

55 Seligmann, *Churchill and Social Reform*,
pp. 43–62.

56 Lavery, *Able Seamen*, pp. 172–3. *BND*, pp.
969–72. Spector, *At War at Sea*, p. 58.
Knock, *Clear Lower Deck*, pp. 95–108.

McKee, *Sober Men*, pp. 73–92 and 239–
40. Carew, *Lower Deck*, pp. 18–27.

57 Capper, *Aft – from the Hawsehole*, p. 131.

58 Carew, *Lower Deck*, pp. 1–46. Davison,
Challenges of Command, pp. 33–7. Farr,
McKenna, pp. 174–5. Baynham, *Men
from the Dreadnoughts*, p. 21.

59 Carew, *Lower Deck*, pp. 56–7.

60 Carew, *Lower Deck*, pp. 67–72. Beckett
and Jeffery, 'Curragh Incident'.
Seligmann, *Churchill and Social Reform*,
pp. 10–19. Lavery, *Able Seamen*, pp.
181–3.

Chapter 7

1 Fuller, *Empire, Technology and Seapower*,
p. 96.

2 Lambert, 'Politics, Technology and
Policy-Making', quoting Palmerston, p.
14. Beeler, *Milne Papers* I, 608–9 and
677–748. Battesti *La Marine de Napoléon
III* I, 163–73. Hamilton, *Anglo-French
Naval Rivalry*, pp. 279–99. Fuller, *Empire,
Technology and Seapower*, pp. 84–92 and
122–32. Alfaro Zaforteza, 'Collapse of the
Congress System', pp. 116–17. Friedman,
British Cruisers I, 306–7, prints Walker's
1858 paper.

3 Buckinghamshire RO: Ramsden
Collection, Somerset Papers
A.R.41/62(L) No. 66, W.E. Gladstone to
Somerset, 13 Dec 1864.

4 Beeler, *Naval Policy*, pp. 6–7 and 18–20.
Hamilton, *Anglo-French Naval Rivalry*,
pp. 127–31. Fuller, *Empire, Technology and
Seapower*, pp. 118–30. Morgan-Owen,
Fear of Invasion, pp. 13–14. Lambert,
'Development of Education', pp. 40–45;
and 'Politics, Technology and Policy-
Making', pp. 16–19. Hamilton, *Portsmouth
Dockyard Papers*, pp. 270–22 and 362.
Rodger, 'Change and Decay', p. 41. The
report of the Royal Commission on the
Defences of the United Kingdom (C.2682)
is printed in HC 1860 XXIII, pp. 431–523.

5 Fuller, *Clad in Iron*, p. 65, quoting the
New York Herald.

6 Davis and Engerman, *Naval Blockades*,
pp. 124–30. Lambert, 'Winning without
Fighting', pp. 179–81. Cook, *Alabama*

Claims, pp. 124–7. Fuller, 'Ericsson, the Monitors and Union Naval Strategy', quoted p. 5.

7 Davis and Engerman, *Naval Blockades*, pp. 109–21 and 130–58. Beeler, *Milne Papers* II, 306, 329 and 332. Bernath, *Squall across the Atlantic*, pp. 4–31. Lambert, 'Great Britain and Maritime Law', pp. 15–17. Coates, 'Trusteeship of International Law', pp. 37–8. Merli, 'The American Way with Blockades'.

8 Baxter, *Ironclad Warship*, pp. 226–37, 255–66 and 290–302. Roberts, 'Political Engineering'. Fuller, *Clad in Iron*, pp. 51–9, 71–9, 88–105, 128–36, 178–80 and 231–62. Fuller, *Empire, Technology and Seapower*, pp. 234–7. Battesti, *La Marine de Napoléon III* I, 240–41. The *Virginia* had been rebuilt on the salvaged hull of the former USS *Merrimack*, which is the name used by older histories.

9 Fuller, *Clad in Iron*, p. 217. Cook, *Alabama Claims*, p. 15. Tracy, *Attack on Maritime Trade*, pp. 90–95. Lemnitzer, *Power, Law and the End of Privateering*, pp. 179–81. Rodney Carlisle, 'Flagging-Out in the American Civil War', *NM* XXII (2012), pp. 53–65. Benjamin W. Labaree et al., *America and the Sea: A Maritime History* (Mystic, CT, 1998), p. 366. Note that the *Alabama* was not a privateer but a regular warship of the Confederate States Navy.

10 Cook, *Alabama Claims*, and English, *The Laird Rams*, are the best studies of this episode.

11 Semmel, *Liberalism and Naval Strategy*, pp. 74–89. Friedman, *British Cruisers* I, 10. Davis and Engerman, *Naval Blockades*, pp. 109–19. Bernath, *Squall across the Atlantic*, pp. 4–31. Lambert, 'Great Britain and Maritime Law', pp. 16–21. Tracy, *Attack on Maritime Trade*, pp. 87–95. Abbenhuis, 'European Hopes for Neutrality', pp. 28–44. Lemnitzer, *Power, Law and the End of Privateering*, pp. 176–81. Lt Sydney M. Eardley-Wilmot, 'Great Britain's Maritime Power . . .', *JRUSI* XXII (1878), pp. 435–60.

12 At least until the arrival of the Dutch ironclad *Koning der Nederlanden* in the East Indies in 1878.

13 Tunstall, 'Imperial Defence' II, 818–19 and 828–38. Burroughs, 'Defence and Imperial Disunity', pp. 320–32. Lambert, 'Unique Global Power'. Darwin, *Empire Project*, pp. 35–6 and 61–2. Fuller, *Empire, Technology and Seapower*, pp. 104–5 and 112. Bach, *Australia Station*, pp. 72–6 and 180. Seymour, 'Colonial Naval Defence Act'.

14 Schurman, *Imperial Defence*, pp. 37–8; cf. Beeler, *Milne Papers* I, 774–7.

15 Beeler, *Birth of the Battleship*, pp. 24–5. Ranft, 'Naval Defence', pp. 145–9.

16 Beeler, *Naval Policy*, pp. 254–7. Beeler, *Birth of the Battleship*, p. 16. Beeler, 'A One Power Standard?', pp. 567–70.

17 Hamilton, *Anglo-French Naval Rivalry*, pp. 314–15. Ropp, *Modern Navy*, pp. 30–33.

18 Bartlett, 'Mid-Victorian Reappraisal', p. 192. Rodger, 'Naval Thought', pp. 143–5.

19 Barry M. Gough, *The Royal Navy and the Northwest Coast of North America, 1810–1914* (Vancouver, 1971), p. 163.

20 *BND*, p. 637.

21 Preston and Major, *Send a Gunboat*, pp. 239–50, printing a list of applications for naval assistance, 1857–61. Mbaeyi, *Military and Naval Forces*, pp. 181–97. Collins, 'Projection of British Power', pp. 94–9.

22 Samson, 'Imperial Benevolence'. Bach, *Australia Station*, pp. 34–60.

23 Beeler, *Naval Policy*, pp. 34–7. Bartlett, 'Mid-Victorian Reappraisal', pp. 191–205. Preston and Major, *Send a Gunboat*, pp. 34–5.

24 Salisbury to Ld Lytton, 9 Mar 1877, in Cecil, *Salisbury* II, 130.

25 Figes, *Crimea*, pp. 454–63. Beeler, *Naval Policy*, pp. 13–15. Lambert, 'Britain and the Baltic', pp. 322–4.

26 Ranft, 'Naval Defence', pp. 150–65. Schurman, *Imperial Defence*, pp. 50–118. Burroughs, 'Defence and Imperial Disunity', pp. 334–5. Ranft, 'The Protection of Seaborne Trade', quoted on pp. 3–4. Smith, 'Public Opinion', p. 30. Gray, *Steam Power*, pp. 26–35. Knight, 'British North Atlantic Convoys', pp. 55–6.

27 Holland, *Blue-Water Empire*, pp. 109–16. Darwin, *Empire Project*, pp. 73–7 and 131. Ferguson, *Cash Nexus*, pp. 299–301.

28 Chilston, *Smith*, pp. 185–8. *BND*, pp. 604–9. Marder, *British Naval Policy*, pp. 121–2. Blumenthal, 'Navy Campaign of 1884', pp. 11–15, 37–40 and 54–75. Mackay, *Fisher*, pp. 179–81. Hamilton, 'The Nation and the Navy', pp. 46–7. Rodger, 'Peace, Retrenchment and Reform', pp. 126–7; and 'Belted Cruisers', p. 32. Parkinson, *Late Victorian Navy*, pp. 89–92.

29 Blumenthal, 'Navy Campaign of 1884', pp. 54–63, 74–5 and 79. Mackay, *Fisher*, pp. 178–81. S. R. B. Smith, 'Public Opinion', p. 37. Beeler, 'In the Shadow of Briggs'. Lambert, *Admirals*, p. 281. Parkinson, *Late Victorian Navy*, pp. 90–92. Bastable, *Arms and the State*, pp. 206–7. Beeler, 'Northbrook's Response'. W. S. Robinson, *Muckraker: The Scandalous Life and Times of W. T. Stead, Britain's First Investigative Journalist* (London, 2012), pp. 63–7. *ODNB* and Gray, *Steam Power*, pp. 43–5, attribute 'The Truth about the Navy' to the young Liberal journalist and politician H. O. Arnold-Foster, who seems to have been one of Stead's informants. Alfaro Zaforteza, 'Age of Empire', pp. 134–5, suggests without citing new evidence that the campaign was politically inspired and conducted by Arnold-Foster and Fisher. This idea of a Liberal attack on a Liberal government is not altogether persuasive in either case.

30 Lambert, 'Britain and the Baltic', pp. 315–27. Berryman, 'Imperial Defence Strategy'. S. R. B. Smith, 'Public Opinion', pp. 32–4. Schurman, *Imperial Defence*, pp. 134–40.

31 Beeler, 'Ploughshares into Swords', pp. 19–25. D. K. Brown, *Warrior to Dreadnought*, pp. 87–8. Cobb, *Preparing for Blockade*, pp. 131–54; and '"In the shadow of the *Alabama*"'. N. Barnaby, 'On the Fighting Power of the Merchant Ship in Naval Warfare', *TINA* XVIII (1877), pp. 1–23. Rodger, 'Change and Decay', pp. 41–5.

32 Ropp, *Modern Navy*, p. 110. Lemnitzer, *Power, Law and the End of Privateering*,

p. 184. Bowen, *Royal Naval Reserve*, pp. 40–45.

33 '. . . comme autrefois le vaisseau de ligne, le cuirassé, c'était Versailles sur l'eau': Motte, *Une Éducation géostratégique*, p. 203.

34 Ropp, *Modern Navy*, pp. 155–78. Motte, *Une Éducation géostratégique*, pp. 160–230. Motte, 'La Jeune École et la généalogie de la guerre totale'. Hobson, *Imperialism at Sea*, pp. 102–9. Michel Depeyre, *Entre vent et eau: Un siècle d'hésitations tactiques et stratégiques, 1790–1890* (Paris, 2003), pp. 429–36. Røksund, 'The *Jeune École*'. Bueb, *Die 'Junge Schule'*. Ceillier, 'Les idées stratégiques'. Monaque, 'L'amiral Aube'. Monaque, *La marine de guerre française*, pp. 327–37. Symcox, 'Admiral Mahan', pp. 681–4. Heuser, *Strategy*, pp. 234–40. Halpern, 'French Navy', pp. 38–40.

35 Friedman, *British Cruisers* I, 25–32. Grimes, *Strategy and War Planning*, pp. 21–3. Gordon, *Rules of the Game*, pp. 193–4. *BND*, pp. 614–17. Taylor, 'Naval Manoeuvres of 1888'. Mullins, 'Sharpening the Trident', pp. 119–20. Morgan-Owen, *Fear of Invasion*, pp. 22–5 and 57–60. 'Extracts from the Report of the Committee on the Naval Manoeuvres, 1888', HC 1889 L, pp. 735–94 [C.5632]. PRO: ADM 231/11, 'Report on the Naval Manoeuvres of 1887'. PRO: ADM 231/14, 'Report on the Naval Manoeuvres of 1888'.

36 Peden, 'Political Economy of Public Expenditure', p. 352. Ferguson, *Cash Nexus*, p. 89. Mullins, 'Sharpening the Trident', pp. 100–18. Friedman, *British Cruisers* I, 218–43. Alfaro Zaforteza, 'Age of Empire', p. 135.

37 To Lord Lytton, 15 Jun 1877, in Cecil, *Salisbury* II, 153.

38 To G. J. Goschen, 10 Feb 1892, in Cecil, *Salisbury* IV, 189.

39 To Lord Selborne, 27 Feb 1901, in Boyce, *Selborne Papers*, p. 112.

40 Ld G. Hamilton to Salisbury, 3 Jul 1888: Hatfield House MSS: 3rd Marquess, Class E, Lord George Hamilton, No. 142.

41 Mullins, *British and American Naval Policy*, pp. 278–81. Mullins, 'Sharpening

the Trident', pp. 52-62 and 118; and 'In the Shadow of Marder', pp. 59-70. Otte, 'Floating Downstream'. Porter, 'Lord Salisbury', pp. 156-67. P. Smith, 'Ruling the Waves', pp. 22 and 36-9. Cecil, *Salisbury* IV, 188-92. Hamilton, *Parliamentary Reminiscences* II, 115-16 and 220-21. Friedman, *British Cruisers* I, 226-43. The key papers in the drafting of the Naval Defence Act are PRO: CAB 37/22/24, 37/22/30, 37/22/36 and 37/22/40; my interpretation of them does not slavishly follow any of the printed authorities.

42 Porter, 'Lord Salisbury', pp. 168-9. P. Smith, 'Ruling the Waves', pp. 35-9. N. A. Lambert, *Fisher's Naval Revolution*, pp. 18-20. Sumida, *Naval Supremacy*, pp. 12-14. Daunton, *Trusting Leviathan*, pp. 69-71. *CO*, p. 108.

43 S. R. B. Smith, 'Public Opinion, the Navy and the City of London'. W. M. Hamilton, 'The "New Navalism" and the British Navy League'. Anne Summers, 'The Character of Edwardian Nationalism: Three Popular Leagues', in *Nationalist and Racialist Movements in Britain and Germany before 1914*, ed. Paul Kennedy and Anthony Nicholls (London, 1981), pp. 68-87.

44 Beeler, *Naval Policy*, pp. 271-7. Beeler, 'Northbrook's Response'. Marder, *British Naval Policy*, p. 162. Mullins, 'In the Shadow of Marder', 'New Ways of Thinking', and *British and American Naval Policy*, pp. 278-81. Salewski, 'Die Wilhelminische Flottengesetze', p. 119. Otte, 'Floating Downstream', pp. 111-17.

Chapter 8

1 Hamilton, 'Childers Admiralty Reforms', pp. 39-42 and 58-9.

2 Beeler, *Naval Policy*, p. 70.

3 Beeler, *Naval Policy*, p. 76.

4 PRO: ADM 116/3453, 1861 Lords' Committee Minutes.

5 Hamilton, 'Policy-Makers and Financial Control', pp. 371-4.

6 Feuchtwanger and Philpott, 'Civil–Military Relations', p. 7.

7 Beeler, *Naval Policy*, p. 72.

8 Beeler, *Naval Policy*, pp. 41-2. Rodger, 'Business Methods', pp. 332-4. C. I. Hamilton, *Modern Admiralty*, pp. 144-7 and 157-8. C. I. Hamilton, 'Phinn Committee', pp. 380, 388-91, 401-2 and 431-2. R. V. Hamilton, *Naval Administration*, p. 25. Haas, *Management Odyssey*, pp. 83, 99-100.

9 Hamilton, *Portsmouth Dockyard Papers*, pp. xxv-xxvi, xxx-xxxii, xl-xli and 259-67. *BND*, pp. 671-4.

10 Fuller, *Clad in Iron*, p. 23.

11 Hamilton, 'Phinn Committee', pp. 418-19.

12 Beeler, *Milne Papers* II, 130-43.

13 Beeler, *Naval Policy*, p. 42.

14 Beeler, *Naval Policy*, p. 45, quoting Seymour's anonymous pamphlet *The Naval Expenditure from 1860 to 1866 and its Results*.

15 Beeler, *Naval Policy*, pp. 80-82. Hamilton, 'Childers Admiralty Reforms', pp. 39-42.

16 Hamilton, *Portsmouth Dockyard Papers*, pp. li, 78-80 and 106. Hamilton, *Modern Admiralty*, pp. 150-55. Hamilton, 'Childers Admiralty Reforms', pp. 44-6. Haas, *Management Odyssey*, pp. 112-13 and 119-20. *BND*, pp. 661-5. Henry Roseveare, *The Treasury: The Evolution of a British Institution* (London, 1969), p. 139.

17 Hamilton, *Modern Admiralty*, pp. 153-8. Beeler, *Naval Policy*, pp. 176-7. R. V. Hamilton, *Naval Administration*, p. 25.

18 Hamilton, *Modern Admiralty*, pp. 139-41 and 149-55. Beeler, *Naval Policy*, pp. 176-83. Rodger, 'Business Methods', pp. 334-9. *BND*, pp. 661-5. Colomb, *Key*, p. 379. Briggs, *Naval Administrations*, pp. 187-9.

19 Rodger, 'Business Methods', pp. 339-40. C. I. Hamilton, *Modern Admiralty*, pp. 153-5. Hamilton, *Anglo-French Naval Rivalry*, pp. 265-6.

20 Hamilton, 'Phinn Committee', pp. 377-8. Leggett, *Shaping the Royal Navy*, pp. 201-4. Brown, *Before the Ironclad*, pp. 85-7 and 92-3. Norman McCord, 'A Naval Scandal of 1871: The Loss of H.M.S. *Megaera*', *MM* LVII (1971), pp. 115-34.

21 Beeler, *Naval Policy*, pp. 133-6.

22 Beeler, *Naval Policy*, pp. 135–9 and 184–9. Hamilton, *Modern Admiralty*, p. 159. *BND*, pp. 666–70.

23 V. Miller to Milne, 14 Nov 1872, in Rodger, 'Business Methods', p. 340.

24 To Rear-Admiral J. W. Tarleton, 10 Apr 1873, in Rodger, 'Business Methods', p. 343.

25 Rodger, 'Business Methods', p. 343.

26 Beeler, *Naval Policy*, pp. 171–2. Egerton, *Hornby*, pp. 183–4 and 192–4.

27 Beeler, *Naval Policy*, pp. 173–4. Egerton, *Hornby*, pp. 183–4 and 192–8. Lambert, *Admirals*, pp. 266 and 278–9. Rodger, 'Change and Decay', pp. 37–8.

28 Colomb, *Key*, pp. 488 and 493 (quoted). Rodger, 'Change and Decay', pp. 39–40.

29 Beeler, *Naval Policy*, pp. 184–5. Colomb, *Key*, pp. 414–89.

30 Allen, 'Foreign Intelligence Committee', pp. 66–8. Rodger, 'Peace, Retrenchment and Reform', pp. 122–5. Colomb, *Key*, p. 455. Hamilton, *Modern Admiralty*, pp. 175–6. Boyd, *Naval Intelligence*, pp. 15–19.

31 PRO: ADM 116/3106, 'Formation of Naval Intelligence Department, 1886–1888', quoting a minute by E. A. Bartlett, Civil Lord, 12 Nov 1886. Allen, 'Foreign Intelligence Committee', p. 70. HC 1888 XII, p. 19/519 QQ.294–303. Gray, *Steam Power*, pp. 56–9.

32 C. I. Hamilton, 'Policy-Makers and Financial Control', pp. 376–8. G. Hamilton, *Parliamentary Reminiscences* I, 278–9.

33 *BND*, pp. 610–14. Allen, 'Foreign Intelligence Committee', pp. 72–3. Boyd, *Naval Intelligence*, pp. 27–30.

34 Beeler, *Naval Policy*, pp. 184–5. G. Hamilton, *Parliamentary Reminiscences* I, 291 and II, 86. On Hood's appetite for paperwork see his evidence to the 1888 Hartington Commission: PRO: HO 73/35/3, p. 148 QQ.1732–1738.

35 HC 1888 XIII, p. 17/231 QQ.4120–4122; pp. 21/235–24/238 QQ.4151–4196, p. 29/243 QQ.4252–4257 (quoted), p. 33/247 QQ.4313–4319, p. 41/255 QQ.4395 and 4404–4405, p. 65/279 Q.4648. To be fair to Hood he really had sketched a war plan fifteen years before at Milne's instruction (cf. Ch. 3); there is a copy in the Milne papers, NMM: MLN/P/B/1(C).

36 PRO: CAB 37/22/24 of July 1888, signed by all the naval lords but evidently written by Hood; he had given his evidence on 13 June.

37 HC 1888 XII, p. 66/566 QQ.906–907, p. 67/567 Q.910 (quoted), p. 74/574 Q.1022.

38 HC 1888 XII, pp. 2/502–40/540, especially p. 19/519 QQ.294–303.

39 Mullins, 'New Ways of Thinking', p. 83. Allen, 'The Foreign Intelligence Committee', pp. 66–71. Hamilton, *Modern Admiralty*, pp. 201–3.

40 *BND*, pp. 673–4. More than sixteen years, in fact: his dockyard service began in 1863 as Superintendent of Chatham.

41 Hamilton, *Portsmouth Dockyard Papers*, pp. xliv–xlvi and liv–lv. Haas, *Management Odyssey*, pp. 89–91 and 107–14.

42 *Politicians and Defence: Studies in the Formulation of British Defence Policy, 1845–1970*, ed. Ian Beckett and John Gooch (Manchester, 1981), Introduction, p. 11.

43 Haas, *Management Odyssey*, pp. 138–40.

44 Hamilton, *Portsmouth Dockyard Papers*, pp. 146–53 and 354. Haas, 'Royal Dockyard Schools', pp. 327–30. Casey, 'Class Rule'. Robertson, 'Technical Education', pp. 228–31. Brown, *Century of Naval Construction*, pp. 32–40, 154–6 and 334–5. Edgerton, *Warfare State*, pp. 111–12 and 135–6. The one exception was Sir Eustace Tennyson d'Eyncourt, DNC 1912–24, who came from Charterhouse and a premium apprenticeship at Armstrong's Elswick yard.

45 Brown, *Century of Naval Construction*, pp. 52–62. Haas, *Management Odyssey*, pp. 116 and 141–5. Haas, 'Royal Dockyard Schools', pp. 331–2.

46 Revealing evidence of this was given to the [Ravensworth] 'Committee Appointed to Enquire into the Conditions Under Which Contracts Are Invited for the Building or Repairing of Ships' (C.4219), printed in HC 1884–5 XIV, pp. 125–364; see especially the evidence of Barnaby (p. 43/171) and

Rear-Admiral Thomas Brandreth the Controller (pp. 34/162–38/166).

47 Minute of 1 February 1887 in *BND*, p. 699.

48 Leggett, 'Naval Architecture'. Leggett, *Shaping the Royal Navy*, pp. 193–5. D. K. Brown, 'British Warship Design Methods 1860–1905', *WI* XXXII (1995), pp. 59–82.

49 Charles Dickens, 'Chatham Dockyard, 29th August 1863', one of the pieces collected in his *The Uncommercial Traveller* (Oxford, 2021), pp. 257–8.

50 Waters, 'Chatham Dockyard Workforce', pp. 55–62. Haas, *Management Odyssey*, p. 115. Evans, *Building the Steam Navy*, pp. 155–65. MacDougall, 'A Demand Fulfilled'.

51 Waters, 'Chatham Dockyard Workforce', p. 166, quoting A. C. Edwards, foreman shipwright of Chatham in 1881.

52 Waters, 'The Dockyardmen Speak Out', pp. 87 and 92.

53 Haas, *Management Odyssey*, pp. 160–66. Waters, 'Chatham Dockyard Workforce', pp. 165–72. Waters, 'The Dockyardmen Speak Out', pp. 94–6. Galliver, 'Trade Unionism in Portsmouth Dockyard'. Haas, 'Low Labour Intensity'.

54 Hamilton, *Portsmouth Dockyard Papers*, pp. xxxvi, 41–7, 62. MacDougall, *Chatham Dockyard*, pp. 53–8. *BND*, pp. 588–91. Coad, *Support for the Fleet*, pp. 171–99. Hamilton, *Anglo-French Naval Rivalry*, p. 201.

55 Coad, *Support for the Fleet*, pp. 83–6 and 225–390. Evans, *Building the Steam Navy*, pp. 170–81 and 189–95. Hamilton, *Portsmouth Dockyard Papers*, pp. 49 and 54.

56 Inglis, 'Imperial Connection', p. 23.

57 Kennedy, 'Imperial Cable Communications', pp. 728–41. Headrick, *Invisible Weapon*, p. 31. Headrick and Griset, 'Submarine Telegraph Cables', pp. 554–6.

58 Boyce, 'Imperial Dreams' and 'Submarine Cables' and 'Pacific Telegraph Cable', p. 57. Headrick, *Invisible Weapon*, pp. 36–9 and 79–80. Headrick, 'Câbles télégraphiques', pp. 140–43. Ferris, 'Whitehall's Black Chamber', pp. 63–4. Allain,

'L'indépendence câblière de la France', p. 119. Pender died in 1896, but his youngest son took over the cable companies and continued his policy.

Chapter 9

1 Lambert, *Warrior*, pp. 12–15. Brown, *Before the Ironclad*, pp. 174–86. C. I. Hamilton, *Anglo-French Naval Rivalry*, pp. 88–97. Baxter, *Ironclad Warship*, pp. 117, 121 and 127–36. Fuller, *Empire, Technology and Seapower*, pp. 138–43. Ropp, *Modern Navy*, pp. 8–10. Dupuy de Lôme, *La construction des bâtiments en fer*. Battesti, *La Marine de Napoléon III* I, 184–7, 202–6, 218–24; II, 681–4. Battesti (I, 220–24) insists that French yards were perfectly capable of building in iron but were prevented by official prejudice.

2 A. D. Lambert, *Warrior*, pp. 16–32. D. K. Brown, *Warrior to Dreadnought*, pp. 12–14. Friedman, *British Battleships* I, 68–78.

3 D. K. Brown, *Warrior to Dreadnought*, pp. 14–17 and 26–38. Ballard, *Black Battlefleet*, pp. 12–97 and 116–201. Sandler, *Modern Capital Ship*, pp. 20–27, 48–51 and 118–52. Baxter, *Ironclad Warship*, pp. 153–80. Friedman, *British Cruisers* I, 87–91.

4 Baxter, *Ironclad Warship*, pp. 245–82.

5 The name 'monitor' could be explained as 'schoolmaster'.

6 Roberts, 'Political Engineering'. Fuller, 'Ericsson, the Monitors, and Union Naval Strategy'. Fuller, *Clad in Iron*, pp. 56–254. Fuller, 'Union Monitors vs. the British Navy', pp. 134–8. Fuller, 'British Reactions to the USS *Monitor*'.

7 Baxter, *Ironclad Warship*, pp. 185–94 and 328–30. Brown, *Warrior to Dreadnought*, pp. 207–12, gives a succinct introduction to stability.

8 Brown, *Warrior to Dreadnought*, pp. 23–4 and 41–51. Brown, 'Design Methods', pp. 67–70. Beeler, *British Naval Policy*, pp. 110–21. Fuller, *Clad in Iron*, pp. 32–4, 143–7 and 164. Leggett, *Shaping the Royal Navy*, pp. 145–62. Sandler, *Modern Capital Ship*, pp. 177–233. Manning, *White*, pp. 30–37. Friedman, *British Battleships* I, 104–15 and 139–44.

9 Leggett, *Shaping the Royal Navy*, pp. 162–72. Brown, *Warrior to Dreadnought*, pp. 58–63. Sandler, *Modern Capital Ship*, pp. 234–9. Friedman, *British Battleship* I, 115–31.

10 Bastable, *Arms and the State*, pp. 72–4 and 92–101. Beeler, *Birth of the Battleship*, pp. 72–4. Hamilton, *Portsmouth Dockyard Papers*, pp. 288–300. Evans, *Arming the Fleet*, pp. 123–5. Battesti, *La Marine de Napoléon III* II, 702–12. Friedman, *British Battleship* I, 32–44.

11 Bastable, *Arms and the State*, pp. 2–3, 19–20, 25–72. Fuller, *Empire, Technology and Seapower*, pp. 108–9. Evans, *Arming the Fleet*, pp. 106–7 and 123–5.

12 Bastable, *Arms and the State*, pp. 23–4, 46, 178–90 and 230–321. Hodges, *Big Gun*, pp. 19–24. Evans, *Arming the Fleet*, pp. 106–7. Friedman, *British Battleship* I, 87–91. Moore, *Greenie*, pp. 31–2.

13 Brown, *Warrior to Dreadnought*, pp. 78–9. Evans, *Arming the Fleet*, p. 124. Bastable, *Arms and the State*, pp. 172–3. Beeler, *Birth of the Battleship*, pp. 76–86. Friedman, *Naval Firepower*, p. 282. Fuller, *Empire, Technology and Seapower*, p. 150. Friedman, *British Battleships* I, 44–7 and 87–91.

14 Beeler, *Birth of the Battleship*, p. 77. Hodges, *Big Gun*, pp. 13–14. Brown, *Warrior to Dreadnought*, p. 64.

15 Sandler, *Modern Capital Ship*, pp. 118–53. W. Laird Clowes, 'Naval Warfare, 1860–1889, and Some of its Lessons', *JRUSI* XXXIV (1890), pp. 719–28, at pp. 720–22.

16 Brown, *Warrior to Dreadnought*, pp. 71–3, and Beeler, *Birth of the Battleship*, pp. 85–6, on British gunnery at Alexandria. Beeler, 'Steam Strategy and Schurman', p. 30, and Dunley, 'Mine Warfare', on ironclads' intended functions. Fuller, *Empire, Technology and Seapower*, pp. 43–51 and 176–80, opposing Beeler and Andrew Lambert. Fuller, 'British Reactions to the USS *Monitor*', pp. 289–90. On the *Glatton* see Dunley, 'Mine Warfare', pp. 392–401; Brown, *Warrior to Dreadnought*, pp. 57–8, and Friedman, *British Battleship* I,

118–26: she drew too much water to get into most fortified harbours and was barely seaworthy, but in good weather she could have attacked Cherbourg or Brest.

17 Allen, 'British Naval Tactics'. A. D. Lambert, *Admirals*, pp. 260–64. Egerton, *Hornby*, pp. 203–4. Gordon, *Rules of the Game*, pp. 183–7, 193–206 and 243–9. *The Journal of George Thomas Mann, Recording the Events of His Service in the Royal Navy 1871–1880*, ed. Maurice Welsh and Avard Mann (Faversham Papers No. 50, Faversham, 1996), p. 8. F. G. H. Bedford, *The Life and Letters of Admiral Sir Frederick George Denham Bedford* [Newcastle upon Tyne, 1961], p. 92. Brown, *Warrior to Dreadnought*, pp. 100–101.

18 Baxter, *Ironclad Warship*, pp. 328–30. Beeler, *Birth of the Battleship*, pp. 159–81 and 194–202. Brown, *Warrior to Dreadnought*, pp. 69, 91 and 95–6. Hodges, *Big Gun*, pp. 33–4. Friedman, *British Battleship* I, 182–5, and 226 n.27.

19 Brown, *Warrior to Dreadnought*, pp. 70–73 and 132.

20 Hovgaard, *Warships*, p. 165.

21 Rodger, 'Inconstant'. Brown, *Warrior to Dreadnought*, pp. 19–23. Dean C. Allard, 'Benjamin Franklin Isherwood: Father of the Modern Steam Navy', in *Captains of the Old Steam Navy: Makers of the American Naval Tradition, 1840–1880*, ed. James C. Bradford (Annapolis, MD, 1986), pp. 301–22; at pp. 309–18 he describes the circumstances in which the *Wampanoag* Class came to be built.

22 NMM: MLN/P/B/1(C), 'Shipbuilding Policy and the State of the Navy, 1858–76', p. 18, printing Admiralty correspondence of April 1874; cf. Rodger, 'Inconstant', pp. 18–21.

23 Thomas Brassey, 'Unarmoured Ships', in Brassey, *The British Navy* II, 262–3. Never an original thinker, Brassey was a reliable echo of conventional wisdom.

24 Brown, *Warrior to Dreadnought*, p. 21. Wood, 'Huascar', pp. 2–11 and 86–8. Manning, *White*, p. 110.

25 Beeler, *Birth of the Battleship*, pp. 182–7 and 193–202. Friedman, *British*

Battleship I, 15. Brown, *Warrior to Dreadnought*, pp. 69–70 and 112–13. Rodger, 'Belted Cruisers', pp. 24–33.

26 Crichton, 'Froude and the Experimental Tank'. Brown, *The Way of the Ship*. Brown, *Grand Fleet*, p. 17. Leggett, *Shaping the Royal Navy*, pp. 175–182. Lyon, 'Admiralty and Private Industry', pp. 44–45. Matsumoto, *Technology Gatekeepers*, pp. 28–33.

27 Brown, *Warrior to Dreadnought*, pp. 74–5 and 79–80. Manning, *White*, pp. 64–5. Slaven, *British Shipbuilding*, p. 48. Parkinson, *Late Victorian Navy*, pp. 130–32. Lindberg and Todd, *Anglo-American Shipbuilding*, p. 23.

28 Beeler, *Birth of the Battleship*, pp. 54–9. Brown, *Warrior to Dreadnought*, pp. 66–9. Brown, 'Marine Engineering', XXXIV, pp. 391, 398–401 and 655–6; XXXV, pp. 92–4. Griffiths, *Steam at Sea*, pp. 47–56 and 65–7. Rippon, *Engineering* I, 69–70. Lyon, 'Admiralty and Private Industry', pp. 47–9. Oram, 'Warship Machinery', pp. 100–106 and 113. Friedman, *British Cruisers* I, 50–54.

29 Rippon, *Engineering* I, 124. Brown, 'Marine Engineering' XXXIV, pp. 648–50. Lavery, *Able Seamen*, p. 104. Moore, *Greenie*, pp. 47–9.

30 MacLaren, 'Electrical Engineering'. Maber, 'Electrical Supply', XXV, pp. 348–52. Rippon, *Engineering* I, 77–9, 84–6 and 181. Moore, *Greenie*, pp. 31–2, 47–9 and 98–9.

31 Beeler, *Milne Papers* I, 668–9. Brown, *Warrior to Dreadnought*, p. 121. Rodger, 'First Light Cruisers', pp. 214–15. Rodger, 'Naval Thought', pp. 140–41. PRO: ADM 231/6, Foreign Intelligence Committee Report No. 73 (May 1885), 'The Protection of Commerce by Patrolling the Ocean Highways and by Convoy'.

32 Rodger, 'First Light Cruisers', pp. 219–22. Brook, *Warships for Export*, pp. 44–7 and 52–5. Manning, *White*, pp. 101 and 107–11. Brown, *Century of Naval Construction*, pp. 61–2. Brown, *Warrior to Dreadnought*, pp. 132–6.

33 Fiume/Rijeka was in those days largely Italian-speaking, but it is in Croatia, then part of the Hungarian fraction of the Dual Monarchy.

34 Briggs, 'Whitehead Torpedo'. Beeler, *Birth of the Battleship*, pp. 65–9. *BND*, pp. 691–3. Brown, *Warrior to Dreadnought*, pp. 81–6. Casali and Cattaruzza, *Sotto i mari*, pp. 15–25. Bedford, *Bedford*, pp. 54 and 73–4. Cowpe, 'Whitehead Torpedo', pp. 23–30. Scheina, *Latin America*, p. 64. Dunley, 'Whitehead Torpedo', pp. 68–9.

35 Brown, *Warrior to Dreadnought*, pp. 85–6 and 116–18. Cowpe, 'Whitehead Torpedo', pp. 28–32. Friedman, *British Destroyers* I, 24–37. Dunley, 'Whitehead Torpedo', pp. 70–82.

Chapter 10

1 Darwin, *Empire Project*, pp. 32–5. Marder, *British Naval Policy*, p. 162. Friedberg, *Weary Titan*, pp. 195–9 and 210–15.

2 To Lord Curzon, 19 April 1901, in Boyce, *Selborne Papers*, p. 115.

3 Morgan-Owen, *Fear of Invasion*, pp. 22–7.

4 Neilson, ' "Greatly Exaggerated" ', pp. 713–14. Marder, *British Naval Policy*, pp. 178–203. Hamilton, *Parliamentary Reminiscences* II, 219–29. Mackay, *Fisher*, pp. 209–10. Morgan-Owen, *Fear of Invasion*, pp. 30–33. Friedman, *British Battleship* I, 250.

5 Morgan-Owen, 'Invasion Question', pp. 19–20, 28–9 and 36–45. Marder, *British Naval Policy*, pp. 216–19 and 235. Grimes, *Strategy and War Planning*, pp. 30–32.

6 Marder, *British Naval Policy*, pp. 242–5. Hamilton, *Parliamentary Reminiscences* II, 223. Gültekin Yıldız, 'How to Defend the Turkish Straits against the Russians: A Century-Long "Eastern Question" in British Defence Planning, 1815–1914', *MM* CV (2019), pp. 40–59, at p. 55.

7 Lt W.C. Crutchley RNR, 'Modern Warfare as Affecting the Mercantile Marine of Great Britain', *JRUSI* XXXVII (1893), pp. 491–511 (quoted p. 495) and subsequent debate. Cf. Crutchley, 'On the Unprotected State of British Commerce at Sea', *JRUSI*

XXXIII (1889), pp. 625ff.; Capt. P. H. Colomb, 'Convoys: Are They Any Longer Possible?', *JRUSI* XXXI (1887), pp. 297–325; Rear-Adm. Samuel Long, 'On the Present Position of Cruisers in Naval Warfare', *TINA* XXXIV (1893), pp. 1–18.

8 Ranft, 'Protection of Seaborne Trade' and 'Parliamentary Debate'. Lambert, 'Deterrence and the Strategy of World Power', p. 77. Beeler, 'Steam, Strategy and Schurman', pp. 43–4. Marder, *British Naval Policy*, pp. 93–5. Between 1880 and 1895 the French and Russian navies completed eight belted cruisers between them; on the broader definition of 1st Class Cruisers (belted or protected) the figures in 1895 were 19 British against 10 French and 5 Russian (Brown, *Warrior to Dreadnought*, p. 157).

9 Cobb, *Preparing for Blockade*, pp. 189–90 and 209–17. Knight, 'British North Atlantic Convoys', pp. 56–8.

10 Ranft, 'Protection of Seaborne Trade'. Ranft, 'Parliamentary Debate'. French, 'Edwardian Crisis', pp. 208–10. Kennedy, *Anglo-German Antagonism*, pp. 307–15. Searle, *National Efficiency*, pp. 54–97. Offer, 'Costs and Benefits', pp. 694–5.

11 P. M. Kennedy, *Anglo-German Antagonism*, p. 309 (written in 1910).

12 N. A. Lambert, *Fisher's Naval Revolution*, p. 23. Friedberg, *Weary Titan*, pp. 162–71.

13 Otte, ' "Floating Downstream"?', pp. 117–19.

14 Boyce, *Selborne Papers*, p. 154; cf. K. Wilson, 'Directions of Travel', p. 270.

15 Lambert, *Fisher's Naval Revolution*, p. 33.

16 Otte, ' "It's What Made Britain Great" ', pp. 14–15. N. A. Lambert, *Fisher's Naval Revolution*, pp. 32–5. R. Williams, *Defending the Empire*, pp. 9–11 and 23–30. Kennedy, *Anglo-German Antagonism*, pp. 251–5 and 342. O'Brien, *Naval Power*, pp. 25–9.

17 More exactly, the railway ran from the port of Lourenço Marques on the shore of Delagoa Bay; the name Maputo is nowadays applied to both.

18 Collins, 'Projection of British Power', pp. 100–101. Searle, *National Efficiency*, p. 38. Coogan, *End of Neutrality*, pp. 30–44

and 52. Darwin, *Empire Project*, pp. 241–7. Burroughs, 'Defence and Imperial Disunity', pp. 343–4. Russell, *Prize Courts and U-boats*, p. 12. Abbenhuis, ' "Too Good to be True?" ', pp. 33–49. Peter Henshaw, 'The "Key to South Africa" in the 1890s: Delagoa Bay and the Origins of the South African War', *Journal of Southern African Studies* XXIV (1998), pp. 527–43.

19 Headrick, 'Câbles télégraphiques', p. 143. Headrick, *Invisible Weapon*, pp. 88–9.

20 *FGDN* I, 172–7. Mackay, *Fisher*, pp. 242–9. Allen, 'Reginald Custance', pp. 62–9. Seligmann, 'Britain's Great Security Mirage', pp. 863–75. Marder, *British Naval Policy*, pp. 393–406. Friedman, *Network-Centric Warfare*, pp. 3–4. Friedman, *British Destroyers* I, 69–72. Lambert, 'Strategic Command and Control', pp. 371–2. Morgan-Owen, 'Invasion Question', pp. 53–4. Morgan-Owen, *Fear of Invasion*, pp. 36–41.

21 Mackay, *Fisher*, pp. 254–6. *FGDN* I, 222.

22 Mackay, *Fisher*, pp. 216–24 and 245–50. Mackay, *Balfour*, pp. 167–8. Sumida, *Naval Supremacy*, pp. 24–7. Williams, *Defending the Empire*, pp. 61–6. Lambert, *Fisher's Naval Revolution*, pp. 30–33, 74–5 and 91–7. Lambert, 'Righting the Scholarship', p. 279. There is no stage of Fisher's career that more urgently justifies a new biography than this period.

23 Mackay, *Fisher*, pp. 306–8, 336–40 and 357–65. Mackay, *Balfour*, pp. 167–8. *FGDN* II, 18–19. Lambert, 'Righting the Scholarship', pp. 278–9. N. A. Lambert, *Planning Armageddon*, pp. 33–4.

24 Seligmann, Nägler and Epkenhans, *Naval Route to the Abyss*, p. 117.

25 Boyce, *Selborne Papers*, p. 142. Balfour was at this date Leader of the House of Commons, but three months later he succeeded his uncle Salisbury as Prime Minister.

26 G. W. Monger, 'The End of Isolation', quoted p. 108; *idem, End of Isolation*, pp. 14–44. Seligmann, 'Switching Horses'. Seligmann, Nägler and Epkenhans, *Naval Route to the Abyss*, p. 154. P. M. Kennedy, 'German World Policy'; *idem, Anglo-German Antagonism*, pp. 228–47;

idem, 'Tirpitz, England and the Second Navy Law'. Wilson, 'Directions of Travel'. Williams, *Defending the Empire*, pp. 70–73. Boyd, *Naval Intelligence*, pp. 44–6. Marder, *British Naval Policy*, pp. 291–301. Rodger, 'Deutsch–Englisch Flottenrivalität', pp. 1–8.

27 Searle, *National Efficiency*, pp. 60–70 and 95–7. French, 'Edwardian Crisis', pp. 209–10. Darwin, *Empire Project*, pp. 102–3. Green, 'Political Economy of Empire', pp. 361–6. Offer, 'Costs and Benefits', pp. 704–7. McCain and Hopkins, *British Imperialism*, pp. 209–22. Friedberg, *Weary Titan*, pp. 69–87.

28 Richard H. Collin, 'The Caribbean Theater Transformed: Britain, France, Germany, and the USA, 1900–1906', *AN* LII (1992), pp. 102–12. *ODNB* sv Pauncefote. Kennedy, *Anglo-German Antagonism*, pp. 265–6. Friedberg, *The Weary Titan*, pp. 169–72. O'Brien, *Naval Power*, pp. 25–9.

29 Enrico Serra, 'L'intesa mediterranea del 1902', *Nuova Antologia* 462 (1954), pp. 307–32 and 483–508; 463 (1955), pp. 97–123. G. W. Monger, 'The End of Isolation'. Friedberg, *The Weary Titan*, pp. 165–7 and 174–6. Neilson, ' "Greatly Exaggerated" ', pp. 698–9.

30 French, *British Strategy and War Aims*, pp. 6–7. Monger, *End of Isolation*, pp. 126–59. Kennedy, *Anglo-German Antagonism*, pp. 265–70. Otte, ' "It's What Made Britain Great" ', p. 15. Stevenson, *Armaments and the Coming of War*, p. 66. Neilson, 'Anglo-Japanese Alliance', pp. 52–4. Gow, 'The Royal Navy and Japan, 1900–1920', pp. 38–40. Holland, *Blue-Water Empire*, pp. 131–3.

31 Neilson, ' "Greatly Exaggerated" ', pp. 715–16.

32 Boyce, *Selborne Papers*, p. 181.

33 Monger, *End of Isolation*, pp. 149–54, 172–4 and 181–3. Steinberg, 'Copenhagen Complex', pp. 32–3. Röhl, *Wilhelm II*, pp. 272–4. Paine, *Japanese Empire*, pp. 67–9. Rotem Kowner, *Great Battles: Tsushima* (Oxford, 2022). Phil Thorne, *Tsushima, Japan's Trafalgar: The Voyage of the Condemned Fleet to the Straits of Korea* (Market Harborough, 2022).

34 O'Brien, *Naval Power*, pp. 29–30.

35 The 'Second Reich', the first having been the Holy Roman Empire, which however was a completely different structure; a supranational confederacy rather than a military superpower.

36 Von Tirpitz from 1900 when he was raised to the nobility. Kelly, *Tirpitz*, is the best modern biography, and the most accessible introduction in English to German naval administration and politics of this era.

37 Fischer, *Admiral des Kaisers*, pp. 29–45. Brézet, 'La pensée navale allemande', pp. 127–30. Kennedy, 'Fisher and Tirpitz', pp. 49–54. Haslop, *Early Naval Air Power*, pp. 59–60.

38 Hobson, *Imperialism at Sea*, pp. 46–7, quoting the title of a book by the Liberal anti-imperialist H. N. Brailsford.

39 Seligmann et al., *Naval Route to the Abyss*, pp. 49–80. Kelly, *Tirpitz*, pp. 11–12, 163–4, 196–9, 227 and 249–51. Röhl, *Wilhelm II*, pp. 20–25, 210, 246, 272–4 and 466–83. Bönker, *Militarism*, pp. 65–78 and 278–87. Epkenhans, *Tirpitz*, pp. 23–34. Herwig, 'Command Decision Making', pp. 112–14. Hobson, *Imperialism at Sea*, pp. 242–52. Kelly, 'Tirpitz and the Oberkommando der Marine', pp. 1037 and 1058–60. Epkenhans, 'Die Tirpitzsche Flottenplanung'. Herwig, 'Luxury' Fleet, pp. 62 and 90–92. Kennedy, 'Fisher and Tirpitz', pp. 53–4. Dash, 'Submarine Policy', pp. 207–12. Gemzell, *German Naval Planning*, pp. 56–61 and 92–103. Strachan, *First World War*, p. 1066. Terrell D. Gottschall, *By Order of the Kaiser: Otto von Diederichs and the Rise of the Imperial German Navy, 1865–1902* (Annapolis, MD, 2003), pp. 223–40. Steinberg, 'Copenhagen Complex', pp. 44–6.

40 Neilson, 'Grey as Foreign Secretary', p. 130. Otte, ' "It's What Made Britain Great" ', p. 16. Kennedy, *Anglo-German Antagonism*, p. 441.

41 Berghahn, 'Des Kaisers Flotte und die Revolutionierung des Mächtesystems', p. 175.

42 Marder, *British Naval Policy*, p. 288. Salewski, 'Die militärische Bedeutung

des Nord-Ostsee-Kanals', p. 107. Goldrick, *Before Jutland*, p. 72. In 1907 the draught limitations were quoted as Kiel Canal 31ft, Little Belt and Sound 24ft, Great Belt 60ft (*BDOW* VIII, 125). Recent British and German battleships drew 26–27ft.

43 For which see *CO*, pp. 469–71 and 549.

44 Dunley, 'Fisher and Strategic Deterrence'. A. D. Lambert, *The British Way of War*, pp. 149 and 169. A. Lambert, 'Thinking about Seapower', p. 315.

45 Morgan-Owen, *Fear of Invasion*, pp. 90–139.

46 Morgan-Owen, *Fear of Invasion*, pp. 86–90. D'Ombrain, *War Machinery and High Policy*. Young, *Balfour*, pp. 224–6 and 269–71. Mackay, *Balfour*, pp. 116–23. French, *Economic and Strategic Planning*, pp. 77–9. Searle, *National Efficiency*, pp. 217–33. Gooch, 'Sir George Clark's Career'. Mackintosh, 'Committee of Imperial Defence'.

47 Morgan-Owen, *Fear of Invasion*, pp. 155–60. Williams, *Defending the Empire*, pp. 79–90 and 120–26. N. A. Lambert, *Fisher's Naval Revolution*, pp. 128–39.

48 N. A. Lambert, *Fisher's Naval Revolution*, p. 142.

49 N. A. Lambert, *Fisher's Naval Revolution*, p. 134. Sidorowicz, 'Armaments Question'. The third battleship for 1907–8 was to be dropped in the very unlikely event of the Hague Peace Conference adopting serious disarmament.

50 Röhl, *Wilhelm II*, pp. 496–7 and 602–5. Kennedy, *Anglo-German Antagonism*, pp. 374 and 442–4. Stevenson, *Armaments and the Coming of War*, pp. 166–7. *DSF* I, 135. O'Brien, *Naval Power*, pp. 31–4. Steinberg, 'German Background', pp. 210–12. Steinberg, 'The Novelle of 1908'. Williams, *Defending the Empire*, pp. 156–73. Brézet, 'Course aux armaments navals', pp. 110–13. Epkenhans, *Die wilhelminische Flottenrüstung*, p. 228.

51 Kennedy, *Anglo-German Antagonism*, pp. 373–4. Williams, *Defending the Empire*, pp. 86–99. French, *Economic and Strategic Planning*, pp. 77–8. Morgan-Owen, *Fear of Invasion*, pp.

155–9, 176–80 and 228–33. W. M. Hamilton, 'The "New Navalism" and the British Navy League'. Anne Summers, 'The Character of Edwardian Nationalism: Three Popular Leagues', in *Nationalist and Racialist Movements in Britain and Germany before 1914*, ed. Paul Kennedy and Anthony Nicholls (London, 1981), pp. 68–87, at pp. 78–80. N. C. Fleming, 'The Imperial Maritime League: British Navalism, Conflict, and the Radical Right, c.1907–1920', *WiH* XXIII (2016), pp. 296–322.

52 Seligmann, Nägler and Epkenhans, *Naval Route to the Abyss*, pp. 361–3 and 372–4. Seligmann, 'Intelligence Information and the 1909 Naval Scare'. Kelly, *Tirpitz*, pp. 300–302. Warren, *Cammell Laird*, p. 146. O'Brien, *Naval Power*, pp. 78–94. *DSF* I, 151–9. Stevenson, *Armaments and the Coming of War*, pp. 166–7. *BDOW* VI, 555–7 and 770–71. Farr, *McKenna*, p. 169. On German industrial weakness see Epkenhans, *Die wilhelminische Flottenrüstung*, and 'Krupp'.

53 Williams, *Defending the Empire*, pp. 156–8. Farr, *McKenna*, pp. 155–62. O'Brien, *Naval Power*, pp. 73–94. *DSF* I, 159–71. Sumida, *Naval Supremacy*, pp. 186–7. Steinberg, 'The Novelle of 1908'.

54 Stevenson, *Armaments and the Coming of War*, pp. 166–7. On 'Dreadnought' battleships, see Ch. 13.

55 Stevenson, *Armaments and the Coming of War*, pp. 166–9. Salewski, 'Die Wilhelminische Flottengesetze', pp. 122–4. Sweet, 'Great Britain and Germany', pp. 223–6. Young, *Balfour*, pp. 271–3. Williams, *Defending the Empire*, pp. 159–73. Daunton, 'Finance of Naval Expansion'. Sumida, *Naval Supremacy*, pp. 188–95. Stürmer, 'Deutscher Flottenbau', pp. 59–64.

56 Mackay, *Fisher*, pp. 360–65 and 371–4. *DSF* I, 88–90 and 102–3. Williams, *Defending the Empire*, pp. 94–9 and 120–37. Goldrick, 'Battleship Fleet', p. 286. Haggie, 'War Planning', p. 115. Sumida, *Naval Supremacy*, p. 54. Boyce, *Selborne Papers*, p. 177. Dunley, *Britain and the Mine*, pp. 61 and 66. A new life of

Beresford would be very welcome; until then we have *ODNB* and Geoffrey Bennett, *Charlie B: A Biography of Admiral Lord Beresford of Metemmeh and Curraghmore* (London, 1968). Gordon, *Rules of the Game*, p. 366, suggests that Beresford may have suffered a minor stroke and some change of personality in 1906 or 1907.

57 Farr, *McKenna*, pp. 178–9. *DSF* I, 189–200. D'Ombrain, *War Machinery and High Policy*, pp. 233–4.

58 *DSF* I, 204, 211–13. Farr, *McKenna*, pp. 208–9. N. Lambert, *Fisher's Naval Revolution*, pp. 204–9. Goldrick, 'Battleship Fleet', p. 289. A. D. Lambert, *The British Way of War*, p. 264.

59 Williamson, *Politics of Grand Strategy*, pp. 139–43, 150–51, 167–71 and 182. Farr, *McKenna*, p. 210. Ferguson, *The Pity of War*, pp. 72–81. D'Ombrain, *War Machinery and High Policy*, pp. 141–50. Seligmann et al., *Naval Route to the Abyss*, pp. 278–83. John W. Coogan and Peter F. Coogan, 'The British Cabinet and the Anglo-French Staff Talks, 1905–1914: Who Knew What and When Did He Know It?', *JBS* XXIV (1985), pp. 110–31.

60 Beckett and Jeffery, 'Curragh Incident'. Nicholas Perry, 'The Irish Landed Class and the British Army, 1850–1950', *WiH* XVIII (2011), pp. 304–32 at p. 324. Anthony Kinsella. 'The Army and Royal Navy in Ireland: Some Statistics', *Irish Sword* XX (1997), No. 81, pp. 234–40, at pp. 234–6. Steven O'Connor, *Irish Officers in the British Forces, 1922–1945* (Basingstoke, 2014), pp. 21 and 34.

61 Jeffery, *Sir Henry Wilson*, pp. 96–7.

62 Farr, *McKenna*, pp. 210–13. D'Ombrain, *War Machinery and High Policy*, pp. 100–107. Jeffery, *Sir Henry Wilson*, pp. 85–97. Keith Neilson, 'Great Britain', in *War Planning 1914*, ed. R. F. Hamilton and H. H. Herwig, pp. 175–97 at pp. 184–7. Williamson, *Politics of Grand Strategy*, pp. 187–204. Stevenson, *Armaments and the Coming of War*, pp. 185–97. Morgan-Owen, *Fear of Invasion*, pp. 197–200. Morgan-Owen, 'Sir Arthur Wilson's War Plan'. Clemmesen, 'North Sea War Plan',

pp. 86–7. French, *British Strategy and War Aims*, pp. 3–4. N. A. Lambert, *Fisher's Naval Revolution*, pp. 204–5. *DSF* I, 243–51 and 388–93. Grimes, *Strategy and War Planning*, pp. 165–7. A. D. Lambert, *The British Way of War*, p. 282.

63 To Balfour's private secretary, 10 Oct 1905, in Morgan-Owen, *Fear of Invasion*, p. 126.

64 To Lord Esher, 19 Nov 1903, in *FGDN* I, 291.

65 Morgan-Owen, *Fear of Invasion*, pp. 43–54, 71–4, 112–14, 143–5, 155–9, 169–70, 176–7, 184–91 and 226–33.

66 Wilson, 'Directions of Travel', pp. 262–6. Steinberg, 'Copenhagen Complex', pp. 25–7 and 41–6. Röhl, *Wilhelm II*, pp. 611–16, 630–43, 789–93 and 992. Bönker, *Militarism*, pp. 64–7 and 76–8. Neilson, 'Grey as Foreign Secretary', pp. 128–35. Williams, *Defending the Empire*, pp. 174–9. Sweet, 'Great Britain and Germany'. Maurer, ' "Ever-Present Danger" ', pp. 15–34. Stevenson, *Armaments and the Coming of War*, pp. 171–4, 209 and 214. Langhorne, 'Naval Question'; *idem*, 'Great Britain and Germany', pp. 299–300. Kennedy, *Anglo-German Antagonism*, pp. 446–7. Epkenhans, *Die wilhelminische Flottenrüstung*, p. 360. For Palmerston's original guarantee of Belgium's frontiers see Ch. 1, pp. 9–10.

67 Röhl, *Wilhelm II*, p. 792.

68 N. Lambert, *Fisher's Naval Revolution*, pp. 249–54. Williams, *Defending the Empire*, pp. 173–5. Stevenson, *Armaments and the Coming of War*, pp. 214 and 336–7. Neilson, 'Grey as Foreign Secretary', pp. 131–4.

69 The phrase used (in English) in the diary of Capt. Albert Hopman of the RMA, 15 Nov 1911: *Das ereignisreiche Leben eines 'Wilhelminers': Tagebücher, Briefe, Aufzeichnungen 1901 bis 1920 von Albert Hopman*, ed. Michael Epkenhans (Munich, 2004), p. 172.

70 Maurer, 'Averting the Great War?' Kennedy, *Anglo-German Antagonism*, pp. 356–8. Stürmer, 'Deutscher Flottenbau', p. 63. Seligmann et al., *Naval Route to the Abyss*, pp. 278–87 and

409–12. Epkenhans, 'A Golden Opportunity', pp. 79–80 and 87–8. Rodger, 'Deutsch-Englisch Flottenrivalität'. On German industrial capacity, see Epkenhans, *Die wilhelminische Flottenrüstung, passim*.

71 Strachan, *First World War*, p. 33. Epkenhans, *Die Wilhelminische Flottenrüstung*, pp. 343 and 396. Brézet, 'Course aux armements navals', pp. 125–7. Seligmann et al., *Naval Route to the Abyss*, pp. 397–401.

72 'Grund, Neidhammelei: Angst unseres zu groß werdens': Fischer, *Admiral des Kaisers*, p. 128. The coarse expression was characteristic of Wilhelm II.

73 Epkenhans, *Die wilhelminische Flottenrüstung*, pp. 391–9; *idem*, 'Die Tirpitzsche Flottenplanung', pp. 129–30. Berghahn, 'Naval Armaments and Social Crisis', pp. 75–84. Kennedy, *Anglo-German Antagonism*, pp. 408–19. Röhl, *Wilhelm II*, pp. 819–23 and 992.

74 Williams, *Defending the Empire*, pp. 195–7 and 227. French, *British Strategy and War Aims*, pp. 3–4. Williamson, *Politics of Grand Strategy*, pp. 197–204, 249–57, 298–9, 330–31 and 365–71.

Chapter 11

1 In his essay 'Heroes and Hero-Worship'.

2 Mackay, *Fisher*, is scholarly and perceptive but now more than forty years old. *ODNB* by Paul G. Halpern, and A. Lambert, *Admirals*, pp. 289–333, are the best recent introductions. Arthur Marder, the most influential twentieth-century naval historian of this period, was an uncritical admirer. Offer, *Agrarian Interpretation*, pp. 249–57, gives an original and sympathetic reading of Fisher's character, not quite the same as mine. A. D. Lambert, *The British Way of War*, is an impressive recent study of Sir Julian Corbett, the strategist and historian who had an important influence on Fisher. In what follows I have drawn also on *DSF* I, 14–16; Kemp, *Fisher Papers* I, xvi–xxvi; C. I. Hamilton, *Modern Admiralty*, pp. 214–21; Marder, *Portrait of an Admiral*, p. 49;

Kennedy, 'Fisher and Tirpitz'; Gordon, *Rules of the Game*, pp. 341–8; Davison, *Challenges of Command*, pp. 9–10, 19 and 49–50; d'Ombrain, *War Machinery and High Policy*, pp. 154–60; and Harley, 'Fisher's Advice to Churchill', pp. 178–82 and 189.

3 E.g. *FGDN* II, 477–8 and 487–8.

4 Rodger, 'Early Career of Sir John Fisher'. Crosbie Smith, '*Dreadnought* Science', pp. 151–2.

5 Rosslyn Wemyss's reason for declining the attractive position of Naval Secretary: Wemyss, *Life and Letters*, pp. 99–100.

6 *FGDN* III, 270, quoting Sir Joseph Thomson, President of the Royal Society, who met Fisher on the Board of Invention and Research.

7 *FGDN* I, 199. Mackay, *Fisher*, p. 252.

8 G. Hamilton, *Parliamentary Reminiscences* II, 132; cf. Mackay, *Fisher*, pp. 277–8, and Crosbie Smith, '*Dreadnought* Science', pp. 201–7.

9 G. Hamilton, *Parliamentary Reminiscences* II, 132–3.

10 Mackay, *Fisher*, pp. 255–6, 323, 330 and 336–40. *FGDN* I, 222. N. Lambert, *Fisher's Naval Revolution*, pp. 111–13. Harley, 'Fisher's Advice to Churchill'.

11 To Mrs Esther Meynell, 20 Jan 1910, and to Gerard Fiennes, 16 Oct 1910, in *FGDN* II, 292 and 341.

12 Sumida, *Naval Supremacy*, Appendix, Tables 3 and 22.

13 Mullins, 'New Ways of Thinking'.

14 Marconi's mother Annie Jameson was an heiress of the Dublin whiskey family; he had excellent English and many contacts in good society in Britain and Ireland.

15 *ODNB* sv Jackson. Bruton, 'Beyond Marconi', pp. 132–53. Blond, 'Technology and Tradition', pp. 9–97. Rippon, *Engineering* I, 87. A. G. E. Jones, 'The Early Days of Wireless Telegraphy at Sea', *NR* LXXIII (1985), pp. 51–5. Pocock and Garratt, *Origins of Maritime Radio*. Hugill, *Global Communications*, pp. 86–93 and 140–42. Priya Satia, 'War, Wireless, and Empire: Marconi and the British Warfare State, 1896–1903', *Technology and Culture* LI (2010), pp. 829–53. Burns,

Communications, pp. 285–99 and 350–51. Moore, *Greenie*, pp. 54–5.

16 N. Lambert, 'Strategic Command and Control', pp. 364–89. Goldrick, 'Battleship Fleet', pp. 286–7. Friedman, *Network-Centric Warfare*, pp. 5–6. W. M. Hamilton, 'The Nation and the Navy', pp. 231–48. Morgan-Owen, 'Invasion Question', pp. 97–117. N. A. Lambert, *Planning Armageddon*, pp. 75–6. Wells, 'Naval Intelligence', pp. 123–5.

17 N. Lambert, 'Transformation and Technology', p. 284, quoting Rear-Admiral Edmond Slade.

18 Grimes, *Strategy and War Planning*, pp. 34–50, 75–6, 83–5, 99–106, 123–37 and 144–5. Partridge, 'End of Close Blockade'. Friedman, *Great War at Sea*, pp. 215–17.

19 Clemmesen, 'North Sea War Plan', p. 79.

20 The Japanese destroyers that attacked the Russian squadron in Port Arthur on the outbreak of war in February 1904 were about 400 miles from their advanced base at Jindo island, off the south-west tip of Korea.

21 Morgan-Owen, 'Fisher and Home Defence', 'Intermediate Blockade' and 'Sir Arthur Wilson's War Plan'. Morgan-Owen, *Fear of Invasion*, pp. 203–20. Morgan-Owen, 'Invasion Question', pp. 150–206. Clemmesen, 'North Sea War Plan', pp. 88–92 and 108. Bell, *Churchill and Sea Power*, pp. 37–9. Seligmann, *Naval Intelligence*, pp. 52–6. *BDOW* VI, 122–4. Friedman, *Great War at Sea*, pp. 108–11. Grimes, *Strategy and War Planning*, pp. 176–81. Gooch, 'Bolt from the Blue', pp. 11–15. Seligmann et al., *Naval Route to the Abyss*, pp. 416–18 and 464–74. Seligmann, 'Role and Function of the Battlecruiser'.

22 Dunley, *Britain and the Mine*, p. 61, quoting a letter to Balfour of 25 May 1904.

23 Dunley, *Britain and the Mine*, pp. 2–3, 10–16, 48–53, 58–66, 73–8, 99–110, 131–2, 136–46 and 151–9.

24 Dunley, *Britain and the Mine*, pp. 167–71, 175–9, 201–20 and 228 (quoted).

25 Brooks, 'Grand Battle-Fleet Tactics', pp. 198–200. Clemmesen, 'North Sea War Plan', p. 96 (quoted).

26 N. Lambert, *Fisher's Naval Revolution*. Friedman, *British Destroyers* I, 74–81. Brooks, 'Grand Battle-Fleet Tactics'. Morgan-Owen, 'Fisher and Home Defence', pp. 555–8. Morgan-Owen, 'Invasion Question', pp. 74–86. Friedman, *Great War at Sea*, pp. 108–9. Friedman, *Naval Weapons of World War One*, p. 324.

27 Herwig, 'Command Decision Making', p. 117. Röhl, *Wilhelm II*, pp. 303–5. P. M. Kennedy, 'The Development of German Naval Operations Plans against England, 1896–1914', in idem, *The War Plans of the Great Powers, 1880–1914* (London, 1979), pp. 171–98. Annika Mombauer, 'German War Plans', in *War Planning 1914*, ed. Richard F. Hamilton and Holger H. Herwig (Cambridge, 2010), pp. 48–78, at pp. 65–6.

28 Bell, *Churchill and Sea Power*, pp. 37–9. Morgan-Owen, *Fear of Invasion*, pp. 215–23. Morgan-Owen, 'Invasion Question', pp. 150, 155–75 and 188–207. Gooch, 'Bolt from the Blue', p. 14.

29 Gooch, 'Adversarial Attitudes', pp. 65–8. Hayes, 'Britain, Germany, and the Admiralty's Plans'. Hans Branner, 'Østersøen og de danske stræder i engelsk krigsplanlægning 1904–14', *Historie* [Aarhus] IX (1970–72), pp. 493–535. N. A. Lambert, *Planning Armageddon*, pp. 41–9. Friedman, *Great War at Sea*, pp. 215–21.

30 Erik Arup, 'Den danske Regerings Forhandlinger og Beslutninger 5 August 1914', ed. Thyge Svenstrup, *Historisk Tidsskrift* [Copenhagen] XCI (1992), pp. 402–27. A. Lambert, *Admirals*, pp. 319–23. Gemzell, *German Naval Planning*, pp. 145–8. *BDOW* VI, 773, and VIII, 123–30. Grimes, *Strategy and War Planning*, pp. 58–61 and 77–109. Salmon, *Scandinavia and the Great Powers*, pp. 104–7 and 125–7. Rahn, 'Strategische Probleme', p. 350. Goldrick, *Before Jutland*, pp. 101–2. Halpern, *World War I*, p. 183. Friedman, *Great War at Sea*, p. 218. Morgan-Owen, *Fear of Invasion*, p. 140. A. Lambert, *The British Way of War*, pp. 316–20.

31 Gordon, *Rules of the Game*, pp. 193–214 (quoting Tryon, p. 195). Hore, *Habit of Victory*, pp. 272–3.

32 Clemmesen, 'North Sea War Plan', p. 86, quoting Sir Archibald Berkeley Milne. Of course this is not a dispassionate judgement but an expression of Milne's dislike of another officer; cf. Andrew Gordon, 'The Transition to War: The *Goeben* Debacle, August 1914', in *The Royal Navy and Maritime Power in the Twentieth Century*, ed. Ian Speller (London, 2005), pp. 13–32 at p. 18.

33 Goldrick, *Before Jutland*, p. 25. Clemmesen, 'North Sea War Plan', pp. 76–89. Friedman, *Network-Centric Warfare*, pp. 11–12. Friedman, *Great War at Sea*, pp. 113–14. N. Lambert, 'Strategic Command and Control', pp. 394–7. N. Lambert, 'Transformation and Technology', pp. 284–5.

34 Coogan, *End of Neutrality*, pp. 17–44 and 52–3. Neilson, 'Naval Policy, Belligerent Rights, and Disarmament'. Davis and Engerman, *Naval Blockades*, pp. 2–14. Partridge, 'End of Close Blockade'. Abbenhuis, 'European Hopes for Neutrality'. Frei, *Maritime Strategic Thought*, pp. 71–4.

35 Coogan, *End of Neutrality*, pp. 56–73 and 83–122. Martin, 'Declaration of London'. Heintschel von Heinegg, 'Naval Blockade and International Law'. Hull, *A Scrap of Paper*, pp. 143–7. N. A. Lambert, *Planning Armageddon*, pp. 63–103. Tracy, *Belligerent Rights*, pp. xix–xxvii and 91–126. Lemnitzer, *Power, Law and the End of Privateering*, pp. 187–8. Stevenson, *Armaments and the Coming of War*, pp. 105–10. A. Lambert, 'Great Britain and Maritime Law', pp. 21–3. Hattendorf, 'Maritime Conflict', pp. 109–11. Offer, 'Morality and Admiralty'. Martin, '1907 Naval War Plans'. Baylen, 'The United States and the London Naval Conference'. *BDOW* VIII, 198, 211, 282–3, 295, 306–7 and 352–64. Seligmann, 'Failing to Prepare', pp. 422–36. Keefer, *Law of Nations*, pp. 241–3. Frei, *Maritime Strategic Thought*, pp. 112–51. Russell, *Prize Courts and U-boats*, pp. 223–35, prints the text of the Declaration of London.

36 Haslop, *Early Naval Air Power*, pp. 18–36. Howlett, *British Naval Aviation*, pp. 26–7.

37 A. Lambert, 'Naval War Course', 'History as Process', pp. 92–7, and 'Development of Education', pp. 50–51. N. Lambert, *Fisher's Naval Revolution*, pp. 170–83. Grimes, *Strategy and War Planning*, pp. 84–7 and 110–11. Dickinson, *Wisdom and War*, pp. 91–5. Cobb, *Preparing for Blockade*, pp. 33–41. *FGDN* II, 21–2. C. I. Hamilton, *Modern Admiralty*, pp. 222–3. Black, *Naval Staff*, pp. 53–5. Roskill, *Hankey*, I, 79. An important new study is Andrew Lambert, *The British Way of War*.

38 Morgan-Owen, 'Intermediate Blockade' and 'Sir Arthur Wilson's War Plan', pp. 878–92.

39 Goldrick, *Before Jutland*, pp. 16–21. C. I. Hamilton, *Modern Admiralty*, pp. 225–6 and 232–4. Black, *Naval Staff*, pp. 53–64. *DSF* I, 265–6, and V, 219–20.

40 Masson, *Histoire de la Marine* II, 229–31. Tristan Lecoq, 'La Grande Guerre sur mer: La Marine et les marins de guerre', *RHM* 22–23 (2017), pp. 369–402, at p. 375. Jean-Philippe Zanco, *Boué de Lapeyrère, 1852–1924: l'amiralissime gascon* (Orthez, 2016). Monaque, *La marine de guerre française*, pp. 358–79. R. F. Hamilton, 'War Planning', pp. 11–14.

41 R. F. Hamilton, 'War Planning', p. 15, translating *Rüstung im Zeichen der wilhelmischen Weltpolitik: grundlegende Dokumente*, ed. Volker R. Berghahn and Wilhelm Deist (Düsseldorf, 1988), p. 334, and *Der Kaiser: Aufzeichnungen des Chefs des Marinekabinetts Admiral Georg Alexander von Müller über die Ära Wilhelms II*, ed. Walter Görlitz (Göttingen, 1965), p. 90.

42 Bönker, *Militarism*, pp. 278–88. Kelly, *Tirpitz*, pp. 163–4. Goldrick, *Before Jutland*, pp. 30–31.

43 Edgerton, *Warfare State*, pp. 1–20, and *Science, Technology and the British Industrial 'Decline'*, pp. 1–12. Supple, 'Fear of Failing'.

44 Robert Tombs, *The English and Their History* (London, 2014), p. 759. O'Rourke and Williamson, *Globalization and History*, pp. 2–5, 15, 29, 36 and 271–82. Darwin, *Empire Project*, p. 116. Findlay and O'Rourke, *Power and Plenty*, p. 323.

45 *BDOW* III, 402–3.

46 *DSF* I, 322–3.

47 Kennedy, *Anglo-German Antagonism*, pp. 467–9. Darwin, *Empire Project*, p. 267. Offer, 'Costs and Benefits', pp. 694 and 707. Findlay and O'Rourke, *Power and Plenty*, p. 392.

48 Howe, 'Restoring Free Trade'. Daunton, *Trusting Leviathan*, pp. 77–81. Trentmann, 'National Identity and Consumer Politics'. Findlay and O'Rourke, *Power and Plenty*, pp. 397–8. Olson, *Wartime Shortage*, pp. 73–5. L. Margaret Barnett, *British Food Policy during the First World War* (London, 1985), pp. 3–4.

49 McCain and Hopkins, *British Imperialism*, pp. 113–15, 122–6, 144–50 and 169–79. P. Kennedy, *Anglo-German Antagonism*, p. 303. Darwin, *Empire Project*, pp. 112–16, 255–6 and 274–7. Peden, *Arms, Economics and British Strategy*, p. 33. Burns, *Communications*, pp. 161–2.

50 Darwin, *Empire Project*, pp. 103–4 and 274–6. Peden, *Arms, Economics and British Strategy*, p. 33. Frei, *Maritime Strategic Thought*, pp. 152–205.

51 Hobson, 'Military-Extraction Gap'. O'Brien, 'The Titan Refreshed' (quoted p. 1). Daunton, *Trusting Leviathan*, p. 23. Peden, *Arms, Economics and British Strategy*, pp. 35 and 38. Peden, 'Political Economy of Public Expenditure', p. 356. Strachan, *First World War*, p. 375.

Chapter 12

1 Hamilton, *Portsmouth Dockyard Papers*, p. 133. Beeler, *Milne Papers* I, 615–16 and 672–3. Dickinson, *Educating the Navy*, pp. 715–17. *BND*, pp. 715–17.

2 Dickinson, *Educating the Navy*, pp. 66–9, 94–5, 104 and 109. Beeler, *Milne Papers* I, 632–3, 637–8, 641, 655–64 and 670. Penn, *Snotty*, pp. 66–7. Payton, 'Naval Education', pp. 192–3.

3 J. R. Soley, 'Report on Foreign Systems of Naval Education' (46th Congress 2nd Sess. Senate Exec. Doc. No. 51, 1880), p. 27.

4 Davison, *Challenges of Command*, pp. 40–45. Walton, 'Corporation and Community', pp. 50–51. Romans, 'Selection and Early Career', p. 31.

5 Jones, *A Naval Life*, pp. 19–20. Dickinson, *Educating the Navy*, pp. 162–3 and 168–9. Wells, *Social History*, pp. 40–41. Dewar, *Navy from Within*, pp. 15–16. Admiral Sir Hugh Tweedie, *The Story of a Naval Life* (London [1939]), pp. 16–19.

6 Jones, 'Hierarchy of Management', pp. 164–7. Jones, 'Naval Officer Corps', pp. 140–47. Dickinson, *Educating the Navy*, pp. 72–4, 105–11, 158–9 and 162–3. Penn, *Snotty*, pp. 76–8. Dawson, *Sound of the Guns*, p. 15 ('The authorities had no wish to fail sub-lieutenants unless it was a very glaring case'), is my source for cheating on the Greenwich sub-lieutenants' course.

7 Vice-Admiral H. H. Smith, *A Yellow Admiral Remembers* (London, 1932), pp. 11 and 19.

8 Lewis, *England's Sea-Officers*, p. 108; Lewis started his career teaching at RNC Osborne in 1913.

9 Dickinson, *Educating the Navy*, pp. 111 and 154–7. Beeler, *Milne Papers* I, 606. Jones, 'Naval Officer Corps', pp. 26–8, 73–4 and 119–21.

10 Rodger, 'Officers, Gentlemen', pp. 147–8. 'Naval Cadets': HC 1882 XL, p. 457.

11 Report of the (Rice) Admiralty Committee on the Training of Naval Cadets (HC 1875 XV, p. 347), evidence of Vice-Admiral A. P. Ryder, Q.1851, p. 75.

12 Mackay, *Fisher*, pp. 2–4. Rodger, 'Fisher's Early Career'. Note that Fisher *père* was a captain in the 78th Regiment, nominally equal in rank to a lieutenant RN but lower in real social status. In the 1870s another coffee planter's son was rejected as a candidate for the Navy: Jones, 'Naval Officer Corps', p. 56.

13 Jones, 'Naval Officer Corps', pp. 19–22 and 41–57, quoting Fig. 4.2, p. 49. Jones,

'Nomination and Patronage'. Rodger, 'Officers, Gentlemen', pp. 146–7. Dickinson, *Educating the Navy*, pp. 164–6.

14 Dewar, *Navy from Within*, p. 58.

15 Dickinson, *Educating the Navy*, pp. 76–8 and 113–39. Dickinson, *Wisdom and War*, pp. 25–48. Davison, *Challenges of Command*, pp. 156–9. Penn, *Snotty*, pp. 66–7 and 115–19. Lloyd, 'Royal Naval Colleges', pp. 149–53. Jones, 'Naval Officer Corps', pp. 72–4, 130–35 and 146–7. Winton, 'Life and Education', pp. 269–70.

16 *Report of the Committee into the Establishment of the Royal Naval College Greenwich* HC 1877 XXXI, p. 415 [C.1733], p. xxi (quoted). Dickinson, *Educating the Navy*, pp. 125–8 and 142–4. Dickinson, *Wisdom and War*, pp. 48–9. Lloyd, 'Royal Naval Colleges', pp. 152–3.

17 Dickinson, *Educating the Navy*, pp. 164–9. Jones, 'Naval Officer Corps', pp. 120–21 and 133–135. A. P. Ryder, 'The Higher Education of Naval Officers', *JRUSI* XV (1871), pp. 734–805.

18 To Somerset, 27 Oct 1862: Buckinghamshire RO: Somerset Papers A.R.41/62(L). Cf. Beeler, *Milne Papers* I, 606.

19 Wells, *Social History*, pp. 16–17 and 47–8. John Wells, *Whaley: The Story of HMS Excellent 1830 to 1980* (Portsmouth, 1980), pp. 31–45. Jones, 'Naval Officer Corps', pp. 137–8 and 152–3. Walton, 'Corporation and Community', p. 240. Warlow, *Pusser*, p. 45. Davison, *Challenges of Command*, p. 145.

20 Wells, *Social History*, pp. 47–8 (quoted p. 48). Jones, 'Naval Officer Corps', p. 189. Moore, *Greenie*, pp. 96–9. Lavery, *Hostilities Only*, p. 60, quoting Sir Ernle Chatfield.

21 Dickinson, *Educating the Navy*, pp. 117 (quoting the 1870 Shadwell Committee) and 195.

22 Davison, *Challenges of Command*, pp. 19–23, 53–63. Colville, 'Interior Design and Identity'.

23 Jones, 'Hierarchy of Management', p. 157. Jones, 'Naval Officer Corps', Table 1:1. Wells, *Social History*, pp. 33 and 42.

BND, pp. 729–30 and 733–4. Lewis, *Navy in Transition*, pp. 120–21. Davison, *Challenges of Command*, pp. 12–13 and 100–103. Winton, *Life on the Lower-Deck*, pp. 225–6. Capper, *Warrant Officers' Annual*, pp. 17–19. Bowen, *Royal Naval Reserve*, pp. 64, 87–9 and 99–100.

24 Romans, 'Selection and Early Career', pp. 96–7. Farquharson-Roberts, 'War to War', pp. 98–9. Beattie, *Churchill Scheme*, pp. 9 and 59.

25 HC 1877 XXI, pp. 5–6 [C.1647, pp. v–vi].

26 Dickinson, *Educating the Navy*, pp. 185–93. Wells, *Social History*, p. 46. Payton, 'Naval Education', p. 194. Penn, *HMS Thunderer*, pp. 16–21 and 35–54. Penn, *Up Funnel*, pp. 125–31. Romans, 'Selection and Early Career', pp. 32–3. Wilson, *Biographical Dictionary*, pp. 38–9. Chamberlain, 'Stokers', p. 312. Rippon, *Engineering* I, 71–7 and 110–11. *FGDN* I, 245 and 266–7. Boyce, *Selborne Papers*, pp. 119–20 and 139–41. Davison, *Challenges of Command*, pp. 259–60, analyses professions of the fathers of engineer students entering the RNEC 1897–1905, showing a slight but distinct social gradient from naval cadets.

27 Boyce, *Selborne Papers*, pp. 119–22. Davison, *Challenges of Command*, pp. 120–21 and 126. Partridge, *Osborne*, pp. 4–5. Mackay, *Fisher*, pp. 274–5.

28 Leggett, *Shaping the Royal Navy*, p. 254; cf. *FGDN* II, 335, 477 and 487–9.

29 Partridge, *Osborne*, p. 13, quoting Engineer Commander H. W. Metcalfe of RNC Osborne.

30 *FGDN* II, 71, 335, 477 and 488. Davison, *Challenges of Command*, pp. 64–5 and 103–4. Penn, *H.M.S. Thunderer*, p. 60. Partridge, *Osborne*, pp. 12–13 and 30–35. Payton, 'Naval Education', p. 195. Beattie, *Churchill Scheme*, pp. 7 and 11. Mackay, *Fisher*, pp. 266–7. Dickinson, *Educating the Navy*, pp. 196–8. *DSF* I, 46–9. Wells, *Social History*, p. 63. Romans, 'Selection and Early Career', pp. 20–25. Baynham, *Men from the Dreadnoughts*, pp. 151–7. Seligmann, *Churchill and Social Reform*, p. 25.

31 Partridge, *Osborne*, pp. 18–20, 30–33, 94, 111–18 and 141–2. *BND*, No. 512, pp. 972–4.

32 On the USN scheme see McBride, *Technological Change*, pp. 24–34, and Chisholm, *Dead Men's Shoes*, pp. 534–5.

33 Mackay, *Fisher*, p. 280.

34 Mackay, *Fisher*, pp. 266–7 and 274–80. Dickinson, *Educating the Navy*, pp. 194–8. McCoy, 'From Selborne to AFO 1/56', pp. 255–6. *FGDN* I, 243–7, 259 and 269; II, 71, 335 and 477. *BND*, pp. 972–4. Davison, *Challenges of Command*, pp. 103–4 and 124–8. Schurman, *Education of a Navy*, pp. 117–20. Beattie, *Churchill Scheme*, pp. 8–10. Penn, *H.M.S. Thunderer*, pp. 60–63. Partridge, *Osborne*, pp. 12–15.

35 Davison, *Challenges of Command*, pp. 141–2. Boyce, *Selborne Papers*, pp. 119–20 and 139–41. *FGDN* I, 245 and 266–9. Romans, 'Selection and Early Career', pp. 82–3. On the IME see Hamblin, 'Marine Engineering', pp. 171–80.

36 Davison, *Challenges of Command*, pp. 83–4, 118–25, 130–34 and 141–2. Hamblin, 'Marine Engineering', p. 195. Boyce, *Selborne Papers*, pp. 139–41 and 153–4.

37 Payton, 'Naval Education', p. 195. Dickinson, *Wisdom and War*, pp. 80–96.

38 Stephen King-Hall, *My Naval Life 1906–1929* (London, 1952), p. 45.

39 Dewar, *Navy from Within*, p. 110.

40 Romans, 'Selection and Early Career', pp. 90–92 and 147–9. Partridge, *Osborne*, pp. 34–6.

41 Seligmann, *Churchill and Social Reform*, pp. 22–3, quoting (from PRO: ADM 1/7875) a paper probably written by Captain Charles Ottley.

42 Seligmann, *Churchill and Social Reform*, p. 29.

43 Capper, *Aft-from the Hawsehole*, p. 94, quoting Captain Lewis Beaumont.

44 Capper, *Aft-from the Hawsehole*, p. 130.

45 Capper, *Aft-from the Hawsehole*, pp. 2, 21 and 74. Capper, *Warrant Officers' Annual*, p. 14. Davison, *Challenges of Command*, pp. 22–9, 82–3 and 108–9. *NRG*, pp. 9–12, prints a table of commissioned warrant ranks.

46 Davison, *Challenges of Command*, pp. 4–5. Farr, *McKenna*, pp. 174–5. Baynham,

Men from the Dreadnoughts, pp. 129–31. *ODNB* sv Archer-Shee. Partridge, *Osborne*, pp. 138–9. Lionel Yexley, *Our Fighting Sea Men* (London [1911]), pp. 195–200.

47 Carew, *Lower Deck*, pp. 47–52. Baynham, *Men from the Dreadnoughts*, pp. 129–31. Romans, 'Selection and Early Career', p. 89. Seligmann, *Churchill and Social Reform*, pp. 38–41.

48 Kerr and Granville, *R.N.V.R.*, p. 63.

49 Howarth, *Royal Navy's Reserves*, pp. 5–10 and 18–26. Kerr and Granville, *R.N.V.R.*, pp. 59–68. Lavery, *Shield of Empire*, pp. 175–7.

50 Robinson, *Fishermen*, pp. 16–20. Howarth, *Royal Navy's Reserves*, pp. 31–4. Bowen, *Royal Naval Reserve*, p. 94. *NRG*, p. 190.

51 Seligmann, *Churchill and Social Reform*, p. 22.

52 Seligmann, *Churchill and Social Reform*, p. 30. 'Annapolis University' refers to the US Naval Academy at Annapolis, Maryland.

53 Davison, *Challenges of Command*, pp. 12–26 and 106–7. Beattie, *Churchill Scheme*, pp. 7–9 and 13–35. Romans, 'Selection and Early Career', pp. 83–6, 107–8 and 201–5. W. S. Galpin, *From Public School to Navy: An Account of the Special Entry Scheme* (Plymouth, 1919), pp. 119–22. Peter H. Liddle, *The Sailor's War, 1914–18* (Poole, 1985), p. 141.

54 Beattie, *Churchill Scheme*, pp. 9 and 13–20. Romans, 'Selection and Early Career', pp. 96–7.

55 Hobson, *Imperialism at Sea*, p. 209.

56 Hobson, *Imperialism at Sea*, pp. 178–215 and 234–7. Epkenhans, 'Die Tirpitzsche Flottenplanung'. Kennedy, *Anglo-German Antagonism*, pp. 221–40.

57 'Weil wir unsere gesamte Kraft konzentrieren müssen auf die Schaffung einer Schlachtflotte gegen England, die uns England gegenüber allein Seegeltung verschaffen kann. Außerdem muß erst die Schlacht geschlagen u[nd] gewonnen sein, ehe man an eine Ausnutzung derselben denken darf'. Berghahn, 'Des Kaisers Flotte und die Revolutionierung des Mächtesystems', p. 175.

58 'Tirpitz aber ging es wie dem Lyderkönig Kroisos, dem das Orakel von Delphi kündete, wenn er den Halys überschreite, werde er ein großes Reich zerstören. Tirpitz tat es, und es war das deutsche'. Stürmer, 'Deutscher Flottenbau', p. 61.

Chapter 13

1 Lautenschläger, 'Dreadnought Revolution', p. 122.
2 Seligmann et al., *Naval Route to the Abyss*, p. 115. Bastable, *Arms and the State*, p. 189. There are significant flaws in the published statistics of shipbuilding, which tend to understate or even omit warship-building: Ian Buxton, Roy Fenton and Hugh Murphy, 'Measuring Britain's Merchant Shipbuilding Output in the Twentieth Century', *MM* CI (2015), pp. 304–22.
3 Johnstone and Buxton, *Battleship Builders*, pp. 13–17, 56–76, 218–20, 227, 235–42 and 298–304. Slaven, *British Shipbuilding*, pp. 53–5. Warren, *Cammell Laird*, pp. 128–33. Peebles, *Warshipbuilding*, pp. 30–39, 46–50 and 158. Arnold, 'Commercial Returns'. Brook, *Warships for Export*, pp. 17–21. Lindberg and Todd, *Anglo-American Shipbuilding*, pp. 24–9 and 43.
4 Brown, *Warrior to Dreadnought*, pp. 126–47; and 'Design Methods'. Friedman, *British Battleship II*, 60–71. Leggett, *Shaping the Royal Navy*, pp. 216–19 and 213–34.
5 Sir Andrew Noble, 'The Rise and Progress of Rifled Naval Artillery', *TINA* XLI (1899), pp. 235–56 at pp. 239–41. Sumida, *Naval Supremacy*, pp. 39–42. Rear-Adm. Samuel Long, 'An Attempt to Estimate the Probable Influence of the Introduction of Q.F. Guns on Naval Tactics and Construction', *JRUSI* XXXVI (1892), pp. 233–59.
6 Sumida, 'Quest for Reach', pp. 51–2; and *Naval Supremacy*, pp. 47, 72–3. Schleihauf, 'Concentrated Effort', p. 118.
7 Grove, 'The Battleship is Dead', p. 416, and 'Battleship *Dreadnought*', pp. 168 and 178. Hodges, *Big Gun*, pp. 40–49. Sumida, 'Quest for Reach', pp. 58–9.

Brooks, 'Preparing for Armageddon', p. 1015. Brooks, *Dreadnought Gunnery*, p. 46. Friedman, *Naval Firepower*, pp. 74–5. Friedman, *British Battleship II*, 43–4.
8 Epstein, *Torpedo*, pp. 5 and 117–18. Friedman, *Naval Firepower*, p. 85; *British Battleship II*, 48–50 and 126–7; and *Naval Weapons of World War I*, pp. 318–23. Brooks, *Jutland*, pp. 91–3. Lambert, *Fisher's Naval Revolution*, pp. 214–21. Compton-Hall, *Submarines and the War at Sea*, pp. 67–9. Goldrick, 'Battleship Fleet', p. 281. Goldrick, *Before Jutland*, pp. 54–5. Hartcup, *War of Invention*, pp. 122–3. Moore, *Greenie*, pp. 44–6. Brooks, 'Grand Battle-Fleet Tactics', p. 190. Brooks, *Jutland*, pp. 91–6. Dodson, *The Kaiser's Battlefleet*, p. 174.
9 Friedman, *Naval Firepower*, pp. 72–80 and 270. Friedman, *Naval Weapons of World War I*, p. 25. Friedman, *British Battleship II*, 43–5. Moore, *Greenie*, pp. 37–8. Brown, *Warrior to Dreadnought*, pp. 142–7.
10 Lambert, *Fisher's Naval Revolution*, p. 23.
11 Dodson, *Before the Battlecruiser*, pp. 47–8 and 73–4. *Dock Book* (Admiralty, 5th edn., 1905), *passim*. Manning, *White*, pp. 109–11. Friedman, *British Cruisers I*, 226–43 and 253. Grove, 'Battleship *Dreadnought*', pp. 171–2. Brown, *Warrior to Dreadnought*, pp. 156–62. Rippon, *Engineering I*, 58 and 71–7.
12 Cobb, ' "In the shadow of the *Alabama*" '. Seligmann, 'Germany's Ocean Greyhounds'.
13 *FGDN* I, 172–7. Grove, 'The Battleship is Dead', pp. 418–21. Friedman, *British Cruisers I*, 36–7. Friedman, *British Battleship II*, 13, 82, 84 and 88. Seligmann, 'New Weapons', pp. 314–15. Epstein, *Torpedo*, pp. 130–32. Brooks, *Dreadnought Gunnery*, p. 296. Sumida, *Naval Supremacy*, pp. 156–61.
14 *DSF* I, 56–66. Kemp, *Fisher Papers I*, 217–21. Brown, *Warrior to Dreadnought*, pp. 169–76. Friedman, *British Battleship II*, 70–88. Friedman, *British Cruisers I*, 266–7. Seligmann, 'New Weapons'. Grove, 'The Battleship is Dead', p. 421. P. A. Towle, 'The Effect of the Russo-Japanese War on British Naval Policy',

MM LX (1974), pp. 383–94 at pp. 386–8. Lambert, 'Righting the Scholarship', pp. 295–7. Friedman, *Naval Firepower*, p. 68. Brown, 'Marine Engineering', pp. 104–5.

15 Smith, '*Dreadnought* Science', pp. 141–5. Scaife, *Galaxies to Turbines*, pp. 293–7. Griffiths, *Steam at Sea*, pp. 140–41. Brown, 'Marine Engineering', pp. 456–7. Brown, *Warrior to Dreadnought*, pp. 180–91. Rippon, *Engineering* I, 124. Brown, *Century of Naval Construction*, pp. 74–5 and 86–7.

16 Carne, *Naval Officer*, p. 31.

17 To Balfour, 23 Aug 1905: Lambert, 'Righting the Scholarship', p. 291.

18 Friedman, *British Battleship* II, 73–84. Brooks, 'Blunder, or Stroke of Genius?' Seligmann, 'New Weapons', and 'Germany's Ocean Greyhounds'. Grove, 'The Battleship is Dead'. Roberts, *The Battleship Dreadnought*, pp. 12–17. Brown, *Warrior to Dreadnought*, pp. 180–93. Brown, 'Marine Engineering', pp. 454–7. Sumida, *Naval Supremacy*, pp. 58–60.

19 Fairbanks, 'Choosing among Technologies', pp. 134–6. Epkenhans, 'Technology, Shipbuilding and Future Combat', pp. 61–2. F. Jorissen, '*Dreadnought/Invincible* en de grote crisis in de Duitse oorlogscheepsbouw', *TvZ* I (1982), pp. 43–60. Breyer, *Battleships*, pp. 51–2. Epkenhans, *Die wilhelminische Flottenrüstung*, pp. 257–60. Röhl, *Wilhelm II*, pp. 473–81 and 493–4.

20 Kemp, *Fisher Papers* I, 217–21. *FGDN* II, 266. Friedman, *British Battleship* II, 92–7. Friedman, *British Cruisers* I, 266–7. Seligmann, 'New Weapons', pp. 316 and 326. Grove, 'The Battleship is Dead', pp. 418, 421 and 424. Fairbanks, '*Dreadnought* Revolution', pp. 257–62.

21 Friedman, *Naval Firepower*, pp. 283–4 and 288. Friedman, *Naval Weapons of World War I*, pp. 18 and 28–30. Friedman, *British Battleship* II, 82–103. Seligmann, 'New Weapons', pp. 324–9. Sumida, *Naval Supremacy*, pp. 158–9. Seligmann, *German Threat*, pp. 79–84. Seligmann, 'Germany's Ocean Greyhounds'. Brown, *Warrior to Dreadnought*, pp. 153–6. Jorissen, '*Dreadnought/Invincible*', pp. 53–8. Hodges, *Big Gun*, pp. 31–2. Noble, 'Rifled Naval Artillery', p. 238.

22 Sumida, *Naval Supremacy*, pp. 256–7 and 262–3. *BND*, pp. 928–33. Lambert, *Fisher's Naval Revolution*, pp. 246–8. Lambert, 'Fleet Unit Concept'. Ranft, *Beatty Papers* I, 59. Peter Overlack, 'Australian Defence Awareness and German Naval Planning in the Pacific, 1900–1914', *W&S* X (1992), 1, pp. 37–51. Christopher M. Bell, 'Sentiment *vs* Strategy: British Naval Policy, Imperial Defence and the Development of Dominion Navies, 1911–1914', *IHR* XXXVII (2014), pp. 262–81. Stephen McLaughlin, 'Battlelines and Fast Wings: Battlefleet Tactics in the Royal Navy, 1900–1914', *JSS* XXXVIII (2015), pp. 985–1005, at pp. 999–1000. Seligmann, 'Role and Function of the Battlecruiser'.

23 Scaife, *From Galaxies to Turbines*, p. 224, quoting Rudyard Kipling's experience of steaming trials in a 30-knotter.

24 Friedman, *British Destroyers* I, 38–59. Brown, *Warrior to Dreadnought*, pp. 137–41. Brown, 'Marine Engineering', pp. 451–2. Rippon, *Engineering* I, 61–2. Brown, *Century of Naval Construction*, pp. 73–5.

25 Brown, *Warrior to Dreadnought*, pp. 139–41 (quoted p. 140).

26 Friedman, *British Destroyers* I, 86–93. Brooks, *Jutland*, p. 3.

27 Epstein, *Torpedo*, pp. 127–30. Friedman, *British Destroyers* I, 74–93 and 99–106. Brown, *Warrior to Dreadnought*, pp. 162–4, and *Grand Fleet*, pp. 61–73.

28 Brown, *Warrior to Dreadnought*, pp. 165–6. Brown, 'Marine Engineering', pp. 96–100. Griffiths, *Steam at Sea*, pp. 127–9. Rippon, *Engineering* I, 71–7. Skelton, 'Marine Engineering', pp. 103–6 and 120. Chamberlain, 'Stokers', pp. 39–46.

29 Friedman, *British Battleship* II, 133 n.1, quoting Groos, *Der Krieg in der Nordsee* IV, 149. Cf. Brooks, *Jutland*, p. 475.

30 Goldrick, *After Jutland*, p. 41.

31 McKee, *Sober Men*, p. 122.

32 Gray, 'Coaling Warships', and *Steam Power*, pp. 69–96, 120–26 and 161–81. Goldrick, 'Coal', *Before Jutland*, pp. 54

and 264, *After Jutland*, pp. 22–3 (quoted p. 41). N. A. Lambert, 'Fleet Unit Concept', n.23. Bach, *Australia Station*, p. 220. Sondhaus, *Great War at Sea*, p. 316. Campbell, *Jutland*, pp. 102 and 384. Philbin, *Hipper*, pp. 52 and 56–7. Friedman, *British Battleship* II, 133 n.1. Goldrick, 'How It Worked', pp. 140–43.

33 Goldrick, 'Coal', pp. 325–7 and 337. Goldrick, *Before Jutland*, p. 58. Brown, *Grand Fleet*, pp. 21–3. *BND*, p. 933. Rippon, *Engineering* I, 80–88 and 177–8. Skelton, 'Marine Engineering', pp. 107–8. Chamberlain, 'Stokers', pp. 229–33. Gibson, 'Oil Fuel'. Friedman, *British Battleship* II, 58–9. Rogan, *Fall of the Ottomans*, pp. 79–87.

34 Sir Reginald Bacon, *From 1900 Onward* (London, 1940), p. 50. The phrase is sometimes ascribed to A. K. Wilson, then Controller of the Navy, but Bacon gives it merely as his own summary of current opinion, and only cites Wilson as one who hoped to see submarines abolished; cf. Lambert, *Submarine Service*, pp. x–xi and 21, and Friedman, *British Submarines* I, 56 n.1.

35 Battesti, *La Marine de Napoléon III* I, 206–15. Marder, *British Naval Policy*, pp. 356–70. Rippon, *Engineering* I, 204–11. Dash, 'Submarine Policy', pp. 85–151. Cummins, *Diesel's Engine*, pp. 482–95 and 620–25. Cummins, *Submarine Power 1902–1945*, pp. 179–96, 547–8 and 562–7. Lambert, *Fisher's Naval Revolution*, pp. 221–96. Brown, *Grand Fleet*, pp. 78–86. Lambert, *Submarine Service*, pp. x–xi and xxv–xxvi. Redford, 'Naval Culture and the Fleet Submarine', pp. 163–9. Lavery, *Shield of Empire*, pp. 254–6. Morgan-Owen, 'Invasion Question', pp. 208–12. Goldrick, *After Jutland*, pp. 232–3. Friedman, *British Submarines* I, 43–53, 79 and 87–96.

36 Dash, 'Submarine Policy', pp. 179–80.

37 Goldrick, *Before Jutland*, pp. 56–8. *BND*, pp. 915–17. Dash, 'Submarine Policy', pp. 161, 176 and 184–9. Mackay, *Fisher*, pp. 445–53. Jean Meyer, 'La guerre de course de l'Ancien Régime au XXe siècle: essai sur la guerre industrielle', *HES* XVI

(1997), pp. 7–43 at p. 24. Mackay, *Balfour*, pp. 241–2.

38 To Fisher, 1 Jan 1914: *BND*, p. 932; cf. N. A. Lambert, *Submarine Service*, p. 232, and Dash, 'Submarine Policy', p. 161.

39 To Fisher, 20 May 1913: *FGDN* II, 486; cf. Balfour to Fisher, 6 May 1913 and 6 Sep 1915: *FGDN* II, 485, and III, 280.

40 Cummins, *Diesel's Engine*, pp. 77, 179, 184, 188–9 and 547–8. Friedman, *British Submarines*, pp. 10, 29, 43 and 45–7.

41 Grove, 'Seamen or Airmen?', pp. 13–20. Goldrick, *Before Jutland*, p. 57. Layman, *Naval Aviation*, pp. 36–8 and 79–80. Till, *Air Power*, pp. 111–12. Jones, *Origins of Strategic Bombing*, pp. 40–45. Abbatiello, *Anti-Submarine Warfare*, pp. 9–10. *BND*, pp. 922–38. Moore, *Greenie*, p. 70. Price, *Aircraft versus Submarine*, pp. 2–5. Howlett, *British Naval Aviation*, pp. 1–2 and 26–31.

42 Brooks, 'Grand Battle-Fleet Tactics', p. 186. Friedman, *Naval Weapons of World War I*, pp. 19–20 and 31–2. Sumida, 'Battle Fleet Tactical Planning', pp. 102–6. Schleihauf, 'Concentrated Effort', pp. 118–25. McLaughlin, 'Battlelines and Fast Wings'. Dodson, *Kaiser's Battlefleet*, pp. 83, 88–9, 128 and 175.

43 *FGDN* II, 241 n.1. Crosbie Smith, 'Dreadnought Science: The Cultural Construction of Efficiency and Effectiveness', *TNS* LXXVII (2007), pp. 191–215, at p. 206–7.

44 Sumida, 'Quest for Reach', pp. 63–6, 77–81. Sumida, *Naval Supremacy*, pp. 121–50, 168–70, 224–55, 306–16, 332–3. Sumida, 'A Matter of Timing', pp. 88–104. Brooks, *Dreadnought Gunnery*, pp. 102–26 and 177–213. Brooks, *Jutland*, pp. 63–7. Brooks, 'Preparing for Armageddon', pp. 1006–9. Friedman, *Naval Firepower*, pp. 44–61. N. A. Lambert, *Fisher's Naval Revolution*, p. 192. Epstein, *Torpedo*, pp. 208–10. Friedman, *British Battleship* II, 44–7. Of these authorities Sumida speaks for Pollen, and Brooks for Dreyer.

45 Carne, *Naval Officer*, p. 43.

46 Grove, 'The Battleship is Dead', p. 417. Sumida, 'Quest for Reach', pp. 68–9 and 76–7. Brooks, *Jutland*, pp. 68–73; and *Dreadnought Gunnery*, pp. 20–23, 177–8

and 295. Friedman, *Naval Firepower*, pp. 45–7 and 68–71.

47 Friedman, *Naval Firepower*, pp. 68–9 and 86; and *Naval Weapons of World War One*, p. 127. Sumida, 'A Matter of Timing', pp. 122–3. Sumida, *Naval Supremacy*, pp. 251–3. Schleihauf, 'Concentrated Effort', p. 122. Russell, 'Purely by Coincidence', pp. 286–8. Reid, *Barr and Stroud Binoculars*, pp. 18–29 and 57–60. Brooks, *Dreadnought Gunnery*, pp. 10, 248–9. Brooks, *Jutland*, pp. 86–91. Moss and Russell, *Range and Vision*, pp. 55–7, 62–5 and 92–4. Sambrook, 'Optical Munitions', pp. 23, 72–5, 84–7, 105–20 and 125–55. The source of the myth about British optical glass was the unpublished official history of the Ministry of Munitions (Sambrook, 'Optical Munitions', p. 3). The literature on German fire control is unsatisfactory; Paul Schmalenbach, *Die Geschichte der deutschen Schiffsartillerie* (Herford, 1968), adds little, but the memoir of the *Derfflinger*'s gunnery officer at Jutland is informative: Georg von Hase, *Kiel and Jutland*, trans. A. Chambers and F. A. Holt ([London] 1921), p. 83.

48 Goldrick, *Before Jutland*, p. 26. Baynham, *Men from the Dreadnoughts*, pp. 185–8. The Royal Marines took over official naval bands in 1903.

Chapter 14

1 Ranft, *Beatty Papers* I, 113.
2 Offer, *Agrarian Interpretation*, pp. 11–12. French, *Economic and Strategic Planning*, pp. 51–67 and 85–7. N. A. Lambert, *Planning Armageddon*, pp. 191–9. Goldrick, 'Impact of War', pp. 23–4. Ferguson, 'Traditional Finance and "Total" War', p. 409.
3 Williamson, *Politics of Grand Strategy*, p. 359.
4 French, *Economic and Strategic Planning*, pp. 77–8. Williamson, *Politics of Grand Strategy*, pp. 369–71. Steiner, 'The Foreign Office and the War', p. 517. Baugh, 'British Strategy', pp. 104–6.

5 Bell, *Churchill and the Dardanelles*, p. 65, quoting the diary of Mrs Florence Richmond, whose husband Captain Herbert Richmond was then Assistant Director of the Operations Division of the Naval Staff.
6 N. A. Lambert, *Planning Armageddon*, pp. 187–91 and 211–13. French, *Economic and Strategic Planning*, pp. 88–94. Ferguson, 'Traditional Finance and "Total" War', pp. 409–10. Halpern, *World War I*, p. 68.
7 French, *British Strategy and War Aims*, pp. 20–22 and 36. Strachan, *First World War*, p. 374. N. A. Lambert, *Planning Armageddon*, p. 203. Williams, *Defending the Empire*, pp. 228–9. Williamson, *Politics of Grand Strategy*, pp. 354–69. Coogan, *The End of Neutrality*, pp. 148–51. Gray, *Leverage of Sea Power*, pp. 183–4. Morgan-Owen, 'Invasion Question', p. 207.
8 Karau, *Marine Korps Flandern*, pp. 3–11. De Groot, *Van Duitse Bocht tot Scapa Flow*, pp. 531–41. Röhl, *Wilhelm II*, p. 1142. Emmanuel Boulard, 'L'amiral Ronarc'h à Dunkerque (1914–1919)', *CHM* 81 (2016), pp. 105–15.
9 Schröder, *Die U-Boote des Kaisers*, pp. 46–7. Strachan, *First World War*, pp. 380–83. *DSF* II, 37–8. Marder, *Portrait of an Admiral*, p. 128.
10 Sondhaus, *Great War at Sea*, pp. 98–103. Rogan, *Fall of the Ottomans*, pp. 39–45. Panzac, *La marine ottomane*, pp. 466–7. Fotakis, *Greek Naval Strategy*, pp. 102–5. Halpern, *Mediterranean, 1914–1918*, pp. 12–22. *DSF* II, 20–41. Langensiepen, Nottelmann and Krüsmann, *Halbmond und Kaiseradler*, pp. 10–11. Holland, *Blue-Water Empire*, pp. 149–51. Friedman, *British Battleship* II, 148. Gordon, 'Transition to War'. Zanco, *Boué de Lapeyrère*, pp. 131–4. Herwig, *Luxury Fleet*, p. 153.
11 Goldrick, *Before Jutland*, pp. 111–36. Black, *Naval Staff*, pp. 99–101. Halpern, *World War I*, pp. 30–32. Compton-Hall, *Submarines and the War at Sea*, pp. 120–22. Marder, *Portrait of an Admiral*, p. 104. Epkenhans, 'Die Kaiserliche Marine

1914/15', p. 119. *DSF* II, 50–54. Harris, *Harwich Submarines*, pp. 74–96.

12 Dash, 'Submarine Policy', pp. 152–3 and 207–13. Sondhaus, *Great War at Sea*, pp. 141–3. Goldrick, *Before Jutland*, p. 46, and 'Learning to Fight', p. 44. Rössler, *U-boat*, pp. 17–35.

13 Goldrick, *Before Jutland*, pp. 52–3 and 142–51. Compton-Hall, *Submarines and the War at Sea*, pp. 1–2 and 129–32. Schröder, *Die U-Boote des Kaisers*, p. 59. Halpern, *World War I*, p. 33. *DSF* II, 55–9. Hepper, *Warship Losses*, pp. 25–7. Koerver, *German Submarine Warfare*, pp. 238–41. Sondhaus, *German Submarine Warfare*, p. 2.

14 König, *Der U-Bootkrieg*, pp. 126–9, quoting (p. 129) the *Kölnische Zeitung*: 'gegen sie [submarines] kämpfen Gott er selbst vergebens'. Koerver, *Krieg der Zahlen* I, 37.

15 Morgan-Owen, 'Invasion Question', pp. 224–5. Goldrick, *Before Jutland*, pp. 177–80. *DSF* II, 75–6.

16 Goldrick, 'Learning to Fight', p. 44. Compton-Hall, *Submarines and the War at Sea*, pp. 232–4.

17 Sondhaus, *Great War at Sea*, pp. 75–9. *DSF* II, 101–18. Marder, *Portrait of an Admiral*, pp. 112–13. Strachan, *First World War*, pp. 466–74. Bell, *Churchill and the Dardanelles*, pp. 31–2.

18 Roskill, *Beatty*, p. 98. As we have noted, Beatty was commanding the Battle-Cruiser Squadron of the Grand Fleet, but he had previously been Churchill's Naval Secretary and was familiar with the Admiralty and its personalities.

19 *DSF* II, 118–27. Goldrick, *Before Jutland*, pp. 168–71. Strachan, *First World War*, pp. 381–3 and 474–5. Brock and Brock, *Letters to Venetia Stanley*, p. 294.

20 Sondhaus, *Great War at Sea*, pp. 79–82. Strachan, *First World War*, pp. 475–8. Halpern, *World War I*, pp. 93–100. *DSF* II, 119–27. McKee, *Sober Men*, pp. 107–14, prints a vivid narrative of the action by Henry Welch, Captain's Clerk of the *Kent*.

21 Halpern, *World War I*, pp. 76–7. Sondhaus, *Great War at Sea*, pp. 87–92.

22 'Was man mit der Flotte machen werde, wenn die Engländer überhaupt nicht in der Deutschen Bucht erschienen?': Epkenhans, 'Die Kaiserliche Marine 1914/15', p. 117. Ingenohl himself had apparently raised the same question in 1913 without getting an answer: Philbin, *Hipper*, p. 83. The 'German Bight' and the 'Heligoland Bight' are alternative names for the same body of water.

23 Wolz, *Das lange Warten*, is the fullest study, but cf. Rodger, 'The Culture of Naval War', and Mark Jones, 'Graf von Spee's *Untergang* and the Corporate Identity of the Imperial German Navy', in Redford, *Maritime History and Identity*, pp. 183–202.

24 Halpern, *World War I*, pp. 38–9. Goldrick, *Before Jutland*, pp. 156–8 and 177–84. Sumida, 'Battle Fleet Tactical Planning', pp. 108–9. *DSF* II, 43, 75–6 and 152–6. Strachan, *First World War*, pp. 427–8.

25 Epkenhans, 'Die Kaiserliche Marine 1914/15', p. 119. Goldrick, *Before Jutland*, pp. 184–5. Schröder, *Die U-Boote des Kaisers*, pp. 57–8.

26 Goldrick, *Before Jutland*, pp. 173–6, and 'How It worked'. O'Hara and Heinz, *Clash of Fleets*, pp. 50–51.

27 Even naval officers were slow to appreciate the difficulty of accurate navigation in the notoriously foggy North Sea. Goldrick, 'How It worked', gives a good summary of the problems.

28 Goldrick, *Before Jutland*, pp. 197–220, is the fullest and best account of this action; see also Kelly, *Tirpitz*, pp. 384–5; N. Lambert, 'Strategic Command and Control', pp. 403–6; Strachan, *First World War*, pp. 427–30; *DSF* II, 134–48.

29 Goldrick, *Before Jutland*, pp. 255–84. Strachan, *First World War*, pp. 431–7. Kelly, *Tirpitz*, pp. 384–5. Friedman, *Great War at Sea*, pp. 150–51. Sondhaus, *Great War at Sea*, pp. 124–7. *DSF* II, 156–71. Philbin, *Hipper*, pp. 103–6 and 110.

30 French, *British Strategy and War Aims*, pp. 56–7. Darwin, *Empire Project*, p. 310. C. S. Gray, *Leverage of Sea Power*, pp. 185–90. Baugh, 'British Strategy', pp. 94–9.

31 Bell, *Churchill and Sea Power*, p. 61.

32 Bell, *Churchill and Sea Power*, pp. 61–6.
Bell, *Churchill and the Dardanelles*, pp.
70–77. N. A. Lambert, *Planning
Armageddon*, pp. 319–25, 332–7 and 410–
16. Black, *Naval Staff*, pp. 114–30. Halpern,
World War I, pp. 106–9. Mackay, *Balfour*,
pp. 262–7. Brock and Brock, *Letters to
Venetia Stanley*, pp. 373–4. Gray, *Leverage
of Sea Power*, pp. 204–5. *DSF* II, 199–221.
Friedman, *Great War at Sea*, pp. 224–5.
Rogan, *Fall of the Ottomans*, pp. 130 and
189. Moretz, *Thinking Wisely*, p. 452.
Lambert, ' "Ultimate Action in the
Baltic" ', pp. 88–98.

33 Black, *Naval Staff*, p. 132.

34 Bell, *Churchill and Sea Power*, pp. 66–72.
Bell, *Churchill and the Dardanelles*, pp.
112–64 and 361–7. Langensiepen,
Nottelmann and Krüsmann, *Halbmond
und Kaiseradler*, p. 224, print a chart of
the Dardanelles minefields. *DSF* II,
208–65 and 321–9. Mackay, *Balfour*, pp.
258–67. Friedman, *Great War at Sea*, pp.
227–8. Halpern, *World War I*, pp. 115–24.
Halpern, *Mediterranean, 1914–1918*, pp.
68–77 and 183–9. Moretz, *Thinking
Wisely*, p. 452. Robinson, *Fishermen*, pp.
97–102. Colonel Michael Hickey,
'Gallipoli: The Constantinople
Expeditionary Force, April 1915', in
Lovering, *Amphibious Assault*, pp. 7–22,
gives a good brief professional survey of
the operation.

35 Neilson, 'Imperial Defence, the Middle
East and India'. Halpern, *World War I*,
pp. 112–13 and 124–32. French, *British
Strategy and War Aims*, pp. 82–4 and
137–8. Rogan, *Fall of the Ottomans*, pp.
227–31.

36 Seligmann, 'Failing to Prepare', p. 433.

37 Hull, *A Scrap of Paper*, pp. 164–7.
Seligmann, 'Failing to Prepare'. Bell,
Churchill and Sea Power, pp. 42–4.
Seligmann et al., *Naval Route to the
Abyss*, pp. 419–31.

38 Halpern, 'World War I: The Blockade'.
Lavery, *Shield of Empire*, pp. 223–4.
Goldrick, *Before Jutland*, p. 194. Cobb,
Preparing for Blockade, pp. xvii–xx and
241–7. Brown, *Grand Fleet*, pp. 153–4.
Beeler, 'Ploughshares into Swords', pp.
26–7.

39 'England will uns aushungern; wir
können dasselbe Spiel treiben': Schröder,
Die U-Boote des Kaisers, pp. 86–7. Cf.
König, *Der U-Bootkrieg*, pp. 131–46;
Kelly, *Tirpitz*, p. 395, and Sondhaus,
German Submarine Warfare, pp. 23–8.

40 Messimer, *Find and Destroy*, pp. 13–14.
Lundeberg, 'German Naval Critique', pp.
107–8. Sondhaus, *German Submarine
Warfare*, pp. 23–8.

41 Schröder, *Die U-Boote des Kaisers*, p. 428
(referring to *Frontboote*, meaning those
ready for operations). Halpern, *World
War I*, p. 294.

42 Schröder, *Die U-boote des Kaisers* is the
best single-volume history of the
German submarine campaign, and
Halpern, *World War I*, the best naval
history of the war. On the U-boat
campaign it is also worth reading
Sondhaus, *Great War at Sea* and *German
Submarine Warfare*, Friedman, *Great
War at Sea*, Compton-Hall, *Submarines
and the War at Sea*, and Stegemann, *Die
Deutsche Marinepolitik*.

43 *DSF* II, 367–70. Stegemann, *Die
Deutsche Marinepolitik*, p. 99. Friedman,
Great War at Sea, p. 233. Robinson,
Fishermen, pp. 140–43. There is much
interesting detail about the Flanders
Flotilla in Termote, *War beneath the
Waves*.

44 These figures are for the class *U-31* to
U-41, built 1912–15: Gröner, *Die
Deutschen Kriegschiffe* I, 40, and
Schröder, *Die U-Boote des Kaisers*, p.
424. Rössler, *U-boat*, pp. 31–8. Compton-
Hall, *Submarines and the War at Sea*, pp.
67–74. Goldrick, *Before Jutland*, p. 55.

45 Schröder, *Die U-Boote des Kaisers*, pp.
105–7. Messimer, *Find and Destroy*, pp.
15–16. Halpern, *World War I*, p. 292.
Sondhaus, *German Submarine Warfare*,
p. 14.

46 Hull, ' "Military Necessity" '. Hull,
Absolute Destruction, pp. 123–6. Hull, *A
Scrap of Paper*, pp. 214–24, 240–45, 267–
71 and 318–21. Sondhaus, *German
Submarine Warfare*, pp. 23–5.

47 Schröder, *Die U-Boote des Kaisers*, pp.
83–4. Russell, *Prize Courts and U-boats*,
pp. 223–5, prints the text of the

Declaration of London; Articles 48–51 apply here.

48 Schröder, *Die U-Boote des Kaisers*, p. 111.

49 Schröder, *Die U-Boote des Kaisers*, pp. 126–34. Friedman, *Great War at Sea*, pp. 267–8. Sondhaus, *Great War at Sea*, p. 149. Friedman, *Network-Centric Warfare*, p. 16. Koerver, *German Submarine Warfare*, pp. 174, 257–73 and 404. Koerver, *Krieg der Zahlen* I, 90–102 and 200–215. Gregory, *The Last Great War*, pp. 61–2. Sondhaus, *German Submarine Warfare*, pp. 42–6. The sinking of the *Lusitania* has given rise to a luxurious growth of conspiracy theories, all well worth ignoring.

50 'Der große Menschenverlust ist mir ebenso wichtig wie die materielle Einbuße. Die Abschreckung ist das wesentliche beim U-Bootskrieg'. Wolz, *Das lange Warten*, p. 327, quoting Ernst Freiherr von Weizsäcker (and other officers to the same effect). The word *Abschreckung*, which I translate as 'terror', was usually rendered into contemporary English as 'frightfulness'. In some contexts it could be translated as 'deterrence', but that would be too weak here.

51 'Das deutsche Prestige in der Welt schwer leiden würde': Bachmann quoted by Stegemann, *Die Deutsche Marinepolitik*, p. 31. Their resignations were not accepted.

52 Schröder, *Die U-Boote des Kaisers*, pp. 152–4. Halpern, *World War I*, pp. 299–300. Sondhaus, *Great War at Sea*, pp. 152–4. Messimer, *Find and Destroy*, pp. 66–70. Hull, *A Scrap of Paper*, pp. 240–45 and 262.

53 Schröder, *Die U-Boote des Kaisers*, pp. 147–9.

54 Schröder, *Die U-Boote des Kaisers*, pp. 152–3. Davis and Engerman, *Naval Blockades*, pp. 165–71. Sondhaus, *Great War at Sea*, pp. 140–43. Halpern, *World War I*, pp. 293–5 and 302–3. Sondhaus, *German Submarine Warfare*, pp. 42–6.

55 Schröder, *Die U-Boote des Kaisers*, p. 182. Halpern, *Mediterranean, 1914–1918*, pp. 193–200. *DSF* II, 333–9. Compton-Hall, *Submarines and the War at Sea*, pp.

208–21. Messimer, *Find and Destroy*, pp. 194–5. Sondhaus, *German Submarine Warfare*, pp. 49–60.

56 *DSF* II, 350–57. Hull, *A Scrap of Paper*, pp. 245–52. Lavery, *Shield of Empire*, pp. 241–5. Halpern, *Mediterranean, 1915–1918*, p. 28. Compton-Hall, *Submarines and the War at Sea*, pp. 98–9 and 201–5. Messimer, *Find and Destroy*, pp. 36–9 and 106–12. Sondhaus, *Great War at Sea*, p. 265. Sondhaus, *German Submarine Warfare*, pp. 74–8.

57 Howlett, *British Naval Aviation*, pp. 17–20 and 41–2.

58 Grove, 'RNAS at War'. Abbatiello, *Anti-Submarine Warfare*, p. 60. Layman, *Naval Aviation*, p. 101. Jones, *Origins of Strategic Bombing*, pp. 57–9 and 101. Powers, *Strategy without Slide-Rule*, pp. 11–29. Roskill, *Naval Air Service* I, 168–82. *DSF* II, 149–51. Howlett, *British Naval Aviation*, pp. 9, 22–4, 31–2, 129–31 and 162–5.

59 Grove, 'RNAS at War', p. 30. Layman, *Naval Aviation*, p. 101. Roskill, *Naval Air Service*, pp. 186–8. Friedman, *Great War at Sea*, pp. 147–8. Hamer, *Bombers versus Battleships*, p. 8. Howlett, *British Naval Aviation*, pp. 31–2.

60 Cronin, *Shipboard Aircraft*, pp. 170–89. Grove, 'RNAS at War', pp. 34–5. Roskill, *Naval Air Service* I, 206–7. Jones, *Origins of Strategic Bombing*, p. 64. Howlett, *British Naval Aviation*, pp. 37 and 165–7. Layman, *Naval Aviation*, pp. 132–5. Haslop, *Early Naval Air Power*, p. 82.

Chapter 15

1 Scheer, *Germany's High Sea Fleet*, p. 97.

2 Sondhaus, *Great War at Sea*, pp. 205–6. Layman, *Naval Aviation*, p. 173. Sumida, 'Battle Fleet Tactical Planning', p. 116.

3 Brooks, *Jutland*, pp. 180–92 and 534–9.

4 King-Hall, *Sea Saga*, p. 448, quoting Lt Stephen King-Hall of the light cruiser *Southampton*.

5 Brooks, *Jutland*, pp. 80–85, 180–92, 460–67, 497–501 and 534–36. Brooks, *Dreadnought Gunnery*, pp. 232–55 and 284–8. N. A. Lambert, '"Our Bloody

Ships" '. Gordon, *Rules of the Game*, pp. 29–30. Friedman, *Great War at Sea*, pp. 163–4 and 378. Friedman, *British Battleship II*, 191–8. There are numerous narratives of Jutland in addition to these: the most interesting recent contributions include: Rahn, 'Die Seeschlacht vor dem Skagerrak'; Campbell, *Jutland*; Halpern, *World War I*, pp. 310–29; Sondhaus, *Great War at Sea*, pp. 213–25, and Carne, *Naval Officer*, pp. 66–94. Unless otherwise indicated my brief summary of the battle is based on these.

6 Grove, 'Chief Gunner Grant'. Lambert, '"Our Bloody Ships"', pp. 43–4. Friedman, *Great War at Sea*, p. 181. Brown, *Grand Fleet*, pp. 166–71. Gordon, *Rules of the Game*, pp. 29–30.

7 The *Gefechtskertwendung* was a 16-point turn in quick succession, beginning with the last ship in the line; very similar, therefore, to tacking a sailing fleet in succession from the rear, though the word derives from a Prussian army drill movement.

8 Kelly, *Tirpitz*, p. 413.

9 *DSF* III, 93–126. Brooks, *Jutland*, pp. 61–3, 294–8 and 524. Brooks, *Dreadnought Gunnery*, pp. 252–6. Sumida, 'Battle Fleet Tactical Planning'. Friedman, *Naval Weapons of World War One*, p. 22. Goldrick, *After Jutland*, p. 34.

10 Morgan-Owen, 'Invasion Question', pp. 282–4. Brooks, *Jutland*, pp. 98–105 and 525. Friedman, *British Battleship II*, 197–8. On eighteenth-century French naval thinking see *CO*, pp. 272–3.

11 Kelly, 'Tirpitz and the Oberkommando der Marine', p. 1040. Brooks, *Jutland*, pp. 311–20. Bird, *Raeder*, p. 19. Philbin, *Hipper*, pp. 31 and 130–31. Rolf Güth, *Von Revolution zu Revolution: Entwicklung und Führungsprobleme der deutschen Marine, 1848–1918* (Herford, 1978), p. 83. 'Schlachtkreuzer ran an den Feind; voll einsetzen': *DSF* III, 130. The old order 'ran an den Feind' had been revived in 1912 for this purpose; it was not an improvization.

12 *DSF* III, 128 n.50. Halpern, *World War I*, p. 322. Cf. Brooks, *Jutland*, p. 313.

13 Friedman, *Great War at Sea*, pp. 77–8, 170–71 and 359 n.107. Till, *Understanding Victory*, pp. 56–7. Friedman, *Network-Centric Warfare*, pp. 39–40. Friedman, *Naval Weapons of World War I*, 8. Goldrick, *After Jutland*, p. 35. *Iron Duke*'s automatic plot was manufactured by the German company Anschütz, but the German Navy had apparently not adopted it.

14 *DSF* III, 151–91. Brooks, *Jutland*, pp. 331–450 and 496.

15 Haslop, *Early Naval Air Power*, p. 116. King-Hall, *Sea Saga*, p. 495 (quoted).

16 *DSF* III, 235–48.

17 Grove, 'Chief Gunner Grant'. N. A. Lambert, '"Our Bloody Ships"'. Friedman, *Great War at Sea*, pp. 163–4. Ranft, *Beatty Papers* I, 406–7. *DSF* III, 208–15 and 266–8. *Victory in Command: Through the Hawsepipe, the Autobiography of Captain Alexander Grant, 1872–1961*, ed. J. G. Geddes (p. p. Somerset West, South Africa, 2006).

18 '. . . selbst der glücklichste Ausgang einer Hochseeschlacht England in *diesem* Kriege nicht zum Frieden *zwingen* wird'. Rahn, 'Die Seeschlacht vor dem Skagerrak', p. 213, trans. in Scheer, *Germany's High Sea Fleet*, p. 169.

19 Rahn, 'Die Seeschlacht vor dem Skagerrak', p. 194. Friedman, *Network-Centric Warfare*, p. 14.

20 Stegemann, *Die Deutsche Marinepolitik*, pp. 35, 45, 49 and 51–8. Kielmansegg, *Deutschland und der Erste Weltkrieg*, p. 387. Kelly, *Tirpitz*, p. 407. Friedman, *Great War at Sea*, pp. 261–2. Wolz, *Das lange Warten*, pp. 329–32 and 362–6. Messimer, *Find and Destroy*, p. 94. Schröder, *Die U-Boote des Kaisers*, pp. 203 and 208. Goldrick, *After Jutland*, pp. 129–30. Sondhaus, *German Submarine Warfare*, pp. 60–62 and 101–5. König, *Der U-Bootkrieg*, pp. 646–60.

21 Schröder, *Die U-Boote des Kaisers*, pp. 211–19. Messimer, *Find and Destroy*, p. 95. Halpern, *World War I*, pp. 307–9. Hull, *A Scrap of Paper*, p. 266. Carlisle, *Sovereignty at Sea*, pp. 6–160. Koerver, *Krieg der Zahlen* I, 169–78. König, *Der U-Bootkrieg*, pp. 360–81.

22 'Da Fortführung des U-Bootshandelskrieges gemäß Prisenordnung nach bisherigen Erfahrungen nicht durchführbar ist und die Boote unnütz der Vernichtung preisgibt, habe ich alle U-Boote vom Handelskrieg zurückgerufen. Der U-Boothandelskrieg gegen England hört damit auf': Rahn, 'Die Seeschlacht vor dem Skagerrak', p. 145.

23 Hull, *A Scrap of Paper*, p. 266. Lemnitzer, 'Woodrow Wilson's Neutrality', pp. 627–31. Halpern, *World War I*, pp. 308–9, 335 and 340–50. Lundeberg, 'German Naval Critique', pp. 111–12. Schröder, *Die U-Boote des Kaisers*, p. 237. Stegemann, *Die Deutsche Marinepolitik*, p. 49. Karau, *Marine Korps Flandern*, p. 72. *DSF* III, 326–7. Dunn, *Narrow Sea*, pp. 156–62. McCartney, 'First World War U-boat Losses'. Koerver, *Room 40* I, 160. König, *Der U-Bootkrieg*, pp. 360–81. Sondhaus, *German Submarine Warfare*, pp. 64–5. The figures for the 1916 'offensive patrols', which have often been quoted, come originally from Lt-Cdr D. W. Waters' paper, 'A Study in the Philosophy and Conduct of Maritime War', *JRNSS* XIII (1958), pp. 109–19 and 183–92.

24 Halpern, *World War I*, pp. 159–66 and 304–6. Halpern, *Mediterranean, 1914–1918*, pp. 201–5 and 228–59. *DSF* III, 320, and V, 32–6. Messimer, *Find and Destroy*, pp. 195–8. Robinson, *Fishermen*, pp. 104–10.

25 'So war meine Rekordfahrt zum Beispiel ganz zahm und langweilig . . . Trotzdem hatten wir keinerlei besondere Abenteuer erlebt. Alles hatte sich routinemäßig abgespielt. Wir hielten die Schiffe an. Die Besatzung ging in die Boote. Wir prüfing die Schiffspapiere, gaben den Leuten Segelanweisungen zum nächsten Land und versenkt sodann die eroberte Prise . . .': Schröder, *Die U-Boote des Kaisers*, pp. 233 (quoted) and 433–4. Cf. Koerver, *Krieg der Zahlen* II, 22–9, and *German Submarine Warfare*, pp. 218–20; and Sondhaus, *German Submarine Warfare*, pp. 65–8.

26 Halpern, *World War I*, pp. 330, 333 and 346–50. *DSF* III, 290–301, and IV,

202–6. Karau, *Marine Korps Flandern*, pp. 73, 154–6 and 161–2. Schröder, *Die U-Boote des Kaisers*, pp. 247–50. Dunn, *Narrow Sea*, pp. 117–22. Sondhaus, *German Submarine Warfare*, pp. 91–4.

27 Schröder, *Die U-Boote des Kaisers*, pp. 247–8 and 257–82. Stegemann, *Die Deutsche Marinepolitik*, pp. 39–41, 45 and 49. Hull, *A Scrap of Paper*, p. 266. Russell, *Prize Courts and U-boats*, pp. 186–7. Sondhaus, *German Submarine Warfare*, pp. 112–13.

28 Halpern, *World War I*, pp. 335–41. *DSF* III, 330–35, and IV, 49–54 and 112–14. Roskill, *Hankey* I, 315. Schröder, *Die U-Boote des Kaisers*, pp. 325–6. Stegemann, *Die Deutsche Marinepolitik*, p. 97. Terraine, *U-Boat Wars*, pp. 41–8. Simpson, *Anglo-American Naval Relations* I, 6.

29 French, *British Strategy and War Aims*, pp. 230 and 248–9. French, *Lloyd George Coalition*, pp. 5–6. French, 'The Empire and the USA', pp. 84–5 and 93. Larsen, 'War Pessimism', p. 814.

30 Halpern, *Mediterranean, 1914–1918*, p. 325.

31 Halpern, *World War I*, pp. 343–5. *DSF* IV, 69–79 and 86–8. Messimer, *Find and Destroy*, pp. 127–9. Compton-Hall, *Submarines and the War at Sea*, pp. 60–61. Hartcup, *War of Invention*, pp. 129–35. Goldrick, *After Jutland*, p. 258.

32 Gardner, *Decoding History*, pp. 69–72. Messimer, *Find and Destroy*, pp. 127–9 and 147–9.

33 Halpern, *World War I*, pp. 351–6. *DSF* III, 322–3, and IV, 115–51 and 270. *BND*, pp. 761–6. Friedman, *Great War at Sea*, p. 277. Simpson, *Anglo-American Naval Relations* I, 195–8. Halpern, *Mediterranean, 1914–1918*, pp. 317–21.

34 Rodger, 'Culture of Naval War'. Schröder, *Die U-Boote des Kaisers*, pp. 257–82. Stegemann, *Die Deutsche Marinepolitik*, pp. 73–4 and 79. Scheck, 'Der Kampf des Tirpitz-Kreises', pp. 70–75. Black, *Naval Staff*, p. 3. A. D. Lambert, *The British Way of War*, pp. 119–21.

35 'Der Geist, der den U-Krieg beherrscht, übt auf den Gegner und die Neutralen die stärkste Wirkung aus . . . Je näher wir dem Ende des Krieges kommen, desto

größere Bedeutung bekommt der Kraftwille; letzten Endes entscheidet doch das stärkere Gemüt': Stegemann, *Die Deutsche Marinepolitik*, p. 79.

36 'Einmal mehr stoßen wir hier auf das Phänomen, daß die deutsche Strategie aus dem Postulat entwickelt wurde, daß der Sieg möglich sein müsse, weil er notwendig sei': Kielmansegg, *Deutschland und der Erste Weltkrieg*, p. 387.

37 Scheck, 'Der Kampf des Tirpitz-Kreises'.

38 Greenhalgh, *Victory through Coalition*, p. 117, quoting Cdt Pierre Vandier. I have not been able to get sight of the original French publication she cites, but Vandier's remark only makes sense on the assumption that Greenhalgh's 'pirates' is a mistranslation of 'corsaires' (privateers), and that the two occasions he refers to are the French privateering campaigns in the reigns of Louis XIV and Napoleon Bonaparte, which would be familiar to any French naval officer.

39 Halpern, *Mediterranean, 1914–1918*, pp. 446–7. Halpern, *Mediterranean, 1915–1918*, pp. 178–82 and 193–7. Halpern, *World War I*, pp. 204–10 and 351–9. *DSF* IV, 115–66. Messimer, *Find and Destroy*, pp. 147–51. Mackay, *Balfour*, p. 301. Stegemann, *Die Deutsche Marinepolitik*, pp. 68–9. Gardner, *Decoding History*, p. 43. Simpson, *Anglo-American Naval Relations* I, 197–8. Friedman, *Great War at Sea*, p. 314. Goldrick, *After Jutland*, pp. 156–9. Sondhaus, *German Submarine Warfare*, pp. 144–7.

40 Schröder, *Die U-Boote des Kaisers*, pp. 325–8 and 427–30. Compton-Hall, *Submarines and the War at Sea*, p. 266. Stegemann, *Die Deutsche Marinepolitik*, pp. 66, 72–3 and 97. *DSF* V, 85–8. Grove, *Enemy Attack on Shipping*, pp. 3–4. Figures for German submarine strength vary somewhat between authorities, mainly because they take different dates in the month, or do not distinguish between total strength and operational *Frontboote*.

41 Doughty, *Merchant Shipping and War*, pp. 6–7 and 21–39. French, 'Defense of the British Empire', pp. 125–6. Messimer, *Find and Destroy*, pp. 147–55. Halpern,

Mediterranean, 1914–1918, pp. 396–7. *DSF* IV, 63–5. Stegemann, *Die Deutsche Marinepolitik*, pp. 64, 84–9 and 99–102. Schröder, *Die U-Boote des Kaisers*, p. 372. Offer, 'Bounded Rationality', p. 194, and *Agrarian Interpretation*, p. 366. Olson, *Wartime Shortage*, pp. 86–113. Robinson, *Fishermen*, pp. 87–8. An excellent collection of statistical tables relating to convoys and the submarine campaign is in Davis and Engerman, *Naval Blockades*, pp. 163–98.

42 *DSF* V, 22–30 and 36–8. Fotakis, *Greek Naval Strategy*, pp. 141–2. Sondhaus, *German Submarine Warfare*, pp. 144–5, 152–3 and 173–6. Carne, *Naval Officer*, pp. 138–57, gives a good narrative of escorting Mediterranean convoys in 1917.

43 Herwig, 'Total Rhetoric', pp. 204–5. *DSF* IV, 53–4, and V, 81–3. Halpern, *World War I*, pp. 338–40, 346–50 and 422–3. Jeschke, *U-Boottaktik*, pp. 58–60. Karau, *Marine Korps Flandern*, pp. 138 and 167. Rössler, *U-boat*, pp. 75–87. Kielmansegg, *Deutschland und der Erste Weltkrieg*, p. 387. Friedman, *Great War at Sea*, pp. 259–65. Goldrick, *After Jutland*, pp. 129–30. Sondhaus, *German Submarine Warfare*, pp. 190–91.

44 David Kennedy, *Over Here: The First World War and American Society* (New York, 1980), p. 322. Baer, *One Hundred Years of Sea Power*, p. 59, quotes Wilson telling House, 'Let us build a Navy bigger than hers and do what we please'.

45 French, 'Winning the Great War', pp. 205–7. French, 'The Empire and the USA', pp. 94–9. Baer, *One Hundred Years of Sea Power*, pp. 66–7, 73 and 78. Simpson, *Anglo-American Naval Relations* I, 4–5 and 8–9. Stegemann, *Die Deutsche Marinepolitik*, pp. 99–102. Herwig, 'Strategische Unbestimmtheitsrelation', pp. 174–6.

46 Messimer, *Find and Destroy*, pp. 181–8. Halpern, *World War I*, pp. 438–40. Compton-Hall, *Submarines and the War at Sea*, p. 84.

47 Messimer, *Find and Destroy*, pp. 163–76. Halpern, *World War I*, pp. 406–16. Karau, *Marine Korps Flandern*, pp. 186–8 and 199–224. *DSF* V, 39–66. De Groot,

Van Duitse Bocht tot Scapa Flow, pp. 335–8. Friedman, *Great War at Sea*, pp. 242–3. Wolz, *Das lange Warten*, pp. 437–8. Dunn, *Narrow Sea*, pp. 171–95. Goldrick, *After Jutland*, pp. 239–50.

48 Halpern, *World War I*, pp. 422–8. Abbatiello, *Anti-Submarine Warfare*, pp. 151–2. Jeschke, *U-Boottaktik*, pp. 59–64. *DSF* IV, 281, and V, 85–96. Llewellyn-Jones, *Anti-Submarine Warfare*, p. 9. Koerver, *German Submarine Warfare*, p. 131.

49 French, 'Winning the Great War', pp. 206–8. French, *Lloyd George Coalition*, pp. 175–7. Darwin, *Empire Project*, pp. 313–16.

50 Neilson, 'Imperial Defence, the Middle East and India', pp. 109–11. Darwin, *Empire Project*, pp. 313–18. Holland, *Blue-Water Empire*, pp. 175–81. French, *Lloyd George Coalition*, pp. 7–11. Reynolds, *Long Shadow*, pp. 86–104. Michael Head, 'The Caspian Campaign', *WI LIII* (2016), pp. 69–81 and 225–46.

51 James, *Paladins*, p. 60. Pulsipher, 'Aircraft and the Royal Navy', pp. 47–8 and 99–102. Grove, 'RNAS at War', p. 39. Till, *Air Power*, pp. 29–30 and 111–13. Powers, *Strategy without Slide-Rule*, pp. 28–9 and 42. Hore, *Habit of Victory*, p. 290. Hartcup, *War of Invention*, pp. 83–6. Jordan, 'Royal Navy Concepts of Air Power'. Howlett, *British Naval Aviation*, pp. 2–3.

52 Howlett, *British Naval Aviation*, pp. 2–3 and 18–26.

53 Howlett, *British Naval Aviation*, pp. 42–5.

54 Jones, *Origins of Strategic Bombing*, pp. 80–121, 142–6 and 154–9. Grove, 'RNAS at War', p. 43. Goulter, 'Royal Naval Air Service', pp. 58–60. Jordan, 'Royal Navy Concepts of Air Power'. Roskill, *Naval Air Service*, pp. 271–3 and 373. Howlett, *British Naval Aviation*, pp. 128–9 and 139–45.

55 Roskill, *Naval Air Service*, pp. 271–3, 344–79 and 389–432. Grove, 'RNAS at War', p. 40. Layman, *Naval Aviation*, pp. 72–5. Cooper, 'Blueprint for Confusion', p. 439. Mackay, *Balfour*, pp. 292–6. Till, *Air Power*, p. 114. Howlett, *British Naval

Aviation*, pp. 141–3. Haslop, *Early Naval Air Power*, pp. 95–102.

56 Layman, *Naval Aviation*, pp. 42 and 172–81. Price, *Aircraft versus Submarine*, pp. xii–xiv.

57 Howlett, *British Naval Aviation*, pp. 179–80.

58 Roskill, *Naval Air Service* I, 469–73, 529, 549–54 and 610. Haslop, *Early Naval Air Power*, pp. 101–2. Till, *Air Power*, pp. 115–16. Black, *Naval Staff*, pp. 224–5. Cooper, 'Blueprint for Confusion', pp. 441–7. Biddle, *Rhetoric and Reality*, pp. 29–35. Jones, *Origins of Strategic Bombing*, pp. 81–98 and 129–63. Grove, 'RNAS at War'.

59 Haslop. *Early Naval Air Power*, pp. 111–13. Abbatiello, *Anti-Submarine Warfare*, pp. 1–2, 25, 88–91 and 99–114. Till, *Air Power*, pp. 115 and 167. Layman, *Naval Aviation*, pp. 81, 119–24 and 168. Grove, 'RNAS at War', pp. 48–50. Buckley, *RAF and Trade Defence*, p. 17. Howlett, *British Naval Aviation*, pp. 86–108.

60 Wise, 'Origins of Strategic Bombing', pp. 156–8. Grove, 'RNAS at War', pp. 46–8. Jones, *Origins of Strategic Bombing*, pp. 130–34. Powers, *Strategy without Slide-Rule*, pp. 52–61 and 71–2. Howlett, *British Naval Aviation*, pp. 176–83.

61 Layman, *Naval Aviation*, pp. 191–5. *DSF* IV, 3–23. Weir, 'Naval Air Warfare', p. 219. Grove, 'RNAS at War', pp. 53–4. Rippon, *Engineering* I, 193–8. Cronin, *Shipboard Aircraft*, pp. 15–69. Goldrick, *After Jutland*, pp. 165–6 and 267–8. Howlett, *British Naval Aviation*, pp. 42–60.

Chapter 16

1 Hull, *A Scrap of Paper*, pp. 143–7. Bell, *Churchill and Sea Power*, pp. 50–52. Coogan, 'Short-War Illusion', pp. 1052–5. Coogan, *End of Neutrality*, pp. 145–7, 156–7 and 238–41. French, *Economic and Strategic Planning*, pp. 22–30. Offer, 'Morality and Admiralty', pp. 101–10. Davis and Engerman, *Naval Blockades*, pp. 12–17. Offer, 'Blockade of Germany', pp. 171–2. Marsden, 'Blockade', pp. 489–90. N. A. Lambert, *Planning Armageddon*, pp. 211–13 and 270–71.

(Note that the main argument of this book is challenged by Coogan, 'Short-War Illusion'.)

2 Foxton, 'Prize Court', p. 281. Cf. Ferris, 'Pragmatic Hegemony', p. 101.

3 Coogan, *End of Neutrality*, pp. 194–5. Foxton, 'Prize Court', pp. 281–5. Ørvik, *Decline of Neutrality*, p. 44. N. A. Lambert, *Planning Armageddon*, pp. 386–7. Ferris, 'Pragmatic Hegemony' and 'Declaration of London'.

4 N. A. Lambert, *Planning Armageddon*, pp. 210–78 and 341–61. Black, *Naval Staff*, pp. 86–92. Halpern, 'World War I: The Blockade'. G. Kennedy, 'Intelligence and the Blockade'. G. Kennedy, 'North Atlantic Triangle'. Peden, *Arms, Economics and British Strategy*, pp. 78–81. Marsden, 'Blockade'. French, *Economic and Strategic Planning*, pp. 170–75.

5 Sumida, 'Forging the Trident', p. 217.

6 Ehrman, *Cabinet Government*, pp. 55–9. Gordon, *Seapower and Procurement*, pp. 13–15. Peden, *Arms, Economics and British Strategy*, pp. 71–2. Offer, *Agrarian Interpretation*, pp. 313–16. N. A. Lambert, *Planning Armageddon*, p. 235. French, *Economic and Strategic Planning*, pp. 124–65. Friedman, *Great War at Sea*, pp. 284–5.

7 R. A. Smith, 'Strategy of the Economic Weapon', p. 71.

8 Turner, 'Higher Direction of War', pp. 60–62. N. A. Lambert, *Planning Armageddon*, pp. 460–85. French, *Economic and Strategic Planning*, pp. 124–31.

9 Williams, *Defending the Empire*, pp. 231–3. *DSF* II, 278–99. Mackay, *Fisher*, pp. 496–504. *FGDN* III, 149 and 209–15. Bell, *Churchill and Sea Power*, pp. 73–5.

10 Mackay, *Balfour*, p. 276, quoting a character sketch by Selborne in June 1916, with the words in parenthesis added by Mackay.

11 Bell, *Churchill and the Dardanelles*, pp. 2–9 and 353–67. N. A. Lambert, *Planning Armageddon*, pp. 361–493. Black, *Naval Staff*, pp. 138–40. Turner, 'Higher Direction of War', pp. 58–61. French, *Economic and Strategic Planning*,

pp. 124–31 and 166–77. C. I. Hamilton, *Modern Admiralty*, p. 237.

12 R. A. Smith, 'Strategy of the Economic Weapon', pp. 24–56 and 137–69. Tracy, *Attack on Maritime Trade*, pp. 135–39. G. Kennedy, 'Strategy and Power', pp. 197–200. G. Kennedy, 'Intelligence and the Blockade', pp. 707–9 and 715–16; G. Kennedy, 'British Strategic Assessment', pp. 13–20. N. A. Lambert, *Planning Armageddon*, pp. 494–6. Ritschl, 'Germany's Economy at War', pp. 58–9. McKercher and Neilson, 'Sweden and the Allied Blockade', pp. 187–93. Marsden, 'Blockade', pp. 509–15. Ferris, 'To the Hunger Blockade'.

13 Ferris, 'War Trade Intelligence Department'.

14 *Nederlandsche Overzee Trustmaatschappy*, but the name was coined in English.

15 Ørvik, *Decline of Neutrality*, pp. 53–9. Otte, 'Sea Power, Diplomacy and Economic Warfare'. Den Hertog, 'Dutch Neutrality'. Kruizinga, 'NOT Neutrality'. Hull, *A Scrap of Paper*, p. 152.

16 Hull, *A Scrap of Paper*, pp. 269–71 and 318–24. Tracy, *Belligerent Rights*, pp. 231 and 311–18. Tucker, *Wilson*, p. 22. Ferris, 'Declaration of London'.

17 See *CO*, pp. 347–8 and 468–9, for the 'Armed Neutralities' of 1780 and 1800.

18 Tucker, *Wilson*, pp. 1–51 and 194–8. O'Connell, *Influence of Law*, p. 139. Lemnitzer, 'Woodrow Wilson's Neutrality'. Ferris, 'To the Hunger Blockade'. Lemnitzer, *Power, Law and the End of Privateering*, pp. 189–90. O'Brien, *Naval Power*, pp. 115–23. Davis and Engerman, *Naval Blockades*, pp. 168–70. Hull, *Absolute Destruction*, pp. 1–3, 91. Hull, *A Scrap of Paper*, pp. 257–61. Schröder, *Die U-Boote des Kaisers*, pp. 156–8. Lundeberg, 'German Naval Critique', p. 110. Lindberg and Todd, *Anglo-American Shipbuilding*, p. 58. Coogan, *End of Neutrality*, p. 255. Carlisle, *Sovereignty at Sea*, pp. 97–160. Herwig, 'Strategische Unbestimmtheitsrelation', pp. 176–81. Friedman, *British Battleship* II, 216.

19 Ritschl, 'Germany's Economy at War', pp. 46–59. Offer, 'Blockade of Germany', pp. 178–87. Offer, *Agrarian Interpretation*, pp. 27–78. Davis and Engerman, *Naval Blockades*, pp. 198–214. Tracy, *Attack on Maritime Trade*, p. 138. Marsden, 'Blockade', p. 515. Olson, *Wartime Shortage*, pp. 79–81 and 110–15. Broadberry and Harrison, 'Economics of World War I', pp. 18–21.

20 Larsen, 'War Pessimism'. French, *British Strategy and War Aims*, pp. 158–9.

21 Mackay, *Balfour*, p. 276.

22 There is a whole library on Lloyd George; this brief sketch draws heavily on the masterly short life by K. O. Morgan in *ODNB*. Hankey quoted by Turner, 'Higher Direction of War', p. 64.

23 Turner, 'Higher Direction of War', pp. 64–6.

24 Goldrick, *Before Jutland*, pp. 16–18; *After Jutland*, pp. 114–19, 153 and 282. C. I. Hamilton, *Modern Admiralty*, pp. 232–48 and 265–7. C. I. Hamilton, 'Policy-Makers and Financial Control', pp. 389 and 395. C. I. Hamilton, 'Three Cultures at the Admiralty', pp. 90–91; 'Solvitur Ambulando', pp. 77–9. Black, *Naval Staff*, pp. 17–52 and 195–6. N. Lambert, 'Strategic Command and Control', pp. 400–408.

25 Mackay, *Balfour*, pp. 273–4. Roskill, *Naval Air Service* I, xiii. *DSF* II, 8, and IV, 215. *ODNB* sv Greene.

26 C. I. Hamilton, *Modern Admiralty*, pp. 252–7. Ranft, *Beatty Papers* I, 421. *DSF* IV, 56–60 and 134. Black, *Naval Staff*, pp. 190–92. Patterson, *Jellicoe Papers* II, 116 and 120–21. Roskill, 'Dismissal of Admiral Jellicoe', pp. 70–71.

27 C. I. Hamilton, *Modern Admiralty*, p. 261; cf. Wemyss, *Life and Letters*, pp. 370–71, and Beesly, *Very Special Admiral*, p. 15.

28 C. I. Hamilton, *Modern Admiralty*, p. 262.

29 Black, *Naval Staff*, pp. 214–15 and 228–33. C. I. Hamilton, *Modern Admiralty*, pp. 258–63. Roskill, *Naval Air Service* I, xiii. Patterson, *Jellicoe Papers* II, 116–21. *DSF* IV, 175–264. Wemyss, *Life and Letters*, pp. 364–71. Beesly, *Very Special Admiral*, pp. 15 and 44–5. K. G. B. Dewar, *Navy*

from Within, pp. 215–49, is worth reading with a sceptical eye.

30 Afflerbach, 'What Was the Great War About?', p. 3 (quoting Crown Prince Rupert). Strachan, 'Military Operations and National Policies', pp. 14–25.

31 W. S. Churchill, *The World Crisis* (London, 1923–31, 6 vols), IV, 295.

32 Sumida, 'Forging the Trident', pp. 217–21. Friedman, *Great War at Sea*, pp. 284–5.

33 MacLeod and Andrews, 'Board of Invention and Research'. Hamilton, 'Three Cultures at the Admiralty', pp. 91–5. *FGDN* III, 269–70. Hartcup, *War of Invention*, p. 189. Black, *Naval Staff*, p. 212. Compton-Hall, *Submarines and the War at Sea*, pp. 93–7.

34 Sumida, 'Forging the Trident', pp. 223–6. Friedman, *Great War at Sea*, pp. 284–5. Johnston and Buxton, *Battleship Builders*, p. 265. Lindberg and Todd, *Anglo-American Shipbuilding*, pp. 49–57. Peebles, *Warshipbuilding*, pp. 89–92. Scott and Hughes, *War Production*, pp. 140–41. Sumida, 'Operational Logistics', pp. 458–60.

35 Lavery, *Shield of Empire*, pp. 216–19. W. M. Brown, 'Fuel Supplies'. Sumida, 'Operational Logistics'. (My figure of 5½–7½ million tons is from Brown, p. 126, but Sumida, p. 471, claims 41.7 million tons, or roughly 10 million tons a year. His figures for oil consumption are also much higher.)

36 Roskill, *Naval Air Service*, p. 209, quoting Asquith's private secretary Maurice Bonham-Carter.

37 Layman, *Naval Aviation*, pp. 72–6. Jones, *Origins of Strategic Bombing*, pp. 52–3 and 66–9. Grove, 'RNAS at War', pp. 27, 33–6 and 40. Till, *Air Power*, pp. 111–13. Pugh, 'Oil and Water'. Abbatiello, *Anti-Submarine Warfare*, pp. 22–4 and 52. Goulter, 'Royal Naval Air Service'.

38 Goldrick, 'How It Worked', pp. 128–39. Goldrick, *After Jutland*, pp. 32–6, and 'Learning to Fight', p. 47.

39 Headrick, *Invisible Weapon*, pp. 120–33 and 141. Hugill, *Global Communications*, pp. 87–91. Winkler, *Nexus*, pp. 14–16, 22–4, 66 and 85. Hiley, 'Origins of Room 40', pp. 252–5. Beesly, *Room 40*, pp. 30

and 69–72. Beesly, *British Naval Intelligence*, pp. 30–31. Blond, 'Technology and Tradition', pp. 108, 236 and 244. Friedman, *Great War at Sea*, pp. 37 and 93–5. Strachan, *First World War*, pp. 450–51. Friedman, *Network-Centric Warfare*, pp. 9–14.

40 N. A. Lambert, 'Strategic Command and Control', p. 399. Beesly, *Room 40*, pp. 21–3. Ferris, 'British "Enigma"', pp. 139–40. McKay and Beckman, *Swedish Signal Intelligence*, pp. 25–7. Goldrick, *Before Jutland*, p. 50. Friedman, *Network-Centric Warfare*, pp. 9–10. Koerver, *Krieg der Zahlen* I, 194–7.

41 Meaning 'Signal Book of the Imperial Navy', 'Communications Book' and 'Merchant Communications Book' respectively. The first was indeed a visual signal book; the others primarily telegraph codes.

42 *DSF* II, 132–4 and 446 gives the 'classic' story; cf. Headrick, *Invisible Weapon*, p. 159; Grant, *U-boat Hunters* I, 34–8; II, 640–56. The *T-119* is often referred to by her former number as *S-119*.

43 Hammant, '*Magdeburg* Incident', p. 334. Bonatz, *Die deutsche Marine-Funkaufklärung*, pp. 29–30. Beesly, *Room 40*, pp. 3–7 and 24.

44 Hiley, 'Origins of Room 40', pp. 245–8 and 257–65. N. A. Lambert, 'Strategic Command and Control', pp. 408–9. Wells, 'Naval Intelligence', p. 125. Headrick, *Invisible Weapon*, p. 160. Beesly, *Room 40*, pp. 14–15. Ferris, 'The Road to Bletchley Park'. Friedman, *Network-Centric Warfare*, p. 13. Donovan and Mack, *Codebreaking in the Pacific*, p. 76. Batey, *Dilly*, pp. 13–20. Koerver, *Room 40* II, 634–59, prints the unpublished internal history of the organization. Boyd, *Naval Intelligence*, pp. 105–9, the leading modern authority, does not share my unease about this famous cryptographic story.

45 Hiley, 'Origins of Room 40', pp. 245–8. Beesly, *Room 40*, pp. 8–10, 134 and 169–71. Winkler, *Nexus*, pp. 25–6. Blond, 'Technology and Tradition', pp. 269–71. Andrew, *Secret Service*, p. 121. Batey, *Dilly*, p. 13. *DSF* IV, 265–7.

46 Bonatz, *Die deutsche Marine-Funkaufklärung*, pp. 36–7. Headrick, *Invisible Weapon*, pp. 166–7. Blond, 'Technology and Tradition', pp. 244 and 305. Ferris, 'The Road to Bletchley Park', pp. 55–60. Ferris, 'The British "Enigma"', pp. 140–41. Hammant, '*Magdeburg* Incident', pp. 337–8. Beesly, *Room 40*, pp. 21–6, 32–3 and 40–42. Bird and Hinds, 'In the Shadow of Ultra'. Lavery, *Shield of Empire*, p. 219. Friedman, *Great War at Sea*, pp. 96–7. De Groot, *Van Duitse Bocht tot Scapa Flow*, p. 115. Grant, *U-boat Hunters*, pp. 34–8. Koerver, *Room 40* II, 657–9. Innes McCartney, 'The Archaeology of First World War U-boat Losses in the English Channel and its Impact on the Historical Record', *MM* CV (2019), pp. 183–201 at pp. 197–9.

47 Friedman, *Network-Centric Warfare*, pp. 11–15.

Chapter 17

1 Davison, 'Executive Branch', pp. 88–9. Davison, *Challenges of Command*, pp. 11, 97, 101, 219–23 and 234–5.

2 In 1916 the then Captain Plunkett inherited the Charborough estate in Dorset from his mother (née Ernle-Erle-Drax) under a 'name and arms' clause in her will, and changed his surname to Plunkett-Ernle-Erle-Drax, which he usually abbreviated to 'Drax'.

3 Marder, *Portrait of an Admiral*, p. 89.

4 James Goldrick, 'The Founders', in Hore, *Dreadnought to Daring*, pp. 1–17. Davison, *Challenges of Command*, pp. 7–15, 209–10, 231–2, 236–45 and 251–2. Davison, 'Executive Branch'. Marder, *Portrait of an Admiral*, pp. 43, 89, 237 and 240–41. A. D. Lambert, *The British Way of War*.

5 Ranft, *Beatty Papers* I, 275.

6 King-Hall, *Sea Saga*, p. 424.

7 Davison, *Challenges of Command*, p. 254. 'To clear one's yardarm' means to avoid responsibility.

8 Wolz, *Das lange Warten*, p. 103.

9 Wolz, *Das lange Warten*, pp. 103–4, 150–51, 317–19, 426–7 and 443. Davison, *Challenges of Command*, pp. 219–27,

233–7 and 251–2. Davison, 'Executive Branch', pp. 88–9 and 94–104. Spector, *At War at Sea*, p. 102. Roskill, *Beatty*, pp. 273–80. Rüger, *Great Naval Game*, pp. 258–61.

10 Arthur, *Lost Voices*, pp. 15–16, quoting Commander Frank Layard, who was a midshipman in *Indomitable* in 1915.

11 Seligmann, *Churchill and Social Reform*, pp. 138–62. Wolz, *Das lange Warten*, p. 166. Roskill, *Beatty*, p. 247. Davison, *Challenges of Command*, pp. 226–7. J. Wells, *Social History*, p. 115. Rowe, 'Discipline and Morale', pp. 44–7. Farquharson-Roberts, *War to War*, pp. 39–40. Arthur, *True Glory*, p. 10. J. V. P. Goldrick, ed., 'The Memoirs of Captain J. B. Foley', in Rodger, *Naval Miscellany* V, 499–531, at 500–502.

12 Herwig, *German Naval Officer Corps*, pp. 155–70, 187–209 and 253–64. Thomas, *German Navy*, pp. 5–8 and 128–33. Philbin, *Hipper*, pp. 60–63. Epkenhans, 'Red Sailors'. Goldrick, *Before Jutland*, pp. 31–4.

13 Baynham, *Men from the Dreadnoughts*, p. 161, quoting the ERA H. S. Wright.

14 Penn, *HMS Thunderer*, pp. 63–9. McCoy, 'From Selborne to AFO 1/56', pp. 258–9. Romans, 'Selection and Early Career', pp. 27–8. Lewis, *Navy in Transition*, p. 205. Davison, *Challenges of Command*, pp. 103–7.

15 Carne, *Naval Officer*, pp. 22–3.

16 Marder, *Portrait of an Admiral*, p. 335, quoting a 1918 paper by Herbert Richmond.

17 Romans, 'Selection and Early Career', pp. 41–5 and 258. Beattie, *Churchill Scheme*, pp. 7–20. Marder, *Old Friends* I, 280–82.

18 Davison, *Challenges of Command*, p. 145.

19 Gordon, *Rules of the Game*, p. 176.

20 C. I. Hamilton, *Anglo-French Naval Rivalry*, p. 198.

21 K. G. B. Dewar, *Navy from Within*, p. 74.

22 Marder, *Old Friends* I, 282, quoting an anonymous contributor to the *Naval Review*.

23 Dewar, *Navy from Within*, p. 119.

24 Gordon, *Rules of the Game*, is a brilliant book that argues exactly this case at length.

25 NMM: MSS/87/006; to 'Heathcote', 22 Jul 1933, possibly referring to Admiral Field's post-Invergordon reforms, for which see Ch. 21.

26 Jones, 'Naval Officer Corps', pp. 75–87, 193 and 219. Wells, *Social History*, pp. 62–3. Payton, 'Naval Education', p. 195. Romans, 'Selection and Early Career', pp. 149–51. Davison, *Challenges of Command*, pp. 72–3, 110–14 and 201. Goldrick, *Before Jutland*, p. 24. *BND*, pp. 729–30 and 733–4. Spector, *At War at Sea*, p. 68.

27 Goldrick, *Before Jutland*, p. 25. Farquharson-Roberts, 'War to War', pp. 1–2. Seligmann, 'The State of the Royal Navy in July 1914'.

28 *CO*, p. 489.

29 Rowe, 'Their Lordships Regret', p. 45, quoting Beatty.

30 Rowe, 'Discipline and Morale', pp. 56–63, 75–8, 95–6, 115–17, 157–62, 174–6, 180–81 and 227–31. Carew, *Lower Deck*, pp. xix and 72–90. Rowe, 'Their Lordships Regret'. Wolz, *Das lange Warten*, pp. 233–6 and 239–40. McKee, *Sober Men*, pp. 44–7 and 60–70. Chamberlain, 'Stokers', pp. 229–33 and 295–7. Baynham, *Men from the Dreadnoughts*, pp. 169–70. Wells, *Social History*, pp. 86–8. Knock, *Clear Lower Deck*, pp. 40–41.

31 Rowe, 'Discipline and Morale', pp. 204–5, 218 and 221–3. Chamberlain, 'Stokers', pp. 282–4. Sears, 'Discipline'.

32 McKee, *Sober Men*, pp. 73–84, 94–8. Chamberlain, 'Stokers', p. 140. Lavery, *Able Seamen*, pp. 191–4. Knock, *Clear Lower Deck*, pp. 95–106.

33 Chamberlain, 'Stokers', pp. 136–40. McKee, *Sober Men*, pp. 67–70 and 84–8. Romans, 'Internal Economy', pp. 79–86. Knock, *Clear Lower Deck*, pp. 147–8 and 156–63. Arthur, *True Glory*, p. 209.

34 Spector, *At War at Sea*, p. 102. Knock, *Clear Lower Deck*, pp. 174–6. McKee, *Sober Men*, pp. 142–8.

35 Dawson, *Flotillas*, p. 131.

36 Wolz, *Das lange Warten*, p. 185 n.408.

37 Wolz, *Das lange Warten*, p. 196. Frewen is quoting Captain Ronald Hopwood's poem 'The Laws of the Navy' (itself quoting Psalm 139).

38 Till, 'Letters from the First World War', p. 288.

39 Wolz, *Das lange Warten*, pp. 157–60, 183–5. Rowe, 'Discipline and Morale', p. 88. Romans, 'Selection and Early Career', p. 192. Goldrick, *After Jutland*, p. 19. Watson, 'Bloody Orkney'.

40 McKee, *Sober Men*, pp. 89–90. Rowe, 'Discipline and Morale', pp. 86 and 90. *DSF* V, 130. Wolz, *Das lange Warten*, pp. 155 and 161–3. Baynham, *Men from the Dreadnoughts*, pp. 192–3. Goldrick, *After Jutland*, p. 19.

41 Wolz, *Das lange Warten*, p. 162.

42 Lavery, *Shield of Empire*, pp. 196–8. Wolz, *Das lange Warten*, pp. 162, 186–7, 190 and 200–202. *DSF* II, 173 and 431. Gordon, *Rules of the Game*, pp. 23–6 and 30.

43 Arthur, *The True Glory*, p. 100, quoting Brian de Courcy-Ireland of the destroyer *Pellew*.

44 Owen, *Plain Yarns*, p. 71.

45 W. G. Carr, *By Guess and by God: The Story of the British Submarines in the War* (London, 1930), p. 184.

46 McKee, *Sober Men*, pp. 71–3. Compton-Hall, *Submarines and the War at Sea*, pp. 22–7. Chamberlain, 'Stokers', pp. 239–54. Philpott, *Air and Sea Power*, p. 66. Tall, 'Waging the Undersea War', pp. 44–51.

47 Howlett, *British Naval Aviation*, pp. 79, 82, 85, 102 and 199–205. *BND*, pp. 922–8. Layman, *Naval Aviation*, pp. 79–80 and 105–6. Till, *Air Power and the Royal Navy*, pp. 111–13 and 119. Roskill, *Naval Air Service*, pp. 319–20. Haslop, *Early Naval Air Power*, pp. 109–12.

48 Reading any modern British newspaper will confirm this at once – but even before the First World War the army was much the bigger service, and journalists struggled to get naval terminology right.

49 Lavery, *Hostilities Only*, p. 21. J. M. Winter, *The Great War and the British People* (London, 2nd edn., 2003), pp. 72–3. It is notoriously difficult to square statistics taken from different sources.

50 Lavery, *Able Seamen*, pp. 200–204. Lavery, *Shield of Empire*, pp. 202–3. Howarth, *Royal Navy's Reserves*, pp. 24–52. Wells, *Social History*, p. 113. Bowen, *Royal Naval Reserve*, pp. 109–23. Compton-Hall, *Submarines and the War at Sea*, pp. 53–5.

51 Rowe, 'Their Lordships Regret', p. 56.

52 Moretz, *Thinking Wisely*, p. 268. Grove, 'Seamen or Airmen?', pp. 21–4. Abbatiello, *Anti-Submarine Warfare*, p. 176. Jefford, *Observers and Navigators*, p. 66. Pulsipher, 'Aircraft and the Royal Navy', pp. 47–9. Layman, *Naval Aviation*, pp. 197–9. Beattie, *Churchill Scheme*, p. 45. Till, *Air Power and the Royal Navy*, pp. 29–30.

53 Roberts, *WRNS in Wartime*, p. 45.

54 Stanley, *Women and the Navy*, p. 62.

55 Mason, *Britannia's Daughters*, pp. 2–33. *ODNB* sv Elvira Laughton Mathews. Fletcher, *WRNS*, pp. 13–24. Wells, *Social History*, p. 117. Stanley, *Women and the Navy*, pp. 53–75 and 87. Watson, *Fighting Different Wars*, pp. 162–70. *BND*, pp. 982–3. Roberts, *WRNS in Wartime*, pp. 3–4 and 33–61.

Chapter 18

1 Friedman, *Naval Firepower*, pp. 63 and 101–6. Friedman, *Naval Weapons of World War I*, p. 25. Brooks, *Dreadnought Gunnery*, pp. 217–18.

2 Gordon, *Rules of the Game*, p. 591.

3 Friedman, *Great War at Sea*, pp. 150–51. Strachan, *First World War*, pp. 435–6. Goldrick, *Before Jutland*, pp. 219 and 300–302, and 'Learning to Fight'. Friedman, *Naval Firepower*, pp. 107–9. Brooks, *Dreadnought Gunnery*, pp. 218–27.

4 Friedman, *Naval Weapons of World War One*, pp. 13, 28 and 30. Friedman, *Naval Firepower*, pp. 282–4 and 289. Brooks, *Jutland*, pp. 80–81, 89–91 and 460–67. D. K. Brown, *Grand Fleet*, pp. 165–71. Campbell, *Naval Weapons*, p. 5. Parkinson, 'Naval Defence Act', pp. 182–4. Halpern, 'French Navy', p. 46. Hodges, *Big Gun*, pp. 31–2. Garcia y Robertson, 'Failure of the Heavy Gun', p. 553. Sumida, *Naval Supremacy*, pp. 46–8, 300–301, 306–9 and 312–16. Brown and Campbell, 'Attack and Defence', p. 23. Evans, *Arming the Fleet*, pp. 168–70 and 181–5. Campbell, *Jutland*, pp. 368–74.

N. A. Lambert, 'Our Bloody Ships'.
Hartcup, *War of Invention*, pp. 52–4.
Cordite MD of 1901, the British
propellant in use 1914–17, was largely the
work of the biochemist and Zionist
leader Chaim Weizmann, whose
contribution to British naval gunnery is
not widely known.
5 Friedman, *Naval Firepower*, pp. 61–3 and
289–91. Friedman, *Naval Weapons of
World War One*, pp. 30–34. Friedman,
British Battleship II, p. 198. Sumida, 'A
Matter of Timing', pp. 126–7. Sumida,
'Quest for Reach', p. 77. Sumida, *Naval
Supremacy*, pp. 300–304. Brown, *Grand
Fleet*, pp. 96, 158–9 and 167–71. Brooks,
Jutland, pp. 454–67. K. I. McCallum, 'A
Little Neglect: Defective Shell in the
Royal Navy 1914–1918', *JNE* XXXIV
(1993), pp. 408–17.
6 Sumida, *Naval Supremacy*, pp. 262–5 and
290–94. D. K. Brown, *Grand Fleet*, pp.
48–9, 97–8 and 164. Friedman, *British
Battleship* II, pp. 133–8 and 170–80. N. A.
Lambert, 'Our Bloody Ships'.
7 Friedman, *British Cruisers* II, pp. 10–12.
D. K. Brown, *Grand Fleet*, pp. 61–7, 101–5
and 160–65. Brown, *Warrior to
Dreadnought*, pp. 183–5. D. K. Brown,
Century of Naval Construction, p. 120.
Friedman, *British Cruisers* II, 36–65.
Rippon, *Engineering* I, 129–31. Griffiths,
Steam at Sea, pp. 140–41 and 149–52.
8 D. K. Brown, *Grand Fleet*, pp. 89–93, 106–
11 and 194–6. Friedman, *British Destroyers*
I, 125–71. D. K. Brown, *Atlantic Escorts*,
pp. 18–21. D. K. Brown, *Century of Naval
Construction*, pp. 120–21.
9 D. K. Brown, *Grand Fleet*, pp. 136–46.
Goldrick, *After Jutland*, pp. 135–6.
Robinson, *Fishermen*, pp. 11–25 and 86.
Greenacre, 'Interwar Planning with the
British Fishing Industry'.
10 D. K. Brown, *Grand Fleet*, pp. 146–54.
D. K. Brown, *Century of Naval
Construction*, p. 111.
11 D. K. Brown, *Grand Fleet*, pp. 111–13.
Layman, *Naval Aviation*, pp. 102–3 and
191–5. Brooks, *Jutland*, pp. 119–20.
Cronin, *Shipboard Aircraft*, pp. 15–16.
Friedman, *British Carrier Aviation*, pp.
26, 37 and 44–6. *BND*, pp. 933–8.
12 Howlett, *British Naval Aviation*, p. 50.
D. K. Brown, *Grand Fleet*, pp. 115–19.
Lavery, *Shield of Empire*, p. 230. Layman,
Naval Aviation, pp. 103–6. *BND*, pp.
933–8. Friedman, *British Carrier
Aviation*, pp. 61–72. Rippon, *Engineering*
I, 186–93. D. K. Brown, 'Design of
Aircraft Carriers', pp. 358 and 363.
Cronin, *Shipboard Aircraft*, pp. 15–16.
The *Ben-my-Chree* was in civilian life the
flagship of the Isle of Man Steam Packet
Company; her Manx name means 'girl of
my heart'.
13 Howlett, *British Naval Aviation*, pp. 53–7.
Brown, *Grand Fleet*, pp. 113–19. Layman,
Naval Aviation, pp. 61–72 and 103–6.
Friedman, *British Carrier Aviation*, pp.
48–66. Rippon, *Engineering* I, 186–93.
14 Evans and Peattie, *Kaigun*, pp. 340–43.
Peattie, *Sunburst*, pp. 88–91 and 102–23.
15 Hone, Friedman and Mandeles,
*American and British Carrier
Development*, pp. 40, 145, 164–5 and 169.
Wildenberg, *Destined for Glory*, p. 3.
Hone and Mandeles, 'Interwar
Innovation in Three Navies', pp. 72–4.
Reynolds, 'Two-Ocean Navy', pp. 181–4.
Roskill, *Naval Policy* I, 467–72.
16 Till, 'Adopting the Aircraft Carrier', pp.
210–11. Coletta, 'Dirigibles', pp. 214–15
and 222–7. Spector, *At War at Sea*, pp.
142–3. Reynolds, 'William A. Moffett', p.
383. Hone, Friedman and Mandeles,
*American and British Carrier
Development*, pp. 58–60. Biddle, *Rhetoric
and Reality*, pp. 128–9 and 143–4.
Friedman, *US Aircraft Carriers*, pp. 13, 51
and 75. Hone and Hone, *Battle Line*, p.
13. Hone and Mandeles, 'Interwar
Innovation', pp. 65 and 73–4. Epstein,
Torpedo, gives a full account of the
USN's difficulties with torpedo
technology.
17 Friedman, *British Battleship* II, pp. 254–
83. D. K. Brown, *Grand Fleet*, pp. 98–100,
and *Nelson to Vanguard*, pp. 19 and 150–
57. D. K. Brown, 'Rearmament', pp. 20–
29. Lenton, *British and Empire Warships*,
pp. 21–2. Peattie, *Kaigun*, pp. 245–8.
Rippon, *Engineering* I, 235.
18 D. K. Brown, *Nelson to Vanguard*, p. 29,
quoting the words of the Controller of

the Navy, Vice-Admiral Reginald Henderson, from the diary of Sir Stanley Goodall, Director of Naval Construction.

19 D. K. Brown, *Grand Fleet*, pp. 172–83. D. K. Brown, *Nelson to Vanguard*, pp. 32–5. Friedman, *British Battleship* II, 254–97. Lenton, *British and Empire Warships*, pp. 25–6. Jordan, *Warships after Washington*, pp. 74–82. The failure of the underwater protection of the *Prince of Wales* of this class is addressed in Ch. 25.

20 Friedman, *British Cruisers* II, 96–141. Lenton, *British and Empire Warships*, pp. 46–54. D. K. Brown, *Nelson to Vanguard*, pp. 68–71. There were four County classes, all developments of a common design.

21 Friedman, *British Battleship* II, 338–40. Brown, *Nelson to Vanguard*, pp. 74–5 and 155–6. Brown, *Design and Construction* I, 112.

22 Friedman, *British Destroyers* I, 200.

23 Friedman, *British Destroyers* I, 178–99, 201, 207 and 218. Friedman, *Network-Centric Warfare*, pp. 41–2.

24 Friedman, *British Destroyers* I, 178–81. Jordan, *Warships after Washington*, pp. 264–7.

25 Friedman, *British Destroyers* I, 198–202. Brown, *Nelson to Vanguard*, pp. 101–3. Kingcome, 'Marine Engineering', especially pp. 106–18. Goodall, *Diary*, p. 38. Bean, 'Production of Naval Machinery'. Skelton, 'Marine Engineering'. Cf. Ch. 12.

26 Whitley, *German Destroyers*, pp. 22–5. Heinrich, *Warship Builders*, pp. 84–5. Johannesson, *Offizier in kritischer Zeit*, pp. 72–81; quoted p. 81: 'Die *Hermes* war ein reiner "Arbeitszerstörer". Er war nicht störanfällig und brauchte geringere Werftliegezeiten. Um möglichst schnell zum Einsatz zu kommen, lehnte ich alle Änderungen ab . . .'

27 D. K. Brown, *Nelson to Vanguard*, pp. 210–11. McBride, 'Electric Battleship.' Raper, 'Main Machinery'. Griffiths, *Steam at Sea*, p. 176. Friedman, *British Destroyers* I, 201–27. Wildenberg, *Destined for Glory*, p. 119. Heinrich,

Warship Builders, pp. 74–85. By December 1941, 89 new US destroyers of the *Somers*, *Craven*, *Sims*, and *Benson-Livermore* Classes had been launched.

28 On Henderson see *ODNB* and D. K. Brown, *Nelson to Vanguard*, p. 201.

29 Clemmesen, 'The Armoured Commerce Raider', pp. 317–19. Gemzell, *Raeder, Hitler und Skandinavien*, pp. 32–9. Maiolo, *Cry Havoc*, pp. 92–3. Maiolo, *Navy and Nazi Germany*, pp. 13–48. Maiolo, 'Admiralty Technical Intelligence'. Messerschmitt, 'Foreign Policy and Preparation for War', pp. 602–3. Rahn, 'Strategy and Armament'. Rahn, 'German Navies', pp. 31–4. Bräckow, *Marine-Ingenieuroffizierkorps*, pp. 197–200. Friedman, *British Battleship* II, 250–53.

30 Bräckow, *Marine-Ingenieuroffizierkorps*, pp. 183–8, 195–6 and 205–6. Whitley, *German Destroyers*, pp. 22–4.

31 Friedman, *British Destroyers* II, 22–48. Of the 'Tribals' the Canadian *Haida* and her half-sister the Polish *Błyskawica* are still afloat.

32 Friedman, *British Destroyers* I, 211–12, and II, 22–7 and 58–67. Brown, *Nelson to Vanguard*, pp. 121–6. Brown, *Atlantic Escorts*, pp. 85–9. Brown, *Design and Construction* II, 38–45.

33 Brown, *Nelson to Vanguard*, pp. 8–12 and 20–24. Friedman, *Naval Firepower*, pp. 187–91 and 203–5. Sumida, 'Quest for Reach', pp. 77–8. Sumida, 'The Best Laid Plans'. Hartcup, *War of Invention*, pp. 120–23. Friedman, *U.S. Aircraft Carriers*, p. 43.

34 Sumida, 'Quest for Reach', pp. 312–16. Sumida, 'The Best Laid Plans', pp. 686 and 693–4. Friedman, *Naval Firepower*, pp. 137 and 272–3.

35 Campbell, *Naval Weapons*, pp. 202–3 and 207. Evans and Peattie, *Kaigun*, pp. 266–72. The name 'Long Lance' for the Type 93, widely cited in English sources but unknown to the Japanese, was apparently invented by the imaginative Professor Samuel E. Morison of Harvard, official historian of the USN.

Chapter 19

1 Paine, *Wars for Asia*, p. 78.
2 Offer, *Agrarian Interpretation*, pp. 383–92
   and 400. Smith, 'Strategy of the
   Economic Weapon', pp. 272–4. Mary
   Cox, *Hunger in War and Peace: Women
   and Children in Germany, 1914–1924*
   (New York, 2019).
3 Lavery, *Shield of Empire*, pp. 268–71.
   Simpson, *Anglo-American Naval
   Relations* I, 484–5. Roskill, *Naval Policy* I,
   73–8 and 94–5. Doepgen, *Deutsche
   Marinepolitik*, pp. 10–12, 17–18 and 25–
   34. Bird, *Weimar*, pp. 62–4. Rahn,
   'German Navies', pp. 29–30. Rüger, *Great
   Naval Game*, pp. 255–7. Thomas, *German
   Navy*, pp. 26–7. Strictly, the Germans
   were allowed six pre-Dreadnought
   battleships plus two in reserve, but the
   manpower limits in the treaty meant that
   they never had more than four in
   commission.
4 O'Brien, *Naval Power*, pp. 136–52.
   Simpson, *Anglo-American Naval
   Relations* I, 488–94. Ranft, *Beatty Papers*
   II, 125–7. McDonald, 'Washington
   Conference', p. 191. Louis Halewood,
   'Internationalising Sea Power: Ideas of
   World Order and the Maintenance of
   Peace, 1890–1919' (Oxford D.Phil. thesis,
   2019), Ch. 7, has an important new
   interpretation of these negotiations.
5 Goldstein, 'British Official Mind', pp. 67–
   9. O'Brien, *Naval Power*, pp. 149–52 and
   155–7. Simpson, *Anglo-American Naval
   Relations* I, 492. Roskill, *Naval Policy* I, 51.
6 O'Brien, *Naval Power*, pp. 153–65 (quoted
   p. 162).
7 Ferris, 'Symbol and Substance', pp. 69–
   72. Bell, 'Ten Year Rule'. McDonald,
   'Washington Conference', p. 191. Neilson,
   'Unbroken Thread', p. 63. O'Brien, *Naval
   Power*, pp. 153–5 and 161–2. Roskill,
   Naval Policy I, 222–5. Ranft, *Beatty
   Papers* II, 127. Gibson, *Britain's Quest for
   Oil*, pp. 135–6. Doepgen, *Deutsche
   Marinepolitik*, pp. 50–65.
8 Asada, *Mahan to Pearl Harbor*, pp. 56–92
   and 99–100. Ferris, 'The Last Decade',
   pp. 131–4. Ferris, 'Armaments and Allies',
   p. 258. McDonald, 'Washington

Conference', pp. 191–210. Evans and
   Peattie, *Kaigun*, pp. 192–200. O'Brien,
   Naval Power, pp. 158–83. G. Kennedy,
   'Navy and Imperial Defence', pp. 135–6.
   Roskill, *Naval Policy* I, 300–330. Mackay,
   Balfour, pp. 309–32. *BND*, pp. 772–7.
   Birn, 'Washington Naval Conference', pp.
   170 and 176. Gibson, *Britain's Quest for
   Oil*, pp. 162–3. Joel Blatt, 'The Parity that
   Meant Superiority: French Naval Policy
   towards Italy at the Washington
   Conference, 1921–22, and Interwar
   French Foreign Policy', *French Historical
   Studies* XII (1981), pp. 223–48. Kowark,
   'La marine française et la Conférence de
   Washington'. Doepgen, *Deutsche
   Marinepolitik*, pp. 82–3. Sondhaus, *Great
   War at Sea*, p. 369. Maurer, 'Lloyd
   George and Naval Mastery'. Simpson,
   Anglo-American Naval Relations II, 38–
   52, prints key documents.
9 Ferris, 'Armaments and Allies', pp. 255–
   56, quoting a 1920 War Office
   memorandum.
10 Bell, *Churchill and Sea Power*, pp. 86–7
   and 95–6. Bennett, *Policy under Lloyd
   George*, pp. 110–13. Ferris, 'Symbol and
   Substance', p. 63.
11 Asada, *Mahan to Pearl Harbor*, pp. 63–5.
   Ferris, 'Armaments and Allies', p. 258.
12 Paine, *Japanese Empire*, p. 84.
   McKercher, 'Disarmament to
   Rearmament', pp. 23 and 28–30. Ferris,
   'The Last Decade', pp. 127–34. Bell,
   Seapower and Strategy, p. 2. Baer, *One
   Hundred Years of Sea Power*, pp. 98–102.
   Birn, 'Washington Naval Conference', pp.
   168 and 176. Tracy, *Naval Defence of the
   Empire*, p. 249. Offer, *Agrarian
   Interpretation*, pp. 374–6. Gibson,
   Britain's Quest for Oil, pp. 162–3.
13 Kuramatsu, 'Inter-War Naval Limitation',
   p. 130 (quoted). Tracy, *Naval Defence of
   the Empire*, pp. 249 and 317.
14 Roskill, *Naval Policy* I, 144–5.
15 Lavery, *Able Seamen*, pp. 241–5. Roskill,
   Naval Policy I, 131–80. E. Anderson,
   'Undeclared Naval War'. Jeffery, *MI6*, pp.
   175–7. Bennett, *Cowan's War*. Agar, *Baltic
   Episode*, especially pp. 30–31, 80–88 and
   152–79. Dawson, *Sound of the Guns*, pp.
   151–75. *BND*, p. 838. Clayton, *British*

Empire, pp. 510–11. Carew, *Lower Deck*, pp. 110–13. McShane, *Harding Diaries*, pp. 66–7. Ferris, 'Appeasement and the Archive on Intelligence', pp. 541–2.

16 Roskill, *Naval Policy* I, 181–203. Halpern, *Mediterranean Fleet, 1919–1929*, pp. 3–11, 121–32 and 289–301. Ferris, *Behind the Enigma*, pp. 134–40. When surnames were introduced in Turkey in 1935, Kemal adopted the name Atatürk, 'Father of the Turks', by which he is generally referred to today.

17 Bell, *Seapower and Strategy*, pp. xv, 2–13. Ferris, 'Symbol and Substance', pp. 56–60.

18 Biddle, *Rhetoric and Reality*, pp. 13–17, 27–33. Till, 'Competing Visions'. Robertson, *RAF Strategic Bombing Doctrine*, pp. 20–29. M. Smith, *British Air Strategy*, pp. 44–7 and 61–3. Overy, 'Allied Bombing'.

19 Till, 'Competing Visions', pp. 60–63 and 67.

20 Note that 'seaplane' (Churchill's coinage) meant the same as the American 'floatplane', while the American 'seaplane' was the British 'flying boat'.

21 N. Jones, *Beginnings of Strategic Air Power*, pp. xi–xii. It is only the official histories sponsored by the Air Ministry that omit Coastal Command: the naval volumes sponsored by the Admiralty give it full credit for its contribution, especially to the Atlantic campaigns.

22 Robertson, *RAF Strategic Bombing Doctrine*, pp. 38–51, 67–70, 81, 85–7 and 97–103. M. Smith, *British Air Strategy*, pp. 27, 32–3, 72. Biddle, *Rhetoric and Reality*, pp. 87–93. Ferris, 'Catching the Wave', p. 165. Ferris, 'Achieving Air Ascendancy', pp. 23–5. N. Jones, *Beginnings of Strategic Air Power*, pp. 24–59. Franklin, *Anti-Submarine Capability*, pp. 103–9.

23 Sumida, 'Reimagining the History', pp. 171–3.

24 Till, *Air Power and the Royal Navy*, p. 161, quoting the then Air Commodore Robert Brooke-Popham.

25 Weir, 'Naval Air Warfare', pp. 18–21, 26 and 34–6. Till, *Air Power and the Royal Navy*, pp. 98–9 and 118–19. Jefford,

Observers and Navigators, pp. 66 and 123. Hone and Mandeles, 'Interwar Innovation', pp. 65–9. Roskill, *Naval Policy* I, 472.

26 Boyd, *Eastern Waters*, p. 5. Ferris, 'The Last Decade', pp. 136–9. Ferris, 'Symbol and Substance', pp. 59–64. Bell, *Churchill and Sea Power*, pp. 108–11 and 153–4. Bell, *Seapower and Strategy*, pp. 49–56. Bell, 'Ten Year Rule'. Bell, 'Churchill and the Limits of British Power', pp. 51–64. Neilson, 'Defence Requirements Sub-Committee', pp. 653–4.

27 Randolph Churchill and Martin Gilbert, *Winston S. Churchill* (London, 1966–81, 8 vols. in 21) V, 76.

28 Ferris, 'The Last Decade', pp. 125–7 and 143–4. Asada, *Mahan to Pearl Harbor*, pp. 111–24. Marriott, *Treaty Cruisers*, pp. 160–62. Kuehn, 'The General Board and the London Naval Treaty', pp. 18–22. Bell, *Churchill and Sea Power*, pp. 112–18. Bell, 'London Naval Conference', p. 49. Friedman, *British Cruisers* II, 113. Epstein, 'Historians and the Geneva Naval Conference', pp. 132–4. Maurer, 'London Conference', pp. 231 and 236–7. Kuramatsu, 'Cecil, Churchill and Geneva', and 'Geneva Naval Conference'. Fanning, 'Coolidge Conference'. Roskill, *Naval Policy* I, 422–34. O'Brien, 'US Naval Development', p. 154. O'Brien, *Naval Power*, pp. 183–97, blames Britain rather than the US for the failure of the conference. Simpson, *Anglo-American Naval Relations* II, 66–90, and Tracy, *Attack on Maritime Trade*, pp. 157–65, print documents.

29 Bell, 'London Naval Conference', pp. 53–5. Maurer, 'London Conference', pp. 231 and 236–7. O'Brien, *Naval Power*, pp. 198–202. Bell, 'Ten Year Rule', pp. 1098 and 1120–24. *BND*, pp. 777–9. Ferris, 'The Last Decade', pp. 137–40. Neilson, '"Unbroken Thread"', p. 76. Neilson, 'Defence Requirements Sub-Committee', pp. 654–5.

30 Kuehn, 'The General Board and the London Naval Treaty', pp. 35–6. Bell, 'London Naval Conference' (quoted p. 59). Friedman, 'Naval Strategy and Force Structure', pp. 210–19. Maurer,

'London Conference', pp. 229–31 and 245–9. Bell, *Churchill and Sea Power*, pp. 135–7. Friedman, *British Cruisers* II, 142–56. O'Brien, *Naval Power*, pp. 210–20. Tracy, *Belligerent Rights*, pp. 292–7. Tracy, *Attack on Maritime Trade*, pp. 157–63. Ferris, 'The Last Decade', pp. 154–7. Babij, 'The Second Labour Government and British Maritime Security'. Babij, 'Defence of the British Empire', pp. 178–9. G. C. Kennedy, 'London Naval Conference', pp. 150–51 and 161. Baer, *One Hundred Years of Sea Power*, pp. 114–17. Simpson, *Anglo-American Naval Relations* II, 98–149. McKercher, 'Belligerent Rights in 1927–1929'. Allard, 'Naval Rearmament', pp. 37–40.

31 Ferris, 'Information Superiority'. Asada, 'London Conference'. Asada, *Mahan to Pearl Harbor*, pp. 132–57.

32 O'Brien, *Naval Power*, pp. 213–20. G. C. Kennedy, 'London Naval Conference', pp. 154–5. McKercher, 'Great Britain Pre-Eminent', pp. 764–6. Neilson, 'Unbroken Thread', p. 79. Baer, *One Hundred Years of Sea Power*, pp. 113–17. Tracy, *Attack on Maritime Trade*, pp. 162–5. The British had less than double the cruiser tonnage, because their ships were on average smaller than those of the USN.

33 B. L. McKercher, *The Second Baldwin Government and the United States, 1924–1929* (Cambridge, 1984), p. 174.

34 Maurer, 'London Conference', p. 229. O'Brien, *Naval Power*, pp. 213–16.

Chapter 20

1 Reynolds, *Long Shadow*, pp. 129–34. Barnhart, *Japan Prepares for Total War*, pp. 32–3. Paine, *Wars for Asia*, pp. 13–17 and 44–6. Paine, *Japanese Empire*, pp. 97–103 and 112–17. Iguchi, *Demystifying Pearl Harbor*, pp. 40–46.

2 Bell, *Churchill and Sea Power*, pp. 133–40. McKercher, 'The Politician-Strategist', pp. 104–11. Roberts, *Churchill*, pp. 340–74. Ferris, 'Appeasement and the Archive on Intelligence', pp. 553–5.

3 McKercher, 'Disarmament to Rearmament', p. 31.

4 A sub-committee because it was at sub-ministerial level, consisting of the three Chiefs of Staff, the Cabinet Secretary Sir Maurice Hankey, and the Parliamentary Under-Secretaries of the Treasury and Foreign Office.

5 Bell, 'Ten Year Rule', p. 1126. Friedman, 'Naval Strategy and Force Structure', pp. 201–9. G. Kennedy, 'Principles of Anglo-American Strategic Relations', pp. 34–9. Bell, *Churchill and Sea Power*, pp. 141–3. Babij, 'Defence of the British Empire', pp. 179–82. Gordon, *Seapower and Procurement*, pp. 106–12. Murray and Millett, 'Net Assessment on the Eve of World War II', p. 11. Christman, 'Roosevelt and Strategic Assessment'. Utley, 'Roosevelt and Naval Strategy'. Simpson, *Anglo-American Naval Relations* II, 249.

6 Maiolo, *Cry Havoc*, pp. 92–3. Maiolo, *Navy and Nazi Germany*, pp. 13–48. Maiolo, 'Admiralty Technical Intelligence'. Messerschmitt, 'Foreign Policy and Preparation for War', pp. 602–3. Rahn, 'Strategy and Armament'. Rahn, 'German Navies', pp. 31–4. Doepgen, *Deutsche Marinepolitik*, pp. 214–27.

7 Not to be confused (though he sometimes is) with Otto Krüger, an alleged German spy arrested in Britain in 1914; cf. Nicholas Hiley, 'Entering the Lists: MI5's Great Spy Round-Up of August 1914', *I&NS* XXI (2006), pp. 46–76.

8 Maiolo, *Navy and Nazi Germany*, pp. 57–60, 67–72, 147, 168–70, 181, 186–8 and 191. Maiolo, 'The Admiralty and the Anglo-German Naval Agreement'. Scammell, 'Anglo-German Naval Agreement'. Dülffer, *Reichspolitik und Flottenbau*, pp. 392–4 and 413–19. Roskill, *Naval Policy* II, 302–7. Bird, 'German Naval History', pp. 42–52. Bell, *Churchill and Sea Power*, pp. 144–6. Deist, 'Rearmament of the Wehrmacht' I, 451–2 and 460–71. Treue, Möller and Rahn, *Die Gefahren der Tirpitz-Tradition*, pp. 142–3.

9 O'Brien, *Naval Power*, pp. 226–9. Bird, *Raeder*, pp. 113–15, 120–25 and 135. Deist, 'Rearmament of the Wehrmacht', pp.

451–2, 466 and 478–9. Thomas, *German Navy*, p. 179. Hoerber, 'Psychology and Reasoning'. Herwig, 'Failure of German Sea Power', pp. 90–94. Salewski, 'Das maritime Dritte Reich', pp. 113–14. Ottmer, '*Weserübung*', pp. 12–14. Toprani, 'The German Navy's Independent Energy Security Strategy'. Mawdsley, *War for the Seas*, pp. 8–10. Maiolo, *Navy and Nazi Germany*, pp. 58–60 and 72–4. The *Scharnhorst*'s turbines were built by Brown Boveri of Zürich. The new carrier was never formally named, but was referred to as the *Graf Zeppelin*.

10 'Die Leute träumen in Kontinenten': Salewski, 'Das maritime Dritte Reich', p. 114.

11 Darwin, *Empire Project*, pp. 427–9. Gooch, *Mussolini and His Generals*, pp. 267–93. Mallett, 'Breaking Out of Prison', pp. 203–11. Mallett, *Italian Navy*, pp. 14–46 and 74. Ball, *The Bitter Sea*, pp. 4–5. Tracy, *Attack on Maritime Trade*, pp. 176–7. Clayton, *British Empire*, pp. 337–47. Marder, 'Ethiopian Crisis' (revised in *Dardanelles to Oran*, pp. 64–101). Roskill, *Naval Policy* II, 248–63. *BND*, pp. 779–81. Ørvik, *Decline of Neutrality*, pp. 172–94. Omissi, 'The Mediterranean and the Middle East', pp. 4–7. Gordon, 'British Navy, 1918–1945', pp. 166–7. Middlemas and Barnes, *Baldwin*, pp. 876–7, 883–4, 887 and 898–9. Self, *Chamberlain*, pp. 246–50. Davis and Engerman, *Naval Blockades*, pp. 404–5. Ferris, 'Appeasement and the Archive on Intelligence', pp. 553–5 and 558. Hammond, 'British Perceptions of the Italian Navy, 1935–1943'.

12 Clayton, *British Empire*, pp. 349–62. O'Connell, *Influence of Law*, pp. 116–20. Tracy, *Attack on Maritime Trade*, pp. 178–80, and *Belligerent Rights*, pp. 420–29. Mallett, *Italian Navy*, pp. 98–100. Ball, *The Bitter Sea*, p. 14. Santoni, 'La politique navale du fascisme', p. 104. Maiolo, 'Did the Royal Navy Decline?', p. 21. Cable, *Gunboat Diplomacy*, pp. 171–4. Roskill, *Naval Policy* II, 369–91. Tracy, *Belligerent Rights*, pp. 420–29. Franklin, *Anti-Submarine Capability*, pp. 180–81.

De Ninno, *I sommergibili del fascismo*, pp. 226–34.

13 Boyd, *Eastern Waters*, pp. 18–21. O'Brien, *Naval Power*, pp. 230–36. Maiolo, *Navy and Nazi Germany*, pp. 39–40. Berg, 'Protecting National Interests', pp. 209–13 and 220–21. G. Kennedy, *Anglo-American Strategic Relations*, pp. 121–5 and 174–8. Gordon, *British Seapower and Procurement*, p. 172. G. Kennedy, *Imperial Crossroads*, pp. 202–3. Simpson, *Anglo-American Naval Relations* II, 162–212.

14 Maiolo, 'Did the Royal Navy Decline?', pp. 22–3.

15 Bell, *Seapower and Strategy*, pp. 99–105.

16 Bell, *Seapower and Strategy*, p. 109.

17 Peden, *British Rearmament*, p. 163.

18 Bell, *Seapower and Strategy*, pp. 27–47. Boyd, *Eastern Waters*, pp. 25–8 and 48–50. O'Brien, *Naval Power*, pp. 224–5. Maiolo, *Navy and Nazi Germany*, pp. 134–7. Babij, 'Defence of the British Empire', pp. 183–4. Barnett, *Engage the Enemy*, p. 37. Peden, *British Rearmament*, pp. 161–6. Gordon, *Seapower and Procurement*, pp. 233–4 (quoting the First Sea Lord's private secretary). Tracy, *Naval Defence of the Empire*, pp. 560–61.

19 Smith, *British Air Strategy*, pp. 70–76, 135–8, 174, 189, 194, 216 and 224. Biddle, *Rhetoric and Reality*, pp. 125–6. Bialer, *Shadow of the Bomber*, pp. 12–157. Deist, 'Rearmament of the Wehrmacht', pp. 493 and 497. Messerschmidt, 'German Military Effectiveness', p. 241. Posen, *Sources of Military Doctrine*, p. 97. O'Brien, *How the War was Won*, pp. 120–21. Reynolds, *Long Shadow*, pp. 225–6 and 248–9. Edgerton, *Britain's War Machine*, p. 36.

20 'Radar' was a USN neologism, adopted as an Allied standard term in 1943. The British had hitherto used 'RDF' ('Radio Direction-Finding') as a thin cover.

21 Ferris, 'Fighter Defence', and 'Achieving Air Ascendancy'. Moore, *Greenie*, pp. 62–5. Rose, 'Radar and Air Defence'. Brown, *Radar History*, pp. 50–53. Smith, *British Air Strategy*, pp. 46–53 and 78–80. Burns, *Communications*, p. 580. Hugill, *Global Communications*, p. 187.

22 Deist, 'Rearmament of the Wehrmacht', pp. 451–2 and 469–71. Messerschmidt, 'German Military Effectiveness', pp. 232 and 241–2. Maiolo, *Navy and Nazi Germany*, pp. 75–80 and 112–13. Maiolo, 'The Knockout Blow against the Import System', pp. 207–15. Salmon, *Scandinavia and the Great Powers*, pp. 340–41. Brown, *Atlantic Escorts*, pp. 11–13. Bell, *Seapower and Strategy*, pp. 207 and 211–27. Claasen, 'Blood and Iron'.

23 Rössler, *U-Boat*, p. 120; cf. Maiolo, 'Deception and Intelligence Failure', pp. 56–9 (and p. 71, where 'served' should read 'secured'). Friedman, *British Submarines* I, 165 and nn.41 and 43. Hackmann, *Seek and Strike*, p. 126.

24 Herwig, 'Innovation Ignored', pp. 233–40. Maiolo, 'Deception and Intelligence Failure', pp. 56–60 and 65–71. Maiolo, 'The Knockout Blow against the Import System', pp. 211–14 and 227. *BND*, pp. 781–7. Treue, Möller and Rahn, *Die Gefahren der Tirpitz-Tradition*, pp. 21 and 145. Gemzell, *German Naval Planning*, p. 290. Burns, 'Regulating Submarine Warfare'.

25 Hartwig, *Dönitz*, pp. 15–44 and 97–8. Hillmann, 'Der "Mythos" Dönitz'. Maiolo, 'The Knockout Blow against the Import System', and 'Deception and Intelligence Failure', pp. 69–70. Herwig, 'Innovation Ignored', p. 240. Treue, Möller and Rahn, *Die Gefahren der Tirpitz-Tradition*, p. 21. Rust, *Crew 34*, pp. 51 and 121–3. Terraine, *U-Boat Wars*, pp. 161–72. Salewski, 'Das maritime Dritte Reich', pp. 125–9. Koerver, *German Submarine Warfare*, pp. 595–600, prints the 1917 British interrogation report of the captured Oberleutnant Dönitz.

26 Howard, 'A Thirty Years War?', p. 181.

27 Peden, *British Rearmament*, pp. 148–9. Howard, *Continental Commitment*, pp. 125–30. Gibbs, *Grand Strategy* I, 491–529 and 642–9. Mawdsley, *War for the Seas*, pp. 50–51. Gat, 'The Phoney War as Allied Strategy', pp. 11–12. Darwin, *Empire Project*, pp. 489–500. Volkmann, 'National Socialist Economy', I, pp. 356–62.

28 Boyd, *Eastern Waters*, pp. 55–80 (quoted p. 78). Bell, *Churchill and Sea Power*, pp. 153–8. Bell, 'Intelligence Assessments of Japan'. Field, *Strategy in the Far East*, pp. 97–117. Ong, *Operation Matador*, pp. 36–59. Ferris, 'Double-Edged Estimates'. Moretz, *Capital Ship*, pp. 193–6. Omissi, 'The Mediterranean and the Middle East', p. 13. Bell, *Seapower and Strategy*, pp. 59–90. Austin, *Malta*, pp. 1, 34–5, 42, 45 and 53. Santoni, 'La politique navale du fascisme', pp. 110–17. Goldrick, 'Buying Time'. Bell, ' "Singapore Strategy" '. Tracy, *Naval Defence of the Empire*, pp. 466–8 and 475–7. *BND*, pp. 779–81. Anten, *Navalisme nekt Onderzeeboot*, studies Dutch submarine policy.

29 G. Kennedy, 'Symbol of Empire', pp. 43–6. Omissi, 'The Mediterranean and the Middle East', pp. 13–14. Talbott, 'Weapons Development', p. 60. Quinlan, 'Diplomacy, Strategy and the Allocation of Ships', pp. 157–62. Johnson, *Pacific Campaign*, pp. 18–20. Symonds, *World War II at Sea*, p. 184. Leutze, *Bargaining for Supremacy*, pp. 177–85.

30 G. Kennedy, 'Symbol of Empire', pp. 58–60. G. Kennedy, *Imperial Crossroads*, pp. 39–40. Marder, *Old Friends* I, 188–201, and II, 546–7 (quoted I, 197).

31 To H. Chamberlain, 28 Jul 1934, in *The Neville Chamberlain Diary Letters*, ed. Robert Self (Aldershot, 2000–2004, 4 vols.), IV, 94–5.

32 G. Kennedy, *Imperial Crossroads*, pp. 239–47.

33 Ferris, *Behind the Enigma*, pp. 155–9.

34 Gibbs, *Grand Strategy* I, 810. Roberts, *Churchill*, pp. 448–52, 459 and 487.

35 Patalano, 'Feigning Grand Strategy', pp. 163–6. Paine, *Wars for Asia* and *Japanese Empire*.

36 Howard, 'A Thirty Years War?', pp. 172–9. Stegemann, 'Politics and Warfare' II, 7–9. Paine, *Wars for Asia*, pp. 4–11, 92, 123, 127–30, 143–4 and 175. Paine, *Japanese Empire*, pp. 152–3. Murray, 'Net Assessment in Nazi Germany', pp. 86–7. Murray, *Military Adaptation in War*, p. 161 n.26. De Ninno, 'The Italian Navy and Japan'.

37 '. . . mit Anstand zu sterben . . . die Grundlage für eine späteren

Wiederaufbau zu schaffen': Rahn, 'Seestrategisches Denken', p. 73, and Deist, 'Rearmament of the Wehrmacht' I, 480. Bird, *Raeder*, p. 137.

38 Mawdsley, *War for the Seas*, pp. 3–4. Murfett, *Naval Warfare*, pp. 50 and 93. Hessler, *U-Boat War* I, 40–46. Burns, 'Regulating Submarine Warfare', pp. 59–60.

39 O'Brien, *How the War was Won*, p. 125. Milner, *Battle of the Atlantic*, pp. 28–9. Hessler, *U-Boat War* I, 2–10.

40 A. Lambert, 'Sea Power and Strategy, September 1939–June 1940', p. 63. Jeschke, *U-Boottaktik*, p. 73.

41 Stegemann, 'First Phase of the War' II, 177–8. Hessler, *U-Boat War*, I, 7–15. Lavery, *Shield of Empire*, pp. 297–301. Milner, *Battle of the Atlantic*, pp. 31–2. Faulkner, *War at Sea*, p. 10.

42 Stegemann, 'Politics and Warfare' II, 8.

43 Murfett, *Naval Warfare*, pp. 66–7. Levy, *Home Fleet*, pp. 38–9. Stegemann, 'First Phase of the War' II, 175.

44 Clemmesen, 'Armoured Commerce Raider', p. 326. Levy, *Home Fleet*, pp. 41–3. Schuur, 'Unternehmen "Juno"', pp. 17–18. Barnett, *Engage the Enemy*, p. 76.

45 Mawdsley, *War for the Seas*, pp. 25–8. Frieser, 'War in the West', pp. 289–90. Stegemann, 'Politics and Warfare' II, 8. Stegemann, 'First Phase of the War' II, 166–8 and 176–8. Murfett, *Naval Warfare*, pp. 57–60. Roskill, *War at Sea* I, 117–21. Sumida, 'Best Laid Plans', pp. 690–96. Hore, *Habit of Victory*, pp. 352–3. *BND*, No. 466, pp. 840–42. Faulkner, *War at Sea*, pp. 14–15. Roman Kochnowski, 'Bitwa u ujścia La Plata – stare mity, nowe fakty', in *Rola polityki, ekonomii i techniki w działaniach zbrojnych na rzekach, morzach i oceanach*, ed. R. Kochnowski and Jarosław Jastrzębski (Oświęcim, 2019), pp. 101–22, at p. 114.

46 Boog, 'Anglo-American Strategic Air War' VI, 494–5. Claasen, *Hitler's Northern War*, pp. 159–60. Boog, 'Luftwaffe Support of the German Navy', p. 307. Bonatz, *Seekrieg im Äther*, p. 158.

47 A. Lambert, 'Sea Power and Strategy, September 1939–June 1940', p. 66.

Chapter 21

1 Farquharson-Roberts, *War to War*, pp. 26–7, 73 and 101–10. Wells, *Social History*, p. 132. Roskill, *Naval Policy* I, 124–5.

2 Farquharson-Roberts, *War to War*, pp. 26–7, 54, 67–75, 93–4, 102–5 and 113–14. Farquharson-Roberts, 'Officers at Invergordon', pp. 113–15. Romans, 'Selection and Early Career', pp. 214–26.

3 Farquharson-Roberts, *War to War*, pp. 57–60. Franklin, *Anti-Submarine Capability*, p. 37. 'Salt horse' was the old slang for salt beef.

4 So these officers held both the rank and the job of commander, which should be carefully distinguished.

5 Franklin, *Anti-Submarine Capability*, pp. 35–46.

6 Owen, *No More Heroes*, p. 131.

7 Roskill, *Naval Policy* II, 343–4. Romans, 'Selection and Early Career', pp. 152–4. Davison, *Challenges of Command*, pp. 244–5. Hunt, 'Richmond and the Education of the Navy'. McCoy, 'From Selborne to A F O 1/56', pp. 257, 261, 264–5 and 268–70.

8 Romans, 'Selection and Early Career', pp. 153–4.

9 Farquharson-Roberts, *War to War*, pp. 84–5. S. W. Roskill, 'The Navy at Cambridge, 1919–23', *MM* XLIX (1963), pp. 178–93. Roskill, *Naval Policy* II, 341. James Goldrick, 'The Royal Navy's First Mature Age Student? Captain Francis Sandford DSO BA (Oxon) RN (1887–1926)', *MM* XCIII (2007), pp. 352–7.

10 Farquharson-Roberts, *War to War*, pp. 60–66. Lambert, *Admirals*, pp. 383 and 386. *ODNB*. Lavery, *In Which They Served*, p. 276.

11 Romans, 'Selection and Early Career', pp. 47–9. Penn, *Snotty*, pp. 125–9. Penn, *HMS Thunderer*, pp. 69–79. Farquharson-Roberts, *War to War*, pp. 95–7.

12 Farquharson-Roberts, *War to War*, pp. 44–53. Romans, 'Selection and Early Career', p. 207. Beattie, *Churchill Scheme*, pp. 10–11. Penn, *HMS Thunderer*, pp. 73–9 and 89–90.

13 Farquharson-Roberts, *War to War*, pp. 100, 111–13 and 140–41. Farquharson-Roberts, 'Officers at Invergordon', p. 116. Owen, *Plain Yarns*, pp. 64–5. Moretz, *Thinking Wisely*, pp. 98–9.

14 Farquharson-Roberts, *War to War*, pp. 115–19, 141–5 and 169–70. Farquharson-Roberts, 'Officers at Invergordon', p. 112. Wells, *Social History*, p. 126. Roskill, *Naval Policy* I, 118 and 419 n.1. Beattie, *Churchill Scheme*, pp. 63–5. The cadets were aware which of them had been admitted on the reduced pass mark. [*Ex inf.* the author's father, the late Lt-Cdr I. A. Rodger, who was of that generation.]

15 Lavery, *Able Seamen*, pp. 246–55. Carew, *Lower Deck*, pp. 101–41. Carew, 'Invergordon Mutiny', pp. 157–60 and 168–71. *BND*, pp. 986–92.

16 Till, 'Retrenchment, Rethinking, Revival', p. 321, quoting the head of the Naval Personnel Committee.

17 Lavery, *Able Seamen*, pp. 250–58 and 269–70. Carew, *Lower Deck*, pp. 123–6 and 142–54. Carew, 'Invergordon Mutiny', pp. 161–6.

18 Farquharson-Roberts, *War to War*, pp. 119–29 (quoted pp. 128–9). Carew, *Lower Deck*, pp. 105–41.

19 Reynolds, *Long Shadow*, pp. 132–45. Self, 'War Debt Controversy', pp. 286–311.

20 Roskill, *Naval Policy* I, 25, is mistaken here: the First Lord of the Admiralty and his Service colleagues were excluded from the Cabinet not from 1931 to 1935, but only during the first National Government from 27 August to 8 November 1931 (PRO: CAB 23/68 p. 14 and CAB 23/69, p. 2).

21 Bell, 'Invergordon Mutiny', pp. 177 (quoted) and 179. Carew, *Lower Deck*, pp. 154–60. Carew, 'Invergordon Mutiny', pp. 154–60 and 168–76. Roskill, *Naval Policy* II, 90–94. Divine, *Mutiny at Invergordon*, pp. 84–7 and 205–6. Farquharson-Roberts, *War to War*, pp. 131–2. Lavery, *Able Seamen*, pp. 287–94. Pursey, 'Invergordon', pp. 158–9. *The Austen Chamberlain Diary Letters*, ed. Robert C. Self (Camden Soc. 5th S. Vol. 5, 1995), pp. 378–82. A 'wet' canteen served alcohol.

22 Farquharson-Roberts, *War to War*, pp. 117 and 130–33. Bell, 'Invergordon Mutiny', pp. 170–72. Carew, *Lower Deck*, pp. 156–63. Carew, 'Invergordon Mutiny', pp. 170–82. Lavery, *Hostilities Only*, pp. 14–15.

23 Bell, 'Invergordon Mutiny', pp. 180–82. Carew, 'Invergordon Mutiny', pp. 177–84. Pursey, 'Invergordon', pp. 157–64.

24 Carew, 'Invergordon Mutiny', p. 163.

25 Divine, *Mutiny at Invergordon*, p. 142.

26 Farquharson-Roberts, *War to War*, pp. 130–35. Farquharson-Roberts, 'Officers at Invergordon', pp. 118–20. Chamberlain, 'Stokers', pp. 298–304. Carew, *Lower Deck*, pp. 154–71. Lavery, *Able Seamen*, pp. 288–97. Bell, 'Invergordon Mutiny'. *BND*, pp. 993–1001. Carew, 'Invergordon Mutiny', pp. 167–88. Pursey, 'Invergordon'. Roskill, *Naval Policy* II, 122–3. *ODNB* sv Sir Frederick Field.

27 Farquharson-Roberts, *War to War*, p. 134. Arthur, *Lost Voices*, p. 174, quoting Able Seaman Ginger Le Breton of the *Dorsetshire*. 'Going aft' meant to the captain's stern cabin (and office); note the carefully phrased request.

28 Whalley, 'Invergordon Mutiny', p. 17. Andrew, *Defence of the Realm*, pp. 162–6.

29 Report by Captain F. B. Watson of HMS *Nelson*, 16 Sep 1931, *BND*, No. 525.

30 Rear-Admiral R. M. Colvin, Chief of Staff Atlantic Fleet, to Captain G. C. Dickens of HMS *Nelson*, 24 Sep 1931, *BND*, No. 526, p. 997.

31 Andrew, *Defence of the Realm*, pp. 162–4 and 360–66. Andrew, *Secret Service*, pp. 360–62. Hinsley, *British Intelligence* IV, 18. Whalley, 'Invergordon Mutiny'. Carew, *Lower Deck*, pp. 156–67. Carew, 'Invergordon Mutiny', pp. 173–88. *BND*, pp. 993–1001. Clayton, *British Empire*, pp. 512–13. Smith, *Mountbatten* I, 77–8.

32 Bell, 'Invergordon Mutiny', p. 175, quoting a Confidential Fleet Order of 1918.

33 Edward H. Locker, *Memoirs of Celebrated Commanders* (London, 1832) sv Collingwood, pp. 8–9.

34 Wells, *Social History*, pp. 146–7. Lavery, *Hostilities Only*, pp. 14–15.

35 Farquharson-Roberts, *War to War*, pp. 150–51 and 154, quoting A F O 2315 of 1932.
36 Farquharson-Roberts, *War to War*, p. 154.
37 Farquharson-Roberts, *War to War*, pp. 54–6, 121–4, 135, 157 and 162–3. Halpern, *Keyes Papers* II, 239. Roskill, *Naval Policy* II, 125–6 and 457–60. Farquharson-Roberts, 'Officers at Invergordon', pp. 109–11. Prysor, 'Morale', pp. 24–37. Owen, *Plain Yarns*, pp. 64–5. Romans, 'Leadership Training', pp. 180–87. Wells, *Social History*, pp. 146–7. Goldrick, 'Life at Sea', pp. 238–42; cf. Rory O'Conor, *Running a Big Ship on Ten Commandments* (Portsmouth, 1937). The *OED* 's first citation of 'leadership' in the sense of 'capacity to lead' dates from 1870, but it was not widely current until the twentieth century.
38 Pridham's 'Memorandum on Discipline', quoted by Le Bailly, *The Man around the Engine*, p. 107.
39 Romans, 'Leadership Training', pp. 186–9.
40 Hamilton, 'Operational Intelligence Centre', p. 311, quoting the senior N I D officer Frank Birch in 1919 (cf. Beesly, *Very Special Intelligence*, p. 6, with Beesly's italics).
41 *ODNB* sv Monsell. Farquharson-Roberts, *War to War*, pp. 157–9 and 180–81. Chatfield, *The Navy and Defence*, p. 185. Roskill, *Naval Policy* II, 131–2, 191–3 and 243. Note on the Divisional System from the memoir of Admiral J. H. Godfrey, in *BND*, No. 524, pp. 993–4. Lavery, *Hostilities Only*, pp. 14–15. Lavery, *In Which They Served*, pp. 9–44. Owen, *No More Heroes*, pp. 134–5. For the eighteenth-century origins of the divisional system see Rodger, *Wooden World*, pp. 216–17.
42 Carew, *Lower Deck*, pp. 172–87.
43 Carew, *Lower Deck*, pp. 174–6. Farquharson-Roberts, *War to War*, pp. 136–7, 160 and 175–7. Roskill, *Naval Policy* II, 32–4 and 191–3.
44 Lavery, *All Hands*, pp. 70–71. Lavery, *River Class*, pp. 131–5.
45 Lavery, *Able Seamen*, pp. 259–65. Lavery, *River Class*, pp. 131–5. Lavery, *All Hands*, p. 38. McKee, *Sober Men and True*, pp. 102–3.

46 McKee, *Sober Men and True*, pp. 92–3.
47 McKee, *Sober Men and True*, pp. 48–64 and 81–4. Personal acquaintance with many officers of this generation. Leading Telegraphist C. R. Thomas in *BND*, pp. 1001–2, is an example of the discontented minority.
48 Owen, *Plain Yarns*, p. 57.
49 McKee, *Sober Men and True*, p. 225, quoting Mechanician Raymond Dutton.
50 McKee, *Sober Men and True*, pp. 29–33 and 67–70.
51 McKee, *Sober Men and True*, p. 67, quoting Plumber Jock Batters.
52 McKee, *Sober Men and True*, p. 223.
53 Crang, 'Women's Auxiliary Services', pp. 354–6 (quoted p. 355). Roberts, *WRNS in Wartime*, pp. 65–8. Roskill, *Naval Policy* II, 245 and 459–60. Stanley, *Women and the Navy*, pp. 88–90. Mrs Mathews had been christened Elvira by her Spanish mother, but in England she usually signed as 'Vera'.
54 Mathews, *Blue Tapestry*, p. 60.
55 Roberts, *WRNS in Wartime*, pp. 76–9 and 86–93.
56 Mathews, *Blue Tapestry*, p. 29.
57 Roberts, *WRNS in Wartime*, pp. 4, 67, 76–93 and 100–106. Brown, *Fittest of the Fit*, pp. 14–18. Mason, *Britannia's Daughters*, pp. 34–44. Mathews, *Blue Tapestry*, pp. 51–3, 58, 83 and 117–18. Stanley, *Women and the Navy*, pp. 91–3. Fletcher, *WRNS*, pp. 28–30. Wildish, 'Western Approaches', p. 54.
58 Lavery, *Churchill's Navy*, pp. 184 and 224–5.
59 Brown, *Fittest of the Fit*, pp. 14–18. Stanley, *Women and the Navy*, pp. 115–17. Mathews, *Blue Tapestry*, pp. 81–2.
60 Mathews, *Blue Tapestry*, p. 202.
61 Mathews, *Blue Tapestry*, pp. 58 and 136 (quoted p. 136). Roberts, *WRNS in Wartime*, pp. 84–5 and 110–11.
62 Roberts, *WRNS in Wartime*, pp. 92–100 and 109.

Chapter 22

1 Ehrman, *Cabinet Government*, pp. 55–63, 84–6 and 109–10. C. I. Hamilton, 'Policy-Makers and Financial Control', pp.

380–82, 388–9 and 395. Edgerton, *Warfare State*, p. 147. Ferris, *Behind the Enigma*, pp. 134–40.

2 Till, *Air Power and the Royal Navy*, pp. 119–21 (quoted p. 119). Moretz, *Capital Ship*, pp. 41–6.

3 Till, *Air Power and the Royal Navy*, p. 124.

4 Till, *Air Power and the Royal Navy*, pp. 119–25.

5 Scott and Hughes, *War Production*, pp. 151–6.

6 Till, *Air Power and the Royal Navy*, p. 193.

7 Till, 'Airpower and the Battleship', p. 109.

8 Ranft, *Beatty Papers* II, 349.

9 Middlemas and Barnes, *Baldwin*, pp. 321–4. Ranft, *Beatty Papers* II, 223 and 228. Roskill, *Naval Policy* I, 234–9, 267–8 and 390–94. Till, *Air Power and the Royal Navy*, pp. 32–48. Lady Trenchard and Lady Keyes were sisters.

10 Till, 'Airpower and the battleship', p. 108. The paralysis of President Harding and his government must have had something to do with this.

11 Ranft, *Beatty Papers* II, 228.

12 Self, 'War Debt Controversy', pp. 283–5. Ferguson, 'Traditional Finance and "Total" War', pp. 420–27, gives somewhat higher figures.

13 Otte, ' "It's What Made Britain Great" ', pp. 17–18. Reynolds, *Long Shadow*, pp. 132–40. McKercher, 'Great Britain Pre-Eminent', pp. 756–62 and 775–8.

14 D. M. Kennedy, *Over Here*, p. 99. This is the voice of a rural Southerner, always strong in the Democratic Party, but his overtly anti-Semitic tone could have been heard just as frequently among Republicans.

15 D. M. Kennedy, *Over Here*, pp. 340–47. Self, 'War Debt Controversy', pp. 285–311.

16 Findlay and O'Rourke, *Power and Plenty*, pp. 447–58. Reynolds, *Long Shadow*, pp. 238–40. Tooze, *Wages of Destruction*, pp. 14–28 and 52–8. Peden, *British Rearmament*, p. 86. Self, 'War Debt Controversy', pp. 284–91.

17 Reynolds, *Long Shadow*, pp. 141–50. Peden, *British Rearmament*, p. 76.

18 Gordon, *Seapower and Procurement*, p. 195.

19 Peden, *British Rearmament*, pp. 36–48, 62–6, 71–85, 96–103, 113–17, 151, 156 and

164–5. Peden, *Arms, Economics and British Strategy*, pp. 139–40. Edgerton, *Warfare State*, p. 152. Lindberg and Todd, *Anglo-American Shipbuilding*, pp. 80–85. Edgerton, *England and the Aeroplane*, p. 75. Gordon, *Seapower and Procurement*, pp. 82–5, 133, 145–8, 161–4, 193–5, 202–14, 235 and 285. Reader, *Weir*, pp. 193–4.

20 Miller, *Planning and Profits*, pp. 17–23. Miller, 'Clydeside Cabal', pp. 341–2. Gibbs, *Grand Strategy* I, 777–9. Gordon, *Seapower and Procurement*, pp. 52–62, 100, 129, and 232–3. Peden, *British Rearmament*, p. 30. Reader, *Weir*, pp. 191–4.

21 Lynch, 'The Peace Movement and British Arms Policy'. Gordon, *Seapower and Procurement*, pp. 52–62 and 129–33. Miller, *Planning and Profits*, pp. 83–107 and 143–7.

22 Gibson, *Britain's Quest for Oil*, pp. xix, 54–70, 87–94, 136–42, 180–82 and 194–5. Brown, 'Fuel Supplies', pp. 141–5, 176, 197, 204–5 and 212–13. Tracy, *Naval Defence of the Empire*, pp. 282–5 and 290–95.

23 Miller, *Planning and Profits*, pp. 47–67, 106–7 and 162–3. Miller, 'Clydeside Cabal', p. 346 (quoted). Gordon, *Seapower and Procurement*, pp. 82–5. Peebles, *Warshipbuilding*, pp. 111, 136 and 142–3.

24 Miller, *Planning and Profits*, p. 70.

25 Gordon, *Seapower and Procurement*, p. 77; and 'Naval Procurement', pp. 108–13. Miller, *Planning and Profits*, pp. 69–76, 92–105, 117–21, 132, 136–7 and 162–71. Miller, 'Clydeside Cabal'. Smith, 'The Choice "Between Lithgow and Hitler" ', pp. 52–3. Slaven, *British Shipbuilding*, p. 102. Lindberg and Todd, *Anglo-American Shipbuilding*, pp. 76–83. Johnston and Buxton, *Battleship Builders*, pp. 38–9. *ODNB* sv Lithgow Family. Published figures for the NSS scheme vary somewhat.

26 Gordon, *Seapower and Procurement*, pp. 123–4, 136–7 and 165–7. Anderson, 'British Re-Armament'. Peden, 'The Navy and Grand Strategy', pp. 149–57. Peden, *British Rearmament*, p. 8.

27 Peden, *British Rearmament*, pp. 32–5, 57–8 and 65–79 (quoted pp. 32 and 55).

Peden, *Arms, Economics and British Strategy*, p. 121.

28 Gordon, *Seapower and Procurement*, p. 139, referring to the Abyssinian Crisis of 1935.

29 Peden, *British Rearmament*, pp. 17–18.

30 Peden, *British Rearmament*, p. 31.

31 The fullest study of the Bullock affair is in Richard A. Chapman, *Ethics in the British Civil Service* (London, 1988), pp. 142–85. See also Roskill, *Naval Policy* II, 203–5; O'Halpin, *Warren Fisher*, pp. 206–15; Roskill, *Hankey* III, 209; *BND*, pp. 943–9; and Cross, *Swinton*, pp. 151–2.

32 Reader, *Weir*, pp. 202–3 and 226–7.

33 Peden, *British Rearmament*, p. 28.

34 O'Halpin, *Warren Fisher*, p. 242.

35 *ODNB* sv Newall (quoted). Cross, *Swinton*, p. 137. O'Halpin, *Warren Fisher*, p. 242. Sebastian Ritchie, 'A Political Intrigue Against the Chief of the Air Staff: The Downfall of Air Chief Marshal Sir Cyril Newall', *W&S* XVI (1998), pp. 83–104, offers a half-hearted defence of Newall.

36 Roskill, *Naval Policy* II, 221–2. Peden, *British Rearmament*, pp. 19–20. Roskill, *Hankey* III, 206–7. Reader, *Weir*, p. 270. Grove, *Royal Navy since 1815*, p. 172. O'Halpin, *Warren Fisher*, p. 244.

37 Weir, 'Naval Air Warfare', pp. 270–72, quoting PRO: ADM 116/3725.

38 To Sir John Simon, 28 Jul 1937, in Peden, *British Rearmament*, p. 32.

39 Cross, *Swinton*, pp. 181–7. Till, *Air Power and the Royal Navy*, pp. 49–53. Reader, *Weir*, pp. 270–79. *ODNB* sv Cunliffe-Lister. Middlemas and Barnes, *Baldwin*, pp. 816 and 1020–21. Roskill, *Naval Policy* II, 395–404. Gibbs, *Grand Strategy* I, 363–70. Meilinger, 'Fleet Air Arm before the War', p. 76 (quoted).

40 Roskill, *Naval Policy* II, 245 (quoted). Jones, *Fleet Air Arm* II, 445–9.

41 Notes by the official historian Professor M. M. Postan (author of *British War Production* [1952]) of an interview with Commodore M. S. Slattery, Chief Naval Representative at the Ministry of Aircraft Production, 25 Jun 1943, in Jones, *Fleet Air Arm* II, 446. Scott and Hughes, *War Production*, pp. 151–6. Roskill, *Naval*

Policy II, 245 and 412. O'Brien, *How the War was Won*, pp. 161–6. *ODNB* sv Portal. Brodhurst, *Churchill's Anchor*, p. 125. Buckley, 'Maritime Air Power', pp. 128–9.

42 Buckley, *RAF and Trade Defence*, pp. 47–52, 81, 91, 95–100, 104, 106, 111–14, 118 and 121–5. Price, *Aircraft versus Submarine*, pp. 23 and 36. Layman, *Naval Aviation*, pp. 82–3. Weir, 'Naval Air Warfare', pp. 198–9.

43 P. Kennedy, 'British "Net Assessment"', p. 29.

44 Robertson, *RAF Strategic Bombing Doctrine*, p. 149.

45 Smith, *British Air Strategy*, pp. 39, 77–80 and 271–80. Biddle, *Rhetoric and Reality*, pp. 122–5 and 178–80. Robertson, *RAF Strategic Bombing Doctrine*, pp. 88–9, 116–19, 126–7, 136–9 and 144–53. Powers, *Strategy without Slide-Rule*, pp. 107–58. Jones, *Beginnings of Strategic Air Power*, pp. 59–87, 110–13, 121–4 and 146–9. *ODNB* sv Londonderry, Ellington and Newall. Cross, *Swinton*, pp. 137 and 150–52.

46 Jeffery, *MI6*, pp. 115 and 210–11. Ferris, 'Whitehall's Black Chamber', pp. 56–8, 63–9 and 73–5. M. Smith, 'The Government Code and Cypher School', pp. 16–21. Andrew, *Secret Service*, pp. 259–62, 294–5, 342 and 352–4. Andrew, 'Secret Intelligence and British Foreign Policy'. Andrew, 'Bletchley Park in Pre-War Perspective'. Grey, 'Bletchley Park', pp. 785–8. 'Ferris, 'Information Superiority', pp. 181–9. Friedman, *Network-Centric Warfare*, p. 264 n.20. Kuramatsu, 'Inter-War Naval Limitation'. *ODNB* sv Sinclair. Headrick, *Invisible Weapon*, pp. 219–21. Ferris, *Behind the Enigma*, pp. 78–80 and 669–70.

47 Headrick, *Invisible Weapon*, pp. 198–212. Headrick and Griset, 'Submarine Telegraph Cables', pp. 571–7. Hugill, *Global Communications*, pp. 29, 49, 84, 94–5, 118–32 and 139–41. Winkler, *Nexus*, pp. 203–5 and 225–78. Hezlet, *The Submarine and Sea Power*, p. 120. Note that 'short wave' and 'high frequency' are terms describing different dimensions of

the same physical phenomena and can be regarded as practically synonymous.

48 Referred to in French, the language in which the Poles communicated with their Western Allies. The Polish is *bomby*, literally meaning 'bombs', adopted as a cover name at a meeting in a Warsaw café where the participants ate ice-cream 'bombs' (Batey, *Dilly*, p. 95).

49 Headrick, *Invisible Weapon*, p. 220. Hinsley, *British Intelligence* III, ii, 945–59.

50 Enigma with a 'Type X adaptor', hence the name. Perhaps 'X' was originally to be read as the Roman numeral, as in 'Station X', the SIS cover name for Bletchley Park.

51 Ferris, 'Whitehall's Black Chamber', pp. 68–70. Ferris, 'The British "Enigma"', pp. 143–64. Erskine, 'Enigma's Security', p. 371. Erskine, 'The Admiralty and Cipher Machines'. McKay and Beckman, *Swedish Signal Intelligence*, pp. 25–30. Headrick, *Invisible Weapon*, pp. 220–21.

52 This is the code known to the USN and generally to historians as JN25.

53 Smith, *The Emperor's Codes*, pp. 5 and 20–61. Chapman, 'Japanese Intelligence', pp. 149–54. Straczek, 'The Empire Is Listening'. Bath, *Tracking the Axis Enemy*, pp. 138–9. Best, *British Intelligence and the Japanese Challenge*, pp. 93–104. Marder, *Old Friends* I, 356. Chapman, '"Higher Realms of Intelligence"', pp. 155–7. Ferris, 'Far East Combined Bureau'. Donovan and Mack, *Codebreaking in the Pacific*, pp. 31–46, 125–6 and 144–5. The British, US and Dutch were all attacking JN25 independently, and sources differ as to who first broke it.

54 Everest-Phillips, 'The Rutland Naval Spy Case'. Ferris, 'A British "Unofficial" Aviation Mission'. Ferris, 'Student and Master', pp. 98–9. Edgerton, *England and the Aeroplane*, pp. 47–8. Peattie, *Sunburst*, pp. 17–20. Arnd Bauerkämper, *Die 'radikale Rechte' in Großbritannien: Nationalistische, antisemitische und faschiste Bewegungen vom späten 19. Jahrhundert bis 1945* (Göttingen, 1991), p. 137. Richard Griffiths, *Fellow Travellers of the Right: British Enthusiasts for Nazi Germany, 1933–9* (London, 1980), pp. 137–40.

55 Ferris, 'Image and Accident', pp. 125–8. Ferris, 'The Road to Bletchley Park', pp. 53–74. Andrew, *Secret Service*, pp. 402–6. Ball, *The Bitter Sea*, p. 15. Friedman, *Network-Centric Warfare*, pp. 22 and 267 n.1. Hinsley, *British Intelligence* I, 298–309. Cernuschi, *Ultra*, pp. 31–51. Giorgerini, *La guerra italiana sul mare*, pp. 105–21, describes the *Supermarina*.

56 Beesly, *Very Special Intelligence*, pp. 11–23 and 258. McLachlan, *Room 39*, pp. 54–9. Roskill, *Naval Policy* II, 388 and 461. Hamilton, 'Operational Intelligence Centre'. Lamb, *Beyond the Sea*, p. 95. Grey, 'Bletchley Park'. Hinsley, 'Bletchley Park', pp. 78–9. Thomas, 'Joint Intelligence System'. *BND*, No. 488, 894–7, outlines the structure of the interwar Naval Staff.

57 Hinsley, *British Intelligence* II, 631–5. Erskine, 'The Admiralty and Cipher Machines', pp. 62–7. Ferris, 'The British "Enigma"', p. 142. Ferris, 'The Road to Bletchley Park', pp. 66–76. Ferris, 'Image and Accident', pp. 125–8. Friedman, *Network-Centric Warfare*, pp. 275–7 n.1. Faulkner, 'Signals Intelligence and the Development of the B-Dienst'.

Chapter 23

1 Kristiansen, 'A German Menace to Norway'. Stegemann, 'Politics and Warfare' II, 8–9 and 15–16. Gemzell, *German Naval Planning*, pp. 278–84, 319–31 and 362–3. Maier, 'German Strategy' II, 184–5 and 191–2. Rahn, 'Seestrategisches Denken', pp. 70–71. Riste, 'War Comes to Norway', pp. 14–25. Claasen, 'Blood and Iron'.

2 'Die Unternehmung verstößt gegen alle Regeln der Seekriegslehre': Ottmer, 'Weserübung', p. 3.

3 'Die britische Überlegenheit an allen Typen war so ungeheuer groß, daß diese eine Operation mit dem Verlust der gesamten Marine enden konnte': Ottmer, 'Weserübung', p. 49, quoting Captain

Theodor Krancke, the principal naval planner of the operation.

4 Moretz, *Towards a Wider War*, pp. 36–45, 53–7, 66–80 and 112–18. Peden, *Arms, Economics and British Strategy*, pp. 199–202. Mawdsley, *War for the Seas*, pp. 32–3. Bell, *Churchill and Sea Power*, pp. 171–8. Salmon, *Scandinavia and the Great Powers*, pp. 320–30, 340–41. Claasen, 'Blood and Iron', pp. 73–80. Stegemann, 'First Phase of the War' II, 185–91. Haarr, *Norway* I, 26–7. Meier, 'German Strategy' II, 185–9.

5 Roskill, *War at Sea* I, 151–3. Moretz, *Towards a Wider War*, pp. 69–71. Ottmer, '*Weserübung*', pp. 27–8. O'Connell, *Influence of Law*, pp. 40–44. Cable, *Gunboat Diplomacy*, pp. 15–25. Riste, 'War Comes to Norway', pp. 18–19 and 40. Ørvik, *Decline of Neutrality*, pp. 216–23. Haarr, *Norway* I, 6–9. Stegemann, 'Politics and Warfare', pp. 15–16. Clemmesen, 'Armoured Commerce Raider', pp. 325–7.

6 Haarr, *Norway* I, 18–58 and 63–5. Levy, *Home Fleet*, pp. 47–53. Faulkner, *War at Sea*, pp. 18–19.

7 Haarr, *Norway* I, 129–41. Ottmer, '*Weserübung*', pp. 114–23 and 128–9. Kersaudy, *Norway 1940*, pp. 59–62 and 68. Munthe-Kaas, 'Campaign in Norway', pp. 38–45. Riste, 'War Comes to Norway', pp. 38–48. Kristiansen, 'A German Menace to Norway'. Johan Jörgen Holst, 'Surprise, Signals and Reaction: The Attack on Norway April 9th 1940 – Some Observations', *Cooperation and Conflict: Nordic Studies in International Politics* I (1965–6), No. 1 for 1966, pp. 31–45. There is now a detailed account of the sinking of the *Blücher* and its consequences: Geirr Haarr and Tor Jørgen Melien, *The Sinking of the Blücher: The Battle of Drøbak Narrows, April 1940* (Barnsley, 2023).

8 Bell, *Churchill and Sea Power*, p. 184 and n.103. Mawdsley, *War for the Seas*, pp. 38–9. Stegemann, 'First Phase of the War' I, 159.

9 Haarr, *Norway* II, 32–8, 69–71 and 175–7. Mawdsley, *War for the Seas*, p. 24. Claasen, *Hitler's Northern War*, pp.

46–52. Clemmesen, 'Armoured Commerce Raider', pp. 326–8. D. Brown, *Campaign in Norway*, pp. 56–7 and 138–41. Lambert, 'Sea Power and Strategy, September 1939–June 1940', pp. 67–8. Kristiansen, 'A German Menace to Norway'. Levy, *Home Fleet*, pp. 50–56. Faulkner, *War at Sea*, pp. 20–21.

10 Haarr, *Norway* I, 273–8 and 309–13. Stegemann, '*Weserübung*' II, 208. Till, *Air Power and the Royal Navy*, p. 16. Friedman, *Naval Firepower*, p. 150. Friedman, *British Carrier Aviation*, p. 213 n.36.

11 *Second World War* (1st edn., 1949) II, 384.

12 Haarr, *Norway* II, 13–15, 32–7, 82–3, 115, 136–7, 202–3, 222 and 237.

13 Haarr, *Norway*, I, 320–50. Levy, *Home Fleet*, pp. 54–6. Faulkner, *War at Sea*, pp. 20–21. The Norwegian pilots were correct about the greater size of German destroyers, which was in most cases of the order of 1,811 tons against 1,350 tons (standard displacement) and five 12.7cm guns against four 4.47in guns, though Warburton-Lee's *Hardy*, as the flotilla leader, displaced 1,450 tons with a fifth gun.

14 Haarr, *Norway* I, 351–71. The circumstances in which Bey met his death in 1943 are sketched in Ch. 30.

15 Haarr, *Norway* II, 190–275. Moretz, *Towards a Wider War*, pp. 155–90.

16 Salmon, *Scandinavia and the Great Powers*, pp. 104 and 118–19. Friedman, *Naval Anti-Aircraft Guns*, pp. 136–7 and 192 nn.16–17.

17 Hinsley, *British Intelligence* II, 631–5. Erskine, 'The Admiralty and Cipher Machines', pp. 62–7. Ferris, 'The British "Enigma" ', p. 142. Ferris, 'The Road to Bletchley Park', pp. 66–76. Ferris, 'Image and Accident', pp. 125–8. Friedman, *Network-Centric Warfare*, pp. 275–7 n.1. Faulkner, 'Signals Intelligence and the Development of the B-Dienst'.

18 Haarr, *Norway* I, 180–84. Salmon, *Scandinavia and the Great Powers*, pp. 94–6.

19 Haarr, *Norway* II, 115, 202, 222 and 292–5.

20 Haarr, *Norway* II, 309 and 318–66.
Schuur, 'Unternehmen "Juno"'. Weir,
'Naval Air Warfare', pp. 142–4, 155–6 and
169–70. Mawdsley, *War for the Seas*, p.
45. Bird, *Raeder*, pp. 150–52. Stegemann,
'Weserübung' II, 217. Levy, *Home Fleet*,
pp. 64–7. Moretz, *Thinking Wisely*, p.
496. Jones, *Fleet Air Arm* I, 181, translates
Admiral Marschall's report of this action:
he opened fire at 27,800 yards.

21 Ottmer, 'Weserübung', p. 145. Herwig,
'Failure of German Sea Power', p. 97.
Gemzell, *German Naval Planning*, p. 414.
Stegemann, 'Weserübung' II, 218, offers
slightly different figures of German
strength, no doubt for a different date.

22 Haarr, *Norway* II, 28. Salmon,
Scandinavia and the Great Powers, pp.
143–7 and 330.

23 Jackson, *Fall of France*, pp. 24–50 and
215–22. Tooze, *Wages of Destruction*, pp.
368–80. Weinberg, 'German Strategy',
pp. 115–16. Frieser, 'War in the West', pp.
290–310. Posen, *Sources of Military
Doctrine*, pp. 86–114. Reynolds, *Long
Shadow*, pp. 253–4. Umbreit, 'Battle for
Hegemony' II, 233, 264 and 290–94. Bell,
Twelve Turning Points, pp. 2–3. The first
citation of the word *Blitzkrieg* in the
OED is from the magazine *War
Illustrated* in October 1939; the concept,
developed after the event, is thoroughly
explored by Karl-Heinz Frieser,
Blitzkrieg-Legende: Der Westfeldzug 1940
(Munich, 1996, 2 vols.), now translated
as *The Blitzkrieg Legend: The 1940
Campaign in the West* (Annapolis, MD,
2005).

24 Roberts, *Churchill*, p. 471, quoting
Harold Nicolson.

25 Roberts, *Churchill*, pp. 494–511, is the
best and most detailed analysis of these
momentous (and in some respects still
obscure) events. Modern historians still
anxious to blame Churchill for
everything include Levy, *Home Fleet*, pp.
62–3, and John D. Fair, 'The Norwegian
Campaign and Winston Churchill's Rise
to Power in 1940', *IHR* IX (1987), pp.
410–37.

26 Roberts, *Churchill*, p. 524, quoting the
MP Bob Boothby.

27 Roberts, *Masters and Commanders*, pp.
35–6, quoting Air Marshal Charles
Portal, then commanding Bomber
Command, and soon afterwards Chief of
the Air Staff.

28 Roberts, *Churchill*, pp. 524–5.

29 Roberts, *Masters and Commanders*, p.
111, quoting Sir George Mallaby of the
War Cabinet Military Secretariat.

30 Roberts, *Churchill*, pp. 490–93. Roberts,
Masters and Commanders, p. 43. Bell,
Churchill and Sea Power, pp. 194–6.
Moretz, *Towards a Wider War*, pp. 235–
45 and 299–301. Mawdsley, *War for the
Seas*, p. 42. Kersaudy, *Norway 1940*, pp.
188–91 and 226.

31 Jackson, *Fall of France*, p. 97. Bell, *Twelve
Turning Points*, p. 7. Weinberg, 'German
Strategy', pp. 115–16. Frieser, 'War in the
West', pp. 308–13. Umbreit, 'Battle for
Hegemony' II, 289–94.

32 Hore, *Habit of Victory*, p. 363, quoting
NMM: TEN/21.

33 Roskill, *War at Sea* I, 216–28 and 603.
Barnett, *Engage the Enemy*, pp. 141–61.
Umbreit, 'Battle for Hegemony' II, 289–
94. Frieser, 'War in the West', pp. 308–13.
Arthur, *1939 to the Present*, pp. 45–6.
Mawdsley, *War for the Seas*, pp. 47–53.
Murfett, *Naval Warfare*, pp. 78–9.
Simpson, *Somerville Papers*, p. 31.
Masson, *Histoire de la Marine* II, 386–8.
Hore, *Habit of Victory*, p. 363, quoting
Captain Tennant. Prysor, *Citizen Sailors*,
pp. 74–82, has a vivid collection of
personal experiences. Faulkner, *War at
Sea*, pp. 22–3, has excellent maps.

34 Umbreit, 'Landing in England' II, 367–9.
Bell, *Churchill and Sea Power*, pp. 199–
201 and 216.

35 Ferris and Mawdsley, 'Battle of Britain',
pp. 316–27. Bennett and Bennett, *Hitler's
Admirals*, pp. 79–82. O'Brien, *How the
War was Won*, pp. 123–4. Bell, *Twelve
Turning Points*, pp. 13–15 and 22–5.
Schreiber, 'The Mediterranean in Hitler's
Strategy in 1940', pp. 245–6. Faulkner,
War at Sea, pp. 34–5. Hellwinkel,
Kriegsmarinestützpunkt Brest, p. 45.

36 O'Brien, *How the War was Won*, pp. 95–
7. Ferris, 'Fighter Defence'.

37 Mallett, *Italian Navy*, p. 176.

38 Brescia, *Mussolini's Navy*, pp. 57–68, is more useful than the official history; Giorgio Giorgerini and Augusto Nani, *Le Navi di Linea Italiane* (Rome, 3rd edn., 1969). Mallett, *Italian Navy*, pp. 155–94. De Ninno, *I sommergibili del fascismo*, pp. 206–7.

39 O'Hara, *Six Victories*, pp. 5, 11, 14–17 and 33–5. Austin, *Malta*, pp. 53 and 131. Bell, *Churchill and Sea Power*, p. 216. Giorgerini, *La battaglia dei convogli*, pp. 63–5. Faulkner, *War at Sea*, pp. 24–5. Robb-Webb, 'Sea Control in Narrow Waters', pp. 36–7. Giorgerini, *La guerra italiana sul mare*, pp. 50–51. Simpson, 'Wings over the Sea', p. 135. Boyd, *Naval Intelligence*, p. 440.

40 O'Hara, *Six Victories*, pp. 5, 11 and 14–17. Austin, *Malta*, pp. 53 and 131. Bell, *Churchill and Sea Power*, p. 216. Faulkner, *War at Sea*, pp. 24–5. Robb-Webb, 'Sea Control in Narrow Waters', pp. 36–7. Giorgerini, *La guerra italiana sul mare*, pp. 50–51. Simpson, 'Wings over the Sea', p. 135. Boyd, *Naval Intelligence*, p. 440. Carne, *Naval Officer*, p. 230.

41 Reynolds, *Long Shadow*, p. 256.

42 Simpson, *Somerville Papers*, p. 110 (quoted). Martin Gilbert, *Second World War* (London, 1989), p. 107.

43 Costagliola, *Darlan*, pp. 46–110. In my view this is the only trustworthy life of the admiral. Coutau-Bégarie and Huan, *Darlan*, is useful for detail but quasi-fascist in sympathy. Masson, *Histoire de la Marine* II, 386–8 and 415, is always worth reading, but he was an eccentric historian and an unrepentant fascist. Dupont and Taillemite, *Les guerres navales françaises*, pp. 282–9, give a temperate account of the Franco-British negotiations. Other narratives of the Mers-el-Kébir tragedy are: Marder, 'Oran', Coutau-Bégarie and Huan, *Mers-el Kébir*, the unfinished posthumous study by David Brown, *Road to Oran*, Philippe Lasterle, 'Could Admiral Gensoul Have Averted the Tragedy of Mers el-Kebir?', *JMilH* LXVII (2003), pp. 835–44, and Canuel, *French Sea Power*, pp. 16–28. Faulkner, *War at Sea*,

pp. 28–9, has as usual an excellent map. Simpson, *Cunningham Papers* I, 57–8 and 86–97, covers the Alexandria negotiations.

44 Mawdsley, *War for the Seas*, p. 115.

45 Giorgerini, *La guerra italiana sul mare*, pp. 170–84. Faulkner, *War at Sea*, pp. 30–31. Schreiber, 'Mediterranean Area, 1939–1940' III, 255–6. Mawdsley, *War for the Seas*, pp. 111–22. Hinsley, *British Intelligence* I, 208–9. Cernuschi, *Ultra*, pp. 45–6. Simpson, *Cunningham Papers* I, 58–9 and 99–111. Ball, *The Bitter Sea*, pp. 44 and 52. Till, *Air Power and the Royal Navy*, p. 179. Knox, *Hitler's Italian Allies*, pp. 158–9. Mallett, *Italian Navy*, pp. 184–5. Gooch, *Mussolini's War*, pp. 137–8 and 405–10. Bagnasco, *In guerra sul mare*, pp. 102–7, prints some excellent photographs of this action.

46 'Del resto ciò doveva cosituire una della pratiche dimostrazioni dell'illusione del bombardamento in quota; illusione che doveva in seguito ricevere ben altri colpi su tutti i fronti e presso tutti i belligeranti': Giorgerini, *La guerra italiana sul mare*, p. 192, quoting General Giuseppe Santoro, Deputy Chief of Staff of the *Regia Aeronautica*.

47 [La Marina] 'mancato la sua ora decisiva': De Ninno, *Fascisti sul mare*, p. 235. Carne, *Naval Officer*, pp. 242–62. Cf. Ch. 22, p. 391

48 Stegemann, 'Politics and Warfare' II, 25–8. Schreiber, 'Mediterranean Area, 1939–1940' III, 187–222. Clemmesen, 'Armoured Commerce Raider', p. 327.

49 Mawdsley, *War for the Seas*, pp. 71–3. Benbow, ' "Menace" to "Ironclad" ', pp. 771–90. Masson, *Histoire de la Marine* II, 421 and 432. Barnett, *Engage the Enemy*, pp. 203–5. Campbell, *Naval Weapons*, p. 280. Canuel, *French Sea Power*, pp. 30–31. Garzke and Dulin, *Battleships* II, 86–93, provides details of the complicated damage the *Richelieu* sustained in the July and September attacks.

50 Goodall, *Diary*, p. 64. D. K. Brown, *Atlantic Escorts*, pp. 61–5. Connell, *Jack's War*, p. 83.

51 Leutze, *Bargaining for Supremacy*, pp. 43–4, 78–9, 86–90 and 115–26. Symonds,

World War II at Sea, pp. 111–14 and 179–80. Ørvik, *Decline of Neutrality*, p. 205.

52 Boyd, *Naval Intelligence*, p. 441. Simpson, *Cunningham Papers* I, 141–6.

53 Boyd, *Naval Intelligence*, pp. 441–2. Weir, 'Naval Air Warfare', pp. 202–3 and 258–9. Caravaggio, 'Attack at Taranto', pp. 111–12. Howlett, *British Naval Aviation*, p. 27. English readers should remember that there are almost no tides in the Mediterranean.

54 Gooch, *Mussolini's War*, pp. 451–2. Jones, *Fleet Air Arm* I, 314–29. Simpson, *Cunningham Papers* I, 174–90. Caravaggio, 'Attack at Taranto', pp. 107–10. Giorgerini, *La guerra italiana sul mare*, pp. 213–28. Map in Faulkner, *War at Sea*, pp. 42–3; excellent photographs in Bagnasco, *In guerra sul mare*, pp. 129–33, 162, 189 and 207.

55 Giorgerini, *La guerra italiana sul mare*, pp. 230–43. Simpson, *Cunningham Papers* I, 195–203. Mawdsley, *War for the Seas*, pp. 121–2. Hammond, 'British Perceptions of the Italian Navy, 1935–1943', p. 825. Gooch, *Mussolini's War*, p. 156. Maps in Faulkner, *War at Sea*, pp. 44–5. Santarini, 'Gunfire Dispersion', analyses the ballistics.

56 Hague, *Allied Convoy System*, pp. 126–7 and 131–6. Blair, *Hitler's U-Boat War* I, 424–5.

57 Levy, *Home Fleet*, pp. 77–81. Mawdsley, *War for the Seas*, pp. 99–101. Clemmesen, 'Armoured Commerce Raider', p. 327. Faulkner, *War at Sea*, pp. 38–9 and 46–7, has excellent maps of German raiders' and warships' cruises in 1940.

Chapter 24

1 Sumida, 'Reimagining the History', pp. 167–71. Schurman, *Education of a Navy*, pp. 20–21. Gat, *Origins of Military Thought*, pp. 205–7. Rodger, 'Change and Decay', pp. 41–2. Wolz, *Das lange Warten*, pp. 279–80. Offer, 'Bounded Rationality', p. 192. Rodger, 'Culture of Naval War'.

2 Bell, *Seapower and Strategy*, p. 126.

3 Paul M. Kennedy, 'The Relevance of the Prewar British and American Maritime Strategies to the First World War and its Aftermath, 1898–1920', in *Maritime Strategy and the Balance of Power*, ed. Hattendorf and Jordan, pp. 165–88. Ross, 'French Net Assessments'. Hobson, *Imperialism at Sea*, p. 79. *DSF* III, 263–8. Rodger, 'Culture of Naval War', pp. 112–13. MacGregor, 'Operational Lessons', pp. 608–10. Sumida, 'Best Laid Plans', pp. 683–96. Field, *Strategy in the Far East*, pp. 123–71. Maiolo, 'The Knockout Blow against the Import System', p. 206. Moretz, 'Legacy of Jutland'.

4 Herwig, 'Strategische Unbestimmtheitsrelation', and 'Influence of Mahan', pp. 70–72. Hagan, 'Apotheosis of Mahan'. Simpson, *Anglo-American Naval Relations* I, 61, 64 and 195–9. Halpern, *World War I*, pp. 357–69. Rahn, 'Seestrategisches Denken', pp. 58–64. Rödel, *Tirpitz*, pp. 12–20. Goldrick, *After Jutland*, pp. 160–62. Bönker, *Militarism*, pp. 6–7.

5 'Durch den geistig-seelischen Zusammenbruch der Heimat und der Etappe': Michael Salewski, 'Menschenführung in der deutschen Kriegsmarine 1939–1945', in *Menschenführung in der Marine* (Herford, 1981), pp. 83–103, quoting Karl Dönitz at p. 99.

6 Bird, 'German Naval History', quoted pp. 46–7. Bird, *Raeder*, pp. 36–45, 62–6, 83–5, 94–5 and 100–109. Jones, 'War Culture and the Imperial German Navy', pp. 249–72, and Sondhaus, *German Submarine Warfare*, pp. 221–2, on the German naval 'death squad' *Organisation Consul*.

7 Schröder, *Die U-Boote des Kaisers*, p. 17. Fischer, *Admiral des Kaisers*, pp. 231 and 244–5. Offer, 'Bounded Rationality'. Lundeberg, 'German Naval Critique'. Herwig, *Naval Officer Corps*, pp. 203–14. Wolz, *Das Lange Warten*, pp. 362–5. Bönker, *Militarism*, pp. 308–10. Bird, *Raeder*, pp. 34–45. Bird, 'German Naval History'. Dülffer, 'German Naval Policy, 1920–1939', p. 160. Deist, *The Wehrmacht and German Rearmament*, pp. 71–9, quoted p. 79 ('autistic thinking'). Salewski, 'Das maritime Dritte Reich'.

Gemzell, *Raeder, Hitler und Skandinavien*. Gemzell, *Organization, Conflict, and Innovation*, pp. 278–84.

8 Baer, *One Hundred Years of Sea Power*, p. 182, quoting a calculation by Captain Edward L. Beach, USN (which must surely rest on a narrow definition of the word 'fought', applying it to battles alone).

9 Asada, 'Japanese Navy's Road to Pearl Harbor'. Coox, 'Japanese Military Establishment'. Evans and Peattie, *Kaigun*, pp. 131–2, 212 and 515. Hone and Hone, *Battle Line*, pp. 74–5 and 84–8. T. C. Hone, 'Evolution of the U.S. Fleet, 1933–1941', pp. 69–72. Vlahos, *The Blue Sword*, pp. 70–71, 107–12 and 136–49. Spector, *Eagle against the Sun*, pp. 478–9.

10 Bönker, *Militarism*, pp. 175–7, 187–99, 235–40 and 289–91. Karsten, *Naval Aristocracy*, pp. 204–9 and 355–6. O'Connell, *Sacred Vessels*, pp. 122–5 and 192–4. Leutze, *Bargaining for Supremacy*, pp. 12–13. Kuehn, 'The General Board and the London Naval Treaty', pp. 10–15. Hone and Hone, *Battle Line*, pp. 126–33. O'Brien, 'US Naval Development', pp. 151–2. O'Brien, *Naval Power*, pp. 16–17. Christman, 'Roosevelt and Strategic Assessment', pp. 224–5. Spector, 'Military Effectiveness of the U.S.', p. 79. Hattendorf, 'Changing American Perceptions', n.56.

11 O'Brien, 'US Naval Development', p. 151. Hone and Hone, *Battle Line*, pp. 173–5. T. C. Hone, 'Evolution of the U.S. Fleet, 1933–1941', pp. 78–80. O'Brien, *Naval Power*, pp. 18–20. Roskill, *Naval Policy*, II, 468–9. Reardon, '"Gun Club" Mentality', pp. 537–9. Felker, *Testing American Sea Power*, pp. 79–85. Epstein, *Torpedo*, tells the unhappy story of the USN and the torpedo.

12 Baer, *One Hundred Years of Sea Power*, pp. 120–21 and 128. Johnson, *Pacific Campaign*, pp. 17, 25, 35–8. Utley, 'Roosevelt and Naval Strategy', pp. 50–56. Paine, 'Allied Embargo of Japan', pp. 75–86. Iguchi, *Demystifying Pearl Harbor*, pp. 79–91. Spector, 'Military Effectiveness of the U.S.', p. 82. Asada, *Mahan to Pearl*

Harbor, pp. 259–60. Symonds, *World War II at Sea*, pp. 193–4. Casey, 'Roosevelt', pp. 217–18. Murray and Millett, 'Net Assessment on the Eve of World War II', p. 11. Christman, 'Roosevelt and Strategic Assessment', pp. 216–17, 224–7 and 238–41. Tracy, *Attack on Maritime Trade*, pp. 181–90. Roberts, *Masters and Commanders*, p. 128.

13 Paine, *Wars for Asia*, pp. 4–11, 92, 103 and 127–47. Paine, *Japanese Empire*, pp. 121, 133–4, 138 and 143. Coox, 'Japanese Net Assessment', p. 266. Aizawa, '"Anti-British" Strategy', pp. 145–8. G. Kennedy, *Imperial Crossroads*, pp. 80–82. Murfett, 'Living in the Past', p. 92.

14 Asada, 'Japanese Navy's Road to Pearl Harbor', pp. 152–72. Barnhart, 'Roosevelt to Pearl Harbor', pp. 42–5. Ong, *Operation Matador*, pp. 60–76, 100–101 and 123–5. Best, *British Intelligence and the Japanese Challenge*, p. 139. Aizawa, '"Anti-British" Strategy', pp. 144–6. Evans and Peattie, *Kaigun*, p. 451. Marder, *Old Friends* I, 45.

15 W. R. Louis, 'American Anti-Colonialism and the Dissolution of the British Empire', *International Affairs* LXI (1985), pp. 395–420 at pp. 399–404. Leutze, *Bargaining for Supremacy*, pp. 259–62. Mawdsley, *War for the Seas*, p. 165.

16 Milner, *Battle of the Atlantic*, pp. 71–81, 'Atlantic War' and 'Anglo-American Naval Co-operation'. Glover, 'Manning and Training', pp. 199–201. Spector, *At War at Sea*, pp. 229–38. Gardner, *Decoding History*, p. 148.

17 Milner, *Battle of the Atlantic*, pp. 53–4. Lyon, 'British Order of Battle', p. 266. Barnett, *Engage the Enemy*, pp. 259–65. Faulkner, *War at Sea*, pp. 62–3. Neitzel, 'Deployment of the U-boats', p. 277. Hellwinkel, *Kriegsmarinestützpunkt Brest*, p. 142.

18 J. D. Brown, *Carrier Operations*, pp. 50–51. Hammond, 'British Aero-Naval Co-operation', pp. 234–41.

19 To Sir Dudley Pound, 18 Sep 1941, in Simpson, *Cunningham Papers* I, 509.

20 Simpson, *Cunningham Papers* I, 516.

21 To Sir A. Willis, 20 Nov 1941, in Simpson, *Cunningham Papers* I, 533.

22 Milner, *Battle of the Atlantic*, pp. 53–4.
Lyon, 'British Order of Battle', p. 266.
Barnett, *Engage the Enemy*, pp. 259–65.
Faulkner, *War at Sea*, pp. 62–3. Neitzel,
'Deployment of the U-boats', p. 277.
Hellwinkel, *Kriegsmarinestützpunkt
Brest*, p. 142. Goodall, *Diary*, p. 77.

23 A. Smith, *Fairey*, p. 222.

24 Postan, *War Production*, pp. 137–8, 160–
61 and 322–5. Scott and Hughes, *War
Production*, pp. 291–6. Peden, *Arms,
Economics and British Strategy*, pp. 189–
90. Robertson, 'Beaverbrook and the
Supply of Aircraft'. *ODNB* sv
Beaverbrook. A. Smith, *Fairey*, quoted p.
223. Brown, *Duels in the Sky*, pp. 146–7.
Postan, Hay and Scott, *Design and
Development of Weapons*, p. 135. Hobbs,
'Naval Aviation, 1930–2000', pp. 75–6.
Rippon, *Engineering* II, 99–100. Jones,
Fleet Air Arm II, 381–2.

25 A. Smith, *Fairey*, pp. 139–45, 160, 176–9,
227–8 and 238–46. *ODNB* sv Fairey.

26 A. Smith, *Fairey*, pp. 230, 254–7. Jones,
Fleet Air Arm II, 5–6 and 270–72.

27 Laurence to Admiral Dreyer, 27 Nov
1942, in Jones, *Fleet Air Arm* II, 269.
'These aircraft' refers to the delayed
Fairey Barracuda.

28 Jones, *Fleet Air Arm* II, 382–3.

29 Hone, Friedman and Mandeles,
Innovation in Carrier Aviation, pp. 102–5,
117–25, and 134–41. Zeitlin, 'Flexibility
and Mass Production', pp. 48–55.
Edgerton, *England and the Aeroplane*,
pp. 69–79. Scott and Hughes, *War
Production*, pp. 77–86 and 151–6.

30 Hague, *Allied Convoy System*, pp. 29–37
and 55–6. Mawdsley, *War for the Seas*,
pp. 93 and 96. Bell, *Churchill and Sea
Power*, pp. 218–19. Milner, *Battle of the
Atlantic*, pp. 53–4. Pugh, 'Military Need',
pp. 35–6. Lavery, *Shield of Empire*, pp.
318–38. Doughty, *Merchant Shipping and
War*, pp. 158–76. Bennett, 'Eclipse of the
Schnellboote', pp. 227–8.

31 Using 'operational U-boats' to translate
the German *Frontboote*, meaning U-boats
available for immediate operations, not
including those on trials or training.

32 Milner, *Battle of the Atlantic*, pp. 31–2.
Mawdsley, *War for the Seas*, p. 89. Anten,

Navalisme nekt Onderzeeboot, pp. 310–
24. J. Bosma, 'Zur U-Bootstaktik', *Marine
Rundschau* XLI (1936), pp. 117–23.
Jeschke, *U-Boottaktik*, pp. 65–6 and 75.
Bennett and Bennett, *Hitler's Admirals*,
pp. 92–5. Hessler, *U-boat War* I, 68–81.
Gardner, *Decoding History*, p. 159. Boog,
'Luftwaffe Support of the German Navy',
pp. 307–8. Claasen, *Hitler's Northern
War*, pp. 175–7. Stegemann, 'Second
Phase of the War' II, 347.

33 Boyd, *Naval Intelligence*, pp. 392–401.
Milner, *Battle of the Atlantic*, pp. 50–51.
Friedman, *Network-Centric Warfare*, p.
33 and n.1, pp. 275–7. Hinsley, *British
Intelligence* I, 403. Todman, *Into Battle*, p.
579. Howse, *Radar at Sea*, p. 79.

34 Boyd, *Naval Intelligence*, pp. 362 and
366–7. Erskine, 'The First Naval Enigma
Decrypts', pp. 42–3. Erskine, 'The
Breaking of Heimisch and Triton'.
Hinsley, *British Intelligence* II, 639, and
III, ii, 945–59. Rohwer, 'Operational Use
of "Ultra" ', pp. 279–80. Steury, 'Sinking
of the *Bismarck*', pp. 219–22.

35 Boyd, *Naval Intelligence*, pp. 402–4.
Milner, *Battle of the Atlantic*, pp. 63–4.
Murfett, *Naval Warfare*, pp. 109–10.
Beesly, *Very Special Intelligence*, pp. 71–2.
Rohwer, 'Operational Use of "Ultra" ', pp.
280–81. *ODNB* sv Baker-Cresswell
(quoted).

36 Mawdsley, *War for the Seas*, pp. 97–98.
Milner, *Battle of the Atlantic*, p. 68.
O'Brien, *How the War was Won*, pp.
241–2. Gardner, *Decoding History*, pp.
171–7. Cf. Hinsley, *British Intelligence*
III, ii, 945–59, printing a revised and
more generous account of the
contribution of pre-war Polish and
French cryptography than that given in
earlier volumes.

37 Mawdsley, *War for the Seas*, pp. 97–8 and
nn.24–6. Milner, *Battle of the Atlantic*, p.
68. Hamer, *Bombers versus Battleships*, p.
205. Schoenfeld, 'Battle of the Atlantic
Committee, 1941'. Friedman, *British
Carrier Aviation*, pp. 178–81. Bell,
'Churchill and the Battle of the Atlantic',
p. 24. Gilbert, *Churchill War Papers* II,
xv–xvii. Bell, *Churchill and Sea Power*,
pp. 218–19.

38 Friedman, *British Carrier Aviation*, pp. 182–3. Hobbs, 'Ship-borne Air Anti-Submarine Warfare', pp. 391–2. Jones, 'Fleet Air Arm and Trade Defense', p. 134. Milner, *Battle of the Atlantic*, pp. 85–6. Heitmann, 'Convoy HG76'. Westwood, *U-Boat War*, pp. 253–4. Jones, *Fleet Air Arm* I, 543–52. Brown, *Carrier Operations*, p. 38.

39 Hague, *Allied Convoy System*, pp. 26–8. Lavery, *Shield of Empire*, pp. 332–41. Franklin, *Anti-Submarine Capability*, pp. 189–95. Hackmann, *Seek and Strike*, pp. 233–4 and 276–7. Rohwer, *Critical Convoy Battles*, pp. 196–7. Kingsley, 'German Maritime Radar'. Franklin, 'Surfaced Night U-Boat Attack', pp. 73–8, shows that Asdic could detect surfaced submarines in favourable conditions.

40 Milner, *Battle of the Atlantic*, pp. 46, 61–4 and 101. Brown, *Radar History*, pp. 62–3, 101–2, 208 and 336. Howse, *Radar at Sea*, pp. 58 and 79. Price, *Aircraft versus Submarine*, pp. 49–53. Jones, *Fleet Air Arm* II, 15–20. Austin, *Malta*, pp. 132 and 135. O'Hara, *Six Victories*, p. 21. Zimmerman, 'Technology and Tactics', pp. 480–81. Jones, *Fleet Air Arm* II, 15–20.

41 Howse, *Radar at Sea*, p. 79. Barnett, *Engage the Enemy*, p. 262. Bonatz, *Seekrieg im Äther*, p. 214. Gardner, *Decoding History*, p. 140. Hessler, *U-Boat War* II, 25–6.

42 Erskine, 'U-Boats, Homing Signals and HFDF', p. 327. Rahn, 'Atlantic and Arctic Ocean' VI, 344. Brown, 'Atlantic Escorts', p. 574, and *Atlantic Escorts*, pp. 71–6. Gardner, *Decoding History*, pp. 105 and 124–8. Rohwer, 'Operational Use of "Ultra"', p. 289. Rohwer, *Critical Convoy Battles*, pp. 187, 193 and 198–9. Bonatz, *Seekrieg im Äther*, p. 214. Erskine, 'Shore H/F D/F'. Boyd, *Naval Intelligence*, pp. 342–3 and 413–14. Zimmerman, 'Technology and Tactics', pp. 480–81.

43 Howse, *Radar at Sea*, pp. 143–4. Moore, *Greenie*, pp. 109–10. Boyd, *Naval Intelligence*, pp. 342–3 and 414. Redgement, 'High-Frequency Direction Finding'. Herwig, 'Germany and the Battle of the Atlantic', pp. 76–9. Gardner,

Decoding History, pp. 60–61, 105, 124–5, 140–41 and 155. Syrett, *The Defeat of the German U-Boats*, pp. 11–12. Rhys-Jones, 'The German System'. Rohwer, 'Operational Use of "Ultra"', pp. 280–81 and 289. Rohwer, *Critical Convoy Battles*, pp. 37 and 197. Llewellyn-Jones, *Anti-Submarine Warfare*, p. 28. Hessler, *U-Boat War* I, 77–86. Friedman, *Network-Centric Warfare*, pp. 27–33. Zimmerman, 'Technology and Tactics', pp. 480–81.

44 Milner, *Battle of the Atlantic*, pp. 55–64. Moore, *Greenie*, pp. 115–17. Howse, *Radar at Sea*, pp. 66–71, 83–7 and 156–7. L. Brown, *Radar History*, pp. 150–56. D. K. Brown, *Atlantic Escorts*, pp. 71–6. Murfett, *Naval Warfare*, p. 166. Edgerton, *Warfare State*, p. 142. Postan, Hay and Scott, *Design and Development of Weapons*, pp. 379–80. Scott and Hughes, *War Production*, p. 115. Burns, *Communications*, pp. 582–93. Friedman, *British Destroyers* II, 104. Redgement, 'High-Frequency Direction Finding'.

45 A good study of the social history of the nineteenth-century Italian navy is Francesco Zampieri, *Marinai con le stellette: Storia sociale della Regia Marina nell'Italia liberale (1861–1914)* (Rome, 2008).

46 De Ninno, *I sommergibili del fascismo*, pp. 14, 45–7, 63–78, 218–20, 232–7 and 244–56. De Ninno, *Fascisti sul mare*, pp. 144–7.

47 'Il tecnico è un uomo di tavolino, ed è un uomo de azione di minor grado di quello che non sia il combattente; il combattente deve avere come qualità eccelente del carattere la serena prontezza di decisione di fronte al pericolo . . .': De Ninno, *Fascisti sul mare*, p. 79, quoting a lecture by Admiral Giuseppe Fioravanzo.

48 De Ninno, *Fascisti sul mare*, pp. 35–8 and 144–8. De Ninno, *I sommergibili del fascismo*, pp. 14, 47 and 63–78. Knox, *Hitler's Italian Allies*, pp. 44–5 and 63.

49 De Ninno, *I sommergibili del fascismo*, pp. 79–84. De Ninno, *Fascisti sul mare*, pp. 179–86 and 206–34. Giorgerini, *La guerra italiana sul mare*, pp. 105–19.

Knox, *Hitler's Italian Allies*, pp. 128–9. There is a company history of Whitehead's original Hungarian firm and its modern Italian descendant: Antonio Casali and Marina Cattaruzza, *Sotto i mari del mondo: La Whitehead 1875–1990* (Rome, 1990).

50 De Ninno, *Fascisti sul mare*, pp. 62 (quoted) and 194–6. De Ninno, *I sommergibili del fascismo*, pp. 247–51. Knox, *Hitler's Italian Allies*, p. 62. Cernuschi, *Marinelettro*, pp. 42–4 and 55–7. Santoni, 'I rapporti tra la Regia Aeronautica e la Regia Marina'.

51 De Ninno, *I sommergibili del fascismo*, pp. 244–56.

52 Paine, *Japanese Empire*, pp. 95–102 (quoted p. 96).

53 Paine, *Wars for Asia*, pp. 7–41, 92–103 and 130. Paine, *Japanese Empire*, pp. 115–21 and 133–8. Asada, 'Road to Pearl Harbor', pp. 137–49 and 159–63. Berg, 'Protecting National Interests', pp. 207–9. Pelz, *Race to Pearl Harbour*, pp. 11–16.

54 Benesch, *Way of the Samurai*, p. 2.

55 Benesch, *Way of the Samurai*, pp. 2–7.

56 Hatashin Omi, 'Japanese Organisational Decision Making in 1941', *International Journal of Management and Decision Making* XII, No. 1 (2012), pp. 69–84.

Chapter 25

1 Roberts, *Churchill*, p. 619.

2 Reynolds, *Anglo-American Alliance*, pp. 63–75, quoted p. 74.

3 Stegemann, 'Second Phase of the War' II, 356–7. Rahn, 'Atlantic and Arctic Ocean' VI, 407–9. Simpson, *Cunningham Papers* I, 303. Mawdsley, *War for the Seas*, pp. 99–101.

4 Hellwinkel, *Kriegsmarinestützpunkt Brest*, pp. 94–8, 104–21, 163–7, 170, 179, 186–8 and 197 (quoted p. 166: 'willig und fleißig', 'einwandfrei'; p. 188 'besonders gut'.) These contemporary German reports are an important corrective to post-war French narratives anxious to avoid the subject of collaboration.

5 Hellwinkel, *Kriegsmarinestützpunkt Brest*, pp. 103–4, 109–11, 116 and 121. Boyd, *Eastern Waters*, pp. 265–6.

6 Gooch, *Mussolini's War*, pp. 169–70. Mawdsley, *War for the Seas*, p. 123. Jones, *Fleet Air Arm* I, 313–14 and 342–56. Simpson, *Cunningham Papers* I, 231. Friedman, *Naval Anti-Aircraft Guns*, pp. 34 and 193. Grove, 'Carrier Fighter Control', p. 363. Murfett, *Naval Warfare*, pp. 100–101. Robb-Webb, 'Sea Control in Narrow Waters', p. 45. Hore, *Habit of Victory*, p. 374. Stegemann, 'Italo-German War in the Mediterranean' III, 661. Santoni and Mattesini, *La partecipazione tedesca*, pp. 28–31. Faulkner, *War at Sea*, pp. 52–3. Hinsley, *British Intelligence* I, 384–5. Ball, *The Bitter Sea*, pp. 67–8. Gray, 'History for Strategists', pp. 10–18.

7 Gooch, *Mussolini's War*, pp. 194–7. Simpson, *Cunningham Papers* I, 232–40. Faulkner, *War at Sea*, pp. 56–7. Murfett, *Naval Warfare*, pp. 103–6. Jones, *Fleet Air Arm* I, 374–91. Lambert, *Admirals*, pp. 400–401. Robb-Webb, 'Sea Control in Narrow Waters', pp. 46–7. Giorgerini, *La guerra italiana sul mare*, pp. 52, 98, 270–322 and 338–40. Stegemann, 'The Italo-German War in the Mediterranean' III, 664–70. Santoni, *Il Vero Traditore*, pp. 71–88 and 301–12. Mattesini, *Il giallo di Matapan*, pp. 21–5, 30, 81–2 and 120–21.

8 Jones, *Fleet Air Arm* I, 412. The telegraphic style is from the original signal.

9 O'Hara, *Six Victories*, pp. 18–20. Prince, 'Crete 1941', pp. 72–83. Vogel, 'German Intervention in the Balkans' III, 513–55. Boyd, *Eastern Waters*, pp. 275 and 131–6. Mawdsley, *War for the Seas*, pp. 124–6. Simpson, *Cunningham Papers* I, 242–52, 370–94, 409–46, 479–80 and 490. Ball, 'Mediterranean and North Africa', p. 380. Weinberg, 'German Strategy', p. 119. Schreiber, 'South-East Europe' III, 454–5. Bennett and Bennett, *Hitler's Admirals*, pp. 156–7. G. Kennedy, 'Sea Denial, Interdiction and Diplomacy', p. 56. Murfett, *Naval Warfare*, p. 115.

10 Roberts, *Churchill*, p. 648.

11 Stegemann, 'Italo-German War in the Mediterranean' III, 671–88. Gooch, 'Mussolini's Strategy, 1939–43', pp. 149–50. O'Hara, *Six Victories*, pp. 15–21.

Simpson, 'Wings over the Sea', pp. 138–44. Roberts, *Churchill*, p. 647. Ball, *The Bitter Sea*, pp. 81–96. Santoni and Mattesini, *La partecipazione tedesca*, p. 61.

12 Simpson, *Cunningham Papers* I, 480, to Rear-Admiral A. Willis, 12 Jun 1941. The Fairey Fulmars were the carrier fighters.

13 Prince, 'Crete, 1941', p. 106.

14 Giorgerini, *La guerra italiana sul mare*, pp. 327–8. Roberts, *Churchill*, p. 647. Austin, *Malta*, p. 120.

15 Gorodetsky, *Grand Delusion*, pp. 6–12, 52–8, 73–5, 89–95, 105, 120–37, 150–72, 179–80, 188–9, 202–32, 281–6 and 311–15. Boyd, *Eastern Waters*, pp. 158–9. Schreiber, 'South-East Europe' III, 454–5. Schreiber, 'Politics and Warfare in 1941' III, 593–617. G. Kennedy, 'Navy and the Role of Malta, 1939–1943', pp. 50–54. Ball, *The Bitter Sea*, pp. 81–5 and 96. Tooze, *Wages of Destruction*, pp. 319–20. Prince, 'Crete, 1941', pp. 75 and 106. Austin, *Malta*, pp. 120–22. Murfett, *Naval Warfare*, pp. 116–17. Roberts, *Masters and Commanders*, p. 127.

16 Milner, 'Atlantic War', p. 7. Mawdsley, *War for the Seas*, pp. 99–101. Levy, *Home Fleet*, pp. 77–85. Grove, *Enemy Attack on Shipping*, pp. 213–27. Steury, 'Sinking of the *Bismarck*', pp. 219–24.

17 Simpson, *Cunningham Papers* I, 303. Steury, 'Sinking of the *Bismarck*', pp. 219–24. Levy, *Home Fleet*, pp. 82–5. Bird, *Raeder*, pp. 177–9. Rahn, 'Atlantic and Arctic Ocean' VI, 413.

18 I follow the analysis of Santarini, *Bismarck and Hood*, pp. 35–109; cf. Friedman, *Naval Firepower*, pp. 137, 149 and 154; Friedman, *British Battleships* II, 318–20 and 348–52; W. J. Jurens, 'The Loss of HMS *Hood* – A Re-examination', *WI* XXIV, No. 2 (1987), pp. 122–61, and David L. I. Kirkpatrick, 'Sink the Bismarck (with luck?)', *Defence and Peace Economics*, VII (2007), pp. 351–6.

19 Jones, *Fleet Air Arm* I, 421–4 and 502–11. *BND*, No. 467, pp. 842–4. Steury, 'Sinking of the *Bismarck*', pp. 226–31. Simpson, *Somerville Papers*, pp. 267–78. Garzke and Duilin, *Battleships* III, 276–309. Santarini, *Bismarck and Hood*, pp. 9,

20 and 36. Levy, *Home Fleet*, pp. 91–103. Rahn, 'Atlantic and Arctic Ocean' VI, 411–18. Oels, 'Der Einsatz des Schlachtschiffe *Bismarck*'. Rodger, *CO*, p. 145, gives the context of Torrington's original remark. Giorgerini, *La guerra italiana sul mare*, p. 119, quotes Admiral Romeo Bernotti: 'In sostanza la flotta italiana era una *fleet in being* che al momento di agire constatava di *non potere*, essenzialmente per manca di cooperazione aerea'.

20 Faulkner, *War at Sea*, pp. 70–71 and 78–9. Grove, *Enemy Attack on Shipping*, pp. 213–27. Rahn, 'Atlantic and Arctic Ocean' VI, 426–31. Most of the uncertainty that surrounded the fate of the *Sydney* has been dispelled since her wreck was located and explored.

21 Mawdsley, *War for the Seas*, pp. 108–10. Murfett, *Naval Warfare*, p. 116. Bird, *Raeder*, p. 177. Hinsley, *British Intelligence* II, 165.

22 To Sir H. Ismay, in Till, 'Competing Visions', pp. 69–70.

23 Murfett, 'Living in the Past', pp. 81–96. Faulkner, *War at Sea*, p. 90, prints a plan of Singapore Naval Base in 1941.

24 Boog, 'Strategic Air War in Europe' VII, 380.

25 Rahn, 'Atlantic and Arctic Ocean' VI, 312. Weinberg, 'German Strategy', pp. 120–21. Gorodetsky, *Grand Delusion*, pp. 179–89, 222–7, 246–7 and 267–318.

26 Stegemann, 'Italo-German War in the Mediterranean' III, 688, 708–9, 712–22, 752–3. Santoni, *Il Vero Traditore*, pp. 130–36. Santoni and Mattesini, *La partecipazione tedesca*, p. 61. Giorgerini, *La battaglia dei convogli*, pp. 133, 136–40, 151–7, 161–2. Simpson, 'Wings over the Sea', pp. 142–4. Ball, *The Bitter Sea*, pp. 109–10 and 122. Giorgerini, *La guerra italiana sul mare*, pp. 450–52 and 483–90. Gooch, *Mussolini's War*, pp. 209–11. Murfett, *Naval Warfare*, pp. 123–4. Faulkner, *War at Sea*, pp. 82 and 95. *Hinsley, British Intelligence* II, 287 and 320–23 (as corrected by O'Hara, *Six Victories*, pp. 41–53).

27 Stegemann, 'Italo-German War in the Mediterranean' III, 714. Hinsley,

British Intelligence II, 325. Ball, *The Bitter Sea*, pp. 109–10. Boyd, *Naval Intelligence*, p. 446.

28 Giorgerini, *La guerra italiana sul mare*, pp. 162, 206–7, 334. Ball, *The Bitter Sea*, p. 108 (quoted) and pp. 109–10. Brown, *Nelson to Vanguard*, pp. 168–9. Jones, *Fleet Air Arm* I, 522–3, 540–41 and 554–9. O'Hara, *Six Victories*, p. 55. Faulkner, *War at Sea*, pp. 76–7. Friedman, *British Carrier Aviation*, pp. 126–7. Goodall, *Diary*, p. 97.

29 O'Hara, *Six Victories*, pp. 70–71. Ball, *The Bitter Sea*, p. 122. Cunningham to Pound, 4 Dec 1941 (quoted) in Simpson, *Cunningham Papers* I, 544. Friedman, *British Battleships* II, 352–353. *Barham* had been bombarding German targets ashore; she was certainly sunk by the torpedoes, but it seems likely that her final explosion was caused by fused HE shells falling out of their bins as the ship turned over.

30 Giorgerini, *La guerra italiana sul mare*, pp. 342–4. Faulkner, *War at Sea*, pp. 94–5. Hinsley, *British Intelligence* II, 323–4. O'Hara, *Six Victories*, pp. 109–13. Hammond, 'British Perceptions of the Italian Navy, 1935–43', p. 826 (quoted).

31 Giorgerini, *La guerra italiana sul mare*, p. 346. Knox, *Hitler's Italian Allies*, p. 134. Hinsley, *British Intelligence* II, 324. Boyd, *Naval Intelligence*, p. 447. Simpson, *Cunningham Papers* I, 66–7 and 73. O'Hara, *Six Victories*, pp. 114–19.

32 Hammond, 'British Perceptions of the Italian Navy, 1935–43', p. 826.

33 O'Hara and Cernuschi, 'Italian Attack on Alexandria'. Friedman, *British Submarines* I, 337. Brescia, *Mussolini's Navy*, pp. 190–91. Hinsley, *British Intelligence* II, 329. Friedman, *British Battleships* II, 356. Stegemann, 'Italo-German War in the Mediterranean' III, 723–4. Giorgerini, *La guerra italiana sul mare*, pp. 223 and 346. Simpson, *Cunningham Papers* I, 551–4. O'Hara, *Six Victories*, pp. 119–27. Friedman, *British Submarines* I, 397 n.8, is worth consulting on the origins of the SLC.

34 Giorgerini, *La guerra italiana sul mare*, pp. 19–21. De Ninno, *Fascisti sul mare*,

pp. ix–xv. Santoni, 'La politique navale du fascisme', pp. 99–100. Not surprisingly, Italian official histories steer clear of this subject, though an Anglo-Italian film, 'The Valiant', was made about it in 1962. Borghese's father really was a prince of the Roman nobility, though as a younger son he himself was not.

35 Cowman, *Dominion or Decline*, p. 246.

36 Mainly Boyd, *Eastern Waters* and *Naval Intelligence*, seconded by Bell, *Churchill and Sea Power*, and the neglected earlier work of Cowman, *Dominion or Decline*, and 'Defence of the Malay Barrier'.

37 There was no post mortem after Pound's death and little hard evidence of how long he had been ill, but his habit of dozing during meetings had been apparent for some time.

38 Boyd, *Eastern Waters*, pp. 252–3, 285–6, 298–305 and 311–13. Faulkner, *War at Sea*, pp. 76–7.

39 Boyd, *Eastern Waters*, pp. 295–8, 311–17 and 338–40. Memorandum by Pound on the loss of the *Prince of Wales* and *Repulse* in *BND*, No. 469, pp. 847–52.

40 Boyd, *Eastern Waters*, pp. 276–98. Christman, 'Roosevelt and Strategic Assessment', pp. 252–3. In reality neither the B-17 nor the B-24 had the range to bomb Japan from Luzon (Johnson, *Pacific Campaign*, pp. 30–31).

41 Boyd, *Eastern Waters*, pp. 287–90.

42 Boyd, *Eastern Waters*, pp. 291–3. Chapman, 'Higher Realms of Intelligence', p. 160. M. Smith, *The Emperor's Codes*, pp. 45–7 and 67–72.

43 Caravaggio, 'Winning the Pacific War'. Reynolds, *Fast Carriers*, pp. 6–8. Ferris, 'Student and Master', p. 116.

44 Ike Nobutaka, *Japan's Decision for War: Records of the 1941 Policy Conferences* (Stanford, 1967), p. 139 (both quotations).

45 Mawdsley, *War for the Seas*, pp. 178–80. Barnhart, 'Roosevelt to Pearl Harbor'. Evans and Peattie, *Kaigun*, pp. 471–86.

46 Mawdsley, *War for the Seas*, pp. 180–83. Caravaggio, 'Winning the Pacific War', pp. 102–3. Evans and Peattie, *Kaigun*, pp. 344–52. Dull, *Imperial Japanese Navy*, pp. 7–8. Reynolds, *Fast Carriers*, pp. 6–9. Hanyok, 'Catching the Fox Unaware', pp.

99–119. Faulkner, *War at Sea*, pp. 88–9, has a detailed plan of the attack. Peattie, *Sunburst*, pp. 144–6, with a diagram of the IJNAF shallow-water air tail.

47 Symonds, *World War II at Sea*, pp. 193–4.

48 Mawdsley, *War for the Seas*, p. 182. Donovan and Mack, *Codebreaking in the Pacific*, pp. 83–6. Caravaggio, 'Winning the Pacific War', pp. 103–11. Johnson, *Pacific Campaign*, pp. 29–31. Coletta, 'Admiral Bellinger and General Martin', pp. 263–9. Boyd, *Eastern Waters*, p. 248. Hanyok, 'Catching the Fox Unaware', pp. 102–7. Peattie, *Sunburst*, pp. 144–6. Haslach, *Nederlands-Indische inlichtingsdienst*, pp. 9–10 and 178–87. The battleship moorings of Taranto and Pearl Harbor were in fact in about the same depth, but the Americans do not seem to have consulted an Italian chart.

49 Dull, *Imperial Japanese Navy*, pp. 8–20. Morison, *Naval Operations* III, 88–127. Faulkner, *War at Sea*, pp. 88–9. Friedman, *US Battleships*, p. 415. I have not attempted a detailed treatment of this action (in which no British forces were directly involved); the most complete narrative, with extensive Japanese sources, is Gordon W. Prange, *At Dawn We Slept: The Untold Story of Pearl Harbor* (New York, 1981).

50 Boyd, *Eastern Waters*, pp. 320–28. Till, *Understanding Victory*, pp. 124–5. Gow, 'Royal Navy and Japan, 1921–1941', pp. 122–4. Bell, 'Singapore Strategy', pp. 614–16 and 621–9.

51 To Cunningham, 20 Oct 1941, and to Sir Dudley North, 11 Dec 1941, in Simpson, *Somerville Papers*, pp. 328 and 341.

52 Brown, *Nelson to Vanguard*, pp. 159–60. Boyd, *Eastern Waters*, pp. 250–53. Murfett, *Naval Warfare*, pp. 139–40. Garzke, Dulin and Denlay, 'Loss of HMS *Prince of Wales*'. Hamer, *Bombers versus Battleships*, pp. 118–36. Marder, *Old Friends* I, 398–443. Peattie, *Sunburst*, pp. 169–70. Brown, *Nelson to Vanguard*, pp. 158–63. Friedman, *British Battleship* II, 302 and 355–6. Friedman, *Naval Anti-Aircraft Guns*, pp. 196–7. Goodall, *Diary*, pp. 99 (quoted), 103–7 and 111–13.

Barnett, *Engage the Enemy*, p. 415, is mistaken in claiming that the Japanese aircraft dropped 24-inch heavy torpedoes, which they could not possibly have lifted. The Japanese Navy's Type 91 17.7-inch air torpedo (Mod.1 with a 300lb warhead, some aircraft carried Mod.2 with the heavier 450lb warhead) was very similar to the British Mk.XII torpedo (the same calibre, though rated as '18-inch'), with a 388-lb warhead (Campbell, *Naval Weapons*, pp. 87 and 209. Evans and Peattie, *Kaigun*, pp. 577–8. Peattie, *Sunburst*, pp. 35–6).

53 Boyd, *Eastern Waters*, pp. 348–408. Mawdsley, *War for the Seas*, p. 188. Murfett, *Naval Warfare*, pp. 139–40. Peattie, *Sunburst*, pp. 169–70. Bell, 'Singapore Strategy', pp. 604–6. Ferris, ' "Ground of our own Choosing" ', pp. 186–9.

54 Mawdsley, *War for the Seas*, pp. 184–5. Roberts, *Churchill*, pp. 692–5. Johnson, *Pacific Campaign*, pp. 91–3. Hamer, *Bombers versus Battleships*, pp. 91–2. Paine, *Wars for Asia*, pp. 197–9. Boyd, *Eastern Waters*, pp. 401–2, 407–8 and 461–3. Dull, *Imperial Japanese Navy*, pp. 28–9, 35–6, 49–54 and 66–104. Marder, *Old Friends* II, 9–10 and 33–4. Harvey, 'Japanese Aviation', p. 189.

55 Bell, *Churchill and Sea Power*, pp. 246–52. Roberts, *Churchill*, pp. 692–3. Paine, *Wars for Asia*, pp. 190–91. Simpson, *Anglo-American-Canadian Naval Relations*, p. 4. This theme has now been taken up by Brendan Simms and Charlie Laderman, *Hitler's American Gamble: Pearl Harbor and the German March to Global War* (New York and London, 2021).

Chapter 26

1 Roberts, *Masters and Commanders*, p. 28. Mawdsley, *War for the Seas*, pp. 189–90. Murfett, *Naval Warfare 1919–1945*, pp. 151–2. Boer, *Loss of Java*, pp. xxi–xxix, 81–6, 162–5, 209–12 and 509. Charrier, 'Japanese Naval Tactics and Strategy', p. 241. Marder, *Old Friends* II, 560–66. Murfett, *Naval Warfare*, pp. 151–2. Paine, *Wars for Asia*, p.

188. Christman, 'Roosevelt and Strategic Assessment', p. 243.

2 'Of the True Greatness of Kingdoms and Estates', in *Essays* (1625).

3 Mawdsley, *War for the Seas*, pp. 204–5. Krebs, 'War in the Pacific', VII, 706–9. Ross, *American War Plans*, pp. 24–30. Lacey, 'Creating an American Strategy', pp. 192–5. Simpson, *Anglo-American Naval Relations* III, 4.

4 Fuquea, 'Task Force One'. Zimm, 'Battleline Strength', pp. 294–6 and 310–14. Blewett, 'Fuel and U.S. Naval Operations'. Wildenberg, *Gray Steel and Black Oil*, pp. 170–73 and 180–81. Wildenberg, *Destined for Glory*, pp. 177–82. Hone, *Learning War*, p. 165. Hone, 'Replacing Battleships with Aircraft Carriers', pp. 56–8. Dull, *Imperial Japanese Navy*, pp. 100–102. Johnson, *Pacific Campaign*, pp. 89–90. Spector, *Eagle against the Sun*, p. 149. IFF is explained in Ch. 29.

5 Simpson, *Somerville Papers*, pp. 357–61. Chapman, 'Higher Realms of Intelligence', pp. 166–8. Baer, *One Hundred Years of Sea Power*, pp. 215–16. Williamson, 'Somerville and Anglo-American Naval Relations', p. 312. Bath, *Tracking the Axis Enemy*, pp. 176–80. M. Smith, *The Emperor's Codes*, pp. 106–11, 128–33 and 166–9. Chapman, 'Higher Realms of Intelligence', pp. 166–8.

6 Boyd, *Eastern Waters*, pp. 363–85. Dull, *Imperial Japanese Navy*, pp. 104–11. Boyd, *Naval Intelligence*, p. 471. Mawdsley, *War for the Seas,* pp. 191–4. Faulkner, *War at Sea*, pp. 114–15. Simpson, *Somerville Papers*, pp. 357–67 and 400–408. Tully and Yu, 'A Question of Estimates', pp. 86–91 and n.11. Marder, *Old Friends* II, 123–5 and 145. Brown, *Carrier Fighters*, pp. 64–6. Chapman, 'Higher Realms of Intelligence', p. 167.

7 Benbow, ' "Menace" to "Ironclad" '. Mawdsley, *War for the Seas*, pp. 278–9. Marder, *Old Friends* II, 88–92. Williamson, 'Somerville and Anglo-American Naval Relations', pp. 312–13. Faulkner, *War at Sea*, pp. 116–17. Roskill, *War at Sea* II, 185–92. Jones, *Fleet Air Arm* II, 106–10.

8 Buckley, *RAF and Trade Defence*, p. 196.

9 Roskill, *War at Sea* II, 148–61. Bennett and Bennett, *Hitler's Admirals*, p. 141. Murfett, *Naval Warfare*, pp. 155–7. Buckley, *RAF and Trade Defence*, pp. 196–204. Hinsley, *British Intelligence* II, 180–88. Hamer, *Bombers versus Battleships*, pp. 137–49. Vego, 'Operation Cerberus' (quoted p. 128), the most recent study, gives a full and only slightly muddled narrative of the whole affair.

10 Mawdsley, *War for the Seas*, pp. 278–9. Martens, 'Operation "Chariot" '. Roskill, *War at Sea* II, 168–73. Faulkner, *War at Sea*, pp. 112–13. I cannot agree with Murfett, *Naval Warfare*, p. 163, who describes the raid as a 'grisly failure'.

11 Jones, *Fleet Air Arm* II, 72–5 (quoted p. 74). Hinsley, *British Intelligence* II, 227.

12 Boyd, *Naval Intelligence*, pp. 495–9. Llewellyn-Jones, *Arctic Convoys*, pp. 2 and 8–20. Levy, *Home Fleet*, pp. 113–17. Claasen, *Hitler's Northern War*, pp. 195–205. Woodman, *Arctic Convoys*, pp. 43–4 and 77–9. Hinsley, *British Intelligence* II, 202–11. Roskill, *War at Sea* II, 130–32.

13 Llewellyn-Jones, *Arctic Convoys*, p. 46.

14 The British did not yet know that the *Lützow* had grounded heavily in the Grimsøystraumen trying to take a short cut through the Lofoten Islands (Murfett, *Naval Warfare*, p. 197).

15 Lacey, 'Creating an American Strategy', pp. 192–3. Boyd, *Naval Intelligence*, pp. 500–504. Levy, 'Opposition to the Arctic Convoys'. Claasen, *Hitler's Northern War*, pp. 190–94 and 206–9. Woodman, *Arctic Convoys*, pp. 187–93. Hinsley, *British Intelligence* II, 213–22 and 686–9. Llewellyn-Jones, *Arctic Convoys*, pp. 55–69.

16 Boyd, *Naval Intelligence*, pp. 415–16. McKay and Beckman, *Swedish Signal Intelligence*, pp. 133–54 and 219–28. Hinsley, *British Intelligence* II, 211–22. Beesly, *Very Special Intelligence*, pp. 126–7. *Geheimschreiber* means 'secret writer', but the Siemens & Halske machine was very insecure.

17 Llewellyn-Jones, *Arctic Convoys*, pp. 73–4. Boyd, *Naval Intelligence*, pp. 504–5. Claasen, *Hitler's Northern War*, pp.

219–20. Hinsley, *British Intelligence* II, 227. Friedman, *Fighters over the Fleet*, p. 148. Levy, *Home Fleet*, pp. 125–7. Woodman, *Arctic Convoys*, pp. 260, 282–3 and 295. J. D. Brown, *Carrier Operations*, pp. 22–3.

18 Murfett, *Naval Warfare*, pp. 244–7. Llewellyn-Jones, *Arctic Convoys*, pp. 90–103. Bird, *Raeder*, pp. 191–2. Levy, *Home Fleet*, pp. 128–32. Woodman, *Arctic Convoys*, pp. 316–33. L. Brown, *Radar History*, p. 350. Rahn, 'Atlantic and Arctic Ocean' VI, 458–66. Bess, 'Operation "Regenbogen"', pp. 193–5. Owen, *No More Heroes*, pp. 167–70, describes this action, in which he fought as 1st Lieutenant of the destroyer *Obdurate*.

19 Mawdsley, *War for the Seas*, pp. 211–15. Hamer, *Bombers versus Battleships*, pp. 165–9. Friedman, *Fighters over the Fleet*, p. 102. Dull, *Imperial Japanese Navy*, pp. 115–31. Nofi, *US Navy Fleet Problems*, p. 305. J. D. Brown, *Carrier Operations*, pp. 138–43. J. D. Brown, *Carrier Fighters*, pp. 67–9. Wildenberg, *Destined for Glory*, pp. 183–99. Faulkner, *War at Sea*, pp. 122–3.

20 Mawdsley, *War for the Seas*, pp. 215–23. Tully and Yu, 'A Question of Estimates'. Isom, *Midway Inquest*, pp. 5–17 and 183–202. Peattie, *Sunburst*, pp. 175–6. Hamer, *Bombers versus Battleships*, pp. 185–203. Wildenberg, *Destined for Glory*, pp. 199–215. Dull, *Imperial Japanese Navy*, pp. 139–68. J. D. Brown, *Carrier Fighters*, pp. 72–80. Faulkner, *War at Sea*, pp. 124–7. Spector, *Eagle against the Sun*, pp. 166–78. Older US accounts of this battle are influenced by Mitscher's artfully vague report and need to be treated with caution; Parshall, 'What WAS Nimitz Thinking?' Isom, *Midway Inquest*, and Simms and McGregor, *Silver Waterfall*, are particularly interesting on the historiography. Jones, *Fleet Air Arm* II, 183–4, records the Fleet Air Arm's comments on Midway.

21 Ugaki, *Fading Victory*, p. 155.

22 Peattie, *Sunburst*, p. 180. Hughes, *Fleet Tactics*, pp. 96–102. Mawdsley, *War for the Seas*, pp. 224–36. Hone, *Learning War*, pp. 165–203. Donovan and Mack,

Codebreaking in the Pacific, pp. 346 and 354–56. T. C. Hone, 'Replacing Battleships with Aircraft Carriers'. J. D. Brown, *Carrier Operations*, pp. 163–76. O'Brien, *How the War was Won*, p. 391. Levy, 'Race for the Decisive Weapon', pp. 137–41. Dulin and Garzke, *Battleships* I, 73–4.

23 Johnson, *Pacific Campaign*, pp. 137–200 and 258–61. Blewett, 'Fuel and U.S. Naval Operations', pp. 77–8. Murfett, *Naval Warfare*, pp. 205–9. Godspeed, 'Carrier-Based Close Air Support', pp. 226–8. Reynolds, *Fast Carriers*, pp. 31–3. Dull, *Imperial Japanese Navy*, pp. 180–207. Spector, *Eagle against the Sun*, pp. 186–92 and 209. On US carrier doctrine see T. C. Hone, 'Replacing Battleships with Aircraft Carriers'; Symonds, *World War II at Sea*, p. 311.

24 Spector, *Eagle against the Sun*, p. 208. King's affected ignorance of US army terminology was no doubt intended to annoy, but in 1942 the word 'logistics' was still little used in English outside the US Army, which had borrowed it in 1918 from a half-understood French military term whose correct meaning was roughly equivalent to the English 'billets'.

25 Rear-Admiral Sir Victor Crutchley, VC, who was on loan to the RAN and flew his flag in the cruiser *Australia*.

26 Spector, *Eagle against the Sun*, p. 148, quoting the then Captain Arleigh Burke, USN.

27 Reardon, ' "Gun Club" Mentality', pp. 534–50. Hone, *Learning War*, pp. 167–209. Murfett, *Naval Warfare*, pp. 205–9 and 231–51. Friedman, *Network-Centric Warfare*, pp. 43–7. Charrier, 'Japanese Naval Tactics and Strategy'. Dull, *Imperial Japanese Navy*, pp. 237–58. Marder, *Old Friends* I, 292–5. Hughes, *Fleet Tactics*, pp. 118–30 (quoted pp. 129–30).

28 Marshall quoted from Stimson's diary in Lacey, 'Creating an American Strategy', p. 195.

29 Baer, *One Hundred Years of Sea Power*, pp. 222–6. Ross, *American War Plans*, pp. 24–34. Stoler, 'American Perception of British Mediterranean Strategy', pp.

327–34. Symonds, *World War II at Sea*, pp. 324–5. O'Hara, *Torch*, p. 41. Lacey, 'Creating an American Strategy', pp. 192–7. French, 'British Military Strategy', pp. 41–2.

30 Milner, *Battle of the Atlantic*, pp. 124–33. Hague, *Allied Convoy System*, pp. 57–8. Boyd, *Naval Intelligence*, p. 514.

31 Buckley, *RAF and Trade Defence*, pp. 136–7 and 147–52. Rahn, 'Atlantic and Arctic Ocean' VI, 379–89.

32 O'Brien, *How the War was Won*, pp. 243–8 – which however muddles the argument by failing to distinguish fleet destroyers from destroyer escorts.

33 Rahn, 'Atlantic and Arctic Ocean' VI, 378–9. Friedman, *Network-Centric Warfare*, p. 34.

34 Stumpf, 'North Africa and the Central Mediterranean, 1942–43' VI, 829. O'Hara, *Six Victories*, pp. 127, 135, 155, 157, 163–6, 177–82, 186–7 and 249–57. Faulkner, *War at Sea*, pp. 110–11. Mawdsley, *War for the Seas*, pp. 286–9. Murfett, *Naval Warfare*, p. 159. Llewellyn-Jones, *Mediterranean Convoys*, pp. 36–53. Ball, *The Bitter Sea*, pp. 126–35. Giorgerini, *La guerra italiana sul mare*, pp. 350–57 and 384–7. Hezlet, *The Submarine and Sea Power*, pp. 146–8 and 157–8. Simpson, *Cunningham Papers* I, 466–70 and 570–71. Hinsley, *British Intelligence* II, 330–49. Bennett and Bennett, *Hitler's Admirals*, pp. 152–5.

35 Hammond, 'British Perceptions of the Italian Navy', p. 827, quoting Sir Henry Harwood the new Commander-in-Chief Mediterranean. Cf. Jones, *Fleet Air Arm* II, 228, and Llewellyn-Jones, *Mediterranean Convoys*, p. 102, who attribute almost the same phrase to Cunningham.

36 Mawdsley, *War for the Seas*, pp. 293–4. Murfett, *Naval Warfare*, pp. 201–2. Llewellyn-Jones, *Mediterranean Convoys*, pp. 55–79. Ball, *The Bitter Sea*, pp. 135–6 and 145. Giorgerini, *La guerra italiana sul mare*, pp. 369–77. Roberts, *Churchill*, pp. 741–2. Austin, *Malta*, pp. 151–8 and 166. Hinsley, *British Intelligence* II, 330–49. Bennett and Bennett, *Hitler's Admirals*, pp. 152–5. Howard, *Grand Strategy* IV, 63. Austin, *Malta*, pp. 159–60. Barnett, *Engage the Enemy*, p. 516.

37 Boyd, *Naval Intelligence*, p. 448. Jones, *Fleet Air Arm* II, 52–3. Austin, *Malta*, pp. 141–2, 149–53 and 159. Llewellyn-Jones, *Mediterranean Convoys*, pp. 55–6 and 103. Roskill, *War at Sea* II, 302–8. Hastings, *Operation Pedestal*, pp. 52–4. These new *motosiluranti* are to be to be distinguished from the older and smaller *MAS*.

38 Boyd, *Naval Intelligence*, pp. 448–50. Boyd, *Eastern Waters*, pp. 388–90. Jones, *Fleet Air Arm* II, 170–81 and 359–60. Giorgerini, *La guerra italiana sul mare*, pp. 378–83. Stumpf, 'North Africa and the Central Mediterranean, 1942–43' VI, 831. Mattesini, *La battaglia di mezzo agosto*, pp. 405–8, 429–30 and 441–6. Llewellyn-Jones, *Mediterranean Convoys*, pp. 89–92 and 101–2. Mawdsley, *War for the Seas*, pp. 295–6. Hamer, *Bombers versus Battleships*, pp. 204–20. Hastings, *Operation Pedestal*. Faulkner, *War at Sea*, pp. 134–5. *BND*, pp. 852–6, prints eyewitness narratives.

39 Mattesini, *La battaglia di mezzo agosto*, pp. 411 and 444–6. Cernuschi, '*Ultra*', pp. 166–76. Giorgerini, *La guerra italiana sul mare*, pp. 532–4. Austin, *Malta*, pp. 162–7. Hinsley, *British Intelligence* II, 419–24. Bennett and Bennett, *Hitler's Admirals*, pp. 156–7. Ralph Bennett, *Ultra and Mediterranean Strategy*, p. 121. Howard, *Grand Strategy* IV, 64 (quoted).

40 Gooch, 'Mussolini's Strategy, 1918–1945', pp. 155–8. Mattesini, *La battaglia di mezzo agosto*, p. 411. Giorgerini, *La guerra italiana sul mare*, pp. 388–91. Mawdsley, *War for the Seas*, pp. 297–300. Austin, *Malta*, pp. 169–89. Roberts, *Churchill*, p. 761. Rommel was off sick and von Thoma was his deputy.

41 Boyd, *Naval Intelligence*, pp. 510–14. Mawdsley, *War for the Seas*, pp. 283–5. Monaque, *La marine de guerre française*, pp. 423–33. O'Hara, *Torch*, pp. 57–82 and 282–9. Murfett, *Naval Warfare*, pp. 234–9. Bennett and Bennett, *Hitler's Admirals*, p. 160. Hessler, *U-Boat War* II, 60–61. Hinsley, *British Intelligence* II, 476–7.

Chapter 27

1 From his 1887 story 'The Canterville Ghost'; the customary attribution to George Bernard Shaw is mistaken.

2 O'Brien, *How the War was Won*, pp. 131–46.

3 O'Brien, *How the War was Won*, pp. 154–7. Reynolds, *Anglo-American Alliance*, pp. 179–80. Roberts, *Churchill*, p. 631.

4 Roberts, *Masters and Commanders*, pp. 2–4. Cohen, 'War Planning', pp. 548–52.

5 Ramsey, 'Professor Wilkinson and Admiral Sims', p. 223.

6 Lacey, 'Creating an American Strategy', pp. 187–97. Spector, *Eagle against the Sun*, pp. 124–5. Roberts, *Masters and Commanders*, pp. 175–6, 190–94, 203–4 and 253–4.

7 Spector, *Eagle against the Sun*, p. 126.

8 Mawdsley, *War for the Seas*, pp. 206–7. O'Brien, *How the War was Won*, pp. 146–9. Baer, *One Hundred Years of Sea Power*, pp. 184–7 and 196–8. Christman, 'Roosevelt and Strategic Assessment', pp. 216–27. Cohen, 'War Planning', pp. 548–52. Buell, *King*, pp. 162–79. Reynolds, *Fast Carriers*, p. 40. Brodhurst, *Churchill's Anchor*, pp. 216–17. Spector, *Eagle against the Sun*, p. 126.

9 Bath, *Tracking the Axis Enemy*, p. 229. Buckley, *RAF and Trade Defence*, pp. 139–64. Lewis, 'Admiral Hewitt', pp. 265–6.

10 Wildenberg, *Destined for Glory*, pp. 87–93. Reynolds, *Fast Carriers*, pp. 19, 36–49, 73, 303 and 307. Bath, *Tracking the Axis Enemy*, pp. 103–4. Coles, 'King and the British Pacific Fleet'. Johnson, *Pacific Campaign*, pp. 94–5 and 144–7. O'Brien, *How the War was Won*, pp. 166–7. Boyd, *Naval Intelligence*, p. 482. Spector, *At War at Sea*, pp. 220–23.

11 Bath, *Tracking the Axis Enemy*, p. 70. I am not sure which of King's six daughters this was.

12 C. I. Hamilton, 'Operational Intelligence Centre', p. 312, quoting the then Cdr Rodger Winn RNVR, head of the Submarine Tracking Room in the Admiralty Operational Intelligence Centre (and later a Lord Justice of Appeal), who went to Washington in 1942 to teach the USN anti-submarine organization.

13 John Wukovits, *Eisenhower: A Biography* (New York, 2015), p. 66.

14 Buell's biography *Master of Sea Power*, though published after its subject's death, offers only discreet hints (e.g. p. 89), and later writers have steered well clear of the shoals. Clark G. Reynolds, 'Admiral Ernest J. King and the Strategy for Victory in the Pacific', *NWCR* XXVIII, No. 3 (Winter 1976), pp. 57–64, sums up the literature then available. Love, 'King', is convincing in some respects, but skirts the more embarrassing episodes. The most candid assessment of King's character I have met is an unpublished thesis by a US Army officer: Maj. James R. Hill, USAR, 'A Comparative Analysis of the Military Leadership Styles of Ernest J. King and Chester W. Nimitz' (Master's thesis, School of Advanced Military Studies, US Army Command and General Staff College, Fort Leavenworth, Kansas, 2009) [found Nov 2021 at https://apps.dtic.mil/dtic/tr/fulltext/u2/a505406.pdf]. The *Wikipedia* entry on King is also worth reading.

15 Paine, *Wars for Asia*, pp. 197–8. Spector, *Eagle against the Sun*, pp. 324–30 and 341–50.

16 Johnson, *Pacific Campaign*, p. 22. Smith, *Ultra-Magic Deals*, p. 68. Schreiber, 'Politics and Warfare in 1941' III, 562–8.

17 Roberts, *Churchill*, p. 639.

18 Roberts, *Masters and Commanders*, p. 45. Darwin, *Empire Project*, pp. 509–11. Pugh, 'Military Need', p. 35. Mahnken, 'US Grand Strategy', p. 198. Mawdsley, *War for the Seas*, pp. 163–4. Broadberry and Howlett, 'Victory at All Costs', p. 53. Simpson, *Anglo-American Naval Relations* III, 30.

19 Tooze, *Wages of Destruction*, pp. 403–10. Peden, *Arms, Economics and British Strategy*, pp. 197–8 and 245. Reynolds, *Long Shadow*, pp. 265–6. Darwin, *Empire Project*, pp. 511–12. Mawdsley, *War for the Seas*, pp. 163–4. Rockoff, 'United States', pp. 94–5. B. F. Smith, *Ultra-Magic Deals*, p. 68. Pugh, *Cost of Seapower*, pp. 14–20.

Reynolds, *Anglo-American Alliance*, pp. 156–66, 213–15 and 283.

20 Hill, 'British Lend Lease Aid'. Todman, *Into Battle*, pp. 692–3.

21 Tooze, *Wages of Destruction*, pp. 404–10. Harrison, 'Economics of World War II', p. 22. Postan, *War Production*, pp. 231–2 and 236.

22 Weir, 'A Truly Allied Undertaking', pp. 102–13. Edgerton, *Britain's War Machine*, pp. 81–4. Lindberg and Todd, *Anglo-American Shipbuilding*, pp. 99–103 and 155. Johnman and Murphy, *British Shipbuilding and the State*, pp. 85–6. Adams, *Mr Kaiser goes to Washington*, pp. 95–7 and 114–15. Postan, *War Production*, p. 231. The US name was 'Liberty Ship' not 'Empire Liberty', which to American ears sounded like an uncomfortable contradiction.

23 Bell, 'Churchill and the Battle of the Atlantic', p. 44.

24 Bell, *Churchill and Sea Power*, pp. 262–3.

25 Milner, *Battle of the Atlantic*, pp. 118–19. Niestlé, 'German Technical and Electronic Development', p. 442. Hessler, *U-Boat War* II, 42–3. Price, *Aircraft versus Submarine*, pp. 81–9. The *Funkmessbeobachtungsgerät* ('wireless reporting device') was a German design usually known by the name of its French manufacturer Métox.

26 Bell, 'Very Long Range Aircraft'. Bell, *Churchill and Sea Power*, pp. 256–72. Grove, *Enemy Attack on Shipping*, p. 74. Buckley, *RAF and Trade Defence*, pp. 128–47. The post-war maritime patrol aircraft the Avro Shackleton was developed from the Lancaster.

27 Rahn, 'Atlantic and Arctic Ocean' VI, 379–89. Murfett, *Naval Warfare*, pp. 240 and 258–9. Bell, 'Very Long Range Aircraft', pp. 710–15. Buckley, *RAF and Trade Defence*, pp. 129–35. Goette, 'Closing the Mid-Atlantic "Air Gap"'.

28 Sebastian Cox, 'The Sources and Organization of RAF Intelligence', in *The Conduct of the Air War in the Second World War*, ed. Horst Boog (New York, 1992), p. 577.

29 Jones, *Fleet Air Arm* II, 148–9, despatch of 2 Aug 1942.

30 Benbow, 'Brothers in Arms'. Peden, *Arms, Economics and British Strategy*, pp. 209–16. Biddle, *Rhetoric and Reality*, pp. 197–208. Biddle, 'Anglo-American Strategic Bombing', pp. 493–501. Bell, *Churchill and Sea Power*, pp. 225–79. Edgerton, *Britain's War Machine*, pp. 124–9. Barnett, *Engage the Enemy*, pp. 454–79. Boog, 'Anglo-American Strategic Air War' VI, 561–627. O'Brien, *How the War was Won*, pp. 207–8.

31 G. Kennedy, 'Anglo-American Diplomatic Relations', pp. 42–8.

32 Tracy, *Attack on Maritime Trade*, pp. 195 (quoted) and 200–203. Pugh, 'Military Need', pp. 32–4 and 41.

33 Milner, *Battle of the Atlantic*, pp. 78–92. Milner, 'Atlantic War', pp. 10–13. Mawdsley, *War for the Seas*, pp. 253–60. O'Brien, *How the War was Won*, pp. 234–7.

34 Milner, 'Atlantic War', pp. 10–13, and *Battle of the Atlantic*, pp. 80–92. Mawdsley, *War for the Seas*, pp. 253–60. Roberts, *Churchill*, p. 713. Boyd, *Naval Intelligence*, p. 478. Murfett, *Naval Warfare 1919–1945*, p. 154. Rohwer, 'Operational Use of "Ultra"', p. 285. O'Brien, *How the War was Won*, pp. 231–41. Bell, *Churchill and Sea Power*, p. 270.

35 Biddle, *Rhetoric and Reality*, p. 205, quoting Air Vice-Marshal John Slessor.

36 Simpson, *Cunningham Papers* II, 14–15.

37 Buckley, *RAF and Trade Defence*, pp. 139–46. Mawdsley, *War for the Seas*, pp. 256–60. Simpson, *Cunningham Papers* II, 13.

38 Mawdsley, *War for the Seas*, pp. 253–60. Rahn, 'Atlantic and Arctic Ocean' VI, 378–80. O'Brien, *How the War was Won*, pp. 234–7 and 250–56. Boyd, *Naval Intelligence*, p. 478. Hessler, *U-boat War* II, 11–13. Milner, *Battle of the Atlantic*, pp. 78 and 90–92. Milner, 'Atlantic War', p. 13. Murfett, *Naval Warfare*, p. 154. Roberts, *Churchill*, p. 713.

39 Morison, *Naval Operations* I, 200–201 (quoted). Reynolds, *Fast Carriers*, pp. 168–9. Johnson, *Pacific Campaign*, pp. 94–5. Buckley, *RAF and Trade Defence*, pp. 140–64. Bath, *Tracking the Axis Enemy*, pp. 88–90.

40 Westwood, *U-Boat War*, p. 259. Rössler, *U-Boat*, pp. 103–5 and 161–3. Hessler, *U-Boat War* II, 5–25 and 109–10. Gröner, *Die Deutschen Kriegschiffe* I, 415–17. Taylor, *German Warships of World War II*, pp. 115–17. Rahn, 'The Atlantic in the Strategic Perspective of Hitler', p. 163. Terraine, *U-Boat Wars*, p. 409. O'Brien, *How the War was Won*, pp. 231–50. Hezlet, *Submarine and Sea Power*, pp. 179–81. Neitzel, 'Deployment of the U-boats', pp. 277–91. Mawdsley, *War for the Seas*, pp. 255–60. Milner, *Battle of the Atlantic*, pp. 80–92. Murfett, *Naval Warfare*, p. 154. Rahn, 'Atlantic and Arctic Ocean' VI, 369–73. Hinsley, *British Intelligence* III, i, 212.

41 Ziegler, *Mountbatten*, p. 156.

42 Ziegler, *Mountbatten*, pp. 186–96. A. Smith, *Mountbatten*, pp. 193–244.

43 Boyd, *Naval Intelligence*, pp. 405 and 477–8. Mulligan, 'German Cryptographic Security'. Erskine, 'The Breaking of Heimisch and Triton'. Rohwer, 'Operational Use of "Ultra"'. Beesly, *Very Special Intelligence*, pp. 110–13. Bath, *Tracking the Axis Enemy*, p. 74. Hinsley, *British Intelligence* II, 636–9.

44 Ferris, *Behind the Enigma*, pp. 102–7 and 165–83. Batey, *Dilly*, pp. ix–xi, xxiii, 59–63 and 95–6 (a good life of Dillwyn Knox by a leading member of his group).

45 Hinsley, *British Intelligence* II, 655–7, and III, i, 477–82.

46 Ferris, *Behind the Enigma*, p. 441, quoting an unsigned memorandum.

47 Ferris, *Behind the Enigma*, pp. 102–7 and 164–213. Hinsley, *British Intelligence* III, i, 480–81. Beesly, *Very Special Intelligence*, pp. 151 and 230. Stanley, *Women and the Navy*, p. 100. Roberts, *WRNS in Wartime*, p. 125. Grey, 'Bletchley Park', pp. 785–8.

48 Winkler, *Nexus*, p. 106. Roskill, *Naval Policy* II, 265. Boyd, *Naval Intelligence*, p. 104. Friedman, *British Submarines* I, 397 n.7.

49 O'Hara, *Six Victories*, pp. 26–31 and 210–11. Cernuschi, *Ultra*, pp. 19–37, 51–78 and 110–15. Headrick, *Invisible Weapon*, pp. 219–30.

50 Roberts, *Masters and Commanders*, pp. 205–7. Jenner, 'Turning the Hinge of Fate', pp. 165–79 and 190–97. Santoni, *Il Vero Traditore*, pp. 38–9. Ferris, *Behind the Enigma*, pp. 247–54. Smith, *Ultra-Magic Deals*, pp. 111–12. Gooch, *Mussolini's War*, p. 213. Knox, *Hitler's Italian Allies*, pp. 72 and 122. Mawdsley, *War for the Seas*, pp. 289–90.

51 Ferris, *Behind the Enigma*, p. 335. Erskine, 'Holden Agreement'. Cohen, 'War Planning', pp. 548–50. Buckley, *RAF and Trade Defence*, pp. 140–64. Boyd, *Naval Intelligence*, pp. 480–86. Bath, *Tracking the Axis Enemy*, pp. 76–8, 176–91. Donovan and Mack, *Codebreaking in the Pacific*, pp. 150–52. M. Smith, *The Emperor's Codes*, pp. 148–69. *ODNB* sv Winn, who had studied at both Yale and Harvard.

Chapter 28

1 Most Commonwealth citizens were subjects of the British Crown and eligible to serve in British forces, but only their own governments exercised any power of conscription over them.

2 Lavery, *Hostilities Only*, pp. 29–35. Lavery, *All Hands*, pp. 15–16. K. Brown, *Poxed and Scurvied*, p. 189. K. Brown, *Fittest of the Fit*, pp. 1–6. Kerr and Granville, *R.N.V.R.*, pp. 138–9, give a breakdown of the manning situation at the end of 1938.

3 Lavery, *Hostilities Only*, pp. 10–11 and 36. Pugh, 'Military Need', p. 34. Arthur, *1939 to the Present*, pp. 38–9.

4 Kerr and Granville, *R.N.V.R.*, p. 151.

5 D. K. Brown, *Design and Construction* II, 51. D. K. Brown, *Atlantic Escorts*, pp. 47–9. Lavery, *In Which They Served*, pp. 20, 45–9 and 186. Lavery, *Hostilities Only*, p. 243. Howarth, *Royal Navy's Reserves*, p. 77.

6 Meaning potential officers, the responsibility of the Commission and Warrant Branch of the Admiralty, which in spite of its name normally dealt with warrant and not commissioned officers.

7 Lavery, *Hostilities Only*, pp. 36–8, 63–4, 149–54 and 159–67. Lavery, *In Which*

They Served, pp. 25–42, 72 and 133–7. Prysor, 'Morale', pp. 67–8. Howarth, *Royal Navy's Reserves*, pp. 59 and 96. Kerr and Granville, *R.N.V.R.*, pp. 160–62 and 174–7. Glover, 'Manning and Training', p. 194.

8 Prysor, *Citizen Sailors*, p. 320. A 'Salvationist' refers to a member of the 'Salvation Army'.

9 Kerr and Granville, *R.N.V.R.*, p. 160. Howarth, *Royal Navy's Reserves*, p. 91.

10 Lavery, *All Hands*, pp. 25–6. Lavery, *Hostilities Only*, pp. 36–8, 149–54 and 159–67. Lavery, *In Which They Served*, pp. 25–42, 72 and 133–7. Prysor, 'Morale', pp. 67–8. Howarth, *Royal Navy's Reserves*, pp. 59 and 96. Kerr and Granville, *R.N.V.R.*, pp. 160–62 and 174–7. Glover, 'Manning and Training', p. 194.

11 Farquharson-Roberts, *War to War*, pp. 180–81, 198 and 226. Howarth, *Royal Navy's Reserves*, pp. 77, 83, 86 and 91–6. Kerr and Granville, *R.N.V.R.*, pp. 133–77.

12 Monsarrat, *H.M. Frigate*, p. 7.

13 Lavery, *Hostilities Only*, pp. 36–7 and 134–41. In 1943 the RN College was compelled by bomb damage to move from Dartmouth to the Duke of Westminster's palatial country house of Eaton Hall, Cheshire.

14 Lavery, *Hostilities Only*, pp. 143–7. Lavery, *In Which They Served*, pp. 77–81. Farquharson-Roberts, *War to War*, p. 194. Personal knowledge (Trowbridge was the author's uncle).

15 Prysor, 'Morale', p. 241.

16 Prysor, 'Morale', pp. 159–66, 217–19 and 241–6.

17 Brown, *Fittest of the Fit*, pp. 126–7.

18 Farquharson-Roberts, *War to War*, pp. 188–207.

19 Farquharson-Roberts, *War to War*, p. 35.

20 Dickinson, *Wisdom and War*, pp. 185–6. Kerr and Granville, *R.N.V.R.*, pp. 158–9. Moore, *Greenie*, pp. 135–8.

21 Edgerton, *Britain's War Machine*, pp. 56–7. Lavery, *Churchill's Navy*, pp. 190–206. Hone, Friedman and Mandeles, *Innovation in Carrier Aviation*, pp. 3–4. D. Brown, *Carrier Fighters*, pp. 38–40. Friedman, *British Carrier Aviation*, p. 205. Lavery, *Hostilities Only*, pp. 176–81.

Jones, *Fleet Air Arm* II, 357. Simpson, *Anglo-American-Canadian Naval Relations*, pp. 93–5.

22 Hennessy and Jinks, *Silent Deep*, p. 45. Lavery, *Hostilities Only*, p. 63, quotes overall RN casualties as 50,758 killed (ca. 1 in 20), 14,663 wounded, 820 missing and 7,401 prisoners of war.

23 Arthur, *1939 to the Present*, pp. 16–17. Hezlet duly rose fast as a submariner, getting his first command at 26, becoming the youngest captain in the Navy at 36, and later the youngest admiral at 45.

24 Tall, 'Waging the Undersea War', pp. 45–6, quoting Captain W. R. Fell.

25 Chalmers, *Max Horton*, p. 106.

26 Lavery, *All Hands*, p. 93. Lavery, *Churchill's Navy*, pp. 212–14. Tall, 'Waging the Undersea War', pp. 44–51. Moretz, *Towards a Wider War*, p. 384. Brown, *Fittest of the Fit*, pp. 114 and 123–31. Topp, 'Manning and Training the U-boat Fleet', pp. 215–16. De Ninno, *I sommergibili del fascismo*, pp. 251–2. On US submarines see Spector, *At War at Sea*, pp. 225 and 287–9.

27 Moore, *Greenie*, pp. 133–9. Lavery, *All Hands*, pp. 46–7. Lavery, *Hostilities Only*, pp. 129 and 174. Howse, *Radar at Sea*, pp. 112–13. Patrick, 'Radar Fitting Policy' I, 344–6. Laws, 'Radar Maintenance at Sea' I, 306.

28 Gavin Douglas, 'Tell us about D-Day', in Kerr and James, *Wavy Navy*, pp. 223–35, quoted p. 223.

29 Lavery, *Hostilities Only*, pp. 190–206. The novelist Evelyn Waugh was one of the 1939 'Temporary Officers', and his fictional trilogy *Sword of Honour* draws on his experience of the 'Royal Corps of Halbardiers'.

30 Grove, *Enemy Attack on Shipping*, p. 186.

31 Lavery, *Hostilities Only*, pp. 44–9. Lavery, *Shield of Empire*, pp. 358–86.

32 Glover, 'Manning and Training', p. 192. Goldrick, 'Work-Up', pp. 221–4. Lavery, *In Which They Served*, pp. 282–97. Lavery, *Shield of Empire*, pp. 372–4. *ODNB* sv Stephenson. Bailey, *Corvettes and Their Crews*, pp. 11–20. Baker, *Terror of Tobermory*.

33 Lavery, *In Which They Served*, p. 287, quoting an article Stephenson contributed to the *Monthly Anti-Submarine Report* in 1944.
34 Baker, *Terror of Tobermory*, p. 120.
35 Lavery, *In Which They Served*, pp. 296–7. Christopher Marlowe's *Doctor Faustus* calls up Helen of Troy from the underworld and exclaims 'Was this the face that launch'd a thousand ships, / And burnt the topless towers of Ilium?'
36 Lavery, *River Class Frigates*, pp. 163–5. Goldrick, 'Work-Up', pp. 222–3.
37 Goldrick, 'Work-Up', pp. 224–9. Goldrick, ' "A" Teams', p. 12. Lavery, *Hostilities Only*, pp. 254–67.
38 Monsarrat, *H.M. Frigate*, pp. 21–2.
39 Goldrick, 'Work-Up', pp. 227–9. Williams, *Gilbert Roberts*, pp. 85–6 and 100–101. Parkin, *Birds and Wolves*, pp. 94–7.
40 Campbell, *Naval Weapons*, pp. 260–63. Parkin, *Birds and Wolves*, pp. 63, 85, 93–102, 122–4, 128–30, 142–61, 248 and 253. Magnozzi, 'Kretschmer's U-Boat Tactics'.
41 Williams, *Gilbert Roberts*, pp. 86–97 (quoted p. 95). Parkin, *Birds and Wolves*, pp. 94–7 and 156–61. Campbell, *Naval Weapons*, p. 263.
42 Gretton, *Convoy Escort Commander*, pp. 100–101.
43 Goldrick, ' "A" Teams' (quoted p. 10), and 'Work-Up'.
44 Williams, *Gilbert Roberts*, pp. 101–5. Westwood, *U-Boat War*, pp. 167–9. Parkin, *Birds and Wolves*, pp. 162–73.
45 Mathews, *Blue Tapestry*, pp. 146–8. Roberts, *WRNS in Wartime*, pp. 101–2. Fletcher, *WRNS*, p. 80.
46 Roberts, *WRNS in Wartime*, pp. 7–8, 92–3 and 128–41. Dickinson, *Wisdom and War*, p. 178. Lavery, *Churchill's Navy*, pp. 153–9.
47 Lavery, *Churchill's Navy*, p. 155. Stanley, *Women and the Navy*, pp. 117–18 and 124.
48 Roberts, *WRNS in Wartime*, pp. 111–18. Parkin, *Birds and Wolves*, p. 194.
49 Parkin, *Birds and Wolves*, p. 194, quoting Monsarrat.
50 Roberts, *WRNS in Wartime*, pp. 208–9.
51 Simpson, *Cunningham Papers* I, 530.
52 Roberts, *WRNS in Wartime*, pp. 144–6.
53 Mathews, *Blue Tapestry*, p. 136.
54 Howse, *Radar at Sea*, p. 112.
55 Lamb, *Beyond the Sea*, pp. 134–7.
56 Lavery, *Hostilities Only*, p. 236.
57 Mathews, *Blue Tapestry*, p. 187. Roberts, *WRNS in Wartime*, p. 129.
58 Mathews, *Blue Tapestry*, p. 227. Roberts, *WRNS in Wartime*, pp. 110, 128–9, 153–5 and 174–80. Fletcher, *WRNS*, pp. 31–45. Mason, *Britannia's Daughters*, pp. 70 and 75. Jones, *Fleet Air Arm* II, 344. Wildish, 'Western Approaches Command', p. 54.

Chapter 29

1 Cronin, *Shipboard Aircraft*, pp. 70–82. Thetford, *British Naval Aircraft*, pp. 125–36.
2 Biddle, *Rhetoric and Reality*, pp. 84–98. Robertson, *RAF Strategic Bombing Doctrine*, pp. 62–160. M. Smith, *British Air Strategy*, pp. 28–33. Meilinger, 'Fleet Air Arm before the War', p. 76. Howlett, *British Naval Aviation*, pp. 102, 109–10 and 174–5. Ferris, 'Student and Master', p. 107.
3 Ferris, 'Achieving Air Ascendancy', pp. 40–45. Edgerton, *Warfare State*, pp. 42–4. Lund, 'Industrial History of Strategy', pp. 75–83. Zeitlin, 'Flexibility and Mass Production', pp. 76–8. Edgerton, *England and the Aeroplane*, pp. 17–34. Friedman, *Fighters over the Fleet*, p. 14. Friedman, *British Carrier Aviation*, pp. 16–17 and 162–4.
4 Cronin, *Shipboard Aircraft*, pp. 70–122. D. K. Brown, *Nelson to Vanguard*, pp. 45–6. Friedman, *Naval Anti-Aircraft Guns*, p. 21 n.7. Thetford, *British Naval Aircraft*, pp. 138–42. Horsley, *Find, Fix and Strike*, quoted p. 22 ('man on a bicycle'). E. M. Brown, *Duels in the Sky*, pp. 9–11, quoted p. 9 ('negligible performance'). E. M. Brown, *Wings of the Navy*, pp. 7–19.
5 Friedman, *Naval Anti-Aircraft Guns*, pp. 22–4 and n.18. Jones, *Fleet Air Arm* II, 443. The British Mk.XII 18-inch torpedo of 1937 weighed 1,548 lbs; its late-war successor the Mk.XV weighed 1,801 lbs (Campbell, *Naval Weapons*, p. 87).

6 Friedman, *Naval Anti-Aircraft Guns*, pp. 23–4 and nn.10–12. Hayward, 'Air-Dropped Depth Charges and Torpedoes', pp. 124–30. Friedman, *British Carrier Aviation*, p. 216. Campbell, *Naval Weapons*, p. 87.

7 Horsley, *Find, Fix and Strike*, p. 33. The seaplanes of the day were almost all powered by air-cooled radial engines whose exposed hot cylinder heads were liable to be cracked by cold spray thrown up by the floats.

8 Thetford, *British Naval Aircraft*, pp. 322–7. *ODNB* sv R. J. Mitchell. Friedman, *British Cruisers* II, 88–93.

9 Friedman, *Fighters Over the Fleet*, p. 14. Friedman, *British Carrier Aviation*, pp. 15–17, 155, 158 and 162–4.

10 Jones, *Fleet Air Arm* I, 211.

11 Friedman, *British Carrier Aviation*, pp. 166, 209–10 and 369–70. Friedman, *Fighters Over the Fleet*, pp. 145–6. Jones, *Fleet Air Arm* I, 72–4, 83–6, 115–18, 167, 209–12, 306 and 496–501; *Fleet Air Arm* II, 11–12, 360, 381–3 and 443–4. Thetford, *British Naval Aircraft*, pp. 159–64 and 237–42. J. D. Brown, *Carrier Fighters*, pp. 15–18 and 43–4. E. M. Brown, *Wings of the Navy*, pp. 40–50 and 108–16. These best speeds were at high altitude; lower was always slower.

12 To the Secretary of the Chiefs of Staff Committee, 30 Sep 1941, in Jones, *Fleet Air Arm* I, 499.

13 Jones, *Fleet Air Arm* I, 83–6. Thetford, *British Naval Aircraft*, pp. 209–13. Friedman, *Fighters Over the Fleet*, p. 146. Jones, 'Struggle for the Mediterranean', pp. 93–5. D. Brown, *Carrier Fighters*, pp. 21–2. E. Brown, *Wings of the Navy*, pp. 40–51. Friedman, *British Carrier Aviation*, p. 209. When the US Navy started naming aircraft in 1941, the F4F became the Wildcat, but the FAA did not adopt the US name until January 1944.

14 Thetford, *British Naval Aircraft*, pp. 171–8. J. D. Brown, *Carrier Fighters*, pp. 17–18 and 103–6. E. Brown, *Wings of the Navy*, pp. 145–50. E. Brown, *Duels in the Sky*, pp. 158–60. Friedman, *Fighters over the Fleet*, pp. 142–4.

15 Friedman, *British Carrier Aviation*, p. 19.

16 Friedman, *British Carrier Aviation*, pp. 19, 110–15, 155. Weir, 'Naval Air Warfare', p. 224.

17 Peattie, *Sunburst*, pp. 86–93, 113 and 281–2. Horikoshi, *Eagles of Mitsubishi*, pp. 26–57. J. D. Brown, *Carrier Fighters*, pp. 18–23. Hirama, 'Japanese Naval Preparations', p. 72. Best, *British Intelligence and the Japanese Challenge*, p. 167. Marder, *Old Friends* I, 307–8. Boyd, *Eastern Waters*, pp. 225–30. Mahnken, *Uncovering Ways of War*, pp. 78–80. Aldrich, *Intelligence and the War against Japan*, p. 65.

18 Peattie, *Sunburst*, pp. 92–3 and 157. Hone and Mandeles, 'Interwar Innovation', p. 78. E. M. Brown, *Duels in the Sky*, pp. 69–71. Isom, *Midway Inquest*, p. 201. J. D. Brown, *Carrier Fighters*, pp. 22–3. Harvey, 'Japanese Aviation', pp. 175–9. Till, 'Adopting the Aircraft Carrier', pp. 212–23.

19 Peattie, *Sunburst*, pp. 86–7 and 94–7. E. M. Brown, *Duels in the Sky*, pp. 71–3. Lautenschläger, 'Technology and Naval Warfare', pp. 28–30.

20 Peattie, *Sunburst*, pp. 102–34.

21 Peattie, *Sunburst*, pp. 133–7, 166–7, 177–84 and 190–99. Evans and Peattie, *Kaigun*, p. 501. O'Brien, *How the War was Won*, pp. 82–3.

22 Horikoshi, *Eagles of Mitsubishi*, pp. 64–5. Peattie, *Sunburst*, pp. 98–101.

23 Jones, *Fleet Air Arm* I, 30–34, 50 and 211. Llewellyn-Jones, *Mediterranean Convoys*, pp. 136–7. E. M. Brown, *Duels in the Sky*, pp. 49–51 and 56. E. M. Brown, *Wings of the Navy*, pp. 60–68. Friedman, *British Carrier Aviation*, p. 170.

24 Hobbs, 'Naval Aviation, 1930–2000', pp. 75–6. Brown, *Wings of the Navy*, pp. 100, 106–7 and 146–50. Thetford, *British Naval Aircraft*, pp. 165–70. Hill, *Duty Free*, p. 30. Friedman, *British Carrier Aviation*, pp. 170 and 214–15. Friedman, *Naval Anti-Aircraft Guns*, pp. 30–33. Brown, *Duels in the Sky*, pp. 146–7. Jones, *Fleet Air Arm* II, 356. Friedman, *Fighters over the Fleet*, p. 142.

25 Jones, *Fleet Air Arm* II, 356.

26 *ODNB* sv Dreyer. Jones, *Fleet Air Arm* II, 3 ('controversial', 'unsatisfactory'), 136

and 284. Goodall, *Diary*, p. 143 ('Myself'). Hone, Friedman and Mandeles, *Innovation in Carrier Aviation*, pp. 65 and 134. Roskill, *Naval Policy* II, 119–20. Roskill, *Churchill and the Admirals*, pp. 231–2.

27 Jones, *Fleet Air Arm* II, 441–9. Cf. Ch. 24.

28 Jones, *Fleet Air Arm* II, 27–30. Thetford, *British Naval Aircraft*, pp. 217–22. E. Brown, *Wings of the Navy*, pp. 117–25. Friedman, *Naval Anti-Aircraft Guns*, pp. 24–25. Friedman, *British Carrier Aviation*, pp. 214–15. J. D. Brown, *Carrier Operations*, p. 40.

29 E. Brown, *Wings of the Navy*, p. 87.

30 E. Brown, *Wings of the Navy*, pp. 78–9, and *Duels in the Sky*, pp. 121–3. Friedman, *Fighters over the Fleet*, pp. 133–9. J. D. Brown, *Carrier Fighters*, pp. 99–101. Wildenberg, *Destined for Glory*, p. 154. Jones, *Fleet Air Arm* I, 306. Thetford, *British Naval Aircraft*, pp. 79–84.

31 Minute by 1st Lord to Cabinet Defence Committee (Supply), 20 Mar 1943, in Jones, *Fleet Air Arm* II, 371,

32 Nofi, *US Navy Fleet Problems*, pp. 24 and 279. Wildenberg, *Destined for Glory*, pp. 92–3.

33 Friedman, *Naval Anti-Aircraft Guns*, pp. 30–31. Weir, 'Naval Air Warfare', pp. 224, 230–34 and 240–46.

34 Friedman, *Naval Anti-Aircraft Guns*, pp. 193–200, and Hamer, *Bombers versus Battleships*, pp. 41–7. Pugh, 'Managing the Aerial Threat', is good on the science of the 1931 committee, but weak on the history.

35 L. Brown, *Radar History*, pp. 50–54, 63 and 205–8. Zimmerman, 'Technology and Tactics', pp. 477–9. Friedman, *Fighters over the Fleet*, pp. 70–71 and 110. Friedman, *Network-Centric Warfare*, pp. 51–2.

36 L. Brown, *Radar History*, pp. 129–40 and 423. Friedman, *Fighters over the Fleet*, p. 107. Howse, *Radar at Sea*, p. 141. J. D. Brown, *Carrier Fighters*, p. 60.

37 L. Brown, *Radar History*, pp. 456–65.

38 L. Brown, *Radar History*, pp. 460–65. Friedman, *Fighters over the Fleet*, pp. 104–5 and 110–13. Howse, *Radar at Sea*,

pp. 64–5 and 112–13. Friedman, *Network-Centric Warfare*, p. 54. Grove, 'Carrier Fighter Control', pp. 360–62.

39 Grove, 'Carrier Fighter Control', pp. 363–8. Friedman, *Fighters over the Fleet*, pp. 107–18. Friedman, *Network-Centric Warfare*, pp. 56–9. Woolrych, 'Fighter-Direction Matériel' II, 177–8. J. D. Brown, *Carrier Fighters*, p. 63. Jones, 'Struggle for the Mediterranean', p. 89. L. Brown, *Radar History*, pp. 129–34.

Chapter 30

1 Roberts, *Masters and Commanders*, p. 879. Spector, *Eagle against the Sun*, pp. 220–24. Lacey, 'Creating an American Strategy', pp. 190–206.

2 Jones, *Mediterranean War*, p. 21.

3 G. Kennedy, 'Anglo-American Diplomatic Relations', pp. 42–5. Spector, *Eagle against the Sun*, pp. 324–30. O'Brien, *How the War was Won*, pp. 208–14. Bath, *Tracking the Axis Enemy*, p. 108. Ross, *American War Plans*, pp. 39–44 and 50–57. Stoler, 'American Perception of British Mediterranean Strategy', p. 327.

4 Blair, *U-Boat War* II, 145–8. Boyd, *Naval Intelligence*, p. 492. Murfett, *Naval Warfare*, pp. 259–60. Milner, *Battle of the Atlantic*, pp. 136–40. Gardner, *Decoding History*, pp. 182–7. Syrett, *Defeat of the German U-Boats*, p. 25. Rahn, 'Atlantic and Arctic Ocean' VI, 340 and 394–6. Hessler, *U-Boat War* II, 88–100. Roskill, *War at Sea* II, 367–8. Hinsley, *British Intelligence* II, 553 and 562–4. Faulkner, *War at Sea*, p. 169. P. Kennedy, *Engineers of Victory*, p. 40 (quoted).

5 Faulkner, *War at Sea*, pp. 161 and 172–3. Milner, 'Atlantic War', pp. 16–17. Murfett, *Naval Warfare*, p. 265. Goette, 'Closing the Mid-Atlantic "Air Gap"', pp. 33–40. Milner, *Battle of the Atlantic*, pp. 143–5. Hague, *Allied Convoy System*, pp. 57–8. Grove, *Enemy Attack on Shipping*, pp. 113–14. Rahn, 'Atlantic and Arctic Ocean' VI, pp. 394–403. Rahn, 'Die Deutsche Seekriegführung 1943 bis 1945' X, 3–11 and 112–14. Hessler, *U-Boat War* II, 100–113.

6 Mawdsley, *War for the Seas*, pp. 328–35. Barnett, *Engage the Enemy*, pp. 625–6. L. Brown, *Radar History*, p. 355. Edgerton, *Britain's War Machine*, p. 155. Simpson, *Anglo-American Naval Relations* III, 5–12. Ball, *The Bitter Sea*, pp. 209–10, quotes 210,000 Axis prisoners taken on the surrender of Tunisia, and 2,000 who escaped.

7 Mawdsley, *War for the Seas*, p. 333.

8 Mawdsley, *War for the Seas*, pp. 334 and 376–7. Ross, *American War Plans*, pp. 39–52. Lacey, 'Creating an American Strategy', pp. 199–206. Murfett, *Naval Warfare*, p. 271. Barnett, *Engage the Enemy*, pp. 628–33 and 651–4. A. Smith, *Mountbatten*, pp. 260–62.

9 Kowner, 'Inter-Axis Connections', pp. 241–50. Rahn, 'Die Deutsche Seekriegführung 1943 bis 1945' X, 115–16. Marder, *Old Friends* II, 202–14. Symonds, *World War II at Sea*, p. 398.

10 Mawdsley, *War for the Seas*, pp. 245–7. Dull, *Imperial Japanese Navy*, pp. 259–60 and 267–70. J. D. Brown, *Carrier Operations*, p. 203. Faulkner, *War at Sea*, p. 176.

11 Dull, *Imperial Japanese Navy*, pp. 261–5. Faulkner, *War at Sea*, pp. 170–71.

12 O'Brien, *How the War was Won*, pp. 393–4. J. D. Brown, *Carrier Operations*, pp. 77–8, 202 and 207–8. Milner, 'Anglo-American Naval Co-operation'. Reynolds, *Fast Carriers*, pp. 34–5. Trent Hone, 'US Navy Surface Battle Doctrine'. Hone, 'Replacing Battleships with Aircraft Carriers', pp. 60–63.

13 Reardon, '"Gun Club" Mentality'. Murfett, *Naval Warfare*, p. 282. Hughes, *Fleet Tactics*, pp. 124–31. Dull, *Imperial Japanese Navy*, pp. 274–9. J. D. Brown, *Carrier Operations*, p. 210. Spector, *Eagle against the Sun*, pp. 200–201. Reynolds, *Fast Carriers*, p. 72. Robb-Webb, *British Pacific Fleet*, p. 84. Faulkner, *War at Sea*, p. 185.

14 T. C. Hone, 'Replacing Battleships with Aircraft Carriers', pp. 64–5.

15 Buckley, *RAF and Trade Defence*, pp. 154–8. Bell, *Churchill and Sea Power*, p. 279. Jones, *Fleet Air Arm* II, 427–31. Murfett, *Naval Warfare*, p. 275. Milner,

Battle of the Atlantic, pp. 146–9. Faulkner, *War at Sea*, p. 169. Mawdsley, *War for the Seas*, pp. 316–17. Bell, 'Very Long Range Aircraft'. Hinsley, *British Intelligence* III, i, 214–16.

16 Report of Proceedings, dated 6 June 1943, by courtesy of Commander J. A. A. McCoy, RN, *ex inf.* Rear-Admiral James Goldrick RAN.

17 Milner, *Battle of the Atlantic*, pp. 150–52. Blair, *Hitler's U-Boat War* II, 288–93. Hague, *Allied Convoy System*, p. 21. Syrett, *Defeat of the German U-Boats*, pp. 94–5 and 133–42. *BND*, pp. 856–63.

18 Campbell, *Naval Weapons*, pp. 101 and 162. Milner, *Battle of the Atlantic*, pp. 148–55. Syrett, *Defeat of the German U-Boats*, pp. 116–19 and 133–46. Hinsley, *British Intelligence* III, i, 212–14. Faulkner, *War at Sea*, p. 184.

19 'Dann werden wir siegen, das sagt mir mein Glaube an unsere Waffe und an Euch': Rahn, 'Die Deutsche Seekriegführung 1943 bis 1945' X, 97.

20 Simpson, *Cunningham Papers* II, 103. Faulkner, *War at Sea*, pp. 180–83 and 187. D. K. Brown, *Design and Construction* III, 70–78. Mawdsley, *War for the Seas*, pp. 336–7. P. Kennedy, *Engineers of Victory*, pp. 215–82. Symonds, *World War II at Sea*, pp. 424–40. A. Smith, *Mountbatten*, pp. 260–63. Hammond, 'British Perceptions of the Italian Navy, 1935–1943', pp. 828–9. Murfett, *Naval Warfare*, pp. 278–80 and 292–4. Ball, *The Bitter Sea*, pp. 217–18. *ODNB* sv Ramsay.

21 Faulkner, *War at Sea*, pp. 186–7. Hinsley, *British Intelligence* III, i, 95–9 and 337–40. Murfett, *Naval Warfare*, pp. 279–80 and 292–6. Mawdsley, *War for the Seas*, pp. 336–45. Ball, *The Bitter Sea*, pp. 233 and 238–9. Weinberg, 'German Strategy' I, 129 (in *CH2WW* I, 107–31). Barnett, *Engage the Enemy*, pp. 681–5.

22 Jones, *Mediterranean War*, pp. 97–102. Ball, *The Bitter Sea*, p. 248. Murfett, *Naval Warfare*, pp. 300–301 and 307–8. Peden, *Arms, Economics and British Strategy*, p. 222.

23 Krebs, 'War in the Pacific' VII, 726–33. Marder, *Old Friends* II, 202–9 and 216–36. Kowner, 'Inter-Axis Connections'.

Simpson, *Somerville Papers*, pp. 366–9.
Ross, *American War Plans*, pp. 68–74.

24 Mawdsley, *War for the Seas*, pp. 370–73 and 386–8. O'Brien, *How the War was Won*, pp. 413–14.

25 Murfett, *Naval Warfare*, pp. 302–3. Howse, *Radar at Sea*, pp. 66–8. Hessler, *U-Boat War* III, 32–5. Hinsley, *British Intelligence* III, i, 222–3. Vogel, 'War in the West' VII, 484.

26 Hessler, *U-Boat War* III, 26.

27 'Der Feind schaut uns in die Karten und nicht wir Ihn': Rahn, 'Die Deutsche Seekriegführung 1943 bis 1945' X, 125, quoting the *BdU* war diary.

28 Rahn, 'Die Deutsche Seekriegführung 1943 bis 1945' X, 122–5. Hessler, *U-Boat War* III, 25–7. Hinsley, *British Intelligence* III, i, 224. Syrett, *Defeat of the German U-Boats*, p. 256.

29 'Die Überwassertaktik des U-Bootes ist vorbei': Rahn, 'Die Deutsche Seekriegführung 1943 bis 1945' X, 126–30 at 130. Milner, *Battle of the Atlantic*, pp. 178–9. Syrett, *Defeat of the German U-Boats*, pp. 227–31 and 256–7. Hessler, *U-Boat War* III, 46. Hinsley, *British Intelligence* III, i, 226.

30 Boyd, *Naval Intelligence*, pp. 505–9. Rahn, 'Die Deutsche Seekriegführung 1943 bis 1945' X, 210–11. Levy, *Home Fleet*, pp. 136–7. Hinsley, *British Intelligence* III, i, 252–3.

31 '. . . sich irgendwelche Blößen gibt oder große Fehler macht': Rahn, 'Die Deutsche Seekriegführung 1943 bis 1945' X, 214. This was the Bey who had been promoted admiral for his lacklustre performance at Narvik in 1940.

32 Rahn, 'Die Deutsche Seekriegführung 1943 bis 1945' X, 211 and 213–19. Boyd, *Naval Intelligence*, pp. 507–9. Murfett, *Naval Warfare*, pp. 311–16. *BND*, pp. 861–3. Mawdsley, *War for the Seas*, pp. 318–19. Llewellyn-Jones, *Arctic Convoys*, pp. 110–14. Claasen, *Hitler's Northern War*, pp. 229–33. Woodman, *Arctic Convoys*, pp. 352–72. Levy, *Home Fleet*, pp. 136–43. Hinsley, *British Intelligence* III, i, 252–3, 263–9 and 537–41. Koehler, 'Operation "Ostfront"', p. 120. Faulkner, *War at Sea*, pp. 206–7.

Chapter 31

1 'Der Schiffsraum die Grundlage und Voraussetzung seiner operativer Freiheit [ist]': Rahn, 'Die Deutsche Seekriegführung 1943 bis 1945', p. 20.

2 Edgerton, *Britain's War Machine*, pp. xvii, 15–20 and 158–74.

3 Faulkner, *War at Sea*, pp. 168–9.

4 Tracy, *Attack on Maritime Trade*, pp. 195–203. K. Smith, 'Maritime Powers in Transition', p. 169. O'Hara, *Six Victories*, p. 185.

5 See further A Note on Conventions, p. xiv.

6 Mawdsley, *War for the Seas*, pp. 252–3. Edgerton, *Britain's War Machine*, p. xvii.

7 Bell, *Churchill and Sea Power*, pp. 274–7. G. Kennedy, 'Anglo-American Diplomatic Relations', pp. 42–4. Ross, *American War Plans*, pp. 46–52. M. Jones, *Mediterranean War*, pp. 54–7. Baer, *One Hundred Years of Sea Power*, p. 229.

8 M. Jones, *Mediterranean War*, p. 63.

9 Stoler, 'American Perception of British Mediterranean Strategy', pp. 325–37 (quoted pp. 327 and 334). Roberts, *Churchill*, p. 745. The J W P C's comment was probably drafted by its chairman, General Albert C. Wedemeyer, a graduate of the German *Kriegsakademie* and an important influence on General Marshall.

10 Stoler, 'American Perceptions of British Mediterranean Strategy', pp. 336–7. M. Jones, *Mediterranean War*, pp. 218–19. Roberts, *Churchill*, pp. 850–53. Simpson, *Cunningham Papers* II, 167.

11 Mawdsley, *War for the Seas*, pp. 376–9. Krebs, 'War in the Pacific' VII, 713–14 and 720–33. Goodman, *Joint Intelligence Committee* I, 125–6.

12 Simpson, *Anglo-American-Canadian Naval Relations*, pp. 46–8. Goodall, *Diary*, pp. 19–20 and 187. Postan, *British War Production*, pp. 47–66.

13 Simpson, *Anglo-American-Canadian Naval Relations*, pp. 9–12. Mawdsley, *War for the Seas,* pp. 376–7. Jones, *Mediterranean War*, pp. 139 and 147–8. Baer, *One Hundred Years of Sea Power*,

pp. 237–8. Krebs, 'War in the Pacific', pp. 713–14 and 726. Ross, *American War Plans*, pp. 46–52. Bath, *Tracking the Axis Enemy*, p. 108.

14 Simpson, *Anglo-American-Canadian Naval Relations*, pp. 5–6. Simpson, *Cunningham Papers* II, 141–65.

15 Simpson, *Anglo-American-Canadian Naval Relations*, pp. 11–12 and 16–18.

16 Spector, *Eagle against the Sun*, p. 207, quoting Arnold's diary.

17 Konvitz, 'Allied Bombing of French Ports'. Boog, 'Strategic Air War in Europe' VII, 11–20, 30–40, 50 and 74–82. O'Brien, *How the War was Won*, pp. 276–93. Biddle, *Rhetoric and Reality*, pp. 223–4.

18 Campbell, *Naval Weapons*, pp. 156–7 and 260–65. Baer, *One Hundred Years of Sea Power*, pp. 233–4. Mawdsley, *War for the Seas*, pp. 350–60. Krebs, 'War in the Pacific', p. 718. Smith, *Ultra-Magic Deals*, pp. 146–7. Donovan and Mack, *Codebreaking in the Pacific*, p. 331.

19 Vogel, 'War in the West', p. 498.

20 'Das deutsche Uboot ist in seiner Gesamtplanung, schiffbaulich und maschinenbaulich, die beste Leistung, die in der Entwicklungslinie dieses Uboots-Grundtyps, der auf 2 Antriebsarten, für Überwasser- und Unterwasserfahrt angewiesen ist, hat errichtet werden können'. To Erich Raeder, 24 Jun 1942, in Rahn, 'Einsatzbereitschaft und Kampfkraft deutscher U-Boote 1942', pp. 107–8. '1918 standards': Müller, 'Speer and Armament Policy', p. 646.

21 Rössler, 'U-boat Development and Building', pp. 127–35. Rössler, *U-Boat*, pp. 122–42. Herwig, 'Germany and the Battle of the Atlantic', pp. 80–83. Rahn, 'Die Deutsche Seekriegführung 1943 bis 1945', pp. 41–2.

22 Rössler, 'U-boat Development and Building', pp. 133–6. Rhys-Jones, 'The German System', pp. 138–57. Rahn, 'Einsatzbereitschaft und Kampfkraft deutscher U-Boote', pp. 82–110. Müller, 'Speer and Armaments Policy', pp. 659–60. Campbell, *Naval Weapons*, pp. 261–2. The most recent victim was the Russian submarine *Kursk*, sunk with all hands in the Barents Sea in 2000 by the explosion of an HTP torpedo.

23 Rössler, *U-Boat*, pp. 168–87, 214–31 and 240–65. Mawdsley, *War for the Seas*, pp. 322–3. Weinberg, 'German Strategy', p. 128.

24 Müller, 'Speer and Armament Policy', pp. 401–6, 649–50 and 713–20. Rahn, 'Die Deutsche Seekriegführung 1943 bis 1945', pp. 77–82. Wegner, 'Hitler's Grand Strategy', p. 142. Tooze, *Wages of Destruction*, pp. 614–15. Heinrich, *Warship Builders*, pp. 223–5. Hessler, *U-Boat War* III, 84–5.

25 Herwig, 'Germany and the Battle of the Atlantic', pp. 81–4. Müller, 'Speer and Armament Policy', pp. 404–8, 651 and 713. Tooze, *Wages of Destruction*, pp. 552–6.

26 Edgerton, *Warfare State*, p. 211.

27 Mawdsley, *War for the Seas*, pp. 313–14. Sutcliffe, 'Operational Research'. Edgerton, *Britain's War Machine*, pp. 140–47. Price, *Aircraft versus Submarine*, pp. 62–4. Boyd, *Naval Intelligence*, p. 488.

27A Sutcliffe, 'Operational Research', p. 423.

28 Edgerton, *Warfare State*, p. 211.

29 L. Brown, *Radar History*, p. 64.

30 Gardner, *Decoding History*, pp. 117–18. Hore, *Habit of Victory*, pp. 382–4. Edgerton, *Warfare State*, pp. 210–20. Hamilton, 'Three Cultures at the Admiralty', pp. 94–5. O'Brien, *How the War was Won*, pp. 256–8. Milner, *Battle of the Atlantic*, p. 184. Niestlé, 'Technical and Electronic Development', pp. 443–4. Lavery, *River Class Frigates*, pp. 179–81.

Chapter 32

1 Friedman, *British Battleship* II, 254–321 and 431–2. Bell, *Churchill and Sea Power*, pp. 304–5.

2 Goodall, *Diary*, p. 209.

3 J. D. Brown, *Carrier Operations*, pp. 293–4. D. K. Brown, *Nelson to Vanguard*, pp. 49–56. Friedman, *British Carrier Aviation*, pp. 19 and 110–40.

4 Friedman, *British Carrier Aviation*, pp. 110–54 and 254–67.

5 Friedman, *Naval Anti-Aircraft Guns*, pp. 227–9. Friedman, *Fighters over the Fleet*, p. 34.

6 Brown, *Carrier Fighters*, pp. 67 and 72–5. Reynolds, *Fast Carriers*, p. 72. Friedman, *British Carrier Aviation*, pp. 110–15 and 131–5. T. C. Hone, 'Replacing Battleships with Aircraft Carriers', pp. 60–65. Hone, *Learning War*, p. 165. J. D. Brown, *Carrier Operations*, pp. 200–210.

7 Mawdsley, *War for the Seas*, pp. 347–9. Jones, 'Fleet Air Arm and Trade Defense', pp. 142–7. Jones, *Fleet Air Arm* II, 580–85. J. D. Brown, *Carrier Operations*, pp. 35 and 40. Simpson, *Cunningham Papers* I, 516.

8 Hill, *Duty Free*, p. 138.

9 Hobbs, 'Naval Aviation, 1930–2000', pp. 81–2. Simpson, *Cunningham Papers* II, 163. Rahn, 'Atlantic and Arctic Ocean' VI, 397.

10 Friedman, *British Carrier Aviation*, pp. 177–82. D. K. Brown, *Nelson to Vanguard*, pp. 61–6. J. D. Brown, *Carrier Operations*, pp. 34–41 and 395–6. Hobbs, 'Naval Aviation, 1930–2000', p. 81. Grove, *Enemy Attack on Shipping*, pp. 291–7. Woodman, *Arctic Convoys*, pp. 382–447.

11 Hobbs, 'Ship-Borne Air Anti-Submarine Warfare' (quoted pp. 393–4). Hague, *Allied Convoy System*, pp. 83–8 and 97–9. Grove, *Enemy Attack on Shipping*, pp. 291–7. Friedman, *British Carrier Aviation*, pp. 193–4. Jones, *Fleet Air Arm* II, 384–6.

12 Friedman, *British Cruisers* II, 156–71 and 186–93.

13 Friedman, *British Cruisers* II, 142–92 and 200–39. Lacroix and Wells, *Japanese Cruisers*, p. 451. D. K. Brown, *Nelson to Vanguard*, pp. 74–7. These Colony Class cruisers were named after larger British colonies, whereas the American-built Colony Class frigates were named after smaller British colonies.

14 Brown, *Design and Construction* III, 132–9.

15 Lavery, *River-Class Frigates*, p. 20, quoting Lt-Cdr Robert Bower of HMS *Fleur de Lys*. Fraser quoted in Goodall, *Diary*, p. 64.

16 Friedman, *British Destroyers* II, 133–8. A. Lambert, 'Seapower 1939–1940', pp. 92–4. D. K. Brown, *Atlantic Escorts*, pp. 41–51, 134–5 and 148–9. D. K. Brown,

Design and Construction II, 48–51. D. K. Brown, 'Weather and Warships', p. 615. Lavery, *Churchill's Navy*, pp. 226–7. Endurance from Wildish, 'Western Approaches Command', p. 53. The class was oddly named in that the sailing corvettes of the eighteenth and nineteenth centuries had been bigger than the sloops of that day, but these were smaller than the 1930s sloop classes.

17 Goodall, *Diary*, pp. 161–2 (written in 1939).

18 Goodall, *Diary*, p. 69 (both quotations). Friedman, *British Destroyers* I, 69–79, and II, 69–77. D. K. Brown, *Nelson to Vanguard*, pp. 103–6. D. K. Brown, *Design and Construction* I, 10–11, offers more criticism from the standpoint of a senior constructor of a later generation.

19 D. K. Brown, *Century of Naval Construction*, p. 163. D. K. Brown, 'Naval Rearmament', p. 22. Goodall, *Diary*, pp. 7–8, 22–4 and 163. Scott and Hughes, *War Production*, p. 93.

20 Lavery, *River Class Frigates*, pp. 21–72. D. K. Brown, *Atlantic Escorts*, pp. 77–80 and 126–7. D. K. Brown, *Official Record* II, 47 and 51–5. Goodall, *Diary*, pp. 198 and 297. Buxton, 'Warship Building and Repair'.

21 Gardiner, *Fighting Ships 1922–1946*, pp. 61–2 and 135–41. D. K. Brown, *Atlantic Escorts*, pp. 90–107 and 128–37. D. K. Brown, *Nelson to Vanguard*, pp. 129–37. Friedman, *British Destroyers* II, 69–85 and 138–45.

22 D. K. Brown, *Nelson to Vanguard*, pp. 129–31, and *Official Record* II, 55–62. D. K. Brown, *Atlantic Escorts*, pp. 120–26, and 'Atlantic Escorts 1939–45', p. 569. Buxton, 'Warship Building and Repair', pp. 87–8. Friedman, *British Destroyers* II, 144–51. Lindberg and Todd, *Anglo-American Shipbuilding*, pp. 105–15.

23 Friedman, *British Destroyers* II, 142–5. D. K. Brown, *Atlantic Escorts*, pp. 36–40; and 'Atlantic Escorts 1939–45', pp. 571–3. Franklin, *Anti-Submarine Capability*, pp. 153–62.

24 Friedman, *British Destroyers* II, 138–45. Lavery, *Shield of Empire*, pp. 348–9.

Edgerton, *Warfare State*, p. 351. Lavery, *River Class Frigates*, pp. 88–95.
25 Friedman, *British Destroyers* II, 146–52. Gardner, *Decoding History*, p. 109. Llewellyn-Jones, *Anti-Submarine Warfare*, p. 34. D. K. Brown, *Atlantic Escorts*, pp. 114–20. Zimmerman, 'Technology and Tactics', pp. 484–6. D. K. Brown, *Official Record* II, 55–60. Rawling, 'Challenge of Modernization'. Lavery, *Shield of Empire*, pp. 348–9.
26 McLean, 'Technological and Tactical Change'. Llewellyn-Jones, 'Anti-Submarine Warfare', pp. 68–80. Sarty, 'Limits of Ultra'.
27 Hague, *Allied Convoy System*, pp. 89–99. D. K. Brown, *Design and Construction* III, 13–39 and 153–61. D. B. Fisher, 'Fleet Train', pp. 411–12.
28 Reuter, *Funkmess*, pp. 23–31 and 54. Kingsley, *Radar* II, 192 and 274–5. Howse, *Radar at Sea*, pp. 45–9, 55 and 73. Hezlet, *Electron and Sea Power*, p. 193. L. Brown, *Radar History*, pp. 1, 73, 76, 105–6 and 122–8. Cernuschi, *Marinelettro*, pp. 14–16, 45–6 and 52–3. Friedman, *Naval Firepower*, pp. 144–5. Llewellyn-Jones, *Arctic Convoys*, pp. 110–14. Rahn, 'Die Deutsche Seekriegführung 1943 bis 1945' X, 213–19. Mawdsley, *War for the Seas*, pp. 318–19. Murfett, *Naval Warfare*, pp. 311–16.
29 Lavery, *River Class*, pp. 98–9. Campbell, *Naval Weapons*, p. 264. Hackmann, *Seek and Strike*, pp. 310–13. D. K. Brown, *Atlantic Escorts*, pp. 108–14. Milner, *Battle of the Atlantic*, pp. 171–5. Hessler, *U-Boat War* III, 25–7. Hinsley, *British Intelligence* III, i, 222–3.
30 Boyd, *Naval Intelligence*, p. 519. Rahn, 'Die Deutsche Seekriegführung 1943 bis 1945' X, 121–3. Campbell, *Naval Weapons*, pp. 276–7. Mawdsley, *War for the Seas*, pp. 322–3. Gardner, *Decoding History*, pp. 207–8.
31 Rahn, 'Die Deutsche Seekriegführung 1943 bis 1945' X, 100.
32 Hessler, *U-Boat War* III, 4–5. Hinsley, *British Intelligence* III, i, 222–3. Campbell, *Naval Weapons*, pp. 264–5. Milner, *Battle of the Atlantic*, pp. 171–5. Westwood, *U-boat War*, pp. 265–6.

Hackmann, *Seek and Strike*, pp. 320–22. Gardner, *Decoding History*, p. 105.

Chapter 33

1 Lavery, *All Hands*, pp. 25 and 50–53. Lavery, *Hostilities Only*, pp. 26–8.
2 Lavery, *Hostilities Only*, pp. 33–6. Owen, *Plain Yarns*, pp. 184–7. The Senior Psychologist was Alec Rodger (1907–82), later Professor of Occupational Psychology at Birkbeck College, London; no kin of the author as far as he knows.
3 Lavery, *Hostilities Only*, pp. 63 and 108–17. Moore, *Greenie*, pp. 135–8. Lavery, *All Hands*, pp. 57–9. Lavery, *Churchill's Navy*, pp. 143–8. Lavery, *River Class Frigates*, pp. 141–4.
4 Moore, *Greenie*, pp. 134–43.
5 Lavery, *Hostilities Only*, p. 279.
6 Parkin, *Birds and Wolves*, p. 258.
7 Lavery, *Hostilities Only*, p. 69.
8 Lavery, *Hostilities Only*, p. 69, quoting Oram's diary.
9 Lavery, *Hostilities Only*, pp. 23, 69 (quoted), 127 and 154–7. Owen, *Plain Yarns from the Fleet*, pp. 184–7. Brown, *Fittest of the Fit*, pp. 11–13. Lavery, *In Which They Served*, p. 147. Prysor, 'Morale', p. 66.
10 Howarth, *Royal Navy's Reserves*, p. 83. Lavery, *Hostilities Only*, p. 69. J. D. Brown, *Carrier Fighters*, p. 40.
11 Kerr and Granville, *R.N.V.R.*, p. 195.
12 Lavery, *Churchill's Navy*, p. 136, quoting an Admiralty handbook for First Lieutenants, ca. 1932.
13 Officer of the Deck, equivalent to a British Officer of the Watch.
14 Wellings, *On His Majesty's Service*, p. 67. Written late in 1941 when Wellings was Assistant US Naval Attaché in London but spent much time afloat in British ships.
15 Lavery, *Churchill's Navy*, pp. 136–7. Lavery, *All Hands*, pp. 51–5 and 70–71. Lavery, *Hostilities Only*, pp. 131–3. Hone, *Learning War*, pp. 304–7. Spector, *At War at Sea*, p. 263. Godspeed, 'Carrier-Based Close Air Support', p. 229.
16 Lavery, *Churchill's Navy*, p. 138, quoting PRO: ADM 231/235.

17 A. H. Cherry, *Yankee RN* (London, 1951), p. 385. Cherry was an American who illegally enlisted in the RNVR before the US entered the war and served through to 1945 when he retired as a Commander RNVR. Cf. Lavery, *In Which They Served*, p. 264, and Lavery, *River Class Frigates*, pp. 131–5.

18 Connell, *Jack's War*, p. 177.

19 Lavery, *Hostilities Only*, p. 24.

20 Hill, *Duty Free*, pp. 125–6.

21 Hanson, *Carrier Pilot*, p. 146.

22 Brown, *Fittest of the Fit*, pp. 106–10. Jones, *Fleet Air Arm* I, 267–70. Goddard, 'Operational Fatigue'.

23 Hill, *Duty Free*, p. 91.

24 Hill, *Duty Free*, p. 57.

25 Le Bailly, *The Man around the Engine*, pp. 107, 113 and 127–34.

26 Hennessy and Jinks, *Silent Deep*, pp. 45–63 (quoted p. 62).

27 Hennessy and Jinks, *Silent Deep*, pp. 8 (quoting Commodore Martin Macpherson) and 67.

28 Hennessy and Jinks, *Silent Deep*, p. 63, quoting Admiral Sir John 'Sandy' Woodward, who joined the Submarine Service in 1954.

29 Prysor, *Citizen Sailors*, p. 323.

30 *BND*, p. 1002.

31 Prysor, *Citizen Sailor*, pp. 170–71.

32 Brown, *Fittest of the Fit*, p. 72 ('East Indies' referring to the experience of the author's father aboard *Emerald* in 1941; quotation referring to 1943 when she was back in home waters).

33 Brown, *Fittest of the Fit*, pp. 70–81. Lavery, *River Class Frigates*, pp. 150–58. Lavery, *Churchill's Navy*, p. 230. Goldrick, 'Life at Sea', p. 243. Connell, *Jack's War*, p. 58. Bailey, *Corvettes and Their Crews*, pp. 90–96. D. K. Brown, *Atlantic Escorts*, pp. 128–37, and 'Atlantic Escorts, 1939–45', pp. 574–82.

34 Connell, *Jack's War*, pp. 24–5. Warlow, *Pusser*, p. 56. Lavery, *Churchill's Navy*, pp. 44–5.

35 S. Gorley Putt, *Men Dressed as Seamen* (London, 1943), pp. 80–81.

36 Connell, *Jack's War*, p. 79.

37 Brown, *Fittest of the Fit*, pp. 82–5. *BND*, No. 532.

38 Goldrick, ' "A" Teams', pp. 14–15. Friedman, *British Submarines* I, 277.

39 Moore, *Greenie*, pp. 144–61.

40 Lavery, *All Hands*, pp. 54–5. Dull, *Imperial Japanese Navy*, pp. 332–3. Murfett, *Naval Warfare*, p. 444.

41 Brown, *Fittest of the Fit*, pp. 175–7. Prysor, *Citizen Sailors*, pp. 133–41. Goldrick, 'Life at Sea'. Connell, *Jack's War*, p. 32. D. K. Brown, 'Weather and Warships'. Bailey, *Corvettes and Their Crews*, pp. 115–18.

42 Hague, *Allied Convoy System*, pp. 89–95 and 101–5. Lavery, *Hostilities Only*, pp. 245–8. Lane, 'Human Economy of the Merchant Navy', p. 50. Dickinson, *Wisdom and War*, p. 174.

43 Lavery, *Hostilities Only*, pp. 272–3. Lavery, *In Which They Served*, p. 273. Prysor, 'Morale at Sea', pp. 266–75.

44 Prysor, 'Morale at Sea', pp. 277–305.

Chapter 34

1 Also the smaller *Ranger*, which was never regarded as fit for the front line. Mawdsley, *War for the Seas*, pp. 386–8 and 392–4. Ross, *American War Plans*, pp. 216–19. Faulkner, *War at Sea*, pp. 204–5 and 213–15. O'Brien, *How the War was Won*, pp. 391–2 and 413–14. Trent Hone, 'US Navy Surface Battle Doctrine', pp. 79–81. T. C. Hone, 'Replacing Battleships with Aircraft Carriers', pp. 66–73.

2 Paine, *Japanese Empire*, pp. 162–4. Spector, *Eagle against the Sun*, pp. 365–9. Faulkner, *War at Sea*, pp. 234–5.

3 Krebs, 'War in the Pacific' VII, 713–14. Baer, *One Hundred Years of Sea Power*, pp. 237–45. O'Brien, *How the War was Won*, pp. 392–402. Spector, *Eagle against the Sun*, pp. 237–45. Davis and Engerman, *Naval Blockades*, pp. 381–2. Ross, *American War Plans*, pp. 112–13.

4 Symonds, *World War II at Sea*, pp. 538–52. O'Brien, *How the War was Won*, pp. 374–7 and 420–21. Murfett, *Naval Warfare*, pp. 350–53. Trent Hone, 'US Navy Surface Battle Doctrine', pp. 83–6. Hamer, *Bombers versus Battleships*, pp. 247–69. Spector, *At War at Sea*, pp.

280–86. Spector, *Eagle against the Sun*, pp. 302–12 and 368–9. Baer, *One Hundred Years of Sea Power*, pp. 246–50. Marder, *Old Friends* II, 340–42 and 379–80. Dull, *Imperial Japanese Navy*, pp. 303–11. Reynolds, *Fast Carriers*, pp. 151–206 and 400–406. Faulkner, *War at Sea*, pp. 234–5. Friedman, *Fighters over the Fleet*, pp. 124–5.

5 French, 'British Military Strategy' (in *CH2WW* I, 45). O'Brien, *How the War was Won*, pp. 276–89, 323–5 and 469–70. Boog, 'Strategic Air War in Europe' VII, 85–102. Vogel, 'War in the West' VII, 556.

6 Roskill, *War at Sea* III, ii, 32–3. L. Brown, *Radar History*, pp. 340–43. Woodman, *Arctic Convoys*, pp. 382–94. Blair, *Hitler's U-Boat War* II, 516–18. Claasen, *Hitler's Northern War*, p. 233. Hinsley, *British Intelligence* III, i, 282–5. Gardner, 'Smart Mining without Smart Mines'.

7 Rahn, 'Die Deutsche Seekriegführung 1943 bis 1945' X, 219–22. Roskill, *War at Sea* III, ii, 169. John Asmussen and Kjetil Åkra, *Tirpitz: Hitlers siste Slagskip* (Mid-Troms Museum, 2006), pp. 158–65. Barnett, *Engage the Enemy*, p. 825.

8 Woodman, *Arctic Convoys*, pp. 409 and 418. Hinsley, *British Intelligence* III, ii, 491–5. Milner, *Battle of the Atlantic*, pp. 216–17. Symonds, *World War II at Sea*, p. 463. Murfett, *Naval Warfare*, pp. 374 and 407–8. Levy, *Home Fleet*, pp. 148–9 and 154. Rahn, 'Die Deutsche Seekriegführung 1943 bis 1945' X, 89.

9 Roberts, *Masters and Commanders*, pp. 190–94, 361–71. Hastings, *Overlord*, pp. 26–8, 60. Jones, *Mediterranean War*, pp. 237–41. Bell, *Twelve Turning Points*, pp. 166–8. Roskill, *War at Sea* III, ii, 8–10.

10 Roskill, *War at Sea* III, ii, 8–10.

11 Lavery, *Shield of Empire*, pp. 364–70. Lavery, *Hostilities Only*, pp. 207–22. Mahnken, 'US Grand Strategy', p. 209. Lewis, 'Planning and Doctrine for Operation Overlord'. Roskill, *War at Sea* III, ii, 10.

12 Faulkner, *War at Sea*, pp. 228–31. Vogel, 'War in the West', VII, 498–507. Andrew, *Defence of the Realm*, pp. 306–7. Roskill, *War at Sea* III, ii, 12–14, 41–2.

13 Hastings, *Overlord*, pp. 31–4, 335–48 (Allied Order of Battle). Mawdsley, *War for the Seas*, pp. 419–22. O'Brien, *How the War was Won*, pp. 212–15, 224–7. Roberts, *Masters and Commanders*, pp. 361–71, 437. Symonds, *World War II at Sea*, pp. 498–509. Barnett, *Engage the Enemy*, pp. 754–5. Lavery, *Shield of Empire*, pp. 365–8. Jones, *Mediterranean War*, pp. 151, 182. Lavery, *Hostilities Only*, pp. 207–22. Harding, 'Amphibious Warfare, 1930–1939'. Simpson, *Anglo-American-Canadian Naval Relations*, pp. 175–8, 263–7. Farquharson-Roberts, *War to War*, p. 208. Fletcher, *WRNS*, p. 59. Roskill, *War at Sea* III, ii, 12–23, 33–7, 53.

14 Faulkner, *War at Sea*, pp. 228–31. Lambert, *Admirals*, p. 257. Gordon, *Rules of the Game*, pp. 183–7. Brooks, *Jutland*, pp. 54–6.

15 Boog, 'Strategic Air War in Europe', VII, 81–102. Biddle, *Rhetoric and Reality*, pp. 233–5. Vogel, 'War in the West', VII, 556. Hastings, *Overlord*, pp. 41–5.

16 Hastings, *Overlord*, pp. 70–77, 89–104, 348. Roskill, *War at Sea* III, ii, 35–6, 39–40, 47–53, 63, 71. Vogel, 'War in the West', VII, 585–6. Mawdsley, *War for the Seas*, pp. 422–6. Murfett, *Naval Warfare*, pp. 339–45. Lewis, 'Planning and Doctrine for Operation Overlord'.

17 Roskill, *War at Sea* III, ii, 73.

18 O'Brien, *How the War was Won*, pp. 212–18. Boyd, *Naval Intelligence*, pp. 529–35. Simpson, *Anglo-American-Canadian Naval Relations*, pp. 175–92, 263–7. Mawdsley, *War for the Seas*, pp. 419–27. Murfett, *Naval Warfare*, pp. 339–45. Rahn, 'Die Deutsche Seekriegführung 1943 bis 1945' X, 139–45. Vogel, 'War in the West' VII, 505–7, 534, 556, 576, 582–6. Hinsley, *British Intelligence* III, ii, 125–32. Lewis, 'Planning and Doctrine for Operation Overlord'. Bell, *Twelve Turning Points*, pp. 166–8. Barnett, *Engage the Enemy*, pp. 834–5. Milner, *Battle of the Atlantic*, pp. 197–201. McLean, 'Technological and Tactical Change', pp. 88–92.

19 Simpson, *Anglo-American-Canadian Naval Relations*, pp. 191–2, 313–24.

Mawdsley, *War for the Seas*, p. 430.
Barnett, *Engage the Enemy*, pp. 849–52.

20 Faulkner, *War at Sea*, pp. 221, 224, 236–7. Simpson, *Anglo-American-Canadian Naval Relations*, pp. 351–3. Bell, *Churchill and Sea Power*, pp. 292–3. Robb-Webb, *British Pacific Fleet*, pp. 89–91, and 'Light Two Lanterns', p. 129. J. D. Brown, *Carrier Operations*, p. 93. Marder, *Old Friends* II, 305–28, 381–7.

21 Marder, *Old Friends* II, 259–81, 311–29. Simpson, *Somerville Papers*, pp. 366–77. O'Brien, *How the War was Won*, pp. 427–9.

22 Day, 'Britain's Pacific Pledge', p. 76, quoting Captain Charles Lambe.

23 Bell, *Churchill and Sea Power*, pp. 292–5. Robb-Webb, 'Light Two Lanterns', pp. 129–32. Robb-Webb, *British Pacific Fleet*, pp. 11, 27, 30–35. Marder, *Old Friends* I, 334–9. Day, 'Promise and Performance', pp. 75–80. Simpson, *Cunningham Papers* II, 320 (quoted). Simpson, *Anglo-American-Canadian Naval Relations*, p. 54.

24 Marder, *Old Friends* II, 347, quoting Brooke's diary. Roberts, *Churchill*, pp. 837–8. Bell, *Churchill and Sea Power*, p. 301. Sarantakes, 'One Last Crusade', pp. 432–8. Simpson, *Anglo-American-Canadian Naval Relations, 1943–1945*, pp. 67–70, 329–38. Hall, 'Final Defeat of Japan', pp. 97–8.

25 Simpson, *Anglo-American Canadian Naval Relations*, p. 362, quoting Captain C. J. Wheeler USN, reporting to Admiral Nimitz from Colombo in November 1944.

26 Robb-Webb, *British Pacific Fleet*, p. 11 (quoting Fraser), pp. 56–7, 66–8. Robb-Webb, 'Light Two Lanterns', pp. 135–9. Hall, 'Final Defeat of Japan', pp. 96–8. Baxter, 'British Planning for the Defeat of Japan', pp. 259–62. Marder, *Old Friends* II, 343–8, 510–11. Simpson, *Anglo-American-Canadian Naval Relations*, pp. 329–38, 370–87. Mawdsley, *War for the Seas*, pp. 411–12. Sarantakes, 'One Last Crusade', p. 450.

27 Reynolds, *Fast Carriers*, pp. 292–3, 347–9. Symonds, *World War II at Sea*, pp. 601–3. Murfett, *Naval Warfare*

1919–1945, p. 442. Marder, *Old Friends* II, 510–12.

28 Spector, *Eagle against the Sun*, pp. 365–9. Ross, *American War Plans*, p. 80. Reynolds, *Fast Carriers*, p. 64. Marder, *Old Friends* II, 291–6. Johnson, *Pacific Campaign*, p. 147 (quoted).

29 Symonds, *World War II at Sea*, pp. 554–7. Baer, *One Hundred Years of Sea Power*, pp. 253–4. Reynolds, *Fast Carriers*, pp. 255–8. Hone, 'US Navy Surface Battle Doctrine', pp. 87–90. Hone, *Learning War*, pp. 280–81, 295–8. Spector, *Eagle against the Sun*, pp. 422–3. Murfett, *Naval Warfare*, pp. 350–53. Mawdsley, *War for the Seas*, pp. 443–5. Marder, *Old Friends* II, 511–12.

30 Symonds, *World War II at Sea*, pp. 572–8, 586. Mawdsley, *War for the Seas*, pp. 446–56. Spector, *Eagle against the Sun*, pp. 424–39. Hone, *Learning War*, pp. 280–81, 295–8. Murfett, *Naval Warfare*, pp. 377–401. Charrier, 'Japanese Naval Tactics and Strategy', pp. 221–3. Dull, *Imperial Japanese Navy*, pp. 313–31. Reynolds, *Fast Carriers*, pp. 254–83. Faulkner, *War at Sea*, pp. 240–47. Even more than usual in naval warfare, these complex actions can only be understood with good maps.

31 Hessler, *U-Boat War* III, 97.

32 Rahn, 'Die Deutsche Seekriegführung 1943 bis 1945' X, 5 ('fanatischste Hingabe', 'härtesten Siegeswillen', 'bedingungslosen Gehorsam' and 'Hingabe bis zum letzten Atemzug').

33 Rahn, 'Die Deutsche Seekriegführung 1943 bis 1945' X, 93: 'Einer bei Dönitz noch anhaltenden trügerischen Flucht in Illusionen, da er – im Banne Hitlers stehend – nicht in Alternativen denken wollte od konnte.'

34 Rahn, 'Die Deutsche Seekriegführung 1943 bis 1945' X, 29–53, 92–3. McLean, 'Technological and Tactical Change'. Milner, *Battle of the Atlantic*, pp. 200–201. Hinsley, *British Intelligence* III, ii, 466–74. Sarty, 'Limits of Ultra'.

35 Rahn, 'Die Deutsche Seekriegführung 1943 bis 1945' X, 136–42, 181–205. Simpson, *Anglo-American-Canadian Naval Relations*, pp. 222–3. Müller, 'Speer and Armament Policy' II, 735.

36 Hinsley, *British Intelligence* III, ii, 475–87, 625–8. Milner, *Battle of the Atlantic*, pp. 220–33. Murfett, *Naval Warfare*, pp. 428–37. Rahn, 'Die Deutsche Seekriegführung 1943 bis 1945' X, 159–75, 268–73. Faulkner, *War at Sea*, pp. 249, 254–5. Llewellyn-Jones, *Arctic Convoys*, pp. xi–xv. Hartwig, *Dönitz*, pp. 118–19. U-boat statistics from Rahn X, 169, with somewhat different figures in Milner, p. 230.

37 Symonds, *World War II at Sea*, pp. 595–6, 604–11. Baer, *One Hundred Years of Sea Power*, pp. 264–5. Reynolds, *Fast Carriers*, p. 248. Faulkner, *War at Sea*, pp. 260–61.

38 Meaning 'divine wind' and referring to the 1281 typhoon that destroyed a Mongol invasion fleet. The parallel with Japan's situation in 1944 is obvious, but although *kamikaze* is a Japanese word and a Japanese historical allusion, it was not officially adopted by the Japanese services during the war.

39 Symonds, *World War II at Sea*, pp. 608–9. J. D. Brown, *Carrier Fighters*, p. 151.

40 Robb-Webb, *British Pacific Fleet*, p. 45. Faulkner, *War at Sea*, pp. 262–3.

41 Robb-Webb, *British Pacific Fleet*, pp. 117–19. Sarantakes, 'One Last Crusade', pp. 451–8. Mawdsley, *War for the Seas*, pp. 464–9. Hall, 'Final Defeat of Japan', p. 99. Baxter, 'British Planning for the Defeat of Japan', pp. 265–70.

42 Hall, 'Final Defeat of Japan', pp. 99–108. Baxter, 'British Planning for the Defeat of Japan', pp. 265–70. Ross, *American War Plans*, pp. 154–5. Baer, *One Hundred Years of Sea Power*, pp. 264–8. Howse, *Radar at Sea*, pp. 248–51. Simpson, *Anglo-American-Canadian Naval Relations*, pp. 422–5, 441–2. Hobbs, *British Pacific Fleet*, pp. 129–30, 145–7. Robb-Webb, 'New Tricks for Old Sea Dogs', pp. 121–4. Faulkner, *War at Sea*, p. 264. J. D. Brown, *Carrier Operations*, pp. 94–100. Sarantakes, 'One Last Crusade', pp. 454–7.

43 Marder, *Old Friends* II, 412–28. Reynolds, *Fast Carriers*, p. 346. Reynolds, *Long Shadow*, p. 303.

44 Mawdsley, *War for the Seas*, pp. 464–5. Symonds, *World War II at Sea*, pp.

625–9. Murfett, *Naval Warfare*, p. 441. Reynolds, *Fast Carriers*, p. 341. Dull, *Imperial Japanese Navy*, pp. 332–5.

45 Mawdsley, *War for the Seas*, p. 411. Murfett, *Naval Warfare*, p. 444.

46 Sarantakes, 'One Last Crusade', pp. 459–65. *BND*, No. 475, 'British Pacific Fleet: Tactical Lessons'. Reynolds, *Fast Carriers*, pp. 372–4.

Chapter 35

1 Overy, *Why the Allies Won*, pp. 372–4 and 395. Müller, 'Speer and Armament Policy' II, 715–24, 735, 747 and 811–17. Rahn, 'Die Deutsche Seekriegführung 1943 bis 1945', p. 84.

2 Bonatz, *Seekrieg im Äther*, p. 214. Erskine, 'U-Boats, Homing Signals and HFDF', p. 327. Hessler, *U-Boat War* III, 81. Rahn, 'Die Deutsche Seekriegführung 1943 bis 1945', pp. 100–107. Hinsley, *British Intelligence* III, ii, 852–3.

3 Müller, 'Speer and Armament Policy', p. 713.

4 Overy, *Why the Allies Won*, pp. 372–3.

5 'Einer bei Dönitz noch anhaltenden trügerischen Flucht in Illusionen, da er – im Banne Hitlers stehend – nicht in Alternativen denken wollte oder konnte': Rahn, 'Die Deutsche Seekriegführung 1943 bis 1945', pp. 92–3.

6 'Ich muß es nochmal als mein innerste Überzeugung sagen, der Führer hat immer recht. Er hat in allen Plänen und Maßnahmen recht behalten gegen den Widerspruch der Generale, die nur ihren kleinen Kreis übersehen . . .' Rahn, 'Die Deutsche Seekriegführung 1943 bis 1945', p. 55.

7 Herwig, 'Germany and the Battle of the Atlantic', p. 84.

8 Rawlings to Fraser, 28 Apr 1945, in Simpson, *Anglo-American-Canadian Naval Relations*, p. 403.

9 Sarantakes, 'One Last Crusade', p. 442, quoting Fraser's formal despatch to the Admiralty covering November 1944 to November 1945 from PRO: ADM 199/118.

10 The origin of the phrase 'fleet train' seems to be unknown to the standard

means of reference, but it is evidently
parallel to the military sense of 'train', as
in 'waggon train' or 'artillery train'.

11 Fisher, 'Fleet Train', p. 425.

12 Postan, *British War Production*, pp. 370–
80. Robb-Webb, 'Light Two Lanterns',
pp. 131–2. John Curtin suffered a heart
attack in November 1944 and died in
July 1945.

13 Fisher, 'Fleet Train', quoted p. 426. D. K.
Brown, 'Official Record' III, 34–7.

14 Fisher, 'Fleet Train'. D. K. Brown, *Design
and Construction* III, 13–39. D. K.
Brown, *Century of Naval Construction*,
pp. 186–7. Hobbs, *British Pacific Fleet*, p.
171. Wells, *Social History*, p. 210. D. K.
Brown, *Nelson to Vanguard*, pp. 147–9.

15 Hobbs, *British Pacific Fleet*, pp. 108–9
and 120–21. Simpson, *Somerville Papers*,
pp. 470 and 539. Tom Frame, *No Pleasure
Cruise: The Story of the Royal Australian
Navy* (Crows Nest, NSW, 2004) pp. 194–
5. Goodall, *Diary*, pp. 75 and 238–9.

16 Hobbs, *British Pacific Fleet*, pp. 125, 131
and 156–8. Marder, *Old Friends* II, 405–
8. 'Neurotic' was also Rawlings'
description of Vian (Simpson, *Anglo-
American-Canadian Naval Relations*,
p. 402).

17 Nash, *Mobile Logistic Support*, pp. 36–42.
Marder, *Old Friends* II, 357–70. Pugh,
'Military Need', pp. 39–43. Simpson,
*Anglo-American-Canadian Naval
Relations*, pp. 17–18, 27–35 and 85–91.

18 Coles, 'King and the British Pacific Fleet',
pp. 117–18. Robb-Webb, 'New Tricks for
Old Sea Dogs'. Lindberg and Todd,
Anglo-American Shipbuilding, pp. 116–19.
Postan, *British War Production*, pp. 381–
7. Boyd, *Naval Intelligence*, pp. 545–7.
Hobbs, *British Pacific Fleet*, p. 156.
Simpson, *Anglo-American-Canadian
Naval Relations*, pp. 333–8, 369, 403–6,
412–13, 434–5 and 448. Roskill, *War at
Sea* III, ii, 426–30.

19 Sarantakes, 'One Last Crusade', pp. 447
and 449.

20 Simpson, *Cunningham Papers* II, 175–81.
Peden, *Arms, Economics and British
Strategy*, pp. 218–19. Vogel, 'War in the
West' VII, 576. Owen, *No More Heroes*,
p. 177.

21 Mawdsley, *War for the Seas*, pp. 392–3.

22 Faulkner, *War at Sea*, pp. 205 and 212–
13. T. C. Hone, 'Replacing Battleships
with Aircraft Carriers', pp. 66–73.
Hobbs, *British Pacific Fleet*, pp. 25–7.
Reynolds, *Fast Carriers*, pp. 128–9, 135–7
and 251. Mawdsley, *War for the Seas*, pp.
386–92.

23 Robb-Webb, *British Pacific Fleet*, pp.
96–112.

24 Reynolds, *The Fast Carriers*, p. 251.
Hobbs, *British Pacific Fleet*, pp. 120–21.
Mawdsley, *War for the Seas*, pp. 389–92.
Spector, *Eagle against the Sun*, pp. 300
and 426–7.

25 Marder, *Old Friends* II, 357–9 and 364–
70. Nash, *Mobile Logistic Support*, p. 37.
Weir, 'A Truly Allied Undertaking', pp.
111–13. Baer, *One Hundred Years of Sea
Power*, p. 228. Pugh, 'Military Need', pp.
42–3.

26 Reynolds, *Fast Carriers*, p. 251. Faulkner,
War at Sea, pp. 240–41. Spector, *Eagle
against the Sun*, p. 300. Mawdsley, *War
for the Seas*, pp. 391–2.

27 Reynolds, *Fast Carriers*, pp. 121–5
and 213.

28 Boyd, *Naval Intelligence*, pp. 541–7.
Kohnen, 'Group Monsoon', pp. 254–6.
B. F. Smith, *Ultra-Magic Deals*, pp. 146–
55 and 170–226. Erskine, 'The 1944 Naval
BRUSA Agreement'. Aldrich,
Intelligence and the War against Japan,
pp. 241–56. M. Smith, *The Emperor's
Codes*, pp. 111, 148–9, 160–69, 226–8 and
264–77. Krebs, 'War in the Pacific', VII,
717–18. Donovan and Mack,
Codebreaking in the Pacific, pp. 38 and
323–31. Bath, *Tracking the Axis Enemy*,
pp. 223–4.

29 Benesch, *Way of the Samurai*, pp. 82–8,
104–9, 174–6 and 242–5. Evans and
Peattie, *Kaigun*, p. 4 and n.4. Marder, *Old
Friends* II, 477–94 and 503–4. Krebs,
'War in the Pacific', pp. 763–81 and 822–
34. Overy, *Why the Allies Won*, p. 370.

Epilogue

1 Paine, *Wars for Asia*, pp. 123–270.

2 Perkins, 'Unequal Partners', p. 52, quoting
The Economist of 15 December 1945.

3 P. M. Kennedy, 'Mahan versus Mackinder', pp. 81–2. Broadberry and Howlett, 'Blood, Sweat and Tears', pp. 175–6. Hall, 'Mere Drops in the Ocean', pp. 109–10. Peden, *Arms, Economics and British Strategy*, pp. 198 and 245. Darwin, *Empire Project*, pp. 509–19 and 531–2. Friedman, *Fifty-Year War*, pp. 30–31. Hancock and Gowing, *British War Economy* (rev. edn. 1975), p. 548. Pugh, 'Military Need and Civil Necessity', pp. 38–43. Robb-Webb, *British Pacific Fleet*, p. 136. Crowe, 'Policy Roots', pp. 61–8.

4 Baylis, *Anglo-American Defence Relations*, pp. 23–41. Perkins, 'Unequal Partners', pp. 43–53. May and Treverton, 'Defence Relationships', pp. 165–72. Friedman, *Fifty-Year War*, pp. 57 and 83.

5 Bell, *Churchill and Sea Power*, pp. 309–10. Edgerton, *Britain's War Machine*, pp. 118–21. Roberts, *Churchill*, pp. 664–5, 686, 791 and 841. Friedman, *Fifty-Year War*, pp. 36–50. Baylis, *Anglo-American Defence Relations*, pp. 49–50.

6 Baer, *One Hundred Years of Sea Power*, pp. 267–78. Marder, *Old Friends*, II, 542. Miller, *Nuclear Weapons and Aircraft Carriers*, pp. 33–4.

7 Barlow, *Revolt of the Admirals*, pp. 23–89. Dorwart, 'Forrestal and the Navy Plan of 1945'.

8 Baer, *One Hundred Years of Sea Power*, p. 313.

9 Baer, *One Hundred Years of Sea Power*, pp. 303–10. Barlow, *Revolt of the Admirals*, pp. 107–276.

10 Barlow, *Revolt of the Admirals*, pp. 145–57, 254–76 and 283–9. Friedman, *Fifty-Year War*, pp. 124–9.

11 Peden, *Arms, Economics and British Strategy*, pp. 249–54. Grove, *Vanguard to Trident*, pp. 67–79. Crowe, 'Policy Roots', pp. 104–7. Friedman, *Fifty-Year War*, pp. 154–70. Johnman and Murphy, *British Shipbuilding and the State*, p. 137.

12 Grove, *Vanguard to Trident*, pp. 137–52. Baer, *One Hundred Years of Sea Power*, pp. 324–5.

13 Hone et al., *Innovation in Carrier Aviation*, pp. 11, 32 and 45–67.

14 Hone et al., *Innovation in Carrier Aviation*, pp. 69–87, 99–121 and 126–7. Friedman, 'Royal Navy and the Post-War Naval Revolution', pp. 427–8.

15 Hone et al., *Innovation in Carrier Aviation*, pp. 96–7. Grove, *Vanguard to Trident*, p. 116. Friedman, 'Royal Navy and the Post-War Naval Revolution', pp. 427–8.

16 Hone et al., *Innovation in Carrier Aviation*, pp. 123–45, 165–7 and 181. Friedman, 'Royal Navy and the Post-War Naval Revolution', pp. 427–8.

17 Louis, 'Dulles, Suez and the British'. Bowie, 'Eisenhower, Dulles, and the Suez Crisis'. Friedman, *Fifty-Year War*, pp. 221–3.

18 Bowie, 'Eisenhower, Dulles and the Suez Crisis', pp. 208–13. Baylis, *Anglo-American Defence Relations*, pp. 53–4 and 59–75. Hennessy and Jinks, *The Silent Deep*, pp. 140–52, 165–70, 179–82, and 202–22. Crowe, 'Policy Roots', pp. 252–65. Perkins, 'Unequal Partners', p. 43. Speller, 'Amphibious Operations 1945–1998', pp. 224–6. Eberle, 'Military Relationship', pp. 154–5.

19 Baylis, *Anglo-American Defence Relations*, p. 58.

20 Ferris, *Behind the Enigma*, pp. 580–606. Speller, 'Limited War and Crisis Management', pp. 167–8. Grove, *Vanguard to Trident*, pp. 150–52 and 262–7. Crowe, 'Policy Roots', pp. 108–10.

21 Grove, *Vanguard to Trident*, p. 361, quoting Max Hastings and Simon Jenkins, *The Battle for the Falklands* (London, 1983), p. 67.

22 Grove, *Vanguard to Trident*, pp. 276–81. Edward Hampshire, 'The Battle for CVA01', in *British Naval Aviation*, ed. Benbow, pp. 177–96. Geoffrey Till, 'The Return to Globalism: The Royal Navy East of Suez, 1975–2003', in *British Naval Strategy East of Suez, 1900–2000*, ed. G. Kennedy (Abingdon, 2005), pp. 244–68, at pp. 246–58. Speller, 'Limited War and Crisis Management', pp. 170–71.

23 His poem 'Mandalay' of 1890.

24 Till, 'Return to Globalism', pp. 260–66, quoted pp. 261 and 265.

abeam, adj.   In the direction at right angles to the ship's centreline.

able seaman, sb.   The rating of a fully trained sailor in the Royal Navy.

Adcock aerial, sb.   An antenna used for direction-finding, consisting of a pair of vertical dipoles (20th century).

admiral, sb.   1. The officer commanding a squadron of ships. 2. **The Lord (High) –**, an officer of the Crown with jurisdiction over Admiralty and naval affairs. 3. **Rear –**, A flag-officer of the rank of Rear-Admiral. 4. **Yellow –**, colloquial term for 'Rear-Admiral without distinction of squadron', a notional promotion established in 1747 allowing a captain to retire with the nominal rank of Rear-Admiral.

Admiralty, sb.   1. The government department in charge of the administration of the British Royal Navy. 2. **First Lord of the –**, the political head of the Royal Navy. 3. **– Board**, governing board responsible for the administration and planning of the Royal Navy. 4. **– War Group**, a committee of the First Lord, First Sea Lord, Chief of War Staff and Secretary of the Admiralty, responsible for directing wartime operation, WWI. 5. **– War Staff**, early form of Naval Staff, WWI.

Admiralty Fire Control Table, sb.   An electromechanical analogue computer fire-control system which calculated the correct elevation and deflection of the main gun armament of a warship to improve accuracy of shells striking a surface target (20th century).

aft, abaft, adj., adv.   Towards the stern or after part of the ship.

ahead, adj., adv.   Relating to the ship's head or direction of forward movement.

air brake, sb.   A wing flap used to slow a diving aircraft.

air compressor, sb.   An air pump that increases the pressure of a gas by reducing its volume.

air rudder, sb.   A primary flight control surface, mounted on the trailing edge of the vertical stabilizer or fin, which controls rotation about the vertical axis of an aircraft.

airship, sb.   A power-driven aircraft kept aloft by a body of gas which is lighter than air.

Allied powers, sb.   Alliance during WWII, led by Great Britain, the United States of America and the Soviet Union. Five additional nations joined during the course of the war: Hungary, Romania, Bulgaria, Slovakia and Croatia.

altitude, sb.   The angle of elevation of an object or point above the horizon.

amenity ship, sb.   A ship outfitted with recreational facilities as part of a mobile naval base.

amidship(s), adj.   Along or relating to the central section or centreline of the ship.

amphibious operations, sb.   Also known as combined operations, where naval, military and air forces work in combination to secure a landing site and land troops.

anchor, sb., vb.   1. A heavy object attached to a cable or chain and used to moor a ship to the sea bottom, typically a metal shank with a pair of curved barbed flukes at one end. 2. vb. To moor a ship to the sea bottom with an anchor. 3. **Weigh** –, to lift the anchor off the bottom to allow the ship to move.

anchorage, sb.   An area off the coast which is suitable for a ship to anchor.

anti-flash gear, sb.   Personal protective equipment usually consisting of fire-resistant hood and gloves to protect naval personnel from short duration flame exposure and heat.

anti-flash shutters, sb.   Used to close the space between explosives and gun turrets to minimize the risk of a flash explosion.

anti-fouling, sb.   A coating, paint, surface treatment, process or device used on a ship to control or prevent the attachment of unwanted organisms to the hull.

anti-submarine nets, sb.   Heavy steel nets hung from buoys to prevent enemy submarines penetrating a harbour or strait.

anti-torpedo bulges, sb.   Watertight external bulges fitted below the waterline to protect against torpedo attack.

Argo Clock, sb.   An electrically powered analogue computer developed by Arthur Pollen. A differential analyser which enabled big guns to engage with long-range targets when both ships were moving at speed in different directions. A component within the Mark II Dreyer Table for Fire Control.

armour, sb.   1. Protective metal plating (usually iron or steel) applied to a ship's structure to resist enemy gunfire. 1. **Face-hardened** —, armour treated to give it a specially resistant outer layer.

artificer, sb.   1. A craftsman, a skilled man. 2. **Engine Room** –, Engineer Petty Officer's rating (from 1868). 3. **Air** –, air-engineering equivalent to an ERA (from 1938).

artillerist, sb.	A person skilled in the use of artillery.
Asdic, sb.	An underwater sound ranging and detection device (equivalent to the US 'sonar').
ashore, adj., adv.	1. (Of a ship) beached, aground. 2. (Of a person) on shore.
astern, adj.	Behind a ship, in the direction from which she is moving.
athwartships, adj.	Across, at right angles to the ship's centreline.
atoll, sb.	A ring-shaped reef, island or chain of islands formed of coral.
auxiliaries, sb.	1. Volunteers giving supplementary support to the Navy. 2. A ship designed to support combatant ships and other naval operations. 3. – **machinery**, secondary machinery, usually run off a smaller engine, which does not provide the main propulsion for the vessel but other important services such as pumps, compressors, cooling, electrical power and sewage treatment.
avgas, sb.	Aircraft fuel (US, 20th century).
Axis powers, sb.	Alliance during WWII comprising Nazi Germany, the Kingdom of Italy and the Empire of Japan
bacca, sb.	(colloquial) Tobacco, especially the official-issue tobacco leaf.
banjo-frame, sb.	A device for raising and lowering the propeller of an auxiliary screw steamer (19th century).
bar, sb.	A build-up of sand and silt at a river mouth.
Barbary powers, sb.	Collective term for three semi-independent North African satellites of the Ottoman Empire, namely Algiers, Tunis and Tripoli (16th–19th century).
barbette, sb.	A fixed armoured breastwork protecting a gun mounting.
barnacle, sb.	A marine crustacean which attaches itself to a rock or the underwater hull of a ship.
barrage, sb.	1. A concentrated artillery bombardment over a wide area. 2. **North Sea Mine** –, a large minefield laid between the Orkney Islands and Norway to inhibit U-boat movement (WWI).
basin, sb.	A body of water enclosed by quays, especially one impounding the water to allow ships to lie afloat regardless of the state of the tide.
battery, sb.	1. The broadside guns mounted on one deck, or on one side, of the ship. 2. **floating** –, a stationary raft or hulk mounting heavy guns.
battlecruiser, sb.	A type of capital ship (20th century); a light, fast battleship.

battleship, sb.   1. A heavy warship of a type built chiefly in the late nineteenth and early twentieth centuries, with extensive armour protection and large-calibre guns. 2. **Pocket –**, a small heavily armoured and armed battle cruiser built to conform with treaty limitations on tonnage and armament, particularly built in Germany during the 1930s.

bauxite, sb.   Aluminium ore.

beach, vb.   To ground a ship, or haul a boat out of the water.

beakhead, sb.   A projection at the prow of a ship serving to support the base of the bowsprit (15th–18th century).

beam, sb.   1. The width of a ship at its widest point. 2. A heavy timber spanning the ship from side to side, serving to support decks and hatches.

bearing, sb.   1. A part of a machine that allows one part to rotate or move in contact with another part with as little friction as possible. 2. The direction or position of something, or the direction of movement, relative to a fixed point, often North.

bell-bottoms, sb.   Flared trousers worn as ratings' uniform in the RN.

belligerent, sb.   1. A person or country engaged in fighting a war. 2. – **rights**, legal rights exercised during the conduct of a war.

Benthamite, sb.   Relating to the utilitarian philosophy of Jeremy Bentham, who taught that the greatest happiness of the greatest number should be the ultimate goal of both society and the individual.

berth, sb.   1. Where a vessel is moored or secured alongside. 2. Sleeping-place of a member of the ship's company.

Bessemer process, sb.   A steel-making process in which carbon, silicon and other impurities are removed from molten pig iron by oxidation.

Beta Search, sb.   A tactic developed by WATU to eliminate a shadowing U-boat before it could home in on other U-boats.

bilge, sb.   1. The area at the base of a ship's hull where the bottom curves to meet the vertical sides. 2. The lowest levels inside the ship's hull, where water tends to accumulate. 3. – **keel**, fins or fixed stabilizers, fitted to the underwater hull to reduce rolling. 4. – **pump**, a water pump used to remove water which has collected in the bilge. 2. vb. To open the underwater hull of the ship, by grounding or battle damage, causing it to leak.

biplane, sb.   An early type of aircraft with two pairs of wings, one above the other.

birdcage, sb.   High-frequency wireless aerial (WWII).

Black Code, sb.   A US State Department code book (WWII).

black shoe, sb.   (USN colloquial, WWII) A battleship officer.

blackbirding, sb.   Casual slave-raiding (Pacific Ocean, 19th century).

bleeding, vb.   Phlebotomy, drawing blood from a patient, formerly a common medical treatment.

blimp, sb.   A non-rigid airship.

blind fire, sb.   Gunnery at an unseen target, in darkness or thick weather.

blockade, sb., vb.   1. An act or means of sealing off a place to prevent goods or people from entering or leaving. 2. **Paper** –, a distant or notional rather than physical blockade.

blockship, sb.   A ship moored or grounded in a channel to prevent ships moving along it.

Board of Trade, sb.   A British government department concerned with commerce and industry.

boat-hook, sb.   A hook mounted at the end of a pole used to pull or push boats towards or away from a landing, or to pick up a mooring.

boatswain, sb.   1. A petty officer on a merchant ship or a warrant officer on a warship particularly responsible for the maintenance of masts, sails and rigging. 2. **Custard** – (colloquial), the Warrant Instructor in Cookery, head of one of the three RN Cookery Schools (from 1910).

boiler, sb.   1. A pressure vessel for generating steam under pressure to drive a steam engine. 2. **– blowdown**, water intentionally wasted from a boiler to avoid a build-up of concentrated impurities during the continuous evaporation of steam. The water is blown out of the boiler with force by steam pressure within the boiler. 3. **forced draught** –, a boiler system where the air pressure in the stokehold is maintained above atmospheric pressure by the use of a fan or blower. 4. **water-tube** –, a high-pressure boiler in which water circulates in tubes heated externally by the fire.

bombe, sb.   (Cover-name, WWII) Electromagnetic deciphering machine used to work fast through possible readings.

bomb-sight, sb.   A device used by military aircraft to drop bombs accurately (20th century).

boom, sb.   A floating barrier used to contain oil spills or to prevent entry to a harbour or river.

bore, sb.   1. The internal diameter of a gun barrel. 2. A tidal wave generated by the flood tide in some estuaries. 3. **smooth** –, a gun with an unrifled barrel.

bottom, sb.	1. The lower surface of a ship's hull. 2. A cargo-ship.
bounty, sb.	A sum of money payable as an inducement, a reward or compensation.
bow, sb.	1. The foremost end of a ship, the opposite of the stern. 2. – **tubes**, submarine torpedo tubes mounted forward-facing in the bow.
boy, sb.	Rate of those aged fifteen and a half to eighteen aboard Royal Navy vessels.
branches, sb.	Trades and skills serving to divide the ship's company into groups.
breakwater, sb.	A barrier built out into the sea to protect a coast or harbour from the force of the waves.
breastwork, sb.	An armoured superstructure not extending to the ship's side.
breech, sb.	1. The rear or inboard end of a gun barrel. 2. -**loader**, a gun designed to have ammunition inserted at the breech rather than through the muzzle.
brew, sb.	(Colloquial, 20th century) a pot of tea.
bridge, sb.	1. A platform aboard a ship (originally spanning the paddle-boxes) from which the vessel may be navigated and commanded. 2. **open** –, one unenclosed and open to the elements.
broadside, sb.	1. The side of the ship. 2. The number of guns mounted or bearing on one side. 3. The simultaneous fire of these guns. 4. The total weight of shot fired by all the guns of the ship.
BRUSA, sb.	British-American intelligence-sharing agreement, initially negotiated in 1943 to facilitate cooperation between the US War Department and the GC&CS.
bulkhead, sb.	A vertical barrier dividing compartments of the ship.
bulwark, sb.	A barrier around the side of a deck.
bunker, sb.	1. A large container or compartment for storing fuel. 2. – **oil** (otherwise 'Heavy Fuel Oil'), oil fuel of suitably quality to be burned in a marine boiler.
bunker, vb.	To fill the fuel containers of a ship.
buoy, sb.	A float, anchored as a navigational marker or as a means of mooring ships.
Buttercup, sb.	Tactic developed by Commander F. J. 'Johnny' Walker for sinking U-boats attacking convoys.
cadet, sb.	A student officer in the armed forces.
caisson, sb.	A watertight boxlike structure used in construction work underwater or as a lock gate.
calibre, sb.	The bore or internal diameter of a gun.
call-sign, sb.	A combination of letters and numbers used to identify a radio transmitter.

canal effect, sb.	Phenomenon which affects vessels steaming on parallel courses close abreast, sucking the ships together.
cannon, sb.	1. A heavy smooth-bore gun, usually firing solid shot (15th–19th century). 2. A heavy machine gun firing explosive ammunition (20th-century aircraft).
capstan, sb.	A machine with a drum that rotates around a vertical spindle turned by a motor, used for hauling in heavy ropes.
captain, sb.	1. The form of address of the commanding officer of any ship or vessel. 2. **– of the fleet**, a captain or rear-admiral assisting the commander-in-chief. 3. **post- –**, an officer of the rank of captain.
carpetbagger, sb.	A political candidate who seeks election in an area where they have no local connections.
carrier, sb.	1. Aircraft carrier, a large warship with a deck from which aircraft can take off and land. 2. **fleet –**, an aircraft carrier designed to operate with the main fleet of a nation's navy. 3. **light fleet –**, smaller than the standard carriers of a navy. 4. **escort –**, small carrier often converted from a merchant ship, used for providing air cover to convoy escorts, amphibious operations, etc.
Catapult-Armed Merchantman, sb.	A merchant ship fitted with a catapult carrying a fighter as a one-shot defence of a convoy.
caulker, sb.	A shipyard worker who makes seams watertight by driving in oakum and applying melted pitch.
cavity magnetron, sb.	High-power vacuum tube used in early radar systems.
centimetric, adj.	Radio or radar equipment working on frequencies of less than one metre.
Central Powers, sb.	One of the two main alliances which fought the First World War, comprising Germany, Austria-Hungary, the Ottoman Empire and Bulgaria (also known as the Quadruple Alliance).
centre-line, sb.	An imaginary line from bow to stern of a ship, used to locate parts of the ship.
Channel, sb.	1. A length of water joining two larger bodies of water. 2. **– Fleet**, originally known as the Channel Squadron, this formation of Royal Navy warships defended the waters of the English Channel, 1854–1909 and 1914–15.
chaplain, sb.	A member of the clergy attached to a private chapel, institution, ship or regiment.
chart, sb.	A map that depicts the configuration of the shoreline and the seafloor.

Chartism, sb.   A political movement aiming to advance the interests of the working classes (19th century).

check, vb.   To stop some motion or activity.

chronometer, sb.   A clock or watch designed to keep accurate time at sea

civil, sb.   1. Non-military. 2. – **officer**, generic term for any RN officer without general command authority (including surgeons, pursers and chaplains).

class, sb.   Collective term for ships or vessels, particularly warships, built to a common design.

clockwork mice, sb.   Practice submarines for escorts to hunt (colloquial).

clutter, sb.   Spurious radar echoes and false returns from waves.

coarse pitch (screw), sb.   A propeller with a high blade angle.

Coast Volunteers, sb.   Naval reserve force (1853 to 1873).

Coastguard, sb.   An organization keeping watch on coastal waters to assist ships and to prevent smuggling.

Cobdenism, sb.   An economic ideology which perceives international free trade and a non-interventionist foreign policy as the key requirements for prosperity and world peace (19th century).

cochineal, sb.   A scarlet dye used for colouring food.

coffer dam, sb.   A watertight enclosure pumped dry to permit the construction of a pier, dock, etc.

collaborationist, adj.   Relating to a person or government collaborating with the German invaders of France (1940–45).

collier, sb.   A ship designed to carry coal.

Colossus, sb.   An electromagnetic machine often referred to as the first computer, applied to cryptanalysis of intercepted messages transmitted by the German Lorenz cypher teleprinter.

combined operations, sb.   A British term first coined in WWII to denote multi-service activities involving air, land and naval forces acting together and co-ordinated by a Combined Operations headquarters.

commander, sb.   1. (in RN usage) the executive officer, second in command of a large ship. 2. (In loose or civilian usage) the senior officer commanding an operation. 3. **-in-chief**, a senior officer in command of a squadron or station.

commando, sb.   A light-infantry or special-operations force, trained to carry out raids and operating in small teams behind enemy lines (WWII, but title borrowed from the Boer mounted units of the South African War, 1899–1904).

commission, vb.   To set up a ship or naval establishment as an active unit for command, administrative and financial purposes.

commodore, sb.   A post-captain appointed in command of a squadron or station with the temporary rank of a rear-admiral.

compass, sb.   1. **magnetic** –, a navigational instrument indicating the bearing of the magnetic poles. 2. **gyro** –, a navigational instrument driven by a gyroscope providing a constant bearing on true north.

con, vb.   To steer or pilot a ship in confined waters.

conning-tower, sb.   The superstructure of a submarine from which it can be conned when on the surface.

conscript, sb.   A person enlisted compulsorily.

Constitutionalist, sb.   An adherent of the (Spanish, Portuguese, etc.) constitution.

constructor, sb.   A naval architect in government employment. A member of the Royal Corps of Naval Constructors (founded 1883).

continuous voyage, sb.   Legal doctrine defining the circumstances which make a cargo liable to capture as enemy property in wartime.

contraband, sb.   Goods imported or exported illegally.

convoy, sb.   A body of merchant ships under escort.

coppering (copper sheathing), sb.   The sheathing of a wooden hulled vessel below the water-line in copper plating to protect and extend the lifespan of the hull by inhibiting marine growth and deter worms from destroying the wood.

coppersmith, sb.   An artificer who works with copper and brass.

cordite, sb.   A family of smokeless propellants developed and produced in Britain from 1889 for use in military firearms.

corvette, sb.   1. A warship smaller than a frigate, usually employed as a convoy escort. 2. **twin-screw** –, a larger class of convoy escort, later named frigate.

court martial, sb.   A court held under naval or military law.

coxswain, sb.   A petty officer or leading hand in charge of a boat's crew.

craft, sb.   A boat or vessel.

crank, sb.   A part of an axle or shaft bent out at right angles for converting reciprocal to circular motion and vice versa.

crossing the line, sb.   An initiation ceremony commemorating a person's first crossing of the equator.

crown and anchor, sb.   A dice-based gambling game traditionally played in the Royal Navy

cruiser, sb.   1. (Battlev-cruiser) a fast, lightly armed form of battleship (20th century). 2. **armed merchant** –, merchant ship taken up and armed for naval service (20th century). 3. **heavy** –, a cruiser defined by the London Naval Treaty of 1930 as carrying guns not over 8 inches. 4. **light** –, defined by the London Naval Treaty as carrying guns not over 6 inches.

cupola furnace, sb.   A vertical cylindrical furnace capable of melting iron.

CW candidate, sb.   Potential officer candidate, the responsibility of the Commission and Warrant Branch of the Admiralty.

cypher, sb., vb.   1. A key which allows one to convert plain text into letters or numbers. 2. **de-**, to convert from code into plain text. 3. **long subtractor book –**, method of constructing a code book.

Dart, sb.   Officer educated at the RNC Dartmouth (colloquial).

davit, sb.   A light spar used as a crane, particularly to lower ship's boats into the water.

dead-reckoning, sb.   A position estimated by combining course, distance run and leeway.

deadwood (stern), sb.   Narrowing of the underwater hull of a ship as it is faired into the sternpost and keel.

deflagration, sb.   An intense fire, characteristic of explosives allowed to burn in air.

deflection, sb.   A measure of the degree by which the gunner's aim is offset to hit a moving target.

degaussing, sb.   The neutralization of the magnetic field of a ship by encircling it with a conductor carrying electric current.

demarcation, sb.   The practice of reserving specific jobs to members of particular trades unions.

dengue fever, sb.   A mosquito-borne viral disease widely spread in tropical and subtropical regions.

depot ship, sb.   An auxiliary ship used as a floating base for submarines or other smaller vessels.

depth charge, sb.   An anti-submarine weapon dropped by surface vessels or aircraft and designed to detonate in the water around a submerged submarine.

derrick, sb.   A type of small shipboard crane with a pivoting arm.

desertion, sb.   The action of illegally leaving the armed forces.

destroyer, sb.   1. (Originally 'Torpedo Boat Destroyer' or 'TBD') A small, fast warship intended to counter attacks by torpedo boats. 2. **– leader**, a larger destroyer fitted to accommodate the captain commanding the destroyer flotilla and his staff (WWI).

dhobey, dhobi, sb.   A lower-deck washing firm.

dilutee, sb.   A semi-skilled man, a craftsman with diluted skill (1941).

direct entry, sb.   A method of recruiting officer cadets from older schoolboys.

direction-finding, sb.   The act or process of finding the direction of a radio source by comparing the signal strength of antennae pointing in different directions.

(gunnery) director, sb.	A mechanical or electronic computer that continuously calculates trigonometric firing solutions for use against a moving target and transmits targeting data to the gun.
displacement, sb.	1. The tonnage of a ship as measured indirectly using Archimedes' Principle, by first calculating and weighing the volume of water displaced by the vessel. 2. **standard –**, definition adopted by the Washington Naval Treaty of 1922 as the displacement of a ship fully stored and armed but without fuel, lubricants or boiler feed water.
disrate, vb.	To demote a sailor to a lower rate.
Distinguished Service Order, sb.	A British military decoration awarded to officers 'for distinguished services during active operations against the enemy'.
ditty box, sb.	1. A small wooden box used by sailors to accommodate their personal belongings. 2. Title of a naval magazine (*The Dittybox*).
dock, sb.	1. An excavation or basin for ships. 2. **dry-**, a dock with gates allowing it to be drained of water to expose the underwater hulls of ships within it. 3. **-master**, a person in charge of a dock. 4. **-yard**, a naval yard with one or more drydocks. 5. **floating –**, a large box-like structure that can be submerged to allow a vessel to enter it and then floated to raise the vessel out of the water for maintenance or repair.
domestic, sb.	One of the ratings who did not enlist for continuous service but signed on for each voyage.
drag, sb.	The slowing force acting on a body moving through a fluid parallel and opposite to the direction of motion.
draught, sb.	1. The depth of water required to float a ship. 2. The drawings showing the design of a ship.
draughtsman, sb.	One skilled in engineering drawing employed as assistant to a constructor.
Dreadnought, sb.	A British battleship launched in 1906, which became the archetype for the all-big-gun fast battleship, older designs being referred to as 'Pre-Dreadnoughts'.
dredger, sb.	A vessel equipped to remove silt from the bottom of a channel to keep it free for navigation.
drifter, sb.	A type of fishing vessel used to catch fish in a drift net, often taken up to serve as a naval auxiliary.
dry, adj.	Referring to a ship carrying no alcohol.

dual purpose, adj.	(Of a gun) capable of being aimed at either surface or air targets.
duff, sb.	A boiled or steamed pudding, often containing dried fruit.
duplex pistol, sb.	A torpedo-firing mechanism combining contact and magnetic triggers.
E-boat, sb.	'Enemy boat', British term for German or Italian motor torpedo boats.
echo sounder, sb.	A device for determining the depth of the seabed by measuring the time taken for sound echoes to return to the listener. Cf. Asdic.
electrolytic corrosion, sb.	The process in which one metal corrodes preferentially when in electrical contact with another in the presence of an electrolyte.
electromagnetic radiation, sb.	A form of radiation that propagates as either electrical or magnetic waves.
embargo, sb.	An official ban on trade or commercial relations with a particular country.
embark, vb.	To go aboard a ship or aircraft.
engine-room telegraph/ engine order telegraph, sb.	A communications device between the bridge and the engine room transmitting orders relating to engine speed.
engineer officer, sb.	1. An officer of the engine room in charge of operating and maintaining the ship's machinery. 2. RN (1st, 2nd and 3rd class) commissioned officer in charge of the engineering department (from 1847).
Enlightenment, sb.	A European intellectual movement of the late 17th and 18th centuries emphasizing reason and individualism rather than tradition.
equal-speed man- oeuvre, sb.	A system of tactics allowing ships of different design to be handled in close company.
Equator, sb.	An imaginary line around the middle of the earth at an equal distance from the North and South Poles.
escort, sb.	A warship employed to protect merchant ships.
Estimates (Navy Estimates), sb.	British Parliamentary procedure for voting money to the Navy.
estuary, sb.	The tidal mouth of a river, where the tide meets the stream.
ethereal vapour, ether, sb.	An early general anaesthetic (1840s).
evaporator, sb.	A machine for distilling fresh water from salt water.
executive branch, sb.	Collective title for sea officers having general command authority (formerly known as 'Military Officers').

face-hardened armour, sb.	A type of steel naval armour developed in the 1890s in which the face of the plate was heated to a high temperature for a week or two before cooling it quickly, resulting in a very hard high-carbon steel face.
fathom, sb.	A unit of length or depth equal to six feet.
fetch, sb.	The distance over which the ocean wind blows unobstructed and the waves are free to grow in strength and size, hence the force of the sea.
filibuster, sb.	A person engaging in private warfare against a foreign state (19th century, US).
Filter Room, sb.	A control room in which reports of enemy aircraft were plotted and orders to British aircraft issued (RAF, 1940s).
fire-control table, sb.	An instrument to calculate the elevation, deflection, etc., to be applied to a gun to hit an observed target.
fireman, sb.	A stoker.
firm, sb.	An association of two or more men of the ship's company providing goods and services as part of the domestic economy of the ship.
First Lord, sb.	The First Lord of the Admiralty, the political head of the Royal Navy.
First Sea Lord, sb.	The First Sea Lord (from 1917 also Chief of the Naval Staff) is the professional head of the Royal Navy.
First (Second, Third) Rates, sb.	Classification of ships of the line (early 19th century).
fish-head	(Colloquial) non-flying officer aboard aircraft carrier.
flag, sb.	1. An admiral's distinguishing flag. 2. – **captain**, the captain of a flagship. 3. – **rank**, admiral's rank. 4. **-ship**, the admiral's ship.
flare, sb.	A firework used for signalling at sea.
fleet, sb.	1. A body of warships, or of warships and merchant ships in company. 2. – **train**, a mobile base capable of accompanying or following a fleet and supplying it with fuel, ammunition, stores and repairs.
Fleet Engineer, sb.	A RN engineer's rank, created 1886 (formerly Chief Engineer 1st Class), renamed Engineer Commander 1903.
fleet in being, sb.	Phrase coined by Lord Torrington in 1690 to explain the strategic influence of even an inferior fleet so long as it avoided defeat.
Flower Class, sb.	A class of small anti-submarine escorts, built 1940–43.
flush-deck, sb., adj.	A weather deck running unbroken from stem to stern; a ship distinguished by being flush-decked.

forced draught, adj. Relating to a boiler supplied with air under pressure.

'fore and aft' rig, sb. (Colloquial) officer-style uniform with collar and tie (as worn by, e.g., petty officers, distinguished from ratings wearing 'square rig', with square collar and no tie).

forecastle, sb. (Fo'c'scle) A raised deck over the forward part of the ship, beneath which ratings may berth.

(foreign) bottom, sb. 1. The outside surface of a ship's hull below the waterline. 2. A cargo ship (often in the phrase 'foreign bottoms').

forward, adj., adv. Relating to the fore part of the ship, or motion towards the bow.

fouling, sb. 1. The process whereby a ship's underwater hull becomes coated with weed, barnacles, etc. 2. The growths, etc., responsible.

Free French, sb. The would-be government of France established in London, 1940–44.

free trade, sb. International trade left to its natural course without tariffs, quotas or other restrictions.

freeboard, sb. The height of a ship's weather deck above the waterline.

friendly society, sb. A mutual association providing sickness benefits, life assurance and pensions to members before the existence of modern insurance or the welfare state in Britain.

frigate, sb. 1. A cruising warship with an unarmed lower deck, mounting her battery on a single main deck (18th century). 2. An escort intermediate in size between a corvette and a destroyer (WWII).

frogmen, sb. Military personnel trained in swimming or scuba diving for tactical underwater operations.

fruit machine, sb. (Colloquial) a mechanical analogue computer aboard a submarine, fed with target information and submarine depth etc., and used to calculate torpedo firing conditions.

galley, sb. A ship's kitchen.

George Cross, sb. A decoration instituted in 1940 for civilians or service personnel for 'acts of conspicuous courage in circumstances of extreme danger' not encountered in combat.

glass, sb. A barometer.

glider bomb, sb. Pilotless aircraft or radio-controlled missile.

goffer, sb. An iced lemonade stall on board ship.

Grand Fleet, sb. The main battlefleet of the Royal Navy during the First World War.

graphite, sb. A form of carbon essential to waging war due to its use as a solid lubricant as well as a moderator in nuclear reactors.

Great Circle course, sb. The shortest navigational course between two points on the surface of the globe.

green sea, sb. — A solid wave or mass of water breaking over the bow or bulwark of a ship.

Greenland Air Gap, sb. — A wide swath of open ocean 600–800 miles wide south-west of Iceland that lay outside the maximum range of most Allied patrol planes, and in which convoys had no air cover.

gross domestic product, sb. — The total value of goods produced and services provided in a country.

gross register tonnage, sb. — A measure of the total internal capacity of a ship.

ground, vb. — To run aground on a beach or seabed.

ground wave, sb. — A secondary, ground-level propagation of a high-frequency transmitter.

guano, sb. — The excrement of seabirds and bats, often used as a fertilizer.

guinea worm, sb. — A long parasitic nematode worm which lives under the skin in infected humans in rural Africa and Asia.

gunboat, sb. — A small ship mounting one or two heavy guns, for use in shallow coastal waters and rivers.

guncotton, sb. — Cellulose nitrate explosive.

gunfounding, sb. — The process of casting a gun from molten metal.

gunnery, sb. — 1. The firing of heavy guns. 2. Specialist branch of the Royal Navy (from 1876). 3. **helm-free** –, means of keeping guns continuously trained on a target while a ship manoeuvred to avoid incoming fire or torpedoes. 4. **quick-firing** –, a light gun with a quick-acting breech mechanism.

gunroom, sb. — The mess allocated to midshipmen and junior officers in the Royal Navy.

gutta percha, sb. — An electrically non-conductive thermoplastic latex derived from the tree of the same name, used as an insulator of underwater cables.

hammock, sb. — A hanging canvas bed.

head sea, sb. — Waves coming from directly ahead.

heads, sb. — Ship's latrines.

heel, sb. — The inclination of a vessel to one side or the other.

helm, sb. — The wheel, tiller or entire apparatus by which a vessel is steered.

Hemisphere, sb. — A half of the Earth, usually divided into Northern and Southern by the Equator, or into Eastern and Western halves by an imaginary line passing through the poles.

Herzian waves, sb. — Electromagnetic radiation (19th century).

high water, sb. — High tide.

high-angle, adj.	Used of anti-aircraft guns mounted to engage targets overhead.
high-frequency, adj.	Describing radio or electromagnetic waves of high frequency or short wave, particularly in the context of wireless signals.
hoist, sb.	A purchase or mechanical lifting device.
hoist, vb.	To lift or raise with a purchase, usually with ropes and pulleys.
Home Fleet, sb.	The principal unit of British warships in home waters. Cf. Channel Fleet.
horsepower, sb.	A measure of the power generated by a rotary engine, or the rate at which work is done, in units notionally equal to the force of a draught horse. Different methods of measuring horsepower are indicated by **brake horsepower, indicated horsepower, nominal horsepower, shaft horsepower**.
Hostilities Only, sb.	Designation of naval or military personnel conscripted to serve in wartime only.
huff-duff, sb.	(Colloquial) rendering of HF/DF (high-frequency direction-finding).
hull, sb.	The body or main structure of a ship or vessel.
hull-down, adj.	Of a ship showing only her masts or upperworks above the horizon.
hydrodynamics, sb.	The branch of physics concerned with the mechanical properties of fluids.
hydrogen peroxide, sb.	A liquid explosive (H_2O_2), usable as a rocket or turbine fuel.
hydrography, sb.	The science of surveying and charting bodies of water.
hydrophone, sb.	An underwater microphone.
hydrostatic valve, sb.	A pressure-activated hydraulic valve.
hydrovane, sb.	A fin rudder or stabilizer fitted below the waterline to a boat, seaplane or torpedo (WWI).
Identification/ Identify Friend or Foe, sb.	An electronic signature identifying a friendly radar transmission.
impressment, sb.	The recruitment of men into the Navy by force.
inclining experiment, sb.	Test performed to determine the stability of a vessel and its vertical centre of gravity, by shifting a series of known weights transversally across the deck and measuring the angle of heel.
indenture, sb.	Legal document engaging someone to work for a defined period of time.
inshore, adj., adv.	Near, towards the shore.

Inspector of Machinery Afloat, sb.	Engineer officer's rank created 1847, renamed Engineer Captain 1903.
ionosphere, sb.	An electrically charged layer of the Earth's upper atmosphere capable of reflecting short-wave radio signals.
ironclad, sb.	A steam warship protected by iron or steel plates (1860s–1890s).
Jago's System, sb.	The system of cooking and serving meals known as 'General Messing', introduced by Mr Alphonso Jago, Warrant Instructor in Cookery, in 1918.
jewing, sb.	The work of tailoring aboard ship.
Kampfgruppe, sb.	'Battle Group', i.e. air squadron.
keel, sb.	The longitudinal timber or steel structure along the base of the ship's hull and supporting the framework of the whole.
kipper, vb.	(Colloquial) to cut a ship in half lengthways and open her up to increase her beam and stability.
kite balloon, sb.	A barrage balloon towed by a ship, supporting an observer connected by telephone (WWI and WWII).
knot, sb.	A unit of speed equivalent to one nautical mile per hour.
Laird Rams, sb.	Ironclads built in Britain for the Confederacy.
landfall, sb.	The position on the coast where a ship first sights (or intends to sight) the land.
landing craft, sb.	A boat or vessel designed for putting troops and military equipment ashore on a beach.
landsman, sb.	Rating of an unskilled member of a ship's company (abolished as a rating in 1853).
lantern, sb.	(Colloquial) lantern-shaped wooden and Perspex housing of a Type 271 radar.
lay down, vb.	To 'lay the keel', as the formal start of a ship's construction.
lay up, vb.	To put a ship or boat in dock or out of commission.
leading hand, sb.	A rating of 'Leading Seaman', senior to Able Seaman and Junior to a Petty Officer, or the equivalent rate in other branches (Leading Signalman, Leading Telegraphist, etc.).
leeward, adj.	Relating to the direction towards which the wind is blowing.
Liberty Ship, sb.	A class of cargo ship built to a British design by the United States (WWII).
libertyman, sb.	A sailor having permission to go ashore.
lieutenant, sb.	1. A commissioned sea officer's rank. 2. **-commander**, a rank created in 1914 for lieutenants of eight years' seniority and above. 3. **sub-**, the most junior commissioned rank in the RN. 4. **'salt horse'** – (colloquial, 20th century), a lieutenant who has not elected to train as a specialist in gunnery, torpedoes, navigation, etc.

line of battle, sb   Tactical formation of warships arranged in line ahead.

LL sweep, sb.   Electrically charged wire sweep to detonate magnetic mines.

Loa-Loa, sb.   (African Eye Worm) A roundworm prevalent in central and west Africa, causing Loiasis disease.

long subtractor book, sb.   A type of code.

lower-deck, adj.   Relating to the ratings of the ship's company as a whole.

lyddite, sb.   The first British 'high explosive', introduced as a shell-filler in 1896.

MAC-ships, sb.   'Merchant Aircraft Carrier' tankers and grain carriers with a flight deck fitted over their hulls to fly off anti-submarine aircraft, but still able to load or discharge cargo by hose.

magazine, sb.   1. A storehouse. 2. A compartment in the ship for storing explosives.

make and mend, sb.   A naval half-holiday.

Manchester Party/ School, sb.   A political school of thought influential in the British Liberal Party in the mid-nineteenth century. Its followers believed in laissez-faire economic policies, including free trade and free competition and were isolationist in foreign affairs.

marines, sb.   Naval infantry, specializing in operating in littoral zones.

master ship, sb.   A capital ship with advanced fire-control for long-range shooting which would lead each three-ship division for concentration firing (from 1939).

master-at-arms, sb.   A warrant officer responsible for police duties aboard a ship.

mate, sb.   1. A deck officer of a merchant ship. 2. A petty officer assisting a warrant officer or more senior petty officer. 3. – **Scheme**, scheme for advancing ratings for promotion to commissioned rank via the revived rank of 'Mate' (1912–31), succeeded by the Upper Yardman Scheme (1931).

mean low water, sb.   The mean water level at low tide.

mechanic, sb.   An engineering rating of 'dilutee' skill level (1941).

mechanician, sb.   A warrant rank for stokers (1903).

Mercantile Marine, sb.   A collective title for merchant ships, in Britain formally awarded in 1928.

mercurial, sb.   A drug or other compound containing mercury.

mess, sb.   1. A unit of some number of men, a division of the ship's company for the distribution of victuals. 2. – **deck**, a compartment of a ship allotted to the members of a mess to relax, sleep and eat.

messing, sb. 1. The act or system of feeding the ship's crew. 2. **general** –, see 'Jago's System'. 3. **canteen** –, messing system under which messes had to prepare their own meals and carry them to the galley to be cooked.

metacentric height, sb. A measurement of the initial static stability of a floating body. It is defined as the distance between the centre of gravity of a ship and its metacentre.

meteorology, sb. The science of atmospheric phenomena, particularly with a view to forecasting the weather.

MI5 Cover name for the British Security Service.

MI6 Cover name for the British Secret Intelligence Service (SIS).

midshipman, sb. 1. A former Naval Cadet, rated petty officer. 2. A young man training to become a commissioned officer.

mine, sb. 1. A submerged explosive charge laid on the bottom or moored in a channel to sink passing ships. 2. **magnetic** –, a mine detonated by the magnetic field of a passing iron- or steel-hulled ship

minesweeper, sb. A ship equipped to sweep sea mines.

missionary, sb. A person sent on a religious mission, especially one sent to promote Christianity in a foreign country.

mole, sb. A masonry pier protecting a harbour from the force of the sea.

monoplane, sb. An aeroplane having only one wing on each side of the fuselage.

Monsters, sb. (Colloquial) fast liners serving as troopships (1939–45).

mooring, sb. 1. The act of making a ship fast to a fixed anchor or to a pair of ship's anchors. 2. A permanent mooring buoy to which a ship may secure. 3. A quay, wharf, jetty or other permanent structure to which vessels may make fast.

Morse code, sb. A method of visual or wireless signalling in which letters and numbers are represented by combinations of long and short light flashes or sounds.

multiplexing, sb. Electronic system of carrying up to eight simultaneous channels on a single cable.

muster book, sb. A record of the names of the ship's company or dockyard workforce.

mutiny, sb, vb. Open rebellion by sailors or soldiers refusing to obey their officers' orders.

muzzle, sb. 1. The open end of the barrel of a firearm. 2. **-loader**, a gun that is loaded through its muzzle.

National Grid, sb. British national high-voltage electrical distribution system.

naval architecture, sb. The science of designing ships and vessels.
naval attaché, sb. A naval officer serving as a diplomatic representative in a foreign state.
navicert, sb. A certificate issued in time of war by a blockading power certifying a neutral ship's cargo as meeting blockade regulations.
navigation lights, sb. A set of lights shown by a ship or aircraft at night to indicate its position and orientation.
Navy, Army and Air Force Institutes The amalgamated Expeditionary Force Canteens and Navy and Army Canteen Board from 1920, which ran recreational establishments for the British armed forces.
Navy Bill, sb. (and/or) **Victualling Bill**, negotiable payment orders issued by the Navy and Victualling Boards in payment for goods or services (to 1829).
Navy Board, sb. Government board responsible for shipbuilding and the dockyards. Abolished in 1832 when its functions were absorbed into the Admiralty.
Navy List, sb. Official listing of ships and officers (published from 1814).
neap, neap tide, sb. Tides falling after the first and third quarters of the moon, when the tidal range is least.
neutral, sb. A non-belligerent state.
nitroglycerine, sb. A powerful explosive and an important ingredient in most forms of dynamite.
non-combatant, sb. A person legally exempt from any obligation to fight.
'Notices to Mariners', sb. Public bulletins issued by the Hydrographic Office (or equivalent authorities in other countries) circulating navigational information including chart updates, changes in buoyage and prior warning of dangers or activities (from 1834).
obturator, sb. A cap or pad used to seal the breech of a gun when firing.
officer, sb. 1. A person having rank and authority in a disciplined service. 2. **commanding** –, the senior officer of a squadron of warships. 3. **commissioned** –, a sea officer appointed by Admiralty commission: a captain, commander or lieutenant. 4. **naval** –, an officer of the Navy. 5. **petty** –, a senior rating. 6. **warrant** –, a sea or subordinate officer appointed by warrant from one of the naval boards. 7. **military** (later **executive**) Officer, member of the body of naval officers bearing general command authority. 8. – **of the watch**, officer primarily responsible for the navigation of the ship, in the absence of the captain, during a certain watch. 9. **flag** –, an admiral. 10. US **line** –, member of the body of naval officers bearing general command authority. 11. **liaison** –, officer of a foreign navy or allied service attached to advance inter-service communication.

oilskins, sb.	Foul-weather clothes.
one-time pad, sb.	A unique cypher used once and then discarded.
open water, sb.	A stretch of sea not enclosed by land, ice or other barriers.
operational research, sb.	The application of sophisticated mathematics to analyse plans and projects.
Order in Council, sb.	Legislative order issued by the Privy Council with the assent of the monarch.
ordinary seaman, sb.	Rating of a seaman with only basic training.
ordnance, sb.	1. Heavy guns. 2. **Board of –**, the British government body originally established in the Tudor period responsible for the supply of munitions and equipment to the Army and Navy (abolished 1855).
out to out, adv.	From one extremity to the other of a range of movement.
outrank, vb.	To assume authority over an officer of lower rank.
packet, sb.	A vessel employed under Post Office contract to carry mails.
paddle-box, sb.	A structure enclosing the upper part of a paddle wheel.
paddle steamer, sb.	A steamboat or steamship propelled by a paddle wheel or wheels.
Palliser system, sb.	System of converting smooth-bore guns to rifling developed by William Palliser (1860s).
pay, sb.	1. Remuneration for service provided or work done, goods received, or debt incurred. 2. **half-**, reduced pay. 3. **harbour –**, reduced pay for non-seagoing service. 4. **- master**, rank of an administrative officer originally responsible for paying the ship's company. 5. **sea –**, full pay for service at sea.
pay off, vb.	To put a ship out of commission, to pay the ship's company their accumulated wages.
Peelite, sb.	A follower of Sir Robert Peel, a member of Peel's Parliamentary faction (1846–59).
pilotage, sb.	The navigation and safe conduct of ships, especially in coastal waters.
pistol, sb.	1. Firing mechanism of a mine or torpedo. 2. **duplex –**, firing mechanism actuated by a magnetic field or physical contact. 3. **magnetic –**, firing mechanism actuated by the magnetic field of a passing ship.
pitch, vb.	(Of a ship) to plunge the bows and stern alternately into the waves, to oscillate about a lateral axis.
Plan Position Indicator, sb.	Type of radar display using an oscilloscope to represent the transmitter in the centre and a rotating trace to show the radar beam.
plenipotentiary, sb.	A diplomat invested with full power to negotiate on behalf of their government.

792 · ENGLISH GLOSSARY

plot, sb.   A graphic display showing collated data from a ship's instruments; a chart marked with the positions of nearby ships.

port, sb.   The left-hand side of a vessel, looking forward.

poundage, sb.   A payment for handling money by deducting a percentage of the sum handled.

pounder, sb.   A gun classed by the weight of projectile it fires.

powder, sb.   1. Gunpowder. 2. **black –**, earliest chemical explosive, known as 'black' to distinguish it from modern smokeless powder. 3. **prismatic –**, slow-burning propellant for heavy guns (1870s–1890s).

prefabrication, sb.   The construction of ships by assembling pre-made components.

press, sb.   1. Recruitment of men for the Navy by force. 2. **– gang**, a party of men employed on impressment.

privateer, sb.   A privately owned warship licensed by letter of marque to capture enemy shipping for profit.

prize, sb.   1. A captured enemy ship. 2. **International – Court**, the first ever international court, initially proposed at the Second Hague Conference in 1907, to which decisions made by national prize courts could be appealed. 3. **– money**, the proceeds of selling a prize.

protectionism, sb.   Policy of using tariffs or other measures to shelter home industries from foreign competition.

protectorate, sb.   A territory controlled and protected by another.

Pub, sb.   (Colloquial) a young officer recruited from school by the 'Special Entry' scheme (from 1918).

purser, sb.   1. An officer responsible for victuals. 2. **– and paymaster**, an officer responsible for handling public money aboard ship (from 1852). 3. **pusser** (colloquial), a purser.

Q-ship, sb.   Armed merchant ship with concealed weaponry and disguised naval crew designed to decoy U-boats into making surface attacks.

quartermaster, sb.   A senior Petty Officer.

Queen Bee, sb.   A wireless-controlled version of the Tiger Moth light aircraft used as a drone target for anti-aircraft guns.

quick-firing (gun), sb.   A light breech-loading gun with fixed ammunition.

quinine, sb.   An antimalarial drug derived from cinchona bark.

radar, sb.   1. A system for discovering the presence and position of aircraft, ships, etc., by detecting reflected electromagnetic waves. 2. **centimetric –**, radar transmitting on a wavelength between 1cm and 10cm (from 1941). 3. **Chain Home –**, British home-defence radar system (1939–45).

radial engine, sb.
A type of internal combustion engine used chiefly in aircraft, having cylinders fixed radially around a rotating crankshaft.

radio physics, sb.
The study of electromagnetic radiation (1940s).

radio valve, sb.
(Otherwise 'vacuum tube') A glass vacuum tube containing electrodes generating a wireless signal of a defined wavelength; an essential component of radio and radar sets.

raider, sb.
RN term for an enemy surface warship or disguised armed merchantman (WWII).

ram, sb.
A naval weapon comprising an underwater prolongation of the bow of a ship to form an armoured beak which could be driven into the hull of an enemy ship.

range, sb.
1. The maximum distance to which a gun will shoot or over which a missile will travel. 2. The maximum distance at which a radio transmission can be effectively received.

range-finder, sb.
1. An instrument for estimating the distance of a target. 2. **stereoscopic –**, an optical range-finder with two eyepieces that measures the distance from observer to target using the observer's capability of binocular vision.

rank, sb.
1. A permanent status conferred by an officer's commission or warrant. 2. **post –**, the rank of full captain.

rate, sb.
A title combining the trade and status of a member of a ship's company.

rating, sb.
1. A man's rate. 2. A man so rated, one of the 'common men' of a ship's company having no rank.

reciprocating engine, sb.
A steam engine driven by steam admitted on each side of the piston in turn.

recommission, vb.
To bring a ship back into service.

reconnaissance, sb.
Observation of a region to locate an enemy or ascertain strategic features.

redoubt, sb.
A small detached or external fortification.

reef, sb.
A line of submerged rocks.

reflector sight, sb.
An optical sight of various types of gun that allows the user to look through a partially reflecting glass element and see an illuminated projection of a target.

regatta, sb.
A sporting event consisting of a series of boat or yacht races.

reserved occupation, sb.
An essential employment whose workers are protected from military service.

reversing cradle, sb.
A device which allowed paddle-box boats (stowed upside-down on top of the paddle wheels) to be reversed and launched into the water (19th century).

rig, sb.

1. The design or arrangement of the masts and sails of a sailing vessel or boat. 2. **fore-and-aft –**, a rig predominantly made up of sails attached by the luff or windward edge to the ship's masts. 3. **square –**, a rig predominantly made up of quadrangular sails suspended from horizontal spars. 4. (Colloquial) a naval uniform or working dress.

rigger, sb.

One who sets up ships' masts and sails, a seaman employed in a dockyard.

rigging, sb.

The ropes supporting and controlling the masts and spars.

righting, righting moment, sb.

Terms of naval architecture for the forces acting to return a ship to the vertical.

river blindness, sb.

A tropical skin disease caused by a parasitic worm and transmitted by blackflies which breed in fast-flowing rivers.

roll, vb.

(Of a ship) to heel from one side to the other under the pressure of the waves.

royal commission, sb.

An official inquiry set up under government authority.

Royal Naval Coast Volunteers, sb.

Unsuccessful scheme to recruit a reserve organization from fishermen (1852).

Royal Naval Reserve, sb.

A naval reserve drawn from the British Mercantile Marine and fishing fleets (established 1859).

Royal Naval Volunteer Reserve, sb.

A naval reserve recruited from volunteers not employed at sea (established 1903). **Supplementary Reserve**, a list of potential officers recruited from boat-owners and others possessing skills useful to the Navy (created 1936).

Royal Naval Volunteer Reserve (Special Branch), sb.

Special branch of talented administrators largely recruited to work ashore in staff and intelligence.

safety interlocks, sb.

Safety mechanisms which lock to prevent machine operation or start-up in an unsafe situation. Interlocks were used to seal off the hoists which carried propellant from the magazines to the guns.

safety line, sb.

A length of cordage connecting a crew member's safety harness to a strong point.

salvo, sb.

A half broadside.

scantling, sb.

1. A timber beam of small cross section. 2. A set of standard dimensions for parts of a structure, particularly in shipbuilding.

scarecrow patrols, sb.

(Colloquial) unarmed obsolete aircraft flown over convoys to frighten U-boats into submerging (WWI).

scout, sb.

A ship or aircraft intended for reconnaissance.

screen, sb.

A defensive tactic, arranging warships around a fleet or convoy to protect against various forms of attack.

screw, sb.   A helical ship's propeller.

scupper, sb.   A hole in a ship's side to carry water overboard from the deck.

scuttle, vb.   To sink one's own ship deliberately by holing it or opening its seacocks to let water in.

sea trials, sb.   The tests applied to establish the qualities of a new vessel.

Seabees, sb.   US Navy's Construction Battalions.

seakeeping, sb.   The ability of a vessel to withstand rough conditions at sea.

seaplane, sb.   1. An aircraft fitted with floats to land on water (British). 2. An aircraft with a waterborne hull (US), i.e. a flying-boat (British).

sea-time, sb.   Accumulated experience at sea, a requirement for a naval officer's promotion.

sextant, sb.   A navigational instrument capable of taking sights or angles up to 120°.

shadow, vb.   To locate and follow enemy ships or aircraft, if possible undetected.

shadow factory, sb.   A factory financed by the 1935 'Shadow Factories' scheme, which provided for new manufacturing capacity for the motor and other mechanical engineering trades, but intended to be easily converted if necessary to the manufacture of aircraft.

Shark, sb.   British term for the German naval cypher *Triton*, first issued in February 1942.

shell, sb.   A hollow shot containing an explosive or incendiary charge.

ship, sb.   1. A seagoing vessel. 2. **capital** –, a warship of the largest size, a battleship. 3. **convict** –, a ship engaged in carrying convicted criminals under sentence of penal transportation to their place of exile. 4. – **handling**, the skill of manoeuvring a vessel. 5. -**master**, the master of a merchant ship. 6. -**mate**, a fellow member of a ship's company. 7. – **of the line**, a warship large enough to form part of the line of battle. 8. -**'s company**, the crew of a ship. 9. **troop**-, a ship used to carry soldiers. 10. **war**-, an armed ship or vessel.

shipwright, sb.   1. A carpenter or craftsman skilled in shipbuilding. 2. **master** –, the yard officer responsible for all building and repairs (19th century).

shoal, sb.   A bank or bar of water too shallow for ships to pass.

shot, sb.   A bullet or (non-explosive) projectile fired from a great gun.

sick berth, sb.   1. A compartment of a ship fitted to accommodate the sick or injured. 2. – **attendant**, RN rating trained in simple care or first aid of the wounded (from 1833).

side-lever engine, sb.
A marine steam engine, developed from the beam engine, which powered many early paddle steamers (1830s–1860s).

Siemens–Martin (otherwise 'open hearth') process, sb.
A steelmaking process (1860s–1890s).

sight, sb.
1. An observation of a star or planet, to calculate a ship's position. 2. An optical instrument allowing a gun to be aimed at its target.

signal-book, sb.
A compilation of signals by either flag, light or radio.

signalman, sb.
A seaman trained to communicate between ships with flags, lamps or other communication systems.

skid, sb.
A coal box.

Skipper RNR, sb.
Warrant officer's rank used in the RNR Trawler Branch.

sky wave, sb.
Electromagnetic radiation propagated or refracted back towards earth from the ionosphere.

slide rule, sb.
A ruler with a sliding central strip, marked with logarithmic scales and used for making rapid mathematical calculations.

slinging billet, sb.
The space or berth allocated for slinging a hammock.

slip, **slipway**, sb.
An inclined plane by which ships and boats may be hauled out of the water or launched into it.

sloop, sb.
A warship of destroyer size, armed as an anti-submarine or anti-aircraft escort (WWII).

smith, sb.
An artificer trained in metal-working (often in compounds such as 'blacksmith' or 'coppersmith').

snobbing, sb.
Bootmaking, repair of footwear.

snorkel, sb.
Air mast used by a submarine to allow prolonged periods submerged (from the German *Schnorchel*, Dutch *snuiver*, both meaning 'snorer').

sound, sb.
An inlet, fjord or strait communicating with the open sea.

sound, vb.
To measure the depth of water.

sounding, sb.
A measurement of water depth.

sovereign, sb.
A former British gold coin worth one pound sterling.

Special Entry scheme, sb.
A system (instituted in 1913) of recruiting young men as future officers at 17½–18½.

specie, sb.
Money in the form of gold or silver coin.

sponson, sb.
1. A projection on the side of a boat, ship or seaplane. 2. A gun platform standing out from a warship's side. 3. A short subsidiary wing that serves to stabilize a seaplane.

spotter, sb.
An aircraft 'spotting' for a ship's gunfire, i.e. reporting the fall of shot.

spring, sb.	A hawser laid to slew a ship or to prevent a ship surging along a quayside.
springs, **spring tides**, sb.	Tides falling at the new and full moons, when the tidal range is greatest.
squadron, sb.	A group of warships detached on a particular duty or under the command of a flag officer.
squall, sb.	A sudden violent gust of wind or localized storm.
stability, sb.	The ability of a ship to float in an upright position and, if inclined under action of an external force, to return to this position after the external force has ceased acting.
standard displacement, sb.	*See* displacement.
starboard, sb.	The right-hand side of a vessel, looking forward.
starshell, sb.	A naval pyrotechnic used for night illumination.
State Shinto, sb.	Imperial Japan's ideological use of the Japanese religion and traditions of Shinto.
station, sb.	A geographical area assigned to a particular ship or squadron.
station-keeping, sb.	Keeping a ship in a position relative to other ships in company.
steam, sb.	1. Heated water vapour. 2. **saturated** –, steam generated at but not above the boiling point of water at the ambient pressure. 3. **superheated** –, steam heated above boiling point at the ambient pressure.
steel, sb.	An iron alloy containing a proportion of carbon or other elements giving higher tensile strength.
stencil subtractor frame, sb.	A ciphered text recyphering tool (introduced by GC&CS in 1943).
stern, sb.	1. The rearmost part of a ship or boat. 2. -**gland**, a sleeve around the propeller shaft packed with compressible material to allow the shaft to turn without admitting water. 3. -**post**, central upright support at the stern of a boat, traditionally bearing the rudder.
stocks, sb.	External framework in a shipyard used to support a ship under construction.
stokehold, sb.	The working platform from which stokers or firemen fuel and maintain the furnace of a boiler.
stoker, sb.	1. One employed to tend to a furnace and supply it with fuel, specifically a rating who tends a marine steam boiler. 2. **chief** –, Petty Officer's rating (abolished 1868).
stowage, sb.	Storage space aboard a ship.
straits, sb.	A narrow passage of water connecting two seas or two other large areas of water.

strike down, vb.   To stow something below decks.

submarine, sb.   1. A seagoing craft capable of independent operation underwater. 2. **anti – nets**, a net boom placed across the mouth of a harbour or strait for protection against submarines. 3. **midget –**, small submarine, usually used for harbour penetration or reconnaissance.

substantive (pay), sb.   Pay for service in a substantive (i.e. permanent) rating.

suffragette, sb.   A member of the Women's Social and Political Union, founded in 1903 to campaign by radical or illegal means for women's right to vote.

superannuated, adj.   Outdated or obsolete through age or new developments.

superannuation, sb.   Regular payment made into a fund by an employee towards a future pension.

super-encypherment, sb.   A process of encrypting an already encrypted message one or more times either using the same or a different algorithm.

superfiring, adj.   Referring to guns mounted to fire over other mountings at a lower level.

Sweeney Todd, sb.   (Colloquial) a ship's barber.

T124 Articles, sb.   Named after a Board of Trade form for signing conscripts on as members of a merchant ship's company, under naval discipline but retaining mercantile pay rates (WWII).

tachymetric system, sb.   US and German anti-aircraft fire-control system using observed or calculated values of target speed, bearing and range rate.

telegraph, sb.   (Otherwise 'Engine Order Telegraph'). Communication devices enabling the pilot or captain on the bridge of a ship to transmit speed and other orders to the engine room.

telegraphist, sb.   A wireless operator.

terraqueous, adj.   Consisting or formed of land and water.

terrestrial magnetism, sb.   The properties of the Earth's magnetic field.

territorial waters, sb.   The waters under the jurisdiction of a coastal state, normally defined as those within a stated distance of the shore.

testing tank, sb.   A tank used to carry out hydrodynamic tests on model ships for the purpose of designing full-sized ships (1870).

'The Branch', sb.   (colloquial) The Fleet Air Arm.

theodolite, sb.   A surveying instrument incorporating a telescope, used for measuring horizontal and vertical angles.

tidal range, sb.   The vertical difference in height between high and low water at spring tides.

tidal stream, sb.   A current generated by the ebbing or flowing tide.

tiddly suits, sb.   (Colloquial) rating's uniform with unauthorized alterations.

tiddlyvated, adj.	(Colloquial) of an unofficially altered uniform.
tide, sb.	The diurnal rise and fall of the sea level responding to the gravitational influence of the moon.
tide gauge, sb.	A device for recording changes in sea level generated by the tides.
ton, sb.	1. One of a number of measures of volume used to calculate ships' tonnage, commonly 100 cubic feet for gross or net tonnage and 40 cubic feet for stowage of cargo. 2. A weight equal to 2,240lbs (US 2,000lbs).
torpedo, Whitehead torpedo, sb.	1. A cylindrical self-propelled underwater missile. 2. **aerial –**, a torpedo launched from an aircraft into the water. 3. **– boat**, a small fast vessel designed to launch torpedoes (late 19th century). 4. **homing –**, a torpedo able to identify and steer towards its target. 5. **– tube**, a cylinder from which torpedoes are launched.
transmitting station, sb.	An armoured compartment housing fire-control instruments for the main armament.
transom, sb.	A transverse timber crossing the sternpost of a ship and supporting the planking of the stern.
trawler, sb.	A fishing vessel which tows bags made of netting to capture fish.
trim, sb.	The attitude of a ship in the water, normally adjusted to keep her load-line parallel to the waterline.
trimmer, sb.	A stoker whose task is to level the coal stowed in the bunkers and facilitate the supply of coal to the stokehold.
triple-expansion engine, sb.	A steam engine in which steam is expanded in three stages in cylinders of increasing diameter to accommodate the increasing volume of the steam.
trunk, sb.	A vertical or inclined space or passage within the structure of a ship providing ventilation or access to other compartments.
trunnion, sb.	A cylindrical protrusion used as a mounting or pivoting point for a gun.
tug, sb.	1. A small powerful vessel used for towing larger vessels into harbour. 2. **salvage –**, a specialized seagoing tug equipped to rescue ships in distress.
turbine engine, sb.	A rotary engine that converts the kinetic energy of a moving fluid (water, steam, air or burning fuel) into mechanical energy.
turbo-electric, adj.	Describing a machine combining a turbine driving an electric generator.
turner, sb.	A person skilled in turning wood or metal on a lathe.
turret ship, sb.	A ship mounting her main armament in revolving turrets (19th century).

twin-screw, adj. — Of a ship with two shafts and two screw propellers.

two-power standard, sb. — A loosely defined policy adopted in 1889, determining that British naval strength be based on maintaining a navy at least larger than the fleets of the next two largest navies combined.

Typex, sb. — A British cypher machine adapted from the German Enigma machine (1937).

U-boat, sb. — Anglicized version of the German term *U-Boot*, officially used in the RN to refer to enemy submarines of all nationalities.

uckers, sb. — A board game resembling Ludo, played in the Navy.

Ultra, adj. — Special security classification (more than Most Secret) used for material obtained from enemy signals by cryptography (WWII).

under way, adj. — Of a ship in motion.

upper yardman, sb. — A rating identified as a candidate for accelerated promotion to officer rank (1932).

upperworks, sb. — All parts of the hull of a ship above the load waterline.

uptake, sb. — Piping serving to discharge a ship's exhaust gases into the atmosphere.

variable-geometry wing — A type of aeroplane wing whose performance can be changed by extending or retracting flaps to change its shape.

Vichy France, sb. — The French government established in the city of Vichy, which adopted a policy of collaboration with the occupying Germans (1940–44).

Victoria Cross, sb. — The highest decoration for valour in the British armed forces, awarded for 'conspicuous courage in the face of the enemy'.

victuals, sb. — Foodstuffs and/or provisions.

voice-pipe, sb. — A tube (often copper) connecting the bridge with other parts of the ship to pass orders and reports.

volunteer, sb. — 1. A person volunteering to serve. 2. A 'Boy 1st Class', an officer cadet. 3. A pupil of the Royal Naval Academy, Portsmouth (1731–1812).

War Office, sb. — The administrative headquarters of the British army.

wardroom, sb. — A compartment in which a warship's officers messed.

warp, sb. — A rope or hawser used to warp or heave a ship across a basin by manpower.

warrant officer, sb. — An officer promoted from a senior technical rating, and appointed by a warrant rather than a commission.

watch, sb. — 1. One of the seven divisions of the nautical day. 2. One of the two or three divisions of the ship's company, taking turns to be on duty. 3. The length of one watch, a spell of duty on deck.

waterline, sb. — The level reached by the water on the side of a ship afloat.

water-tube boiler, sb. A type of boiler in which water circulates in tubes heated externally by a furnace.

Wavy Navy, sb. (Colloquial) the Royal Naval Volunteer Reserve (so nicknamed from its officers' wavy rank stripes).

way, sb. 1. **make –**, vb., (of a ship or vessel) to move through the water under her own power. 2. **under –**, adj., moving through the water.

weather-ship, sb. A ship stationed at a designated position in the ocean to make meteorological observations for use in weather forecasting.

Western Approaches, sb. 1. The area of the Atlantic Ocean lying immediately to the west of the British Isles. 2. **– Command**, Naval command at Plymouth, later (1941) Liverpool, responsible for the Eastern Atlantic.

wet canteen, sb. A naval ratings' canteen serving alcohol.

wharf, sb. A quayside to which ships may be moored to load and unload.

Whigs, sb. A British political movement claiming descent from the authors of the 'Glorious Revolution' of 1688 (17th–19th century).

white-out, sb. Low visibility caused by driving snow.

winch, sb. A hauling or lifting device consisting of a rope or chain winding round a rotating drum, turned by manpower or machinery.

windage, sb. The force exerted by the wind to deflect a ship from her course.

wireless, sb. 1. An apparatus for wireless telegraphy, a radio. 2. **long-wave –**, radio signals on a wavelength longer than 1,000 metres and below 300 kiloherz in frequency. 3. **short-wave –**, high-frequency radio signal having a wavelength between 10 and 100 metres.

work up, vb. To train a newly commissioned ship's company to full efficiency.

wrecker, sb. A person who tries to bring about a shipwreck in order to plunder or profit from the wreckage.

Wren, sb. A member of the Women's Royal Naval Service (1917–19, 1939–96).

yardarm, sb. The outer ends of a ship's yard.

yaw, sb., vb. (Of a ship) to wander to one side or the other of a straight course.

yeoman of signals, sb. A petty officer signalman.

Youngman flap, sb. An early form of variable-geometry wing (1940s).

Zeppelin, sb. A large dirigible airship with a rigid framework and inflated by hydrogen (1900–1930s).

FOREIGN GLOSSARY

Abwehr, sb. (German)	Counter-intelligence (literally 'resistance' or 'defence').
Admiralstab, sb. (German)	German naval planning staff, personally dependent on the Kaiser (1899–1918).
amae, sb. (Japanese)	A dependent or infantile relationship with a person of rank with the moral authority to demand frank answers to difficult questions.
Befehlshaber der Unterseeboote; BdU, sb. (German)	Rear-Admiral and Flag Officer, Submarines (Karl Dönitz, 1939–43), 'Flag Officer Submarines' or German Submarine Command.
Beobachtungsdienst (B-Dienst), sb. (German)	'Observation Service', cryptographic department of German Naval Intelligence.
Blitzkrieg, sb. (German)	'Lightning War'. A style of offensive warfare characterized by a concentrated attack on a narrow front by mobile, usually armoured, forces with strong air support.
bushidō, sb. (Japanese)	An anachronistic portmanteau word covering imported foreign ideas, notably those based on European concepts of chivalry (19th–20th century).
Chasseurs Alpins, sb. (French)	French regiment specializing in mountain warfare.
Comando Supremo della Marina ('Supermarina'), sb. (Italian)	Italian naval headquarters in Rome.
Decima Flottiglia MAS, sb. (Italian)	'10th MTB Flotilla', cover name of a secret naval unit formed to mount attacks using 'stealth weapons'.
Directeur du matériel, sb. (French)	Director of French naval construction (Stanislas Dupuy de Lôme).
Electro-boote, sb. (German)	(Colloquial) German fast U-boats of Types XXI and XXIII (1943–5).
Entente Cordiale, sb. (French)	Anglo-French 'friendly agreement' of 8 April 1904 co-ordinating British and French strategy and foreign policy against Germany.

Entscheidungs-schlacht, sb. (German)	'Decisive battle'.
Entzifferungsdienst, sb. (German)	German Naval Cypher Service.
Fliegerkorps X, sb. (German)	10th Air Corps, a formation of the German Luftwaffe, specializing in operations against shipping.
Flottengesetz, sb. (German)	German Naval Law.
Freikorps, sb. (German)	Collective term for paramilitary militias formed by former servicemen, fighting to overthrow the Weimar Republic and restore militarist government (1918–1920s).
Frontboote, sb. (German)	Fully operational U-boats.
Führer, sb. (German)	Leader.
Führerstaat, sb. (German)	The Nazi concept of a 'Leader state' in which all state power is concentrated in the hands of a single individual.
Funkmessbeobach-tungsgerät, sb. (German)	'Wireless reporting device', i.e. radar detector.
Geheimscheiber, sb. (German)	Siemens & Halske cypher teleprinter or 'secret writer'.
Génie Maritime, sb. (French)	1. Naval engineers' corps. 2. Marine engineering.
genro, sb. (Japanese)	The elder statesmen of the Japanese Imperial Court.
Handelsverkehrs-buch, sb. (German)	'Transport [code] book'. One of the German Navy's three main code books, used by merchant ships, U-boats and Zeppelins (WWI).
Heimische (Gewässer), sb. (German)	Cypher for German vessels in 'Home Waters'. Known to GC&CS as 'Dolphin'.
honne, sb. (Japanese)	A personal inner conviction of the truth, which may be revealed at the demand of the *Tenno* (Emperor) or a person with dominant moral authority.
Immediatstellung/ Immediatvortrag, sb. (German)	The power allowed to the most senior admirals and generals to demand a private audience with the Kaiser to present their requirements.
Jeune École, sb. (French)	'Young School'. A radical French naval movement proposing to replace ironclads with torpedo boats (late 19th century).
jus in bello, sb. (Latin)	Laws governing the conduct of war.

Kaiserliche Marine, sb. (German)	Title of the German 'Imperial Navy', 1871–1919.
kamikaze, sb. (Japanese)	'Divine wind', a reference to the hurricane which destroyed the Mongol invasion fleet of 1281, applied to the suicide bombers of 1944–5.
Kampfgruppe, sb. (German)	'Battle Group', i.e. air squadron.
kana, sb. (Japanese)	Characters in one of the Japanese syllabic alphabets, *katakana* and *hiragana*.
Kempetai, sb. (Japanese)	Military police.
Kidō Butai, sb. (Japanese)	'Mobile force', the principal carrier force (1941–4).
Kriegsmarine, sb. (German)	Title of the German Navy, 1935–45.
Kriegsspiele, sb. (German)	'War games', table-top exercises developed by the German army and navy for tactical training (19th–20th century).
Kurzsignale, sb. (German)	Short signals.
Luftflotte, sb. (German)	'Air fleet' (Luftwaffe formation corresponding to an Army corps).
Luftwaffe, sb. (German)	German airforce.
maiali, sb. (Italian)	'Swine', divers' nickname for 'Slow-Running Torpedoes' or underwater powered sleds.
maistrance, sb. (French)	Collective term for specialist Petty Officers of the French Navy.
Marine Rundschau, sb. (German)	Official journal of the German Navy.
Marinekabinett, sb. (German)	Kaiser's naval private office, controlling officers' promotions (1889–1918).
Marinekorps Flandern, sb. (German)	Flanders Naval Division (1915–18).
Métox, sb. (French)	French radio company, manufacturer of the German radar detector FuMB 2 (*Funkmessbeobachtungsgerät*), colloquially named after it.
mezzi insidiosi, sb. (Italian)	Stealth weapons.
Milchkühe, sb. (German)	'Milch cows' – Type XIV submarine tankers for refuelling U-boats.
Motobarca Armata con Siluranti, sb. (Italian)	Motor torpedo boats.

motosiluranti, sb. (Italian)	Motor torpedo boats (seagoing, 1941 type).
Novellen, sb. (German)	Supplementary Parliamentary bills.
Oberkommando der Marine, sb. (German)	'Naval High Command', 1. Naval headquarters (abolished 1899). 2. Naval Staff (renamed *Marineleitung*, 1935).
Oberkommando der Wehrmacht, sb. (German)	German Armed Forces High Command.
Panzerschiff, sb. (German)	'Armoured ship', small battlecruiser.
Paukenschlag, sb. (German)	'Drumroll'. Code name for the German U-boat offensive against Allied merchant shipping on the East Coast of America (January–August 1942).
Plasmodium falciparum, sb. (Latin)	Malarial parasite (African variety).
Plasmodium vivax, sb. (Latin)	Malarial parasite (West Indian variety).
Quai d'Orsay, sb. (French)	French Foreign Ministry.
Regenbogen, sb. (German)	'Rainbow'.
Regia Aeronautica Italiana, sb. (Italian)	Royal (Italian) Airforce (1923–46).
Reichsmarine, sb. (German)	Title of the German Navy (1913–35).
Reichsmarineamt, sb. (German)	The Imperial Naval Office, one of three separate offices comprising the German Admiralty from 1889.
Reichstag, sb. (German)	The German parliament.
Rudeltaktik, sb. (German)	'Herd tactics', used by German U-boats in WWII, often mistranslated as 'Wolf Pack'.
S-Boot, sb. (German)	German *Schnellboot* ('fast boat', i.e. motor torpedo boat).
Schicksalzone, sb. (German)	The 'fateful area' – the waters of northern Norway, where Hitler was convinced the war at sea would be settled.
schuit, sb. (Dutch)	Barge or small coastal vessel.
Seegeltung, sb. (German)	Naval status or reputation.
Seekriegsleitung, sb. (German)	German Naval High Command/Headquarters (WWII). (SKL).
Seetakt, sb. (German)	'Naval tactical' (radar set) (1938–45).

Signalbuch der Kaiserlichen Marine, sb. (German)	German naval code book, used by major warships (WWI).
Siluri Lenta Corsa, sb. (Italian)	'Slow-running torpedoes'.
Snorkel, sb. (German)	Anglicized form of German *Schnorchel* (from Dutch *snuiver*), both meaning 'snorer'. An air-mast allowing a submarine to run on diesel engines at periscope depth.
Sonderschlüssel, sb. (German)	Private Enigma keys used by German U-boats (1944–5).
Staatssekretär, sb. (German)	Permanent secretary.
tatemae, sb. (Japanese)	Conventional wisdom a subordinate feels obliged to adopt in public as a loyal member of a community or an organization.
tenno, sb. (Japanese)	The Emperor, the 'King of Heaven'.
ten-no-koye, sb. (Japanese)	The 'voice of heaven', the decision of the Emperor or other authority figure.
tokkōtai, sb. (Japanese)	'Special attack' units of suicide bombers, more commonly known as *Kamikaze*.
torpilleurs de haute mer, sb. (French)	Torpedo-boat destroyers or deep-sea torpedo boats.
UB, sb. (German)	Coastal torpedo- and gun-armed submarines (WWI).
UC, sb. (German)	Minelaying submarines (WWI).
un effort de sang, sb. (French)	'A commitment in blood'.
uneingeschränkt, adj. (German)	Unrestricted or unlimited (submarine warfare).
Verkehrsbuch (der Kaiserlichen Marine), sb. (German)	'Transport Book', German naval code book used by flag officers (WWI).
viva voce, adj. (Latin)	Using the spoken word.
Wanze, sb. (German)	Type of German radar detector (WWII).
Wehrmacht, sb. (German)	Collective term for the armed forces of Germany (WWII).
Wirkungsgrad, sb. (German)	'Performance indicator' based on tonnage sunk per U-boat day at sea.
Zaunkönig, sb. (German)	'Wren'. Cover name of German T5 homing torpedo.

ABBREVIATIONS (IN MAIN TEXT)

AA	Anti-Aircraft
ACNS	Assistant Chief of the Naval Staff
AFD	Admiralty Floating Dock
AFO	Admiralty Fleet Order
AMC	Armed Merchant Cruiser
AOC	Air Officer Commanding
AP	Armour-piercing
AS	Anti-Submarine
ASV	Air to Surface Vessel [radar]
BASF	Badische Anilin- und Sodafabrik [German chemical firm]
B-Dienst	*Beobachtungsdienst* ['Reporting Service', i.e. German Naval Intelligence]
BdU	*Befehlshaber der Untersee Boote* ['Flag Officer Submarines']
BEF	British Expeditionary Force
BPF	British Pacific Fleet
BRUSA	British-American [Intelligence-sharing agreement]
BTM	British Tabulating Machines
CAM	Catapult-Armed Merchantman
CID	Committee of Imperial Defence
CIGS	Chief of the Imperial General Staff
CINCUS	Commander-in-Chief US Fleet [to 1941]
CMB	Coastal Motor Boat
CNO	Chief of Naval Operations [USN]
CO	Commanding Officer
COMINCH	Commander-in-Chief US Fleet [from 1942]
CPO	Chief Petty Officer
D/F	Direction-finding [by wireless]
DNC	Director of Naval Construction
DRC	[Cabinet] Defence Requirements Sub-Committee
DSO	Distinguished Service Order
ERA	Engine Room Artificer
FAA	Fleet Air Arm
GC&CS	Government Code and Cypher School
GDP	Gross Domestic Product
GNP	Gross National Product
GRT	Gross Register Tonnage

HE	High Explosive
H/F D/F	High-Frequency Direction-Finding, 'Huff-Duff'
HMS	His/Her Majesty's Ship
HO	Hostilities Only
HP	Horse Power
HTP	High-Test Peroxide
HVB	*Handelsverkehrsbuch* [i.e. 'Transport [code] book'.]
IBM	International Business Machines
IFF	Interrogate Friend or Foe
IHP	Indicated Horse Power
IJN	Imperial Japanese Navy
IJNAF	Imperial Japanese Naval Air Force
IME	Institute of Marine Engineers
JWPC	[US] Joint War Plans Committee
KG	*Kampfgruppe* ['Battle Group', i.e. air squadron]
LCT	Landing Craft, Tank
MAS	*Motobarca Armata con Siluranti* [i.e. MTB]
MI5	Cover name for the Security Service
MI6	Cover name for the Secret Intelligence Service
MP	Member of Parliament
mph	miles per hour
MTB	Motor Torpedo-Boat
NID	Naval Intelligence Department, Naval Intelligence Division [of the Naval Staff]
NMM	National Maritime Museum
NSS	National Shipbuilders' Security
OIC	[Admiralty] Operational Intelligence Centre
OKM	*Oberkommando der Marine* [German Naval High Command]
OKW	*Oberkommando der Wehrmacht* [German Armed Forces High Command]
PM	Prime Minister
PPI	Plan Position Indicator [circular cathode-ray tube radar display]
psi	pounds per square inch
PSOC	Principal Supply Officers' Committee
QARNNS	Queen Alexandra's Royal Naval Nursing Service
QF	Quick-Firing [gun]
RAAF	Royal Australian Air Force
RAF	Royal Air Force
RAN	Royal Australian Navy
RCAF	Royal Canadian Air Force
RCN	Royal Canadian Navy
RCNVR	Royal Canadian Naval Volunteer Reserve

RDF	'Radio Direction-Finding' [i.e. radar]
RFC	Royal Flying Corps
RGF	Royal Gun Factory [in Woolwich Arsenal]
RMA	*Reichsmarineamt* [German Imperial Navy Office]
RML	Rifled Muzzle-Loader
RN	Royal Navy, Royal Naval
RNAS	Royal Naval Air Service, Royal Naval Air Station
RNC	Royal Naval College
RNEC	Royal Naval Engineering College
RNR	Royal Naval Reserve
RNVR	Royal Naval Volunteer Reserve
RNVSR	Royal Naval Volunteer (Supplementary) Reserve
SBML	Smooth-Bore Muzzle-loader
SHP	Shaft Horse Power
SKL	*Seekriegsleitung* [German naval headquarters]
SKM	*Signalbuch der Kaiserlichen Marine*
SLC	*Siluri Lenta Corsa* [Italian 'slow-running torpedoes']
SNO	Senior Naval Officer
TNT	Trinitrotoluene
UB	Coastal torpedo- and gun-armed submarines (WWI)
UC	Coastal minelaying submarines (WWI)
US, USA	United States of America
USAAF	United States Army Air Forces
USN	United States Navy
USS	United States Ship
VB	*Verkehrsbuch [der Kaiserlichen Marine]*
VC	Victoria Cross
VD	Venereal disease
VHF	Very High Frequency
VLR	Very Long Range [aircraft]
WAAF	Women's Auxiliary Air Force
WATU	Western Approaches Tactical Unit
WRNS	Women's Royal Naval Service
WSPU	Women's Social and Political Union
WTID	War Trade Intelligence Department

ABBREVIATIONS (IN REFERENCES)

AHR	*American Historical Review*
AN	*American Neptune*
BDOW	Gooch and Temperley, *British Documents on the Origins of the War*
BND	Hattendorf, *British Naval Documents*
CH2WW	Ferris et al., *Cambridge History of the Second World War*
CHM	*Chronique d'Histoire Maritime*
CO	Rodger, *Command of the Ocean*
D&S	*Diplomacy and Statecraft*
DH	*Diplomatic History*
DR2WK	Deist et al., *Das Deutsche Reich und der Zweiten Weltkrieg*
DSF	Marder, *Dreadnought to Scapa Flow*
EcHR	*Economic History Review*
EHR	*English Historical Review*
FGDN	Marder, *Fear God and Dread Nought*
G2WW	Deist et al., *Germany in the Second World War*
GBSP	Bartlett, *Great Britain and Sea Power*
GWS	*Global War Studies*
HC	House of Commons Sessional Papers
HES	*Histoire, Économie et Société*
HJ	*Historical Journal*
HR	*Historical Research*
I&NS	*Intelligence & National Security*
IHR	*International History Review*
IJNH	*International Journal of Naval History*
IRSH	*International Review of Social History*
JBS	*Journal of British Studies*
JCH	*Journal of Contemporary History*
JEEH	*Journal of European Economic History*
JGH	*Journal of Global History*
JICH	*Journal of Imperial and Commonwealth History*
JIH	*Journal of Intelligence History*
JMH	*Journal of Modern History*
JMilH	*Journal of Military History*
JMR	*Journal of Maritime Research*
JNE	*Journal of Naval Engineering*

JRNMS	*Journal of the Royal Naval Medical Service*
JRNSS	*Journal of the Royal Naval Scientific Service*
JRUSI	*Journal of the Royal United Service Institution [later Royal United Services Institute]*
JSS	*Journal of Strategic Studies*
MGM	*Militärgeschichtliche Mitteilungen*
MM	*Mariner's Mirror*
NM	*Northern Mariner*
NMM	National Maritime Museum
NR	*Naval Review*
NRG	Rodger, *Naval Records for Genealogists*
NRS	Navy Records Society
NWCR	*Naval War College Review*
PRO	Public Record Office (now National Archives)
ODNB	*Oxford Dictionary of National Biography*
OED	*Oxford English Dictionary*
OHBE	*Oxford History of the British Empire* [i.e. Vol. III, ed. Andrew Porter, Oxford, 1999]
P&P	*Past & Present*
p.p.	privately printed
RIHM	*Revue Internationale d'Histoire Militaire*
RHM	*Revue d'Histoire Maritime*
RO	Record Office
S.	Series
Soc.	Society
T&C	*Technology and Culture*
TINA	*Transactions of the Institute of Naval Architects*
TNS	*Transactions of the Newcomen Society*
TRHS	*Transactions of the Royal Historical Society*
TvZ	*Tijdschrift voor Zeegeschiedenis*
W&S	*War and Society*
WI	*Warship International*
WiH	*War in History*

BIBLIOGRAPHY

Abbatiello, John J., *Anti-Submarine Warfare in World War I: British Naval Aviation and the Defeat of the U-Boats* (Abingdon, 2006).

Abbenhuis, M. M., ' "Too Good to be True?" European Hopes for Neutrality before 1914', in *European Hopes for Neutrality before 1914*, ed. Herman Amersfoort and Wim Klinkert (Leiden, 2011).

Ackroyd, Markus, Laurence Brockliss, Michael Moss, Kate Retford and John Stevenson, *Advancing with the Army: Medicine, the Professions and Social Mobility in the British Isles, 1790–1850* (Oxford, 2006).

Adams, Stephen B., *Mr Kaiser Goes to Washington: The Rise of a Government Entrepreneur* (Chapel Hill, NC, 1997).

Adams, Thomas, 'A Standard Caliber: The Genesis of the French 30-Pounder', in Freeman, *Les empires en guerre et paix*, pp. 195–203.

Afflerbach, Holger, 'What Was the Great War About?', in Afflerbach, ed., *The Purpose of the First World War: War Aims and Military Strategies* (Berlin, 2015), pp. 3–6.

Agar, Captain Augustus, *Baltic Episode: A Classic of Secret Service in Russian Waters* (London, 1963). Agar wrote this in 1935, from secret and official papers, but was forbidden to publish it for almost thirty years.

Aizawa, Yoshio, 'The Path Towards an "Anti-British" Strategy by the Japanese Navy between the Wars', in Gow, Hirama and Chapman, *The History of Anglo-Japanese Relations, 1600–2000, Vol. 3: The Military Dimension*, pp. 139–50.

Akiyama, Yuriko, *Feeding the Nation: Nutrition and Health in Britain before World War One* (London, 2008).

Akrigg, G. P. V. and Helen B. Akrigg, *HMS Virago in the Pacific, 1851–1855* (Victoria, BC, 1992).

Aldrich, Richard J., *Intelligence and the War against Japan* (Cambridge, 2000).

Alfaro Zaforteza, Carlos, 'The Vienna Settlement, 1815–1854', in James, Alfaro Zaforteza and Murfett, *European Navies and the Conduct of War*, pp. 87–112.

—'The Collapse of the Congress System, 1854–1870', *ibid.*, pp. 113–29.

—'The Age of Empire, 1870–1914', *ibid.*, pp. 130–56.

Allain, Jean-Claude, 'L'indépendance câblière de la France au début du XXe siècle', *Guerres mondiales et conflits contemporains* 166 (1992), pp. 115–31.

Allard, Dean C., 'Naval Rearmament, 1930–1941: An American Perspective', *RIHM* 73 (1991), pp. 35–50.

Allen, Matthew, 'Rear Admiral Reginald Custance: Director of Naval Intelligence', *MM* LXXVIII (1992), pp. 61–75.

—'The Foreign Intelligence Committee and the Origins of the Naval Intelligence Department of the Admiralty', *MM* LXXXI (1995), pp. 65–78.

—'The Deployment of Untried Technology: British Naval Tactics in the Ironclad Era', *WiH* XV (2008), pp. 269–93.

Al-Qasimi, Sultan Muhammad, *The Myth of Arab Piracy in the Gulf* (London, 1986).

Anderson, David G., 'British Re-Armament and the Merchants of Death: The 1935–36 Royal Commission on the Manufacture and Trade in Armaments', *JCH* 29 (1994), pp. 5–37.

Anderson, Edgar, 'An Undeclared Naval War: The British-Soviet Naval Struggle in the Baltic, 1918–1920', *Journal of Central European Affairs* XXII (1962), pp. 43–78.

—*A Liberal State at War: English Politics and Economics during the Crimean War* (London, 1967).

Anderson, Olive, 'Economic Warfare in the Crimean War', *EcHR* 2nd S. XIV (1961), pp. 34–47.

Anderson, R. C., *Naval Wars in the Levant 1559–1853* (Liverpool, 1952).

Andrew, Christopher, *Secret Service: The Making of the British Intelligence Community* (London, 1985).

—*The Defence of the Realm: The Authorized History of MI5* (London, 2009).

—'Secret Intelligence and British Foreign Policy 1900–1939', in Andrew and Noakes, *Intelligence and International Relations, 1900–1945*, pp. 9–28.

—'Bletchley Park in Pre-War Perspective', in *Action this Day*, ed. Ralph Erskine and Michael Smith (London, 2001).

Andrew, Christopher and Jeremy Noakes, eds., *Intelligence and International Relations, 1900–1945* (Exeter, 1987).

Angster, Julia, *Erdbeeren und Piraten: Die Royal Navy und die Ordnung der Welt 1770–1860* (Göttingen, 2012). More about naval policy and empire than strawberries and pirates.

Anten, Jaap, *Navalisme nekt Onderzeeboot. De invloed van buitenlandse zeestrategieën op de Nederlandse zeestrategic voor de defensie van Nederlands-Indië, 1912–1942* (Leiden doctoral thesis, 2010). Recommended for its ideas, though not for its style.

Arnold, A. J., *Iron Shipbuilding on the Thames, 1832–1915: An Economic and Business History* (Aldershot, 2000).

—'"Riches beyond the dreams of avarice"? Commercial Returns on British Warship Construction', *EcHR* LIV (2001), pp. 267–89.

Arthur, Max, *The True Glory: The Royal Navy, 1914–1939* (London, 1996).

—*The Navy, 1939 to the Present Day* (London, 1997).

—*Lost Voices of the Royal Navy: Vivid Eyewitness Accounts of Life in the Royal Navy 1914–1945* (London, 2005). Anthologies of personal experience.

Asada, Sadao, *From Mahan to Pearl Harbor: The Imperial Japanese Navy and the United States* (Annapolis, Md., 2006).

—'The Japanese Navy's Road to Pearl Harbor, 1931–1941', in *Culture Shock and Japanese-American Relations: Historical Essays* (Columbia, MO, 2007), pp. 137–73.

—'The London Conference and the Tragedy of the Imperial Japanese Navy', in Maurer and Bell, *At the Crossroads between Peace and War: Naval Rivalries and Arms Control between the World Wars; The London Conference of 1930* (Annapolis, Md., 2014). One of the few Japanese scholars to write serious naval history in good English.

Ashcroft, William, 'The Reminiscences of William Petty Ashcroft', *NR* LII (1964), pp. 59–66, 194–202, 310–19 and 437–46, continued LIII (1965), pp. 62–70, 157–65, 272–8 and 358–65. Intelligent memoir of a mid-Victorian petty officer.

Austin, Douglas, *Malta and British Strategic Policy, 1925–43* (London, 2004).

Avenel, Jean David, *L'Affaire de Rio de la Plata 1838–1852* (Paris, 1998).

Babij, Orest M., 'The Second Labour Government and British Maritime Security, 1929–31', *D&S* VI (1995), pp. 645–71.

—'The Royal Navy and the Defence of the British Empire, 1928–1934', in Kennedy and Neilson, *Far-Flung Lines*, pp. 171–89.

Bach, John, *The Australia Station: A History of the Royal Navy in the South West Pacific, 1821–1913* (Kensington, NSW, 1986).

Badem, Candam, *The Ottoman Crimean War (1853–1856)* (Leiden, 2010).

Baer, George W., *One Hundred Years of Sea Power: The U.S. Navy, 1890–1990* (Stanford, CA, 1994). Intelligent and informative.

Bagnasco, Erminio, *In guerra sul mare: navi e marinai italiani nel secondo conflitto mondiale* (Parma, 2005). Excellent pictorial history and chronology.

Bailey, Chris Howard, *The Battle of the Atlantic: The Corvettes and Their Crews, an Oral History* (Stroud, 1994).

Baker, Richard, *The Terror of Tobermory: An Informal Biography of Vice-Admiral Sir Gilbert Stephenson, KBE, CB, CMG* (London, 1972).

Balano, Randy Carol and Craig L. Symonds, *New Interpretations in Naval History: Selected Papers from the Fourteenth Naval History Symposium* (Annapolis, Md., 2001).

Ball, Simon, *The Bitter Sea: The Struggle for Mastery in the Mediterranean, 1935–1949* (London, 2009).

—'Mediterranean and North Africa, 1940–1944', in *CH2WW* I, 358–88.

Banbury, Philip, *Shipbuilders of the Thames and Medway* (Newton Abbot, 1971).

Barlow, Jeffrey G., *Revolt of the Admirals: The Fight for Naval Aviation, 1945–1950* (Washington, 1994).

Barnett, Correlli, *Engage the Enemy More Closely: The Royal Navy in the Second World War* (London, 1991). Spirited history, but now showing its age.

Barnhart, Michael, *Japan Prepares for Total War: The Search for Economic Security, 1919–1941* (Ithaca, NY, 1987).

—'"Making It Easy For Him": The Imperial Japanese Navy and Franklin D. Roosevelt to Pearl Harbor', in Marolda, *FDR and the U.S. Navy*, pp. 35–46.

Barrow, Sir John, *An Auto-Biographical Memoir* . . . (London, 1847).

Bartlett, C. J., *Great Britain and Sea Power 1815–53* (Oxford, 1963).

—'The Mid-Victorian Reappraisal of Naval Policy', in *Studies in International History Presented to W. N. Medlicott*, ed. K. Bourne and D. C. Watt (London, 1967), pp. 189–208.

—'Statecraft, Power and Influence', in Bartlett, *Britain Pre-eminent* (London, 1969).

—'Castlereagh, 1812–22', in *The Makers of British Foreign Policy*, ed. T. G. Otte (Basingstoke, 2002), pp. 52–74.

Bastable, Marshall J., *Arms and the State: Sir William Armstrong and the Remaking of British Naval Power, 1854–1914* (Aldershot, 2004).

Batey, Mavis, *Dilly: The Man Who Broke Enigmas* (London, 2010). A life of the cryptographer Dillwyn Knox by a leading member of his group.

Bath, Alan Harris. *Tracking the Axis Enemy: The Triumph of Anglo-American Naval Intelligence* (Lawrence, KS, 1998).

Battesti, Michèle, *La Marine de Napoléon III* (Service Historique de la Marine, Vincennes, 1997, 2 vols.).

Baugh, Daniel A., 'British Strategy during the First World War in the Context of Four Centuries: Blue-Water versus Continental Commitment', in Masterson, *Naval History* . . . *Sixth Symposium*, pp. 85–110.

Baumgart, Winfried, ed., *Englische Akten zur Geschichte des Krimkriegs* (Munich, 2005–6, 4 vols.). A full collection of political and diplomatic documents of the Crimean War calendared in German.

Baxter, Christopher, 'In Pursuit of a Pacific Strategy: British Planning for the Defeat of Japan, 1943–45', *D&S* XV (2004), pp. 253–77.

Baxter, James P., *The Introduction of the Ironclad Warship* (Cambridge, Mass., 1933).

Baylen, Joseph O., 'The United States and the London Naval Conference of 1908–1909: A Study in Anglo-American Unity', *Historia* [Puerto Rico] V (1955), pp. 62–90.

Baylis, John, *Anglo-American Defence Relations 1939–1980: The Special Relationship* (London, 1981).

Baynham, Henry, *Men from the Dreadnoughts* (London, 1976). Sailors' reminiscences.

Beachey, R. W., 'The Anti-Slave Patrol on the East African Coast in the Nineteenth Century', in *Foreign Relations of African States*, ed. Kenneth Ingham (London, 1974), pp. 85–108.

Bean, C. W. C., 'The Production of Naval Machinery from 1935 to 1945', *JNE* VII (1954), pp. 180–95.

Beattie, John H., *The Churchill Scheme: The Royal Naval Special Entry Cadet Scheme 1913–1955* (p.p. Cobham, 2011).

[Bechervaise, John], *Thirty-Six Years of a Seafaring Life by an Old Quarter Master* (Southsea, 1839).

—*A Farewell to my old Shipmates and Messmates* (Portsea, 1847).

Beckett, Ian F. W. and Keith Jeffery, 'The Royal Navy and the Curragh Incident', *HR* LXII (1989), pp. 54–69.

Bedford, F. G. H., *The Life and Letters of Admiral Sir Frederick George Denham Bedford* (p.p. nd [ca. 1960]).

Beeler, John F., *British Naval Policy in the Gladstone-Disraeli Era 1866–1880* (Stanford, CA, 1997).

—*Birth of the Battleship: British Capital Ship Design 1870–1881* (London, 2001).

—ed., *The Milne Papers: The Papers of Admiral of the Fleet Sir Alexander Milne, Bt., K.C.B. (1806–1896)*, Vols. I–III (NRS Vols. 147, 162 and 170, 2004–23 *et seq.*).

—'A One Power Standard? Great Britain and the Balance of Naval Power, 1860–1880', *JSS* XV (1992), pp. 548–75.

—'Fit for Service Abroad: Promotion, Retirement and Royal Navy Officers 1830–1890', *MM* LXXXI (1995), pp. 300–312.

—'Steam, Strategy and Schurman: Imperial Defence in the Post-Crimean Era, 1856–1905', in G. Kennedy and K. Neilson, *Far-Flung Lines*, pp. 27–54.

—'Ploughshares into Swords: The Royal Navy and Merchant Marine Auxiliaries in the Late Nineteenth Century', in G. Kennedy, *The Merchant Marine in International Affairs, 1850–1950*, pp. 5–30.

—' "A Whig Private Secretary is in itself fatal": Benjamin Disraeli, Lord Derby, Party Politics and Naval Administration, 1852', in *Splendidly Victorian: Essays in Nineteenth- and Twentieth-Century British History in Honour of Walter L. Arnstein*, ed. Michael H. Shirley and Todd E. A. Larson (Aldershot, 2001), pp. 109–28.

—'In the Shadow of Briggs: A New Perspective on British Naval Administration and W. T. Stead's 1884 "Truth about the Navy" Campaign', *IJNH* I (2002).

—ed., 'Lord Northbrook's 1885 Response to William T. Stead's Criticisms of Naval Preparedness in the *Pall Mall Gazette*', in *Naval Miscellany* VIII, ed. Brian Vale.

Beesly, *Very Special Intelligence: The Story of the Admiralty's Operational Intelligence Centre 1939–1945* (London, 1977).

—*Very Special Admiral: The Life of Admiral J. H. Godfrey* (London, 1980).

—*Room 40: British Naval Intelligence 1914–18* (London, 1982).

Bell, Christopher M., *The Royal Navy, Seapower and Strategy between the Wars* (Basingstoke, 2000).

—*Churchill and Sea Power* (Oxford, 2013).

—*Churchill and the Dardanelles* (Oxford, 2017).

—'The "Singapore Strategy" and the Deterrence of Japan: Winston Churchill, the Admiralty and the Dispatch of Force Z', *EHR* CXVI (2001), pp. 604–34.

—'Winston Churchill, Pacific Security, and the Limits of British Power, 1921–41', in *Churchill and Strategic Dilemmas before the World Wars: Essays in Honour of Michael J. Handel*, ed. John H. Maurer (London, 2003), pp. 51–87.

—'The Invergordon Mutiny, 1931', in Bell and Elleman, *Naval Mutinies of the Twentieth Century*, pp. 170–92.

—'The Royal Navy and the Lessons of the Invergordon Mutiny', *WiH* XII (2005), pp. 75–92.

—'The Royal Navy, War Planning, and Intelligence Assessments of Japan, 1921–1941', in *Intelligence and Statecraft: The Use and Limits of Intelligence in International Society*, ed. Peter Jackson and Jennifer L. Sieger (Westport, Conn., 2005), pp. 139–56.

—'Winston Churchill and the Ten Year Rule', *JMH* LXXIV (2010), pp. 1097–128.

—'Great Britain and the London Naval Conference, 1929–1930', in Maurer and Bell, *At the Crossroads between Peace and War*, pp. 49–87.

—'Air Power and the Battle of the Atlantic: Very Long Range Aircraft and the Delay in Closing the Atlantic "Air Gap"', *JMH* LXXIX (2015), pp. 691–719.

—'The View from the Top: Winston Churchill, British Grand Strategy, and the Battle of the Atlantic', in Bell and Faulkner, *Decision in the Atlantic*, pp. 20–45.

Bell, Christopher M. and Bruce A. Elleman, *Naval Mutinies of the Twentieth Century: An International Perspective* (London, 2003).

Bell, Christopher M. and Marcus Faulkner, *Decision in the Atlantic* (Lexington, Ky., 2019).

Bell, P. M. H., *Twelve Turning Points of the Second World War* (London, 2011).

Benbow, Tim, ed., *British Naval Aviation: The First 100 Years* (Farnham, 2011).

—'British Uses of Aircraft Carriers and Amphibious Ships, 1945–2010' (King's College London, *Corbett Paper No. 9*, 2012).

—'British Naval Aviation and the "Radical Review", 1953–55', in *British Naval Aviation*, ed. Benbow, pp. 125–50.

—'Brothers in Arms: The Admiralty, the Air Ministry, and the Battle of the Atlantic', in Bell and Faulkner, *Decision in the Atlantic*, pp. 78–124.

—'"Menace" to "Ironclad": The British Operations against Dakar (1940) and Madagascar (1942)', *JMH* LXXV (2011), pp. 769–809.

Benesch, Oleg, *Inventing the Way of the Samurai: Nationalism, Internationalism and Bushidō in Modern Japan* (Oxford, 2014).

Bennett, Geoffrey, *Cowan's War: The Story of British Naval Operations in the Baltic, 1918–20* (London, 1964).

Bennett, George Henry, *The Royal Navy in the Age of Austerity 1919–22: Naval and Foreign Policy under Lloyd George* (London, 2016).

—'The Other Critical Convoy Battles of 1943: The Eclipse of the *Schnellboote* in the English Channel and the North Sea', in Bell and Faulkner, *Decision in the Atlantic*, pp. 225–51.

Bennett, George Henry and Roy Bennett, *Hitler's Admirals* (Annapolis, Md., 2004).

Bennett, Ralph, *Ultra and Mediterranean Strategy, 1941–1945* (London, 1989).

Berg, M. W., 'Protecting National Interests by Treaty: The Second London Naval Conference, 1934–36', in McKercher, *Arms Limitation and Disarmament*, pp. 203–27.

Berghahn, Volker R., *Der Tirpitz-Plan: Genesis und Verfall einer innenpolitischen Krisenstrategie unter Wilhelm II.* (Düsseldorf, 1971).

—'Naval Armaments and Social Crisis: Germany before 1914', in *War, Economy and the Military Mind*, ed. Geoffrey Best and Andrew Wheatcroft (London, 1976), pp. 61–88.

—'Des Kaisers Flotte und die Revolutionierung des Mächtesystems vor 1914', in *Der Ort Kaiser Wilhelms II in der deutschen Geschichte*, ed. John C. G. Röhl (Munich, 1991), pp. 173–88.

Bernath, Stuart L., *Squall across the Atlantic: American Civil War Prize Cases and Diplomacy* (Berkeley, CA, 1970).

Berryman, John, 'British Imperial Defence Strategy and Russia: The Role of the Royal Navy in the Far East, 1878–1898', *IJNH* I (2002), 1 (n.p.).

Bess, Henning, 'Probleme der Gefechtsführung im Verlauf der Operation "Regenbogen" Ende Dezember 1942', in *Der Marineoffizier als Führer im Gefecht*, ed. Heinrich Walle (Hamburg, 1984), pp. 177–200.

Best, Anthony, *British Intelligence and the Japanese Challenge in Asia, 1914–1941* (Basingstoke, 2002).

Bethell, Leslie, *Britain, Brazil and the Slave Trade Question, 1807–1869* (Cambridge, 1970).

Bialer, Uri, *The Shadow of the Bomber: The Fear of Air Attack and British Politics, 1932–1939* (London, 1980).

Biddle, Tami Davis, *Rhetoric and Reality in Air Warfare: The Evolution of British and American Ideas about Strategic Bombing, 1914–1945* (Princeton, NJ, 2002).

—'Anglo-American Strategic Bombing, 1940–1945', in *CH2WW* I, 485–526.

Bird, Keith W., *Weimar, the German Naval Officer Corps and the Rise of National Socialism* (Amsterdam, 1977).

—*Erich Raeder, Admiral of the Third Reich* (London, 2006).

—'The Origins and Role of German Naval History in the Inter-War Period 1918–1939', *NWCR* XXXII, 2(1979), pp. 42–58.

Bird, K. W. and Hinds, Jason, 'In the Shadow of Ultra: A Reappraisal of German Naval Communications Intelligence in 1914–1918', *NM* XXVIII (2018), pp. 97–117.

Birn, Donald S., 'The Washington Naval Conference of 1921–22 in Anglo-French Relations', in Masterson, *Naval History . . . Sixth Symposium*, pp. 167–78.

Black, Nicholas, *The British Naval Staff in the First World War* (Woodbridge, 2009).

Blair, Clay, *Hitler's U-Boat War: The Hunters, 1939–1942* (London, 1997).

—*Hitler's U-Boat War: The Hunted, 1942–1945* (London, 1999).

Blake, Richard, *Religion in the British Navy 1815–1879: Piety and Professionalism* (Woodbridge, 2014).

Blewett, Daniel K., 'Fuel and U.S. Naval Operations in the Pacific, 1942', in *The Pacific War Revisited*, ed. Günther Bischof and Robert L. Dupont (London and Baton Rouge, 1997), pp. 57–80.

Blond, A. J. L., 'Technology and Tradition: Wireless Telegraphy and the Royal Navy, 1895–1920' (Lancaster University PhD thesis, 1993).

Blumenthal, Harvey, 'W. T. Stead's Role in Shaping Official Policy: The Navy Campaign of 1884' (George Washington University PhD thesis, 1984).

822 · BIBLIOGRAPHY

Blyth, Robert, Jan Rüger and Andrew Lambert, eds., *The Dreadnought and the Edwardian Age* (Farnham, 2011).

Boer, P. C., trans. H. Kirkels, *The Loss of Java* (Singapore, 2011): revised trans. of *Het verlies van Java: een kwestie van air power* (Amsterdam, 2006).

Bonatz, Heinz, *Die deutsche Marine-Funkaufklärung 1914–1945* (Darmstadt, 1970).

—*Seekrieg im Äther: Die Leistungen der Marine Funkaufklärung 1939–1945* (Herford, 1981).

Bönker, Dirk, *Militarism in a Global Age: Naval Ambitions in Germany and the United States before World War I* (Ithaca, NY, 2012).

Bonner-Smith, David, ed., *Russian War 1855, Baltic* (NRS Vol. 84, 1944).

Bonner-Smith, David and A. C. Dewar, eds., *Russian War 1854: Baltic and Black Sea* (NRS Vol. 83, 1943).

Bonner-Smith, David and E. W. R. Lumby, eds., *The Second China War 1856–1860* (NRS Vol. 95, 1954).

Boog, Horst, 'The Anglo-American Strategic Air War over Europe and the German Air Defence', in *G2WW* VI, 467–628.

—'The Strategic Air War in Europe and Air Defence of the Reich, 1943–1944', in *G2WW* VII, 7–458.

—'Luftwaffe Support of the German Navy', in Howarth and Law, *The Battle of the Atlantic*, pp. 302–22.

Boteler, John Harvey, *Recollections of my Sea Life from 1808 to 1830*, ed. David Bonner-Smith (NRS Vol. 82, 1942; originally p.p. 1883).

Boudriot, Jean and Hubert Berti, *L'artillerie de mer: Marine française 1650–1850* (Paris, 1992).

Bourchier, Jane Lady, *Memoir of the Life of Admiral Sir Edward Codrington* (London, 1873, 2 vols.).

—*Letters of Sir Henry Codrington* (London, 1880). Useful life of the admiral and correspondence of his son, both edited by the admiral's daughter.

Bowen, Frank C., *History of the Royal Naval Reserve* (London, 1926).

Bowie, Robert R., 'Eisenhower, Dulles, and the Suez Crisis', in *Suez 1956: The Crisis and its Consequences*, ed. William Roger Louis and Roger Owen (Oxford, 1989), pp. 189–214.

Boyce, D. George, ed., *The Crisis of British Power: The Imperial and Naval Papers of the Second Earl of Selborne, 1895–1910* (London, 1990).

Boyce, Robert W. D., 'Submarine Cables as a Factor in Britain's Ascendency as a World Power', in *Kommunikationsrevolutionen: Die neuen Medien des 16. und 19. Jahrhunderts*, ed. Michael North (Cologne, 1995), pp. 81–99.

—'Imperial Dreams and National Realities: Britain, Canada and the Struggle for a Pacific Telegraph Cable', *EHR* CXV (2000), pp. 39–70.

Boyd, Andrew, *The Royal Navy in Eastern Waters: Linchpin of Victory 1935–1942* (Barnsley, 2017).

—*British Naval Intelligence through the Twentieth Century* (Barnsley, 2020). Important new studies.

Bräckow, Werner, *Die Geschichte des deutschen Marine-Ingenieuroffizierkorps* (Oldenburg and Hamburg, 1974). Essential corrective to the naive enthusiasm of many writers in English.

Brassey, Sir Thomas, *The British Navy, Its Strength, Resources and Administration* (London, 1882–3, 5 vols.). Brassey's collected articles are a reliable source of the conventional wisdom of their day.

Brescia, Maurizio, *Mussolini's Navy: A Reference Guide to the Regia Marina 1930–1945* (Barnsley, 2012). Excellent and well-illustrated.

Breyer, Siegfried, *Battleships and Battle-Cruisers 1905–1970*, trans. Alfred Kurti (London, 1973).

Brézet, François-Emmanuel, 'Course aux armements navals ou accord de limitation: le dilemme des relations anglo-allemandes de 1905 à 1914', in *Aspects du désarmement naval*, ed. Hervé Coutau-Bégarie (Paris, 1994), pp. 109–30.

Briggs, Mark, 'Innovation and the Mid-Victorian Royal Navy: The Case of the Whitehead Torpedo', *MM* LXXXVIII (2002), pp. 447–55.

Briggs, Sir John Henry, *Naval Administrations 1827 to 1892: The Experience of 65 Years* (London, 1897). Unreliable posthumous work nominally by a senior Admiralty clerk, but (it seems) largely written by his widow.

Brisou, Dominique, *Accueil, introduction et développement de l'énergie vapeur dans la Marine militaire française au XIXe siècle* (Vincennes, 2001, 2 vols.).

Broadberry, Stephen and Mark Harrison, eds., *The Economics of World War I* (Cambridge, 2005).

Broadberry, Stephen and Peter Howlett, 'The United Kingdom: "Victory at all costs"', in *The Economics of World War II: Six Great Powers in International Comparison*, ed. Broadberry (Cambridge, 1998), pp. 43–80.

—'Blood, Sweat and Tears: British Mobilization for World War II', in *A World at Total War: Global Conflict and the Politics of Destruction*, ed. Roger Chickering, Stig Förster and Bernd Greiner (Cambridge, 2005), pp. 157–76.

Broadhead, Augustus G., *The Navy as it is; or the Memoirs of a Midshipman* (Portsea, 1854, 2 vols.). Jaundiced but acute survey of the mid-Victorian Navy, offering candid portraits of serving senior officers with lightly disguised names.

Brock, Michael and Brock, Eleanor, eds., *H. H. Asquith: Letters to Venetia Stanley.* Many of these were written during wartime Cabinet meetings and form the best or only record of their proceedings.

Brodhurst, Robin, *Churchill's Anchor: Admiral of the Fleet Sir Dudley Pound* (Barnsley, 2000).

Bromley, J. S., ed., *The Manning of the Royal Navy: Selected Public Pamphlets, 1693–1873* (NRS Vol. 119, 1974).

Brook, Peter, *Warships for Export: Armstrong Warships 1867–1927* (Gravesend, 1999).

Brooks, John, *Dreadnought Gunnery and the Battle of Jutland: The Question of Fire Control* (London, 2005).

—*The Battle of Jutland* (Cambridge, 2016). Important studies of still-controversial subjects.

—'*Dreadnought*: Blunder, or Stroke of Genius?', *WiH* XIV (2007), pp. 157–78.

—'Grand Battle-Fleet Tactics: From the Edwardian Age to Jutland', in Blyth, Rüger and Lambert, *The Dreadnought and the Edwardian Age*, pp. 183–211.

—'Preparing for Armageddon: Gunnery Practices and Exercises in the Grand Fleet Prior to Jutland', *JSS* XXXVIII (2015), pp. 1006–23.

Brown, David, *Palmerston: A Biography* (New Haven, Conn., 2010).

Brown, David [i.e. J. D.], *Carrier Fighters 1939–1945* (London, 1975).

—ed., *Naval Operations of the Campaign in Norway, April–June 1940* (London, 2000).

—*The Road to Oran: Anglo-French Naval Relations September 1939–July 1940* (Abingdon, 2004).

—*Carrier Operations in World War II*, ed. David Hobbs (Barnsley, 2009). [This reprints the first two volumes by Brown, originally issued in 1968 and 1974, together with the posthumous (and unreliable) text of his intended third volume.]

Brown, D. K. [i.e. David K.], *A Century of Naval Construction: The History of the Royal Corps of Naval Constructors* (London, 1983).

—*Before the Ironclad: Development of Ship Design, Propulsion and Armament in the Royal Navy, 1815–60* (London, 1990).

—*Paddle Warships: The Earliest Steam Powered Fighting Ships 1815–1850* (London, 1993).

—*The Design and Construction of British Warships 1939–1945: The Official Record* (London, 1995–96, 3 vols.).

—*Warrior to Dreadnought: Warship Development 1860–1905* (London, 1997).

—*The Grand Fleet: Warship Design and Development 1906–1922* (London, 1999).

—*Nelson to Vanguard: Warship Design and Development, 1923–1945* (London, 2000).

—*The Way of the Ship in the Midst of the Sea: The Life and Work of William Froude* (Penzance, 2006).

—*Atlantic Escorts: Ships, Weapons and Tactics in World War II* (Barnsley, 2007).

—'The Introduction of Iron Warships into the Royal Navy', *Naval Architect* XXI (1977), pp. 49–51.

—'*Nemesis*, the First Iron Warship', *Warship* VIII (1978), pp. 283–5.

—'The Design of Aircraft Carriers prior to World War II', *Interdisciplinary Science Reviews* VIII (1983), pp. 358–70.

—'Naval Re-Armament 1930–41: The Royal Navy', *RIHM* LXXIII (1991), pp. 11–30.

—'Atlantic Escorts, 1939–45', *JNE* XXXIV (1993), pp. 562–87.

—'Marine Engineering in the RN 1860–1905', *JNE* XXXIV (1993), pp. 391–407 and 647–58; XXV (1994), pp. 92–108 and 448–63.

—'Weather and Warships, Past, Present and Future', *JNE* XXXV (1994), pp. 612–27.

—'British Warship Design Methods 1860–1905', *WI* XXXII (1995), pp. 59–82.

Brown, D. K. and N. J. M. Campbell, 'Attack and Defence', in *Metals and the Sea: Papers presented at the March 1990 conference of the Historical Metallurgy Society*, ed. J. Lang (London, 1990), pp. 16–24.

Brown, E. M., *Wings of the Navy: Flying Allied Carrier Aircraft of World War Two* (London, 1980).

—*Duels in the Sky: World War II Naval Aircraft in Combat* (Annapolis, Md., 1988). [This is Captain Eric 'Winkle' Brown, wartime Chief RN test pilot.]

Brown, Kevin, *Poxed and Scurvied: The Story of Sickness and Health at Sea* (Barnsley, 2011).

—*Fittest of the Fit: Health and Morale in the Royal Navy, 1939–1945* (Barnsley, 2019).

Brown, Louis, *A Radar History of World War II: Technical and Military Imperatives* (Bristol, 1999).

Brown, Warwick M., 'The Royal Navy's Fuel Supplies, 1898–1939: The Transition from Coal to Oil' (King's College London PhD thesis, 2003).

Bruton, Elizabeth, 'Beyond Marconi: The Roles of the Admiralty, the Post Office, and the Institution of Electrical Engineers in the Invention and Development of Wireless Communication up to 1908' (Leeds PhD thesis, 2010).

Buchanan, R. A. and M. W. Doughty, 'The Choice of Steam Engine Manufacturers by the British Admiralty, 1822–1852', *MM* LXIV (1978), pp. 327–47.

Buckley, John, *The RAF and Trade Defence, 1919–1945: Constant Endeavour* (Keele, 1995).

—'Maritime Air Power and the Second World War: Britain, the USA and Japan', in *Air Power History: Turning Points from Kitty Hawk to Kosovo*, ed. Sebastian Cox and Peter Gray (London, 2002), pp. 125–41.

Bueb, Volkmar, *Die 'Junge Schule' der Französischen Marine. Strategie und Politik 1875–1900* (Munich, 1971). The *Jeune École*.

Buell, Thomas B., *Master of Sea Power: A Biography of Fleet Admiral Ernest J. King* (Boston, Mass., 1980). Even after his death King intimidated his biographers.

Burns, Richard Dean, 'Regulating Submarine Warfare, 1921–1941: A Case Study in Arms Control and Limited War', *Military Affairs* XXXV (1971), pp. 56–63.

Burns, Russell W., ed., *Radar Development to 1945* (London, 1988).

—*Communications: An International History of the Formative Years* (Institute of Electrical Engineers, London, 2004).

Burroughs, Peter, 'Defence and Imperial Disunity', in *OHBE* III, 320–45.

Burrows, Montagu, *Autobiography*, ed. Stephen Burrows (London, 1908). An improbable career, from naval officer to Oxford professor.

Cable, James, *Gunboat Diplomacy 1919–1991* (Basingstoke, 3rd edn., 1994).

Cain, P. J. and A. G. Hopkins, *British Imperialism: Innovation and Expansion 1688–1914* (London, 1993).

Campbell, N. J. M., *Naval Weapons of World War Two* (London, 1985).

—*Jutland: An Analysis of the Fighting* (London, 1986).

Canney, Donald L., *Africa Squadron: The U.S. Navy and the Slave Trade, 1843–1861* (Washington, DC, 2006).

Canuel, Hugues, *The Fall and Rise of French Sea Power: France's Quest for an Independent Naval Policy, 1940–1963* (Annapolis, Md., 2021).

Capper, Henry D., ed., *Royal Naval Warrant Officers' Annual 1894–95* (London, 1894).

—*Aft-from the Hawsehole: Sixty-Two Years of Sailors' Evolution* (London, 1927).

Caravaggio, Angelo N., 'The Attack at Taranto: Tactical Success, Operational Failure', *NWCR* LIX, no. 3 (2006), pp. 103–27.

Carew, Anthony, *The Lower Deck of the Royal Navy 1900–1939* (Manchester, 1981).

—'The Invergordon Mutiny, 1931: Long-Term Causes, Organisation and Leadership', *IRSH* XXIV (1979), pp. 157–88.

Carlisle, Rodney, *Sovereignty at Sea: U.S. Merchant Ships and American Entry into World War I* (Gainesville, FL, 2009).

Carne, W. P., *The Making of a Royal Naval Officer* (London, 2021).

Casali, Antonio and Marina Cattaruzza, *Sotto i mari del mondo: La Whitehead 1875–1990* (Rome, 1990). A business history of the Hungarian, later Italian, branch of the Whitehead torpedo company.

Casey, Neil, 'Class Rule: The Hegemonic Role of the Royal Dockyard Schools, 1840–1914', in *History of Work and Labour Relations in the Royal Dockyards*, ed. Kenneth Lunn and Ann Day (London, 1999), pp. 66–86.

Casey, Steven, 'Franklin D. Roosevelt', in *Mental Maps in the Era of Two World Wars*, ed. Casey and Jonathan Wright (Basingstoke, 2008), pp. 216–39.

Cavell, S. A., *Midshipmen and Quarterdeck Boys in the British Navy, 1771–1831* (Woodbridge, 2012).

Cawood, John, 'Terrestrial Magnetism and the Development of International Collaboration in the Early 19th Century', *Annals of Science* XXXIV (1977), pp. 551–87.

—'The Magnetic Crusade: Science and Politics in Early Victorian Britain', *Isis* LXX (1979), pp. 493–518.

Cecil, Lady Gwendolen, *Life of Robert, Marquis of Salisbury* (London, 1921–34, 4 vols.).

Ceillier, Marie-Raymonde, 'Les idées stratégiques en France de 1870 à 1914: La Jeune École', in *L'évolution de la pensée navale*, ed. Hervé Coutau-Bégarie (Paris, 1990–2007, 10 vols.), I, 195–231.

Cernuschi, Enrico, *Marinelettro e il radiotelemetro Italiano: Lo sviluppo e l'evoluzione del radar navale (1933–1943)* (Supplement to *Rivista Marittima*, 1997).

—'Ultra': *La fine de un mito. La guerra dei codici tra gli inglesi e le Marine italiane, 1934–1945* (Milan, 2014).

Chalmers, W. S., *Max Horton and the Western Approaches* (London, 2nd edn., 1957).

Chamberlain, Tony, 'Stokers – the lowest of the low? A Social History of Royal Navy Stokers, 1850–1950' (Exeter PhD thesis, 2013).

Chapman, J. W. M., 'Japanese Intelligence 1919–1945: A Suitable Case for Treatment', in Andrew and Noakes, *Intelligence and International Relations*, pp. 145–90.

—'Britain, Japan and the "Higher Realms of Intelligence", 1918–1945', in Gow, Hirama and Chapman, *Anglo-Japanese Relations*, Vol. 3, pp. 151–72.

Charrier, Philip, 'British Assessments of Japanese Naval Tactics and Strategy, 1941–1945', in Gow, Hirama and Chapman, *Anglo-Japanese Relations*, Vol. 3, pp. 222–31.

Chatfield, A. E. M. Lord, *The Navy and Defence* (London, 1942).

Chickering, Roger and Stig Förster, eds., *Great War, Total War: Combat and Mobilization on the Western Front, 1914–1918* (Annapolis, Md., 2000).

Chilston, Eric Akers-Douglas, Viscount, *W. H. Smith* (London, 1965).

Chisholm, Donald, *Waiting for Dead Men's Shoes: Origins and Development of the U.S. Navy's Officer Personnel System, 1793–1941* (Stanford, CA, 2001).

Christman, C. L., 'Franklin D. Roosevelt and the Craft of Strategic Assessment', in Murray and Millett, *Calculations: Net Assessments and the Coming of World War II*, pp. 216–57.

Churchill, W. S., *The Second World War* (London, 1948–54, 6 vols.).

Claasen, Adam R. A., *Hitler's Northern War: The Luftwaffe's Ill-Fated Campaign 1940–1945* (Lawrence, KS, 2001).

—'Blood and Iron, and *der Geist des Atlantiks*: Assessing Hitler's Decision to invade Norway', *JSS* XX, no. 3 (1997), pp. 71–96.

Clayton, Anthony, *The British Empire as a Superpower, 1919–39* (London, 1986).

Clemmesen, Michael H., 'The Armoured Commerce Raider: The Concept that Guided German Naval Lobbying for Control of Norway', in *Northern European Overture to War, 1939–1941: From Memel to Barbarossa*, ed. Clemmesen and Marcus S. Faulkner (Leiden, 2013), pp. 307–30.

—'The Royal Navy North Sea War Plan 1907–1914', *Fra Krig og Fred* I (2014), pp. 59–115.

Clowes, William Laird, *The Royal Navy: A History from the Earliest Times to the Present* (London, 1897–1903, 7 vols.).

Coad, Jonathan, *Support for the Fleet: Architecture and Engineering of the Royal Navy's Bases 1700–1914* (Swindon, 2013).

Coates, Benjamin, ' "Upon the Neutral Rests the Trusteeship of International Law": Legal Advisers and American Unneutrality', in *Caught in the Middle: Neutrality and the First World War*, ed. Johan Den Hertog and Samuël Kruizinga (Amsterdam, 2011), pp. 35–51.

Cobb, Stephen, *Preparing for Blockade 1885–1914: Naval Contingency for Economic Warfare* (Farnham, 2013).

—' "In the shadow of the *Alabama*": Royal Navy Appreciations of the Role of Armed Merchant Cruisers, 1900–1918', in Greg Kennedy, *Britain's War at Sea*, pp. 110–26.

Cock, Randolph, 'Rear-Admiral Sir Francis Beaufort, RN, FRS: "The Authorized Channel of Scientific Communication in England", 1829–1855', in *Science and the French and British Navies, 1700–1850*, ed. Pieter van der Merwe (National Maritime Museum, 2003), pp. 99–116.

—'Scientific Servicemen in the Royal Navy and the Professionalisation of Science, 1816–55', in *Science and Beliefs: From Natural Philosophy to Natural Science, 1700–1900*, ed. David M. Knight and Matthew D. Eddy (Aldershot, 2005), pp. 95–111.

Cock, Randolph and N. A. M. Rodger, eds., *A Guide to the Naval Records in the National Archives of the UK* (London, 2006).

Cogar, William B., ed., *Naval History: The Seventh Symposium of the U.S. Naval Academy* (Wilmington, DE, 1988).

—*New Interpretations in Naval History: Selected Papers from the Eighth Naval History Symposium* (Annapolis, Md., 1989).

Cohen, Eliot A., 'War Planning', in *CH2WW* I, 533–55.

Coleman, E. C., *Rank and Rate: Royal Naval Officers' Insignia since 1856* (Marlborough, 2009).

Coles, Howard E., 'The Contribution of British Defence Departments to Technical Education and Instruction from about 1700' (Manchester PhD thesis, 1984).

Coles, Michael, 'Ernest King and the British Pacific Fleet: The Conference at Quebec, 1944 ("Octagon")', *JMH* LXV (2001), pp. 105–29.

Coletta, Paolo E., 'Rear Admiral Patrick N. L. Bellinger, Commander Patrol Wing Two, and General Frederick L. Martin, Air Commander, Hawaii', in Cogar, *Eighth Naval History Symposium*, pp. 263–78.

—'Dirigibles in the US Navy', in Sweetman et al., *Tenth Naval History Symposium*, pp. 213–30.

Collinge, J. M., ed., *Office-Holders in Modern Britain VII: Navy Board Officials 1660–1832* (London, 1978).

Collins, Bruce, 'The Royal Navy and the Projection of British Power, 1863–1900', in Cogar, *Seventh Symposium*, pp. 89–106.

Colomb, P. H., *Memoirs of Sir Astley Cooper Key* (London, 1898). A perceptive life of a not very perceptive Senior Naval Lord.

Colville, Quintin, 'Jack Tar and the Gentleman Officer: The Role of Uniform in Shaping the Class- and Gender-Related Identities of British Naval Personnel, 1930–1939', *TRHS* 6th S. XIII (2003), pp. 105–29.

—'The Role of the Interior in Constructing Notions of Class and Status: A Case Study of Britannia Royal Naval College Dartmouth, 1905–39', in *Interior Design and Identity*, ed. Susie McKellar and Penny Sparke (Manchester, 2004), pp. 114–32.

Compton-Hall, Richard, *Submarines and the War at Sea, 1914–18* (London, 1991).

Conacher, J. B., *Britain and the Crimea, 1855–1856: Problems of War and Peace* (London, 1987).

Conley, Mary A., *From Jack Tar to Union Jack: Representing Naval Manhood in the British Empire, 1870–1918* (Manchester, 2009).

Connell, G. G., *Jack's War: Lower-Deck Recollections from World War II* (Bristol, 2nd edn., 1995), III (2003), pp. 105–30.

Coogan, John W., *The End of Neutrality: The United States, Britain and Maritime Rights, 1899–1915* (Ithaca, NY, 1981).

—'The Short-War Illusion Resurrected: The Myth of Economic Warfare as the British Schlieffen Plan', *JSS* XXXVII (2015), pp. 1045–64.

Cook, Adrian, *The Alabama Claims: American Politics and Anglo-American Relations, 1865–1872* (Ithaca, NY, 1975).

Cooper, Malcolm, 'Blueprint for Confusion: The Administrative Background to the Formation of the Royal Air Force, 1912–1919', *JCH* XXII (1987), pp. 437–53.

Coox, Alvin D., 'The Effectiveness of the Japanese Military Establishment in the Second World War', in *Military Effectiveness*, ed. A. R. Millett and W. Murray (London, 1988), III, 1–44.

—'Japanese Net Assessment in the Era before Pearl Harbor', in Murray and Millett, *Calculations: Net Assessment and the Coming of World War II*, pp. 258–98.

Costagliola, Bernard, *Darlan: La collaboration à tout prix* (Paris, 2015). In my opinion the only trustworthy life of a very untrustworthy admiral.

Coutau-Bégarie, Hervé and Claude Huan, *Darlan* (Paris, 1989).

—*Mers-el-Kébir (1940): La Rupture Franco-Britannique* (Paris, 1994).

Cowman, Ian, *Dominion or Decline: Anglo-American Naval Relations in the Pacific, 1937–1941* (Oxford, 1997).

—'Defence of the Malay Barrier? The Place of the Philippines in Admiralty Naval War Planning, 1925–1941', *WiH* III (1996), pp. 398–417.

Cowpe, Alan, 'The Royal Navy and the Whitehead Torpedo', in Ranft, *Technical Change and British Naval Policy*, pp. 23–36.

Crang, Jeremy A., 'The Revival of the British Women's Auxiliary Services in the Late Nineteen-Thirties', *HR* LXXXIII (2010), pp. 343–57.

Crichton, A. T., 'William and Robert Edmund Froude and the Evolution of the Ship-Model Experimental Tank', *TNS* LXI (1989–90), pp. 33–49.

Crimmin, P. K., 'The Supply of Timber for the Royal Navy, c.1803–c.1830', in *The Naval Miscellany VII*, ed. Susan Rose (NRS Vol. 153, 2008), pp. 191–234.

Cronin, Dick, *Royal Navy Shipboard Aircraft Developments 1912–31* (Tonbridge, 1990).

Cross, J. A., *Lord Swinton* (Oxford, 1982).

Crowe, W. J., 'The Policy Roots of the Modern Royal Navy, 1946–1963' (Princeton PhD thesis, 1965). An important source, based on extensive interviews with statesmen and senior officers who spoke under Chatham House rules (i.e. anonymously with no verbatim quotation).

Cummins, C. Lyle, *Diesel's Engine* (Wilsonville, OR, 1993).

—*Diesels for the First Stealth Weapon: Submarine Power 1902–1945* (Wilsonville, OR, 2007).

Curtiss, John Shelton, *Russia's Crimean War* (Durham, NC, 1979).

Daly, John C., *Russian Seapower and the 'Eastern Question', 1827–41* (London, 1991).

Dandeker, Christopher, 'Patronage and Bureaucratic Control: The Case of the Naval Officer in English Society 1780–1850', *British Journal of Sociology* XXIX (1978), pp. 300–320.

Darwin, John, *The Empire Project: The Rise and Fall of the British World-System, 1830–1970* (Cambridge, 2009).

Dash, Michael W., 'British Submarine Policy 1853–1918' (King's College London PhD thesis, 1990).

Daunton, Martin, *Trusting Leviathan: The Politics of Taxation in Britain, 1799–1914* (Cambridge, 2001).

—'"The Greatest and Richest Sacrifice Ever Made on the Altar of Militarism": The Finance of Naval Expansion, c.1890–1914', in Blyth, Rüger and Lambert, *The Dreadnought and the Edwardian Age*, pp. 31–49.

Davies, Charles E., *The Blood-Red Arab Flag: An Investigation into Qasimi Piracy 1797–1820* (Exeter, 1997).

Davis, Lance E. and Stanley L. Engerman, *Naval Blockades in Peace and War: An Economic History since 1750* (New York, 2006).

Davison, Robert L., *The Challenges of Command: The Royal Navy's Executive Branch Officers, 1880–1919* (Farnham, 2011).

—'"*Auxillium ab Alto*" – The Royal Navy Executive Branch and the Experience of War', *NM* XV, no. 3 (2005), pp. 87–105.

Dawson, Lionel, *Sound of the Guns: Being an Account of the Wars and Service of Admiral Sir Walter Cowan* (Oxford, 1949).

Day, Vice-Admiral Sir Archibald, *The Admiralty Hydrographic Service, 1795–1919* (London, 1967).

Day, David A., 'Promise and Performance: Britain's Pacific Pledge, 1943–5', *W&S* IV (1986), 2, pp. 71–93.

de Groot, Bas, *Van Duitse Bocht tot Scapa Flow: De oorlog ter zee 1914–1918* (Soesterberg, 2012).

Deist, Wilhelm, *The Wehrmacht and German Rearmament* (London, 1981).

—'The Rearmament of the Wehrmacht', in *G2WW* I, 373–540.

Deist, Wilhelm et al., *Das Deutsche Reich und der Zweiten Weltkrieg* (Stuttgart, 1979–2008, 10 vols. in 12 parts). This magnificent multinational history of the Second World War, compiled by the German Armed Forces Historical Service (*Militärgeschichtliche Forschungsamt*) from the archives of all the belligerents, is easily the most comprehensive and impartial single work on the war, widely cited by all serious scholars. An English translation, *Germany in the Second World War*, was begun by Oxford University Press in 1990 and initially made good progress, but the death of the principal editor has seriously retarded its completion, and at the time of going to press the tenth volume, including Werner Rahn's important essay on the German naval high command in the last years of the war ('Die Deutsche Seekriegführung 1943 bis 1945'), has yet to appear. I have cited the English translation as far as it is yet available (as *G2WW*), and the original German thereafter (as *DR2WK*).

den Hertog, Johan, 'Dutch Neutrality and the Value of Legal Argumentation', in Johan den Hertog and Samuël Kruizinga, eds., *Caught in the Middle: Neutrality and the First World War* (Amsterdam, 2011), pp. 15–33.

De Ninno, Fabio, *I sommergibili del fascismo. Politica navale, strategia e uomini tra le due guerre mondiali* (Milan, 2014).

—*Fascisti sul mare. La Marina e gli ammiragli di Mussolini* (Bari, 2017).

—'The Italian Navy and Japan, the Indian Ocean, Failed Cooperation and Tripartite Relations (1935–1943)', *WiH* XXVII (2020), pp. 224–48.

Dewar, A. C., ed., *Russian War, 1855: Black Sea, Official Correspondence* (NRS Vol. 85, 1945).

Dewar, K. G. B., *The Navy from Within* (London, 1939).

Dickinson, H. W., *Educating the Royal Navy 1702–1902* (Abingdon, 2007).

—*Wisdom and War: The Royal Naval College Greenwich 1873–1998* (Farnham, 2012). How the Navy divided the inhabitants of the naval world into warriors and bookworms.

Divine, David, *Mutiny at Invergordon* (London, 1970).

Dodson, Aidan, *The Kaiser's Battlefleet: German Capital Ships 1871–1918* (Barnsley, 2016).

—*Before the Battlecruiser: The Big Cruiser in the World's Navies 1865–1910* (Barnsley, 2017).

Doe, Helen and Richard Harding, eds., *Naval Leadership and Management, 1650–1950* (Woodbridge, 2012).

Doepgen, Peter, *Die Washingtoner Konferenz, das deutsche Reich und die Reichsmarine. Deutsche Marinepolitik 1921 bis 1935* (Bremen, 2005).

d'Ombrain, Nicholas, *War Machinery and High Policy: Defence Administration in Peacetime Britain, 1902–1914* (London, 1973).

Don, W. G., *Reminiscences of the Baltic Fleet, 1855* (p.p. Brechin, 1894).

Donovan, Peter and John Mack, *Codebreaking in the Pacific* (New York, 2014).

Dorwart, Jeffery M., 'Forrestal and the Navy Plan of 1945: Mahanian Doctrine or Corporatist Blueprint?', in Cogar, *New Interpretations in Naval History . . . 8th Symposium*, pp. 209–23.

Doughty, Martin, *Merchant Shipping and War: A Study of Defence Planning in Twentieth-Century Britain* (London, 1982).

Douglas, General Sir Howard, *A Treatise on Naval Gunnery* (London, 4th edn., 1855).

Douin, Georges, *Navarin (6 juillet–20 octobre 1827)* (Cairo, 1927). Still the most complete account of the Navarino campaign, using French, British and Egyptian archives.

Drayton, Richard, *Nature's Government: Science, Imperial Britain, and the 'Improvement' of the World* (New Haven, Conn., 2000).

Drescher, Seymour, 'British Abolitionism and Imperialism', in *Abolitionism and Imperialism in Britain, Africa, and the Atlantic*, ed. Derek R. Peterson (Athens, OH, 2010), pp. 129–49.

Dülffer, Jost, *Weimar, Hitler und die Marine: Reichspolitik und Flottenbau 1920–1939* (Düsseldorf, 1973).

—'Determinants of German Naval Policy, 1920–1939', in *The German Military in the Age of Total War*, ed. Wilhelm Deist (Leamington Spa, 1985), pp. 152–70.

Dull, Paul S., *A Battle History of the Imperial Japanese Navy (1941–1945)* (Annapolis, Md., 1978).

Dunley, Richard, *Britain and the Mine 1900–1915: Culture, Strategy and International Law* (Basingstoke, 2018).

—' "The Most Resistless and Revolutionary Weapon of Naval Warfare that has Ever Been Introduced": The Royal Navy and the Whitehead Torpedo, 1870–1900', in Lo Cicero, Mahoney and Mitchell, *A Military Transformed?*, pp. 68–82.

—'Sir John Fisher and the Policy of Strategic Deterrence, 1904–1908', *WiH* XXII (2015), pp. 155–73.

—'Technology and Tradition: Mine Warfare and the Royal Navy's Strategy of Coastal Assault, 1870–1890', *JMilH* LXXX (2016), pp. 389–409.

Dunn, Emma, ' "The Cement of Mediocrity": The Experience of the Royal Naval Transport Service during Britain's War with Russia in the Crimea from 1854–1856', in *New Researchers 2004: Papers Presented at the Twelfth Annual New Researchers in Maritime History Conference*, ed. Paul Rees (Liverpool, 2004), pp. 19–29.

Dunn, Steve R., *Securing the Narrow Sea: The Dover Patrol 1914–1918* (Barnsley, 2017).

Dupont, Maurice and Étienne Taillemite, *Les Guerres navales françaises du Moyen Âge à la guerre du Golfe* (Paris, 1995).

Dupuy de Lôme, Stanislas, *Mémoire sur la construction des bâtiments en fer* (Paris, 1844).

Eardley-Wilmot, Arthur, *The Midshipman's Friend: or, Hints for the Cockpit* (London, 2nd edn., 1845).

Eardley-Wilmot, Sydney, *Life of Vice-Admiral Edmund, Lord Lyons* (London, 1898).

Eberle, Admiral Sir James, 'The Military Relationship', in Louis and Bull, *The 'Special Relationship'*, pp. 151–9.

Edgerton, David, *England and the Aeroplane: An Essay on a Militant and Technological Nation* (London, 1991).

—*Science, Technology and the British Industrial 'Decline' 1870–1970* (Cambridge, 1996).

—*Warfare State: Britain, 1920–1970* (Cambridge, 2005).

—*Britain's War Machine: Weapons, Resources and Experts in the Second World War* (London, 2011).

Edgerton, Mrs Frederick [Mary Augusta], *Admiral of the Fleet Sir Geoffrey Phipps Hornby, A Biography* (Edinburgh, 1896).

Ehrman, John, *Cabinet Government and War, 1890–1940* (Cambridge, 1958).

Eltis, David, *Economic Growth and the Ending of the Transatlantic Slave Trade* (Oxford, 1987).

Engerman, Stanley L. and Patrick K. O'Brien, 'The Industrial Revolution in Global Perspective', in *The Cambridge Economic History of Modern Britain*, ed. Roderick Floud and Paul Johnson (Cambridge, 2004, 3 vols.), I, 451–64.

English, Andrew R., *The Laird Rams: Britain's Ironclads Built for the Confederacy, 1862–1923* (Jefferson, NC, 2021).

Epkenhans, Michael, *Die wilhelminische Flottenrüstung 1908–1914: Weltmacht-streben, industrieller Fortschritt, soziale Integration* (Munich, 1991). Many false trails in historical scholarship could have been avoided if this book had been translated into English.

—*Tirpitz: Architect of the German High Seas Fleet* (Washington, DC, 2008). Until recently this short book was the only useful life of Tirpitz in English.

—'Die kaiserliche Marine im Ersten Weltkrieg: Weltmacht oder Untergang?', in *Der Erste Weltkrieg. Wirkung, Wahrnehmung, Analyse*, ed. Wolfgang Michalka (Munich, 1994), pp. 319–40.

—'Der Deutschen Griff Nach der Weltmacht: Die Tirpitzsche Flottenplanung 1897–1914', in *Seemacht und Seestrategie im 19. und 20. Jahrhundert*, ed. Jörg Duppler (Hamburg, 1999), pp. 121–31.

—'Krupp and the Imperial German Navy, 1898–1914: A Reassessment', *JMilH* LXIV (2000), pp. 335–69.

—'Technology, Shipbuilding and Future Combat in Germany, 1880–1914', in O'Brien, *Technology and Naval Combat*, pp. 53–68.

—' "Red Sailors" and the Demise of the German Empire, 1918', in Bell and Elleman, *Naval Mutinies of the Twentieth Century*, pp. 80–105.

—'*Dreadnought*: A "Golden Opportunity" for Germany's Naval Aspirations?', in Blyth, Rüger and Lambert, *The Dreadnought and the Edwardian Age*, pp. 79–91.

Epkenhans, Michael and Stephan Huck, eds., *Der erste Weltkrieg zur See* (Berlin, 2017), pp. 41–8.

Epstein, Katherine C., *Torpedo: Inventing the Military-Industrial Complex in the United States and Great Britain* (Cambridge, Mass., 2014).

Epstein, Marc, 'The Historians and the Geneva Naval Conference', in McKercher, *Arms Limitation and Disarmament*, pp. 1–19.

Erskine, Ralph, 'U-Boats, Homing Signals and HFDF', *I&NS* II (1987), pp. 324–30.

—'Naval Enigma: The Breaking of Heimisch and Triton', *I&NS* III (1988), pp. 162–83.

—'The First Naval Enigma Decrypts of World War II', *Cryptologia* XXI (1997), 1, 42–6.

—'The Holden Agreement on Naval Sigint: The First BRUSA?', *I&NS* XIV (1999), 2, 187–97.

—'Enigma's Security', in *Action this Day*, ed. Ralph Erskine and Michael Smith (London, 2001), pp. 370–85.

—'The Admiralty and Cipher Machines during the Second World War: Not So Stupid After All', *JIH* II, no. 2 (2002), pp. 49–68.

—'Shore High-Frequency Direction-Finding in the Battle of the Atlantic: An Undervalued Intelligence Asset', *JIH* IV, no. 2 (2004), pp. 1–32.

—'The 1944 Naval BRUSA Agreement and its Aftermath', *Cryptologia* XXX (2006), 1, 1–22.

Evans, David, *Building the Steam Navy: Dockyards, Technology and the Creation of the Victorian Battle Fleet 1830–1906* (London, 2004).

—*Arming the Fleet: The Development of the Royal Ordnance Yards, 1770–1945* (Gosport, 2007).

Evans, David C. and Mark R. Peattie, *Kaigun: Strategy, Tactics and Technology in the Imperial Japanese Navy 1887–1941* (Annapolis, Md., 1997).

Everest-Phillips, Max, 'Reassessing Pre-War Japanese Espionage: The Rutland Naval Spy Case and the Japanese Intelligence Threat before Pearl Harbor', *I&NS* XXI (2006), 2, 258–85.

Fairbanks, Charles H., 'Choosing among Technologies in the Anglo-German Naval Arms Competition, 1898–1915', in Cogar, *Seventh Symposium*, pp. 127–42.

—'The Origins of the *Dreadnought* Revolution: A Historiographical Essay', *IHR* XIII (1991), pp. 246–72.

Fanning, R. W., 'The Coolidge Conference of 1927: Disarmament in Disarray', in McKercher, *Arms Limitation and Disarmament*, pp. 105–27.

Fanshawe, Alice, *Admiral Sir Edward Gennys Fanshawe* (London, p.p. 1904).

Farquharson-Roberts, Mike, *Royal Naval Officers from War to War, 1918–1939* (Basingstoke, 2015).

—'Forgotten or Ignored, the Officers at Invergordon: "We are doing this for you as well you know"', in Doe and Harding, *Naval Leadership and Management*, pp. 109–22.

Farr, Martin, *Reginald McKenna: Financier among Statesmen, 1863–1916* (London, 2008).

Faulkner, Marcus, *War at Sea: A Naval Atlas 1939–1945*. An essential work of reference.

—'The *Kriegsmarine*, Signals Intelligence and the Development of the *B-Dienst* before the Second World War', *I&NS* XXV (2010), pp. 521–46.

Fay, Peter Ward, *The Opium War, 1840–42* (Chapel Hill, NC, 1975).

Felker, Craig C., *Testing American Sea Power: U.S. Navy Strategic Exercises, 1923–1940* (College Station, Tx., 2007).

Ferguson, Niall, *The Pity of War* (London, 1998).

—*Cash Nexus: Money and Power in the Modern World 1700–2000* (London, 2001).

—'How (Not) to Pay for the War: Traditional Finance and "Total" War', in Chickering and Förster, *Great War, Total War*, pp. 409–434.

Ferns, H. S., *Britain and Argentina in the Nineteenth Century* (Oxford, 1960).

Ferris, John, *Behind the Enigma: The Authorised History of GCHQ, Britain's Secret Cyber-Intelligence Agency* (London, 2020).

—'A British "Unofficial" Aviation Mission and Japanese Naval Developments, 1919–29', *JSS* V (1982), pp. 416–39.

—'Whitehall's Black Chamber: British Cryptology and the Government Code and Cypher School, 1919–29', *I&NS* II, no. 1 (1987), pp. 54–91.

—'The Symbol and the Substance: Great Britain, the United States, and the One-Power Standard, 1919–1921', in *Anglo-American Relations in the 1920s: The Struggle for Supremacy*, ed. B. J. C. McKercher (Basingstoke, 1991), pp. 55–80.

—' "It is our Business in the Navy to Command the Seas": The Last Decade of British Maritime Supremacy, 1919–1929', in Kennedy and Neilson, *Far-Flung Lines*, pp. 124–70.

—'Fighter Defence before Fighter Command: The Rise of Strategic Air Defence in Great Britain, 1917–1934', *JMilH* LXIII (1999), pp. 845–84.

—'Achieving Air Ascendancy: Challenge and Response in British Air Defence, 1915–1940', in *Air Power History: Turning Points from Kitty Hawk to Kosovo*, ed. Sebastian Cox and Peter Gray (London, 2002), pp. 21–50.

—'The Road to Bletchley Park: The British Experience with Signals Intelligence, 1892–1945', *I&NS* XVII (2002), 1, 53–84.

—'Student and Master: The United Kingdom, Japan, Airpower and the Fall of Singapore', in *Singapore, Sixty Years On*, ed. Brian Farrell and Sandy Hunter (Singapore, 2002), pp. 94–121.

—' "Double-Edged Estimates: Japan in the Eyes of the British Army and the Royal Air Force, 1900–1939', in Gow, Hirama and Chapman, *Anglo-Japanese Relations*, pp. 91–108.

—' "Ground of our own Choosing": The Anglo-Japanese War in Asia, 1941–1945', in Gow, Hirama and Chapman, *Anglo-Japanese Relations*, pp. 186–201.

—'Armaments and Allies: The Anglo-Japanese Strategic Relationship, 1911–1921', in *The Anglo-Japanese Alliance, 1902–1922*, ed. P. P. O'Brien (London, 2004), pp. 249–66.

—'Image and Accident: Intelligence and the Origins of the Second World War, 1933–41', in John Ferris *Intelligence and Strategy: Selected Essays* (Abingdon, 2005), pp. 99–137.

—'The British "Enigma": Britain, Signals Security and Cipher Machines, 1906–1953', in John Ferris *Intelligence and Strategy: Selected Essays* (Abingdon, 2005), pp. 138–80.

—'Catching the Wave: The RAF pursues a RMA, 1918–39', in *The Fog of Peace and War Planning: Military and Strategic Planning under Uncertainty*, ed. Talbot C. Imlay and Monica Duffy Toft (Abingdon, 2006), pp. 159–78.

—' "Now that the Milk is Spilt": Appeasement and the Archive on Intelligence', *D&S* XIX (2008), pp. 527–656.

—'Information Superiority: British Intelligence at London', in Maurer and Bell, *At the Crossroads between Peace and War*, pp. 181–200.

—'The War in the West, 1939–1940: The Battle of Britain?', in *CH2WW* I, 315–30.

—'Pragmatic Hegemony and British Economic Warfare, 1900–1918: Preparations and Practice', in Greg Kennedy, *Britain's War at Sea*, pp. 87–109.

—'To the Hunger Blockade: The Evolution of British Economic Warfare, 1914–1915', in *Der erste Weltkrieg zur See*, ed. Michael Epkenhans and Stephan Huck (Berlin, 2017), pp. 41–8.

—'Doing the Necessary: The Declaration of London and British Strategy, 1905–1915', in *The Civilianization of War: The Changing Civil-Military Divide, 1914–2014*, ed. Andrew Barros and Martin Thomas (Cambridge, 2018), pp. 23–46.

—'The War Trade Intelligence Department and British Economic Warfare during the First World War', in *British World Policy and the Projection of Global Power, c.1830–1960*, ed. T. G. Otte (Cambridge, 2019), pp. 24–45.

Ferris, John et al., eds., *The Cambridge History of the Second World War* (Cambridge, 2015–17, 3 vols.) [cited as *CH2WW*].

Feuchtwanger, Edgar and William J. Philpott, 'Civil–Military Relations in a Period without Major Wars', in *Government and the Armed Forces in Britain 1856–1990*, ed. Paul Smith (London, 1996), pp. 1–19.

Field, Andrew, *Royal Navy Strategy in the Far East, 1919–1939: Preparing for War against Japan* (London, 2004).

Figes, Orlando, *Crimea: The Last Crusade* (London, 2010).

Findlay, Ronald and Kevin O'Rourke, *Power and Plenty: Trade, War, and the World Economy in the Second Millennium* (Princeton, NJ, 2007).

Fischer, Jörg-Uwe, *Admiral des Kaisers: Georg Alexander von Müller als Chef des Marinekabinetts Wilhelms II* (Frankfurt am Main, 1992).

Fisher, Douglas B., 'The Fleet Train in the Pacific War', *JNE* VII (1954), pp. 411–27.

Fletcher, M. H., *The WRNS: A History of the Women's Royal Naval Service* (London, 1989).

Fotakis, Zisis, *Greek Naval Strategy and Policy, 1910–1919* (Abingdon, 2005).

—'Sea Power and the Establishment of the Modern Greek State, 1821–1829', in *Following the Nereids: Sea Routes and Maritime Business, 16th–20th Centuries*, ed. Maria Christina Chatziioannou and Gelina Harlaftis (Athens, 2006), pp. 217–22.

Fox, Grace, *British Admirals and Chinese Pirates 1832–1869* (London, 1940).

Foxton, David, 'International Law in Domestic Courts: Some Lessons from the Prize Court in the Great War', *British Yearbook of International Law* LXXIII (2002), pp. 261–91.

Franklin, George, *Britain's Anti-Submarine Capability 1919–1939* (London, 2003).

—'The Origins of the Royal Navy's Vulnerability to Surfaced Night U-Boat Attack 1939–40', *MM* XC (2004), pp. 73–84.

Freeman, Edward, ed., *Les Empires en guerre et paix, 1793–1860: Journées franco-anglaises d'histoire de la Marine, Portsmouth, 23–26 mars 1988* (Vincennes, Service Historique de la Marine, 1990).

Frei, Gabriela A., *Great Britain, International Law, and the Evolution of Maritime Strategic Thought, 1856–1914* (Oxford, 2020).

French, David, *British Economic and Strategic Planning, 1905–1915* (London, 1982).

—*British Strategy and War Aims, 1914–1916* (London, 1986).

—*The Strategy of the Lloyd George Coalition, 1916–1918* (Oxford, 1995).

—'The Edwardian Crisis and the Origins of the First World War', *IHR* IV (1982), pp. 207–21.

—'The Royal Navy and the Defense of the British Empire, 1914–1918', in Neilson and Errington, *Navies and Global Defense*, pp. 117–37.

—'The Empire and the USA in British Strategy in the Spring of 1917', in Kennedy and Neilson, *Far-Flung Lines*, pp. 84–102.

—'British Strategy and Winning the Great War', in *Strategic Logic and Political Rationality: Essays in Honour of Michael J. Handel*, ed. Bradford A. Lee and Karl F. Walling (Newport, RI, 2003), pp. 196–219.

—'British Military Strategy', in *CH2WW* I, 28–50.

Friedberg, Aaron L., *The Weary Titan: Britain and the Experience of Relative Decline, 1895–1905* (Princeton, NJ, 1988).

Friedman, Norman, *U.S. Aircraft Carriers: An Illustrated Design History* (London, 1983).

—*U.S. Battleships: An Illustrated Design History* (London, 1986).

—*British Carrier Aviation: The Evolution of the Ships and their Aircraft* (London, 1988).

—*The Fifty-Year War: Conflict and Strategy in the Cold War* (London, 2000).

—*British Destroyers, from Earliest Days to the Second World War* (London, 2006).

—*British Destroyers and Frigates: The Second World War and After* (London, 2006) [cited as *British Destroyers* I and II].

—*Naval Firepower: Battleship Guns and Gunnery in the Dreadnought Era* (Barnsley, 2007).

—*Network-Centric Warfare: How Navies Learned to Fight Smarter through Three World Wars* (Annapolis, Md., 2009).

—*British Cruisers of the Victorian Era* (Barnsley, 2012).

—*British Cruisers: Two World Wars and After* (Barnsley, 2010) [cited as *British Cruisers* I and II].

—*Naval Weapons of World War I* (Barnsley, 2011).

—*Naval Anti-Aircraft Guns and Gunnery* (Barnsley, 2013).

—*Fighting the Great War at Sea: Strategy, Tactics and Technology* (Barnsley, 2014).

—*Fighters over the Fleet: Naval Air Defence from Biplanes to the Cold War* (Barnsley, 2016).

—*British Battleships of the Victorian Era* (Barnsley, 2018).

—*The British Battleship, 1906–1946* (Barnsley, 2015) [cited as *British Battleship* I and II].

—*British Submarines in Two World Wars* (Barnsley, 2019).

—*British Submarines in the Cold War Era* (Barnsley, 2021) [cited as *British Submarines* I and II].

—'The Royal Navy and the Post-War Naval Revolution, 1946 to the Present', in Hill, *Oxford Illustrated History*, pp. 409–33.

—'Naval Strategy and Force Structure', in Maurer and Bell, *At the Crossroads between Peace and War*, pp. 201–28.

Frieser, Karl-Heinz, 'The War in the West, 1939–1940', in *CH2WW* I, 287–314.

Fuller, Howard J., *Clad in Iron: The American Civil War and the Challenge of British Naval Power* (Westport, Conn., 2007).

—*Empire, Technology and Seapower: Royal Navy Crisis in the Age of Palmerston* (Abingdon, 2014).

—'"This Country Now Occupies the Vantage Ground": Understanding John Ericsson's Monitors and the American Union's War against British Naval Supremacy', *AN* LXII (2002), pp. 91–110.

—'"The Whole Character of Maritime Life": British Reactions to the USS *Monitor* and the American Ironclad Experience', *MM* LXXXVIII (2002), pp. 285–300.

—'John Ericsson, the Monitors and Union Naval Strategy', *IJNH* II (2004).

Fuquea, David C., 'Task Force One: The Wasted Assets of the United States Pacific Battleship Fleet, 1942', *JMilH* LXI (1997), pp. 707–34.

Galliver, Peter, 'Trade Unionism in Portsmouth Dockyard, 1880–1914: Change and Continuity', in Lunn and Day, *Labour Relations in the Royal Dockyards*, pp. 99–126.

Garcia y Robertson, Rodrigo, 'Failure of the Heavy Gun at Sea, 1898–1922', *T&C* XXVIII (1987), pp. 539–57.

Gardner, Richard N., 'Sterling-Dollar Diplomacy in Current Perspective', in Louis and Bull, *The 'Special Relationship'*, pp. 185–200.

Gardner, W. J. R., *Decoding History: The Battle of the Atlantic and ULTRA* (London, 1999).

—'Smart Mining without Smart Mines: Second World War British Operations in the Baltic', *IJNH* VI (2007).

Garzke, William H. and Robert O. Dulin, *Battleships of World War II* (London 1976–85, 3 vols.).

Garzke, William H., Robert O. Dulin and Kevin V. Denlay, 'Death of a Battleship: The Loss of HMS *Prince of Wales* December 10, 1941: A Marine Forensics Analysis of the Sinking' (www.pacificwrecks.com 2009, updated 2010 and 2012).

Gash, Norman, *Mr Secretary Peel: The Life of Sir Robert Peel to 1830* (London, 2nd edn., 1985).

Gat, Azar, *The Development of Military Thought: The Nineteenth Century* (Oxford, 1992).

—'Containment and Cold War before the Nuclear Age: The Phoney War as Allied Strategy According to Liddell Hart', in Clemmesen and Faulkner, *Northern European Overture to War*, pp. 9–21.

Gemzell, Carl-Axel, *Raeder, Hitler und Skandinavien: Der Kampf für einen maritimen Operationsplan* (Lund, 1965).

—*Organization, Conflict, and Innovation: A Study of German Naval Strategic Planning, 1888–1940* (Lund, 1973).

Gibbs, N. H., *History of the Second World War, Military Series: Grand Strategy, Vol. I, Rearmament Policy* (London, 1976).

Gibson, Martin, *Britain's Quest for Oil: The First World War and the Peace Conferences* (Solihull, 2017).

—'"Oil Fuel Will Absolutely Revolutionize Naval Strategy": The Royal Navy's Adoption of Oil before the First World War', in Lo Cicero, Mahoney and Mitchell, *A Military Transformed?*, pp. 110–23.

Gilbert, Martin, ed., *The Churchill War Papers* (London, 1993–2000, 3 vols.).

Giorgerini, Giorgio, *La battaglia dei convogli nel Mediterraneo* (Milan, 1977).

—*La guerra italiana sul mare: La Marina tra vittoria e sconfitta, 1940–1943* (Milan, 2001).

Glover, William, 'Manning and Training the Allied Navies', in Howarth and Law, *Battle of the Atlantic*, pp. 188–213.

Goddard, A. H., 'Operational Fatigue: The Air Branch of the Royal Navy's Experience during the Second World War', *MM* XCI (2005), pp. 52–66.

Godspeed, Hill, 'Doyle's Dauntless Dory: USS *Nassau* and the Evolution of Carrier-Based Close Air Support', in Balano and Symonds, *Fourteenth Naval History Symposium*, pp. 217–50.

Goette, Richard, 'Britain and the Delay in Closing the Mid-Atlantic "Air Gap" during the Battle of the Atlantic', *NM* XV (2005), 4, 19–41.

Goldfrank, D. M., *The Origins of the Crimean War* (London, 1994).

Goldrick, James, *Before Jutland: The Naval War in Northern European Waters, August 1914–February 1915* (Annapolis, Md., 2015).

—*After Jutland: The Naval War in Northern European Waters, June 1916–November 1918* (Barnsley, 2018).

—'Work-Up', in Howarth and Law, *Battle of the Atlantic* (1994), pp. 220–39.

—'The Battleship Fleet: The Test of War, 1895–1919', in *The Oxford Illustrated History of the Royal Navy*, ed. J. R. Hill (Oxford, 1995), pp. 280–318.

—'The Impact of War: Matching Expectations with Reality in the Royal Navy in the First Months of the Great War at Sea', *WiH* XIV (2007), pp. 22–35.

—'Life at Sea and Ship Organisation', in Hore, *Dreadnought to Daring*, pp. 236–53.

—'Buying Time: British Submarine Capability in the Far East, 1919–1940', *GWS* XI (2014), 3, 33–50.

—'Coal and the Advent of the First World War at Sea', *WiH* XXI (2014), pp. 322–37.

—'How it Worked: Understanding the Interaction of Some Environmental and Technological Realities of Naval Operations in the Opening Years of the First World War, 1914–1916', in Greg Kennedy, *Britain's War at Sea*, pp. 127–48.

—'Learning to Fight On, Above and Below the Water: Operational Challenges of the Royal Navy, 1914–1916', in Epkenhans and Huck, *Der erste Weltkrieg zur See*, pp. 41–8.

—'All Should be "A" Teams: The Development of Group Anti-Submarine Escort Training in the British and Canadian Navies during the Atlantic Campaign', in Bell and Faulkner, *Decision in the Atlantic*, pp. 150–68.

Goldstein, Erik, 'The British Official Mind and the United States, 1919–42', in *Personalities, War and Diplomacy: Essays in International History*, ed. T. G. Otte and Constantine A. Pagedas (London, 1997), pp. 66–80.

Gooch, John, *Mussolini and His Generals: The Armed Forces and Fascist Foreign Policy, 1922–1940* (Cambridge, 2007).

—*Mussolini's War: Fascist Italy from Triumph to Collapse 1935–1943* (London, 2020).

—'The Bolt from the Blue', in John Gooch, *The Prospect of War: Studies in British Defence Policy 1847–1942* (London, 1981), pp. 1–34.

—'Sir George Clarke's Career at the Committee of Imperial Defence, 1904–1907', in Gooch *The Prospect of War*, pp. 73–91.

—'Adversarial Attitudes: Servicemen, Politicians and Strategic Policy in Edwardian England, 1899–1914', in *Government and the Armed Forces in Britain 1856–1990*, ed. Paul Smith (London, 1996), pp. 53–74.

—'Mussolini's Strategy, 1939–1943', in *CH2WW* I, 132–58.

Gooch, G. P., ed., *The Later Correspondence of Lord John Russell* (London, 1925, 2 vols.).

Gooch, G. P. and Harold Temperley, eds., *British Documents on the Origins of the War, 1898–1914* (London, 1926–38, 11 vols. in 13) [cited as *BDOW*].

[Goodall, Sir Stanley], *Diary of a Naval Constructor: Sir Stanley Goodall*, ed. Ian Buxton (Barnsley, 2022).

Goodman, Michael, *The Official History of the Joint Intelligence Committee. Vol. 1: From the Approach of the Second World War to the Suez Crisis* (Abingdon, 2014).

Gordon, Andrew, *The Rules of the Game: Jutland and British Naval Command* (London, 1996).

—'The Transition to War: The *Goeben* Debacle, August 1914', in Speller, *The Royal Navy and Maritime Power in the Twentieth Century*, pp. 13–32.

Gordon, G. A. H., *British Seapower and Procurement between the Wars: A Reappraisial of Rearmament* (London, 1988).

—'The British Navy, 1918–1945', in Neilson and Errington, *Navies and Global Defense*, pp. 161–80.

Gorodetsky, Gabriel, *Grand Delusion: Stalin and the German Invasion of Russia* (London, 1999).

Gough, Barry M., ed., *To the Pacific and Arctic with Beechey: The Journal of Lieutenant George Peard of H.M.S. Blossom, 1825–1828* (Hakluyt Soc. 2nd. S. 143, 1973).

—'Specie Conveyance from the West Coast of Mexico in British Warships c.1820–1870: An Aspect of the *Pax Britannica*', *MM* LXIX (1983), pp. 419–33.

Goulter, Christina J. M., 'The Royal Naval Air Service: A Very Modern Force', in *Air Power History: Turning Points from Kitty Hawk to Kosovo*, ed. Sebastian Cox and Peter Gray (London, 2002), pp. 51–65.

Gow, Ian T. M., 'The Royal Navy and Japan, 1900–1920: Strategic Re-Evaluation of the IJN', in *The History of Anglo-Japanese Relations, 1600–2000. Vol. 3: The Military Dimension*, ed. Ian T. M. Gow, Y. Hirama and J. W. M. Chapman (Basingstoke, 2003), pp. 35–50.

Graham, G. S., *The Politics of Naval Supremacy* (Cambridge, 1965).

—*Great Britain in the Indian Ocean: A Study of Maritime Enterprise 1810–1850* (Oxford, 1967).

—*The China Station: War and Diplomacy 1830–1860* (Oxford, 1978).

Graham, G. S. and R. A. Humphreys, eds., *The Navy and South America, 1807–23* (NRS Vol. 104, 1962).

Grainger, John D., *The First Pacific War: Britain and Russia, 1854–1856* (Woodbridge, 2007).

Grant, Robert M., *U-Boat Hunters: Code Breakers, Divers and the Defeat of the U-Boats, 1914–1918* (Penzance and Annapolis, Md., 2003).

Gray, Colin S., *The Leverage of Sea Power: The Strategic Advantage of Navies in War* (New York, 1992).

—'History for Strategists: British Seapower as a Relevant Past', *JSS* XVII (1994), pp. 7–32.

Gray, Steven, *Steam Power and Sea Power: Coal, the Royal Navy and the British Empire, c. 1870–1914* (Cham, Switzerland, 2017).

—'Coaling Warships with Naval Labour, 1870–1914: "I wish I could get hold of the man who first found coal"', *MM* CI (2015), pp. 168–83.

Green, E. H. H., 'The Political Economy of Empire, 1880–1914', in *OHBE* III, 346–68.

Greenacre, John, 'The Admiralty's Interwar Planning with the British Fishing Industry, 1925–1940', *JMR* XXII (2020), pp. 139–56.

Greenhalgh, Elizabeth, *Victory through Coalition: Britain and France during the First World War* (Cambridge, 2005).

Greenhill, Basil and Ann Giffard, *The British Assault on Finland 1854–1855: A Forgotten Naval War* (London, 1988).

—*Steam, Politics and Patronage: The Transformation of the Royal Navy 1815–54* (London, 1994).

Gregory, Adrian, *The Last Great War: British Society and the First World War* (Cambridge: 2008).

Gretton, Peter, *Convoy Escort Commander* (London, 1964).

Grey, Christopher, 'The Making of Bletchley Park and Signals Intelligence, 1939–42', *I&NS* XXVIII (2013), pp. 787–807.

Griffiths, Denis, *Two Centuries of Steam-Powered Ships* (London, 1997).

Grimes, Shawn T., *Strategy and War Planning in the British Navy, 1887–1918* (Woodbridge, 2012).

Grindal, Peter, *Opposing the Slavers: The Royal Navy's Campaign against the Atlantic Slave Trade* (London, 2016).

Gröner, Erich, *Die deutschen Kriegschiffe 1815–1945* (Munich, 1966–8, 2 vols.). There are several later editions of this invaluable reference book.

Groos, Otto and Walter Gladisch, *Der Krieg zur See 1914–18: Der Krieg in der Nordsee* (Berlin, 1920–65, 6 vols.). [Part of the German Navy's official history series. There is a second edition, 2006, of Vol. VI.]

Grove, Eric, *Vanguard to Trident: British Naval Policy since World War II* (London, 1987).

—ed., *The Defeat of the Enemy Attack on Shipping, 1939–1945* (NRS Vol. 137, 1997).

—*The Royal Navy since 1815: A New Short History* (Basingstoke, 2005).

—'The Battleship is Dead; Long Live the Battleship. HMS *Dreadnought* and the Limits of Technological Innovation', *MM* XCIII (2007), pp. 415–27.

—'The Autobiography of Chief Gunner Alexander Grant: H.M.S. *Lion* at the Battle of Jutland, 1916', in *The Naval Miscellany* VII, ed. Susan Rose (NRS Vol. 153, 2008), pp. 379–406.

—'The Battleship *Dreadnought*: Technological, Economic and Strategic Contexts', in Blyth, Rüger and Lambert, *The Dreadnought and the Edwardian Age*, pp. 165–81.

—'Seamen or Airmen? The Early Days of British Naval Flying', in Benbow, *British Naval Aviation*, pp. 7–26.

—'Air Force, Fleet Air Arm – or Armoured Corps? The Royal Naval Air Service at War', in Benbow, *British Naval Aviation*, pp. 27–55.

—'The Aircraft Carrier Fighter Control Revolution: How the Aircraft Carrier Became an Effective Anti-Air Warfare System', in David Stevens, ed., *Naval Networks: The Dominance of Communications in Maritime Operations* (Canberra, 2012), pp. 359–74.

Haarr, Geirr H., *The German Invasion of Norway* (Barnsley, 2009).

—*The Battle for Norway April–June 1940* (Barnsley, 2010) [cited as *Norway* I and II].

Haas, J. M., *A Management Odyssey: The Royal Dockyards, 1714–1914* (London, 1994).

—'The Best Investment Ever Made: The Royal Dockyard Schools, Technical Education and the British Shipbuilding Industry, 1800–1914', *MM* LXXVI (1990), pp. 325–35.

—'Low Labour Intensity and Overmanning in the Royal Dockyards, 1815–1914', *MM* CII (2016), pp. 426–41.

Hackmann, Willem, *Seek & Strike: Sonar, Anti-Submarine Warfare and the Royal Navy 1914–54* (London, 1984).

Hagan, Kenneth J., 'The Apotheosis of Mahan: American Naval Strategy, 1889–1922', in Neilson and Errington, *Navies and Global Defense*, pp. 93–115.

Haggie, Paul, 'The Royal Navy and War Planning in the Fisher Era', in *The War Plans of the Great Powers, 1880–1914*, ed. Paul M. Kennedy (London, 1979), pp. 118–32.

Hague, Arnold, *The Allied Convoy System 1939–1945: Its Organization, Defence and Operation* (St Catherine's, Ont., 2000).

Hall, Thomas, ' "Mere drops in the Ocean": The Politics and Planning of the Contribution of the British Commonwealth to the Final Defeat of Japan, 1944–45', *D&S* XVI (2005), pp. 93–115.

Halpern, Paul G., ed., *The Keyes Papers* (NRS Vols. 117, 121 and 122, 1972–81).

—*The Naval War in the Mediterranean, 1914–1918* (London, 1987).

—ed., *The Royal Navy in the Mediterranean, 1915–1918* (NRS Vol. 126, 1987).

—*A Naval History of World War I* (London, 1994).

—*The Mediterranean Fleet, 1919–1929* (NRS Vol. 158, 2011).

—'The French Navy, 1880–1914', in O'Brien, *Technology and Naval Combat*, pp. 36–52.

Hamblin, K. J., ' "Men of brain and brawn and guts": The Professionalization of Marine Engineering in Britain, France and Germany 1830–1914' (Exeter PhD thesis, 2013).

Hamer, David, *Bombers versus Battleships: The Struggle between Ships and Aircraft for the Control of the Surface of the Sea* (London, 1998).

Hamilton, C. I. [Ian], *Anglo-French Naval Rivalry 1840–1870* (Oxford, 1993).

—ed., *Portsmouth Dockyard Papers 1852–1869: From Wood to Iron* (Portsmouth Record Series X, Winchester, 2005).

—*The Making of the Modern Admiralty: British Naval Policy-Making, 1805–1927* (Cambridge, 2011).

—'Sir James Graham, the Baltic Campaign and War-Planning at the Admiralty in 1854', *HJ* XIX (1976), pp. 89–112.

—'Anglo-French Seapower and the Declaration of Paris', *IHR* IV (1982), pp. 166–90.

—'Selections from the Phinn Committee of Inquiry of October–November 1855 into the State of the Office of Secretary to the Admiralty', in Rodger, *The Naval Miscellany* V (NRS Vol. 125, 1984), pp. 371–438.

—'The Diplomatic and Naval Effects of the Prince de Joinville's *Note sur l'Etat des Forces Navales de la France* of 1844', *HJ* XXXII (1989), pp. 675–87.

—'The Childers Admiralty Reforms and the Nineteenth-Century "Revolution" in British Government', *WiH* V (1998), pp. 37–61.

—'The Character and Organization of the Admiralty Operational Intelligence Centre during the Second World War', *WiH* VII (2000), pp. 295–324.

—'John Wilson Croker: Patronage and Clientage at the Admiralty, 1809–1857', *HJ* XLIII (2000), pp. 49–77.

—'British Naval Policy, Policy-Makers and Financial Control, 1860–1945', *WiH* XII (2005), pp. 371–95.

—'Three Cultures at the Admiralty, c.1800–1945: Naval Staff, the Secretariat and the Arrival of Scientists', *JMR* XVI (2014), pp. 89–102.

—'*Solvitur Ambulando*: The Admiralty Administration Reacts to War, 1914–1918', in Greg Kennedy, *Britain's War at Sea*, pp. 70–86.

Hamilton, Lord George, *Parliamentary Reminiscences and Reflections, 1868–1906* (London, 1917–22, 2 vols.).

Hamilton, Richard F., 'War Planning: Obvious Needs, Not So Obvious Solutions', in *War Planning 1914*, ed. R. D. Hamilton and Holger H. Herwig (Cambridge, 2009), pp. 1–23.

Hamilton, Sir Richard V., *Naval Administration* (London, 1896).

Hamilton, W. Mark, 'The Nation and the Navy: Methods and Organisation of British Navalist Propaganda, 1889–1914' (London PhD thesis, 1977).

—'The "New Navalism" and the British Navy League, 1895–1914', *MM* LXIV (1978), pp. 37–44.

Hammant, Thomas R., 'Russian and Soviet Cryptology: II, The *Magdeburg* Incident; the Russian View', *Cryptologia* XXIV (2000), pp. 333–8.

Hammond, Richard, 'British Aero-Naval Co-operation in the Mediterranean, 1940–45, and the Creation of RAF No. 201 (Naval Co-operation) Group', in Lo Cicero, Mahoney and Mitchell, *A Military Transformed?*, pp. 229–45.

—'An Enduring Influence on Imperial Defence and Grand Strategy: British Perceptions of the Italian Navy, 1935–1943', *IHR* XXXIX (2017), pp. 810–35.

Hampshire, Edward, 'The Battle for CVA 01', in *British Naval Aviation*, ed. Benbow, pp. 177–96.

Hancock, W. K. and Margaret Gowing, *British War Economy* (London, rev. edn., 1975).

Hanson, Norman, *Carrier Pilot* (Cambridge, 1979).

Hanyok, Robert J., ' "Catching the Fox Unaware": Japanese Radio Denial and Deception and the Attack on Pearl Harbor', *NWCR* LXI, no. 4 (2008), pp. 99–124.

Harding, Richard, ed., *The Royal Navy, 1930–2000: Innovation and Defence* (London, 2005).

Harding, Richard and Agustín Guimerá, eds., *Naval Leadership in the Atlantic World: The Age of Reform and Revolution, 1700–1850* (London, 2017).

Harland, Kathleen, *A History of Queen Alexandra's Royal Naval Nursing Service* (London, 1990).

Harley, Simon, ' "It's a Case of All or None": "Jacky" Fisher's Advice to Winston Churchill, 1911', *MM* CII (2016), pp. 174–90.

Harling, Philip, *The Waning of the 'Old Corruption': The Politics of Economical Reform in Britain, 1779–1846* (Oxford, 1996).

Harling, Philip and Peter Mandler, 'From "Fiscal-Military" State to Laissez-Faire State, 1760–1850', *JBS* XXXII (1993), pp. 44–70.

Harris, Mark, *Harwich Submarines in the Great War: The First Submarine Campaign of the Royal Navy in 1914* (Warwick, 2021).

Harrison, Mark, ed., *The Economics of World War II* (Cambridge, 1998).

—'An "Important and Truly National Subject": The West African Service and the Health of the Royal Navy in the Mid-Nineteenth Century', in *Health and Medicine at Sea, 1700–1900*, ed. David Boyd Haycock and Sally Archer (Woodbridge, 2009), pp. 108–27.

Hartcup, Guy, *The War of Invention: Scientific Developments, 1914–1918* (London, 1988).

Hartwig, Dieter, *Großadmiral Karl Dönitz: Legende und Wirklichkeit* (Paderborn, 2010).

Harvey, A. D., 'Army Air Force and Navy Air Force: Japanese Aviation and the Opening Phase of the War in the Far East', *WiH* VI (1999), pp. 174–204.

Haslach, Robert D., *Nishi no kaze, hare: Nederlands-Indische inlichtingendienst contra agressor Japan* (Weesp, 1985).

Haslop, Dennis, *Early Naval Air Power: British and German Approaches* (Abingdon, 2018).

Hastings, Max, *Overlord: D-Day and the Battle for Normandy 1944* (London, 1984).

—*Operation Pedestal: The Fleet that Battled to Malta 1942* (London, 2021). Spirited narrative of a decisive naval battle in the 20th-century style.

Hatashin, Omi, 'Japanese Organisational Decision Making in 1941', *International Journal of Management and Decision Making* 12, 1 (2012), pp. 69–84. An important article which should be better known.

Hattendorf, John B., 'The Bombardment of Acre, 1840: A Case Study in the Use of Naval Force for Deterrence', in Edward Freeman, ed., *'Les Empires en guerre et paix, 1793–1860'* (Vincennes, Service Historique de la Marine, 1990), pp. 205–23.

—'Maritime Conflict', in *The Laws of War: Constraints on Warfare in the Western World*, ed. Michael Howard, George J. Andreopoulos and Mark R. Shulman (New Haven, Conn., 1994), pp. 98–115.

—'Changing American Perceptions of the Royal Navy since 1775', *IJNH* XI (July 2014), no. 1.

Hattendorf, John B. and Robert S. Jordan, eds., *Maritime Strategy and the Balance of Power: Britain and America in the Twentieth Century* (Basingstoke, 1989).

Hayes, Paul, 'Britain, Germany, and the Admiralty's Plans for Attacking German Territory, 1860–1905', in *War, Strategy and International Politics: Essays in Honour of Sir Michael Howard*, ed. Lawrence Freedman, Paul Hayes and Robert O'Neill (Oxford, 1992), pp. 95–116.

Hayward, Roger, 'British Air-Dropped Depth Charges and Anti-Ship Torpedoes', *Royal Air Force Historical Society Journal* XLV (2009), pp. 122–36.

Headrick, Daniel R., *The Invisible Weapon: Telecommunications and International Politics 1851–1945* (Oxford, 1991).

—'Câbles télégraphiques et rivalité franco-britannique avant 1914', *Guerres Mondiales et Conflits Contemporains* 166 (1992), pp. 133–47.

Headrick, Daniel R. and Pascal Griset, 'Submarine Telegraph Cables: Business and Politics, 1838–1939', *Business History Review* LXXV (2001), pp. 543–78.

Heath, Admiral Sir Leopold, *Letters from the Black Sea during the Crimean War, 1854–1855* (London, 1897).

Heinrich, Thomas, *Warship Builders: An Industrial History of U.S. Naval Shipbuilding, 1922–1945* (Annapolis, Md., 2020).

Heintschel von Heinegg, Wolf, 'Naval Blockade and International Law', in *Naval Blockades and Seapower: Strategies and Counter-Strategies, 1805–2005*, ed. Bruce A. Elleman and S. C. M. Paine (London, 2006), pp. 10–22.

Heitmann, Jan G., 'The Front Line: Convoy HG76 – The Offence', in Howarth and Law, *Battle of the Atlantic*, pp. 490–507.

Hellwinkel, Lars, *Der deutsche Kriegsmarinestützpunkt Brest* (Bochum, 2010).

Hennessy, Peter and James Jinks, *The Silent Deep: The Royal Navy Submarine Service since 1945* (London, 2015).

Hepper, David J., *British Warship Losses in the Age of Sail, 1650–1859* (Rotherfield, E. Sussex, 1994).

Herschel, Sir John F. W., ed., *A Manual of Scientific Enquiry prepared for the Use of Officers in Her Majesty's Navy and Travellers in General* (London, 1851).

[Often cited, not quite correctly, as *The Admiralty Manual of Scientific Enquiry.*]

Herwig, Holger, *The German Naval Officer Corps: A Social and Political History, 1890–1914* (London, 1973).

—'*Luxury' Fleet: The Imperial German Navy 1888–1918* (London, 1980).

—'The Failure of German Sea Power, 1914–1945: Mahan, Tirpitz and Raeder Reconsidered', *IHR* X (1988), pp. 68–105.

—'Innovation Ignored: The Submarine Problem – Germany, Britain and the United States, 1919–1939', in Williamson Murray and Allan R. Millett, eds., *Military Innovation in the Interwar Period* (Cambridge, 1996), pp. 227–64.

—'Strategische Unbestimmtheitsrelation? Die US-Navy im Ersten Weltkrieg', in *Seemacht und Seestrategie im 19. und 20. Jahrhundert*, ed. Jörg Duppler (Hamburg, 1999), pp. 173–83.

—'Total Rhetoric, Limited War: Germany's U-Boat Campaign, 1917–1918', in Chickering and Förster, *Great War, Total War*, pp. 189–206.

—'Germany and the Battle of the Atlantic', in *A World at Total War: Global Conflict and the Politics of Destruction*, ed. Roger Chickering, Stig Förster and Bernd Greiner (Cambridge, 2005), pp. 71–87.

—'Command Decision Making: Imperial Germany, 1871–1914', in *The Fog of Peace and War Planning: Military and Strategic Planning under Uncertainty*, ed. Talbot C. Imlay and Monica Duffy Toft (Abingdon, 2006), pp. 100–125.

[Hessler, Günter], *The U-Boat War in the Atlantic* (London, 1989, 4 vols. in 2). A survey of the war from the German point of view, written for the Admiralty after the war by Commander Hessler, who was Dönitz's staff officer and son-in-law.

Heuser, Beatrice, *The Evolution of Strategy: Thinking War from Antiquity to the Present* (Cambridge, 2010).

Hezlet, Sir Arthur, *The Submarine and Sea Power* (London, 1967).

—*The Electron and Sea Power* (London, 1970).

—*British and Allied Submarine Operations in World War II* (Gosport, 2001, 2 vols.). Excellent operational history with detailed appendices and good illustrations.

Hiley, Nicholas, 'The Strategic Origins of Room 40', *I&NS* II (1987), pp. 245–73.

Hill, Alexander, 'British Lend-Lease Aid and the Soviet War Effort, June 1941–June 1942', *JMilH* LXXI (2007), pp. 773–808.

Hill, J. R., ed., *The Oxford Illustrated History of the Royal Navy* (Oxford, 1995).

—'The Realities of Medium Power, 1946 to the Present', in Hill, *Oxford Illustrated History*, pp. 381–408.

Hill, Michael, *Duty Free: Fleet Air Arm Days* (Deal, 2003).

Hillmann, Jörg, 'Der "Mythos" Dönitz: Annäherungen an ein Geschichtsbild', in *Nordlichter: Geschichtsbewußtsein und Geschichtsmythen nördlich der Elbe*, ed. Bea Lundt (Cologne, 2004), pp. 243–67.

Hilton, Boyd, *A Mad, Bad and Dangerous People? England 1783–1846* (Oxford, 2006).

Hinsley, F. H. ed., *British Foreign Policy under Sir Edward Grey* (Cambridge, 1977).

—'Bletchley Park, the Admiralty and Naval Enigma', in *Code Breakers: The Inside Story of Bletchley Park*, ed. Hinsley and Alan Stripp (Oxford, 1994), pp. 77–80.

Hinsley, F. H. et al., *British Intelligence in the Second World War* (London 1979–90, 5 vols.).

Hirama, Yōichi, 'Japanese Naval Preparations for World War II', *NWCR* XLIV (1991), no. 2, pp. 63–81.

Hobbs, David, *The British Pacific Fleet* (Barnsley, 2011).

—'Ship-Borne Air Anti-Submarine Warfare', in Howarth and Law, *The Battle of the Atlantic*, pp. 388–407.

—'Naval Aviation, 1930–2000', in Harding, *The Royal Navy, 1930–2000*, pp. 69–88.

Hobson, John M., 'The Military-Extraction Gap and the Weary Titan: The Fiscal Sociology of British Defence Policy, 1870–1913', *JEEH* XXII (1993), pp. 461–506.

Hobson, Rolf, *Imperialism at Sea: Naval Strategic Thought, the Ideology of Sea Power and the Tirpitz Plan, 1875–1914* (Leiden, 2002).

Hodges, Peter, *The Big Gun: Battleship Main Armament 1860–1945* (Greenwich, 1981).

Hoerber, Thomas, 'Psychology and Reasoning in the Anglo-German Naval Agreement, 1935–39', *HJ* LII (2009), pp. 153–74.

Holland, Robert, *Blue-Water Empire: The British in the Mediterranean since 1800* (London, 2012).

Hone, Thomas C., 'The Evolution of the U.S. Fleet, 1933–1941: How the President Mattered', in Marolda, *FDR and the U.S. Navy*, pp. 65–114.

—'Replacing Battleships with Aircraft Carriers in the Pacific in World War II', *NWCR* LXVI (2013), no. 1, pp. 56–76.

Hone, Thomas C. and Mark D. Mandeles, 'Interwar Innovation in Three Navies: U.S. Navy, Royal Navy, Imperial Japanese Navy', *NWCR* XL (1987), no. 2, pp. 63–83.

Hone, Thomas C. and Norman Friedman and Mark D. Mandeles, *American and British Aircraft Carrier Development, 1919–1941* (Annapolis, Md., 1999).

Hone, Thomas C. and Trent Hone, *Battle Line: The United States Navy, 1919–1939* (Annapolis, Md., 2006).

Hone, Trent, *Learning War: The Evolution of Fighting Doctrine in the US Navy, 1898–1945* (Annapolis, Md., 2018).

—'US Navy Surface Battle Doctrine and Victory in the Pacific', *NWCR* LXII (2009), no. 1, pp. 66–115.

Hoock, Holger, *Empires of the Imagination: Politics, War, and the Arts in the British World, 1750–1850* (London, 2010).

Hore, Peter, *The Habit of Victory: The Story of the Royal Navy 1545 to 1945* (London, 2005).

—ed., *Dreadnought to Daring: 100 Years of Comment, Controversy and Debate in The Naval Review* (Barnsley, 2012).

Horikoshi, Jirō, *Eagles of Mitsubishi: The Story of the Zero Fighter*, trans. S. Shindo and H. N. Wantiez (Seattle, 1981).

Horsley, Terence, *Find, Fix and Strike: The Work of the Fleet Air Arm* (London, 1943).

Hovgaard, William, *Modern History of Warships* (London, 1920).

Howard, Sir Michael, *The Continental Commitment: The Dilemma of British Defence Policy in the Era of the Two World Wars* (London, 1972).

—'A Thirty Years War? The Two World Wars in Historical Perspective', *TRHS* 6th Series III (1993), pp. 171–84.

Howarth, Stephen, *The Royal Navy's Reserves in War and Peace 1902–2003* (Barnsley, 2003).

Howarth, Stephen and Derek G. Law, eds., *The Battle of the Atlantic, 1939–1945: 50th Anniversary International Naval Conference* (London, 1994).

Howe, Anthony, 'Restoring Free Trade: The British Experience, 1776–1873', in *The Political Economy of British Historical Experience, 1688–1914*, ed. Donald Winch and P. K. O'Brien (Oxford, 2002), pp. 193–214.

Howell, R. C., *The Royal Navy and the Slave Trade* (London, 1987).

Howlett, Alexander, *The Development of British Naval Aviation, 1914–1918* (Abingdon, 2021).

Howse, Derek, *Radar at Sea: The Royal Navy in World War 2* (Basingstoke, 1993).

Huddie, Paul, 'Recruiting the Royal Naval Coast Volunteers in Britain and Ireland, 1854–6', *MM* CVII (2021), pp. 420–34.

Hughes, Wayne P., *Fleet Tactics: Theory and Practice* (Annapolis, Md., 1986).

Hugill, Peter J., *Global Communications since 1844: Geopolitics and Technology* (Baltimore, Md., 1999).

Hull, Isabel V., *Absolute Destruction: Military Culture and the Practices of War in Imperial Germany* (Ithaca, NY, 2005).

—*A Scrap of Paper: Breaking and Making International Law during the Great War* (Ithaca, NY, 2014).

—'"Military Necessity" and the Laws of War in Imperial Germany', in *Order, Conflict, and Violence*, ed. Stathis N. Kalyvas, Ian Shapiro and Tarek Masoud (Cambridge, 2008), pp. 352–77.

Hunt, Barry D., 'Richmond and the Education of the Royal Navy', in *Mahan is Not Enough: The Proceedings of a Conference on the Works of Sir Julian Corbett and Admiral Sir Herbert Richmond*, ed. James Goldrick and John B. Hattendorf (Newport, RI, 1993), pp. 65–81.

Hunter, Mark C., *Policing the Seas: Anglo-American Relations and the Equatorial Atlantic, 1819–1865* (St John's, Newfoundland, 2008: Research in Maritime History, no. 36).

Hyde, H. Montgomery, *British Air Policy between the Wars, 1918–1939* (London, 1976).

Iguchi Takeo, *Demystifying Pearl Harbor: A New Perspective from Japan*, trans. David Noble (Tokyo, 2010).

Inglis, K. S., 'The Imperial Connection: Telegraphic Communication between England and Australia, 1872–1902', in *Australia and Britain: Studies in a Changing Relationship*, ed. A. F. Madden and W. H. Morris-Jones (London, 1980), pp. 21–38.

Isom, Dallas Woodbury, *Midway Inquest: Why the Japanese Lost the Battle of Midway* (Bloomington, Ind., 2007).

Jackson, Julian, *The Fall of France: The Nazi Invasion of 1940* (Oxford, 2004).

James, Alan, Carlos Alfaro Zaforteza and Malcolm Murfett, eds., *European Navies and the Conduct of War* (Abingdon, 2019).

James, Frank A. J. L., 'Davy in the Dockyard: Humphry Davy, the Royal Society and the Electrochemical Protection of the Copper Sheeting of His Majesty's Ships in the mid-1820s', *Physis: Rivista Internazionale di Storia della Scienza* XXIX (1992), pp. 205–25.

—'Faraday in the Pits, Faraday at Sea', *Proceedings of the Royal Institution* LXVIII (1997), pp. 277–301.

James, John, *The Paladins: A Social History of the RAF up to the Outbreak of World War II* (London, 1990).

Jarrett, Dudley, *British Naval Dress* (London, 1960).

Jeffery, Keith, *Field Marshal Sir Henry Wilson: A Political Soldier* (Oxford, 2006).

—*MI6: The History of the Secret Intelligence Service 1909–1949* (London, 2010).

Jefford, C. G., *Observers & Navigators, and Other Non-Pilot Aircrew in the RFC, RNAS & RAF* (Shrewsbury, 2001).

Jenner, C. J., 'Turning the Hinge of Fate: Good Source and the UK-U.S. Intelligence Alliance, 1940–1942', *DH* XXXII (2008), pp. 165–205.

Jeschke, Hubert, *U-Boottaktik: Zur deutschen U-boottaktik 1900–1945* (Freiburg-im Breisgau, 1972).

Johannesson, Rolf, *Offizier in kritischer Zeit* (Herford & Bonn, 1989).

Johnman, Lewis and Hugh Murphy, *British Shipbuilding and the State since 1918: A Political Economy of Decline* (Exeter, 2002).

Johnson, William Bruce, *The Pacific Campaign in World War II: From Pearl Harbor to Guadalcanal* (Abingdon, 2006).

Johnston, Ian and Ian Buxton, *The Battleship Builders: Constructing and Arming British Capital Ships* (Barnsley, 2013).

Jones, Ben, ed., *The Fleet Air Arm in the Second World War* (NRS Vols. 159 and 166, 2012–18).

—'The Fleet Air Arm and the Struggle for the Mediterranean, 1940–44', in Benbow, *British Naval Aviation* (2011), pp. 79–98.

—'The Fleet Air Arm and Trade Defense, 1939–1944', in Bell and Faulkner, *Decision in the Atlantic*, pp. 125–49.

Jones, C. G. Pitcairn, ed., *Piracy in the Levant 1827–8: Selected from the Papers of Admiral Sir Edward Codrington* (NRS Vol. 72, 1934).

Jones, Mark, 'From "Skagerrak" to the "Organisation Consul": War Culture and the Imperial German Navy, 1914–22', in *Other Combatants, Other Fronts:*

Competing Histories of the First World War, ed. James E. Kitchen, Alisa Miller and Laura Rowe (Newcastle upon Tyne, 2011), pp. 249–74.

Jones, Mary, ed., *A Naval Life: The Edited Diaries and Papers of Admiral John Locke Marx 1852–1939* (Dulverton, Somerset, 2007).

—'The Making of the Royal Naval Officer Corps 1860–1914' (Exeter PhD thesis, 1999).

—'Towards a Hierarchy of Management: The Victorian and Edwardian Navy, 1860–1918', in Doe and Harding, *Naval Leadership and Management*, pp. 157–72. [See also her valuable website: 'Nomination and Patronage' (http://www.personanavalpress.co.uk/nomination_database.htm).]

Jones, Matthew, *Britain, the United States and the Mediterranean War, 1942–44* (Basingstoke, 1996).

Jones, Neville, *The Origins of Strategic Bombing: A Study of the Development of British Air Strategic Thought and Practice up to 1918* (London, 1973).

—*The Beginnings of Strategic Air Power: A History of the British Bomber Force 1923–1939* (London, 1987).

Jones, Wilbur D., *The American Problem in British Diplomacy, 1841–1861* (London, 1974).

Jordan, David, 'Royal Navy Concepts of Air Power in the Maritime Environment 1900–1918', in Greg Kennedy, *Britain's War at Sea*, pp. 183–203.

Jordan, John, *Warships after Washington: The Development of the Five Major Navies, 1922–1930* (Barnsley, 2011).

Karau, Mark D., *'Wielding the Dagger': The Marine Korps Flandern and the German War Effort, 1914–1918* (Westport, Conn., 2013). [Reprinted as *The Naval Flank of the Western Front* (Barnsley, 2015).]

Karsten, Peter, *The Naval Aristocracy: The Golden Age of Annapolis and the Emergence of Modern American Navalism* (Annapolis, Md., 1972, 2nd edn 2008, reprinted Barnsley, 2015). A clever, richly researched, Vietnam-War era view from the common room.

Keefer, Scott Andrew, *The Law of Nations and Britain's Quest for Naval Security: International Law and Arms Control, 1898–1914* (Cham, 2016).

Keevil, J. J., C. C. Lloyd and J. L. S. Coulter, *Medicine and the Navy, 1200–1900* (Edinburgh, 1957–63, 4 vols.). Vol. IV skims the 19th century.

Kelly, J. B., *Britain and the Persian Gulf 1795–1880* (Oxford, 1968).

Kelly, Patrick J., *Tirpitz and the Imperial German Navy* (Bloomington, Ind., 2011).

—'Strategy, Tactics, and Turf Wars: Tirpitz and the Oberkommando der Marine, 1892–1895', *JMilH* LXVI (2002), pp. 1033–60.

Kemp, Peter, ed., *The Papers of Admiral Sir John Fisher* (NRS Vols. 102 and 106, 1960–64).

—*The British Sailor: A Social History of the Lower Deck* (London, 1970). Now showing its age.

Kennedy, David M., *Over Here: The First World War and American Society* (New York, 1980).

—ed., *British Naval Strategy East of Suez 1900–2000: Influences and Actions* (London, 2005).

—ed., *Imperial Defence: The Old World Order, 1856–1956* (London, 2008).

—ed., *Britain's War at Sea, 1914–1918: The War they Thought and the War they Fought* (Abingdon, 2016).

Kennedy, Greg and Keith Neilson, eds., *Far-Flung Lines: Essays on Imperial Defence in Honour of Donald Mackenzie Schurman* (London, 1997).

Kennedy, Gregory C., 'The 1930 London Naval Conference and Anglo-American Maritime Strength, 1927–1930', in McKercher, *Arms Limitation and Disarmament*, pp. 149–71.

—' "Rat in Power": Neville Chamberlain and the Creation of British Foreign Policy, 1931–39', in Otte, *The Makers of British Foreign Policy*, pp. 173–95.

—'Symbol of Empire: Singapore and Anglo-American Strategic Relations in the Far East, 1924–1941', in *Singapore, Sixty Years On*, ed. Brian Farrell and Sandy Hunter (Singapore, 2002), pp. 42–67.

—'Sea Denial, Interdiction and Diplomacy: The Royal Navy and the Role of Malta, 1939–1943', in Speller, *The Royal Navy and Maritime Power in the Twentieth Century*, pp. 50–66.

—'Intelligence and the Blockade, 1914–17: A Study in Administration, Friction and Command', *I&NS* XXII (2007), pp. 699–721.

—'Anglo-American Diplomatic Relations, 1939–1945', in *War & Diplomacy: From World War I to the War on Terrorism*, ed. Andrew Dorman and G. Kennedy (Washington D.C., 2008), pp. 41–57.

—'The North Atlantic Triangle and the Blockade, 1914–1916', *Journal of Transatlantic History* VI (2008), pp. 22–33.

—'The Royal Navy and Imperial Defence, 1919–1956', in *Imperial Defence: The Old World Order*, pp. 133–51.

—'Strategy and Power: The Royal Navy, the Foreign Office and the Blockade, 1914–1917', *Defence Studies* VIII (2008), pp. 190–206.

—'Some Principles of Anglo-American Strategic Relations, 1900–1945', in *The British Way in Warfare: Power and the International System, 1856–1956*, ed. Keith Neilson and Greg Kennedy (Farnham, 2010), pp. 29–57.

—ed., *The Merchant Marine in International Affairs, 1850–1950* (London, 2000).

Kennedy, Greg, *Anglo-American Strategic Relations and the Far East 1933–1939: Imperial Crossroads* (London, 2002).

Kennedy, Paul M., *The Rise of the Anglo-German Antagonism, 1860–1914* (London, 1980).

—*Engineers of Victory: The Problem Solvers who Turned the Tide in the Second World War* (London, 2013).

—'Tirpitz, England and the Second Navy Law of 1900: A Strategical Critique', *MGM* II (1970), pp. 33–58.

—'Imperial Cable Communications and Strategy, 1870–1914', *EHR* LXXXVI (1971), pp. 728–52.

—'German World Policy and the Alliance Negotiations with England, 1897–1900', *JMH* LXV (1973), pp. 605–25.

—'Fisher and Tirpitz: Political Admirals in the Age of Imperialism', in *Naval Warfare in the Twentieth Century: Essays in Honour of Arthur Marder*, ed. Gerald Jordan (London, 1977), pp. 45–59.

—'Mahan versus Mackinder: Two Interpretations of British Sea Power', in Paul M. Kennedy, *Strategy and Diplomacy 1870–1945: Eight Studies* (London, 1983), pp. 41–85 [originally in *MGM* 1974, no. 2, pp. 39–66].

—'British "Net Assessment" and the Coming of the Second World War', in *Calculations: Net Assessment and the Coming of World War II*, ed. Williamson Murray and Alan R. Millett (New York, 1992), pp. 19–59.

Keppel, Henry, *The Expedition to Borneo of H.M.S. Dido* (London, 1847, 2 vols.).

—*A Sailor's Life under Four Sovereigns* (London, 1899, 3 vols.).

Kerr, J. Lennox and Wilfred Granville, *The R.N.V.R: A Record of Achievement* (London, 1957).

Kerr, J. Lennox and David James, eds., *Wavy Navy, by Some who Served* (London, 1950).

Kersaudy, François, *Norway 1940* (London, 1990; originally *Churchill contre Hitler: Norvège 1940, la victoire fatale*, Paris, 1987, 2nd edn. 2002).

Kielmansegg, Peter, *Deutschland und der Erste Weltkrieg* (Frankfurt am Main, 1968).

Kingcome, John, 'Marine Engineering in the Royal Navy: A Review of Progress in the Last Twenty-Five Years', *JNE* III (1949), pp. 103–24.

King-Hall, Louise, ed., *Sea Saga, being the Naval Diaries of Four Generations of the King-Hall Family* (London, 1935).

Kingsley, F. A., 'Review of German Maritime Radar Developments', in *The Applications of Radar and Other Electronic Systems in the Royal Navy in World War 2* (Basingstoke, 1995), II, pp. 267–308.

Knight, Roger, *William IV: A King at Sea* (London, 2015).

—'The Battle for Control of the Royal Navy, 1801–1835' [2014] (www.GlobalMaritimeHistory.com). An important but regrettably obscure article which has never been printed.

—'British North Atlantic Convoys, 1812–14, and the Subsequent Rejection of the Convoy System', in *Navies in Multipolar Worlds: From the Age of Sail to the Present*, ed. Paul Kennedy and Evan Wilson (London, 2021), pp. 47–61.

Knock, Sidney, *Clear Lower Deck: An Intimate Study of the Men of the Royal Navy* (London, 1932).

Knox, MacGregor, *Hitler's Italian Allies: Royal Armed Forces, Fascist Regime, and the War of 1940–43* (Cambridge, 2000).

Koehler, Wolfgang, 'Der Einsatz der Führungsdienste bei der Operation "Ostfront" vom 25 bis 27 Dezember 1943', in *Führungsprobleme der Marine im Zweiten Weltkrieg*, ed. Heinrich Schuur, Rolf Martens and Wolfgang Koehler (Freiburg im Breisgau, 1973), pp. 95–148.

Koerver, Hans Joachim, ed., *Room 40: German Naval Warfare 1914–1918* (Steinbach, 2 vols., 2007, 2009).

—ed., *German Submarine Warfare 1914–1918 in the Eyes of British Intelligence: Selected Sources from the British National Archives, Kew* (Steinbach, 2nd edn., 2012).

—*Krieg der Zahlen: Deutscher Ubootkrieg, britische Blockade und Wilsons Amerika 1914–1919. Band 1: Die Ära Tirpitz 1914–1916; Band II: Frieden oder Uboote?* (Steinbach, 2015, 2017).

Kohnen, David, 'The Cruise of *U-188*: Special Intelligence and the "Liquidation" of Group Monsoon, 1943–1944', in Bell and Faulkner, *Decision in the Atlantic*, pp. 252–88.

König, Markus, *Agitation – Zensur – Propaganda. Der U-Bootkrieg und die deutsche Öffentlichkeit im Ersten Weltkrieg* (Stuttgart, 2014).

Konvitz, Josef W., 'Bombs, Cities and Submarines: Allied Bombing of the French Ports, 1942–1943', *IHR* XIV (1992), pp. 23–44.

Kowark, Hannsjörg, 'La marine française et la Conférence de Washington, 1921– 1922', in *Aspects du désarmement naval*, ed. Hervé Coutau-Bégarie (Paris, 1994), pp. 151–229. [Cf. his *Die französische Marinepolitik 1919–1924 und die Washingtoner Konferenz* (Stuttgart, 1979).]

Kowner, Rotem, 'When Economics, Strategy, and Racial Ideology Meet: Inter-Axis Connections in the Wartime Indian Ocean', *JGH* XII (2017), pp. 228–50.

Krebs, Gerhard, 'The War in the Pacific 1943–1945', in *G2WW* VII, 703–840.

Kristiansen, Tom, 'A German Menace to Norway: The Evolution of Threat Perceptions and Strategy between the Wars', in Clemmesen and Faulkner, *Northern European Overture to War, 1939–41*, pp. 271–94.

Kruizinga, Samuël, 'NOT Neutrality: The Dutch Government, the Netherlands Oversea Trust Company and the Entente Blockade of Germany, 1914–1918', in *Caught in the Middle: Neutrality and the First World War*, ed. Johan den Hertog and S. Kruizinga (Amsterdam, 2011), pp. 85–103.

Kuehn, John T., 'A Turning Point in Anglo-American Relations? The General Board of the Navy and the London Naval Treaty', in Maurer and Bell, *At the Crossroads between Peace and War*, pp. 7–47.

Kuramatsu, Tadashi, 'The Geneva Naval Conference of 1927: The British Preparation for the Conference, December 1926 to June 1927', *JSS* XIX (1996), pp. 104–21.

—'Viscount Cecil, Winston Churchill and the Geneva Naval Conference of 1927: *Si vis pacem para pacem* versus *si vis pacem para bellum*', in *Personalities, War and Diplomacy: Essays in International History*, ed. T. G. Otte and Constantine A. Pagedas (London, 1997), pp. 105–26.

—'Britain, Japan and Inter-War Naval Limitation, 1921–1936', in Gow, Hirama and Chapman, *The History of Anglo-Japanese Relations, 1600–2000*, pp. 127–38.

Lacey, James, 'Towards a Strategy: Creating an American Strategy for Global War, 1940–1943', in *The Shaping of Grand Strategy: Policy, Diplomacy, and War*, ed. Williamson Murray, Richard S. Sinnreich and J. Lacey (Cambridge, 2011), pp. 182–209.

Lacroix, Eric and Linton Wells, *Japanese Cruisers of the Pacific War* (Annapolis, Md., 1997).

Laing, E. A. M., *Steam Wooden Warship Building in Portsmouth Dockyard 1832–52* (Portsmouth Papers, no. 42; Portsmouth, 1985).

Lamb, Christian, *Beyond the Sea: A Wren at War* (London, 2021).

Lambert, Andrew, *Battleships in Transition: The Creation of the Steam Battlefleet 1815–1860* (London, 1984).

—*Warrior: Restoring the World's First Ironclad* (London, 1987).

—*The Crimean War: British Grand Strategy against Russia, 1853–56* (Manchester, 1990; reprinted Farnham, 2011, with a new introduction surveying the literature).

—*The Last Sailing Battlefleet: Maintaining Naval Mastery 1815–1850* (London, 1991).

—*Admirals: The Naval Commanders who Made Britain Great* (London, 2008).

—*Franklin: Tragic Hero of Polar Exploration* (London, 2009).

—*The British Way of War: Julian Corbett and the Battle for a National Strategy* (London, 2021).

—ed., 'Sir Henry Keppel's Account *Capture of Bomarsund, August 1854*', in Rodger, *The Naval Miscellany V* (NRS Vol. 125, 1984), pp. 354–70.

—' "Part of a Long Line of Circumvallation to Confine the Future Expansion of Russia": Great Britain and the Baltic, 1809–1890', in *In Quest of Trade and Security: The Baltic in Power Politics 1500–1900*, ed. Göran Rystad, Klaus-Richard Böhme and Wilhelm M. Carlgren (Stockholm, 1994–5, 2 vols.), I, 297–334.

—'The Royal Navy 1856–1914: Deterrence and the Strategy of World Power', in Neilson and Errington, *Navies and Global Defense*, pp. 69–92.

—'The British Naval Strategic Revolution, 1815–1854', in *Shipping, Technology and Imperialism: Papers Presented to the Third British-Dutch Maritime History Conference*, ed. Gordon Jackson and David M. Williams (Aldershot, 1996), pp. 145–61.

—'Preparing for the Long Peace: The Reconstruction of the Royal Navy 1815–1830', *MM* LXXXII (1996), pp. 41–54.

—'Politics, Technology and Policy-Making, 1859–1865: Palmerston, Gladstone and the Management of the Ironclad Naval Race', *NM* VIII (1998), no. 3, pp. 9–38.

—'Responding to the Nineteenth Century: The Royal Navy and the Introduction of the Screw Propeller', *History of Technology* XXI (2000), pp. 1–28.

—'Making the Modern Naval Rating: From the *Shannon-Chesapeake* Action of 1813 to "Continuous Service" in 1853', in *Människan i Flottans Tjänst. Sjöhistorisk jubileumssymposium i Åbo, 24 November 2000*, ed. C. H. Ericsson and K. Montin (Åbo, 2001), pp. 23–40.

—'Under the Heel of Britannia: The Bombardment of Sweaborg 9–11 August 1855', in *Seapower Ashore: 200 Years of Royal Navy Operations on Land*, ed. Peter Hore (London, 2001), pp. 96–129.

—' "Within Cannon Shot of Deep Water": The Syrian Campaign of 1840', in *Seapower Ashore: 200 Years of Royal Navy Operations on Land*, ed. Peter Hore (London, 2001), pp. 79–95.

—' "Good, while it lasts": Great Britain and the Crimean War Coalition, 1854–1856', in *Future Wars: Coalition Operations in Global Strategy*, ed. D. E. Showalter (Chicago, Il., 2002), pp. 29–47.

—'History as Process and Record: The Royal Navy and Officer Education', in *Military Education: Past, Present, and Future*, ed. Greg Kennedy and Keith Neilson (Westport, Conn., 2002), pp. 83–104.

—'The Royal Navy, John Ericsson, and the Challenges of New Technology', *IJNH* II (2003), no. 3.

—'Winning without Fighting: British Grand Strategy and its Application to the United States, 1815–1865', in *Strategic Logic and Political Rationality: Essays in Honour of Michael J. Handel*, ed. Bradford A. Lee and Karl F. Walling (Newport RI, 2003), pp. 164–95.

—'Great Britain and Maritime Law from the Declaration of Paris to the Era of Total War', in *Navies in Northern Waters 1721–2000*, ed. Rolf Hobson and Tom Kristiansen (London, 2004), pp. 11–38.

—'Looking for Gunboats: British Naval Operations in the Gulf of Bothnia, 1854–55', *JMR* VI (2004), pp. 65–86.

—'The Crimean War Blockade, 1854-56', in *Naval Blockades and Seapower: Strategies and Counter-Strategies, 1805–1005*, ed. Bruce A. Elleman and S. C. M. Paine (London, 2006), pp. 46–60.

—'The Development of Education in the Royal Navy: 1854–1914', in *The Development of British Naval Thinking: Essays in Memory of Bryan McLaren Ranft*, ed. Geoffrey Till (London, 2006), pp. 34–59.

—'Economic Power, Technological Advantage, and Imperial Strength: Britain as a Unique Global Power, 1860–1890', *IJNH* V (2006), no. 2. [originally 'Wirtschaftliche Macht, technologischer Vorsprung und Imperiale Stärke: Grossbritannien als einzigartige globale Macht: 1860 bis 1890', in M. Epkenhans and G. P. Gross, *Das Militär und der Aufbruch die Moderne 1860 bis 1890* (Munich 2003)].

—'Science and Sea Power: The Navy Board, the Royal Society and the Structural Reforms of Sir Robert Seppings', *Transactions of the Naval Dockyards Society* I (2006), pp. 9–20.

—'Palmerston and Sea Power', in *Palmerston Studies*, ed. David Brown and Miles Taylor (Southampton, 2007, 2 vols.), II, 39–65.

—'Politics, Administration and Decision-Making: Wellington and the Navy, 1828–1830', in *Wellington Studies* IV, ed. C. M. Woolgar (Southampton, 2008), pp. 185–243.

—'Slavery, Free Trade and Naval Strategy, 1840–1860', in *Slavery, Diplomacy and Empire: Britain and the Suppression of the Slave Trade, 1807–1975*, ed. Keith Hamilton and Patrick Salmon (Brighton, 2009), pp. 65–80.

—'The Naval War Course, *Some Principles of Maritime Strategy* and the Origins of "The British Way in Warfare"', in *The British Way in Warfare: Power and the International System, 1856–1956*, ed. Keith Neilson and Greg Kennedy (Farnham, 2010), pp. 219–55.

—'The Only British Advantage: Sea Power and Strategy, September 1939–June 1940', in Clemmesen and Faulkner, *Northern European Overture to War, 1939–41*, pp. 45–73.

—' "The Possibility of Ultimate Action in the Baltic": The Royal Navy at War, 1914–1916', in *Jutland: World War I's Greatest Naval Battle*, ed. Michael Epkenhans, Jörg Hillmann and Frank Nägler (Lexington, Ky., 2015), pp. 79–116. [Originally *Skagerrakschlacht: Vorgeschichte, Ereignis, Verarbeitung* (Munich, 2009).]

—'Napier, Palmerston and Palmella in 1833: The Unofficial Arm of British Diplomacy', in *Naval Leadership in the Atlantic World: The Age of Reform and Revolution, 1700–1850*, ed. Richard Harding and Agustín Guimerá (London, 2017), pp. 141–56.

—'Thinking about Seapower: Navies, the Academic and Strategic Choice', *NR* CX (2022), pp. 310–19.

Lambert, Nicholas A., *Sir John Fisher's Naval Revolution* (Columbia, SC, 1999).

—*The Submarine Service, 1900–1918* (NRS Vol. 142, 2001).

—*Planning Armageddon: British Economic Warfare and the First World War* (Cambridge, Mass., 2012).

—' "Our bloody ships" or "Our bloody system"? Jutland and the Loss of the Battle Cruisers, 1916', *JMilH* LXII (1998), pp. 29–56.

—'Sir John Fisher, the Fleet Unit Concept, and the Creation of the Royal Australian Navy', in *Southern Trident: Strategy, History and the Rise of Australian Naval Power*, ed. David Stevens and John Reeve (Crows Nest, NSW, 2001), pp. 214–24.

—'Transformation and Technology in the Fisher Era: The Impact of the Communications Revolution', *JSS* XXVII (2004), pp. 272–97.

—'Strategic Command and Control for Manoeuvre Warfare: Creation of the Royal Navy's "War Room" System', *JMilH* LIX (2005), pp. 361–410.

—'Righting the Scholarship: The Battlecruiser in History and Historiography', *HJ* LVIII (2015), pp. 275–307.

Lane, Tony, 'The Human Economy of the British Merchant Navy', in Howarth and Law, *Battle of the Atlantic*, pp. 45–59.

Langensiepen, Bernd, Dirk Nottelmann and Jochen Krüsmann, *Halbmond und Kaiseradler: Goeben und Breslau am Bosporus, 1914–1918* (Hamburg, 1999).

Langhorne, Richard, 'The Naval Question in Anglo-German Relations, 1912–14', *HJ* XIV (1971), pp. 259–370.

—'Great Britain and Germany, 1905–1911', in *British Foreign Policy under Sir Edward Grey*, ed. F. H. Hinsley (Cambridge, 1977), pp. 288–314.

Larsen, Daniel, 'War Pessimism in Britain and an American Peace in Early 1916', *IHR* XXXIV (2012), pp. 795–817.

Lautenschläger, Karl, 'Technology and the Evolution of Naval Warfare', *International Security* VIII (1983), pp. 3–51.

—'The Dreadnought Revolution Reconsidered', in Masterson, *Naval History . . . Sixth Symposium*, pp. 121–45.

Lavery, Brian, *Hostilities Only: Training the Wartime Royal Navy* (London, 2004).

—*Churchill's Navy: The Ships, Men and Organisation 1939–1945* (London, 2006).

—*River Class Frigates and the Battle of the Atlantic* (London, 2006).

—*Shield of Empire: The Royal Navy and Scotland* (Edinburgh, 2007).

—*In Which They Served: The Royal Navy Officer Experience in the Second World War* (London, 2008).

—*Royal Tars: The Lower Deck of the Royal Navy, 875–1850* (London, 2010).

—*Able Seamen: The Lower Deck of the Royal Navy 1850–1939* (London, 2011).

—*All Hands: The Lower Deck of the Royal Navy since 1939* (London, 2012).

Law, Robin, 'International Law and the British Suppression of the Atlantic Slave Trade', in *Abolitionism and Imperialism in Britain, Africa, and the Atlantic*, ed. Derek R. Peterson (Athens, Oh., 2010), pp. 129–49.

Laws, R. A., 'Radar Maintenance at Sea: A Personal Story, 1940–45', in *The Development of Radar Equipments for the Royal Navy, 1935–45*, ed. F. A. Kingsley (Basingstoke, 1995), pp. 305–24.

Layman, R. D., *Naval Aviation in the First World War: Its Impact and Influence* (London, 1996).

Le Bailly, Vice-Admiral Sir Louis, *The Man around the Engine: Life below the Waterline* (Emsworth, 1990).

Leggett, Don, *Shaping the Royal Navy: Technology, Authority and Naval Architecture, c.1830–1906* (Manchester, 2015).

—'Neptune's New Clothes: Actors, Iron and the Identity of the Mid-Victorian Warship', in *Re-inventing the Ship: Science, Technology and the Maritime World, 1800–1918*, ed. Leggett and Richard Dunn (Farnham, 2012), pp. 71–91.

—'Naval Architecture, Expertise and Navigating Authority in the British Admiralty, c.1885–1906', *JMR* XVI (2014), pp. 73–88.

Lemnitzer, Jan Martin, *Power, Law and the End of Privateering* (London, 2014).

—' "That Moral League of Nations against the United States"– The Origins of the 1856 Declaration of Paris and the Abolition of Privateering', *IHR* XXXV (2013), pp. 1068–88.

—'Woodrow Wilson's Neutrality, the Freedom of the Seas, and the Myth of the "Civil War Precedents" ', *D&S* XXVII (2016), pp. 615–38.

Lenton, H. T., *British and Empire Warships of the Second World War* (London, 1998).

Leutze, James R., *Bargaining for Supremacy: Anglo-American Naval Collaboration, 1937–1941* (Chapel Hill, NC, 1977).

Levy, James P., *The Royal Navy's Home Fleet in World War II* (Basingstoke, 2003).

—'The Needs of Political Policy versus the Reality of Military Operations: Royal Navy Opposition to the Arctic Convoys, 1942', *JSS* XXVI (2003), no. 1, pp. 36–52.

—'Race for the Decisive Weapon: British, American and Japanese Carrier Fleets, 1942–1943', *NWCR* LVIII (2005), no. 1, pp. 137–50.

Lewis, Adrian, 'The Failure of Allied Planning and Doctrine for Operation Overlord: The Case of Minefield and Obstacle Clearance', *JMilH* LXII (1998), pp. 787–808.

—'Admiral Henry Kent Hewitt: The Powerless Expert', in Balano and Symonds, *Fourteenth Naval History Symposium*, pp. 265–79.

Lewis, Michael, *England's Sea-Officers: The Story of the Naval Profession* (London, 1939).

—*The Navy in Transition, 1814–1864* (London, 1965).

Lindberg, Michael and Daniel Todd, *Anglo-American Shipbuilding in World War II: A Geographical Perspective* (Westport, Conn., 2004).

Llewellyn-Jones, Malcolm, *The Royal Navy and Anti-Submarine Warfare, 1917–49* (Abingdon, 2006).

—*The Royal Navy and the Arctic Convoys* (London, 2007).

—*The Royal Navy and the Mediterranean Convoys, 1941–42* (London, 2007). Post-war Naval Staff studies.

Lloyd, Christopher C., *The Navy and the Slave Trade* (London, 1949).

—'The Royal Naval Colleges at Portsmouth and Greenwich', *MM* LII (1956), pp. 145–56.

Lo Cicero, Michael, Ross Mahoney and Stuart Mitchell, eds., *A Military Transformed? Adaptation and Innovation in the British Military, 1792–1945* (Solihull, 2014).

Louis, Wm. Roger, 'Dulles, Suez and the British', in *John Foster Dulles and the Diplomacy of the Cold War*, ed. Richard H. Immermann (Princeton, NJ, 1990), pp. 133–58.

Louis, Wm. Roger and Hedley Bull, eds., *The 'Special Relationship': Anglo-American Relations since 1945* (Oxford, 1986).

Louis, Wm. Roger and Roger Owen, eds., *Suez 1956: The Crisis and its Consequences* (Oxford, 1989).

Louvier, Patrick, *La puissance navale et militaire britannique en Méditerranée 1840–1871* (Paris, Service Historique de la Défense, 2006).

—'Les officiers de marine britannique et la Méditerranée au XIXe siècle: un regard intime et singulier?', *RHM* XXII–XXIII (2017), pp. 277–302.

Lovell, Julia, *The Opium War: Drugs, Dreams and the Making of China* (London, 2011).

Lovering, Tristan T. A., ed., *Amphibious Assault: Manoeuvre from the Sea. Amphibious Operations from the Last Century* (Ministry of Defence, 2005).

Lund, Erik, 'The Industrial History of Strategy: Reevaluating the Wartime Record of the British Aviation Industry in Comparative Perspective, 1919–1945', *JMilH* LXII (1998), pp. 75–99.

Lunderberg, Philip K., 'The German Naval Critique of the U-Boat Campaign, 1915–1918', *Military Affairs* XXVII (1963), pp. 105–18.

Lunn, Kenneth and Ann Day, eds., *History of Work and Labour Relations in the Royal Dockyards* (London, 1999).

Lynch, Cecilia, 'A Matter of Controversy: The Peace Movement and British Arms Policy in the Interwar Period', in McKercher, *Arms Limitation and Disarmament*, pp. 61–82.

Lynn, Martin, 'British Policy, Trade, and Informal Empire in the Mid-Nineteenth Century', in *OHBE* III, 101–21.

Lyon, David J., 'The British Order of Battle', in Howarth and Law, *Battle of the Atlantic*, pp. 266–75.

Lyon, Hugh, 'The Relations between the Admiralty and Private Industry in the Development of Warships', in Ranft, *Technical Change and British Naval Policy*, pp. 37–64.

Maber, John M., 'Electrical Supply in Warships: A Brief History', *JNE* XXV (1980), pp. 348–60.

MacDougall, Philip, ed., *Chatham Dockyard, 1815–1865: The Industrial Transformation* (NRS Vol. 154, 2009).

—'A Demand Fulfilled: Analysis of an Industrial Dispute between the Admiralty and the Civilian Work Force Employed in the Naval Dockyards of Southern England, 1833–41', *Southern History* XIX (1997), pp. 112–34.

MacGregor, David, 'The Use, Misuse, and Non-Use of History: The Royal Navy and the Operational Lessons of the First World War', *JMilH* LVI (1992), pp. 603–16.

Mackay, Ruddock F., *Fisher of Kilverstone* (Oxford, 1973).

—*Balfour: Intellectual Statesman* (Oxford, 1985).

Mackintosh, John P., 'The Role of the Committee of Imperial Defence before 1914', *EHR* LXXVII (1962), pp. 490–503.

MacLaren, Hamish D., 'Electrical Engineering in the Royal Navy', *JNE* XIII (1961), pp. 68–73.

MacLeod, Christine, Jeremy Stein, Jennifer Tann and James Andrew, 'Making Waves: The Royal Navy's Management of Invention and Innovation in Steam Shipping, 1815–1832', *History and Technology* XVI (2000), pp. 307–33.

MacLeod, Roy M. and E. Kay Andrews, 'Scientific Advice in the War at Sea, 1915–17: The Board of Invention and Research', *JCH* VI, no. 2 (1971) pp. 3–40.

MacMillan, D. F., 'The Development of British Naval Gunnery, 1815–53' (London PhD thesis, 1967).

Mahnken, Thomas C., *Uncovering Ways of War: U.S. Intelligence and Foreign Military Innovation, 1918–1941* (Ithaca, NY, 2002).

—'US Grand Strategy, 1939–1945', in *CH2WW* I, 189–212.

Maier, Klaus A., 'German Strategy', in *G2WW* II, 181–96.

Maiolo, Joseph A., *The Royal Navy and Nazi Germany, 1933–39: A Study in Appeasement and the Origins of the Second World War* (London, 1998).

—*Cry Havoc: The Arms Race and the Second World War, 1931–1941* (London, 2010).

—' "I believe the Hun is cheating": British Admiralty Technical Intelligence and the German Navy, 1936–39', *I&NS* XI (1996), pp. 32–58.

—'The Admiralty and the Anglo-German Naval Agreement of 18 June 1935', *D&S* X (1999), pp. 87–126.

—'Deception and Intelligence Failure: Anglo-German Preparation for U-Boat Warfare in the 1930s', *JSS* XXII, no. 4 (1999), pp. 55–76.

—'The Knockout Blow against the Import System: Admiralty Expectations of Nazi Germany's Naval Strategy, 1934–9', *HR* LXXII (1999), pp. 202–28.

—'Did the Royal Navy Decline between the Two World Wars?', *JRUSI* CLIX (2014), pp. 18–24.

Magnozzi, Michele, ' "One Torpedo, One Ship": An Appraisal of Otto Kretschmer's U-Boat Tactics, 1939–1941', *MM* CVII (2021), pp. 202–15.

Mallett, Robert, *The Italian Navy and Fascist Expansionism 1935–1940* (London, 1998).

Mandler, Peter, *Aristocratic Government in the Age of Reform: Whigs and Liberals, 1830–1852* (Oxford, 1990).

Manning, Frederic, *The Life of Sir William White* (London, 1923).

Marder, Arthur J., *British Naval Policy, 1880–1905* (London, 1940).

—*Portrait of an Admiral: The Life and Papers of Sir Herbert Richmond* (London, 1952)

—ed., *Fear God and Dread Nought: The Correspondence of Admiral of the Fleet Lord Fisher of Kilverstone* (London, 1952–9, 3 vols.).

—*From the Dreadnought to Scapa Flow: The Royal Navy in the Fisher Era, 1904–19* (London, 1961–70, 5 vols. [with a second edition of vol. 3, Oxford 1978]). Once standard works, now largely superseded.

—'The Royal Navy and the Ethiopian Crisis of 1935–36', *AHR* LXXV (1970), pp. 1327–56; but I have cited the revised version in Marder, *From the Dardanelles to Oran: Studies of the Royal Navy in War and Peace 1915–1940* (London, 1974), pp. 64–104.

—'Oran, 3 July 1940: Mistaken Judgement, Tragic Misunderstanding, or Cruel Necessity?', in Marder, *From the Dardanelles to Oran*, pp. 179–288.

—(completed by Mark Jacobsen and John Horsfield) *Old Friends, New Enemies: The Royal Navy and the Imperial Japanese Navy* (Oxford, 1981–90, 2 vols.).

Marolda, Edward J., ed., *FDR and the U.S. Navy* (New York, 1998).

Marriott, Leo, *Treaty Cruisers: The First International Warship Building Competition* (London, 2005).

Marsden, Arthur, 'The Blockade', in Hinsley, *British Foreign Policy under Sir Edward Grey*, pp. 488–515.

Marshall, Adrian G., *'Nemesis': The First Iron Warship and her World* (Singapore, 2016).

Martens, Rolf, 'Operation "Chariot": Die Abwehr eines Kommandounternehmens auf St. Nazaire am 27 und 28 März 1942', in *Führungsprobleme der Marine im Zweiten Weltkrieg*, ed. Heinrich Schuur, Rolf Martens and Wolfgang Koehler (Freiburg im Breisgau, 1973), pp. 55–93.

Martin, Christopher, 'The 1907 Naval War Plans and the Second Hague Peace Conference: A Case of Propaganda', *JSS* XXVIII (2005), pp. 833–56.

—'The Declaration of London: A Matter of Operational Capability', *HR* LXXXII (2009), pp. 731–55.

Mason, Ursula Stuart, *Britannia's Daughters: The Story of the WRNS* (London, 2nd edn., 1992). [The first edition had a different title: *The Wrens, 1917–77* (Reading, 1977).]

Masson, Philippe, *Histoire de la Marine* (Paris, 2nd edn., 1992, 2 vols.). Erratic but knowledgeable and entertaining.

Masterson, Daniel M., ed., *Naval History: The Sixth Symposium of the U.S. Naval Academy* (Wilmington, Del., 1987).

Mathews, Dame Vera Laughton, *Blue Tapestry* (London, 1948). Memoir of the head of the WRNS in the Second World War.

Matsumoto, Miwao, *Technology Gatekeepers for War and Peace: The British Ship Revolution and Japanese Industrialization* (Basingstoke, 2006).

Mattesini, Francesco, *Il giallo di Matapan: Revisione di giudizi* (Rome, 1985, 2 pts.).

—*La battaglia aeronavale di mezzo agosto* (Rome, 1986). Excellent detailed operational studies, much superior to the Italian official histories.

Matzke, Rebecca Berens, *Deterrence through Strength: British Naval Power and Foreign Policy under Pax Britannica* (Lincoln, Nb., 2011).

Maurer, John H., 'The London Conference: A Strategic Reassessment', in *At the Crossroads between Peace and War: Naval Rivalries and Arms Control between the World Wars; The London Conference of 1930*, ed. Maurer and Christopher M. Bell (Annapolis, Md., 2014), pp. 229–55.

—'Averting the Great War? Churchill's Naval Holiday', *NWCR* LXVII, no. 3 (2014), pp. 25–42.

—'David Lloyd George and the Contest for Naval Mastery: The American Challenge', in *Navies in Multipolar Worlds: From the Age of Sail to the Present*, ed. Paul Kennedy and Evan Wilson (London, 2021), pp. 82–100.

Mawdsley, Evan, *The War for the Seas: A Maritime History of World War II* (New Haven, Conn., 2019).

May, Ernest R. and Gregory F. Treverton, 'Defence Relationships: American Perspectives', in Louis and Bull, *The 'Special Relationship'*, pp. 161–82.

May, W. E., *A History of Marine Navigation* (Henley on Thames, 1973).

Mbaeyi, Paul Mmegha, *British Military and Naval Forces in West African History, 1807–1874* (New York and London, 1978).

McBride, William M., *Technological Change and the United States Navy, 1865–1945* (Baltimore, Md., 2000).

—'Strategic Determinism in Technology Selection: The Electric Battleship and U.S. Naval-Industrial Relations', *T&C* XXXIII (1992), pp. 248–77.

McCartney, Innes, 'The Archaeology of First World War U-Boat Losses in the English Channel and its Impact on the Historical Record', *MM* CV (2019), pp. 183–201.

McCord, Norman, 'Cobden and Bright in Politics, 1846–1857', in *Ideas and Institutions of Victorian Britain*, ed. Robert Robson (London, 1967), pp. 87–114.

McCoy, James, 'From Selborne to AFO 1/56', in Hore, *Dreadnought to Daring*, pp. 254–83.

McDonald, J. Kenneth, 'The Washington Conference and the Naval Balance of Power', in *Maritime Strategy and the Balance of Power: Britain and America in the Twentieth Century*, ed. John B. Hattendorf and Robert S. Jordan (Basingstoke, 1989), pp. 189–213.

McKay, C. G. and Bengt Beckman, *Swedish Signal Intelligence, 1900–1945* (London, 2003).

McKee, Christopher, *Sober Men and True: Sailor Lives in the Royal Navy 1900–1945* (Cambridge, Mass., 2002).

McKercher, B. J. C., ed., *Arms Limitation and Disarmament: Restraints on War, 1899–1939* (Westport, Conn., 1992).

—'Belligerent Rights in 1927–1929: Foreign Policy versus Naval Policy in the Second Baldwin Government', *HJ* XXIX (1986), pp. 963–74.

—' "Our Most Dangerous Enemy": Great Britain Pre-Eminent in the 1930s', *IHR* XIII (1991), pp. 751–83.

—'From Disarmament to Rearmament: British Civil-Military Relations and Policy-Making, 1933–1934', *Defence Studies* I (2001), pp. 21–48.

—'The Limitations of the Politician-Strategist: Winston Churchill and the German Threat, 1933–39', in *Churchill and Strategic Dilemmas before the World Wars: Essays in Honor of Michael I. Handel*, ed. McKercher (London, 2003), pp. 51–87.

McKercher, B. J. C. and Keith Neilson, ' "The Triumph of Unarmed Force": Sweden and the Allied Blockade of Germany 1914–17', *JSS* VII (1984), pp. 178–99.

McLachlan, Donald, *Room 39: Naval Intelligence in Action 1939–45* (London, 1968).

McLaughlin, Stephen, 'Battlelines and Fast Wings: Battlefleet Tactics in the Royal Navy, 1900–1914', *JSS* XXXVIII (2015), pp. 985–1005.

McLean, David, *Surgeons of the Fleet: The Royal Navy and its Medics from Trafalgar to Jutland* (London, 2010).

—'Trade, Politics and the Navy in Latin America: The British in the Paraná, 1845–46', *JICH* XXXV (2007), pp. 351–70.

McLean, Douglas M., 'Confronting Technological and Tactical Change: Allied Antisubmarine Warfare in the Last Year of the Battle of the Atlantic', *NWCR* XLVII, no. 1 (1994), pp. 87–104.

McShane, Gregor, *From Archangel to New Zealand: The Diaries of Robert Henry Harding* (Hamilton, NZ, 1985).

Meilinger, Phillip S., 'Between the Devil and the Deep Blue Sea: The Fleet Air Arm before the Second World War', *JRUSI* CXLIV (1999), pp. 73–8.

Melancon, G., *Britain's China Policy and the Opium Crisis: Balancing Drugs, Violence and National Honour, 1833–1840* (Aldershot, 2003).

Mends, Bowen Stilon, *Life of Admiral Sir William Robert Mends* (London, 1899).

Merli, Frank J., 'The American Way with Blockades: Reflections on the Union Blockade of the South', in Sweetman et al., *Tenth Naval History Symposium*, pp. 44–64.

Messerschmidt, Manfred, 'German Military Effectiveness between 1919 and 1939', in Millett and Murray, *Military Effectiveness* II, 218–55.

—'Foreign Policy and Preparation for War', in *G2WW* I, 541–717.

Messimer, Dwight R., *Find and Destroy: Antisubmarine Warfare in World War I* (Annapolis, Md., 2001).

Middlemas, Keith and John Barnes, *Baldwin: A Biography* (London, 1969).

Miller, Amy, *Dressed to Kill: British Naval Uniform, Masculinity and Contemporary Fashions, 1748–1857* (National Maritime Museum, 2007).

Miller, Christopher W., *Planning and Profits: British Naval Armaments Manufacture and the Military Industrial Complex, 1918–1941* (Liverpool, 2018).

—'The Clydeside Cabal: The Influence of Lord Weir, Sir James Lithgow, and Sir Andrew Rae Duncan on Naval and Defence Policy, around 1918–1940', *MM* CVII (2021), pp. 338–57.

Miller, Graeme A., ' "From Jack Tar to Bluejacket": Impressment, Manning and the Development of Continuous Service in the Royal Navy, 1815–1853' (London PhD thesis, 2012).

Miller, Jerry, *Nuclear Weapons and Aircraft Carriers: How the Bomb Saved Naval Aviation* (Washington, DC, 2001).

Millett, Alan R. and Williamson Murray, eds., *Military Effectiveness* (London, 1988, 3 vols.).

Milner, Marc, *Battle of the Atlantic* (Stroud, 2003).

—'Anglo-American Naval Co-operation in the Second World War, 1939–45', in *Maritime Strategy and the Balance of Power: Britain and America in the Twentieth Century*, ed. John B. Hattendorf and Robert S. Jordan (Basingstoke, 1989), pp. 243–68.

Mitcham, John C., 'Patrolling the White Man's Grave: The Impact of Disease on Anglo-American Naval Operations against the Slave Trade, 1841–1862', *NM* XX (2010), pp. 37–56.

Mitchell, Leslie, *The Whig World, 1760–1837* (London, 2005).

Mokyr, Joel, 'The Industrial Revolution and the New Economic History', in *The Economics of the Industrial Revolution*, ed. Mokyr (London, 1985), pp. 1–51.

Monaque, Rémi, *Une histoire de la marine de guerre française* (Paris, 2016).

—'L'amiral Aube, ses idées, son action', in *L'évolution de la pensée navale* IV, ed. Hervé Coutau-Bégarie (Paris, 1994), pp. 133–43.

Monger, George, *The End of Isolation: British Foreign Policy 1900–1907* (London, 1963).

—'The End of Isolation: Britain, Germany and Japan, 1900–1902', *TRHS* 5th S. XIII (1963), pp. 103–21.

Monod, Paul Kléber, *Imperial Island: A History of Britain and its Empire, 1660–1837* (Oxford, 2009).

Monsarrat, Nicholas, *H.M. Frigate* (London, 1946). Autobiographical novel by a noted escort officer and post-war author.

Moore, Patrick A., *The Greenie: The History of Warfare Technology in the Royal Navy* (Stroud, 2011).

Moretz, Joseph, *The Royal Navy and the Capital Ship in the Interwar Period* (London, 2002).

—*Thinking Wisely, Planning Boldly: The Higher Education and Training of Royal Navy Officers, 1919–1939* (Solihull, 2014).

—*Towards a Wider War: British Strategic Decision-Making and Military Effectiveness in Scandinavia, 1939–40* (Solihull, 2017).

—'The Legacy of Jutland: Expectation, Reality and Learning from the Experience of Battle in the Royal Navy, 1913–1939', in Greg Kennedy, *Britain's War at Sea*, pp. 149–64.

Morgan-Owen, David G., *The Fear of Invasion: Strategy, Politics and British War Planning, 1880–1914* (Oxford, 2017).

—'The Invasion Question: Admiralty Plans to Defend the British Isles, 1888–1918' (Exeter PhD thesis, 2013).

—' "History is a Record of Exploded Ideas": Sir John Fisher and Home Defence, 1904–10', *IHR* XXXVI (2014), pp. 550–72.

—'Cooked Up in the Dinner Hour? Sir Arthur Wilson's War Plan, Reconsidered', *EHR* CXXX (2015), pp. 865–906.

—'An "Intermediate" Blockade? British North Sea Strategy, 1912–1914', *WiH* XXII (2015), pp. 478–502.

Morison, Samuel Eliot, *History of United States Naval Operations in World War II* (Boston, Mass., 1947–62, 15 vols.).

Morriss, Roger, *Cockburn and the British Navy in Transition: Admiral Sir George Cockburn 1772–1853* (Exeter, 1997).

—*Naval Power and British Culture, 1760–1850: Public Trust and Government Ideology* (Aldershot, 2004).

—'Military Men Fall Out: Wellington, Cockburn and the Last Lord High Admiral, 1827–8', in *Wellington Studies* III, ed. C. M. Woolgar (Southampton, 1999), pp. 116–35.

Moss, Michael and Iain Russell, *Range and Vision: The First Hundred Years of Barr & Stroud* (Edinburgh, 1988).

Motte, Martin, *Une éducation géostratégique: La pensée navale française de la Jeune École à 1914* (Paris, 2004).

—'La Jeune École et la généalogie de la guerre totale', in *L'évolution de la pensée navale* VIII, ed. Hervé Coutau-Bégarie (Paris, 2007), pp. 131–82.

Müller, Rolf-Dieter, 'Albert Speer and Armaments Policy in Total War', in *G2WW* V 2, pp. 293–831.

Mulligan, Timothy, 'The German Navy Evaluates its Cryptographic Security, October 1941', *Military Affairs* XLIX (1985), pp. 75–79.

Mulligan, William, 'British Anti-Slave Trade and Anti-Slavery Policy in East Africa, Arabia, and Turkey in the Late Nineteenth Century', in *Humanitarian Intervention: A History*, ed. Brendan Simms and D. J. B. Trim (Cambridge, 2011), pp. 256–80.

Mullins, Robert E., *The Transformation of British and American Naval Policy in the Pre-Dreadnought Era: Ideas, Culture and Strategy*, ed. John Beeler (Cham, 2016).

—'New Ways of Thinking: The Intelligence Function and Strategic Calculations in the Admiralty, 1882–1889', *I&NS* XV (2000), No. 3, pp. 77–97.

—'Sharpening the Trident: The Decisions of 1889 and the Creation of Modern Seapower' (King's College London PhD thesis, 2000).

—'In the Shadow of Marder: A New Perspective of British Naval Administration and the Naval Defense Act of 1889', in Balano and Symonds, *Fourteenth Naval History Symposium*, pp. 44–81.

Munthe-Kaas, O. U., 'The Campaign in Norway in 1940 and the Norwegian and British War Direction Machineries', *RIHM* XLVII (1980), pp. 36–59.

Murfett, Malcolm, *Naval Warfare, 1919–1945: An Operational History of the Volatile War at Sea* (London, 2009).

—'Living in the Past: A Critical Re-Examination of the Singapore Naval Strategy, 1918–1941', *W&S* XI, no. 1 (1993), pp. 73–104.

Murray, Williamson, *Military Adaptation in War: With Fear of Change* (Cambridge, 2011).

—'Net Assessment in Nazi Germany in the 1930s', in Murray and Millett, *Calculations*, pp. 60–96.

Murray, Williamson and Alan R. Millett, eds., *Calculations: Net Assessment and the Coming of World War II* (New York, 1992).

—'Net Assessment on the Eve of World War II', in Murray and Millett, *Calculations*, pp. 1–18.

Napier, Elers, *The Life and Correspondence of Admiral Sir Charles Napier* (London, 1862, 2 vols.).

Nash, Peter V., *The Development of Mobile Logistics Support in Anglo-American Naval Policy, 1900–1953* (Gainesville, Fl., 2009).

Neilson, Keith, ' "Greatly Exaggerated": The Myth of the Decline of Great Britain before 1914', *IHR* XIII (1991), pp. 695–725.

—' "The British Empire Floats on the British Navy": British Naval Policy, Belligerent Rights, and Disarmament, 1902–1909', in McKercher, *Arms Limitation and Disarmament*, pp. 21–41.

—' "For Diplomatic, Economic, Strategic and Telegraphic Reasons": British Imperial Defence, the Middle East and India, 1914–1918', in Kennedy and Neilson, *Far-Flung Lines*, pp. 103–23.

—' "Control the Whirlwind": Sir Edward Grey as Foreign Secretary, 1906–16', in Otte, *The Makers of British Foreign Policy*, pp. 128–49.

—'The Defence Requirements Sub-Committee, British Strategic Foreign Policy, Neville Chamberlain, and the Path to Appeasement', *EHR* CXVIII (2003), pp. 651–84.

—'The Anglo-Japanese Alliance and British Strategic Foreign Policy, 1902–1914', in O'Brien, *The Anglo-Japanese Alliance, 1902–1922*, pp. 48–63.

—' "Unbroken Thread": Japan, Maritime Power and British Imperial Defence, 1920–32', in Greg Kennedy, *British Naval Strategy East of Suez 1900–2000*, pp. 62–89.

Neilson, Keith and Elizabeth Jane Errington, eds., *Navies and Global Defense: Theories and Strategy* (Kingston, Ont., 1995).

Neilson, Keith, and Greg Kennedy, eds., *The British Way in Warfare: Power and the International System, 1856–1956. Essays in Honour of David French* (Farnham, 2010).

Neitzel, Sönke, 'The Deployment of the U-Boats', in Howarth and Law, *The Battle of the Atlantic*, pp. 276–301.

Niestlé, Axel, 'German Technical and Electronic Development', in Howarth and Law, *The Battle of the Atlantic*, pp. 430–51.

Noble, Sir Andrew, 'The Rise and Progress of Rifled Naval Artillery', *TINA* XLI (1899), pp. 235–57.

Noble, Samuel, *Sam Noble, A.B.: 'Tween Decks in the 'Seventies* (London, [1925]). Evocative memoir of a South Atlantic commission, beautifully written.

Nofi, A. A., *To Train the Fleet for War: The U.S. Navy Fleet Problems, 1923–1940* (Newport, RI, 2010).

[Norman, F. M.] 'Martello Tower', *At School and at Sea: or Life and Character at Harrow, in the Royal Navy and in the Trenches before Sebastopol* (London, 1899).

O'Brien, Phillips Payson, *British and American Naval Power: Politics and Policy, 1900–1936* (London, 1998).

—ed., *Technology and Naval Combat in the Twentieth Century and Beyond* (London, 2001).

—ed. *The Anglo-Japanese Alliance, 1902–1922* (London, 2004).

—*How the War was Won: Air Power and Allied Victory in World War II* (Cambridge, 2015).

—'Politics, Arms Control and US Naval Development in the Interwar Period', in O'Brien, *Technology and Naval Combat*, pp. 148–61.

—'The Titan Refreshed: Imperial Overstretch and the British Navy before the First World War', *P&P* 172 (2001), pp. 146–69.

O'Connell, D. P., *The Influence of Law upon Sea Power* (Manchester, 1975).

O'Connell, Robert L., *Sacred Vessels: The Cult of the Battleship and the Rise of the U.S. Navy* (Boulder, Col., 1991).

Oels, Hans Joachim, 'Der Einsatz des Schlachtschiffe *Bismarck* unter dem Blickwinkel der Operations- und Schiffsführung', in *Der Marineoffizier als Führer im Gefecht*, ed. Heinrich Walle (Hamburg, 1984), pp. 104–35.

Offer, Avner, *The First World War: An Agrarian Interpretation* (Oxford, 1989).

—'Morality and Admiralty: "Jacky" Fisher, Economic Warfare and the Laws of War', *JCH* XXIII (1988), pp. 99–118.

—'Bounded Rationality in Action: The German Submarine Campaign, 1915–18', in *The Economics of Rationality*, ed. Bill Gerrard (London, 1993), pp. 179–202.

—'Costs and Benefits', in *OHBE* III, 690–711.

—'The Blockade of Germany and the Strategy of Starvation, 1914–1918: An Agency Perspective', in Chickering and Förster, *Great War, Total War*, pp. 169–88.

O'Halpin, Eunan, *Head of the Civil Service. A Study of Sir Warren Fisher* (London, 1989).

O'Hara, Vincent P., *Torch: North Africa and the Allied Path to Victory* (Annapolis, Md., 2015).

—*Six Victories: North Africa, Malta, and the Mediterranean Convoy War, November 1941–March 1942* (Annapolis, Md., 2019).

O'Hara, Vincent P. and Enrico Cernuschi, 'Frogmen against a Fleet: The Italian Attack on Alexandria 18/19 December 1941', *NWCR* LXVIII, no. 3 (2015), pp. 119–37.

O'Hara, Vincent P. and Leonard R. Heinz, *Clash of Fleets: Naval Battles of the Great War, 1914–18* (Annapolis, Md., 2017).

Oldfield, John, 'After Emancipation: Slavery, Freedom and the Victorian Empire', in *The Victorian Empire and Britain's Maritime World, 1837–1901: The Sea and Global History*, ed. Miles Taylor (Basingstoke, 2013), pp. 49–63.

Olson, Mancur, *The Economics of the Wartime Shortage: A History of British Food Supplies in the Napoleonic Wars and in World Wars I and II* (Durham, NC, 1963).

Omissi, David, 'The Mediterranean and the Middle East in British Global Strategy', in *Britain and the Middle East in the 1930s: Security Problems, 1935–1939*, ed. Michael J. Cohen and Martin Kolinsky (Basingstoke, 1992), pp. 3–20.

Ong Chit Chung, *Operation Matador: Britain's War Plans against the Japanese 1918–1941* (Singapore, 1997).

Oram, Vice-Admiral Sir Henry, 'Fifty Years' Changes in British Warship Machinery', *TINA* LIII (1911), pp. 66–120.

O'Rourke, Kevin and Jeffrey Williamson, *Globalization and History: The Evolution of a Nineteenth-Century Atlantic Economy* (Cambridge, Mass., 1999).

Ørvik, Nils, *The Decline of Neutrality 1914–1941: With special Reference to the United States and the Northern Neutrals* (London, 2nd edn., 1971).

Otte, T. G., '"It's What Made Britain Great": Reflections on British Foreign Policy, from Malplaquet to Maastricht', in Otte, *The Makers of British Foreign Policy: From Pitt to Thatcher* (Basingstoke, 2002), pp. 1–34.

— '"Floating Downstream"?: Lord Salisbury and British Foreign Policy, 1878–1902', *ibid.*, pp. 98–127.

— '"Allah is great and the NOT is his prophet": Sea Power, Diplomacy and Economic Warfare. The Case of the Netherlands, 1900–1918', in Greg Kennedy, *Britain's War at Sea*, pp. 38–69.

Ottmer, Hans-Martin, *'Weserübung'. Der deutsche Angriff auf Dänemark und Norwegen im April 1940* (Munich, 1994).

Otway, Sir Arthur, ed., *Autobiography and Journals of Admiral Lord Clarence E. Paget* (London, 1896).

Overy, Richard, *Why the Allies Won* (London, 1995; 2nd edn., 2006).

— 'Allied Bombing and the Destruction of German Cities', in *A World at Total War: Global Conflict and the Politics of Destruction*, ed. Chickering, Förster and Greiner (Cambridge, 2005), pp. 277–95.

Owen, Charles, *No More Heroes: The Royal Navy in the Twentieth Century: Anatomy of a Legend* (London, 1975).

— *Plain Yarns from the Fleet: The Spirit of the Royal Navy during its Twentieth-Century Heyday* (Stroud, 1997).

Owen, J. R., 'The Post Office Packet Service, 1821–37: Development of a Steam-Powered Fleet', *MM* LXXXVIII (2002), pp. 155–75.

Paine, S .C. M., *The Wars for Asia, 1911–1949* (Cambridge, 2012).

— *The Japanese Empire: Grand Strategy from the Meiji Restoration to the Pacific War* (Cambridge, 2017). Essential works based on extensive reading in Chinese and Japanese sources.

—'The Allied Embargo of Japan, 1939–1941: From Rollback to Deterrence to Boomerang', in *Navies and Soft Power: Historical Case Studies of Naval Power and the Non-Use of Military Force*, ed. Bruce A. Elleman and Paine (Newport, RI, 2015), pp. 69–89.

Palmer, Sarah, *Politics, Shipping and the Repeal of the Navigation Laws* (Manchester, 1990).

Panzac, Daniel, *Les corsaires barbaresques: La fin d'une épopée 1800–1820* (Paris, 1999).

—*La marine ottomane: De l'apogée à la chute de l'Empire (1572–1923)* (Paris, 2009).

Parker, C. S., *The Life and Letters of Sir James Graham* (London, 1907, 2 vols.).

Parkin, Simon, *A Game of Birds and Wolves: The Secret Game that Won the War* (London, 2019).

Parkinson, Roger, *The Late Victorian Navy: The Pre-Dreadnought Era and the Origins of the First World War* (Woodbridge, 2008).

—'The Origins of the Naval Defence Act of 1889 and the New Navalism of the 1890s' (Exeter PhD thesis, 2006).

Parry, Ann, *Parry of the Arctic: The Life Story of Admiral Sir Edward Parry 1790–1855* (London, 1963).

Parshall, Jonathan B., 'What *WAS* Nimitz Thinking?', *NWCR* LXXV, no. 2 (2022), pp. 92–122.

Partridge, M. S., *Military Planning for the Defense of the United Kingdom, 1814–1870* (New York, 1989).

—*The Royal Naval College Osborne: A History 1903–21* (Stroud, 1999).

—'The Russell Cabinet and National Defence, 1846–1852', *History* LXXII (1987), pp. 231–50.

—'The Royal Navy and the End of Close Blockade, 1885–1905: A Revolution in Naval Strategy?', *MM* LXXV (1989), pp. 119–36.

Patalano, Alessio, 'Feigning Grand Strategy: Japan, 1927–1945', in *CH2WW* I, 159–88.

Patrick, A. M., 'Naval Radar Fitting Policy, Matériel Procurement, Installation, Sea Trials and Shore-Based Maintenance 1939–45', in *The Applications of Radar and Other Electronic Systems in the Royal Navy in World War 2*, ed. F. A. Kingsley (Basingstoke, 1995).

Patterson, A. Temple, ed., *The Jellicoe Papers* (NRS Vols. 108 and 111, 1966–8).

Payton, Philip and Derek Oakley, 'Naval Education and Training in Devon', in *The New Maritime History of Devon*, ed. Michael Duffy, Stephen Fisher, Basil Greenhill, David J. Starkey and Joyce Youings (Exeter, 1992–4), II, 191–203.

Peattie, Mark R., *Sunburst: The Rise of Japanese Naval Air Power, 1909–1941* (London, 2002).

Peden, G. C., *British Rearmament and the Treasury, 1932–1939* (Edinburgh, 1979).

—*The Treasury and British Public Policy 1906–1959* (Oxford, 2000).

—*Arms, Economics and British Strategy: From Dreadnoughts to Hydrogen Bombs* (Cambridge, 2007).

—'From Cheap Government to Efficient Government: The Political Economy of Public Expenditure in the United Kingdom, 1832–1914', in *The Political Economy of British Historical Experience, 1688–1914*, ed. Donald Winch and P. K. O'Brien (Oxford, 2002), pp. 351–78.

—'The Royal Navy and Grand Strategy, 1937–1941', in *Strategy and the Sea: Essays in Honour of John B. Hattendorf*, ed. N. A. M. Rodger, J. Ross Dancy, Benjamin Darnell and Evan Wilson (Woodbridge, 2016), pp. 148–58.

Peebles, Hugh B., *Warshipbuilding on the Clyde: Naval Orders and the Prosperity of the Clyde Shipbuilding Industry, 1889–1939* (Edinburgh, 1987).

Pelz, Stephen E., *Race to Pearl Harbor: The Failure of the Second London Naval Conference and the Onset of World War II* (Cambridge, Mass., 1974).

Penn, Geoffrey, *'Up Funnel, Down Screw!' The Story of the Naval Engineer* (London, 1955).

—*Snotty: The Story of the Midshipman* (London, 1957).

—*HMS Thunderer: The Story of the Royal Naval Engineering College Keyham and Manadon* (Havant, 1974).

Perkins, Bradford, 'Unequal Partners: The Truman Administration and Great Britain', in Louis and Bull, *The 'Special Relationship'*, pp. 43–64.

Philbin, Tobias R., *Admiral von Hipper: The Inconvenient Hero* (Amsterdam, 1982).

Phillimore, Augustus, *The Life of Admiral of the Fleet Sir William Parker* . . . (London, 1876–80, 3 vols.), prints much valuable correspondence.

Philpott, Maryam, *Air and Sea Power in World War I: Combat and Experience in the Royal Flying Corps and the Royal Navy* (London, 2013).

Pocock, R. F. and G. R. M. Garratt, *The Origins of Maritime Radio: The Story of the Royal Navy between 1896 and 1900* (Science Museum, 1972).

Porter, A. N., 'Lord Salisbury, Foreign Policy and Domestic Finance, 1860–1900', in *Salisbury: The Man and his Policies*, ed. Robert Blake and Hugh Cecil (Basingstoke, 1987), pp. 148–84.

Posen, B. R., *The Sources of Military Doctrine: France, Britain and Germany between the World Wars* (London, 1984).

Postan, M. M., *British War Production* (London, 1952).

Postan, M. M., D. Hay and J. D. Scott, *Design and Development of Weapons* (London, 1964).

Powers, Barry D., *Strategy without Slide-Rule: British Air Strategy, 1914–1939* (London, 1976).

Preston, Anthony and John Major, *Send a Gunboat: A Study of the Gunboat and its Role in British policy, 1854–1904* (London, 1967).

Preston, Virginia, 'Constructing Communities: Living and Working in the Royal Navy, c.1830–1860' (Greenwich University PhD thesis, 2009).

Price, Alfred, *Aircraft versus Submarine in Two World Wars* (Barnsley, 3rd edn., 2004). A useful work, but the first and second editions (1973 and 1980) have only sketchy references and the third none at all.

Prince, Stephen, 'Air Power and Evacuations: Crete 1941', in Speller, *The Royal Navy and Maritime Power*, pp. 67–87.

Prysor, Glyn, *Citizen Sailors: The Royal Navy in the Second World War* (London, 2011).

—'Morale at Sea: Personnel Policy and Operational Experience in the British Navy, 1939–45' (Oxford DPhil thesis, 2008).

Pugh, Hugh, 'Oil and Water: A Comparison of Military and Naval Aviation Doctrine in Britain, 1912–1914', in Lo Cicero, Mahony and Mitchell, *A Military Transformed*, pp. 124–38.

Pugh, Philip, 'Military Need and Civil Necessity', in Howarth and Law, *The Battle of the Atlantic*, pp. 30–44.

—'Managing the Aerial Threat: Provisions for Anti-Aircraft Warfare during the 1930s', in Harding, *The Royal Navy, 1930–2000*', pp. 19–41.

Pulsipher, Lewis E., 'Aircraft and the Royal Navy, 1908–18' (Duke University PhD thesis, 1981).

Pursey, Harry, 'Invergordon: First Hand – Last Word?', *NR* LXIV (1976), pp. 157–64.

Quinlan, Robert J., 'The United States Fleet: Diplomacy, Strategy and the Allocation of Ships (1940–1941)', in *American Civil-Military Decisions: A Book of Case Studies*, ed. Harold Stein (Birmingham, Al., 1963), pp. 153–201.

Quinn, Paul, 'The Mexican Frigate *Guadalupe*', *MM* XCVI (2010), pp. 323–9.

Rahn, Werner, ed., *Die Deutsche Flotte im Spannungsfeld der Politik 1848–1985* (Hamburg, 1985).

—'Einsatzbereitschaft und Kampfkraft deutscher U-Boote 1942. Eine Dokumentation zu den materiallen Voraussetzungen und Problemen des U-Boot-Krieges nach dem Kriegseintritt der USA', *MGM* XLVII (1990), pp. 73–132.

—'Strategische Probleme des deutschen Seekriegführung, 1914–1918', in *Der Erste Weltkrieg. Wirkung, Wahrnehmung, Analyse*, ed. Wolfgang Michalka (Munich, 1994), pp. 341–65.

—'Seestrategisches Denken in deutschen Marinen von 1848–1990', in *Seemacht und Seestrategie im 19. und 20. Jahrhundert*, ed. Jörg Duppler (Hamburg, 1999), pp. 53–79.

—'German Naval Strategy and Armament, 1919–39', in O'Brien, *Technology and Naval Combat*, pp. 109–27.

—'The War at Sea in the Atlantic and in the Arctic Ocean', in *G2WW* VI, 301–466.

—'Die Deutsche Seekriegführung 1943 bis 1945', in *DR2WK* X, 3–273.

—'Die Seeschlacht vor dem Skagerrak: Verlauf und Analyse aus deutscher Perspektive', in *Skagerrakschlacht: Vorgeschichte – Ereignis – Verarbeitung*, ed. Michael Epkenhans, Jörg Hillmann and Frank Nägler (Munich, 2009), pp. 139–286.

—'The Atlantic in the Strategic Perspective of Hitler and his Admirals, 1939–44', in Rodger, Dancy, Darnell and Wilson, *Strategy and the Sea*, pp. 159–68.

—'German Navies from 1848 to 2016: Their Development and Courses from Confrontation to Cooperation', *NWCR* LXX, no. 4 (2017), pp. 13–47.

Ramsey, Paul M., 'Professor Spenser Wilkinson, Admiral William Sims and the Teaching of Strategy and Sea Power at the University of Oxford and the United

States Naval War College, 1909–1927', in Rodger, Dancy, Darnell and Wilson, *Strategy and the Sea*, pp. 213–25.

Ranft, Bryan, ed., *Technical Change and British Naval Policy, 1860–1939* (London, 1977).

—ed., *The Beatty Papers: Selections from the Private and Official Correspondence of Admiral of the Fleet Earl Beatty* (NRS Vols. 128 and 132, 1989–93).

—'The Naval Defence of British Sea-Borne Trade, 1860–1905' (Oxford DPhil thesis, 1967).

—'The Protection of British Seaborne Trade and the Development of Systematic Planning for War, 1860–1906', in Ranft, *Technical Change and British Naval Policy*.

—'Parliamentary Debate, Economic Vulnerability, and British Naval Expansion, 1860–1905', in *War, Strategy and International Politics: Essays in Honour of Sir Michael Howard*, ed. Lawrence Freedman, Paul Hayes and Robert O'Neill (Oxford, 1992), pp. 75–93.

Raper, R. G., 'Main Machinery: How Do We Stand?', *Papers on Engineering Subjects* XXI (1946), pp. 66–76. [These Papers were the predecessor of the *Journal of Naval Engineering*.]

Rasor, Eugene L., *Reform in the Royal Navy: A Social History of the Lower Deck, 1850–1880* (Hamden, Conn., 1976).

Rath, Andrew C., *The Crimean War in Imperial Context, 1854–1856* (Basingstoke, 2015).

Reader, W. J., *Architect of Air Power: The Life of the First Viscount Weir of Eastwood, 1877–1959* (London, 1968).

Reardon, Jeff, 'Breaking the U.S. Navy's "Gun Club" Mentality in the South Pacific', *JMilH* LXXV (2011), pp. 533–64.

Redford, Duncan, ed., *Maritime History and Identity: The Sea and Culture in the Modern World* (London, 2014).

—'Naval Culture and the Fleet Submarine', in *Re-Inventing the Ship: Science, Technology and the Maritime World, 1800–1918*, ed. Don Leggett and Richard Dunn (Farnham, 2012), pp. 157–72.

Redgement, P. G., 'High-Frequency Direction Finding in the Royal Navy: Development of Anti-U-Boat Equipment, 1941–5', in *The Applications of Radar and Other Electronic Systems in the Royal Navy in World War 2*, ed. F. A. Kingsley (Basingstoke, 1995), pp. 229–66.

Reid, William, *'We're certainly not afraid of Zeiss': Barr and Stroud Binoculars and the Royal Navy* (Edinburgh: National Museums of Scotland, 2001).

Reidy, Michael S., *Tides of History: Ocean Science and Her Majesty's Navy* (Chicago, Il., 2008).

Reuter, Frank, *Funkmess: die Entwicklung und der Einsatz des RADAR-Verfahrens in Deutschland bis zum Ende des Zweiten Weltkrieges* (Opladen, 1971).

Reynolds, Clark G., *The Fast Carriers* (New York, 2nd edn., 1978).

—'William A. Moffett: Steward of the Air Revolution', in *Admirals of the New Steel Navy: Makers of the American Naval Tradition 1880–1930*, ed. James C. Bradford (Annapolis, Md., 1990), pp. 374–92.

—'Carl Vinson, Admiral John H. Towers, and the Creation of the Two-Ocean Navy', in Sweetman et al., *Tenth Naval History Symposium*, pp. 181–9.

Reynolds, David, *The Creation of the Anglo-American Alliance, 1937–1941: A Study in Competitive Co-operation* (London, 1981).

—*The Long Shadow: The Great War and the Twentieth Century* (London, 2013).

Rhys-Jones, Graham, 'The German System: A Staff Perspective', in Howarth and Law, *The Battle of the Atlantic*, pp. 138–57.

Riley, Patrick, *Memories of a Blue-Jacket, 1872–1918* (London, [1927]).

Rippon, P. M., *Evolution of Engineering in the Royal Navy* (Tunbridge Wells, 1988, and London, 1994, 2 vols.).

Riste, Olav, 'War Comes to Norway', in *Norway and the Second World War*, ed. Johannes Andenæs, Olav Riste and Magne Skodvin (Oslo, 1966), pp. 9–53.

Ritschl, Albrecht, 'The Pity of Peace: Germany's Economy at War, 1914–1918 and Beyond', in *The Economics of World War I*, ed. Stephen Broadberry and Mark Harrison (Cambridge, 2005), pp. 41–76.

Robb-Webb, Jon, *The British Pacific Fleet Experience and Legacy, 1944–1950* (Farnham, 2013).

—'Light Two Lanterns, the British are Coming by Sea': Royal Navy Participation in the Pacific 1944–1945', in Greg Kennedy, *British Naval Strategy East of Suez 1900–2000*, pp. 128–53.

—'Sea Control in Narrow Waters: The Battles of Taranto and Matapan', in Speller, *The Royal Navy and Maritime Power in the Twentieth Century*, pp. 33–49.

—'New Tricks for Old Sea Dogs: British Naval Aviation in the Pacific, 1944–45', in *British Naval Aviation: The First 100 Years*, ed. Tim Benbow (Farnham, 2011), pp. 99–124.

Roberts, Andrew, *Masters and Commanders: How Roosevelt, Churchill, Marshall and Alanbrooke Won the War in the West* (London, 2008).

—*Churchill: Walking with Destiny* (London, 2018).

Roberts, Hannah, *The WRNS in Wartime: The Women's Royal Naval Service 1917–1945* (London, 2018).

Roberts, John, *The Battleship Dreadnought* (London, 1992).

Roberts, William H., ' "The Name of Ericsson": Political Engineering in the Union Ironclad Program, 1861–1863', *JMilH* LXIII (1999), pp. 823–43.

Robertson, A. J., 'Lord Beaverbrook and the Supply of Aircraft, 1940–1941', in *Business, Banking and Urban History: Essays in Honour of S. G. Checkland*, ed. Anthony Slaven and Derek H. Aldcroft (Edinburgh, 1982), pp. 80–100.

Robertson, Paul L., 'Technical Education in the British Shipbuilding and Marine Engineering Industries, 1863–1914', *EcHR* XXVII (1974), pp. 222–35.

Robertson, Scot, *The Development of R.A.F. Strategic Bombing Doctrine 1919–1939* (London, 1995).

Robinson, Robb, *Fishermen, the Fishing Industry and the Great War at Sea: A Forgotten History?* (Liverpool, 2019; Research in Maritime History, no. 54).

Rockoff, Hugh, 'The United States: From Ploughshares to Swords', in *The Economics of World War II: Six Great Powers in International Comparison*, ed. Mark Harrison (Cambridge, 1998), pp. 81–121.

Rödel, Christian, *Krieger, Denker, Amateure: Alfred von Tirpitz und das Seekriegsbild vor dem Ersten Weltkrieg* (Stuttgart, 2003).

Rodger, N. A. M., ed., *The Naval Miscellany, Vol. V* (NRS Vol. 125, 1985).

—*The Wooden World: An Anatomy of the Georgian Navy* (London, 1986).

—*Naval Records for Genealogists* (Public Record Office, Richmond, Surrey, 2nd edn., 1988).

—*The Safeguard of the Sea: A Naval History of Great Britain, Vol. 1, 660–1649* (London, 1997).

—*The Command of the Ocean: A Naval History of Britain, Vol. 2, 1649–1815* (London, 2004).

—'The Design of the *Inconstant*', *MM* LXI (1975), pp. 9–22.

—'The Dark Ages of the Admiralty, 1869–1885; Pt. I, Business Methods, 1869–74', *MM* LXI (1975), pp. 331–44.

—'The Dark Ages of the Admiralty; Pt. II, Change and Decay, 1874–1880', *MM* LXII (1976), pp. 33–46.

—'The Dark Ages of the Admiralty; Pt. III, Peace, Retrenchment and Reform, 1880–1885', *MM* LXII (1976), pp. 121–8.

—'British Belted Cruisers', *MM* LXIV (1978), pp. 23–36.

—'The First Light Cruisers', *MM* LXV (1979), pp. 209–30.

—'British Naval Thought and Naval Policy, 1820–1890', in *New Aspects of Naval History*, ed. Craig L. Symonds (Annapolis, Md., 1981), pp. 140–52.

—'Officers, Gentlemen and their Education, 1793–1860', in Freeman, *Les Empires en guerre et paix, 1793–1860*, pp. 139–51.

—'Commissioned Officers' Careers in the Royal Navy, 1690–1815', *JMR* III (2001), pp. 85–129.

—'Deutsch-Englisch Flottenrivalität, 1860–1914', in *Skagerrakschlacht: Vorgeschichte – Ereignis – Verarbeitung*, ed. Michael Epkenhans, Jörg Hillmann and Frank Nägler (Munich, 2009, pp. 1–18. [Later translated as 'Anglo-German Naval Rivalry, 1860–1914', in *Jutland: World War I's Greatest Naval Battle*, ed. Epkenhans, Hillmann and Nägler (Lexington, Ky., 2015), pp. 25–62.]

—'The Early Career of Sir John Fisher', *Trafalgar Chronicle* 20 (2010), pp. 188–95.

—'The Culture of Naval War, ca 1860–1945', in Epkenhans and Huck, *Der Erste Weltkrieg zur See* (Berlin 2017), pp. 99–114.

Rodger, N. A. M., J. Ross Dancy, Benjamin Darnell and Evan Wilson, eds., *Strategy and the Sea: Essays in Honour of John B. Hattendorf* (Woodbridge, 2016).

Rogan, Eugene, *The Fall of the Ottomans: The Great War in the Middle East* (London, 2015).

Röhl, John C. G., *Wilhelm II: Into the Abyss of War and Exile* (Cambridge, 2014), trans. Sheila de Bellaigue and Roy Bridge; originally *Wilhelm II. Der Weg in den Abgrund 1900–1941* (Munich, 2008).

Rohwer, Jürgen, *The Critical Convoy Battles of March 1943: The Battle for HX.229/SC122*, trans. Derek Masters (London, 1977); originally *Geleitzugschlachten im März 1943; Führungsprobleme im Höhepunkt der Schlacht im Atlantik* (Stuttgart, 1975).

—'The Operational Use of "Ultra" in the Battle of the Atlantic', in *Intelligence and International Relations, 1900–1945*, ed. Christopher Andrew and Jeremy Noakes (Exeter, 1987), pp. 275–92.

Røksund, Arne, *The Jeune École: The Strategy of the Weak* (Leiden, 2007).

Romans, Elinor, 'Selection and Early Career Education of Executive Officers in the Royal Navy c.1902–1939' (Exeter PhD thesis, 2012).

—'Leadership Training for Midshipmen, c.1919–1939', in Doe and Harding, *Naval Leadership and Management*, pp. 172–91.

Ropp, Theodore, *The Development of a Modern Navy: French Naval Policy 1871–1904*, ed. Stephen S. Roberts (Annapolis, Md., 1987).

Rose, Alexander, 'Radar and Air Defence in the 1930s', *20th Century British History* IX (1998), pp. 219–45.

Roskill, S. W., *The War at Sea* (London, 1954–61, 3 vols. in 4). The Admiralty's Official History of the Second World War.

—'The Dismissal of Admiral Jellicoe', *JCH* I (1966), pp. 69–93.

—*Naval Policy between the Wars* (London, 1968–76, 2 vols.).

—ed., *Documents Relating to the Naval Air Service, Vol. I, 1908–1918* (NRS Vol. 113, 1969).

—*Hankey, Man of Secrets* (London, 1970–74, 3 vols.).

—*Churchill and the Admirals* (London, 1977).

—*Admiral of the Fleet Earl Beatty* (London, 1980).

Ross, Steven T., *American War Plans 1941–1945: The Test of Battle* (London, 1997).

—'French Net Assessments', in Murray and Millett, *Calculations*, pp. 136–74.

Rössler, Eberhard, *The U-Boat: The Evolution and Technical History of German Submarines*, trans. Harold Erenberg (London, 1981); originally *Geschichte des deutschen U-bootbaus* (Munich, 1975).

—'U-Boat Development and Building', in Howarth and Law, *Battle of the Atlantic*, pp. 118–37.

Rowbotham, W. B., ed., *The Naval Brigades in the Indian Mutiny, 1857–58* (NRS Vol. 87, 1947).

Rowe, Laura, 'At the Sign of the Foul Anchor: Discipline and Morale in the Royal Navy during the First World War' (King's College London PhD thesis, 2008). Since I read it this thesis has been published as *Morale and Discipline in the Royal Navy during the First World War* (Cambridge, 2018).

—'"Their Lordships Regret That . . .": Admiralty Perceptions of and Responses to Allegations of Lower Deck Disquiet', in *Finding Common Ground: New Directions in First World War Studies*, ed. Jennifer D. Keene and Michael S. Neiberg (Leiden, 2011), pp. 43–65.

Rubin, Alfred P., *The Law of Piracy* (Irvington-on-Hudson, 2nd edn., 1998).

Rüger, Jan, *The Great Naval Game: Britain and Germany in the Age of Empire* (Cambridge, 2007).

Russell, Bruce, *Prize Courts and U-Boats: International Law at Sea and Economic Warfare during the First World War* (Dordrecht, 2009).

Russell, Iain, 'Purely by Coincidence: The Rangefinders of Barr and Stroud at the Battle of Jutland, 1916', in *Studies in the History of Scientific Instruments*, ed. Christine Blondel et al. (London, 1989), pp. 283–90.

Rust, Eric C., *Naval Officers under Hitler: The Story of Crew 34* (New York, 1991).

Ryan, Maeve, 'The Price of Legitimacy in Humanitarian Intervention: Britain, the Right of Search, and the Abolition of the West African Slave Trade, 1807–1867', in *Humanitarian Intervention: A History*, ed. Brendan Simms and D. J. B. Trim (Cambridge, 2011), pp. 231–55.

Sainty, J. C., ed., *Office-Holders in Modern Britain IV: Admiralty Officials 1660–1870* (London, 1975).

Salewski, Michael, 'Menschenführung in der deutschen Kriegsmarine 1939–1945', in *Menschenführung in der Marine?* ed. (Herford, 1981).

—'Das maritime Dritte Reich: Ideologie und Wirklichkeit 1933–1945', in Rahn, *Die Deutsche Flotte im Spannungsfeld der Politik 1848–1985*, pp. 113–38.

—'Die militärische Bedeutung des Nord-Ostsee-Kanals', in Salewski, *Die Deutschen und die See: Studien zur deutschen Marinegeschichte des 19. und 20. Jahrhunderts II* (Stuttgart, 2002, 2 vols.), I, 96–118.

—'Die Wilhelminische Flottengesetze: Realität und Illusion', *idem*, I, 119–26.

Salmon, Patrick, *Scandinavia and the Great Powers 1890–1940* (Cambridge, 1997).

Sambrook, Stephen, 'The Optical Munitions Industry in Great Britain, 1888–1923' (Glasgow PhD thesis, 2005).

Samson, Jane, 'Imperial Benevolence: The Royal Navy and the South Pacific Labour Trade 1867–1872', *Great Circle XVIII* (1996), pp. 14–29.

—'An Empire of Science: The Voyage of HMS *Herald*, 1845–1851', in *Pacific Empires: Essays in Honour of Glyndwr Williams*, ed. Jane Samson and Alan Frost (Vancouver, 1999), pp. 69–85.

Sandler, Stanley, *The Emergence of the Modern Capital Ship* (Newark, Del., 1979).

Santarini, Marco, *Bismarck and Hood: The Battle of the Denmark Strait: A Technical Analysis for a New Perspective* (Stroud, 2013).

—'Gunfire Dispersion of Large Italian Naval Guns: The Strange Case of the 381/50 ANSALDO-OTO mod. 1934 Gun', *WI LVII* (2020), pp. 303–27.

Santoni, Alberto, *Il Vero Traditore: Il ruolo documentato di ULTRA nella guerra del Mediterraneo* (Milan, 1981).

—'I rapporti tra la Regia Aeronautica e la Regia Marina', in *Italo Balbo: aviazione e potere aereo: atti del Convegno internazionale nel centenario della nascita*, ed. Carlo Maria Santoro (Rome, 1998), pp. 331–40.

—'La politique navale du fascisme et les stratégies méditerranéennes dans les années trente', in *La Marine Italienne de l'unité à nos jours*, ed. Michel Ostenc (Paris, 2005), pp. 87–124.

Santoni, Alberto and Francesco Mattesini, *La partecipazione tedesca alla guerra aeronavale nel Mediterraneo (1940–45)* (Rome, 1980).

Sarantakes, Nicholas, 'One Last Crusade: The British Pacific Fleet and its Impact on the Anglo-American Alliance', *EHR* CXXI (2006), pp. 429–66.

Sarty, Roger, 'The Limits of Ultra: The Schnorkel U-Boat Offensive against North America, November 1944–January 1945', *I&NS* XII (1997), pp. 44–68.

Scaife, W. G., *From Galaxies to Turbines: Science, Technology and the Parsons Family* (Bristol, 2000).

Scammell, Claire M., 'The Royal Navy and the Strategic Origins of the Anglo-German Naval Agreement of 1935', *JSS* XX, no. 2 (1997), pp. 92–118.

Scheck, Raffael, 'Der Kampf des Tirpitz-Kreises für ein uneingeschränkten U-boot-Krieg im deutschen Kaiserreich 1916–1917', *MGM* LV (1996), pp. 69–91.

Scheer, Reinhard, *Germany's High Sea Fleet in the World War* (London, 1920); originally *Deutschlands Hochseeflotte im Weltkrieg, persönliche Erinnerungen* (Berlin, 1920).

Scheina, Robert L., *Latin America: A Naval History, 1810–1987* (Annapolis, Md., 1987).

Schleihauf, William, 'A Concentrated Effort: Royal Navy Gunnery Exercises at the End of the Great War', *WI* XXXV (1998), pp. 117–39.

Schoenfeld, Max, 'Winston Churchill as War Manager: The Battle of the Atlantic Committee, 1941', *Military Affairs* LII (1988), pp. 122–7.

Schreiber, Gerhard, *Revisionismus und Weltmachtstreben. Marineführung und deutsch-italienische Beziehungen 1919 bis 1944* (Stuttgart, 1978).

—'The Mediterranean in Hitler's Strategy in 1940: "Programme" and Military Planning', in *The German Military in the Age of Total War*, ed. Wilhelm Deist (Leamington Spa, 1985), pp. 240–81.

—'Political and Military Developments in the Mediterranean Area, 1939–1940', in *G2WW* III, 5–301.

—'Germany, Italy, and South-East Europe: From Political and Economic Hegemony to Military Aggression', in *G2WW* III, 303–448.

—'Politics and Warfare in 1941', in *G2WW* III, 557–640.

Schröder, Joachim, *Die U-Boote des Kaisers: die Geschichte des deutschen U-Boot-Krieges gegen Grossbritannien im Ersten Weltkrieg* (Lauf a.d. Pegnitz, 2000). The best single-volume history of the German U-boat campaigns of 1915–18.

Schurman, D. M., *The Education of a Navy* (London, 1965).

—*Imperial Defence, 1868–1887*, ed. John Beeler (London, 2000).

Schuur, Heinrich, 'Auftragserteilung und Auftragsdurchführung beim Unternehmen "Juno" vom 4 bis 10 Juni 1940', in *Führungsprobleme der Marine im Zweiten Weltkrieg*, ed. Heinrich Schuur, Rolf Martens and Wolfgang Koehler (Freiburg im Breisgau, 1973).

Scott, J. D. and Richard Hughes, *The Administration of War Production* (London, 1955).

Scrimgeour, Alexander, *The Complete Scrimgeour: From Dartmouth to Jutland 1913–16*, ed. Richard Hallam and Mark Benyon (London, 2016). Correspondence of a midshipman.

Searle, G. R., *The Quest for National Efficiency 1899–1914: A Study in British Politics and Political Thought, 1899–1914* (Oxford, 1971).

Sears, Jason, 'Discipline in the Royal Navy, 1913–1946', *W&S* IX, no. 2 (1991), pp. 39–60.

Self, Robert, *Neville Chamberlain: A Biography* (Aldershot, 2006).

—'Perception and Posture in Anglo-American Relations: The War Debt Controversy in the "Official Mind", 1919–1940', *IHR* XXIX (2007), pp. 282–312.

Seligmann, Matthew S., ed., *Naval Intelligence from Germany: The Reports of the British Naval Attachés in Berlin, 1906–1914* (NRS Vol. 152, 2007).

—*The Royal Navy and the German Threat 1901–1914: Admiralty Plans to Protect British Trade in a War against Germany* (Oxford, 2012).

—*Rum, Sodomy, Prayers, and the Lash Revisited: Winston Churchill and Social Reform in the Royal Navy, 1900–1915* (Oxford, 2018).

—'A Service Ready for Total War? The State of the Royal Navy in July 1914', *EHR* CXXXIII (2003), pp. 98–122.

—'New Weapons for New Targets: Sir John Fisher, the Threat from Germany, and the Building of H.M.S. *Dreadnought* and H.M.S. *Invincible*, 1902–1907', *IHR* XXX (2008), pp. 303–31.

—'Switching Horses: The Admiralty's Recognition of the Threat from Germany, 1900–1905', *IHR* XXX (2008), pp. 239–58.

—'Intelligence Information and the 1909 Naval Scare: The Secret Foundations of a Public Panic', *WiH* XVII (2010), pp. 37–59.

—'Britain's Great Security Mirage: The Royal Navy and the Franco-Russian Naval Threat, 1898–1906', *JSS* XXXV (2012), pp. 861–86.

—'The Evolution of a Warship Type: The Role and Function of the Battlecruiser in Admiralty Plans on the Eve of the First World War', in Rodger, Dancy, Darnell and Wilson, *Strategy and the Sea*, pp. 138–47.

—'Germany's Ocean Greyhounds and the Royal Navy's First Battle Cruisers: An Historiographical Problem', *D&S* XXVII (2016), pp. 162–82.

—'Failing to Prepare for the Great War? The Absence of Grand Strategy in British War Planning before 1914', *WiH* XXIV (2017), pp. 414–37.

Seligmann, Matthew S., Frank Nägler and Michael Epkenhans, eds., *The Naval Route to the Abyss: The Anglo-German Naval Race 1895–1914* (NRS Vol. 161, 2015).

Semmel, Bernard, *The Rise of Free Trade Imperialism: Classical Political Economy, the Empire of Free Trade, and Imperialism, 1750–1850* (Cambridge, 1970).

—*Liberalism and Naval Strategy: Ideology, Interest and Sea Power during the Pax Britannica* (London, 1981).

Senior, William, *Naval History in the Law Courts* (London, 1927).

Seymour, John, 'The Colonial Naval Defence Act 1865 and its Impact in Australia', *MM* CVII (2021), pp. 435–52.

Sharp, James A., *Memoirs of the Life and Services of Rear-Admiral Sir William Symonds* . . . (London, 1858).

Sidorowicz, Andre T., 'The British Government, the Hague Peace Conference of 1907, and the Armaments Question', in McKercher, *Arms Limitation and Disarmament*, pp. 1–19.

Simms, Brendan and Steven, McGregor, *The Silver Waterfall: How America Won the War in the Pacific at Midway* (New York, 2022).

Simpson, Michael, ed., *Anglo-American Naval Relations, 1917–1939* (NRS Vols. 130 and 155, 1991 and 2010).

— *The Somerville Papers* (NRS Vol. 134, 1995).

— *The Cunningham Papers* (NRS Vols. 140 and 150, 1999 and 2006).

— *A Life of Admiral of the Fleet Andrew Cunningham: A Twentieth-Century Naval Leader* (London, 2004).

— *Anglo-American-Canadian Naval Relations, 1943–45* (NRS Vol. 168, 2021).

— 'Wings over the Sea: The Interaction of Air and Sea Power in the Mediterranean, 1940–42', in *Naval Power in the Twentieth Century*, ed. N. A. M. Rodger (London, 1996), pp. 134–50.

Skelton, R. W., 'Progress in Marine Engineering', *Papers on Engineering Subjects* XI (1930), pp. 85–141.

Slaven, Anthony, *British Shipbuilding 1500–2010: A History* (Lancaster, 2013).

Smith, Adrian, *Mountbatten: Apprentice War Lord* (London, 2010).

— *The Man who Built the Swordfish: The Life of Sir Richard Fairey* (London, 2018).

Smith, Bradley F., *The Ultra-Magic Deals and the Most Secret Special Relationship, 1940–1946* (Novato, Ca., and Shrewsbury, 1993).

Smith, Crosbie, '*Dreadnought* Science: The Cultural Construction of Efficiency and Effectiveness', in Blyth, Rüger and Lambert, *The Dreadnought and the Edwardian Age*, pp. 135–64.

Smith, Kevin, 'Maritime Powers in Transition: Britain's Shipping Capacity Crisis and the Mobilization of Neutral American Power, 1940–41', in G. Kennedy, *The Merchant Marine in International Affairs*, pp. 155–75.

— ' "Immobilized by Reason of Repair" and by the Choice "Between Lithgow and Hitler": Class Conflict in Britain's Wartime Merchant Shipping Repair Yards', in Bell and Faulkner, *Decision in the Atlantic*, pp. 46–77.

Smith, Malcolm, *British Air Strategy between the Wars* (Oxford, 1984).

Smith, Michael, *The Emperor's Codes: Bletchley Park and the Breaking of Japan's Secret Ciphers* (London, 2000).

— 'The Government Code and Cypher School and the First World War', in Erskine and Smith, *Action this Day*, pp. 15–40.

Smith, Paul, 'Ruling the Waves: Government, the Service and the Cost of Naval Supremacy, 1885–99', in Paul Smith, ed., *Government and the Armed Forces in Britain 1856–1990* (London, 1996).

Smith, Richard A., 'Britain and the Strategy of the Economic Weapon in the War against Germany, 1914–19' (Newcastle PhD thesis, 2000).

Smith, Steven R. B., 'Public Opinion, the Navy and the City of London: The Drive for British Naval Expansion in the Late Nineteenth Century', *W&S* IX, no. 1 (1991), pp. 29–50.

Sondhaus, Lawrence, *The Great War at Sea: A Naval History of the First World War* (Cambridge, 2014).

—*German Submarine Warfare in World War I: The Onset of Total War at Sea* (Lanham, Md., 2017).

Spector, Ronald, *Eagle against the Sun: The American War with Japan* (New York, 1984).

—*At War at Sea: Sailors and Naval Combat in the Twentieth Century* (New York, 2001).

—'The Military Effectiveness of the U.S. Armed Forces, 1919–39', in Millett and Murray, *Military Effectiveness* II, 70–97.

Speller, Ian, ed., *The Royal Navy and Maritime Power in the Twentieth Century* (London, 2005).

—'Amphibious Operations, 1945–1998', in Harding, *The Royal Navy, 1930–2000*, pp. 213–45.

—'Limited War and Crisis Management: Naval Aviation in Action from the Korean War to the Falklands Conflict', in Benbow, *British Naval Aviation*, pp. 151–75.

Stafford, Robert A., 'Scientific Exploration and Empire', in *OHBE* III, 294–319.

Stanley, Jo, *A History of the Royal Navy: Women and the Royal Navy* (London, 2018).

Stegemann, Bernd, *Die Deutsche Marinepolitik 1916–1918* (Berlin, 1970).

—'Politics and Warfare in the First Phase of the German Offensive', in *G2WW* II, 3–29.

—'The First Phase of the War at Sea up to the Spring of 1940', in *G2WW* II, 151–78.

—'Operation Weserübung', in *G2WW* II, 206–19.

—'The Second Phase of the War at Sea (until the Spring of 1941)', in *G2WW* II, 341–60.

—'The Italo-German Conduct of the War in the Mediterranean and North Africa', in *G2WW* III, 641–754.

Steinberg, Jonathan, 'The Copenhagen Complex', *JCH* I, no. 3 (1966), pp. 23–46.

—'The Novelle of 1908: Necessities and Choices in the Anglo-German Naval Arms Race', *TRHS* 5th S. XXI (1971), pp. 25–44.

—'The German Background to Anglo-German Relations, 1905–1914', in Hinsley, *British Foreign Policy under Sir Edward Grey*, pp. 193–215.

Steiner, Zara, 'The Foreign Office and the War', in Hinsley, *British Foreign Policy under Sir Edward Grey*, pp. 516–31.

Steury, Donald P., 'Naval Intelligence, the Atlantic Campaign and the Sinking of the *Bismarck*: A Study in the Integration of Intelligence into the Conduct of Naval Warfare', *JCH* XXII (1987), pp. 209–33.

Stevenson, David, *Armaments and the Coming of War: Europe, 1904–1914* (Oxford, 1996).

Stoler, Mark A., 'The American Perception of British Mediterranean Strategy, 1941–45', in Symonds, *New Aspects of Naval History*, pp. 325–39.

Stone, I. R. and R. J. Crampton, ' "A Disastrous Affair"; The Franco-British Attack on Petropavlovsk, 1854', *Polar Record* XXII (1985), pp. 629–41. A full account from British, French and Russian sources.

Strachan, Hew, *The First World War. Vol. I: To Arms* (London, 2003).

—'Military Operations and National Policies, 1914–1918', in Afflerbach, *The Purpose of the Great War*, pp. 7–26.

Straczek, Jozef, 'The Empire is Listening: Naval Signals Intelligence in the Far East to 1942', *Journal of the Australian War Memorial* 35 (2001). [Read online in unpaginated form at www.awm.gov.au/journal/.]

Stumpf, Reinhard, 'The War in the Mediterranean Area 1942–1943: Operations in North Africa and the Central Mediterranean', in *G2WW* VI, 627–840.

Stürmer, Michael, 'Deutscher Flottenbau und europäische Weltpolitik vor dem Ersten Weltkrieg', in Rahn, *Die Deutsche Flotte im Spannungsfeld der Politik 1848–1985* (Hamburg, 1985), pp. 53–65.

Sulivan, H. N., ed., *Life and Letters of the Late Admiral Sir Bartholomew James Sulivan* (London, 1896).

Sumida, Jon Tetsuro, *In Defence of Naval Supremacy: Finance, Technology and British Naval Policy, 1889–1914* (London, 1988).

—'The Best Laid Plans: The Development of British Battle-Fleet Tactics, 1919–1942', *IHR* XIV (1992), pp. 681–700.

—'British Naval Operational Logistics, 1914–1918', *JMilH* LVII (1993), pp. 447–80.

—'Forging the Trident: British Naval Industrial Logistics, 1914–1918', in *Feeding Mars: Logistics Western Warfare from the Middle Ages to the Present*, ed. Jhon A. Lynn (Boulder, CO, 1993), pp. 217–49.

—'The Quest for Reach: The Development of Long-Range Gunnery in the Royal Navy, 1901–1912', in *Tooling for War: Military Transformation in the Industrial Age*, ed. Stephen D. Chiabotti (Chicago, Il., 1996), pp. 49–97.

—'A Matter of Timing: The Royal Navy and the Tactics of Decisive Battle, 1912–1916', *JMilH*, LXVII (2003), pp. 85–136.

—'Reimagining the History of Twentieth-Century Navies', in *Maritime History as World History*, ed. Daniel Finamore (Gainesville, FL, 2004), pp. 167–82.

—'Expectation, Adaptation, and Resignation: British Battle Fleet Tactical Planning, August 1914–April 1916', *NWCR* LX, no. 3 (2007), pp. 101–22.

Supple, Barry, 'Fear of Failing: Economic History and the Decline of Britain', *EcHR*, 2nd. S., XLVII (1994), pp. 441–58.

Sutcliffe, Paul M., 'Operational Research in the Battle of the Atlantic', in Howarth and Law, *The Battle of the Atlantic*, pp. 418–29.

Sweet, D. W., 'Great Britain and Germany, 1905–1911', in Hinsley, *British Foreign Policy under Sir Edward Grey*, pp. 216–35.

Sweetman, Jack et al., eds., *New Interpretations in Naval History: Selected Papers from the Tenth Naval History Symposium* (Annapolis, Md., 1993).

Symcox, Geoffrey, 'Admiral Mahan, the *Jeune Ecole* and the *Guerre de Course*', in Michel Mollat, *Course et Piraterie* (Paris, 1975, 2 vols.), II, 676–701.

Symonds, Craig L., *Navalists and Anti-Navalists: The Navy Policy Debate in the United States, 1785–1827* (Newark, NJ, 1980).

—*New Aspects of Naval History* (Annapolis, Md., 1981).

—*World War II at Sea: A Global History* (Oxford, 2018).

Syrett, David, *The Defeat of the German U-Boats: The Battle of the Atlantic* (Columbia, SC, 1994).

Talbott, J. E., 'Weapons Development, War Planning and Policy: The U.S. Navy and the Submarine, 1917–1941', *NWCR* XXXVII, no. 3 (1984), pp. 53–71.

Tall, Jeff, 'Waging the Undersea War: A British Perspective', in *The Great World War, 1914–1945*, ed. Peter Liddle, John Bourne and Ian Whitehead (London, 2000–2001, 2 vols.), I, 44–59.

Taylor, J. C., *German Warships of World War II* (London, 1966).

Taylor, Nicholas, 'The Impact of the Naval Manoeuvres of 1888 on British Naval Policy' (Exeter MA dissertation, 2006).

Taylor, R., 'Manning the Royal Navy: The Reform of the Recruiting System, 1852–62', *MM* XLIV (1958), pp. 302–13, and XLV (1959), pp. 46–58.

Termote, Tomas, *War beneath the Waves: U-Boat Flotilla Flandern 1915–1918* (London, 2017).

Terraine, John, *Business in Great Waters: The U-Boat Wars, 1916–1945* (London, 1989).

Thetford, Owen, *British Naval Aircraft since 1912* (London, 6th edn., 1991).

Thomas, Charles S., *The German Navy in the Nazi Era* (London, 1990).

Thomas, Edward, 'The Evolution of the Joint Intelligence System up to and during World War II', in Andrew and Noakes, *Intelligence and International Relations*, pp. 219–34.

Till, Geoffrey, *Air Power and the Royal Navy 1914–1945: A Historical Survey* (London, 1979).

—*Understanding Victory: Naval Operations from Trafalgar to the Falklands* (Santa Barbara, Ca., 2014).

—'Letters from the First World War', *MM* LXIII (1977), pp. 285–92.

—'Adopting the Aircraft Carrier: The British, American and Japanese Case Studies', in Williamson Murray and Allan R. Millett, eds., *Military Innovation in the Interwar Period* (Cambridge, 1996), pp. 191–226.

—'Airpower and the Battleship in the 1920s', in Ranft, *Technical Change and British Naval Policy*, pp. 108–22.

—'Competing Visions: The Admiralty, the Air Ministry and the Role of Air Power', in Benbow, *British Naval Aviation*, pp. 57–78.

—'Retrenchment, Rethinking, Revival, 1919–1939', in Hill, *The Oxford Illustrated History of the Royal Navy*, pp. 319–47.

—'The Return to Globalism: The Royal Navy East of Suez, 1975–2003', in Greg Kennedy, *British Naval Strategy East of Suez 1900–2000*, pp. 244–68.

Todman, Daniel, *Britain's War: Into Battle 1937–1941* (London, 2016).

Tooze, Adam, *Wages of Destruction: The Making and Breaking of the Nazi Economy* (London, 2006).

Topp, Erich, 'Manning and Training the U-Boat Fleet', in Howarth and Law, *The Battle of the Atlantic*, pp. 214–19.

Toprani, Anand, ' "The Navy's Success Speaks for Itself"? The German Navy's Independent Energy Security Strategy, 1932–1940', *NWCR* LXVIII, no. 3 (2015), pp. 91–118.

Tracy, Nicholas, *Attack on Maritime Trade* (London, 1991).

—ed., *The Collective Naval Defence of the Empire, 1900–1940* (NRS Vol. 136, 1997).

—ed., *Sea Power and the Control of Trade: Belligerent Rights from the Russian War to the Beira Patrol, 1854–1970* (NRS Vol. 149, 2005).

Trentmann, Frank, 'National Identity and Consumer Politics: Free Trade and Tariff Reform', in *The Political Economy of British Historical Experience, 1688–1914*, ed. Donald Winch and P. K. O'Brien (Oxford, 2002), pp. 215–42.

Treue, Wilhelm, Eberhard Möller and Werner Rahn, *Deutsche Marinerüstung 1919–1942: Die Gefahren der Tirpitz-Tradition* (Herford and Bonn, 1992). A study by Eberhard Möller based on a wartime paper by his later supervisor Wilhelm Treue, with an introduction by Werner Rahn, asking awkward questions about pre-war design decisions.

Tucker, Robert W., *Woodrow Wilson and the Great War: Reconsidering America's Neutrality, 1914–1917* (Charlottesville, Va., 2007).

Tully, Anthony and Lu Yu, 'A Question of Estimates: How Faulty Intelligence Drove Scouting at the Battle of Midway', *NWCR* LXVIII, no. 2 (2015), pp. 85–100.

Tunstall, W. C. B., 'Imperial Defence 1815–70', in *The Cambridge History of the British Empire*, ed. J. Holland Rose et al. (Cambridge, 1929–36, 8 vols.), II, 806–41.

Turner, John, 'Cabinets, Committees and Secretariats: The Higher Direction of War', in *War and the State: The Transformation of British Government, 1914–1919*, ed. Kathleen Burk (London, 1982), pp. 57–83.

Ugaki Matome, *Fading Victory: The Diary of Admiral Matome Ugaki 1941–1945*, trans. Masataka Chihaya, ed. D. M. Goldstein and K. V. Dillon (Pittsburgh, N.J., 1991).

Umbreit, Hans, 'The Battle for Hegemony in Western Europe', in *G2WW* II, 227–326.

—'Plans and Preparations for a Landing in England', in *G2WW* II, pp. 366–73.

Utley, Jonathan G., 'Franklin Roosevelt and Naval Strategy, 1933–1941', in Marolda, *FDR and the U.S. Navy*, pp. 47–64.

Vale, Brian, *A War betwixt Englishmen: Brazil against Argentina on the River Plate, 1825–1830* (London, 2000).

—*A Frigate of King George: Life and Duty on a British Man-of-War* (London, 2001).

—ed., *Naval Miscellany* VIII (NRS Vol. 164, 2017).

—'Appointment, Promotion and "Interest" in the British South American Squadron, 1821–3', *MM* LXXXVIII (2002), pp. 61–8.

—'Lord Cochrane in Chile: Heroism, Plots and Paranoia', *Age of Sail* I (2002), pp. 59–68.

Vego, Milan, 'Redeployment of the German Brest Group through the English Channel, 11–13 February 1942 (Operation Cerberus)', *NWCR* LXXIV, no. 3 (2021), pp. 100–161.

Vlahos, Michael J., *The Blue Sword: The Naval War College and the American Mission, 1919–1941* (Newport, R.I., 1980).

Vogel, Detlev, 'German Intervention in the Balkans', in *G2WW* III, 449–555.

—'German and Allied Conduct of the War in the West', in *G2WW* VII, 459–702.

Volkmann, Hans-Erich, 'The National Socialist Economy in Preparation for War', in *G2WW* I, 157–372.

Von Grafenstein, Johanna, 'Corso y piratería en el Golfo Caribe durante las guerras de independencia hispanoamericanas', in *La Violence et la Mer dans l'espace atlantique (XIIe-XIXe Siècle)*, ed. Michaël Augeron and Mathias Tranchant (Rennes, 2004), pp. 269–82.

Walton, Oliver, 'Social History of the Royal Navy 1856–1900: Corporation and Community' (Exeter PhD thesis, 2003).

—'Officers or Engineers? The Integration and Status of Engineers in the Royal Navy, 1847–60', *HR* LXXVII (2004), pp. 178–201.

—'"A great improvement in the sailor's feeling towards the naval service": Recruiting Seamen for the Royal Navy, 1815–1853', *JMR* XII (2010), pp. 27–57.

—'New Kinds of Discipline: The Royal Navy in the Second Half of the Nineteenth Century', in Doe and Harding, *Naval Leadership and Management*, pp. 134–56.

Ward, J. T., *Sir James Graham* (London, 1967).

Waring, Sophie, 'The Board of Longitude and the Funding of Scientific Work: Negotiating Authority and Expertise in the Early Nineteenth Century', *JMR* XVI (2014), pp. 55–71.

Warlow, Ben, *The Pusser and his Men: A History of the Supply and Secretarial Branch of the Royal Navy* (Salisbury, 1984).

Warren, Kenneth, *Ships, Steel and Men: Cammell Laird, 1824–1993* (Liverpool, 1998).

Waters, Mavis, 'Changes in the Chatham Dockyard Workforce, 1860–1890', *MM* LXIX (1983), pp. 55–63, 165–73.

—'The Dockyardmen Speak Out: Petition and Tradition in Chatham Dockyard, 1860–1906', in Lunn and Day, *History of Work and Labour Relations*, pp. 87–98.

Watson, Ian, 'Bloody Orkney? A Comparison of the Perceptions Held by Sailors and the Reality of Leisure and Recreational Opportunities at Scapa Flow during the First World War', *MM* CVIII (2022), pp. 323–36.

Watson, Janet S. K., *Fighting Different Wars: Experience, Memory and the First World War in Britain* (Cambridge, 2004).

Watt, Sir James, 'The Health of Seamen in Anti-Slavery Squadrons', *MM* LXXXVIII (2002), pp. 69–78.

Webster, Sir Charles, *The Foreign Policy of Lord Palmerston, 1830–41* (London, 1951, 2 vols. paginated as one).

Wegner, Bernd, 'Hitler's Grand Strategy between Pearl Harbor and Stalingrad', in *G2WW* VI, 112–44.

Weinberg, Gerhard, 'German Strategy, 1939–1945', in *CH2WW* I, pp. 107–31.

Weir, Gary E., 'A Truly Allied Undertaking: The Progeny of Britain's *Empire Liberty*, 1931–43', in Howarth and Law, *The Battle of the Atlantic*, pp. 101–17.

Weir, P. A., 'The Development of Naval Air Warfare by the Royal Navy and Fleet Air Arm between the Two World Wars' (Exeter PhD thesis, 2006).

Wellings, Joseph H., *On His Majesty's Service*, ed. John B. Hattendorf (Newport, RI, 1983).

Wells, Anthony, 'Naval Intelligence and Decision Making in an Era of Technical Change', in Ranft, *Technical Change and British Naval Policy*, pp. 123–46.

Wells, John, *The Royal Navy: An Illustrated Social History 1870–1982* (Stroud, 1994).

Wemyss, Victoria, Lady Wester Wemyss, *The Life and Letters of Lord Wester Wemyss* (London, 1935).

Westwood, David, *The U-Boat War: The German Submarine Service and the Battle of the Atlantic, 1935–45* (London, 2005).

Whalley, Philip, 'The Invergordon Mutiny and the National Economic Crisis of 1931: A Media and Parliamentary Perspective', *JMR* XI (2009), pp. 1–23.

Whitley, M. J., *German Destroyers of World War Two* (London, 1991).

Wilcox, Martin, ' "These peaceable times are the devil": Royal Navy Officers in the Post-War Slump, 1815–1825', *IJMH* XXVI, no. 3 (2014), pp. 471–88.

Wildenberg, Thomas, *Gray Steel and Black Oil: Fast Tankers and Replenishment at Sea in the U.S. Navy, 1912–1995* (Annapolis, Md., 1996).

—*Destined for Glory: Dive Bombing, Midway, and the Evolution of Carrier Airpower* (Annapolis, Md., 1998).

Wildish, Engineer Rear-Admiral Sir H. W., 'Some Maintenance Aspects of the Western Approaches Command in the Second World War', *JNE* IV (1950), pp. 42–58.

Williams, H. Noel, *The Life and Letters of Admiral Sir Charles Napier* (London, 1917).

Williams, Mark, *Captain Gilbert Roberts R.N. and the Anti-U-Boat School* (London, 1979).

Williams, Rhodri, *Defending the Empire: The Conservative Party and British Defence Policy 1899–1915* (New Haven, Conn., 1991).

Williamson, Corbin, 'A One-Way Street? Admiral James Somerville and Anglo-American Naval Relations, 1942', *MM* CVI (2020), pp. 307–19.

Williamson, Samuel R., *The Politics of Grand Strategy: Britain and France Prepare for War, 1904–1914* (Cambridge, Mass., 1969).

Wilson, Alastair, *A Biographical Dictionary of the Twentieth-Century Royal Navy, Vol. 1, Admirals of the Fleet and Admirals* (Barnsley, 2013).

Wilson, Keith, 'Directions of Travel: The Earl of Selborne, the Cabinet, and the Threat from Germany, 1900–1904', *IHR* XXX (2008), pp. 259–72.

Winch, Donald, and P. K. O'Brien, *The Political Economy of British Historical Experience* (Oxford, 2002).

Winkler, Jonathan Reed, *Nexus: Strategic Communications and American Security in World War I* (Cambridge, Mass., 2008).

Winton, John, ed., *Hurrah for the Life of a Sailor! Life on the Lower-Deck of the Victorian Navy* (London, 1977).

—'Life and Education in a Technically Evolving Navy, 1815–1925', in Hill, *The Oxford Illustrated History of the Royal Navy*, pp. 250–79.

Wise, Sydney, 'The Royal Air Force and the Origins of Strategic Bombing', in *Men at War: Politics, Technology and Innovation in the Twentieth Century*, ed. Timothy Travers and Christon Archer (Chicago, Il., 1982, 2011), pp. 149–72.

Wolz, Nicolas, *Das lange Warten: Kriegserfahrungen deutscher und britischer Seeoffiziere 1914 bis 1918* (Paderborn, 2008). A rare and praiseworthy essay in comparative naval social history.

Wong, John Yue-Wo, *Deadly Dreams: Opium, Imperialism, and the Arrow War (1856–1860) in China* (Cambridge, 1998).

Wood, Gerald L., 'The Ironclad Turret Ship *Huascar*', *Warship* 37 (1986), pp. 2–11, and 38 (1986), pp. 86–94.

Woodman, Richard, *The Arctic Convoys 1941–45* (London, 1991).

Woolrych, Lt-Cdr R. S., 'Fighter-Direction Matériel and Technique', in Kingsley, *Radar* II, 173–88.

Wright, Thomas, 'Thomas Young and Robert Seppings: Science and Ship Construction in the Early Nineteenth Century', *TNS* LIII (1981–2), pp. 55–72.

Yexley, Lionel, *The Inner Life of the Navy* (London, 1908).

Young, Kenneth, *Arthur James Balfour: The Happy Life of the Politician, Prime Minister, Statesman, and Philosopher, 1843–1930* (London, 1963).

Zanco, Jean-Philippe, *Boué de Lapeyrère, 1852–1924: l'amiralissime gascon* (Orthez, 2016).

Zeitlin, Jonathan, 'Flexibility and Mass Production at War: Aircraft Manufacture in Britain, the United States, and Germany, 1939–1945', *T&C* XXXVI (1995), pp. 46–79.

Ziegler, Philip, *Mountbatten: The Official Biography* (London, 1985).

Zimm, Alan D., 'American Calculations of Battleline Strength, 1941–2', *NM* XIX (2009), pp. 291–317.

Zimmerman, David, 'Technology and Tactics', in Howarth and Law, *The Battle of the Atlantic*, pp. 476–89.

INDEX

Ben-my-Chree, HMS 306, 607
Bengal *541–2*
Benghazi *xxvii*, 392, 407, 443, 447, 448
Benin expedition (1897) 99
Bentham, Jeremy 21, 22, 26, 27, 31, 123, 772
Beobachtungsdienst (*B-Dienst*) 282–3,
    389, 400, 414, 428, 432, 461, 492, 533,
    801, 807
Beresford, Captain Lord Charles 644;
    Asquith and 269; Channel Fleet command
    160, 169; failures of British training and
    249; Fisher and *169–70*, 178, 186; leaves
    Admiralty 131; mines, on 180; Naval
    Intelligence Department and 131;
    politicized faction-fighting of 284; Pollen
    and 223; retires *169–70*; RNR Trawler
    Section and 204; Selborne Scheme and
    200; South African War and 158; Sturdee
    and 231
Bergen *xxii*, 394, 396, *397–8*
Berkeley, Admiral, Sir Maurice 94, 124, 673
Berlin: Congress (1878) *114–15*; Crisis
    (*1948–9*) 624
Bermuda *xvii, xxiv, xxv*, 6, 23, 111, 412
Bessemer process *148–9*, 772
Beta Search 513, 772
Bethlehem Steel 305
Bethmann Hollweg, Theobald von 242, 256
Bevin, Ernest 371
Bey, Commander Erich 399, 543
biplanes 518, 520, 521, 525, 560, 772
birdcage 433, 772
Birmingham University 433
Bismarck xxiv, 444–5, 462, 652
Bismarck Sea, USS 606
Bismarck Sea, battle of (1943) 536, 653
Bismarck, Prince Otto von 160, 163, 435
Björnstjerna, Colonel Carl *465–6*
Black Code 495, 773
Black Prince, HMS 139, 145
Black Sea 111, 114, 155, 158, 159, 162, 182, 192,
    235, 325, 440, 647; Russian War (*1853–56*)
    and *xix*, 30, *43–4, 46–7*, 49, 63, 74, 640
black shoe 467, 528, 773
blackbirding 114, 773
Blackburn 518; Kangaroo 387; Skua *397–8*,
    520, *521–2*, 529
Blackett, Patrick *554–5*
Blackwood, Rear-Admiral Sir Henry 19
Blair, Tony 634
Blanco Encalada 152
blind fire 466, 471, *543*, 773

blockade 7, 8, 165, 265, 268, 319; American
    Civil War and 109, *110–11*; Berehaven,
    Hornby practices in *118–19*; close
    blockade 119, 178, 179, 182, 184, 266;
    Declaration of London and 185; Delagoa
    Bay 158; Dutch ports 9, 638; First World
    War and *237–8*, 241, 242, 256, *266–70*, 273,
    319, 342, 648; legality of *184–5*; London
    Treaty and 333; meanings of 154, 184;
    Ministry of Blockade *269–70*; Peking 35;
    Piraeus 42, 639; Russian War and 49, 50,
    640; sea mines and 180, 181; Second
    World War and 344, *394–5*, 416, 419, 443,
    607–8; slaving coasts *40–41*; Spanish Civil
    War and 339; tactic of 154, 156; torpedo
    craft and *178–9*
blockships 62–3, 631
Blohm, Rudolf 553
Blücher 216, *234–5*, 342, *396–7*
Bluejacket, The 105
Board of Invention and Research *277–8*
Board of Trade 89, 267, 268, 269, 499, 585,
    773, 796
boatswain 82, 92, 97, *99–100*, 581, 773
Boeing: B-17 *451–2*, 524, 538, 550; B-29 590,
    602, 606, 626
Bogue Forts 34
boilers 151, 304, 313, 314, 439, 455, 510, 579,
    614, 629, 774, 779, 782, 795, 799; boiler
    rooms 95, 96, 220, 293, 572; boilermakers'
    union *134–5*; coal-fired 214; definition of
    773; explosions 95, 643; forced draught
    149, 209, 773, 782; oil-fired 219; steamers
    and 58, 149, 309, 310, 312, 315; steel 149;
    stokers and *see* stokers; Thornycroft 313;
    water-tube 198, 212, 218, 565, 773, 799
Bomarsund, capture of fortress (1854) 47, 49,
    640
Bombay *xvii, xxviii*, *11–12*, 642; Bombay
    Dockyard 615
bombes 389, 492, 493, 494, 773
Bonaparte, Napoleon 1, 9, 42
Bonar Law, Andrew 273, 373
Bonham-Carter, Rear-Admiral Stuart *464–5*
Bonte, Commodore Friedrich 398, 399
Borghese, Commander Junio Valerio 339,
    450
Borneo *xxx*, 12, 454, 632, 633
botany 14, 15, 55, 83
Bougainville Island 536, 542, 654
Boulton & Watt 24, 25
Bounty Act (1825) 12

Bowles, Commodore William 6
Bowring, Sir John 51
boys: 'Boy 1st class, called Volunteer' 65;
Royal Navy and 65, 78, 79, 84, *91–4*, 103,
193, 194, 195, 201, 203, 205, *286–7*, 295, 297,
352, 358, 498, *501–2*, 506, 778
Bradley, General Omar 597, *626–7*
Braithwaite Burn & Jessop of Bombay 615
Brassey, Thomas 147
Brazil 6, 7, 10, 14, 39, 40, 613, 637, 670
Breconshire 448
breech-loading guns *142–6*, 151, *209–10*, 774,
783, 788, 790
Bremen *xx*, 165, 238, 553, 575
Bremen 315
Breslau 228, 646
Brest 179, 410, 439, 446, *462–3*, 653
Brest-Litovsk, Treaty (1918) 260, 318, 647
Bretagne xxvi, 409
bridge, ship's 59, 304, 307, 310, 427, 433, 560,
563, 581, 582, 584, 606
Bridges, Edward 341
Bright, John *3–4*, 51, 89
Brind, Rear-Admiral Patrick 486
Bristol: Beaufort, Rear-Admiral Sir F. 439,
473; Blenheim 439
Bristol, Rear-Admiral Arthur L. 421
Britain: Act of Union (1707) xxxiii; Act of
Union (1801) 4; AUKUS partnership
634–5; balance of payments 190, 267, 383,
623, 633, 656; Battle of the Atlantic
Committee *429–30*; Cabinet *see* Cabinet;
chiefs of staff, rising importance and
influence of 373; Combined Operations
491, 501, 507, 540, 599, 776; conferences/
treaties *see individual conference and
treaty name*; defence review (1997) 634;
defence spending 38, 191, 378, *382–3*, 387,
627–8; Defence White Papers and *see*
Defence White Papers; devaluation 378,
624, 633; 'East of Suez', withdrawal from
633–5, 658; empire 1, 16, 37, 53, 112, 157, 161,
243, 259, 260, 324, 346, 348, 380, 406, 456,
477, 487, 546, 547, 549, 598, 599, 600, 617,
656; exports 108, *190–91*, 256, *267–8*, 270,
419, 623; Far East Combined Bureau 390,
496; fiscal-military state 2; general
elections, British *see* general elections,
British; gold standard and 190, 362, 378,
649, 650; Great Depression and *359–60*;
gross domestic product 190, 191; imports
111, 156, 189, *257–8*, 266, 427, *438–9*, 486,

487, *544–5*, 546, 623; Keynesian economic
principles and 378; legislation *see
individual title of legislation*; loans,
wartime 344, *376–7*, 378, 482, *623–4*, 656;
malnutrition in, post-war 624; ministries
see individual ministry name; national
debt 17, *319–20*, 334, *376–8*, 482, 600, 623,
789; national decline, narrative of 156,
188–91; political parties within *see
individual party name*; public spending
120, 378; Royal Navy and *see* Royal Navy;
shipbuilding *see* Royal Navy; slave trade
and *see* slavery; sterling and *see* sterling;
suffrage in 2, 3, 4, 119; Suez Canal and *see*
Suez Canal; taxation *see* taxation; Three
Power Standard and 157, 162; Treasury *see*
Treasury, British; trade *see* trade; treaties
and *see individual treaty name*; Two-
Power Standard and 6, 119, 121, 157, 158,
162, 172, 322, 323, 644; underwater cable
manufacture 136; wars/conflicts/battle *see
individual service and war/conflict/battle
name*
Britannia, HMS (training ship) 174, *192–4*,
199, 201, 641
British Admiralty Delegation, Washington
526, 549, 599
British Army 1, *30–31*, *44–6*, 47, 158, 166, 170,
176, 182, 227, 798; British Expeditionary
Force (BEF) 227, 235, 244, 260, 402, 404,
405, 479, 651, 807. *See also individual battle
and campaign name*
British Association for the Advancement of
Science 13
British Dominions 168, 312, 547, 612, 613, 638,
649
British Joint Staff Mission, Washington 510
British Merchant Navy 197, 206, 245, 465,
499, 539, 545, 561, 569, 585, 648
British Merchant Shipping Mission,
Washington 487
British Museum 14
British Naval Cyphers 282; No. 3 492; No. 5
542
British Purchasing Commission,
Washington 425
British Tabulating Machines 493, 807
broad front formation 430
Broad Fourteens 229
Bromley, Richard 29
Brooke, Field-Marshal Sir Alan 479, 600
Brooke, James 'Rajah' 12